The
**POSEN LIBRARY OF JEWISH
CULTURE AND CIVILIZATION**

The Posen Library of Jewish Culture and Civilization

A monumental project many years in the making, the Posen Library collects more than three thousand years of Jewish primary texts, documents, images, and cultural artifacts into ten encyclopedic volumes, with selections made by 150 internationally recognized scholars. When complete, the library will include the following volumes:

Volume 1: Ancient Israel, from Its Beginnings through 332 BCE, edited by Jeffrey H. Tigay and Adele Berlin

Volume 2: Emerging Judaism, 332 BCE–600 CE, edited by Carol Bakhos

Volume 3: Encountering Christianity and Islam, 600–1200, edited by Arnold E. Franklin

Volume 4: Late Medieval Era, 1200–1500, edited by Jonathan S. Ray

Volume 5: Early Modern Era, 1500–1750, edited by Yosef Kaplan

Volume 6: Confronting Modernity, 1750–1880, edited by Elisheva Carlebach

Volume 7: National Renaissance and International Horizons, 1880–1918, edited by Israel Bartal and Kenneth B. Moss

Volume 8: Crisis and Creativity between World Wars, 1918–1939, edited by Todd M. Endelman and Zvi Gitelman

Volume 9: Catastrophe and Rebirth, 1939–1973, edited by Samuel D. Kassow and David G. Roskies

Volume 10: Late Twentieth Century, 1973–2005, edited by Deborah Dash Moore and Nurith Gertz

The Posen Foundation's mission is rooted in the belief that Jewish education can make a meaningful difference in Jewish life, and should be available to all who are interested. To this end, the Foundation works internationally to promote Jewish learning, support academic research into Jewish history and culture, and encourage participation in Jewish cultural life.

The Posen Library of Jewish Culture and Civilization

Deborah Dash Moore, *Editor in Chief*

Volume 6: Confronting Modernity, 1750–1880

Elisheva Carlebach, *Editor*

Yale UNIVERSITY PRESS   New Haven and London

The Posen Foundation   Lucerne

Copyright © 2019 by the Posen Foundation.

All rights reserved.

This book may not be reproduced, in whole or in part, including illustrations, in any form (beyond that copying permitted by Sections 107 and 108 of the U.S. Copyright Law and except by reviewers for the public press), without written permission from the publishers.

Yale University Press books may be purchased in quantity for educational, business, or promotional use. For information, please e-mail sales.press@yale.edu (U.S. office) or sales@yaleup.co.uk (U.K. office).

Designed by George Whipple Design
for Westchester Publishing Services.

Set in Bulmer MT type by Newgen.

Printed in the United States of America.

Library of Congress Control Number: 2011043318
ISBN 978-0-300-19000-7 (hardcover)

A catalogue record for this book is available from the British Library.

This paper meets the requirements of ANSI/NISO Z39.48-1992 (Permanence of Paper).

10 9 8 7 6 5 4 3 2 1

Contents

Advisory Boards xxi

Project Staff xxii

Acknowledgments xxiii

Introduction to the Posen Library of Jewish Culture and Civilization, *by Deborah Dash Moore and James E. Young* xxv

How to Read This Book xxxii

Introduction to Volume 6, *by Elisheva Carlebach* xxxiii

LITERATURE

Introduction 1

LIFE WRITING 2

1752
Abraham Mendes de Castro, "Last Will and Testament" 2

1753–1767
Aaron Lopez and Benjamin Gomez, "Correspondence Re: Circumcision of Babies and Marranos" 3

1760
Pinchas Katzenellenbogen, *Sefer yesh manḥilin (Those Who Bequeath)* 4

CA. 1762–1770
Jacob Emden, *Megilat sefer (The Scroll of the Book)* 6

1771
Rebecca Henriquez da Costa, "Epitaph, from the Tombstone of Rebecca Henriquez da Costa" 7

1777
Fromet Guggenheim, "Letter from Fromet to Moses Mendelssohn" 7

1778
David Attias, *The Golden Garden* 9

1781
Rebecca Franks, "Letter to Abigail Franks" 10

1783
Michael Joseph Edler von Arnstein, "Letter to His Parents after His Conversion" 11

1787
Raphael Laniado, *Sefer kise Shelomoh (Solomon's Throne)* 12

1788
Isaac Euchel, *Toldot rabenu he-hakham Mosheh ben Menaḥem (Biography of Our Wise Teacher, Moses, Son of Menachem)* 13

1789
Daniel Mendoza, *The Art of Boxing*, Preface 14

1790
Aaron Hart, "Aaron Hart and His Children" 15

CA. 1790–1800
Ber of Bolechów, *Zikhronot (Memoirs)* 15

CA. 1792
Rebecca Samuel, "Letter from Rebecca Samuel to Her Parents" 16

1792–1793
Solomon Maimon, *Solomon Maimon: An Autobiography* 17

1793
Fanny von Arnstein, "First Will" 19
Family of Richea Gratz, "Letters to Richea Gratz" 20

1794
Relle Luzzatto Morschene, "A Letter to Chief Rabbi Raffael Natan Tedesco of Trieste" 21

1794–1832
Roza, Wife of Leyzer ben Moses Judah, *Register of a Jewish Midwife* 22

1796
Akiva Eger, "Statement of Mourning" 22

1799
Rahel Levin Varnhagen, *Letters* 24

1801–1802
Aaron Isaac, *Autobiography* 26

1809
Moses Sofer, *Sefer ha-zikaron (The Book of Memory)* 28

1814
Akiva Eger, "Letter of Rabbinic Appointment to the City of Posen" 30

1815
Rachel Mordecai Lazarus, "The Education of the Heart" 32
Isaac Judah Yehiel Safrin of Komarno, "Account of His Visit to Lublin" 33

1816
Daniel Mendoza, *Memoirs of the Life of Daniel Mendoza* 33

CA. 1820
Moses Wasserzug, *Memoirs* 35

1821
Judah Jeitteles, *Bene ha-ne'urim (The Youth)* 37

1822–1823
Emanuele Levi, *Journal* 38

1832
Sheftall Sheftall, "Description of His Career as a Revolutionary Soldier, 1777–1783" 39

1839
Peter Beer, *The Childhood and Youth of a Man of the Enlightenment* 40

1842
Abraham Kohn, *A Jewish Peddler's Diary* 43

1846
Judith Cohen Montefiore, *The Jewish Manual of Practical Information in Jewish and Modern Cookery with a Collection of Valuable Recipes & Hints Relating to the Toilette* 45

1849
Mordecai Manuel Noah, "Ziprah Nunez's Account of the Family Escape" 45

MID-19TH CENTURY
Leopold Zunz, "My First Lessons in Wolfenbüttel" 47

1850
Henriette de Lemos Herz, *Her Life and Her Memories* 47

CA. 1855
Daniel Khvolson, "Letter on His Conversion" 48

1859–1861
Salomon de Rothschild, "Correspondence from the United States, 1859–1861" 49

1864
Abraham Rosanes, *Diary* 51

1864–1865
Emma Mordecai, *Letters and Diary* 53

1866
Oro Arieh, "Correspondence with Moses Montefiore" 56
J. A. Joel, "A Union Soldier's Passover" 56

1868
Samuel Siegfried Karl von Basch, *Memories of Mexico* 58
Miriam Markel-Mosessohn, "Letter to Judah Leib Gordon" 58

1871
Esther Levy, *Jewish Cookery Book* 60

1873
Ignác Goldziher, *My Oriental Diary*   61
Moses Leib Lilienblum, *The Sins of My Youth*   62

1880
Abraham Ber Gottlober, *Zikhronot u-masaʿot (Memoir and Journeys)*   64

1881–1902
Saʿadi Besalel a-Levi, *Memoir*   65

Travel Writing   66

1792
Samuel Romanelli, *Travail in an Arab Land*   66

1836
Judith Cohen Montefiore, *Private Journal of a Visit to Egypt and Palestine*   67

1840
Joseph Solomon Lutski, *Epistle of Israel's Deliverance*   68

1856
Solomon Nunes Carvalho, *Travel Journal*   70

Date Unknown
Ḥayim Joseph David Azulai, *Maʿagal tov ha-shalem (The Good Journey)*   72

Folktales and Fiction   74

1790
Isaac Euchel, *Igrot Meshulam (Epistles of Meshulam)*   74

1794–1797
Aaron Halle-Wolfsohn, *Siḥah be-erets ha-ḥayim (A Conversation in the Afterlife)*   75

1814
Anonymous, *In Praise of the Baʿal Shem Tov*   77

1815
Nachman of Bratslav, "The Tale of a Rabbi and His Only Son"   79

CA. 1824
Heinrich Heine, "A Seder Night"   80

1826
Benjamin Disraeli, *Vivian Grey*   82

1833
Benjamin Disraeli, *The Wondrous Tale of Alroy*   84
Eugénie Foa, "Rachel; or, The Inheritance"   85

1836
Ludwig A. Frankl, *Ancestral Tales and Legends*   86

1841
Godchaux Baruch Weil (Ben-Lévi), "The Rise and Fall of a Polish Tallis"   87

CA. 1843
Jonah ben Gabriel, *Folktales of the Kurdistani Jews*   88

1844
Grace Aguilar, "The Escape: A Tale of 1755"   89

1847
Leopold Weisel, "Die Pinchasgasse"   91

CA. 1847
Wolf Pascheles, "The Kamzan" ("The Miser")   93

1848
Leopold Kompert, "The Death of the Tavern Keeper's Wife"   94

1849–1853
Auguste Widal (Daniel Stauben), *Scenes of Jewish Life in Alsace*   95

1853
Abraham Mapu, *The Love of Zion*   97

1854
Ludwig Philippson, "The Three Brothers"   98

1857–1864
Abraham Mapu, *The Hypocrite*   99

1859
Salomon Formstecher, "The Stolen Son: A Contemporary Tale"   100
Osip Rabinovich, "The Penal Recruit"   102

1860
Alexandre Weill, "Braendel"   103

1861
Israel Aksenfeld, "The Headband"   106

1863–1864
Sara Hirsch Guggenheim, "Aurelie Werner"   108

1864
David Schornstein, "The Tithe"   109

1864–1865
Sholem Yankev Abramovitsh (Mendele Mokher Sforim), *The Little Man; or, Portrait of a Life*   111

1865
Isaac Meyer Dik, *The Women Shopkeepers, or, Golde-Mine, the Abandoned Wife of Brod*   112

1867
Jorge Isaacs, *María*   113

1867–1869
Isaac Joel Linetski, *The Polish Lad*   115

1868
Isaac Meyer Dik, "The Panic, or, The Town of Hérres"   116

1871–1873
Lev Levanda, *Seething Times*   117

1873
Karl Emil Franzos, "The Jews of Barnow"   119

Poetry   122

1768
Ephraim Luzzatto, "The Doctor Who Fell Prey to Love"   122

1789–1802
Naphtali Herts Wessely, "Shire tiferet" ("Songs of Glory")   122

CA. 1820
Anonymous, "A Story of What Happened to Rav Moshe Danon and the Elders of the Jewish Community of Sarajevo on 20 October 1819"   123

1827
Heinrich Heine, "Donna Clara"   124

CA. 1827
Anonymous, "A Dirge for the Ninth of Av"   125

1833
Penina Moïse, "Miriam"   127

1835
Heinrich Heine, "Farewell, You Cheerful Folk of France"   128

1842
Abraham Dov (Adam) ha-Kohen Lebensohn, "Lament of the Daughter of Judah"   128

Abraham Dov (Adam) ha-Kohen Lebensohn, "Seeker of Truth"   129

1846
Siegfried Kapper, "Ben-Oni" ("Son of Sorrow")   130

1847
Afanasy Fet, "Sheltered by a Crimson Awning..."   130
Rachel Luzzatto Morpurgo, "On Hearing She Had Been Praised in the Journals"   131

1863
Abraham Jacob Paperna, "Emet ve-emunah" ("Truth and Faith")   131

1866
Judah Leib Gordon, "Awake My People!"   132

1875
Judah Leib Gordon, "The Tip of the Yod"   133

CA. 1875
Emma Lazarus, *Epochs*   134

1877
Salomón López Fonseca, "Love and Illusion"   135

CA. 1880
Solomon Ettinger, "The Assembly"   136

1883
Emma Lazarus, "The New Colossus"   137

INTELLECTUAL CULTURE

Introduction   139

Rabbinic and Religious Thought   140

1744
Jonathan Eybeschütz, "Sermon of Ethical Rebuke Preached... during the Penitential Period Preceding the New Year's Day, 5505 [1744], to the Congregation of Metz"   140

1751
Angelo (Mordechai) de Soria, "A Public Speech on Temptation, Composed by Mordechai de Abraham de Soria, and Which Was Delivered by a Student of His on His Bar Mitzvah, on the First Day of Sukkot"   142

1752
Ba'al Shem Tov, "Igeret aliyat ha-neshamah" ("Epistle on the Ascent of the Soul")   143

1755
Jonathan Eybeschütz, *Sefer luḥot edut (Tablets of Testimony)*   144

1757
Samuel Mendes de Sola, "License Authorizing Daniel da Costa Gomez to Be a Ritual Slaughterer"   146

1760
Ezekiel Landau, *Derushe ha-tselaḥ (Sermons* [of Landau])   147

CA. 1760
Jacob Frank, *Collection of the Words of the Lord*   148

1761
Jacob Emden, *Mor u-ketsiyah (Myrrh and Cassia)*   150

1762
Jacob Emden, *Sefer hitavkut (Book of Struggle)*   151

1766
Zeraḥ Eidlitz, *Or la-yesharim (Light for the Righteous)*   152

1772
Elijah ben Solomon Zalman, Gaon of Vilna, "Epistle against the Hasidim"   153
Rabbis of Schwerin, "Rabbis of Schwerin to Moses Mendelssohn"   154

1775
Jonathan Eybeschütz, *Urim ve-tumim (The Urim and Thummim)*   156

1776
Ezekiel Landau, *Noda bi-Yehudah (Known in Judah)*   158

1780
Jacob Joseph of Polnoye, *Toldot Ya'akov Yosef (The Offshoots of Jacob Joseph)*   159

1781
Dov Ber of Mezritsh, *Magid devarav le-Ya'akov (He Declares His Word to Jacob)*   159

1782
Ezekiel Landau, "Sermon for the Sabbath Preceding Passover"   160

David Tevele, "A Sermon contra Naphtali Herts Wessely"   161

1784
Saul Berlin, *Ketav yosher (Epistle of Justice)*   162

1788
Elimelech of Lizhensk, *No'am Elimelekh (Pleasing Qualities of Elimelech)*   163

CA. 1790
David Hisquiau Baruch Louzada, "Anti-Slave Prayer"   163

1793
Ba'al Shem Tov, *Tsava'at ha-Rivash (Testament of Rabbi Israel Ba'al Shem Tov)*   164
Saul Berlin, "Besamim rosh" ("Scent of a Bitter Spice")   164

1797
Shneur Zalman of Liady, *Tanya*   166

CA. 1797
Elijah ben Solomon, Gaon of Vilna, "Ethical Will"   166

1798
Levi Isaac of Berdichev, *Kedushat Levi (Sanctity of Levi)*   168

1799–1800
Eleazer Fleckeles, *Kuntres ahavat David (Treatise: The Love of David)*   168

CA. 1800
Yom Tov ben Israel Jacob Algazi, *Kedushat Yom Tov (The Sanctity of Yom Tov)*   169

1803
Ḥayim of Volozhin, "Igeret ha-yeshiva" (Epistle on the Yeshiva)   172

CA. 1803
Elijah ben Solomon, Gaon of Vilna, *Bi'ur ha-Gra: Glosses to Shulḥan arukh*   173

1805
Ezekiel Paneth, *Sefer mar'eh Yeḥezkel (The Vision of Ezekiel)*   174

1807
Grand Sanhedrin (France), "Declaration Adopted by the Assembly and the Answers to the First Three Questions"   176

1808

Menachem Mendel Lefin, *Sefer ḥeshbon ha-nefesh (Book of Moral Accounting)* 177

1809

Nachman of Bratslav, "Tiku emunah" 179

Moses Sofer, *Derashot Ḥatam Sofer (Sermons of Ḥatam Sofer)* 179

1810

Jacob Landau, "From the Introduction to His Father's Book, *Noda bi-Yehudah*" 180

Moses Sofer, "Responsa Ḥatam Sofer: *Oraḥ ḥayim* 154" 180

1814

Menachem Mendel of Vitebsk, *Peri ha-arets (Fruit of the Earth)* 180

1818

Aaron Chorin, *Nogah ha-tsedek (Radiance of Justice)* 181

1819

Bet Din of Hamburg, *Eleh divre ha-berit (These Are the Words of the Covenant)* 182

1820

Jacob de la Motta, "Discourse Delivered at the Consecration of the Synagogue of the Hebrew Congregation Mickve Israel, in the City of Savannah, Georgia, 21 July 1820" 183

Jonathan Eybeschütz, *Tiferet Yonatan (The Splendor of Jonathan)* 184

1822

Eduard Gans, "A Society to Further Jewish Integration" 185

CA. 1820S

Moses Sofer, *Ḥut ha-meshulash (Threefold Cord)* 186

1831

Aaron Worms of Metz, *Me'ore or (Luminescence of Light)* 186

1835

Moses Sofer, "Responsa Ḥatam Sofer: *Oraḥ ḥayim* 51" 188

1836

Samson Raphael Hirsch, *Nineteen Letters on Judaism* 188

Israel ben Samuel of Shklov, *Pe'at ha-shulḥan (Edge of the Table)* 190

1839

Moses Sofer, "Responsa Ḥatam Sofer, *Oraḥ ḥayim* 36" 191

1840

Judah Alkalai, *Shalom Yerushalayim (Peace of Jerusalem)* 192

Isaac Asher Francolm, *Rational Judaism* 192

1842

Kalonimos Kalman Epstein, *Ma'or va-shemesh (Light and Sun)* 193

Samuel Hirsch, *The Religious Philosophy of the Jews* 194

Bonaventura Mayer, *The Jews in Our Time* 195

1844

Grace Aguilar, *Women of Israel, or, Characters and Sketches from the Holy Scriptures* 196

Jacob Ettlinger, "Rabbinic Reports on Circumcision" 197

1845

Zechariah Fraenkel, *The Symptoms of the Time* 197

Solomon Judah Rapoport, *Open Rebuke* 199

1850

Jacob Ettlinger, *Arukh la-ner* 200

1854

Fanny Neuda, "On the Approach of Childbirth" 200

Isaac Mayer Wise, *History of the Israelite Nation, from Abraham to the Present Time* 201

1855

Fanny Neuda, "For a Mother Whose Son Is in Military Service" 202

1860

Joseph Salvador, *Paris, Rome, Jerusalem, or the Religious Question in the Nineteenth Century* 203

1862

Samuel David Luzzatto, *Lessons of Jewish Moral Theology* 204

1863

Elijah Benamozegh, "Israel and Humanity" 205

1864

Akiva Joseph Schlesinger, *Lev ha-Ivri (The Heart of a Jew)* 206

1865

Elissa Lisbonne, "On the Emancipation of Women in Jewish Worship"   208

1867

Penina Moïse, *Hymns Written for the Use of Hebrew Congregations. Charleston, Congregation Beth Elohim*   209

1870

Judah Papo, "Is the Printing Press Harmful? A Rabbi from Sarajevo Responds"   210

CA. 1870

Simon Sofer, *Shem ha-gedolim ha-shalem (Names of the Great Ones, Complete)*   211

1874

Jacob Ettlinger, *Responsa binyan tsiyon (Responsa: Building Zion)*   211

1902

Elimelech of Lizhensk and Zusya of Annopol (Hanipoli), *Menorat zahav (Golden Menorah)*   213

1911

Uri of Strelisk, *On the Seer of Lublin's Court*   214

Date Unknown

Isaac Judah Yehiel Safrin of Komarno, *Notser ḥesed to Avot (Preserving Mercy [Commentary to* Ethics of the Fathers*])*   214

Israel Salanter, *Be'ure ha-midot (Clarification of the Virtues)*   214

Shneur Zalman of Liady, *Igrot ha-kodesh (Holy Epistles)*   217

Haskalah and Pedagogy   218

1761

Moses Mendelssohn, *On the Religious Legitimacy of Studying Logic (Commentary on Maimonides'* Milot ha-higayon*)*   218

1764

Me'am Lo'ez, "Introduction to the Commentary on Numbers—*Me'am Lo'ez*," by Isaac Magriso   219

1767

Moses Mendelssohn, *Phaedon*   220

1779

David Friedländer, *Reader for Jewish Children*   222

1780

Baruch ben Jacob (Baruch of Shklov) Schick, *Introduction to Euclid*   223

1782

Naphtali Herts Wessely, *Words of Peace and Truth*   223

1783

Moses Mendelssohn, *Light for the Path*   224

1784

Benedetto Frizzi, *Defense against the Attacks Leveled against the Jewish Nation in the Book Entitled* On the Ghetto's Influence on the State   226

1786

Moses Mendelssohn, "Letter to the Friends of Lessing (On the Spinoza Conversations between Lessing and Jacobi)"   226

1787–1790

Benedetto Frizzi, *Dissertation on Medical Policy Concerning Certain Foods Which Are Prohibited in the Pentateuch*   230

CA. 1780s

Naphtali Herts Wessely, *Sefer ha-midot (Book of Virtues)*   231

1792

Saul Ascher, *Leviathan*   231

Solomon Maimon, *Givat ha-moreh* [Commentary to Maimonides' *Moreh nevukhim*, Guide for the Perplexed]   233

1792–1793

Solomon Maimon, *The Autobiography of Solomon Maimon: Maskilic View of Heder*   234

1793

Lazarus Bendavid, *Notes Regarding the Characteristics of the Jews*   235

1796

Aaron Halle-Wolfsohn, *Silliness and Sanctimony*   236

CA. 1798

David of Makev, *Shever poshe'im: The Court of R. Ḥayim Ḥaykl of Amdur*   239

1799

David Friedländer, "Open Letter"   241

1809
Menachem Mendel Lefin, "Prayer against the Hasidim"   242

1819
Joseph Perl, *Megaleh temirin (The Revealer of Secrets)*   243

1827
Anania Coen, "An Essay on Hebrew Eloquence, Exposed in a Practical Lesson by Doctor Anania Coen, First Rabbi of the Jewish Community of Florence"   244

1834
Lelio Della Torre, *Five Orations Given in Padua by Lelio Della Torre*   245

1837
Abraham Ber Gottlober, *Pirḥe he-aviv (Spring Flowers)*   246

1839
Isaac Leeser, *Catechism for Jewish Children: Designed as a Religious Manual for House and School*   248

1840
Isaac Erter, *Ha-tsofeh le-vet Yisra'el: Tashlikh (The Observer of the House of Israel: Tashlikh)*   248
Pinḥas de Segura, "A Sermon Delivered at the Great Synagogue of Smyrna on the Arrival of Sir Moses and Lady Montefiore in that City after His Successful Mission on Behalf of His Persecuted Brethren in Damascus"   250

1843
Isaac Bekhor Amarachi and Joseph ben Meir Sason, *Sefer musar haskel (Book of Moral Lessons)*   252

SECOND HALF OF THE NINETEENTH CENTURY
S. Beilin, "Heder Riddles and Puzzles among Lithuanian Jews"   253

1853
Isaac Samuel Reggio, "The Religious Instruction of Jewish Youth"   254

1858
Isaac Akrish, *Sefer kiryat arba*   255

1859
Emmanuil Borisovich Levin, "Note on the Emancipation of the Jews of Russia"   256

1863
Grigory Bogrov, "Notes of a Jew"   257
Mordechai Aaron Gintsburg, *Aviezer*   259

CA. 1863
Mikhail Morgulis, "Toward a History of the Education of Russian Jews"   263

1867
Isaac Ber Levinzon, *Emek refa'im (Valley of Giants)*   265

1868
Abraham Uri Kovner, *Tseror peraḥim (A Bouquet of Flowers)*   266

1871
Rosa Gabbay, *Courtesy, or Rules of Comportment*   269

1872–1874
Eliezer Shem-Tov Papo, *The Book of the Governing of My Household*   269

1873
Eliezer Zweifel, *Shalom al Yisra'el (Peace upon Israel)*   271

1879
Samuel Joseph Fuenn, *Dor ve-dorshav (A Generation and Its Seekers)*   273

SCHOLARSHIP AND SCIENCE   277

CA. 1750
Simhah Isaac ben Moses Lutski, *Me'irat enayim (Light of the Eyes)*   277

1774
Joseph Vita Castelli, "Medical-Critical Letter Written by Doctor Joseph Vita Castelli to His Friend, a Doctor, Regarding a Serious and Complicated Case of Acute Fever"   278

1812
Herz Homberg, *Bene Zion: A Religious-Moralistic Textbook for the Youth of the Israelite Nation*   280

1828
Léon Halévy, *A Summary of Modern Jewish History*   280

1832
Isaac Markus Jost, *The Rigors of Jewish Historiography*   281

Leopold Zunz, "The Liturgical Addresses of the Jews" 283

1843
Adolphe Franck, *The Kabbalah, or The Religious Philosophy of the Hebrews* 285

1844
Leopold Dukes, *Rabbinical Anthology* 286

1846
Heinrich Graetz, "The Diaspora: Construction of Jewish History" 287

1851
Nachman Krochmal, *Moreh nevukhe ha-zeman (Guide for the Perplexed of Our Time)* 290
Samuel David Luzzatto, *Igerot Shadal (Letters of Samuel David Luzzatto)* 291

1860
Samuel Joseph Fuenn, *Kiryah ne'emanah (Faithful City)* 291

1864
Abraham Geiger, *Judaism and Its History* 292

1866
Abraham Harkavy, "On the Language of the Jews Who Lived in Ancient Russia" 294

1869
Jacob Brafman, *Book of the Kahal: Materials for the Study of the Jewish Life* 296

1870
Samuel David Luzzatto, *Introduction to the Pentateuch* 297

1872
Daniel Khvolson, *The Semitic Nations* 299

1883
Ignác Goldziher, *The Zahiris* 299

POLITICAL LIFE AND THOUGHT 301

1757–1758
Shearith Israel, "The Earliest Extant Minute Books of the Spanish and Portuguese Congregation Shearith Israel in New York, 1728–1786" 301

CA. 1778–1779
Mordecai Sheftall, "In the Hands of the British" 301

1780
Ezekiel Landau, "Eulogy for Empress Maria Theresa" 303

1782
Moses Mendelssohn, "Preface to *Vindiciae Judaeorum*" 304

1783
Moses Mendelssohn, *Jerusalem* 304

1787
Jonas Phillips, "Letter to Federal Constitutional Convention" 305

1788
David de Isaac Cohen Nassy, *History of the Colony of Suriname* 306

1789
Zalkind Hourwitz, "Vindication of the Jews" 308

1790
Moses Seixas, "Letter to George Washington" 309

1792
David Franco Mendes, "Note of Royalty Who Visited the Sephardic Synagogue of Amsterdam between 1642 and 1781" 310

1799
Isaac Sasportas, "Plan for the Invasion of Jamaica to Emancipate Slaves and Interrogation Testimony to British Authorities Following His Arrest for the Plan to Emancipate Slaves in Jamaica" 311

1803
Lev Nevakhovich, *Lament of the Daughter of Judah* 313

1835
Benjamin Disraeli, "Utilitarian Follies" 315

1841
Isaac Leeser, *The Claims of the Jews to an Equality of Rights* 318

1842
Jacques-Isaac Altaras and Joseph Cohen, "Report on the Moral and Political State of the Israelites of Algeria and on the Means to Improve It" 319

1843
Karl Marx, *On the Jewish Question* 320

1847
Anonymous, "The Cry of the Poor Jews of Izmir" 321
1848
Karl Marx, "Manifesto of the Communist Party" 322
1849
Reuben Kulisher, "An Answer to the Slav" 324
1852
Ernestine Potovsky Rose, "An Address on Women's Rights" 325
1860
Alliance Israélite Universelle, "Proclamation of the Alliance Israélite Universelle" 327
1861
Morris Jacob Raphall, "The Bible View of Slavery" 328
David Einhorn, "Response to 'A Bible View of Slavery'" 330
1862
Moses Hess, *Rome and Jerusalem* 331
1864–1867
Judah Scheindling of Shkudy, *Excerpts from the Minute Book of a Psalms Society in the Russian Army* 332

JOURNALISM 335

1815
Jacob Samuel Bick, "Letter to Tuvie Feder" 335
1840
Löw Schwab, *The Jews* 336
1841
Godchaux Baruch Weil (Ben-Lévi), "The March 17th Decree" 337
1842
Die Allgemeine Zeitung des Judentums, "La Buena Esperansa" ("The Good Hope") 339
1844
David Kuh, "A Word to Jews and Slavs" 339
1846
Rafael Uziel, "Editor's Note in *Sha'are mizraḥ*" (*Gates of the East*) 341
Rafael Uziel, "On the Discords among the Jews of Izmir" 341
1853
Giuseppe Levi and Esdra Pontremoli, "*L'educatore Israelita*: A Newspaper of Readings for Jewish Families. Compiled by the Teachers Giuseppe Levi and Esdra Pontremoli" 342
1860
Ezekiel Gabay, "From the Editor, *El Jurnal israelit*" 343
1861
Daniel Neufeld, "Editorial about Jews in the American Civil War" 344
Daniel Neufeld, "The Hebrew Crusading Newspaper" 345
1862
Al. K., "Response to a Writer's Letter in *Jutrzenka*, January 3, 1862" 346
Shiye Mordkhe Lifshits, *Yudl and Yehudis* 347
1863
Urye Kahan and Alexander Zederbaum, "A Few Remarks Regarding the Education of Women" 349
Shiye Mordkhe Lifshits, "The Four Classes" 351
Daniel Neufeld, "Progress: The Meaning of Passover" 352
Alexander Zederbaum, "A Great Announcement" 353
1864
Abraham Harkavy, "A Few Words Concerning Literary Criticism" 354
Berish Rozenblum and Menashe Margolis, "A Story about a Rabbi, Followed by a Letter (in *Kol mevaser*)" 358
1865
Sholem Yankev Abramovitsh (Mendele Mokher Sforim), "The Association 'Concern for the Needy'" 360
1866
A. Grodner, "Yidishe Mitsves" ("Jewish Good Deeds") 361
1867
Alexander Zederbaum, "Keter Kehunah: On the Seer's Fall" 362
1868
Fabius Mieses, "Milḥemet ha-dat" ("Religious War") 362

1869

Sholem Yankev Abramovitsh (Mendele Mokher Sforim), "Fishke the Lame"   363

Israel Leon Grosglik, "Letters of a Young Ex-Hasid"   365

1874

Moritz Hartmann, "Impressions of the Prague Revolution"   367

1875

Isidoro Epstein, "Why Our Forefather Adam Had to Bite the Apple"   369

1877

Sa'adi Besalel a-Levi, "How Does a Newspaper Survive?"   369

Anonymous, "Letter Addressed to the Conference of Constantinople in Favor of the Jews of the Orient"   370

Ilya Orshanski, "The Russification of Jews"   371

1878

Sholem Yankev Abramovitsh (Mendele Mokher Sforim), *The Brief Travels of Benjamin the Third*   372

James Sanua, "The Journey of the Holy Man Abou Naddara Zarqa from Cairo the Victorious to Paris the Glorious"   374

VISUAL AND MATERIAL CULTURE

Introduction   377

MATERIAL CULTURE   378

EIGHTEENTH CENTURY

Amulet for the Protection of Pregnant Women and Newborn Children (Artist Unknown)   378

Omer Calendar (Artist Unknown)   379

1748

Huppah (Artist Unknown)   380

1753

Inventory of Household Goods of Nathan Levy   381

1754

Ketubah (Artist Unknown)   382

1760–1770

Snuff Box (Myer Myers)   383

1765–1776

Torah Finials (Myer Myers)   383

1766

Torah Shield (Ze'ev, Son of Abraham [?])   384

CA. 1769–1776

Hanukkah Lamp (Rötger Herfurth)   385

CA. 1770

Wedding Riddle (Artist Unknown)   386

1772–1773

Curtain and Valance for Torah Ark (Jacob Koppel Gans)   387

1775

Torah Crown (Wilhelmus Angenendt)   388

CA. 1775

Sukkah Decoration (Israel David Luzzatto)   389

1778

Henriette Herz as Hebe (Anna Dorothea Lisiewska-Therbusch)   390

CA. 1780

Jewish Burial Society (Artists Unknown)   391

1794

Portrait of Benjamin S. Judah (Ralph Earl)   392

1795

Cup and Saucer with Portrait of Isaac Daniel Itzig and His Residence (Artist Unknown)   393

1798

Oldest Jewish Cemetery in America (Photographer Unknown)   394

LATE EIGHTEENTH–EARLY NINETEENTH CENTURY

Torah Ark Curtain, Gördes, Turkey (Artist Unknown)   395

CA. 1800

Hand-Washing Basin (Artist Unknown)   396

1802

Portrait of Giacomo Meyerbeer as a Boy (Friedrich Georg Weitsch)   397

1803

Portrait of Amalie Beer (Johann Karl Kretschmar)   398

CA. 1805
Circumcision Bench (Artist Unknown)   399

1806
Medal in Honor of the Grand Sanhedrin of Napoleon (Alexis Joseph Depaulis and Augustin Dupré)   399

1814
Torah Binder (Koppel ben Moses Heller)   400

CA. 1819
Alms Container (Artist Unknown)   400

1820
Illustrated Daily Prayer Book (Hijman [Ḥayim ben Mordecai] Binger, with Marcus and Antonie Binger)   401

CA. 1824
Grace Mendes Seixas Nathan (Mrs. Simon Nathan) and Her Son Seixas Nathan (William James Hubard)   401

1826
Medal from Dedication of the Munich Synagogue in 1826 (I. W. Loewenbach)   402
Torah Curtain (Artist Unknown)   402

1830
Jewish Women from Izmir Whitewashing (Artist Unknown)   403

1832
Portrait of Cecilie Freiin von Eskeles (Friedrich von Amerling)   403
Saada, the Wife of Abraham Benchimol and Preciada, One of Their Daughters (Eugène Delacroix)   404

1837
Feuchtwanger Cent (Lewis Feuchtwanger)   404

1838
Chart of Gems from *A Popular Treatise on Gems* (Lewis Feuchtwanger)   405
Wedding Sofa (Artist Unknown)   406

1838–1839
Shiviti (Moses Ganbash)   406

1840
Medal Commemorating Sir Moses Montefiore (Artist Unknown)   407

CA. 1845
Ewer and Basin (Artist Unknown)   407

1847
Ketubah (Artist Unknown)   408

1848
Paper Cut—Mizraḥ (Moses Michael Rosenboim)   409

1849
H. M. King Leopold I Stamp, Belgium (Jacques Wiener)   410
The Music Room of Fanny Hensel (Julius Helfft)   410

CA. 1850
Esther Scroll (Artist Unknown)   411

1855
Tombstone (Artist Unknown)   411

1855–1856
Burial Comb and Nail Pick of the Bischitz Burial Society   412

1858–1859
Paper Cut—Shiviti Sign (Artist Unknown)   412

1859
Ketubah (Artist Unknown)   413

1860
Medal of Appreciation (Wenzel Seidan)   413
Torah Scroll and Case (Artist Unknown)   414

CA. 1860
Kiddush Cup and Wine Carafe (Daniel Henriques de Castro)   415

1861
Postage Stamp (Jacob Abraham Jesurun)   415

1861–1862
Amulet for Bitoul Ada (Artist Unknown)   416

1862
Medal—St. Stephanskirche (Jacques Wiener)   416
Paper Cut—Brit Milah (Nachman ha-Kohen Bialsker)   417

1863
Ketubah (Zemah Davidsohn)   417

1864
Alms Plate (Artist Unknown)   418
A Jewish Tailor (Mark Antokolski)   418

Medal with the Image of Judith and Moses Montefiore (Charles Wiener)   419

1864–1867
Minute Book of Psalms Society Serving in the Russian Army   420

1865
Medal Commemorating the Opening of the Dutch Jewish Orphanage in Amsterdam (Jacques Elion)   421

1867–1880
Paper Cut—Yortsayt (Artist Unknown)   422

1871
Ivan the Terrible (Mark Antokolski)   423

1876
Religious Liberty Monument (Moses Ezekiel)   424

1887
Ketubah (Artist Unknown)   425

SYNAGOGUE ARCHITECTURE   426

1730 AND 1818
Shearith Israel Synagogue   426

1763
Touro Synagogue, Newport, Rhode Island   427

1789–1790
Synagogue in the Park at Wörlitz, Germany   428

EIGHTEENTH CENTURY
Janów Sokólski Synagogue   429

1820–1821
Óbuda Synagogue   430

1838
Interior of the Beth Elohim Synagogue, Charleston, South Carolina (Solomon Nunes Carvalho)   431

1854–1859
Dohány Street Synagogue   432

1863–1864
Grand Synagogue of Lyon (Abraham Hirsch)   433

1867–1876
Grand Synagogue of Paris (Alfred-Philibert Aldrophe)   434

FINE ART   435

1745
Theresa Concordia Mengs, *Self-Portrait*   435

1765
Martha Isaacs (Attributed), *Portrait of David Tevele Schiff, Chief Rabbi of London*   435

1767
Anton Raphael Mengs, *Annunciation*   436

1770
Anton Raphael Mengs, *Portrait of the Marquesa de Llano*   436

1812
Charles Towne, *Landscape with Figures*   437

1813
Henschel Brothers (Gebrüder Henschel), *Triumph des Jahres 1813 (Triumph of the Year 1813)*   438

1819
Philipp Veit, *Religion*   439

CA. 1820S
Jeremiah David Alexander Fiorino, *Portrait of a Girl with a Red Belt*   439

1833–1834
Moritz Daniel Oppenheim, *The Return of the Jewish Volunteer from the Wars of Liberation to His Family Still Living in Accordance with Old Customs*   440

1838
Solomon Alexander Hart, *An Early Reading of Shakespeare*   440

1842
Charlotte von Rothschild, *Passover Haggadah with German Translation*   441

1850
Solomon Alexander Hart, *The Feast of the Rejoicing of the Law at the Synagogue in Leghorn, Italy*   442

1851
Rudolf Lehmann, *Portrait of Leo Lehmann*   443
Salomon Leonardus Verveer, *Townview with Bell Tower in the Background*   443

1854
Solomon Nunes Carvalho, *Portrait of Wakara*　444

1855
Abraham Solomon, *First Class—The Meeting*　444

1857
Abraham Solomon, *Waiting for the Verdict*　445

1859
Friedrich Friedländer, *People Pouring out of a Public Building into the Street*　445

1860
Henry Mosler, *Canal Street Market*　446

1861
Aleksander Lesser, *The Funeral of the Five Victims*　446
Rebecca Solomon, *The Arrest of the Deserter*　447

CA. 1865–1870
Maurits Leon, *Spinoza before His Judges*　448

1867
Jacques-Émile-Édouard Brandon, *Sermon of the Fast of Av (Synagogue of Amsterdam)*　449
Édouard Moyse, *The Grand Sanhedrin*　450
Simeon Solomon, *Carrying the Scrolls of the Law*　451

1869
Moritz Daniel Oppenheim, *The Bar Mitzvah Discourse*　451

CA. 1869
Alberto Henschel, *Negersklavin Bahia (Black Slave Bahia)*　452

CA. 1860S
Julius Muhr, *Fisherman's Wife Mourning at the Shore*　452

1870
Jacques-Émile-Édouard Brandon, *Heder (Jewish Children's School)*　453

1870–1871
Alphonse Lévy, *"L'aigle déplumé! . . ." (The Bald Eagle!)*　453

1872
Eduard Julius Friedrich Bendemann, *Jeremiah and the Fall of Jerusalem*　454

Jozef Israëls, *The Last Breath*　454

1873
Camille Pissarro, *Factory near Pontoise*　455
Camille Pissarro, *Self-Portrait*　456

1875–1876
Tina Blau, *Jewish Street in Amsterdam*　457

1876
Max Liebermann, *The Dutch Sewing School*　458

1877
Camille Pissarro, *A Road in the Woods in Summer*　458

1878
Maurycy Gottlieb, *Jews Praying in the Synagogue on Yom Kippur*　459
Ernst Josephson, *David and Saul*　459

1878–1879
Maurycy Gottlieb, *Christ Preaching at Capernaum*　460

1879
Max Liebermann, *The Twelve-Year-Old Jesus in the Temple with the Scholars*　460
Henry Mosler, *Return of the Prodigal Son*　461

CA. 1880
Camille Pissarro, *The Avenue de l'Opéra, Sunlight, Winter Morning*　462

DATE UNKNOWN
Benjamin-Eugène Fichel, *At the Restaurant*　463
Friedrich Friedländer, *The Death of Tasso*　463
Henry Mosler, *Drawings Published in Harper's*　464
Geskel Salomon, *Ferdinand II, 1810–1859 Bourbon King of Two Sicilies*　464

THE PERFORMING ARTS

Introduction　465

THEATER　466

1819
Isaac Harby, *Alberti: A Play in Five Acts*　466
Mordecai Manuel Noah, *She Would Be a Soldier, or, the Plain of Chippewa; An Historical Drama in Three Acts*　467

1823
Michael Beer, *The Paria: A Tragedy in One Act* 468

1826
Joseph Ha-Efrati, *Melukhat Sha'ul (The Kingdom of Saul)* 470

1839
Solomon Ettinger, *Serkele* 470

1847
Abraham Daninos, *The Pleasure Trip of Sweethearts Reunited after the Agonies of Love Unrequited in the City of Tiryaq in Iraq* 471

CA. 1848
Poster of Rachel Félix 473

1862
Moses Samuel Konfino, *The Song of Our Forefather Jacob and His Sons* 473

1866
Adah Isaacs Menken, *Portrait of Adah Isaacs Menken* 476

1873
Anonymous, *The Fake Doctor* 476

1881
Abraham Goldfaden, *Shulamis* 479

DATE UNKNOWN
Israel Aksenfeld, *Recruits* 481

OPERA 484

1790
Lorenzo Da Ponte, *Così Fan Tutte* 484

1831
Giacomo Meyerbeer, *Robert le diable* 485

1835
Jacques-François-Fromental-Élie Halévy, *La juive* 486

1841
Jacques-François-Fromental-Élie Halévy, *La reine de Chypre* 487

1846
Eduard Magnus, *Portrait of the Singer Jenny Lind (the "Swedish Nightingale")* 487

1849
Giacomo Meyerbeer, *Le prophète* 488

1866
Jacques Offenbach, The Brazilian's Song from the Opera *La vie parisienne* 488

1867
Jacques Offenbach, *La Grande-Duchesse de Gérolstein* 489

1870
Anton Rubinstein, *Der Thurm zu Babel (The Tower of Babel)* 490

CA. 1870
Adolf Gustaw Sonnenfeld, "Kantorzysta: Polka na fortepiano, op. 68" 490

1875
Karl Goldmark, *The Queen of Sheba* 491

1880–1881
Jacques Offenbach, *Tales of Hoffmann* 491

DATE UNKNOWN
Geskel Salomon, *Drawing of Costume for Vitka in the First Production of the Opera Dalibor by Bedřich Smetana* 492

MUSIC 493

CA. 1790
Levi Isaac of Berdichev, "A Din Toyre mit Gott/Der kadish fun rabi Levi Yitshok" ("A Court Case with God/The Kaddish of Rabbi Levi Isaac") 493

CA. 1800
Anonymous, "La vocación de Abraham" 493
Shneur Zalman of Liady, "Niggun of Four Stanzas" 493

1815
Isaac Nathan, "Song Settings for the Poet Lord Byron's *Hebrew Melodies*" 494

1827
Michael Joseph Guzikov, "Shir hama'alot" ("Song of Ascents") 494

CA. 1831
Artist Unknown, *Marsch der Israelitischen national Garde in Warschau* 495

1841
Fanny Mendelssohn Hensel, with Wilhelm Hensel, "Duette: Mein Liebchen, wir sassen beisammen (Duet: My Sweetheart, We Sat Together)" 495

1844
Charles-Valentin Alkan, "Ancienne melodie de la synagogue" 496

1847
Giacomo Meyerbeer, "Hallelujah: Eine Cantatine für 4 Männerstimmen mit begleitung einer obligaten orgel und des chores ad libitum" 496
Samuel Naumbourg, "Seu Shearim (Lift Up Your Heads, O Gates)" 497
Moses L. Penha, "Esther's Triumph" 497

1850
Israel Moses Ḥazan, "Kerakh shel romi" ("City of Rome") 497

1853
Louis Gottschalk, "The Water Sprite—Polka" 499

1859
Charles-Valentin Alkan, *Super flumina Babylonis,* 499

CA. 1868
Mikhl Gordon, "Whisky" 500

1871
Pesach-Elijah Badkhn, "Songbird, or Six Folk Songs" 501

1874
Samuel Naumbourg, *Aggudat Shirim* 502

1875
Elyokum Tsunzer, "Song of the Railway" 502

1876
Louis Lewandowski, "Psalm 92, Od yenuvun" ("They Shall Still Bring Forth") 503
Samuel Naumbourg, Title Page for His Version of Salamone de Rossi's *Hashirim asher le-Shelomoh (The Songs of Solomon)* 504

1877
Abraham Baer, "Baal T'fillah: Oder, Der practische Vorbeter" ("Prayer Leader: Or The Practical Litanist") 504

1886
Salomon Sulzer, "Statement upon the Publication of *Denkschrift an die hochgeehrte Wiener israelitische Cultus-Gemeinde (Memorandum to the Esteemed Viennese Israelite Religious Community)*" 505

DATE UNKNOWN
Elyokum Tsunzer, "The Flower" 505

Credits 507

Index of Authors and Artists 521

Advisory Boards

General Advisory Board

    Deborah Dash Moore, Editor in Chief
    James E. Young, Founding Editor
    Michel Abitbol
    Robert Alter
    Yehuda Bauer
    Menachem Brinker z"l
    Rachel Elior
    Moshe Halbertal
    Paula E. Hyman z"l
    Sara Japhet
    Yosef Kaplan
    Nadav Na'aman
    Fania Oz-Salzberger
    Antony Polonsky
    Jonathan D. Sarna
    Anita Shapira
    A. B. Yehoshua
    Steven J. Zipperstein

Advisory Board for Volume 6

    David Assaf
    Emily D. Bilski
    Michah Gottlieb
    Hillel J. Kieval
    James Loeffler
    Maurice Samuels
    Jeffrey Veidlinger
    Beth S. Wenger

Project Staff

Posen Library of Jewish Culture and Civilization, Volume 6

Editor in Chief	Deborah Dash Moore
Founding Editor	James E. Young
Volume Editor	Elisheva Carlebach
Executive Editor	Joyce Rappaport
Managing Editor	Rachel M. Weinstein
Senior Editor	Alison Joseph
Senior Editor	Maud Kozodoy
Senior Editorial Assistant	Avery Robinson
Editorial and Operations Assistant	Henry Rosen
Manuscript Coordinator	Marsha Lustigman
Text Permissions Manager	Melissa Flamson
Art Permissions Managers	Fred Wasserman
	Elisa Frohlich Gallagher

Posen Foundation

President and Founder	Felix Posen
Managing Director	Daniel Posen

Yale University Press

Executive Editor	Sarah Miller
Commissioning Editor	Jonathan Brent
Managing Editor	Ann-Marie Imbornoni
Editorial Assistant	Ashley E. Lago
Production Controller	Maureen Noonan
Production Editor, Newgen North America	Charlie Clark

Acknowledgments

This volume began with the vision of Felix Posen to open the Jewish cultural panorama in all its aspects to those who wished to learn more about it but were deterred by barriers of language and the fragmented nature of the sources. The Posen Library would represent Jewish culture broadly conceived in an accessible format. His unwavering commitment to the project, to excellence in all its dimensions, and to editorial freedom have allowed me to embark on an unparalleled adventure of learning and discovery. I thank him and Danny Posen for their steadfast interest and support. Jesse Tisch at the Posen Foundation turned conferences of editors from a chore into a pleasure.

Over the many years that this project required, I have benefited from the wisdom and interest of many colleagues. I thank James E. Young, the first editor in chief of the Posen Library, and the advisory board of the project for paving the way. Many colleagues encouraged me when I first set out: Shmuel Feiner, Michael Stanislawski, Jonathan D. Sarna, and the late and much-missed Paula E. Hyman urged me to persevere and provided valuable advice. I could not have done this volume without the extraordinary group of scholars who made up its board of advisors. Professors David Assaf, Emily D. Bilski, Michah Gottlieb, Hillel J. Kieval, James Loeffler, Maurice Samuels, Jeffrey Veidlinger, and Beth S. Wenger gave unstintingly from their storehouses of knowledge, assisting with selections and with the introduction to the volume. Francesca Bregoli, Maoz Kahana, and Julia Phillips Cohen served as consultants; and Mayer Juni, Gosha Zaremba, David Bunis, Philippe Girard, Jacob J. Schacter, and Nancy Sinkoff contributed to the volume in their areas of specialization, greatly enriching its scope with their knowledge and linguistic expertise.

Jordan Katz, Gilana Keller, Roni Meiseles, Daniel Nerenberg, Aliza Tanzar, Haley Wodenshek, and Rishauna Zumberg provided valuable research assistance at various stages of this volume. The staffs at the Library of the Jewish Theological Seminary, the New York Public Library Dorot Jewish Division, the Center for Jewish History, and the Columbia University Libraries provided gracious assistance in tracking down materials for this volume.

In the past few years, the Posen Library project acquired a top-notch team of specialists in various areas. I am grateful for their professionalism, their dedication, and their keen attention to detail. Marsha Lustigman served as manuscript coordinator, no small task in a manuscript of this complexity. Melissa Flamson and her team at With Permission tracked down the copyright holders for the many texts in this volume, while Fred Wasserman and Elisa Frohlich Gallagher served as art permissions managers. Tracking down permissions sometimes required the skills of a detective. Their wise suggestions of replacements for items for which permission was not forthcoming saved the volume from many omissions. Michele McKay Aynesworth, Amanda Burstein, David E. Cohen, Dina Danon, Maia Evrona, Sonia Gollance, Alyssa Hauer, Magdalene Klassen, Katke Reszke, Yosef Robinson, Sebastian Schulman, and Fred Wasserman wrote most of the biographies for the volume. Michele McKay Aynesworth, Olga Borovaya, and David E. Cohen went out of their way to provide excellent translations of difficult texts. Katharine Halls translated and helped select the Arabic materials.

I owe very special and heartfelt thanks to Rachel Weinstein. Just as I was beginning to despair of completing the project, Rachel was brought on. Her enthusiasm, her willingness to help me surmount every problem, her organizational brilliance, and her tenacity and good cheer were the pivot for this project, moving from the stage of vague dream to completion. For teaching me many valuable lessons that will outlive the production of a volume, I want to say, "Elef todot, Rachel!"

Joyce Rappaport had the unenviable task of coordinating every part of the volume—assigning translations and biographies, editing and coordinating the styles of dozens of different contributors, and editing and polishing the manuscript into a coherent whole. Her skill and devotion, her patience and prodding, are evident on every page.

Deborah Dash Moore has been an energetic and responsive editor in chief of the Posen Library. Her wise counsel and detailed comments serve as a model for how this work is done.

Despite the efforts of this wonderful team, errors and omissions will surely remain. It is the hope of all those who labored over this Library that the value of having these materials accessible in one volume will transcend any flaws that remain.

Elisheva Carlebach
New York City

Introduction to the Posen Library of Jewish Culture and Civilization

Deborah Dash Moore and James E. Young

In 2003 Felix Posen had an audacious idea and the wherewithal to explore it. Born in Berlin, he subsequently abandoned the religious strictures of his youth in the face of the evil of the Holocaust. Then, in his fifties, he decided to learn about the antisemitism that had threatened his life. He began to read about it. "I learned; I listened; I attended lectures," he recalled. "I had the good fortune of befriending one of the world's greatest experts, Yehuda Bauer, who also happened to be the head of something I had never heard of—an Israeli movement in secular Judaism." Those years of reading and learning and that particular encounter ultimately prompted Felix Posen to convene a conference of prominent Jewish scholars and intellectuals. Having prospered in business, he possessed the wherewithal to establish the Posen Foundation to further Jewish education. Thus Felix Posen began a new life in philanthropy. He was able to underwrite not only a conference but also an ambitious project that imagined anchoring Jewish unity in the very multiplicity of the Jewish past. "Each generation must struggle to make sense of its legacy," he reflected. Out of that initial conference emerged a vision of an anthology of Jewish culture and civilization, one that would make more apparent Judaism's immense diversity over the centuries, extending far beyond the parameters of religious orthodoxy. In short, he came to share an understanding of Judaism articulated by the influential biblical scholar Israel Friedländer. In 1907 Friedländer, a recent immigrant to New York City, had observed that American Jews possessed the opportunity to return to Judaism's "original function as a culture, as the expression of the Jewish spirit and of the whole life of the Jews."

The idea of an anthology implicitly drew upon a long and rich Jewish history dating back to the Bible itself, the most influential of Jewish anthologies, and including many classic Jewish texts, such as Mishnah and Talmud, as well as the prayer book. Anthologizing can be seen as a quintessential Jewish practice because of the ways it extends Jewish conversations backward and forward in time. Backward, because anthologizers must read and judge Jewish texts from previous eras, selecting some, rejecting others. And forward, because anthologizers seek to create new understandings that will shape the Jewish future, contributing to an ongoing dialogue. David Stern, editor of *The Anthol-*

ogy in Jewish Literature, argues that the anthology is a ubiquitous presence in Jewish literature—arguably its oldest literary genre. Jewish literature reflects what Stern calls an "anthological habit," that is, a tendency to gather together "discrete and sometimes conflicting stories or traditions." David Roskies dubs this Jewish predilection "the anthological imagination." The *Posen Library of Jewish Culture and Civilization* partakes of both "habit" and "imagination," with the latter often transforming the former. Unlike some past Jewish anthologies, the Posen Library makes no effort to weave together its varied components into a teleological whole.

During the Jewish Middle Ages, anthologies became primary mediums for recording stories, poems, and interpretations of classical texts. They also preserved and transmitted textual traditions across generations. For example, every year at Passover when Jews sat down to conduct a seder, they read from the Haggadah. This Jewish creation is a wonderful anthology that has been continually reinvented—illustrated, translated, modified—to reach new generations.

Yet even as the *Posen Library of Jewish Culture and Civilization* shares in a long and venerable anthological tradition, it also participates in its own moment in time. It is a product of the twenty-first century and the flowering of secular academic Jewish studies in Israel, the United States, and around the world. Its approach to Jewish culture and civilization reflects a new appreciation of Jewish diversity that, for example, embraces women alongside men. Unlike most previous Jewish anthologies, the Posen Library recognizes that both women and men created Jewish culture, although the contributions of women have largely been unacknowledged. The Posen Library's distinguished editorial board reflects contemporary Jewish diversity and includes many of this generation's leading scholars and thinkers in Jewish culture: Michel Abitbol, Robert Alter, Yehuda Bauer, Menachem Brinker (z"l), Rachel Elior, Moshe Halbertal, Paula E. Hyman (z"l), Yosef Kaplan, Sara Japhet, Nadav Na'aman, Fania Oz-Salzberger, Antony Polonsky, Jonathan D. Sarna, Anita Shapira, A. B. Yehoshua, and Steven J. Zipperstein. Together with Felix Posen, this eminent editorial board invited James E. Young to serve as editor in chief of an ambitious anthology project dedicated to the collection of primary texts, documents, images, and artifacts constituting Jewish culture and civilization, from ancient times to the present.

In consultation with the editorial board, James Young prepared a working project outline and précis and appointed individual volume editors with special expertise in particular eras. The précis articulated three important criteria:

1. to gather into a single, usable collection all that the current generation of scholars agrees best represents Jewish culture and civilization in its historical and global entirety;
2. to establish an inclusive and pluralistic definition of Jewish culture and civilization in all of its rich diversity, an evolving amalgam of religious and secular experience;
3. to provide a working anthological legacy by which new generations will come to recover, know, and organize past, present, and future Jewish cultures and civilizations.

While this mandate appeared broad and compelling, the actual task of fulfilling it proved daunting. Gradually, the passing years revealed the immensity of the *Posen Library of Jewish Culture and*

Civilization, involving enormous challenges to find, select, translate, organize, conceptualize, and introduce artifacts and documents that constituted Jewish culture over the ages. The tasks produced changes in leadership. In 2016 James Young assumed the position of founding editor in chief, having launched the Posen Library, and Deborah Dash Moore accepted responsibilities of editor in chief. Current editors of the ten volumes of the *Posen Library of Jewish Culture and Civilization* are Jeffrey H. Tigay and Adele Berlin (Volume 1); Seth Schwartz (founding editor), Carol Bakhos (Volume 2); Menahem Ben-Sasson (founding editor), Ora Limor and Israel Jacob Yuval (founding coeditors), Arnold E. Franklin (Volume 3); Ora Limor and Israel Jacob Yuval (founding coeditors), Yaacov Deutsch (past coeditor), Jonathan S. Ray (Volume 4); Yosef Kaplan (Volume 5); Elisheva Carlebach (Volume 6); Eli Lederhendler (founding editor), Israel Bartal and Kenneth B. Moss (Volume 7); Todd M. Endelman and Zvi Gitelman (Volume 8); Samuel D. Kassow and David G. Roskies (Volume 9); and Deborah Dash Moore and Nurith Gertz (Volume 10). These volume editors invited specialists from across diverse genres and geographies in varied disciplines and eras to serve as members of their respective volumes' advisory boards. This collective of some 150 of the world's leading scholars of Jewish culture continues to cull examples of expressions of Jewish culture and civilization from around the world, from antiquity to the twenty-first century.

It is with great pleasure on behalf of all who are assembling the *Posen Library of Jewish Culture and Civilization* to present *Confronting Modernity, 1750–1880*, edited by Elisheva Carlebach, one of ten volumes constituting the massive *Posen Library of Jewish Culture and Civilization* to be published with Yale University Press.

The job of the anthologizer is far from easy. Not only does it involve sifting through many potential historical, philosophical, religious, legal, literary, exegetical, political, folkloristic, popular, and artistic documents, images, and artifacts that might be chosen and extracted. It also requires conceptualizing key themes that characterize each period under consideration. And that process introduces questions about the production of Jewish culture and civilization. Is Jewish culture global, or is it an aggregate of many local Jewish cultures, each of them formed and defined in the interaction between Jewish and surrounding non-Jewish cultures? Are there essential Jewish qualities to Jewish culture, or is Jewish culture itself a dialectic between "adaptation and resistance to surrounding non-Jewish cultures," as David Biale has suggested in his *Cultures of the Jews*? Or should Jewish culture be regarded as something that is produced mostly in relationship to itself, its own traditions and texts, as David G. Roskies argued in his review of Biale's volume of essays?

Each volume editor has proffered somewhat different answers to those questions. Some have stressed the experience of Judaism as a minority culture in constant contact and occasional conflict with majority civilizations. Others have emphasized the remarkable internal dynamic of Jewish creativity, responding to developments across time and space. Still others have noted the importance of geography and related political structures, dividing Jews from one another and fostering rather separate and even insular modes of cultural creativity. Historically, any number of distinctive and parallel Jewish civilizations have flourished, some sharing cultural practices and traditions, some with little in common beyond core religious laws and beliefs. Working answers to such fundamental questions as, What is Jewish culture and civilization? are embedded in the multitude of entries selected by individual volume editors and their expert advisory boards. Each volume's extracts allow a reader to savor myriad juxtapositions of materials that often illuminate the familiar through the unfamiliar, or, conversely, introduce what is new and unexpected by placing it in conversation with what is well known. Insofar as any culture is itself a composite of multiple peoples, nations, languages, traditions, and beliefs, the Posen Library's volume editors have emphasized the heterogeneity of Jewish culture and civilization.

The Posen Library builds upon the efflorescence of university-based Jewish scholarship of the twentieth century, especially in Israel and the United States. It is heir to debates on the meanings of Jewish culture and Jewish civilization. In the United States, those debates often pictured culture as gendered female and civilization as masculine. Thus civilization evoked machines, work, politics, and technology often associated with cities. Culture suggested nonutilitarian activities, such as the arts, personal refinement, formal higher education, and religion. Nations produced civilizations; peoples nourished cultures. The fact that the title of the Posen Library references both culture and civilization indicates a critical openness to aspects of this binary formulation. It implicitly reflects a consciousness that Jews often had to struggle to gain recognition from others that they possessed a civilization. And it envisions a measure of reciprocity. The Posen anthology project aims for inclusivity and pluralism—"culture" understood both in its anthropological and in its literary senses, referring to products of everyday life as well as to religious and elite artistic and philosophical work. The inclusion of "civilization" refers to an interest in political, economic, and social dimensions of Jewish life. The Posen Library champions a perspective that is less hierarchical and more egalitarian, one that embraces multiple points of view.

Heterogeneous and pluralist, the Posen Library nonetheless presents Jewish culture and civilization in the English language, the lingua franca of our age. This means that in addition to being an exercise in Jewish anthologizing, it is an exercise in translation. As does anthologizing, translating has a long and distinguished Jewish history as a means of conveying sacred and secular texts to generations unfamiliar with their original source languages. As Anita Norich has observed in *Writing in Tongues*, "The need for translation in Western culture, and among Jews, is commonly traced to the familiar Tower of Babel story, which is to say that it is traced to the human desire to understand and interpret and the hubris implied in that desire." Translation has kept Jewish traditions alive as Jews have acquired new languages in the various parts of the globe where they have lived. In the twelfth century, the great Jewish scholar Maimonides, in a letter to his translator, Samuel Ibn Tibbon, wrote: "Whoever wishes to translate and purports to render each word literally, and at the same time to adhere slavishly to the order of the word and sentences in the original, will meet with much difficulty. This is not the right method." Rather "the translator should first try to grasp the sense of the subject thoroughly, and then state the theme with perfect clarity in the other language." Creating a Jewish anthology in English means wrestling with the implications of translating Jewish sources into the current world's universal language.

Time, space, and genre are the fundamental organizational units of the Posen Library. These units reflect debates and a measure of consensus that emerged from conferences among the editors. As much as all members of the editorial board admired the intellectual and interpretive insights into Jewish culture and civilization occasioned by a purely thematic organization of these volumes, most also agreed that consistency across all of the volumes, readability, and proper historicization required subordinating thematic interpretations to broad categories of chronology and genre while also taking into account the significance of the diasporic dispersion of Jews around the globe. As a means of "telling" history, thematic chapter heads are clearly the preferred method of historian-authors. But as a means of "showing" what exists in its historical time and place, in the immediate context of other works in a given genre (e.g., art, literature, theater, architecture), thematic categories remain inadequate on their own. Such genres as literature, visual and material culture, and intellectual culture provide an immediate context for comprehension and can be found in all of the volumes. The Posen Library aims not to unify or homogenize Jewish culture. Rather, the anthology reflects as closely as possible multiple, even competing, manifestations of Jewish culture and civilization as they existed in their own temporal and geographic contexts. It recognizes, for example, that while poetry as a genre exists across all the many centuries of Jewish civilization, significant differences separate medieval Hebrew poetry from Yiddish poetry.

The volume editors' responsibility here is to research all that has been regarded as representative of Jewish culture over time, even as they may nominate new expressions of Jewish culture. Perhaps a particular editor thinks that Soutine or Pissarro made Jewish art, or that Kafka wrote Jewish parables, or that Heine wrote Jewish poetry, or that Freud or the Marx brothers or Al Jolson or any of hundreds of others added to Jewish culture. However, editors also have to consider what the Jewish cultural worlds of museums, libraries, and other institutional and scholarly arbiters of culture have decided over time in their exhibitions, archives, and anthologies. As the editors of Volume 10 observed, "Jews make culture and make it Jewish in a variety of ways: through language, references, reception, uses, debates, and performances." Texts chosen can reflect "a broad understanding of culture, including high and low, elite and popular, folk and mass." Examples can be "chosen as representative, illuminating, unusual, influential, or excellent." Accordingly, volume editors looked closely at how previous anthologizers arrived at their lists of Jewish literature, art, and philosophy in their particular times and places. Volume editors engaged in the anthological task in part by consulting other anthologies. Here is evidence of the anthological imagination at work.

How should the issue of non-Jews' participation and even the creation of Jewish culture be answered? This challenging question remained in the hands of the volume editors and their advisory boards. For some members of the advisory board, it was obvious, as Yehuda Bauer insisted, that Jesus' Sermon on the Mount is "so similar to a Jewish text that it is absolutely clear to [him] that this was a Jew speaking to Jews" and would have to be included, even if the original words were subsequently Christianized in the context of their redaction as part of the New Testament and depleted of Jewish meaning. Others, of course, disagreed. Or, consider adaptations that have moved the other way. When Jews employ the products of non-Jewish creativity for Jewish purposes—for example, illuminated Hebrew manuscripts, synagogue architecture, and headstone reliefs—these cultural works take their place as part of Jewish civilization and can be found in the Posen Library.

Thus, the Posen Library presents a model for defining "national culture" as distinct from "nationalist culture." In this approach, a national culture defines itself by its differences and reciprocal exchanges with other cultures, whereas "nationalist culture" portrays itself as sui generis and self-generated. National cultures grow in reciprocal exchanges with others; nationalist cultures partake in a myth of self-containment and self-creation. Unfortunately, we know too well what happens when nations and cultures attempt to purge themselves of all supposedly foreign elements. They become small and sometimes so depleted of inspiration and imagination that they collapse inwardly like hollow shells. By contrast, national cultures continually reinvent and reinvigorate themselves, extending their creativity across new modes of expression.

"No single volume can address the entire sweep of a multifaceted culture and hope to render it in full, in all its layered complexity and dynamism," writes the editor of Volume 6 with a compelling blend of modesty and insight. However, a volume can "trace a trajectory." This volume of the *Posen Library of Jewish Culture and Civilization* takes up the challenge by adopting a perspective that embraces the extraordinary breadth of Jewish cultural creativity during years of rapid transformation. This period saw the expansion of Jewish writers, artists, and thinkers into new arenas, where they produced work often considered lacking in explicit Jewish "content." Instead, they shared a sense of openness and curiosity about possibilities previously unavailable to their Jewish forbears.

The anthologist's task, in this case, is to introduce readers to this exciting, complicated new Jewish world. As Elisheva Carlebach astutely notes, "This volume appears in a series whose title is the *Posen Library*, the latter an apt word, as it intends to provide readers with an experience similar to that of browsing through a curated library collection." She continues: "Regardless of their previous knowledge, readers will encounter familiar landmarks, well-known touchstones of Jewish culture, perhaps even 'usual suspects' previously anthologized. By reverse token," she explains, "all readers are bound to find new treasures, unexpected juxtapositions, previously unknown texts, and objects that will enrich their understanding of the role Jews played in world culture of the period." Both individually and collectively, each volume "tells the tale of a people who refused to sit on the sidelines while others did the work of culture, be it literary, visual, material, musical, or intellectual." Recognition of such energies has inspired the editors of the Posen Library.

All of the editors agreed that visual culture constitutes a major part of Jewish culture and civilization and must be included throughout these volumes, in all its forms. From early synagogue architecture and iconography of ancient texts to later illuminated manuscripts and Haggadahs, Jewish visual culture in its many forms appears in every volume. It ranges from folk art to costume design and eventually encompasses painting, sculpture, photography, film, installation and performance art, as well as museum and later synagogue architecture. In some cases, images may be used to illustrate nonvisual texts; but in most cases, they will be either the actual work (e.g., a painting) itself or images of objects and artifacts being anthologized.

As difficult and complex as it may be to select, extract, and translate every textual entry from its original language into English, or as expensive as it may be to secure the rights to reprint "flat art" images of paintings, sculpture, and architecture, it can also be said that the book form of the volumes itself made the compilation of these literary and visual expressions of culture possible. Unfortunately for the Posen Library, a traditional book excludes motion and sound, and therefore audiovisual works—whether orchestral, theatrical, performative, or cinematic—cannot be heard or seen. Reducing a musical composition to its score, or a theatrical presentation to its written script, or any kind of film performance to still photos radically transforms these pieces into something they simply are not. As a consequence, the Posen Library represents audiovisual media with what amount to annotated lists of music and titles of film and theater presentations.

What strategic purposes animate this effort to collect in a ten-volume anthology all that this generation deems to constitute Jewish culture and civilization? First, the Posen Library seeks to restore consciousness of the diversity and richness of Jewish culture and civilization across many centuries in many lands. Second, it aims to democratize Jewish knowledge, facilitating readers' encounters with varied texts produced by Jewish thinkers, writers, and artists in dozens of languages around the globe. Third, the Posen Library implicitly demonstrates that like Jewish national and diasporic culture, other national and diasporic cultures consist of multiple, often-competing constituent subcultures. Just as Jews express themselves in, participate in, and engage with cultures around the world, and just as those cultures bear the imprint of Jewish culture and experience, so too do many of these other cultures nourish and shape Jewish culture and civilization. Jewish literature and poetry, religious thought and Talmudic commentaries, and even treatises on what constitutes Jewish culture are written in many of the world's languages—in English, Arabic, French, German, Russian, Spanish, Italian, and Persian—as well as in Hebrew, Yiddish, Ladino, Aramaic, and Judeo-Arabic. Jewish culture and civilization live in and are shaped by these cultural and linguistic contexts. Finally, the Posen Library offers otherwise disaffected and disengaged Jews opportunities to restore their cultural identification as Jews. It demonstrates that Jews produced Jewish culture in part through struggles with Jewish identity and tradition, and not only through an embrace of Judaism.

How to Read This Book

This volume includes examples of Jewish cultural and intellectual creativity in the years 1750–1880, by artists, writers, and thinkers who created during that period. The selections appeared originally in many languages—Arabic, Czech, French, German, Hebrew, Hungarian, Italian, Ladino, Polish, Russian, and Yiddish, as well as English—and are published here in English translation. The volume is organized by genre. Within each genre, the selections appear chronologically and within each year alphabetically according to the author's last name. Readers may wish to read the selections sequentially within each genre, as they are presented, or, alternatively, they may wish to move back and forth between the different genres, selecting texts from a particular year or group of years. The former offers perspectives on how Jewish cultural and intellectual life developed over several decades; the latter samples Jewish cultural activity at a particular point in time in the major Jewish communities of the world, allowing for comparative perspectives.

A brief biography of each author accompanies each selection. Some of the authors are well known; many more are familiar only to specialists, and a few are so little known that the details of their lives cannot be recovered. Because a number of writers are represented by more than one selection, this biographical information appears only the first time a writer is included. The index lists multiple selections by a writer, thus enabling readers to find any biography and read all the works by any given author. In addition, each biography ends with a short list of other works by the author. If a work has not been published previously in English, the title of the work is given in its original language with its date of first publication.

This collection focuses on presenting the original works to the English-language reader in the most straightforward manner. Notes and other scholarly apparatus have been kept to a minimum. Editorial deletions are indicated by bracketed ellipsis points. Most of the selections here are brief excerpts from much longer works; we have not included ellipses at the beginning and end of each selection so as not to encumber the reader.

Introduction to Volume 6

Elisheva Carlebach

All of us who were still children thirty years ago can testify to the incredible changes that have occurred both within and outside us. We have traversed, or better still flown through a thousand-year history.
—Isaac Markus Jost, 1833

No single volume can address the entire sweep of a multifaceted culture and hope to render it in full, in all its layered complexity and dynamism. This is particularly true of a volume covering almost a century and a half in which every aspect of Jewish life underwent the most profound changes to have occurred since antiquity. Rather than attempting to be exhaustive, this volume intends to trace a trajectory. Each item, as well as the collection in the aggregate, tells the tale of a people who refused to sit on the sidelines while others did the work of culture, be it literary, visual, material, musical, or intellectual. There is virtually no field of human culture in this period in which Jews only participated enthusiastically; they often pioneered, introducing new techniques, innovative approaches, and fresh ways of looking at the world.

Most often, Jews were able to do this out of the deep wellsprings of Jewish identity and creativity itself. It is no exaggeration to claim that the very concept of a Jewish culture that was not primarily religious arose and was articulated first in the period covered in this volume. A truly Jewish total culture that was secular at heart while incorporating some traditional elements did not come to fruition until the advent of Jewish nationalisms (Zionism and diaspora nationalism), beyond the scope of this volume. What we have before us is a more inchoate and, in some ways, more interesting picture. The breakaway from traditional patterns took place both in the form of an embrace of non-Jewish cultural idioms and forms, on the one hand, and in the conscious reshaping of Jewish traditional culture into something modern, on the other. Both of these movements are in full evidence in this volume. They are intertwined and cannot, and ought not, be easily separated. Often the same artist or writer who made his or her mark in a fully neutral vein also pioneered new modes of representing aspects of Jewish culture. The cultural production of Jewish women and men was often distinctive and original because they were among the first Jews to participate creatively in their fields. This allowed them to bring fresh perspectives into the larger culture. Simultaneously, their efforts remade the very concept of Jewish culture. Thus, the volume does not include only material that looks or sounds "Jewish," however that might be defined. To the contrary, it attempts to represent the full range of cultural creation by Jews regardless of whether such expressions contain identifiably Jewish content. As Richard I. Cohen writes with great insight, "Artists were so involved in their own radical break with Jewish traditional society and pattern, so concerned with coming to grips with the new surroundings into which they had been thrown [...] that much time was needed before a return to the past could be contemplated."[1] Even when writers and artists "returned" to a Jewish past, it was not the same as the primal and original engagement. In the words of Ammiel Alcalay, "The 'Jewish' world depicted becomes just that: subject matter, and not the very material of a way of life that is simply practiced from within."[2]

If there is one thread that connects the multifarious entries in this volume, it is the sense of great possibility and openness. In some parts of the world civil barriers to equality before the law had begun to fall, Jews of the West had finally been granted citizenship, and others believed they would soon follow suit. Jews not only ventured into the world around them but also allowed the world to penetrate their thinking, their dreams, their very definitions of self, in ways they had scarcely done before. In places with large concentrations of Jews, the Jewish population continued to face hostility and prejudice in this period. This volume closes just before some of the worst depredations of the late nineteenth and twentieth centuries were unleashed with violent fury upon the world in general and on the Jews in particular. Thus, this period was one of creativity borne aloft by hope, a sense that the gates of the broader world of culture were finally opening to Jews, that their voices and their contributions could be judged on the basis of merit alone. European Jews embraced the opportunities with dazzling results.

Jews living in the Ottoman Empire, whether in North Africa, the Middle East, or the Balkans, encountered European culture in a far more complex set of circumstances. Just as Western powers spread their imperial message through their culture, their Jewish citizens, newly acculturated themselves, attempted to "enlighten" their indigenous coreligionists in colonial and semicolonial contexts. The synthesis of cultural strands they wove is multilayered and complex. Jewish culture in the Ottoman Empire in the nineteenth century emerged newly invigorated, drawing on the Middle Eastern and Iberian cultures to which it was heir. As European states expanded their footholds within the Ottoman Empire, growing numbers of European merchants settled in the empire, missionaries traveled its length and breadth, and scholars took to the study of its languages and texts.

The effect of Westernization coupled with new avenues for professional advancement changed the face of Ottoman Jewish culture. Although the political and economic fortunes of Jews in Islamic lands declined in the eighteenth century, the classes of merchants whose services were necessary for the Europeans seized the opportunity to advance. They became translators, intermediaries, and agents for European interests. They supported European-style education and vocational training for Jews. French Jews established a vigorous defense organization, the Alliance Israélite Universelle, in 1860 to protect the interests of Jews. This organization established a chain of schools that sought to intensify the Westernization process, opening a rift between Europeanized "francos" and native Jews, who often held different legal status and cultural positions. These developments ultimately accelerated the cultural gap between Jews and local Muslims in much of North Africa and the Middle East.[3]

During the period covered in this volume, Jews lived in and between a changing cast of ambitious empires built at the expense of weaker empires, whether neighbors or distant colonial outposts. The Polish–Lithuanian Commonwealth fell prey to its expanding imperialist neighbors, as Russia, Prussia, and Austria partitioned it out of existence in the last decade of the eighteenth century. As a result, the three-quarters of a million Polish Jews were divided among these empires, with the largest number falling to the tsarist Russian Empire. The Ottoman Empire, which predated all of these, began to sustain serious losses during this period, although it continued to rule over much of the Middle East, North Africa, and southeastern Europe throughout the period covered in this volume. The sun never set on the British Empire in this period; the ambitious French Empire expanded its borders to distant shores, touching Egypt and conquering Algeria by 1830. The Netherlands, Spain, and Portugal engaged in empire building across the Atlantic and in the Pacific, gaining and losing colonies in Asia and the Americas. Cultural and linguistic shifts accompanied each political turn in every one of these polyglot and multiethnic societies. Jews, never a majority and often a marginal minority, were often caught between the shifting borders. Their decisions regarding choice of language, which to write in, or to educate their children in, often had serious political ramifications. What might seem like a curricular preference could easily lead to alienation or even charges of treasonous departure.

When the partition of Poland brought the region of Galicia under Habsburg Austrian rule in 1772, a great population of Yiddish-speaking Polish Jews found themselves virtually overnight in a very different cultural sphere: German-speaking, Enlightenment-influenced, and Catholic rather than Christian Orthodox. Under Austrian influence, many Galician Jews adopted German language and culture, which Poles regarded as a shameful and traitorous choice, and Jewish culture increasingly came under Enlightenment influences, parallel to that of modernizing German Jews. A far greater rupture befell the Polish, Lithuanian, and Ukrainian Jews whose fate was to come under Russian rule. Largely restricted to the western frontier that came to be called the Pale of Settlement, the population of largely Yiddish-speaking Jews suffered the vagaries of an inconsistent and ambivalent government whose policies shifted among measures designed to forcibly integrate, convert, or segregate them.

Beyond the political transfers triggered by imperial brinkmanship, another ubiquitous change supported the emergence of new cultural forms. In the period under consideration, Jews underwent demographic shifts of staggering proportions. In some parts of the world Jewish populations declined while in others, the numbers soared. Particularly noteworthy is the growing number of cities in the Russian and Ottoman empires whose Jewish populations accounted for as much as one-third of the overall population. As Jews left the countryside and small villages for expanding cities, this had a great effect on their cultural production. The urban bustle, the proximity to stimulating images and ideas, the public sphere offered by cafés, parks, boulevards, and taverns in which to exchange views and learn about the lives of others—all these nurtured multiple forms of cultural productivity, both intensely Jewish and decidedly not.

This volume spans the two most foundational events in United States history, the American Revolution of 1776, which liberated the states from British colonial domination, and the Civil War, of 1861–1865, which was fought to unify the states and abolish the way of life made possible by slavery. As Jonathan Sarna and Jonathan Golden say of the American Revolution, it was a turning point not only in world and U.S. history, but in Jewish history as well: "Never before had a major nation committed itself so definitively to the principles of freedom and democracy in general and to religious freedom in particular. Jews and members of other minority religions could dissent from the religious views of the majority without fear of persecution."[4] The years between and around these events saw two primary waves of Jewish immigration to the United States, although no group was exclusive in either period. The first small group of North American Jews arrived as refugees from Recife, Brazil, in 1654. When Brazil fell to Portugal, these Sephardic Jews fled the Inquisition and headed for greater religious freedom in New Amsterdam (later, New York). Others soon followed. The Sephardic pioneers profoundly shaped public Jewish culture through the early nineteenth century. The second wave (ca. 1820–1880) is loosely dubbed the "Central European" migration. Jews fleeing Europe often came from socially disadvantaged classes and adjusting to the opportunities of America took time. Women often ventured beyond home and hearth to help with family finances and ultimately found independent voices in public forums.[5] This created a unique space for cultural production that differed in context and content from the European models.

At the outset of the period covered by this volume, most Jews lived within the framework of religious tradition. Religion constituted one of the primary components of Jewish identity and the central modes of Jewish cultural expression. With some notable exceptions, this had not changed profoundly since the medieval period. Similarly, most Jews lived within Jewish communal structures that governed many aspects of their social lives and civil status. By the end of the nineteenth century, the pillars of these institutions were greatly weakened; in parts of the world they were completely shattered. In the West, as Jews were socially integrated and legally emancipated, community lost its holistic and authoritative structure. In Russia, particularly under the reign of Tsar Nicholas I (1825–1855), conscription of Jewish boys into Cantonist camps at very young ages, and the cooperation of Jewish leaders in providing recruits, made Jews fear and distrust the Jewish communal elite. Although for some Jews breaks with the past occurred almost overnight, for others changes took place far more gradually and imperceptibly. Improvements in the standard of living in the West toward the beginning of the nineteenth century also spurred changes in the cultural lives of Jews. A prosperous middle class that included lawyers, doctors, entrepreneurs, and civic leaders soon emerged as a new type of patron of the arts. In Eastern Europe, Hasidic Jews supported lavish courts for their leaders while deeply traditional Jews continued to support hundreds of yeshivot and study halls where rabbinic scholarship was advanced.

In many parts of the world, as cultural endeavors by Jews were no longer rooted in religion, Jews experimented with different definitions of Jewish identity. The quest to find a positive Jewish identification that was not exclusively religious yielded fascinating and varied new results. This volume traces the course of Jewish culture during a period of constant transformation. For some Jews, this period was marked by the transition into modernity, for others into a new form of colonial rule, and for others yet, a growing confidence that they could put down roots in lands of relative civic equality and freedom. Many of those who steadfastly championed religious tradition could nevertheless be seen as making conscious religious and cultural choices within the marketplace of competing identities, options that were themselves creations of modern times.

The dizzying array of choices about their very identity and the means of expressing it, as well as continuing hostility to Jews and Jewish culture through the nineteenth century, propelled some Jews to abandon their Jewish identities entirely. For others, social, religious, and cultural bonds to Jews and Judaism diminished over the course of generations, leading to a process that Todd M. Endelman has called "drift and defection."[6] This happened frequently enough that conversion out of Judaism in this period can be seen as one of an array of choices made by Jews, one that characterized the Jewish experience in this period no less than intense attachments. Religious conversion to another faith generally led to a historical dead end for an individual's progeny as members of the Jewish people. The volume nevertheless includes the contributions of converts if their work could be seen as having been nourished in some way by their Jewish background. The poet Heinrich Heine, statesman Benjamin Disraeli, composer Felix Mendelssohn Bartholdy, *salonnière* Rahel Varnhagen, Russian schoolteacher Jacob Brafman, and founder of communism Karl Marx provide some of the more renowned examples of this category. In many cases converts knew and interacted with one another, sometimes over several generations, and many placed the struggle to define themselves at the center of their creative work. Familial ties ran strong in convert families who often socialized with one another both out of preference and as a result of subtle discrimination. Their transformations of Jewish identity and the allusive references to it allow us to include such figures in this volume not just because of the accident of their birth, but also because their Jewishness remained an elemental and enduring aspect of their lives, their art, and their work.

Developments over the eighteenth and nineteenth centuries provided more than new opportunities for Jewish encounters with non-Jewish cultures: they completely transformed the fields on which these interactions played out. The traditional templates of Jewish culture as existing within the framework of majority–minority relations, of those who belonged and barely tolerated aliens, receded. Instead, a growing Jewish self-consciousness emerged, with new definitions and articulations of the self. Where premodern life writing by Jews located the self firmly within the communal sphere, Western, and later Eastern European Jewish, autobiography emphasized the individual's break from community and tradition.[7]

Jews embarked on this odyssey along utterly different pathways depending on national community, geography, and individual proclivities. For some Jews, this passage meant mobility from village to urban settings, from economic margins to bourgeois prosperity, from old world to new, and in some parts of the world, from pariah to civic equal. In Western Europe, the demise of the *kehilah* (structured Jewish community) and its traditional authority, largely accomplished over the course of our period, meant the disappearance of a holistic Jewish life and culture that did not depend on the world outside it for validation. It opened the way for Jews to embrace the culture of the majority directly and consciously, and to do so in ways that ranged from the superficial to the profound, from head coverings, facial hair, and dress style to social, linguistic, economic, and occupational choices. Introduced to European philosophy, scientific and intellectual achievements, art, music, and theater, Jews immersed themselves in, and soon mastered, these genres. In nineteenth-century Russia, deep fissures characterized Jewish society. The vast majority of Jews became increasingly impoverished, with limited access to economic and educational means to improve their lot. Wealthier Jews migrated to St. Petersburg, where they lived like urban elites. The best of the Talmud scholars flocked to cities with famous yeshivot, as in Vilna, while a cadre of official rabbis administered to the religious needs of their often disenchanted flocks. By the second half of the nineteenth century, as Nicholas I's reign ended, Jewish ideologues embraced multiple paths designed to bring Russia's Jews to a more dignified existence.

In the Ottoman Empire, a different cultural pathway appeared. Within the Jewish court system traditional rabbinic leaders had to compete with state-supported (or appointed) rabbis. While state backing would appear to have strengthened these rabbinic courts, this was not the case. The rise of new "mixed" state courts alongside the existing Islamic and consular courts, where Jews also historically went to adjudicate various cases, made for a system of legal pluralism that weakened the hold of the Jewish courts over Jews in the empire. Nevertheless, religion resided far more closely with features of modern Western life and this is reflected in the cultural production of the period. The comfortable accommodation of state, religion, and culture in the Muslim sphere contrasted with the antagonistic relationship of state, religion, and culture in the Christian world.[8]

New models of Jewish leadership emerged in this period: maskilic intellectuals, Hasidic rebbes, writers, artists, and a secular intelligentsia. They shared a rejection of the traditional model in which a combination of piety and rabbinic scholarship, with emphasis on the latter, formed the primary basis of authority. By overturning models of leadership, Jews challenged long-standing traditions of hierarchical values in Jewish society.

Two central themes intersect at the very foundations of the Jewish experience in this period. In the West they are traditionally termed Enlightenment and Emancipation. This volume construes these concepts in the broadest possible way, such that they embrace the Jewish experience without borders. The former term refers here to engagement with the larger culture, the adoption of new modes of Jewish self-definition, and a reconfigured relationship to the larger culture. The strong and varied forms of resistance, in many parts of the Jewish world, to such engagement were inextricably intertwined with these developments. The term *emancipation* refers broadly to the constantly shifting relationship of Jews to their states and to the societies of which they formed an integral part. This volume traces the emergence of cultural, religious, and political movements, as well as new individual identities, representations, and expressions of the Jewish self vis-à-vis the community and within the non-Jewish world. These movements and choices often appeared in innovative configurations that had little precedent in Jewish culture. They alternately embraced, rejected, or revised the Jewish elements that emerged from the crucible of self-examination, public deliberation, and the private agony of modernization.

Organization

This volume appears in a series whose title is the Posen Library, the latter an apt word, as it intends to provide readers with an experience similar to that of browsing through a curated library collection. Regardless of their previous knowledge, readers will encounter familiar landmarks, well-known touchstones of Jewish culture, perhaps even "usual suspects" previously anthologized. By reverse token, all readers are bound to find new treasures, unexpected juxtapositions, previously unknown texts, and objects that will enrich their understanding of the role Jews played in world culture of the period. The volume includes culture and civilization both high and low, the familiar and the strange, the exquisite alongside the coarse. It includes voices of women and men calling out to us from the past. They are rich and poor, learned and simple, thrilling or dull—all elements in a glorious collection.

The decision to organize material primarily by genre allows the volume to defy hierarchical and well-known cultural clusters and to encourage readers to make new connections. For example, Nachman of Bratslav, charismatic Hasidic leader in Ukraine; French classicist Auguste Widal (writing under the name Daniel Stauben); and Jacob Frank, Podolian charlatan and messianic pretender, all used inventive tales as the creative vehicle for their teachings. Each set of tales belongs to a different worldview and finds its first context within its own cultural milieu. Yet their juxtaposition in this volume allows us to see something of the appeal of complex storytelling in very different settings of the same period.

Language

One of the complicating and constitutive elements in any discussion of Jewish culture is the question of language and how to convey it in a volume of translated texts. Jews have always been multilingual, but in this period the very choice of languages Jews employed became freighted with ideological weight as never before. Which languages Jews should employ, in which contexts, became the subject of contentious debate and discussion. Most Jews through the eighteenth century employed as the language of their daily discourse, written and oral, a form of the vernacular that differed slightly or entirely from that of their non-Jewish neighbors. The Jewish variation on these vernaculars often contained elements from all strata of classical Jewish culture, including biblical and rabbinic literature, and were sometimes written in Hebrew characters. As the speakers of these languages migrated, they often incorporated new layers and new colorations. Names such as *Judezmo* (another name for Ladino) and *Yiddish* testify to the fact that both Jews and non-Jews viewed these languages as Jewish. Such vernacular Jewish languages, which had been molded and shaped unselfconsciously by Jews, became the subject of fierce public polemic. This contention turned on whether hyphenated or hybrid languages were legitimate in their own right or were imagined versions of some "pure" main language. Some Jews advocated a return to Hebrew, and the argument centered on whether Hebrew, which had been preserved as a sacred language of prayer and rabbinic scholarship, could be adapted for nonsacred writing. Could a language that had been used primarily by rote for prayers, and with comprehension by a small number of scholars, be revived to express the fullness of modern life? If Jewish languages did not suffice for communication in modern times, which would be the best non-Jewish language to employ? In an age of crumbling empires and emerging nationalisms these choices were laden with political and cultural consequences.

As Jewish culture modernized and Westernized, distinctive Jewish languages began to lose their special features, and ultimately many ceased to be used altogether. But their existence is central to the narrative in this volume, because the embrace of these hyphenated Jewish languages, and their acceptance by the writers and literati as languages of literary discourse, opened the way for a secular and vernacular literature that could be understood by more Jews. Thus, as Yiddish became a literary language and secular works were written in it, more traditional Jews had access to these ideas. Similarly, as Ladino became a respectable medium for both religious and secular writers, their ideas could reach a far broader audience.

Just as Yiddish itself was spoken in many regional variants, Sephardic Jews used a rich variety of Judeo-Spanish dialects. In Ottoman southeastern Europe and the Levant, Sephardic Jews spoke a Judeo-Spanish dialect known variously as Ladino and Judezmo, with admixtures from different Romance languages, Hebrew, and other neighboring tongues, such as Turkish, Greek, and Bulgarian. Some variants were even identified with particular cities, such as Salonika and Adrianople (Edirne). Sephardim in northern Morocco spoke their own version of Judeo-Spanish known as Haketia, which had a greater number of Arabic borrowings. Ladino presses arose in mid-eighteenth-century Greece, Turkey, Bulgaria, Mexico, Argentina, and the Middle East; the standardization of the languages began to erase some of the most distinctive variants. The arrival of the Alliance Israélite Universelle introduced French into the mix, although the presses flourished in Ladino throughout the Ottoman era. Linguistic acrobatics characterized Jewish life across the globe. Kurdish Jews used Hebrew for liturgy, neo-Aramaic for paraliturgical occasions such as weddings, and Kurdish for folklore. As they modernized, Arabic became their dominant language.[9]

Another important element in our period is the enormous amount of cultural energy that went into translating non-Jewish texts into and between Jewish languages. The texts in this volume (aside from those that appeared in English first) originally appeared in Hebrew, in hybrid Jewish languages such as Yiddish and Ladino, and in a host of other languages and dialects, including Arabic, Czech, French, German, Hungarian, Italian, Polish, and Russian. The enterprise of translation represents one of the important channels of cross-fertilization and intercultural exchange. The difficulty of conveying language in a volume in which all the texts are presented in translation also provides one of the justifications of this enterprise. Here, for the very first time, these Jewish voices of the past exist in proximity and in conversation with one another and with us.

Literature

Life Writing: Biography, Autobiography, and Ego Documents

The section "Life Writing" can be thought of as snapshots in words, glancing testimonies to Jewish lives.[10] Although first-person accounts are mediated in multiple ways, these excerpts provide us some insight into what it meant to live, and to live as a Jew, in this period. The entries are arranged chronologically. This allows for precisely the unexpected juxtapositions that this volume intends to provoke. The famous and the obscure, women and men, in epitaphs and private letters, ethical wills, cookbooks, and religious reflections, all reflect aspects of Jewish life in a period of great transition.

The literary genre we call autobiography is one of the signal innovations in this period among Jews across the spectrum.[11] The "Life Writing" section includes many accounts that chart the development of the self; an individual's coming of age; his or her realization that the self is formed, in positive and negative ways, by the culture into which it was born; and revelations about the inner journey of the self to become the character who writes. In particular, the self-conscious use of the narrative of a life came into its own as a signature of Enlightenment writing and moved quickly from the European world into Jewish literature. While many Jews continued to write about their private lives in traditional modes, in letters, travel accounts, and rabbinic introductions, the maskilic (Jewish Enlightenment) autobiography in both Western and Eastern Europe became a virtually formulaic literary genre in which the writer depicted, often with humor and pathos, the journey from childhood into adult awareness as parallel to his awakening out of the world of backward and superstitious traditional Jewish life to one of reason and beauty. Haskalah writers targeted the one-room schoolhouse, its boorish teachers and exclusive emphasis on Talmud study, as a failed pedagogical system. They skewered the traditional system of arranged marriages at a young age as contrary to nature and lampooned the general level of ignorance, even as it served as backdrop for their emergence into the light of reason.

Just as the individual figured in writings about the self, so, too, did the genre of biography and admiring hagiography arise in this period. Thus, the philosopher Moses Mendelssohn's acolyte wrote about his life, and Hasidic followers wrote about their masters. Ostensibly worlds apart, the two movements shared a literary genre that elevated the exemplary life of a leader.

Life writing as defined in this volume includes far more than formal narrations of a life in history. It includes every genre of writing that reveals something of the individual life: letters, diaries, and reminiscences of every kind. Jews plied every trade, from the expected (peddler, teacher, homemaker, midwife) to the surprising (Civil War soldier, pugilist, wine merchant). From wealthy merchant slaveholders to the starving and destitute, Jews around the world belonged to every class and expressed something of their lives in their written legacies. Learned philosophers poured out their souls in their personal correspondence while boxers recalled learning their art and women wrote about keeping house on the American frontier. Salon hostesses in Berlin and Vienna, brilliant conversationalists who broke social and class barriers by inviting people of every background into their homes, agonized over their tortured decision to convert out of Judaism. A superb rabbinic scholar erupted in incredulous fury when someone proposed a new match for him shortly after the death of his beloved wife. (Not to worry, dear reader: he recovered and had nine children with the next wife.) Each excerpt presented here provides us with a distant glimpse of the contours of a unique life, a Jewish life, at once greatly removed from our time, yet always human and somehow familiar.

Travel Writing

The proliferation of the press and travel by steamship (and toward the end of the period, railroad) brought descriptions of far-flung parts of the world and reports about Jews living in them from one corner of the globe to another. Accounts in this section were primarily written by people who traveled for the joy of expanding their horizons. They acted on dreams of exploring different civilizations and unfamiliar climates with exotic flora and fauna, accumulating rich experience and colorful impressions that they then recorded in their enduringly appealing works. Jews had always been highly mobile, traveling for commerce, for scholarship, for refuge, and for adventure. As the expense and danger of travel diminished, motives for traveling increased. New forms of pilgrimage arose not only to stone monuments but to human ones as well. People traveled to visit the great savants, even briefly, and bask in their aura. Some had excuses for their peripatetic lives. Rabbi Ḥayim Joseph David Azulai was an emissary, collecting and channeling funds for destitute Jews in his native Holy Land. This did not stop him from visiting zoos, palaces, and gardens as he traversed Europe, Africa, and the Middle East and recorded the details of each place and its people.[12] Samuel Romanelli left Italy, where he was born, and traveled through England and Germany, distinguishing himself as a man of letters in many languages. He is best known for his detailed account of his journey through Morocco. His language drips with condescension when he regards the primitive and exotic Jews of North Africa, but he preserved a priceless picture of their lifeways. Judith Cohen Montefiore traveled the world to advocate for Jews in trouble. She accompanied her husband, Moses, to Russia to protest the expulsion of Jews from Polish border areas. Her travel diary preserves a sense of what the Holy Land was like in the nineteenth century, as she sought to alleviate the neediness of its impoverished Jewish community.

Joseph Solomon Lutski was a leader of nineteenth-century Karaites, venerable Jewish sectarians. He petitioned the tsar to exempt the Karaites from the Cantonist decrees (1825) that required Jews to deliver young boys to be trained in the tsarist army. Most never returned home. His *Epistle* recounting his travels opens the panorama of the Russian Empire, with St. Petersburg and its fabulous palaces. His Hebrew account was published along with a Judeo-Tatar translation, the vernacular of his Crimean people.[13]

Christian Hebraists with interest and curiosity in antiquities and exploration contributed as well to the impetus for contact and research into the conditions of Jewish communities that had grown apart from the mainstream Jewish world. Among the former we may count the Samaritans (who figured prominently in the Christian Bible), Karaites, Khazars, as well as the Falasha of Ethiopia and the Jews of Kai Feng in China. Jews traveled for many reasons, and travel brought with it a sense of Jewish lifeways that differed radically around the world. In the farthest outposts, new permutations of Jewish identity remained to be discovered.

Folktales and Fiction

The "return to history" of Jews in the eighteenth and nineteenth centuries and engagement between Jews and their majority cultures offered new models for imaginative writing beyond those within their ancestral traditions. Belles lettres were cultivated by Jews in many cultural milieus in the past, but perhaps none with the ardor and all-encompassing passion of this period in which literature became one of the chief ways of entering (as well as countering) modernity. Far more than in other realms of cultural creativity, such as visual fine arts and music, Jewish writers tended to engage with openly Jewish characters, themes, and stories. Jews of the past wrote polemics and poetry, midrash and miracle tales, scholarship and manuals, but they had not yet written novels.

Scholars of literature differ over how and where to locate the origins of the novel, the literary genre most closely identified with European modernity itself. Some argue for unbroken continuity since antiquity, whereas others name Cervantes, Defoe, or Richardson as the first modern novelists. Early novels tended to mimic existing prose genres such as diaries, epistolary exchanges, or travel writing. Richardson's *Pamela* (one candidate for the first "real" novel) was an epistolary novel, as is the first selection in this section. Isaac Euchel's *Igrot Meshulam* (1790; *Epistles of Meshulam*) modeled after Montesquieu's *Lettres persanes* (1721) embodies the search for new genres by writers in Hebrew. The first attempts by Jews tended to serve didactic or ideological ends. The "realistic" novel, the genre whose purpose was to transport the reader to an alternative yet familiar world for the sake of the imagination alone, emerged gradually as a mature field of Jewish creativity. By the later decades of the nineteenth century, Jewish authors had mastered the art of novel writing in European languages.

Writers faced questions not only concerning the best language to reach their readers but also on how to shape their story, how to portray their characters, and how to balance their message with the aesthetic value of their prose. Ruth Wisse has argued that while European novelists exalted the "man of action" who influenced his own and others' destiny, Jewish writers could not easily "acclaim the man of action as their authentic Jewish hero."[14] They did not have the political or military experience that European Christians had, and so they ended up creating what she calls the comic hero, a compromise of sorts. Apropos of her remarks, it is notable that one of the most accomplished statesmen represented in the volume, both as political thinker and as writer, Benjamin Disraeli, often did choose "men of action" as his literary heroes.

Writing a novel requires an author to conjure an entire world with language. This was a daring venture in any language, but it was doubly so for Hebrew and the Jewish vernaculars, each for different reasons. As Robert Alter notes, "To write a novel in Hebrew . . . was to constitute a whole world in a language not actually spoken in the real-life equivalent of that world, yet treated by the writer as if it were really spoken."[15] The first Hebrew novels were written in biblical idiom, some even based on biblical characters, as authors searched for the noblest language in which to create, then reached back several millennia to find usable precedents. Decades later, as authors added rabbinic and other registers of Hebrew to the literary palette, Hebrew novels lost their stiff diction and became far more linguistically rich and supple. Still, novels written in the Hebrew of the nineteenth century would always remain the province of a very small and committed readership, mainly educated, secular, yet Hebraically literate young men.

In Eastern Europe, the lingua franca of the masses was Yiddish, and to create fine literature in that language presented its own challenges. For all its widespread use in the daily life of millions of Jews in Ashkenazic Europe, west and east, Yiddish was thought of by literary arbiters as a lowly jargon, a coarse pidgin dialect with no grammatical structure, no beauty, no literary past, and no future. Isaac Meyer Dik was one of the first enlightened writers to seize on Yiddish narrative as a way to rival and combat what he saw as twin problems: the ignorance of the masses and Hasidism. His stories have a direct, unadorned, and sometimes heavily didactic style, yet his descriptive power and sense of humor made them enormously popular. "The Panic, or The Town of Hérres" (*hérres* meaning "havoc" in Hebrew) describes the tumult when an "evil" decree prohibiting child marriages hits the town and the parents rush to avert it by marrying off all their children at once. Sholem Yankev Abramovitsh pioneered writing in Yiddish as a creative, exuberant, and lively literary language. His story "Dos kleyne menshele" ("The Little Man," 1864–1865) introduced his literary alter ego Mendele Mokher Sforim (Mendele the Book Peddler). In a language dense with Jewish literary allusions, Abramovitsh (Mendele) conjured entire fictional worlds with vivid characters whose foibles evoked both sympathy and ridicule. Abramovitsh opened the way for others who wove the unpromising language into a literary fabric of unanticipated depth and richness.

Folktales reappeared in the nineteenth century, sometimes as sophisticated replicas of their naïve early selves, having been appropriated by savvy masters to play their nostalgia value for ideological ends. Writers and storytellers living in (or trying to capture the bygone flavor of) traditional societies used folktales as a means to reach the largest readership and to convey lofty messages with their stories.

Jewish writers used literature not only to reckon with a Jewish past many wished to jettison or reshape; they also addressed the multiple and entangled aspects of their new reality. Thus the figure of Jews serving in the military appears in the art and letters of this period. Reversing a centuries-long aversion on both sides, Jews entered the armed services of various nations and distinguished themselves in combat, learning to graft their military training onto their Jewish identities. Some writers and artists evoked the pride felt by Jewish families in the West for whom serving in the military signaled the most honorable place in society. Moritz Oppenheim's now-iconic painting *The Return of the Jewish Volunteer from the Wars of Liberation to His Family Still Living in Accordance with Old Customs* (1833–1834) portrays a range of emotions from pride to ambivalence as various family members regard their young man just returned from the front. This one painting conveys many messages about the benefits of integration and emancipation as well as the inner conflicts they provoked. Although the painting itself is a positive portrayal, and some of the family members admire the act of sacrifice and patriotism of the son, the father looks up from the text he is studying on the Sabbath with consternation. Other artists evoked a darker side, particularly of the horrors of forced conscription of young children in tsarist Russia.[16]

Novels and short stories advanced a host of ideologies through their characters, from enlightenment to nationalisms in all their complexity, as well as socialism and communism. They explored the consequences of romantic love, class disparity, and the glories of the natural world as they invented a vocabulary for a reality that had seemed beyond their grasp only a short while earlier. Heinrich Heine, one of the most versatile and gifted stylists writing in German in the nineteenth century, left no subject untouched, although he frequently returned to Jewish themes.

Jewish women played important roles in the creation of Jewish literature in the vernacular. Eugénie Foa of Bordeaux, France, was one of the first Jewish French fiction writers, one of the first Jewish women to publish fiction in any language, and the first to support herself entirely from her writings. Foa's novels featured strong protagonists, Jewish women who forged their own way, independent of fathers or husbands. Scion of a prominent Sephardic family, abolitionist, feminist, and champion of children's rights, Foa lived the paradox of so many Jews of this period. She championed strong-willed women who refused to convert in her novels; she converted to Christianity later in her life.[17] In England, Grace Aguilar wrote poems, stories, and histories, with special emphasis on the *converso* experience, Sephardic history, and Jewish women. In the United States, Emma Lazarus produced an astonishing bounty of literary works in multiple genres. Although she is remembered today primarily for her famous sonnet "The New Colossus," inscribed on the Statue of Liberty, she and Aguilar can be considered among the most important nineteenth-century Sephardic writers in English.

Poetry

Poetry is the literary genre that most defies translation. If the elasticity of meaning is lost in translation of prose, how much more so for poetry, built from the marrow of words: their sounds, their cadences, their accents, their meters, lost in the journey to a different tongue. Allusion, intertext, the music of language—all but one plain meaning out of many are sloughed off by the necessity of translation. So why include poetry in this anthology if so much of it is anglicized from the original? Despite the caveats, poetry in this volume reaches places that prose cannot: from personal emotion—love, despair, joy, shame, rage; to the political—triumph and disaster of a people as well as calls to ideological arms. Masterful poetry conferred authority on its writers as tellers of deep truths and as seers of penetrating vision. Even in translation we can sense the stiffness of the first attempts to breathe new life into Hebrew, as well as its subsequent growth and maturation over time and place. Jewish poets throughout Europe and the Americas created in the languages of their native tongues. From folk-song lyrics to wedding riddles and synagogue hymns, poetry, even in translation, allows us access to voices and moments, particular and collective, that we would otherwise not hear.[18] To Rachel Luzzatto Morpurgo's plaintive cry—"I've looked to the north, to the south and east, and west; // in each a woman's word is lighter than dust. // Years hence, will anyone really remember // her name, in city, province, any more // than a dead dog's?"[19]—Emma Lazarus's confident voice provides the ultimate rejoinder. It continues to echo in millions of ears even today.

Intellectual Culture

The emergence of new definitions of citizenship, of state, and of individual identities within them, along with ideas formulated by the leading European philosophers and statesmen of the age, presented a direct challenge to Jewish educated elites—writers, thinkers, teachers, and rabbis. Western European states offered inclusion into the polity if Jews changed enough about themselves to lose their distinctiveness. Governments would reverse centuries-long policies of discrimination that kept Jews from acculturating. In return, the states expected Jews to abandon their intense devotion to a distinctive Jewish culture, although they would be allowed to retain their religious identity. Russia fluctuated between promoting strategies aimed at pressuring the Jewish masses to convert to Orthodox Christianity and policies designed to turn them into enlightened subjects, however defined. They were to be educated alongside everyone else, to speak and write the language of the nations, and to pursue economic and professional activities that were deemed "productive." Russian society itself was deeply polarized between aristocrats and peasants, with a scant middle class for Jews to integrate into.[20] Nevertheless, Jewish thinkers of all stripes saw this offer of redemption as a momentous turning point, away from a past filled with persecution and segregation, toward a new age of acceptance and inclusion. Most felt that this was an offer they could not refuse, and they were filled with a sense of urgency. They penned hundreds of passionate essays, each claiming to have the very formula that would change Jews sufficiently to enable them to participate in the new society while retaining aspects of their Jewish identities.

In their manifold works, European Jewish writers addressed several readerships. They wrote to convince themselves, to persuade their fellow Jews, and to prove to the gentile intellectuals that they were serious about transforming a people whose habits, religion, and culture had been shaped for millennia as a society apart. In contrast to the "drift and defection" pattern of disengagement, members of the literate vanguards were the first to articulate their struggle to define precisely which elements of Jewishness and Judaism were worth conserving, which needed transformation in order to remain vital, and which should be consigned to oblivion.[21] Some proponents of change advocated for their vision with conscious deliberation and programmatic manifestos; others advocated resistance to all changes with equal awareness and staunch positions that nevertheless signaled that they were responding to a new set of circumstances. Jewish responses to the conditional welcome into equality in the legal, civic, and social spheres included total abandonment of Judaism (in the nineteenth century this still usually meant conversion to another religion), programs to enlighten the Jewish masses, movements of spiritual renewal, and the division of Western Judaism into different denominations. These positions mattered immensely to those who advocated for them; they articulated and disseminated their ideas with ferocious zeal. They hoped to reshape the very concepts and images of Jews and Judaism for all time. Many believed that they were the first to face such a radically reconfigured world, the first to take the measure of all of Jewish culture in all the preceding ages and judge it on the altar of the future unknown.

This volume aims to include an array of voices, the well known alongside the obscure, ranging across an eventful century and a half, across diverse contexts and political circumstances. German Jews were perhaps the most self-conscious and highly articulate in this period; although there was often a time lag of decades before their work was translated and taken up, their writings were hugely influential in distant parts of the Jewish world. Access to education and literacy—academic, scientific, rabbinic—was very limited for women. They are less present in this section of the volume than in others because in every one of the ideological movements, from Hasidic thought and rabbinic scholarship to religious denominationalism and pedagogical reform, men's voices dominated the discourse.

Rabbinic and Religious Thought

Rabbinic scholarship stood at the apex of the hierarchy of values of traditional Jewish society. Despite the challenges to its status and the erosion of its authority beginning in the early modern period, it flourished with figures of coruscating brilliance in Central and Eastern Europe in the latter half of the eighteenth century and the first half of the nineteenth century. The period opened with a spectacular controversy when, in 1751, noted rabbi Jacob Emden accused Jonathan Eybeschütz, chief rabbi of Altona-Hamburg-Wandsbek, of secretly harboring heretical tendencies. Eybeschütz was then one of the most renowned rabbinic scholars of his time, author of brilliant Talmudic novellae. When Emden accused him of writing amulets that called upon the spiritual powers of Shabetai Tsevi, heresiarch and leader of a failed messianic movement a century earlier, their clash riveted the traditional Jewish world and provoked interest in the European Christian press as well. Pressured to defend his honor, Eybeschütz reproduced an affidavit from the burial society of Metz attesting to the efficacy of his amulets in reducing the number of Jewish women who died in childbirth.

Other rabbinic figures in this volume, such as Elijah, Gaon of Vilna; Jacob Ettlinger in Altona; and Akiva Eger of Posen, commanded the respect of learned Jews across Europe for their mastery of the entire Jewish corpus and their pathbreaking scholarly interventions. They are represented in this volume not by the highly technical works of rabbinic scholarship for which they are best known but by works that expand our understanding of these eminent religious leaders. Far from being rigid and monolithic legalists, as their opponents caricatured them, the rabbis themselves presented multifaceted profiles to their publics. Rabbinic scholarship remained a creative magnet for some of the best minds in the traditional Jewish world. This vitality enables us to better contextualize the ferocity of the polemics in this era. Many of the most important movements envisioned an alternative to the rabbinate as Jewish leadership and to rabbinic scholarship as the apex of valued knowledge.

HASIDISM

Hasidism, with its focus on pietism and spirituality, is one among the genuinely new forms of Jewish identity to develop in the period covered by this volume. It burgeoned in Eastern Europe into a popular mass movement that offered alternative leadership models, new social organization, and a hierarchy of spiritual ideals different from rabbinic values.[22] Earlier scholarly assessments of the Hasidic movement as appealing to semiliterate Jewish masses and led by leaders lacking scholarly bona fides have now been revised by scholars. Israel ben Eliezer (1700–1760), known as the Ba'al Shem Tov (often known by the Hebrew acronym *Besht*) considered the founder of the movement, left few writings but was on the community payroll as a scholar, and many of his early adherents were rabbinic scholars as well.[23] Thus, the movement was deeply rooted in the communities and included the elite from the outset.

Hasidism's rapid spread and the deep roots it struck throughout the nineteenth century cannot be pinned down to one factor.[24] By the late eighteenth century, Poland was a polity in crisis, and the Jewish communal structure that depended on its kings and magnates either folded completely, as did the supraregional organization known as the Council of Four Lands in 1764, or lost the respect of the people as did the magnate-appointed rabbis. Many Jews, across classes and in every corner of Eastern Europe, were attracted to the Hasidic emphasis on joy in the worship of God and the power of every Jew to create a relationship with the divine creator. Eventually, Hasidism built its own institutions, with dozens of spiritual leaders known as tsadikim or *admorim*. Each one built a center, known as a court, that attracted male adherents to celebrate the holidays together. Each Hasidic court emphasized a slightly different spiritual approach in prayer, thought, and song. Collectively, Hasidic thinkers produced a ramified homiletic literature that reflected their individual interpretation of Hasidic ideas and integrated and popularized elements of Jewish mystical teachings.

As the movement grew in popularity, it was attacked from many sides. Adherents of Haskalah saw it as a regression from rationalism as well as from the progress Jews were making toward integration into the civic sphere. Rabbinic opponents (beginning with the ban of Elijah ben Solomon, Gaon of Vilna, in 1772) condemned it as a deviation from the ideal of Torah study as the highest expression of Jewish values. Given that the Jewish population in Poland on the eve of the partition (in the 1760s, approximately three-quarters of a million) was the largest population of Jews in the world at the time, its religious and cultural character was highly consequential. Such numbers, coupled with high concentrations of Jews in large cities and many villages, shaped the posture of East European Jewry as a powerful and confident minority.[25] At a time when Enlightenment ideals became the yardstick of human progress in the West, the appearance and success of a Jewish movement that looked inward to Jewish tradition for its inspiration came as a surprise to its contemporaries. It remains something of a challenge for historians to the present day.[26]

The strength of Hasidism sparked an outpouring of writing critical of the movement. From the hilariously satirical *Revealer of Secrets* by the *maskil* Joseph Perl, to the bitter reminiscences of an ex-Hasid such as Abraham Ber Gottlober, to the denunciations of Hasidism as a suspicious cult by rabbinic leaders beginning with Elijah, Gaon of Vilna, Hasidism came under attack from many quarters. It stimulated countermovements within rabbinic circles.[27] That despite these attacks it remained a powerful magnet for generations of Jews throughout Eastern Europe testified to its power as a meaningful response to the challenges of modernization.

In the West, and particularly among German-speaking Jews, in the nineteenth century, Jewish rituals, synagogue spaces, and the prayer service itself came under increasing scrutiny in light of the call for modernization. A search for the "essence of Judaism" prompted an outpouring of religious writings and a spectrum of responses that left Western Ashkenazic Jewry religiously divided along rigid lines: Reform or Liberal, Positive Historical (closely aligned with American Conservative), Neo-Orthodox, and Ultra-Orthodox were just some of the movements that crystallized the varied positions. In addition, many Jews belonged to no formal denomination. In rural areas, filial pietism dominated, whereas in many urban areas some Jews chose the path of radical assimilation.

Unlike these divisions in the West, Jewish modernization in the Ottoman Empire followed a different and distinctive trajectory.[28] Just as Muslim societies, even as they modernized, did not radically reconfigure Islam, Jews in the Muslim world adapted in ways that were far less anticlerical.[29] Jews who drifted from the traditional ways did not seek to establish formal denominations. The community remained on the surface religiously cohesive. Many Sephardic rabbinic thinkers of the nineteenth and twentieth centuries saw the Torah as sufficiently capacious to incorporate features of modern life.

The effect of Westernization, coupled with new avenues for professional advancement, changed the face of Jewish culture, generally beginning with the highest socioeconomic classes. Study of religious texts and the prestige of the rabbinate as a career declined. With some exceptions, such as the Baghdad yeshiva Bet Zilkha, founded in 1840 by a towering figure in nineteenth-century Iraqi Jewry, Abdullah Somekh, the cultural focus of the communities in the Islamic orbit shifted. Paradoxically, efforts to revive and sustain Torah study by the late nineteenth century often stemmed from European rabbis traveling east whose published works were circulating more broadly. During this period of flourishing religious productivity, the Karaite community in Crimea continued to produce significant work as well. Its thinkers authored some of the last great compilations of Karaite law, commentary, and theology as well as the last major metanarrative of Karaite history.[30]

Haskalah and Pedagogy

Until the latter half of the eighteenth century, religious skepticism and calls for reform of various aspects of Jewish life remained individual expressions. They did not coalesce into movements that would overturn the structure of Jewish life and its hierarchy of values. When such movements began to take shape, they developed against an efflorescence of traditional rabbinic culture determined to hold the forces of innovation at bay.

One of the first programmatic statements came from the pen of Naphtali Herts Wessely. Reacting to the Toleranzpatent issued by the "enlightened despot" Joseph II of Austria, Wessely issued an epistle, *Divre shalom v'emet* (*Words of Peace and Truth*, 1782), calling upon Jews to abandon the deadened rabbinic culture with its talmudo-centrism and to reorient Jewish culture toward the full range of Hebraic knowledge as well as other languages, and the natural and exact sciences. He urged a complete change of attitude toward non-Jews. Wessely was a practicing Jew whose significance lay in his call to reimagine Ashkenazi Jewish society and culture from the top down. His epistle was a gauntlet thrown down to traditional rabbinic authority and was widely seen as the text that crystallized the aims of the Haskalah (Jewish Enlightenment) movement.

The Haskalah's influential embodiment and philosophical icon was Moses Mendelssohn. An accomplished philosopher celebrated as the "Socrates of Berlin," Mendelssohn addressed many conundrums of his time while adhering to and defending observant Judaism. Although he hoped to provide the intellectual infrastructure for Judaism in an enlightened society, and he clearly approved of the founding of the Jüdische Freischule (a free Jewish school in the maskilic spirit) in 1778, he did not establish schools or institutions to realize these goals.

The first official maskilic circle and the first printed journal for *maskilim* were founded by Isaac Euchel in Königsberg. Over the late eighteenth and early nineteenth centuries, Haskalah ideals and pedagogy slowly expanded and provided intellectual underpinnings for further movements of Jewish modernization.[31] In formerly Polish (then Austrian) Galicia, in cities such as Brody, Tarnopol, and Lemberg (present-day Lviv), maskilic culture saw the traditionalist Hasidic movement as the foremost obstacle to Jewish modernization. In Russia, maskilic ideals, formulated in a programmatic essay by Isaac Ber Levinzon (1828), took root first in cities such as Odessa and Vilna. Yet the illiberalism of the society itself, from the tsar down, made it far more difficult for even for the most committed enlighteners to effect meaningful change. While the scholarly circles around the Gaon of Vilna and his disciples embraced a rabbinic rationalism and openness to the sciences as bold as those of any enlightened figures, Jews in Eastern Europe did not turn to the larger culture en masse until the late nineteenth century.[32]

The first *maskilim* ransacked both Jewish and European tradition to find new and better platforms for creating and transmitting the Jewish cultural ideal they conceived. From translations of sacred Jewish texts to autobiographies and "dialogues of the dead," Jews enlisted diverse literary genres to call for social, educational, and economic change. By the late nineteenth century, they had stimulated a profound recasting of Jewish literary culture in Hebrew and in Yiddish.

Questions of language were always political and deeply intertwined with those of Jewish education. A basic component of the traditional Jewish educational system (mainly for boys) had been the translation of the Bible into a stylized form of the vernacular—Yiddish-taytsh, Ladino, and Sharkh (Judeo-Arabic). In the Islamic world, Western Jewish, as well as non-Jewish, imperial and colonial cultural influences broadened educational choices. European Jewish schools, Christian missionary schools, and Russian and Ottoman state schools all competed with traditional Jewish schools in the nineteenth century. The modernization of curricula in Western-influenced schools was essential to the realization of maskilic goals.

Scholarship and Science

As more academic institutions opened their doors to Jews, scientific method and professions in the social and natural sciences and medicine became more accessible to Jews. The first efforts in the sciences in this period were often works of translation by individuals hoping to share their knowledge with Jews who could not directly learn about the latest advances in hygiene, medicine, and nutrition. With the advance of the nineteenth century, medicine (alongside the law) became one of the more popular professional choices for educated Jews, who soon began to contribute to myriad aspects of medical and scientific fields as well as to the social sciences. From Joseph Vita Castelli's letter to a physician friend describing the symptoms of an acute illness to Ignác Goldziher's foundational work on Islamic history and society, the scholarly and scientific ethos permeated Jewish intellectual life in the late eighteenth and nineteenth centuries and resulted in contributions obscure and renowned. The foundations of the astonishing breakthroughs of Jews in the sciences in the twentieth century were laid in this period.

Perhaps as significant as Jewish scholars' contributions to their respective fields was their application of scientific methods to their own culture and history. The advent of critical historical thinking about the Jewish past and Jewish texts constituted a monumental break from traditional modes. With rare exceptions, even modern Jews had accepted the narratives and materials of their past uncritically. Neither the German term *Wissenschaft* nor its incomplete English translation, "science," do adequate justice to the breadth, rigor, dedication, and manifold materials that this term embraced. "More than footnotes, variant readings and bibliographies," writes historian Ismar Schorsch, "At the core of modern Jewish scholarship there is a new way of thinking about Judaism. . . . A religious tradition indifferent to the category of time in comprehending itself . . . was suddenly confronted with a mode of cognition that rested on contextual interpretation."[33] The establishment in Berlin, in 1819, of a society to study the materials of Jewish history set off a search for sources and revision of narratives whose repercussions remain with us until this day. On the occasion of the first anniversary of this society, Eduard Gans remarked, "No revolution is more difficult than the overturning and recasting of a state of mind."[34]

The university-trained Jewish men (and they were virtually all men), rejected for employment by the very institutions that nurtured them, brought their academic training to the study of Judaism. They hoped to wrest the "curatorship" of Jewish culture from the hands of its Christian antagonists and its traditional rabbinic Jewish guardians.[35] Attempting to fit the materials of the Jewish past into the European academic format was no easy task. It took decades to turn these studies into a new Jewish narrative that would appeal to a broad readership. Not until Heinrich Graetz produced his engrossing and dramatic multivolume history of the Jews, subsequently translated into many languages, did the products of the academic world become popular among Jews around the globe in the nineteenth century.[36]

Over the course of the nineteenth century, these ideas and ideals radiated out toward other circles of Jewish intellectuals with differences specific to their context. "Études juives" circles in France, for example, saw themselves in a different light than the German Jewish scholars. A notable development was the adoption of scholarly approaches within more traditional circles. Because these practitioners saw themselves as continuing traditions of Jewish scholarship rather than as products of a rupture, they were less apt to distance themselves from more traditional Jewish values. Their contributions in Hebrew came to be known collectively as Ḥokhmat Yisrael.

Political Life and Thought

During the period 1750–1880, the political status of Jews changed dramatically from England and its colonies in the West to Jews of the Ottoman East and points beyond.[37] At the beginning of this period, most Jews were organized in self-governing units within the larger polity. While they never had full political autonomy and were always subject to local as well as distant political powers, they functioned as many smaller units tended to in the early modern period: running their own affairs, employing their own language, and educating their children while paying taxes and homage to the princes, dukes, bishops, kings, and emperors who granted them the right to dwell and pursue commerce in their domains. This internal political life should be seen within the framework of variable local political practices of the early modern period that only later came to be subsumed under nation-states.[38] Local Jewish political governance and its regulation abounded.

Jews expressed fealty to their political overlords. In 1780, Rabbi Ezekiel Landau of Prague delivered a eulogy for Empress Maria Theresa. Remembered for her cruel banishment of Bohemian Jews from her domains in 1745, she seems an unlikely candidate for such a demonstration of grief and loyalty. The text testifies to the status and meaning of the Jews as *subjects* in the Habsburg Empire. Over the course of the nineteenth century, this began to change. Local politics gave way to stronger centralizing nation-states that granted citizenship while insisting on the right to create a unified nationality, inclusive of cultural and educational dimensions. An intense debate ensued in the European sphere regarding the place of Christianity within the new national identities. If it remained central, then Jews would continue to remain unequal. In eloquent pleas to the governing bodies of nation-states, Jews argued that nation-states must extend equal rights under the law to all citizens regardless of religion in order to be faithful to their own stated ideals.

Jews debated all sides of the major political issues of their day. Some welcomed the idea of equality, whereas others feared the loss of their religious-institutional distinctiveness. Some defended and others repudiated the notion of private property and capital. Some defended and others repudiated the institution of slavery. Jewish women advocated for gender equality long before any nation was ready to entertain it. In the mid-nineteenth century, the first Jew elected to the U.S. Congress, Lewis

Charles Levin, ran on a platform of temperance, nativism, and anti-Catholicism, and Benjamin Disraeli served in the British Parliament. Jews formed transnational societies, such as Alliance Israélite Universelle, to aid Jews in trouble and laid the first foundations for Zionist thinking when antisemitism grew to threaten the dream of political equality.

Much of the political discourse by and about Jews was disseminated via the press. While this volume has generally privileged the message over the medium, journalism is an exception. Its ubiquitous growth and presence, particularly in Central and Eastern Europe (later in the Ottoman Empire), profoundly shaped political debates and created a new sense of a Jewish public sphere.[39]

Journalism

From the second half of the eighteenth century, journalism in all forms became the significant medium for the creation of an engaged public, the instrument for debating and shaping local politics and consolidating middle-class identity. This period marks the explosive rise of Jewish newspapers, dailies and weeklies, yearbooks and almanacs, feuilletons and other time-bound printed media throughout the Western world. Newspapers and journals of the nineteenth century disseminated far more than news and advertisements. They kept Jews aware of events affecting other Jews around the world, creating a new vehicle for their collective identity as Jews and as members of a far-flung community.

To cite one example, Shukr Kuhayl II, a messianic pretender, arose in Tan'im, Yemen, in 1868; he was arrested in 1871 by the Ottomans. Primary texts of the movement were published while it was at its apogee, including one set of letters in Kraków. What did the messiah of Yemen have to do with the Jews of Kraków? The letters were likely to have been published by a Galician *maskil* as a means of satirizing local Jews' gullibility in following wonder workers.[40] They testify to the power of the press to link Jews from far-flung regions.

As party organs and cultural platforms, periodicals become the forum of choice for a new intelligentsia. Their choices of language, of register, and of audience were politically consequential. Journals served as springboards for writing by Jews not just of opinion and politics but also of belles lettres in Hebrew, in the Jewish vernaculars, and in many European languages. Although political borders in this period shifted frequently, journals employed a common language to unite politically dispersed Jews.

The first European Jewish periodicals appeared haltingly in the eighteenth century (earlier attempts were extremely short lived). With the emergence of the German Haskalah and its subscriber base, however, Jewish journals such as *Ha-me'asef* and *Shulamith* became more sustainable. The former was published in Hebrew, with the goal of fostering its use as a literary language among German Jews.

Through the first half of the nineteenth century, German-speaking Jewry remained at the forefront of periodical literature. The medium gradually expanded into the Austro-Hungarian Empire, at first with particular emphasis on the literature and criticism that were hallmarks of Haskalah.[41] By the 1840s, Jews were printing journals and newspapers in Hebrew, Yiddish, and German, as well as in Hungarian, French, Ladino, Italian, Polish, Spanish, and, of course, English.

As soon as the number of Jews in the United States reached a critical mass of potential readers, the Jewish press emerged to educate, entertain, and exhort them. Isaac Leeser, *ḥazan* of Congregation Mikveh Israel in Philadelphia, founded the first successful Jewish paper, *The Occident* (1843), a monthly. Within a few years, its success spurred several other journals. In 1854, in Cincinnati, Reform rabbinic leader Isaac Mayer Wise established the long-lived and lively *The Israelite*. American Jewish papers tended to focus on local news and events, and came to be printed not only in English but also in German, Yiddish, Russian, and Ladino, following the needs of each wave of immigrants and increasing in circulation accordingly. Fearful that criticism would reflect poorly on the Jews who struggled to make their place in a new environment, many of the papers presented a relentlessly positive view of their communities.

In 1823, one of the first European Jewish newspapers, *Dostrzegacz Nadwiślański (Observer over the Vistula)*, appeared in Polish, containing articles in German in Hebrew letters and in Polish in parallel columns. It was short lived, possibly because Jews who read and spoke Yiddish had difficulty relating to the Germanized Yiddish, and they may not have been able to follow the Polish-language news. *Izraelita*, founded in Warsaw in 1866, was the first Jewish newspaper printed in Poland to succeed over several decades. It originally championed the ideal of polonization of Jews; later it adopted a more Zionist posture.[42] A Hebrew-language journal founded by Eliezer Silverman, *Ha-magid*, appeared in Lyck in East Prussia in 1856. Its formula of moderate enlightenment and conservative religious stance granted it longevity through the end of the nineteenth century.

In Russia, the reign of Tsar Alexander II (1855–1881) ushered in an era of great reforms. The serfs were liberated, and the economy began a transformation from rural and agrarian to urban and industrial. Along with these momentous changes, such a stark contrast to the preceding reign of Nicholas I, hope sprung that Russia had finally started on a path of political and social liberalism. Against this background, the need to prepare Jews for the new era stimulated a proliferation of opinions and journals. Five newspapers were founded in the 1860s and 1870s in Odessa alone.

One of the great entrepreneurs of Jewish journalism in the later nineteenth century was Alexander Zederbaum (1816–1893), who championed Russian rather than German as the language of modernization. Adopting the railroad as a symbol of modernization, he urged Jews not to miss the train of modernity. During the 1863 Polish insurrection against Russia, Zederbaum's newspapers supported the tsar against the Polish rebels, unlike the Polish Jewish papers that supported the Poles. Zederbaum founded *Ha-melits* (1860–1905), one of the most successful journals, attuned to all aspects of interest for its readers rather than advancing one didactic agenda. To succeed, Zederbaum had to navigate many obstacles. His statement of purpose declared that he hoped to carve a path between Jewish interests and those of the Russian government. He published imperial decrees relating to Jews and news of Jews advancing in the public sphere. By reverse token, his papers carried news affecting Jews around the world. He had to tread carefully between Russophiles who disdained the paper as too Jewish and traditionalists who rejected its advocacy of modernization. Zederbaum also founded and edited a Yiddish paper, *Kol mevasser*, in whose pages he introduced "Sholem Aleichem" to readers. Many other luminaries of Jewish life and letters appeared in its pages.

By eschewing the stilted German in Hebrew letters for a more colloquial Yiddish, the paper attracted broad readership from all classes and was particularly noted for attracting women as readers in large numbers. Its pages carried the debates that raged in Jewish society, from questions about migration, about science, and literature to the critical social issues of the day. Indeed, the paper encountered fierce resistance to its reports of social problems, for Jews feared oppressive reaction from the Russian government and people if problems such as poverty and internal discord were aired. The 1881 assassination of Alexander II, followed by pogroms and mass emigration to the United States, signaled the extinction of hope for liberalization of Russian society and a retreat from the elusive cultural and national acceptance that many Jews had worked so hard to achieve. Despite this dark turn, the extraordinary liveliness of the intellectual exchanges and cultural contributions of the journalistic press made it one of the signal arenas of nineteenth-century Jewish creativity.

Visual and Material Culture

Material Culture

Borrowed from the fields of anthropology and ethnography, the term *material culture* signifies objects and built physical environments that tell us how people navigated, related to, or shaped their material world. Many types of objects—furnishings and clothing, jewels and medals, wares crafted by Jews or specifically for use by Jews—are included in this section. "In portraying patterns of life in the modern period, changes in the ways Jews lived privately and publicly, their dress, manners, social customs and behavior, physical possessions and space and their attitudes to them, need to be integrated. For wherever Jews lived they possessed objects, and . . . those from the modern period are many, bearing the stamp of a Jew's identity, relationship to the outside world, and sense of self."[43]

There are precious few material objects shaped by human hands that do not convey the character of the individual creator as well as that of the larger society and culture in which it was made. A humble spoon, a chair, an item of clothing—each can be made of many materials, in so many patterns and shapes. As universal as they might appear to be, each exemplar is unique in the age before mass production. In addition to many single objects, we have tried to convey a sense of the material surroundings of Jewish spaces. When objects or environments proved impossible to include in this volume, we have relied on the "next best thing." An inventory of household goods from Jews in colonial America, although technically a text, gives a sense of the material possessions considered significant in their time and place. The delicate watercolor of Fanny Hensel's music room likewise allows us to perceive the furnishings and sensibility of the physical space in which her music composition and private rehearsals took place.

Ritual objects constitute one of the enduring platforms for Jewish artistic creativity and patronage through the ages. Each piece manifests its creator's responsibility to the purpose of the object and its prescribed forms, alongside the desire to transcend its physical limitations and create an artifact of surpassing meaning. Ritual objects have one of the longest trails in Jewish art history. Indeed, in the not-too-recent past the very term *Jewish art* would conjure silver Kiddush cups and Havdalah spice boxes, Seder plates and illuminated manuscript Haggadahs. Artisans worked from the most precious to the most base of materials, from refined gold and silver to wood and paper. They created ritually necessary items, such as menorahs, as well as decorative objects, such as *mizraḥ* and *shiviti* signs, each invested with individual beauty, yet reflecting the larger culture of the time. *Mizraḥ* (east) designated the wall in the house that faced east, whereas *shiviti* was the starting word of the verse "I place God before me always" (Psalm 16:8). Neither of these signs was ritually obligatory in any way. They migrated from synagogue walls, where they served to concentrate worshipers' attention, to broadsheet pages, to home decorations, marking spaces as Jewish abodes.

It is worth pausing to note that depending on Jewish political status in a given time and place, the craftsmen and artisans may or may not have been Jews. In many Muslim lands in the nineteenth century, metalworkers were Jews because Muslims were forbidden to engage in the craft. In Poland, the Czech lands, and later Russia, Jews often organized themselves into craft guilds that played an important social and economic role. In Western Europe, through the first part of the nineteenth century, Jews were excluded from guilds and often commissioned Christians to create ritual pieces in silver to their specifications. In colonial America, by contrast, Jews were free to choose to work in silver, as Myer Myers's works attest. Beyond political status, each work exemplifies the interplay between local artistic traditions, Jewish customs and requirements, the economic status of the parties, and of course individual artistic imaginations and abilities.[44] Many items in this section were used and beloved even by Jews whose attachment to religious tradition was marginal at best. The ritual objects can be divided into two types. The first category contains objects that were used to mark life-cycle events in a Jewish key.

For every stage of life from birth to death, for every life-cycle ritual, the embellished artifacts speak to the values their makers held dear. Jews all over the world sought every protection for children yet to be born and for newborns by invoking angelic names on amulets and ordering evil spirits, often embodied in the name Lilith, to stay away. Some amulets designated a specific child to be the beneficiary of special protection. Circumcision was practiced to represent the bond between God and male Jews since Abraham. Special seats, often beautifully decorated, were set aside at circumcision ceremonies for the invisible presence of Elijah. Special implements to care for the infant and adornments were created to commemorate the event. In Ashkenazic communities, mothers would embroider a cloth sash (wimple) with the new baby boy's name and blessings for the future. When he was old enough to attend synagogue, he ceremonially brought the sash to serve as a Torah binder. The sermon for the bar mitzvah child coming of age cannot be captured by an object, but as photography grew in popularity, pictures of the bar mitzvah boy marked this rite of passage.

Marriages were celebrated with greater embellishment than any other life-cycle ritual. During his sojourn in Tangier, Morocco, the French painter Eugène Delacroix was moved by the way a Jewish mother lovingly prepared her daughter for marriage. His painting *Saada, the Wife of Abraham Ben-Chimol and Préciada, One of Their Daughters* (1832) immortalized the moment and captures a larger sense of the interior space as background for the rich life that unfolded within it. Delacroix's visit to Tangier and his friendship with the Jews of the city gained him entry to a Jewish wedding that made a deep impression on him; he made a painting of it almost a decade later.[45] A huppah (wedding canopy) represented the home that the newlyweds would build, as did the wedding sofa. The ketubah (marriage contract) emerged as a locus for artistic embellishment all over the Jewish world. Some were written on parchment with exquisite decoration and illustrations that referred to the bride and groom's families.

The end of life's journey, too, was invested with dignified ritual. Jewish shrouds and coffins were to be plain, as the soul journeyed into a world where wealth and material matters fell away. But the "holy society," members of the community who attended to the dead and prepared them for burial, marked their work with lasting images. Even the implements they used to prepare the dead were specially marked. Finally, while poor and rural Jews could not always afford lasting markers, many Jews were able to set carved and engraved headstones that served as durable memorials to the departed. These became and remained platforms for artistic creativity, with traditional signs indicating priestly or Levite birth or the person's occupation.

The second category of ritual objects consists of those whose primary purpose was to carry out religious ritual related to the Jewish calendar, governed by a long tradition of *hidur mitsvah*, carrying out a religious ritual in the most beautiful manner. These objects spanned the gamut from humble to exquisite. They were used on Sabbath and holidays, some designed for private domestic use and others intended for the synagogue.

As has been practiced through the ages, every married woman blessed the Sabbath on special candlesticks or hanging lamps, the Sabbath day sanctified by a blessing over wine and special challah loaves presented on platters. The New Year included honey dishes to symbolize sweetness and the blowing of the shofar (ram's horn) in the synagogue. Its plaintive notes would arouse the congregation to introspection and penitence. The sukkah (tabernacle) brought Jews outdoors into temporary shelters that reminded them of the transience of the material structures in their lives, of their desert sojourn when clouds and fire were their only protection. Jews built architecturally innovative sukkahs and decorated them to be as inviting as possible. Hanukkah brought lamps in many different materials and an astonishing profusion of decorative styles. The lamps were supposed to be seen by the public as reminders of the miracle of light against the forces of darkness. The daily prayer book, special prayer books for holidays, along with the Scroll of Esther and various accoutrements for Purim provided additional opportunities for lively illustration. Passover was the high point of the ceremonial year, and the Haggadah, its text the foundation story of the Jewish people, the story of the exodus from Egypt, was one of the most beloved, adapted, commented-on, and decorated Jewish books. Over the centuries its style and illustration reflected the Jewish historical experience.[46] The Seder plate, matzo covers, pitcher and basin for ceremonial washing of hands—indeed, every aspect of the Seder—was fair game for artistic embellishment.

The adornments inside synagogues, from the Torah vessels to charity boxes, the Ark and its hangings, the gates and the walls, all provided opportunities for Jews to affirm, "This is my God and I will beautify Him" (Exodus 15:2). Because they protect and adorn the most sacred object in Jewish religious life, the Torah scroll, Jews created a rich array of accoutrements in the finest materials and craftsmanship to adorn the Torah.[47] The Jewish calendar itself merited an embellished form of material representation.[48] Jews even had special subcalendars, such as the Omer calendar, to count the days from the exodus from slavery to the epiphany at Sinai. In the period covered by this volume, many of the objects transitioned from their original and intended use to become mementos of the past. Even then, they continued to exert their power as objects of inherent dignity. They were witnesses to, if not participants in, a living culture.

SPECIAL SPACES: SALONS

The term *salon* originated in France and refers to an unofficial, often domestic space that is devoted to crossing social boundaries in order to foster great conversation, appreciation of the arts, and social mingling across classes. It is difficult to capture its ephemeral spirit in any material medium for its central legacy is the very fact of its existence and its spirit of a safe yet adventurous space.[49] By allowing people who were often doubly marginalized in this society, as women and as Jews, to shine by virtue of their social skills, these private spaces came to exert powerful influence on the imagination of their time. Salons fostered a new class of social leaders, a space for ideas and art appreciation to grow without fear of political reprisals. In a society still constrained by social and legal boundaries, salons and their hosts created a miniature world in which social taboos were temporarily cast off and members of different religious, artistic, and professional groups could mingle for the joy of their mutual company. The interiors and objects from these homes reflected a rarified setting of the luxury items and furnishings of the wealthiest Jews. Yet their purpose went far beyond a conspicuous display of consumption. These Jews used their homes to draw in a world that had excluded them for centuries, to host the political nobility in a style to which they were accustomed, and to announce that Jews had triumphed over centuries of discrimination in a society that still regarded them warily.

When in 1795 the wealthy Berlin merchant Isaac Daniel Itzig commissioned a porcelain teacup and saucer bearing his portrait and that of his palatial residence, he accomplished several goals with one object. He perpetuated his likeness, he showed off his princely residence as a Jew who had "arrived" in Berlin, and he projected a quasi-royal signal of power and wealth to those who frequented his household. Portraiture became a significant medium to signal social status, and Jewish subjects commissioned portraits from prominent artists. They presented themselves wearing special clothes and holding particular objects with coded significance in settings of their choosing, thus projecting themselves within a material environment that distilled their sense of their status in the social world. Portraits announced to the world that their subjects were comfortable with who they were, that they had arrived into the bourgeois life and were claiming their place in that world. Richard Brilliant noted the contrast between the ubiquitous lack of overtly Jewish identity in the paintings of American Jews and the strong ties to Jewishness that we know most of the subjects affirmed.[50] The seeming contradiction resolves when we consider that these portraits were almost always hung in the semiprivate quarters of a family home. Anyone who entered, coreligionist or not, knew the Jewish identity of the family. The painting did not need to proclaim the obvious. Instead, portraits served as affirmations of class and of belonging to the larger society even while their commitment to Jewish identity was strong.[51]

Not all portraits of Jews projected high status. Some "portraits" convey the opposite impression. The lithograph of Jewish washerwomen from Izmir (1830) portrays their poverty and drudgery as it conveys their inner dignity, and Delacroix's painting of his Jewish translator's wife, Saada, expresses the artist's orientalist perspective while providing a sense of the circumstances of a North African Jewish woman in her home.

Synagogue Architecture

Through this period, the built environment inhabited by Jews—neighborhoods, individual dwellings, and buildings used for communal social and welfare purposes—was created in the style of the surrounding environment. "Jewish architecture" is a more difficult category to define, for as a professional trade architecture was not practiced by Jews until later in this period. Yet, all over the world, Jews commissioned, patronized, planned, and built structures for their use, sometimes with the specific intention of making them identifiable as Jewish structures. This is obviously true for buildings intended for religious use such as synagogues, *mikva'ot* (ritual baths), or mausoleums. Our section includes religious buildings, but it goes well beyond them.

Just as the changing interest in ritual objects that had been in continuous use among Jews was spurred in part by the European fascination with antiquities and the archeological discoveries in the Middle East, so, too, interest in a "Jewish" architectural history was sparked in the nineteenth century in the West in part by archeology fever. The discovery of remains of synagogues from the Byzantine period in Israel and the architectural models of the Jerusalem Temple piqued the interest of Jews and non-Jews alike in questioning the character of synagogue architecture. If Jews would be free to build the best structure they could afford, what would it, what should it, look like? Synagogues built in Europe in the age of Emancipation had somewhat contradictory goals. On the one hand, they were to articulate a proud Jewishness, which by definition meant a distinctive style. On the other hand, they wanted to announce that they were deeply embedded in the European cityscape.

One distinctive type of building associated with Jewish culture in the earlier part of the period covered in this volume is the wooden synagogue of Poland. Very few survived the Nazi period, but these buildings, dating from the seventeenth and eighteenth centuries, bespeak a confident relationship of Jews within their environment.[52] The synagogues were intended to stand out from surrounding buildings both by their height and by their design. They were often located on the outskirts of the original settlement, close to the water. Their exuberant interior decoration testifies to an important and original form of folk art.

Why wood? Laws made it difficult for Jews in that period to obtain permission for masonry synagogue structures, and timber abounded in the rich forests of Poland and Lithuania. Polish synagogues were largely built and decorated by Jewish craftsmen. Prayer spaces for women in the synagogue evolved over time, from small slits in the wall to elaborate galleries with latticed woodwork and separate entrances, possibly indicating an increased presence of women in the synagogues in this period. The large wooden synagogues often functioned as study halls as well as places of worship.[53]

As Jews settled in Western Europe and the Americas, they built synagogues that reflected the spirit of houses of worship of their time and place while also distinguishing the buildings with emblems denoting its Jewish character.[54] (Surprisingly, Stars of David came very late as synagogue adornments.) The second synagogue built in colonial America was the Touro Synagogue of Newport (1763). Its Christian architect designed other noted buildings in Newport, Cambridge, and Boston. Among its many features, the Touro Synagogue has a "secret" trapdoor in the floor of the reading platform, a feature of many colonial American buildings that may have resonated with a Sephardic congregation descended from Iberian refugees. Many of the most elegant synagogue buildings had their main entrances behind gates or facing away from the street.

Synagogues in the Western world went through several stylistic phases, with some elements overlapping or mingling in each. Greco-Roman classicism was replaced by references to Egyptian antiquity; from the mid-nineteenth century there was a pronounced turn to orientalism. The "Moorish" style for synagogues, influenced by the Alhambra and by fantasy, took hold particularly powerfully in Central European lands.[55] It also became popular in the United States and in England and France where Jews' embrace of a "Moorish" style reinforced the argument that they did not truly belong in Europe. This perspective held many positive as well as negative connotations; however, Jews of the time used these tropes to convey their pride in their unique history.[56]

By the early nineteenth century, Jews in large urban areas of Western Europe and the United States commissioned synagogues from the most prominent architects of their time. While the architects of Western synagogues were generally non-Jews in the eighteenth and early nineteenth century, Jewish architects were more common in the second half of the nineteenth century.

Some of the same principles governing Jewish buildings for daily life were echoed in cemeteries. Jews not only designed and decorated gravestones; wealthier individuals and families also constructed monuments and mausoleums that resembled small buildings and expressed their Jewish identity. Jewish grave sites were adorned with Stars of David, candelabra, tablets of the Law, and similar icons identifying the dead as Jews.[57]

Any discussion of built environment must include the central role that Jewish entrepreneurs and industrialists had in building the modern cities of Europe. Often least invested in preserving memories of a difficult past from which they had been excluded, Jews hoped to leave an ordered and beautiful stamp on the shape of the cities themselves. They participated in and sometimes led the construction of railroads and stations, shopping arcades and department stores, new neighborhoods with grand boulevards and elegant apartment buildings, not to mention their own residential quarters. In Paris, the bankers James de Rothschild and Louis Fould, and the developers Émile and Isaac Pereire, left an indelible stamp on the city as they commissioned and built banks, hotels, and entire neighborhoods, buildings that today still signal "quintessential Paris."[58] An age of fathomless aesthetic possibility dawned for a people whose horizons had been so greatly circumscribed until the nineteenth century.

Fine Art: Painting and Sculpture

For the longest time, scholars of the visual arts and built environment discounted the very notion of Jewish fine art, not to mention architecture. "Jewish art" conjured primarily objects intended for ritual purposes. The material included in this section embraces the ever-growing body of scholarship that demonstrates that contrary to earlier assumptions, Jews pursued artistic expression in many media wherever they lived. As new gateways to artistic education and freedom opened, Jews flocked to the arts and made them their own. All over the world, Jewish art reflected the hybrid nature of Jewishness, including the material circumstances and cultural milieu of the larger environment. Individual artisans and artists selected and created according to their personal and Jewish experiences.[59]

The pursuit and nurturing of the fine arts (primarily painting and sculpture) required elaborate educational, social, economic, and institutional frameworks. This context scarcely existed for Jews until the later decades of the nineteenth century (although the myth that Jewish culture shunned visual expression has long been put to rest).[60] Unlike music, to which Jews had at least some basic approach in synagogue settings, no framework in premodern society existed within which Jews could pursue the fine arts. The emergence of Jews as painters and sculptors involved more of a creation de novo than any of the other fields of culture in which Jews participated. Visual artists included painters, sculptors, photographers, engravers of medals and coins, miniaturists, and muralists. It is difficult to name even one serious sculptor of Jewish origins who worked before the nineteenth century, and although Jews had been making craft items of exquisite beauty through the ages, other than synagogue decoration, manuscript illustration, and metal engraving, it is difficult to find them painting and drawing much earlier than the period that this volume addresses.

To speak of the opening of the world to art made by Jews and the opening of Jewish eyes to the world of art, a new framework as well as a new mind-set had to come into being on both sides. Fine arts required access into social circles that cultivated and appreciated secular art. Gradual exposure of more Jews to more Western art meant that more of them were able to contemplate and appreciate it. Academies and circles of painters where art could be studied and learned began to accept Jewish students. Salons at which art could be exhibited and analyzed, homes in which it could be commissioned and hung, and museums that could acquire, display, and validate it, each of these formed a necessary link for the cycle of artistic affirmation to be perpetuated. To earn a livelihood, artists needed to cultivate the commercial side of art, to befriend agents and dealers who would introduce them to the parts of society that could afford to cultivate their talent. Art could be criticized in journals, replicated in print for popular consumption, and collected for private and public appreciation. As the nineteenth century progressed, Jews moved from the margins to the center of the art world, both as creators of first-rank art and as entrepreneurs.

Yet a label such as "Jewish art" is neither helpful nor relevant. Certainly, there is nothing inherently Jewish about many of the images included in this volume, and readers may be surprised by some of the choices. The guiding principle for inclusion has been the identity of the artist (with the exception of certain portraits), based on the concept that art expresses the experience and personality of the artist, even if that connection is not immediately obvious. The artists exhibited the world they knew best, in all its particularity, as a subject just as worthy of artistic depiction as any other. To illustrate this, we can look at the trajectories of a few of the artists encountered in these pages.

Moritz Daniel Oppenheim is one of the best-recognized "Jewish" artists of nineteenth-century Europe.[61] A prodigy who trained at the Munich Academy at a young age, his work embraces his own Jewish identity and that of his people. It fully engages the experiences of German Jews who entered comfortable middle-class life while maintaining their traditions. His work overturned stereotypes of Jewish life held by most non-Jews and many enlightened Jews of his age. Yet by virtue of his own distance from the subject and his great talent, his paintings transcend the particulars. Oppenheim's success was unique: most Jewish artists found that despite the growth of an art-consuming middle class of Jews, if they were confined to a Jewish market by genre or subject, they could not earn a livelihood as artists.

Such was the case with Abraham Jacob Pizzaro. Born to Sephardic parents in the Caribbean colony of St. Thomas, he led a peripatetic life from a young age, with stints in France and Venezuela. Reaching Paris in the mid-nineteenth century, he styled himself Camille Pissarro. His work reflects his embrace of the rural countryside and its peasants as a space of warmth, natural beauty, and harmony (plein air was in vogue then), and he rejected as dark and malevolent the forces of industrialization and capitalism. Although not directly present in his paintings, Pissarro's Jewish origins and family circles remained a presence throughout his life. The schools and salons judged his work on its merits and accepted him without any distinction from the others. Yet he was sometimes teased for his Jewishness, called Abraham or Moses because of his hair and beard (see his self-portrait).

Galician-born Maurycy Gottlieb went to study art in Kraków as a teen, and his immense talent was nurtured at the Academy there. A Polish patriot, Gottlieb presented his Jewish subjects in their full humanity and depth. His *Jews Praying in the Synagogue on Yom Kippur* is perhaps the most iconic of his paintings, while he depicted subjects that ranged from Jesus to Shylock to Ahasuerus as contemporary Jews (frequently including Gottlieb himself). His premature death at age twenty-three cut off a brilliant talent, but he had already earned a place in the history of representing Jews in art for his warm, direct, and unapologetic images.

While histories of Jews and the fine arts often survey the national or stylistic clusters of artists, this tends to obscure some of the remarkable commonalities that many of the Jewish artists shared. The number of family members who shared some roots or orientation in cognate fields is striking. Three brothers of the Dutch Verveer family became renowned artists. Salamon Leonardus Verveer and his brother Elchanon Leonardus Verveer were famed for iconic depictions of the Dutch landscape. A third brother, Maurits, was a skillful painter as well; by the mid-1850s he had turned to photography, one of the first in the Netherlands to do so. Henschel, Solomon, Meyerbeer (Beer), and Weiner represent just a few of the family clusters of Jewish artists productive in this period.

Every one of the selections in this volume represents a personal, and Jewish, odyssey. In some cases, this is addressed overtly in the works of art themselves, whereas in many others, the artist or his or her work did not represent conventional Jewishness or Jewish identity. The very ordinariness of some of these images and their lack of any particularly Jewish content reflects ways in which the artist embraced the world. In other cases, the work is deeply Jewish in theme and here the general message is the reverse. The artist is exhibiting the world he or she knows best, in all its particularity, as a subject just as worthy of artistic depiction as any other.

PHOTOGRAPHY

As a new technology, photography caught the imagination of young Jews. Louis Daguerre invented his eponymous process using chemicals to capture an image on a silver plate in 1839, and within a few years the technique had spread through Europe and the United States. Initially used for portraiture, one of the first to employ the technology to capture the great outdoors was Solomon Nunes Carvalho. Carvalho accompanied explorer John Fremont on an expedition across the United States in 1853. Despite the demanding challenges of the process itself, not to mention the need to adapt it to freezing conditions, they captured some three hundred daguerreotype images, a historic achievement. This traditional Jew of Sephardic descent penned a riveting and best-selling account of his adventures. Through his images and his account of their expedition, *Incidents of Travel and Adventure in the Far West*, Carvalho became the lens through which many Americans first encountered the western frontier, its magnificent and rugged landscapes, and its Native Americans.

Jews served the art world as prominent and influential critics, patrons, collectors, and exhibitors of the arts. They collected, displayed, and donated art to eminent institutions. Jews used their collections to announce their aesthetic discernment and financial success. Thus, Lesser Gieldzinski (1830–1910) collected furniture, paintings, and Judaica, objects that collectively affirmed his Jewish identity as well as his citizenship and rootedness in the city of Danzig. Isaac Straus of Strasbourg exhibited (perhaps for the first time in modern history) his collection of Jewish ceremonial objects at the Palais de Trocadéro in Paris in 1878. The exhibit marked a new turn toward the nostalgic appreciation of explicitly Jewish art, a turn that was not fully realized until the end of the nineteenth century. The Rothschild, Sassoon, and Goldsmid families began to amass collections that became synonymous with Jewish art collecting. Their donation of collections to central institutions to exhibit under their names in perpetuity expressed their desire to be remembered in association with the features of the art they collected.[62]

Although most of these collections did not focus primarily on Jewish art, by the late nineteenth century many European Jews regarded artistically crafted Jewish ceremonial objects with a new gaze, as exotic reminders of a lost past. By then, European interest in the art and archeology of ancient Palestine demonstrated to the world that the modern emergence of Jews in the art world was no anomaly but rather the recovery of a lost patrimony.

The Performing Arts

Jews had always cherished lofty liturgical traditions, and popular occasions for musical and theatrical expression abounded. Torah cantillation and cantorial tunes that dated to medieval times continued in synagogue tradition. In the early modern period, many synagogues supported a musical team, with cantor, bass, and *meshorer* (voice accompanist) harmonizing the music. Weddings, *purimshpils*, and the dramatization of Bible stories provided entertainment over the centuries. One of the most striking changes in European Jewish culture toward the later eighteenth century was marked by the entry of Jews into art music, opera houses, and the stage.

The pathbreaking turn in this period lies in the Jewish entry into artistic spheres previously considered beyond Jews' abilities, "belonging" instead to European social strata where Jews were not welcome.[63] Like many other elite arts, music, opera, and theater required special training, lifelong exposure and appreciation, cultivated patrons, and appropriate performance settings. The business of what we call today "classical music," "classical opera," and professional theater changed dramatically in the eighteenth century. In this period, it stepped away from its ecclesiastical roots and was reinvented as public entertainment. Such innovation created spaces that had hitherto been closed to Jews.

This entrepreneurial spirit was evident on all types of public stages. Theaters presented plays written by Jews, featuring Jewish characters, or acted by Jewish professionals. Rachel Félix maintained classical tragedy on the French stage as a singular presence against the prevailing trend of romantic comedy, and Sarah Bernhardt achieved her early international acclaim on the stage in this period. The first Arabic-language secular script for a play, written by Abraham Daninos, was published in the mid-nineteenth century.

Conservatories of music established neutral standards for judging talent, opening their doors to those without social connections. Technical innovations in instruments and acoustics enabled music and voices that had been played in small spaces to be projected powerfully to large audiences in grand halls. Instead of being sponsored by churches, royals, or small elite circles, patronage of artistic performance expanded to public "audiences," and this required an entirely new economic model for the giant productions.[64]

Once the doors began to open, music by Jews ceased to be "Jewish music." It entered and belonged to the broader world. In some cases, the Jewish (or born Jewish) composers bridged both worlds, but this volume includes all manner of musical creation by Jews without distinguishing whether the form and content overtly indicate Jewishness. The role of Jews as critics, journalists, and printers of music and of librettos contributed immeasurably to its popularization as one of the accoutrements for accomplished educated citizens.

The first half of the nineteenth century saw the breakthrough of Jewish composers and performers to the greatest renown on the European stage. In the 1830s and 1940s, Felix Mendelssohn Bartholdy, Fromental-Halévy, and Giacomo Meyerbeer, each with strong ties to his Jewish origins, were the most celebrated composers in France and in German lands and were renowned throughout Europe. Jews brought aspects of Jewish synagogue music into the larger world of classical music, while progressive synagogues took contemporaneous Western music into their services.[65] Cantors began to collect and transcribe arrangements of synagogue music, and many introduced Western elements into their arrangements. In the late nineteenth century, professional Yiddish theater and opera matured in Eastern Europe and opened a new chapter in modern Yiddish culture.

Jews stood at the forefront of a movement to integrate "indigenous" music into the Western canon. Mordechai Rosenthal (Ròszavölgyi) advanced the cause of "gypsy" music in Hungary, and British composer Isaac Nathan championed Australian aboriginal music later in his life. Joseph Gusikov of Shklov enthralled Jewish and non-Jewish audiences with ingenious devices on which he played a form of klezmer folk music while dressed in Hasidic garb. The integration of traditional elements of Jewish folk music and theater into performances intended for modern audiences symbolizes the journey of Jewish performing arts that had come full circle.

This volume concludes, then, on a high note. The most distressing turns in nineteenth-century European history, Russian pogroms, and the Dreyfus affair in France had not yet occurred. Their effects, including mass migrations to the United States, Canada, and Latin America, and the founding of Zionism, were not yet imaginable. The Ottoman Empire, the Austro-Hungarian Empire, and the tsarist Russian Empire still governed their subjects. I often remind students that the key to entering the past sometimes resides not in remembering but in forgetting. If we are to enter the world of our subjects, we must forget what we know came "after." What may seem to be fragile victory from a contemporary perspective appeared to the Jews of the nineteenth century as inexorable progress. They seized opportunities regardless of how hesitantly offered and turned them into achievements of enduring value, deep humanity, and surpassing beauty. What opens before you, dear reader, is a panorama of hope and of passion for the world. There are many entry points. Each selection stands in its own right. Taken as a whole, I hope you find these riches from the past as provocative, amusing, and moving as I did.

Notes

1. Richard I. Cohen, *Jewish Icons: Art and Society in Modern Europe* (Berkeley: University of California Press, 1998), 158.

2. Ammiel Alcalay, *After Jews and Arabs: Remaking Levantine Culture* (Minneapolis: University of Minnesota Press, 1993), 213.

3. Aron Rodrigue, *Jews and Muslims: Images of Sephardi and Eastern Jewries in Modern Times* (Seattle: University of Washington Press, 2003).

4. Jonathan D. Sarna and Jonathan Golden, "The American Jewish Experience through the Nineteenth Century: Immigration and Acculturation," National Humanities Center, Brandeis University, http://www.bjpa.org/Publications/details.cfm?PublicationID=4067.

5. On the German migration and the role of women in it, see Hasia Diner, "German Immigrant Period in the United States," *Jewish Women's Archive*, https://jwa.org/encyclopedia/article/german-immigrant-period-in-united-states.

6. Todd M. Endelman, "German Jews in Victorian England: A Study in Drift and Defection," in *Assimilation and Community: The Jews in Nineteenth-Century Europe*, ed. Jonathan Frankel and Steven J. Zipperstein (Cambridge: Cambridge University Press, 1992), 57–87.

7. For early modern examples, see Debra Kaplan, "The Self in Social Context: Asher ha-Levi of Reichshofen's *Sefer Zikhronot*," *Jewish Quarterly Review* 97, no. 2 (2007): 210–36; Leon Modena, *The Autobiography of a Seventeenth-Century Venetian Rabbi*, ed. Mark Cohen (Princeton, N.J.: Princeton University Press, 1988); Beth-Zion Abrahams, *The Life of Glueckel of Hameln (1646–1724) Written by Herself* (New York: T. Yoseloff, 1962; repr., Philadelphia: Jewish Publication Society of America, 2010) or the full text in Yiddish with Hebrew translation, *Glikl, Zikhroynes 1691–1719*, ed. and trans. Chava Turniansky (Jerusalem: Mercaz Shazar and Mercaz Dinur, 2006). For an analysis of Western life writing that emphasizes rupture, see Alan L. Mintz, *Banished from Their Father's Table: Loss of Faith and Hebrew Autobiography* (Bloomington: Indiana University Press, 1989).

8. For an acute analysis of the cultural and legal pluralism in nineteenth-century Morocco and the turn away from it under French influence, see Jessica M. Marglin, *Across Legal Lines: Jews and Muslims in Modern Morocco* (New Haven, Conn.: Yale University Press, 2016).

9. Edith Gerson-Kiwi, "The Music of the Kurdistan Jews," *Yuval* 2 (1971): 59–72.

10. For the most recent assessment of this term, see Zachary Leader, introduction to *On Life-Writing*, ed. Zachary Leader (Oxford: Oxford University Press, 2015), 1–6.

11. Marcus Moseley, *Being for Myself Alone: Origins of Jewish Autobiography* (Stanford, Calif.: Stanford University Press, 2005).

12. Matthias B. Lehmann, *Emissaries from the Holy Land: The Sephardic Diaspora and the Practice of Pan-Judaism in the Eighteenth Century* (Stanford, Calif.: Stanford University Press, 2014).

13. Phillip E. Miller, *Karaite Separatism in Nineteenth-Century Russia: Joseph Solomon Lutski's Epistle of Israel's Deliverance* (Cincinnati, Ohio: Hebrew Union College Press, 1993), 4.

14. Ruth R. Wisse, *The Modern Jewish Canon: Journey through Language and Culture* (Chicago: University of Chicago Press, 2000), 31.

15. Robert Alter, *The Invention of Hebrew Prose: Modern Fiction and the Language of Realism* (Seattle: University of Washington Press, 1988), 5.

16. On Jews in the military of this period, see Derek J. Penslar, *Jews and the Military: A History* (Princeton, N.J.: Princeton University Press, 2013), chaps. 1–4; Yohanan Petrovsky-Shtern, *Jews in the Russian Army, 1827–1917: Drafted into Modernity* (Cambridge: Cambridge University Press, 2009).

17. Lisa Moses Leff, "Eugénie Foa," *Jewish Women: A Comprehensive Historical Encyclopedia*, *Jewish Women's Archive*, http://jwa.org/encyclopedia/article/foa-eugenie.

18. For introductions, see T. Carmi, *The Penguin Book of Hebrew Verse* (London: Penguin Books, 1981), 13–55; Irving Howe, Ruth R. Wisse, and Khone Shmeruk, *The Penguin Book of Modern Yiddish Verse* (New York: Penguin Books, 1987), 1–50.

19. Richard I. Cohen, "Urban Visibility and Biblical Visions," in *Cultures of the Jews*, ed. David Biale (New York: Schocken Books, 2002), 756.

20. Eliyahu Stern, *Jewish Materialism: The Intellectual Revolution of the 1870s* (New Haven, Conn.: Yale University Press, 2018).

21. Endelman, "German Jews."

22. For an overview of the growth and development of Hasidism, see David Assaf, "Hasidism," in *YIVO Encyclopedia of Jews in Eastern Europe* (New Haven, Conn.: Yale University Press, 2008), 1:659–70.

23. Moshe Rosman, *Founder of Hasidism: A Quest for the Historical Ba'al Shem Tov* (Oxford: Littman Library of Jewish Civilization, 1996).

24. For the best recent account of the rise of Hasidism, see *Hasidism: A New History,* ed. David Biale et al. (Princeton, N.J.: Princeton University Press, 2017).

25. On this argument, see Gershon David Hundert, *Jews in Poland-Lithuania in the Eighteenth Century: A Genealogy of Modernity* (Berkeley: University of California Press, 2004).

26. Marcin Wodziński, *Haskalah and Hasidism in the Kingdom of Poland: A History of Conflict*, trans. Sarah Cozens, with Agnieszka Mirowska (Oxford: Littman Library of Jewish Civilization, 2005), analyzes how the conflict between *maskilim* and Hasidim played out in the Kingdom of Poland.

27. On the opponents of Hasidism (Mitnagdim), see Allan Nadler, *The Faith of the Mithnagdim: Rabbinic Responses to Hasidic Rapture* (Baltimore: Johns Hopkins University Press, 1999); Yehudah Mirsky, "Musar Movement," in *YIVO Encyclopedia of Jews in Eastern Europe* (New Haven, Conn.: Yale University Press, 2008), 2:1214–16.

28. Zvi Zohar, "Religion: Rabbinic Tradition and the Response to Modernity," in *The Jews of the Middle East and North Africa in Modern Times*, ed. Reeva Spector Simon, Michael Menachem Laskier, and Sara Reguer (New York: Columbia University Press, 2002), 71.

29. On the impact of scientific thought on late nineteenth-century Muslim society, see Marwa Elshakry, *Reading Darwin in Arabic, 1860–1950* (Chicago: University of Chicago Press, 2013).

30. See further Fred Astren, *Karaite Judaism and Historical Understanding* (Columbia: University of South Carolina Press, 2004).

31. Michael Graetz, "The Jewish Enlightenment," in *German Jewish History in Modern Times*, ed. Michael Meyer (London: Leo Baeck Institute, 1996), 1:261–375.

32. Eliyahu Stern, *The Genius: Elijah of Vilna and the Making of Modern Jewry* (New Haven, Conn.: Yale University Press, 2013), 63–82.

33. Ismar Schorsch, *From Text to Context: The Turn to History in Modern Judaism* (Hanover, N.H.: Brandeis University Press, and University Press of New England, 2003), 152.

34. The society was called Verein für Kultur und Wissenschaft der Juden. Schorsch, *Text to Context*, 213.

35. On the multiple tensions inherent in the Wissenschaft enterprise, see David Myers, *Re-inventing the Jewish Past: European Jewish Intellectuals and the Zionist Return to History* (Oxford: Oxford University Press, 1995), 15.

36. Heinrich Graetz, *Geschichte der Juden von den ältesten Zeiten bis auf die Gegenwart*, 11 vols. (Leipzig: Oskar Leiner, 1853–1870). For a recent review of the primary and secondary literature by and about Graetz, see Amos Bitzan, "Heinrich Graetz," *Oxford Bibliographies Online,* http://www.oxfordbibliographies.com/view/document/obo-9780199840731/obo-9780199840731-0047.xml.

37. For a comprehensive discussion of the changes in the Ottoman Empire during the nineteenth-century Tanzimat reforms and their cultural and political impact on Jews, see Julia Phillips Cohen, *Becoming Ottomans: Sephardi Jews and Imperial Citizenship in the Modern Era* (Oxford: Oxford University Press, 2014).

38. Wim Blockmans, "Citizens and Their Rulers," in *Empowering Interactions: Political Cultures and the Emergence of the State in Europe, 1300–1900*, ed. Wim Blockmans, Andre Holenstein, and Jon Mathieu (Farnham, U.K.: Ashgate, 2009), 281–92, provides a corrective to the teleological conception of nations states as the inevitable outcome of political consolidation. I thank David Sorkin for alerting me to this collection.

39. On the Ottoman Jewish press in the last decades of the nineteenth and the early ones of the twentieth century, see Sarah Abrevaya Stein, *Making Jews Modern: The Yiddish and Ladino Press in the Russian and Ottoman Empires* (Bloomington: Indiana University Press, 2003).

40. Philip E. Miller, "Shukr Kuhayl in Galicia: An Anti-Hasidic Ruse?" in *Judaeo-Yemenite Studies: Proceedings of the Second International Congress,* ed. Ephraim Isaac and Yosef Tobi (Princeton, N.J.: Princeton University Press, 1999), 65–69; Bat-Zion Eraqi-Klorman, *The Jews of Yemen in the Nineteenth Century: A Portrait of a Messianic Community* (Leiden: Brill, 1993).

41. Avraham Greenbaum, "Newspapers and Periodicals," in in *YIVO Encyclopedia of Jews in Eastern Europe* (New Haven, Conn.: Yale University Press, 2008), 2:1260–68.

42. Natan Cohen, "Itonut yomit yehudit be-Folin," in Israel Bartal and Israel Gutman, eds., *Kiyyum ve-shever: Yehudei Polin le-doroteihem* (Jerusalem: Merkaz Zalman Shazar le-toledot Yisra'el, 1997), 2: 301–2.

43. Isaiah Shachar, *Jewish Tradition in Art: The Feuchtwanger Collection of Judaica*, trans. Rafi Grafman (Jerusalem: Israel Museum, 1981), 12–14, cited in Cohen, *Jewish Icons*, 70.

44. I thank Emily D. Bilski for this observation and her astute comments throughout this section.

45. Vivian B. Mann, ed., *Morocco: Jews and Art in a Muslim Land* (New York: Merrell, 2000), fig. 77, p. 127.

46. Yosef Yerushalmi, *Haggadah and History: A Panorama in Facsimile of Five Centuries of the Printed Haggadahs from the Collections of Harvard University and the Jewish Theological Seminary of America* (Philadelphia: Jewish Publication Society of America, 1997).

47. Rafi Grafman and Vivian Mann, eds., *Crowning Glory: Silver Torah Ornaments of the Jewish Museum* (Boston: David R. Godine, 1996).

48. Elisheva Carlebach, *Palaces of Time: Jewish Calendar and Culture in Early Modern Europe* (Cambridge, Mass.: Harvard University Press, 2011).

49. Emily D. Bilski and Emily Braun, *Jewish Women and Their Salons: The Power of Conversation* (New York: Jewish Museum, 2005).

50. See similar patterns described in Laura Arnold Leibman, *Messianism, Secrecy and Mysticism: A New Interpretation of Early American Jewish Life* (London: Vallentine Mitchell, 2012). I thank Prof. Julia Phillips Cohen for pointing this out.

51. Richard Brilliant, "Portraits as Silent Claimants: Jewish Class Aspirations and Representational Strategies in Colonial and Federal America," in *Facing the New World: Jewish Portraits in Colonial and Federal America* (Munich: Jewish Museum, 1997), 2.

52. Maria Piechotka and Kazimierz Piechotka, *Wooden Synagogues* (Warsaw: Arkady, 1959), and the expanded edition, *Heaven's Gates: Wooden Synagogues in the Territories of the Former Polish–Lithuanian Commonwealth* (Warsaw: Wydawn. Krupski i S-ka, 2004); Rachel Wischnitzer, *The Architecture of the European Synagogue* (Philadelphia: Jewish Publication Society of America, 1964), 125–47.

53. Thomas C. Hubka, *Resplendent Synagogue: Architecture and Worship in an Eighteenth-Century Polish Community* (Lebanon, N.H.: Brandeis University Press and University Press of New England, 2003), 41.

54. Barry Stiefel, *Jewish Sanctuary in the Atlantic World: A Social and Architectural History* (Columbia: University of South Carolina Press, 2014).

55. Ivan D. Kalmar, "Moorish Style: Orientalism, the Jews, and Synagogue Architecture," *Jewish Social Studies* 7, no. 3 (2001): 68–100.

56. Kalmar, 76–84; and John Efron, *German Jewry and the Allure of the Sephardic* (Princeton, N.J.: Princeton University Press, 2015), 112–60.

57. Fredric Bedoire, *The Jewish Contribution to Modern Architecture: 1830–1930* (Jersey City, N.J.: Ktav, 2004), 157–63.

58. Bedoire, 152–209.

59. Cohen, *Jewish Icons*, 7, concludes that Jewish art is "an elusive entity that can be best encapsulated by a general definition as that which reflects the Jewish experience." Bezalel Narkiss, "Introduction," *Journal of Jewish Art* 1 (1974): 5, preferred to avoid any definition.

60. Archaeological discoveries such as the Dura Europos synagogue and Byzantine-era synagogue floors paved the way for modern scholars' realization that Jews created rich figurative art in antiquity. For a survey of visual imagination in medieval Jewish culture, see Kalman P. Bland, *The Artless Jew: Medieval and Modern Affirmations and Denials of the Visual* (Princeton, N.J.: Princeton University Press, 2002).

61. For a fuller picture of Oppenheim's oeuvre, see George Heuberger and Anton Merk, eds., *Moritz Daniel Oppenheim: Jewish Identity in 19th Century Art* (Cologne: Wienand Verlag, 1999) and his memoir, *Erinnerungen eines deutsch-jüdischen Malers* (Heidelberg: Manitius, 1999).

62. Richard I. Cohen, "The Visual Revolution in Jewish Life—An Overview," in *Visualizing and Exhibiting Jewish Space and History*, ed. Richard I. Cohen, Studies in Contemporary Jewry 26 (New York: Oxford University Press, 2012), 4–11.

63. My discussion of Jews in Western music is indebted to David Conway, *Jewry in Music: Entry to the Profession from the Enlightenment to Richard Wagner* (Cambridge: Cambridge University Press, 2012), and to James Loeffler, *Posen Library* volume board member.
64. Conway, *Jewry in Music*, 11.
65. Conway, 133.

Bibliography

Alcalay, Ammiel. *After Jews and Arabs: Remaking Levantine Culture.* Minneapolis: University of Minnesota Press, 1993.

Alter, Robert. *The Invention of Hebrew Prose: Modern Fiction and the Language of Realism.* Seattle: University of Washington Press, 1988.

Assaf, David. "Hasidism." In *YIVO Encyclopedia of Jews in Eastern Europe*, 1:659–70. New Haven, Conn.: Yale University Press, 2008.

Astren, Fred. *Karaite Judaism and Historical Understanding.* Columbia: University of South Carolina Press, 2004.

Bartal, Israel, and Israel Gutman, eds. *Kiyyum ve-shever: Yehudei Polin le-doroteihem.* Jerusalem: Merkaz Zalman Shazar le-toledot Yisra'el, 1997.

Bedoire, Fredric. *The Jewish Contribution to Modern Architecture: 1830–1930.* Jersey City, N.J.: Ktav, 2004.

Biale, David, ed. *Cultures of the Jews.* New York: Schocken Books, 2002.

Bilski, Emily D., and Emily Braun, *Jewish Women and Their Salons: The Power of Conversation.* New York: Jewish Museum, 2005.

Bland, Kalman P. *The Artless Jew: Medieval and Modern Affirmations and Denials of the Visual.* Princeton, N.J.: Princeton University Press, 2002.

Borovaya, Olga. *Modern Ladino Culture: Press, Belles Lettres and Theater in the Late Ottoman Empire.* Bloomington: Indiana University Press, 2011.

Brilliant, Richard, ed. *Facing the New World: Jewish Portraits in Colonial and Federal America.* Munich: Jewish Museum, 1997.

Carlebach, Elisheva. *Palaces of Time: Jewish Calendar and Culture in Early Modern Europe.* Cambridge, Mass: Harvard University Press, 2011.

Carmi, T. *The Penguin Book of Hebrew Verse.* London: Penguin Books, 1981.

Cohen, Julia Phillips. *Becoming Ottomans: Sephardic Jews and Imperial Citizenship in the Modern Era.* Oxford: Oxford University Press, 2014.

Cohen, Richard I. *Jewish Icons: Art and Society in Modern Europe.* Berkeley: University of California Press, 1998.

——, ed. *Visualizing and Exhibiting Jewish Space and History.* Studies in Contemporary Jewry 26. New York: Oxford University Press, 2012.

Conway, David. *Jewry in Music: Entry to the Profession from the Enlightenment to Richard Wagner.* Cambridge: Cambridge University Press, 2012.

Diner, Hasia. "German Immigrant Period in the United States." *Jewish Women's Archive.* http://jwa.org/encyclopedia.

Efron, John M. *German Jewry and the Allure of the Sephardic.* Princeton, N.J.: Princeton University Press, 2015.

Endelman, Todd M. *The Jews of Georgian England, 1740–1830: Tradition and Change in a Liberal Society.* Philadelphia: Jewish Publication Society of America, 1979.

Eraqi-Klorman, Bat-Zion. *The Jews of Yemen in the Nineteenth Century: A Portrait of a Messianic Community.* Leiden: Brill, 1993.

Gerson-Kiwi, Edith. "The Music of the Kurdistan Jews." *Yuval* 2 (1971): 59–72.

Grafman, Rafi, and Vivian B. Mann, eds. *Crowning Glory: Silver Torah Ornaments of the Jewish Museum.* Boston: David R. Godine, 1996.

Greenbaum, Avraham. "Newspapers and Periodicals." In *YIVO Encyclopedia of Jews in Eastern Europe,* 2:1260–68. New Haven, Conn.: Yale University Press, 2008.

Hess, Jonathan M., Maurice Samuels, and Nadia Valman, eds. *Nineteenth-Century Jewish Literature: A Reader.* Stanford, Calif.: Stanford University Press, 2013.

Heuberger, George. *Erinnerungen eines deutsch-jüdischen Malers.* Heidelberg: Manutius Verlag, 1999.

Heuberger, George, and Anton Merk, eds., *Moritz Daniel Oppenheim: Jewish Identity in 19th-Century Art.* Cologne: Wienand Verlag, 2004.

Howe, Irving, Ruth R. Wisse, and Khone Shmeruk. *The Penguin Book of Modern Yiddish Verse.* New York: Penguin Books, 1987.

Hubka, Thomas C. *Resplendent Synagogue: Architecture and Worship in an Eighteenth-Century Polish Community.* Hanover, N.H.: Brandeis University Press and University Press of New England, 2003.

Hundert, Gershon David. *Jews in Poland-Lithuania in the Eighteenth Century: A Genealogy of Modernity.* Berkeley: University of California Press, 2004.

Hyman, Paula E. *The Emancipation of the Jews of Alsace: Acculturation and Tradition in the Nineteenth Century.* New Haven, Conn.: Yale University Press, 1991.

Kalmar, Ivan D. "Moorish Style: Orientalism, the Jews, and Synagogue Architecture." *Jewish Social Studies,* n.s. 7, no. 3 (2001): 68–100.

Leff, Lisa Moses. "Eugénie Foa." *Jewish Women: A Comprehensive Historical Encyclopedia.* https://jwa.org/encyclopedia/article/foa-eugenie.

Lehmann, Matthias B. *Emissaries from the Holy Land: The Sephardic Diaspora and the Practice of Pan-Judaism in the Eighteenth Century.* Stanford, Calif.: Stanford University Press, 2014.

Leibman, Laura Arnold. *Messianism, Secrecy and Mysticism: A New Interpretation of Early American Jewish Life.* London: Vallentine Mitchell, 2012.

Mann, Vivian B., ed. *Morocco: Jews and Art in a Muslim Land.* New York: Merrell, 2000.

Marglin, Jessica M. *Across Legal Lines: Jews and Muslims in Modern Morocco.* New Haven, Conn.: Yale University Press, 2016.

Mendes-Flohr, Paul, and Jehuda Reinharz, eds. *The Jew in the Modern World: A Documentary History.* Oxford: Oxford University Press, 2010.

Meyer, Michael A., ed. *German Jewish History in Modern Times.* Vols. 1–2. London: Leo Baeck Institute, 1996.

Miller, Phillip E. *Karaite Separatism in Nineteenth-Century Russia: Joseph Solomon Lutski's Epistle of Israel's Deliverance.* Cincinnati, Ohio: Hebrew Union College Press, 1993.

Mirsky, Yehudah. "Musar Movement." In *YIVO Encyclopedia of Jews in Eastern Europe,* 2:1214–16. New Haven, Conn.: Yale University Press, 2008.

Moseley, Marcus. *Being for Myself Alone: Origins of Jewish Autobiography.* Stanford, Calif.: Stanford University Press, 2005.

Nadler, Allan. *The Faith of the Mithnagdim: Rabbinic Responses to Hasidic Rapture.* Baltimore: Johns Hopkins University Press, 1999.

Narkiss, Bezalel. "Introduction." *Journal of Jewish Art* 1 (1974): 5.

Penslar, Derek J. *Jews and the Military: A History.* Princeton, N.J.: Princeton University Press, 2013.

Petrovsky-Shtern, Yohanan. *Jews in the Russian Army, 1827–1917: Drafted into Modernity.* Cambridge: Cambridge University Press, 2009.

Piechotka, Maria, and Kazimierz Piechotka. *Wooden Synagogues.* Warsaw: Arkady, 1959. Expanded edition, *Heaven's Gates: Wooden Synagogues in the Territories of the Former Polish–Lithuanian Commonwealth.* Warsaw: Wydawn. Krupski i S-ka, 2004.

Rodrigue, Aron. *Jews and Muslims: Images of Sephardi and Eastern Jewries in Modern Times.* Seattle: University of Washington Press, 2003.

Rosman, Moshe. *Founder of Hasidism: A Quest for the Historical Ba'al Shem Tov.* Oxford: Littman Library of Jewish Civilization, 1996.

Sarna, Jonathan D., and Jonathan Golden. "The American Jewish Experience through the Nineteenth Century: Immigration and Acculturation." Waltham, Mass.: National Humanities Center, Brandeis University, 2000. http://www.bjpa.org/Publications/details.cfm?PublicationID=4067.

Schorsch, Ismar. *From Text to Context: The Turn to History in Modern Judaism.* Hanover, N.H.: Brandeis University Press and University Press of New England, 2003.

———. *Leopold Zunz: Creativity in Adversity.* Philadelphia: University of Pennsylvania Press, 2016.

Shachar, Isaiah. *Jewish Tradition in Art: The Feuchtwanger Collection of Judaica.* Translated by Rafi Grafman. Jerusalem: Israel Museum, 1981.

Simon, Reeva Spector, Michael Menachem Laskier, and Sara Reguer, eds. *The Jews of the Middle East and North Africa in Modern Times.* New York: Columbia University Press, 2002.

Stanislawski, Michael. *Psalms for the Tsar: A Minute-Book of a Psalms-Society in the Russian Army, 1864–1867.* New York: Yeshiva University Press, 1988.

———. *Tsar Nicholas I and the Jews: The Transformation of Jewish Society in Russia, 1825–1855.* Philadelphia: Jewish Publication Society of America, 1983.

Stein, Sarah Abrevaya. *Making Jews Modern: The Yiddish and Ladino Press in the Russian and Ottoman Empires.* Bloomington: Indiana University Press, 2003.

Stiefel, Barry L. *Jewish Sanctuary in the Atlantic World: A Social and Architectural History.* Columbia: University of South Carolina Press, 2014.

Wischnitzer, Rachel. *The Architecture of the European Synagogue.* Philadelphia: Jewish Publication Society of America, 1964.

Wisse, Ruth R. *The Modern Jewish Canon: Journey through Language and Culture.* Chicago: University of Chicago Press, 2000.

Wodziński, Marcin. *Haskalah and Hasidism in the Kingdom of Poland: A History of Conflict.* Translated by Sarah Cozens, with Agnieszka Mirowska. Oxford, U.K.: Littman Library of Jewish Civilization, 2005.

Literature

Jewish writing in this section reflects the profound changes that confronted Jews in the eighteenth and nineteenth centuries. It includes writing in many genres and styles, both formal and informal, literary and colloquial, across language, gender, class, and profession. Some writers self-consciously broke with traditional and religious models; others defiantly embraced it. The section, and this volume, opens with "Life Writing." This genre introduces the volume as a whole in two ways: first, it allows the reader a glimpse into individual lives as their writers presented them, a way for the reader to step into the world of the past as it was recollected by those who lived it. Second, writing about the self emerged as a literary form in this period. While not all life writing is self-consciously literary, each selection opens a small window into the contours of an individual Jewish life. It is followed by a section on "Travel Writing." Mobility of Jews as individuals as well as in large numbers was a hallmark of this period. Unlike migration for the purpose of settling in a new place, travelers intended to return home with impressions and reports of the marvels they had seen abroad. Their writing allows us to reflect both on their own cultures as well as the ones they visited, to see the world through their eyes.

A key concept in this volume is the rise of a Jewish-inflected culture that is not primarily religious. The expansion of belles lettres in many genres in Jewish and in vernacular languages, literature written for its aesthetic rather than primarily utilitarian value, is another *novum* in Jewish culture of this period. For the final sections, "Folktales and Fiction" and "Poetry," Jews wrote in their local vernaculars, or in Jewish vernaculars; they revived Hebrew as a modern literary language. The chronological order of the entries in each section allows the reader to trace the development of new forms of writing. These progressed from the first wooden and stumbling efforts to literary mastery that eventually allowed modern Jewish writers to renew Jewish culture and to secure their place in modern world literature.

Life Writing: Biography, Autobiography, and Ego Documents

Abraham Mendes de Castro
1689–1762

In 1751, Abraham Mendes de Castro, a Sephardic Jew who lived on the island of Curaçao, donated the wooden beams needed to expand the Holy Ark in the Mikvé Israel-Emanuel Synagogue, the oldest continuously used synagogue in the Western Hemisphere. In 1760, de Castro commissioned the first bilingual Hebrew–Spanish Bible from publishers in Amsterdam. While the proceeds from sales of this edition were intended to go to Jewish communities in Hebron and Jerusalem, he died before the work was completed.

Last Will and Testament
1752

Realizing that life is not in the hands of man but is governed by the only living God Almighty in whom I believe and adore, whose Divine Mosaic Law I, His slave, follow and venerate with all my heart and soul and His greatness and mercy profess, I Ab^m [Abraham] Mendez de Castro, son of Ab^m Mendez de Castro and Mrs. Ester Mendez de Castro, of Jewish origin, in full possession of my senses, declare this to be my last will and testament, irrevocable by virtue of divine and human laws.

I leave all that I possess and what He has granted to me and is [therefore] His, to my heir, the Almighty God of Ysrael, disowning all sorts of blood relations on earth; and so with His permission and Divine help I make these bequests and testament in His Holy Name as I submit to His Divine will, amen. [. . .]

I bequeath to the Hebra [Guemiluth Hasadim] of this island the house purchased from Marcos Basarne located between [that of] the Widow Jacob Fos [Vos] and [of] Mr. Jan Amaño opposite the worthy Haham's house. It shall be rented to tenants approved by the Messrs. Parnassim who shall pay the rent regularly and deliver same to the parnas of the Hebra to help maintain the sick poor under its care. The Hebra shall not distribute said rents to any other charity or mortgage or sell said house. For carrying out this objective, God will approve the work and grant complete health and prosperity to the Congregation for many years.

The house purchased from Yshak Pereira and that from the wife of Elias Dubernar and the one located on Pi[e]ter de May (Maai) Road where the wood is, I bequeath to Daniel and Jacob Mendez de Castro (equally) for them and their legitimate heirs through marriage. The deeds to said houses shall remain in the Chest of Documents at the Synagogue. Neither the said Mendez nor their heirs shall be able to mortgage, transfer or sell said houses to anyone. In the event of the death of the abovenamed [nephews], God forbid, one-third of the rent or value of said houses shall go to the Hebra [Guemiluth Hasadim] of this island, another third to the Congregation of Jerusalem and the remaining third to the Congregation of Hebron, without prejudice. [. . .]

The canuco [cunuco] shall not be sold while Serafiña lives; afterwards, the earnings therefrom shall become part of my residuary estate. [. . .]

I order the following gifts and escaboth [bequests for memorial prayers] to be made: For memorial prayers for my father, Ab^m Mendez de Castro, who died on the 10th of Kislev, forty pesos; for my mother, Mrs. Ester Mendez de Castro, who died on the 15th of Kislev, forty pesos; for my brother Yshak Mendez de Castro, forty pesos; one hundred pesos for my memorial services that God may receive me. To the Esiva [Yeshiva] of the elderly [Misheneth Zekenim] of Amsterdam, eighty pesos which shall be remitted by bill of exchange to the parnassim then presiding; to the three esibot [Yeshivot of Curaçao] of which I am a member, namely, the Honen Dalyn [Dalim], Pene Sabat and the Esiba of Semuel de Casseres, twenty-five pesos each; to the daughter of Benjamin de Rosa, to the daughter of Aron Machado and to the daughter of Ysaque [Mendez?] de Castro, twenty-five pesos each; fifty pesos to be distributed monthly among the poor of the Sedaca, I repeat, fifty pesos.

I also order that all work started by my negroes shall be finished and supplied with what I would have adjusted. Any lumber then remaining, white or mahogany, shall be sold at public auction for the benefit of my estate. Each of my negroes and negresses shall take his chest without opposition. Certificates of manumission shall be given to those hereinbelow named: Serafiña, children, grandchildren and her entire family; Esperanza, children, grandchildren and her entire family. Sesilia, Bastiaan and Inguito are discharged and shall be given a certificate of manumission. Acara owes forty pesos for his freedom while Agustin owes fifty (50) pesos. Caba must pay one hundred seventy pesos for his freedom; Sire, his brother, one hundred fifty pesos, and Sape, one hundred twenty pesos; said three brothers to look for the money [namely], four hundred forty pesos on which they shall meanwhile pay interest at 8 pc. per year until fully paid off. The rest [of the slaves] are mentioned in my inventory.

After the settlement of my accounts and payment of my debts, funeral expenses and legacies, I leave half of the remainder of my estate to the Community of Jerusalem and the other half to the Community of Hebron, to be remitted by the Messrs. Parnassim, in my name, for the purpose of buying several houses and annually distributing the rent realized therefrom among the poor of said communities, as the monies are received. And may God be judge and witness over the work that will receive my gift. [The Parnassim of Curaçao] shall send over whomever they wish to said communities to make certain that neither the Hahamim nor the Parnassim of those communities [i.e., Jerusalem and Hebron] sell, transfer or mortgage said houses, their mission being only to keep the deeds to such investment, in my name, in the Poor Chest. And should there not be enough after costs, insurance, postage or loss of money, then there shall be added the value of the house on Pi[e]ter de May (Maai) Road to make up the deficit. [. . .]

In the event that the balance of my account set aside for Hebron and Jerusalem does not reach 2,000 pesos net (free of all costs), the house of Pi[e]ter de May (Maai) Road shall be sold to make up the deficit for such charity. [. . .]

The Messrs. Parnassim and adjuntos in charge of the administration of my estate and execution of my last will and testament shall also see that my body is buried in the betahayn [Beth Hahaim] in the prepaid grave recorded in the Cemetery Register, and they shall send away for a tombstone on which shall be engraved Ab[raha]m's Sacrifice, with the verse: "And the angel of the Lord called unto him out of heaven, and said: 'Abraham, Abraham.' And he said: 'Here am I.'" May God gather me unto Him, amen.

To my nephews I recommend the love and reverence of God and the observance of His Holy Law. I also order that the apartment from whence God will call me unto Him should not be rented until eleven months after my death, and that the members of the esibot [yeshivot] to which I belong shall send someone to pray during that period, and every Saturday one real shall be offered for each [yeshiva].

Finally, I commend my soul to Adonay, God of Heaven and Earth, our God, our Father, our Creator in whom I believe and hope under the wings of His Divinity to be forgiven for all my sins, as promised us by the Merciful Father in the verse: "You the People, and I Adonay, your God." [. . .]

NOTE

Words in brackets appear in the original translation.

Translated by Isaac S. Emmanuel and Suzanne A. Emmanuel.

Aaron Lopez and Benjamin Gomez

Lopez, 1731–1782

Aaron Lopez was a prominent figure in colonial-era Rhode Island. Born Duarte Lopez in Lisbon to a family of conversos, Lopez changed his given name to Aaron after immigrating to North America, where he began living openly as a Jew. He settled in Newport and built a fortune on the trade of spermaceti, a wax derived from whale oil, though he had a range of mercantile interests, including involvement in the slave trade. When Lopez was denied citizenship of the colony of Rhode Island, he relocated for a time to Massachusetts, where his application for citizenship was successful. Though his fortunes were severely damaged during the Revolutionary War, Lopez supported the war effort. He was buried in the Jewish cemetery in Newport.

Gomez, 1710–1772

Benjamin Gomez was a member of one of the first prominent Jewish families in New York and colonial America. His father, Luis Gomez, born in Madrid to a wealthy converso, had married his mother, a Sephardic Jew from Jamaica, by prearrangement on his way to America. In New York, the Gomez family made a living trading with Native Americans. Their home, known today as the Gomez Mill House, is considered the oldest Jewish building in North America. The family also helped secure funding for the Shearith Israel Synagogue in Manhattan. Each member of the

Gomez family served an important role in the observance of Jewish ritual: Benjamin was the family mohel.

Correspondence Re: Circumcision of Babies and Marranos
1753-1767

New York, 28 May, 1753
Mr. Aaron Lopez
Dear Sir:

I have received your esteemed letter, in which you so kindly inform me that our Lord has given you a son. For this I extend the due felicitations to you, to your wife, my cousin, and to the rest of the family. May God permit you to rear him in great joy, together with the rest of your dear ones.

I am very grateful for the favor that you do me in offering me a part in the circumcision ceremony. I would accept most willingly, were it not that my business affairs do not permit it. I have no doubt that my brother Daniel will try to send someone who can. I, on my part, shall do what I can in this regard, and I shall always be honored to serve you in anything within my power.

Praying to God that this letter finds you and your wife, my cousin, and the rest of the family enjoying perfect health—may it come to me [also] soon—and may God preserve you for many years.

Yours sincerely,
Benjamin Gomez

New York, September 28th, 1767
Sir:

The inclosed [letter for a Mr. Mendes] received this week from Jamaica. As there is no person of that name here, conclude it must be intended for your son in law, who, am informed, is gone to Jamaica. Wish him safe there, and that this may find you in health in company of your spows [spouse], his, and the rest of your famley [family], as mine is at present.

Announcing you the compliments of the [Holiday] season, and that you may all be recorded in the books of life, I am, sir,
Your most humble servant,
Benjamin Gomez

I congratulate you on the safe arrival of your brothers, whome, I understand, intend to undergo the [circumcision] operation. Pray take care to have a good surgeon present, as it will require some judgment to stop the blood and cure the wound. My compliments to them, allso to Mr. Reveira and famley.

Mr. Aaron Lopez

Newport, September 30th, 1767
Mr. Benjamin Gomez
Sir:

I received your esteemed favour of the 28th inst., covering a letter for my son in law, Mr. Mendes, who left this port the 24th ult. for Jamaica and hope is safe arrived there before now. Your forwarding his letter lays me under an obligation, as also the good wishes and kind expressions you are pleased to pronounce on the arrival of my brother and his family from Portugal.

I duly notice the hints you are good enough to give in regard to the safety of the operation.

May you enjoy the approaching holy days and many others to come with perfect health and uninterrupted felicities, in which sincere wishes Mrs. Lopez and rest of my family joins me. Being most respectfully, sir,
Your very humble servant,
[Aaron Lopez]

NOTE

Words in brackets appear in the source text.

Other work by Aaron Lopez: "Letter Book: Manuscript" (date unknown).

Pinchas Katzenellenbogen
1691-1767

Scion of an illustrious rabbinical family, Pinchas (Pinḥas) Katzenellenbogen served as a rabbi in Moravia and Bavaria. He wrote his mainly autobiographical book, *Sefer yesh manḥilin*, between 1758 and 1764. The book sheds light on everyday Jewish life in Eastern and Central Europe in the 1700s, including detailed descriptions of remedies Katzenellenbogen presumably utilized in his practice as a *baʻal shem* (kabbalist healer).

Sefer yesh manḥilin (Those Who Bequeath)
1760

Section 230

Behold, I am aged and my eyes are dim and my hands heavy and shaky, and at a time when my strength, enabling me to remain standing upon my watch, is ebbing away—with the yoke of the rabbinate to carry out my task. Moreover, the divine attribute of judgment has struck at me, and my splendor and glory were taken from me on the evening of Thursday, the thirteenth day of Tishri last; I have dwelt alone—my wife, who had been my crown of beauty and the treasured mistress of the household, died on me—and it is an amazing thing that Wednesday, the twelfth, was the occasion of the *yortsayt* of the precious jewel that had formerly been in my hand, the lady Esther—may her soul rest in Paradise—my beloved daughter, who was of such surpassing excellence; and thus I was left all alone, and what can we say? etc.; for by this Divine decree I was cut off—and I lovingly accepted everything decreed against me by Heaven, in the year five thousand five hundred and twenty, [1760][1] in my abundant sorrow, as having occurred on account of my own guilt. Accordingly I said to myself: "What is there for me here?" and I became minded to settle in the city of Fürth, the place where I had grown up, and thereby to fulfill the verse: "I shall lie with my forefathers," in such manner as to be at table with one of our relatives, either with my brother's son, R. Saadya Isaiah—may his Rock and Redeemer preserve him—or with R. Zalman Ber, the husband of my sister, the lady Gittel—long may she live—while I was still able to manage—with God's help—being in a state of good bodily health, on just two or three gold coins from week to week, if God so willed it, for so long as the Almighty, blessed be He, has ordained that I remain alive and in fine physical health, with His assistance, blessed be He. And my son, the beloved of my soul, is in agreement concerning this, and, through God's help, he is my glory and the one who raises my head. My heart tells me that the most excellent mind of my beloved brother-in-law, our noble Master, R. Leib Fürth of Vienna, will likewise be in agreement, and I am expecting his reply to my inquiry shortly, if the Almighty so wills it. Now that being the case, what difference does it make whether I am living here or there, since all that matters is for me to prepare myself and to write to my aforementioned relatives in Fürth?

However, all new beginnings are fraught with difficulty, and my heart is pounding in relation to this matter—to uproot myself from the place where, with God's help, there is relief, and which is pleasant both toward Heaven and toward human beings, all of whom are beloved, and so forth, and to go to another place, which is wearisome, by reason of its great distance, and to sit at the table of others, and the like—and who knows what events a day may produce? However, may the All-Present cause everything to turn out favorably! Thus I said to myself that, in any event, I should seek the advice of the Master, the Rabbi—may the All-Merciful guard him and redeem him—as I had heard from his own mouth that his father-in-law, the illustrious head of the ecclesiastical court, the Maharitkh[2] of blessed memory, was in the habit of seeking the counsel of a wise man who was straightforward in his ways, upon which he would rely. Hence I make enquiry of you, my esteemed brother—may the All-Merciful guard and redeem you—sage of perfection and man of truth; it will be regarded as the equivalent of someone inquiring of the Urim and Tumim, representing truth and perfection. Now there is one thing that I request, and that I seek, given that his wide-ranging mind is on the verge of agreeing to that fine proposal mentioned above, which is, from a rational perspective, the appropriate and correct way for me to go—with Divine assistance—at the time of my old age, as aforementioned; may my esteemed brother—may the All-Merciful guard and redeem him—kindly forgive me for requesting him to send an introductory message to my aforesaid relatives in Fürth on my behalf along the lines mentioned above, to prepare the goodly way before me in advance—that is to say, whichever way he deems most appropriate—on the basis that I need to have a special room for my own use, containing a bed, a table, a chair and books, as well as an oven that I can heat up at times when the weather is cold; and the expenses of the wood are to be my responsibility, as the lodger, as I am aware that they are extremely high over there. And, as regards eating arrangements, these are—with God's help—to be like those of a righteous man eating to full satisfaction—I have no strength whatsoever for fasting; for even on the *yortsayt* of our mother, my most honored righteous rebbetzin, may her soul rest in Paradise—I have not fasted for the past four or five years, as I said to myself: "The vow I made to fast has duly been annulled by reason of 'subsequent regret,' just like other vows, in accordance with the decisions appearing in the responsa literature; albeit I was initially reluctant to annul it, because of what the Maharshal [R. Solomon Luria] has written in this regard, and because of what the Shakh [R. Shabetai Kohen] has written on *Yoreh de'ah* (section 214: para. 104) [and also at section 46 above] [. . .] until such time as I proved, in my own responsa, as aforementioned (at section 46), that one may annul a vow [to fast on] a *yortsayt* by reason of subsequent regret, just as one may annul other sorts of vows."

Now in the mornings, I drink coffee with milk, together with a breakfast loaf, a penny or a half and for lunch I eat as everyone else does; that is to say, on Sundays, the leftovers of the cooked Sabbath meals, and on Mondays and Thursdays, I habitually eat dairy foods, and on occasion also meaty liquid dishes without meat, pursuant to what we have learned in a Mishnah [m.Nedarim 6:6]: "One who takes a vow not to eat meat is permitted to eat the gravy and the skimmed-off portions" [. . .] for I am accustomed to do this, not having taken any vow concerning it; and on Tuesdays and Wednesdays, I eat meaty soups plus meat [. . .] and on Fridays, whatever is available to me, so as to avoid getting hungry [. . .] and at night I eat nothing, except for on the nights of the New Moon and special seasons and Festivals; and with this detailed description one will know the amount it is appropriate to allocate by way of expenses for food [. . .] besides the cost of the firewood [for heating the oven], which I shall be defraying personally, with God's help. And I am more inclined to go to the home of my sister's daughter, the lady Gittel, who is chaste and God-fearing, though I do not know her husband [. . .] Mr. Zalman Ber; and ever since he became connected to us by marriage, he has not enquired about me; although I have enquired as to his welfare in my letters addressed to my brother's son, R. Saadya Isaiah, he has never sent me a single letter in reply, and because of this [. . .] my soul is exceedingly bitter, and I have no inclination to write to him. In addition, I must take into consideration that it is quite a distance to travel from here to there, and that two or three months are required for a letter to reach its destination and for a reply to be received, and thus the entire summer will pass without my enjoying any peace of mind. But the main point is that, I have, willy-nilly, become an idle laborer, and I do not have it within my power to speed up my work in composition of letters so as to complete them in a single day, and at times, I have become preoccupied by unavoidable constraints for several days, and even weeks. It is for this reason that I request my esteemed brother—may the All-Merciful guard and redeem him—to write to Fürth on my behalf to the two individuals mentioned above, and in the light of their replies he should write again, with his hands battling for him, twice or three times more, to negotiate with them in relation to such matters as are necessary for achievement of the desired objective, until such time as he concludes the matter favorably on my behalf, God willing! And he will then be in a position fully to restore my soul, and may God, Who accomplishes all things, conclude matters favorably on our behalf and be as a help unto us—Selah—blessed be He, Amen! Moreover, my soul yearns for that room to be especially designated for me to hold a regular minyan there, even on Sabbaths and Festivals, just as I do here, with Divine assistance, seeing that it is hard for me to move from the walls of my home to the House of Prayer, on account of a number of ailments and so forth; for this too, the owners' knowledge is required, so that they have knowledge of my requirements from start to finish.

NOTES

1. [The numerical value of which equates in Hebrew to "The True Judge."—Trans.]
2. [Jacob ben Benjamin Kohen Poppers, author of *Responsa Shav Ya'akov*, Frankfurt, 1741–1742.—Trans.]

Translated by David E. Cohen.

Other works by Katzenellenbogen: Sermons, Pentateuch commentaries, Talmudic novellae, responsa (all extant in manuscript at Oxford).

Jacob Emden
1697–1776

Jacob (Ya'akov) Emden, also known as Ya'avets (Ya'akov ben Tsevi), was a renowned rabbinic scholar who lived in Altona, then in Denmark, near Hamburg, for most of his life, though he spent some time in Amsterdam, Moravia, and Emden. Except during his time in Emden, he held no official rabbinic post. Emden was a prolific writer; many of his works, including *Sefer hitabkut* (1762–1767), were related to his controversies. He owned a small printing press in Altona. A temperamental and controversial figure, he leveled accusations against many rabbinic figures, that they were secret believers in Shabetai Tsevi, including against Jonathan Eybeschütz, whom he accused of creating Sabbatian amulets.

Megilat sefer (The Scroll of the Book)
ca. 1762–1770

I was the fourth [child] born and the first son, a tender darling to my father and my mother (cf. Prov. 4:3) after my mother had given birth to three daughters. My parents were worriers and trembled over me a great deal. I was reared on their knees as a delightful child (cf. Jer. 31:19), with great daintiness and delicacy (cf. Isa. 47:1), and yearning. With it all, my father, may his memory be for a blessing, hastened to bring me to school when I had completed three years so that, by the fifth year after my birth, I had already completed studying the tractate *Bezah*. I was so diligent in my studies that my friends, my peers, followed behind me and, by that time, had not [even] reached the ability to read the prayers. (Afterwards, however, he [i.e., my father] refrained from bringing my brothers who were born to him after me to the teacher's house while they were tender children because, he said, that he had weakened me thereby.)

Were I to say I will tell how it is (Ps. 73:15), everything that occurred to me in the years of [my] childhood, the story would be exceedingly long, aside from what is hidden and forgotten from me. I will only mention several tidbits, three frightful things that happened to me in the days of my tender childhood. The first was a rash that appeared on the flesh of my face, in particular, which covered it from side to side in a manner that I was in great jeopardy, almost beyond despair. God sent His word and healed me (cf. Ps. 107:20) without there being left [. . .] any trace of damage on my face and no scars at all. Secondly, a leprous boil appeared on my penis and it blocked the urinary hole for some time in a manner that caused my parents great worry, sadness and sighing (Isa. 35:10) because of me. Thirdly, onerous boils covered all of my legs, similar to the boils of Job (cf. Job 2:7), with ugly pain. God delivered me from all these, aside from other evil and serious maladies (cf. Deut. 28:59) found in all children, like pimples, pox, measles [and] teething. In particular, I was especially prone to swollen tonsils, colds, coughing and burning urine, and sometimes also small blisters and red speckles. [All this was] aside from the blows with which *I was beaten in the house of those who loved me* (Zekh. 13:6), the teachers into whose hands I was placed to study, who were generally cruel [and] who mercilessly hit me. [All this] aside from other aches and pains which have affected me *in the days of my prime* (Job 29:4). *Much have they afflicted me since my youth, but they have never conquered me* (Ps. 129:2).

NOTE

Words in brackets appear in the original translation.

Translated by Jacob J. Schacter.

Other works by Emden: *Leḥem shamayim* (1728); *She'elat Ya'avets* (1739–1759); *Sefer shimush* (1758–1762); *Mor u-ketsiyah* (1761–1768); *Tsitsim u-feraḥim* (1768).

Rebecca Henriquez da Costa
d. 1771

Rebecca Henriquez da Costa died in childbirth and was buried in Cassipora cemetery, Suriname. Her epitaph was written in Hebrew and Portuguese.

Epitaph, from the Tombstone of Rebecca Henriquez da Costa
1771

> On the day of my abundant joy
> illness suddenly overcame me
> Birth pangs and rupture
> overwhelmed me
> I gave birth and died, like a blossom
> I turned away
> And the fruit of my womb was
> brought with me to the grave
> Woe alongside joy, birth pangs
> alongside song was what I brought
> My kin mourned for me, as did all
>   passers-by
> You who pass by, if you have a
>   human heart,
> Shed your tears upon my bones.

Translated by Aviva Ben-Ur.

Fromet Guggenheim
1737–1812

Eldest daughter of a merchant from Hamburg, Fromet Guggenheim married the philosopher Moses Mendelssohn in 1762. Exceptional for the time, theirs was not an arranged marriage. As was the case with many premodern Jewish couples, when Mendelssohn was away, he relied on his wife to maintain his business correspondence. A great lover of the theater, Fromet Mendelssohn was acquainted with some German playwrights, Lessing among them. Felix Mendelssohn Bartholdy and Fanny Mendelssohn Hensel were her grandchildren. The square in front of the Jewish Museum in Berlin was named for the couple in 2013.

Letter from Fromet to Moses Mendelssohn
1777

Berlin, 18 July 1777   Berlin, 13 Tammuz 5537
Dear Moses, may you live,[1]

I hope that my letter will find you happy and in good spirits in Königsberg. We are all, thank G-d, well and alive, and when you will receive this reassurance more often from me, you will also be happy and in good spirits on your journey.

There is very little news here. With the exception of Madame Flißen[2] having been delivered of a young daughter, everything is on the same old footing as when you left Berlin. So in order to tell you anything, I will have to make it a journal about how I am spending my time. That evening, when you left us, I was completely out of sorts. I quarreled with everybody in the house, until, eventually, Meyer Warburg arrived and wanted to say good-bye to you. When I told him that you had already left, you should have seen the expression on the face of fat Meyer. He stood before me like a pillar and displayed such anxiety that I had to laugh about it. Finally, after many pleas that he should get a grip on himself, I asked him to join me at table. After he had consumed a few pieces of fish and other good things his astonishment subsided and now he is wishing you, like all other people, a happy journey. After dinner our Brendel[3] played for us on the piano for an hour. My brother-in-law R. Selig[4] also came by that evening; and since it doesn't cost him anything to pretend to me that he had come to say good-bye to you, I had to accept the compliment.

On Thursday, when I got up, many good friends were already with me to inquire if I had slept well. In the afternoon Mr. Lessing[5] arrived and took me and Brendel and Reikl[6] to have coffee with his wife. Professor Engel[7] was there too. So we drank coffee and argued about the German and French troupes. Everyone claimed that it wouldn't be right to be amused by such miserable actors.[8] What do you think, dear Moses, did we do after coffee? We ladies went to the French comedy, the gentlemen to the German [theater]. And best of all, both parties were wonderfully entertained. I will even make an effort to go there more often with the children. I think this will be useful for our children. Brendel understood the comedy pretty well. And Reikl will now make an effort to learn to understand it, at least today she is sitting already with a French book. Yes, dear Moses, received visitors, went on a visit, went to the comedy, and yet, despite all of that: boredom, which I don't feel at all when you are with me. You can believe that in these three days this is the first joyful hour that I am spending, speaking with you now. Give me the opportunity for such joy more often and write to me a lot. At the moment you can do nothing more beneficial for your Fromet.

NOTES

1. [Fromet addresses her husband by his Hebrew name משה (Mosheh) and she adds לעב, probably a brief form of *lebn* in the sense of "may you live."—Trans.]

2. [German spelling could be *Flißen* or *Fliessen*, or *Fließen*.—Trans.]

3. [Brendel Mendelssohn, 1764–1839, oldest daughter; after her marriage to Friedrich von Schlegel in 1799, she became Dorothea von Schlegel.—Trans.]

4. [Selig Moses Bacher, husband of Fromet's sister.—Trans.]

Unknown artist, *Portrait of Fromet Guggenheim*, 1867.

5. [Gotthold Ephraim Lessing, 1729–1781.—Trans.]
6. [Recha Mendelssohn, 1767–1781, second daughter.—Trans.]
7. [Johann Jakob Engel, 1741–1802, writer and important theater man in Berlin.—Trans.]
8. [Meaning somewhat unclear in original.—Trans.]

Translated by Susanne Klingenstein.

David Attias
Mid- to Late Eighteenth Century

Merchant and writer David Attias championed the use of Ladino, the vernacular language common among Jews of the Ottoman Empire. Born in Sarajevo, he moved to Livorno (Leghorn) in 1769. As part of the vibrant Sephardic community in the Ottoman Empire, he decried the lack of historical, scientific, and popular literature written in Ladino. Blaming conservatism and traditionalism for this lack, Attias's *La güerta de oro* (The Golden Garden), an education anthology covering a variety of practical topics, sought to fill this void and was likely the first secular work written in Ladino. His views on modernization, education, and language reform would inspire later Haskalah thinkers.

The Golden Garden
1778

[The lessons a mother should give her son]: My son, you should know that before your body looked the way it does now, it was nothing. You were formed in my belly from the drops of fertility that came from me and your father, and thus you grew in my belly, and nine months later I gave birth to you and delivered you into this world. But you should know that this body of yours has grown because it consists of the following four things: the earth on which you walk, the heat that you feel, which is sent to you by the sun, water, and air. My son, you would not have been born or grown up if we did not eat the things that come from the earth, nor would you live if your body did not receive the heat sent to the earth and to all of us by the sun. You would not exist if from time to time you did not counter this heat and fire that you feel through thirst with water used to cook our food. We could not even breathe if we did not have air, which also refreshes our bodies. And all the birds you see flying and all the animals you see walking on four legs on earth are made of these things. All of this, as I told you, is the image of God, who is One and his name is One.

My son, do not get sad or upset when you learn that someone has died. For the reason I have explained, you should not be frightened or saddened by death, because before you were conceived you were nothing and dead. And from the moment I conceived you, you began to die, and every hour of your life was deadly. And thus at the moment I gave birth to you, time—or rather, God—condemned you to death and to return to your original place, which was nothingness, where you will soon be again. So do not be surprised or afraid of this path that will take you to nothingness because, whether you like it or not, time is pushing you and years will fly by until you reach the point where you will have to pay back what time has lent you so that you could live. Why should you get angry and upset about something that you never owned? If someone lends you something why should you get angry when you have to return it? Thirty or forty years ago you did not exist in this world. Time lent you these years and the world lent itself to you so that you could live and die in it. So why do you get angry when you have to pay it back, knowing that none of this is yours? And thus you will give back everything. Time will take back the years that passed; the earth will take back your life; the sun will take back its heat from your body and will absorb its humidity to return it to the water in clouds; the air will take back your breath; God will take back your true holy and wise soul; and fortune or people will take back the clothes and garments they gave you. And thus, having returned everything, you will rest in that place where you had been before you were born, which is nothingness. So you should live in peace and not worry about anything because things are going as they should and cannot go any better. And if you want to understand this better, look at a new candle. What is it before it is lit? It does not do anything, and it is nothing and darkness. But when it is lit, it begins to shine and shrivel, killing itself, and eventually this candle becomes what it had been before it was lit, which is nothing and darkness. The same is true of human beings before and after they are born, when they live and die, and even when they are dead. There is only one difference: we have to make sure that the light of our lives is bright and full in our existence, both in what we do and how we live, and that it shines both before God and people. And as for the fear of Gehenna, if you want to free yourself from this fear, follow what reason tells you and, above all, know that God is neither cruel nor vindictive like people, but merciful and forgiving. In addition, he will see that you used the soul he gave you to do good.

My son, do not lie, because otherwise, even when you tell the truth, nobody will believe you. But I do not recommend that you tell the truth that can hurt you. Keep silent and, rather than lying or telling the truth, say, "I do not know," and thus you will not do good to anybody or hurt anybody.

My son, to make a living learn a profession that is indispensable for the world, thus you will not depend on fortune. And try to be useful to people and the world, which will make people and the world useful to you. The shop said to the merchant, "If you maintain me and take care of me, I will maintain you and take care of you. But if you do not do this for me, I will not do anything for you either."

My son, stay close to wise people in order to refine your mind. And when this is not possible, be with yourself and enjoy it. And from time to time get to know the wicked and the lost and all sorts of people and talk to them, but be careful not to make them your friends, because eventually they will damage or hurt you. Keep your eyes open and observe their ways and the evils that befall them, and thus you will learn to avoid their ways. All of this will help you to refine your mind.

My son, if you want to have a long life, live like the poor, which means eat little, just enough to sate the hunger, but not too much. This way you will cure yourself of all diseases.

My son, study as much as possible and day and night ask God to give you wisdom and understanding in the matters you must handle as well as courage and patience in misfortunes and humility in prosperity and wealth.

Translated by Olga Borovaya.

Rebecca Franks
1760–1823

The daughter of a Jewish father and Christian mother, Rebecca Franks was raised in privilege, as a Protestant, in Philadelphia. Despite her Christian upbringing, Franks was known by many as the "Jewish belle" of Philadelphia, though she does not appear to have experienced a great deal of antisemitism as a result of this insistence on her Jewish heritage. She was a popular socialite celebrated for her intelligence and wit. She wrote poetry and maintained correspondence with numerous important men of her era. Sympathetic to the Royalists, she and her father were expelled from Philadelphia to New York during the Revolutionary War. She eventually married a lieutenant colonel in the British army and moved to England, where in her later years, she expressed regret for her Royalist sympathies.

Letter to Abigail Franks
1781

Flat Bush, Saturday, 10 o'c[lock]., August 10th, [17]'81

My dear Abby: [. . .]

[. . .] By the by, few N.York ladies know how to entertain company in their own houses unless they introduce the card tables, except this family (who are remarkable for their good sense and ease). I don't know a woman or girl that can chat above half an hour, and that's on the form of a cap, the colour of a ribbon, or the set of a hoop stay or *jupon* [petticoat]. I will do our ladies, that is Phila'ans, the justice to say they have more cleverness in the turn of an eye than the N.Y. girls have in their whole composition. With what ease, have I seen a Chew, a Penn, Oswald, Allen, and a thousand others entertain a large circle of both sexes, and the conversation without the aid of cards not flag or seem the least strain'd of [or] stupid.

Here, or more properly speaking in N.Y., you enter the room with a formal set curtesy and after the how do's, 'tis a fine or a bad day, and those triffling nothings are finish'd, [then] all's a dead calm 'till the cards are introduc'd when you see pleasure dancing in the eyes of all the matrons, and they seem to gain new life. The misses, if they have a fav'rite swain, frequently decline playing for the pleasure of making love, for to all appearances 'tis the ladies and not the gentlemen that shew a preference now adays. 'Tis here, I fancy, always leap year. For my part that am us'd to quite an other mode of behaviour, cannot help shewing my surprize, perhaps they call it ignorance, when I see a lady single out her *pet* to lean all most in his arms at an assembly or play house (which I give my honor I have too often seen both in married and single), and to hear a lady confess a partiality for a man who perhaps she has not seen three times. [These women say] "Well, I declare, such a gentleman is a delightfull creature, and I could love him for my husband," or "I could marry such or such a person." And scandle sais [with respect to] most who have been married, the advances have first come from the ladies side. Or she has got a male friend to introduce him and puff her off. 'Tis really the case, and with me they loose half their charms; and I fancy there wou'd be more marriage was an other mode adopted. But they've made the men so saucy that I sincerely believe the lowest ensign thinks 'tis but ask and have; a red coat and smart epaulet is sufficient to secure a female heart. . . .

And now, my d'r Abby, I am going to tell you a piece of news that you'll dislike as much as I do. What do you think of Moses [our brother in London] coming out with a cockcade [an officer's insignia]! He writes to papa and me 'tis his serious resolve, and we must not be surpriz'd if we see him this summer. The idea of ent'ring an ensign at his time of life [he was probably close to thirty] distresses [me] more then any thing I've met with since I left you. All the comfort I have is that his Uncle M[oses]. will not allow him. I have not had an oppor[tuni]'ty of asking papa's opinion of it, as I receiv'd the letter's since I've been here, but I am certain he must disapprove of it as much as I do. Was he ten or twelve years younger, I should not have the smallest objection, but 'tis too late for him to enter into such a life, and after the indulgence he's ever been us'd to he'll never brook being commanded from post to pillow by ev'ry brat of [or] boy who may chance to be longer in the service. Tomorrow I shall write to him and make use of ev'ry argument I am misstress of to disuade him from so mad a project, which I hope will arrive in time to prevent it, for if he once enter's I wou'd be the first to oppose his quiting it, as I ever lov'd a steady character. The danger of the war I have in a measure reconcil'd myself to. 'Tis only his age I object to and the disagreeable idea of his being sent the L[or]'d knows where. If he does enter (which I hope to God he may not), I wish he may join the 17th, or els get into the dragoons; the latter I think he'll prefer on account of his lameness. He has not, I believe, wrote to you by this oppor[tuni]'ty; Aunt [Moses?] Franks and Aunt Richa [father's sister], I believe, have. . . .

Nanny VaHorn and self employ'd yesterday morn'g in trying to dress a rag baby [doll] in the fashion, but cou'd not succeed. It shall however go, as 'twill in some degree give you an idea of the fashion as to the jacket and pinning on of the handkerchief. . . .

Yesterday the granadiers had a race at the Flatlands [Long Island], and in the afternoon this house swarm'd with beaus and some very smart ones. How the girls wou'd have envy'd me cou'd they have peep'd and seen how I was surrounded, and yet I shou'd have [felt] as happy if not much more to have spent the afternoon with the Thursday Party at the W[oo]'dlands. I am happy to hear you'r out there as the town must be dreadfull this hot summer. N.Y. is bad enough tho' I do not think 'tis as warm as Phil'a. . . .

Well, this is sufficiently long; love to everybody. . . .
Y[ou]'rs,
[R.F.]

NOTE

Words in brackets appear in the source text.

Michael Joseph Edler von Arnstein
1756–1811

The youngest of his parents' five sons, Austrian Michael Joseph Arnstein converted to Catholicism in 1778, whereupon they disowned him. Deeply saddened at this turn of events, he attempted to reconcile with his parents, from whom, in the course of time, he received property and a sum of money. At his own request, and in order to develop his property, he was ennobled, receiving successively the titles *Edler*, *Freiherr*, and *Reichsfreiherr*, that is, nobleman, baron, and imperial baron.

Letter to His Parents after His Conversion
1783

Certainly, dearest parents, I know what is commonly the result of the influence of education and of misunderstood religion, but is it possible that you could hate your son because he harbors other principles of faith than yours? In these times of enlightenment, under the government of our most gracious monarch, who exhibits his tolerance and general forbearance in all his dealings as an example to all his subjects, who allows each one to *believe* that which he will, if he only *behaves* as he should; under such a government, under which you, subject to Jewish law, enjoy the same protection, the same rights as any of your fellow-citizens, where you have gathered your treasures and may consume them in peace, without fear of any pressure or compulsion; under such a tolerant government, should you hate an innocent, irreproachable son, cast him aside, who implores only to be received by his parents and to have their blessing, because he does not share your theoretical principles? and banish from your sight forever your innocent grandchild, not yet of age, who did no other, could do no other, than to obey the well-intentioned will of her father! Herein I appeal to my brother, who is still Jewish, and to his wife my sister-in-law, who go so often into the great world, and see from their own experience that among the numerous members of the established religion they are received with love and respect, at the same time as you, out of religious hatred, banish from your sight a once beloved son! Your religion itself, dearest parents! damns nobody for eternity, and yet you would be relentlessly severe even in this temporal life!

Accordingly, once more, most worthy parents, I beseech you, hear my request, which has no selfish or ulterior motive, allow me and my dear child, your grandchild, to approach you, even to visit you daily, to kiss your hands and receive your blessing. We are human, dearest parents! Human beings who flourish today and fade tomorrow—what a terrible thought is this not for me, and I may add, must it be for you too, if one of us should be snatched away from this earthly life without a full and heartfelt reconciliation and reunion.

Appoint the hour for myself and my child at which we may betake ourselves to our parents, and believe me, to the last breath in my body,
your dearest son
Michael Joseph Edler von Arnsteiner

Translated by Christine Shuttleworth.

Raphael Laniado
d. 1793

An Aleppo-born rabbi, Raphael Solomon ben Samuel Laniado came from a prominent Sephardic family of scholars and judges; he compiled a family history to stress the eminence of his lineage. Laniado served as chief rabbi of Aleppo from 1740 until his death and was known for his firm and uncompromising stance toward Sephardic tradition. For example, in the 1760s, he attempted to impose his authority and community customs on the "Francos," a group of Jewish merchants originally from France and Italy who had neither paid taxes to nor recognized the authority of the Aleppo Jewish community. He defends here the local custom of chief rabbi serving as lone judge rather than the traditional three-member rabbinic court. His opponent, Rabbi Judah Kassin, defended the Francos, and the controversy lasted for a number of years.

Sefer kise Shelomoh (Solomon's Throne)
1787

When our teacher Rabbi Solomon, who was a rabbi here in Aleppo, passed away without any male children, the rabbis [of the city] consulted among themselves, and with the elders of the people and the ministers who were the great and magnificent masters, elected as the chosen among the fathers my father, the wonderful rabbi who was full of God's respect, our esteemed rabbi and teacher Samuel Laniado of blessed memory, as he was a descendant of the father and a fifth generation to the rabbi "Ba'al ha-kelim" [author of a series of rabbinic works titled *Kelim*, vessels]. And they appointed him to be the head and the judge, and he presided over [the people of] Israel [in Aleppo] for fifty years. When he passed away, just like Rosh [Asher ben Yehiel], of blessed memory, he left five ordained scholars: I, the eldest, inherited his crown. I have thus been presiding over monetary laws as a sole judge for about forty years, as this was the custom of the elders, the Rishonim, to preside over monetary laws as a sole judge. And there were a few of them at the time of the Rishonim, rabbis before and after who were the strongest in the world, righteous, and greater than lions [who presided solely over monetary issues]. And nowadays too, there are many righteous and strong [who do so] and no one speaks up or even wonders whether such matters should not be decided by one alone. This is because these were the practices of the Rishonim from the times of our forefathers, as I have already mentioned. And [in our city] everyone accepted happily and wholeheartedly that the rabbi of the city would preside over cases as a sole judge.

Yet despite all my work I have faced poverty, as the people are in great need and they turn to me [for counsel] day and night. Furthermore, the hands of the ministers and their deputies have all been involved in embezzling. Therefore, due to the demands of the ministers of the country, and because I am also old and frail, and "Joseph could no longer control himself before all his attendants," I have for years trained my dear son Ephraim, the perfect sage, the excellent judge, may God protect him, to replace me. Now it is time for him to teach and judge, as he has reached his standing through his education, wisdom, and age, thanks to God's glory. Then, on a full-moon day, one *talmid hakham* [Torah scholar] stood up to Ephraim and challenged him like a man, saying that according to what we read in *Mishnat Hasidim*, one shall not issue rulings by himself, as no one except the One [God] has the right to serve as a sole judge. [The *talmid hakham* continued by suggesting that] we learn from this that if there are fewer than three [judges] at the tribunal, the ruling is not binding and a person may do as he pleases. He [the *talmid hakham*] was babbling to himself about this issue wherever he went, but no one informed me about it. He himself did not talk to me directly, and I was busy studying Torah. Then I learned that his intention was not [to please] God but rather to annoy and vex [us] due to his baseless hatred and his jealousy. Jealousy is the anger of men, and his problem was not with my son but rather with me, as I had issued, as a sole judge, a ruling that affected him. [Yet] this is my reward—a father is rewarded with a son, so that my son can replace me as [judge]. Therefore he [Ephraim] is entrusted with my duties and he accepts them. All we do is act justly and judge righteously. [. . .]

NOTE

Words in brackets appear in the original translation.

Translated by Yaron Ayalon.

Other work by Laniado: *Bet dino shel Shelomoh* (1775).

Isaac Euchel
1756–1804

Born in Copenhagen, Isaac Euchel moved to Berlin when he was thirteen. He remained in Germany and became a significant figure in the Haskalah, organizing circles of young Jewish scholars. In Königsberg, he studied under Immanuel Kant. A Hebraist, Euchel was one of the editors of the journal *Ha-me'asef*. His Hebrew style is at its most brilliant in his biography of Moses Mendelssohn, which he wrote partly to introduce Mendelssohn's ideas, hitherto published in German, to a Hebrew-reading audience.

Toldot rabenu he-ḥakham Mosheh ben Menahem (Biography of Our Wise Teacher, Moses, Son of Menachem)
1788

On the twelfth of the month of Elul in the year five thousand four hundred and eighty-nine, Menaḥem the scribe and teacher of young children in the community of Dessau, became the father of Moses, [Menaḥem's] wife's name being Sara. May their name remain as an everlasting memorial, proclaiming: "Happy are you, parents of the righteous one, how pleasant is your lot! Understand this, you who love Truth!" The father of Moses was a teacher of young children—as you will be aware, this is the lowliest of positions and a repugnant occupation, into which only the most feeble of men, who are seeking refuge from the raging heat of famine, will put themselves. Such men as these enjoyed neither wealth nor honor, and were reduced to the status of those departed from the world in this bitter exile: what person of upright heart, worthy of honor and of receipt of blessings, can witness the evil nature of this situation without feeling grief at the lack of knowledge displayed by those who despise it? But notwithstanding all this, [Moses' father] shared his bread with him and gave him to drink from his waters until such time as he had left the city of his birth; and he did not allow him to depart until Moses pressed him strongly to let him do so. "Proclaim concerning the righteous that he is good, and may he consume the fruits of his fine deeds!"

Moses was taken to school and studied in the manner of all the youth of our nation, who merrily chirp away the laws pertaining to divorce and to marriage, to those suffering and those causing damage, and numerous topics of a similar kind that are far beyond their ability to grasp, before having even learned to read a single verse of scripture properly; and by the age of six, he was already studying halakhah and Tosafot. (Now it is only right to make mention here of the words of one with a close spiritual bonding to him—of his friend and disciple, R. David Friedländer—who related what he had heard from the mouth of the most honorable sage, that even in wintertime, his father used to get up early to bring him to the *bet midrash*, while he was still but a young lad of seven years of age, of a delicate temperament and disposition, carrying him on his shoulder, wrapped in his cloak, at three or four o'clock in the morning, after having given him a little hot water to drink.) But this young lad, Moses, was like no ordinary boy—while still in the freshness of youth, the spirit of discernment possessed him, and he perceived that this was not the way to grasp the essence even of a single item of knowledge, as it is impossible to understand clearly the contents of a single statement without possessing prior knowledge of the grammatical structure of language, and that it is not within an individual's capacity to master the laws and customs that the authorities of later times have established without first having examined the landmarks set down by earlier authorities. Accordingly, he set his mind to study the books of the Bible with great diligence, and would accustom himself to write in a pure and unadulterated Hebrew; and when he was ten years of age, he composed several poems, though later, after having subjected them to proper scrutiny, they found no favor in his sight, and he declared: "My soul lacks this power—it does not contain within it the talents required for composing poetry; it is better suited for sharpening the intellect than for toying with diverse images through the power of the imagination!" Accordingly, he composed no more Hebrew poetry throughout his life. Now although we ourselves can see, from his translation of the Book of Psalms and the other poems that he translated, that he possessed great talent in the art of poetry too, he nonetheless regarded himself as only mediocre in this field, as is apparent from a letter that he wrote, when publishing the translation of the Psalms, to the renowned poet Rommler, requesting him to examine his work and to assess its worth. With the same degree of diligence, he learned the Talmud from the mouth of his splendid teacher, R. David Fraenkel—may the memory of the righteous be for a blessing—author of the work *Korban ha-edah* who was the head of the ecclesiastical court in the holy community of Dessau at that time. He studied the books of the Bible without the assistance of any teacher, and I have been informed by a trustworthy individual, who was his friend during his early youth in Berlin, that he literally knew all the books of the Bible by heart!

Translated by David E. Cohen.

Other work by Euchel: *Igrot Meshulam* (1790).

Daniel Mendoza
1764–1836

Born in Aldgate, London, bare-knuckle pugilist Daniel Mendoza was the first Jew to become an English heavyweight champion, a title that he defended twice before losing it to John Jackson on a ninth-round knockout in 1795. Although he was a natural middleweight, Mendoza developed defensive moves and a technique of rapid rather than hard punching to fight against much heavier opponents. He has been called the father of scientific boxing. Proudly billed as "Mendoza the Jew," he was the first boxer to receive royal patronage. He opened his own boxing academy and gave boxing exhibitions throughout the United Kingdom. Mendoza was selected for the inaugural group in the United States Boxing Hall of Fame in 1954.

The Art of Boxing, Preface
1789

After the many marks of encouragement bestowed on me by a generous publick, I thought that I could not better evince my gratitude for such favours, than by disseminating to as wide an extent, and at as cheap a rate as possible, the knowledge of an ART, which though not perhaps the most elegant, is certainly the most useful species of defence. To render it not totally devoid of elegance has, however, been my present aim, and the ideas of coarseness and vulgarity which are naturally attached to the science of pugilism, will, I trust, in a great measure, be done away, by a candid perusal of the following pages. *Boxing* is a national mode of combat, and is as peculiar to the inhabitants of this country as *Fencing* to the French; [. . .] I flatter myself that I have deprived Boxing of any appearance of brutality to the learner, and reduced it into so regular a system, as to render it equal to fencing, in point of neatness, activity, and grace.

The Science of Pugilism may, therefore, with great propriety, be acquired, even tho' the scholar should feel actuated by no desire of engaging in a contest, or defending himself from an insult. Those who are unwilling to risque any derangement of features in a real boxing match, may, at least, venture to practise the Art from sportiveness; and sparring is productive of health and spirits, as it is both an exercise and an amusement.

The *two great objects* of my present publication have been to explain with perspicuity, the Science of Pugilism, and to lay before my readers, a fair statement of facts, relative to the battle which is shortly about to take place between Mr. Humphreys and myself. In the first, it has been my endeavour to offer no precepts which will not be brought to bear in practice, and found useful in fighting; and, in the second, I trust, I have not displayed any thing like untruth of illiberality: and it will give me peculiar satisfaction and pleasure to understand that I have attained my first object, by having taught any man an easy regular System of so useful an Art as that of Boxing; and that I have proved successful in my *second*, by having removed any prejudices which, from the mistatement of others, might have been unfavourable to my character.

Aaron Hart
1724–1800

Often considered to be the founder of Canadian Jewry, Aaron Hart was one of several Jewish traders who arrived in Quebec following the British takeover. Hart was likely born in London, though some sources claim Germany; we find him in Montreal, by way of Jamaica and New York, in 1760. A supplier of goods for the British troops, he accompanied them to the city of Trois-Rivières and settled there. He became a successful fur trader, acquired land, and was even appointed the town's postmaster, notable given that just a few years before, non-Catholics had not even been permitted to live in New France. While Hart maintained connections to the Jewish communities in New York and Montreal, his wish was to keep his family in Trois-Rivières.

Aaron Hart and His Children
1790

Dear Mo:

I se no way for you to keep *Pesah* at William Hanry thear fore you had batter come over hear the Sunday before than you neat not due any thing to your house to git the *hamez* out of your house. It will be attanted with no lass as its all holy dayes that pople boy noting.

I have wrote to H. Judah and to Ben and Alex to sett of for New York the 1st of May next as I am determent to have tham hear. If you cane at any rate go across the lakes for tham I will pay all expence you may be at. As I hope you well not faile being hear *Pesah* than shall say more to you on that jurny. It well save you truble and expence of baking of *mazot* to come heur.

I had only one letter by December pachit of pes of 5th December. Noting new the full not than arrived haveng further to mention tell I se you and am d[ea]r Mo your loveng father

Aaron Hart

NOTE
Letters in brackets appear in the source text.

Ber of Bolechów
1723–1805

Dov Ber Birkenthal, also known as Ber of Bolechów (his native town in Galicia), was a merchant of Hungarian wine, Hebrew memoirist, and arbitrator. Combining extensive Jewish traditional and secular knowledge and tutored in Polish, German, French, and Latin, he is most noted for his memoirs (*Zikhronot*), written in the 1790s but published only in the twentieth century. The chronicle of his life describes both religious and secular activities and delves into historical and political events. They also portray Jews' prominent roles in Polish economic life.

Zikhronot (Memoirs)
ca. 1790–1800

The new Rabbi pleased everybody, because he was beyond all doubt a righteous man. I was then a boy of twelve. My father received two letters from Rabbi Yukel on the subject of a good match for me in Brody, and as a consequence I had to visit R. Mordechai every Saturday after the midday meal and read *Gemara* with him, in order that I might become familiar with Talmudic disputation and law. The Rabbi's sister, the virtuous Leah, renowned for her learning was living in the house, where she remained after her parents had departed for Brody. She was married to the learned R. Aryeh Loeb, son of the Rabbi of Dobromil. Rabbi Mordechai used to point out to me the passage I was to read, and then took his afternoon sleep; he was of a delicate constitution all his life. His sister Leah, sitting by us, looked on and saw that I did not understand the passages from the *Gemara* and the commentaries of Rashi. She would say to me: "Why are you puzzled? Tell me the text of the *Gemara* over which you are in doubt." So I would read to her the difficult passage in the *Gemara* or in Rashi's commentary on it, and she would repeat the passage correctly from memory and explain it to me. Thus assisted by her I was able, when the Rabbi awoke, to read the passage aright. This continued during a whole year, so long R. Mordechai lived. For our many sins the illness of the Rabbi became more serious, and he died in 496 [1736]. The community decreed a week's mourning and lamentations, and they honoured his memory by not appointing for the space of one year and more another Rabbi in his stead. His widow, the daughter of the Rabbi of Sniatyn, remained for a whole year at Bolechow, receiving the revenues of the Rabbinate, and she went away to her father only after the year of mourning had come to an end.

The next Rabbi at Bolechow was Moses, son of R. Aaron Segal. His eldest brother, R. Mordechai, was the son-in-law of R. Kalman, Elder of the Council of Four Lands, a native of Tysmienica. The younger brother of the new Rabbi at Bolechow occupied the Rabbinical chair at Olesko. After R. Moses had resigned the position at Bolechow, he became Rabbi at Olesko, whilst his brother, his predecessor at the latter place, moved to Brody, where he survived his elder brother for many years, until the accession to the throne of our Lord the Emperor Joseph II. Later he was made Chief Rabbi of the district of Brody, though during the whole time he lived at Lemberg.

R. Moses, who was Rabbi at Bolechow for ten years, enjoyed great respect, for he carried out his duties with wisdom, in face of the opposition of some leading people of the community. Then he left us with two sons borne to him by his wife, the daughter of the Rabbi of Stryi, R. Berish, son of R. Moses Harif. These two boys grew up at Bolechow.

In 499 [1739] I was married to a young girl who did not prove to be my destined wife. R. Moses Segal performed the sacred ceremony. This ill-assorted match was due to our great sins. I was forced into this marriage, which was arranged by my stepmother Feige. I lived with my wife for two and a half years, but we had no children, and by the loving-kindness of God, be He praised, I divorced her. And behold, through the providence of His name, be He praised. I was given the right wife who was predestined for me from eternity, after having spent the time as a "widower" in my father's house. I conducted myself as a God-fearing man, attending every morning and evening the service of the synagogue and praying with great devotion. I was deeply engaged in studying the Bible, the *Mishnah*, the *Gemara* and the laws of the *Shulchan Aruch*, besides other ethical works. As a rule I hastened to become acquainted with every book which came to my hand, and to understand the meaning of the author. I learned also the Polish language to please my father, who wanted me to know it.

Translated by Mark Vishnitzer.

Other work by Ber of Bolechów: *Divre binah* (ca. 1780–1800).

Rebecca Samuel
Late 1700s

Originally from a vibrant Jewish community in Hamburg, Rebecca Samuel immigrated to America in the 1780s to escape the guild restrictions her husband was subject to as a watchmaker in Germany. Though they welcomed the increased economic opportunities they found in the United States, and the absence of antisemitism in the small town of Petersburg, where they originally settled in Virginia, Samuel was disappointed by the lack of Jewish communal life in the town. She and her husband eventually moved to Charleston, South Carolina, home to the largest Jewish community in America at that time.

Letter from Rebecca Samuel to Her Parents
ca. 1792

Dear Parents:

I hope my letter will ease your mind. You can now be reassured and send me one of the family to Charleston, South Carolina. This is the place to which, with God's help, we will go after Passover. The whole reason why we are leaving this place is because of [its lack of] *Yehudishkeit* [Jewishness].

Dear Parents, I know quite well you will not want me to bring up my children like Gentiles. Here they cannot become anything else. Jewishness is pushed aside here. There are here [in Petersburg] ten or twelve Jews, and they are not worthy of being called Jews. We have a shohet [slaughterer of animals and poultry] here who goes to market and buys terefah [nonkosher] meat and then brings it home. On Rosh Ha-Shanah [New Year] and on Yom Kippur [the Day of Atonement] the people worshipped here without one sefer torah [pentateuchal scroll] and not one of them wore the tallit [a larger prayer shawl worn in the synagogue] or the *arba kanfot* [the small set of fringe worn on the body], except Hyman and my Sammy's godfather. The latter is an old man of sixty, a man from Holland. He has been in America for thirty years already; for twenty years he was in Charleston, and he has been living here for four years. He does not want to remain here any longer and will go with us to Charleston. In that place there is a blessed community of three hundred Jews.

You can believe me that I crave to see a synagogue to which I can go. The way we live now is no life at all. We do not know what the Sabbath and the holidays are. On the Sabbath all the Jewish shops are open; and they do business on that day as they do throughout the whole week. But ours we do not allow to open. With us there is still some Sabbath. You must believe me that in our house we all live as Jews as much as we can.

As for the Gentiles, we have nothing to complain about. For the sake of a livelihood we do not have to leave here. Nor do we have to leave because of debts. I believe ever since Hyman has grown up that he has not had it so good. You cannot know what a wonderful country this is for the common man. One can live here peacefully. Hyman made a clock that goes very accurately, just like the one in the Buchenstrasse in Hamburg. Now you can imagine what honors Hyman has been getting here. In all Virginia there is no clock [like this one], and Virginia is the greatest province in the whole of America, and America is the largest section of the world. Now you know what sort of country this is. It is not too long since Virginia was discovered. It is a young country. And it is amazing to see the business they do in this little Petersburg. At times as many as a thousand hogsheads of tobacco arrive at one time, and each hogshead contains 1,000 and sometimes 1,200 pounds of tobacco. The tobacco is shipped from here to the whole world.

When Judah [my brother] comes here, he can become a watchmaker and a goldsmith, if he so desires. Here it is not like Germany where a watchmaker is not permitted to sell silverware. [The contrary is true in this country.] They do not know otherwise here. They expect a watchmaker to be a silversmith here. Hyman has more to do in making silverware than with watchmaking. He has a journeyman, a silversmith, a very good artisan, and he, Hyman, takes care of the watches. This work is well paid here, but in Charleston, it pays even better.

All the people who hear that we are leaving give us their blessings. They say that it is sinful that such blessed children should be brought up here in Petersburg. My children cannot learn anything here, nothing Jewish, nothing of general culture. My Schoene [my daughter], God bless her, is already three years old; I think it is time that she should learn something, and she has a good head to learn. I have taught her the bedtime prayers and grace after meals in just two lessons. I believe that no one among the Jews here can do as well as she. And my Sammy [born in 1790], God bless him, is already beginning to talk.

I could write more. However, I do not have any more paper.

I remain, your devoted daughter and servant, Rebecca, the wife of Hayyim, the son of Samuel the Levite, I send my family, my . . . [mother-in-law] and all my friends and good friends, my regards.

NOTE

Words in brackets appear in the original translation.

Translator unknown.

Solomon Maimon
1753/4–1800

Born Solomon ben Joshua (Shelomoh ben Yehoshu'a) in Nieśwież (Polish–Lithuanian Commonwealth; now Nyasvizh, Belarus), Solomon Maimon received a traditional Talmudic education and married at age eleven. He studied secular German-language books on Jewish philosophy (including Maimonides, whose surname he adopted), and on Kabbalah and Hasidism. His secular and philosophical interests pushed him to move to Germany and Holland in the 1770s. There he became part of a circle of *maskilim* and later became a foremost interpreter of the philosophy of Immanuel Kant. Maimon wrote several works, including an autobiography, which opened up a new genre for Jewish writers and portrayed the traditions of Polish Jewish life in a mocking tone.

Solomon Maimon: An Autobiography
1792–1793

I was sent to school at Iwenez, about fifteen miles from our abode, and here I began to study Talmud. The study of the Talmud is the chief object of a learned education among our people. Riches, bodily advantages, and talents of every kind have indeed in their eyes a certain worth, and are esteemed in proportion; but nothing stands among them above the dignity of a good Talmudist. He has the first claim upon all offices and positions of honour in the community. If he enters an assembly,—he may be of any age or rank,—every one rises before him most respectfully, and the most honourable place is assigned to him. He is director of the conscience, lawgiver and judge of the common man. He, who does not meet such a scholar with sufficient respect, is, according to the judgement of the Talmudists, damned to all eternity. The common man dare not enter upon the most trivial undertaking, if, in the judgement of the scholar, it is not according to law. Religious usages, allowed and forbidden meats, marriage and divorce are determined not only by the rabbinical laws which have already accumulated to an enormous mass, but also by special rabbinical judgments which profess to deduce all special cases from the general laws. A wealthy merchant, farmer or professional man, who has a daughter, does everything in his power to get a good Talmudist for his son-in-law. As far as other matters are concerned, the scholar may be as deformed, diseased, and ignorant as possible, he will still have the advantage over others. The future father-in-law of such a phoenix is obliged, at the betrothal, to pay to the parents of the youth a sum fixed by previous agreement; and besides the dowry for his daughter, he is further obliged to provide her and her husband with food, clothing, and lodging, for six or eight years after their marriage, during which time the interest on the dowry is paid, so that the learned son-in-law may continue his studies at his father-in-law's expense. After this period he receives the dowry in hand, and then he is either promoted to some learned office, or he spends his whole life in learned leisure. In either case the wife undertakes the management of the household and the conduct of business; and she is content if only in return for all her toils she becomes in some measure a partaker of her husband's fame and future blessedness. [. . .]

Chapter XI

Here I must mention a little anecdote. I had read in a Hebrew book of an approved plan for a husband to secure lordship over his better half for life. He was to tread on her foot at the marriage ceremony; and if both hit on the stratagem, the first to succeed would retain the upper hand. Accordingly, when my bride and I were placed side by side at the ceremony this trick occurred to me, and I said to myself, Now you must not let the opportunity pass of securing for your whole lifetime lordship over your wife. I was just going to tread on her foot, but a certain *Je ne sais quoi*, whether fear, shame, or love, held me back. While I was in this irresolute state, all at once I felt the slipper of my wife on my foot with such an impression that I should almost have screamed aloud if I had not been checked by shame. I took this for a bad omen and said to myself, Providence has destined you to be the slave of your wife, you must not try to slip out of her fetters. From my faint-heartedness and the heroic mettle of my wife, the reader may easily conceive why this prophecy had to be actually realised.

I stood, however, not only under the slipper of my wife, but—what was very much worse—under the lash of my mother-in-law. Nothing of all that she had promised was fulfilled. Her house, which she had settled on her daughter as a dowry, was burdened with debt. Of the six years' board which she had promised me I enjoyed scarcely half a year's, and this amid constant brawls and squabbles. She even, trusting to my youth and want of spirit, ventured now and then to lay hands on me, but this I repaid not infrequently with compound interest. Scarcely a meal passed during which we did not fling at each other's head, bowls, plates, spoons, and similar articles. [. . .]

As far as rabbinical morals in other respects are concerned, I know in truth nothing that can be urged against them, except perhaps their excessive strictness in many cases. They form in fact genuine Stoicism, but without excluding other serviceable principles, such as perfection, universal benevolence, and the like. Holiness with them extends even to the thoughts. This principle is, in the usual fashion, referred to the following passage in the Psalms, "Thou shalt have no strange God in thee"; for in the human heart, it is argued, no strange God can dwell, except evil desires. It is not allowed to deceive even a heathen either by deeds or by words—not even in cases where he could lose nothing by the deceit. For example, the common form of courtesy, "I am glad to see you well," is not to be used, if it does not express the real sentiments of the heart. The examples of Jews who cheat Christians and heathens, which are commonly adduced against this statement, prove nothing, inasmuch as these Jews do not act in accordance with the principles of their own morals.

The commandment, "Thou shalt not covet anything that is thy neighbour's," is so expounded by the Talmudists, that we must guard against even the wish to possess any such thing. In short, I should require to write a whole book, if I were to adduce all the excellent doctrines of rabbinical morals.

The influence of these doctrines in practical life also is unmistakable. The Polish Jews, who have always been allowed to adopt any means of gain, and have not, like the Jews of other countries, been restricted to the pitiful occupation of *Schacher* or usurer, seldom hear the reproach of cheating. They remain loyal to the country in which they live, and support themselves in an honourable way.

Their charity and care for poor, their institutions for nursing the sick, their special societies for burial of the dead, are well enough known. It is not nurses and grave-diggers *hired for money*, but the *elders of the people*, who are eager to perform these acts. The Polish Jews are indeed for the most part not yet enlightened by science, their manners and way of life are still rude; but they are loyal to the religion of their fathers and the laws of their country. They do not come before you with courtesies, but their promise is sacred. They are not gallants, but your women are safe from any snares with them. Woman, indeed, after the manner of the Orientals in general, is by them not particularly esteemed; but all the more on that account are they resolved on fulfilling their duties towards her. Their children do not learn by heart any *forms* for expressing love and respect for their parents—for they do not keep French *demoiselles*;—but they show that love and respect all the more heartily.

Translated by John Clark Murray.

Other works by Maimon: *Versuch über die Transcendentalphilosophie* (1790); *Philosophisches Wörterbuch* (1791); *Über die Progressen der Philosophie* (1792).

Fanny von Arnstein
1758–1818

Born into a prominent Jewish banking family in Berlin and married to a leading Viennese financier, Fanny von Arnstein (b. Itzig) entertained many luminaries at her famous salon. Having received an excellent education, von Arnstein was interested in art and culture and was a cofounder of the Music Society of Austria. She was a prominent hostess during the Congress of Vienna (1814–1815), and delegates such as Metternich and Talleyrand attended her receptions, which were sites of political negotiations and intrigues. Although famed for her engagement in non-Jewish society and culture, including introducing the custom of the Christmas tree to Vienna, von Arnstein never converted and remained committed to helping needy Jews.

First Will
1793

I request my husband to dispose as follows:

I would wish to be able to give my family in Berlin the capital of 10,000 gulden held for me by my husband . . . my pearls, as my favorite pieces of jewelery, I ask to be divided into necklaces for each of my sisters, and whichever of them shall first be snatched away from this life / which God forbid should happen for a long time / let her bequeath this necklace which has been made her portion to another sister, so that these pearls, as a cherished present from my husband, shall never pass out of my family——my jewelery I give as a present to my daughter, and of my trinkets, as well as of part of the jewelery, if the trinkets should not suffice, she shall make a choice to give as keepsakes to her male and female cousins on her mother's side, according to her own judgment . . .

For what concerns my remaining disposable possessions, . . . let my husband leave a small pension to our remaining domestic servants, or indeed give them a present, at the same time assuring them that if I had been richer I would gladly have done more for them and the services they have rendered . . .

What can I leave to my husband but boundless gratitude for his love and consideration which he has given me from the hour in which we were united by fate, if he needs a trifle to revive my memory in him, then let him be the first to choose, everything in any case is his—and the right to dispose of these things is mine only through his kindness, with which, as I live, he has never denied me anything, and therefore he will certainly not refuse me at this moment.

I request that Pepi as my tenth sister shall be given a tenth string of pearls with the same proviso that she shall bequeath it after her death to one of my sisters, moreover all my necklaces, hair rings and keepsakes of my sisters shall be her portion, because she certainly rates them at double their worth, moreover all my Wedgwood, and porcelain cups as well as the furniture embroidered by my sister Wulff—for this she shall take over all my papers, and if my family request it shall supply to them all the letters addressed to me by them, . . . let her forgive me this last heavy charge as well as the ill-humor which she has had to suffer from me from time to time, and which were certainly not the consequence of an ill-natured heart . . .

Finally, I request my husband, if it should please God to let me end my life before the education of my daughter should be complete, to entrust her to the care of my sisters in Berlin, and when she has reached a riper age, to marry her only to the man she has chosen, if it is otherwise according to her wish, yet not to allow her to take this step either in the heat of passion, or against her will, should my husband grant me this last request, to entrust my daughter to my sisters, he will heap up my gratitude, and if it is permitted for the blessed in heaven to pray for those left behind, and to care for their well-being, then he will never be lacking in the happiness for which my grateful soul will entreat on his behalf—

Fanny Arnstein
née Itzig
5th August 1793

From my daughter's attachment to her father as well as to me I promise myself a blind obedience to his will, as he will certainly demand nothing of her but what will be for her own good, and I also request her to support me towards him in the request to entrust her to my Berlin family, and to be obedient to them as to her parents, and also to remain true to the laws of her forefathers, as one can have no good opinion of the manner of thinking of a person who changes the religion into which chance has allowed her to be born. It is not prejudice that allows me to make this request to her, but rather the intention that she should not lose the esteem of the thinking world.

Fanny

Translated by Christine Shuttleworth.

Family of Richea Gratz
Richea Gratz, 1774–1858

As the first Jewish woman to attend college in the United States, Richea Gratz was shaped by the privilege of an upper-middle-class upbringing and liberal arts education, and by an equally strong rearing in Jewish tradition. Her father was a successful Philadelphia-based merchant, originally from Germany, and the descendant of a long line of rabbis, while her maternal grandfather was a wealthy Pennsylvania fur trader. In 1784, Richea married Samuel Hays, a trustee of the Mikveh Israel congregation in Philadelphia. She became a dedicated philanthropist and a patron of the arts and education. Her son, Isaac Hays, would become an important scientist and writer.

Letters to Richea Gratz
1793

> Lancaster, August 5th 1793
> Miss Richea Gratz,
> Philadelphia
>
> The letter of the 1st instant from my dear sister I now seat myself to accknowledge. Its contents I duly note. The subject it treats on is of the most interesting nature, and I hope dear sister gave it the consideration due.
>
> You are now about to enter into a state wherein I hope and pray you may experience nothing to give you pain but, on the contrary, enjoy perfect happiness and tranquillity. But, my dear, you must remember that to ensure to yourself and to the man you love a lasting continuance of happiness, you must ever make it your constant duty and study to please. In short, copy our

Vincenz Georg Kininger, *Portrait of Fanny von Arnstein.*

amiable and virtuous mother; act as she does, and you will ensure to yourself and to all about you contentment. But as a preliminary to all happiness, lett a due sence of religion, and a proper attention to the precepts and commands of the great God always actuate you, and place your sole confidence and trust in him.

Be pleased to remember me affectionately to Mr. Hays. I shall be down at Philadelphia immediately after the [Jewish] hollowdays, and shall then spend some time with you. Grandpa [Joseph Simon] desires his love to you and begs you would write and inform him how Aunt Leah [his daughter] is, as his greatful son-in-law, Mr. [Levi] Phillips, has not thought proper to write him a line this 5 months.

I shall write to you again shortly, but in the intrem, belive me to be, with constant prayers of your happiness,
Your ever affectionate brother and well wisher,
Simon Gratz

Hyman [our brother] desires his love to you and can't write this week.

Philadelphia, Friday, 22nd November, 1793
Miss Richea Gratz,
at Mr. Joseph Simon's Merchant,
Lancaster

Have just time, before Shabath sets in, to acquaint my dear and amiable girl of our getting here this forenoon in good health. The city seems more lively then I ever remember it, all the shops open, and business transacted as usual. I have heard nothing mentioned of the fever.

[Benjamin] Nones and family are in town and is just the same as ever, much benefitted in his looks. They insist on Simmy and me supping with them tonight. He has shewed us a rock [a precious stone?] of 20 odd pound [worth 20 odd pounds].

The markets lookt to me today as if it had been market day. In short, nothing is thought more of the past disorder, and I should entirely forget it, was but my d[ear] girl here [if only you were here]. I anticipate the moment. Interim, am in haste hers, etc.
S. Hays

My respects to your honored parent, Fanny, etc. Nancy opened the house to day. I wrote from Mrs. Miller's per F. Lauman. Have a great deal to say, but Shabath will not admit [permit it].

NOTE

Words in brackets appear in the source text.

Relle Luzzatto Morschene
1770–1844

When Relle Luzzatto Morschene discovered that her husband had a venereal disease, she decided to divorce him and wished ultimately to marry her physician, Benedetto Frizzi. As a resident of Trieste, she was a subject of the Habsburg monarch, Joseph II, a man deeply affected by the Enlightenment quest for a more rational world of intellectual and religious tolerance. In secular society, Morschene thus had rights founded in natural law to protect her, and she was granted a civil divorce. Morschene's legal problem was complicated, however, by halakhic stipulations that prevented Frizzi, a *kohen*, or member of the priestly class, from marrying a divorced woman. How this conflict proceeded was expressed, in part, by the letter she wrote to the chief rabbi of Trieste, a letter that might in fact have been penned by a legal expert but which she herself signed.

A Letter to Chief Rabbi Raffael Natan Tedesco of Trieste
1794

Most Distinguished Sir,

The undersigned, your most humble servant, is a wretched woman of twenty-three years of age. I was married for five and a half years to this Mr. Lucio Luzzatto, [but] I was unexpectedly abandoned by him by means of a vile stratagem about three months ago. He believed that with threats he could thus force me to live as his wife in actuality and continue under the mantle of husband to be the instrument of my death. [. . .]

But I cannot refrain from humbly submitting myself to your judgment in order to restate in writing what I have already told you verbally about my failing health. For more than twenty months I have not enjoyed good health for [even] a moment, besides suffering from other ailments that developed at the time I nursed my daughter. An almost fatal illness, nervous [literally, hysterical] fevers, horrible pains in my head similar to those experienced in the region of the uterus and stomach, and a thousand other discomforts, all continue to oppress me even now. For more than two years my husband [has suffered] from a virulent [case of the] French contagion, which causes the uncontrolled flow of urine and feces, thus reducing our conjugal bed to a latrine from which at time I was forced to remove myself. The complete breakdown of my husband's humors unfortunately altered mine, which were initially without exception of the highest order; he was certainly the principal cause of my ailments. My life would be in danger if I continued to live any longer as the wife of such a man. That is the opinion of the most respected doctors, copies of whose reports I attach. I too know, though I am a woman, that a marriage is a serious matter, as is its dissolution, but I know even more that the first duty of nature is to preserve life. My husband's excesses and his case of French disease are widely known, and you can certainly find out about them. Moreover, you yourself with your own eyes indubitably saw the stockings, the underwear, and the bed linen of my miserable husband covered with filth and foul matter, besides which my former domestic servants themselves will be able to attest to it. The uncertainty of a cure, even if possible in the future for either the symptoms or the underlying disease, and still more then the impossibility of ensuring no relapse are of the greatest certainty. I therefore most respectfully appeal to your wisdom along with your humanity to rule on the matter in question [divorce], so that you then, with your authority as Chief Judge, will prescribe [a solution] that will accord with reason, and with religion to which you will always find me obedient.

Trieste, 24 January 1794
Relle Luzzatto Morschene

NOTE
Words in brackets appear in the original translation.
Translated by Lois Dubin.

Roza, Wife of Leyzer ben Moses Judah
Dates Unknown

Roza, wife of Leyzer ben Moses Judah, was a midwife in the Dutch city of Groningen who served both Jewish and non-Jewish women and their families. While little is known of her life, she left behind a detailed bilingual Hebrew-Yiddish register of her activities in the Jewish community in the years 1794–1832. The register itself provides basic information about the households she served, in turn shedding light on the social structure of the Jewish community in the Netherlands at the time and on the vital role played by midwives in Jewish society. Roza also produced a register of births in Dutch documenting her work among non-Jews, an indication of a long-standing tradition of Jewish midwives working across communal boundaries as well as evidence of Jewish midwives' literacy, status, and level of education (this latter register in Dutch does not seemed to have survived).

Register of a Jewish Midwife
1794–1832

This is the book of the generations/children of man, those that were born by my hands among the Hebrew women. I came to them, I the midwife, for they are vital [Exodus 1:15–19] and give birth to a son or daughter. I took this book as my possession, and I recorded in it the name of those giving birth with the name of the newborn, with the date of birth, so that it should be a remembrance from the day I began this occupation and forward. And I prayed to the Lord above that he should strengthen me and give me courage and not let my hands falter while I am engaged in this profession, and may no obstruction be caused by my hands, heaven forbid, neither to the woman sitting on the birthing stool nor to the newborn about to be born: Only let it be expelled from the uterus like an egg from a hen. And these are the children of Israel who were born by my hands. In addition to this, I took another book and there I wrote in Dutch script the names of those born by my hand among gentile women here in Groningen, Sunday, 1 Kislev in the year **"I am the midwife."** Roza wife of Leizer bar Moshe Yehuda, long may he live. [16 November 1794]

Translated by Elisheva Carlebach.

Akiva Eger
1761–1837

Born in Eisenstadt (in Burgenland) and educated in Mattersdorf and Breslau, Akiva Eger was a prominent rabbinic and halakhic leader. After living in Lissa, Prussia, he served as rabbi in Märkisch Friedland (1791–1815) and Posen (1815–1837; his letter of appointment is reproduced in this volume). While a

Title page of the register of Jewish midwife Roza, wife of Leyzer ben Moses Judah, in Yiddish (L) and Hebrew (R).

bitter opponent of Reform Judaism, Eger was more accommodating to modernity than was Moses Sofer, his son-in-law. He wrote numerous works on the Talmud and *Shulḥan arukh* that have become mainstays of rabbinical literature.

Statement of Mourning
1796

Do you deem me to be hard and evil-hearted in that I should hasten to do a match during my period of mourning? Am I to forget the love of the wife of my youth, my pure dove, whom God graciously gave to His servant? [. . .] She was my helpmeet enabling me to acquire the little bit of divine Torah within me. [. . .] It was she who preserved my person, by taking care of my enfeebled and miserable body; she it was who sheltered me from the worries of earning a livelihood, so that I would not cease serving the Almighty, as I can only now perceive and appreciate, on account of my many sins. [. . .] What mortal being is more aware of her abundant righteousness and her modesty than I? On numerous occasions I engaged in dialogues with her on

[. . .] My righteous marriage partner—may her soul rest in Paradise—agreed with me on this matter, and it was agreed between us that if the Almighty were to grant us the merit of rearing our children and marrying them off, we should then live tranquilly, contenting ourselves with dry bread and a little water, and so serve the Almighty. [. . .] For my part, I would choose to be a sexton in a synagogue or a night-watchman, so as to earn my livelihood from the labor of my hands, and to study [Torah] for the most of the day.

Translated by David E. Cohen.

Other works by Eger: *Ḥiluka de-rabanan* (1822); *Gilyon ha-shas* (1830–1834); *She'elot u-teshuvot* (1834, 1839); *Tosafot* (1841–1848); *Hagahot* (1862).

Rahel Levin Varnhagen
1771–1833

The influence of Rahel Varnhagen on German culture owed much to the salon society of the late eighteenth and early nineteenth centuries. Hostess of a noted salon in Berlin, she was greatly interested in philosophical exchanges, though she also had an impressive command of imaginative literature and knew important writers, including Goethe. What we know of her intellectual and emotional life derives primarily from the thousands of letters she wrote to her many correspondents. She converted to Christianity in 1810, but championed the cause of Jews during the outbreak of German antisemitism in 1819. The German Jewish political philosopher Hannah Arendt identified strongly with Varnhagen and wrote a biography of her.

Letters
1799

Diary, April 1799

I often said to a younger girl friend: "If you are marrying without love, after all, do not talk to your husband. Please him as much as your nature can tolerate; do not argue with him; never prove that you are right and that he is wrong. Look at F., she owes the tranquility of her life and her freedom to her *silence*. —I will explain it to you. One can do pretty much anything one pleases as long as one leaves the law intact—, but one must never insist on one's point of view. Immediately they go on the attack and start proving; one is driven to defend oneself, the less one agrees with them. This is

Unknown Artist, *Portrait of R. Akiva Eger.*

matters of spirituality through half the night [. . .]. I shall not yet focus my mind and set my heart upon contemplation of a marriage partner, whether it be a single girl or someone else; and whether I bow my head like a bulrush to function as a rabbinic leader, or whether to seek a path to find repose, to remove the yoke of the rabbinate and live as an ordinary person, for it is well-known to you that I have despised rabbinic leadership greatly. You, O Lord, know all this; quite apart from the constant fear of issuing halakhic guidance by someone as deficient in knowledge as myself, it is always like having *gehenna* lying open beneath me, and the necessity of presenting public lectures on dialectic, which, on occasion, create an unavoidable joy in my heart. Further, the question of earning my livelihood is difficult for me—to impose a burden upon the community for doing nothing, no physical labor, and to take money from individuals, some of whom may be giving it involuntarily, out of embarrassment. I assure you, the major focus of my prayers during the Holy Days concerns removing me—prisoner that I am—from confinement.

sufficient to disturb what you love most. Learn from the stupid and wicked how they achieve their advantage! What is their advantage? You may prove to them whatever you want; they may concede to you whatever they want, but afterwards they will behave just as they did before; and it is for naught that they appeared to change; it wasn't true when you believed it. They just couldn't offer you any good reasons for their behavior or lacked the courage to reveal to you its wicked causes, or they were unaware of them. You are hoping in vain; they are indestructible in their wickedness. In this you must become like them: they do not talk, they simply do as they wish; one never succeeds with them by talking to them; and that is how you should act too—; so much about love, do what you can manage—and for the love of yourself, remain silent."

[Section in French:] What fate is comparable to that of man! His imagination deceives him and leads him astray; it depicts *evils* for him and pleasures that never come true. He who writes the history of a man only as a sequence of events does not teach us whether he was happy or unhappy. Beyond our feelings, it is the development of our ideas and thinking that determines our destiny. If one leaves to life only true happiness and the misfortunes that befall us, one will almost always curtail our sweetest pleasures and your most intolerable sorrows.

[She continues in German:] Time and again I made sacrifices for him, he did not turn to me; even among human beings one chooses for oneself a god; and they withdraw from us like gods.

Diary, Autumn 1799

What would that be like to become unhappy in one's happiness? Would that be the most terrible of occurrences? There are even more painful sorrows; *those* I do not even know.

Diary, January 1800

This breast will never be completely healed, because it yearns for new duties. Victory!—Pooh! Being victorious. What does one gain by it? One's own misfortune; and one must—one *has* to work for a world that one doesn't know and that demands *everything, everything* one loves irresistibly for itself.

From a letter to Brinckmann, March 16, 1800

Whom am I expecting now? Dull Friend! Whom! "My significant person." He is a Roman, twenty-two years old, commander of a brigade, wounds on neck and leg, and beautiful like a god. He is not coming here for the first time. He is proud, but that does not help him *in the least*. After all—isn't he already coming to see me? Didn't he lead me during the entire opera ball? Won't he—if circumstances aren't entirely unfavorable—have to do what I want him to do? Am I creating sorrows for myself? Yes. But I no longer shrink from them. How beautiful he is! You know him. Everyone fights at the beginning, and *then*—Pauline thinks he is divine.[1] Her charitable instinct always made her say in the Tuileries, when I did not know him yet: "Just like a bear, don't you think, Levin, just like a bear." She had an inkling of the divine race and called it bear. To my brother I wrote recently: "I am also in love, but in a pleasant way." I did not yet know him back then; now it's no longer pleasant. Because, when he entered the ballroom, where I had already been for two hours for the concert, or, rather, when I became aware of his presence, since I had not seen him come in, I did not believe it; I examined it once more, and when it was truly he, I felt all my blood *hard* inside my chest; and then my heart surely beat for an hour in *such a way* that I can say I was passing through an illness. Then I fell into a drowsiness[2] that was very much like ill-humor; for three half hours I sat on a chair; would have loved, right then and there, to tear off my bonnet, pearls, dress, everything and hide in the deepest depth of bed: God, how hideous I appeared to myself,—I have not yet been able to recover from that feeling,—and I would indeed have gone home, if it had been possible to suggest that to my companion. He saw me too, when I saw him, and the most flattering element of our acquaintance is for now *the* look, which conveyed his astonishment to see me. After that he was *very* proud. I wasn't, but yet—. It was *more* than pride. Serendipity and his lady conducted him eventually onto an armchair so close in front of me that I had to remain seated; he looked at me only a few times and *seemed* to want to annoy me; I did not pay the least attention and looked about as *I* pleased; that was a better sort of pride, and more Roman than his; he began to take the fan away from his lady and to court her out of all proportion, because she appeared not to understand any of it; moreover she didn't fit at all into his usual rhythm[3] of moving. So I took *that* as a point in my favor and smiled *for real*; but that did *not* lighten my heart, which is *still* heavy. Suddenly the lady got up, said it was too crowded and left against his will, which he expressed gallantly in words and by walking with considerable hesitation. But he did *not* look at me

Unknown Artist, *Portrait of Rahel Levin Varnhagen.*

and left. He was *gone*:—and I had stayed, deader than my chair, for an hour and a half. Finally I became furious, went looking for my escort in another room, wanted to go straight home and not to another carnival ball,[4] but find my significant person in the company of my escort, who had been talking to him the entire time, almost alone—except for a game table, at which the lady was seated—and in excellent agreement. They exchange their addresses. Visits are planned and I am being introduced. Gregori is his name. Now it begins. Immensely respectful, eternally lovely, but proud; but I haven't spoken with him alone. Do I please you? I am writing all of this because we are not together; and since you do not have me even piecemeal, I am letting you have a good chunk at one time. I am presenting myself black on white as a spectacle. And how right. But I have sense of foreboding: because I will have to bear the brunt of it and that never ends well,—or rather, that ends in nothing good,—because in such matters every ending *must* always be bad, and when they don't end, that is the right end,—so "with courage, captain." The[5]

NOTES

1. [Pauline Wiesel (1778–1848).—Trans.]
2. [RV uses the French word *assoupissement*.—Trans.]
3. [RV uses *Mensur*, a form of fencing that is performed within a measured area (Latin *mensura*: measure).—Trans.]
4. [RV uses *Maskenball*—a masked ball.—Trans.]
5. [The hanging "The" is explained at the beginning of the next letter: RV breaks off when the Roman enters the room.—Trans.]

Translated by Susanne Klingenstein.

Aaron Isaac
1730–1817

Born to a Yiddish-speaking family in Brandenburg, Aaron Isaac (Aron Isak; Arn Yitskhok) was a seal engraver and merchant invited to settle in Sweden by King Gustav III. Relocating to Stockholm in 1774, Isaac and his family, through the economic benefit their skills brought to Sweden, became the conduit through which Jews settled in the kingdom on a large scale. His memoirs depict a period of transition for Jews in Sweden, from a persecuted minority with few rights to a burgeoning community with an established place in the country's commerce, crafts, and trade.

Autobiography
1801–1802

When the Seven Years War broke out in 1756, I was the father of four children, and the cost of living was high. I had tried to make my way in the world like an honourable man. When the enemy Prussians seized Mecklenburg, I did a brisk business with them, selling mostly fancy goods. The following year the Swedes entered Mecklenburg as friends. They gave me a lot of work and I sold them huge quantities of fancy goods. Indeed, within a short time I earned 500 reichsthalers, which I used to purchase more of the same stock at the fair in Frankfort-on-the-Oder. That is how I suddenly became a fancy goods dealer, a trade that was much more profitable than seal-engraving. So I packed my tools away in a trunk, and as a prosperous merchant I bought a house and garden. Within five years I had a fortune of several thousand reichsthalers and a fine establishment filled with good furniture and beautiful silverware. [. . .]

We took a stroll. I felt towards him like a brother. When I inquired about the state of his affairs, he complained bitterly.

"It serves you right," I observed. "It is incredible that an artist of your talent should remain in Mecklenburg where you can't make a living. Come to Sweden with me. We shall be the only practitioners of our craft there, and we shall have more work than we can handle. Why, you admitted that you haven't earned ten reichsthalers in ten weeks!"

I impressed upon him that I knew the fancy goods business, but he was hesitant.

"I have never been away from home," he replied. "How can I leave my wife and children? Besides, how can we succeed when Jews are not permitted to live there? You say that because there are no craftsmen of our kind in Sweden, it will be possible to secure the right of residence. Very well, then. Suppose you make the trip. I will share the traveling expenses with you, and as soon as you secure permission to live and work there, I will join you."

I replied, "Brother, I agree. Keep this a secret. Tell it to nobody, not even your wife."

He likewise asked me not to mention our plan, even to my brother.

"Brother," I continued, "I will give you my answer tomorrow."

Then I went to the house of my brother Abraham, who was the richest Jew in Schwerin and was said to be worth 100,000 thalers. He knew nothing of my difficult circumstances. I owned some serviceable silver worth about 200 thalers, and on the next morning I sold it to him. After lunch I returned to Herr Abraham and said, "I accept your proposition. But we must put it into writing and have it notarized."

He agreed wholeheartedly. As we did not want any one to learn of our plan, we were at a loss as to where we could have the agreement drawn up.

At length Herr Abraham said, "I have a very good friend who works at the grinding-mill less than a quarter of a mile outside the city where we will not easily be seen. I also know a notary who will accompany us."

We returned to his house and drank coffee.

"I must go out for a while," he said. "Please stay here in the company of my wife, I'll be back soon and we shall take a stroll by the City Gate."

He left and arranged with the notary to go to an inn outside the Gate, order a bottle of wine and await us. He returned home, we left together, met the notary, paid for the wine, and walked further. We found a room where we enjoyed privacy and wrote down our agreement in the form of a contract, taking a sacred oath to observe it faithfully. It could be broken only by mutual agreement; all profits, whether from work or trade, were to be shared equally. [. . .]

However, I had made my decision and refused to be deterred. I made no reply to my brother's letter. A few days before my departure, my eldest daughter came to Stralsund with a piteous letter from my wife pleading that I should not sail. My daughter was more precious to me than anything.

"Dear father," she pleaded tearfully, "if you leave us now, we will never see you again."

I was aware that this had unfortunately happened in other instances. Nevertheless, I explained the state of my affairs to her and how this was an opportunity to make my fortune again. Then I gave her some gifts and set her mind at peace. The next day she went home on the mail-coach.

I had made a reservation on a packet-boat and paid my passage to Ystadt. All the Stralsund Jews came and reproached me and urged me not to sail. But I never was a poltroon. I always stuck to my decisions. As I went down to the bridge to embark, the householders, including some of the women, accompanied me. They continued to discourage me even when I was on the ship. The women lamented as though I were leaving for America. But I was determined to carry out my plan. When they saw that the anchor was about to be lifted, they left the ship, shouting and waving their blessings as long as the ship was in sight. [. . .]

The Secretary of State was most cordial when I saw him again the following morning. He told me that he had had a satisfactory conversation about me with the Lord Mayor. The protest, however, required some revision. He volunteered to attend to this and suggested that I return the following day to sign the new document. After I had done this, he asked whether I had spoken to the councillors. I told him that I had seen some of them. He suggested that I intensify my efforts. "Tomorrow the King will hold council in Ulrichsdal and four councillors [he named them] will be present. If you know any of them, go to see them immediately and ask their assistance." He added that he would be away for four or five days but would be glad to see me upon his return.

It so happened that two of these councillors were among those to whom I had letters of recommendation. I had seen them often and won their favor. I went to them once more, and to the other two as well, and told them the story. All of them promised to do everything in their power and assured me that I need have no fears about the outcome.

At the appointed time I again went to see Secretary of State Heland. As I entered his office, he congratulated me. He told me that my request had been granted and I would find the papers at the Lord Mayor's. I thanked him more than a thousand times and said that I hoped I would have the privilege of repaying this great obligation. Then I hurried to the Lord Mayor's. He instructed me to go to Chancery at the royal castle and ask for the royal secretary, von Sieverts. Off I went to the castle. The secretary gave me the privilege papers and I paid the required fee.

When I visited the Lord Mayor with the intention of expressing my deep appreciation, he spoke to me abruptly. "I've done the Devil's work and prefer not to hear of it. If you must thank some one, thank the King. But be sure to go to the Town Hall tomorrow with your attorney and have the papers officially recorded."

The councillor there requested that I leave the papers and return for them in a week. I hesitated to let them out of my hands, but as my attorney assured me, in German, that there was no reason for worrying about their return, I left them. The papers were certified in Ulrichsdal on May 2, 1775. They granted me, my brother Mordecai, and Herr Abraham Pach the right of residence with our wives and children provided we paid the regular levies.

A week later I returned to the councillor and received my papers. I wrote forthwith to Herr Pach asking him to join me, and to my wife, whom I told to sell the house and garden and to bring the children.

NOTE

Words in brackets appear in the original translation.

Translated by Leo W. Schwarz.

Moses Sofer

1762–1839

Moses (Mosheh) Sofer (also Schreiber) was a major rabbinic leader who did much to shape Orthodox Judaism and Hungarian Jewry. Born and educated in Frankfurt, he first held rabbinic positions in Moravia and Burgenland. In 1806, he accepted the position of rabbi of Pressburg (now Bratislava, Slovakia); there, he founded a major and influential yeshiva, where numerous significant Hungarian rabbis received their training. Sofer was famous for his uncompromising opposition to Reform Judaism. He published very little during his lifetime, but his roughly 1,500 responsa were published posthumously (some included in this volume) under the title of *Ḥatam Sofer*.

Sefer ha-zikaron (The Book of Memory)
1809

I have written this down in connection with all that befell us during that year five thousand five hundred and sixty-nine [1809] here, in our holy community of Pressburg. Now an omen of this had already been vouchsafed to us by way of alarming dreams, in regard to which I was seized on several occasions with quaking and trembling, which agitated all my bones with fright, and sometimes this also occurred when I was awake—despite there being no such thing as magic, there is such a thing as "an omen."[1] Although I knew that I was unworthy, I made haste to act stringently, pursuant to the words of R. Joseph—as the divine hand was still stretched out against us, I acted in accordance with whatever was within the realms of possibility for a lowly person such as myself.

As our vicissitudes were too numerous for time and space to allow us to place them all on record, I shall describe them in abridged form, but I shall, in any event, in passing, commit to writing everything that befell us.

[. . .] Now during that winter the cold was exceedingly great, and the waters of the River Danube had frozen, remaining in that state for several months, which was regarded as quite astonishing. And it so happened that on the morning of Sunday, the twelfth of Shevat, all of a sudden, the ice and the ice-floes vanished, and the waters flowed at a tranquil pace and not with fury, as they had previously, in accordance with their normal way in the aforesaid River Danube. But things had scarcely settled down, so as to enable us to rejoice in pleasant fashion, when the frosts arrived, like an overwhelming flood, from the city of Linz and the city of Vienna, together in one go, and with quite substantial fury, and blocked up the water exits; and the ice stood several palm-breadths in height, standing upright as a heap, and due to the overwhelming swiftness of the arrival of the awesome frost, the waters overflowed into the center of our city, on the opposite side of the city from here; it then changed course, proceeding onward and overflowing, up to the center of the city, to that place where delightful things are planted, which we call *Allei*; and likewise, through the streets of the city, passage was only possible by boats. And the flood damaged houses by the hundreds, rising higher and higher, and it also swept away the lives of many humans and animals. The greatest cause of damage was that the flood carried along with it many large boats, and bridges, and beams, from other locations, in that, when these made contact with the walls, their foundations were destroyed, and quite a number of storehouses and commercial wares suffered damage; the Jews too suffered losses in the thousands. The overriding point is, however, that it was on account of our great iniquities—of our sins—that "the hand of the Almighty was against us and against our ancestors"—which refers to the exhumation of the dead,[2] in that, as a result of the flood, the wall of the cemetery was destroyed, and tombstones were smashed, and in addition, the abodes of the most elevated and holy men, the place where the graves of the rabbis were situated—may their merit serve as a shield for us—over whose graves monuments had been erected, everything was destroyed, and the water overflowed and passed by them, in combination with the awesome ice, for many days.

[. . .] On the next day, the old man ascended to the roof of the attic and cried out in a bitter voice and with much weeping, to the point where his voice could be heard inside our city, and the inhabitants sensed that there was a Jew there in the midst of the troubles; and the chief members of the community, its leaders and fine men, dispatched a certain seaman and gave him fifty gold coins by way of remuneration for his trouble, and together with him they sent the esteemed Feivel, sexton of the burial society, to save the Jews, if that were possible. And they went over there in great peril and returned on the Tuesday toward evening, bringing with them no one other than a woman and her two sons, as the boat could not fit a larger number; and on the following day, they dispatched the seaman again and gave him thirty gold coins by way of remuneration, and this time they brought back the father too, on the Wednesday, the fifteenth of Shevat. We then heard that in the village of Ave, there was a Jew stuck on the roof of one of the houses who had not eaten bread for the past three days, and they sent to fetch him as well, and brought him, sick with tuberculosis by reason of the cold, and they occupied themselves with medical treatment for him until such time as the Almighty had healed him and restored him to his former state of health—praise be unto the most blessed God! May the Almighty remember for good the men of our holy community, for they have always been men of a kindly nature; and meanwhile, the seaman sailed over to the other side of the river to save the gentiles, the residents of the village mentioned above, and saved the majority of them, bringing them into the city in an impoverished and wretched state; and the Jews acted with kindness toward them and took them into their own homes and gave them to eat and to drink, as a result of which they gained a good name among the peoples and the princes. They also dispatched a boat filled with bread and all goodly things to the holy community of Kitza, although—praise be unto the most blessed God—they had not suffered harm to such a great extent—praise be unto the Almighty, Who performed such wondrous kindness among us amidst all this!

Almost immediately afterwards, the fair at Pest took place, and many of the residents of our city sailed over to the fair at Pest on a boat, along the River Danube, and they encountered a stormy wind and gale, which threatened to sink the boat, and the surplus ropes had already been torn away from the helm, and the sailors had abandoned hope. The boat was filled with great, fine, and distinguished individuals—their children too were with them, and the parents did not even turn their attention toward their children by reason of their great distress. They confessed their sins in a loud voice and prepared themselves for drowning—may the All-Merciful deliver us from such a fate!—but the Almighty saved them in a miraculous manner; however, I know this not from any written accounts, but rather, only from verbal reports, and I will therefore not elaborate further.

[. . .] On the New Moon of Sivan, the third month, the French army appeared on the other bank of the River Danube, and called upon the city to provide them with ferryboats to cross over to us, and threatened that if we did not do so, they would bring burning shafts with ballistic stones to attack us. The citizens, however, paid no heed to them, nor did they listen to what they said, and the enemies were treated by them with scornful laughter. But as regards myself, as my heart was well acquainted with the bitterness of my soul, I was extremely frightened and in a state of trembling, though indeed all the ordinary folk, and our own brethren, the Jews, laughed scornfully at them, declaring: "They will not cast a mound against it or come before it with shield," and they considered me to be unjustifiably fearful in regard to the issue of defense. Now the French army remained standing at the ready on their watch, doing no harm for the time being, but on the holy Sabbath, the eve of Shavuot, in the morning, they proceeded onward, abandoning their positions—it was not known what had happened to them; and there was great rejoicing in the city and "You shall rejoice on your Festival" was fulfilled.[3]

Now during that period of time, I had an inner feeling of worry every day, and I summoned my dear friend, the great sage, the communal leader, the man in overall charge of the place, Mr. Moses Schreiber, and requested him to hand over to me some of the funds designated to a charity in respect of which all the members of the community participated, amounting to a total of five hundred and forty-one "entreaties," corresponding to the numerical value of ISRAEL, whereupon I would perform the ritual of "ransom for life" on behalf of the community, under the name *Israel*, pursuant to the "ransom for life" ritual proceeding recommended by Naḥmanides of blessed memory; and I told him in private not to disclose anything of this, and he acted accordingly. I then joined ten men of distinction to be together with me, most of whom were from my trustworthy students, who would not publicize the matter. This is the text of the prayer which we then recited—commencing with the letter *yod*, followed by *sin*, followed by *resh*, and then *alef* and *lamed*.

For the sake of the Unity of the Holy One, blessed be He, and His Divine Presence, in fear and love, to unite the Name *Y-H* with *V-H*, I hereby donate these ten coins as agent for all of Israel, and in particular, for the local Jewish community of Pressburg, to unify righteousness with the righteous nation, as a ransom for the lives of all Your people, the House of Israel; and these coins shall be a ransom for the letter *yod* of the name *Yisrael*. May it be Your will, O Lord our God and God of our fathers, that these ten coins may serve as ransom for the lives of all Your people, the House of Israel, and in particular of the local Jewish community of Pressburg; and may the act of donation to charity bring peace, and the performance of charity bring about quietude and security henceforth and for ever. I implore You, O God, have pity; grant pardon, I beseech You, have mercy now upon Your entire nation, the Children of Israel, and deliver them from the sword and from captivity and from the confusion caused by the invading armies, and from all punishments that afflict the world, and from the collapse of siege walls and from conflagrations—"charity will save from death"—not only from an abnormal type of death, but from death itself: "If there be for him an angel, an intercessor, even one among a thousand, to vouch for man's righteousness, then He is gracious unto him, and says: 'Deliver him from going down to the pit: I have found a ransom!'"[4] "It is He Who forgives all your sins, Who heals all your sicknesses, Who redeems your life from the pit, Who crowns you with favor and mercy, Who satiates you with goodness—may your youth be renewed like that of the eagle." We then recited the verses comprising the priestly blessing: "May He bless you"—"May He make His face shine"—"May He lift up," followed by the psalm "May He answer you"—and then the verse: "May the pleasantness," continuing [with Psalm 91] up to: "With long life will I satisfy him"—then we recited the prayer *Ana be-Koaḥ*—then "A Song of Ascents" [Psalm 121]—and after that the requisite rituals for the letter *sin*, and then for the letter *resh*, etc.

[. . .] Within two or three hours, the land was at rest from war, and that night, the sleep of the entire city was indeed disturbed, but, praise be to God, nothing could be heard; only at daybreak were a few sounds heard, but they ceased, and we remained at ease on the eve of the holy Sabbath and on the Sabbath day until the time of the Afternoon Service.

NOTES

1. [Akin to that referred to in tractate *Ḥulin* 95b.—Ed.]
2. [b.*Yevamot* 63b.—Ed.]
3. [Deuteronomy 16:14.—Ed.]
4. [Job 33:24.—Ed.]

Translated by David E. Cohen.

Other works by Sofer are found in this volume.

Akiva Eger

Letter of Rabbinic Appointment to the City of Posen
1814

When the leaders of the people were assembled, all the tribes of Israel together, on the evening of the twenty-first day of Adar 5572, to oversee the affairs of the general community and the needs of the Jews here in the holy community of Posen, each one a prince among men, the outstanding Rabbis, the Sages, the Torah scholars [. . .] the communal overseers and leaders, the merit of whose ancestors sustains them and whose righteousness is like the mountains of God; joining them were the rest of the sacred congregation, the elect of the assembly, men of renown throughout the Jewish Diaspora—then did they who feared the Almighty speak with one another, saying: "How long shall the assembly of the Lord be like sheep without a shepherd? Let us appoint a leader, a man over the community, a faithful shepherd to tend Jacob in accordance with the simplicity of his heart, to teach the people the statutes of God and His laws, that they may know what ought to be done in Israel! Let us now search and make enquiry to find a man who has the Divine spirit within him—the spirit of wisdom and understanding—a discerning heart attuned to justice—and within whom He has placed the ability to issue halakhic rulings, and who actually does so." And one of the group responded and said: "Behold, there is a holy man, a perfectly righteous individual, who reveals hidden things, residing in the holy community of Friedland, whose name is the Illustrious Master and Teacher, Akiva Güns, unto whom truth, peace, and the law of the Torah have been transmitted, and from whom no mystery is concealed. He is well known in Judah, and his name is great in Israel on account of the fact that the divine spirit and the Torah that he possesses, in wisdom and in understanding and in knowledge, is equal to that of Akiva, son of Joseph in his generation; his fame goes forth throughout all the provinces, and they declare his praise in the isles. Let us now issue a call to the man of God to be a prince of God within our midst, to act as a rabbi and teacher, a lamp at the feet of the people and a light unto their path. Let him execute the righteousness of the Lord and His ordinances with Israel!" And the people answered with one voice and said: "The thing you have suggested is good, as we are acquainted with the man and his speech, that he seeks the welfare of his nation and that he is great among the Jews. He is the man who has been elevated on high, and upon him shall shine the crown of rabbinic leadership. However, we will consent to his appointment only on the following condition; namely, that he is agreeable to observing the points set forth in our *Book of Memorial*, as was discussed with the prior illustrious authorities—and these are the details thereof:

1. The rabbi—may his light shine brightly—is to accept responsibility for responding to questions involving ritually prohibited and permitted matters; he is to set aside one day each week for matters of controversy; should quarrels arise between individuals within the community and they submit themselves to judgment, then, in the event that they expressly desire to litigate in front of him, he is to suspend his other existing activities to designate a certain, definite date to judge between a man and his neighbor; and the rabbi is entitled to take for himself one-half of the remuneration due for the time he has lost by reason of enforced cancelation of his other activities, while the remaining half is to be taken by the other ecclesiastical judges by way of remuneration for their lost time.
2. As the counsel tendered by the Illustrious rabbi—may his light shine brightly—is as serious a matter as if a man were seeking counsel as to the word of God, and his counsel is faithfulness, accordingly, in the event that the chief overseers and leaders of the community need to take sweet, secret counsel together and to ask his advice, he is to suspend all his other existing activities, taking time to focus upon listening to what the chief overseers and leaders of the community have to say.
3. The weekly salary of the rabbi is to be 10 *Reichsthalers*, and double that amount at festival seasons.
4. The rabbi—may his light shine brightly—is to have six unmarried young men who will come from afar to listen to the learned discourses, to study with the illustrious rabbi—may his light shine brightly.
5. The financial entitlements due to the rabbi, the cantor, and the sexton given by bridegrooms on the day of their wedding and the gladness of their hearts shall be deemed to be satisfied as and when the rabbi is given 2 percent out of every hundred *Reichsthalers* that the bride's family bring into the marriage by way of dowry. However, if she brings inherited estates for the dowry on a permanent basis, he is to be given merely 1

percent of their value. All of the above is to apply where the value of the dowry is below a thousand *Reichsthalers*, but where the value of the dowry is above a thousand *Reichsthalers*, the rabbi may only take 1/2 of 1 percent from such amount as is in excess of a thousand *Reichsthalers*; and from inherited estates, he may take 1/4 of 1 percent of such amount as is in excess of a thousand *Reichsthalers*.

6. The rabbi and all those associated with him shall refrain from business activities, except that he shall be permitted to use the *shetar iskah* device.[1]
7. Regarding the matter of being called up to the reading of the Torah, he is to have an absolute entitlement—he must be called up every Sabbath; and on festivals, he has an absolute entitlement on the first day, while on the second day, should his honor acquiesce in going to the *bet midrash* of the chief members of the community—may it be built speedily in our days—to exercise his entitlement there, he may do so if he wishes.
8. Regarding the matter of acting as *sandek* [godfather] for newly born boys when they are circumcised in the flesh of their foreskins, the first two cases of this that occur in each week constitute the entitlement of the rabbi, and in regard to the remaining cases, the head of the family in question may give the honor to anyone he wishes."

These words were spoken and stipulated as terms and conditions of the appointment on the day of the assembly, and the terms and conditions were written out, under separate subject-headings, for the benefit of the renowned illustrious rabbi. He undertook and affirmed that he would ratify and uphold them, and that he would serve as rabbi and halakhic guide in accordance with these terms and conditions, just as the former illustrious rabbis had done. The people rejoiced, and blew the *shofar* loudly, and exclaimed: "Long live our Master! May he come with joy to our community, and may our hearts rejoice and our souls be glad—and let us render thanks and praise unto our Creator for all the goodness that He has bestowed upon us, and for His abundant goodness unto the House of Israel; and we give thanks for the past and cry out in supplication in regard to the future. May it be the divine will that our master, our teacher and our rabbi come at a propitious hour, for our enduring welfare. To all this we make a firm covenant, and our Levites, our priests, and our princes, the outstanding rabbis and the leaders and the noblemen, the rulers, the lay and spiritual leaders, and the rest of the holy community set their seal upon it below.

Executed here, in Posen.

(One hundred and thirty-three signatures appear from the honorable members of the community.)

NOTE

1. [A rabbinically approved type of deed to allow engagement in lending and borrowing for commercial purposes, with interest being payable.—Trans.]

Translated by David E. Cohen.

Rachel Mordecai Lazarus
1788–1838

A teacher and early champion of women's rights, Rachel Mordecai Lazarus was born in Virginia; she grew up in the small town of Warrenton, North Carolina, where she and her family were the only Jews. While she had little formal education, Rachel's father Jacob Mordecai was a prominent scholar and she herself loved learning, and taught at the nonsectarian boarding school her father directed. In 1821, she married Aaron Lazarus, a widower from Wilmington. Though she was drawn to Christianity—going so far as to be baptized shortly before her death—she was distressed by antisemitism and began a correspondence with a favorite author, Maria Edgeworth, to protest the antisemitic depiction of a character in one of the latter's novels. Their correspondence was published in a full edition in 1977.

The Education of the Heart
1815

Warrenton, North Carolina
U.S. of America
August 7th, 1815

A young American lady who has long felt towards Miss Edgeworth those sentiments of respect and admiration which superior talents exerted in the cause of virtue and morality never fail to excite. [. . .]

With all my confidence in the benignant goodness of Miss Edgeworth I tremble at having said so much, and trespassed so very greatly on her patience and indulgence; still must I entreat that they may be extended to me yet a little longer.

Relying on the good sense and candour of Miss Edgeworth I would ask, how it can be that she, who on all other subjects shows such justice and liberality, should on one alone appear biased by prejudice; should even instill that prejudice into the minds of youth! Can my allusion be mistaken? It is to the species of character which wherever a *Jew* is introduced is invariably attached to him. Can it be believed that this race of men are by nature mean, avaricious, and unprincipled? Forbid it, mercy. Yet this is more than insinuated by the stigma usually affixed to the *name*. In those parts of the world where these people are oppressed and made continually the subject of scorn and derision, they may in many instances deserve censure; but in this happy country, where religious distinctions are scarcely known, where character and talents are all sufficient to attain advancement, we find the Jews to form a respectable part of the community. They are in most instances liberally educated, many following the honourable professions of the Law, and Physick, with credit and ability, and associating with the best society our country affords. The penetration of Miss Edgeworth has already conjectured that it is a Jewess who addresses her; it is so, but one who thinks she does not flatter herself in believing that were she not, her opinion on this subject would be exactly what it is now. Living in a small village, her father's the only family of Israelites who reside in or near it, all her juvenile friendships and attachments have been formed with those of persuasions different from her own; yet each has looked upon the variations of the other as things of course—differences which take place in every society. Again and again I beg pardon for thus intruding myself on Miss Edgeworth's notice; yet even now is my temerity about to appear in a new form while I give utterance to a very imperfect hope, that these lines may be honoured with a reply, and their author thus taught to believe herself not wholly unpardonable, in the liberty she takes in writing them. Should she be thus highly favoured, Miss Edgeworth will have the goodness to direct the letter according to the address, which a brother of the writer's, now in England, will annex.

With sentiments of admiration, esteem, and gratitude, Miss Edgeworth's most respectful and obedient servant
Rachel Mordecai

Isaac Judah Yehiel Safrin of Komarno
1806–1874

Isaac Judah Yehiel (Yitsḥak Yehudah Yeḥi'el) Safrin was the first rebbe of the Komarno dynasty of Hasidism, based in the town of that name in Galicia and an offshoot of the Zhidachov dynasty. He attracted thousands of followers upon the death of his uncle (Zvi Hirsh of Zhidachov) in 1831, with whom he studied and by whom he was raised after his father's passing in 1818. Deeply inspired by Kabbalah and early Hasidic philosophy, he wrote prolifically, expounding on the Torah, Mishnah, Jewish law, and the Zohar. Among these works was *Notser ḥesed*, a commentary on *Pirke avot* (an excerpt is included in this volume). At one point, he hinted that he might be the Messiah.

Account of His Visit to Lublin
1815

I was privileged to visit Lublin with my late father when I was a boy of nine, and I saw his [the Seer's] face illuminated like torches. And when he opened the door to recite *Ke-gavnah* [An Aramaic text from the Zohar recited in the hasidic prayer rite on Friday nights] I saw a flame hovering over his head. I was there for the Passover holiday and I witnessed several matters of the holy spirit and of the highest spirituality and his intensely wonderful prayer, a leaping flame.

NOTE
Words in brackets appear in the original translation.
Translated by Dena Ordan.

Other works by Safrin: *Derekh emunah* (1850); *Zohar ḥai* (1875).

Daniel Mendoza

Memoirs of the Life of Daniel Mendoza
1816

Few events of a similar kind ever attracted the attention of the public, in such a degree, as the contests between Mr. Humphreys and myself. The long correspondence which passed between us previous to our second contest, the skill which, as was candidly acknowledged by the friends of both parties, was mutually displayed; these and various other circumstances contributed to excite, in an extraordinary manner, the attention not only of spotting men, but of all ranks and descriptions of persons, generally; and I found, on my return to London, that our contests were the general subject of conversation all over the town. I had even the almost unprecedented honour of being frequently alluded to and mentioned in many dramatic performances; for instance, *The Duenna*, *The Farmer*, *The Road to Ruin* and others.

Many of my friends who had been rallied for their want of judgment in supporting me in the first contest with Mr. Humphreys, had now a fair opportunity of retorting, which they did not fail to avail themselves of. Several songs were made on the subject of the late victory; among others, the following was sung with great applause at several convivial meetings.

Unknown Artist, *Humphreys and Mendoza; Their Third Public Contest for Superiority, on Sept. 29, 1790.*

Song

On The Battle Fought Between

HUMPHREYS AND MENDOZA

at Stilton in Huntingdonshire

O my Dicky, my Dicky, and O my Dicky my dear,
Such a wonderful Dicky is not to be found far nor near;
For Dicky was up, up, up, and Dicky was down, down, down,
And Dicky was backwards and forwards, and Dicky was round, round, round.

My Dicky was all the delight of half the genteels in the town;
Their tables were scarcely compleat, unless my Dicky sat down;
So very polite, so genteel, such a soft complaisant face,
What a damnable shame to be spoil'd by a curst little Jew from Duke's Place!

My Dicky he went to the school, that was kept by this Danny Mendoza,
And swore if the Jew would not fight, he would ring his Mosaical nose, Sir,
His friends exclaimed, go-it, my Dicky, my terrible, give him a derry;
You've only to sport your position, and quickly the Levite will sherry.

Elate with false pride and conceit, superciliously prone to his ruin,
He haughtily stalk'd on the spot, which was turf'd for his utter undoing;
While the Jew's humble bow seem'd to please, my Dicky's eyes flash'd vivid fire;
He contemptuously viewed his opponent, as David was viewed by Goliath.

Now Fortune, the whimsical goddess, resolving to open men's eyes;
To draw from their senses the screen, and excite just contempt and surprise,
Produced to their view, this great hero, who promis'd Mendoza to beat,
When he proved but a boasting imposter, his promises all a mere cheat.

For Dicky, he stopt with his head,
Was hit through his guard ev'ry round, Sir,
Was fonder of falling than fighting,
And therefore gave out on the ground, Sir.

Moses Wasserzug

ca. 1750–ca. 1825

Born near Posen, the son of a clothes merchant, Moses (Mosheh) Wasserzug (Wassercug) received a traditional Jewish education and worked as a ritual slaughterer. He lived mainly in the Polish city of Płock during the Prussian occupation, where he owned a prosperous tavern. Wasserzug is noted for writing his memoir, vividly describing life in Poland and Germany, in the first decade of the nineteenth century. Of particular interest is his recounting of his attendance at a Polish theater.

Memoirs

ca. 1820

For the two reasons specified below, I have given myself the surname "Wasserzug"; the first reason is that when I was five or six years of age, I was playing with some young children, I believe, in a house [. . .] near our home [. . .] in the holy community of Skoki [Schoken], at a distance of four parasangs from the holy community of Posen; behind the synagogue there was a river, and upon the bank of the river were planted some non-fruit-bearing trees, and each of the children who were playing climbed up to the top of a tree to cut off a branch for himself to play with it. I too, like them, climbed up to the top of a particular tree where I had seen a branch that I had found to my liking. However, the tree up which I had climbed had its roots in the riverbank and its branches were curved in a crooked manner, and the top of the tree extended out right to the center of that river, but the bough on which I was standing to cut off the branch snapped beneath me, and I fell headlong into that river; and since there was no one who knew anything about my fall, as the other children had become detached from me, and prior to my fall [. . .] they saw [. . .] that an object was floating on the water and realized that something with the appearance of a child's hand was visible in the water, and they started shouting: "Jews! A human being is floating in the water!"—and they made their voices heard by the multitude of people who happened to be present. Now at some distance from there was a flour mill, and at that time, its grinder and its wheel had become entangled as a result of the flooding of the river—and this was an act of God, as they ran swiftly with the one whom they had delegated to shut off the flooding with a water-lock, and several of them skimmed over the water in a little boat to search [. . .] and they discovered me not far away from the millstones, close by the lock [. . .] and they hauled me out of the water, the Almighty having saved me in His mercy; and blessed be the man who saved me from death—and for that reason I gave myself the surname "Wasserzug."

The second reason for my choice of surname is that it is well-known that Moses tended cattle, and was called by that particular name, "For, said Pharaoh's daughter, I drew him [Heb. *meshitihu*] out of the water": Now it so happened that on a certain day, when the King of Prussia had decreed that every Jewish man would have to choose a surname for himself, besides that given to him on the occasion of his circumcision, I chose the aforesaid name to serve as a memorial to the kindness of the Almighty, for what God wrought on my behalf by saving me from the mighty waters—and for the second reason, which involves the source for the name "Moses"; and I was thereby able to satisfy the king's officials without transgressing the words of the Torah that commanded us not to alter our names; for that was one of the merits of our holy ancestors who went forth from slavery to freedom—may the Almighty, in His mercy, redeem us, speedily in our days. Amen, Selah. [. . .]

And now, dear reader, I shall unfold before you the essence of the character and the ways of my late father of blessed memory. He was one of the merchants in the town in which the holy community of Skoki resided, as his home was there; and because that place afforded insufficient opportunities for the merchants to provide adequately for their households, they were compelled to travel to the fairs held around the town in order to sell their wares—and the custom—an upright one—prevailing in my family home was that they would not eat any proper meal until such time as all the menservants and maidservants had gathered around and encircled the table, and then the head of the family, together with them, in identical fashion, sat down to eat food—everything that the Almighty had provided for them. And on those days when the head of the family traveled from his home to the fair, they would delay eating their meal until their master had returned to his house. On one particular day, when my father had traveled to a certain fair, and my mother of blessed memory was sitting at home, a certain pauper, a Jewish child of tender years, knocked at the door of her house in wintertime, barefooted and virtually naked; my mother of blessed memory stretched out her hand to that pauper to give him his due portion, but he refused to take it, and said: "If I have found favor in the sight of my lady, can an order be given to provide me with some soup from the samovar, to enable me to warm myself up from the fierce cold going through my bones?" My mother of blessed memory issued an order that he was to be given to eat from the family's left-over food. While he was eating, he turned toward my mother of blessed memory and said to her: "It seems to me that my lady hails from the natives of the holy community of Waranik"—and this was indeed the case—and without a doubt, my father of blessed memory, Mr. Raphael, who had, throughout his life, been the overseer and lay leader of the community, had known her and been closely acquainted with her. He went on to say, "My father of blessed memory passed on, and I was left alone with my mother, who had not the means either to maintain me, to provide me with my daily portion of food, or to support me financially in my studies, as a result of which I wandered away from my home in the hope that maybe the Almighty would have mercy upon me and grant me favor in the sight of some kind gentlemen with a view to rendering me financial assistance." Now when she heard what the youth was saying, her eyes streamed with tears, as she had known his father, who had once been a wealthy man and a distinguished Torah scholar, and had, throughout his life, been the overseer and lay leader of the community; but she said nothing to him, merely promising him that when her husband came back safely to his home from the fair she would endeavor to appeal to her husband's heart regarding this matter. Then this poor fellow, whose name was Asher Judah Leib, went to the inn where he was lodging, and at around midnight, my father of blessed memory returned to his home, and after they had unloaded the merchandise he had brought, they prepared the table and set it ready for eating a meal, my father of blessed memory and all the members of the family gathering around the table in accordance with his custom. After the benediction *ha-motsi* had been recited she turned her face toward the fireplace, upon which a pile of firewood had been placed. Her seat at the table became vacant, and my father of blessed memory called out to her: "Zipporah! Why is your countenance sad? Tell me, I pray you, why are you crestfallen? What has happened to you today?" But she did not answer him a single word, but began to sigh and weep. At that juncture, my father of blessed memory was seized with fear and trembling and said to her a second time: "What is all this about?" Then she replied to him in a voice of weeping and in bitterness of heart: "If only you had been at home and seen a certain young man from among the natives of the holy community of Waranik, the son of Mr. Raphael of blessed memory, who is now a fugitive and a wanderer upon the earth, seeking bread and also support for his studies, and not a single human being has pity upon him, and he walks around barefooted and has no clothes to wear! And what are *we* to do, in that God has favored us with a male child and we do not know what his ultimate fate is to be when we pass on—and unto the man to whom these things in this house belong, I will have conceived nothing but travail and anger!"

My father of blessed memory replied and said: "What is the meaning of this sound of commotion and trembling with which you are bombarding the world in such great measure? I shall wait till the morning, and I shall send a message to the young lad, and have him put to the test before the rabbi, the head of the ecclesiastical court; if he finds him ready and sufficiently talented to study Torah, I will then support him and he will be like a member of our own household, and the time of proof will be tomorrow! But as far as you are concerned, keep silent and cast the cloak of sadness from off you; arise, eat your food which you have prepared!" Now I, the writer, knew nothing of this entire episode, as I was already asleep in my bed; moreover, my father of blessed memory had ordered all the members of the family not to tell me anything of what had taken place. At dawn, I went to my teacher, and from there, went on to prayers—and my father of blessed memory meanwhile sent a message to the wayfarers' inn to bring the youth to him. After my father of blessed memory had made enquiry of him regarding this matter, and he had responded in the same way as he had done to my mother of blessed memory, my father of blessed memory then said to him: "Go to your inn, and at about ten o'clock in the morning, you are to go to the rabbi for testing, to ascertain whether any sparks of Torah still remain within you, and in the event of your responding positively to the test, I will support you and will watch over you until the days of evil have passed."— While my father of blessed memory was in the synagogue, after the morning service, he went up to the rabbi and said to him: "May I request His Excellency to test the young man whom I shall send to him on matters of Torah, and to report back to me as to this individual's essential character in the evening, between the afternoon and the evening service." So it happened that at the time when the students were gathering around the rabbi, this youth too came along, and said to the rabbi: "Reb Itterl ordered me to attend before the rabbi with a view to his testing me in relation to my studies." However, we, the other students knew nothing whatsoever of all this, but rather, this man who had come along with his clothes all torn and worn out, and bare-footed, was simply an object of scorn among us, thinking to ourselves, as we did: "If he is indeed a Torah scholar, how would it be possible for him to have sunk to such a lowly and inferior state as he has?" The rabbi showed him a certain place in some tractate on which to test him—and the lad took the Gemara, seating himself by the side of the oven with the Gemara in his hand; and within about half an hour, he greeted the rabbi once more and declared that he had completed his task—the task of looking through and considering the passage in the Gemara: but when he started speaking, he stuttered over the perusal of the idiom of the Talmud—even over the most straightforward words appearing in the Gemara text—and he appeared as someone to whom the idiom of the Talmud was unfamiliar: however, after the rabbi had read over to him the text of the Gemara in the correct manner, and had engaged with him in the analytical dialectics of the Talmud, he grasped it with rapidity and responded to everything the rabbi asked him—and after he had concluded his task, he went off to his inn, as this was what my father of blessed memory had ordered him to do. So it came about on that day, at the time when the congregation went out of the synagogue after the evening service, that my father of blessed memory enquired of the rabbi as to the character of the lad—what he was and what he did, and, in regard to the question of his studies, whether he would still be capable of achieving success in the field of learning; and the rabbi replied: "He possesses plenty of wisdom and understanding, but on account of his abandonment of his studies, he has virtually forgotten the linguistic idiom of the Talmud, though if he persists with his learning, he is fit and ready to succeed." My father of blessed memory delayed not a moment in sending instantly for the lad, with a view to bringing him into his household, and he ordered all his patched-up clothes and everything contained inside them to be committed to the flames; and he ordered that he be dressed in my pleated garments; and he ordered that the tailor R. Aryeh be summoned, as he was the especially designated tailor in my father's household, and the most delightful garments were made by him. Then he went with him to the shop and handed him material with which to sew for the youth from the soles of his feet right up to his head, and he ordered him to complete his task by that very night, in order that the clothes would be ready for the next day, by the time that they would be summoned to prayers in the synagogue—and so the tailor did. At dawn, he brought the clothes, and they dressed the man in his holiday clothes, and as a result he became a different person, so that he was no longer recognizable.—And I went to the prayers and seated him at my side, by the eastern wall, for my place was there—and after the prayers were concluded, the rabbi beckoned to me to approach him, and he asked me: "Who is this young man?" Whereupon I said to him: "He is the young man with whom His Excellency learned yesterday in order to test him."—Then the rabbi raised his voice aloud in the gladness of his heart—so it came about, when the young man, R. Leib, had grown ever greater in learning, that he became one of the students of the aforementioned rabbi, the head of the ecclesiastical court, and he circulated freely within the household of my father of blessed memory for roughly three consecutive years, and he ate his meals at the table of my father of blessed memory throughout the time when he was resident in the town of Skoki.

Translated by David E. Cohen.

Judah Jeitteles
1773–1838

Judah Jeitteles, a Hebrew writer, poet, and advocate of the Haskalah, was the son of the prominent physician Jonas Jeitteles in Prague. Although Judah Jeitteles had a traditional Jewish education, he advocated for the abolition of heders and the integration of religious Jewish studies into the secular curriculum. Among his writings was a book on Aramaic grammar. He became a Jewish communal leader in Prague and also supervised the German-language Jewish school there. His *Bene ha-ne'urim* is largely a biography of his father, including a recounting of Jonas Jeitteles's efforts in distributing Jenner's smallpox vaccine. For the last eight years of his life, Jeitteles lived in Vienna.

Bene ha-ne'urim (The Youth)
1821

Jonas saw that he was successful in the study of these sciences and that he had mastered the Latin tongue; in addition, his younger brother, who would be taking over his role in the family had grown to adulthood, and his sisters had become young maidens and would now be capable of being of benefit to their father by engaging in commerce and acquisitions of property, so Jonas directed his attention to the science of medicine—his true love—with a view to studying it in all its different aspects—as this was the path whereby he could attain the loftiest peaks of that science, and in addition, he would thereby find sufficient means to support himself and his household. Through this, his yearning for honor, which burned ardently within him, would be alleviated; through this, he would satisfy his powerful longing to benefit human society! At that time, it was not permitted for the Jewish people to enter gentile places of learning; the halls of academia were locked in their faces, and non-Jews would not even let them pass over the threshold of the academies—they were expelled, thus preventing them from becoming a part of the abodes of understanding—accordingly, the luminaries darkened, and all the Jewish people could see only gloom staring in their faces; for if a Jew indeed desired to draw sustenance from the font of knowledge, where would he be able to find a sufficiently broad well? Where was the path along which light dwelt?

[. . .] This matter constituted an impediment and an obstacle for Jonas; he realized that it was a stumbling block to him, and that it would deprive him of the hope of hearing the exposition of the science of medicine and of the other branches of knowledge from the mouths of the savants of the gentile schools of learning. He had made investigation into this, and further understood that it was better to hear the orderly presentation of the words of wisdom and knowledge while among the assemblies of students, the dispositions of whose minds differed from one another's, than to study in his own home, in the privacy of his abode, where he would be residing all alone, without any companion—for a student can acquire more wisdom and gain a greater amount of knowledge when among a group of students, as the topic becomes ever clearer through the ongoing questions and answers, the arguments and the discussions, the doubts and the resolutions; and it is also better for the public, who make enquiries on the theme and receive replies as appropriate—in addition, the natural mutual jealousy existing among the experts in the field increases, and inspires the mind of the student to fortify himself with wisdom, to magnify it and make it glorious. Accordingly, it was this aspect that constituted the primary reason for his decision to leave his native land and travel to another country.

Translated by David E. Cohen.

Other work by Jeitteles: *Mevo ha-lashon ha-aramit* (1813).

Emanuele Levi
ca. 1811–?

Emanuele Levi is known to us through his precocious diary, written during the Restoration period of early nineteenth-century Italy. For a year and a half, Emanuele wrote about life as he experienced it in Asti, where he was sent at age eleven to attend the Jewish school. The diary was written in a copybook, reviewed by his tutor Lazzaro Artom, and forwarded each week to Emanuele's parents.

Journal
1822–1823

We will compose a little book that will also serve as an amusement when, in ten years' time, we want to look back into the past and observe what we lived through. All people have a weakness for remembering the past, as if they want to take up the thread of their lives again and return to their first youth. (28 January, 1822) [. . .]

Another piece of news that upset us very much and that I do not wish to omit telling you concerns the loss of our puppy Tesor. Having departed from there with Signor Abramino, he arrived in Turin perhaps too tired, not being used to such a long journey, and he was not able to keep up with his master, who did not notice and abandoned him on the road. Or perhaps he had just stopped to talk to a canine friend, to ask him, as strangers to a city usually do, if there was much riff-raff in Turin, and how dogs were treated. . . . But in whichever way it happened, he is lost, and who knows in what desperate confusion this poor little animal finds himself, without his master, or his friends, and not knowing a relative there, should he have any. It could be that prompted by necessity, which often produces virtue, he may have made an effort, managed to disentangle himself from the midst of the complicated backstreets of Turin, and get himself back to Chieri as best as he could on the same road as his outward journey, where I pray that someone gives aid to this poor animal, who is so faithful to his master and who had the skill to know undesirables by their smell, so that when an honest gentleman went past the shop he would not be silent, but if he saw a crook he would follow him for a long way hurling insults at him. It may be that this is a skill common to all dogs, but it is well known that when we talk about matters of personal concern, we always find there singular virtues that our self-esteem magnifies as though we view them through a microscope. In short, however, what does it matter? This dog if he is passing through there has need of help, not of my useless moralizing observations, and I pray for him to be given food and shelter, as innkeepers who lack discretion when someone arrives without money, grant no favor apart from a piece of moldy bread and poor Tesor, tired and downcast from his journey, would not even be able to digest that. (24 April) [. . .]

In the Piazza d'Armi we have already enjoyed a carnival entertainment. A Genoese horse merchant allowed the son of his hotel owner to dress up a young foal, at least twenty-four years old, twenty inches high or a little less, and with an ass's hair, who was so adorned with other suchlike virtues, that antique dealers imagined that they were seeing the famous Rocinante of *Don Quixote* being brought back to life. Some young men pretended to be the groom Sancho Panza jumping onto him, and the nag showed his bravery by doing extraordinary jumps on his back, and putting his head between his legs in such a polite and casual manner that he made all the bystanders laugh, and in this way he kept all those who had come to the piazza for entertainment well amused. [. . .]

A lady about to give birth, who was so tiny but of such monstrous shape that the doctors had predicted a dangerous birth, miserably lost her life after twenty-four hours of terrible agony surrounded by obstetricians, surgeons, and many pious people. She had meanwhile brought into this world—and simultaneously into the grave—a poor infant without the knowledge of the surgeon and the others standing around. There was lots of whispering—as there always is in unusual cases. People criticized the inexperience of the attendants. Both bodies were buried in an enormous and deep trench after being transported to the distant cemetery with much difficulty over streets covered in snow a foot deep. All of this kept Signor Tedeschi very busy, and I have had, as I said, the freedom to write all day. [29 January, 1823 . . .]

Translated by Alberto Cavaglion.

Sheftall Sheftall
1762–1847

The son of Mordecai Sheftall, an important member of Georgia's early Jewish community, and Frances Hart Sheftall, a housewife originally from the Hague, Sheftall Sheftall was born in Savannah. He joined his father in supporting the Revolutionary War, serving as Assistant Deputy Commissioner of Issues for the Continental Troops, in Georgia. Both Sheftall and his father were captured in 1778, during the fall of Savannah, and held as prisoners of war for more than a year in the West Indies. Following a prisoner exchange, Sheftall Sheftall continued to serve until the end of the war and eventually returned to Savannah.

Description of His Career as a Revolutionary Soldier, 1777–1783
1832

Georgia
City of Savannah
Sheftall Sheftall of the said city, being duly sworn, saith:

That some time in the latter part of the year one thousand seven hundred and seventy seven, or the beginning of the year seventeen hundred and seventy eight, this deponent was appointed by John B. Geredeau [Geradieu] Esquire, Deputy Commissary General of Issues of the Continental troops in Georgia, to be an Assistant Deputy Commissary of Issues in his office;

That he continued in that station for some months when Mr. Geredeau resigned, and this deponent's father, the late Mordecai Sheftall, Esquire, was appointed Mr. Geredeau's successor; that this deponent was reappointed to his said office by his father, and that he continued in the office untill the British troops took Savannah, which was on the twenty ninth day of December of the said year seventeen hundred and seventy eight, when they took this deponent and his father prisoners, and a few days after put them on board of a prison ship, say, the second day of January, seventeen hundred seventy nine;

That on the twenty sixth day of March following, his father was admitted to his parole; that on the twenty-sixth day of June of the same year, this deponent was admitted also on his parole. On his landing, he was sent to the town of Sunbury, a distance of forty miles from

Savannah, where his father and a number of Continentall officers were on parole; that they continued theire [there] until the month of October following (the British garrison having been previously withdrawn to reinforce Savannah);

That the American and French army, under the command of General Lincoln and Count D'Estaing, laid siege to Savannah; that while in that situation, a Tory armed party that was hovering about the country threatened to Kill the American officers and did actually kill Captain Hornby of the Fourth Georgia Continental regiment; that in this situation, the officers applied to the commanders of the Allied army, what they were to do, who, in reply, recommended to them to remove to a place of safety, but to consider themselves as still on parole;

That this deponent, his father, and several officers embarked [October, 1779] on board of a brig in the harbour of Sunbury, which had been taken in the said harbour by a small American privateer, for to proceed in her to Charles Ton [Charlestown], in South Carolina; that on their passage, they were taken by a British frigate called the *Gaudaloupe*, who bore away and carried them and landed them in the island of Antigua; that some time in the month of November, that after being their [there] between five and six months, their [they] were admitted to a parole to return to America;

That this deponent and his father arrived in Philadelphia (via St. Eustatia) on the twentieth day of June, seventeen hundred and eighty; that a few days after their arrival, they were introduced to the Board of War, which consisted of General Thomas Mifflin, Colonel Timothy Pickering, Colonel [Robert Hanson] Harrison, and Richard Peters, Esquire, their secretary, by Colonel George Walton, one of the signers of the Declaration of Independence;

That the Board of War directed Mr. [Thomas] Bradford, Commissary of Prisoners, to send away two Englishmen, natives of Antigua, by the name of Jacob Jarvis and his brother, John Swinton Jarvis, for to be exchanged for this deponent and his father;

That some time in the early part of the month of December following, certified copies of their paroles, with certificates of their exchange for the said gentlemen, were received by this deponent and his father, by which means they were released from being prisoners of war;

That a few days thereafter, this deponent was sent for by the Board of War, and informed that he must proceed in a sloop called the *Caroline Packett*, commanded by Captain John Derry, [under] a flag of truce, as flag master to Charles Ton in South Carolina, for to carry goods, flour, and money for to be delivered to General Moultrie or the senior officer of the Continentall troops, prisoners of war at that place;

That he proceeded on the voyage agreeable to his instructions; that owing to storms and head winds, he did not arrive in Charles Ton harbour untill the seventh day of February following, when the aforesaid articles were delivered to a person appointed by General Moultrie and by his order; that he was detained by the British untill some time in April, when he was permitted to pursue his voyage back;

That he arrived in Philadelphia on the twenty third day of April; that on his arrival, he delivered up to the Board of War all his papers and vouchers, and, in particular, got a receipt acknowledging the delivery of the money, agreeable to the orders of General Moultrie, which receipt was signed by a Mr. Charlton or Carlton [Joseph Carlton], Paymaster of the Board of War and Ordinance;

That about three years agoe, a fire broke out in this city, in his neighbourhood; that he moved his furniture and things for safety into the street; that among them was the certificate of his exchange, the instructions from the Board of War, and the receipt for the money, [all of which] was unfortunately lost;

That the deponent continued in the service untill the close of the Revolutionary War, and that this deponent's pay was sixty dollars per month, exclusive of rations, and that on the eight[h] day of September last past, he was seventy years of age.

NOTE

Words in brackets appear in the source text.

Peter Beer

ca. 1758–1838

Born in Nový Bydžov, Bohemia, Peter (Perez) Beer was an educator, author, and religious reformer. He attended yeshivas in Prague and Pressburg (Bratislava); he also learned Latin and German. Beer was one of the first Habsburg Jews to study in a teaching seminary, and he taught at the German Jewish school in Prague from 1811 until his death. Beer wrote Jewish and biblical histories, as well as religious manuals, a prayer book for women, and a commentary on the Book of Genesis 1–24 (1815). He contributed to periodicals such as *Sulamith* and *Ha-me'asef*. Valued by Austrian authorities and controversial among Jews, Beer was a founder of the Reform synagogue in Prague.

The Childhood and Youth of a Man of the Enlightenment
1839

I was born on 19 February 1758 in Nový Bydžov [in Bohemia] of well-to-do parents who destined me at birth to be a rabbi, a common practice among the Israelites then. For at that time, when all institutions of higher learning were closed to Israelites, and every scholarly discipline remained unknown to them, the Talmud touched upon scholarly subjects such as geometry, astronomy, biology, etc., to the extent that they were understood in those days, and it was the epitome of all human knowledge. . . . So, as was then the custom, I was encouraged to read Hebrew when I turned three. . . .

In my fifth year I was encouraged to translate the Pentateuch in the so-called Judaeo-German dialect and, following a cabalistic opinion (in other words, following the advice of a cabalist), I began my Biblical career with the Third Book of Moses . . . with a Polish teacher. . . . The common method was for the teacher to translate one or more verses from the Pentateuch orally for the pupil, and to repeat them and have the pupil repeat them again and again the whole week until he was able to recite the text and the translation on the Sabbath. . . . I found these completely meaningless and absurd lessons, especially about subjects of which I had and could have no understanding, very boring, but I had to learn because my wise *orbil* [teacher] pressured me with his "forceful" arguments. Thus passed my fifth and sixth years, during which I learned to translate fragments of the Pentateuch, the Proverbs of Solomon, and parts of the so-called Early Prophets, without, however, understanding their contents.

I was encouraged to continue with the Talmud, and at the beginning of my seventh year I had to start out on this steep path, whether I liked it or not. However, the subject matter appealed to my ambitious mind because it is closer to practical life. My introduction to the study of the Talmud consisted of the tractate "Baba Mezia," which on the very first page relates a legal dispute between two people who had found a piece of cloth. When they appeared before the judge, each claimed to have found it sooner than the other, and thus claimed possession of it, according to the legal decision: *res derelicta* (or *res nullius*) *coelit primo occupanti* [an abandoned thing (or a thing belonging to nobody) belongs to the one who takes it first].

My father could read and write German, which was unusual among the Israelites in those days, and this advantage helped him to get a position as district manager of the tobacco administration in Moravia. Therefore he also wanted me to learn to read and write the German language. But as he did not have time to teach me himself, and no other Israelite was suited for it, the local Christian schoolmaster was chosen. For lack of another book, he taught me using a German breviary and from it I learned to write and read German moderately well, and also learned the five rules of arithmetic.

This good old man became fond of me, and since he had studied theology in his youth and was a very good Latin scholar, he also offered to instruct me in Latin. My parents resisted this proposal for a long time, because they were worried that this profane subject (as they called it) might keep me from my main occupation, the Talmud, and be detrimental to it. But they gave in on the condition that I devote eight hours daily to the study of the Talmud, and instruction in Latin began in my tenth year, although I still did not know pure German, or pure Hebrew.

My Latin teacher used the same method as my Hebrew teacher, but with more success. He first had me learn Amos Comenius's *Orbis Pictus* by heart and then selected an easy sentence from Cornelius Nepos. This sentence I had to copy in Latin. He dictated the German translation of every word to me, which I then wrote above the text. Then I had to memorize this sentence in both languages and had to recite the Latin text together with the German translation, both word for word and in its full context. Since my teacher simultaneously familiarized me with the circumstances connected with the story that the author tells, as well as with other related subjects, the instruction became more attractive and interesting for me. . . .

As soon as I was thirteen, my parents sent me to Prague, where at that time there was a very famous Talmudic college, a so-called *yeshiva*. For four years I very industriously heard the lectures of Chief Rabbi Ezechiel Landau, recognized as the greatest Talmudist of his time, as well as other renowned rabbis, and made good progress. The first German book I came across was Dusch's moral letters. I had hardly begun to read it when a fellow student complained to the rabbi about me, and the latter forbade me to read German books, adding that I would be excluded from Talmudic lectures if I disobeyed.

After four years in Prague, I went to Pressburg [Bratislava], where there was a rabbinical school at that time directed by Rabbi Meyer Barbi, who was known as the best mind among all the rabbis of his time. There I devoted myself industriously to the study of the Talmud. The Talmud was my element; I immersed myself in it exclusively, and I continued to be unfamiliar with the rest of human knowledge....

To become a rabbi, it was usual for a student of the Talmud without means to become a private tutor in a house and to wait until a well-to-do man chose him for his son-in-law. The latter usually gave him a considerable dowry and free board and lodging for several years. During these years the student perfected himself in the Talmud, its commentaries and epitomes, acquired a reputation for Talmudic learning and scholarship, and then received a *morenu*, or rabbinical doctoral diploma, from an accredited rabbi. Finally, with these qualifications, he was received as a rabbi by a congregation. I also followed this path, and became a tutor....

My first position was in a village in Hungary, on the Upper Danube, named Nagyssek. There was not a single person who spoke German in that village, and even in the house where I was a tutor the language of conversation was Hungarian, so that I was able to teach my pupils the Pentateuch in the usual so-called Judaeo-German dialect only with the greatest difficulty. Since I did not know Hungarian, my pupils did not feel like studying, and apart from the Pentateuch and the book of daily prayers there was no book in Hebrew or in any other language in the house. I, being accustomed to reading and thinking, although only in the Talmudic way—that is to say, in a way that requires astuteness and sharp wits—was very much plagued by boredom....

In order to while away time, I searched through all the nooks and crannies of the house. On one of these expeditions I found a treasure that was worth its weight in gold, given my situation at that time. It was a dust-covered package of books, which lay in a corner under the roof. My joy over this important find can only be compared with the joy that one feels when one sees a well with pure water after thirsting in a waterless desert for several days.

Jubilantly I took the package to my room. The people in the house told me that the books had belonged to a teacher who had died in the house.... I quickly opened the package and found a Hebrew grammar book ... a *More Nebuchim* [The Guide of the Perplexed] by Rabbi Moses ben Maimon, three volumes of the Hebrew Bible with the title *Zohar Hatovah* with a commentary to the Hebrew text by Rashi along with a translation in the so-called Judaeo-German dialect, and, finally, the story of the adventures of Don Quixote, Knight of la Mancha.

The first of the books that attracted me was the Hebrew grammar, which made me recall much that I had known from Latin. This book was especially pleasing to me because it was not dry, as grammar books usually are, but was written with much rabbinical wit, and delighted me as a reminder of my study of the Talmud. The Judaeo-German Bible, from which, as already mentioned, I had only known a few historical fragments (apart from the Pentateuch), occupied my attention to such an extent that I could recite the total Hebrew text, along with the Judaeo-German translation, from memory within a year.... Though I read a few easier passages in *More Nebuchim*, those passages that dealt with philosophy in general (or metaphysics or rational philosophy in particular) were beyond my understanding because, as far as religion was concerned, I was only familiar with a faith according to Talmudic tradition and could not imagine rational knowledge, not to speak of doubts.

Therefore I put aside this work, like a sealed book. However, through these books I realized that there are other writings worth knowing apart from the Talmud, in Hebrew as well as in other languages, and the idea of investigating them awoke in me.

Moreover a strange era began for the Jews at this time, both in regard to science and to politics. In politics it was caused by Emperor Joseph and science by Mendelssohn, for he brought about a great change of ideas in this nation, the news of which even penetrated into my remote little village. I heard of Mendelssohn's translation of the Pentateuch, bought it with half of my savings, and instantly devoured the contents. Then it dawned on me that it was not enough to depend on old legends (which are often contradictory in themselves) to understand this book of books, but that it can be brought closer to the mind and heart through Hebrew grammar, classical studies, and religious and moral thought. It was fortunate that just at this time, Joseph the Unforgettable [Joseph II] took over the government of the Austrian State. The news of his Toleration Edict, which would take away the Jews' yoke that had weighed sorely on their bodies and souls up till then and had excluded them from civic society so that they had had to concentrate on themselves, filled me with such an enthusiastic love for this monarch who valued everyone's human rights, that I decided to risk everything to see this crowned benefactor. Therefore, as soon as my period of service was over, I started for Vienna.

Arriving there in 1780, good fortune took me to a very respectable, very advanced household where I was hired as tutor. There I found a large collection of books in Hebrew, in German, and in other languages, which were put in my charge. But since there were so many books and I did not know which of them to choose, I put my hand in the cupboard as into a Lucky Dip and took the first book that chance placed in my hands. . . . Fortunately several Viennese scholars often visited my master as friends of the house, among them Hofrat [Court Councilor] Jos. Ritter von Sonnenfels, one of the most active patrons of Austrian culture, whose acquaintance I made. This noble philanthropist noticed my exuberant chaos and advised me to go to work systematically and to organize my knowledge. At his suggestion I therefore chose Ch. Wolf as my guide, began with his arithmetic, and successively went through all his mathematical, philosophical, and theological works. Out of the goodness of his heart Herr von Sonnenfels explained the most difficult passages to me. At the same time, I read the writings of Mendelssohn, Lessing, Wieland, Herder, Kant, and Göthe [sic], which were being published at that time, and thus the tangle was partially unraveled. . . .

The Emperor now decreed that German schools on the pattern of the *Normalschulen* [elementary schools] should be introduced among the Jews. My eagerness to add my mite to the regeneration of my fellow believers, and to advance the plan of the noble monarch as much as lay in my power, made me decide to become a public teacher. I attended lectures on educational theory, methodology, catechetics, and the like at the University of Vienna, and especially at the *Hauptmusterschule* in Vienna. In 1783 I took up teaching at the newly founded German school at Mattersdorf in Hungary and was its principal for two years. During this time I began my career as a writer by translating Ebert's book on natural sciences. . . .

In 1787 I married my wife, Rebecca Hlawatsch, also born in my hometown Nový Bydžov, who is still living. She is a woman whose mind was not formed, or rather deformed, by fashionable education, novels, and plays, but who was endowed by nature with a direct and healthy common sense and a noble heart, so that she fulfilled all duties as wife, mother, and housewife in our 47 years of marriage, and I believe I can call her, as Solomon did, "A wife among thousands." The small dowry she brought me in cash I used primarily to buy theological, philosophical, and educational books, and my time was divided between my teaching profession and educating myself, even though my annual income hardly amounted to 300 florins and God soon blessed me with six children.

From my own experience I recognized the inappropriate method of teaching Jewish youth, especially the teaching of the Bible, and when my first boy was ready to be taught, I wrote a Biblical story for him in Hebrew with a German translation accompanied by moral comments and published this in 1796 in Prague under the title *Toldot Jisrael*.

NOTE

Words in brackets appear in the original translation.

Translated by Wilma Abeles Iggers, Káča Poláčková-Henley, and Kathrine Talbot.

Other works by Beer: *Toldot Yisra'el* (1796); *Gebetbuch für gebildete Frauenzimmer mosaischer Religion* (1815 in Hebrew letters; 1843 in German); *Geschichte, Lehren und Meinungen aller bestandenen und noch bestehenden religiösen Sekten der Juden und der Geheimlehre oder Cabbalah* (1822–1823).

Abraham Kohn

1819–1871

Born in Bavaria, Abraham Kohn arrived in the United States in 1842, first working as a peddler in New England and then settling in Chicago, where he owned a prosperous store and helped to found Chicago's first synagogue, Kehilath Anshe Ma'arav. A loyal Republican supporter of Abraham Lincoln, Kohn advocated for Jewish equal rights. He was elected city clerk of Chicago.

A Jewish Peddler's Diary
1842

On the eve of the New Year I found myself with a new career before me. What kind of career? "I don't know"—the American's customary reply to every difficult question. . . . I was in New York, trying in vain to find a job as clerk in a store. But business was too slow, and I had to do as all the others; with a bundle on my back I had to go out into the country, peddling various articles. This, then, is the vaunted luck of the immigrants from Bavaria! O misguided fools, led astray by avarice and cupidity! You have left your friends and acquaintances, your relatives and your parents, your home and your fatherland, your language and your customs, your faith and your religion—only to sell your wares in the wild places of America, in isolated farmhouses and tiny hamlets. . . .

Only rarely do you succeed, and then only in the smallest way. Is this fate worth the losses you have suffered, the dangers you have met on land and sea? Is this an equal exchange for the parents and kinsmen you have given up? Is this the celebrated freedom of America's soil? Is it liberty of thought and action, when, in order to do business in a single state, one has to buy a license for a hundred dollars? When one must profane the holy Sabbath, observing Sunday instead? In such matters are life and thought more or less confined than in the fatherland? True, one does hear the name "Jew," but only because one does not utter it. Can a man, in fact, be said to be "living" as he plods through the vast, remote country, uncertain even as to which farmer will provide him shelter for the coming night?

In such an existence the single man gets along far better than the father of a family. Such fools as are married not only suffer themselves, but bring suffering to their women. How must an educated woman feel when, after a brief stay at home, her supporter and shelterer leaves with his pack on his back, not knowing where he will find lodging on the next night or the night after? On how many winter evenings must such a woman sit forlornly with her children at the fireplace, like a widow, wondering where this night finds the head of her family, which homestead in the forest of Ohio will offer him a poor night's shelter? O, that I had never seen this land, but had remained in Germany, apprenticed to a humble country craftsman! Though oppressed by taxes and discriminated against as a Jew, I should still be happier than in the great capital of America, free from royal taxes and every man's religious equal though I am! . . .

Today, Sunday, October 16th, we are here in North Bridgewater, and I am not so downcast as I was two weeks ago. The devil has settled 20,000 shoemakers here, who do not have a cent of money. Suppose, after all, I were a soldier in Bavaria; that would have been a bad lot. I will accept three years in America instead. But I could not stand it any longer.

As far as the language is concerned, I am getting along pretty well. But I don't like to be alone. The Americans are funny people. Although they sit together by the dozen in taverns, they turn their backs to each other, and no one talks to anybody else. Is this supposed to be the custom of a republic? I don't like it. Is this supposed to be the fashion of the nineteenth century? I don't like it either. . . .

On Wednesday, November 9th, Moses and I went to Holden, where we stayed until Sunday with Mr. How. On Monday, we went on, arriving on Tuesday at Rutland. In the morning our packs seemed very heavy, and we had to rest every half-mile. In the afternoon a buggy was offered to us and, thank Heaven, it was within our means. We took off our bundles and anticipated thriving business. Wednesday we proceeded to Barre by horse and carriage, and on Thursday went to Worcester to meet Juda. Here we stayed together until Friday, November 25th, when we left for West Boylston, staying for the night at Mr. Stuart's, two miles from Sterling. We stayed on Saturday night and over Sunday at the home of Mr. Blaube where I met the most beautiful girl I have ever seen. Her name is Helena Brown and she is from Boston. But despite this girl, I do not yet like America as well as I might wish. But if Heaven causes us to prosper we may yet be entirely satisfied.

Last Thursday was Thanksgiving Day, a general holiday, fixed by the governor for the inhabitants of Massachusetts. Yet it seems to be merely a formal observance, coldly carried through with nothing genuine about it. To the American one day is like another, and even Sunday, their only holiday, is a mere form. They often go to church here, but only to show the neighbor's wife a new veil or dress.

Winter has come. . . . We were at Sterling and Leominster on Monday, November 28th, and we went from there to Lunenburg.

Not far from here we were forced to stop on Wednesday because of the heavy snow. We sought to spend the night with a cooper, a Mr. Spaulding, but his wife did not wish to take us in. She was afraid of strangers, she might not sleep well; we should go our way. And outside there raged the worst blizzard I have ever seen. O God, I thought, is this the land of liberty and hospitality and tolerance? Why have I been led here? After we had talked to this woman for half an hour, after repeatedly pointing out that to turn us forth into the blizzard would be sinful, we were allowed to stay. She became friendlier, indeed, after a few hours, and at night she even joined us in singing. But now often I remembered during that evening how my poor mother treated strangers at all times. Every poor man, every traveler who entered the house, was welcomed hospitably and given the best at our table. Her motto, even for strangers, was, "Who throws stones at me shall be, in turn, pelted by me with bread." Now her own children beg for shelter in a foreign land....

Translated by Abram Vossen Goodman.

Judith Cohen Montefiore
1784–1862

"First Lady of Anglo-Jewry," Lady Judith Cohen Montefiore was highly educated in languages, literature, and the arts. She was an influential force for Sir Moses Montefiore, whom she married in 1812. She kept a diary of their first trip to Palestine in 1827 and published an account of their second visit in her *Private Journal of a Visit to Egypt and Palestine* (an excerpt of which appears in this volume). In 1846 she wrote (or cowrote) the first Anglo-Jewish cookbook, *The Jewish Manual* by "A Lady." Montefiore was an active philanthropist who supported Jewish communal organizations. Although not strictly observant in her youth, she later became Orthodox in her practice. Her husband founded Lady Judith Montefiore College in her honor.

The Jewish Manual of Practical Information in Jewish and Modern Cookery with a Collection of Valuable Recipes & Hints Relating to the Toilette
1846

Hands

Nothing contributes more to the elegance and refinement of a lady's appearance than delicate hands; and it is surprising how much it is in the power of all, by proper care and attention, to improve them. Gloves should be worn at every opportunity, and these should invariably be of kid; silk gloves and mittens, although pretty and tasteful, are far from fulfilling the same object. The hands should be regularly washed in tepid water, as cold water hardens, and renders them liable to chap, while hot water wrinkles them. All stains of ink, &c., should be immediately removed with lemon-juice and salt: every lady should have a bottle of this mixture on her toilette ready prepared for the purpose. The receipts which we have already given as emollients for the skin are suitable for softening the hands and rendering them smooth and delicate. The nails require daily attention: they should be cut every two or three days in an oval form. A piece of flannel is better than a nail-brush to clean them with, as it does not separate the nail from the finger.

When dried, a little pummice-stone, finely powered, with powdered orris-root, in the proportion of a quarter of a tea-spoonful to a tea-spoonful of the former, mixed together, and rubbed on the nails gently, gives them a fine polish, and removes all inequalities.

A piece of sponge, dipped in oil of roses and emery, may be used for the same purpose.

When the nails are disposed to break, a little oil or cold cream should be applied at night.

Sand-balls are excellent for removing hardness of the hands. Palm soap, Castille soap, and those which are the least perfumed, should always be preferred. Night-gloves are considered to make the hands white and soft, but they are attended with inconvenience, besides being very unwholesome; and the hands may be rendered as white as the nature of the complexion will allow, by constantly wearing gloves in the day-time, and using any of the emollients we have recommended for softening and improving the skin.

Mordecai Manuel Noah
1785–1851

Mordecai Manuel Noah was born in Philadelphia to parents of mixed Sephardic and Ashkenazic heritage. He lived for some years in Charleston, where he studied law, before settling in New York. His father had served in the Revolutionary War and, as a young man, Noah also wished to serve his country. However, he became disillusioned with the prospects for Jews in the United States when, acting as the U.S. consul in Tunis, he was recalled for the given reason that his religion had proven an obstacle to his consular duties. Thereafter, Noah became a proponent of Zionism, even purchasing land on Grand Island, in upstate New York, to serve as a temporary refuge for persecuted

Jews until they could go to the Land of Israel. He named this proposed refuge Ararat. In addition to these activities, Noah was a dramatist, writer, and speaker. (An excerpt from his *She Would Be a Soldier* appears in this volume.)

Ziprah Nunez's Account of the Family Escape
1849

On page 101, reference is made to the history of the Jews in this State. Since that part of the work was printed, M. M. Noah, Esquire, of New-York, has kindly favoured us with the following additional items:

Dr. Samuel Nunez, whose name belonged to a distinguished family in Lisbon, was a physician of eminence, and had an extensive practice, even in times when Jews of that city were under the surveillance of the Inquisition. Jealousy and rivalry, however, caused him to be denounced to that dreadful tribunal, and himself and family were arrested as heretics, and thrown into the dungeons of the Inquisition. At that period the Jews were not permitted openly to follow their religion; they had no synagogues or places of public worship, but assembled for devotional purposes in each others' houses, and their prayer-books were concealed in the sets of chairs, and opened by springs. It had long been observed that the families never ventured abroad on Friday evenings, being the evening of the Sabbath, and suspicions were awakened as to their real faith, although for form sake they all attended mass. The familiars of the Inquisition, who were generally spies, were set to work to discover what their pursuits were on the Sabbath, and detecting them at prayers, seized their Hebrew prayer-books, and threw them all into prison.

Doctor Nunez, who was a most popular and skilful man, was physician to the Grand Inquisitor, who was anxious to save him. He did all in his power to alleviate the sufferings of his family; but one of them, Abby de Lyon, who died in Savannah, carried to her grave the marks of the ropes on her wrists when put to the question. They remained for some time in prison; but as the medical services of Doctor Nunez were very much in demand in Lisbon, the ecclesiastical council, under the advice of the Grand Inquisitor, agreed to set him and family at liberty, on condition that two officials of the Inquisition should reside constantly in the family, to guard against their relapsing again into Judaism. The doctor had a large and elegant mansion on the banks of the Tagus, and being a man of large fortune, he was in the habit of entertaining the principal families of Lisbon. On a pleasant summer day he invited a party to dinner; and among the guests was the Captain of an English brigantine, anchored at some distance in the river. While the company were amusing themselves on the lawn, the captain invited the family and part of the company to accompany him on board the brigantine, and partake of a lunch prepared for the occasion. All the family, together with the spies of the Inquisition, and a portion of the guests, repaired on board the vessel; and while they were below in the cabin, enjoying the hospitality of the captain, the anchor was weighed, the sails unfurled, and the wind being fair, the brigantine shot out of the Tagus, was soon at sea, and carried the whole party to England. It had been previously arranged between the doctor and the captain, who had agreed, for a thousand moidores in gold, to convey the family to England, and who were under the painful necessity of adopting this plan of escape to avoid detection. The ladies had secreted all their diamonds and jewels, which were quilted in their dresses, and the doctor having previously changed all his securities into gold, it was distributed among the gentlemen of the family, and carried around them in leather belts. His house, plate, furniture, servants, equipage, and even the dinner cooked for the occasion, were all left, and were subsequently seized by the Inquisition and confiscated to the State.

On the arrival of Doctor Nunez and family in London, the settlement of Georgia, and the fine climate and soil of that country, were the subjects of much speculation. The celebrated John Wesley, and his brother Charles, had resolved to embrace the occasion of visiting this El Dorado; and when the ship which conveyed Governor Oglethorpe to that new settlement was about sailing, the doctor and his whole family embarked as passengers, not one of whom could speak the English language; and from them the families have descended, already named in the body of this work. After a few years, a number sailed for New York; and Zipra Nunez married the Rev. David Machado, Minister of the Hebrew congregation of that city. Major Noah states that he remembers his great-grandmother, Zipra Nunez, as a very remarkable personage. She died at nearly ninety years of age, and was celebrated for her beauty and accomplishments. She spoke several languages—preserved to the last a beautiful set of teeth, unimpaired, and was observed, whenever the clock struck, to repeat a silent prayer, which had some reference to her imprisonment in the Inquisition. The whole family were rigid in their attachment to the doctrines of their faith. Two of her brothers, who arrived in the same vessel from London, lie buried in the Jewish cemetery in Chatham Square, New York; and from them has sprung a long list of highly respectable descendants in Savannah, Charleston, Philadelphia, and New York, all of them of the Hebrew persuasion at this day.

Other works by Noah: *Marion; or, The Hero of Lake George. A Drama in Three Acts, Founded on Events of the Revolutionary War* (1822); *Discourse on the Restoration of the Jews* (1845); *The Selected Writings of Mordecai Noah* (1999).

Leopold Zunz
1794–1886

Raised in Hamburg, Germany, Leopold Zunz helped found the discipline of *Wissenschaft des Judenthums* (academic Jewish studies), and indeed edited and wrote for the periodical *Zeitschrift für die Wissenschaft des Judenthums*. From 1815 to 1819 he attended the University of Berlin, and obtained his doctorate in 1821 from the University of Halle. Ordained by Rabbi Aaron Chorin, Zunz served at the Reform New Synagogue in Berlin, though his thinking was not always in accord with Reform Judaism. Zunz's major works included an analysis of Jewish preaching, *Die gottesdienstlichen Vorträge der Juden historisch entwickelt* and his *Namen der Juden*, a work defending, against government decree, the adoption of German names for Jews. In 1840, Zunz became director of the Berlin Jewish Teachers' Seminary. As a scholar, he oversaw biblical translations and wrote a number of historical works.

My First Lessons in Wolfenbüttel
Mid-19th Century

In the year 1803, on Sunday afternoon the 5th of June, I and my uncle, accompanied—from the town gate onwards—by a soldier, arrived at the *bet midrash*, located at the Zimmerhofe. The soldier left us when Mr. Ruben (Polli) came out to receive us (Polli was my grandmother's natural cousin, and so my uncle's second cousin, once removed) and brought us to the home of Ph. Samson, on the opposite side of the street. There I was given something to eat—it was brown cabbage. Mr. Samson interviewed me, and around 2:00 we marched to Harz Street, in front of the old *bet midrash*. Mr. Kalman (born in 1733, I believe) stood in front of the door, a gray cap over the white and so forth. From the next day on, the Talmud-learning began; since I was not yet 9 years old, I was spared the *leinen* [reading out loud]. We were kept busy every afternoon until 5:00, in winter until around 4:00. Only Friday morning was devoted to the *ḥumash*. Mr. Kalman had Mendelssohn's translation of the Bible in front of him; in addition Mr. Benlevy from Sandersleben (now in Hildesheim) taught two periods of Jewish writing (until April 1804; later Polli); G. Bertrand (a novelist who died in 1811) taught German writing, reading, and math for four or five periods a week. The other or higher rabbi, who lived one story above, was R. Lik from Burg-Ebrach (near Bamberg) who had studied in Poland and therefore dressed in Polish style, a gentle man, but married to a devil named Miriam. He was a kabbalist, stayed later than everyone else in the synagogue, and sat in on the morning Talmud lesson wearing tallit and tefillin. I found the following fellow students: 1) with R. Lik: Meier Gumpel (b. 1786), who left the Institute in November 1804 and died in Braunschweig; Moses from Burg-Ebrach who wore a three-cornered hat and left in 1804—I think he went to Ballenstadt; 2) with R. Kalman: Salomon from Altona (a brother of David Berlin who left in April 1808), who was around 14 or 15 years old; Hirsch from Hamburg, who was the same age and in 1805 was sent home because of illness; Jakob Frensdorf from Hannover, born in August 1792, who was in the *bet midrash* from 1802 until May 1805.—There were no school rules, no guidelines and hardly any pedagogy. Friday afternoons we picked over the beans and peas; in our games and scuffles we were left to ourselves.

Translated by Carola Murray-Seegert.

Other works by Zunz: *Etwas über die rabbinische Literatur* (1818); *Die gottesdienstlichen Vorträge der Juden historisch entwickelt* (1832); *Synagogale Poesie des Mittelalters* (1855); *Literaturgeschichte der synagogalen Poesie* (1865).

Henriette de Lemos Herz
1764–1847

Henriette de Lemos Herz was a Berlin *salonnière* famed for her beauty and literary engagement. She was highly educated, especially in ancient and modern languages. Following her marriage in 1779 to physician and philosopher Marcus Herz, the couple started a salon that attracted Prussian nobles, romantic writers, and Jewish reformers. Along with Dorothea Schlegel, Wilhelm and Alexander von Humboldt, and others, she founded a *Tugendbund* (Society of Virtue) to foster friendship and learning. She translated two English travel books into German. After her husband's death in 1803, the salon declined. Herz then lived in reduced circumstances, working as a governess and teacher, and converted to Protestantism. Although she began her memoir in the 1820s, it was not published until 1850.

Her Life and Her Memories
1850

But was it surprising, when in the midst of such social circumstances or actually disarray, an intellectual sociability was offered, despite the prejudices that prevailed against the Jews at that time, that it was hungrily taken up by those who were looking for intellectual stimulation through the conversational exchange of ideas? It is no less comprehensible, however, that among the men, it was the younger ones who first approached these circles. For the spirit that prevailed in them was that of a new era, and also the representatives of it, by fortunate coincidence, were in part very beautiful young girls and women. Also, it was under these circumstances that the aspiring element of the noble youth was the first to join, for the nobility itself was too distant from the Jews in bourgeois society to mingle with them and so appear to be their peers.

But of course, the conditions within our circle changed soon enough. The spirit is a great equalizer, and love, which every now and again did not hesitate to interfere, often transformed pride into humility. Courtly behavior would have been fully subject to satire here, where informality was a condition of life. It was already directed against the entire class of the court nobility with its cold, stiff formality. Since the court at that time was much in mourning for all sorts of princes and minor princes that no one knew, not even the court itself, and because one therefore hardly saw them except with so-called *Pleureusen*,[1] so the nobility in our circle were usually referred to as *Pleureusenmenschen*.[2]

Into this circle was gradually drawn, as if by magic, every significant youth and young man who lived in Berlin, and even those who only came to visit. For self-awareness and vitality would not allow the once-kindled light to be placed again under the basket, and therefore it soon shone far into the distance. Congenial female relatives and friends of those young men also began gradually to join. Soon, too, the free-spirited among the more mature men followed, once word of such socializing reached their circles. I mean, *pour comble* (to top it all), we were finally fashionable—even foreign diplomats did not spurn us.

And so I believe I do not exaggerate when I claim that, at that time in Berlin, there was neither a man nor a woman who later somehow distinguished themselves, who, for a longer or shorter time as allowed by their position in life, was not a member of these circles. Yes, the boundary is scarcely to be drawn at the royal household, for even the undoubtedly brilliant Prince Louis Ferdinand later moved in them. Rahel's [Varnhagen] correspondence, as far as it has been published, may reasonably serve to support my assertion. I say "reasonably" for were not the male and female friends to whom she addressed her letters, and those who are mentioned in them, more or less also the members of this society? So the full publication of the correspondence would certainly be more significant in presenting the personalities who were her friends, and furthermore, she had no relationship to some who belonged to an earlier period. Yes, and I also do not fear to exaggerate if I declare that the spirit that emerged from these circles penetrated even the most elevated of Berlin's spheres, as explained by the social position of those who adopted it. Otherwise, however, this spirit had almost no effect elsewhere.

NOTES

1. [Black ribbons, worn on the shoulder as a sign of mourning.—Trans.]
2. [Mourners.—Trans.]

Translated by Carola Murray-Seegert.

Daniel Khvolson
1819–1911

Born in Vilna (Vilnius), Daniel Khvolson (Khvol'son) received a traditional Jewish religious education. He moved to Riga and then was invited to complete his studies in Breslau, where he learned German, French, and Russian. Upon converting to Christianity in 1855, he became a professor of Hebrew and Syriac studies at the University of St. Petersburg. His *Die Sabier un der Sabismus* (1856) not only established his expertise in Semitic studies, but also helped shape Russian-language scholarship in that field. Despite his conversion, he defended Jews against blood libels and helped to win their acquittal in numerous cases.

Letter on His Conversion
ca. 1855

A few days after receiving your precious letter of 5 November 1854, I began collating [the pages of my book], which took me until New Year's eve to finish. But what a chasm in between! I began the work as a Jew and finished as a Christian [. . .]! As my first child lay dying from his circumcision, I made the initial decision to convert to Christianity, and after two years of vacillating the decision had ripened sufficiently to carry out. The pale face of my poor, wretched and sickly child admonished me constantly and thus fourteen days ago, I, my wife and my two small children (the second is only ten weeks old and not circumcised) converted to Christianity. We would have preferred to become Protestants . . . but a variety of circumstances, which I cannot spell out here, prompted me to convert to the Greek [Orthodox] Church. This step is judged differently by different people, though God alone knows what was in my heart.

NOTE
Words in brackets appear in the original translation.
Translated by Ephraim M. Epstein and D. Khvolson.

Other works by Khvolson: *Corpus inscriptionum hebraicarum* (1882); *Die Blutanklage und sonstige mittelalterliche Beschuldigungen der Juden* (1901).

Salomon de Rothschild
1835–1864

One of the more reckless scions of the famous Rothschild family, Salomon James de Rothschild was born in Paris in 1835. His father, James Meyer, had brought the Rothschild banking empire to France and expected his children, in turn, to expand the sphere of the family's influence. Instead, Salomon lost vast sums of money on the stock exchange. As punishment, he was assigned a tedious apprenticeship with another branch of the family in Frankfurt, where he met his cousin and future wife, Adèle. His father later sent him to tour the United States on the eve of the Civil War, where Salomon sympathized with the Confederate cause. Despite these sympathies, and his proclivity for gambling—the cause, the Goncourt brothers claimed, of his relatively early death at the age of twenty-nine—he was known to have a philanthropic side. He was buried in the family vault at Père-Lachaise Cemetery in France.

Correspondence from the United States, 1859–1861
1859–1861

New York, October 17, [18]59

People are rather preoccupied with the internal politics of the country. The abortive attempt of [the abolitionist John] Brown and his accomplices, and their execution, have again aroused the hatreds of the two great parties which divide America, and there are some who go so far as to fear a complete schism between the states of the South and those of the North. The prudent men of the North, in order to avoid any such extreme, declare themselves in favour of maintaining the *status quo*, but the population is enraged against slavery, and it is aroused in this feeling by skilful ringleaders.

At their head is [the Reverend Henry Ward] Beecher, the brother of Mrs. [Harriet] Beecher Stowe, author of *Uncle Tom's Cabin*. Every day he delivers the most fiery speeches, and since he is a clergyman, he generally chooses Sunday and the churches to give vent to his eloquence.

In Washington, the Congress is so divided that it has not as yet been able to name a president [Speaker of the House]. In Philadelphia there have been disturbances, and in South Carolina $200,000 have been put aside in case of war with the Northern states. A pathetic union! But I think that all this excitement will go up in smoke!

I am beginning to become popular in this new life; everyone is very polite to me and I have been getting invitations by the dozen. . . . In my travels I'm frequently amused by the sight of fires. They are so frequent here that people pay no attention to them, and even the people next door are not even disturbed. Fire-fighting services are admirably organized; the fire engines are magnificent and manned by volunteers who vie with one another to arrive at the scene of the misfortune first. So it happens that if two companies of firemen arrive at the same time, the one that arrives first has the right to command the other, but they begin to battle about precedence. Anyway, the fires generally don't last long; the fire engines are well-suited to the task. Some of the engines are run by steam and they travel by themselves in the streets. But they have the disadvantage that each time that they move, they crush several people and overturn carriages. Outside of that, they are very useful. . . .

I can assure you that the Americans are skillful thieves. I had just gotten some money from the office, and I went into a shop to pay a bill. I had no sooner put my pocketbook back into my pocket and gone a hundred steps, than it disappeared with the hundred dollars in it.

But there is an event here more serious than most important political happenings: it is the construction and the establishment of a garden or park which will be nine miles in circumference. Thus all Americans tell me we are going to have a part more beautiful than the Bois de Boulogne [in Paris]. It will cost $10,000,000. [This was Central Park.]

New York, October 19, 1859

I must confess that New York has made upon me an altogether different impression from what I expected. In it I found the most aristocratic sentiments side by side with the most thoroughly democratic institutions. I have seen few countries where society was more exclusive, and yet this exclusiveness is founded on nothing. Wealth, political position, education are not the criteria that get you admitted. You are fashionable or you are not, and the reason is completely unknown to those who are the object of this preference and to those who bestow it. It is, in my opinion, the most peculiar and often the most unjust structure of society possible.

I found the men infinitely better informed and more worldly than I expected, and I would find them perfectly all right, if they didn't have a constant tendency to exaggerate the faults of their motherland. The financial and industrial activity has rather disappointed me, and with the exception of the unbelievable expansion of the dry goods trade (importing of manufactured goods), and the immense scale on which these houses are established, business seems to me quite limited at this time.

It is true that the difficulties arising in European politics, and the fears conceived in this country of a dissolution of the American union, were dominant in the slowdown of commerce and long-term enterprises. Now I suppose that everything will resume again here, for the Italian question has been considered entirely resolved since the Congress announcement [of Villafranca di Verona, July, 1859, whereby the emperors of Austria and France settled, as they thought, the Italian Question], and the differences between France and England completely ended by the union of the forces of the two countries in the Chinese expedition [in 1859 to bring that country into the sphere of European influence]. As for the internal politics of the country, judicious people have been so frightened by the consequences of a rupture between the North and South that a strong reaction will suddenly arise from all the sides. Meetings have been held in favor of the Union, at the same time as people are expecting to see the anti-slavery (Republican) candidate named president of Congress [Speaker of the House]. Nevertheless, the understanding between the North and South will be re-established, and the great problem of the slaves will be left dormant until next year.

Meanwhile, however, the Republican party vanguard bustles about quite a bit. Its leaders, Beecher and [Wendell] Phillips, give such fiery speeches that prudent Americans say they deserve to be hanged, but in this land of extravagant liberty you can attack the property of your neighbor, and the law protects the thief infinitely more than the honest man.

Another thing that astonishes me very much is that, with rare exceptions, statesmen in public office or in Congress are so lightly esteemed, and people pay so little attention to them. Yet there are some that possess great eloquence, and if there are some interesting matters under discussion, I shall go to Washington next month to attend some of the debates.

New York, January 3, '60

It is bitter cold. A snowstorm has made sledding possible, but I don't find that pleasant—you risk coming back with your nose or your ears frozen, but what is really nice is ice skating, and Central Park offers a strange spectacle with its 4,000 skaters, going to and fro, jostling one another and failing. This park will certainly be one of the most beautiful in the world, and Americans are as proud of it as of Washington.

Speaking of Washington, I think I'll go next week to see the city that bears this name, for then Congress will be organized and the assembly [the House of Representatives] will be interesting to see. Right now political passions have reached their peak, and the problem of slavery will be forever buried, or there will be a rupture between the Southern and Northern states, and perhaps a civil war will follow as a result of the breach. To know what political passions are, you must see them here, and it is a strange sight for a foreigner.

After studying the problem on its own terrain, I must tell you something that will make you jump and make me fall considerably in your estimation. If I were an American and had to give my opinion, I would be as much a "staunch slavery man" as the oldest plantation owner in the South. . . .

New York, January 12, '60

. . . . The negligence of the government in preventing all sorts of accidents is shameful, and I am surprised that even greater disasters don't happen. An engineer who, through his fault, negligence, and inability, caused the death of a number of people, went unpunished. But I hope that the latest frightful accident that has just occurred will bring about increased supervision.

A manufacturer had built cotton mills at Lawrence [Massachusetts]. In order to save a couple of thousand dollars, however, he did not have the buildings constructed as sturdily as they should have been. Public opinion was aroused over it, but the government claimed it had nothing to do with it as long as no misfortune occurred. The day before yesterday the building suddenly collapsed on 800 workers who were working at their looms and almost buried them under the debris. The work of salvage was immediately begun, when, on top of everything, fire broke out among the ruins and burned to death the unfortunate people who had not been crushed. More than 300 perished in this catastrophe and 150 were injured, some seriously.

It would really be a good deed for humanity if European newspapers took this unfortunate accident as an opportunity to attack American government, which is infinitely more concerned with its political influence than with the welfare and the security of those whom it was supposed to govern paternally. The word *liberty* means here, as in all democracies, being able to do anything to hurt one's neighbor or to inconvenience him.

NOTE
Words in brackets appear in the source text.

Abraham Rosanes
1838–1879

A scholar and merchant, Abraham Rosanes was a chronicler and leader in the Ottoman Jewish community. Hailing from Rusçuk (now Ruse, Bulgaria), he was part of a prominent Sephardic family. In 1867 he traveled to Palestine, recording his experiences. His travelogue and letters home were translated from their original Solitreo—a form of Ladino—to Hebrew and published under Rosanes's acronym Abir (or HeAbir). Returning to Rusçuk, he founded a secular Jewish school in 1869. He engaged in a nonacademic but valuable ethnographic study of the Ottoman Jewry. His commitment to Jewish education and history were taken up by his son, Solomon, with whom Rosanes sought refuge in Istanbul during the Russo-Ottoman War (1877–1878).

Diary
1864

In the month of Tevet of the same year I entered that school and began studying Greek with tremendous dedication. I repented of all my previous actions and habits, just as I had promised my father (of blessed memory) that I would. My desire to learn that language was immense, so much so that I turned night into day, sleeping only very little and reviewing my lessons. I would rise early in the morning and go immediately to school after prayers, staying there until nightfall. It was a long distance from my house to the school and bitter cold that winter, but none of it impeded my attendance every single day. My Jewish friends on the other hand were often absent because of these impediments.

At lunchtime one day, after I had been there about four months, my friends began to converse with some of the Armenian students there concerning their messiah [Jesus]. Over the course of their conversation they began to mock and curse each other until they became embroiled in a full-blown fight. They brought the matter before the teacher, who informed the school principal. A decision was made to expel the Jewish children, and I alone would remain because I had not spoken a word. This was the truth and this was what those students told the principal. It was extremely difficult to be the lone Jew among all those Christians in addition to the long distance I needed to travel every morning and evening and the other distractions. My enthusiasm, however, overcame them all, and I never missed a day of attendance for an entire year. In this manner I acquired an excellent knowledge of that language.

When this period has passed, I was no longer able to attend the school. This is because a war raged in those days . . . so that most days the shops in our city were shuttered, because the townspeople were called to the duty of the king. Another issue was that they would bring cattle through the marketplaces and I was scared of them. I therefore requested of my father (may his soul dwell in Eden) that he hire a tutor who could come to our house every day and teach me. Now my father (may his soul dwell in Eden), having seen that I kept my promise to give up my wayward life, did not refuse me in this matter. At great expense he hired for me the very same teacher with whom I had studied at the school! He would come each day for about an hour, by which means I continued my studies for about another eight months. I almost completed my studies of that modern language, and I therefore began to learn the ancient language called *Ellin-nana*,[1] but after a short time the teacher did not wish to come any more and I did not learn more.

In the month of Sivan 5615 [June 1855], my father (may his soul dwell in Eden) brought me to Vienna (may God preserve it) along with my mother (may God preserve her forever) and my sister, and we stayed through the whole summer in the village of Baden. I then commenced studying the German language with *Hakham* Jacob Ashkenazi, but after two months he left me to travel to Belgrade, and I could find no other Jew to instruct me in this language.

In the month of Rahamim [Elul, in early fall] of that year my brother Isaac (may his light shine) also came there because he had decided to divorce his first wife. We remained in Baden until after the holiday of Sukkot, at which time we returned to Vienna. In the month of Marheshvan in the year 5716 [late fall of 1855], after my father (may his soul dwell in Eden) had opened a store in Vienna, he decided to place it in the hands of my brother Isaac (may his lamp shine) while he, my mother (may she be blessed above all the women of the tent), I, and my sister would return to our city. When I heard this my face fell and I was deeply saddened, for I wanted to remain there to learn German as well as ancient Greek. I spoke about this with my honored mother and begged her to intercede with my father (may his soul dwell in Eden), [asking] that he leave me there with my brother. My father (may his soul dwell in Eden), being very anxious to see me successfully educated, did not refuse my request even though it caused him to incur great expense. He put out the costs of clothing and other needs with a glad heart, knowing with certainty that my mind was made up to search out and pursue wisdom. I would not even mention my past deeds of three [wasted] years, let alone repeat them.

Now since no one could be found who knew the Greek language to instruct me—for I preferred it to the German tongue—[my father] was compelled to entreat the principal and Greek [Orthodox] priest who were there to accept me into their school and add me to the list of students. They acceded to his request and promised to receive me on certain conditions. My father (may his soul dwell in Eden) placed me in the charge of friends he had there and of my brother, and he returned to our city.

In the month of Kislev I began to attend that school with great joy, and I studied with devotion. To my enormous sorrow, however, I was not able to continue there for long, for the teacher was a man who hated the religion [of Judaism] and did not supervise me properly. He would show me the anger in his face in order that I leave and never return. At first I thought he might be doing this to me because he was being forced to teach me for free under instructions of the principals, and I therefore tried to appease him in a different way. One day I said to him, "Sir, if you are interested in teaching me the German language during the afternoon when you are free I will pay you as much money for it as you require." He replied,. "But you should know that I will take a florin every day." I answered him, "Fine, I will pay you as you wish."

He did begin to teach me every day, and as soon as we finished learning, I would give him the florin. None of this helped me though, for my real desire was to learn Greek, that to which my soul aspired. But it was not long until I saw that this was also in vain; I was paying him this enormous sum every day and yet his evil attitude did not change. I then fully understood that he harboured nothing but profound hatred for the [Jewish] religion. He could not even look me in the face. I was therefore forced to leave that school and move on. [. . .]

NOTE

Words in brackets appear in the original translation.

1. Most likely Ellinika, i.e., Greek.

Translated by Matt Goldish.

Emma Mordecai
1812–1906

The youngest daughter of Jacob Mordecai, a prominent Hebraist and founder of the Warrenton Female Academy, a boarding school, and the younger half-sister of Rachel Mordecai Lazarus, Emma Mordecai was born in Warrenton, North Carolina. At the outbreak of the Civil War, Mordecai was living in Richmond, where she taught children at a synagogue's Sunday school. Due to the intense hostilities, she was forced to leave town to live on her late brother's plantation in North Carolina, with her Christian sister-in-law Rosina. There Mordecai kept a diary and continued to practice Judaism in private, while she nursed wounded Confederate soldiers in local hospitals. In addition to her diary and correspondence, she published various short works, often under the byline "American Jewess."

Letters and Diary
1864–1865

Exeunt the Slaves

The negro movement is still a most vexatious and mischievous one, and its effects are painfully felt in every Southern household. This morning Cy came to high words with George and John, insisting he had a right to stay here, to bring here whom he pleases, to keep his family here. He was, he said, entitled to a part of the farm after all the work he had done on it. The kitchen belonged to him because he had helped cut the timber to build it. He also insists that the land belongs to the U.[nited] States, and that it is to be divided among the negroes, etc. Willie told him that he would give him three days to find a place to move to, a thing which he declared this intention of doing three weeks ago.

Georgiana continues for the most part sullen and perverse. Lizzy, though she has resumed her duties in the house, is still in an uncertain position and devotes much time to her maternal cares and, though not impertinent, is rather too independent to be satisfactory. . . .

May 5th. This morning, without giving any warning of their intentions, *all* the servants were discovered to be packing up to go. Lizzy, whom we considered *engaged* for a month, was the first to get ready. Her husband told Rose he was mighty sorry to take her away from her, but that he liked to have his friends to visit him, and as this as not liked by the family, he had rented a room at Mr. Harwood's and was going to move there. Of course, this was a false pretext, as this place has always been run over with negro visitors. Cyrus has rented a house on the turnpike, near the battery, and is moving there with the rest of this family. They all seem anything but joyous at the change, and Rosina is really and greatly distressed at parting with the foolish creatures. She thinks Cy already repents of his late improper conduct, which alone has brought about this change. Rose gave them all presents of old dresses, etc., and also some meat, meal, and potatoes, for all of which they seemed very grateful.

We shall not be left *entirely* [without] a servant, as Willie told Cy he wanted Georgiana to stay a few days, until we had found someone to take her place, and Elick to mind the cows, to which Cy willingly consented, for which condension [condescension] on his part, Willie gave him leave to pick up firewood about here for his own use for a few days longer.

His wife, Sarah, has behaved as well as possible the whole time, and we all respect her for it. She does not seem to approve of Cy's arrangements. They will now begin to find out how easy their life as *slaves* had been, and to feel the slavery of their freedom. Rose has walked over to Mr. Taylor's to make enquiries after other servants. The afternoon is lovely. I forgot to mention that when in town last, I met Mrs. John N. Gordon, a lady who has a very large family, and who was entirely burnt out in the conflagration of the fourth of April. She saved nothing but her beds. She told me all her servants [slaves] have since left her, but she found it a great relief, as there were so many children among them to provide for. She now has a woman to cook for her, who was living at the place to which the family had gone (a furnished house, from which the owners had fled on the approach of the enemy), and she gets a woman to come and wash for them one day in the week, and they dispense with other service. I told her I had heard how wonderfully she bore her misfortunes. She replied: "I don't regard my private troubles as of the slightest importance. It is public calamity, the loss of our cause and the misfortunes of the country that distress me. If that was all right, I should not care, and I *do* not care for my losses!"

May 6th. The servants *all* went Friday evening [yesterday]. Georgiana and Martha returned at dusk and are still with us. They behave well so far and are very useful. Willie milked the cows that evening and I strained the milk. Susan, one of the former Gardner servants [Negro], came up from the mill and engaged to milk and to get breakfast every day until we get supplied with a cook. A niece of hers, a very nice girl who is out of a place, thinks of hiring herself here. She got dinner yesterday and cooked it very nicely.

Poor Rose is miserably depressed. She scarcely slept at all Friday night. She is not only entirely upset in her domestic affairs, but she is grieved to part with Cy and Sarah and Lizzy. She said: "If they felt as *I* do, they could not possibly leave me."

Cy came back yesterday after his fowls and sought an opportunity to take leave of his "Mistiss" (as he still calls her, in spite of his declaration to me to the contrary) and of the boys. He expressed to Rose his regret for his improper conduct the other morning, and was very much affected at parting with her. She could not take leave of him without emotion and has felt miserable ever since.

What an uprooting of social ties and tearing asunder of almost kindred associations and destruction of true loyalty, this strange, new state of things produced! The disturbance to the Whites and the privations it will at first entail upon the poor, improvident negroes is incalculable. . . .

The End of the Old South

Several corps of Grant's Army had been passing up the turnpike all day, returning to Washington, there to be disbanded. I went on top of the house to see the living stream, in one compact mass, pouring up the road as far as the eye could reach in both directions. An admirably disciplined and well-organized force: no straggling, no uproar; a quiet, steady stream, moving in an almost unbroken current. They have finished their work of destruction and subjugation, and are going in triumph to uninjured, undisturbed homes and customs, only ruining a few more farms in their progress, the owners of which have just returned from our army destitute of everything and having some hope of making something to live on, as the surrender took place in time to plant. They camped all over the farms above Mr. Stuart's, as far as the eye could reach, burning fences to make their camp fires and treading down the wheat and oats. It is said Sherman's Army is also to pass this way. If so, all farming operations on their line of march had as well be suspended.

Last night the coops with setting hens and these with broods of young chickens were robbed of seven hens. Three large broods are thus left to shift for themselves, and four settings of eggs, two of the nests being duck eggs for which a high price was paid, all probably rendered useless. The eggs were left behind the pigpen. This was doubtless done by Yankee soldiers who were prowling about the place yesterday.

May 7th, P.M. Martha (one of Cy's [children]) left us this morning and Georgiana and Elick, this afternoon. Susan was sick and could not come up to milk. So Willie milked, I set the supper table, and Rose fed the fowls and attended to everything. . . .

May 11th. A day of rare beauty, following a stormy night. The air so clear and cool, the sky so blue, and the slopes of the leafy woods so green. The birds are numerous and the air is filled with their warbling. Thus it is in the outer world. Within, there is no beauty, no enjoyment, no harmony. Rose has had two days of nervous suffering and mental torture. She is still unsupplied with servants and we have no definite prospect of getting any. I have been doing drudgery for the greater part of the week, assisted unwillingly and inefficiently by a little white girl from town, who is so miserable at being in the country, that she thinks of nothing but how to get home again. My efforts do not meet with the only compensation I desire for them, the satisfaction of knowing that they afford one ray of comfort, or are in any way appreciated.

The events of the last two days have arisen from the moving of Sherman's Army from Richmond to Washington. Last night a general (perhaps Sherman himself) and his staff were camped at Westbrook, and the troops are moving up the turnpike today, leaving behind then [them] the ruin and desolation and misery they have spread through our land, to return to their own and find it untouched by these four years of cruel war. Sherman's Army is perfectly ruthless, and now that the War is over, are as destructive as other armies are when engaged in hostilities. They . . . camped in the yard under the dining room windows, turned the horses out of the stables to put theirs in, put their horses in the carriage house, and parked their wagons before the kitchen. I only hope they may continue such practices north of the Potomac [River].

May 13th. . . . I must here record two anecdotes told me by an eye and *ear* witness, illustrative of the new *dis*order of things. My informant was working in his garden, which lies on the public road.

He heard a negro man, who was passing by, thus soliloquizing: "Dis what you call freedom? No wuk [work] to do, and got to feed and clothe yourself." The same person was in town a few days ago, talking to an acquaintance on the street. A negro girl passed them, *with her books on her way to school*. They stopped her and asked what she was studying. She replied: "I studyin' dis here book." Let me look at it," said the gentleman. It was a *French grammar!* He returned it to her, gravely remarking that it was a very suitable book for her to study.

The fifteenth. Corps of Sherman's Army (the last, they say) passed up the Brook Turnpike yesterday, exciting admiration, even among our own soldiers, by their numbers, equipment, and discipline. How is it that we have sustained a four-years' war with an enemy who can present such armies at its close? The men boast of the destruction they have spread through So. Carolina and Georgia. They say they left nothing standing but houses, and [they] destroyed many of them. They have in their train cows that they have driven all the way from Georgia, mules, splendid horses, and handsome equipages, all taken from once wealthy Southerners, whom they have left stript of even the necessities of life. Doubtless the officers' baggage wagons are loaded with stolen family plate and other valuables. . . .

Wednesday [May 17th]. . . . I met with Moses, my former slave, who was at work (he is a bricklayer) on Broad St. No servant could behave better than he has done. He showed great interest in me and all of us, and begged me to call upon him whenever he could do anything for me. His freedom will be little to me, nor gain to him, for as his wife, who also belonged to me, is a very sickly woman and the children only an expense, it took nearly the whole of the wages he paid me [for the privilege of being allowed to hire himself out], to pay the d[octo]r's and druggist's bills and to clothe them. . . .

Heard of President Davis' capture. Only hope it is not true that he was disguised in Mrs. Davis' clothes! . . .

Got up very soon, made fire, and took up the ashes in R's [Rose's] room while Gusta swept, and then I dressed, strained the milk, swept back and front porch, fixed things on the table, got ice water in the pitcher, by wh.[ich] time breakfast was ready. After breakfast we cleared away the table, washed up, and I cleaned knives while she [Gusta] swept and dusted the dining room.

Then she practiced while I gathered strawberries. Willie went to town servant hunting and returned with a woman and two little boys, the only one he could find willing to come to the country. Rose says she is an untaught field hand. She certainly cannot cook well, but is said to wash and iron well. At any rate, her being here relieves Gusta and me from housework, as Ellen, the girl whom I omitted to record, was cooking, [and] can now come in the house. [The kitchen was separate from the house.] The new woman expresses willingness to learn what she does not know. Had a visit from Mrs. Oscar Taylor. All the talk, everywhere now, is servants. . . .

May 21st. There was a tremendous rainstorm at night, doing much damage in town and country, cellars overflowed, etc. Out here the milldam broke and the pond was emptied. Corn on hillsides washed up, Sunday, while I was in town. Before coming home on Monday I succeeded in getting some whiskey for Rose at $1.15 a quart. I went to see Gen'l Patrick, the provost marshal, who won my heart by his kindness, courtesy, and attention. He gave me unsolicited an order to get a mule or horse, in place of Charlie the stolen horse, and an order on the commissary to let me have two qts. whiskey for R.[osina]. Came home in triumph. . . .

May 23rd, Tuesday, I rose early. After our early breakfast, did some mending, heard Gusta her French, and gathered about ten qts. strawberries for market. R. helped me wash them (the heavy rains making this necessary), and this took till near dinner time. Then changed my dress and lay down to rest until dinner was ready. Willie and George went to town after the promised mule and returned while we were at dinner with the mule and a cowboy, having also seen bl[ac]k George [the former slave], who told them where the stolen cart was. So we are making up for our losses. . . .

May 24th. The Fifth [Sixth?] Army Corps, Gen'l [H. G.] Wright, passed up the turnpike, occupying the whole day in the transit, consequently Gusta was detained at Brook Hill. We hear that many of the troops that have passed here to be disbanded have been sent to Texas, Kirby-Smith refusing to surrender and, it is said, being still in command of a large army. Some think the Trans-Miss.[issippi] country will still achieve its independence. Willie went this A.M. after the stolen cart and succeeded in getting not only it, but the harness and cover. In our misfortunes we have been wonderfully fortunate. . . .

May 30th. Got a note from Caroline [Myers, my niece, in Richmond] on Saturday, telling me that brother Alfred [Major Alfred Mordecai] was in town! [He] arrived Thursday afternoon. Felt very much agitated at learning this. Got Willie to walk in with me Sunday (the cars not running) to see him. On reaching my cousins' found that he had gone the day before on his way to Raleigh [to see the family]. . . . I felt at once disappointed and relieved, so much had I dreaded seeing him. They told me he was very sad, though he looked well. [Major Alfred Mordecai resigned from the United States Army in 1861. He would not fight against the South nor turn against the Union.]

I staid in town till Monday afternoon, when I returned in the cars. Got interesting letters from Raleigh while in town. They have suffered much more in the vicinity of Raleigh than we have near Richmond. In the town, property was protected, but in the country, destroyed wantonly. [Nephew] Jacob Mordecai's place six or eight miles north of Raleigh—*ruined*. These letters contained the first direct information we have received of my dear, good brother Sam's death. He died on Sunday, April 9th [1865], of erysipelas, after a painful illness of a week's duration. His old friends in Richmond express the highest admiration of his character and intellect, and sincere regret at his loss. [He was the author of *Richmond in By-Gone Days*.] For himself he had little left to make life desirable. Although age had not rendered him incapable of enjoyment, circumstances deprived him of all its opportunities. . . .

The tattered sheet containing this sad record is the last I can find of those containing my diary.

NOTE

Words in brackets appear in the source text.

Oro Arieh
Dates Unknown

Oro Arieh was a Jewish widow in Palestine; the details of her life are unknown, but her plea to Moses Montefiore in her Hebrew-language letter illustrates the respectful tone his munificence engendered.

Correspondence with Moses Montefiore
1866

"*The Sorrows of a Woman*": *A Jewish Widow Faces Eviction*

To Sir Moses Montefiore, from Oro, the widow of Hayim Arieh, 1866

[Oh] one who gives light to the earth and to them that dwell thereon, who is full of good deeds, the father of orphans, the champion of widows, the poor and needy, Moses, the faithful shepherd, the doer of good deeds, the minister and officer, his great lordship . . . our teacher and rabbi Sir Moses Montefiore, may his candle shine on forever . . . and in our times and in his days, Judah shall be delivered and Israel shall dwell secure. He shall come as redeemer to Zion, amen.

I come to his highness bowing low with a prayer, that he shall live long to reign upon his kingdom. . . . I come begging, in tears, to inform his royal highness of the magnitude of my oppression and sorrows, the sorrows of a woman. For it has been some two years since my husband died and I was left a widow with three children, two nursing twin boys and one five-year-old daughter, naked and destitute, wandering about [searching] for bread and water. My cry has risen to the very skies, and my eyes, my eyes run with tears over my misfortune, the dire straits of the poor. What is more, I owe the rent of the house and I am being pressed every day in these times of disturbances, and there is no one to save me. And so I go unto the king to beg him and ask that he will keep his compassionate eye on us. Act for the orphans and widows. Act for the nursing infants. Act for the sake of the weaned babes. As a father has compassion for his children, so have compassion upon . . . as is becoming of his good virtue, his hand as good as a king's hand. For it is a great deed to revive four souls from Israel. Indeed it is like reviving the dead. And for that his glory shall live forever. Great is the charity that brings salvation closer. . . .

NOTE

Words in brackets appear in the original translation.

Translated by Yali Hashash.

J. A. Joel
Mid-1800s to Late 1800s

J. A. Joel was a private in the Union Army during the Civil War. He was one of roughly seven thousand to eight thousand Jews who fought for the Union cause.

A Union Soldier's Passover
1866

The approaching feast of Passover, reminds me of an incident which, transpired in 1862,[1] and which as an index of the times, no doubt, will prove interesting to a number of your readers. In the commencement of the war of 1861, I enlisted from Cleveland, Ohio, in the Union cause, to sustain intact the Government of the United States, and became attached to the 23rd Regiment, one of the first sent from the "Buckeye State." Our destination was West Virginia,—a portion of the wildest and most mountainous region of that State, well adapted for the guerrillas who infested that part, and caused such trouble to our pickets all through the war. After an arduous march of several hundred miles through Clarksburgh, Weston, Sommerville, and several other places of less note, which have become famous during the war, we encountered on the 10th of September, 1861, at Carnifax Ferry, the forces under the rebel Gen. Floyd. After this, we were ordered to take up our position at the foot of Sewell Mountain, and we remained there until we marched to the village of Fayette, to take it, and to establish there our Winter-quarters, having again routed Gen. Floyd and his forces. While lying there, our camp duties were not of an arduous character, and being apprised of the approaching Feast of Passover, twenty of my comrades and co-religionists belonging to the Regiment, united in a request to our commanding officer for relief from duty, in order that we might keep the holydays, which he readily acceded to. The first point was gained, and, as the Paymaster had lately visited the Regiment, he had left us plenty of greenbacks. Our next business was to find some suitable person to proceed to Cincinnati, Ohio, to buy *Matzos*. Our sutler being a co-religionist and going home to that city, readily undertook to send them. We were anxiously awaiting to receive our *Matzos*, and about the middle of the morning of the eve of Passover a supply train arrived in camp, and to our delight seven barrels of *Matzos*. On opening them, we were surprised and pleased to find that our thoughtful sutler had enclosed two *Hagedahs* and prayer-books. We were now able to keep the *seder* nights, if we could only obtain the other requisites for that occasion. We held a consultation and decided to send parties to forage in the country while a party stayed to build a log hut for the services. About the middle of the afternoon the foragers arrived, having been quite successful. We obtained two kegs of cider, a lamb, several chickens and some eggs. Horseradish or parsley we could not obtain, but in lieu we found a weed, whose bitterness, I apprehend, exceeded anything our forefathers "enjoyed." We were still in a great quandary; we were like the man who drew the elephant in the lottery. We had the lamb, but did not know what part was to represent it at the table: but Yankee ingenuity prevailed, and it was decided to cook the whole and put it on the table, then we could dine off it, and be sure we had the right part. The necessaries for the *choroutzes* we could not obtain, so we got a brick which, rather hard to digest, reminded us, by looking at it, for what purpose it was intended.

At dark we had all prepared, and were ready to commence the service. There being no *hazan* present, I was selected to read the services, which I commenced by asking the blessing of the Almighty on the food before us, and to preserve our lives from danger. The ceremonies were passing off very nicely, until we arrived at the part where the bitter herb was to be taken. We all had a large portion of the herb ready to eat at the moment I said the blessing; each eat his portion, when horrors! what a scene ensued in our little congregation, it is impossible for my pen to describe. The herb was very bitter and very fiery like Cayenne pepper, and excited our thirst to such a degree, that we forgot the law authorizing us to drink only four cups, and the consequence was we drank up all the cider. Those that drank the more freely became excited, and one thought he was Moses, another Aaron, and one had the audacity to call himself a Pharaoh. The consequence was a skirmish, with nobody hurt, only Moses, Aaron and Pharaoh, had to be carried to the camp, and there left in the arms of Morpheus. This slight incident did not take away our appetite, and, after doing justice to our lamb, chickens and eggs, we resumed the second portion of the service without anything occurring worthy of note.

There, in the wild woods of West Virginia, away from home and friends, we consecrated and offered up to the ever-loving God of Israel our prayers and sacrifice. I doubt whether the spirits of our forefathers, had they been looking down on us, standing there with our arms by our side ready for an attack, faithful to our God and our cause, would have imagined themselves amongst mortals, enacting this commemoration of the scene that transpired in Egypt.

Since then a number of my comrades have fallen in battle defending the flag, they have volunteered to protect with their lives. I have myself received a number of wounds all but mortal, but there is no occasion in my life that gives me more pleasure and satisfaction than when I remember the celebration of Passover of 1862.

NOTE

1. [This letter, written in 1866, describes events that occurred in 1862.—Ed.]

Samuel Siegfried Karl von Basch
1837–1905

Physician Samuel Siegfried Karl von Basch was born in Prague and studied medicine in his hometown and in Vienna. In 1865 he took the position of chief surgeon at the military hospital in Puebla, Mexico. He then became the personal physician of Emperor Maximilian I, until the latter's defeat and execution in 1867. Von Basch's memoirs of Mexico provide a window into the region's final, tumultuous months under Habsburg rule. Von Basch returned to Austria to teach at the University of Vienna and was granted a knighthood for his service in Mexico—an honor rarely bestowed upon Jews at the time. A medical researcher, he is noted for having developed a new means to measure blood pressure: the sphygmomanometer.

Memories of Mexico
1868

All this heavy misfortune persuaded Maximilian to think earnestly and independently about the problem of Mexico and his throne. I say independently and lay particular emphasis on the word because I can give the best explanation of the sovereign's intentions, perhaps even the only one. At this time I already enjoyed his closest confidence and was the first whom he let in on his thoughts. The evening of the same day the news of the Empress's illness arrived, on his usual walk on the *azotea* (the flat roof) of the palace, he informed me of his tentative plans by asking whether or not he should leave the county.

My clear conviction, created by the unpromising state of affairs, drew me to his way of thinking, and since I considered it a holy duty to make no secret of my opinion, I answered him candidly. "I do not think Your Majesty will be able to remain in the country."

The Emperor asked, "Will anybody really believe that I am going to Europe because of the Empress's illness?"

I answered, "Your Majesty has reasons enough, and Europe will admit that you are no longer obligated to stay in Mexico since France prematurely cancelled its agreements." He then exclaimed "What do you think will be Herzfeld and Fischer's opinion about this?"

"I believe," I openly explained, "that Herzfeld will share my view. As for Father Fischer, as a matter of fact, he does not inspire much confidence in me. He is a cleric, and in all honesty, which I assume he has, his party's gain will come before Your Majesty's special interests."

Translated by Hugh McAden Oechler.

Miriam Markel-Mosessohn
1839–1920

Brought up in Suwałki, Poland, in a wealthy merchant's family, Miriam Wierzbolowska was driven by a passion for learning encouraged by her family. Her mastery of literary and journalistic Hebrew was complemented by her knowledge of French and German. In 1863 she married Anshel Markel-Mosessohn, who shared her interest in Jewish cultural revival. Markel-Mosessohn was encouraged in her literary efforts by men involved in Jewish letters. These included Judah (Yehudah) Leib Gordon (Yalag), who responded enthusiastically to her Hebrew translation of a German poem about English Jews in the time of Richard the Lionheart. At Gordon's insistence she became a Viennese correspondent for the Hebrew newspaper *Ha-melits*. She is most known for her translation, in two volumes, of Eugen Rispart's *Ha-yehudim be Angliyah* (1859 and 1895).

Letter to Judah Leib Gordon
1868

Letter 5

Kovno, Thursday, 20 Heshvan 5629 [5 November 1868]

His Honor, the Great Sage and Sweet Singer of Israel,

Judah Leib Gordon, greetings!

My dear esteemed gentleman! While I was still in Suwałki, the city where my parents resided, your three letters, which you hastened to bring to me and to my husband accompanied by your precious compositions *Shire Yehudah*, reached me, and also my poor translation has been returned to me with its head covered in mourning, and in shame, for, poor woman that I am, I have borne the sin of my husband; and when I returned home a few days ago, my primary obligation was to thank you for all the benefits you have conferred on me, and, jointly with my husband, to seek your pardon for his having angered you in his haste, and thereby triggered the rage that was directed at us regardless of his lack of intent to cause offense. However, sir, I swear by my life that there is no end to my sadness and sorrow over this affair, and my heart is moaning within me because this incident has set up a partition wall blocking our close mutual friendship, which, to my joy and pride, had been formed so recently; and I will not conceal from you that anguish is also intermingled with my distress, and that my heart cries out with regret for the sake of my translation, for had we not angered you and embittered your spirit, you might well have looked upon the poor woman that I am with a pitiful eye, obliterating from her every fault and defect in love and mercy, in accordance with your generous disposition, and you might have responded to me with generosity, to instruct me, and to teach me what I should select and what I should reject. And I wait upon your word, and the ordinances of your mouth are to me as the prophecy of a seer; and why, then, should I conceal this from you, my dear sir? I admit, and am not ashamed to say so, that as a result of your kind words, with which you initially paid honor to me, the hope was engendered within me that you would do even more for me, and that you would proceed forth, as a defending angel, at the opening page of my work, to advise our nation of its pleasing quality and to honor me in the public domain; for I have read and reiterated your original words seven times each day, that the translation is exceptionally good, and that the linguistic style is simple and beautiful, and easy to understand. And these fine words of yours had emboldened me to impose upon you the burden of composing an all-encompassing review of my work, and I was no longer afraid of a harsh verdict. But now, I have made myself heir only to a false hope. Perhaps, over a period of time—to my sorrow—you have withdrawn from your close relationship, which I have valued so highly, and thus have not passed the entire translation under your reviewer's rod, and have merely returned it to me in silence, without comment, either favorable or critical, and have merely scattered some literary thorns, a little here and a little there, in your letter, which have caused me great pain; and I would have preferred to have heard reproof from a person of discernment such as yourself had you said to me in plain words: "Do yourself a favor, and remain sitting at home; why should you fret yourself by getting involved with the literati, over whom you will not prevail?" than to hear your wearisome statements that have dissolved my substance, and whose nature I do not understand. I am not, indeed, distressed—Heaven forbid—about your criticisms that you have noted in my book—in truth, they are very good and fully justified; and blessed be your discretion, and may you too be blessed on account of this kindness that you have accorded me, but my heart is nonetheless grieved insofar as you have made no constructive suggestions, but have merely wounded me, in indirect fashion, with statements, that harsh phrases and numerous Germanic constructions are to be found in my translation, and that if I duly carried out a search, I would find such-and-such examples; Alas, my God! Would that I knew where to find them, for I have now begun refining and polishing my work, and have scattered all thorns to the winds, as though they were unclean, and have sent it to you, complete in its splendor, without any defects. I have, moreover, openly requested you kindly to honor me with a small portion of your pearl-like verses, which are worthy of being bound as a wreath upon its head, but I am unaware of my literary sins, and have relied upon you, as a savant, to serve as someone appropriately directing my attention, to assist me in getting rid of all the thorns contained within my work, and to tell me the plain, honest truth, as to whether it is worthy of publication, as I have no desire to add both my hands, which are filled with emptiness, to the piles of emptiness that have already been heaped up within Hebrew literature, and whose time for disposal by burning has already arrived; and I have no wish to justify myself to the readers of my variety of literary work, as I am only a woman, and accordingly, let them not expect excessive linguistic talent from me, for that would be unworthy of the reader! From whose bowels can material be excreted if a person were merely to taste it with his palate? And if his teeth are set on edge by it, he will not cease protesting vehemently against me, saying: "Who required this of you, to trample the courtyards of the literati? A woman's wisdom lies only in the spinning-wheel!"

And now, after having poured out my complaint before you, my dear sir, I beg your forgiveness for having dared to say all these things to you, for what right do I have to complain about you—for what relationship do I have with you? However, it is the destiny of the sages in every generation to suffer distress at witnessing the distress of others, and it is to them that all those thirsty for good counsel and hungry for wisdom flee for assistance; and if *they* are not on our side, who then will be? And so, on this occasion too, I shall not despair, and I shall place my hope in you that you will render me advice from afar!

My heart moans heavily within me when I see, from your latest letter, the unfortunate lot of the sages and literati among our nation, and that you can see no reward for your enormous toil in the sacred work. Alas for that shame! Will the faces of the leaders of our people in Russia not be covered with embarrassment when they contemplate the lot of the gentile writers in other countries, for besides the glory and the honor that are accorded to them, every knee bowing to them, and their boasting in their glory, the public also enrich them with capital and wealth, and they are regarded as princes and lords. If you, sir, had heeded my advice, you would by now have begun to demonstrate your literary power in other languages, in accordance with the benevolent hand of the Almighty guarding over you; for then your labor would not be in vain, neither would you be producing work for futility, for the majority of *our* nation will not understand you, and most of them lack that sense of glory that would allow them to pride themselves in the wisdom of their few sages and writers—which constitutes our entire honor and glory in the estimation of the gentile nations; and all their virtues are merely like the chewing of the cud, and they revere and hallow the golden calf. I swear by my life, my dear sir, that my heart becomes soured when recalling your sublime poems *Shire Yehudah*, every single idea within which is beyond comparison even with pearls and precious stones, and yet you have sown them on desolate land which will bear you no fruit—not even a single handful in volume—and accordingly, for what purpose are you toiling? It can only be in order that your elegant words, appearing in your first poem, should be given credence, for it was for this purpose that you were created, and you will not retain the strength required to restrain the wind of the spirit!

Kindly let me know, dear sir, whether you are still ready to bless our ungrateful nation with the treasury of your wisdom, and what you will be offering them this time round; and, should a few of the samples from your booklet *Olam ke-minhago* [the world proceeds as usual] come into your hands, kindly honor me with one of these, and it will serve as a sign to me that you have pardoned our transgression and that my honor is now renewed insofar as you are concerned. Regarding your request that I send you a photograph of myself as a memento, I cannot yet comply with it, despite my wish to do so, as I currently have not even a single photograph in my possession, but in a few days' time, I shall be most honored to dispatch it to you. And in the meanwhile, I shall inwardly dare to preempt you with a request that you first send me a photograph of yourself, which will serve me as a double sign that you seek my welfare.

Enclosed herewith, sir, you will receive the price for eleven samples that I have distributed among my acquaintances in Suwałki, because, over and above the ten that you sent to me, I took another one from our dear friend, the esteemed Mr. Prozer, which I had for the purpose of honoring one of my female friends over here.

Farewell to you, my dear sir and friend, and greetings to your wife, the refined adornment of your household, and to your delightful children. Ride on prosperously upon the wings of the heights of happiness and wisdom, in accordance with your desire, and with that of your friend who honors you in measure commensurate with your lofty worth.

Miriam Markel

Translated by David E. Cohen.

Esther Levy
Dates Unknown

Esther Levy's *Jewish Cookery Book* was the first American Jewish cookbook to be publicly available in the United States, and only the second to be written in English. The book offers a breadth of information about topics related to Jewish home life, including menu suggestions as well as housekeeping advice, medicinal recipes, and a Jewish calendar. Little is known about Esther Levy (b. Jacoby) beyond the fact that she was raised within Philadelphia's German Jewish community and that she personally registered her Jewish cookbook with the Library of Congress. The book focuses mainly on German dishes in addition to providing recipes that combine contemporary tastes with kosher preparations. Both a culinary and historical volume, Levy's book functioned as a comprehensive guide to keeping a Jewish home, written to help new European immigrants adapt to

Jewish Cookery Book
1871

Mock Turtle Soup

Get a calf's head, with the skin on, but cleaned from the hair. Half boil it; take all the meat off in square pieces; break the bones of the head, and boil them in some good veal and beef broth to make it richer; fry some shalot and flour enough to thicken the gravy; stir this into the browning, and give it one or two boils; skim it carefully, and then put in the head; put in a pint of Madeira wine, and simmer till the meat is quite tender. About ten minutes before you serve, put in some chives, parsley, cayenne pepper, and salt to your taste; also, two squeezes of lemon, two spoonfuls of mushroom ketchup, and one of soy. Pour the soup into the tureen. Forcemeat balls and yolks of hard boiled eggs. There are various ways of making this soup, but I choose this as preferable.

To Make a Good Frimsel (or Noodle) Soup

Take a piece of thick brisket, about five or six pounds for a large family, and a knuckle of veal, and put in a saucepan, with water sufficient to cover the meat, about, for that quantity of meat, two and a half quarts of water, with an onion, celery, parsley, a little pepper, ginger, and mace. Some persons use saffron, dried and pounded, just a small pinch; boil for three hours. Take out the meat, and strain the soup; then return it to the saucepan. Have ready some vermicelli or frimsels, and let the soup come up to a boil; then throw in, lightly, the frimsels, and boil for ten minutes. Two ounces of flour and one egg, with a pinch of salt and ginger, will make sufficient frimsels; or two eggs and a quarter of a pound of flour, for a large family.

Ignác Goldziher
1850–1921

Hungarian orientalist Ignác Goldziher was born in Székesfehérvár and studied in Berlin and Leiden. He traveled in Egypt, Palestine, and Syria. For nearly thirty years Goldziher was an unpaid university lecturer who supported himself by working as secretary of the Neolog Jewish community, facing American culture while retaining their religious traditions and values.

antisemitism until he finally was appointed professor at Budapest University. Even before achieving the rank of professor, Goldziher was elected a member of the Hungarian Academy of Sciences and was offered professorships abroad. In addition to his pioneering Islamic studies scholarship, Goldziher wrote about relations between Islam and Judaism and served on the editorial board of *Jewish Encyclopedia* (1901–1906).

My Oriental Diary
1873

I did not sleep; I let myself be rocked by the inexorable battle of the waves; soon the monster of seasickness flashed in my innards, but I overcame it. A god held sway in me; he triumphed: it was the dreamlike idealism of the last night, the noble spirit which held sway and dwelt in me. Never before had I felt in such complete harmony. For years I had struggled for this moment, and for the what and how which I now feel. The study chamber could not inspire me with it: self-torturing asceticism could never win for me this congenial Being. But now I was all soul, all feelings. My childhood awoke again in me, I saw the beautiful days of my youth, and when I awoke from my light slumber, which had fallen upon me on the foredeck after unutterable exhaustion, I was on the pulpit of the synagogue of Stuhlweissenburg[1] and, as a youth of thirteen, was preaching to the dense crowd. [. . .]

On the last day of my presence on the Black Sea I got in closer touch with several of the forty Turks from Rumelia who were on their pilgrimage to Mecca. They were aboard with us, and after the initial *idhān* [call to prayer] recited by the twenty-three-year-old *ḥāfiẓ*.[2] Muḥammad Mustapha, performed their five daily prayers, I spoke with them much in Turkish and thus refreshed memories from the earliest times of my Oriental studies. One of the *ḥājjīs* [pilgrims], the most fanatical among them, spoke a little Arabic as well; through this plus his knowledgeability he became, so to speak, the center of my contact with the Turks. We entered into a theological conversation, and when the most learned of the Rumelian pilgrims saw that I had quite a thorough knowledge of the Koran and the Sunna, he opined that '*ilm bilā 'amal* [knowledge without practice] had *lā fā' ida fīhī* [no profit in it]. Nay, it was even *ḍawr* [harmful]. He demonstrated to me that, although I acknowledged to him the *lā ilāha illa 'llāh* [there is no God but Allah] as true, I was still a *kāfir ashadda kufran* [unbeliever who holds fast to unbelief] as long as I did not acknowledge with body and soul also the second credo, *wa'ashhadu anna Muḥammad rasūlu 'llah* [and I testify that Mohammed is the messenger of Allah], for *al-inkār bi-'l-anbiyā kufr* [the denial of the prophets is unbelief]. Further, he demonstrated to me that *al-shābqa wal-zunnār* [the hat and the belt] were the *two 'alāmāt al-kufr* [signs of unbelief]. Therefore, if I wanted to count as a true believer, his *ceterum censeo* would be *shābqa at* [the hat's throw]. These last words became actually the refrain of my two hours' conversation with the Muslims, from which I profited quite a few practical and valuable things.

It made an overpowering impression on my mind when the aforementioned colleague of Bilāl called out his monotheistic confession into the endless sea. It seemed as if this young Muslim with his sonorous voice represented the fast and unshakable faith combating the storms of the world. [. . .]

Unknown Photographer, *Ignác Goldziher Speaking at His Bar Mitzvah*, 1863.

NOTES

Words in brackets appear in the original translation.

1. Hungarian Székesfehévár, a town in Hungary, about thirty-eight miles southeast of Budapest, Goldziher's birthplace, where he and his family lived until his sixteenth year. He gave his Bar Mitzvah sermon in the synagogue there.
2. A Muslim scholar who knows the entire Koran by heart.

Translated by Raphael Patai.

Other works by Goldziher: *Der Mythos bei den Hebräen* (1876); *A zsidóság lényege és fejlödése* (1887); *Muhammedanische Studien*, 2 vols. (1888–1890); *Die Richtungen der islamischen Koranauslegungen* (1920).

Moses Leib Lilienblum
1843–1910

Born in Kaidan (Kėdainiai), Lithuania, Moses (Mosheh) Leib Lilienblum rebelled against his traditional upbringing, left his home in Wilkomir for Odessa, and became a journalist, social activist, and a Zionist who tried to temper halakhic Judaism and make it compatible with modern life. He wrote and edited for Alexander Zederbaum's Yiddish newspaper *Kol mevaser*, and in 1873 published his autobiography, showing his attempts to reconcile religion with secular life; the work was enormously popular. Pogroms in the 1880s persuaded Lilienblum to adopt Jewish nationalism; he became active in the Ḥovevei Zion organization and advocated settlement in the Land of Israel.

The Sins of My Youth
1873

There are two sorts of biography: the biography a famous person writes for his admirers, because the public likes to know everything about celebrities, and [the] autobiography, usually written because the events are worth recording for themselves, not because of the person to whom they have happened.

Of biographies of famous people written in Hebrew we have many, but I know of only two autobiographies—Luzzatto's and Mordechai Aaron Guenzburg's *Aviezer*. Luzzatto's autobiography is as hollow as the parched ears of corn in Pharaoh's dream, whereas *Aviezer* was written to tell about events—the system of Jewish education in our country. But *Aviezer* is limited to the author's childhood and boyhood, and tells nothing of his later life, which might have been instructive for the young people of my native land. This defect I wish to repair: I want here to set down events in my life, from my childhood until I became a mature man.

I am an ordinary man. Hebrew is the only language [in which] I have written—some articles in periodicals and a few books. I have no particular distinction, yet my experiences can be instructive, even though they are not spiced with tall tales and extraordinary accomplishments. My life is a sort of Jewish drama. I came on stage and played it for my readers. They ridiculed me, shook their heads in disapproval, and held me up as a horrible example. [. . .]

My troubles did not arise from passion or evil, as in a French drama, but out of foolishness, for that is the basis of Jewish drama. A *maskil* once wrote, "The life of the Jew begins in triviality and foolishness and ends in sorrow and woe; the beginning a comedy and the end a tragedy." My life was a tapestry woven of small and large errors my parents made and I myself made, of idle dreams that I dreamed about myself and that others dreamed about me. The threads became warped and tangled round my neck, sapping my strength.

Now I am twenty-nine, and old age has already overtaken me. I have given up the idea of living a vital life. My eyes have become heavy with weeping, and the source of my tears has dried. But my self-esteem does not let me rest. Perhaps my tears and despair can serve as a lesson to others. That is why I am writing the story of my life. [. . .]

I passed through four periods: the days of chaos in my native town when I was still unformed clay waiting to be shaped; the days of darkness and the beginning of the transition, when I lived in Miroslav with my in-laws.[1] There I stuffed my head with harmful nonsense. The world became dark, and its monstrous darkness began to oppress me. Then came the time of disbelief, when I thought I had discovered the truth and fought for it, as Don Quixote fought the windmills. I was satisfied with myself, though I had nothing with which to be satisfied. Finally came the time of crisis and despair, when I traveled and discovered a new world that I had never known in dream or reality. [. . .]

I have written this book for myself and for others: for me—to lighten my heart's burden with this funeral oration on my wasted life; and to show others the mistakes and the sins of my youth that they should avoid. For others—to show the readers all the sins of my youth, so that they may avoid them based on the experiences they find in this book. Perhaps my desire to benefit my readers is only my residual intoxication, since, in truth, it is hard to accept the experiences of others as a guide; some things one needs to experience for oneself. Still, it is hard for me to believe that my book will make no impression on its readers. [. . .]

I hope that copies of my book will not be eaten by the moths in the bookstores but sold and read by parents and children. Some parents, I suppose, will draw an a fortiori conclusion: see what has become of this writer who had studied all of the Talmud by the age of eighteen, was steeped in the responsa literature at nineteen, and at twenty, subject to judgment of the Heavenly Court, he fasted and studied all day in prayer shawl and phylacteries so that he might enter the fifty gates of holiness. Though he lived among Talmudic sages and God-fearing men, where no one doubted God, yet even his Torah study and piety could not resist the Devil, and he became an unbeliever. How much easier, then—these parents will think—for their children to be corrupted?

If parents understand me, they will not prevent their children from becoming educated out of fear that they will be ruined, nor will they marry them off prematurely. If parents want to protect their children from heresy, they should keep them from speculative thought, bar them from studying even a page of Talmud, and teach them a trade instead. [. . .] Otherwise their children will come to the same end as I.

I would like to think that my book will influence the young people who have become absorbed in the futile chaos our writers call Haskalah. They must learn from my fate and turn to more practical things: learn living languages (I do not mean Hebrew—those reading this book know it already), mathematics, penmanship, natural sciences, and a trade by which they can live. [. . .]

Boys ought to be prepared for the world while they are still young. Anything that cannot be understood as preparing them for life and does not provide them with real treasures—such as languages, the sciences, or vocational skills—should be strictly forbidden. [Now] those who flee from the Talmud run toward the chaos of the new literature. This flight has been going on for about a hundred years. [. . .] All the younger generation is fleeing, but they do not know to where. It is high time for us to stop a moment and ponder where we are running and why. Are we not fleeing into a bottomless pit? Have we no other way except flight? [. . .]

I am not the first victim of the Haskalah; many writers and *maskilim* secretly bewail the sins of their youth for it is too late to correct them. But they continue to lead new enthusiasts on the same futile path along which they went, calling on young people to build and repair the Hebrew language, raise the walls of Zion, serve in the temple of the Haskalah, and other such meaningless phrases. But I hide only my face, not my ruination, neither the sins of my youth nor the afflictions and sorrows that destroyed my life.

NOTES

Words in brackets appear in the original translation.

1. Lilienblum's in-laws' home was actually in Vil'komir; however, in the text, he calls the town Miroslav.

Translated by Jay Harris and Saadya Sternberg.

Other works by Lilienblum: *Al teḥiyat Yisra'el al admat erets-avotenu* (1884); *Zerubavel* (1887); *Derekh laavor golim* (1899); *Derekh teshuvah* (1899).

Abraham Ber Gottlober
1811–1899

The Volhynia-born Abraham (Avraham) Ber Gottlober was an important Haskalah figure in Eastern Europe. A poet, satirist, playwright, historian, journalist, translator, and Talmud teacher, he wrote mainly in Hebrew and Yiddish. Despite his initial interest in Hasidism and Kabbalah, he became widely acquainted with Haskalah figures and philosophy in the course of his travels throughout Eastern Europe. When he lived briefly in Odessa, he also studied Karaite culture and literature. He chronicled tales from his youth in his *Zikhronot u-masa'ot*. This excerpt begins with a recollection of the *khappers*, Jewish communal officials charged with filling quotas of Jewish boys for the tsarist army.

Zikhronot u-masa'ot (Memoir and Journeys)
1880

4. On the Way to Iași

Those who seized the youths to put them into the army in the city where I was born, desired to have, as a residence for themselves, a house adjacent to the one in which my father lived; it was there that these hardhearted and cruel men assembled and transacted business with the souls of the Jewish children. They seized them and incarcerated them, and when their fathers came along, weeping and wailing, and gave them ransom monies in exchange for the children's lives, they set them free and took others in their stead. And in this house, the sound of weeping and crying, and the wailing of fathers and children jointly together, could be heard each day—the sound of a great tumult. My father of blessed memory, whose heart melted like wax at the sound of these weeping souls, was weary of his life, and all his days were a painful ordeal, and he was heartbroken. Even at night time, he allowed his eyes no sleep and his eyelids no slumber, and besides the fact that it was his regular habit to arise at midnight to give thanks to the Almighty and to lament the destruction of our Holy Temple, he added on further lamentations during these days, and meditations and dirges, and he fasted almost every day, and each night he wept and chanted lamentations.

Now it once happened that one Wednesday, on the thirteenth of Tammuz in the year five thousand five hundred and eighty-eight [1828], that my father arose early in the morning, and went to the synagogue to pour out his complaint before the Almighty. And when he returned home from there, he took his clothes and his pillows and cushions and put them in his suitcase, and ordered me likewise to get myself ready, as we had a journey in front of us. And even before I was able to inquire of him as to where we were going and what his destination was, there was a wagon standing outside, harnessed to two horses, and a non-Jewish man, a villager, was driving them. And my father made haste, and issued an order that the packed suitcase be put onto the wagon—and he blessed his wife—that is to say, my mother, and his daughters; and there was much crying, and they all fell lovingly upon his neck and asked him: "Where are you going?"—however, he answered them not a single word, but simply blessed them a second time, and said: "The Lord is my Shepherd. He will lead me in the paths of righteousness for His name's sake!" So we turned away, and began our journey; I too had wept profusely upon the neck of my mother and my sisters; moreover, the recollection of my wife and my sons whom she had borne to me, entered my mind—but I too trusted in the Almighty and in the righteousness of my father—may the memory of the righteous be for a blessing—and I remained silent. I had no idea as to the proposed destination of my father of blessed memory until we arrived at a large city, when I asked him what it was called, and my father said to me: "Satanov."

Translated by David E. Cohen.

Other works by Gottlober: *Dos lid funem kugl* (1863); *Bikoret le-toldot ha-Kara'im* (1865); *Tiferet li-vene binah* (1867); *Toldot ha-Kabalah veha-ḥasidut* (1869); *Kol shire Mahalal'el* (1890).

Sa'adi Besalel a-Levi
1820–1903

Sa'adi Besalel a-Levi was a publisher, journalist, and singer in Salonika. Although his formal education was limited to a few weeks of traditional schooling, he was a passionate *maskil* who was instrumental in establishing the first Alliance Israélite Universelle school in Salonika (1873). In addition to publishing religious and secular texts, including his own poems and songs composed for holidays and special occasions, he founded two long-lasting periodicals. In 1875, he started a Ladino newspaper, *La epoka*, and in 1895, the French-language *Le journal de Salonique*. In 1874, a-Levi was excommunicated by local rabbis on false charges. In his memoir he presents himself as a victim of the ignorant masses and a heroic fighter for progress.

Memoir
1881–1902

These high officials were not accustomed to wearing European-style shirts. When they decided to dress in the European style, they asked a certain *ham*,[1] Daniel Andjel, whose shop at the Women's Market was their meeting place, to help them get such shirts. He inquired about who sold such shirts, but he didn't find any, simply because sewing machines were not available. And those worn by *frankos* had been hand-sewn by my *sinyora* mother, who inherited this craft from her mother and her grandmother.[2] Then, *ham* Daniel needed to call on my *sinyora* mother to sew a dozen shirts for each one of them, and he tried to take my *sinyora* mother to see these gentlemen. My *sinyora* mother replied that she was unwilling to go to a Turkish home, but anyone who wished was welcome to her house to be measured for her to sew the shirts. The *sinyor* Daniel asked how much she charged for sewing a shirt. She answered that she charges all consuls and businessmen one *altılık* to sew a shirt.[3] *Ham* Daniel replied that he would charge a 100 percent commission on the total amount of her sale to these gentlemen.

My *sinyora* mother replied, "Fine, if they pay me two *altılıks*, you will get the second one." This *sinyor* said to her, "I'll bring here three people for you to sew a dozen for each one." My *sinyora* mother thought that only three people would be coming; yet by the time she heard the sound of the twenty armed horsemen who accompanied each one of them, the streets were filled to capacity with all these people. To be precise, streets around our home were alleys rather than streets, varying between three and two *pikos* in width.[4] As soon as mother looked through the window and caught a glimpse of the gold-embroidered uniforms and the hanging swords, she immediately hid my three maiden sisters in one of the rooms. In came the three top military officers, accompanied by four to five majors. She didn't even have enough chairs for sitting! She had to borrow extra chairs to seat them all—tall, hefty, and covered in golden embroidery. *Sinyor* Daniel was no less impressive: He was quite fat and tall, wore a silk turban around his head, and his body was wrapped in a loose robe of red damascene fabric, an alpaca robe with a sash from Tripoli. He sent his employees to the market to bring bolts of embroidered fabric. They brought in about forty to fifty bolts of this fabric to make about a dozen shirts each. When my *sinyora* mother took a look at this fabric, she reacted by saying that her original price was inadequate because this is a thicker fabric, hard to sew. *Ham* Daniel agreed on three *altılıks* to get half of it for himself. As for the customers, they had no interest in these price changes, beyond what he told them, especially because *Chilibi* Menahem's coffers paid any bill that came.[5] My *sinyora* mother took the measurements of every one of them for the fabrics they chose, making sure to set aside one-tenth of the fabric from each dozen shirts, [all of which equaled a] sum total [of] two robes, five half-shirts, and five jackets for my wedding. As soon as they left, my *sinyora* mother with her three daughters and three helpers started the work, and within a month they finished eight dozen shirts.

NOTES

1. Shortened form of *hakham*, used for ordinary Jews who are not rabbis.
2. *Frankos*, or "Franks," meaning Europeans.
3. An Ottoman unit of currency, one *altılık* equaled six kuruş, or piasters.
4. One *piko* is approximately thirty inches
5. *Chilibi*, or Çelebi, a title of respect for men.

Translated by Isaac Jerusalmi.

Travel Writing

Samuel Romanelli
1757–1814

Italian Hebrew poet, translator, and playwright Samuel Aaron Romanelli was born in Mantua and traveled extensively throughout his life. He is best known for his Hebrew travelogue *Masa ba-arav*, which describes Jewish life in Morocco from a Western perspective. While living in Germany, Romanelli befriended Berlin *maskilim* such as Isaac Euchel and David Friedländer. He worked as a proofreader in Vienna and published his play *Alot ha-minḥah* in honor of the marriage of Charlotte Arnstein. A number of his Hebrew works appeared with Italian translations. He returned to Mantua in 1807 and died in Casale Monferrato.

Travail in an Arab Land
1792

Free of any preoccupations, I allowed myself to seek out and investigate the Jews, their manners and customs. They are good-hearted folk, charitable and hospitable to strangers. They honor the Torah and study it. They hold the European Jews who come there in high esteem and call them "freemen."

The lack of books and news mires their hearts in the mud of ignorance and superstition. They tend to view all new and mysterious things previously unknown to them as miracles. The sciences are too lofty for them. Their ignorance is bliss, for they say that many victims have been thrown into the pits of heresy and atheism by science. The light of knowledge does not shine upon them, nor has it even reached them until now to eradicate their moral failings and their immature vanities. A veil of obscurantist faith corrupts their hearts and blinds their eyes. They cling steadfastly to their ancestral customs even to the point of transgressing the laws of God, rather than violating their own laws. One of the proverbs they are fond of quoting (which befits them as do legs on a cripple) is "the customary practice of our forefathers is Torah." They will not examine who their forefathers were and what were their customs, if they have something on which they rely—even if it is like the customary practice of Jehu b. Nimshi. They do not understand that in so doing they have gone against the intent of the Torah which seeks to set us apart by its laws from the practices of the other nations. With the Moroccan Jews it is the opposite, because they follow their ways completely. Either they interpret rhetorical hyperbole in Scripture literally, saying that under no circumstances should it be taken in the abstract, or they imagine secrets and read mysteries into matters that are as clear as day. They lean upon the dictum that "for every thorny point mountains upon mountains of laws may be derived." They are awed by dreams and terrified by visions. They will fast on account of bad ones and feast as a consequence of good ones. They are besotted by dread apparitions and by fear of night. No man would dare sleep alone in a room at night, nor would any woman dare to go alone from house to house. They swear by a burning lamp and say: "By this angel," thinking that the lights of a fire are celestial angels, an error that has come to them from a misinterpretation of the verse "He makes the winds His messengers, fiery flames His servants." The end result is that the might of even an intelligent man is dried up, and they become like light-minded women. Despite all this, their minds are not entirely blocked from reason, because they comprehend other matters perfectly well. In fact, sometimes their intelligence emits flashes of insight that reveal that it is not thick by nature, but only held down and mired in thick muck, like the sun when it is covered by a very dense cloud. [. . .]

During that period, I also had the leisure to discover things that I did not know before and that enlightened me so that I understood things about which I had been mistaken. While I was passing in the street, I heard a great tumult coming from a Jewish house. I approached the gate leading to the inner court, and there I beheld a crowd of women, their heads enveloped in a white shawl. I imagined they were dancing girls. I was indeed mistaken; they were mourning a dead man. The two who stood in the middle were the deceased's kin. They were beating their breasts and wailing in Arabic, while all the women around them clapped their hands together in grief. Between each verse they would scratch their faces and cry out each time: "*waw, waw*" (that is, "alas, alack"). It was then that I understood the biblical verse "You shall not gash yourselves," which should be compared with "And they gashed themselves . . . according to *their custom*" (the latter being forbidden to us according to the prohibition against following Gentile practices). This custom is mentioned four times in Jeremiah, and is referred to in two verses in Amos, the first being: "Her maidens escort her with voices like doves, beating their breasts." The second is: "In every street cries of 'Ah, woe!'" Still another reference is the verse in the Mishna about women who wail and clap their hands. All this is called in Arabic *geshdūr*.

When they come to a graveyard, they say to the diggers, "May God be with you," just as Boaz said to the reapers. Until all the preparations are made, they lay the bier on the ground and pull on each others dresses imploring one another to give money for charity. Women also come and sit at the graves of their relatives, calling upon them for their aid, discussing their private matters with the dead, even arguing with them, just as a person talks with his friend who is still alive. All of these things—this entire scene—are also performed on the Ninth of Av.

Translated by Yedida K. Stillman and Norman A. Stillman.

Other works by Romanelli: *Ha-kolot yeḥdalun* (1791); *Ruaḥ nakhon* (1791); *Alot ha-minḥah* (1793); *Maḥazeh shaddai . . . Illusione felice ossia visione sentimentale* (1818).

Unknown Artist, *Moroccan Peddler in London*, ca. 1800.

Judith Cohen Montefiore

Private Journal of a Visit to Egypt and Palestine
1836

Thursday, October 18. Jerusalem.

There is no city in the world which can bear comparison in point of interest with Jerusalem,—fallen, desolate, and abject even as it appears—changed as it has been since the days of its glory. The capitals of the ancient world inspire us, at the sight of their decaying monuments, with thoughts that lead us far back into the history of our race, with feelings that enlarge the sphere of our sympathies, by uniting our recollections of the past with the substantial forms of things present: but there is a power in the human mind by which it is capable of renewing scenes as vividly without external aids, as when they are most abundant. There are no marble records on the plain of Marathon, to aid the enthusiasm of the traveller, but he feels no want of them: and thus it is, whenever any strong and definite feeling of our moral nature is concerned; we need but be present on the spot where great events occurred, and if they were intimately connected with the fate of multitudes, or with the history of our religion, we shall experience a sentiment of veneration and interest amounting to awe, and one above all comparison nobler than that which is excited chiefly by the pomp or wonders of antiquity. It is hence that Jerusalem, notwithstanding the ploughshare of the heathen, infinitely exceeds in interest Rome, Athens, and even the cities of Egypt, still abounding, as they do, in monuments of their former grandeur, and wonderful and venerable as they are, above all other places on which the mere temporal history of mankind can bestow a sanctity. No place has ever suffered like Jerusalem:—it is more than probable that not a single relic exists of the city that was the joy of the whole earth; but the most careful and enthusiastic of travellers confess, that when they have endeavoured to find particular marks for their footsteps, there was little to encourage them in the investigation. But it depends not for its power of inspiring veneration on the remains of temples and palaces; and were there even a less chance of speculating with success respecting the sites of its ancient edifices, it would still be the city towards which every religious and meditative mind would turn with the deepest longing. It is with Jerusalem as it would be with the home of our youth, were it levelled with the earth, and we returned after many years and found the spot on which it stood a ploughed field, or a deserted waste: the same thoughts would arise in our hearts as if the building was still before us, and would probably be rendered still more impressive from the very circumstance that the ruin which had taken place was complete. [. . .]

After an hour's ride we came to Rachael's tomb, which stands in a valley on the right, near to which is a well at present without water. We dismounted to view this most interesting monument of sacred history. It is formed of four square walls, with Gothic arches bricked up, and is covered by a dome-roof. On entering I was deeply impressed with a feeling of awe and respect, standing, as I thus did, in the sepulchre of a mother in Israel. The walls of the interior are covered with names and phrases chiefly in Hebrew and other Eastern characters; but some few English are to be found among them, and to these I added the names of Montefiore and myself. My feelings of gratitude on this occasion were not a little increased by a knowledge of the circumstance, that only six European females are said to have visited Palestine in the course of a century.

Joseph Solomon Lutski
ca. 1777–1844

Born near Lemberg (present-day Lviv) and later living in Lutsk, Volhynia, Joseph Solomon Lutski was a Karaite leader and scholar. He moved to Yevpatoria, in Crimea, in 1802 to serve as ḥazan (in Karaite communities, a community leader) and teacher. In 1827, he traveled with the ḥakham (spiritual leader) Simhah Babovich to St. Petersburg, where they successfully lobbied the Russian government to exempt Karaites from the compulsory military service imposed by Nicholas I on Jews. These developments are described in his *Igeret teshu'at Yisra'el* (1840), originally published in Hebrew and translated into Judeo-Tatar by his brother-in-law, Abraham (Avraam) Firkovich. Several of Lutski's prayers, liturgical poems, and religious hymns were included in the Karaite prayer book.

Epistle of Israel's Deliverance
1840

Chapter One: The Lord Is Good, a Stronghold in the Day of Trouble, and He Knoweth Them That Take Refuge in Him

In the days of Nicholas the First, the great tsar and emperor (May he live forever!) who ruled all the Russias and other places—in the year 1827 according to the Christians, and in the year 5588 since Creation according to us, the children of Israel—in the third year of his reign, a royal order was given. Written in the name of the king and sealed with his seal, it was a new law to be established for generations to come, one unknown in earlier days.

It was the king's express command that letters be sent by messenger to all the officials in his kingdom in which it was explicitely stated that men from among the Jews be taken for military service in equal measure to other nations and tongues under his rule. The tsar's order was made stronger by repeated warnings in copies of his decree that were sent to all officials that they be diligent in fulfilling the king's order in every detail, and not to lighten the weight of this decree for the Jews: they were not to accept from them either payment for a substitute or an apportionment tax, as was done previously. Instead, the Jews should give over their own sons to be soldiers rather than the sons of other nations. That is, the Jews would not be permitted to buy men of other nations or to give substitutes other than their own nation's sons; sending a person bought to serve in the tsar's army in place of one's own sons would be a violation.

Great was the mourning, fasting, and weeping among the Jews when the king's order reached each province. The hearts of all were broken, spirits were faint, and knees dripped with water. They stripped themselves of their ornaments and took off their robes. Rabbinic courts decreed that the women of Israel should take off their beautiful ornaments and not beautify themselves with gold, silver, jewels, or pearls. Our Rabbanite brethren did this in all their communities.

With the passage of each day, as the force of the decree grew in strength, the [Rabbanite] Jews gathered to take counsel with one another. They sent duly appointed emissaries to the royal city of St. Petersburg to stand before the tsar (May he live forever!) to seek mercy and to petition on behalf of their nation and themselves that he rescind this decree and be pleased to receive money in their stead, as was the customary practice of earlier years; this was as apportionment tax paid by everyone. Were the tsar to have doubled the amount of money each person had previously given, the Jews would have accepted this with glad hearts and peace of mind. They hoped only for God's mercy and kindness from the tsar, that he be pleased to rescind the decree and to receive gold and silver instead.

The emissaries strove to have the king's order put aside in order to make the nation's lot easier, but they were unsuccessful in their mission. The tsar would not lend an ear to their words. Instead, they left hurriedly, in terror and empty-handed. The order remained in place, in full force upon all Jews, with none exempted.

As the word "Jews" was written in the text of the decree, and as it was understood afterwards in some places that the decree was to include each and every Jewish sect and did not exclude the Karaites, the officials of the Crimean towns included us Karaites in this decree as well. Thus empowered, they so concluded the matter. They sent copies of the decree to all the towns in the Crimea, to the officials and to those in charge at each and every town, determining absolutely to include us Karaites in this decree in a measure equal to the Rabbanites. To implement the king's decree, two young men between the ages of twelve and twenty-five were to be selected for every five hundred males of the population for the time fixed in the text of the decree.

When the king's order was heard in the Crimean communities of [Chufut-] Kale, Közlävä, and Käfä as well as the other places where our Karaite brethren dwelt and were engaged in business, such as Or, and outside the Crimea, in cities such as Odessa, Kherson, and Nikolaev, their lips and ears trembled in fear constantly; they became upset and sick. Frightened, they were seized with trembling and were in pain, just like a woman in labor. The news came during the Sukkot festival. Days of joy were turned into sadness and moaning; sackcloth was upon all loins and baldness upon every head, at a time of harvest and treading grapes, [when there ought to have been] happy voices in the vineyards. How we were filled with terror! In the year: "How the city was broken," mourning and moaning increased in a tumultuous and joyous city. A loud and bitter cry was heard in its quarters and streets. In the vineyards there was no singing, for the terror-filled messengers and representatives went hurriedly from community to community and from vineyard to vineyard crying aloud: "Listen now and come, for this is a day of sadness and chastisement. Officials are bearing rule over people and the taskmasters are urgent, saying: 'Complete your work' and bring forth the quota of men who are selected to be turned over to the military to be soldiers according to royal decree. That time is near. The day is short and the task is great."

Chapter Six: From Vitebsk to St. Petersburg

Our master Prince Simḥah took Solomon Michri and me in his sleigh and we set out from the town while it was still daytime, our purpose being to arrive at the first postal station and not desecrate the Sabbath. We departed Vitebsk and traveled 20 versts, coming before sunset to the postal station at a place called Gaponovshchina, where we welcomed the Sabbath at the appropriate time, without desecration. The second wagon arrived after us during the evening, and we rested there comfortably.

Snow fell the entire Sabbath day and the cold became more intense, which suited the sleigh. We left there on Saturday night, going 19.5 versts to a small town, Surazh, where we went over the Tver River, which flows into the Dvina River. Since the river was frozen, local residents brought the wagons across by pulling them; the horses were unhitched and the wagons were pulled across by men on foot. They then brought the horses across separately, for they were afraid the ice would break.

Thanks be to God who watched over us and brought us across safely, for the descent to the river's port and the ascent afterwards on the other side was done with great effort and much labor. The river flows between two mountains which are very high, and the descent to its shore and the ascent after are almost in a straight line, not in a spiral. For this reason, fifty men were involved in the task, in front of and behind the wagons, pulling by means of ropes and pulleys. Consequently, the cost of hiring the labor was great. [. . .]

Chapter Thirteen: Letters Home

On Tuesday, 21 Kislev/November 29, we sent letters containing the good news to all the Crimean communities, to all the towns where our Karaite brethren reside and are engaged in business: Kale, Közlävä, Käfä, Or, Kherson, Nikolaev, [and] Odessa. [We wrote] each place an individual letter with the exact text copied from the ukase sent at the command of our lord, the great tsar (May his rule be exalted!) from Minister Lanskoi to Akmedjid, the capital of the Crimea, regarding the release of our people from having to supply men for military service: seven letters with seven [copies of the] text of the ukase, sent by special delivery so that the words of the good news would safely reach each person in his place and so that they could rest from the pain in their heart and from the broken spirit, hardships, and moans which they had borne for some time. And when they heard [the good news] they were comforted, and blessed the Lord and our lord the great tsar (May his rule be exalted!). [. . .]

Chapter Fifteen: The Hermitage

We also went to the royal treasure-house called the Hermitage, where there are valuable and rare choice possessions of Kings. Our eyes saw high buildings of every kind of ornamentation, first, second, and third stories. [There were] tables of multi-colored marble and jasper, large mirrors three cubits high, surrounded by braided gilded engravings and designs, lamps on precious bases, items of great value made of pure marble and polished jasper which shone with different colors, forms of great value done by expert masters such that one seeing them would think that they possessed life, are capable of movement, or have eyes which can look at those [people standing] before them. In one room there were precious stones, gold vessels, rings and precious objects, priceless and without number.

Royal gifts have been sent by many rulers from other treasure-houses to the rulers of Russia since antiquity, and up to this day there are many, precious and valuable. We saw, among them, one quill pen around whose length and breadth was the palm of a hand, with the palm and fingers set with pure diamonds of great value which shone like lightning. The official in charge of the treasure-house told us that this pen was a gift sent to our lord the tsar (May his reign be exalted!) from the sultan of the Ishmaelites' kingdom.

We also saw there one pearl as large as the size of a small egg from a one-year old hen. We saw a songbird, called "pavlin" in another language, and "tavus kush" in the language of the Meads, made of gold which sat upon a base made of gold. Near this songbird there was a hen, also made of gold, and a third bird called "yanshuf" in Hebrew, "sova" in Russian, and "yapalak" in the language of the Meads. The feathers upon the birds were of gold [but] in natural colors. These birds were made by artists in workshops, and by means of different devices, implements, and wheels, the birds can move, such that the songbird stood on its legs, spread its wings and its tail feathers, made a full circle as is its manner, and crowed. The hen cried out in a customary voice and acted according to its nature. The owl, which did likewise, was a gift sent from the English kingdom.

There were two gold trays set upon one table made of precious wood. On the gold trays there were two golden egg-shaped cups. The trays were for bread and the cups for salt. These two trays and two cups were a gift to our lord the late Tsar Alexander (May he rest in peace!) when he returned safely from the French War in the year 574 according to the short reckoning, with which one of the Muscovite merchants and two Muscovite officials and their assistants, that is, the nobility greeted him with bread and salt. Similar to them, there was a third gold tray upon which was a gold cup, also a gift of that time to our master the above-mentioned tsar (May he rest in peace!) from the merchants of St. Petersburg.

I have written about only a fraction of what we saw there. This book cannot contain the rest, for the eye is not satisfied with seeing, nor the ear filled with hearing, nor does the memory recall.

NOTE

Words in brackets appear in the original translation.

Translated by Philip E. Miller.

Other works by Lutski: *Petaḥ ha-tevah* (1831); *Tirat kesef* (1835).

Solomon Nunes Carvalho
1815–1897

Solomon Nunes Carvalho, the son of a prominent Sephardic family in Charleston, South Carolina (his father was a founder of the first Reform congregation in the United States), had a career as both a painter and a photographer. Carvalho painted allegorical portraits, biblical paintings, and landscapes. His portrait *Child with Rabbits* was reproduced on the U.S. one-, two-, five-, and ten-dollar bills. An early user of daguerreotype photography, Carvalho was the official photographer for an exploratory expedition through the Kansas, Colorado, and Utah territories to map out a route for a transcontinental railway. Unable to support himself from his art, Carvalho invented two steam heaters. He was an elected officer of the Hebrew Education Society in Philadelphia and a founder of the short-lived Sephardi congregation Beth Israel in Baltimore.

Travel Journal
1856

The River Jordan runs through the valley and empties into Great Salt Lake. The city is thirty miles from the Lake, and the valley is entirely surrounded with high mountains topped with snow, winter and summer.

The governor's residence, a large wooden building of sufficient capacity to contain his extensive family—nineteen wives and thirty-three citizens, was nearly finished. I made a daguerreotype view of it, and also a drawing.

The court house is a large square building, on the east side, opposite the Temple square.

The post office occupies the corner on the south side.

The Tabernacle, an unpretending one story building, occupies a portion of the Temple square.

The Temple is in course of building—the foundation is laid—and I was allowed to see the plan projected by a Mr. Angell, who by inspiration has succeeded in producing an exact model of the one used by the Melchizedek Priesthood, in older times.

The theatre, a well built modern building, is opposite to the governor's house on the north, and is the property of the church as are all the public buildings. I may say all the real estate in the valley is the property of the church, for proprietors have only an interest in property so long as they are members of the Mormon Church, and reside in the valley. The moment they leave or apostatize, they are obliged to abandon their property, and are precluded from selling it, or if they do give the bill of sale it is not valid—it is not tenable by the purchaser. This arrangement was proposed by the governor and council, at the conference which took place during my residence among them in 1854, and thousands of property holders subsequently deeded their houses and lands to the church, in perpetuity.

Under the operation of this law, nobody but Mormons can hold property in Great Salt Lake City. There are numbers of citizens who are not Mormons, who rent properties; but there is no property for sale—a most politic course on the part of the Mormons—for in case of a railroad being established between the two oceans, Great Salt Lake City must be the half way stopping place, and the city will be kept purified from taverns and grog shops at every corner of the street. Another city will have to be built some distance from them, for they have determined to keep themselves distinct from the vices of civilization. During a residence of ten weeks in Great Salt Lake City, and my observations in all their various settlements, amongst a homogeneous population of over seventy-five thousand inhabitants, it is worthy of record, that I never heard any obscene or improper language; never saw a man drunk; never had my attention called to the exhibition of vice of any sort. There are no gambling houses, grog shops, or buildings of ill fame, in all their settlements. They preach morality in their churches and from their stands, and what is as strange as it is true, the people practise it, and religiously believe their salvation depends on fulfilling the behests of the religion they have adopted.

The masses are sincere in their belief, if they are incredulous, and have been deceived by their leaders, the sin, if any, rests on them. I firmly believe the people to be honest, and imbued with true religious feelings,—and when we take into consideration their general character previously, we cannot but believe in their sincerity. Nine-tenths of this vast population are the peasantry of Scotland, England and Wales, originally brought up with religious feelings at Protestant parish churches. I observed no Catholic proselytes. They have been induced to emigrate, by the offers of the Mormon missionaries to take them free of expense, to their land flowing with milk and honey, where, they are told, the Protestant Christian religion is inculcated in all its purity, and where a farm and house are bestowed gratuitously upon each family. Seduced by this independence from the state of poverty which surrounds them at home, they take advantage of the opportunity and are baptized into the faith of the "latter day saints," and it is only after their arrival in the Valley that the spiritual wife system is even mentioned to

Attributed to Samuel Nunes Carvalho, *Self-Portrait of S. N. Carvalho*, ca. 1850.

them. Thousands of families are now in Utah who are as much horrified at the name of polygamy, as the most carefully educated in the enlightened circles of Europe and America. More than two-thirds of this population (at least, this is the ratio of my experience) cannot read or write, and they place implicit faith in their leaders, who, in a pecuniary point of view, have fulfilled their promise; each and all of them are comfortably provided with land and tenements. The first year they, of course, suffer privations, until they build their houses and reap their crops, yet all their necessities in the meantime are provided for by the church, and in a social point of view, they are much happier than they could ever hope to have been at their native homes. From being tenants at will of an imperious and exacting landlord, they suddenly become land holders, in their own right—free men, living on free soil, under a free and enlightened government.

Their religious teachers of Mormonism preach to them, as they call it, "Christianity in its purity." With their perfect right to imbibe new religious ideas, I have no wish to interfere, nor has any one. All religions are tolerated, or ought to be, in the United States, and I offer these remarks as an apology for the masses of honest men, many of whom have personally told me, that they were ignorant of the practice of polygamy before their arrival in the Valley, and surrounded as they are, by hostile tribes of Indians, and almost unsurmountable mountains of snow, they are precluded from returning home, but live among themselves, practicing as well they know how, the strict principles of virtue and morality.

Ḥayim Joseph David Azulai
1724–1806

Born in Jerusalem to a Sephardic rabbinical family, Ḥayim Joseph David Azulai was a prominent rabbinic scholar, proficient in Talmud, Kabbalah, and Jewish history. He was sent as an emissary to Europe and North Africa starting in 1753 or 1755, to raise funds for the small and beleaguered Jewish communities of Palestine. Interested in the history of rabbinical literature, he wrote prolifically; his works included a literary diary, in which he recorded ideas in Jewish history, scholarship, and folklore that occurred to him on his travels. From 1778 (after one of his missions) until his death, he lived in Livorno (Leghorn), Italy.

Ma'agal tov ha-shalem (The Good Journey)
Date Unknown

And in the City of London we went to the Fort which is called the Tower, and there I saw lions and an eagle one hundred years old and a great snake from India and another snake and other wild beasts in iron chains, and I also saw a room perhaps fifty cubits long and more, divided into many chambers, the walls between which are guns and weapons most beautifully made, then another wall, with an open door in the middle, the sides and the roof wondrously decorated with thousands and tens of thousands and more weapons. I also saw effigies of all the Kings of England in armour riding on armoured horses and anyone, to look at them, would think that they are alive. I also saw many coats of mail of different kinds arranged in rows, and many kinds of large cannons and weapons of war and shields and lances, which they had captured from their enemies from the time when England first existed and all kinds of strange vessels fearful and big. And in a room, somewhat dark, with an iron rail round inside, was shown the royal crown and sparkling precious stones, full of fire, giving light and flashing, and a golden cup, from which the King drank, and other precious vessels and royal treasure of precious stones and pearls. All this I saw with a sad heart, praying that if He does thus for those who break His commandments, may He do so to those who keep them. May the days come for the glory and grandeur and deliverance of the house of Israel and may our eyes see it and witness the saviour shining forth like the sunlight seven times, crowned with the crown of crown and the holy of holies; thus may it be His will! I delivered a sermon on Sabbath. [. . .]

This city [Paris], the capital of France, is of great size, it is said to be fifteen miles round. Its streets and squares are wide enough for two coaches to pass each other with ease, even though foot passengers are walking along the sides of the roads. The city is served by its river, the Seine, over which there is a great bridge, long and wide, called the "Pont Neuf," that is to say, the "New Bridge." All day long, and all through the night, without ceasing, pedestrians are wending their way over it. Here stands the clock "la Samaritaine," which is surrounded by water. There is a saying that never in the twenty-four hours is there an instant without a white horse, a monk and a prostitute at this spot. The city is of great beauty and everything is to be found in it, but all at a very high price, except prostitution, which is very cheap and openly dis-

"Voleti," *Prayers at the Tomb of Rabbi Isaac ben Sheshet at Algiers,* ca. 1870.
Rabbi Isaac ben Sheshet Perfet, a fourteenth-century Spanish scholar and codifier of Jewish law, fled the violent depredations against Jews of Spain in 1391 and settled in Algiers, where he died in 1408. His tomb became a site of pilgrimage for Jews who traveled there for contemplation and prayer through the twentieth century. Pilgrimage to sites of cultural and religious importance remained a key motive for Jewish travelers throughout the period covered in this volume.

played; there are said to be thirty thousand public prostitutes inscribed on the registers, without counting the thousands who are not public and offered to all comers. There are academies in great numbers, and every kind of manufacture is carried on. The Jews enjoy tranquillity, there are many Germans, many Portuguese from Bordeaux and Bayonne, and many who hail from Avignon. People pray together every Saturday, but there is no fixed community, birds of passage for the most part resorting hither for trading purposes. The synagogues are without "privilege," and exist only by a miracle.

Translated by Elkan Nathan Adler.

Other works by Azulai: *Shem ha-gedolim* (part 1, 1774; part 2, 1786); *Va'ad la-ḥakhamim* (1796).

Folktales and Fiction

Isaac Euchel

Igrot Meshulam (Epistles of Meshulam)
1790

Letter 5

    Sivan, 5529 Livorno [1769]
    In the name of G-d, the G-d of mercy!

In such measure as light exceeds darkness, such is the superiority of the people of this country over the people of Spain, where I lived for a while. The Spaniards are proud and haughty, and are too lazy to engage in work and manual labor, to such an extent that they choose to beg for bread from other paupers besides themselves rather than doing some work to alleviate their hunger through the labor of their hands. This is not the case in regard to the Italians—they are humble, and they welcome other human beings, each individual being accorded the honor properly due to him, and they are diligent in all manner of work, and in business; they adore science, and engage in the arts of song and melody, and drawing and construction, and they accord honor and render greatness to wisdom and its practitioners above all else. And notwithstanding their religion being the same as that of the Spaniards, their fine traits of character have nonetheless not been corrupted as a result of it; they do not detest those who oppose their religion, nor do they expel from their territories any other nation to prevent them having a share in their inheritance, nor do they afflict the alien dwelling among them.

Now in this large city, the population of which is roughly fifty thousand, almost one-half of that number are Jews; the majority of them adopt the customs of the Spanish Jews, while some of them are of Judeo German or Polish extraction; and they have splendid synagogues. They dwell in tranquility and at ease, and are engaged in all types of trades and businesses, in accordance with their desire. My heart is glad, and my glory rejoices, when I see my brethren living in security among their captors without impediment or mishap.

I have already informed you in one of my letters that I wrote to you in Madrid that you should not be astounded when you hear of the etiquette of the men of Europe when they are in the company of women for the purpose of eating and drinking with them; but in this country, even I was astounded at the sight; there is no company, no feast and no joyous occasion without the men and the women—young men and young maidens—mingling together; and the men honor the women, standing up in their presence and being ready to serve them, in contrast to the situation in our own lands, where the women are as handmaids to the menfolk. When I first witnessed this, I said to myself: "How corrupt this manner of etiquette is, and there will be no restraint upon the increase in lewdness amongst the people!" However, I later had second thoughts as to the harm of which I had spoken once I had been in their company on two or three occasions. And indeed the very opposite was the case, as this is the proper way to correct manners, and it is by such means that character traits within the young men can be reformed. And I then said: "This sort of conduct is indeed a brain-child of wisdom!" You know, my dear brother! You must surely be aware that the trait of self-shame constitutes the cornerstone of all the worthy traits of character that an individual can choose to possess, for so long as the saplings of wisdom and of ethics—of knowing the difference between good and evil—have not yet sprouted forth within his soul, there is nothing to fence him in, to guard him against doing something unbecoming, other than self-shame. And it is in this connection that our Sages, of blessed memory, declared: "The shamefaced are destined for Paradise!"—this being on account of the end result, for it is by virtue of this trait that he renders his general character wholesome, and he will be just in respect of his actions.

Now regarding this exalted character trait, the Creator, elevated be He, placed the charge of it upon the shoulders of women; namely, that a sense of shame should govern their lives and prevail over all their feelings, so that it guards the paths they pursue, to save them from the hands of the arrogant and of those who lead others astray, to prevent them from sinning. And accordingly, the more men accord honor to a woman, the more they strengthen within her soul the roots of the trait of self-shame, and she will be most afraid of debasing her honor in the estimation of man when lending her ear to the sound of lovemaking and paying attention to lustful words. And thus it is good for a man if, while still in his youth, he is in the company of chaste women such as these, who will serve as a wall of fortification and of strength to his mouth and his tongue, to protect him from uttering obscene expressions, let alone from committing any lewd acts, which would be regarded as outrageous and as a cause of derision among the circle of his friends. He will accustom himself to reflect wisely on everything issuing from his mouth, and be careful not to follow vile individuals, and to be concerned about his speech, lest the words that he utters become known and he will be put to shame. And it is by virtue of such acclimatization on his part that the worthy character traits will come to the fore within his soul—that is to say, of chastity, of humility, and of the good manners that raise the stature of a person and elevate his honor, and he will accordingly find favor and good understanding in the sight of all who see him. And now I will tell you of the general principle that I have learned: man is fashioned out of clay, and from his youth, the imagination of the thoughts of his heart chooses the physical and the material, and therefore the fundamental basis of the experimentation of man is man himself! And it was in relation to this that King Solomon declared: "Iron sharpens iron, and a man sharpens the countenance of his friend!" The etiquette and character traits of a man who has been sitting at home throughout his life and who has not come into contact with human society are of little significance to me; and even if he is possessed of a clear intellect and of goodwill, he is comparable, in my estimation, to bdellium that has just come from the source from which it was quarried, around which no light will shine until the hand of the furbisher and the polisher has been put to it, to work at it. This is the reality, my dear brother; the sages in every generation have tried and tested it, and the latter-day sages have complemented it by saying: "And a gracious wife sharpens the countenance of a young man!"

Translated by David E. Cohen.

Aaron Halle-Wolfsohn
1754–1835

A Prussian-born *maskil* from Halle, Aaron Halle-Wolfsohn joined Moses Mendelssohn's circle in Berlin. He edited Mendelssohn's German Bible translation and produced his own translations of and commentaries on scripture. Wolfsohn was an editor of the Hebrew journal *Ha-me'asef*, to which he also contributed. He embraced the educational ideas of the Enlightenment in his pioneering Hebrew primer, *Avtalyon*, and as a teacher at the Königliche Wilhelmsschule, a Jewish public school in Breslau (now Wrocław, Poland). Wolfsohn's *Laykhtzin und fremelay* has been called one of the first modern Yiddish plays, although it relies heavily on German dialogue to promote a maskilic message.

Sihah be-erets ha-ḥayim (A Conversation in the Afterlife)
1794–1797

A dialogue in the land of the living between our teacher, R. Moses Maimonides, the Spaniard, and our Teacher Moses, son of Menaḥem [Mendelssohn] of Dessau, and an anonymous third person.

On the day of arrival of the soul of our Master, our Teacher Moses, son of Menaḥem, of Dessau, in the land of the living.

[*A large and spacious area, all around which are planted all types of fruit-bearing trees of desirable appearance and good for food, and beneath their shade, many souls are seated to amuse and enjoy themselves.* MOSES MAIMONIDES *is walking along, when, lo and behold, a certain individual runs toward him and stands opposite him.*]

ANON: Moses! Moses! Please stop and listen to what I . . .

MAIM: For how long will you behave aggressively toward me? Have I not already told you two or three times "Leave me alone"? See over there, beneath the verdant oak-trees, there is a band of men sitting and enjoying themselves in an affectionate manner; go there, I beg you, if you desire to develop friendships, but leave me alone and let me go on my way.

ANON: Do not let your anger be kindled against me, and allow me to speak just this once! Are you that man, Moses, whose name is renowned still today amongst Judah and Israel? Are you the man in regard to whom those dwelling on earth declare: "From Moses unto Moses, no one has arisen like unto Moses"? I trust that my words bespeak only goodness and mercy; I had hoped to see your face as one sees the face of God, and now I have seen you as a human being, as one of us—is this what is called "the path of holiness"—to pour scorn on a man before having enquired into and examined his inner thoughts? Do you possess the eyes of the Almighty to perceive what is within my heart, in that you have shut your ears to my words? What have I done to you and how have I wearied you? Testify against me!

Maim: You are correct! I am indeed not God to be able to penetrate the imaginings of your heart, but I have eyes to see to what sort of people you belong. I know the men of your place of origin and your birthplace—I know them well, for they are children lacking in faith and without any decent order in their laws and their deeds; moreover, they have not trained their tongues to speak with rectitude and with purity, as is appropriate. My soul was fully sated with sorrow on each occasion when I was here amid their assemblies. And I have accordingly made a covenant with myself these many days to store myself away from this generation for eternity! [. . .]

Maim: If that is the case, why do we need to go to the end of my work to speak about matters existent in former times that have now passed away? Let us go to the beginning of my work to hear what you have to say, with words remaining constant forever—speak, I beg you! Look, I stated in the section "*Halakhot* relating to Opinions and Beliefs": "Anyone saying that the Creator, blessed be He, has a body and a material form is a heretic"; and I heard that, after its publication, there arose an individual who became my intellectual opponent, a certain Abraham, son of David, whom you have mentioned, and who said as follows: "Why has he called such a person a heretic? Were there not men greater and better than he who held this belief?" Now tell me, I pray you, what is your view on this? How can a single man have the audacity to harbor thoughts of such a vile nature as this, and to affirm two opposites in relation to the identical theme? For if the Creator has a body, He is also blended and conjoined from various different parts; and if He is conjoined from different parts, He would also necessarily be something novel, for prior to His blending, He was not what He is now, and He would also, by this token, be existent within space and time—and what man of intelligence could conceivably believe something like that?

Anon [*to himself*]: Conjoined, novel, existent in space!—My ears are hearing novel and bizarre things; I do not understand a single word that he has spoken! Is he philosophizing? Moses! How you have changed your tune! Look, I came to you to give you to drink of the spiced wine of Torah, with words both sweet and pleasant, and you revert with words of a trivial nature, the knowledge of which will neither benefit nor add anything to you. I swear by my life, in a little while he will also be asking me questions based upon his work *The Guide to the Perplexed*! What shall I do?

Maim: Why are you silent and do not open your mouth? Do you too believe what my intellectual opponent says, that the Creator has a body and a material form?

Anon: Heaven forbid that I should believe something like that, which lacks the light of reason!

Maim: But why? How have you refuted his arguments? And from where have you adduced proof against him?

Anon: Proof? Is not the negation of material form within the Creator, blessed be He, readily apparent from the Torah of Moses our Teacher, for there it is stated that the Lord is a consuming fire?

Maim [*laughing*]: But what you have adduced as a proof actually refutes your words rather than supporting them, for this verse too materializes the Creator, blessed be He, by describing Him as "a consuming fire"; whereas in reality, our Master, Moses, said this merely as a figure of speech; for fire is a lofty substance, pure and elevated above all the other elements, and anyone daring to approach it will not escape unscathed; the Lord your God is comparable to this metaphorical image—a zealous God, Who will not acquit anyone who rebels against His words or transgresses His covenant. And had our Master, Moses, spoken only in the presence of sages and men of discernment, he would have depicted the Creator, blessed be He, through the employment of lofty metaphors, far removed from any traces of materiality; but as it was, he was speaking in the presence of the masses, whose hearts were "plastered over" in such manner as to impede their comprehension of elevated notions—hence he employed a physical description.

Anon [*to himself*]: By my life, he is philosophizing; how cast down is my soul and how it moans within me!

Maim: Now what if we were to say that what is absent here in the verse is the letter *kaph*, denoting comparison, as is the custom of scripture on frequent occasions, in which case the verse, in its perfected form, would read: "For the Lord your God is *like* a consuming fire"?

Anon [*to himself*]: He comes to challenge me with grammar too! I can no longer hold my peace; no longer will I place a bridle on my mouth, come what may, but I will speak in accordance with whatever is in my heart, for zeal for the Lord of Hosts and His holy Torah is fueling this! [*To* Maim, *in a spirit of pride*]: I am neither a philosopher nor the son of a philosopher, but rather, I have meditated upon the Torah of the Almighty, and have constantly been attracted to it, and when I stated that I have studied your work from start to finish, I meant only as regards those matters as are of the greatest importance, such as the laws concerning the sacrifices of birds and the purification of menstruating women, or laws relating to sacred objects and monetary matters and the like, so as to enable me to provide guidance as between plea and plea and as between blood and blood. So of what interest to me are those things which you have asked me? What will I gain by knowing them and what will I lose by not knowing them? Accordingly, I have not studied the *halakhot* relating to theological beliefs and opinions at all!

Maim [*to himself*]: It is exactly as I said: I yearn for pride such as this to be manifested within Jacob! Now he has unveiled the mask from himself and has appeared before me as naked as when he came forth from his mother's womb! But now, what shall I do? Shall I leave him and proceed on my way? Will he then not remain entrenched in his false opinions—no! For the honor of the Almighty, I shall hold myself back from acting thus, and direct him as to the way on which he should go; perhaps his heart will understand, and he will return and be healed! [*To* Anon]: Was it for nothing that I placed the *halakhot* relating to theological opinions and beliefs at the beginning of my work? Was it not through this means that I demonstrated to people, that they might realize that this theme emerges promptly, at first instance, to greet anyone desirous of studying my work, and that without it, he cannot penetrate into the interior of my work. And in similar vein, our Sages of the Talmud have declared: "Any Talmudic scholar who is deficient in theological knowledge, a carcass is better than he!"

Anon: I am not unaware of this Talmudic dictum, and the sages and Torah scholars of my own era have already explained it well, when they stated that the meaning of this statement is: any Talmudic scholar who is lacking in knowledge, that is to say, lacking in the fear of the Almighty included within it, to appreciate his own lowliness, such an individual is worse than a carcass, because, in regard to a carcass, wherever it is thrown and laid to rest on the surface of the dung, everyone will maintain his distance from it so as to avoid having to walk around it; and thus it will never, in any event, constitute a stumbling-block to human beings. This is, however, not the case in regard to a Talmudic scholar who is lacking in knowledge—such a person will be loathsome and will accustom others to conduct themselves in ways that are not beneficial, and hence he will be the cause of stumbling on the part of other human beings who neither see nor know him.—And blessed be God, Who inclined his lovingkindness toward me to make me worthy of possessing knowledge, for I know how low is my worth, and my spirit has never raised me up to ascend to the heights with lofty philosophical explorations, but on the contrary, I have been wholehearted with the Lord my God!

Translated by David E. Cohen.

Other works by Halle-Wolfsohn: *Avtalyon* (1790); *Jeschurun* (1804).

Anonymous, In Praise of the Ba'al Shem Tov
The Ba'al Shem Tov, ca. 1700–1760

Regarded as the founder of Hasidism, Israel ben Eliezer (Yisra'el ben Eli'ezer) (known as the Ba'al Shem Tov or Besht, "master of the good name") was likely born in Okopy, Ukraine. Of humble background, he mastered Kabbalah and meditation, and as a healer was skilled at communicating with people from many walks of life, applying kabbalistic principles to everyday affairs. He settled in Mezhbizh (now Medzhybizh, Ukraine), where he led a circle that promoted dedication to God characterized by joy, ecstatic prayer, and levels of emotional communion. Although he did not establish a dynasty, he is considered the role model for later Hasidic teachers. Records of his life and deeds were compiled by Dov Ber of Linits and printed as *Shivḥei ha-Besht* by the Lubavitch Hasid Israel Yoffe.

In Praise of the Ba'al Shem Tov
1814

The Birth of the Besht

While he was on his journey, Elijah the Prophet revealed himself to him and said: "Because of the merit of your behavior a son will be born to you who will bring light to Israel, and in him this saying will be fulfilled: *Israel in whom I will be glorified.*"

He came home and with God's help he found his wife still alive. The Besht was born to them in their old age, when both of them were close to a hundred. (The Besht said that it had been impossible for his father to draw his soul from heaven until he had lost his sexual desire.)

The boy grew up and was weaned. The time came for his father to die, and he took his son in his arms and he said," I see that you will light my candle, and I will not enjoy the pleasure of raising you. My beloved son, remember this all your days: God is with you. Do not fear anything." (In the name of *Admor*, I heard that it is natural for a son and a father to be closely bound, for as our sages, God bless their memory, have said: "The talk of the child in the market place is either that of his father or of his mother." How much closer then are ties between parents and children who are born to them in their old age. For example, Jacob loved Joseph because he was born to him in his old age, and the ties between them were very great, as it is said in the holy Zohar. And it was true here. Although the Besht was a small child, because of the intensity and sincerity of the tie, the words were fixed in his heart.)

The Besht's Education and Youth

After the death of his father the child grew up. Because the people of the town revered the memory of his father, they favored the child and sent him to study with a melamed. And he succeeded in his studies. But it was his way to study for a few days and then to run away from school. They would search for him and find him sitting alone in the forest. They would attribute this to his being an orphan. There was no one to look after him and he was a footloose child. Though they brought him again and again to the melamed, he would run away to the forest to be in solitude. In the course of time they gave up in despair and no longer returned him to the melamed. He did not grow up in the accustomed way.

He hired himself out as the melamed's assistant, to take the children to school and to the synagogue, to teach them to say in a pleasant voice, "Amen, let His great name be blessed forever and to all eternity, kedushah, and amen." This was his work—holy work with school children whose conversations are without sin. While he walked with the children he would sing with them enthusiastically in a pleasant voice that could be heard far away. His prayers were elevated higher and higher, and there was great satisfaction above, as there was with the songs that the Levites had sung in the Temple. And it was time of rejoicing in heaven.

And Satan came also among them. Since Satan understood what must come to pass, he was afraid that the time was approaching when he would disappear from the earth. He transformed himself into the sorcerer. Once while the Besht was walking with the children, singing enthusiastically with pleasure, the sorcerer transformed himself into a beast, a werewolf. He attacked and frightened them, and they ran away. Some of them became sick, and, heaven help us, could not continue their studies.

Afterwards, the Besht recalled the words of his father, God bless his memory, not to fear anything since God is with him. He took strength in the Lord, his God, and went to the householders of the community, the fathers of the children, and urged them to return the children to his care. He would fight with the beast and kill it in the name of God.

"Should school children go idle when idleness is a great sin?" They were convinced by his words. He took a good sturdy club with him. While he walked with the children, singing pleasantly, chanting with joy, this beast attacked them. He ran toward it, hit it on its forehead, and killed it. The next morning the corpse of the gentile sorcerer was found lying on the ground.

After that the Besht became the watchman of the beth-hamidrash. This was his way: while all the people of the house of study were awake, he slept; and while they slept, he was awake, doing his pure works of study and prayer until the time came when people would awaken. Then he would go back to sleep. They thought that he slept from the beginning until the end of the night.

The Besht's Seclusion

Now I will relate the great events, which I heard from my father-in-law, God bless his memory, concerning how the Besht was revealed.

He lived in a small village and made his living by keeping a tavern. After he brought brandy to his wife he would cross the river Prut and retire into seclusion in a house-like crevice that was cut into the mountain. He used to take one loaf of bread for one meal and eat once a week. He endured this way of life for several years. On the eve of the holy Sabbath he used to return home. His brother-in-law, Rabbi Gershon of Kuty, thought him to be an ignorant and boorish person, and he used to try to persuade his sister to obtain a divorce from him. But she refused since she knew his secret but did not reveal it to anybody.

Translated by Dan Ben-Amos and Jerome Mintz.

Nachman of Bratslav
1772–1810

Rabbi Nachman of Bratslav (or Breslov) was the great-grandson of the Ba'al Shem Tov. As a young man, Nachman felt drawn to commune with God and reveled in the outdoors; his religious identity and antipathy toward other Hasidic leaders strengthened after his visit to the Land of Israel in 1798–1799. In 1802, he moved to Bratslav in Ukraine and attracted followers to a new, introspective form of Hasidism. He later settled in the town of Uman, leaving no successor after his death to lead Bratslav Hasidism. Rabbi Nathan Sternhartz, his disciple and amanuensis, published Nachman's teachings. Nachman's most significant writings are his *Sipure ma'asiyot*, fantasy tales with kabbalistic and folkloristic elements; and his *Likute MoHaRaN*, an anthology of his homiletic teachings.

The Tale of a Rabbi and His Only Son
1815

Once there was a rabbi who had no children. Finally, he had an only son. He raised him and married him off. The son used to sit in an attic room and study in the manner of rich men and he always studied and prayed. The son had already performed a commandment by which he reached the aspect of "the small light." And yet he felt that there was some imperfection in himself, but he did not know what it was, so he felt no delight in his study and prayer. He told it to two young men and they advised him to go to a certain *zadik*. And the only son went to tell his father that since he did not feel any delight in his worship (his praying, his study, and other commandments) and felt something missing but did not know what, he wanted to go to the *zadik*. And his father answered him: "Why should you want to go to him? You are a greater scholar than he, and of a better family than he. It is not fitting that you should go to him. Turn away from this road!" Thus he prevented him from going.

The son returned to his study and again he felt that imperfection. Again he took counsel with those men, and they advised him as they had before to go to the *zadik*. And again he went to his father. His father dissuaded him and prevented him as before. And so it happened several times. The son felt he was missing something and he longed very much to fulfill this imperfection but did not know what it was. So he came once more to his father and implored him till his father was forced to go with him, because he did not want to let him go by himself since he was an only son. And his father told him: "I shall go with you, and show you there is nothing real in him." They harnessed the carriage and set out.

His father said to him: "This is how I shall test. If the journey proceeds without mishap, it is from heaven. And if not, it is not from heaven and we shall return." They set out. They came to a small bridge and one horse fell down and the carriage turned over and they almost drowned. The father said: "You see that this journey does not proceed without mishap and it is not from heaven." And they returned home.

The son went back to his studies and again he saw his imperfection and did not know why. He came again and implored his father as he had done before and the father was forced to go with him again. When they set out his father established the former test: "If it proceeds without mishap. . . ." And it happened that while they were traveling, the two axles broke. And his father told him: "You see that it does not proceed as if we should go, since, is it natural for two axles to break? They have traveled so many times with this carriage and nothing like that has happened!" And they returned home.

The son returned to his way of life, that is, to his studies, etc., and again felt that imperfection. And the men advised him to travel. The son told his father that they should not establish such a test, since it is natural for a horse to fall sometimes or for axles to break, unless there is something very bizarre.

They set out and came to an inn to spend the night. They found a merchant there, and they started talking to him like merchants, but they did not reveal to him where they were going, because the rabbi was ashamed to say that he was going to the *zadik*. They talked about the affairs of the world, until in the course of the conversation, they reached the subject of *zadikim*, and where *zadikim* were to be found. The merchant told them there was a *zadik* there, and there and there so they started talking about the *zadik* they were traveling to. Then the other answered, in amazement, "But he is frivolous! I am coming from him now, and I was there when he committed a sin." The father answered and said to his son: "Did you see, my son, what this merchant has reported while speaking plainly with no intention to malign? And he is coming from there." And they returned home.

And the son died. And he came to his father, the rabbi, in a dream. When he saw his son standing in great anger, he asked him: "Why are you so angry?" He answered him that he should go to the *zadik* whom they had intended to go to, "and he will tell you why I am angry." The father woke up and said it was just a coincidence. Afterwards he dreamt again as before, and he said this, too, was an idle dream. And this happened a third time. Then he understood that there was something in it and he traveled there.

On the way he met the merchant whom he had met before when he had traveled with his son, and recognizing him said to him: "Aren't you the one whom I saw in that inn?"

He answered him: "Of course you saw me."

The merchant opened his mouth and told him: "I can swallow you if I want to."

He said to him: "What are you talking about?"

And he replied: "Do you remember? When you traveled with your son, first the horse fell on the bridge, and you returned. Then the axles broke. Then you met me and I told you that the *zadik* was frivolous. And now that I have done away with your son you are allowed to go on. For your son was in the aspect of 'the small light,' and that *zadik* is in the aspect of 'the great light,' and if they had united the Messiah would have come. But now that I have done away with him, you are allowed to travel."

In the middle of his words he disappeared, and the rabbi had no one to talk to. The rabbi traveled to the *zadik* and he cried: "What a pity, what a pity! A pity on those who are lost and will never be found! May the Lord, blessed be He, return our exiles shortly, Amen."

(That merchant was Samael himself, who disguised himself as a merchant and led them astray. Afterwards, when he met the rabbi again, he tested him for having heeded his advice, because this is Samael's manner, as is known. May the Lord, blessed be He, save us!)

Translated by Arnold J. Band.

Heinrich Heine
1797–1856

A German romantic poet and essayist, Heinrich Heine was born in Düsseldorf. Unsuccessful in his early business career, he studied law, and settled in Berlin in 1821. There he met with success as a poet and was influenced by the founders of *Wissenschaft des Judentums*; he became acquainted with Rahel Varnhagen, Moses Mendelssohn, and Leopold Zunz. In 1825, Heine converted to Christianity, apparently for the career opportunities that such a conversion might have afforded. Heine's life was dominated by enthusiasm for the French Revolutionary ideals and Napoleon in their liberal treatment of Jews; he spent the last twenty-five years of his life in Paris. (Several of Heine's poetry and prose works appear in this volume.)

A Seder Night
ca. 1824

In the large room of his house sat Rabbi Abraham and commenced the celebration of the Passover Eve, in company with his relatives and pupils and other guests. Everything in the room was brighter than usual. The table was covered with a silk-embroidered cloth, with golden fringe trailing to the ground. The little plates glittered pleasantly with their symbolic food, as did also the high goblets filled up with wine, and graven entirely with sacred subjects. The men sat in black mantles, and flat black hats and white ruffs. The women wore marvellous shimmering stuffs of Lombardy, and on their head and neck ornaments of gold and pearls; and the silver Sabbath lamp shed its festive light upon the devoutly happy faces of young and old. On a raised seat, leaning against a cushion of purple velvet, reclined Rabbi Abraham and read and chanted the *Hagadah*, and the gay choir joined in or responded at the appointed places. The Rabbi, too, was attired in a gala dress of stately black, his noble, yet somewhat severe features looked milder than usual, the lips smiled out of his brown beard as though they wished to tell many charming things, and his eyes seemed to swim with beatific memories and anticipations. The beauteous Sara, who sat on another raised chair by his side, wore, as hostess, no jewellery; only white linen enfolded her slender form and devout features. Her face was touchingly beautiful, as indeed the beauty of all Jewesses is of a strangely moving sort. The consciousness of the deep misery, bitter insult, and unhappy state in which their relations and friends live, spreads over their graceful faces a certain painful earnestness and watchful affectionate anxiety, that wondrously bewitch our hearts. So sat to-day beauteous Sara, for ever gazing into her husband's eyes. Now and then she looked at the *Hagadah* which lay before her, a beautiful book bound in gold and velvet, an old heirloom with aged wine-spots from her grandfather's days. There were ever so many bold and brightly-painted pictures in it, which, even as a child, she had been happy to look at on the Pesach night, and which represented all sorts of bible stories. Such as Abraham, with his hammer, smashing his father's stone idols, and the angels coming to visit him, and Moses killing the Egyptian, and Pharaoh sitting on his throne, and the frogs which gave him no rest even at table, and he, thank God, drowning while the children of Israel carefully walked through the Red Sea, and they, standing open-mouthed, at the foot of Mount Sinai with their sheep and kine and oxen, and then pious King David playing the harp, and last, Jerusalem, with the towers and minarets of the Temple illumined by the sun.

The second Cup had been filled, faces and voices were growing more cheerful, and the Rabbi, as he seized one of the unleavened cakes, and with a happy greeting held it up, read out from the *Hagadah* the following words: "Behold! This is the bread our fathers have eaten in Egypt! Let everyone who is hungry come and eat! Everyone who is sad, let him come and join in our Pesach feast. This year we celebrate it here, but next year in the land of Israel. This year we are still slaves, but next year we shall celebrate it as the sons of freedom."

Here the door opened, and two tall pale men entered, wrapped in big cloaks. "Peace be with you, "said one of them." We are co-religionists on our travels, and would like to keep Pesach with you." And the Rabbi answered quick and friendly. "With you be peace. Seat yourselves near me." The two strangers sat down to table and the Rabbi proceeded with his reading. Sometimes while the others were repeating the responses after him, he whispered affectionate words to his wife. Playing on the old saw that on that night every Jewish housefather thinks himself a king, he said "Be joyful, oh my Queen!" But she answered with a melancholy smile, "Our prince is missing," and by that she meant a son of the house who, as a passage in the *Hagadah* requires, has in fixed phraseology to ask his father the meaning of the feast. The Rabbi made no answer, but with his finger pointed at one of the pictures on the open page of the *Hagadah*, which portrayed very agreeably how the three angels came to Abraham to announce that he would have a son born to his wife Sara, and Sara standing behind the door of the tent listening with womanly artfulness to the conversation. The hint brought a fiery blush to the cheeks of the lovely woman. She cast down her eyes and then looked up again lovingly at her husband, who was now chanting the wondrous tale of how Rabbi Joshua, Rabbi Eliezer, Rabbi Azaria, Rabbi Akiba and Rabbi Tarphon sat reclining in Bene Brak, and conversed all night about the exodus of the Children of Israel from Egypt, until their pupils came and announced to them that it was day, and the people were already saying the morning prayer in the Synagogue. As the lovely Sara listened reverently with her eyes on her husband, she saw his face suddenly transfixed with horror and the blood leave his cheeks and lips, and his eyes start out like icicles. Yet almost at the same moment his features resumed their former repose and cheerfulness, his lips and cheeks grew red again, his eyes sparkled joyously once more, and he himself seemed mastered by a mad mood, most strange in him. Sara was terrified as she had never been terrified in her life before, and an icy shudder ran though her, less because of those signs of blank horror she had observed in her husband's face for a single instant than for this present exhilaration of his, which gradually turned to roaring merriment. The Rabbi jocosely shifted his beret from ear to ear, pulled at his beard and curled it waggishly, and sang the text of the *Hagadah* like a street song. When recounting the Egyptian plagues, where the index finger is dipped into the full glasses and the drops of wine shaken off on to the floor, the Rabbi besprinkled the younger girls with the red wine, and there was much grumbling for spoiled ruffs, and much resounding laughter. To Sara this boisterous but forced merriment seemed more and more uncanny, and seized by unmentionable fear she stared at the crowd of guests rocking themselves to and fro or nibbling the crisp cakes, or gulping down the wine, or chatting with each other, or singing out aloud, all very merry.

Then came time for supper, and everybody stood up to wash the hands, and beauteous Sara brought in a large silver basin, richly chased with golden figures and held it before each of the guests, while the water was poured over their hands. When she came to offer the Rabbi this service, he looked meaningly at her and slung out of the door. Sara followed him, and the Rabbi hastily seized his wife's hand. Hastily he dragged her through the dark streets of Bacherach, hastily through the city gate to the high road which leads along the Rhine to Bingen.

The Rabbi then stood still a while, he moved his lips several times, but they uttered no sound. At last he exclaimed: "Do you see the Angel of Death? Down there, he hovers over Bacherach. But we have escaped his sword. Praise be to God!" And then, in a voice still quivering with horror, he related how he was cheerfully singing the *Hagadah* as he sat there, reclining, when suddenly he glanced by chance beneath the table and saw at his feet the blood-stained body of a child. "Then I noticed," added the Rabbi, "that our two last guests did not belong to the community of Israel, but to the congregation of the ungodly, and they had contrived to introduce the corpse into our house in order to accuse us of the child murder, so as to rouse the populace, and to plunder and murder us. I dared not let it be noticed that I had seen through the hellish plot. I should have only hastened our destruction; only craft has saved us both. Praise be to God! Do not fear, Sara. Our friends and relations will be safe. It was only my blood for which the villains thirsted. I have escaped them, and they will content themselves with my silver and gold. Come with me, Sara, to another land! The God of our fathers will not forsake us!"

Translated by Elkan N. Adler, from Heine's novel *The Rabbi of Bacherach*.

Other works by Heine: *Gedichte* (1821); *Reisebilder*, 4 vols. (1826–1831); *Buch der Lieder* (1827); *Die romantische Schule* (1833–1835); *Neue Gedichte* (1844); *Romanzero* (1851).

Benjamin Disraeli
1804–1881

Twice elected prime minister of Britain, Benjamin Disraeli initially turned to writing in an effort to repay his debts; his early works were fashionable "silver-fork novels" depicting an aristocratic lifestyle he had yet to attain. When he entered politics, he soon became a prominent member of the emerging Conservative Party and was elected prime minister of Britain in 1868. The only person of Jewish birth to have held this office (he converted to Christianity at age twelve), Disraeli wrote throughout his life, often romances that reflected on political issues and the relationship between Christianity and Judaism.

Vivian Grey
1826

Book the First

CHAP. I. THE CONSULTATION

I am not aware that the infancy of Vivian Grey was distinguished by any extraordinary incident. The solicitude of the most affectionate of mothers, and the care of the most attentive of nurses, did their best to injure an excellent constitution. But Vivian was an only child, and these exertions were therefore excusable. For the first five years of his life, Master Vivian, with his curly locks and his fancy dress, was the pride of his own, and the envy of all neighbouring establishments; but, in process of time, the horrible spirit of *boyism* began to develope itself, and Vivian not only would brush his

Moritz Daniel Oppenheim, *Portrait of Heinrich Heine*, 1831.

hair "strait," and rebel against his nurse, but actually insisted upon being—breeched! At this crisis it was discovered that he had been *spoiled*, and it was determined that he should be sent to school. Mr. Grey observed, also, that the child was nearly ten years old, and did not know his alphabet, and Mrs. Grey remarked, that he was getting very ugly. The fate of Vivian was decided.

"I am told, my dear," observed Mrs. Grey, one day after dinner to her husband, "I am told, my dear, that Dr. Flummery's would do very well for Vivian. Nothing can exceed the attention which is paid to the pupils. There are sixteen young ladies, all the daughters of clergymen, merely to attend to the morals and the linen— terms very moderate—100 guineas per annum, for all under six years of age, and few extras, only for fencing, pure milk, and the guitar. Mrs. Metcalfe has both her boys there, and she says their progress is *astonishing*. Percy Metcalfe, she assures me, was quite as backward as Vivian. Ah! indeed, much backwarder; and so was Dudley Metcalfe, who was taught at home on the new system, by a pictorial alphabet, and who persisted to the last, notwithstanding all the exertions of Miss Barnett, in spelling A-P-E—monkey, merely because over the word, there was a monster munching an apple."

"And, quite right in the child, my dear—*Pictorial* alphabet!—pictorial fool's head!"

"But what do you say to Flummery's, Grey?"

"My dear, do what you like. I never trouble myself, you know, about these matters"; and Mr. Grey refreshed himself, after this domestic attack, with a glass of claret.

Mr. Grey was a gentleman who had succeeded, when the heat of youth was over, to the enjoyment of a life-interest in an estate of about £2000 per annum. He was a man of distinguished literary abilities, and he had hailed with no slight pleasure, his succession to a fortune, which, though limited in its duration, was still a very great thing for a young *littérateur* about town; not only with no profession, but with a mind utterly unfitted for every species of business. Grey, to the astonishment of his former friends, the wits, made an excellent domestic match; and, leaving the whole management of his household to his lady, felt himself as independent in his magnificent library, as if he had never ceased to be that true freeman, A MAN OF CHAMBERS.

CHAPTER VIII. SOCIETY

In England, personal distinction is the only passport to the society of the great. Whether this distinction arise from fortune, family, or talent, is immaterial; but certain it is, to enter into high society, a man must either have blood, a million, or a genius.

Neither the fortune nor the family of Mr. Grey entitled him to mix in any other society than that of, what is, in common parlance, termed, the middling classes, but from his distinguished literary abilities he had always found himself an honoured guest among the powerful and the great. It was for this reason that he had always been anxious that his son should be at home as little as possible; for he feared for a youth the fascination of London society. Although busied with his studies, and professing "not to visit," Vivian could not avoid occasionally finding himself in company, in which *boys* should never be seen; and, what was still worse, from a certain *esprit de société*, an indefinable *tact*, with which Nature had endowed him, this boy of nineteen began to think this society very delightful. Most persons of his age would have passed through the ordeals with perfect safety: they would have entered certain rooms, at certain hours, with stiff cravats, and Nugee coats, and black velvet waistcoats; and after having annoyed all those who condescended to know of their existence, with their red hands, and their white kid gloves, they would have retired to a corner of the room, and conversationised with any stray four year oldest not yet sent to bed.

But Vivian Grey was an elegant, lively lad, with just enough of dandyism to preserve him from committing *gaucheries*, and with a devil of a tongue. All men, I am sure, will agree with me when I say, that the only rival to be feared by a man of spirit is—a clever boy.—What makes them so popular with the women, it is not for me to explain; however, Lady Julia Knighton, and Mrs. Frank Delmington, and half a score of dames of fashion, (and some of them very pretty!) were always patronizing our hero, who really found an evening spent in their company not altogether dull; for there is no fascination so irresistible to a boy, as the smile of a married woman. Vivian had really passed such a recluse life for the last two years and a half, that he had quite forgotten that he was once considered a very fascinating fellow; and so, determined to discover what right he ever had to such a reputation, master Vivian entered into all those amourettes in very beautiful style.

But Vivian Grey was a young and tender plant in a moral hot-house. His character was developing itself too soon. Although his evenings were now generally passed in the manner we have alluded to, this boy was, during the rest of the day, a hard and indefatigable student; and having now got though an immense series of historical reading, he had stumbled upon a branch of study certainly the most delightful in the world—but, for a boy, as certainly the most pernicious—THE STUDY OF POLITICS.

And now every thing was solved: the inexplicable longings of his soul, which had so often perplexed him, were at length explained. The *want*, the indefinable *want*; which he had so constantly experienced, was at last supplied; the grand object on which to bring the powers of his mind to bear and work was at last provided. He paced his chamber in an agitated spirit, and panted for the Senate.

It will be asked, what was the evil of all this? and the reader will, perhaps, murmur something about an honourable spirit and youthful ambition. Ah! I once thought so myself—but the evil is *too* apparent. The time drew nigh for Vivian to leave for Oxford—that is, for him to *commence* his long preparation for entering on his career in life. And now this person, who was about to be a *pupil*—this boy, this stripling, who was going to begin his education,—had all the feelings of a matured mind—of an experienced man; was already a cunning reader of human hearts; and felt conscious, from experience that his was a tongue which was born to guide human beings. The idea of Oxford to such an individual was an insult!

Other works by Disraeli: *Sybil, or the Two Nations* (1845); *Tancred, or the New Crusade* (1847); *Endymion* (1880).

Benjamin Disraeli

The Wondrous Tale of Alroy
1833

Preface

And now for my style. I must frankly confess that I have invented a new one. I am conscious of the hazard of such innovation, but I have not adopted my system without long meditation, and a severe examination of its qualities. I have in another work already ventured to express my opinion that the age of Versification has past. I have there observed, "The mode of composition must ever be greatly determined by the manner in which the composition can be made public. In ancient days, the voice was the medium by which we became acquainted with the inventions of a poet. In such a method, where those who listened had no time to pause, and no opportunity to think, it was necessary that everything should be obvious. The audience who were perplexed would soon become wearied. The spirit of ancient poetry, therefore, is rather material than metaphysical. Superficial, not internal; there is much simplicity and much nature, but little passion, and less philosophy.["...]

Part III

I

It was midnight. Alroy slept upon the couch: his sleep was troubled. Jabaster stood by his side motionless, and gazing intently upon his slumbering guest.

"The only hope of Israel," murmured the Cabalist, "my pupil and my prince! I have long perceived in his young mind the seed of mighty deeds; and o'er his future life have often mused with a prophetic hope. The blood of David, the sacred offspring of a solemn race. There is a magic in his flowing veins my science cannot reach.

Francis Grant, *The Right Hon. B. Disraeli M.P., Chancellor of the Exchequer*, 1852.

"When in my youth I raised our standard by my native Tigris, and called our nation to restore their ark, why we were numerous, wealthy, potent; we were a people then, and they flocked to it boldly." Did we lack counsel? did we need a leader? Who can aver Jabaster's brain or arm was ever wanting? And yet the dream dissolved, the glorious vision. Oh! when I struck down Marvan, and the Caliph's camp flung its blazing shadow o'er the bloody river—ah! then indeed I lived. Twenty years of vigil may gain a pardon that I then forgot we lacked the chief ingredient in the spell—the blood that sleeps beside me.

"I recall the glorious rapture of that sacred strife amid the rocks of Caucasus. A fugitive, a proscribed and outlawed wretch, whose life is common sport, and whom the vilest hind may slay without a bidding. I who would have been Messiah!"

Eugénie Foa
1796–1853

Born in Bordeaux into an influential French Sephardic family, Eugénie Foa wrote on Jewish themes for the general public, as well as for children. Sympathetic to many ideals of the 1848 revolutions, she also contributed to early feminist publications such as *La voix des femmes* that year. Foa was the first woman in France to support herself on her own writings. Although she herself converted to Catholicism, her works are notable for their Jewish heroines who, despite loving Christian men, retain pride in their heritage.

Rachel; or, The Inheritance
1833

April 1833

We had spent the summer at Enghien, in the pleasant Montmorency valley, where every year spring brings along with its fragrant greenery, the choicest Parisian society. Situated on the shore of a small lake, a spa offering sulphurous baths draws as many foreigners as Parisians to this beautiful area, thanks to the healing powers of its waters. As in all such thermal bathing establishments, people live in what could be called a communal manner, almost like a family. And whosoever would refuse such familiarity arouses curiosity, or perhaps a stronger sentiment, in the other inhabitants of the spa.

This did not fail to happen to a young woman who tried to live apart in the establishment. Alone among this boisterous and animated crowd, who continually seek pleasure and often find it without looking, she carefully avoided the gardens, the shores of the lake, and the other public spaces. We used to see her, always alone, searching out the most solitary sports, the most out-of-the-way sites. Whenever one of us, of whichever sex, approached her, she would quickly move away. If you greeted her, however, she would politely return the greeting, blushing, and pass you by so quickly that she discouraged you from attempting to continue the conversation.

Was this arrogance or pride? The sweetness of her physiognomy gave the lie to such a thought. Was she punishing herself for some secret sin? The nobility and modesty of her bearing quickly dispelled this idea and proved, beyond a shadow of a doubt, that she would not have been out of place in the very highest society. Was it therefore a secret sorrow or a deep disgust with life? Alas! Everything about her came to confirm this sad conjecture.

This woman seemed quite young. Without being exactly pretty, her features, which were hollowed out by suffering, bore an expression of indefinable sadness. Long curls of black hair framed her pale, slightly oval face, which made you suspect she might be of Jewish origin. Her big black eyes, with their soft and melancholy expression, seemed to fear the light of day and to shade themselves on purpose beneath a row of long brown lashes, through which pierced from time to time the rays of her shining pupil. Her frail figure had a remarkable elegance and suppleness. This woman inspired interest in all who saw her. It was more than a banal curiosity, however, that attracted people to her. It was a deep and intimate feeling, but one that was hard to pin down, which took you by the soul and seemed to cry out: "This is an unhappy person! A sufferer! Who knows but that one of your tears would perhaps make hers less bitter? A welcoming smile, a word of friendship, would surely lessen the pain of this poor young woman." And if you didn't cede to this heartfelt instinct that attracted you to her, that made you want to mingle your tears with hers, to take her hand, to call her by her name, it was because you did not dare. It was because you understood that often an unwanted consolation bruises or tears the soul instead of calming its pain.

After few days, the remarks and conjectures became increasingly consistent and plausible. The young woman's modest clothing, although always clean and in good taste, implied a total lack of fortune, as did her simple and frugal manner of living. Thus the pretense of always wanting to be alone, the fear, the terror even, that overtook her at the approach of a happy and brilliant young person, explained itself: the suffering of a tender soul is more sensitive to pity than insult. It is defenseless against the first of these sentiments and too far superior to the second for it to affect her.

She inhabited a little house that was isolated at the far end of the garden of the establishment. An old woman served her. A young and pretty girl, Madeleine, who worked at the dairy, brought her milk every morning and evening. The presence of that young girl, her naïve and happy chatter, were the only distractions of the *pale lady*, as she came to be called by everyone.

She received no visitors with the sole exception of an old man in oriental dress whose grave and venerable face was adorned by a long white beard. But his great age didn't allow him to make the trip from Paris to Enghien very often. We only saw him arrive on Friday morning and he would always return before sundown.

Did this young woman have a family? Sisters? Brothers? People said so but we didn't know for sure. The horrible thing about misfortune is that it often breaks the bonds of nature and cools the very hearts that should be the most devoted to us. It is necessary to have experienced such cruelty to understand how much bitterness and truth this observation contains.

Autumn was approaching and little by little the woman's thinness became more frightening. A dry cough that at first we barely noticed acquired daily a sharper and more penetrating intensity. Her misfortunes were stifling her bit by bit. Each morning another trace of life would disappear from her face. Each evening found her more worn down and more resigned to her suffering.

One afternoon, after I had received some awful news, I fled my usual company to go and weep on my own. Before I knew it, night had fallen. Thinking myself alone, I gave way to my sadness and allowed the sighs that were tearing my breast apart to escape.

"Are you crying?" said a voice in my ear. "Are you suffering? Oh! Madame, excuse my question! From anyone else it would be indiscreet, but not from me!"

I turned around. The mysterious woman from the garden was at my side. Her look, the sweet expression of her face in the moonlight, said so clearly: *I myself am suffering too much not to sympathize with your pain*, that, giving way to a desire I could not control, I threw myself into her arms. "I lost my best friend!" I cried. And I wept at her breast. This was how our relationship began.

Thus I came to know that her name was Rachel, and that she was married very young to an unworthy man who abandoned her to the most dire poverty. That man's family, who were rich and powerful, had abandoned her as well. One of her uncles took her in. But that uncle was not rich. Formerly the chief rabbi of Jerusalem, now a cantor in Paris, he lived on his wages alone. This was the old man with the white beard who would come to see her on Fridays. I thus learned that she was Jewish.

While Rachel told me that story that was at once so sad and at the same so typical of the lives of certain of us weak women whom relatives often sacrifice for money or propriety, I looked at that poor victim of marriage: she had been fresh and beautiful, but although she was still young, tears had already left their mark on her. Her frail and thin figure, which had once had healthy curves but was now dried out by sorrow, seemed hardly able to withstand the least little shock. And yet she never complained! She never said how much she suffered. But what words could express more eloquently than her physical decay the moral suffering of that unfortunate woman! Tears had scarred her chest. She was dying of consumption. Still so young, she who was not yet twenty would not see the beginning of winter nor the end of the fine days of autumn. Her fate was sealed, and it was approaching so fast!

"Do you see the leaves that protect us from the sun?" she said to me one day. Today, they offer me shade. Tomorrow, perhaps, they will wither on my tomb!"

"Rachel! You could still have hope?"

"Oh! It's all over for me!" she said, with a melancholy shake of her head. "All over! And yet, if my heart had not been broken, I would have been able to live a few more years! I used to feel such a strong and vigorous sap in my breast! But now death! . . . Don't pity me, Eugénie! Death is but a respite for a suffering soul. And I have suffered so much!"

Translated by Maurice Samuels.

Other works by Foa: *Le kidouschim* (1830); *Le petit Robinson de Paris, ou le triomphe de l'industrie* (1840).

Ludwig A. Frankl
1810–1894

Born in Chrast, Bohemia, Ludwig August Frankl was educated in Prague and Vienna; he studied medicine in Italy. He became a poet, editor of the *Sonntagsblät-*

ter, secretary of the Vienna Jewish community, and founder of the Laemel School in Jerusalem and the Vienna Jewish Institute for the Blind. Frankl was a political liberal who supported the 1848 revolution through his journal and his verse. He used his position in Vienna's literary elite to encourage new writers and was ennobled as Ritter von Frankl-Hochwart in recognition of his philanthropic activities. His is one of the earliest Prague golem tales.

Ancestral Tales and Legends
1836

Under the roof of the oldest synagogue in Prague (the Altneuschul), because of the belief that misfortune would meet the workers, there is preserved, in its primeval form and color, a piece of trunk-like clay, which is known by the name "*Golem.*"

A wise rabbi (still called High-Reb Leb by the Jews), who diligently occupied himself with the *Kabbalah* on every secret, silent night, formed a human-like figure and put a secret name ("*Schem*") of God under its tongue. Thus it was brought to life and performed the duties of a servant. But when the first three stars appeared in the sky on Friday evening, and the beadle (*Schames*, usually called *Mulassim* by the peoples of the Orient) announced the Sabbath, the rabbi, because even the damned spirits (only the Lord God creates a blessed one) are permitted to rest on the Sabbath, took the secret name of God from under his servant's tongue, so that he became again a lifeless piece of clay. Once, it is told, the rabbi suffered the pain of the loss of his beloved son and forgot to de-animate his servant, when the beadle again proclaimed the peace of the Sabbath. Then this one was seized as if by madness; his eyes rolled and burned like flaming wheels, his breath was visible and sparkled with wonderful colors, and he began a terrible destruction in the house. Everyone was very terrified and cried with anxious horror for the rabbi. However, he was not in any condition to restrain the creature in order to take the secret name from under his tongue. So he spoke a deep-cutting curse, and the servant became again what it was before, a piece of clay. The rabbi never dared again to practice the secret science.

Translated by Edan Dekel and David Gantt Gurley.

Other works by Frankl: *Das Habsburgerlied* (1832); *Morgenländische Sagen* (1834); *Elegien* (1842); *Die Universität* (1848); *Libanon* (1855); *Nach Jerusalem*, 2 vols. (1858–1860); *Ahnenbilder* (1864).

Godchaux Baruch Weil (Ben-Lévi)
1806–1878

Godchaux Baruch Weil (Ben-Lévi) was among the first generation of Jews to have grown up as French citizens, and his writing reflects a loyalty to French ideals of pluralism and universalism. The son of a prominent Parisian businessman, Weil received a traditional Jewish education and was something of a prodigy, publishing a refutation of a reformist article at age fifteen. After his father died, he became dedicated to modernizing Jewish institutions and traditions in France. To this end, Weil (under the pseudonym Ben-Lévi) wrote dozens of short stories and social commentaries in *Les archives israélites*.

The Rise and Fall of a Polish Tallis
1841

Sixty years ago, Jacob, who was known in his quarter as *Old Jacob*, was living in the rue de la Mortellerie. He ran a successful business selling old clothes, scrap metal and even, on occasion, old watches. Old Jacob was loved and respected, and he was renowned for his piety in the neighborhood.

For the occasion of his marriage, he sent away to Poland, at great expense, for a magnificent tallis of fine white wool, embellished with azure stripes, surrounded by a large border of white satin, and adorned with gold fringe, fantastical embroidery, and delicate tsisit in braided silk. On the day of the wedding, the rabbi spread this beautiful new tallis over the heads of Jacob and his fiancée, and he covered it with handfuls of golden wheat, a mysterious symbol of fertility. From that day forward, the beautiful woolen tallis became a precious talisman for Old Jacob, a sacred relic, a family heirloom that he would not have parted with at any price. The religious hearts of our fathers endowed everything with a sacred significance, and the naïve souls of our mothers attached great importance to the ceremonies of a religion that they loved.

The tallis played an especially big role in the religious life of that time: at the high holidays, it served as an obligatory accompaniment to prayer; it did the honors when a stranger was called to the Torah; it acted as a canopy at weddings; it covered the cradle of newborns at their naming ceremonies; fathers spread it like a shield over their sons when they blessed them at temple; and when it belonged to a wise and pious man, it was placed in his coffin, like a veil between this world and the next. . . .

When Jacob died, his beautiful tallis was passed down as a legacy to his son *Jacobi*. This son started as a simple soldier and wound up as a supplier of Napoleon's armies. He grew rich by supplying as little as possible and he Italianized his name, as much to lend himself a Corsican air as to erase its overly Biblical traces. Jacobi was frank and obliging in business and a *bon vivant* like all old soldiers. But he was much less religious than his father: military life had stifled his religious feeling and he frequently violated the principles he had learned in his father's house. And yet, whenever there was a solemn religious occasion, Jacobi celebrated it conscientiously. He gave to charity, attended services at temple, dressed himself carefully, and his dwelling (he lived in the rue Montmartre) took on a joyous holiday appearance.

Jacobi above all retained a special respect for the memory of his father, and the tallis that he inherited was precious to him. When he donned it for the morning service on Yom Kippur, he draped it about himself with pride, and when he wore it on the anniversary of the death of his father or of his mother, he would kiss it fervently, large tears welling up in his eyes. Even in war, Jacobi was not separated from the sacred tallis. Rolled in his sack, it served in numerous campaigns alongside him. With filial superstition, he credited it with helping him to escape unharmed from battles.

Today Jacobi is dead and his son, a handsome young man of twenty, has inherited his fortune and his tallis. This son calls himself Jacoubé in order to conceal his Israelite origin. He works as a stock broker, dwells in the Chaussée-d'Antin, wears polished boots, long hair, a collar shaped like the alleys of the Trianon, and an eyeglass that holds itself in place between the eyebrow and the eye. In a word, he is a *lion*. No need to add that Jacoubé is only Jewish by birth, that he knows nothing of the Israelite religion, and that he would blush to be seen in the synagogue. If he is asked about Old Jacob, he responds dismissively, "What is that?"

And what has become of the beautiful woolen tallis, which came from Poland sixty years ago? Do you know what our fashionable chap has done with the holy veil that was so precious to Old Jacob and so dear to the late Jacobi? Alas! Yesterday at the Opera's first masked ball of the season, amid an infernal galop and the roar of Musard's orchestra, I noticed the wild dancing of a handsome young man wearing the costume of a post boy from Longjumeau and a pretty working-class girl disguised as a stevedore. Her jacket struck me: it was made of a fine woolen cloth streaked with azure stripes, adorned with fantastical embroidery and gold fringe. It appeared strange and old, and yet, bizarre as it was, it had a certain pleasing *je ne sais quoi*.

Alas! Alas! The handsome post boy from Longjumeau was the ungrateful Jacoubé, son of Jacobi, and the jacket of the pretty working-class girl was made of the beautiful tallis, which came, sixty years ago, from Poland for the wedding of Old Jacob! Alas! Alas! Alas! In this all too truthful tale, is there not an entire religious epic?

Translated by Maurice Samuels.

Other work by Weil: *Les matinées du samedi* (1842).

Jonah ben Gabriel
1772–ca. 1850s

What we know about Jonah ben Gabriel comes largely from his *Folktales of the Kurdistani Jews*, written around 1843, as the book includes numerous digressions on current events, superstitions, and other phenomena affecting life in his hometown Arbil—the capital of today's Iraqi Kurdistan. A pious Jew, ben Gabriel played a prominent role in Arbil, including overseeing the building of a synagogue and negotiating the purchase of a town area from the Turkish governor to allow Jews to carry items on the Sabbath.

Folktales of the Kurdistani Jews
ca. 1843

The Plague of Hailstones

The year 5573 (1813) was a leap year (in the Jewish calendar). On the twenty-fourth of Nisan, the Sabbath right after Passover, after midday, the skies became overcast and rain fell. Afterward it hailed for about half an hour. The hailstones were large and small, some as big as walnuts. However, a few people came forth afterward and claimed that they had seen hailstones as big as hens' eggs. Thereupon the floodwater surrounded the town wall and destroyed about three hundred houses—some say about four hundred—and killed some Gentiles. Some died indoors and others were carried away by the flood. The hailstones remained in the fields for about fifteen days. The Gentiles would bring them and sell them in the marketplace. On that Sabbath, in the morning, the governor's palace (*sarāy*) collapsed and about eight Gentiles died beneath it. Ten days later the Gentiles brought a hailstone (to town) and weighed it, and it weighed one *waqīyah* (about

1½ lbs.). Moreover, before the Passover a Jew (from another town) came forth and declared that in his town it had hailed (so heavily) that the hailstones killed several people, and that each hailstone that was weighed came to one *huqqah* (about 2¾ lbs.). May it be (God's) will to have peace in the world. Amen, so be it.

The Plague of Locusts

In the year 5584 (1824) there was (so) much blessing and abundance in the world that one Arbil bushel of wheat cost (only) one *akilej* and a half. However, in the year 5585 (1825), (although) crops were good, locusts appeared but did not do much damage, except that one Arbil bushel now rose in price to eight akilej. In the year 5586 (1826) crops were also good, but (this time) locusts ate up half of the grain, and one Arbil bushel sold for twelve akilej. In the year 5587 (1827) there was little rain, crops were poor, and locusts ate up all the greenery in the fields. As a result, one Arbil bushel rose to sixty akilej, and the people in all the villages around Arbil fled (elsewhere). Some died of starvation, and some kept fleeing further on. The villages, with no people left in them, went to ruin. In the holy (Jewish) congregation of Arbil about two hundred Jews died—men, women, and children, having had nothing to eat. Horses and cattle died (as well). The Gentiles ate the flesh of (dead) donkeys, horses, dogs, and cats. People offered to sell their household belongings very cheaply but found no buyers. In the year 5588 (1828) the area surrounding Arbil was replanted, but one Arbil bushel (still) cost twenty-five akilej, for locusts remained active. However, they ate only some (of the crops) and left others (untouched), so that later on one Arbil bushel cost (only) eight akilej. May the Holy One, blessed be He, send us our righteous Messiah and resurrect our dead. Amen, so be it.

The Plague of Pestilence

In that year (1828) there was also a horrible pestilence (which spread) from the gates of Diyarbakir to the gates of Qantara and carried away several thousand Gentiles, (so many) that they could not be counted. Also, from among the Jews (of Arbil) about a hundred and fifty died. The Jews fled to the villages, but even there some people died. In the year 5591 (1831) there was (another) pestilence in all the provinces as well as in Arbil. On the first day after Passover the (Jewish) community fled again to the villages and remained there for about three months, returning on the first day of the month of Tammuz. About seventy people from among the Jews died (this time). May the Holy One, blessed be He, deliver us from all kinds of misfortunes. Amen, so be it.

The Pillar of Cloud

In the year 5603 (1843), in the month of Second Adar, a white pillar shaped like a long cloud appeared (nightly in the sky), beginning with the first hour of the night. It would appear in the west and turn to the south, remain there for about two hours of the night, and then gradually diminish. The pillar appeared every night until the first night of Passover, but (afterward) did not appear again. Scripture says, *And be not dismayed at the signs of heaven* (Jer. 10:2). May the Holy One, blessed be He, send us our righteous Messiah and swiftly and soon resurrect our dead. Amen, so be it.

On the Borrowing of Books

An emissary from the Land of Israel, (named) Joseph Uzziel, borrowed from me the book *Midrash Samuel*, the book *Bet Peres*, and the book *The Joy of the Festival*. He (promised that he) would send them back to me from (the town of) Kirkuk or from Baghdad, but he never did.

Translated by Yona Sabar.

Grace Aguilar
1816–1847

Grace Aguilar was born in London and lived in Devon and Brighton before returning to her city of birth. A celebrated writer, she was mainly educated at home by her Sephardic family, whose cultural history often inspired her work. She was prolific in a variety of literary genres, including historical novels, poetry, religious works, and translations. Though she supported Jewish reform—notably religious education for Jewish women—she opposed assimilation; her views invited a wide and varied readership; of note was her intellectual relationship with American editor Isaac Leeser. In poor health for most of her life, Aguilar died on a convalescent trip to Frankfurt, where she is buried.

The Escape: A Tale of 1755
1844

A moment of agonized suspense and Alvar Rodriguez stood at the window, the bar he had removed in his hand. He let down the string, to which Hassan's now trembling hands secured the ladder and drew it to the wall. His descent could not have occupied two minutes, at the extent; but to that solitary watcher what eternity of suffering did they seem! Alvar was at his side, had clasped his hands, had called him "Hassan! brother!" in tones of intense feeling, but no word replied. He sought to fly, to point to the desired haven, but his feet seemed suddenly rooted to the earth. Alvar threw his arm around him, and drew him forwards. A sudden and unnatural strength returned. Noiselessly and fleetly as their feet could go, they sped beneath the shadow of the wall. A hundred yards alone divided them from the secret door. A sudden sound broke the oppressive stillness. It was the tramp of heavy feet and the clash of arms; the light of many torches flashed upon the darkness. They darted forward in the fearful excitement of despair; but the effort was void and vain. A wild shout of challenge—of alarm—and they were surrounded, captured, so suddenly, so rapidly, Alvar's very senses seemed to reel; but frightfully they were recalled. A shriek, so piercing, it seemed to rend the very heavens, burst through the still air. The figure of the Moor rushed from the detaining grasp of the soldiers, regardless of bared steel and pointed guns, and flung himself at the feet of Alvar.

"O God, my husband—I have murdered him!" were the strange appalling words which burst upon his ear, and the lights flashing upon his face, as he sank prostrate and lifeless on the earth, revealed to Alvar's tortured senses the features of his WIFE.

How long that dead faint continued Almah knew not, but when sense returned she found herself in a dark and dismal cell, her upper garment and turban removed, while the plentiful supply of water, which had partially restored life, had removed in a great degree the dye which had given her countenance its Moorish hue. Had she wished to continue concealment, one glance around her would have proved the effort vain. Her sex was already known, and the stern dark countenances near her breathed but ruthlessness and rage. Some brief questions were asked relative to her name, intent, and faith, which she answered calmly.

"In revealing my name," she said, "my intention must also be disclosed. The wife of Alvar Rodriguez had not sought these realms of torture and death, had not undergone all the miseries of disguise and servitude, but for one hope, one intent—the liberty of her husband."

"Thus proving his guilt," was the rejoinder. "Had you known him innocent, you would have waited the justice of the Holy Office to give him freedom."

"Justice," she repeated, bitterly. "Had the innocent never suffered, I might have trusted. But I know accusation was synonymous with death, and therefore came I here. For my faith, mine is my husband's."

"And know you the doom of all who attempt or abet escape? Death—death by burning! and this you have hurled upon him and yourself. It is not the Holy Office, but his wife who has condemned him"; and with gibing laugh they left her, securing with heavy bolt and bar the iron door. She darted forwards, beseeching them, as they hoped for mercy, to take her to her husband, to confine them underground a thousand fathoms deep, so that they might but be together; but only the hollow echo of her own voice replied, and the wretched girl sunk back upon the ground, relieved from present suffering by long hours of utter insensibility.

It was not till brought from their respective prisons to hear pronounced on them the sentence of death, that Alvar Rodriguez and his heroic wife once more gazed upon each other.

They had provided Almah, at her own entreaty, with female habiliments; for, in the bewildering agony of her spirit, she attributed the failure of her scheme for the rescue of her husband to her having disobeyed the positive command of God and adopted a male disguise, which in His eyes was abomination, but which in her wild desire to save Alvar she had completely overlooked, and she now in consequence shrunk from the fatal garb with agony and loathing. Yet despite the haggard look of intense mental and bodily suffering, the loss of her lovely hair, which she had cut close her head, lest by the merest chance its length and luxuriance should discover her, so exquisite, so touching, was her delicate loveliness, that her very judges, stern, unbending as was their nature, looked on her with an admiration almost softening them to mercy.

And now, for the first time, Alvar's manly composure seemed about to desert him. He, too, had suffered almost as herself, save that her devotedness, her love, appeared to give strength, to endow him with courage, even to look upon her fate, blended as it now was with his own, with calm trust in the merciful God who called him thus early to Himself. Almah could not realise such thoughts. But one image was ever present, seeming to mock her very misery to madness. Her effort had failed; had she not so wildly sought her husband's escape—had she but waited—they might have released him, and now, what was she but his murderess?

Little passed between the prisoners and their judges. Their guilt was all sufficiently proved by their endeavours to escape, which in itself was a crime always visited by death; and for these manifold sins and misdemeanours they were sentenced to be burnt alive, on All Saints' day, in the grand square of the Inquisition, at nine o'clock in the morning, and proclamation commanded to be made throughout Lisbon, that all who sought to witness and assist at the ceremony should receive remission of sins, and be accounted worthy servants of Jesus Christ. The lesser severity of strangling the victims before burning was denied them, as they neither repented nor had trusted to the Justice and clemency of the Holy Office, but had attempted to avert a deserved fate by flight.

Not a muscle of Alvar's fine countenance moved during this awful sentence. He stood proudly and loftily erect, regarding those that spake with an eye, bright, stern, unflinching as their own; but a change passed over it as, breaking from the guard around, Almah flung herself on her knees at his feet.

"Alvar! Alvar! I have murdered—my husband, oh, my husband, say you forgive—forgive—"

"Hush, hush, beloved! mine own heroic Almah, fail not now!" he answered with a calm and tender seriousness, which to still that crushing agony, strengthened her to bear and raising her, he pressed her to his breast.

"We have but to die as we have lived, my own! True to that God whose chosen and whose first-born we are, have been, and shall be unto death, aye, and *beyond* it. He will protect our poor orphan, for He has promised the fatherless shall be His care. Look up, my beloved, and say you can face death with Alvar, calmly, faithfully, as you sought to live for him. God has chosen for us a better heritage than one of earth."

She raised her head from his bosom; the terror and the agony had passed from that sweet face—it was tranquil as his own.

"It was not my own death I feared," she said, unfalteringly, "it was but the weakness of human love; but it is over now. Love is mightier than death; there is only love in heaven."

Other works by Aguilar: *Woman's Friendship: A Story of Domestic Life* (1844); *The Women of Israel* (1845); *Home Influence: A Tale for Mothers and Daughters* (1847); *The Vale of Cedars or, The Martyr* (1850).

Leopold Weisel
1804-1873

The physician Leopold Weisel, born in the Czech city of Prestitz (Přeštice), was among the first to collect the Jewish folktales of his homeland, a project he worked on with the non-Jewish folklorist Franz Klutschak. The proto–oral histories became the foundation for the popular "ghetto fiction" genre. In addition to being a gifted storyteller, Weisel wrote several articles in support of Czech national freedom during the upheavals of 1848. Although he converted to Christianity upon his marriage to a Catholic woman, Weisel continued to preserve and popularize stories of traditional Bohemian and Czech Jewish life.

Die Pinchasgasse
1847

"What you spend in honor of the holy days, the Lord will richly reward!" says the Talmud, and pious Pinchas granted everything his wife demanded. Clothes for the children and ornaments for herself were bought, pure white linens, golden headpieces and other treasures: neither the best wines nor the fattest meats were lacking, and in the home, where yesterday there was only the most oppressive need, today was found only joy and wellbeing. Never since the Israelites fled Egypt has a Passover been celebrated with such joyful spirits and pious devotion as it was this time at Reb Pinchas's home. The eight-pointed lamp over the table and the candelabra on the walls with their circular, polished backing plates spread a bright halo of light in the clean, warm room. Next to the table, a divan of cushions decorated with large flowers had been built for the master of the house who, dressed in his finest robes, stretched out on it like a Pasha. The housewife sat opposite her husband and filled the glasses with red wine. She was clothed in a long, plentifully pleated white gown and wore a golden head covering decorated with stiffened lace and silk ribbons. The children sat around the table with happy faces, impatiently waiting for what was to come. Only the youngest enjoyed the privilege of sitting on the throne-bed at his father's feet. On the table was a round tin dish, on which lay three unleavened loaves wrapped in a long hand-towel, as well as horseradish, watercress, cooked eggs, a piece of roasted meat, and a vessel with saltwater. Now the whole family raised the dish, and spoke with one voice the words: "This is the poor bread that our forefathers ate in the Land of Egypt; he who is hungry, let him come in and eat with us."

Just then, the sound of wagon wheels was heard in the lane, and before Reb Pinchas could finish the blessing, someone was knocking on the window (their dwelling was on the ground floor). Pale with shock and all a-tremble, Reb Pinchas rose from his divan to see what was causing the disturbance. With a quaking voice, he went to the window and asked who was there. A voice from outside could be heard saying, "Just open up, Pinchas! I am here to celebrate Passover with you." For a moment, everyone thought that the latecomer must be no other than the Prophet Elijah who at this time appears in the home of pious people, which is why a special glass, filled with wine, must be placed on the table. The bolt was quickly slid back; the door was opened, and in walked—Count B., Pinchas's patron. "Almighty God! Can this be possible? Your Honor! Children—remove your caps, kiss his hand!" cried Reb Pinchas, totally beside himself, tearing the caps from the amazed children's heads. "Don't mind me, Pinchas, go on with your devotions! But what do I see?" cried the count in amazement, as he looked around the room, "Have you suddenly become a wealthy man?" "Yes, Your Honor!" said the Jew with a joyful smile. "Yes, God the Almighty has helped me! Just a few days ago, I was still a poor man and did not know whether I would be able to celebrate this Passover as a believer should; God's help came just at the right time, and I am now a wealthy man."

"Will you not tell me," said the count, "how your situation changed so quickly?" "Yes, Your Honor, I can tell you of the miracle God bestowed upon his servant, for Your Honor always acted like an angel, heaping beneficence upon me," replied Pinchas, and then truthfully began to tell the story. The count listened carefully, but when the Jew mentioned the monkey, he could no longer contain his amazement and cried out "What, a dead monkey! It must be mine! Truly, that would be amazing! My monkey died suddenly, three days ago and, so as not to see the animal anymore, I immediately had it removed from the house; but go on—how is that connected to your good fortune?" When Reb Pinchas heard these words, his anxiety peaked, his whole body began to tremble, his face turned deathly white, and he could not utter a single word. Silently he went to the cupboard, opened it, took out a pouch, and handed it to the count with the words "Your Honor! Here is all of it, except for a few pieces that I spent to honor the holy days." "What do you want with that pouch?" asked the count in astonishment. "Well, this gold was in the monkey and if the monkey is Your Honor's property, then so is the gold," replied the frightened Jew. "Ach! The beautiful golden ducats!" sighed Pinchas's wife. "Be quiet, woman. The Lord gave and the Lord hath taken away; blessed be his name!" cried Pinchas. The count turned to his servant, who stood, pale-faced, at some distance from him, and asked "Do you perhaps know something more specific about this? Speak, I want to hear it; what happened with the dead monkey?" "Forgive me, Your Excellency," replied the frightened servant. "Jakob wanted to play a trick on poor Pinchas, and he threw the animal into his chamber—several other servants knew about it." "What, Jakob? The joke turned out strangely," said the count with a smile, "So, it seems that I had the poor boy locked up unjustly—but it might be a penalty for the misdeed that he committed against Pinchas. It is very likely that the foolish animal, with its instinct to imitate, ate the gold that was taken from my desk. It saw that I took the small gold coins and bent them between my teeth to mark them, so it thought that gold was edible." "Yes indeed, Your Honor! The monkey died from eating the ducats—here is the gold," Pinchas chimed in, as he extended the pouch to the count. "But no, honest Pinchas! The God of your fathers bestowed this treasure upon you, and it remains with you. I denied you the usual gift this year to see whether your God alone would help you, for you always said, 'God has helped me.' Now I realize that trust in God is worthwhile." Who could now describe the joy of Reb Pinchas who again saw himself in possession of such a sum? "Children! Woman! Kiss the feet of your benefactor, kneel before the Angel of the Lord!" cried the happy man who seized the hand of the noble count and kissed it many times. The children fell down, embraced the knees of the magnanimous man, and kissed his coat. The count smiled down on the group with genuine pleasure, his truly noble spirits rose and found sweet recompense in the gallant deed. "I wish to spend this evening with you," he said, "and watch the ceremonies that you conduct today; don't worry about it, just act as though I were not here. My lady must also come quickly to learn of this wonderful coincidence." Indeed, the wagon was sent off, and after a short time, the countess arrived. The noble couple stayed almost until midnight in the home of Reb Pinchas, who was not allowed to omit even the least important ceremony, and the two only departed after the so-called Seder came to an end and Reb Pinchas concluded with the verse "One day God will strike down the Angel of Death."

Through hard work and intelligence, and with the count's money, Rabbi Pinchas earned a great fortune after some years. Just as his money continuously increased, so, too, increased his reputation among his people: he was soon elected head of the Israelite community. But he remained as pious, honest, and modest as when he was in poverty. His house was a meeting place for the wisest rabbis, his purse was open to every request, and every day the hungry ate at his table. He also had several dwellings built for poor fellow-religionists in the lane where he lived, and on the same narrow street, he built with his own money a grand synagogue, which today still bears the name of its patron, so that the lane also is known as the "Pinchasgasse" (Pinchas Lane). Rabbi Pinchas died at a blessedly advanced age, after all his children had been married off and provided for.

Translated by Carola Murray-Seegert.

Wolf Pascheles
1814–1857

Wolf Pascheles, the son of impoverished parents, lived his entire life in Prague. At first a tutor, he soon became a publisher and bookseller. In 1828, he edited and published a small German-language prayer book for women. During the cholera epidemic in his city in 1832, he printed a book of penitential prayers by Rabbi Eliezer Ashkenazi. In 1836, he opened Prague's first Hebrew bookshop; he opened another one in Brünn (present-day Brno) in 1844. Beginning in 1846, he edited a popular anthology under the title *Sippurim*; the collection included biographies of medieval and later Jewish figures as well as imaginative Jewish literature (such as "The Kamzan").

The Kamzan (The Miser)
ca. 1847

There was once a Mohel, who was very avaricious. He had inherited some money, and his sole pleasure was to augment his wealth, and count his gold and silver coin. In his own opinion he was a religious man, for he observed all the ceremonies prescribed by the law, and believed himself especially pleasing to God, in performing the office of Mohel without asking any remuneration from the poor. His love of money increased with age, and he would sit for many hours before his coffer, gazing at his heaps of gold, riveted to the metal by a singular fascination, whilst he felt acute pain whenever he was obliged to part with even a farthing. People observing how difficult it was to get any money from him, called him "Kamzan," "the tongs," because he kept fast hold of what he grasped.

One day a stranger came and asked him to perform the office of Mohel to a son that had been born to him. As the carriage and horses of the stranger indicated wealth, the Mohel had a special pleasure in accepting the invitation, thus at the same time serving God and himself.

They drove on until dusk, when the stranger suddenly turning into a wild country, hurried madly on over the trackless heath. In vain the Mohel cried, "Stop!" and entreated the stranger to set him down; the more he cried and entreated, the more furiously the stranger whipped his horses, so that the Mohel at last was more dead than alive, and completely unable to pay any attention to the direction in which he was carried. Suddenly the carriage stopped at the gate of a park leading to mansion, the splendour of which formed a singular contrast to the surrounding desolate landscape.

The Mohel was led to the chamber of the mother and infant, and when he for a moment was left alone with her, she said, "For God's sake do not eat or drink anything here, nor accept any gift; my husband is a spirit, and all here are spirits excepting myself." Her husband now returned, and they talked of other matters.

Next morning, when the ceremony was to be performed, a large and merry party gathered round a plentiful breakfast table. The Mohel was led to the seat of honour, and the most delicate of the dishes were offered him; but under the pretext that he always fasted on such a day, he declined to eat, although it cost him great pain, accustomed as he was to satisfy his appetite at other people's tables. His pain was very much prolonged, for the party prolonged their breakfast to a late hour, during which the host never seemed to resign the hope of seeing his guest, the Mohel, break his fast.

At length the religious ceremony was performed. When it was finished, the host took the Mohel aside and said to him, "I am very much indebted to you for the great service you have shown me, and I beg you will accept a little token of gratitude." So speaking, he opened a door leading into a large room, the walls of which were silver, and where immense piles of silver coin reached from the floor to the ceiling.

"Please take as much as you like," said the host.

The Mohel had involuntarily stretched out both hands towards the glittering piles, but remembering what the woman had said, he as quickly let them drop and replied, "You owe me nothing."

"I beg your pardon for having offered you a gift unworthy of your acceptance," said his host, opening the door into another room, the walls of which were of gold, while piles of gold coin reached from the floor to the ceiling.

"Please take as much as you like," said the host.

The Mohel's head turned in the enchanted atmosphere, and it was only with greatest effort that he could repeat to himself the woman's warning. He faintly said, "You owe me nothing; pray, let me go."

"Oh! I see," said his host, "you spurn anything like payment, and again I ask your pardon. This perhaps will be more to your taste."

So saying, he opened the door of a third room, where precious stones in large heaps, symmetrically arranged, dazzled the Mohel's eyes with a promise of that unspeakable pleasure of which he had only faintly dreamed, when brooding over his own coffer. But having resisted temptation in the silver and gold rooms, he found it easier now, and it cost him comparatively little effort to shake off the spell and to repeat: "You owe me nothing; only let me get home."

"Well, then, this way, if you please," said the host, leading him through an empty room, where only a number of keys were seen hanging on the walls. Instinctively the Mohel felt attracted by these keys and looked at them, until suddenly to his amazement he fancied he recognized the key of his own coffer. He turned to his host, who said smiling, "Yes, Mohel, it is the key of thy coffer."

The Mohel became pale as death, and said, "How does it come here?"

"Why, Mohel," said his host, "this is easily explained. Thou art at present among spirits, servants of the Lord. When a man orders a coffer, there are always two keys made: one is the man's, the other is God's. If God's key is not made use of, He delivers it over to us, and then the man is not himself master of his money, nor his coffer. He can put in, but cannot take out; and at last his own soul is locked up therein. Remember this; and since thou hast gone through thy trial here, take God's key with thee, and try to make use of it, that thou mayest thyself be master of thy money."

Translated by Claud Field.

Other works by Pascheles: *Deutsche Gebete für Frauen* (1828); *Pascheles' illustrierter jüdischer Volkskalender* (from 1852).

Leopold Kompert
1822–1886

Leopold Kompert grew up on the "Gasse"—the one street in small Bohemian towns where Jews were allowed to live. The son of a poor wool merchant in Münchengrätz (Mnichovo Hradiště), he left home at age seventeen, and supported himself as a tutor and journalist while traveling throughout the Austro-Hungarian Empire. Kompert's nostalgic stories of small-town Bohemian Jewish life are foundational texts of the "ghetto fiction" genre, and in his later years he was a significant figure in the Viennese Jewish community.

The Death of the Tavern Keeper's Wife
1848

With every stone that was set in the new barn, another drop of life seemed to ebb from the wife of the *randar* or tavern keeper. When she looked out at the building, she often said that she would not eat the bread that would come from it next summer. Sometimes she was not able to leave her bed for several days. Moritz crept away with tears in his eyes when he saw his mother's debilitating infirmity increase day by day. Pain engulfed his soul.

Meanwhile, the church fair had arrived. The usual preparations were made in the house. The floor was scrubbed, candles were put in the wall sconces and, above all, bottles were filled. Despite his unhappy situation, Moritz could not suppress the thought that his father, a Jew, had to host the celebration of a Christian saint's feast. . . .

The tavern keeper's wife suddenly became critically ill. Her illness has worsened so much that death seemed imminent. The doctor was summoned and in the courtyard the stableboy harnessed the horses to drive to the nearby ghetto to fetch the "devout women" who laid out the dead. Slowly, the shadow of death spread over the house! . . .

Her fight for life lasted all night. Her soul did not want to leave the rooms to which it was so closely attached. But toward morning she became calmer. The women who had prayed with her all night were tired and wanted to sleep briefly. The tavern keeper's wife herself lay in a serene, almost healthy sleep.

In the village the church fair began.

Processions of pilgrims came from all directions. Fluttering red flags preceded them. The music started, and from the house one could plainly hear the first strains of the choir leaders clashing with the singing of the people. At the same time, the bells rang and salutes were fired. The hills and valleys seemed drunk with life. Everything seemed to lift its voice to praise the saint. Then the village fell silent. Mass had begun. Occasionally a little bell tinkled, or the congregation's chant swelled like a mighty ocean. The sound of the organ, trumpets, and kettledrums flooded forth as though to prove they were stronger than the feeble human sounds.

It was during one of these moments filled with resounding noise that the tavern keeper's wife awoke from her sleep. She saw only Moritz beside her, sitting with his arms crossed in silent grief by her bed. She called his name softly, startling him.

"There are a lot of things I want to tell you," she began in a weak voice.

Moritz begged her to save her strength.

"One word more or less," she smiled bleakly, "will not stop death. I'd just like to know something."

"What, dear Mother?"

"Whether you'll remain Jewish."

"I swear to you, I will."

It was midday. The sermon was over, and everyone who had come to glorify the saint had been granted absolution. After church they moved to the house of the "Jew," and within seconds the taproom was filled with thirsty guests. There was nothing separating the sacred and the profane any more. It seemed as if the priest and the tavern keeper held the fair at each end; the morning belonged to the former, and the much more important afternoon to the latter.

At first the tavern keeper had decided to stop the celebration. He did not want to let anyone enter his house while his wife was dying. But his resistance was too weak to stand up to the people excited by wine, prayer, and sensual enjoyment. He had no choice but, despairingly, to accept the inevitable. Hannele had to tear herself away from her mother's bedside to serve the guests. The tavern keeper went about among them and asked everyone to be quiet, but in the frenzy and the pleasure of the moment his plea went unheeded.

And then the band arrived. The tavern keeper had booked it some days before; now he did not want it to play. But the musicians had already entered the room, and the village magistrate's son, wild young Pavel, called, "Strike up!" and threw them several twenties. The tavern keeper grew angry and shouted, "I won't allow it!" But Pavel repeated his request for a dance tune and pushed the burly man aside. The mighty trumpet was the first to attempt opposition; it began to play through all the talk. The fiddles, double bass, and clarinets followed hesitantly. Finally, all the instruments were playing in harmony, and wild young Pavel led off the dancing.

Moritz had not left his mother's bedside, and dark curses involuntarily entered his mind between tears and prayers. He cursed his father's profession, which would not let his mother die in peace. It seemed so terrible that his mother had to depart this life amid the sounds of excited passions. . . .

The wailing of the father and the servants could be heard through the noise of music and fighting. By the time the daughter Hannele entered the room, the tavern keeper's wife was already dead. The "devout women" were making preparations to lay her out.

The tavern keeper now felt an enormous strength within himself, enough to break up the fair. Blood had already been spilled, for Pavel's temple had been cut by a heavy beer mug. Now it was easier to persuade the others. The music ceased, the room emptied gradually.

The deceased could rest in peace.

Translated by Wilma Abeles Iggers, Káča Poláčková-Henley, and Kathrine Talbot.

Other works by Kompert: *Aus dem Ghetto: Geschichten* (1848); *Am Pflug* (1855); *Zwischen Ruinen* (1875).

Auguste Widal (Daniel Stauben)
1822–1875

Auguste Widal's fictional accounts of trips to his native Alsace are early French examples of the immensely popular genre of "ghetto fiction." His picturesque descriptions of the customs and traditions of small-town Alsatian Jews helped popularize ghetto nostalgia, as did his translations of the works of his Czech contemporary Leopold Kompert. A classicist, Widal wrote under the pseudonym Daniel Stauben, perhaps to preserve his somewhat precarious position as one of the few Jews teaching in French universities at this time. In 1873 he was appointed inspector general for French primary and secondary schools.

Scenes of Jewish Life in Alsace
1849–1853

After an absence of many years, I returned to Alsace in November 1856, in response to the invitation of an old friend. During this first and short visit, I was greatly moved in recovering all the familiar village scenes which I had known since my most tender age. By chance, I was also lucky to meet some extraordinary Jewish characters and to participate in a number of solemnities. The Friday night and Sabbath celebration was followed by a wedding, and then by a funeral; events which I have faithfully recorded as they occurred, with no additions of my own.

The village of Bollwiller near Mulhouse harbors a sizable Jewish population. It is the home of my host, père Salomon, a handsome old man with a good-natured, fine face. I left Mulhouse for Bollwiller on a Friday afternoon, to arrive around four o'clock, so as not to disturb the preparations for Sabbath which, for a Jewish woman, are a double chore. Since one is not allowed to cook on holidays, she must prepare the meals for Saturday as well. All work stops at sunset, and with it the one rare and peaceful break of the week begins, the Sabbath, when all worries and humdrum preoccupations are cast aside, and everyone is cheerful and relaxed. Even the poorest peddler drops stick and pack to have a slice of *barches* (white twisted bread), a glass of wine, and a small piece of meat or fish. Stretching his tired limbs as he sits on the door-step in his clean shirt in summer, and near the hot stove in a warm cap and jacket in winter, this poorest of the poor would not, at such a moment, change his existence for a kingdom.

I reached Bollwiller just as everyone was getting ready for synagogue; mothers and daughters dressing up after a day's work in the kitchen, and fathers all set to go, preparing wicks for the seven-branched Sabbath lamps, while waiting for the ladies.

As I was walking down the street, I saw many such lamps through the windows. Then, suddenly, a man appeared and, with a big wooden hammer, he started knocking at doors, gates and shutters. It was the *Schule-Klopfer* (synagogue convoker) in full regalia calling the congregation to the services. No church bell could have been more effective. Men and women were promptly pouring into the streets to go to synagogue in their Sabbath fineries. The men were wearing black, bulky trousers reaching down to shiny boots, heavy, short-waisted blue frock coats with very large lapels and cuffs, and their hats were wider on top than at the bottom. The huge collars of their coarse, though meticulously white, shirts hid their faces, and were so stiff that the poor fellows could not turn their heads without contortions. Women in dark dresses had red and green leaf-patterned scarves over their shoulders and red-ribboned tulle bonnets to cover their hair. Each held a prayer-book clasped proudly against her stomach, showing off the magnificent green leather binding of her Rödelheim [noted imprint in Germany] edition.

I soon found myself alone in the street. Afraid of being late, I rushed toward the synagogue, and saw my host come down its steps with a most cordial "*solem alechem.*" Seeing my embarrassment, he reassured me that I was not late. "Knowing you were on the way, my dear Parisian," he said, "I have asked our cantor to hold his *Boi Besolem* for a few moments until your arrival." This courtesy was very touching, and I thanked him for it.

Père Salomon's home, like all others of that region, is divided between the business quarters on the ground floor and the family apartment one flight up. A steep, narrow staircase, lit by an iron lamp bracket, took us to the flat, with a *mezuzah* on the doorframe. My hostess was there to greet me, surrounded by her children, two pretty dark-haired girls with big brown eyes, and three husky boys. They all received me laughingly, as it the custom in Alsatian villages where many do not speak a perfect French, and thus try to hide their self-consciousness behind a cheerful front. But since I pride myself on knowing our Alsatian-Jewish dialect, so picturesque with all its fine contortions and deviations, I quickly put them all at ease.

While the rest of the family was listening with rapt attention to père Salomon and his sons singing the *Malke Solem*, my eyes were wandering around the room, embracing with delight all the familiar objects which can be found in almost every well-to-do Jewish home; objects I had grown up with, and which had kept their primitive simplicity: the indispensable seven-branched lamp hanging from the ceiling, the red embroidered Persian tapestry over two *barches* on the table, and on a chest reserved for ritual objects and talmudic books, a red copper water jug in a basin. On the Eastern wall a framed white sheet of paper with the Hebrew word *Mizrach* (East) indicated to strangers the direction to face when addressing the Almighty. Next to it were two engravings, one of Moses holding in his right hand the Ten Commandments and in his left hand a staff; the other of the High Priest Aaron wearing a pontifical turban, a *choshen* and an *ephod* (breast-plate and apron). The huge head of a stag above a small mirror carried, alternatively, the master's hat when he was in, or his skull cap when he was out of doors.

After the succulent meal of Jewish Alsatian dishes, preceded and followed by prayers, père Salomon told me of his nephew's wedding on the following Wednesday. The son of his brother Yekel was to marry the daughter of the *parness* of Wintzenheim, a village near Colmar.

"My brother will personally invite you to the wedding," said my host. "Tonight though, in your honor, I've planned for us to stay at home around the fire to listen to the stories of our friend Reb Samuel. He often comes to us on Friday night. Does he know stories! Just ask my wife and children. The things he reads, the things he remembers about legends, adventures, witchcraft! You name it! I hope you have not lost your taste for this sort of things, dear Sir. And above all, do me one favor, please. You Parisians may not believe in supernatural matters. That's your good right, of course. But should Reb Samuel tell such a story tonight, I beg you not to show your incredulity, or he may stop and be offended. In his own way, he is quite proud."

At that very moment, we heard some heavy steps outside and, without knocking, in came Reb Samuel with a hearty "A good Shabbes to all of you!" He was a man of about fifty, with an intelligent, somewhat plumpish face framed by a pair of bushy whiskers; a typical rural character as one often sees them in our Alsatian countryside. This worthy neighbour of père Salomon is a Jack-of-all-trades, performing with equal fervor and success the most diverse and delicate functions. He assists the cantor of the synagogue, serves as male nurse, barber, matchmaker, and general factotum, besides being a story teller.

The newcomer, self-assured and at home, installed himself quite naturally next to the master of the house. "Samuel," said my host without preamble, "since it is Friday night and we cannot play cards, you'll tell us one of your stories. But a real good one that will please our friend from Paris."

Samuel nodded at me without touching his hat. "As you know," he answered, "I don't have to be urged. Just let me think. What shall I tell you?"

The whole clan immediately assaulted him with wishes and suggestions. The mistress of the house asked for the legend about the Queen of Sheba who, it was said, had come to Bollwiller once after midnight, riding a golden chariot without harness, and wearing a white gown, her hair let down and fluttering in the wind.

Her two daughters wished to hear the tragic story about little Rebecca and how she died from a shock after she ventured, on a Saturday, to look out of her little kitchen window, and saw the *Mohkalb* crouching under a stone and howling.

The sons of my host opted for the adventures of old Jacob who had gone astray on his way to the market of St. Dié. After erring about all night, he found himself at three o'clock in the morning back at the very spot from where he had started out the previous evening. There he was haunted by a horde of *fiery men* (ghosts) who followed him to his house, leaving the imprints of their burning hands on his door, like a sinister threat.

Père Salomon, last but not least, would have preferred a story about Nathan the Devil. He was the terror and scandal of the pious community of Grusenheim. Thanks to his pact with hell, and in front of everybody, he would ring chimes in his attick, pour mysterious letters from all ceilings, and conjure up blazing flames to come through the walls of his parlor without burning him or anything around him.

"You have heard all this already," said Samuel, giving himself some airs. "Today I will tell you a story no one has ever told before. As a matter of fact, I must ask you to keep it strictly to yourself, so as not to attract the evil spirit."

My host passed him a glass of wine. "Before you begin," he said, "I want you and our Parisian gentleman to drink to each other's health."

Then he addressed the mistress of the house: "Yedele," he said, "tell the *Shabbes goye* to add some oil to all the lamps, to rearrange the wicks, and stir the fire." When all was done, he finally reclined, and turning towards Samuel, asked him to start his story.

Translated by Rose Choron.

Other works by Widal (Stauben): *Études sur trois tragédies de Sénèque imitees d'Euripide* (1854); *Juvénal et ses satires; études littéraires et morales* (1870).

Abraham Mapu
1808–1867

Abraham (Avraham) Mapu, the first Hebrew novelist, was born in Slobodka near Kovno and was known as a brilliant Talmud scholar. He studied Latin, modern languages and literature, and Hebrew grammar on his own. While living apart from his family and working as a tutor, he began following the Haskalah, becoming one of its major figures in Eastern Europe due to his popular and widely translated novels. His fiction combined European romanticism with works set in ancient Israel, influencing both maskilic writers and Zionists. Mapu also wrote several language textbooks. In his later years he struggled with poverty, infirmity, and censorship.

The Love of Zion
1853

Azrikam grew in his father's house like a thorn, becoming uglier as he grew. Tamar, however, grew more beautiful day by day. The contrast between these two children was not only noticeable in their looks but also in their actions. While Tamar was all that was good and noble, sweet and gentle, Azrikam was cruel, quarrelsome and disagreeable; he was unkind to his servants and would not stretch out a helping hand to the poor and needy. Tamar was kind to her servants and ever ready to comfort the sick and help the poor. Azrikam continually bragged of his birth and looked down upon those who were not of noble birth and not as wealthy as he; but Tamar was meek and gentle with her mates and associated even with the poorest of them. Azrikam was like a wooden image that had to be bedecked with gold and jewels to make it look presentable; Tamar on the other hand was like a sapphire set in gold, which did not increase the value of the jewel but only enhanced its beauty. At the age of sixteen, Azrikam was still of small stature and was peculiarly built. His head was small and set deeply between his shoulders. He had red hair and his face was covered with freckles. Tamar was like a rose in her beauty, and when she was sixteen she was a woman, both in looks and actions. She was not only a joy to her parents but was loved by everyone with whom she came in contact. She and Azrikam were as different from each other as day is from night.

There would have been no thought of uniting these two had not Yedidiah wished to fulfill his promise to Yoram. He refused, therefore, to listen to all the suitors for Tamar's hand.

Tirzah kept her father's letter, and Tamar, finding it one day, read its contents. She mused over the dream of her grandfather, and the more she pondered over it, the dearer the vision of the youth became to her. He was continually in her thoughts by day, and at night she saw him in her dreams. She had studied the description of the youth in the letter so carefully that she could see him in her mind's eye. Tamar came to love this lad of her dreams, and the more she saw Azrikam the more she came to despise him, and she shuddered when he approached. Her whole mind was intent upon her dream-lad and no one else could please her.

Azrikam noticed Tamar's aversion and ascribed it to the reading of Hananeel's letter. Azrikam was in despair, and calling Zimri to his house said to him, "Look here, you have turned Tamar's heart away from me through the letter you bought from Hananeel. She despises me and thinks only of the youth that her grandfather saw in his dream. You unwittingly wronged me; therefore, you must use your wit and your wisdom to remedy it. I will reward you generously."

"I know," said Zimri, "that Tamar is dearer to you than all the treasures, and I also know that her heart is far away from you and that with no wealth can you buy it. But anything can be done with scheming; without money, however, you cannot scheme. Therefore, if you will open your purse, I am ready to be your accomplice and supply you with my advice. Wait for me three days, and in that time I will devise some plan of action."

After three days Azrikam inquired of Zimri what plan he had made, and Zimri answered: "The first thing you must do is to put your confidence in me. Make Tamar disbelieve the reality of this dream, which is the cause of her aversion to you. Then I will try to bring her affections back to you. Now, give me three hundred shekels for the one who will accomplish our purpose; I assure you I will succeed."

"You know," said Azrikam, "money is dear to me, but Tamar is dearer. Tenfold the amount you shall receive from me when you fulfill your promise."

Translated by Joseph Marymount.

Other works by Mapu: *Ashmat shomron* (1865); *Amon pedagog* (1867).

Ludwig Philippson
1811–1898

A writer and rabbi from a family of rabbis and writers, Ludwig Philippson published biblical translations, philosophical commentaries, poetry, and fiction. In 1837, he founded the *Allgemeine Zeitung des Judentums* (Journal of Judaism) billed as a "nonpartisan organ for all Jewish interests." In response to the political turmoil of 1848, Philippson advocated for moderate liberalism and became a leader of Saxony's Social Reform Party. Later in life he published a German translation of the Hebrew Bible with controversial illustrations by the French artist Gustave Doré.

The Three Brothers
1854

"Back at home, I pulled myself together and reflected on what had happened. Given how the people had behaved when they heard the wrongheaded and hateful rabbi's curse of excommunication, I realized that I could only continue my lectures if something were done explicitly to redress what had happened. But was this really to be expected? There weren't enough Spaniards for me to lecture just to them. And who was the one who dealt me this blow? The father of my future wife! Could this have happened without the firm intent to destroy the bond that connected me to him? The more I thought about what the angry rabbi had said, the more I became sure of it. Both my honor and my love were about to become the casualties of a shipwreck caused by the folly of a wounded spirit who could not bear being challenged. I couldn't make sense of all this. But when a courier came and handed me a letter that had been composed the day before, on Friday, things began to make more sense. The letter contained the final words of the rabbi's sermon and his signature, nothing else. This little man had carefully thought through his maneuvers. Everything he did had been prepared in advance!

"I was outraged. I felt I had only one choice, to publish an open letter to the man who had hurled the curse of excommunication at me. I would publicly accuse him of the crudest ignorance and claim that he was not capable of occupying a rabbi's post with honor. I had plenty of proof for this. I would also challenge him to a public disputation and invite him to have a tribunal of other rabbis judge our case. I had resolved to take this route. But how did Dina feel about all this? Hadn't she also already destroyed the bonds that connected her to me? I spent an entire day in unspeakable anguish. No one came by. But then I pulled myself together. I paid a visit to my bride's aunt, who had always been good to me. She took me in, and what is more, she accepted me with tears and deep pain. She was a woman full of proper feeling. She recognized what had motivated her brother-in-law's actions, and she did not just assume that he was mistaken. She knew he was going after me intentionally. But this was bitter consolation for me. She acquainted me with the pitiful situation in which Dina and her good mother found themselves. Dina was caught between her love for her fiancé and her father's threat of excommunication. What could she do? She was suffering so under this cruelty. I asked the aunt whether I might have an audience with Dina in her home, and she agreed.

"We met at dusk in the honorable woman's home. I had forged and hatched so many plans by then. It was a painful reunion. For a long time, Dina lay at my breast without being able to compose herself. She apologized for her father, who had behaved so poorly toward the homeless stranger in their midst and who had chosen such an awful way to show his gratitude to the man who saved his wife and child. She assured me of her deep and eternal love for me. The girl's desperation brought me to my senses. I spoke clearly and simply to her. Either she could honor the sacred vow she had made and go with me, or she could respect her father's orders and we would have to go our separate ways. There was no third choice, I explained, and it was time to make a decision. I could not remain any longer in this town, where I had had such sweet but also such bitter experiences. She understood what I was saying, but what could she do? She threw herself again into my arms, saying she could not leave me and did not want for us to be apart. We were still deep in conversation thinking things through and reassuring each other when we heard a screeching voice coming after us with execrations and threats. Somehow the old rabbi had learned of our meeting. He grabbed his daughter with arms of iron and took her away. He would not listen to my objections and my words of wrath. And Dina! The presence of her father broke her courage. I left."

Translated by Jonathan M. Hess.

Other works by Philippson: *Saron* (1843); *Die israelitische Bibel* (1858).

Abraham Mapu

The Hypocrite
1857–1864

After finishing the letter, Elisheva handed it back to Hogeh and gracefully added: "Would that letters such as this might appear more often in our literature! For only such refinement of language will teach the youth of Israel good taste and fine understanding, and inspire their minds. But not so the harsh style which ruins the taste of the learned, and robs the language of its beauty. Azriel writes in an exalted style and the words of his letter might well be counted among the holy things of Israel."

"The holy things of Israel?" replied Shubal indignantly. "It is not for women to declare what is good or what is holy. Such judgements can be given only by the pious men of the community, and they pour out their wrath against these refined and polished writings, condemning both the literary gems and their noisy authors equally to perdition. Yet you, Elisheva, declare that they may be counted among the holy things of Israel. Who then is destroying holiness with worthless phrases?"

"What is all this quarrelling?" the old man asked.

"It is no quarrel," Shubal replied. "But a slip of the tongue. Your daughter erred in thinking that fine language might be counted among the holy things of Israel, while I condemned all such authors and everything to do with them out of hand."

"Why do you persecute them so relentlessly?" replied Yair. "Once you defended them. Have you changed so much that you can cruelly assign them all to hell? Do you not hear their bitter cries?"

"Even from the depths of hell they would still cry out in elegant phrases!" Shubal retorted caustically. "Nor will they be there alone, for those who honour them, will accompany them down. But why should I joke about things which are so serious? In my youth I toyed with their glowing coals, and so scorched my fingers that even today I feel the scars. All who look for righteousness in them are deluded; for their fine words are like deadly flies that hover boldly about the flowers of paradise, daring even to penetrate the sanctuary and pollute the fragrant oil. They are saturated with lies, they shoot out their lips against both God and man, and tear out holy ideas root and branch, leaving not a shred, and rejecting them utterly. But what I always say to these slanderers is this: Do not malign in secret, but bring forth your arguments, and show them squarely to our brethren who remain faithful to Israel. Put them before us naked, without shrouding their faces in a mantle of righteousness, as Azriel has done in this letter. Then they can see their nakedness and be ashamed. For even Azriel covers himself with fig leaves which he has sewn together in this letter, and the secrets of ancient days he has moulded into a healing salve to hide the truth."

Translated by Joseph Marymount.

Salomon Formstecher
1808–1889

Salomon Formstecher was among the first generation of university-trained rabbis in Germany. In his influential reformist work *Religion des Geistes* (Religion of the Spirit, 1841), he attempted a systematized, modern explanation of Jewish thought. His efforts to harmonize Jewish religious and social life with modern society included his work as editor of *Der Freitagabend: Eine Familienschrift*, which published popular literature on Jewish themes. Formstecher served his native community of Offenbach am Main as chief rabbi for nearly fifty years.

The Stolen Son: A Contemporary Tale
1859

VI. The Confession

The Israelites spent the rest of the day celebrating this festival of thanksgiving in their homes as a second Purim, with tears of sadness and joy, and by the time the sun set, the Jewish quarter was permeated by this mood of bliss. That evening the rabbi and his wife were entertaining several friends in their home, and here too the atmosphere was one of religious elation. Outside, the weather was harsh and a storm was raging, with the mix of rain and snow showers that was typical for April. Inside the rabbi's well-heated home, however, the conversation was cozy and warm. Someone had just told an amusing anecdote when the maid came in and announced to the rabbi's wife that an unknown man had come to speak to the rabbi. The hospitable old man did not like to leave his cheerful surroundings. Just a moment later he returned to his company, however, reassuring them that he would be back as soon as he had the chance to have a brief conversation with the stranger who had come by. He then made his way to his study, a room that was dimly lit by a covered lamp; once there, he started to help his guest take off his wet coat. Suddenly he exclaimed, "Dr. Basilides! What brings you, Reverend Father, to my home, so late and in such stormy weather? To what do I owe this great honor?"

"The reason why I'm coming to you so late and hidden in my coat like this, venerable rabbi, is that I am no longer a 'reverend father.' The monastery officials have excommunicated me. They have publicly declared me a renegade son of the holy order and a traitor. That's why I have to remain in hiding. I creep through secluded streets at night so as not to incite the mob's anger. And why am I being so impertinent as to take you away from your family now? There's a request I would like to make of you. I would like you to tell me, namely, under what conditions I can enter the covenant of the Israelite religion."

Aghast at this statement, the rabbi quickly rose up from his armchair and exclaimed, "Are you trying to create even more hardship for us, when the wounds of the calamity we've just escaped from haven't even yet scarred over? Think of all the people who hate us. Once they decide that we caused a friar to convert to our religion, they will only persecute us with renewed anger. Yes, the state authorities themselves would punish us, perhaps even drive us out of the country. You've probably not thought through this decision of yours thoroughly. Perhaps you're just trying to convince us how much you care about what has happened to us. Remain true to your paternal faith, for according to the teachings of our sages the pious of all nations have a share in the world to come. You can find the grace of God and eternal bliss through your own faith."

"No, honored rabbi, I have no choice. I owe the world a public declaration of the religion that I carry in my heart."

"This isn't necessary," the rabbi pointed out once again. "You are only accountable to the eternal one for what you believe and feel. And why would you want to submit yourself to all those difficult religious laws? You're not obligated to follow them by birth."

"Well, now you must learn my secret," the doctor responded. "I was born a Jew, thus according to my ancestry I am your coreligionist."

Once again the rabbi got up from his chair in shock. He entreated the doctor to share with him all the details of his life secret.

"Certainly, but that will have to wait for another occasion," the doctor responded. "I've already kept you longer than I should today, and you should return to your family."

"I shall hurry back to them," the rabbi responded, "but only to tell them that our conversation will go on for longer than I originally anticipated. Then you shall unfold your entire life's story for me. And don't think about giving me anything less than a full report, I'm always in this room well past midnight."

Soon the elderly man returned from his adoring family and sat back down with youthful swiftness, eager to listen to Dr. Basilides, who told him the following: "You know that Dr. Apollonios, of blessed memory, raised me with all the care of a loving father. It was in my arms that his soul passed away into the hereafter. Before he left this earth, he entrusted me with a holy relic, a hidden black box in which much to my surprise I found an incredibly detailed diary he had kept. This life chronicle of that noble man did not only paint a picture of *his* existence on this earth. It also shed light on mine. Yes, I could see that this work was written especially for me. For at many times there would be several pages in a row that addressed me affectionately, speaking of the supreme truths to be known and felt. When I now read these speeches directed at me, I hear the voice of the spirit of my departed friend speaking to me from the peaceful world of the heavenly hereafter.

As for my life story, I learned that it is much richer than I could have imagined. But I'll skip over all the unessential events to sketch out for you just its general contours. In M——, the important Russian commercial town, there was a man named Samuel Rabbinowicz who enjoyed domestic bliss alongside his faithful and dearly beloved wife, Rachel. This honest couple—my parents—worked hard and managed to secure a fine livelihood for themselves, and there was no other wish in their hearts than to be able to enjoy the joys of parenthood. It was I who was supposed to bring them this joy in the sixth year of their marriage, for this is when I was born, their little son, Raphael. I remained the only child of these joyful parents, and I had all the parental care and tender maternal love in the world to show for it. They hired a nurse for me, to look after me, and they compensated her well. They intentionally hired a Christian woman so that someone could prepare food for me on the Sabbath. To the joy and delight of my happy parents, I grew big and strong. When I was three years old, however, a treacherous case of scarlet fever confined me to bed. My parents' family doctor, Dr. Leander, did everything in his power to strengthen the little flame of life that was quivering weakly at the wick. But to no avail. My fearful parents donated significant alms to the most needy to buy my young life, but this too was in vain. The weak little spark of life in me was glowing more feebly every day. My mother was worn out and she took to desperate measures. She made a vow to fast for two days straight, and she fulfilled her scared oath with steadfast resolve. On the second evening, lo and behold, she had just said a devout prayer to end her solemn fasting and was about to eat some bread and drink some water when my burning fever finally broke. At last, I broke out in a sweat, as they had been hoping for for so long. I recovered my childlike vitality, and my health improved from day to day. My dear mother was comforted by her conviction that her pious fasting had stolen me out of the arms of the angel of death. A rapidly as children's health can deteriorate, children often recover just as quickly, and after several months I was once again able truly to enjoy life. Once again, my father happily placed his hands in blessing on my head with its black locks of hair on the Sabbath. My mother's gaze was even more drunk with bliss than before when she would stare at me, saying, 'This is the boy I prayed for.' But alas, the higher mortals climb up the mountain of happiness, the more easily this bliss can break into smithereens when nefarious hands conspire to hurl it into shallow waters. It was the evening of the Day of Atonement, and after a long day of fasting and praying, my parents were returning home from synagogue. They expected to come home to find their chipper Raphael, holding his nurse's hand, jumping out to meet them with joy, as he always did. Much to their surprise, they saw that there were no lights burning in their home, and the front door of the house was locked. They knocked, they called out, they screamed, and they ran around in desperation. None of the neighbors could provide them with any information about the whereabouts of their son and his nurse. Finally, the postman joined the crowd in front of their house. This man, who was well known in my parents' house, told them that that afternoon he had seen Ursula traveling off in a mail coach with little Raphael and a suitcase. In the meantime, my parents had managed to get a locksmith to open the door. On the table they found a note that Ursula had written. Its content was as follows:

"'By the time you return home this evening, I will be far away from you, and I will have taken Raphael, the son who was yours, with me. From now on, his name will be Christopher, and it is my intent that he be brought up in a monastery as a pious Christian. When your son was sick, I was concerned for his good soul. Worried that he would die and enter into eternal damnation, I sat at his bedside crying. But then I convinced a pious Christian man, who happened to be sitting alone with me, to baptize the child quickly so that his soul could be saved for heaven; it had already been lost for earth. This God-fearing man—I am bound by an oath not to reveal his name—completed the holy baptism according to protocol, and with this act your son was taken into the fold of the Holy Church. The good Lord soon brought him back to health, for he wanted your son to live and act on this earth as a Christian, and it was thus for me a sacred duty to have him raised as a Christian. Do not bother looking for me or for the dear Christopher, for other than that man who baptized him there is no one on earth who knows where I am going with the child. But do not be worried, you should know that the young Christian boy will be raised conscientiously and will be made to fear God. One day he will pray for you. Your servant, Ursula.'"

Translated by Jonathan Hess.

Other work by Formstecher: *Buchenstein und Cohnberg* (1863).

Osip Rabinovich
1817–1869

Born into a prominent Russified family in Ukraine, Osip Rabinovich was an important early writer on Jewish themes in the Russian language. Moving to Odessa in 1845, Rabinovich worked as a lawyer and writer, contributing essays and short stories to literary journals. In fiction and essays, Rabinovich simultaneously attacked what he saw as Jewish passivity and traditionalism while defending Jewish rights and depicting the cruelties of the tsarist regime. He is perhaps best remembered as the editor of the influential but short-lived journal *Rassvet*, an important organ for promoting Westernization among Russia's Jews. While he wrote little after the journal was forced to close in 1861, a three-volume edition of his collected works was published in St. Petersburg and Odessa in 1880–1888.

The Penal Recruit
1859

"One morning—it was the fourth day of Hanukkah (the holiday of the Maccabees), when we were readying ourselves to celebrate the victory of our heroic ancestors, which was the capture of Antioch—the sound of many bells rang out through the town. Our hearts sank. Government officials came from the provincial and district recruitment offices. A detachment of armed soldiers entered the town. A few troika carriages rode straight to the synagogue. Our people were herded to the synagogue like sheep. They drove the old and young, women and children, drove everyone with their rifle butts. They ordered the entire population of the town to gather together. We, *kahal* representatives, tax collectors, and elders, all those who held a position, were immediately placed in chains and pushed along with everyone else. A lot of people were collected. Not only were the men's and women's sections filled, but so was the entire courtyard and street in front of the synagogue. An official stepped onto the podium and began to read from a piece of paper. He read for a long time and berated us for persistently disobeying the government. When he finished reading, he began to curse us. He abused everyone, everyone without distinction. Everyone silently listened with anxiety and trepidation. But when in conclusion he yelled out threateningly, 'You've picked the wrong people to trifle with! You know, you contemptuous and insignificant people, that in an instant we can wipe you from the face of the earth, crush you underfoot like a foul worm!'—when he pronounced these words, loud weeping broke out from the listeners' breasts. And those who were in the courtyard and those in the street, hearing the sobs of their brothers in the synagogue, also began to weep, having a premonition of something terrible. Shrieks filled the air. It was terrible to see how the entire population sobbed controllably. It seemed that the deaf walls of the houses were also ready to break out in tears. [. . .]

"But here I am, you see, I have not gone crazy, and I'm still alive," he continued after a short silence and as though responding to my hidden thought. "I am a useless vessel, a broken dish, and must endure all the torments of a mind that has not become muddled; but *she*, such a beautiful and innocent girl, who had just begun to blossom, had to say goodbye to her dreams and hopes. . . . What can one do? God is just. He gave and He took away, let His name be blessed!"

"So what happened then?" I asked, seeing that he had calmed down a bit.

"What could happen then?" he responded bitterly. "Wasn't this alone enough for me? I was sent far to the north; there I spent several months. With the help of good people I was later transferred to the garrison here and given good recommendations. With the help of these same people, my business was properly closed down, since my misfortune came upon me suddenly and my affairs were in disorder. Whatever could be collected from my property and whatever remained after my wife's last large expenditures and theft by various clerks they turned into cash and transferred into trustworthy hands. They assigned an old female relative to care for my youngest daughter and from the interest on the money give her enough for her needs. My eldest daughter, as I was informed in the letter, is at death's door in a hospital in the provincial capital. I pray to heaven to take her away quickly. I am also often sent money here, and for that reason I don't lack for funds; anyway I don't need much here. The officers treat me well. They allow me to rent an apartment and are not too concerned with the service. Let God, the patron of all unfortunates, give them their due. They are respectful toward me, the senior officials that is. The younger ones sometimes give me trouble, although I know what I have to do and to whom I should give my offerings. Anyway, nothing can be done, I endure. Sometimes I even become energetic and reconcile myself to my situation, but this does not last long. The thought of my unfortunate child, the only dear being who is left to me, torments me constantly. The girl is growing up, developing . . . what is going to happen to her, an orphan, without a mother, twelve hundred versts away from me!"

He dropped his head onto his chest and yielded to his heavy sorrow. For a long time I walked back and forth in the room, at times glancing at the penal recruit. He continued to sit in the same position and seemed to have forgotten entirely about my presence. I came up to the window and opened it. The summer evening was at the height of its charming beauty. In the dark-blue sky full of millions of stars, now sparkling with brilliant blinding light, now barely glimmering as though shaking in the unimaginable distance, there swam a barely visible full moon, which gave off a pale, calming light. The town was long since asleep. Everything in nature was quiet and triumphal.

I approached the old man and placed my hand on his shoulder. He got up. I took his hand and led him over to the window.

"Look how beautiful everything is here," I said to him. "Is even this not capable of consoling you?"

"You are speaking of the beauty of nature," he answered, "and asking whether it consoles me. No . . . You are young, you have still not encountered misfortune. Your eyes perceive differently and send their impressions to your heart in a different way. I was young, too, and I looked at the world and nature differently then . . . but not now, I remember," he added, pointing at the horizon, "I remember that there should be happiness and brightness here, but my eyes don't see it, and my heart doesn't feel it. The sky is dressed in the colors of mourning, the moon is a funeral candle for me, the stars seem to me open gaping ulcers on a tormented body from which blood is about to start pouring out, and the trees seem to be whispering about the horrors that occur in silence . . . No, whatever is visible is black for me, and what is *beyond*, what is ahead, what is invisible to my earthly eyes, what is covered by mystery of all of us—that is what consoles me. *There*, beyond what appears to you as bright images, beyond what appears to me as dark ghosts, *there*, where thought does not dare to reach—there it is, my consolation."

Translated by Brian Horowitz.

Other works by Rabinovich: *Morits Sefardi* (1850); *Kaleidoscope* (1860).

Alexandre Weill

1811–1899

Born in Alsace, Alexandre Weill is said to have been destined for a rabbinical career. Instead, he abandoned his studies in Frankfurt and moved to Paris, where he was quickly received in the literary and journalistic scenes, thanks to a letter of introduction from Jewish-born German author Heinrich Heine. A natural polemicist, Weill wrote countless articles and pamphlets on the topics of his day, which were published in French and German newspapers as well as Jewish journals. In addition to these commentaries, he also wrote widely on religious and historical subjects.

Braendel
1860

IX

[. . .] Braendel dragged the poor woman into the smoky room, which stank of sweat, beer, and wine, and cried out in a loud voice, "Aren't you ashamed, you children of honest Jews, to drink and dance when one of you, the best of you, is missing and nobody knows what has become of him?"

"Well then, here is the prophetess who is going to give us a sermon," exclaimed a lad with outstretched arms. "Let her marry her Joël and be done with it. I don't know if he's good student, but he's certainly a poor horseman and as an infantryman he's not worth five hundred francs."

"For you, Dotter, who weigh men on scales," responded Braendel, "you certainly tell the truth, since you're the heaviest boy in the village." Then, turning to the others: "Who among you saw Joël in Haguenau?"

"Didn't Joël come back from the market?" they asked each other.

"Clearly nobody saw him," responded the distressed mother. "You have to go look for him, my children."

"I'm pretty sure," said a young girl, "that Lemah the Redhead gave me pralines and said that they came from Joël."

"You wretch!" Braendel cried out, dragging Lemah out of the corner. "You saw Joël in Haguenau?"

"Yes," groaned the drunkard.

"Where did you leave him?"

"In the forest."

"In the forest!" exclaimed several voices. "And you didn't help him?"

"Let Braendel go help him," mumbled the calf merchant. "He's lying near Croix-Neuve."

"Keep an eye on that man!" cried Braendel. "Eight days ago, when I saw him at the little fountain, he said he would play a nasty trick on Joël."

"What did you do to Joël?" exclaimed twenty voices! And twenty arms came down on Lemah's head.

"Is it any of your business?"

"Lemah," said the fat Dotter, gripping him by the throat. "Tell us right away where Joël is and what you did to him or five minutes from now you will be a dead man."

These words and gestures little by little sobered up the young man. "I didn't do anything to him," he mumbled. "Let me go, Dotter, I'm not a murderer. I'm not a goy."

"Swear on the name of the Lord that you did him no harm."

"Joël fell," responded Lemah. "He wanted me to carry him on my back. I was too tired. I left him near Croix-Neuve. Then I didn't give him another thought."

"Wretch! Pagan! Barbarian!" exclaimed twenty voices. "You abandoned your brother, a Jew, in distress." And within the blink of an eye, the back that Lemah hadn't wanted to lend to Joël was riddled with blows.

"Mercy! Have mercy!" exclaimed Braendel. "We don't need to punish him. We need to go find Joël. Arise, children of Israel, on your feet. There is a soul to save. Get on your horses and scour the forest."

"Scour the forest!" said Dotter. "It's thirty leagues around and it's black as night. It's midnight."

"If you're too cowardly to venture into the forest, and you should be, then give me a horse and I will go by myself," responded Braendel.

"What a girl! God save her!" said the mother. "With her, God will be on our side."

"She's capable of doing as she says," said a very young man. "However, Braendel, I haven't seen you on horseback for a long time."

"A horse, a horse!" she kept repeating. "Do I have to go to the stable myself and saddle one? Which one of you owns a horse?"

"Monsieur Heiser the mayor has two magnificent stallions," Dotter replied. "Go get them, Braendel."

"Alright then, I'm going. Monsieur the mayor, who is Catholic, has more heart than any of you craven drunkards!" With this, she was off as fast as her legs would carry her, leaving behind Joël's mother and all the young cowards who were still deliberating about what to do to save their friend.

"Bah!" Dotter said. "Joël is sleeping on the grass. Better to wait for day and to bring him home in a carriage."

"It's not very much fun," another said, "to wait at two o'clock in the morning near Croix-Neuve."

"Let's go to bed," said a third. "Joël is probably home by now. Braendel is making up stories. She likes people to talk about her."

"But we can't just go to bed as long as one of us is missing and in mortal danger," added Dotter. "Joël is delicate. Plus he's a *bachor*. If we abandon him, the rabbi will banish us and not one of us will be able to mount the *alménor* (the platform in the synagogue) when it is his turn to be called to say the blessing for the reading of a chapter of the Bible. If we're banned, the young girls will scorn us. Come on, brothers, we have to go look for Joël. But before leaving, let's say a prayer."

At this moment, Braendel passed by like lightning on the mayor's beautiful stallion. She was followed by the younger son of Monsieur Heiser who was mounted on the second stallion.

Braendel, like all the young village girls who work, rode a horse like a boy, which is to say straddling it.

No sooner had he been told what brought Braendel to him than the mayor saddled the horse himself. But full of admiration for the young girl, he ordered one of his sons to follow her and watch out for her.

Ashamed to be surpassed in devotion by a young girl and by a Catholic, the most courageous young Jews also mounted on horseback and took off with lanterns and pine torches.

X

In villages, the relation between man and beast is more intimate than in cities. When an animal distinguishes itself either through beauty or intelligence, the whole village adopts it and sees it as its property. The bay stallion of the mayor was one of these. He was as sweet tempered as he was proud. A child could guide him and ride him. Moreover, he seemed to know all the inhabitants of the village who never passed before him without giving him some friendly caress accompanied by flattering words. Like all intelligent animals, the stallion was an original. This is to say that a few oddities distinguished him from other examples of his species. For example, he hated spurs. A child could mount him easily and make him feed, but the instant a rider with spurs tried to jump on his back he would rear up and jump around until the weary rider got back down again, unless the horse preferred to throw him thirty feet away. The stallion had another trick. Even through his comrade was of the same breed, he made it a point of honor never to be overtaken by him. Harnessed together (which happened rarely), he was always, and no matter how he was attached, two steps ahead of him. Saddled separately, you could never make him walk behind his rival. In one leap, he would take the lead and obstinately keep it.

Braendel had stopped riding at the age of twelve, the time of life when the villagers no longer permit young girls this type of amusement. She therefore had to trust the goodness and the intelligence of the animal whose mane she stroked, saying: "My friend, go to Croix-Neuve." The horse, as if he understood the words of the girl, took off at a gallop. But seeing himself followed by his rival, the gallop quickly turned into a furious race. In the blink of an eye, he was on the way to the forest. At first, Braendel cried with all her might: "Joël! Joël!" but soon the unbridled rapidity of her mount took her breath away. She dug in her heels, leaning her head over the neck of the stallion, who once on his way and feeling himself followed closely by his competition, didn't want to stop. The more Braendel's companion attempted to keep up with her, the more the stallion, fearing he was about to be overtaken, increased his pace.

They were followed, but distantly, by a few other young riders. All of a sudden, a black shadow passed in front of these latter horsemen. A second later, that shadow retraced its steps, stopped and whinnied. It was the bay stallion coming back to look for help.

"The stallion returns alone!" they cried. "Something bad has happened to Braendel!" And they all headed toward the spot from which the horse had come. To be safer, the young people dismounted and led their horses by the bridle, moving forward with caution by the light of their resin torches. They marched like that for a half hour, when fifty feet from Croix-Neuve, they found the unlucky young girl stretched out unconscious by a tree, all bloody. While some of them attempted to bring Braendel back to life, others found the unlucky Joël in the bottom of the ditch into which he had fallen, delirious and calling for Braendel. Alas! The poor girl was barely breathing. It was clear that some essential organ had been bruised. Blood was pouring in torrents out of her nose and mouth. Her chest was covered in blood. It seemed as if she had been thrown and broken in two by a tree.

"I told her," cried the mayor's son, "to let me go alone. She didn't want to. Poor girl!" And the young man burst into sobs.

Next to Joël, they found the package containing the new dress destined for his fiancée. They tore it to bandage Braendel. After this first aid, she was bundled in a coat and placed on a bed of grass and pine branches, next to Joël, whom they had to tie up to keep from thrashing about in his delirium. Then the sad cortège, preceded by funereal torches, set off toward the village.

It is said that bad news travels fast. Perhaps the unexpected return of the stallion had alerted the townspeople that a tragedy had occurred, or perhaps some of the young people had alerted them by their cries, but before the lifeless body of Braendel had entered the village, all the inhabitants, men and women, old people and children, were standing in the street, crying in despair. Some thought that Joël had been devoured by a wolf, others talked of a broken leg. Nobody guessed the terrible truth. When it became known, there was a single cry of sadness.

"The crown of the village has fallen," exclaimed the rabbi. "Let all the Jews put on mourning!" And not only the Jews, but all the Catholics also cried over the premature end of that valiant girl. Only her grandmother was calm, saying: "Whatever God has done is good. Soon, dear soul, your grandmother will join you in paradise. I would have wanted to live to see you have a son who would have walked in the footsteps of our ancestor. But since the Lord above did not want it, let His will be done!"

As for Joël, nobody paid him any attention except his mother. The fever didn't leave him for two days. He was the last one in the village to learn of the death of Braendel.

XI

The following day, all the Jewish women gathered in the house of the dead girl, to make her a wedding dress and to wash her with warm water and lay her out properly. For the Jews wash and dress their dead so that they can appear worthy in front of the King of Kings.

The men assembled at the same time to make the coffin. The Jews always make their coffins themselves, the same for all regardless of fortune or birth. This coffin is composed of six unsanded boards. The next day, they placed the body in the bier without covering it. The Jews claim that the dead person hears everything that is said until the moment when the last nail is hammered into the cover of the coffin. That belief is a guarantee against premature burial. An hour before the body is taken away, all who know the dead person approach, touch the body's toes, and ask for forgiveness for all the offenses that they committed against the person.

Since the cemetery was located in the forest, not very far from Croix-Neuve, they needed a wagon. The mayor of the village offered his, and the stallion was harnessed to it. The poor animal was so sweet and sad that it seemed like he was stricken with regret. A child led him by the bridle. All the inhabitants, without distinction of age or sex, followed the coffin. The Jewish women, however, followed behind, their heads covered in veils as a sign of mourning. At the edge of the village, they stopped the wagon and everyone said a prayer, a sort of *De profundis*, mixed with cries and sobs. All the young people of the village followed Braendel's body all the way to the cemetery.

As for Joël, as soon as he was cured, he left for Metz in order to grant Braendel her final wish. Soon the study of profane subjects shook his Talmudic faith. He almost converted on a few occasions. But the image of Braendel would always appear between his heart and his head. Although he now enjoys a high social position, Joël never forgets, whenever he returns to Alsace, to place a little stone on the tomb of Braendel, his childhood friend. According to Jewish belief, when the soul comes down from on high to glide above the tomb of the body, that little stone announces that a friend has come to visit.

Translated by Maurice Samuels.

Other works by Weill: *Questions brulantes: République et monarchie* (1848); *Histoire de la guerre des anabaptistes* (1874); *Souvenirs intimes de Henri Heine* (1883).

Israel Aksenfeld
1787–1866

Born in Nemirov, Ukraine, Israel (Yisroel) Aksenfeld is considered to be the first novelist in Yiddish. Despite being raised in a prominent Bratslaver Hasidic family, Aksenfeld became a committed *maskil*, promoting the Enlightenment and Westernization of Russian Jewry from the intellectual center of Odessa; he was also an attorney. His Yiddish-language novels and plays emulated the style of Western European genres. While much of his work went unpublished in his lifetime due to tsarist censorship, Aksenfeld succeeded in publishing *Dos shterntikhl (The Headband)* in 1861 in Leipzig. The novel was noteworthy for its blend of satire with thick description of Jewish life in Eastern Europe together with a rich use of authentic Yiddish dialogue. Aksenfeld's dramatic works, few of which have survived, are similarly described by critics as notable for their use of comic, but authentic Yiddish speech within a context of weak narration, thin plotlines, and a tendency toward melodrama. Aksenfeld spent the last year of his life living with his son in Paris.

The Headband
1861

I

Anyone familiar with our Russian Poland knows what Jews mean by a small *shtetl*, a little town.

A small shtetl has a few small cabins, and a fair every other Sunday. The Jews deal in liquor, grain, burlap, or tar. Usually, there's one man striving to be a Hassidic rebbe.

A *shtot*, on the other hand, a town, contains several hundred wooden homes (that's what they call a house: a *home*) and a row of brick shops. There are: a very rich man (a parvenu), several well-to-do storekeepers, a few dealers in fields, hareskins, wax, honey, some big money-lenders, who use cash belonging either to the rich man, going halves on the profits, or to the tenant farmers and tenant innkeepers in the surrounding area. Such a town has a Polish landowner (the *porits*) with his manor. He owns the town and some ten villages, this entire district being known as a *shlisl*. Some prominent Jew, who is held in esteem at the manor, leases the entire town or even the entire district. Such a town also has a Jewish VIP, who is a big shot with the district police chief. Such a town has an intriguer, who is always litigating with the town and the Jewish community administration, even on the level of the provincial government. In such a town, the landowner tries to get a Hassidic rebbe to take up residence, because if Jews come to him from all over, you can sell them vodka, ale, and mead. All these goods belong to the landowner, and so up goes his income. Such a town has a winehouse keeper, a watchmaker, and a doctor, a past cantor and a present cantor, a broker, a madman, and an abandoned wife (an *agunah*), community beadles, and a caterer. Such a town has tailors' association, a burial association, a Talmud association, and a free-loan association. Such a town has various kinds of synagogues: a *shul* (mainly for the Sabbath and holidays), a *bes-medresh* (the house of study, for everyday use), and sometimes even a *klaizl* (a smaller house of worship) or a *shtibl* (a small Hassidic synagogue). God forbid that anyone should accidently blurt out the wrong word and call the town a *shtetl*! He'll instantly be branded as the local smartass or madman.

A town is called a *big town* if there are a couple of thousand householders and a few brick buildings aside from the wooden homes. This is a horse of a different color. Here, everyone boasts that he greeted someone from the next street because he mistook him for an out-of-towner. After all: In such a big town like this, how can you tell if a stranger is a local? There are tons of people whom you don't know from Adam. [. . .]

In a town like Nosuchville, who isn't doing well? Only the bes-medresh beadle, the shul beadle or the community beadles aren't so well off, because ever since the Hassidim came along, the Cold Shul has remained empty. At Rosh Hashanah (New Year's) and Yom Kippur (Day of Atonement), the tenant farmers come from the countryside with their wives and children to pray in the shul. But the rest of the year, you'll hardly ever see the *minyan*, the quorum of ten men, there. They have to rely on the "ten idlers," the ten pious men maintained by a congregation to ensure a minyan. Hence, the standing joke: "Who goes to shul? The rain, because the roof is full of holes." But no worshipers go to the shul. [. . .]

V

Rabbi N., the rabbi's son, who had come to Nosuchville to make money, knew nothing of the Talmud or the talmudic literature. Since his father was a scholar, the son hadn't wanted to study in his boyhood, and so he knew absolutely nothing, poor man. And he knew even less about the Cabala. Now a Hassidic rebbe's son has heard enough chatting since his childhood to at least spout some wisdom at a Sabbath repast, but Rabbi N. couldn't even do that. You can lead a horse to water but you can't make it drink. Despite his deficiencies, he was still the rabbi's son. That was all. He didn't have the talent to become anything else, or he didn't want to work very hard. He felt it wouldn't do to work for someone else or become a village merchant. Even though our Talmud says: "It is better to flay a carcass in the street than to ask for charity." But that's one homily Jews like to ignore. And so the rabbi's son traveled abut from town to town, from shtetl to shtetl: "Give him money, he's the rabbi's son!"

The rabbi did something that other Hassidic rabbis do. He lied and told falsehoods in a different way. He prophesized no miracles—he told stories. He had bagloads and sackloads of tales about his grandfather, strange tales that weren't in *In Praise of the Baal Shem Tov*. This was a collection gathered by a slaughterer from all the liars in his generation, stories about the Baal Shem Tov and the rebbe, which were printed before Rabbi N. had begun spinning his yarns. He told the biggest whoppers with earnest, pious grimaces as though they were God's own truth and had really happened.

There were some twenty-odd tales, which he kept telling and retelling everywhere and anywhere, over and over again, over and over. When the flock of Hassids get together to hear the stories, that's the time when young husbands try to join the Hassidic ranks themselves. While the older Hassids know the stories from having heard them a dozen times from Rabbi N., they're a novelty for the young pups. They make crazy grimaces, whether they understand the stories or not, whether the stories are probable or not, believable or not, the Baal Shem Tov's grandson has told the stories, and so they must be true, and God forbid that anyone shouldn't swallow them whole—that man could only be a heretic.

However, the Hassidic flock and the young men never give any money, or if they do hand in a small coin, it's never enough for Rabbi N. So he carries his tales to the rich Jews, hoping to unload his wares and make more cash. Some of these rich men give him money just to get him out of the house and avoid listening to his disgusting stories. Some have to suffer through them, after which they fork something over.

Translated by Joachim Neugroschel.

Other works by Aksenfeld: *Der ershter yidisher rekrut* (1862); *Man un vayb, shvester un brider* (1867).

Sara Hirsch Guggenheim
1834–1909

At a time when many Jewish authors turned to fiction to argue that Judaism needed to be altered in order to harmonize with modern life, Sara Hirsch Guggenheim's stories of contemporary Orthodox families emphasized the delights of tradition. The daughter of Rabbi Samson Raphael Hirsch, the founder of the neo-Orthodox movement, Guggenheim was born in Oldenburg, Germany, and began her literary career by publishing serialized stories in her father's journal *Jeschurun*. Written under pseudonyms, Guggenheim's fiction provided enthusiastic support for Orthodoxy.

Aurelie Werner
1863–1864

The relationship between the lovers had already lost much of its intimacy when the couple was blessed with a thriving son. This event reawakened the count's feelings of tenderness for the mother of his child, and once again several months of pure and unadulterated happiness went by. But then Aurelie caught a cold at a masquerade ball and had to spend a great deal of time confined to her room. She thus had to forsake for some time all the distractions and pleasures that had been the couple's main activities. Given that her illness was not serious, the count saw no reason not to go out in society himself, and he soon discovered the allures of going out alone. Unhampered, he could now travel in circles that for the sake of propriety he had had to avoid while in the company of the woman he called his wife. He also had access to many of the houses of the very highest nobility, people who had refused outright to receive the Jewish banker's daughter into their homes but who now greeted the likeable young aristocrat with the utmost politeness. As many pleasantries as the latter offered him, he found himself attracted far more to the former.

Ravenously, he enjoyed the freedom that Aurelie's absence afforded him. He threw himself into the maelstrom of the wildest pleasures and started up an affair with a beautiful ballerina. This relationship became more and more passionate as each day went by, sinking deeper and deeper into debauchery of the most wanton type.

When Aurelie recovered and was ready to partake of the pleasures of the world again, the count made up all sorts of excuses either to keep her at home or to leave her alone at social gatherings. Aurelie keenly perceived this change in their lifestyle, and it gave her great pain. But this was just the beginning. Soon, entire days went by when she would not even see the count, and it was only a matter of time before she learned about his relationship with the dancer. When she first got wind of the count's infidelity, she erupted like an enraged lioness. She had sacrificed so much for this man. He was the reason she had brought her father's curse on herself. She burst into his room and found him staring at the dancer's picture. The couple soon entered into a dreadful fight in which they each harkened back to the sacrifices they had each made for the other. To be sure, they both had made many sacrifices, for they had loved each other passionately. But it had not been true love, but merely a form of selfishness: they made sacrifices in order to be happy, not to make each other happy.

Once the count had been found out, maintaining appearances for the sake of propriety came to an end. He freely and openly gave in to his debauchery. The dancer gave way to another lover, and then to another, and he paid no consideration at all to his child or his mother.

Aurelie found herself completely alone in her grandiose rooms, her breast full of the pain and desperation of an abandoned woman. She had lost touch with all her earlier friends, whether because of the count's pride or her own, and she only had acquaintances in the circles in which she now traveled. She had not made any real friends. And when she saw the count's indifference toward his own child, she remembered all the love that her father always showed her. How had she repaid all this? Her heart was full of bitterest remorse. And the more she felt neglected, the more she heard the words of her father: "There is no power on the earth that can make a Jewess the wife of a Christian man."

"And I'm thus no different than those vile creatures that stole him away from me," she would then cry out, "and I have no right to complain." Full of despair, she would throw herself onto the sumptuous divan and find comfort only in her tears.

The one person who could have kept her company was her mother, for immediately following his daughter's baptism Werner had separated from his wife. Her mother would have loved to have spent time with her daughter the countess. After the wedding, however, the courtesies that the count had shown Mrs. Werner came to an abrupt halt, and he began treating her with condescension and arrogance. Mrs. Werner was hurt deeply by this, and as a result, she seldom visited her daughter in her palace. But her daughter hardly missed her, and she would have been the last person to whom she would have turned now for consolation. She recognized the difference between the tenderness of her mother and that of her father much too late.

As it turned out, Mrs. Werner was also in B—— at the time, and one morning she came to pay her daughter a visit. "Good morning, Countess," she exclaimed with a smile. Aurelie slowly rose to greet her mother, who easily recognized that her daughter had been crying. "Child, child, your eternal mourning and crying will sap away at your beauty," she warned, shaking her head. "Oh, if I only had never possessed this unfortunate beauty which has stolen everything from me," Aurelie sighed.

Her mother looked at her in wonder. "Your beauty stole everything from you? Wasn't it your beauty that made you a countess?"

"And that's precisely what has made me so unhappy, being a countess!"

"A countess cannot be unhappy," her mother smiled.

Just then the count came in. "Good morning, Aurelie," he called out happily to her, "we've not seen each other for so long, my dear. But I'm coming now to tell you that we won't be seeing each other again for quite some time. I've got to take the next train to V——. If letters should come for me here, won't you be so kind as to forward them to me?" Aurelie responded merely by nodding her head. "Au revoir, ma belle," the count said, humming an aria to himself as he went off.

"Do you know," Aurelie asked her mother in a monotone, "why he has to set off for V—— so suddenly?" Her mother gave her a questioning look. "It's because his mistress, the singer Pauline H——, is going to be performing there."

"And he has the audacity to ask you to forward his mail, that's outrageous!" exclaimed Mrs. Werner.

"Oh, but a countess can't be unhappy," Aurelie responded bitterly.

"But it's your own fault you're unhappy," her mother continued impetuously, "why do you let him get away with all this?"

"What am I supposed to do?"

"Pay him back in kind, tit for tat. Why don't you have some affairs, or at least pretend to, to make him jealous?"

"I should make Ferdinand jealous?" Aurelie exclaimed with a raucous laugh. "That would be difficult! After all, he's told me himself that I should love whomever I like. As long as I don't create a public scandal, he's fine with whatever I do." She covered her trembling, pain-stricken face with her hands and groaned loudly. "This is what he tells me, the mother of his child, his wife . . ." She could not finish. Again she was hearing those words of her father in her ears. "Oh, my father, oh, my father," she sighed.

Mrs. Werner got up, insulted. "Why are you calling out for your father? Didn't he leave me just the way Ferdinand is leaving you?"

"Mother," Aurelie exclaimed, "do not compare my noble father with the vile creature that has betrayed me."

"Then why not go to your noble father and ask him for help and consolation?" Mrs. Werner responded angrily, leaving her daughter's garden in haste.

Translated by Jonathan Hess.

Other work by Guggenheim: *Licht und Schattenbilder* (1865).

David Schornstein
1826–1879

Born in an Alsatian village in 1826, the son of a cantor, David Schornstein trained for several years to be a teacher. He then moved to Paris, where he pursued a career in journalism and, at the same time, developed his literary interests as a playwright and novelist. His stories, centering on themes drawn from Jewish life, range from graphic accounts of suffering and persecution to nostalgic tales of traditional life in small towns. In the latter, the subjects are often idealized. "The Tithe" is one such story.

The Tithe
1864

[. . .] The sofer's work is poorly compensated. There is an old proverb about how the *soferim* never grow wealthy in the land of Israel. I don't know who gave birth to that pearl detached from the necklace of the world's wisdom, but in the case of Reb Auscher, the proverb's truth was amply confirmed: the sofer was not rich.

Nevertheless he was the happiest man in the community, next to the cantor of the synagogue that is, who was just as poor as the sofer but much more animated. Always occupied with his transcriptions of the divine word, Reb Auscher naturally possessed a great store of piety and submission to the will of God, the Talmud having long since taught him that the man who is content with his lot is truly rich. Moreover, if heaven had denied him a fortune, it had accorded him other favors. He had an excellent wife and two children, a boy and a girl, who were his joy and his consolation.

The boy was named Samuel. He was twenty-two years old and already a cantor in Berguen. Everyone agreed that he had talent and a remarkable way of officiating in the synagogue. Even if his situation was still modest, his parents could reasonably hope that he might one day aspire to one of the best cantorial positions in the Upper or Lower Rhine.

The girl was named Perle and she was indeed the pearl of all Wertheim. She was seventeen years old, her hair as blond as wheat, and her blue eyes lit up her fine face, which was expressive and full of candor.

Perle was kind and affectionate to a fault with her parents. It was she who prepared her father's work table each day and kept it in order. It was she who would bring him his pipe and tobacco after dinner, and would pour him his cup of coffee. It was also she would interrupt him gently when he had been working too long and urge him to rest. The mother busied herself with making things, both the tools for her husband's work and religious objects whose sale supplemented the family's meager income. Perle alone took care of the household chores. The charming young girl devoted herself to her different occupations with such agility and so little noise that in her hands a task seemed to accomplish itself, as if by magic.

The hazan of Wertheim and the sofer were old friends. Together they had frequented the different Talmudic academies of Alsace and Germany, for in the old days these institutions where Jewish youth get a bit of learning still flourished. Endowed with totally opposite characters, the two young Talmudists were linked by a common trait; neither had ever had any fortune or success. The apathy of the one and the flightiness of the other hampered their studies. Thus when their fellow students were successively getting placed as rabbis or as tutors to wealthy families, neither of our two friends could obtain the Morenu or rabbinical diploma. It was even said that their title of Haber, which gives them the right to the honorific Reb, was due to the extreme indulgence of Rabbi Thias Weill of Karlsruhe. But such gossip can be considered slander, for Rabbi Thias Weill was not someone who would grant a Haber without it being merited. The descendents of that famous Talmudist, who today are living in Paris, can testify to that if necessary. Unable to arrive at the rabbinate, our two friends had to think of other careers: Reb Gerson sang well, Reb Auscher had fine penmanship. The latter therefore became a sofer, the former a hazan. Friendship had long kept them in the same schools; now chance brought them both to the same community of Wertheim, a few leagues from Strasbourg.

Nothing had ever troubled the friendly relations of the hazan and the sofer and of their families, who saw each other quite often. Reb Gerson had only one son: Gabriel. He was a vigorous lad, handsome, and well built. He was not the smartest boy, but he made up for it with a good heart and an honest character. He didn't like studying or singing in the synagogue. The precarious situation his father held in the little community hardly gave the young man a pronounced taste for the hazan's life, and he preferred instead to become a cloth merchant. Reb Gerson was sorry about this, but the mother was very proud to have a son who supported himself and wasn't dependent, like the father, first on the *parnass*, then on the four assessors, and finally on each head of household.

Which is not to say that Gabriel's profession was so pleasing: far from it. His commerce took him for weeks at a time to villages spread throughout the valleys of the

Vosges. He would leave on Sunday and stay in the mountains until Friday, peddling heavy bundles of cloth from hamlet to hamlet, from farm to farm, and living in an extremely sober manner. There are no Israelite establishments in these localities, and since Christian cooking is forbidden, traveling salesman live like real anchorites in the mountains, eating only bread, eggs, salad, fruit, and potatoes cooked in hot coals. But neither pain nor privation hindered Gabriel, and after a long week of hiking and exertion, he would return to Wertheim, his heart beating joyously when he saw the first house of the village through the hawthorn bushes and the willows that bordered the stream. Not only because he was bringing home the small earnings of the week, not only because he was going to rest and enjoy Saturday, but because it was Friday, the night his family would go to Reb Auscher's house, and Gabriel would be near Perle, whom he had already greeted when passing by the modest house of the sofer.

How was the natural affection between the two young people born? They themselves didn't know. They had always loved each other without even a question.

Translated by Maurice Samuels.

Other work by Schornstein: *Perle* (1877).

Sholem Yankev Abramovitsh (Mendele Mokher Sforim)
1836-1917

The so-called father of modern Hebrew and Yiddish literature, Sholem Yankev Abramovitsh is a monumental figure in East European Jewish literature. He was born in Kapulye, Belorussia, began his literary career in Hebrew, and produced maskilic works that sought to educate readers about the natural world and the sciences. He then reached out to a broader readership by writing in Yiddish, adopting the persona of a simple book peddler, Mendele Mokher Sforim, the name by which Abramovitsh himself is most commonly known. Abramovitsh moved to Odessa in the early 1880s where he not only completed several new works of short Hebrew and Yiddish fiction, but also retooled his entire previous oeuvre, adapting and translating his work to better fit the new political and cultural moment. It was at this time that he, in the guise of Mendele, became a venerated figure and, in some circles, a household name who concretized his reputation as the original master of both literatures.

The Little Man; or, Portrait of a Life
1864-1865

As for me, I was born in Tsviatshits and my name is Mendele the Book Peddler. Most of the year I'm on the road, travelling from one place to another, so people know me everywhere. I ride all over Poland with a full stock of books printed in Zhitomir, and apart from that I carry prayer shawls, fringed undergarments, tassels, shofars, tefillin, amulets, mezuzas, wolf tooth charms, and sometimes you can even get brass and copper goods from me. Truth is, since the Yiddish newspaper *Kol mevasser* started coming out a couple years back, I've also taken to carrying a few issues. But actually that's not what I'm driving at—I'm getting off the point. I want to tell you about something else entirely.

Last year, just before Hanukah in 1863, I rode into Glupsk, where I reckoned on selling some candlesticks and wax candles. Well, actually that's not what I'm driving at either. On Tuesday after morning prayers I came to Glupsk and, as I often do, I went straight to the House of Study. But I'm getting off the point again. When I arrived at the House of Study, I saw groups of people standing around arguing, shmoozing, laughing, and looking worried. The people didn't stand still—three circles would join and then split up again into three. How does the saying go, eh? My heart isn't made of stone, and I'm also flesh and bone.

Well, you can imagine that I was curious to know what was going on. In this world you've got to know everything, hear everything, because you never know when it will come in handy. But I'm getting off the point. I had scarcely unhitched my horse when the groups of people moseyed over toward me. One person greeted me, another took a look into my wagon, and others started poking and groping around at my goods, as we Jews are wont to do. The street urchins and schoolboys even managed to pluck hairs from my horse's tail. But I'm getting off the point. In the meantime, I heard the following conversation:

"*Oy, vey! Oy, vey!* Blessed be the true Judge. He was just a young man. I think about forty. *Oy, vey!* How could this happen? And to such a good man!"

"Why are you getting all worked up, Reb Avromtshe? As if you care! What's it to you? Who was he, after all is said and done?"

"Nothing matters to you, Yosl. Reb Avromtshe is right—how could this happen to such a man? Have mercy! As sure as I'm a Jew, have mercy!"

"Lookit the new minister of mercy, Leybtshe Temes! Now he's agreeing with Reb Avromtshe. What was it that you said a little while ago, Leybtshe?"

"Who, me? Yosl, what did I say? I mean it, Yosl, what did I say?"

"You and nobody else, Leybtshe. You, with your kosher mouth, said: 'Big deal! It's just Isaac Abraham Takif.' Whether he'll forgive me for saying so or not, he was a coarse fellow, heartless and a bit of a fool."

"What? Who? Yosl, you mean me? Good day, I'm in a hurry."

"Good day, Leybtshe, and a good year at that, too. Come on, Reb Avromtshe, into the House of Study, let's take a drop of brandy. Today the shammes has very good brandy."

"You know, Yosl, a little brandy never hurt anyone, eh? You sure outsmarted that liar Leybtshe. Gave it to him good, Yosl. What nonsense he was talking! The man, may he rest in peace, was an ignoramus, a meddler, and a bloodsucker. And he left behind a pile of money."

"That's why, Reb Avromtshe, I like you so much. Because you always insist on telling the truth."

I heard all this and more, but now I'm getting off the point again. It was time to unpack my wares. I shifted my horse around in the harness so she faced the wagon, to cheer her up with a bit of straw; as for me, I went to work. As soon as I had pulled out a candlestick, a prayer shawl, and a package of tassels, the assistant to the rabbinical court ran up panting like a goose and said:

"*Oy, gevalt*, Reb Mendele! Sholem aleykhem, Reb Mendele! The Rebbe kindly requests that you come to him as fast as you can."

I told that rabbi's assistant that I'd come right away. Left by myself, I began to wonder what it could mean that the rabbi had called for me in such a hurry; I knew that he used oil wicks instead of candles for Hanukah, because he'd bought his menorah from me the year before. So why did the assistant come running all out of breath? Whatever it was he wanted, I had to go. I thought it over and brought along a few candlesticks, some amulets, and a women's prayer book that was hot off the press, which might be of use to the rebbetzin. But I'm getting off the point.

As I entered the rabbi's house, he ran to meet me and cried out;

"Oy, Reb Mendele! Oy, sholem aleykhem, Reb Mendele! God must have sent you, dear, kind Reb Mendele! This must be a miracle, Reb Mendele, really and truly a miracle from Heaven!" But I'm getting off the point again.

Another bookseller would surely have thought that they were anxious to see my wares, but I'm no babe in the cradle. And I wasn't hatched yesterday, like a chick that has no idea what's going on. You should know that, as a rule, the world consists of deception. When a person needs to buy something essential, he pretends that it has no value to him at all. That way he can buy it for a song. When he urgently needs a prayer book, he haggles over a pamphlet of penitential prayers, lamentations, or a package of tassels. Then he picks up the prayer book as if on a whim, glances at it and puts it down, furrows his brow and smiles, saying: "For a small sum I might have bought this, too." Believe me, all the world is a marketplace. Everyone wants the other guy to lose so he can gain. Everyone is looking for bargains. But I'm getting off the point. I guessed from the rabbi's face that he didn't want to buy anything; otherwise, he wouldn't have let on that he was waiting for me. It's true that the rabbi is a fine and honest man—I should only have his good name—although still, in this world, one has to deceive people. Even the angels had to follow the way of the world and put one over on Abraham, when the Torah says that they ate, although they only pretended to eat.[1] But that's really not at all what I'm driving at. The rabbi led me into his house. There sat the rabbinical judges and all the wealthy men in town, looking lost in thought. Rich people always seem a little bit lost and worried, I don't know why. If you've got money, what's there to worry about? Seems to me that you don't need any fancy ideas to spend money. But I'm getting off the point.

NOTE

1. In Genesis 18:8 Abraham feeds three men who visit him. Rabbinic tradition interprets these visitors as divine messengers, angels who could have only pretended to eat.

Translated by Ken Frieden.

Other works by Abramovitsh: *Toldot ha-teva* (1862); *Dos vintshfingerl* (1865); *Fishke der krumer* (1869); *Di klyatshe* (1873); *Yudl* (1875); *Kitser masoes Binyomin hashlishi* (1878).

Isaac Meyer Dik

ca. 1807–1893

Considered the first popular writer of Yiddish fiction, Isaac (Ayzik) Meyer Dik (also known by the acronym *Amad*) was born in Vilna. A *maskil* who encouraged

Jewish educational and sartorial reform and admired Tsar Alexander II for his liberalism, Dik observed Jewish practice throughout his life. He initially began writing in Hebrew around 1838 but later wrote exclusively in Yiddish. His more than three hundred widely circulated stories and short novels (generally issued by Vilna's Romm publishing house) were designed both to entertain readers and to instruct them in moral values and the teachings of the Haskalah, often through parody, satire, sentimentality, and melodrama. Despite their wide circulation and influence on later Yiddish writers, many of his works have not survived.

The Women Shopkeepers, or, Golde-Mine, the Abandoned Wife of Brod
1865

In short, in addition to being affluent, our Reb Hoshea Heffler was also steeped in the holy books. He was a traditional Jew, who could not abide the *maskilim*, the enlightened ones. He always used to ridicule them by commenting that they might know how to say the word *chair* in ten languages but had no idea how to sit, and in the same way, they might know how to say *bread* in twenty languages, but they had nothing to eat. Nonetheless, he permitted his two lovely daughters, Golde-Mine and Eyge, to be highly educated. In those days it was customary for Jewish males not to receive a secular education, which could harm their sacred studies, but for females, actually, it was another matter because this was necessary for business. Then, as now, we had the terrible custom of making our young women and wives operate shops and restaurants and conduct business both within the local neighborhoods and at the fairs. Well, they needed to know German and Russian, and those who ran hotels had to speak French as well.

And what shall be said? . . . So what can we say about Heffler's two daughters? One managed a wine shop or a restaurant, and the other ran the hotel *because their father, Reb Hoshea, owned his own building complex, which, though purchased for over forty thousand thaler, was worth much more, and in it he introduced a fashionable modern hostelry, and he also established a wineshop with a restaurant. These enriched him considerably.*

Here there was a constant flow of the most distinguished travelers—Germans, Russians, Poles, Frenchmen, and Englishmen. Because this was the time of the war with France, military personnel were everywhere—officers, generals and ambassadors—all passing through Brod. Therefore, our Reb Hoshea Heffler's two daughters needed to be very accommodating to these aforementioned travelers. They were always dressed elegantly and conversed with everyone in his own language. And in this manner they acquired an excellent reputation in town. They were considered extremely competent women, highly regarded by the most important people as being capable, in due time, of supporting husbands. [. . .]

The letter struck Hershele like a spark of fire in an arsenal. He had already been feeling greatly disturbed by Golde-Mine's remarks, and the kernel of suspicion that had lain dormant in his heart for the past two years, in a single moment, like a huge thornbush, put forth all of its bitter, poisonous and galling fruit.

"Faithless, false Golde-Mine, woe to you," he began shouting, "and woe to me, your cuckolded husband, and woe to your children, the fruit of your terrible transgression. At last I understand what you meant when you said that you had heavy sins to atone for. Oh, how stupid I've been until now not to realize that La-hira is your lover. No, one doesn't bestow expensive gifts in exchange for nothing. He was well rewarded by you. And were it not for your own words and this letter, I would have remained in the dark. But heaven and earth have decreed that no mystery can remain buried forever. Well, enough of this! She has incriminated herself. She has trespassed against the Almighty's Seventh Commandment. No, even if she were ten times as wealthy, beautiful and intelligent than she is, I will leave her, her and her two bastards. As long as she lives, she must remain an *agune*, and because they led this tavernkeeper to me, let my parents suffer right along with her."

As he spoke, he stuffed the letter into his pocket. He placed the instructions regarding child support on the table and left the house, slamming the door behind him. He never returned.

Translated by Paul Azaroff and Lillian Schanfield.

Other works by Dik: *Ha-'oreaḥ* (1860); *Der idisher poslonik* (1880); *Note ganif* (1887); *Geklibene verk fun A. M. Dik* (1954).

Jorge Isaacs
1837–1895

The son of an English Jew who had converted to Christianity and famously bought his Colombian citizenship from Simón Bolívar by paying him with cows, Jorge Isaacs was perhaps the most famous Latin

American novelist of the nineteenth century. His father, at first a successful merchant, lost his fortune in the Colombian upheavals, and Isaacs was forced to work a variety of odd jobs to support himself, in addition to taking up arms in Colombia's numerous wars and revolts. Originally a poet, Isaac's novel *María* is considered a seminal work in Latin American literature and Spanish romanticism. He later pursued a career in journalism and politics.

María
1867

VII

When my father made his last trip to the Antilles, Salomón, a cousin of his whom he had loved since childhood, had just lost his wife. At a very young age, they had come together to South America, and on one of their voyages my father fell in love with the daughter of a Spaniard, an intrepid ship captain who, having left the service for a few years, found himself obliged in 1819 to take up arms once more in defense of Spain's king and queen. He was executed in Majagual on May 20, 1820, shot to death.

As a condition for allowing the girl to marry him, her mother insisted that he renounce the Judaic faith. My father became a Christian at the age of twenty. During that time his cousin was becoming interested in the Catholic religion without, however, giving in to requests that he be baptized, for he knew that what had gained the wife he wanted for my father would keep him from being accepted by the woman he loved in Jamaica.

The two friends, then, after several years of separation, saw each other once again. Salomón was now a widower. Sara, his wife, had left him with a three-year-old daughter. My father, who found his cousin ravaged by grief, both physically and mentally, found in his new religion the consoling words their relatives had sought in vain. He urged Salomón to give him his daughter so she could be brought up with his own children, and he dared to propose that he would have her become a Christian. Salomón agreed, saying, "It's true that only my daughter has kept me from making a journey to India that would raise my spirits and ease my poverty. She also has been my only comfort after Sara's death. But you wish it, let her be yours. Christian women are sweet and kind, and your wife must be a saintly mother. If Christianity, in times of greatest misfortune, can lighten one's burden as you have mine, perhaps I would have done a disservice to my daughter if I had let her remain Jewish. Don't tell our relatives, but when you reach the first shore with a Catholic priest, have her baptized and have them change her name from Ester to María." He shed many tears as he spoke these words.

The schooner that was to take my father to the shores of New Granada set sail a few days later from Montego Bay. The swift boat was testing its white wings, as a heron in our woods will do before undertaking a long flight. When Salomón entered the cabin with his daughter held in one arm and a trunk with her things hanging from the other, my father had just finished adjusting his shipboard suit. The girl stretched out her little arms toward her uncle, and Salomón, placing her in his friend's arms, broke down sobbing over the small trunk. The little one, whose precious head had been bathed in a flood of tears by the baptism of grief rather than that of Jesus' religion, was a sacred treasure; my father well knew it, and never did he forget it. As Salomón jumped to the launch that was about to separate them, his friend reminded him of a promise, and Salomón responded in a choked voice, "The prayers of my daughter for me, and those of my own for her and her mother, shall rise together to the feet of the crucified one."

I was seven when my father returned, and I spurned the precious gifts he had brought me from his trip, preferring to admire that child, so beautiful, so sweet and smiling. My mother covered her with caresses, and my sisters lavished her with tenderness from the moment my father placed her on his wife's lap and said, "This is Salomón's daughter, he has sent her to you."

During our games, her lips began to form the sounds of Spanish, so harmonious and seductive when coming from a woman's pretty mouth or that of a happy child.

Some six years must have passed. One afternoon when I walked into my father's room, I heard him sobbing. His arms were crossed upon the table, supporting his forehead. My mother was next to him, crying, with María's head resting on her knees. María was unable to understand such grief and was almost indifferent to her uncle's lamentations. That day there had been a letter from Kingston bearing news of Salomón's death. I just remember something my father said: "If everyone is leaving me with no final good-byes, why should I return to my country?" Alas! His ashes were destined to rest in a foreign land where the winds of the ocean, on whose beaches he had played as a boy, whose vastness he had crossed as a passionate young man, could not sweep away from his tombstone the dried acacia blossoms and the dust of years!

Few among our family's acquaintances could have suspected that María was not my parents' child. She spoke our language well, she was well-mannered, lively, and intelligent. When my mother would caress her head at the same time she was caressing my sisters' and mine, no one could have guessed which of us was the orphan.

She was nine years old. Her flowing locks, still a light chestnut color, hanging loosely and playfully about her svelte, sinuous waist; her expressive eyes; that melancholy way of speaking—such was the image I carried with me when I left my parents' home. And this is how she looked on the morning of that sad day, under the vines of my mother's windows.

Translated by Michele McKay Aynesworth.

Other works by Isaacs: *La revolución radical en Antioquia* (1880); *Poesías completas de Jorge Isaacs* (1920).

Isaac Joel Linetski
1839–1915

Isaac Joel (Yitskhok Yoyel) Linetski was a prolific Yiddish writer, essayist, and literary translator, and an active *maskil* in Russia. After breaking with his Hasidic family, Linetski turned toward the Haskalah and was closely associated with the leading periodicals and figures in Hebrew and Yiddish culture, including Alexander Zederbaum and Abraham (Avrom) Goldfaden. Linetski's most successful work was the satiric novel *Dos poylishe yingl* (The Polish Lad), first serialized in the Yiddish paper *Kol mevaser* beginning in 1867 and published in book form for the first time in 1869. The book, a humorous critique of Hasidic life written as a fictional autobiography, reached a mass audience, going through at least thirty editions. Linetski eventually settled in Odessa and became involved in the city's early Zionist circles as both a critic and prolific translator of Hebrew literature.

The Polish Lad
1867–1869

By Way of Foreword

If my father had been able to foresee even a thousandth part of the trials I was to endure he might have been rather less ardent on the night my mother conceived me. . . . Now, of course, that is all water over the dam. [. . .]

Once on the eve of Tisha be-Av, the fast day commemorating the destruction of the First and Second Temples, my angel was sleeping soundly—since on this day the study of the Torah is forbidden—while my parents-to-be sat on the ledge outside the house. I could not help hearing what they said.

"Do you think, Yossel, that it will really be a boy?" my mother asked.

"What are you babbling about, you fool?" my father irritably returned. "The rebbe has positively said it will be a girl—and you still have your doubts?" [. . .]

Overhearing such a disagreement made my blood run cold. What woe for me if, God forbid, I should be transformed into a girl! I remembered the appalling thing I witnessed through my casement in paradise whenever the Jewish girls in Poland were being dragged down to Sheol—unkempt, slovenly, and downcast everyone of them, every one of them with carious teeth and with her head shaved, according to the marriage ritual of all strictly Orthodox Jews. When called to account for their actions on earth, they would stare out of their beady eyes, like startled mice after an earthquake. Even during my stay in paradise I was in mortal fear of just one thing—of coming into the world as the daughter of a Polish Hasid. But I would take heart in the thought that even if I were doomed to be born female, perhaps it was my destiny to be a genteel lady in some aristocratic Jewish home—one of those very noblewomen who were rarely ushered into paradise, but who were so well-bred, so exquisitely dainty, and so clever that a mere glimpse of them was like a feast for the soul.

Now that I heard the woeful prediction that I was to be born a girl, you can well imagine my anxiety. True enough, there was hardly anything attractive or admirable about the Polish Jews who were likewise relegated to Sheol. They, too, were unkempt, as full of ill will and vindictiveness as any fiend from Sheol, that abode of the dead; still, they were less contemptible than the so-called fair sex. They may have been good-for-nothing ne'er-do-wells and rascals, as well as walking skeletons—but all the same, they were *men*! Though a Polish Jew may be a miserable louse, a stammerer, and a booby, among his fellows he is still considered a man, the lord and master over the prettiest, the most erudite and accomplished woman. Be that as it may, I was scared out of my wits by the tzaddik and the doctor, and found myself between Scylla and Charybdis, between the devil and the deep blue sea. Now that I think of it, surprisingly, I never heard during my interval in paradise any such terms of address as rebbe, or preacher, or righteous Jew. Who knows—perhaps all these professional doers of good were busy in Gehenna purging and condemning the wicked souls of the Jewish damsels from Poland.... In short, throughout those nine painful months I suffered mortal fear of coming into this world as a girl!

Translated by Moshe Spiegel.

Other works by Linetski: *Der beyzer marshelik* (1869); *Der velt-luekh fun yohr eyn kesef* (1872); *Der litvisher bokher* (1875–1876); *Funem yarid* (1909).

Isaac Meyer Dik

The Panic, or, The Town of Hérres
1868

The Sad Letter in the Synagogue

In the year 5594 (1834) it was the Ninth of Av, the holy day commemorating the Destruction of the Temple. In the morning, when the worshipers were lamenting at the synagogue, one of the foremost anti-Hasidim came in. Now in the Jewish towns, the common people usually pray in the great *shul*, while the scholars pray only in the *bes-médresh* and never set foot in the synagogue—it wouldn't be proper. The householder who entered the synagogue was one of those who prayed only here.

The newcomer, holding a letter, made a beeline for the town trustee, who was the leader of the congregation—a respectable man, versed in both secular and religious law. (This trustee had prospects of earning the official title of Great Scholar this year; you see, the rabbi, out of weakness, had formed a minyan—ten-man quorum—in his home.) The worshipers were just ending the lamentation known as "Turn Thine ear to me."

The newcomer, who seemed about to weep, said breathlessly: "Hurry up, my dear Benyómin! Hurry up and read this letter! It's no simple letter, it concerns the very essence of the Jewish nation."

Those words hit the Jews like a two-ton boulder plunging into the middle of a still lake. The news spread from one worshiper to the next, growing and fanning out through the town with a tenfold impact.

And it came to pass—and when the trustee finished reading the letter, he burst into hot tears, wringing his hands, tearing his clothes, pulling out his hair, and twisting his face like the victim of the worst disaster.

"We're doomed! Doomed! We're all doomed!" he exclaimed over and over. And the worshipers were terrified—too upset to recite the Lamentations. The trustee, who just minutes ago had looked forward to seeing the householder, forgot all about the title of Great Scholar. The congregants, not knowing the contents of the letter, went crazy. Their eyes were riveted on the two men: the trustee and the esteemed gentleman who had brought the letter. The Jews were trying to read their faces, hoping to fathom the scope of the disaster, but without much luck. Skipping the Lamentations the way you skip the second half of the Hagada on the second night of Passover, they barely managed to pour into the street. Clusters formed outside every house, people whispered to one another—and yet nobody knew what to tell them.

The Great Assembly in the Rabbi's Home

And it came to pass—the Jews were standing around in small bunches, trying to figure out what the bad news could be. The ragged and unshod beadles and attendants (of whom, as we have pointed out, there were many) were dashing along the houses, calling to a meeting. They summoned the judges, the scholars, the most solid citizens, and especially the tavernkeepers, who are the wisest Jews because they often confound everyone with their liquor. They also rallied a few of the very simple people in the street, partly because they pitied them for being terribly poor—and the poor made up most of the population.

The whole town was then summoned, and the few stay-at-homes were people in mourning. Once everybody was present, they closed the door, and the trustee addressed them on behalf of the rabbi, who was under the weather:

"You ought to know, brothers, that at any moment now we can expect a ukaze that will cut to our very quick, a ukaze that doesn't concern just a single moral precept, but that touches the sheer survival of the Jewish nation, so that there will be no one left who can call himself a Jew: 'Woe unto us for we have sinned!' The evil decree stipulates that no Jewish girl can marry before the age of sixteen and no Jewish boy before the age of eighteen. This edict is far worse than Pharaoh's edict to kill all the male babies of the Jews, for that ukaze was aimed only at boys, but this one includes girls." He then quoted a Hebrew saying: "'Without kids there shall be no wethers.'" Which he translated: "'If there are no baby goats in town, then pretty soon there won't be any rams either.' If you don't make sure you have kids when you're young, then no one'll take care of you when you're old. And Jews will gradually die out."

He then read them the letter from his relative in the big city—the letter revealing the great secret: the ukaze was about to be issued, so he should marry off his daughter immediately. The congregants were so deeply agitated by both the trustee and the letter that they wept and wailed—there wasn't a dry eye among them. They thought it was the start of the trials and tribulations heralding the coming of the Messiah. The trustee told them it was top secret, they mustn't breathe a word to the townsfolk.

They then sat down around the table and mulled for a couple of hours until the Supreme Jewish Court handed down its ruling: Every Jew who cared about God and about His nation, the people of Israel, should marry off his son, his daughter, or some poor orphans this very day, the Ninth of Av. For the ukaze might easily arrive tomorrow, and then the congregant would "cry out in distress" (as is written in the sacred writings)—that is, he would lament, but it would be too late. And the matter had to remain strictly confidential, a guarded secret, so the townsfolk wouldn't find out (God forbid), especially the crooks and connivers, and then who could tell what damage it might cause.

The Great Turmoil in Town

As we know, the whole town had attended the meeting, so you can imagine that the whole town was not oblivious to the great secret. Indeed, before the crowd even broke up, the hubbub and brouhaha had spread to every last home plus the mill, the bath house, and the poorhouse—and with dozens of lies to boot. That was because a couple of tailors among the beadles had sneaked out for a while during the meeting, and during that while those rumormongers had blabbed everything to a certain wadding maker who happened to be around, and he, in turn, had padded the news a little and carried it to a couple of shops. The town was utterly devastated. Within an hour, everyone had heard the story, together with a lot of added drivel. Within another half hour, scholars pointed out allusions to this decree in ancient tomes, and the Hasids said that their rebbe had known about this drivel long since and had married off his little Shmuel in the nick of time.

However, I'd like to briefly describe what concerns us. No sooner had the flock left the meeting than it split into two parties. One party consisted of matchmakers, the second of in-laws. Ignoring the fact that it was raining, they plodded along the muddy road in their stocking feet, whispering and muttering, depicting how sensible and fortunate this marriage or that marriage would be. By evening, half the town was engaged.

The very first victims were the poor, mostly Hasids, for even the non-Hasidic town rabbi observed a few Hasidic customs. He sometimes took a fee, gave an amulet, showed off his wisdom—no ignoramus he and certainly no fool. He dealt in prayer shawls and knew how to hawk his wares. So however great a fuss the rabbi made among the men, his wife made an even greater fuss among the women, who were far more terror-stricken by the edict than the men were. You see, each woman recalled that she had been divorced by the age of sixteen or at least that her marriage had been on the rocks. And now her daughter wouldn't even be married by that age.

And no sooner did the day turn away—the instant the day ended and the evening star began to twinkle, and before people even ate supper, they had weddings in their homes—silent festivities, no clowns, no klezmers, no rituals: no seating of the bride on the bridal seat, no veiling of the bride prior to the ceremony—the only veil was the veil of secrecy. For that was what the rabbi had ordered, and for two reasons. First of all, it was the Ninth of Av, and secondly, the townsfolk were not to get wind of the wedding. But they didn't dare have a marriage without a license and without a rabbi, a cantor, and a beadle.

Because so many weddings took place that night, they couldn't drum up a *minyan* (quorum of ten men) for reciting the nuptial benedictions. I had the misfortune of living near the synagogue courtyard where the stampede had begun, and so that night I was forced to attend a dozen or so weddings in order to complete the *minyan*. At each wedding they served only a single schnapps plus a roll with herring. The weddings were like funerals in the throes of an epidemic—God forbid!—when short shrift is given to the burial rites.

Translated by Joachim Neugroschel.

Lev Levanda
1835–1888

Lev Levanda was a Russian-language journalist and author, born and educated in Minsk. A strong supporter of the Haskalah, Levanda worked for the tsarist government and held the title Jewish Expert, overseeing the development of curricula for state-run Jewish schools. He wrote extensively for Jewish periodicals, including *Rassvet*, *Sion*, *Evreiskaia biblioteka*, *Russkii evrei*, and *Voskhod*, advocating against both traditionalism and assimilation, and promoting Jewish self-defense and early Zionism. While his fiction was considered stylistically subpar both in its day and by later critics, its sophisticated political engagement earned him recognition by contemporaries and later scholars alike. His *Seething Times* depicted reactions by Jews to the Polish uprising of 1863.

Seething Times
1871–1873

This morning I met Vaclav on the street.

"God himself has arranged our meeting," he continued after the usual greetings and inquiries about health. "Walking here, I thought of you."

"Might I be able to find out the reason for your thinking of me?" I asked.

"I wanted to convey to you an interesting piece of news," he replied, twisting his thin moustache.

"News, and even interesting news! That's very interesting. Speak without further delay."

"Aha! So you are curious as well!"

"Surely I am! Am I not Eve's daughter? Do please go on, do not torment me."

"Fine, I shall not. But allow me first to ask if you read newspapers."

"No," I replied. "What is the use in reading them, particularly for women?"

"You at least find out what happens in the whole wide world."

"In the whole wide world everything happens without us," I objected.

"How could it be without us?" Vaclav asked, hurt. "Not angels, but people do everything in the world, the same kinds of creatures as us. It stands to reason that we, too, can do something—and we shall do it. Please believe me that we shall do it and do it well! The sky will be feeling the heat!"

"Oh, Jesus and Mary! How terrifying!" I said jokingly, wringing my arms.

"Have you the pleasure of joking, Panna Sofia?" Vaclav remarked with reproach.

"Why then are you tormenting me? Where is the news you promised?"

"Here it is," he said, removing from his side pocket a folded issue of a Polish newspaper. "In here you will find, marked with a red pencil, an article that I recommend you read carefully."

"And who is the author of this article, not Pan Vaclav Zaremba by any chance?" I asked slyly.

"I don't know," he replied with an author's modesty. It is unsigned,"

"Never mind. I promise to read it with great attention."

"And if you like it," Vaclav added, "then please do read it to your girlfriends, and especially the ones whom I had the good fortune of meeting at your birthday party."

"And to Panna Polina Krants?" I asked suggestively.

"Naturally," he responded, blushing and starting to bid me adieu.

Upon returning home, I pored over the newspaper. The article marked with a pencil was a long contribution from our city, in which—whoever would have expected it!—the celebration of my birthday was described with all the details and in such colors! Names were not revealed, only identified with initials. Even conversations, even jokes were not forgotten. Pan Vaclav must have an excellent memory and also must be quite observant. At the forefront is, of course, Panna P.[1] He calls her now a "pearl in an eastern princess's diadem," now the "main flower in the arrangement." The correspondent comments with delight on our pure Polish pronunciation. Our purely Polish *dowcip*.[2] But even more than by the article itself, I was struck by the following editorial commentary:

> In this interesting article, which, we hope, every good Pole will read with contentment, the unharmonious word *starozakonni*[3] has unpleasantly struck our ears. Does not our esteemed contributor know that we do not have and should not have *starozakonni* but only *Poles of Mosaic persuasion*? If he does not know, then be it known to him and to all *those who ought to know*, that the word *starozakonny* is as old as are those harmful prejudices that we must repudiate forever if we want to go apace with the century, if we want the enlightened world to be with us and not against us. Do you understand, brothers of ours in Poland, Lithuania, Volhynia, and Podolia? . . . If you obstinately persecute an honest man with the label "thief," he will become a thief, not because of his nature but through your doing. If you continue to call Israelites

Yids, *starozakonni*, they will never become Poles. We do not intend here to enter into an inquest about which of you are right and which are wrong. Maybe they are at fault, but maybe we ourselves are even more at fault than they are. We nullify the old scores and extend our hands to them in *zgoda, jedność, braterstwo*.[4] Those to whom we feed our bread must not be and cannot be our enemy. Jews are a historical people, tremendously capable and energetic, not a crowd of gypsies but a civilized society with a significant culture. In them there is an abyss of patriotic feelings. The proof is their two-thousand-year-long attachment to their former fatherland, religion, customs. If we succeed in taking advantage of this feeling, we shall not lose. If we make this land a second Palestine for them, they will go through fire to lay down their lives for it, they will shed their blood for it. With what self-sacrifice, worthy of imitation, did they defend their holy city from the victorious Roman legions! Read Josephus Flavius, and you will be convinced of how much military valor, courage, and fearlessness this people had. Reaching our hands out to today's Israelites, we extend our hands not to heirs of the despicable Russians or to the traitors of their fatherland but to the successors of brave knights, defeated only by the will of Providence. *Sapienti sat* . . .[5]

It is difficult for me to express in words what I felt when I read these fiery lines. My heart began to pound. . . . My head was spinning. . . . I kept reading and rereading it, and I could not believe my eyes. . . . A language completely new to me. . . . It arouses my blood. . . . I am all atremble. . . . And a Pole saying this? And he is not joking, not teasing?. . . Go away, doubts! . . . . I want to believe, I want to love! . . . Cannot we indeed grow to love our motherland the way our ancestors loved Palestine? Yes we can! A thousand times we can!. . . Are we monsters of some kind? We are "successors of brave knights, defeated only by the will of Providence!" Does this mean we have not always been greedy buyers and sellers, spendthrifts, egoists? Give us a chance to love, and we will not be calculating everything in cold blood. Do you think we enjoy not loving anything, not belonging anywhere, always feeling ourselves among strangers? The old generation may have found pleasure in this, but it burdens us, the young. Belonging to our people alone does not satisfy us: we do not find in it that which our parents did. Our needs are entirely different. . . . They must be satisfied. So satisfy them! Do not push us away with words, glances, for we so morbidly understand your words and glances. Give us a fatherland, give us a nationhood! . . . We are loathe to be Germans on Polish soil. . . . I want to be, must be, and can be Polish woman. A Pole just like my fellow countrywomen! . . . Do you hear what your elder brother is telling you? "If we succeed in taking advantage of this feeling, we shall not lose. If we make this land a second Palestine for them, they will go through fire to lay down their lives for it, they will shed their blood for it." Yes. We shall show you that a Jewess can be no less of a patriot than an aristocratic Polish lady. And woe be unto you if you take away from us the chance to love our fatherland the way you love it! . . .

My hand trembles . . . I cannot go on . . .

NOTES

Words in brackets appear in the source text.

1. Polina Krants, Sofia Aronson's friend who, in their Vilna circle of young Jewish women and men, is most taken with Polish patriotism.

2. *Dowcip* (Pol.) = wit.

3. *Starozakonny* (sing.), *starozakonni* (pl.) (Pol.; cf. Russ. *starozakonnyi*) = lit. "of the old law"; a traditional supersessionist Polish-Catholic reference to the Jews ("those of the Old Testament").

4. *Zgoda, jedność, braterstwo* (Pol.) = concord, unity, brotherhood.

5. *Sapienti sat* (Lat.) = [This] will suffice for the intelligent.

Translated by Maxim D. Shrayer.

Other works by Levanda: *Ha-markolet: otsar markolet megrim: o temunat ha-yahadut* (1874); *In shturm* (1900); *A groyser remiz* (1914).

Karl Emil Franzos
1848–1904

Karl Emil Franzos was notable not just for his stature as a prominent nineteenth-century author and journalist, but also for having focused on the scenes and conflicts of small-town Jewish life. First in Austria, then in Germany, he wrote prolifically, often setting his stories in "Barnow," the name he gave his childhood home of Czortków, Galicia. He was educated in Bucovina and spent his adult years in Vienna and Berlin, establishing a publishing house in 1895.

Though he was highly educated and knew several languages, he found that positions as teacher or judge were closed to him because he was Jewish. Since he refused to convert, he became a journalist. He championed reform and opposed oppression; he saw the latter coming as much from Orthodox Judaism as from external forces.

The Jews of Barnow
1873

"Well, as you know already, the story is about Esterka, the daughter of the Jew to whom this house belongs. She was ten years old when he came here, and tall of her age, with black hair and large blue eyes. She was scarcely ever to be seen, and never to be heard: she used to sit over her books all day long, and often far into the night. My daughter Malvina, who was about the same age, used to ask her to come and play with her; but the proud little Jewish girl wouldn't accept any of her invitations, she was so taken up with her reading. It was very foolish of her, and her uncle Grünstein was at the bottom of it all. Old Grünstein is a very queer sort of man—most disagreeable to have anything to do with, I should say: he's neither Jew nor Christian—quite an infidel, in fact; indeed, some people go so far as to say that he can raise the dead when he likes. Yes, I mean what I say! He can raise the very dead from their graves! And he was Esterka's teacher. He must have given her a nice sort of education, for at the end of these three years she was every bit as foolish and godless as himself. To give you an example of this, let me tell you what happened one very hot August afternoon when she was with us. You must know that she embroidered beautifully, so we had asked her to come and help Malvina to finish a bit of work. As we sat at our sewing the clouds began to come up thick and fast, and soon afterward there was a terrible storm; it thundered, lightened, and hailed with the greatest possible fury. My daughter, who, thank God, had received the education of a good Catholic, began to pray aloud; but the Jewess remained calm and cool. 'Esther,' I said, aren't you afraid of the judgment of God?'—'A thunder-storm isn't a judgment of God,' answered the conceited little thing—'Well, then, what do you call the lightening?' I asked.—'A discharge of atmospheric electricity,' was her reply.—'Aren't you afraid of the lightening, then?'—'Oh, yes,' she answered, 'because we haven't a lightning-conductor on the house!'—I couldn't possibly allow such godless sentiments to pass unreproved, as Malvina was there, so I said very sternly; 'You're a little infidel, child; remember this, the good God guides every flash of lightning!'—'How can that be?' answered Miss Impudence. 'The poor peddler, Berisch Katz, was killed by lightning last year, when he was crossing the open fields, although he was a very good man; now that he is dead, his children haven't enough to eat.'—I said nothing more at the time, but next day, when I happened to see old Moses, I told him the whole story. 'The child is having a nice sort of education,' I said in conclusion, 'and if this kind of thing goes on, who knows what the end of it will be?'—'It shall not go on,' he replied; 'I had made up my mind to put a stop to it before, and what you tell me determines me to do so at once.'—He was as good as his word, and took away all of Esther's books. Then he put her in the shop, and made her weigh the sugar and sell the groceries. As for Schlome, he turned him out of the house.

"All this took place nine years ago last summer. One Sabbath afternoon in the following autumn Esther came to my daughter and entreated her with tears to lend her a German book, or else she would die. She said that her father had taken away every one of her books, and looked after her so strictly that she couldn't herself get any to take their place. He did not, however, go so far as to prevent her visiting us. Our acquaintance was an honor to the girl, and besides that, he knew that I was a woman of principle. Well, as I said before, Esther wept and entreated in such a heart-rending manner that I was touched. So I lent her some German books that I happened to have in the house: Heine's 'Reisebilder,' Klopstock's 'Messiade,' 'Kaiser Joseph,' by Louise Mühlbach, the new 'Pitaval,' Eichendorf's poems, and the novels of Paul de Kock. She read them all, devouring them much as a hungry wolf does a lamb. She read them in the shop whenever her father's back was turned, and at night when she went to her room. The only book she didn't like was the first novel of Paul de Kock; she brought it back to me, and asked me to find her something else. But I hadn't time to do so then, so I said: 'Read it, child, read it; you'll like it when once you've fairly begun.' I was right; she liked it so much that she never offered to give back the second novel, and after the third, she wanted to finish all by that author before reading anything else. I was able to gratify her, as we have the whole of his works. She devoured the hundred and eighty volumes in the course of one winter. For, I can assure you, these Jewish girls have no moral feeling . . . !"

The ladies all agree in regarding this statement as true. The estate-agent's wife is the only one who does not join in the chorus. For though she is very fat and rather stupid, she has a good heart.

"It wasn't right," she says very distinctly and very gravely. "You have a great deal to answer for."

The Frau Kasimira looks at her in silent astonishment. If she were not a very courteous woman, a woman of the world, and, above all, if it were not her own house, she would smile sarcastically and shrug her shoulders. As it is, she contents herself with saying apologetically, "Mon Dieu! she was only a Jewess!"

"Only a Jewess!" repeats the chorus of ladies aloud, and also in a whisper. Many of them laugh as they say . . . "only a Jewess!"

"Only a Jewess!" is echoed in a grave deep voice. The games in the ante-room are finished, and the gentlemen have rejoined the ladies unnoticed. "You have made a great mistake, madam."

It is the doctor of Barnow who speaks, a tall stately man. He is a Jew by birth. He is hated because of his religion, and feared because of his power of sarcasm. His position obliges these people to receive him into their society, and he accepts their invitations because theirs is the only society to be had in the dull little country town.

"You have made a mistake," he repeats, addressing the estate-agent's wife. "You have never been able to throw off the prejudices of your German home, where people look upon a Jew as a human being. It is very foolish of you not to have learned to look upon the subject from the Podolian point of the view!"

"Laugh as much as you like," says his hostess quickly. "I still maintain that an uneducated Jewess has very little moral feeling!"

"Yes," is the dry answer, "especially when she has been put through a course of Paul de Kock—has been given the whole of his works without exception. "But, pray, don't let me interrupt you; go on with your story."

Frau Kasimira continues:

"Very well; where did I leave off? Oh, I remember now. She had finished Kock by the spring. I had no more German books to lend her; so she begged me to subscribe to the Tarnapol lending library for her, and I at length consented to do so. I didn't like it at all, but she entreated me to do it, so piteously, that I must have had a heart of stone to refuse. She read every one of the books in the library, beginning with About and ending with Zschokke. Her father had no suspicion of the truth, and he never know it. She used only to read in the night when she went to her bedroom. The exertion did not hurt her eyes at all. She had most beautiful eyes, large and blue—blue as the sky. As to her figure, it was queenly, slender, upright, and rounded. In short, she was lovely—very lovely. But at the same time she was a silly romantic girl, who thought that real life was like the novels she used to devour. When she was sixteen her father told her that he wished her to marry a son of Moschko Fränkel from Chorostko, a handsome Jewish lad of about her own age. She said she would rather die than marry him. But old Freudenthal isn't a man to jest with. The betrothal took place, and beautiful Esther sat at the feast pale and trembling as though she were about to die. I had gone down-stairs to see the ceremony from curiosity. My heart is not a very soft one, but when I saw Esther looking so miserable, I really felt for the girl. 'Why are you forcing your daughter to marry against her will?' I asked the old man. He answered me abruptly, almost rudely, I thought: 'Pardon me; you don't understand; our ways are different from your ways. We don't look upon the chicken as wiser than the hen. And, thank God, we know nothing of love and of all that kind of nonsense. We consider that two things are alone requisite when arranging a marriage, and these are health and wealth. The bride and bridegroom in this case possess both. I've given in to Esther so far as to consent that the marriage should be put off for a year. That will give her time to learn to do her duty. Many changes take place in a year.'["]

Translated by M. W. Macdowall.

Other works by Franzos: *Aus Halb-Asien* (1876); *Vom Don zur Donau* (1878); *Moschko von Parma* (1880); *Ein Kampf ums Recht* (1882); *Der Pojaz* (1905).

Poetry

Ephraim Luzzatto
1725–1792

By profession a medical doctor and, by avocation, a poet, Ephraim Luzzatto was born into a family of physicians in San Daniele, Italy. After graduating from the University of Padua and having worked for some years in that city, Luzzatto settled in London, where he practiced at the hospital of the Portuguese Congregation. He was a gifted poet whose verse sometimes took a satirical bent, occasionally targeting medical practitioners. The range and power of his poetry made him an influential figure among modern poets writing in Hebrew. In religion, Luzzatto appears to have been a man at odds with himself, torn between the Jewish faith and atheism.

The Doctor Who Fell Prey to Love
1768

> A beautiful girl, very much in love, came to the doctor's house, seeking a cure. These many days, she said, her soul had been in pain and even at night peace had eluded her.
>
> Now, as this queenly girl stood beside him, he put his hand out to discover if she had a fever. And, suddenly, a flame was kindled in his heart. He, too, fell in love, and into the pit.
>
> The gentleman was overcome and dumbstruck, until the patient again spoke up discreetly: "Please, sir, is there no cure for my complaint?"
>
> Then he: "O my dearest, do not hold back! *You* dress *my* wound, for this once—I am not the doctor, but the patient."

Translated by T. Carmi.

Other work by Luzzatto: *Eleh bene ha-ne'urim* (1766).

Naphtali Herts Wessely
1725–1805

Born in Hamburg and raised in Copenhagen, Naphtali Herts Wessely was a pioneering Haskalah figure and a contemporary of Moses Mendelssohn. He studied religious subjects under Jonathan Eybeschütz, but also studied modern languages and eventually became a poet and linguist, exploring biblical Hebrew and writing biblical commentaries. As a representative of the Feitel Bank, Wessely moved to Berlin, where he met Mendelssohn. He strongly advocated for the social and educational reforms laid out in Joseph II of Austria's Edict of Toleration, writing *Divre shalom ve-emet* (1782) to advocate for Jews in German-speaking lands to accept these reforms. (Selections from Wessely's *Divre shalom ve-emet* and his *Sefer ha-midot* appear in this volume.)

Shire tiferet (Songs of Glory)
1789–1802

> How could the wise of heart envisage the final outcome of the matter,
> Seeing that, when he was just a quarter of a year old, they placed him in the bulrushes?
> None has arisen like him amongst the thousands of Your seers!
> Even if You become wroth, You do not bear a grudge forever.
> For those suffering Your terrors have raised their foreheads,
> The nation that labored with bricks has witnessed Your might!
>
> When Your eyes perceived the distress of Jacob,
> You formed in the womb the redeemer of Your children
> From the hands of strangers, who devoured them like bread.
> O God! Teach me, I pray you, to tell of Your glory—the great things You have wrought with Your servant,
> From the very day of his birth, from the moment he emerged from the womb.

When the heart of Jacob had melted, and no spirit stirred in anyone,
They did not approach a woman, even the graceful does were despised,
The spirit came upon a man, the Almighty's aid was with a man of valor,
He was Amram the Levite, light shone forth for him in the darkness,
He spoke comfortingly unto his wife, and by means of wisdom he captured her soul.
"Lady of grace, strengthen yourself, daughter of Levi, give ear!
Do not continue to turn your eye away from me,
Return unto me and have no fear of destruction, I pray you,
I am not a cruel man in that I would raise up offspring for nought,
To watch the delights of my eyes being brought forth to be slain:
My heart is overflowing with a goodly matter, I am not one who invents vain things,
You are to be a mother of Jacob, you shall turn darkness into light."
Yokheved was enthused with joy, for she knew the righteousness of her husband,
That his wisdom was great, and how pleasant were his ways,
For the spirit of God spoke through him—his eye would tolerate no falsehood:
So she took the words of his mouth on board, she returned to him and conceived.
Merry of heart was she throughout her pregnancy,
And at the appointed time, she gave birth to a son of goodly appearance—
While still naked inside her belly, she perceived special signs within the child,
That he was a gift from God and the one chosen by the Almighty from the womb,
After about three months together with her, she hid him.

Translated by David E. Cohen.

Other works by Wessely: *Levanon* (*Gan naʿul*) (1765–1766); *Die Moseide in achtzehn Gesängen* (1806).

Anonymous

These *koplas* (couplets), among many other literary compositions in Ladino, celebrate the Purim of Sarajevo and the averted disaster of 1819, related in detail in the *Sarajevo meguila* (1900). Moshe Haviyo, a Jew from Travnik, converted to Islam, and under the name "Dervish Ahmed" preached against Jews. As he was soon killed, Mehmed Ruşdi Pasha, governor of Bosnia, accused the Jews of ritual murder and arrested ten elders and the chief rabbi, Moshe Danon (d. 1830). On pain of death, they were required to pay an enormous fine within three days. Members of their community managed to secure the support of Sarajevo's Muslims, who liberated the prisoners and achieved the governor's dismissal. Danon's burial place in Stolach became a pilgrimage site for Balkan Jews because many attributed this liberation to divine intervention brought about due to the rabbi's righteousness.

A Story of What Happened to Rav Moshe Danon and the Elders of the Jewish Community of Sarajevo on 20 October 1819
ca. 1820

Let us recount a story of the old days, of what happened to a great man who lived then.

He was our Rav Danon,
may his name endure forever.
We will not forget him ever,
We will extol him before God,
for the great salvation
he attained for our nation.

He delivered us from a villain
whose name was Ruşdi Pasha.
The Jews were aware
they would live in terror
In the time of this cruel
enemy of Israel.
He was fierce as a snake.
Let his name be erased!

Vicious and haughty man,
he promised to pay
for governing this place
as is the Turkish way.

He concocted a scheme
to get money for the bribe.

Cursed be Moshe Haviyo,
wicked and insane,
enemy of Israel,
who converted to Islam
and then disappeared,
which is what he deserved.

Ruşdi Pasha flew into a rage
like a beast in a cage,
and he used this occasion
to take revenge on our nation.
He said the Jews had murdered him
to wipe out his name.

This scoundrel thought
his time had come.
He was sure his scheme
would work as he dreamed
through a libel he invented,
and the people would accept it.

Israel's evil oppressor
summoned to his palace
the Jewish elders and their crown,
the righteous Rav Moshe Danon.

Viciously he yelled at them,
"Turkey's enemies you are"
How dared you murder him,
a good and venerated man,
beloved by our holy God,
and he was worthy of God's love,
because he understood the truth?"

He didn't let them say a word.
"All of you are going to die,
and this is as certain
as the sun is in the sky!"
He roared like a furious tiger,
"All of you deserve to die."

They were confounded and stunned,
unable to pronounce a word.
He promised he would set them free
if only they agreed to pay
a huge amount he required,
a ransom they would never find.

He wouldn't agree to less than that,
the sum they offered him instead.
He tortured and tormented them,
and finally put them in chains.

He hoped to take revenge on us,
but, like the plotting of Haman,
his devious plan was ill-conceived.
May our merciful king live!

The Sarajevo Muslims heard
of Ruşdi Pasha's brutal deeds.
They rose against the cruel Turk
and set the Jewish captives free.

As they couldn't stand him anymore,
it went a way he hadn't expected.
He got unhinged and lost his head,
And right away to Travnik[1] fled.

NOTE

1. [The capital city of Ottoman governors of Bosnia, fifty-six miles west of Sarajevo.—Trans.]

Translated by Olga Borovaya.

Heinrich Heine

Donna Clara
1827

In the evening through her garden
Wanders the Alcalde's daughter;
Festal sounds of drum and trumpet
Ring out hither from the castle.

"I am weary of the dances,
Honeyed words of adulation
From the knights who still compare me
To the sun,—with dainty phrases.

"Yes, of all the things I am weary,
Since I first beheld by moonlight,
Him my cavalier, whose zither
Nightly draws me to my casement.

"As he stands, so slim and daring,
With his flaming eyes that sparkle
From his nobly-pallid features,
Truly he St. George resembles."

Thus went Donna Clara dreaming,
On the ground her eyes were fastened,
When she raised them, lo! before her
Stood the handsome, knightly stranger.

Pressing hands and whispering passion,
These twain wander in the moonlight.
Gently doth the breeze caress them,
The enchanted roses greet them.

The enchanted roses greet them,
And they glow like love's own heralds;
"Tell me, tell me, my beloved,
Wherefore, all at once thou blushest."

"Gnats were stinging me, my darling,
And I hate these gnats in summer,
E'en as though they were a rabble
Of vile Jews with long, hooked noses."

"Heed not gnats nor Jews, beloved,"
Spake the knight with fond endearments.
From the almond-tree dropped downward
Myriad snowy flakes of blossoms.

Myriad snowy flakes of blossoms
Shed around them fragrant odors.
"Tell me, tell me, my beloved,
Looks thy heart on me with favor?"

"Yes, I love thee, oh my darling,
And I swear it by our Savior,
Whom the accursed Jews did murder
Long ago with wicked malice."

"Heed thou neither Jews nor Savior,"
Spake the knight with fond endearments;
Far-off waved as in a vision
Gleaming lilies bathed in moonlight.

Gleaming lilies bathed in moonlight
Seemed to watch the stars above them.
"Tell me, tell me, my belovèd,
Didst thou not erewhile swear falsely?"

"Naught is false in me, my darling,
E'en as in my bosom floweth
Not a drop of blood that's Moorish,
Neither of foul Jewish current."

"Heed not Moors nor Jews, belovèd,"
Spake the knight with fond endearments.
Then towards a grove of myrtles
Leads he the Alcalde's daughter.

And with love's slight, subtle meshes,
He hath trapped her and entangled;
Brief their words, but long their kisses,
For their hearts are overflowing.

What a melting bridal carol,
Sings the nightingale, the pure one!
How the fire-flies in the grasses
Trip their sparkling, torch-light dances!

In the grove the silence deepens;
Naught is heard save furtive rustling
Of the swaying myrtle branches,
And the breathing of the flowers.

But the sound of drum and trumpet
Burst forth sudden from the castle.
Rudely they awaken Clara,
Pillowed on her lover's bosom.

"Hark, they summon me, my darling.
But before I go, oh tell me,
Tell me what thy precious name is,
Which so closely thou hast hidden."

And the knight, with gentle laughter,
Kissed the fingers of his donna,
Kissed her lips and kissed her forehead,
And at last these words he uttered:

I, Señora, your belovèd,
Am the son of the respected
Worthy, erudite Grand Rabbi,
Israel of Saragossa!"

Translated by Emma Lazarus.

Anonymous

This dirge relates the tragic events that struck the Ottoman Jewish community in July 1826, when two powerful Jewish financiers were murdered in Istanbul on the sultan's orders. They were Isaac Karmona, known as Çelebi Behor Karmona, and Isaiah Aciman (Ajiman). Both had business ties with the Janissary corps, which had been liquidated by the sultan a few weeks earlier, following the revolt mentioned in the dirge. After Karmona was strangled in his mansion, some of his family members were exiled. A few days later, Ajiman was beheaded. The dirge is modeled on traditional *kinot*, particularly *The Seven Sons of Hana*, a story of seven brothers killed by King Antiochus Epiphanes for refusing to renounce Judaism. This is why Ajiman is referred to as "the second one," as if Karmona and Ajiman were brothers. One version of the *kina* talks of the mother witnessing the violent death of one of her sons, which explains the presence of Karmona's mother in the dirge. This lamentation has twenty-two quatrains. As is typical for Sephardi *koplas* (couplets), the first letters of the first line of each stanza form an acrostic that follows the Hebrew alphabet. The need for a particular sequence of letters appears to have affected the logic of the narration. Thus quatrains sixteen and nineteen are evidently switched.

A Dirge for the Ninth of Av
ca. 1827

1

Let us chant, my brothers,
this dirge together,
for God severed our hands
by this disaster.

2

We have become orphans,
fatherless children.
Let's ask God to save us
from greater evils.

3

Çelebi Behor Karmona,
crown of the whole Jewry,
renowned the world over,
and Ajiman, the second one,

4

as we saw them murdered,
one after the other,
Our eyes filled with tears
streaming like torrents.

5

They came to strangle him at home,
while he was still sleeping,
"What is this fury about?"
They did not know, either.

6

"Come, my beloved mother,
to embrace and kiss me.
If you do not come quickly,
you will not see me ever."

7

Gendarmes all over the house,
raging like a tempest.
Watching him through the window,
His mother's agonizing.

8

"My beloved Behorachi,
you did not die of illness,
You left me all of a sudden,
never guilty of wrongdoing.

9

He was loved by everybody,
everyone is in mourning.
They took from me Behorachi,
never guilty of wrongdoing."

10

Let's weep and lament this misfortune,
the horror that befell us.
If we live a thousand years,
we will never forget it.

11

They threw her out of the mansion
and brought her to look at him.
They wanted her to see her son
prostrated dead on the ground.

12

There is no end to our tears,
We shed them day and night,
for we see that we have lost
the best among the Jews.

13

Anguish, wails, and lamentations
shedding tears, fasting, weeping,
is the lot of the Jewish people,
but our lot is the hardest.

14

There was nobody like him
in the whole of the Jewish nation
God deprived us of his presence,
put him in a grave too early.

15

His life was in great danger
because of the account,
that a minister[1] demanded,
which deeply distressed him.

16

Let's keep weeping and mourning,
lamenting this disaster,
let us turn to the heavens
and demand justice

17

for this man who served the empire,
who was merciful and gracious.
Since the Janissary riot
we did not have any respite.

18

His munificence was matchless
and his charity unequaled.
Everyone received his share,
but the Jews had more than others.

19

When he finished his account,
it resulted right and flawless.
Even so he was strangled,
and his brother sent into exile.

20

Let us pray to the Almighty,
that the Messiah might come quickly,
that we have the joy of seeing
the Temple rebuilt in our lifetime.

21

We will offer sacrifices
from now on daily.
We will see the Messiah
seated in his throne.

22

Let us pray to our Father
for the joy of seeing quickly
the Messiah coming in peace
and revealing the miracle.

NOTE

1. Lit., deputy of the country. One of the Carmona's biographers claims that it was the *bostancibaşi* (lit., chief gardener; i.e., a high-ranking palace administrator), who asked him for a financial account and then went to his house with two gendarmes to strangle him.

Translated by Olga Borovaya.

Penina Moïse
1797–1880

Penina Moïse was a poet and educator from Charleston, South Carolina. Even though her formal education ended at age twelve, after her father's death, she wrote poems and sketches for Jewish and non-Jewish newspapers and was the first American Jewish woman to publish a collection of poetry. Moïse was devoted to Charleston's vibrant Jewish community. She was the superintendent of Congregation Beth Elohim's Sunday school and contributed hymns to the congregation's religious services, some of which were included in the Reform movement's *Union Hymnal*.

Miriam
1833

Amid the flexile reeds of Nile a lovely infant slept,
While over the unconscious babe his mother watched and wept,
Nor distant far another stood whose tears flowed fast and free,
'Twas Miriam the beautiful, bright star of the sea.

With breaking heart that parent bids farewell to her doomed child,
Commending to Almighty God his spirit undefiled.
The sister lingers yet to mourn o'er tyranny's decree.
And bitter was thy agony, fair maiden of the sea.

The palace of the Pharaohs now sends forth a noble train,
Thermutis comes, by Heaven led, to break her father's chain.
And who is that homage yields upon her bended knee?
It is the graceful Miriam, the brightener of the sea.

Trembling she rose and timid stood upon the water's edge,
When lo! the princess marks the boy slumbering amid the sedge.
A fairy ark and foundling too? 'Tis Fortune's gift to me,
Joy to the heart of Miriam, the fair star of the sea.

A nurse for this deserted babe, cried Pharaoh's gentle daughter,
Whose name, my nymphs, shall Moses be, thus rescued from the water.
A woman of the stranger's race I'll quickly bring to thee.
Said the delighted Miriam, the day-star of the sea.

She turned aside, nor tarried long, for soon her infant brother,
On the familiar bosom lay of his own Hebrew mother,
And bounding onward by her side, full of triumphant glee,
Went Miriam the beautiful, the bright star of the sea.

Time fleets—the child, to manhood reared, has left his proud abode,
And royalty's bold protegé has broken Egypt's rod.
The oracle of Israel has set his nation free!
Then sung melodious Miriam, enlightener of the sea.

But why hast thou at Hazeroth thy timbrel cast aside,
And dared to lift thy voice against the legislator's bride?
For this shalt thou be smitten, till thy brother's prayer for thee
Restores again thy loveliness, rash lady of the sea.

A wail is in the wilderness, a deep and solemn wail,
The prophetess who soared beyond mortality's dark pale,
Has to the *spirit's promised land* departed pure and free.
Farewell, inspired Miriam, thou lost star of the sea!

Other work by Moïse: *Fancy's Sketch Book* (1833).

Heinrich Heine

Farewell, You Cheerful Folk of France
1835

Farewell, you cheerful folk of France,
My brethren's merry throng,
A foolish nostalgia drives me hence,
I'll be back, though, before long.

Imagine—I yearn beyond belief
For the smell of heather and peat,
For the dear toy sheep of the Lüneburg heath,
For pickled cabbage and beer.

I find I miss tobacco fug,
Black bread, the Low-German cadence,
The knighted, the night-watchmen—why, the boors!
The flaxen-haired parsonage maidens.

And also I am hankering,
Let me confess, for Mother;
I haven't seen the dear old thing
For thirteen years together.

Farewell, my wife, my lovely wife,
You can't fathom my distress;
I press you so firmly to my heart
But must leave you nonetheless.

I am driven away by that panting pain
From my sweetest happiness—
I must breathe German air again
Or draw no other breath.

Translated by Walter W. Arndt.

Abraham Dov (Adam) ha-Kohen Lebensohn
1794–1878

Abraham (Avraham) Dov Lebensohn, a Lithuanian *maskil* and poet also known as Adam ha-Kohen, was born in Vilna, received a traditional Jewish education, but explored the Hebrew language and grammar. He worked as a merchant and as a Jewish legal scholar for several years in small towns, returning to Vilna in 1819, where he taught and worked in commerce. He earned his fame as a poet, often writing poems for commission (including for a visit to Vilna of Moses

Montefiore, and in honor of Russian governmental figures). He advocated for enlightened Jewish education and wrote biblical commentaries.

Lament of the Daughter of Judah
1842

> O God of Hosts, our God from of old,
> Was it for this that You selected our ancestors from days of yore
> That You took their descendants as an inheritance for Yourself
> To set them up as the target of Your blasts of fury,
> So that they run around the world when stricken by the evils inflicted by You?
> Are all Your arrows spent with a view to their annihilation?
> How is it that we have strayed from the path of understanding,
> And how is it that all that is upright within man has become crooked within us?
> How has all righteousness among us been turned into a destructive force,
> Wisdom and morality into an abomination of the soul?
> Is it not You, O Lord, in that You have forsaken us,
> Have placed us in darkness rather than in light?
> By reason of the abundance of the days of affliction, we have lost sight of justice,
> Those marching us along are perplexed, without vision:
> Not a single man among them looks attentively at the nation,
> There is no one among them who knows how to repair their breaches:
> In the place of fences, they build sheepfolds,
> They cannot discern the location where the breaches lie:
> They who fear the Lord are merely in fear of the reproach of man,
> They who love Him are simply lovers of human gifts:
> They who honor the Lord despise the knowledge of Him,
> They who praise Him are the ones profaning the man of understanding, who seeks after God:
> Our God, make Your wisdom known upon earth,
> Open, I pray You, forever the eyes of those who hate it,
> Lo, You have bestowed upon it redemption and salvation,
> Only those acquainted with it have the ability to save, or to be saved, through it!

Translated by David E. Cohen.

Other works by Lebensohn: *Shene luḥot ha-edut* (1856); *Shire sefat kodesh* (1856, 1870); *Emet ve-emunah* (1867).

Abraham Dov (Adam) ha-Kohen Lebensohn

Seeker of Truth
1842

I

> He said: "Show me, I pray You, Your glory!"[1]
>
> Behold, wise men have declared,
> Moreover, the proofs adduced by them have attested,
> That the senses are illusory,
> Mirages are legion,
> Thoughts are liars,
> Cogitations alter,
> The intellect turns foolish,
> Understanding is not steady,
> Opinions err,
> And there is deficiency in every knowledge:
> Everything I perceive
> Is not like a genuine vision,
> And as for what I know,
> My heart has erred in respect thereof.
> As for myself too, who am I?
> Alas! Who has deceived me?
> And who are all these?
> Wonder of wonders!
> Support me, I pray You,
> O God, my Maker!

II

> He said: "You cannot see My face, for no man can see Me and live!"
>
> Understand, O man! Do so like a man, and this should suffice you.
> Do not discern as God does,
> In regard either to lowly or lofty matters,

For then you are no longer man—indeed, you are no
    longer alive!
Sweet is the light of the sun, but not the strength of
    its face;
Delightful is the light of wisdom,
But it has no boundaries.
How comely is the light of truth, but who can see it?
The veil is over its face—do not lift it,
Lest you gaze upon its countenance with your eyes.
Woe! For then the light of life will grow dark for you!

NOTE
1. [Exodus 33.—Ed.]

Translated by David E. Cohen.

Siegfried Kapper
1821–1879

Siegfried (Isaac Salomon) Kapper was a Czech and German poet, writer, translator, and physician. Born on the outskirts of Prague, where he studied philosophy, Kapper received a doctorate in medicine from the University of Vienna. A medical officer during the 1848 revolution in Vienna, he later served as a representative in the Austrian parliament. Kapper was a leading figure in the Czech–Jewish assimilation movement and the first Jewish writer to publish in the Czech language. His works include revolutionary poems, political essays, writings on Slavic culture, as well as translations of poetry and folk songs.

Ben-Oni (Son of Sorrow)
1846

I do not lift my supplicating hands,
O King, O Lord, O Father, yon on high,
To You whose throne dwells in the starry lands,
I neither plead nor yet Your might defy.

I do not ask of You to end my woeful bane,
To guide my steps, to aid me to return
To the distant shrine for which I long in vain,
Where the Star of Zion ne'er again shall burn.

For the Rose of Sharon I no longer pine;
Nor for the fruits from a sloping Jordan hill,
Its milk and honey I gladly will decline,
Its pleasant days, and nights so cool and still.

My plaintive prayer is free from all regret,
For wasted joys and sweetness spent in vain,
If but for once in life I could forget
The bitter drops of my fellow-men's disdain.

Translated by Roderick A. Ginsburg.

Other works by Kapper: *Karel Hynek Mácha und die neuböhmische Literatur* (1842); *Befreite Lieder* (1848); *Falk* (1853); *Herzel und seine Freunde* (1853); *Výbor ze spisů Siegfrieda Kappera* (1921).

Afanasy Fet
1820–1892

Afanasy Fet is considered to be one of the greatest Russian lyric poets. Of unclear origin, Fet was thought to be the illegitimate son of Charlotte Foeth (née Becker), daughter of German Jewish poet Johann Peter Karl Wilhelm Foeth, and the Russian nobleman Afanasy Shenshin. Fet was disinherited from the Shenshin estate, a fact that haunted him even after he was recognized as a member of the nobility and allowed to carry their surname. He was praised by Russian literati, including Leo Tolstoy, Nikolai Nekrasov, and Ivan Turgenev, and worked with the latter two on the prominent journal *Sovremennik*. His poetry was noteworthy for its musicality, sensuality, and overwhelming melancholy. In his later years, he translated literature from Latin, German, and English.

Sheltered by a Crimson Awning . . .
1847

Sheltered by a crimson awning,
All alone, his slaves dismissed,
A lord is bidding farewell fondly
To a black-browed odalisque.

"Sarah, houri of the prophet,
My sunshine, comfort, strength, delight,
Sarah, morning's not far off now—
Azrael will soon alight.

"After battle on the morrow
Will I still walk the earth somewhere,
Or, forever freed from sorrow,
Rest my head without a care?

"Another night and tabernacle
Soon may take the place of these;
Then despite my ardent rapture,
I won't touch your rosebud cheek.

"I won't smoke my lazy hookah
Idly as you bide nearby,
Will not pensively sit looking
Into your gazelle-like eyes.

"Nor will I with weary fingers
Plait and twist your tresses black
Along the scarlet fez and fringes
Into a shining, scaly snake."

Translated by Alissa Dinega Gillespie.

Other works by Fet: *Liricheskii panteon* (1840); *Vechernie ogni* (1883); *Moi vospominaniia* (1890).

Rachel Luzzatto Morpurgo
1790–1871

Rachel Morpurgo (b. Luzzatto) was born to a rabbinic and literary family in Trieste, Italy. Highly educated in Jewish and secular subjects, Morpurgo began writing poetry at age eighteen. She was one of the first women to write modern Hebrew poetry. Despite her parents' disapproval, she married Italian Jewish merchant Jacob Morpurgo. Rachel Morpurgo's work first appeared in print in 1847 in the literary journal *Kokheve Yitshak*, where she ultimately published some fifty poems to wide acclaim, thanks to the advocacy of her well-known cousin Samuel Luzzatto.

On Hearing She Had Been Praised in the Journals
1847

My soul sighs, fate brings only trouble.
My spirit was lifted, and I grew bold.
I heard a voice: 'Your poem is gold.
Who has learned to sing like you, Rachel?'

My spirit in turn replies: I've lost my savor.
Exile after exile has soured my skin.
My taste has faded, my vineyard long grown thin.
For fear of shame, now, I sing no longer.

I've looked to the north, to the south and east and west:

in each a woman's word is lighter than dust.
Years hence, will anyone really remember

her name, in city or province, any more
than a dead dog's? Ask: the people are sure:
a woman's wisdom is only in spinning wool.

Wife of Jacob Morpurgo, stillborn

Translated by Peter Cole.

Other work by Morpurgo: *Ugav Raḥel* (1890).

Abraham Jacob Paperna
1840–1919

A poet and literary critic, Abraham Jacob (Avraham Ya'akov) Paperna was born and raised in Kapyl, present-day Belarus, and embraced the Haskalah from an early age, though he came to observe the movement critically and allegorically in his writings. In the 1860s, he studied at rabbinical seminaries in Zhitomir and Vilna, and then spent his career teaching at the Jewish government school in Zakroczym, Poland, and at the government secondary school in Płock. An integral member of the Russian Haskalah, he wrote poems, both lyrical and satirical. Paperna died in Odessa, where he had fled during World War I.

Emet ve-emunah (Truth and Faith)
1863

There is a certain ḥayah [angelic being] in the firmament, who bears the sign of truth upon its forehead during the daytime, whereby the angels know that it is day, and in the evening, it bears the sign of faith upon its forehead, whereby they know that it is night.

Truth and faith are as the moon is to the sun,
From times of yore they have been compared to each other.
Truth shines its light like the sun,
And as for faith—its face exults for joy like the moon.
Truth is as elevated above us as is the sun in its loftiness
But faith is as close to us as the moon.

It drops down healing and kindness, daily it disperses rays of life and brightness,
And for the moon which constantly longs for it,

It enwraps itself in a mantle of light, binding a headdress of purity,
And consecrates it to minister in its stead
To illuminate the earth, to banish its dark places.

So likewise does truth gaze out from the skies,
Dispensing precious light to the earth below,
With rays at her side for the yearning soul,
Bestowing of her glory upon her only sister,
Upon faith, that majestic sister of hers,
To serve in her stead in absent locations.

The sun and truth march on daily with strength
Around the earthly sphere with splendor, grandeur, and might;
The moon and faith proceed in darkness,
With torches in their hands to drive away the darkness of the night.
Let us go, I pray you, my brothers, toward the light of these two
Lest we be destroyed, and stumble, in the "night" of life!

The light of the moon and of faith are beneficial to the eyes,
The eye of flesh and spirit rejoices at the magnitude of their light;
But in the light of the sun in its position at noontide,
Every eye grows dim, becomes darkened by its fiery flame.
Such, alas, is the light of truth! We do not realize our lowliness,
We do not perceive the brightness of its rising—save through the thick darkness.

Many are our daily adversaries under the sun,
By its light we see only violence and slaughter,
Beleaguerment and distress and anguish that never depart;
But in the brightness of the moon there is eternal delight
In the shadow of the wings of sleep we find repose,
We do not see perversity, nor indeed the spread of violence.

They who see the light of truth, great is their suffering on earth,
Falsehood lurks on the outside, and a sufficiency within,
Causing hurt and pain until the onset of destruction.

But he who befriends faith shall blossom like the olive tree,
And in the shadow of innocence, tranquil and secure, he shall take refuge;
He shall experience neither mental confusion nor a shattering of his spirit.

The moon and faith are close to us,
Many are the sages of the world who have seen them, yea, examined them,
But the sun is too lofty for us,
And the generation yet to be born will not discover its source of light,
And wise men have grown weary over the past two thousand years
In the exploration of its wonders, but have met with no success.

Thus it is with truth, the sun of our spirit;
It lies concealed, alas, amidst the assembly of the heavenly hosts;
We toil and weary ourselves throughout our lives
To discover its pathways, but they remain hidden for eternity;
Hundreds of years have passed, yea, millennia have elapsed,
But the hiding places of truth have still to be laid bare.

Translated by David E. Cohen.

Other work by Paperna: *Kankan ḥadash male yashan* (1867).

Judah Leib Gordon
1831–1892

Judah (Yehudah) Leib Gordon, the most renowned Hebrew-language poet of the nineteenth century, was born and educated in Vilna. After working as a teacher, he moved to St. Petersburg in 1872 to serve as secretary of the Society for the Promotion of Culture among the Jews of Russia. A proponent of Jewish modernization and enhanced status for women, he was denounced for radicalism and briefly imprisoned. Once exonerated, he became the editor of the Hebrew paper *Ha-melits*, continuing to critique Orthodoxy through his writing. Though his mother tongue was Yiddish, he advocated for Jewish acceptance of Hebrew and Russian as a means of Jewish cultural rebirth and emancipation.

Awake My People!
1866

Awake, my people! How long will you slumber?
The night has passed, the sun shines bright.
Awake, lift up your eyes, look around you—
Acknowledge, I pray you, your time and your place....

The land in which now we live and are born—
Is it not thought to be part of Europe?
Europe—the smallest of the Earth's regions,
Yet the greatest of all in wisdom and reason.

This land of Eden [Russia] now opens its gates to you,
Her sons now call you "brother"!
How long will you dwell among them as a guest,
And why do you now affront them?

Already they have removed the weight of suffering from your shoulder,
They have lifted off the yoke from your neck,
They have erased from their hearts gratuitous hatred and folly,
They give you their hand, they greet you with peace.

Raise your head high, straighten your back,
And gaze with loving eyes upon them,
Open your heart to wisdom and knowledge,
Become an enlightened people, and speak their language.

Every man of understanding should try to gain knowledge;
Let others learn all manner of arts and crafts;
Those who are brave should serve in the army;
The farmers should buy ploughs and fields.

To the treasury of the state bring your strength,
Take your share of its possessions, its bounty.
Be a man abroad and a Jew in your tent,
A brother to your countrymen and a servant to your king....

Translated by D. Goldman.

Other works by Gordon: *Ahavat David u-Mikhal* (1856); *Mishle Yehudah* (1859); *Kol shire Yehudah* (1883–1884); *Kol kitve Yehudah* (1889).

Judah Leib Gordon

The Tip of the Yod
1875

Hebrew woman, who knows your life?
You came in darkness and in darkness depart.
Your sorrows and joys, your hopes and desires
Were born within you and die in your heart.
Daughters of other nations
May know comfort and mirth
But the Jewish woman's vocation,
Is endless servitude on earth.
You conceive, bear, nurse and wean in time,
You bake, cook, season and ripen before your prime.

So what if you bear beauty and possess sentiment,
Or if God endowed you with talent and mind!
For you Torah is tasteless, beauty a detriment,
Every gift a flaw, every thought a bind.
Indecent your voice, monstrous your mane,
You are nothing but vessel of blood and of bile!
Inside you the filth of the serpent remains.
Your nation sends you like a mourner to exile,
From the school and the house of the Lord you are thrown,
Banished from rejoicing to bear sorrows alone.

It is the best that you know not the language of your fathers,
That the door to the house of your Lord is shut tight,
For you hear not the morning blessing of your mockers,
"That He did not make me woman" daily they recite.
They regard you as servile, slave and sinner,
As a hen prepared to raise young chicks.
Why then, milking cow, O burdened heifer,
Why are you required to learn all their tricks?
For naught they continue to teach you well,
Though your disciples are sent directly to hell.

God not only denies you the fruit of your womb
And leaves you a prisoner of grief in your youth,
At so young an age deprived of your bridegroom,
Now his brother's shoe you must also remove.

You weep, unlike your brothers, for your father's
    demise,
Yet his estate is entrusted to them and not you,
The blessings of earth they steal before your eyes
Depriving you even of the fresh morning dew.
Two hundred and forty-eight commandments these
    misers obtain,
And for you, wretched female, only three remain.

O Hebrew woman, your heart full of pain!
You long for life and knowledge but end up with
    none—
Like a sprout of the lord in the desert you wane,
You perceive not the spring and know not the sun,
Like a seedling of fruit crop, a small patch of land,
Your meadow left fallow, now you grow wild;
Before you matured or your mind could expand,
A man took you to bear and nurture his child.
Still a child to your parents, not fully grown,
You were wed and became—mother to your own.

Married—did you know him to whom you
    were wed?
Did you love him? Did you see him eye-to-eye?
Did you love? Wretched one, long has it been said
Love from a daughter of Israel is a lie.
Forty days before her awaited birth
The matchmakers a match prepares,
Why see him now, what is it worth?
What would love give her but additional cares?
Our mothers knew not the ways to adore—
Shall then our sister be treated like a whore?

Place a kerchief on your head, your face you must
    hide,
Shear your long tresses and leave your head bald,
Why should you see him who stands at your side,
If he's thin or hunchbacked, youthful or old?
It makes no difference to you! You shall not choose,
Like an object transferred from domain to domain,
Your parents decide—Who are you to refuse?
Like Arameans they should care if the girl shows
    disdain?
Over your virginity rules your father's firm hand,
Later you submit to your husband's command.

Your husband himself was not properly trained,
He planted no vineyard, no house did he build;
When the dowry and wealth of your parents is
    drained,

Your time of lodging in their home fulfilled,
Only then will this man lacking reason and heart,
Venture into the world to seek out his wage,
And leave you abandoned, as one kept apart,
A deserted *agunah* to wilt in your cage.
For all Jewish women is this story I share,
The tale of Bat-Shua and her dreadful despair.

Translated by Rachel Seelig.

Emma Lazarus
1849–1887

The socially conscious writer Emma Lazarus grew up in an established Sephardic family in New York. Lazarus's eloquent essays, emotive poetry, and insightful translations—particularly of the works of Heinrich Heine—garnered her early respect and acclaim. She was a fervent activist against antisemitism and a champion for Jewish immigrants, volunteering and supporting social services. Her efforts reflected her proto-Zionist views advocating Jewish cultural rebirth and settlement in Palestine. The words she is perhaps most remembered by, which encapsulate her views on the importance of immigrant rights and freedom from persecution, were added to the base of the Statue of Liberty in 1903, sixteen years after her death at the age of thirty-eight.

Epochs
ca. 1875

Peace

    The calm outgoing of a long, rich day,
        Checkered with storm and sunshine, gloom and
            light,
    Now passing in pure, cloudless skies away,
    Withdrawing into silence of blank night.
    Thick shadows settle on the landscape bright,
    Like the weird cloud of death that falls apace
    On the still features of the passive face.
    Soothing and gentle as a mother's kiss,
    The touch that stopped the beating of the heart.
    A look so blissfully serene as this,
    Not all the joy of living could impart.
    With dauntless faith and courage therewithal,
    The Master found her ready at his call.

On such a golden evening forth there floats,
Between the grave earth and the glowing sky
In the clear air, unvexed with hazy motes,
The mystic-winged and flickering butterfly,
A human soul, that drifts at liberty,
Ah! who can tell to what strange paradise,
To what undreamed-of fields and lofty skies!

Loneliness

All stupor of surprise hath passed away;
She sees, with clearer vision than before,
A world far off of light and laughter gay,
Herself alone and lonely evermore.
Folk come and go, and reach her in no wise,
Mere flitting phantoms to her heavy eyes.

All outward things, that once seemed part of her,
Fall from her, like the leaves in autumn shed.
She feels as one embalmed in spice and myrrh,
With the heart eaten out, a long time dead;
Unchanged without, the features and the form;
Within, devoured by the thin red worm.

By her own prowess she must stand or fall,
This grief is to be conquered day by day.
Who could befriend her? Who could make this small,
Or her strength great? She meets it as she may.
A weary struggle and a constant pain,
She dreams not they may ever cease nor wane.

Other works by Lazarus: *Poems and Translations* (1867); *Admetus and Other Poems* (1871); *Alide: An Episode of Goethe's Life* (1874); *Songs of a Semite: The Dance to Death and Other Poems* (1882); *Emma Lazarus: Selected Poems and Other Writings* (2002).

Salomón López Fonseca
1853-1935

Salomón López Fonseca was a Sephardic Jew descended from a prominent Sephardic rabbinic family. A businessman, philanthropist, public official, and poet, López Fonseca played an important role in the Jewish community of Coro, Venezuela. He was active in Coro's two literary societies, Alegría (Happiness) and Armonía (Harmony). A prizewinner in South American literary competitions, López Fonseca was admired for his translations of Italian poets as well as for his own poems.

Love and Illusion
1877

Dedicated to my friend Ignacio Móntes de Oca.

Why, if summer strips the garden
Of flowers and verdant foliage,
Does Spring so generously restore
Lush greenery, soft flowers,
And brilliant color;
And to those who've been betrayed,
Putting an end to trust and candor,
Though shedding a river of cruel tears,
Devoid of flowers or rich attire,
Does love not return?

T. Johnson, *Portrait of Emma Lazarus*, 1852.

Why, if night spreads its wings,
Clothing Creation's beauty in mourning,
Does the sun set the sky afire
And the Earth ignite once more
With fresh emotion;
And for him who's lost his heart's delight,
That innocent peace of happier times,
With no light to warm him, no voice to inspire,
Does not sweet illusion return as before,
Festive and smiling?

Could man be the only plant
That shrivels up in summer's heat,
No more revived by April winds,
But broken by time's onslaught,
Robbing him of vigor?
Is the breast the sole abode,
Enfolded in night's horror,
That finds no star whose golden glow
Turns dark to a radiant dawn
Of rosy splendor?

Oh, no! For if we feel our soul is wounded
By horrible doubts—oh cruel deceit—
Let us humbly bear the martyr's palm,
And seek the soothing calm
That comes with prayer.
If everything speaks to us of pain,
If nothing binds us to worldly strife,
Let us kneel before God, the fount
That quenches the thirst of those who yearn
For love and illusion.
    Carora, August 1, 1877

Translated by Michele McKay Aynesworth.

Solomon Ettinger

1803–1856

One of the most influential Yiddish writers of the early nineteenth century, Solomon (Shloyme) Ettinger was a physician, playwright, and poet, born in Warsaw. A descendant of a prominent rabbinical family, but orphaned at a young age, Ettinger moved between Warsaw, Odessa, Zamość, and Lemberg in search of economic stability. Wherever he was based, he was active in maskilic circles and devoted to the use of Yiddish to spread the message of Enlightenment to the Jewish masses. While he never saw any of his work published in his lifetime due to Russian censorship, Ettinger distributed his plays (an excerpt from his *Serkele* appears in this volume), stories, fables, and poems in manuscript form. Although his letters bespeak a life of disappointment and financial hardship, Ettinger was known as "merry Solomon" by his compatriots, an image which has endured in biography and scholarship on the rise of modern Yiddish culture.

The Assembly
ca. 1880

A lion drew his final breath,
And animals were bereft by his death.
There was no one to rule the realm,
So everyone wanted to take the helm.
When the animals realized their quandary,
They discussed it thoroughly
And agreed with one another
That they ought to get together.
  At the assembly the animals wondered
Who should reign—and they pondered.
  The first candidate was the tiger,
He wanted to be king—if you please.
"No," said the animals, "he's a fighter,
And we want to live in peace."
  Then they heard the eldest bear:
He wished to be monarch there.
"This dancer!" the animals did rage.
"All at once in his old age
He decides he wants to be the head!
Let him dance and prance instead!"
  Now the stag came hurrying
With sharpened antlers—fit for a king.
Turning on his charm he did say:
"Who's more beautiful anyway?
My desire you should heed:
I want to command indeed."
  "What good are all your airs?"
Said the animals assembled there.
"Beauty alone is not enough.
Your mind has to be sharp and tough."
  The fox held his tongue zealously,
But speculated silently:
"No matter who may mount the throne,
I'll outfox him on my own!
Whoever is chosen, whoever reigns—
I'll simply work behind the scenes."

The donkey, that dimwit, that fool,
Also had a hankering to rule.
"Well," he volunteered, "let's think.
Why shouldn't I become the king?
There's no need to ask any question,
How can anyone raise an objection?
I have an ancient pedigree:
The grandest people have ridden on me.
When Father Abraham was sent,
According to God's commandment,
To sacrifice Isaac, he did ride
My great-great-grandfather to the site.
And Balaam's donkey, who saw the angel appear,
Was my uncle's relative—I swear!
And my father says we're the blood relations
Of many asses in the Jewish nation."

The horses, who were the donkey's kin,
Agreed one hundred percent with him,
And they all told him that they had
Heard about his great-granddads.

But the fox's dander was up, and he
Snapped at the donkey angrily:
"Go to hell with your pedigree
And your disgusting genealogy.
Saints and rabbis have ridden on donkeys,
But you brazen fools are not better than monkeys.

"My idea will appeal to everyone.
Don't forget the old saying: Like father, like son.
Why cogitate and ruminate?
Why contemplate and deliberate?
It's very simple: Our ruler should be
The old ruler's son—don't you see?"

"Yes! Yes!" the animals yelled that day.
And the donkey didn't even bray.

Just ask the head of any Jewish congregation.
Meetings are alike throughout the Jewish nation.

Translated by Joachim Neugroschel.

Other works by Ettinger: *Mesholim: lidelekh, kleyne mayselekh un kasavoslekh* (1890); *Oysgeklibene shriftn* (1957); *Komedye: lider, mesholim un kataveslekh* (1965).

Emma Lazarus

The New Colossus
1883

Not like the brazen giant of Greek fame
With conquering limbs astride from land to land;
Here at our sea-washed, sunset gates shall stand
A mighty woman with a torch, whose flame
Is the imprisoned lightning, and her name
Mother of Exiles. From her beacon-hand
Glows world-wide welcome; her mild eyes command
The air-bridged harbor that twin cities frame,
"Keep, ancient lands, your storied pomp!" cries she
With silent lips. "Give me your tired, your poor,
Your huddled masses yearning to breathe free,
The wretched refuse of your teeming shore,
Send these, the homeless, tempest-tossed to me,
I lift my lamp beside the golden door!"

Intellectual Culture

The period covered in this volume was a deeply ideological age. Advocates of enlightenment, of liberalism, of revolution against old regimes fought bitter polemics with forces seeking stasis, stability, tradition, and the familiar strata of privilege. The status of Jews, as individuals and as communities, was one of the central stakes in this tug of war. In some parts of the world (e.g., the United States, France), revolutions succeeded in toppling the existing system and ushering in, if not a completely new beginning, then certainly conditions for radically reshaping old hierarchies. In other nations, traditionalists stood firm and repelled most forms of change. Jews were passionately involved in the fray, as they considered the merits and losses of the changes being demanded of them. Jewish enlighteners advocated reshaping the contours and content of Jewish knowledge. They sought to broaden and modernize Jewish school curricula, introduce avenues to training for new types of professions, and expand scientific and humanistic horizons of Jews more generally. Religious leaders debated proposed changes in synagogue services and customs and emerged with polemical literature brimming with ideas about which elements of the Jewish religion were (still) essential and which could be eliminated or modified. New denominations were formed and new forms of ecstatic Judaism were born in this period of religious ferment.

By the first decades of the nineteenth century, as more Jews were admitted to universities, a cadre of academically trained scholars and leaders began to emerge. For a long time, their devotion to scholarship went unreciprocated, as very few appointments in academe were granted to professing Jews. Nevertheless, once the gates had opened, Jews made crucial contributions to many emerging academic fields and turned their critical sense to Jewish history and texts as well.

Jews entered the larger world of politics in myriad ways. They rethought the relationship between capital and society, religion and society, and gender and society; they wrote works on colonialism, slavery, and democracy. Jews stood in the British houses of Parliament, in the U.S. Senate, and in local offices, and served in the militaries of several nations, in each case entering domains that had been barred to them for centuries. They supported a vibrant press in multiple languages and diverse cultural and political tones; the entire spectrum of Jewish life and thought played out on its pages.

Rabbinic and Religious Thought

Jonathan Eybeschütz
ca. 1694–1764

Born in Kraków into a rabbinical family that settled in Moravia, Jonathan (Yonatan) Eybeschütz was regarded as a prodigy who wrote monumental works of rabbinic scholarship. He served as rabbi and head of a yeshiva in Prague circa 1711–1715, taking positions on religious matters that brought him into conflict with the city's powerful chief rabbi, David Oppenheim. In 1741, Eybeschütz moved to Metz, France, and eight years later to Altona-Hamburg-Wandsbek, assuming the position of chief rabbi in the triple community. After amulets he wrote fell into the hands of Jacob Emden, a two-decade-long controversy erupted when Emden accused him of being an adherent of Sabbatianism in secret. Eybeschütz wrote numerous rabbinic works, including collections of sermons. (Excerpts of several of his works appear in this volume.)

Sermon of Ethical Rebuke Preached . . . during the Penitential Period Preceding the New Year's Day, 5505 [1744], to the Congregation of Metz
1744

> The prophet Hosea cried out: *Come, let us turn back to the Lord; He attacked, and He can heal us; He wounded, and He can bind us up. In two days He will make us whole again; on the third day He will raise us up.*
>
> —Hos. 6:1–2

The rabbis have used this last verse to show that the Holy One does not allow the righteous to remain in distress more than three days. But the relevance of this to the preceding verse needs to be explained.

Whether death and suffering can occur independently of sin and transgression, caused merely by the arrows of fortune or the configuration of the stars, is the subject of a well-known dispute. The truth is that this view has led its adherents to the sick and heretical belief that sin never produces punishment in this world. Those who harbor such a belief fail to place their trust in God. And since the eternity of the world to come transcends sense perception, it makes no impact upon the soul that is foolishly immersed in the carnal vanities of this world.

This was the problem with Esau, as I have [elsewhere] explained. Asking "Why these lentils?" he was told that the old man [Abraham] had died. He responded, "If evil has befallen even Abraham, there can be no justice and no Judge." To understand this, we must recall that the rabbis have given two reasons for the custom of eating lentils in connection with mourning: first, their roundness reminds us that death comes in an inexorable cycle to all; and second, their absence of a "mouth" represents the mourner who sits in silence. If we accept the second reason, then we may also prepare eggs for the mourner.

Now according to the view that "there is no death without sin," the first reason—that the round lentil represents the natural cycle of death—does not apply, for the righteous would escape this. Their death would not result from natural causes. This was Esau's opinion at first. He therefore thought the reason for the use of lentils in mourning was that they had no "mouth," and he asked "Why these lentils?" rather than eggs. Jacob's response was to inform him that Abraham had died. Since Abraham was sinless, the conclusion had to be that death occurs independent of sin, and the lentils were to be eaten because [unlike eggs] they are round. When Esau heard that death can come as an accident to the good and the evil alike, he became a heretic.

This explains why the Holy One does not allow a righteous person to remain in distress for more than three days. . . . In order to demonstrate that He watches over every event that pertains to His people, overpowering planetary configurations so that their fate is not governed by the stars, God does not allow the righteous to remain in distress on the third day, which by natural causes should be the most painful. Instead, He fashions a cure to ease the pain. In this way, all peoples can see that God is responsible, not the natural order. All may acknowledge that afflictions occurring to Israel derive not from the stars but from God, who both injures and heals.

This is why the messengers came to heal Abraham on the third day following his circumcision, in the heat of the day, when his pain would naturally be most severe. Yet he was able to run toward them with ease (Gen. 18:1–2). And Isaiah was instructed to tell Hezekiah, *On the third day you will go up to the house of the Lord* (2 Kings 20:5). This was a public miracle.

Likewise, Jacob's sons were in doubt about the men of Shechem, all of whom had entered the covenant through circumcision. They were uncertain whether sincere motivation had made these men acceptable in God's sight, or whether they had been circumcised while remaining inwardly perverse merely out of lust for Jacob's female progeny. Because of this doubt, Jacob's sons were unwilling to harm them until the third day, when they saw these men suffering pain in the natural manner. Had they been sincerely devoted to God, they would not have remained in distress for three days, as we explained. They therefore determined that God's protection had departed from the men of Shechem because of their inner wickedness. That is why they slaughtered them without mercy.

This is what the verse [from Hosea] admonishes. If the people will desist from evil, their afflictions and pain will be suspended, for their suffering is the work of the Almighty. The prophet said, *Come, let us turn back to the Lord; He attacked, and He can heal us, He wounded, and He can bind us up*. All comes from Him, not from the stars. The proof is that *In two days He will make us whole again; on the third day He will raise us up*, for He does not allow one to remain in distress for three full days. This shows that it is not by the stars or by natural causes but by God that we have been stricken, in accordance with our sins. If we would repent, we must return to God, the source of help and deliverance.

This message applies also to us. We too must return in repentance. This season especially should impel us to do so, for these are days of judgment, when the sound of the shofar is heard and our effort at repentance should be great. The most important thing is this: our welfare does not depend upon the kind of "repentance" most people think of, namely, prolonged recitation of liturgical poems and penitential prayers, or even psalms, or fasting, while the basic iniquity remains unchanged. This is not what God wants; this is not the repentance He desires. Such is the essence of my sermon today. It is a message of truth and peace, for lying and deceitful speech enhance the power and prosperity of Esau and the "other side."

According to the rabbis, this season is divided into three parts: "On the day before the New Year, He cancels one third [of Israel's sins], on the New Year's Day another third, and similarly on the Day of Atonement." This statement speaks about three types of sin.

Repentance before the New Year applies to the sins of desire for unnecessary things, for people love to pursue their base passions. This may be diminished by fasting before Rosh Hashanah. Desire for temporal things is generally suppressed as people see the awesome Day of Judgment approaching, knowing that God will review their conduct. How can one fail to cast away such desires?

On the New Year's Day itself, hearing the sound of the shofar, people feel remorse for their sins [in the ritual realm]. Can the shofar be blown, proclaiming God's sovereignty, without instilling dread? What kind of hollow man would not be moved to sincere remorse and firm resolve to act according to the just laws of the Torah?

Yet there remain the transgressions in interpersonal relations: rancor and strife, unwarranted hatred, the falsehoods people say to each other while secretly planning attack, robbery and exploitation, and so forth. These remain buried inside us, sinners that we are, until the arrival of the special fast day. For ten days people examine their conduct; as the Day of Atonement approaches, they try to appease their neighbors by words and by payment, to extirpate their jealous rivalry, their contentiousness, and all such sinful behavior affecting others.

For the Day of Atonement reminds us of the day of death. This is why we wear white. All aspects of its observance are reminders of death. That is its goal. The final third is forgiven on the Day of Atonement. Even at the end of the day, in the liturgy of the closing service, we pray "that we may cease from the exploitation for which we are responsible." All this is hinted in the prophet's words: *In two days He will make us whole again* refers to the two days [of Rosh Hashanah], but *on the third day*, which is the Day of Atonement, the ultimate goal, *He will raise us up to live in His presence*, for this is the essence of repentance.

That is why they said in the Midrash: The community of Israel said, "Master of the universe, repentance is Yours." The Holy One responded, "No, repentance is yours." The meaning relates to what I have just said: a person easily feels remorse for sins against God and is quite ready to repent, but transgressions in interpersonal relations involving financial matters are difficult to renounce, especially where envy and hatred are aroused, as I have frequently explained.

If a man comes to ask an expert on Jewish law about some questionable meat in his home, or about leaven on Passover, and he is told to throw it in the river, he will obey without protesting, even though it involve a substantial loss. But if the same judge should render a decision in a civil dispute, giving the man's adversary ten gold pieces, he will go to a [secular] court and lodge a complaint against the judge, and his enmity toward that judge will be long-lasting. It is not the loss of the money that he cares about—he is willing to bless the Giver of Torah—but the fact that the money goes to his opponent. His envy is so powerful that it pains him to heed the judge's decision.

This is always the pattern. Regarding sins against God, Jews become sanctified through their remorse. Especially during these days of repentance, the time of God's favor, they will repent of their transgressions against Him. But not of transgressions in interpersonal relations, for these are not considered significant. Even if a quarrel subsides during this period, and the opponents speak to each other, they are secretly planning the next attack, waiting a bit until the Days of Awe are ended to decide what to do. They certainly do not give back the money they have robbed or extorted or taken as interest. This truly hinders repentance, as I have said.

NOTE

Words in brackets appear in the original translation.

Translated by Marc Saperstein.

Other works by Eybeschütz: *Kereti u-feleti* (1763); *Ya'arot devash* (1779–1782).

Angelo (Mordechai) de Soria
Dates Unknown

Angelo de Soria lived in Leghorn (Livorno), Italy, and was active in the mid-eighteenth century. After graduating from the University of Pisa's medical school in 1754, he played a key role in the decree issued by the university in 1755—which would last eleven years—making non-Catholic tuition the same as Catholic tuition for that university. His writing was inspired by the Bible, Midrash, and Mishnah, as well as Sephardic philosophers.

A Public Speech on Temptation, Composed by Mordechai de Abraham de Soria, and Which Was Delivered by a Student of His on His Bar Mitzvah, on the First Day of Sukkot
1751

To the Reader

Do not judge me so vain (O Reader) that, to make myself wise, I would publish my efforts for the world to see, especially when they open your eyes to their pathetic titles. For this is a fitting occasion to bring this resolution to the attention of the critical ones, who will hear its recitation, for the political histories and those of the state may be mentioned in speeches of this kind, when it is known that an orator must be well versed in all the liberal as well as the mechanical arts and also in all stories both divine and human as well as moral, political, and profane, so that the doctrines, rulings, examples, and immoralities that may be deduced therefrom may serve as an incentive to persuade the people to be moved to divine service, which is the object that the orator must have in mind in making his speech—namely, presenting them with an image whereby pedantic critics would know that I have complete satisfaction that the erudite have approved of my argument. All is well.

The Author's Protestation

In this small work, the author presents the public with the first fruits of his poorly developed nature: there is no dearth of critics who trenchantly oppose backsliding, even in the most considered of reflections, dismissing the sweat that a composition requires and ignoring the difference in conceptualization—for some have a graciousness of quill, for others it lies in the concept itself, and the rest have no temperament for the universal. They express themselves for the world to see so that the gracious may admit their faults. This work is not directed at the ignorant, because, no matter how much the author apologizes, the former will not be content nor will he be satisfied. If it falls into the hands of the wise, there is much less that can be presented, because nothing satisfies great men. It is well known that the loftiness of their generous talent can never adjust to the coarseness of their lower concepts. However, they do find common ground with their moderate understanding. Thus, it is necessary to discourse on this work at length, because if it is little discussed and little time is devoted to the author's discussion of the military art, then it probably was never practiced in the schools of Mars, and in those of Minerva, one could become apprised of the cunning and dealings that transpire in the courts of the monarchs, and most notably in the recently waged wars. Thus, he expounds on the little that his capacity could attain, even though, in searching for examples of humanity and politics, the holy ones precede him. If he has succeeded in opening it up, the mediocre mind must judge; if one criticizes the method and the order of the discourse, which he has taken, he must say so, for he has always been inclined to explain matters (as best he could) with allegories, emblems, and other devices to sharpen the wits. This is also extremely useful, because allegories provide reasons that clarify the meaning of some precepts and rituals of our Lord which, owing to their obscurity, appear to be superfluous when taken literally.

Translated by Marvin Meital.

Ba'al Shem Tov

Biographical details appear with the text of *In Praise of the Ba'al Shem Tov*, in the section on Life Writing.

Igeret aliyat ha-neshamah (Epistle on the Ascent of the Soul)
1752

You will assuredly regard it as wondrous, and it will gladden your heart that I too regarded as wondrous the vision vouchsafed to me by the Almighty in relation to the *aliyot* "ascents"—wondrous things concerning the rising of the soul, a phenomenon familiar to you. I saw amazing things that I had never seen until now, from the time when I was capable of reason; and what I saw and learned when I ascended there is impossible to relate and to speak of, even directly in words, except what I experienced when I returned to the nether Paradise and saw numerous souls of the living and of the departed—both those known to me and those unknown to me, in countless numbers—running to and fro, to ascend from one world to another by way of the "platform" familiar to those who experience divine grace, with great and intense joy which the mouth tires to recount and to speak of, and which is too hard for the ear, being of a corporeal nature, to hear. Moreover, many evil men repented, and their sins were forgiven them, as the time of divine favor was then so great that I too was most astounded that so many, even of those known to you, had been accepted by virtue of their repentance; and there was very great joy among them likewise, and they too ascended, in the ascent mentioned above. All of them, in unison, requested and even pressed me to the point of embarrassment, saying: "Most exalted and honored one in your Torah scholarship, the Almighty has favored you with extraordinary understanding, enabling you to grasp and to have knowledge of these matters. Ascend with us to be our help and support, as someone upon whom we may place reliance!" On account of the great joy that I witnessed among them, I said that I would ascend with them; I enquired as to the cause of this joy, and as to why this day was different from all others, in that such joy had never before been experienced, and as to the ultimate purpose of this joy. But they were unable to answer me. My teacher, with whom you are acquainted, was also constantly with me. I also saw all the princes of the nations of the world coming and humbling themselves, like slaves before their masters, before the great angel Mikha'el, and great rewards being bestowed upon all the righteous and upon the entire world, thereby enabling them to remain steadfast and experience that true rejoicing and immense delight which had been felt on the occasion of the giving of the Torah—a phenomenon it is impossible to experience in material form. Now I was alarmed and agitated at this vision, for I said to myself: "Perhaps it was staged on my account and—Heaven forbid—my time had come to leave the earthly world, and perhaps it was with that in view that it was appropriate for this to be done"; and this should suffice for one with understanding! My soul was grieved, both on my own account and for the sake of my friends, at the fact that my soul would be departing this earthly world outside the Land of Israel, until such time as I had arrived at, and ascended to, the palace of the Messianic King—in a literal sense—and I literally saw "faces within faces" such as I had never seen until now, ever since the time I was capable of reason. They revealed to me in this connection that this was *not* taking place on my account, and they additionally disclosed to me wondrous and awesome matters contained in the depths of the Torah which I had neither previously seen nor heard, and which no human ear had heard for a good many years. And the idea entered my heart, and it crossed my mind, to enquire of him: "Is it possible that this rejoicing and gladness is on account of the preparation for his goodly advent, and when will the Master [the Messiah] actually come?" But his lofty reply was: "It is not possible to reveal this, but this much you should know: at such time as your teaching will enter the public domain and become revealed within the world, and your wellsprings are scattered abroad—namely, that which I have taught you and you have grasped—and when they too will be able to perform acts of unification of the Almighty and spiritual ascents like you, then all the husks[1] will cease to exist, and it will be a time of favor and salvation." Now I marveled at this, and was most aggrieved at the fact that it would take so long, and pondered when this might conceivably come about. However, as a result of my having heard three special things of mystical significance and three of the sacred names of the Almighty, which were simple to learn and to explain, my mind was set at ease, and I thought: "It is conceivable that by this means, it will be possible for men of exceptional spiritual inclination also to attain the same spiritual degree and level of testing as myself; that is to say, when they are able to transport souls up to Heaven, and when they will learn and grasp such matters just as I do." But permission was not granted to me to reveal this so long as I live; and I made a request on your behalf to learn with you, but was not allowed under any circumstances to do so, and I remain committed to this by oath from that time henceforth.

NOTE

1. [Serving as a barrier to ultimate divine revelation.—Trans.]

Translated by David E. Cohen.

Jonathan Eybeschütz

Sefer luḥot edut (Tablets of Testimony)
1755

Introduction

For it is not against me that these men have sinned, for what am I and what is my life? My days have passed like a transient shadow, and fly away as does a dream—like a dream upon awakening. I am despised, a man of sorrows and acquainted with illness, with men hiding their faces from me, stricken and smitten by God.[1] The Almighty has caused bewilderment to be my lot, on account of my iniquity, and old age has sprung upon me in an untimely manner. My strength has departed and the cord of yearning has snapped, and my desire for ostensible glory has vanished, and that for a surfeit of honor, advised by crooked counsel. Who is it that they have pursued, and against whom have they plotted stratagems that they cannot bring to fruition, to shoot in the dark those of upright heart? Do not my years fly by faster than a weaver's shuttle, and come to an end with no hope? For the destiny of man is but the worm—I despise it, for I shall not live forever. Let me be, for my days are but vanity, and, that being the case, what further evils can they give to me and what can they add to me if they desecrate my crown and bring my glory down to the ground, to the dust, where it will dwell forever?

[. . .] They have become attached to the habit of slandering fellow Jews to the government, and they have accorded advantage to wagging tongues—the more slander a person relates and the more he creates an abhorrent odor, the more praiseworthy he is! And they have approached the gentile authorities and have desecrated the holy name—Israel. Let Zion weep bitterly—ye mountains of majestic peaks—let neither dew nor rain fall upon you, nor may you enjoy fields of bounty, for it is there that the shields of the mighty ones were rejected, anointed with poison! The sound of the cry and the tears of those who are oppressed, who have no one to comfort them, may readily be heard. In order that later generations may be aware of the things that have befallen us, and what the present generation had seen concerning this and what actually took place, from the mouths of the sages of the generation, the perfect ones—may saviors ascend Mount Zion, namely the gates which are distinguished in mastery of halakhah, to judge and to deliver those forsaken and ostracized such as ourselves—I said: "Let me approach the task concisely, providing mere chapter headings, and without leaving any space between the folds, and clarifying the manner in which they transgressed the covenant of the Torah and the laws."

[. . .] It is now five years since I left the Holy Community of Metz for the Holy Communities of Altona, Hamburg, and Wandsbek here, for the sake of Torah and divine testimony. I was at ease, but the Almighty broke me in pieces; for these five years during which there has been no silence—and silence, which is appropriate for the wise, is all the more so for the foolish! I perceived a powerful conspiracy against me, involving both stronger and feebler opponents. I dwelt with those who inhabit the tents of Kedar and the tents of Cushan in the wilderness of falsehood, and several individuals, both from here and from there—Metz—dealt craftily with me; they hatched a conspiracy, saying: "Let us dig a pit for him with traps to ensnare the wise with guile." They found a pretext, in that I am in the habit of writing out amulets for the afflicted ones among my friends who tremble in terror on account of evil spirits and within whom erring spirits, or things of a comparable nature, reside, in accordance with the tradition received by me. I stitched together an amulet that would work for them. They were able to identify them as emanating from my hand, writing, as I did, in an incomplete manner, albeit with craftsmanship in the square Hebrew script—that employed for writing Torah scrolls, phylacteries, and *mezuzot*. They opened up the amulets and discovered within them unknown words and divine names—albeit they are not well acquainted with them or with their names. They arrived, and thought to say: "Here is an opportunity for us to make allegations against him." Accordingly they interpreted the amulets as one interprets dreams; that is to say, with many vain words—like getting an elephant to go through the eye of a needle—and they smoothed their tongues by drawing distinctions and separations of words, with deliberate confusion of expressions, with a simple *alef-bet* and an *alef-bet* based upon the Atbash system;[2] they held me to be an abomination; they had no delight in me; they profaned my name, and they made the letters *alef, yod, kaf* respectively read *bet, kaf, resh*, and *alef, lamed* read *bet, mem*, by recourse to a secret code in which substituted letters [i.e., those next in the Hebrew alphabet] are employed; and they took the words contained in the amulets and, by means of their magic spells, ordered that a rod of strength be turned into a serpent—one letter was to be read as part of a simple *alef-bet* while another was to be read as forming part of the *alef-bet* of the Atbash system, or as one of the remaining *alef-bet* systems mentioned above—and, on occasion, the entire word was to be read as part of the simple *alef-bet*, or alternatively, as part of the *alef-bet* of the Atbash system, in accordance with the way in which the word in question could be compatible with their views and the evil intent that they had devised. And sometimes they omitted letters, and on occasion, added extra ones, but their omissions were the very opposite of being effected out of love for me—it was only in order to bring their design to fruition. They subtracted from the text, they added and arbitrarily expounded the meaning of the amulets to their own advantage, without following any systematic order and mode of writing—on one occasion they would expound the first letter and on another, the second, and on yet a third occasion, the final letter of a word and sometimes the entire word on the basis of the simple *alef-bet* system. There was no logical basis to their "teaching," and their case against me was very weak. They took no care over all that they said, but rather employed for their purposes anything that was agreeable to their designs. They chose work of deceit, and the lot they had picked came up in their left hand—for Azazel! And they removed words from their aura of sanctity, and Shabetai Tsevi—may his name and his memory be blotted out—passed in front of them and the divine names contained within the amulets would be exchanged—they would depart from their sacred position within the text. They would treat phrases intended as requests to the Almighty as nothing other than supplications taken from Jews who were a band of traitors, the oppressive fruit of the uncircumcised, Shabetai Tsevi—may his name and his memory be blotted out—and they converted that which was pure into that which was impure. [. . .]

Below Is Reproduced a Copy of the Record Book of the Ḥevrah Kadisha [Burial Society]

At the mandate of the distinguished heads, the trustees of the Holy Burial Society—may they enjoy long life—this document is tendered by way of proof of the fact that we have seen the original record book and what has been inscribed in it by the trustees in their actual handwriting: all those who have gone to the world-to-come—on what day, and in which month and in which year this occurred. May the Almighty, in His mercy, heal the breaches of His people Israel! We have seen that it has been recorded in authentic handwriting, that from Tammuz 5509 to the end of Elul 5510—for our many sins—sixteen deaths occurred among women in childbirth, and from Tishri 5511, the time when the Holy Master, the Illustrious One, our Teacher, Rabbi Jonathan—may the All-Merciful preserve and redeem him—Head of the ecclesiastical court and spiritual leader of the Holy Communities of Altona, Hamburg, and Wandsbek, arrived here, until Tishri 5512 only three women died in childbirth.[3] May the Almighty say to the Angel of Death: "Stay your hand!" And by way of formal confirmation of the above, we have duly set our seals this New Moon of Tammuz 5515—the insignificant Meir Gerlitz Hofen, sexton of the Holy Burial Society—long may it live:

The insignificant Joseph, son of Rabbi Ber Ḥazan, sexton of the Holy Burial Society—may his Rock and Redeemer preserve them.

NOTES

1. [Isaiah 53:4. The passage from Isaiah is appropriated by Christians as referring to Jesus, the suffering servant.—Ed.]

2. [In the Atbash system, the letter *tav*, the final letter of the *alef-bet*, is substituted for an *alef*, the letter *shin* for a *bet*, and so forth.—Trans.]

3. [Eybeschütz is arguing that the amulets were very effective in reducing the number of women who died in childbirth.—Ed.]

Translated by David E. Cohen.

Samuel Mendes de Sola
1699–1761

Lisbon-born Samuel Mendes de Sola was renowned as an orator and Talmudist. He studied at a seminary in Amsterdam and initially served as rabbi in that city. He first arrived in Curaçao in 1744 as a rabbinical assistant and then served as *ḥakham* of the local synagogue from 1749 until his death. He was a controversial figure within the Curaçao Jewish community. Disputes arose over such issues as biblical interpretation, marriage contracts, burial rights, and commercial issues. Copies of his sermons and ritual decisions still exist.

License Authorizing Daniel da Costa Gomez to Be a Ritual Slaughterer
1757

These letters of mine may be presented by the witnesses of the Lord, and they will be vindicated—to the effect that the young and delightful young man Daniel, whose utterances were genuine, appeared before me, and requested permission from me to perform ritual slaughter on all types of kosher poultry suitable for eating, and after I had examined, investigated, and made inquiry of him in regard to all the laws pertaining to ritual slaughter, and found him to be conversant with and expert in them and with their various names, and, insofar as the manner in which he examined and felt the slaughtering knife was concerned, I likewise found him capable of aiming at the target and not missing. Moreover, he carried out a ritual slaughter in my presence and in that of the local butcher, a trustee of our community [Mikvé Israel and Neve Shalom], in accordance with the law and in proper fashion; I granted him the license which he had requested of me, and certify that anyone calling himself by the name of Israel is permitted to eat from poultry slaughtered by him—such license being granted upon the condition that he reviews all the laws pertaining to ritual slaughter at least once a month. As I had seen that, on account of our many sins, the violators of the laws within our nation have greatly increased—worthless men who shake off the yoke of the fear of Heaven from themselves, in that they partake of the cheese of the gentiles—I determined not to grant an ordination for the purposes of ritual slaughter or for examination of the internal organs to anyone—no matter who he might be—unless he were to undertake, in my presence, on pain of a total ban of excommunication, not to eat from the aforesaid cheeses. And as the aforementioned young man, in my presence, accepted the terms of this imprecatory ban upon himself, I granted him this license of mine upon this condition. If, Heaven forbid, he should transgress the terms of the ban, I hereby annul this license of mine with retrospective effect, as though I had never granted it, and hereby proclaim all fowl ritually slaughtered by him to be carrion. In order that this should serve as valid testimony for him, I have signed my name here, on the island of Curaçao, in the holy community of Mikvé Israel, on Tuesday, the twenty-third day of the month of Adar, in the year five thousand five hundred and seventeen [1757]. These are the words of the one standing to minister in the sanctuary, who lies bent under the toilsome burden of the holy communities; that is to say, the holy community of Mikvé Israel and the holy community of Neve Shalom—may the Almighty preserve them!

—The junior, Samuel, son of my lord, my father David Hezekiah Mendes de Sola, may he be remembered for the life of the World to Come.

Translated by David E. Cohen.

Ezekiel Landau
1713–1793

Ezekiel (Yeḥezkel) Landau was born in Opatów (Apt), Poland, and was part of the kabbalistic *kloyz* in Brody. In 1745, he became the chief rabbi and head of yeshiva in Jampol, Poland. Landau was appointed chief rabbi of Prague in 1754, a position he held until his death. In this public role, he contributed to political decisions concerning education and military service. Landau is most revered for his halakhic scholarship, particularly his *Noda bi-Yehudah* (1776; 1811), a two-volume collection of more than 850 responsa; he became known by the title of that work.

Derushe ha-tselaḥ (Sermons [of Landau])
1760

One who exchanges good for bad and bad for good, and says that transgressions are really virtuous deeds, and that it is by this means that one can bring the Will of the Creator to fruition—such an individual will never repent, and likewise, one who denies the Providence of the Holy One, blessed be He, over earthly creatures, and says: "The Almighty has abandoned the earth!" and who denies that there is divine reward and retribution, it is clear that such a person will not repent; and while these two groups are, in various ways, different from one another, the common factor they share is that they harm all who approach them and pay attention to their statements; they are two distinct groups, both prevalent in our times: the first group is that of Shabetai Tsevi—may his bones rot—they are the ones who declare that that which is evil is really good, and all transgressions are deemed by them to be virtuous deeds; they are sunk in the depths of uncleanness. The second group are the current philosophers who say of the Creator that His ways are exceedingly elevated, that He is high and exalted and has no concern with earthly creatures—and they maintain that everything is governed by natural processes. Now the *Alshikh*[1] has already explained, in connection with the verse (Psalm 139:20): "Who utter Your name with wicked thought: they take it for falsehood, even Your enemies," that "Your enemies" is to be understood thus: they who hate the Almighty are the very ones who elevate Him in a false manner; since, by such means, they have found a way to spurn the entirety of the Torah and the divine commandments, by declaring: "The Torah is not from Heaven," and they deny the prophecy of Moses our Teacher—peace be upon him—and regarding all the miraculous phenomena recorded in scripture, they attribute these to Nature—Heaven forbid—as a result of that viewpoint; anyone pursuing their path destroys his heavenly reward with contempt.

An allusion to these two groups has been made by the prophet [Micah]; in respect of the first group, he has declared: "With the garment, you strip off also the mantle." That is to say, when performing the commandments, one clothes oneself in robes, and through one's commission of transgressions, one strips off the garments of light and clothes oneself in filthy garments. And the expression "with the garment" must be understood to mean: "That from which one will obtain the merit to clothe oneself in a garment"—which, for us, is the observance of the commandments and the protection of the soul from the filth of transgressions, as scripture states: "At all times let your garments be white"—where *you* desire to become worthy of this, *they* do the opposite; "they strip off the mantle"—that is to say, they commit despicable transgressions, incest and the consumption of prohibited foods—and there can indeed be no better example of "stripping off the precious mantle" than this; by doing such things, they think that they are covering themselves with light, as with a garment, for this type of thing is regarded by them as a worthy deed! Woe unto them and unto their souls and unto all who support them! In regard to the second group, the prophet has declared: "From them that pass by securely"—for even the wicked man who is most despicable in his evil—even one who is wicked in his rebellion against the entirety of the Torah—enjoys no rest, and his heart smites him, and he fears the awesome nature of the Judgment, and does not commit a transgression with any sense of security; but these wicked men, who deny Divine Providence, and who deny that the Torah is from Heaven—they commit a transgression with sated soul, and with a sense of security, without any fear or worry, and they do not even experience anxiety in the face of the Day of Judgment. This is what is meant by the phrase: "From them that pass by securely, so that they are as men returning from battle"—i.e., like valiant soldiers when they return from battle after having defeated the enemy, and who are thus in no fear of anything whatsoever.

Now these two groups are not like one another; the group following Shabetai Tsevi have no faith within them; they deny the cardinal principle of belief in the Unique One of the Universe, whereas the group of the philosophers are sound in their belief in the divine Unity, but have fallen into the pit by reason of their declaration that His ways—blessed be He—are too elevated to have any effect upon earthly creatures, and they wish to deprive the Creator of responsibility for those things that they find problematic in relation to the divine conduct of the world. Accordingly, they have falsified the Torah and the faith, but have brought up mere clay in their hands, as they fall into even greater difficulties. The more they display their sophistry in this regard, they fall into various snares consisting of mighty problems and great doubts. May the spirit of those delving into matters too wondrous for them, which they will never be able to grasp, be blown away! Indeed, in regard to their own souls, which are within their bodies, all the philosophers have wearied themselves in their investigation into its exact nature—so how can they make investigation into the nature of the One Who is higher than the Highest! [. . .] Now these two groups differ from each other in regard to the question of the divine Unity, but in any event, the group of philosophers is better than the group of Shabetai Tsevi, which impairs the belief in the Unity; however, insofar as the question of observance of the Torah and the divine commandments is concerned, they are both equal in being total uprooters of the Torah and the commandments.

And when we examine carefully the rabbinic epigram: "Know what is above you, an eye that sees," *etc.* [. . .]

In my humble opinion, it appears that our Holy Master [R. Judah the Prince] has hereby informed us that whatever is wrought above, in the celestial heights, all stems from ourselves, from our deeds and the study of our Torah, and our prayers—it is all required by the Almighty, and there is not a single matter throughout our entire Torah that constitutes just a bare decree, without a reason; although the reasons behind all the statutes are concealed from us, that is only due to the level of our understanding, but in actual fact, everything is governed in accordance with justice. Hence our Holy Master declared: "Know what is above!"—that you should be aware that everything that is wrought in the celestial heights of Heaven stems in its entirety from you, and it is by dint of your own power that everything takes place, and is it not, then, like a ladder stationed on the earth, with our heads reaching to the heavens? And accordingly we, the Jewish people, must guard ourselves against any dross or trouble resulting from any sin, even a minor one.

NOTE

1. [Moses Alsheikh, ca. 1520–1593, Safed rabbi.—Ed.]

Translated by David E. Cohen.

Other works by Landau: *Tsiyun le-nefesh hayah* (1783; 1791; 1799); *Dagul me-revavah* (1794); *Ahavat tsiyon* (1827).

Jacob Frank
ca. 1726–1791

Jacob (Jakob) Frank, born in Podolia, was a controversial and charismatic messianic figure who attracted a significant Jewish following in Eastern Europe. The son of a purported Sabbatian, he was raised in the Ottoman Empire. As a young adult, he became acquainted with Sabbatian leaders in Salonika. In 1755, he returned to Poland, where he formed a movement of local Sabbatians, advocating against the Talmud and for abrogation of Jewish law. His followers were arrested by the authorities and formally converted to Catholicism. In a staged anti-Jewish disputation in Lviv (Lemberg), in 1759, Frank's followers affirmed the libelous claim that the Talmud required Jews to use Christian blood. This shut off any possibility of reconciliation with the Jewish community. Soon, however, Frankists were viewed with suspicion by Christian clergy as well; they led an ostentatious and libertine lifestyle. Frank was arrested in 1760 and imprisoned for thirteen years. After his release, he moved to Moravia and then to Germany. His major work, *Zbiór słów pańskich* (Collection of the Words of the Lord) is a Polish-language collection of his sayings, tales, and parables.

Collection of the Words of the Lord
ca. 1760

I had a vision in Salonika, as though the following words were said to somebody: Go lead Yakov the wise into the rooms and when you and he come to the first room, I admonish you that all the doors and gates be opened to him. When I entered the first room, a rose was given to me as a sign by which I could go on to the next and so on *consequenter* from one room to the next. And so I flew in the air accompanied by two maidens whose beauty the world has never seen. In these rooms I saw, for the most part, women and young ladies. In some, however, there were assembled only groups of students and teachers, and wherever just the first word was spoken to me, I immediately grasped the whole matter from it and the full meaning. There was an innumerable number of these chambers and in the last one of them I saw the First [Shabtai Zvi], who also sat as a teacher with his students, dressed in *frenk* clothing. This one immediately asked me: Are you Yakov the wise? I have heard that you are strong and bravehearted; to this point have I come, but from here further I have not the strength of proceeding; if you want [to proceed], strengthen yourself and may God help you, for very many ancestors took that burden upon themselves, went on this road, but fell; with that he showed me through the window of this chamber an abyss which was like a black sea, hidden in extraordinary darkness, and on the other side of this abyss I saw a mountain whose height seemed to touch the clouds, at that I shouted, Be what may, I will go with God's help. And so I began to fly on a slant through the air into the precipice until I reached its very bottom, where, having felt the ground, I stopped. Walking in the dark, I came upon the edge of the mountain and seeing that because of the steep flatness of the mountain, I had difficulty getting up on it, I was forced to clamber up with my hands and nails and using all my strength until I reached the top. As soon as I stopped there, an extraordinary scent reached me, and there were many Truebelievers [Shabbateans] there. Seized by great joy, I did not want to go up onto the mountain with my whole body, saying to myself: I will rest awhile here, for sweat poured from my head like a river in flood on account of the tortures which I had bore to climb this mountain; but when I am well rested then I will come up on the mountain toward all the good that is found there. And that is what I did, I let my feet hang and sat with my body and hands at rest on the mountain. Then I went up on the mountain.

Drushim ("Lessons Drawn from the Scriptures")

Neither you nor the whole world knows anything of Esau: who he is and what he is. It was not in vain that Jacob bowed down to him 7 times; and concerning the 400 men who were with him, we know nothing of who they are. Pay heed: when those wondrous garments were put into his [Jacob's] hands he was entrusted with that which we pursue. But just because the robes are of a certain nature, should we assume that the one who wears them is of that nature as well? For a fool looks only at the costume; but one who is wise, at the one who wears the costume. Jacob could not receive the blessing except by being dressed incognito in those robes. The proof of which is that Isaac smelled the odor of the clothing and blessed him. I want you to merit coming to Esau and seeing him, so that my children might be like Esau. [. . .]

The 22nd of June [17]84. Two maidens from Poland, daughters, were leaving and wanted to lie down on the bed. I wanted to have intercourse with them; at that one nun came, undressed and also lay on the bed. I lay on the bed. The nun says to me: Lord Franek, what

Frontispiece of Alexander Kraushar, *Frank i frankiści polscy 1726–1816*, v. 2 (Kraków, 1895), Portrait of Eva Frank, daughter of Jakob Frank and his successor as leader of the Frankists.

Unknown Artist, *Eva Frank's House in Offenbach during the Visit of Tsar Alexander I, November 1813.*

are you doing? indeed I am married. I reply: *What of it?*—Exposition: That thing with the nuns was prepared for you, that you do that with them in squares, towns and streets, and that would have been an eternal praise for you, also that the priests would become your servants. But you did not want it.

NOTE

Words in brackets appear in the original translation.

Translated by Harris Lenowitz.

Jacob Emden

Mor u-ketsiyah (Myrrh and Cassia)
1761

Section 493

In times of emergency, all types of *kitniyot* (legumes, pulses) may certainly be permitted to be eaten during Passover, for even our Master, the Ba'al Ha-Turim [Rabbenu Jacob, son of Asher], who was an Ashkenazi, and in whose times the custom of adopting this stringency had already commenced, did not care about it, and indeed wrote: "It is an excessive stringency, which the public have not adopted as a custom"—from which it may be inferred that our Ashkenazic ancestors of blessed memory had not accepted it in his days, and it was not widespread amongst them; several halakhic decisors regard it as nonsense and an erroneous custom. [. . .] This conclusion is compelling from an edited Gemara. [. . .] I can testify concerning my revered father—may the name of the righteous be for a blessing—how much anguish that righteous man suffered in regard to this; throughout the entire festival of Passover, he used to complain and say: "If I had the power to do so, I would abolish this inferior custom, which is a stringency resulting in an undue leniency, and from which ruin, and a stumbling-block, can arise, in relation to the prohibition of eating fully fledged leaven; for since the various types of pulses are not now available to the masses to eat and to satiate themselves with, they need to bake a large quantity of unleavened bread; the poor in particular, as well as those who have large households, where even an abundance of cooked foodstuffs will be insufficient to subdue their pangs of hunger, will be compelled, against their wishes, to provide sufficient quantities of unleavened bread for the members of their households, and the revival of their empty bellies. As a result of this, they are not scrupulous in regard to the dough, as is befitting and obligatory. [. . .] It is thus likely that they will stumble into a prohibition entailing the penalty of *karet* [divine excision]—Heaven forbid! Furthermore, the unleavened bread is expensive for them, and not everyone has the wherewithal to make it in sufficient quantities for the members of his household—and indeed they do not manage to find sufficient amounts even of leavened bread to satisfy their hunger throughout all the rest of the year, while pulses are readily available at cheap prices without any trouble, and they are permissible as Passover food; moreover, such folk will thereby end up being deprived of the joy associated with the festival by virtue of a stringency possessing neither pleasant taste nor aroma. Therefore, I maintain, the righteous man should happily hold on to his path; he should provide food plentifully for others and dash the preposterous claims of such bizarre stringencies against the rocks.

Translated by David E. Cohen.

Jacob Emden

Sefer hitavkut (Book of Struggle)
1762

You should know and believe me, and understand, that I did not become zealous against the scoffers for my own glory, or for the glory of my father's house, but that it was zeal for the Almighty that inspired me, and the flame of God that burned within me. Many waters are incapable of extinguishing love; my entire objective was to create peace between the Jewish people and their heavenly Father; and He it was who decreed upon me to hunt down those hosts who make war against the assembly of the Lord, to make them into a cause of astonishment—Heaven forbid—and to bring about their ruin; thus there burned a flaming fire within Jacob. Now, therefore, men of courageous heart in Teplitz, listen to me, and God will listen to you! Be aware, I pray you, that your limb bears upon it an old leprosy that has broken forth in its stubborn forehead, as has been mentioned in the book entitled *Torat ha-kena'ot*, twenty years ago, in accordance with the testimony of a reliable individual who is an expert in this area, who has no personal involvement whatsoever with the matter. Once again, his shame has shown up in public—his stench has ascended through his son, a son who causes shame and who creates disgrace, as is stated in the testimony taken from the young men who studied in the Talmudic academy of the enemy—may the name of the wicked rot!—the manner in which a child talks in the marketplace is learned from his father—and the Almighty has now revealed his iniquity through you, and it has become a threefold sin, like the ropes attached to a wagon, and he has displayed the shame of his impurity in the public arena before you. What man is there who will be incapable of understanding this? [. . .] Now there are several groups among them: a few of them appear as though they are observant of the Torah, but everything they do is vain, deeds of deceit, for since they acknowledge idol worship, i.e., Shabetai Tsevi—may the name of the wicked rot!—they are like those who deny the Torah in its entirety. [. . .] In particular, so long as they perceive that no heed is paid to what they say, they are compelled to conceal the malady of their impurity and their sensuality within their hearts, out of fear that zealots may set upon them; hence they are forced, willynilly, to display signs of purity, to deceive the hearts of the Jewish people into regarding them as bona fide faithful [. . .] just like all the deeds of the notorious abominable Eybeschütz, whose entire objective is to promote himself as one in charge of a great Talmudic academy and one who admonishes his coreligionists in public. All this is done in order that they should believe in him, and that no one should criticize his repulsive activities, and that they should not sense the uncleanliness of his private parts [. . .] since he has gained such a high reputation with those students who are not worthy, and with boors, that he will get them placed in top positions, as swiftly as a hart that has gone astray, everywhere his control extends, to scatter the seeds of his heresy and so ensure that the leprosy can be unwittingly spread abroad. Such has been the entire objective and intent of this wicked man from start to finish; and even though they curse Shabetai Tsevi, they cannot be trusted. Who has execrated and cursed his king and his god, Shabetai Tsevi, as much as Eybeschütz has? Yet, for all that, it has now been revealed in the open light of day, that he was attached to him like a dog to its master, and indeed there has never been in the world a heretic as crazed as he, a worshiper of vanity and at the same time one seized with terror; against his own wishes, he needed to consent to the persecution of the men of his own sect and of that of his son, and to expel them from here. Accordingly, there is no substance to their deeds, but they are currently akin to the deeds of Esau, who comes along enwrapped in his prayer shawl and sits alongside Jacob, as I have written above.

Translated by David E. Cohen.

Zeraḥ Eidlitz
ca. 1720–1786

A rabbi, preacher, and member of the *bet din* in Prague, Zeraḥ Eidlitz was a student of the controversial rabbi Jonathan Eybeschütz. Although Eidlitz wrote a Hebrew- and Yiddish-language work on mathematics and did not disparage secular education, he considered it inferior to Torah-centered learning. Eidlitz was accused of Sabbatianism by Jacob Emden. A collection of fourteen of Eidlitz's sermons was printed as *Or la-yesharim*.

Or la-yesharim (*Light for the Righteous*)
1766

To explain the verse with which we started, we will set forth another thesis. It is a custom in Israel—and custom has the status of Torah—for preachers to travel from city to city to rebuke the people. Many of the ignorant masses err by not heeding their message because these preachers accept money for their sermons. The fools say that the preachers' rebuke is only a means of enriching themselves, and that their motives are therefore impure.

I once heard a parable about this from Rabbi Joel the Preacher, may the memory of the righteous be for a blessing. In one city of Poland, there were no houses made of hewn stone. All were made of wood from the forest, and the roofs were covered with straw, like the village houses in our country. A man and a woman lived there in a garret under the roof. Once the woman went to bed at night while her husband was still awake, and he had a lighted candle. Before it was extinguished, he too went to bed, leaving the candle burning. His wife berated him: "What are you doing! Don't you know that we sleep under the roof, and the house is made entirely of wood, and the roof is covered with straw, and everything is dry as clippings? A single flying spark could burn down the entire city, God forbid!"

While she was speaking, the night watchman came and, following the universal practice, proclaimed the time. He then made an announcement, warning the people to be careful about their candles and telling them why they should not go to sleep leaving a candle still lit. But the man replied, "This is nonsense. Do you think that the watchman is making this announcement in sincerity? I happen to know that he has no money at all, no estate to bequeath, not even a single stick anywhere. What does he care if there is a fire or not? He makes the announcement only because the town pays him to do so. If they paid him to proclaim that people should burn down their houses, he would do that as well. Since this man does not speak sincerely, I won't pay any attention to what he said. I'm going to sleep, and I'll leave the candle burning."

Just what the woman had predicted actually happened. Soon after the man lay down and fell asleep, the candle fell over on the table, the house started to burn, and there was a great conflagration, destroying most of the city. He and his wife barely escaped alive, having lost all their possessions.

Now think about this fool. Unwilling to heed the words of the watchman because he did not speak sincerely, the man let his house burn down. The same is true of the itinerant preacher, who admonishes the people to abandon their evil deeds, lest they fall into hell, where their bodies will be burned (for the Bible says, *Lo! that day comes, burning like an oven* [Mal. 3:19]; compare the verse *Can a person stir up fire in his breast without burning his clothes?* [Prov. 6:27]). Yet the fools, saying that the preacher rebukes us not for pure reasons but because he is paid, heed him not, until the fire comes upon them. There can be no foolishness greater than this. This is the end of the quotation from Rabbi Joel, may the memory of the righteous be for a blessing.

Now we would say that a preacher who criticizes the people for religious reasons is indeed preferable to one who does so because of the money he earns, for "Words emanating from the heart penetrate to the heart." When the preacher speaks solely for the sake of the money, his words do not emanate from the heart, and they therefore do not have as great an impact. Although it is extremely foolish not to heed the watchman according to the above parable, this may not apply to a substandard preacher. Even worse, sometimes a preacher will come to a town, and the officers will say to him, "You just need the money; take the money and go your way without rebuking us." When the preacher refrains from speaking critically for this reason, he has certainly not done right.

It appears that the Talmud alluded to this in speaking about the shofar. The rabbis said, "A shofar plated with gold in the place where the mouth is set is unfit. If plated on the inside, it is unfit; if on the outside, it is unfit if its sound is changed from what it was, but if its sound is unchanged, it is fit" [B. RH 27b]. Now we find that the Bible compares the preacher to a shofar, saying *Like a shofar raise your voice* (Isa. 58:1). Thus a shofar "plated in the place where the mouth is set" refers to a preacher who sets his mouth because they give him money. Such a man is unfit to preach a sermon of rebuke.

Similarly, "plated on the inside" refers to a preacher who inwardly cares only about the money and has no religious concerns. He too is unfit. "Plated on the outside" refers to one who is inwardly pure, unconcerned about money, but who accepts money for another reason—because he has no other source of sustenance and is like an itinerant pauper. Of such a person it says, "If its sound is changed from what it was," namely, that because of this he refrains from rebuking those who pay him lest they become angry at him, he too is unfit, for he should trust in the Lord and cast his burden upon God, who will provide for his need. But "if his sound does not change," he is fit.

And so, my brothers and friends, when a preacher comes here and accepts money, you may have something of an excuse. Even though the preacher acts for religious reasons, without any special interest, rebuking even the communal leaders, nevertheless you may say that deep within he does have an ulterior motive, and his words are not sincere. This is sheer nonsense, for the message is a true one, as we already explained in the parable. What difference does it make to you what his inner motivation may be? Nevertheless, there is a bit of an argument and an excuse for the evil impulse, that words not emanating from the heart do not penetrate to the heart. But if you pay no heed to *me*, what excuse or rationalization can you have?

NOTE

Words in brackets appear in the original translation.

Translated by Marc Saperstein.

Other work by Eidlitz: *Melekhet maḥashevet* (1785).

Elijah ben Solomon Zalman, Gaon of Vilna
1720–1797

Elijah ben Solomon Zalman (Eliyahu ben Shelomoh Zalman) was born, probably in Vilna, into a rabbinical family. He mastered Jewish scholarly texts at a young age, lived in Poland and Germany for a time, and returned to Vilna in 1748. Despite the fact that he held no formal position in Jewish communal affairs, his followers recognized him as *ha-ga'on he-ḥasid*, a genius, a sage, and an authority on Jewish legal matters; he was additionally called upon to offer opinions on scientific and educational issues. The Gaon was a foe of the early Enlightenment, but he opposed Hasidism even more, wanting to excommunicate its adherents. (Excerpts from several of the Vilna Gaon's works appear in this volume.)

Epistle against the Hasidim
1772

For there are seven abominations in their hearts to ensnare the souls of the innocent, and they abolish public study of the Torah, and they cast off the yoke of the Torah from their necks and from the necks of their precious children, who are comparable to fine gold, who used to sit first in the heavenly kingdom—for, as the Talmud declares: "Who are the true rulers? The rabbis!"—to read the scriptures and to study the Mishnah, and they were the first to arrive at the *bet midrash* in the mornings and the last to leave it at night—albeit the most important thing is not study but practice; they would adopt the practices of the saintly ones upon earth, and no unrighteousness nor the slightest derisory thing was ever heard to exist among them. But ever since the day that this "nation" came into existence, they have cast off the yoke from their necks, and they constantly go and gather together in pairs—each of them, having been invited, they proceed along in their impure state, when the Hasidim tell them, day by day, that Heaven forbid that they should waste their lives on the study of Torah, but that they ought rather to concentrate on the service of God, namely, on prayer; and Heaven forbid that they should ever be sad, but rather be in a perpetual mood of levity and joy, as they maintain that sadness renders void the unity of God. Further, Heaven forbid that they should ever feel anguish over any particular transgression they may have committed, so as to avoid falling into a state of sadness. In addition, they wait two hours before reciting their prayers, which is excessive, until the respective times for recitation of the Shema, and even of the Amidah, have elapsed; and they ruin their lives by reason of the vapidity emitted from their mouths. Indeed, neither the one form of religiosity nor the other has become firmly established with them, for they abandon their Torah study day by day, and their prayers too are an abomination, by reason of the fact that they say: "Heaven forbid that one should understand and focus upon the meaning of the words of the prayers, and that, when one does understand and focus upon the meaning of the words, that constitutes 'extraneous thoughts.'" The divine fury and burning wrath associated with disqualified offerings and with sacrifices offered up outside the precincts of the Temple may justly be laid at their door. Their children learn to be recklessly wanton in their prayers, just like any boorish person, for they are a topsy-turvy generation. They perform somersaults in front of the ark of the covenant of the Lord, akin to those of aliens and gentiles, with their heads underneath and their feet on top. Has any such kind of irreverence ever been heard of or seen before? Moreover, their religious laws are different from those of the entire nation of Israel, and they do not observe the laws of the Supreme King of Kings, the Holy One, blessed be He; but rather, they create for themselves a society of abandonment—whose purpose is to abandon the customs of the early authorities, and they overstep the boundaries set by the early authorities with respect to their prayers; and all the people flee at their cries, at the sound of the uproar and tumult generated by them in their prayers, and from the city being rent asunder thereby. They halt in the middle of their prayers, and pour scorn upon those who study the holy Torah; they continually create noise by reason of their jesting and mockery and their crazy hilarity. These are just some of their ways.

Translated by David E. Cohen.

Rabbis of Schwerin
1770s

The rabbis of the community of Schwerin in northern Germany were under governmental pressure to extend the time between death and burial to three days, against the Jewish tradition of swift burial. They wrote to Moses Mendelssohn, whose response, included in this correspondence, helped them to defend the imposed practice. The topic had been a subject of debate between Mendelssohn and Jacob Emden.

Rabbis of Schwerin to Moses Mendelssohn
1772

Schwerin, 18 May 1772
15 Iyar 5532 to the Jewish counting

To the man possessed of abundant dominion, wisdom, and understanding, renowned for his knowledge, whose name is spoken of in the far-flung isles, whose breath exudes the hallowed traditions of the faith, the one unto whom the deeds detailing the heavenly constellations are revealed, unto whom night is brightness, unto whom the halakhah is clear as the sun, who acts with benevolence towards both good and evil men, the Talmudic savant, the chieftain of Torah and of the rabbinate, the man perfected, the all-embracing Sage, whose most glorious name is lauded, our master and teacher, Rabbi Moses—may the All-Merciful protect and redeem him!

We have heard a rumor among the gentiles, that they intend to make the people of the Lord transgress, to cause them to walk in the ways of the gentiles. They have made enquiry into matters concerning the dead; they have adopted the pattern of their ancestors. They are going to make due investigation, when they rise against us to compel us to trample upon the law instituted by the ancients, to destroy the edifice of the soul so that the spirit cannot return to the place where it originally was until three days have elapsed. They have ceased to bury him, to place his remains in the ground, just in case he might burst forth out of where he has been placed. These decrees are in writing, contained in the valise of the noble, the ruler, the leader and guide of our community, R. Abraham Starelitz, with a view to showing to His Excellency [Moses Mendelssohn] the decree of the governor, the duke, may his majesty be exalted—yet we shall make mention of the Name of the Lord our God that His Excellency may serve as our advocate and protector before the peoples and the princes, to affirm truth and kindness to the nations; this ruinous situation is now under his powerful control, to address them in their language, employing flowing and incisive eloquence; we shall yet be distinguished from the other nations, as in days of yore; although we are aware that they possess some elements of wisdom, their eyes are plastered over to prevent them seeing, and their hearts from discerning; they are deviating from what is clearly stated in the open letter; but it is for this that he is renowned in Israel before all those who behold us, for the greatness of his knowledge, encompassing numerous elevated branches of wisdom which are like closed books in the regions where we reside; perhaps the same degree of desire as was once manifested by King Solomon will be found within him, too, to dissuade the governor from his intent; and there we would explain that this law of swift burial—albeit not laid down in the Law of Moses, and Moses spoke very well—has been expounded throughout the successive generations as a kind of clay firmly fastened with nails; and what man would be so cruel as to squeeze out the clay in such manner as merely to disturb it and not to knead it?

Let him place a furrow and a bridle into the mouths of those rising and standing up against us for the purpose of uttering vain things against the assembly of the elevated ones, those who have been men of renown from ancient times—and this shall be accounted a memorial to him, an act of kindness and an enduring covenant for those who will behold the consolation of the broken-hearted; and his portion will then be unique, as the foremost individual among the nation, in respect of the abundant goodness that is treasured up for those who fear the Almighty. Such is the view of those who lead the community, the aforesaid overseers and lay leaders of the holy congregation, added to whom now are our righteous teachers, the "insignificant" Joseph Nata of Schwerin, Yeḥiel Mikhel, and the "insignificant" Mordechai, son of the late R. Eliezer Jaffe of blessed memory, of Berlin.

I seek a reply as soon as possible from his exalted Excellency—may he enjoy long life—as we have been ordered to furnish a response on the matter within fourteen days. We are most eager and ready, once again, to be of assistance to him in every way, as this Jewish community is duty-bound to see to it that no further delay should occur—Heaven forbid!

To the Jewish Community of Schwerin [from Moses Mendelssohn]

Berlin, 9 June 1772

8 Sivan 5532, Tuesday—after the Feast of Weeks, 5532, Berlin.

Their delightful letter of last month has duly reached me; and I have seen from it that the governor and ruler of that region has imposed a decree upon them that they are to hold onto the corpses of their deceased for three days before burying them, and my masters are anguished and distressed over this, as though—Heaven forbid—he had desired to make them transgress the halakhah, or to cause them to stumble in respect of a sin involving a Torah-based prohibition or a rabbinic decree. I, however, brutish as I am, do not know why the rabbis have adopted this stance, and what the reason for all the great consternation concerning this matter is. Indeed, even if I were to know that our righteous Messiah had sent them a Talmudic scholar to serve as a spiritual leader and minister, who possessed the requisite knowledge to act in a discerning manner and to issue spiritual guidance, I would nonetheless not refrain from expressing my own view on the matter, and if I have erred, let him guide me and present my case before the Almighty. For in my humble opinion, the matter does not involve making the slightest movement in the direction of transgressing the halakhah—Heaven forbid—as *they* have thought. If our Sages of blessed memory stated: "One who holds onto the corpse of his departed overnight transgresses a negative command," they did permit holding on to it—on account of according honor to the dead—for the purpose of fetching a coffin and shrouds and professional mourning women, or so as to enable relatives to inform the adjacent towns (*Yoreh de'ah* par. 357); if they permitted holding on to the corpse overnight for such insignificant purposes, how much more so ought it not to be buried were there, in addition, a slight element of doubt in relation to the matter—that is to say, just in case the breath of life still remains within it—and there is nothing that is allowed to stand in the way of saving life!

Now as for the fact that our Sages of blessed memory did not explicitly mention this concern, this appears quite simple to understand, in my humble opinion, for they had no need of this in their times, as they used to bury their dead in caves and in vaults, and they stood guard over them for three days to see whether they were still alive, or whether their spirit had returned to their innermost parts, as is stated in tractate *Semaḥot*: "We go forth to the graveyard and stand guard over the deceased for up to three days, and we need have no concern that this conduct might be the ways of the Amorites. There was a case where they stood guard over an individual, and he survived for another twenty-five years, after which he died. In another instance, he went on to father five children and died only thereafter." Now, that being so, the Sages declared with full justification: "Anyone who defers his bier is praiseworthy," as one need have no concern whatsoever in this regard: but as for ourselves, since we bury our dead in such a way that it is impossible to stand guard over them (see the *Perishah*), it is most definitely appropriate for us to hold on to the corpses of our departed ones until such time as they have left the category of those who may conceivably still be alive—and were such a thing as is mentioned in tractate *Semaḥot* to befall us—Heaven forbid—how would we be able to justify ourselves?

Consider! All the medical experts testify and declare that they possess no definitive signs of death having occurred, and that, on occasion, a person loses consciousness to such a degree that the heartbeat has stopped and the breath has totally ceased, and the onlookers think that he is dead, whereas, in fact, he is not; but rather, it is necessary to wait until the flesh begins to decompose and become moldy; and it appears from the words of our Sages of blessed memory that they are in agreement in this matter with the medical experts, as is evident from the incident related in tractate *Semaḥot*, where they brought the deceased out to the cemetery and buried him in their vaults, and he subsequently stood up on his feet and lived! And from what we have learnt in a Mishnah in the chapter *Ha-tinokot*: "A man or a woman having an issue, and a menstruating woman, and a woman who has just given birth, who died, convey ritual impurity by carrying them until such time as the flesh has been consumed," and the Gemara stated: "What is the reason for this? Said Rav: 'It is a special rabbinic decree, lest he faints and loses consciousness.'" It is implicit from their words that it is a most difficult task to distinguish between loss of consciousness and death, and that we cannot arrive at a definite conclusion until the flesh has decomposed; and if they had concerns over this in regard to issues of ritual impurity and purity, how much more so, then, would this be applicable when dealing with the question of saving life! Even though one could entertain some doubt on this point by virtue of the fact that the Gemara does not say: "We are concerned that he may have fainted," but rather "It is a special decree, in case he may faint"—implying that there *is* a definitive sign of death, and our Sages of blessed memory merely decreed that ritual impurity will be created in such cases on account of those who are not medical experts—such a feeble and insubstantial piece of reasoning is insufficient to remove ourselves from the general category of obligatory concern for the possible saving of life.

Now their exalted Excellencies will see attached hereto the basic format of the request which, in my view, it is appropriate for them to make of the governor of the region; the likelihood is that he will be agreeable to this, and then everyone will be able to relax peacefully in his bed. If, however, he is not agreeable, there is no better solution than for them to act in the manner of our ancient forebears of blessed memory—to construct a vault inside the precincts of the synagogue for the purpose of carrying out the purification of the departed there in accordance with custom, and to stand guard over them for three days, after which time they are to be buried. And this, in my view, is an obligation devolving upon all the holy communities—not to deviate from the ways of the ancients of blessed memory, either to the right or to the left, for their ways are ways of pleasantness, and it is befitting for all the Sages of our generation to exhort them concerning this. Even if I knew that they will not heed my words, as the force of custom is powerful and strong, and that I might be regarded by them as a mere scoffer, I will have saved my own soul! With peaceful greetings.

The insignificant one, Moses of Dessau.
Translated by David E. Cohen.

Jonathan Eybeschütz

Urim ve-tumim (The Urim and Thummim)
1775

Introduction

This preface represents not a collated anthology but is rather the result of forgetfulness on my part, insofar as I have been terse in the words I have written, which place on record that I participated in a disputation with the sages and the princes of the Christians in order to remove their taunts from us, they who allege concerning us that we mock and blaspheme against them and their religion in our literary works. Yet truth may serve as a witness on its own behalf that this stumbling block, which appears in our literature, is due to the fact that such was the norm, to follow the ancient texts with precision, and whatever they found to be the text there, they retained, regarding it as a sin to effect any alteration or omission in it, without taking into account the fact that everything changes in accordance with the times, and with the nature of the matter in question. There *were* such sentiments expressed in ancient texts, and similarly, evil things were to be found concerning the gentiles at that time, and in particular, concerning idol worshipers, alien nations, since the root of such matters is based on the Amalekites, in relation to whom we are commanded in the Torah to blot out their name and to destroy their memory [. . .]. From there it extended also to other nations who hold fast to the deeds of Amalek and say: "The Almighty does not see, nor does the God of Jacob possess discernment"—they deny Divine Providence and the existence of God, and ascribe all things to nature and to the stars of the heavens, as we find in several instances that they celebrate festivals associated with the planets and the heavenly constellations, such as Kalendia and Saturnalia [. . .]; but in actual fact such disparaging remarks are not directed against the Christians of our own era; for the Christian nations in whose midst we dwell have in general observed the ways of justice and righteousness; they believe in the creation of the universe and in the existence of a deity and in His providence, and in the law of Moses and in His servants the prophets, and they persecute and set themselves in opposition to the Sadducean-type groups who deny the resurrection of the dead and the survival of the soul after death. That being the case, it is fitting to wish the Christian nations well and to praise and to glorify them and to shower blessings upon them rather than curses, Heaven forbid—and in particular, since they deal benevolently with us and treat us graciously by providing us with the opportunity to earn a livelihood within their lands. It has indeed already been declared by the mouth of the prophet Jeremiah that we are "to pray for the welfare of the city, for it is through its welfare that you live." In like vein, our sages of blessed memory have stated: "Pray for the welfare of the government." Accordingly it is an obligation devolving upon every single community, wherever printing presses are to be found, to remove the stumbling block of taunts and blasphemies from our sacred texts [. . .] and duly take note; I pray for the welfare of the government in general, for the monarchs and dukes of Christendom who offer protection to our entire nation beneath the shadow of their wings. May the Almighty bless them and increase their power, and in particular that of our Lord, the great and gracious King of Denmark, Frederick the Fifth, together with the Queen and his children, his family, and his counselors and ministers, chieftains and deputies. He is the kindly ruler who acted as my shield and was a light in the darkness to set my feet straight, directing my steps; and he rebuked the devilish adversary. And behold, the king shall rule in righteousness, to muzzle all mouths uttering base words. May God remember this to him for his good!

AMEN! AMEN!

Kitsur tokfo kohen[1]

For we do not know what the majority is, as we are not experts on all the opinions of the sages of the various generations, or on their reasoning or their statements. By way of illustration, if we were to say: The opinion of the R"if [R. Isaac Alfasi] and that of Moses Maimonides are identical in any particular case: hence, we have two mutually supportive views here! That is fine, but who knows how many sages of the generation living at the time of the R"if, and similarly, how many sages of the generation living at the time of Maimonides may have disagreed with them, to the point where the views of the R"if and of Maimonides would become nullified by reason of their having been in a minority against the majority view? And if the views of such other authorities have never seen the light of day, that is on account of the troubles we have experienced and the heavy burden of forced apostasy and the yoke of the Exile, and incessant migrations, by reason of our many sins—as a result of which many sages failed to commit their words to writing, to serve as "a memorial in the Sanctuary of the Lord," and numerous works were lost, and many works still extant in manuscript were confiscated and are currently hidden away in the abodes of various private individuals, and have not been scrutinized by the eye of the reader; for, as one might say, fresh works are appearing in print each morning, and light thereby shines forth for the upright—works of early authors that have been hidden away until now, such as the novellae of Rashb"a on numerous themes, novellae of Re"ah and Ritv"a, and an anthology of the views of venerable sages collated in *Shitah mekubezet* to a number of Talmudic tractates. By this means we have discovered and realized that what was originally regarded by us as merely the view of an isolated individual actually enjoyed a great deal of additional support from other authorities. Because this is the case, a single individual may be able to argue that his view should be accepted as halakhah, for how can we legitimately remove the matter from the sphere of doubt, as it is by no means clear to us that it does indeed represent only the view of a single dissident individual, as I have stated above? This seems to be what one might advance as an argument on behalf of those who say that one can claim that a person's minority view can still stand against that of the majority. [. . .]

In particular, regarding a law that is mentioned in the *Shulḥan arukh*, where the author and the Rem"a [R. Moses Isserles] have left out the view of any dissenting authority, it is a tradition transmitted to me, and I have witnessed conduct to similar effect on the part of expert religious judges and so too do I myself conduct judgment and proceed without arguing that the halakhah may legitimately be established as being in accordance with the dissenting view, since the Master, the Bet Yosef [R. Joseph Karo], and the Rem"a placed the memory of the dissenter "behind the door"; accordingly we have no obligation to take it into consideration. The sages of succeeding generations have firmly accepted upon themselves to observe and do according to everything stated in the abbreviated format of the *Shulḥan arukh* and the supplementary remarks of the Rem"a thereto. In my view, there can be no doubt that everything that is written down was vouchsafed to them by way of enlightenment from the hand of the Almighty—for there are numerous difficulties that the later authorities raised against them and resolved in an acute and profound manner, and likewise, the many laws that they incorporated within their sweet, pleasant, and succinct phraseology—and yet, there can be no doubt that they did not think of every single point, for how would that have been possible given the heavy labor—Heavenly labor—devolving upon them? Indeed is there any man in existence who is capable of authoring a work on the entire Torah, drawn from all the statements of the earlier and later authorities without such labor—Heavenly labor—being too burdensome for him? Hence we have to conclude that the spirit of the Almighty [resided] within them, so as to make their words accord perfectly with the halakhah, albeit without the specific intent of the author; and the desire of the Almighty came successfully to fruition in their hands. Accordingly, Heaven forbid that one should say: Establish the halakhah against the ruling of the author of the *Shulḥan arukh* and of the Rem"a. Now I recall that upon the death of my father-in-law's father, the most distinguished, righteous, and upstanding rabbi, R. Mikhel Shapira of blessed memory, he had, prior to his passing, bequeathed all his belongings verbally by the method of "gifts made by a person on his deathbed"—and when he died, an alternative document emerged in which a specific sum was recorded, and over which there were numerous disputes; and my father-in-law, the most illustrious rabbi, R. Isaac Shapira [his son], whose light still illuminates us, sought to contend: "Let the halakhah be established in accordance with the view of the Ra"avad and his supporters, that where there is a verbal loan, the lender cannot make a monetary claim from a gift made verbally by someone on his deathbed, since even without that verbal gift one would not think that the alternative document was authentic"; the contemporary sages, the great men of Israel, sat in convocation to consider the correct halakhah in that case. Despite the fact that I was disqualified by reason of my relationship to the parties, they nevertheless discussed the matter back and forth with me, and together they arrived at a consensus that since there was no mention of such a law in the *Ḥoshen mishpat* of the *Shulḥan arukh* or in the Rem"a, there was no room for an argument that the halakhah may be established [as agreeing with the view of the Ra"avad]. Hence they ruled that the money must be paid to the lender out of the gift, down to the very last farthing. Such is the appropriate course to be followed, without any cavil.

Translated by David E. Cohen.

NOTE

1. [An abbreviation of the work on Talmudic laws of possession, whose original author was Shabetai Kohen.—Ed.]

Ezekiel Landau

Noda bi-Yehudah (Known in Judah)
1776

Author's Introduction (to the First Edition)

When I parted from my father and journeyed forth from his home to Brody, I joined up with friends, God-fearing men of purity; we built a *bet midrash* for ourselves, separated and secluded from the community. During the six working days of the week, it lay there closeted away and secluded; despite all this, we did not attain any heavenly vision—rather, our total engagement, with all the force at our command, was with the sea of the Talmud and the halakhic decisors, which we carried out with distinguished students. My wife, who was by my side as a helpmate and not in opposition to me, enjoyed this merit: that she remained at home in solitude while I was in the *bet midrash* throughout the entire six-day period. In honor of my father and teacher, they magnified my reputation with a view to glorifying me, and the rabbis of numerous communities sent me halakhic enquiries; from the age of twenty-four, I opened the gates of responsa—these constitute the identical themes to those set forth in this work. With a view to presenting pleasing words, I have given the work a title incorporating the name of the "father of the testimony"—its name being *Noda bi-Yehudah* [Renowned in Judah].

Translated by David E. Cohen.

Jacob Joseph of Polnoye
d. 1783

Jacob Joseph (Ya'akov Yosef) of Polnoye, whose birthplace is unknown, embraced strict forms of Hasidism after 1741 and became a disciple of the Ba'al Shem Tov (Besht). Subsequently, he preached in Shargorod and other places in Podolia, facing persecution from Misnagdim (opponents of Hasidism). From 1770 until his death, he lived in Polnoye. Jacob Joseph transcribed and disseminated the Besht's ideas, and wrote *Toldot Ya'akov Yosef*, homilies on the Pentateuch. After the Besht died in 1760, Jacob Joseph and Dov Ber, the Magid of Mezritsh, set a pattern for subsequent developments within Hasidism, though no dynasty was established for the Besht.

Toldot Ya'akov Yosef (The Offshoots of Jacob Joseph)
1780

The Other Man's Faults

I heard from the venerable rabbinic scholar, R. Nahman, an interpretation of the words of [the Besht] that one should intend in every word that he utters submissiveness, separateness, and sweetness. [The interpretation is that] one should leave the quality of Strength (Gevurah), in that he should not find fault with people but treat them with compassion and discover good in everyone. Even when he notices something ugly in his friend, he should feel that it is for his good so that he might detect in himself some aspect of [that ugly quality], even if only in his thoughts, and thus he will repent of it. This is all for his own benefit, for were he alone (without this friend whose ugly qualities displease him) he might think that he is pious; now he knows differently.

I believe that this is the meaning of *It is not good that the man should be alone, I will make a help-mate [ezer] for him [ke-negdo]* (Gen. 2:18). [The verse should be understood as follows:] "It is not good that man be alone"—for this reason, that "I will make a help" for him from his "opposite" (*ke-negdo*), by detecting that he too possesses some of that quality that displeases him in the others.

NOTE

Words in brackets appear in the original translation.

Translated by Norman Lamm.

Other works by Jacob Joseph of Polnoye: *Ben Porat Yosef* (1781); *Tsofnat paneaḥ* (1782); *Ketonet pasim* (1866).

Dov Ber of Mezritsh
1704–1772

Dov Ber, the Magid (preacher) of Mezritsh, was the spiritual successor to the Ba'al Shem Tov (Besht). Born in Volhynia, he was a teacher who consulted the Besht to improve his health, and thereafter abandoned his ascetic practices and adopted the more emotional and contemplative expressions of Hasidism. After the Besht's death in 1760, Dov Ber settled in Mezritsh, where he pioneered the role of the tsadik and influenced major Hasidic dynasties. It was from him, more than from the Besht, that Hasidism grew. His teachings were later published by his disciples.

Magid devarav le-Ya'akov (He Declares His Word to Jacob)
1781

Tzimtzum: An Act of Love

"Why did God reveal the account of Creation to Israel? Because they said 'We will do' before 'and we will understand' (Exod. 24:7)."

This may be understood in the light of what the Rabbis said: that God's first thought in Creation was to create Israel. His earliest will was to create the world so that Israel would be righteous in every generation.

Therefore, God contracted (*tzimtzem*) His pure light, as it were, just as a father diminishes (*metzamtzem*) his intelligence and prattles for the sake of his young son. All sorts of other childish qualities are generated in the father, who loves these childish qualities, so that the son may enjoy them, and this is a source of joy to him.

For the Holy One, past and future are the same, and thus the Holy One derived pleasure from the deeds of the righteous even before Creation, and so contracted (*tzimtzem*) Himself.

God's self-contraction (*tzimtzum*) is called Hokhmah, for Wisdom is found as Ayin ("Nothingness"), as it is written, *But hokhmah is found from ayin* (Job 28:12).

The self-contraction was for Israel's sake, and love caused the self-contraction to take place. Thus it is written, *And these are the generations of Isaac, Abraham's son: Abraham begot Isaac* (Gen. 25:19).

Translated by Norman Lamm.

Other works by Dov Ber of Mezritsh: *Or Torah* (1804); *Or ha-emet* (1899).

Ezekiel Landau

Sermon for the Sabbath Preceding Passover
1782

This is therefore followed by a question: since it is so that we are still slaves, why is this night of Egyptian exile different from all the other nights of exile under other kingdoms? Why all this commotion on the night when we went out from Egypt, if we are still slaves? The answer is that there is a great difference, for then in Egypt we were slaves to Pharaoh, a cruel king, a king who made us suffer without benefit to himself, solely in order to humiliate us. But now there is a gracious and compassionate king. Even though we are slaves, he has removed from us the stigma of bondage, removed all externally recognizable signs of servitude. If we inwardly take it upon ourselves to be submissive, this is as it should be.

But all this applies only to the religious realm. Envy of worldly things, such as the wealth of a rich man, or arrogance because of them, is reprehensible. Nothing good results from it. The sages have said, "*Do not compete with the wicked*—to be like them; *do not envy the evil-doers*—to be like them." The Bible also says, *Do not envy sinners in your heart, but only the God-fearing, at all times* (Prov. 23:17). This means that we should envy those who fear the Lord. Yet we pray, "May my soul be like dust to all." Lest the fulfillment of this request prevent one from being worthy of Torah and commandments by keeping him from proper envy of those who fear God and study His Torah, the prayer continues, "Open my heart to Your Torah, and let my soul pursue Your commandments."

But now, because of our many sins, I have seen everything overturned. How can one envy the study of Torah, when an evil man has arisen from our own people and brazenly asserted that the Torah is not at all important, that an animal carcass is worth more than talmudic scholars; that etiquette is more vital than the Torah? This man is certainly blind to his own faults. *He* is worse than an animal carcass, and in the end his corpse will lie like dung upon the field!

Now as to the substance of the matter—the value of etiquette and of grammatical knowledge of the languages spoken by our neighbors—I too esteem these things. The government has done a great favor in deciding to teach our children to speak correctly. Even in the Bible we were criticized for not knowing how to speak the various languages. Do not think that you know how to speak the German language. No one can be said to know a language unless he can speak it grammatically. [. . .]

Therefore, my brothers and friends, hear me, that you may live. To each and every one of you present I say, *Fear the Lord, my son, and the king, and do not mix with the unstable, for disaster comes from them suddenly, the doom of them both who can foreknow?* (Prov. 24:21–22). I admonish you to *Fear the Lord and the king*, to do the will of His Majesty our king, while remaining very careful to fear the Lord. For as you become accustomed to the language, you will also want to read books that are not aids in learning the language but philosophical inquiries pertaining to matters of Torah and faith, which may lead you to harbor doubts about the faith, God forbid! For whoever speaks and writes about matters of faith on the basis of reason cannot help but diminish that faith, which is the root of everything. It is the legacy of our sainted ancestors, from Abraham, peerless among the faithful. More than this, it is based upon the Torah of Moses, from the mouth of God, which should be as a high wall in your hearts.

Do not mix with those who are "unstable"—those who follow arbitrary whims, who cogitate and ponder with their confused intellects, darkening the religion of the Torah, whether they be Jews or from any other people, those who deny individual providence over the affairs of men, who deny the revelation of the Torah and supernatural miracles, who say that religion was not given by the Creator. Now because of our many sins, various strange sects have multiplied among our people, each different from the other—except in their common proclivity to undermine the perfect faith. It was about such sects that Solomon warned: *Do not mix with the unstable, for disaster comes from them suddenly, the doom of them both who can foreknow?* (Prov. 24:21–22). He was alluding to those sects that are alike in their capacity for evil.

But we, God's people, are obliged to sacrifice our lives for our sacred Torah, both the written Torah and the oral one. Whatever we are admonished in the Talmud must be equivalent in our minds to what is written in the Ten Commandments. What do we care if these sects mock us? We shall walk in the name of the Lord, in the path trodden by Alfasi and Maimonides and Rabbenu Asher and the Tosafists, who found bright light as they walked in the path of the Talmud, who had no interest in esoteric doctrines, yet were deemed worthy of eternal life. The foundation of all is faith!

Translated by Marc Saperstein.

David Tevele

d. 1792

Born in Brody, Galicia, David Tevele held a major rabbinic pulpit in Lissa, Silesia. Tevele is best known for his antipathy to the educational reforms of Naphtali Herts Wessely, with whom he had a public controversy over secular education, outlined in Tevele's *A Sermon contra Naphtali Herts Wessely*. Although Tevele sought to ban the publication of Wessely's writings, Moses Mendelssohn and David Friedländer prevented his wishes from being carried out.

A Sermon contra Naphtali Herts Wessely
1782

Beware! This man, Wessely, is an impious man. Beware, do not draw near to him! God, the Lord of Hosts, knows that for the sake of the glory of your Holy Torah I have come this day to hew down he who tramples upon the heads of your Holy People, and to make known to You the evil machinations of this man. In my perusal of his small book I have noted that the spirit of sin animates it. This book seeks to lead the masses astray and to mislead children just out of the womb so that they will not know the paths of Torah and piety. Wessely's counsel is that of a renegade. So that the people should heed him, this imposter associates his sacrilegious ideas with the great and majestic thoughts of His Majesty the Emperor.

What the Emperor actually commanded and what never occurred to Wessely I shall now explain: in His infinite mercy the Lord, the God of Israel, has rendered our people pleasing to His Majesty the Emperor, who now urges each of us to cross the threshold of science and knowledge, [promising] us a place among the royal servants and ministers. The Emperor has commanded all his subjects the following: Every child shall be taught to speak and write the German language so that he will know the language of the land. Everyone shall [also] remain true to the rites and principles of his faith; no part of his faith shall be made alien to him. No Jew will be prevented from fulfilling the fundamentals of our faith, the Written and Oral Torah. (One Torah was spoken by God, although we heard two—may the Lord be blessed that He gave us both of them!) . . . His Majesty the Emperor wishes to teach our children an hour or two a day to speak and read the German language. [But he also wishes] to educate all who spring from the loins of Jacob in the manner of their traditions, for what is primary remains primary and what is secondary remains secondary. How great are his [the Emperor's] works and how precious is his kindness, for indeed all parents wish to provide their children with an education in every type of wisdom, science and craft. [. . .] But this imposter, Wessely, perverts and distorts the counsel of His Majesty, the Emperor, claiming that he commanded that Jewish children shall no longer attend schools [which teach a traditional Jewish curriculum]. [. . .] This is a prevarication. Far be it from any intelligent man to think this of the righteous and sincere lover of mankind and leader of nations, his most pious Majesty the Emperor. In the abundance of his righteousness he actually wishes to strengthen the fortress of religion, each man according to his faith.

Our children shall study the sciences as an adornment; however, the foundations of their education will be in accordance with the command of our ancient sages of the Talmud. Our children shall be taught Torah, ethics, Mishnah and Talmud. Wessely, a foolish and wicked man of coarse spirit, is the one who lacks civility. A carcass is better than he! Whom does he seek to defame and abuse? He has interpreted the thoughts of His Mighty and wise Majesty, the Emperor, in the light of his own schemes. Moreover, he has distorted the teachings of our holy sages. . . . Can his behavior be construed as proper etiquette or any other virtue?

NOTE

Words in brackets appear in the original translation.

Translated by S. Fischer and P. Mendes-Flohr.

Other work by Tevele: *Nefesh David* (1878).

Saul Berlin

1740–1794

Born in Glogau, Germany, Saul Berlin came from a learned rabbinic family; his father had served in the Great Synagogue of London and was the chief rabbi of Berlin. Saul Berlin was himself ordained and served as a rabbi in Frankfurt an der Oder, though he grew dissatisfied with traditional rabbinical authority and embraced the Haskalah, encouraging secular education and admiring such scholars as Naphtali Herts Wessely. Under pseudonyms, Berlin published several biting works against traditional Talmudic teaching methods and their adherents, including Rabbi Raphael Cohen of Altona and Hamburg, and was accused of libel. He was forced to leave his position and died in London.

Ketav yosher (Epistle of Justice)
1784

Has he had the temerity to speak perversely against the foundations of the faith and of the Torah, and mocked the words of our sages of blessed memory recorded in the Mishnah and the Gemara, or has he had the effrontery to raise his head in denial of any one of the Thirteen Principles of the Faith?

The man who was speaking with me responded: "But why is my Master bent upon involving himself in matters of such great import as these? If the individual in question has indeed made it clear by his words that his intent is to spurn the customs of Israel, is it not right to exact vengeance upon him and to remove the evil from the midst of the land?"

But I reverted to the theme of my dialogue and enquired of him: "What then is the matter concerning which he has written an allegation with his pen? Has he—Heaven forbid—spurned the fine and correct customs practiced by us, such as the waving around our heads of the live chickens for atonement on the eve of Yom Kippur, the banging on wood at the mention of Haman on Purim, or the eating of the head of a sheep, and cabbages, dates, and herbs on the New Year, or has he permitted the eating of nuts before the day of Hoshana [the last day of Sukkot]? Has he preached to the people that the Almighty takes no delight in the two white hairs that protrude between the hollow rim of the capsule of the phylacteries worn upon the arm and the place of closure? Has he denied (Heaven forbid that one should even mention it!) the mystical notions associated with the waving of the palm branches during Sukkot, or has he mocked those laws that involve apparently trivial actions, but which in fact are of the utmost spiritual significance, such as putting on one's right shoe first, and wiping one's hands with a pebble, at any rate after touching a part of one's body that is generally covered, or one's head that has just been washed, and such as not passing urine in the public thoroughfare on the Sabbath, or emitting spittle from a high location? If—woe betide—he were to have done any of these things, what you say would be quite correct!

Perhaps he has spoken perversely against the truth of the miracles familiar to all those dwelling in the diaspora, such as those which were performed by our teacher, the master, Rabbi Loew [Maharal], when he invited the Emperor Rudolf to a banquet, and, by invocation of the Divine Name, brought down a castle from heaven, or such as the golem which was fashioned by our teacher, the master, Rabbi Naphtali—may the memory of the righteous be for a blessing—the dust of which still remains hidden away and concealed? Is it perhaps the case that his heart induced him to ascribe deficiencies to the well-known supernatural good-luck charms, and filled his mouth with falsehoods and denials, maintaining that it is impossible to ward off the Evil Eye by means of glowing embers whose flames have become dimmed? If he has sinned in large measure in respect of matters such as these, one may most assuredly not have any mercy upon him and he is not to be saved; his house ought to be burned with fire over his head, and his literary works need to be disposed of by burning.

Translated by David E. Cohen.

Other works by Berlin: *Mitspeh Yekuti'el* (1789); *Besamim rosh* (1793); *Ha-'orev* (1795).

Elimelech of Lizhensk
1717–1787

Born in Tykocin, Poland, Rabbi Elimelech of Lizhensk was the founder of Hasidism in Poland and Galicia. He was the foremost disciple of Dov Ber, the Magid of Mezritsh, whom he succeeded after the latter's death in 1772. The brother of Meshulam Zusya of Annopol, he settled in the Galician town of Lizhensk, where he gathered his own group of disciples, including Jacob Joseph Horowitz (the "Seer of Lublin") and Abraham Joshua Heshel of Apt. Elimelech's magnum opus, *No'am Elimelekh* (1788), emphasizes the roles of a tsadik, or Hasidic rebbe, including praying for the material as well as spiritual welfare of his followers.

No'am Elimelekh (Pleasing Qualities of Elimelech)
1788

The Relationship of Love and Fear

In the blessing "With a great love hast Thou loved us," we say, "and unify our heart to love and fear Thy Name." This is apparently in contradiction to the principle that fear leads to love.

However, both [statements] are correct, for there are two kinds of fear. There is a "lower fear," which is called "Lower Mother," and this is what leads to [that form of] love which is termed "brother," for it is not yet a perfect love. This [inferior] category of love leads to perfect love, which is called "Father." This [superior] category of love leads to "higher fear," known as "[Higher] Mother." Thus, it is written, *Ye shall fear every man his mother and his father* (Lev. 19:3). This refers to the "lower fear," [for which reason] "mother" precedes "father." But with regard to honor, which is love, "father" precedes "mother."

NOTE
Words in brackets appear in the original translation.

Translated by Norman Lamm.

Other work by Elimelech of Lizhensk: *Tsetl katan* (1849).

David Hisquiau Baruch Louzada
1750–ca.1825

David Hisquiau Baruch Louzada was born in the Jewish colonial settlement of Jodensavanne, Suriname. Located outside the former Dutch colony's capital of Paramaribo, Jodensavanne was a Sephardic commu-

David Hisquiau Baruch Louzada, *Hebrew Prayer at the Time of Revolt of the Negroes, Probably in Surinam*, ca. 1790.

nity whose central economy was slave-operated sugar plantations. Louzada took on the position of ḥazan, or cantor, at Jodensavanne's synagogue in 1777. As cantor, he would bless the Jewish troops sent to fight the nearby Maroon communities of runaway slaves. He also undertook the documentation and registration of the race and social status of Jodensavanne's inhabitants; these notes highlight the racism and prejudicial norms governing status and inclusion in the Jewish community in colonial Suriname at the time.

Anti-Slave Prayer
ca. 1790

Blessed and powerful God, eternally [. . .] universal ruler, Lord of Hosts; we have come to beg of you and pray for the safety of the state, as you ordered us through your prophet: "Seek the welfare of the city where I have sent you into exile, and pray to the Lord on its behalf, for in its welfare you will find your welfare." God, the great, mighty, and revered king, creator of all and savior in times of distress, will show mercy to us and pity, save, succor, and protect all those who, going to war against our enemies the cruel and rebellious Blacks, are fearful of the foe.

Translated by Robert Cohen.

Ba'al Shem Tov

Tsava'at ha-Rivash (Testament of Rabbi Israel Ba'al Shem Tov)
1793

Defining Katnut and Gadlut

In order to understand what is *katnut* ("smallness") and what is *gadlut* ("greatness"), consider this example: If one studies Torah without understanding, he is in a state of smallness, for his intellect is not whole. If, however, he studies with understanding and enthusiasm, then he is in a state of greatness, for he is attached to higher levels [of divine service]. The same holds true for prayer. In every mitzvah that one performs, there is *katnut* and *gadlut*.

Devekut in "Smallness"

There are times when a person is incapable of worship except in a state of smallness, i.e., he does not enter the upper worlds at all but thinks that [since] the *whole earth is full of His glory* (Isa. 6:3), that His presence is close to him. At that moment he is like a child whose intellect is underdeveloped. Nevertheless, even though one worships in smallness, he can do so with great *devekut*.

Devekut in "Smallness" (Continued)

One ought to consider that the whole world is full of His glory; that His Shekhinah is always nearby; that He is completely spiritual (lit. "thinner than the thinnest," i.e., not corporeal or tangible); that He is the master of all that exists in the world; that He can do anything which I desire; and therefore it is not proper for me to trust in anyone but Him. [When] one thinks [thus], he beholds the Shekhinah in the same manner that he perceives physical things. This is the service of God in smallness.

NOTE

Words in brackets appear in the original translation.

Translated by Norman Lamm.

Saul Berlin

Besamim rosh (Scent of a Bitter Spice)
1793

Responsum 181

Now in regard to your inquiry as to my view on the question of the halakhic status of the odor of leavened substances on Passover, as there are some authorities who maintain that odor is included within the category of "something concrete" as well:

Response: The Sages stated that odor is not something concrete, insofar as a person is not liable for the consequences of any odor wafting out from his premises onto the public highway—so that it is comparable to mere respiration, which the Talmud maintains possesses no substantive reality. Indeed, if the issue were to be judged on the basis of large versus small quantities, then it would be feasible to incorporate it within the category of something of substance by virtue of the following reasoning: "If a single piece of bread is deemed to emit a minimal level of odor, which possesses a minimal amount of measurable mass, then a thousand loaves of bread would create odor and mass equivalent to the size of an olive [the volume held by the rabbis as rendering someone liable to a penalty were one to consume it on Passover]. Such a conclusion would be absurd, as it is clear that odor is not deemed to be something concrete; and even in regard to divers types of spices, the prime function of which is to produce pleasant odors, here likewise the odor produced is not deemed to be something of a substantive nature, as it is stated in chapter *Ba-meh ishah* (b. *Shabbat* 62): Said Rav Ada bar Ahavah: "That [ruling of R. Eliezer] effectively teaches us that one who on the Sabbath takes out less than the halakhically determined minimum quantity of food in a container into the public thoroughfare would be liable for taking out the container, even though he is not liable for taking out the food, since taking out a spice bundle that has no spice in it is comparable to taking out less than the minimum quantity of food in a container, as the aroma of the spice still remains." Rav Ashi, however, declared: "Generally speaking, I would say to you that such a person should be exempt from liability, but in this instance the position is different, as there is no substance in it at all." Thus we see that it is not regarded as something tangible—and although it would be feasible to argue that the minimal quantity inside the container is not treated as an independent entity, and is halakhically deemed to be nullified when it is measured against the size of the container, Rav Ashi did not say this, but merely that it does not constitute anything substantive; and even Rav Ada bar Ahavah does not require that it be treated as the equivalent of a real, substantive entity, since it has been stated in a mishnah that where there is no spice in a spice bundle, liability is incurred, but where there *are* spices contained therein, one would be exempt from liability. Hence we see that even a minimal quantity would suffice to satisfy the requirements of Rav Ada bar Ahavah, and how could he logically be heard to say that where the foodstuff does not contain a spice bundle, it is as though it did contain it? However, the Tosafists of blessed memory have stated that even a tiny quantity requires a minimum size/volume for liability to be incurred, and they have adduced proof from the statement made in this same chapter: "A woven item of any size whatsoever is susceptible to ritual impurity, and a decorative ornament of any size whatsoever, *etc*." and additional proofs as well. Hence there are distinctions to be drawn between different kinds of minimal quantities, and indeed, when one analyzes the issue down to its finer points of detail, proof may be adduced from there. However, one could perhaps still invalidate such proof by contending that the phrase "There is something contained within it" is applicable only in instances where that thing can be handled physically as an independent entity, in its own right, such as the way in which women wear it, that being the definition of a decorative ornament. Nonetheless, there is a proof contained within the words of Rav Ashi, and proof may also be furnished from what Rav Ada says. However, this is not the appropriate place to elaborate further.

Responsum 259

In regard to a matter involving danger to life, we most certainly rely on the doctors, even where desecration of the Sabbath is concerned, and even in regard to cases where it is implicit from the text of the Talmud that this particular ailment does not involve danger, since we have perceived with our own eyes alterations within nature occurring in different eras insofar as all such matters are concerned. A number of phenomena exist the meaning of which we do not know how to fathom at all. And my teachers did not wish to leave it to people to rely, in the matter of diseases and remedies, on such as are mentioned in the Talmud, for they declared that the physical nature of the successive generations has changed. However, insofar as matters involving foods ritually unfit for consumption are concerned, they have retained the original halakhic status quo, so that a slaughtered animal with an adhesion of the lobes of the lungs to one another or to the chest is deemed unfit for consumption, yet one with an abscess is deemed fit, notwithstanding the fact that a doctor would maintain a contrary view. But we rely upon the doctor, and everyone, when sick, should place himself in the doctor's hands, and ought not to suspect him of being incompetent. Indeed, I have seen no one who disputes this. I have personally witnessed a certain individual when he was a child, whose leg was broken at the top, close to the body, and the whole of the broken portion was severed from him by amputation, and the doctors made wooden supports for him, and he survived for a long time afterwards. Yet there is nothing remarkable about this, as the entire world has literally become altered—it is like a fresh world in all respects!

Translated by David E. Cohen.

Shneur Zalman of Liady
1745–1812

Shneur Zalman of Liady, born in Liozno, present-day Belarus, was the founder of Ḥabad Hasidism. He was first a disciple of Dov Ber, the Magid of Mezritsh, and then of Menachem Mendel of Vitebsk. Shneur Zalman was involved in conflicts with the Vilna Gaon and other Misnagdim, leading to his arrest and brief imprisonments in 1798 and in 1801. After his second release, he moved his court to Liady, also in present-day Belarus. Characteristic of his leadership was his establishment of a court that attracted thousands, with satellite sites in other Eastern European locations; he also listened personally to individual sorrows and requests. His Hasidic philosophy expressed Kabbalah and Hasidism in terms of the rational and intellectual sphere, as reflected in his magnum opus, *Tanya*. (Excerpts of other works by Shneur Zalman appear in this volume.)

Tanya
1797

Tzimtzum: An Infusion of Light

INTRODUCTION

Now, aside from the fact that it is altogether impossible to interpret the matter of *tzimtzum* literally, for that would attribute corporeal events to the Holy One, Who is removed from them by many myriads of separation *ad infinitum*, they also do not speak wisely. Surely they believe, as befits "believers the sons of believers," that the Holy One knows all the created beings in this lowly world and exercises providence over them, and that His knowledge of them adds neither plurality nor novelty to Him, for He knows everything by knowing Himself. His essence, being, and knowledge are, as it were, all one.

That is why it says in *Tikkunim*, tikkun 57: "There is no place empty of Him, neither in the upper worlds nor in the lower worlds." Similarly it is written in *Raya Mehemna* on the portion of Pinhas: "He grasps all and none can grasp Him. . . . He surrounds all the worlds . . . and no one escapes His domain; He fills all the worlds . . . He binds and unites a kind to its kind, upper with lower, and there is no connection among the four elements but through the Holy One, as He is within them."

"None can grasp Him" means that not even one of the supernal intelligences can grasp with his intellect the essence and being of the Holy One. As it says in the introduction to *Tikkunei ha-Zohar*: "You are the Hidden One of all the hidden, and no thought whatsoever can grasp You." So it is in the lower worlds, where, although "He fills all the worlds," He is unlike the soul of man, which is enclosed within the body, affected and influenced by bodily changes, such as pain from blows or cold or the heat of fire, and so forth. The Holy One, however, is not affected by the changes in this world from summer to winter and from day to night, as it is written: *Even darkness is not dark for You, and night shines as day* (Ps. 139:12), for He is not the least bit encompassed within the worlds even though He fills them.

This is also the meaning of "He surrounds all worlds." For example, when man reflects upon an intellectual subject or thinks about a physical matter, his mind encompasses the subject whose image is formed in his mind, but does not embrace it in actual fact. The Holy One, however, of Whom it is written, *For My thoughts are not your thoughts* (Isa. 55:8), actually embraces each and every creature with His thought and His knowledge of all created beings. For His knowledge is indeed its life-force and that which brings it into existence from nothingness into a being of actual reality.

Translated by Norman Lamm.

Other works by Shneur Zalman: *Torah or* (1837); *Likute Torah* (1848).

Elijah ben Solomon, Gaon of Vilna

Ethical Will
ca. 1797

Grieve not at all on my departure for the Land of Israel (may it be built and established!). You gave me indeed a firm promise to that effect. And why should you be anxious? Many men travel years long, in search of money, leaving wives and children, themselves wanderers and strayers in want of all things. But I, thanks be to God, am on my way to the Holy Land, which everyone is eager to behold; the desired of all Israel, the desired of God Himself, the land for which in heaven and on earth all beings yearn. And I journey in peace, blessed be the Lord, though you know that I have torn myself from my children, for whom my heart moans, from all my precious books, and from the glorious splendor of my house, and have become as a stranger in another country. [. . .]

On Sabbaths and festivals speak not at all of matters which are not absolutely essential, and even in such cases be very brief. For the sanctity of the Sabbath is great indeed, and only with reluctance did the authorities allow even the exchange of greetings—so severe were they regarding even a single utterance. Honor then the Sabbath to the utmost, as was done when I was with you. Be in nowise niggardly, for though God determines how much a person shall have, this does not apply to Sabbaths and festivals.

I also make an especial and emphatic request that you train your daughters to the avoidance of objurgations, oaths, lies, or contention. Let their whole conversation be conducted in peace, love, affability and gentleness. I possess many moral books with Yiddish (versions); let them read these regularly; above all on the Sabbath—the holy of holies—they should occupy themselves with these ethical books exclusively. For a curse, an oath, or a lie, strike them; show no softness in the matter. For, (God forbid!) the mother and father are punished for the corruption of the children. Even if you do your best to train them morally and fail, woe to your shame here and hereafter—"she profaneth her father." Therefore use your utmost rigor in their moral training, and may Heaven help you to success! So with other matters, such as the avoidance of slander and gossip; the regular recital of grace before and after meals, the reading of the Shema', all with true devotion. The fundamental rule, however, is that they gad not about in the streets, but incline their ear to your words and honor you and my mother and all their elders. [. . .]

For slander once spoken there is no remedy. Therefore the rule must be: Speak of no man to his praise, still less to his dispraise. For what has a man to do with slander? "The mouth of slander is a deep pit, he that is abhorred of the Lord falleth therein."

Against this offence the most effective hedge is solitude—to avoid ever leaving the house for the streets unless under pressure of extreme necessity or in order to perform an important religious duty. The Scripture hints at this. Even in Synagogue make but a very short stay and depart. It is better to pray at home, for in Synagogue it is impossible to escape envy and the hearing of idle talk. Men have to give account for it; as the Sages say, he who merely listens and is silent is culpable. The more so on Sabbaths and festivals, when people assemble to talk, it would be better not to pray at all. It is also better for your daughter not to go to Synagogue, for there she would see garments of embroidery and similar finery. She would grow envious and speak of it at home, and out of this would come scandal and other ills. Let her seek her glory in her home, cleaving ever to discipline, and showing no jealousy for worldly gauds, vain and delusive as they are, coming up in a night and perishing in a night. [. . .]

My dear mother! I realize that you need no instruction of mine, for I know your modest disposition. Nevertheless, let them read in your presence this Letter, for it contains counsels derived from the words of the living God. And I earnestly implore you not to grieve for my sake, as you have promised. If, by God's grace, I have the privilege to be in Jerusalem, the Holy City, over against the Gates of Heaven, I will pray on your behalf in accordance with my undertaking. If we are so blessed we shall appear (in the City) together all of us, should the Master of Mercy so will it.

I also beg my wife to honor my mother in accordance with the prescript of the Law, especially regarding a widow. 'Tis an indictable offense to distress her, even in the smallest matter. My mother, too, I entreat to live harmoniously with my wife, each bringing happiness to the other by kindly intercourse, for this is a prime duty incumbent on all mankind. Each one is asked, in the hour of judgment: "Hast thou conducted thyself with friendliness towards thy fellow man?" The aim of the Torah, in large part, is to induce this desire of causing happiness. Let there be no dissension of any kind among all the household, men and women, but let love and brotherliness reign. In case of offense, forgive each other, and live for God's sake in amity. Of my mother I also ask that she shall lay her injunctions on my sons and daughters in tender terms so that she may win obedience; that she shall care for them and they shall honor her. Between them there shall be heard no strife or anger, but peace shall prevail. And may the Master of Peace grant unto you, unto my sons and daughters, my sons-in-law and brothers, and unto all Israel, life and peace! These are the words of one who constantly prays for you—Elijah b. Solomon Zalman (be the memory of the righteous for a blessing!).

Translated by Israel Abrams.

Levi Isaac of Berdichev
ca. 1740–1809

Levi Isaac (Yitshak) of Berdichev, born in Hoshakov, Galicia, to a rabbinic family, was introduced to Hasidism by a follower of Dov Ber, the Magid of Mezritsh. As a fervent Hasid, Levi Isaac clashed bitterly with Misnagdim and, living in a hostile environment in Żelechów and Pinsk, found sanctuary in Berdichev in 1785, where he remained until his death. While he neither established a Hasidic court nor had a large number of disciples, he stressed the role of a tsadik as an intermediary between the human and the divine. His teachings influenced later Hasidism; he became a well-loved figure about whom many tales abound.

Kedushat Levi (Sanctity of Levi)
1798

Woman and the Miracles of Purim and Hanukkah

We recite the blessing "Who performed miracles for our forefathers, etc." on Hanukkah and Purim, but we do not do so on Passover, even though the Exodus too was accompanied by miracles. The reason for this seems to be because the miracles of Hanukkah and Purim were accomplished through the activities of women. Moreover, these miracles were performed by natural means, unlike those accompanying the Exodus, when the Egyptians were struck by the Ten Plagues, and the [Red] Sea was split [in order to allow the fleeing Israelites to pass]—all miracles beyond natural means. In contrast, the miracles of Hanukkah and Purim were accomplished naturally. In the case of Hanukkah, Judith fed the Syrian governor milk, and killed him while he lay sleeping; as to Purim, at first Ahasuerus loved Haman and then transferred that love to Esther. These miracles were thus performed *in time*, a natural phenomenon, and we therefore recite the blessing "Who performed miracles for our forefathers in those days *at this time*." The miracles of Passover were supernatural, and thus we do not recite the blessing.

NOTE

Words in brackets appear in the original translation.

Translated by Norman Lamm.

Other works by Levi Isaac of Berdichev: *Sefer ha-zekhirot* (1794); *Shemu'ah tovah* (1938).

Eleazer Fleckeles
1754–1826

Born into a wealthy family in Prague, Eleazer (El'azar) Fleckeles became a rabbi and disciple of Ezekiel Landau. Fleckeles served communities in Moravia before taking a position in Prague in 1783, eventually becoming the community's presiding judge and halakhic authority. In his sermons in the 1780s, he spoke out against the Haskalah, including Moses Mendelssohn's German translation of the Bible; in the 1790s, however, he began to moderate his stance. He took an active role in condemning Sabbatianism and objected to what he regarded as excesses in Hasidic expressions.

Kuntres ahavat David (Treatise: The Love of David)
1799–1800

Says the Author:

O my God! Remember for good my most honorable Master, my father, my teacher in respect of the Divine precepts—may his memory be for a blessing for the life of the World-to-Come! I recall that when I was a little boy riding on my father's shoulders, he implanted in my heart a love for the Torah and for those who study it, and he reared me in faith in, and practice of, delightful things, separating me from those who go astray; and he related tales to me about that dog, Shabbetai Tsevi—may his bones rot—who exchanged his God for another and permitted things that are prohibited. As for anyone who believes in his "traditions," such a person's innermost designs are not of a godly nature. All his deeds were deceitful—both he and all his disciples wicked dogs, an assembly of evil-doers. They say, in relation to this carcass, that he is now hidden and concealed, and that he will shortly reveal himself and that his naked self will become visible in the sight of all; and they pervert the words of the Living God and the King of the Universe; they destroy the walls that are exalted and lofty—and they treat with disdain those observing the Fast Days with their vanities and dreams. [. . .]

Now I know that just as they turned to insanity in regard to the current year [the year 5560; equivalent to 1799–1800] with allusions, secrets, and perversions, there will yet be further occasions and seasons when they will proclaim: "The years predicted by prophecy for the advent of the Messiah have arrived"—and they will adduce signs and set up signposts culled from the mystic lore of the wise and the discerning, such as in connection with the year 5600—may it come to us for good! They will discover an allusion to it in the Zohar, and this is what they will say: "In the sixth hundredth year of the sixth millennium, the fountains of wisdom will be opened," etc.

[. . .] In a generation which breaches all moral boundaries, and residing outside the Land of Israel, where—on account of our many sins—by reason of the study of the wisdom contained in the mystic tradition, much damage and numerous acts of desecration have occurred—in that the Almighty's great Name has been profaned among the gentile nations, who do not know Him, and among the kingdoms who do not call upon His Name. O Hebrew nation, look around, that you may see!—have regard to the era of that wicked one, that man of excessively bold countenance, Shabetai Tsevi—may his bones rot! All those nations who heard of his apostasy rejoiced; we became a reproach and an object of mockery to our neighbors; as in the days of a solemn assembly, our terrors totally encompassed us; we became a byword in the mouth of the nations, suffering scorn from all sides; and the subsequent impostor made his iniquity still heavier and wrought evil to this people—that is to say, the abominable and abhorrent Jacob [Frank], that accursed man, who blasphemed the Almighty with the names of the *Ba'alim* [the ancient Canaanite deities] and the vain idols; he it was who originally emerged all ruddy, his apparel being red; and his evil companions likewise were from this very same reddish hue. He rode upon a red horse, and his servants after him upon red horses, all of them bearing a reddish appearance; and everything that they wrote was inscribed with a reddish dye. And he compiled a religious law for them, which was neither the law of the Hebrews nor the law of the Christians—neither of Israel nor of Ishmael, nor in accordance with the laws of Persia and Media. Their laws were distinct from those of all who were acquainted with law and judgment; and he gave to his law the title: "The Law of Edom." On the surface it was that of Edom, but inwardly, this modern-day Laban sought the *teraphim* and the idols, and adopted all abominations that had appeared in the land—swearing, and lying, and stealing, and committing adultery, breaking all bounds; raising questions concerning, and expounding, the verses of the Torah and the Prophets and the words of the Midrash in ways agreeable to their religious law and their views; they invented meanings, in consonance with their erroneous faith, in regard to diverse matters, which were contrary to reason—and they would not accept normal human logic. The anointed of the Lord was "taken captive" by their speech—namely, the dialogues of demons and the dialogues of ensnarement, of folly and madness. They bored through and strung together all the prophecies of the Prophets and Seers, and all allusions emanating from the savants of the secret lore, concerning the anointed of the Almighty to their own Messiah, who was "anointed" with the fatty tail of a sacrificial animal, and with impure fat!

Translated by David E. Cohen.

Other works by Fleckeles: *Olat ḥodesh*, 4 vols. (1785–1800); *Teshuvah me-ahavah*, 3 vols. (1809; 1815; 1821).

Yom Tov ben Israel Jacob Algazi
1727–1802

Born in Izmir, Yom Tov ben Israel Jacob (Yisra'el Ya'akov) Algazi was a kabbalist who studied under Shalom Sharabi and succeeded him as rabbi of Jerusalem's Bet El yeshiva. He traveled to Europe to collect funds for Jerusalem Jewry and was welcomed by Akiva Eger and Moses Sofer. When it was rumored that the local Jews were planning to aid Napoleon's conquest of Jerusalem, Algazi sided with the Ottomans and played a large role in defending the city. His most famous work, *Kedushat Yom Tov*, is a collection of responsa and sermons.

Kedushat Yom Tov (The Sanctity of Yom Tov)
ca. 1800

Section 8

Reuben spoke in the marketplace with two men, inviting them to come to his house for the purpose of giving them the monies accrued from a business partnership, and they entered his house together, and from there they went in after him to the house of his neighbor, in the belief that he would give them the monies in his neighbor's house. Now when they entered into the house together, there was a young girl, a virgin, there, engaged in her work. And Reuben spoke up and said to these two men: "You, Mr. So-and-so, and you, Mr. So-and-so, be witnesses!" And he instantly seized the hand of the young girl and said to her:

"Behold! You are betrothed to me with this ring," etc. And the witnesses were alarmed at the sight of this, and astounded, and they turned around forthwith and departed from the house, with Reuben likewise following them outside. But as for the young girl, she was seized with a fit of trembling, and she called to her relatives and told them: "Thus and thus did this man do to me!" And her relatives began to cry out regarding these things, and summoned the witnesses before the ecclesiastical court to testify as to what had occurred; and the witnesses stood and testified before the ecclesiastical court, swearing by their own lives and by their Jewish faith that the matter was as follows: that they had not known what was in the mind of Reuben, and thought that it had genuinely been on account of the money that they had been brought [to Reuben's, and subsequently, to his neighbor's house]; that when they had entered the house of his neighbor, the idea had already dawned on them that Reuben had some business dealings with his neighbors, both those of high and of low rank; and they had mentally concluded that it was from the house of his neighbor that he wished to take the money and give it to them. Moreover, when he had said: "You, Mr. So-and-so, and you, Mr. So-and-so, be witnesses!" they had thought that he wished to get them to testify concerning himself—that he had received the money from the young girl; but that when he took hold of the girl's hand, he did so with force, and the young girl had wept and snatched her hand away, and he had grabbed it with force. The ecclesiastical court further enquired of the witnesses as to whether any words exchanged between Reuben and the young girl had taken place earlier, either in connection with the betrothal or concerning some other subject, and they testified, by way of totally formal evidence, that no words whatsoever had been previously exchanged between them, but rather, as soon as he had entered the house and said to the witnesses: "Be witnesses!" he had taken hold of the hand of the young girl and had said to her: "Behold! You are betrothed," etc. They further testified, by way of totally formal evidence, that they had not seen the transferal of the ring from his hand to her hand, and that they did not know with what object he had betrothed her; merely that they had heard, from his mouth, that he had said to her: "Behold! You are betrothed," etc. They testified, in addition, by way of totally formal evidence, that they had left the house forthwith and that they did not know whether the young girl had instantly thrown down the ring from her hand, while he was saying the words, or not. All this was attested to by the witnesses. Now, they are inquiring as to whether or not this betrothal has any validity, and they further say that in regard to this type of matter, there is a consensus of the rabbis of the early generations to the effect that one ought not to effect a betrothal other than in the presence of ten Jewish men, two of whom should be from among the distinguished members of the community, and that the local rabbi, responsible for the dissemination of Torah, should be overseeing them. And it is stated there as follows: "Any man who acts presumptuously, to betroth a woman with two witnesses present, but who does not have with him at that ceremony ten Jewish men, as aforementioned, such betrothal shall not be binding and shall have no force, and it shall be treated as the dust of the earth, and as something without substance; as for the money which he gave to the woman for the purpose of effecting a betrothal, we hereby declare it to be entirely ownerless, by virtue of the valid power of the ecclesiastical court invested in us; and we render his betrothal entirely null and void, with the same power as the ecclesiastical court of Ravina and Rav Ashi, who possessed the power to confiscate people's money." Now since this man Reuben transgressed this consensus, it remains to be considered whether or not any account is to be taken of the betrothal effected by him. [. . .]

A Festival for the Rabbis

[. . .] The supreme virtue of the Land of Israel is well known, and in particular, the supreme virtue of Jerusalem the Holy City—which is possessed of the very utmost virtue; and in the Gemara there exists a difference of opinion as to whether the original sanctity of Jerusalem created a state of sanctity both for its own time and for the future too, and Rabbi Moses [Maimonides] has explained, in chapter 6 of the *halakhot* relating to the Temple, [in his work *Mishneh Torah*] that the original sanctity of the Holy Temple and of Jerusalem created a state of sanctity for its own time and for the future too, that therefore we may offer up all the various sacrifices there notwithstanding the fact that the Temple has not yet been rebuilt, that we may eat the most holy of the offerings throughout the Temple court even though it lies in ruins, that we may eat those offerings enjoying a minor degree of holiness, and the second tithe, throughout the whole of Jerusalem although it has no surrounding walls, as its original state of sanctity created a state of sanctity both for its own time and for the future too. He provided a reason as to why, in the case of the Temple and of Jerusalem, their original state of sanctity created a state of sanctity for the future, whereas, in regard to the sanctity of the remainder of the Land of Israel—insofar as the Sabbatical year and tithes and other matters of a like nature are concerned, it did not create any sanctity for the future. Namely, that the sanctity of the Temple and of Jerusalem came about on account of the divine presence there, and the divine presence can never be canceled, and scripture indeed states: "And I shall make your sanctuaries desolate"—upon which verse the Sages declared: "Despite their being desolate, they still remain in their state of sanctity"—but those obligations imposed upon the land in the Sabbatical year, and in connection with tithes, are applicable only by virtue of a public conquest of the Land having occurred. Once the Land had been taken away from them, that conquest became null and void, and the Land was exempted, by virtue of the law of the Torah, from the obligations of giving tithes and resting during the Sabbatical year, since it was no longer the Land of Israel; but when Ezra came up and sanctified it a second time, it became sanctified both for its own time and for the future as well. Accordingly, the sanctity of Jerusalem and of the Temple experienced no interruption, for the initial sanctity whereby Jerusalem was sanctified by the descendants of those who came up from Egypt, and the sanctity of the Temple, which was sanctified in the days of King Solomon, never ceased, despite their having been exiled and the Temple having been destroyed—unlike the rest of the territory of the Land of Israel, where their sanctity ceased with the first exile, until such time as Ezra came up from Babylon and sanctified it, both for his own times and for the future. And the essential reason for this distinction is that the sanctity of the Temple and of Jerusalem existed because the divine presence resided there, and the divine presence never departed from there, even when they were destroyed, as is stated in Canticles Rabbah, section 282, where it is written as follows: "Another explanation: 'The divine presence never departed from the midst of the Temple, as it is stated in scripture: And My eyes and My heart shall be there for eternity.'" And we find, in similar vein, the verse: "And He has answered me from His holy mountain. Selah!" Hence, although it is a mountain that now lies in ruins, it remains in its original state of sanctity. And moreover, come and have a look at what is written in regard to the proclamation of Cyrus: "He is the God Who is

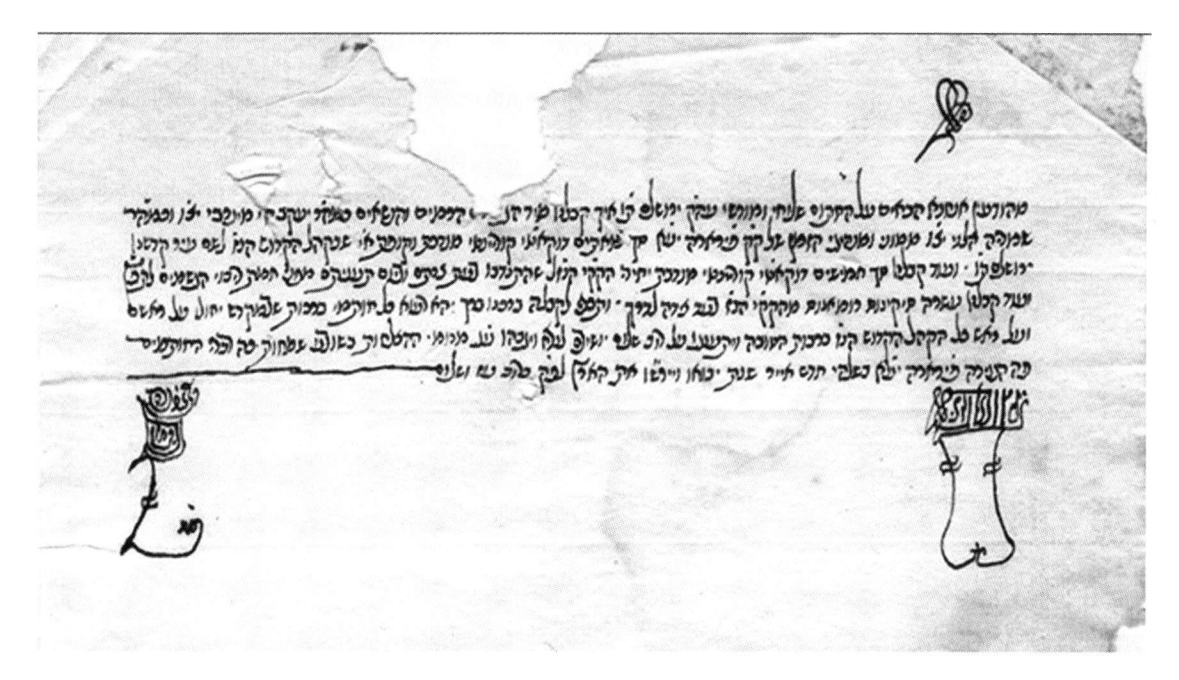

Yom Tov ben Israel Jacob Algazi, *Authorization of Receipt of Donation by "Eretz Israel Contribution Fund" of Ferrara (Italy) Congregation. By "Emissaries of the Holy City of Jerusalem."*

in Jerusalem." He was in effect saying to them: "Even though it lies in ruins, the Almighty God has not departed from there." Moreover, said R. Aha: "The divine presence has never departed from the Western Wall, as it is stated: Behold, He is standing behind our Wall!" The Midrashic citation concludes at this point.

Translated by David E. Cohen.

Other works by Algazi: *Get mekushar* (1767); *Shemot Yom Tov* and *Hilkhot Yom Tov* (1794).

Ḥayim of Volozhin
1749–1821

The foremost disciple of the Vilna Gaon, Ḥayim of Volozhin became the rabbi of Volozhin, his native town. Unlike the Vilna Gaon, Ḥayim did not consider Hasidism heretical but did consider its practices to be misguided. His magnum opus, *Nefesh ha-ḥayim*, published posthumously, is mainly a response to what he regarded as Hasidism's challenges. He considered Torah study to hold the highest religious value for Jews. In 1802, Ḥayim founded the Volozhin yeshiva, drawing on support from throughout Lithuania and setting a model for others to follow, stressing intellectual learning over *yirah* (fear of God). The yeshiva remained prominent until its closing in 1892.

Igeret ha-yeshiva (Epistle on the Yeshiva)
1803

Our dear brethren, Children of Israel, perhaps the time has now come to repair the breaches in our ranks; let us return to uphold the Torah of the Almighty with all our strength. Who will be the volunteers to teach the students? Who to be activists in this meritorious deed? Who to form part of the student body? Who to be supporters of the Torah with their wealth? Every single individual who comes close to the Torah of the Almighty shall be everlasting, for the donation of money is a defense against Divine retribution and the acquisition of wisdom is likewise a defense, and both of these preserve those who possess them in equal measure.

I am going to be the first of those volunteering to be among the teachers—without my taking a solemn vow in this regard; and by the mercies of the Almighty, who has cared abundantly for me throughout my life, in Him do I trust and in Him do I take refuge. He will furnish me generously with the wherewithal to meet the material needs of the students in accordance with each one's requirements.

Now I know that I have not merited possession of the attribute of humility, but it is laid down in the Gemara, in the Palestinian Talmud, at the end of tractate *Shevi'it*, and also adduced by Ra"sh [R. Samson of Sens] *ad loc.* that one who is well-versed in just a single Talmudic tractate and sees that people are according him honor in larger measure than would rightfully be due to him for this is obliged to inform them of the truth; and I have heard that my name is being associated with the name of our teacher, the greatest of our rabbis, whose name is known throughout the Jewish diaspora—our teacher and our master, the holy one of Israel and its light, our most illustrious teacher, Rabbi Elijah—may his soul repose in Paradise—the saint of Vilna; and I have enjoyed the merit of his good name being associated with myself, through people saying that I was his disciple, and hence I acknowledge a personal obligation to make it genuinely known in Israel that far be it from me to diminish the honor due to the master and great and holy rabbi—may his soul repose in paradise—by having my own name associated with his; I know for a certainty that anyone saying that I was his disciple is entirely in error; for our most illustrious master—may his soul repose in paradise—had his learning laid out in perfect order before him, with a crystal-clear knowledge of halakhah throughout the Torah in its entirety, without his entertaining any doubts whatsoever in regard thereto—in scripture, in Mishnah, and in the Babylonian and the Palestinian Talmuds, and the Mekhilta, the Sifra, and the Sifrei and the Tosefta, and Midrashim and Zoharic material, and all the words of the Tanna'im and the Amora'im in our possession; and in all of these, he merited having his due portion among them, enabling him to decide as between the various matters of doubt arising from their statements, and to introduce novel elements into them; to be someone who hears and adds thereto mounds upon mounds of *halakhot* and homiletic items and expositions, as well as the most enigmatic of the divine mysteries; how then can I lift up my face like a flint and not be ashamed to be called his disciple, since I have not had the merit to receive even a small portion of his splendor, neither have I had the merit to possess a clear mastery of the halakhah in respect of even a single tractate, as the instances of doubt are numerous and the final rulings, reconciling differing views, are few. In the short time during which I had the merit of attending upon him, I did not merit obtaining anything from him other than my becoming acquainted with the general thrust of a halakhic discussion, after the exertion of a great deal of mental toil; in this regard, a binding promise has been made to all our brethren, the Children of Israel, in accordance with the assurances of our sages of blessed memory, that if someone were to declare: "I labored hard, but met with no success therein," do not believe him! Furthermore, I did not have the merit of attaining the level of mental toil and effort exerted by our great Master—may his soul repose in paradise—as the immense amount of mental toil and effort expended by our great Master—may his soul repose in paradise—can neither be appreciated nor measured, nor believed by anyone who has not personally witnessed his vast amount of mental exertion over every single detail of the Torah, until such time as he was able to grasp it with full clarity.

Translated by David E. Cohen.

Other works by Ḥayim of Volozhin: *Nefesh ha-ḥayim* (1824); *Ruaḥ Ḥayim* (1859); *Ha-ḥut ha-meshulash* (1882).

Elijah ben Solomon, Gaon of Vilna

Bi'ur ha-Gra: Glosses to Shulḥan arukh
ca. 1803

6. "It is proper," etc. The phraseology employed by the Tur[1] is "And one should cover one's head so that one should not be in a state of bareheadedness"—this is taken from the words of the Ba'al ha-'itur.[2] Now the Bet Yosef[3] has written [commenting on the words in the Tur commencing "One should cover"] the following: "It appears that this does not refer to total bare-headedness, as this has nothing to do with the subject of *tsitsit*." Moreover, how was the person able, therefore, to go to relieve himself and to attend to other matters? Accordingly, it must mean that although his head *is* covered, it is the practice of modest people to place a turban or a prayer shawl on their head, etc. It is conceivable that what was meant is this: that one should not be bareheaded insofar as the wearing of *tsitsit* is concerned, and that this is what the *Shulḥan arukh* meant by stating "It is proper." However, this interpretation is forced, as this is not what one calls "being bareheaded"; we find in the Talmud, in several places, that it was the practice of the Sages to cover their heads with a turban, i.e. in Kiddushin 5a and Berakhot 60b, and in the chapter *Arve Pesaḥim* [101b], and in *Shabbat* ch. 16 [120a] and in *Shabbat* ch. 8 [77b], and in *Mo'ed Katan* ch. 3 [15a] where it is stated: "No! [a person afflicted with leprosy must not have his head covered] with a cap or a turban"; and similarly in ch. 8 of Eruvin [84b], and in the R"if [R. Isaac Alfasi's abridged version of the Talmud], in Berakhot [44b]: "The blessing over the *tsitsit* is recited after the blessing 'Who clothes the naked,' and at the end of the passage: 'When he spreads the turban over his head,'" etc. Moreover, in regard to what the Bet Yosef has written: "How was he able to go to relieve himself?" etc.—it is implicit from what he says that it is halakhically forbidden to walk about with one's head uncovered—but that is not the case, as we see from the fact that it is stated in ch. 16 of *Shabbat* [118b]: "I merit reward," etc.; likewise in the first chapter of *Kiddushin* [31a]: "Rav Huna, son of R. Joshua, did not," etc., and, at [*Kiddushin* 33a]: "How much temerity did that man have?, etc. Perhaps he hails from Mata Mehasya," etc. Thus we see that it is permitted to wear a turban only in the presence of a Talmudic scholar. And likewise in tractate (*Derekh Eretz*) [*Kallah*] in regard to the case of the two small children, and in *Kiddushin* [29b] in connection with Rav Hamnuna, except that there, in *Kiddushin*, it would be feasible to interpret the passage as does the Bet Yosef; [namely, that one ought to wear a head-covering] "on account of modesty." A further instance of this is to be found in *Nedarim* 30b, and similarly, in the instance occurring at the end of *Shabbat* [156b], where the words "Cover your head!" appear, this expression is to be understood in accordance with its plain sense, and in accordance with that which is stated in *Kiddushin* 31a: "Rav Huna, son of R. Joshua, did not have," etc., and in accordance with its usage in the phrase "In the presence of a Talmudic scholar," and in accordance with the mention, in the third chapter of *Megillah*, of a *poheaḥ*, etc., which is interpreted in *Soferim* "With uncovered head," and similarly, the instance in *Kiddushin* 8a is to be understood in accordance with its plain meaning; namely, that anyone else besides a Talmudic scholar does not require a turban at all, and as is mentioned in the eighth chapter of Shabbat [77b] and in the Midrash Rabbah [Vayiqra Rabba, *Emor*, par. 27:6] in relation to the recitation of the Shema, which is cited by the Bet Yosef in section 61: "I have not troubled you," etc. However, it is due to the fact that a person's enwrapping himself in

his prayer shawl is for the purpose of prayer that it states that he should cover his head; and this is in accord with what is written in section 91, subsection 3, and in column 1, subsection 3; and see subsection 5. Now although the Tur has already written in section 2 that one should cover one's head, there it is merely in passing, and in the context of a person displaying "extraordinary piety" until such time as he has enwrapped himself, whereas in the instances cited here, he is stating what is required by strict halakhah—and yet, even this is not, strictly speaking, an absolute halakhic imperative, as he has stated, since, from the strictly halakhic viewpoint, even to pray and to enter the synagogue bareheaded—all of these things are indeed permissible, as I shall state below—albeit here, everyone has an obligation to act stringently, which is not the case in relation to section 2, which is applicable solely to exceptionally modest and God-fearing individuals, in accordance with what is written in *Kiddushin* 8a; and in fact, any form of covering is sufficient until a person covers his head, which, in this context, means: "with a prayer shawl or a turban": but in the *Ra'aya Mehemna* [portion of the Zohar], section 3 122b it is stated: "On account of the fact that he," etc., "for the purposes of prayer and entering the synagogue, and for the rest of the people, who do not possess turbans," and such would appear to be the case in *Shabbat* 147a where reference is made to a doubly folded prayer shawl—see Rashi, and such as would further appear from section 301, subsection 29, which means "After," etc., and likewise from the tractate chapter *Ha-tekhelet* where reference is made to "The prayer shawl with which a minor covers himself"—and see the Zohar, section 3 122b. Furthermore, as to what is stated in *Soferim* 311, to the effect that it is forbidden to pronounce any divine name with uncovered head, that too constitutes an act of extraordinary piety; for, from the Gemara in *Berakhot* 60, this does not appear to be the case, as is evident from section 46, subsection 1; likewise from the Midrash Rabbah cited above, namely: "I have not troubled you," etc. The general principle is that there is no prohibition whatsoever on walking with one's head uncovered, except when one is in the presence of outstanding personages, and similarly, at times of prayer, it is proper to cover one's head out of a sense of propriety and respect for the Almighty; and, as regards the rest of the day, covering one's head is required exclusively for those holy men who stand continuously in the presence of the Almighty.

NOTES

1. [Tur: legal code of Jacob ben Asher (1270–1340).—Ed.]
2. [Ba'al ha-'itur: Isaac ben Abba Mari (ca. 1122–1193), author of *Itur soferim*, masterwork of Jewish law.—Ed.]
3. [Bet Yosef: masterwork of Jewish law, based on the *Tur*, by Rabbi Joseph Karo (1488–1575).—Ed.]

Translated by David E. Cohen.

Ezekiel Paneth
1783–1845

Born into a prominent family in Silesia, Ezekiel (Yeḥezkel) Paneth studied at the Leipnik yeshiva of Baruch Fränkl-Te'omim. Later, in Prague, he encountered pro-Haskalah rabbinic figures such as Judah (Yehudah) Leib Fischeles, the anti-Sabbatian Eleazer Fleckeles, and Baruch Jeitteles. As a result of the restrictions of the Familiants Laws, Paneth moved to Galicia, where he embraced Hasidism largely under the influence of Menachem Mendel of Rimanov. Ultimately Paneth moved to Hungary and from 1823 served as the chief rabbi of the principality of Transylvania, where he worked in rural conditions to serve a variety of Jewish cultures, including Sephardic; he also was on favorable terms with state figures.

Sefer mar'eh Yeḥezkel (The Vision of Ezekiel)
1805

History of Our Rebbe—Letters

Besides these, there are students of outstanding ability in their Torah study seated constantly in his presence—they are swifter than eagles and mightier than lions, each one of whom is able to serve as a shield for the people of his generation—and our rebbe provides them with spiritual and intellectual nourishment to their utmost satisfaction; and they are constantly engaged in the holy service for its own sake, and are filled with humility and lowliness of spirit, loving and honoring one another, and drawing close to the Almighty all those desirous of this—even the most junior individuals such as myself, who was like a mere grasshopper in their estimation; they would all stand trembling when he opened his mouth with words of Torah—they all became like deaf-mutes; and universally acknowledged that they were words which no ear had ever heard before—of a hidden and mysterious nature; each individual would understand and grasp them in accordance with his own spiritual level and the power of his intellect, in such measure as he had previously prepared himself and connected up his thoughts, his comprehension, and his wisdom to walk before the Almighty, and when he had improved his traits of character by "three cubits and seven folds and twelve leaders." Our rebbe—may his light shine brightly—explained that the reason why these are called "the measurements of the soul" is that each person receives his illumination and his flow from the divine intellect in accordance with his own measure of spiritual accomplishment.

Now I have written down all the words that I heard from his mouth precisely as they were uttered, and in identical format, which have amounted to thirty pages, and I have already entertained the idea of recording in writing one discourse selected from those I have to hand, and of explaining his words of purity in a manner commensurate with the paucity of my intellect; although I am keenly aware that I am a mere fledgling whose eyes have not yet opened, and that I am lacking in human understanding and that my power of comprehension is not sufficiently great as to grasp even the simplest statements—namely, the mundane conversation of the students seated before him—I said to myself: "It is the work of heaven—if only to demonstrate to you that the words in question are of ancient origin, emanating from a sacred source, and to prevent the reader from making the error of saying that the words are to be understood in accordance with their plain meaning."

Later on, I said: "This course too is not what the Almighty has chosen; for even if I were to commit to writing the major portion of his teachings, your focus, in studying that material, would not be with a view to learning some fresh manner of fine conduct, and the worthy and upright path which would be acceptable in the sight of the Almighty, and to which the Supreme Ruler would wish to accord honor—i.e., how to study Torah for its own sake and how to concentrate while engaged in prayer, and how to perform the precepts wholeheartedly, with fear and love, so that they ascend toward heaven—but on the contrary, you would focus your attention exclusively on the exposition, as to whether it is sharp and acute, as to whether it is good or bad—one person saying this and another saying that; and perhaps you would incur divine retribution for this—for having laid a blemish upon the sacred property of heaven; and moreover, it is something where the possibility of gaining reward is remote and the likelihood of coming to harm great; in particular, because works on ethical conduct *are* already available, though here it is vital to bear in mind that one cannot compare merely hearing about something to actually seeing it, since the reader will peruse the work in question in his own fashion, and if his mind and intellect are walking in darkness, he will be incapable of perceiving the goodly light lying concealed within such works. For these reasons, when the Creator, blessed be He, will grant His assent to your designs, may you be found worthy of hearing the words of the Living God through the medium of your own vision, emanating from the mouth of holiness as he speaks—from the one who is sitting and expounding as Moses did, from the mouth of the Almighty; then you will gain an understanding of the fear of the Almighty and knowledge of the ways of the feet of his saintly men, so as to prevent your ever returning to folly." [. . .]

Why do you not fortify your yearning for "rejoicing while in a state of trembling," on account of the fear of the Lord and His glorious majesty, to cling to the light of the countenance of the King of Life, the Ruler Who is exalted and extolled by the tongues of His saintly men and His servants? Are your brethren to come and ascend to the House of the royal sanctuary, while you remain here? How will your hearts remain firmly in place, and how will your hands be strengthened, when you witness an exceedingly vast assembly serving His glorious Name with joy and gladness, while you are merely standing by?

How much more—verily, how infinitely more so is this applicable, according to his words, namely, where many are veering away from their habitual ways to obey him, to carry out his work and to perform service for him! One is indeed obligated in regard to this matter, and it is as though one is "commanded and obeys" the command to come in person to the holy community of Frysztak, and to cast behind one's back all such erroneous beliefs and opinions as are within a person, deep-seated within his heart; and one's visit there should not be for no real purpose, but merely to test our rebbe, i.e., to ascertain whether "the Lord is truly in our midst," for then one's departure would constitute no advance on one's arrival—but rather, one's sole objective ought to be to ascend and to appear before the Presence of the Lord, the Lord of Hosts, Who dwells in the midst of

His saintly ones; to learn from their deeds and to cling to their ways and their fine traits of character.

Translated by David E. Cohen.

Grand Sanhedrin (France)

In April 1806, Napoleon Bonaparte convened the Assembly of Jewish Notables in order to consider twelve questions seen as crucial to the legal future of French Jewry. Presided over by David Sinzheim, chief rabbi of Strasbourg, the assembly examined questions ranging from whether halakhah allows polygamy to whether it forbids Jews to take usury from other Jews. Based on the answers to these questions, Napoleon sanctioned the creation of the Grand Sanhedrin, with the intention of emulating the ancient Sanhedrin and of converting these answers to binding decisions. With seventy-one members, religious and lay, the Grand Sanhedrin met several times in 1807.

Declaration Adopted by the Assembly and the Answers to the First Three Questions
1807

Declaration

Resolved, by the French deputies professing the religion of Moses, that the following Declaration shall precede the answers returned to the questions proposed by the Commissioners of His Imperial and Royal Majesty.

> The assembly, impressed with a deep sense of gratitude, love, respect, and admiration for the sacred person of his Imperial and Royal Majesty, declares, in the name of all Frenchmen professing the religion of Moses, that they are fully determined to prove worthy of the favours His Majesty intends for them, by scrupulously conforming to his paternal intentions; that their religion makes it their duty to consider the law of the prince as the supreme law in civil and political matters; that, consequently, should their religious code, or its various interpretations, contain civil or political commands, at variance with those of the French code, those commands would, of course, cease to influence and govern them, since they must, above all, acknowledge and obey the laws of the prince.

> "That, in consequence of this principle, the Jews have, at all times, considered it their duty to obey the laws of the state, and that, since the revolution, they, like all Frenchmen, have acknowledged no other."

First Question

Is it lawful for Jews to marry more than one wife?

Answer

It is not lawful for Jews to marry more than one wife: in all European countries they conform to the general practice of marrying only one.

Moses does not command expressly to take several; but he does not forbid it. He seems even to adopt that custom as generally prevailing, since he settles the rights of inheritance between children of different wives. Although this practice still prevails in the East, yet their ancient doctors have enjoined them to restrain from taking more than one wife, except when the man is enabled by his fortune to maintain several.

The case has been different in the West; the wish of adopting the customs of the inhabitants of this part of the world has induced the Jews to renounce Polygamy. But as several individuals still indulged in that practice, a synod was convened at Worms in the eleventh century, composed of one hundred Rabbies, with Guerson at their head. This assembly pronounced an anathema against every Israelite who should, in future, take more than one wife.

Although this prohibition was not to last for ever, the influence of European manners has universally [p]revailed.

Third Question

Can a Jewess marry a Christian, and a Jew & Christian woman? or does the law allow the Jews to intermarry only among themselves?

Answer

The law does not say that a Jewess cannot marry a Christian, nor a Jew a Christian woman: nor does it state that the Jews can only intermarry among themselves.

The only marriages expressly forbidden by the law, are those with the seven Canaanean nations, with Amon and Moab, and with the Egyptians. The prohibition is absolute concerning the seven Canaanean nations: with regard to Amon and Moab, it is limited, according to many Talmudists, to the men of those nations, and does not extend to the women; it is even thought that these last would have embraced the Jewish religion. As to Egyptians, the prohibition is limited to the third generation. The prohibition in general applies only to nations in idolatry. The Talmud declares formally that modern nations are not to be considered as such, since they worship, like us, the God of heaven and earth. And, accordingly, there has been, at several periods, intermarriages between Jews and Christians in France, in Spain, and in Germany: these marriages were sometimes tolerated, and sometimes forbidden by the laws of those sovereigns, who had received Jews into their dominions.

Unions of this kind are still found in France; but we cannot dissemble that the opinion of the Rabbies is against these marriages. According to their doctrine, although the religion of Moses has not forbidden the Jews from intermarrying with nations not of their religion, yet, as marriage, according to the Talmud, requires religious ceremonies called *Kiduschim*, with the benediction used in such cases, no marriage can be *religiously* valid unless these ceremonies have been performed. This could not be done towards persons who would not both of them consider these ceremonies as sacred; and in that case the married couple could separate without the *religious* divorce; they would then be considered as married *civilly* but not *religiously*.

Such is the opinion of the Rabbies, members of this assembly. In general they would be no more inclined to bless the union of a Jewess with a Christian, or of a Jew with a Christian woman, than Catholic priests themselves would be disposed to sanction unions of this kind. The Rabbies acknowledge, however, that a Jew, who marries a Christian woman, does not cease on that account, to be considered as a Jew by his brethren, any more than if he had married a Jewess *civilly* and not *religiously*.

Translated by F. D. Kirwin.

Menachem Mendel Lefin
1749–1826

Born in Satanów (Satanov), Podolia, Menachem Mendel Lefin was an important Haskalah figure. Raised and educated traditionally, he lived in Berlin in the 1780s, where he met *maskilim* as well as Moses Mendelssohn. Unlike many other East European–born *maskilim* who were attracted to Berlin, he returned to Eastern Europe, adapting Enlightenment features to local conditions. He fiercely opposed Hasidism, advocated the teachings of Maimonides (whose *Guide for the Perplexed* he translated), and promoted the addition of secular subjects to the Jewish school curriculum. Under the patronage of the Polish prince Adam Kazimierz Czartoryski, Lefin published works and received a stipend. Living in Galicia for the last part of his life, he influenced later *maskilim* such as Joseph Perl.

Sefer heshbon ha-nefesh (Book of Moral Accounting)
1808

Introduction

[. . .] 2. When you stroll along the riverbank, you find an entire plain filled with reeds and bulrushes, all of which are standing erect, one adjacent to the other, and none of them possesses the power to shift itself from its position by even a hair's breadth. Yet, within a split second, as a result of just a tiny blast of wind, the entire range of their uppermost surface area appears to be agitated and to be swaying violently from one side to the other like the waves of the sea—for none of them possesses sufficient force to fortify itself against it and to remain in place, even for the instant it takes to utter a single word.

Such is the animal soul, which does not possess a "spirit of counsel and might" either to remain stationary or to move of its own accord, by reason of its own free will. On the contrary, it instantly diminishes and continues to do so as a result of the arousal of some motion of the spirit of desire, or of pain, implanted within it at the very inception of its creation, or because it has acquired automatic characteristics through force of long-time habit, until such time as it has satisfied its desires and all its feelings have ceased, whereupon it becomes frozen stiff in the deep slumber of laziness and is no longer capable of moving of its own accord until some random spirit of sensation and desire arrives and awakens it. When two opposing spirits within it encounter each other, it then succumbs to the one which is the stronger of the two at that moment, because it lacks the understanding to foresee the future, and it lacks the counsel and power required to forego even an insignificant amount of transient physical pleasure on account either of permanent pain or pleasure in the future.

Animals enjoy virtually no superiority over plants and inanimate matter, in that they do not possess the power either to remain stationary or to become mobile, or indeed to defer their movements even in the slightest degree, and their animal soul is instantly pushed to one side, just like the reeds and bulrushes referred to above.

Since the animal's soul, for its part, possesses no free will at all, the notion of "commandment," or of "admonition" in respect to positive and negative precepts, is of no relevance to it whatsoever.

3. Man, however, who possesses knowledge and craft, and who rules over his spirit, is capable of maneuvering the animal's soul toward his own advantage at his will; that is to say, to arouse within it a spirit of genuine desire and pain, for example, to get birds to fly away from the standing corn by ringing a bell, or to entice them with the bait of tasty meat to venture close so as to become trapped in a snare, or to generate within it desires and feelings that become automatic by reason of continuous habit, as mentioned above. And one who is well-versed and expert in the art of training is able to make use of all the diverse kinds of powers with which animals are endowed, just as a human being does with those powers appertaining exclusively to him.

To offer an illustration, a type of bird whose sense of sight is extremely sharp can be trained to hunt wild animals, and birds and fish; the strength of the ox can be harnessed for ploughing, that of the donkey for carrying burdens, and the fleetness of the horse can be harnessed in the service of man.

And even insofar as the gigantic elephant is concerned, a beast in comparison to which the entire body of a human being is like a mere gnat in size, hunters nonetheless employ stratagems against them to capture them, by the hundreds and by the thousands. And the Almighty, blessed be He, who empowered man to utilize the winds of the atmosphere for winnowing the grain in the threshing-floor, for the propulsion of millstones and for the transportation of ships laden with cargo from the ends of the earth for his use and benefit, favored him still further by enabling him to rule also over the animal-like spirits of the soul, as mentioned above; and it is by such means that he is able to exert command over the loftiness of the elephant, and to train it to accept the dominion of its owner, to wait in expectation of his trough and to serve him with all its strength, to the point where, judged from the human perspective, living creatures possess virtually no superiority over inanimate objects and plant-life, etc., as mentioned above.

4. Now, intelligent owners have pity on their animals by not burdening them to excess and by supplying them with all their needs in generous measure, so as to galvanize their strength for the labor they are to perform, and they beat them with rods forthwith upon their doing anything wrong so as to prevent their reverting once more to their perverse behavior—and thus the owners gain in both respects. But the reverse is true of foolish owners. They place an entire world, so to speak, upon their animals' backs and are miserly in regard to the provision of their daily ration of fodder, and as a result of this, they shorten the lifespan of their animals, and accordingly lose the amount of labor they would otherwise have carried out for them; or, in the case of elephants, they cause them to rebel against them, for the power of an elephant's body is far, far greater than that of a man's. It rises up against them to trample on them with its feet and to crush their bones, and they are compelled to fight back with hatchets, in the hope that perhaps they will succeed in striking its nose to kill it, or at any rate to deprive it of a limb and to knock out half of its teeth. And there are other idiotic types who sail on the other side of the spectrum; that is to say, they cosset their animal by allotting it a minimal amount of labor to perform, and by providing it with choice fodder; they degrade themselves to play with it and train it to spurn their favors, so that eventually it will enslave its owner for the feeding of its belly. We find an even more extreme instance of this—there is a species of apes that kidnap little children from human beings and rear them with a view to their adoption of an animal lifestyle, and they eat the same food, and cohabit with them, to the point where they become totally assimilated with them.

In general terms, all those wishing to become intoxicated with the powers of animals need to be experts in the task of training them, and energetic craftsmen in the constant invention of diverse types of cunning tricks, varying in accordance with the particular situation. What they also need is enormous diligence and continual patience for days and even years to break into the mindset of those animals that are now being trained by them before they can succeed in injecting their wisdom into their animal soul, and in extending their rule over them for a lengthy period of time in the manner they desire. [. . .]

21. But it is on account of the fact that they are very relaxed that the entire essence of their activities is dependent upon continual perseverance on their part, as scripture states: "Water erodes stones" (Job 14:19)—from which it is plain that education pursued in a relaxed and diligent manner adds even to the strength of the animal-like body itself. And this may be illustrated by the anecdote related about a certain great pugilist in the land of Greece, who had accustomed himself to carry a bull-calf on his shoulders for several hours day by day, from the moment of its birth until it had developed into a bull three years of age; and yet it remained incapable of becoming a heavier burden for him to bear, even when fully grown, than when it was little, to the point where those who witnessed this phenomenon were astounded, and those who heard about it did not believe it—that is to say, those who did not appreciate the cunning involved in the deceit practiced by his animal-like soul.

Now the following constitutes the program for the preparations: [. . .]

Translated by David E. Cohen.

Other works by Menachem Mendel Lefin: *Igerot ha-ḥokhmah* (1789); *Moda le-vinah* (1789); *Essai d'un plan de réforme ayant pour objet d'éclairer la Nation Juive en Pologne et de redresser par là ses moeurs* (1791); *Sefer refu'at ha-am* (1794).

Nachman of Bratslav

Tiku emunah
1809

Indeed, what is necessary is precisely to "cast away the mind," because it is necessary to cast aside all rational processes and serve God simply. This is because a person's deeds should outweigh his wisdom—and mental understanding is not essential, but rather the deed. And so a person must cast aside his thoughts and serve God simply, without any ideas. And this is not only the case in regard to the foolish ideas entertained by the common folk, but even to ideas that are truly intelligent, even those of a person who has a truly great mind. When a person comes to some type of service of God, he must cast aside all ideas and serve God with utter simplicity. [. . .]

There are some people in the aspect of son, who search through the hidden treasures of their father (see Zohar, B'har IIIb), while others are in the aspect of a slave, who has but one role: that is to do his task, and who may not ask for any reason or explanation. He has one obligation: to do his work that he has been assigned. But there are also people who are the aspect of a son who so loves his father that out of that love he does the work of a slave, of what a simple slave must perform. He leaps from the great rampart, into the very midst of battle; he rolls in all sorts of mud and refuse, if only to please his father, carrying out actions that not even a simple slave would do. And then, when his father sees how strong his love is, so much so that out of his love he acts with total servitude, then he reveals to him even those things that he would not give to a [regular] son. Even the [regular] son, who is able to go through the hidden treasuries of the king, for him too, there are places where he is not allowed—insights that are withheld from him. But when the son sets aside his wisdom, and casts himself into servitude, his father has compassion on him and reveals to him that which is not given over to a [regular] son: why "the righteous suffer and the wicked enjoy well-being"—something that not even Moses was able to understand in his lifetime.

NOTE

Words in brackets appear in the original translation.

Translated by Yaacov David Shulman.

Moses Sofer

Derashot Ḥatam Sofer (Sermons of Ḥatam Sofer)
1809

A sealed Torah was given to us; it is doubtless a Torah of Truth but it is disguised. Every day the Holy One, blessed be He, renews those who study it for its own sake and they find a new taste in it, like a suckling at the breast [. . .] yet those who breach it are not blessed in this manner, for they say there is only one Torah, and scripture merely has its plain meaning.

Translated by Maoz Kahana.

Jacob Landau
ca. 1745–1822

Jacob (Ya'akov) Landau was the oldest son of Ezekiel Landau and was a businessman in the city of Brody, where he was associated with the Haskalah movement.

From the Introduction to His Father's Book, Noda bi-Yehudah
1810

I truly heard a mouth of holiness uttering these words, namely the holy and honored one of the Almighty, the most renowned, illustrious, saintly, and godly kabbalist, our teacher, R. Ḥayim of Sanz of blessed memory, whom we know to have been a worthy companion to him in the study of the secret lore of the Almighty. He used to say that all the sacred writings of the Ari [R. Isaac Luria] of blessed memory, and the other works of Kabbalah which are accepted as authoritative in this country, and also the *Guide for the Perplexed*, were collated together by the Noda bi-Yehudah, and permanently concealed beneath the shelter of his wings; and the other members of the local *kloyz*—who were the elders in that generation—exaggerated in similar vein, claiming that they had experienced the mystical visions of Ezekiel in those days.

Translated by David E. Cohen.

Moses Sofer

Responsa Ḥatam Sofer: Oraḥ ḥayim 154
1810

The reason for this is that if they see Torah scholars, and those who repair the breaches in Jewish religious practice, voiding the Torah in accordance with the exigencies of time and place, they will assemble and debate the matters at issue back and forth, either verbally or in correspondence; and once they have reached a consensus, they will publish it in the form of letters, and the great and glorious individuals of that era will undersign it with the words: "Thus have we determined—to permit such-and-such a rabbinically prohibited matter, for such-and-such a reason, and in the same vein as the special enactments of the communities, and those of Rabbenu Tam to be found at the end of the book of responsa of our teacher, R. Meir, in Prague, and the like." But a single individual in his generation, although he may be as mighty as the oaks and as lofty as the cedars, and although his words are soundly based, like the reflection of a person in a looking-glass, must not dare to permit any prohibited matter even where such prohibition is based purely upon a minor-ranking custom among the customs of Israel. For today he will declare that such-and-such represents the halakhic position, and he will have this duly printed and published, while tomorrow, another individual will declare something else to be the correct halakhah, employing feeble, withered, and lean arguments, to the point where they will ultimately even permit something prohibited by the Torah itself.

Translated by David E. Cohen.

Menachem Mendel of Vitebsk
ca. 1730–1788

A leading disciple of Dov Ber, the Magid of Mezritsh, Menachem Mendel of Vitebsk was instrumental in spreading Hasidism in Lithuania and Russia, and also in Palestine. In 1772, when opposition to Hasidism first appeared, he visited Vilna twice, accompanied during the second visit by Shneur Zalman of Liady, in order to reconcile with the Vilna Gaon, but neither encounter succeeded. The next year, along with Abraham of Kalisk, he left Minsk because of persecutions by opponents of Hasidim (Misnagdim). In 1777, with Abraham as his deputy, he led a group of three hundred followers (many of them Hasidim) to Palestine; they first settled in Safed but relocated to Tiberias a few years later.

Peri ha-arets (Fruit of the Earth)
1814

An Immortal Pleasure

Devekut requires that there be no impediment between man and God; only then is *devekut* possible. As in the parable of the Besht, it is impossible to join silver coins together with glue unless some of the coin is scraped away where the attaching takes place. Only then will they hold well and become as one. If, however, there is rust or some other intervening substance, the pieces cannot be joined together. This indicates the meaning of *If thou seek her as silver, then shalt thou understand the fear of the Lord and find the knowledge of God* (Prov. 2:4–5). Such must be the *devekut* to God. You must scrape away part of your self to make sure that there is no rust or other substance capable of creating an obstructive partition. Only then can *devekut* take effect. However, there is no connection when you hold on to something other than the divine. As is known, attachment to the corporeal causes pleasure so strong that the mind is unable to think about anything else; one's thoughts are focused only upon that one thing. This holds true for every form of pleasure, such as the love of money, which takes up all man's thoughts.

Translated by Norman Lamm.

Other work by Menachem Mendel of Vitebsk (with Abraham of Kalisk): *Igeret ha-kodesh* (1794).

Aaron Chorin
1766–1844

Aaron (Aharon) Chorin, pioneering Reform rabbi, was brought up in Hungary and Prague, where he received a yeshiva education. He studied rabbinic literature, Kabbalah, and general philosophy, and began an unsuccessful business career. Starting his rabbinical career with a position in 1789 in Arad, present-day Romania, he soon proved to be extremely controversial because of his position on a number of halakhic issues. Chorin favored ritualistic innovations such as eliminating Kol Nidre from Yom Kippur services, conducting prayers in the vernacular, and introducing the organ for Sabbath services.

Nogah ha-tsedek (Radiance of Justice)
1818

Better still than this is that they should recite the "Verses of Praise," *Yigdal* and *Adon Olam*, and the other exalted prayers on Sabbaths and festivals to the accompaniment of the harp and the sound of melody, so as to broaden and to enthuse the minds of the worshipers for the strengthening of the spirit of the intellect; and indeed, Rema' [R. Moses Isserles] has already written on [*Shulḥan arukh*] Oraḥ Ḥayim, ch. 560, para. 3, that, for the purposes of performance of a religious precept, it is permitted to play on musical instruments and all types of nonvocal accompaniment, and by such means, relief and deliverance will arise for us to enable us to remove the great stumbling-block and the obstacle concerning which the greatest of the halakhic decisors, both ancient and modern—peace be upon them—have cried out in protest; for even the congregational readers, who present our prayers pleasantly and eloquently, in a loud voice, so as to enable those who are not fluent in the language of the prayers to fulfill their religious obligation in that regard, and to arouse the hearts of the people to hear about the might of His awesome deeds—blessed be His Name—for from the strictly halakhic viewpoint, we are to appoint as congregational reader only that individual who is the greatest in the community in respect of his wisdom and his deeds; but nowadays, on account of our many sins, their strength resides exclusively in their mouths, and those whose mouths are deficient speak without heart!

But only one with a crooked heart would be so embittered as to claim that the accompaniment of the harp and other musical instruments to the songs of praise in our houses of prayer is prohibited on account of the Torah's admonition: "You shall not walk in their statutes." Besides the fact that it is unanimously agreed by all the halakhic decisors that the nations dwelling in Europe are not idol worshipers, as they believe in the majority of the fundamental principles of the Torah of Moses our Teacher—peace be upon him—and they acknowledge the Creator, blessed be He, and His attributes, the most recent of the decisors, from whose words we derive spiritual life, has already written—and this reflects the established consensus—that the prohibition on adoption of the customs of the gentile nations indeed applies only in relation to something that is a custom without any rational basis, where one accordingly has grounds for concern that it is a branch stemming from "a root bearing gall and wormwood," adopted from the ways of the Amorites. However, something acknowledged as being a matter of renown and praise, and with a taste which is sweet unto the eye of the beholder—for it is the norm for a melody chanted to the accompaniment of musical instruments to be especially adapted for the attainment of an arousal of the soul, which will then fly aloft upon the wings of imagination and desire—that apprehension will overpower everything impeding it, to purify its thoughts and to pour out meditation before the Almighty in dread and awe and in love—*that* is not included within the category of "the ways of the gentile nations and of the Amorites," but, on the contrary, it comes under the category of those laws of the gentile nations concerning which was uttered the reproof of Ezekiel the Prophet—peace be upon him—(Ezekiel 5:7), who declared: "You have not walked in My statutes, nor have you performed My laws, neither have you acted in accordance with the laws of the nations dwelling round about you"—and, as R. Joshua, son of Levi, has explained for us (in the Talmudic chapter titled *Eḥad dinei mamonot*): "This means, in accordance with their well-based norms of conduct." Ask your father and he will declare unto you, your elders and they will tell you, that such was the position in the days of our prophets, as is explicitly made clear in a number of biblical verses! Should you say: "Such practices were indeed beloved of the Almighty in the days of our ancestors, but nowadays they are detested by Him—have a look, then, at what the position was long before you, in ancient times; even today there is the custom among holy communities to chant at the inauguration of the Sabbath the hymn *Lekha dodi* to the accompaniment of musical instruments; where the fulfillment of a religious precept is concerned, such as in this instance, it is most certainly permissible to play on musical instruments on Sabbaths and festivals, by employing a non-Jew who has been especially designated for that purpose, as is clearly explained in the comments of the halakhic decisors on Oraḥ Ḥayim, ch. 338 and ch. 339, which do not require to be reproduced here as they are familiar to all.

Translated by David E. Cohen.

Other works by Chorin: *Imre noʻam* (1797–1798); *Shiryon kaskasim* (1799); *Emek ha-shaveh* (1803); *Eleh divre ha-berit* (1819); *Davar be-ito* (1820); *Yeled zekunim* (1839).

Bet Din of Hamburg

In response to changes authorized by the growing Reform movement in Germany, the traditional Bet Din of Hamburg issued warnings and responses to discourage practices such as shortening the prayer cycle, reciting prayers in German, and allowing organs in the synagogue. Leading rabbis contributed from Germany and Eastern Europe, including Eleazer Fleckeles, Moses Sofer, and Akiva Eger.

Eleh divre ha-berit (These Are the Words of the Covenant)
1819

These are the words of the covenant as a statute for Jacob, as an everlasting covenant for Israel; the Almighty spoke but once—and He will never alter His law—through the Torah and the ruling which will issue from the mouth of the righteous religious court of the Holy Community of Hamburg—may God protect it. The great acknowledged religious authorities in the lands of Germany, Poland, France, and Italy, and the lands of Bohemia, Moravia, and Hungary, have supported them. All of these have responded and exclaimed: "The following matter is by the decree of the angelic hosts and by the word of the holy ones—to render null and void the new religion (which some ordinary, simple individuals, who are not Torah scholars, have invented out of their own minds)—to establish fresh customs that are not in accordance with the law of Moses and of Israel. Accordingly, the outstanding halakhic authorities, saintly and holy men, the rabbis of renown, have risen up to drive in a peg in a trustworthy place, finding an unprotected plain and fencing it all around, to establish a prohibition against three sins which they have committed at the cost of their own lives, these being as follows:

It is prohibited to alter the order of prayer established by custom within Israel, from the early morning benedictions up to after the prayer 'It is incumbent upon us to praise'; and *a fortiori*, that one may not abridge it.

It is prohibited to recite this order of prayer in any language other than in the sacred tongue, and any prayer that is printed in a form not in accordance with the established rite, and with our customs, is disqualified from use and it is forbidden to pray from it.

It is prohibited to play on any musical instrument in the synagogue on Sabbaths and festivals, even where the instrumentalist is a non-Jew."

Happy is the man who listens to the decree of the Sages, the righteous religious Court, and to the words of the outstanding saintly and holy religious authorities, and let a person not separate himself from the congregation, so that he may walk in the path of the goodly. He who guards his soul will distance himself from such innovations so as not to transgress their words—Heaven forbid!—in accordance with the adage of our Sages of blessed memory: "Beware of the glowing coals of the wise," etc. What God-fearing man is there who has no fear of the words of the forty saintly and holy ones of the Most High that are sealed in this book, and will not take pity upon his own soul and the souls of his household?

BY ORDER OF THE RIGHTEOUS RELIGIOUS COURT OF THE HOLY COMMUNITY OF HAMBURG.

Printed in Altona in the year 5579 [1819]

By the partners, the brothers Messrs. Samuel and Judah Bon Segal, privileged royal literary printers.

Now we had hoped against hope that those men would pay heed to these words of ours, and that they would listen to the voice of their teachers, to whom alone it is befitting to express an opinion on all topics relating to matters involving prohibited and permitted things, and from times of yore the residents of our city, the joyful city, have listened to the voice of their teachers, who have said to them: "This is the path; travel upon it!" We thought for a certainty that the power we wield now is as it always has been in the past, and that people would not have the temerity to rebel against the words of our mouths.

But we hoped in vain, for these men rebelled against the advice tendered to them and became spiritually impoverished by their sin, and they erected for themselves, in great haste, a house of prayer which they called a "Temple," and they have published a liturgical rite for Sabbaths and festivals, by reason of which all those who are currently sick have become sick; our eyes have streamed with tears for the shattering of our people, for they have added to and derogated from the rites of prayer at their whim; they have omitted the early morning benedictions and the blessing to be recited over the Torah, and they have also canceled "A psalm of praise of David" and the verses of song, and they have wantonly interfered in regard to the texts of the blessing associated with the recital of the Shema; and, in the evil of their hearts, they have abridged the texts of the passages: "There is none to be compared unto You," "To the God Who rested," "God, Who is Lord," and "True and firm." They have, moreover, printed the major part of the prayers in the German language, rather than in the sacred tongue; and worse than all this is an evil malady—that they have omitted all those places where the belief in the ingathering of the exiles is mentioned.

Translated by David E. Cohen.

Jacob de la Motta
1789–1845

Jacob de la Motta, a physician, was born in Savannah, Georgia. Raised in Charleston, he earned his medical degree in Philadelphia and served as an army surgeon during the War of 1812. Discharged in 1814, he lived in New York, returned to Savannah, and spent his final years in Charleston. Active in civic, medical, and Jewish community work, he was president of Charleston's Orthodox synagogue and was appointed South Carolina's receiver general by President Benjamin Harrison. De la Motta's correspondence with Thomas Jefferson and James Madison indicates his advocacy for the protection and maintenance of Jewish rights.

Discourse Delivered at the Consecration of the Synagogue of the Hebrew Congregation Mickve Israel, in the City of Savannah, Georgia, 21 July 1820
1820

Assembled as we are, to re-establish by commemoration, (2) the *Congregation* of this remnant or small portion of the house of Israel; your expectation of a brief sketch of our History, and particularly as connected with a primeval residence in this City, and for many years past, even down to our own time, shall be realized; and may I trust, it will not be uninteresting, as it will include the well known fact, that many Jews struggled, and sacrificed their dearest interest, for the independence of this country.

(3) The emigration of Israelites to this City, from the best records and information, is traced to the earliest period of its settlement. The enterprising adventurers, who accompanied the first Provincial Governor and Commander in Chief, James Edward Oglethorpe, had not long arrived within the River Savannah, when an additional number, including about twenty respectable Jew families, landed on our shores, on the 11th July, 1733, corresponding with the 16th *Tamus*, 5493, of the Hebrew Calender.

Persecution sustained by bigotry, and strengthened by intollerance, compelled many of our nation to abandon their precarious and gloomy abodes, in Spain and Portugal, and leave their possessions, families and friends. Threatened on all sides by a turbulent storm portentous of complete annihilation, no alternative was left, but flight, torture or death; and the most convenient port was their dernier refuge. Stricken by contumely;—assailed by the keenest invectives—the aged and youthful driven from their home; were willing to engage in new adventures, that should promise security, tranquility and liberty. Uniting their destinies and common interest, with many respectable German Jews;

they left Europe to sojourn in a foreign land; inspired by the benefits, that encouraging prospects, and a transatlantic clime, offered their migration. At this period the Government of Great Britain, under George 2nd, was transporting to the new country, many individuals, who were allured by proffered possessions in a rich soil, the luxuriant productions of which by proper cultivation, and a ready exportation, held out the means of amassing wealth; independent of the settlement and extension of a distant section of the habitable Globe. To effect this object, several under the munificence of their sovereign, were sent free of expense. Not so with the Jews. Their easy circumstances and high toned dispositions, placed them above the level of incumbents. They came unassisted by bounty. (4) The distribution of land to the new settlers, gave a portion to each, and certain tracts are still retained by the descendants of those, who possessed the original grants. For respectability—"even tenor of conduct"—correct deportment—and a zealous attachment to the prosperity of the country; the Jews stood on the same eminence with other sects, and by the privileges extended to them in a (5) civil capacity; they were bound by no common ties, for the general weal. Thanks to the protectors of our liberties, *here* we still continue to boast, and enjoy the same rights.

Jonathan Eybeschütz

Tiferet Yonatan (The Splendor of Jonathan)
1820

This is what the episode of the Generation of the Dispersion was all about; that they were afraid of a Flood and accordingly sought to erect a tower up to the heavens. One has, however, to understand—were they really such fools, since if they had indeed wished to do so, they would, in accordance with the principles governing construction, have required a base broader than the circumference of the earth? However, they reasoned that, in accordance with the laws of nature, all rains descend as a result of the steam and the vapors that rise up from the earth and its watery foundation, and that it is from this source that the clouds come into existence, and it is from there that the waters flow, and the waters do not originate in the skies at all. They had already estimated, in accordance with the evidence of their own eyes, that the height of the clouds—that is to say, of the vapors arising from the earth—is no more than five *mil*[1] at most. That being the case, thin vapors formed from segments of water are, perforce, incapable of rising to a higher level than this, for if they were to rise higher, the clouds too would be higher than the earth. Accordingly, they sought to construct a tower higher than the height of those clouds, so that, once that had been done, it would henceforth be impossible for rains to fall upon them. Now the expression used by the Torah: "with its top in the heavens" is employed by way of exaggeration, save that what scientists have written is well-known, namely that the surface of the moon is also a suitable place for habitation, in the same manner as the earthly sphere is. They have already discovered, through the invention of flying balloons, which involves the creation of a mast-like structure set in position above the surface of the earth—and it is thereby demonstrated that the wind rises from the earth. [. . .]

Even if we were to believe that the oceans surround the world from one extremity to the other like a conduit, and that on one side are located three portions of the world—Asia, Africa and Europe—and that on the other side lies the New World, called America, then, that being the case, how did human beings arrive in the New World prior to the Flood without ships? If you wished to retort that there were no human beings there prior to the Flood, it would follow that the Flood could also not have occurred there, as there would have been no need for it. Now that being the case, what special quality would be enjoyed by the Land of Israel in that it is referred to by the rabbis as "pure" because the Flood did not occur there? Plainly, the New World is also "pure" by virtue of the fact that the Flood did not occur there! However, according to what I have written, everything fits in perfectly, for during the Flood, the entire power of the earth was crushed to such an extent that the wind did not emanate in the slightest measure from the earth. Now that being so, it would not have been possible for Noah to sail in a ship upon the ocean, as the wind did not issue forth at the location where he was at the time of the Flood—it being impossible to sail in the absence of wind. Now that being the case, then, in accordance with what I have written, namely that the wind emanates from the earth, from below in an upward direction, it would have been appropriate, regarding the device of a balloon, which operates as a flying device, where the wind blows on the mast, for the wind to lift it up higher and higher, so that it would never again return to earth. However, the fact that it does return to the ground is due to the weight of the powerful and thick atmosphere close to the ground [i.e., the force of gravity] weighs the object down and drives it in a downward direction. And hence the engineers set out on a journey—since the combustible powder, which they call *pilvehr*, through the force of the huge quantity of powder placed in the shaft where the combustion takes place, on the exterior of the balloon, which is positioned inside it, enables it to travel higher and higher—until they searched most carefully in the appropriate location, yet the balloon had not come down at all, as they could find no balloon on the ground—and yet, it *should* normally descend, even by means of natural forces alone, by a short route! As a result of this, they reached the conclusion that the balloon had initially risen higher than the thick and gloomy atmosphere, through the force of the *pilvehr*, and that when it was higher than the atmosphere, it was the atmosphere that impeded it from descending. Now that being so, if it were possible to transport all the balloons above this thick atmosphere, they would be capable of traveling higher and higher in the wind, right up to the surface of the moon—for the wind would be perpetually elevating them, to enable them to journey onward, and, up above, the wind becomes increasingly powerful. Now scientists have already composed works on how to make a spaceship such as this to travel to the surface of the moon; the main point is, however, that this spaceship should initially get above this gloomy atmosphere. This was the intent of the Generation of the Dispersion as well; namely, that they sought to fix their abode on the surface of the moon, where they would be spared from a Flood, and they planned to achieve this by recourse to the type of spaceship mentioned above. However, the problem arose as to how they could elevate the spaceship so as to rise above the gloomy atmosphere, and to this end they endeavored to construct a tower of such height that it could reach a point above that atmosphere; from that vantage point they would be able to utilize the aforementioned spaceship to sail through the air until it reached the surface of the moon.

NOTE

1. [*Mil* is a measure of length used in rabbinic literature. It is equal to two thousand *amot*, approximately three-fourths of a mile.—Ed.]

Translated by David E. Cohen.

Eduard Gans
1798–1839

Eduard Gans, born in Berlin, was a noted jurist. Beginning in 1816, he studied in Berlin, Göttingen, and Heidelberg, where he was influenced by Hegel's philosophy. In 1820, Gans returned to Berlin and taught law at the university. Gans also founded and presided over the short-lived Society for Jewish Culture and Scholarship. In 1825, he converted to Christianity, which made it possible for him to become a professor of law, and he subsequently specialized in the historical school of jurisprudence. His liberal political views aroused the ire of the Prussian government.

A Society to Further Jewish Integration
1822

The way in which the Jewish world will merge into the European follows from the above-mentioned principle. To merge does not mean to perish [*aufgehen ist nicht untergehen*]. Only the obstinate, self-centered independence of the Jews will be destroyed, not that element which becomes a part of the whole, serving the totality, this element shall lose nothing of its independence or substance. The larger entity [which will embrace all Judaism] shall be the richer for the new ingredient, not the poorer for the lost contrast.

[. . .] The wealth of its particularities is the very source of Europe's strength, and it can neither scorn it nor ever have too much of it. No particularity will ever harm Europe; only the single [autonomous] rule of this particularity, its exclusive self-righteousness, must be abolished; it must become a dependent particle among the many. They who see no third alternative between destruction and conspicuous distinction; who consider the eternal substrate of the idea to be its transitory rather than its material [embodiment]; who do not recognize the truth of the whole in every particularity and the truth of every particularity in the whole; who accept their respective viewpoint as the absolute, and reject another as a lie: they have neither understood their age nor the question at hand. This, however, is the consoling lesson of history properly understood: that everything passes without perishing, and yet persists, although it has long been consigned to the past. That is why neither the Jews will perish nor Judaism dissolve; in the larger movement of the whole they will seem to have disappeared, and yet they will live on as the river lives on in the ocean. Remember, gentlemen and friends, remember on this occasion the words of one of the most noble men of the German fatherland, one of its greatest theologians and poets. His words express the intention of my thoughts more concisely: "There will be a time when no one in Europe will ask any longer, who is a Jew and who is a Christian?"[1]

NOTES

Words in brackets appear in the original translation.

1. The citation is from Johann Gottfried von Herder, *Reflections on the Philosophy of the History of Mankind*, trans. T. O. Churchill, abridged and ed. Frank E. Manuel (Chicago: The University of Chicago Press, 1968), p. 15.

Translated by J. Hessing.

Other works by Gans: *Das Erbrecht in Weltgeschichtlicher Entwicklung*, 4 vols. (1824–1835); *Vermischte Schriften* (1832); *Vorlesungen über die Geschichte der letzten fünfzig Jahre* (1833–1834).

Moses Sofer

Ḥut ha-meshulash (Threefold Cord)
ca. 1820s

The Hasid praises the Almighty on the right hand, and the unbeliever tosses away and truncates the principles of faith on the left, while the Torah scholar, standing in the center, maintains silence and mocks both!

Translated by David E. Cohen.

Aaron Worms of Metz
1754–1836

Born into a rabbinical family in the Saarland region of Germany, Aaron (Aharon) Worms first studied with his father, Abraham Aberle, and then at the yeshiva in nearby Metz, present-day France. In 1785 he became principal of the Metz yeshiva and ultimately served as the chief rabbi of that city. Though strictly traditional, Aaron advocated for certain changes: prayer in the vernacular for those who did not understand Hebrew and the insertion of *piyutim* in prayers. Influenced by the ideals of the French Revolution, he was a member of Napoleon's Grand Sanhedrin in 1806–1807. His *Me'ore or*, consisting of commentaries on the Talmud and the *Shulḥan arukh*, was published in seven parts, beginning in 1790.

Me'ore or (Luminescence of Light)
1831

Since the theme of the Noachide commandments has arisen for consideration, I shall mention here what I presented before the assembly of rabbis in the great city [Paris] in the year 5567 [1807], and it was very pleasing to them, since, in the majority of instances of the words of the Sages in the Talmud, they employ the expression *akum* to refer to those nations in ancient times who denied the existence of a Creator, or, in certain cases, where they did believe in a Creator, but denied Divine Providence; there was in addition a sect of Boethusians and Sadducees who denied the validity of the Oral Torah, which is fundamental, as the Sages of blessed memory have expounded, citing the Pentateuchal verse: "Through the *mouthing* of these words have I made a covenant with you" and this is equivalent to that which we have learnt in a Mishnah: "Moses received the Torah on Sinai and transmitted it to Joshua, and Joshua to the elders," etc. Surely, was not the whole of the Pentateuch written down and delivered over to the entire nation? Hence the statement must be referring to the Oral Torah. It is, moreover, stated in the Pentateuch: "If any matter be too hard for you, between plea and plea, or between blood and blood," then you must go up and consult the supreme ecclesiastical court—and liability is imposed in that very same passage upon a rebellious elder for not listening to the priest. Also, in the Pentateuchal weekly portion [*Ve-zot*] *ha-berakhah*: "They shall teach Your judgments unto Jacob and Your Torah unto Israel"—this must necessarily refer to the Oral Torah. Further, we have the exposition, in the first chapter of tractate *Berakhot*: "which I have written to instruct them" whereon the Sages observe: "This refers to Gemara. It teaches us that they were all given at Sinai." But how do we know that the verse is to be expounded in such a manner? It is, quite simply, that the expression "to instruct them" is superfluous, because it is obvious that the Torah was not written in order to be placed obscurely in a corner; furthermore, if it were the case, it would mean that instruction and teaching is to be given in respect of what has been written down, which is already manifestly clear to every young child—hence we must conclude that the reference is to the Oral Torah; and seemingly superfluous phrases or expressions are given a special interpretation throughout the rest of scripture. I have explained this above, in the latest, amended edition of my glosses to tractate *Megillah* 17, and each matter likewise in its appropriate place; I have also discussed Noah taking into the ark those animals that were ritually pure, and Judah performing levirate marriage, and the textual rendition of one sage, in tractate *Zevaḥim* 115: "Of those animals that were subsequently going to be declared ritually pure"—because the righteous men of ancient times voluntarily observed every one of the Divine precepts ordained later, at Sinai, as they were acquainted with the steps needed to be taken to perfect the worlds—for all this is symbolized by the 248 limbs [contained in the human body]—symbolizing the perfection of the 248 positive commandments, and the 365 sinews symbolizing the perfection of the 365 negative commandments; and they knew the specific details of them all—what each limb and each sinew represented, as these spiritual pathways were clear to them to the same degree as they were well-versed in the hermeneutical principles of general propositions and specific particulars.

It is written in the Pentateuch: "You shall not turn aside from any of the words which I command you this day, to the right hand or to the left"—and the meaning of "left" here is: "even if what the Sages tell you appears to you to be 'left'" [i.e., incorrect or unnatural]; or, alternatively, it is possible that the underlying objective of the positive commandments is "doing good," which is symbolized by the "right hand," whereas the underlying objective of the negative commandments is symbolized by the "left hand"—namely, separating oneself from evil. Moreover, the preacher in Ecclesiastes has declared: "That which is written is upright, words of truth"—thereby alluding to the Written Torah; and "The words of the wise are like goads," he is alluding to the Oral Torah, comparable to a goad that guides us in plowing—how to understand the interpretation of scripture in the manner traditionally accepted by the Sages; and when he continues: "and like nails well-fastened are the words of the masters of assemblies"—these refer to the boundaries and fences that were erected by the wise men of the former generations at the assemblies of mutual friends. These too are included within the scope of the Pentateuchal exhortation: "You shall not turn aside," since it is written: "And you shall keep My charge"—whereby we are exhorted not to go so far as to erect "a fence as a protection for the fence"; and this is further explained there, in the interpretation of Ecclesiastes. The meaning of the preacher's admonition: "As regards more than these, be warned!" is: "More than what? More than what one has been commanded"—this can only refer to the Oral Torah, which may be compared to waters that have no end, insofar as its profundity of wisdom and analytical dialectics are concerned—"its breasts will nourish you at all times"—and, as Ecclesiastes has already observed: "it involves much study and is a weariness of the flesh." But the study of the Written Torah is not such a wearisome exercise, and this is likewise the case with the Targum [Onkelos]—and accordingly, the preacher in Ecclesiastes employed the phrase: "of making many books there is no end," as there is indeed no end to the wisdom embedded within the Oral Torah and to the expositions of the inner meanings of the Torah. However, in the "siege" and the dire straits of the Exile, the Sages were compelled to make a portion of the text of the Talmud into a system of analytical dialectics in order that the operative precepts might become familiar; and while they revealed a handbreadth, they concealed two handbreadths of the words of the Sages and their enigmatic statements within the Talmud's homiletical sections, incorporating profound wisdom, and several of them concerning prohibited matters and forbidden sexual relationships. From a strictly legal perspective, it is prohibited to write down any part of the traditional lore, since as the Pentateuch itself states: "For it is exclusively through the *mouthing* of these words" that God has made a covenant with Israel; but it became permissible to do so by virtue of the Sages' realization that "it is now high time to labor for the Almighty!"

But now that the gentiles are most scrupulous concerning such matters, they are to be treated as favorably as Israel, as Rabbenu Nissim [*Ran*] has written in his glosses to Avodah Zarah, *ad loc.*, that the contemporary gentiles sit in judgment upon the perpetrators of these abominations, and deal stringently with them, and accordingly, as for those individuals who have not been stringent about refraining from murder, theft, and adultery, their punishment is that we are to make no effort to save their lives, measure for measure. One view is that it is also permissible to take such a person's material possessions for oneself, while the opposing view holds that since we are not permitted to take positive steps to destroy him, so too are we forbidden to take his material possessions. However, as for the gentiles among whom we live, all the authorities admit that we are duty-bound to save their lives, and their material possessions are prohibited to us, just like those of a Jew.

In any event, it is demonstrable that a gentile falls within the scope of the expression "your fellow man" just as a Jew does; for if he is to be considered a wicked man, is not an offering made by the wicked an abomination? Furthermore, [it is stated] in chapter four of (tractate) *Bava Kamma*: "The expression 'your fellow man' is utilized by the Torah so as to exclude that which has been designated for sacred purposes." In the preface to the first section, I have noted that the meaning of the word *nokhri* [lit., an alien], where it appears without qualification, is an individual who totally denies the existence of the Almighty; the identical conclusion is implicit from the beginning of chapter five of *Bava Metzi'a*, where the Gemara asks: "We do not need to have separate prohibitions, against robbery and against the taking of interest, since charging interest *is* robbery"—but this is amazing, for it is accepted law by us that it is forbidden to rob a gentile, while to charge him interest is permitted, for, as scripture states: "In respect of an alien you may charge interest"! Accordingly, concludes the Gemara, the permission to charge interest must apply only to a gentile who actually denies the existence of the Almighty; and also, the taking of interest from a believing gentile is permissible only to the extent that it is permissible under the law of the land, and it is also permissible to take interest from a Jew through the device of the special permission accorded to business partnerships, where duly documented in a deed indicative of the existence of a business venture as between the lender and the borrower. We ought to add a supplement to this by reference to that which is stated in scripture: "I advise you: keep the king's command, and that in regard to an oath made to God!"—which means, we should observe the royal command not to take interest from the gentiles at a rate higher than is allowed by order of the local earthly ruler, and as for the practice to be adopted vis-à-vis another Jew, we should observe the oath which we swore at Mt. Sinai concerning interest—namely, that we are not to charge interest at all.

Translated by David E. Cohen.

Moses Sofer

Responsa Ḥatam Sofer: Oraḥ ḥayim 51
1835

And likewise I say: Whoever mingles teachings of Kabbalah with rulings of halakhah is liable for *kilayim*—sowing a forbidden mixture of seeds, "Lest the fullness of the seed you have sown be forfeited" (Deuteronomy 22:9). Meanwhile one who mingles philosophy books with Torah transgresses the prohibition against plowing with an ox and a donkey together, and if he is a leader of Israel he leads with a forbidden combination of animals.

Translated by Maoz Kahana.

Samson Raphael Hirsch
1808–1888

The neo-Orthodox rabbi Samson Raphael Hirsch was born and raised in Hamburg. He pursued Jewish studies under rabbis Jacob Ettlinger and Isaac Bernays, and he studied as well at the University of Bonn. From 1830 to 1846, Hirsch was the chief rabbi of several communities in Lower Saxony, and for five years after that in Moravia. From 1851 until his death, he led the Orthodox community of Frankfurt-am-Main, expounding the philosophy of *Torah im derekh erets*, combining strict religious values and traditions while respecting Western values; he nonetheless strongly dissociated himself from the Reform movement. In Frankfurt, Hirsch set up many neo-Orthodox institutions and founded the monthly magazine *Jeschurun*.

Nineteen Letters on Judaism
1836

You ask me for my opinion on the question which at present agitates so greatly the minds of men, emancipation; whether I consider it feasible and desirable, according to the spirit of Judaism, our duty to strive to attain it. [. . .]

When Israel began its great wandering through the ages and nations, Jeremiah proclaimed the following as its duty:

"Build houses and dwell therein; plant gardens and eat the fruit thereof; take wives unto yourselves, and beget sons and daughters, and take wives for your sons and give your daughters in marriage that they bear sons and daughters, and that you multiply there and diminish not. And seek the peace of the city whither I have exiled you, and pray for it to the Lord, for in its peace there will be unto you peace" (Jeremiah 29:5-7).

To be pushed back and limited upon the path of life is, therefore, not an essential condition of the *galut*, Israel's exile state among the nations, but, on the contrary, it is our duty to join ourselves as closely as possible to the state which receives us into its midst, to promote its welfare and not to consider our well-being as in any way separate from that of the state to which we belong.

This close connection with all states is in nowise in contradiction to the spirit of Judaism, for the former independent state life of Israel was not even then the essence or purpose of our national existence; it was only a means of fulfilling our spiritual mission.

Land and soil were never Israel's bond of union, but only the common task of the Torah; therefore, it still forms a united body, though separated from a national soil; nor does this unity lose its reality, though Israel accept everywhere the citizenship of the nations amongst which it is dispersed. This coherence of sympathy, this spiritual union, which may be designated by the Hebrew terms *am* and *goy*, but not by the expression "nation," unless we are able to separate from the term the concept of common territory and political power, is the only communal band we possess, or ever expect to possess, until the great day shall arrive when the Almighty shall see fit, in His inscrutable wisdom, to unite again His scattered servants in one land, and the Torah shall be the guiding principle of a state, an exemplar of the meaning of divine revelation and the mission of humanity.

For this future, which is promised us in the glorious predictions of the inspired prophets, whom God raised up for our ancestors, we hope and pray; but actively to accelerate its coming were sin, and is prohibited to us, while the entire purpose of the Messianic age is that we may, in prosperity, exhibit to mankind a better example of "Israel" than did our ancestors the first time, while, hand in hand with us, the entire race will be joined in universal brotherhood through the recognition of God, the All-One.

Because of this purely spiritual nature of the national character of Israel it is capable of the most intimate union with states, with, perhaps, this difference, that while others seek in the state only the material benefits which it secures, considering possession and enjoyment as the highest good, Israel can only regard it as a means of fulfilling the mission of humanity.

Summon up, I pray you, the picture of such an Israel, dwelling in freedom in the midst of the nations, and striving to attain unto its ideal, every son of Israel a respected and influential exemplar priest of righteousness and love, disseminating among the nations not specific Judaism, for proselytism is interdicted, but pure humanity. What a mighty impulse to progress, what a luminary and staff in the gloomy days of the Middle Ages had not Israel's sin and the insanity of the nations rendered such a *galut* impossible! How impressive, how sublime it would have been, if, in the midst of a race that adored only power, possessions, and enjoyment, and that was oft blinded by superstitious imaginings, there had lived quietly and publicly human beings of a different sort, who beheld in material possessions only the means of practicing justice and love towards all; whose minds, pervaded with the wisdom and truth of the law, maintained simple, straightforward views, and emphasized them for themselves and others in expressive, vivid deed-symbols.

But it would seem as though Israel was to be fitted through the endurance of harsh and cruel exile for the proper appreciation and utilization of its milder and gentler form.

When *galut* will be comprehended and accepted as it should be, when in suffering, the service of God and His Torah will be understood as the only task of life, when even in misery God will be served, and external abundance csteemed only as a means of this service, then, perhaps, Israel will be ready for the greater temptations of prosperity and happiness in dispersion.

Just as it is our duty to endeavor to obtain those material possessions which are the fundamental condition of life, so also is it the duty of every one to take advantage of every alleviation and improvement of his condition open to him in a righteous way; for, the more means, the more opportunity is given to him to fulfill his mission in its broadest sense; and no less than of the individual is it the duty of the community to obtain for all its members the opportunities and privileges of citizenship and liberty. Do I consider it desirable?

I bless emancipation, when I see how the excess of oppression drove Israel away from human intercourse, prevented the cultivation of the mind, limited the free development of the noble sides of character, and compelled many individuals to enter, for the sake of self-support, upon paths which, to be sure men filled with the true spirit of Judaism would have shunned even in the extremest necessity, but the temptation to enter upon which they were too weak to withstand.

I bless emancipation when I notice that no spiritual principle, even such as are born of superstitious self-deception, stands in its way, but only those passions degrading to humanity, lust for gain and narrow selfishness; I rejoice when I perceive that in this concession of emancipation, regard for the inborn rights of men to live as equals among equals, and the principle that whosoever bears the seal of a child of God, unto whom belongs the earth, shall be willingly acknowledged by all as brother, are freely acknowledged without force or compulsion, but purely through the power of their inner truth and demand, as a natural consequence, the sacrifice of the base passions, love of self and gain. I welcome this sacrifice, wherever it is offered, as the dawn of reviving humanity in mankind, as a preliminary step to the universal recognition of God as the only Lord and Father, of all human beings as the children of the All-One, and consequently brethren, and of the earth as soil common to all, and bestowed upon them by God to be administered in accordance with His will.

But for Israel I only bless it if at the same time there awakes in Israel the true spirit, which, independent of emancipation or non-emancipation, strives to fulfill the Israel-mission; to elevate and ennoble ourselves, to implant the spirit of Judaism in our souls, in order that it may produce a life in which that spirit shall be reflected and realized.

I bless it, if Israel does not regard emancipation as the goal of its task, but only as a new condition of its mission, and as a new trial, much severer than the trial of oppression; but I should grieve if Israel understood itself so little, and had so little comprehension of its own spirit that it would welcome emancipation as the end of the *galut*, and the highest goal of its historic mission. If Israel regards this glorious concession merely as a means of securing a greater degree of comfort in life, and greater opportunities for the acquisition of wealth and enjoyments, it would show that Israel had not comprehended the spirit of its own Law, nor learnt aught from the *galut*. But sorrowfully, indeed, would I mourn, if Israel should so far forget itself as to deem emancipation—freedom from unjust oppression and greater opportunity for possession and pleasure—as not too dearly purchased through capricious curtailment of the Torah, capricious abandonment of our inner life. We must become Jews, Jews in the true sense of the word, permitting the spirit of the Law to pervade our entire being, accepting it as the fountain of life spiritual and ethical; then will the spirit of Judaism gladly welcome emancipation as affording a greater chance for the fulfillment of its task, the realization of an ideal life.

Translated by Bernard Drachman.

Other works by Hirsch: *Horeb: Essays on Israel's Duties in the Diaspora* (1838); *Collected Writings of Rabbi Samson Raphael Hirsch* (1984–2012).

Israel ben Samuel of Shklov
ca. 1770–1839

Israel ben Samuel (Yisra'el ben Shemu'el) of Shklov (in present-day Belarus) was among the Talmudists from Shklov to be drawn to the Gaon of Vilna. Israel published the Gaon's commentaries and wrote some of his own, such as *Taklin ḥadtin*. In 1808–1809, he and some other of the Gaon's disciples organized a small migration of Misnagdim to Palestine. He eventually went back to Eastern Europe as an emissary to collect money for impoverished Jews in Palestine. For many years, he served as leader of his community in Safed. His writings there discussed Jewish laws applicable only in the Land of Israel.

Pe'at ha-shulḥan (Edge of the Table)
1836

Author's Introduction

I cannot refrain from relating an amazing, true story that I heard from that mouth of sanctity, the most outstanding disciple of our Holy Master, the rebbe, my dear friend—may the soul of the righteous one repose in peace—the most illustrious and saintly Master, the great Kabbalist, renowned throughout the world, His Honor, our Teacher, Rabbi Menachem Mendel—may his memory be for the life of the world to come—of the holy city of Jerusalem, may it be rebuilt and established, author of ten sacred works in connection with mystical themes that are in print. Now it once happened, during the time when he was serving as assistant to our most illustrious Master—may his soul repose in Paradise—when he was in the holy community of Serhaya, at the time when he had completed his commentary to the

Song of Songs which he received from him, and his demeanor was very merry, rejoicing in the joy of his sacred Torah study, that he summoned the father of his son-in-law, the most illustrious Rabbi of Serhaya, of blessed memory, and his eldest son, our renowned Teacher R— of blessed memory—and ordered that his room be closed off; and the windows were shut in the daytime and they lit many candles; and when he had concluded his commentary, he raised his eyes toward Heaven with immense spiritual attachment, offering blessings and thanks to the great Name of the Almighty, blessed be His Name, for having made him worthy of being able to grasp the light of the entire Torah, both in its internal and its external aspects. This is what he said: "All types of wisdom are required for understanding our holy Torah and are included within it," and that he knew them all to perfection, duly listing them: the science of algebra and that of triangles and geometry, and the art of music, the latter of which he praised greatly. He would then say that the major portion of the logic of the Torah, and of the mysteries underlying the chants of the Levites in the Temple, and the mysteries of the *Tikune zohar*, were impossible to fathom without it, and that through its power, people are even capable of dying, by virtue of their souls being consumed by its melodies, and of reviving the dead by dint of its mysteries, which lie concealed within the Torah. He stated that our Teacher Moses—peace be upon him—had brought down a number of melodies and musical rules from Mount Sinai, and the rest of the tunes we possess are merely grafted blends; he explained the qualities of all the sciences, and said that he had mastered them to perfection, except insofar as the science of medicine was concerned. Although he was acquainted with the science of anatomy and whatever was related to it, he had desired to learn the make-up of pharmaceutical prescriptions and their practical operation from the contemporary medical practitioners, but his father, that righteous man, had ordered him not to study this, so that he would not be wasting time from his study of Torah at times when he needed to go and save lives once he had completed such studies. Likewise, he was acquainted with the art of magic, with which the members of the Sanhedrin and the tana'im had been familiar, and which they taught that one is required to study, as is mentioned in the Talmud in connection with R. Eliezer and R. Joshua concerning the planting of cucumbers and uprooting them—save that he was lacking in knowledge of herbal remedies and how they all work,

as these are the province of non-Jewish villagers. Accordingly, he had been unable to study the subject in its entirety due to its many details. In regard to the science of philosophy, he said that he had studied it to perfection, but that he had extracted only two worthwhile things from it, these being the seventy powers of the human being, as is written in the commentary of our Teacher to Isaiah on the verse: "There shall come forth a shoot out of the stock of Jesse," etc., and one further matter; as to the rest, it ought to be discarded. Later, he said that—blessed be the Lord—he had mastered to perfection the entire Torah that had been given at Sinai, and how the Prophetical Writings and the Hagiographa and the Mishnah and the Oral Torah were concealed within it, and that he had not remained doubtful as to any point relating to any halakhah or theme throughout the entire Torah.

Translated by David E. Cohen.

Other work by Israel ben Samuel of Shklov: *Taklin ḥadtin* (1812).

Moses Sofer

Responsa Ḥatam Sofer, Oraḥ ḥayim 36
1839

17

Indeed, in the countries where we reside, where the gentile women walk about bareheaded, but our mothers did not go out like that and were most careful on that score, concerned as they were about the words of the Zohar on this subject. They were extremely particular in this regard despite the fact that, had we been standing by in the capacity of a religious quorum to fix the halakhah, we would have said that that rule of conduct is interpreted in the Talmud in a permissive manner—that is to say, pursuant to the interpretation of the Arukh [. . .] and that the halakhah is not in accordance with the Zohar. Nonetheless, since our mothers adopted the custom as mentioned in the Zohar, our Teacher, R. Elijah [Stein], has written in relation to this sort of thing that even a foolish custom can uproot a halakhah, and itself attain the status of a fixed halakhah! That is to say, where external works dissent from the view of the Talmud, and by "external works" is meant tractate *Soferim* and the like, or a Midrashic work or the *Pesikta*—and the Zohar falls into a similar category; such a custom has the effect of uprooting the halakhah and becomes a halakhah amongst Israel.

Translated by David E. Cohen.

Judah Alkalai
1798–1878

Born in Sarajevo, Judah ben Solomon (Yehuda ben Shelomoh) Alkalai was a proto-Zionist leader. Studying in Jerusalem, where he grew up, he became influenced by Kabbalah. In 1825, he became a rabbi and teacher in the Sephardic community of Semlin, today a part of Belgrade. The nationalist events occurring in that era in the Balkans stimulated him to develop his Zionist ideas; he is said to have influenced Theodore Herzl. He believed that the Jewish year 5600 (1840) would be the start of the Messianic redemption. The Damascus affair, a blood libel against the Jewish leaders of that city in 1840, spurred him to work more actively in political Zionism.

Shalom Yerushalayim (Peace of Jerusalem)
1840

Hoping for Redemption: Anticipating the Messianic Year 5600 (1840)

For our great sins, a few days later we received the news of the terrible fire, which God caused to happen on the night of Rosh Hashanah in Salonica, city and mother of Israel. . . . Before Tishri was over, we received more bad news: the beacon of Israel went out; we lost God's luminous ark of our diaspora . . . our teacher Moses Sofer . . . may his memory live in the world to come, [and] may his merits protect us. It is written in Genesis that "God said, 'Let there be light,' and there was light." He saw that we are unable to enlighten ourselves with this great light and he saved it for the righteous ones. . . .[1] When I saw these troubles related to one another, fear and terror overcame me. And I said in my mind that it is time to awaken [people] with my words [and] penetrate their hearts. And it happened that precisely in those days I took my book to a printing house in Belgrade: it was *Kuntres darkhe no'am*, a book on grammar. And I wrote in the introduction a few words regarding three things on which the universe is founded. And in order to explain that what is said about the year 5600 is not empty talk, I described some signs concerning its number, 600,[2] in reasonable, pleasant, and truthful words so that we could prepare our hearts for repentance and so that we would not, God forbid, return to falsehood.[3] As our sages say, if Israel does not repent every year in the opportune time, its time will become inopportune.

NOTES

Words in brackets appear in the original translation.

1. According to the Talmud, righteous men are endowed with special privileges and obligations.
2. An abbreviated reference to the Hebrew year 5600.
3. Alkalay uses the Hebrew word *sheker*, whose numeric value is 600. Interpretation of events based on the numeric value of respective Hebrew words is a common kabbalistic device.

Translated by Olga Borovaya.

Other work by Alkalai: *Darkhei no'am* (1839).

Isaac Asher Francolm
1788–1849

Isaac Asher Francolm was a preacher and religious teacher in East Prussia. Born in Breslau, he taught from 1820 to 1826 in Königsberg, during which time he modernized synagogue rituals and introduced the confirmation of girls. In 1826, he returned to Breslau and became headmaster of the local Jewish school, serving until 1847. He wrote on a variety of topics, including religion and history, but also fiction, mathematics, and pedagogy, some under the name Eugen Rispart.

Rational Judaism
1840

According to the rabbinic view, as soon as a boy has completed his thirteenth year he is required to fulfill all the ceremonial laws, although previously he was excused from some, was not permitted to satisfy others, and did not count as a person in religious ceremonies. [. . .]

Therefore, it represents a significant stage in life for boys as well as girls when, due to their acquired knowledge of religion, they are released from their schooling. No particular age can be stipulated for this: it is determined solely by the maturity of understanding. It is, however, appropriate that the studies be concluded with a ceremony at a consecrated place, and that the young mind be grasped and strengthened by a vow to faithfully preserve the acquired knowledge and live according to it.

Such a ceremony, which is not to be confused with the celebration of the completed thirteenth year, was not customary in rabbinism; it is something new but is in accord with the spirit of Judaism. We find the following arrangements to be the most appropriate.

As soon as their schooling is completed, the preacher holds a public examination of the confirmands in any chosen place.

The next day, or a few days later, the confirmands gather in the synagogue at an hour when no service is being held. One of them, in the name of all, makes a simple profession of faith regarding the four articles quoted above. After that, in a hortatory speech, the preacher implores the adherents of the received doctrines to follow their vows to live religiously, to which all attest simultaneously with the words, "Yes, we promise it before God!" The preacher says, "May God stand by you," and all those present cry "Amen." Then the preacher says a prayer and pronounces a blessing. The ceremony can be opened and closed with a psalm, which is either spoken by the cantor, alternating with the members of the choir, or performed by the music choir.

Boys and girls must be confirmed separately.

Where there is neither a newly instituted synagogue nor a preacher, the children are confirmed in the parental home, to which the parents may invite some friends; they must ensure, however, that the religious ceremony does not become a social festivity. In the home, the ceremony begins with an examination, which is followed by the profession of faith and everything else, just as in the synagogue, with the teacher taking the preacher's place. The male or female confirmand must in no case make a speech on this occasion, lest a ceremony that is intended to make a deep impression upon the young mind be profaned by pomp and nihilistic vanity.

Translated by Carola Murray-Seegert.

Other works by Francolm: *Die Grundzüge der Religionslehre aus den zehn Geboten entwickelt* (1826); *Die mosaische Sittenlehre: Zum Gebrauch beim Religionsunterricht* (1831); *Die Juden und die Kreuzfahrer in England unter Richard Löwenherz* (1842).

Kalonimos Kalman Epstein
1754–1823

Born into a rabbinical family in Neustadt (now in Poland), Kalonimos Kalman "Kalmish" Epstein grew up in Kraków and came to be the foremost disciple of Elimelech of Lizhensk, a leading disciple of the Ba'al Shem Tov. Epstein established the first major Hasidic presence in Kraków. His magnum opus, *Ma'or va-shemesh*, is heavily influenced by Kabbalah and contains both his teachings on the Pentateuch as well as his advocacy of the paramount need for tsadikim as role models. He did not establish a Hasidic dynasty, though his son Aaron succeeded him in diffusing Hasidism in western Galicia.

Ma'or va-shemesh (Light and Sun)
1842

Leah and Rachel, the Hidden and Revealed Worlds

Leah's eyes were weak, but Rachel was beautiful of figure and beautiful of appearance (Gen. 29:17). Targum Onkelos renders this verse as "Leah's eyes were lovely (*ya'ayan*), and Rachel was beautiful of form and of lovely appearance." This translation seems difficult, since Targum employs the same Aramaic root, *ya'aya*, "lovely," for two distinct Hebrew words, *rakot*, "weak," and *yefat mar'eh*, "beautiful appearance." Moreover, the *alef* of the Aramaic *ya'ayah* seems superfluous, since it could have been spelled *ya'ey* without the *alef*.

It seems to me that this all is a hint, for it is known from the holy books that Rachel is called *alma de-itgalya*, "the world that is revealed," while Leah is called *alma de-itkasya*, "the world that is concealed." Now, to understand this matter we must appreciate what these terms mean. Submission (*avdut*) involves at first acceptance of the yoke of the Kingdom of Heaven, to know that the Creator is Master and Ruler, and that His Kingship extends to all things. This is called "that which is revealed," since it is apparent and well-known to all that the universe cannot exist without a Ruler. After a person truly accepts the yoke of His Kingdom upon himself, and wishes to serve Him in all sorts of ways as a slave does his master, as befits the Glorious King,[1] God then brings [the servant] close to Him and allows him to enter the Innermost Palace of Palaces.[2] There the servant may better understand the greatness of God so that a spirit of shame and great submission falls upon him, and his heart is broken. From the worship with which he began, that is, the acceptance of the yoke of the Kingdom of Heaven . . . he comes to submission and complete repentance, with a broken heart, and that is called "the world that is concealed." This is because this stage of worship is essentially one which involves the heart and mind, and is totally hidden from the eyes of all.

This is what the Targum hints at by employing the Aramaic word *ya'ayan*, whose letters form the anacronym *yod-alef-heh-nun*—that is "the Lord our God, the Lord is *nun*," i.e., the Tetragrammaton, by which our God is called, is the Being of the world of repentance, the world of Binah, from which issue the fifty (*nun*) Gates of Understanding.

[In contrast,] the Targum employs the Aramaic word *ya'aya* in connection with Rachel, for she represents "the world that is revealed"; the world of [God's] Kingdom, which is also an anacronym: *yod-alef-yod-alef, the Lord our God, the Lord is One*.[3] [This is] the world which the worshipper must unify and tie to the upper world, in the light of the Tetragrammaton, for this is the purpose of our [divine] service.

We may say that this is what the following verses hint at. *I will serve you seven years for your younger daughter, Rachel*, for the essential unification is accomplished by a person's acceptance on himself of the yoke of His Kingdom in the reading of the Shema morning and evening, with the unification [implicit in] *Shema Yisrael*, which contains twenty-five letters in the morning, along with twenty-five letters in the evening, making a total of fifty—in order to tie it to "the world that is concealed," which is hinted at by the *nun* [of *ya'ayan*]. The worshipper must also recite seven blessings—two before the Shema and one after it during the morning prayer, and two before and two after it during the evening prayer—and that is what Jacob hinted at when he offered to serve Laban for seven years for Rachel, his younger daughter—thus accepting upon himself the yoke of the Heavenly Kingdom symbolized by Rachel. Through this acceptance comes the clarity of understanding of "the world that is concealed," which is symbolized by Leah.

[When Jacob asks Laban,] *Why have you cheated me?* (Gen. 29:25), he means to say: Why have you raised me greatly to the world which is hidden from this one [by giving me Leah instead of Rachel]? Laban then answers him, "Fulfill the week of this one, and we will give you this one also by the work which you do for another seven years" (Gen. 29:27). The meaning of this is that you must struggle with great effort in order to rectify the seven gates of the soul, as is noted in *Sefer Yetzirah*, and then you will attain the upper worlds, and you will have the strength and understanding to unify the upper and lower worlds, as we may well understand.

NOTES

Words in brackets appear in the original translation.
1. Allusion to Ps. 24:8–9.
2. Literally, "the palace of the inner palaces."
3. The words of the Shema.

Translated by Norman Lamm.

Samuel Hirsch
1815–1889

Samuel Hirsch, born in Thalfang, Germany, was a major figure in Reform Judaism. In 1838, he served as a rabbi in Dessau, Germany, but was forced to resign in 1841 because of his radical stances. In 1843, he was appointed as Luxembourg's chief rabbi, a position he resigned in 1866 to become rabbi of Congregation Keneseth Israel in Philadelphia; there he advocated observing the Jewish day of rest on Sundays. He served as president of the first Conference of American Reform Rabbis; in that capacity he influenced the movement's famous Pittsburgh Platform of 1885.

The Religious Philosophy of the Jews
1842

Note: The word "religion" is not biblical. It is taken over from paganism, where it does not include the factor of freedom. People disagree as to whether it is derived from *religere* or *relegere*; about whether its basic meaning is *to be bound* under the will of the gods, or amounts to *making present* the *essence* of the gods. It would be a wonder for Holy Scripture, undeniably a treasure of religious expressions and indications, not to contain an equivalent expression for religion. But neither *religere* nor *relegere* correctly and completely expresses what the essence of religion [is for it]. Holy Scripture defines the essence of the human being in terms of *the religious life*. Religion in Holy Scripture means the *essence of the human being*. The two concepts [religion and the essence of the human being] coincide.

The human being ceases to be human as soon as it sets out to be other than religious. How does Holy Scripture express itself about the human being?

[For example]:

> And God said, Let us make man in our image, after our likeness; and let them have dominion over the fish of the sea, and over the fowl of the air, and over the cattle, and over all the earth, and over every creeping thing that creepeth upon the earth. (Genesis 1:26)

Much has been said about the matter of the human being's similarity to God, but the verse makes it clear. The similarity consists of freedom. Not in the *abstract*, but as realized and ever *self-realizing*. The term "let them have dominion" is to be thought of only in terms of true freedom, not external mastery. The author of Genesis obviously knew that the human being never had, nor ever could have, dominion over all the fish in the sea, the fowl of the air, and over all animals including the worm which creeps on the earth. It follows from Genesis 1:29–30 that only vegetation, not animals, are provided for the human being's immediate use.

This creation history is based on the perception that the human being sublimates into itself all prior stages of earthly development (and again, this is not the microcosm of paganism). Intentionally hidden in the verse is the perception that to be truly free the human being must first *turn against itself* the animalistic in *itself*. Not *annihilate* it—not lead a purely spiritual, non-sensual life; not kill off sensuality, but rather *master* the sensual and the animal in itself, using it as a means for *realizing* the human's freedom. This was intentionally hidden in the verse, so *the true meaning of the mastery would become clear for the human being only in the course of subsequent history*. Only the literal, outer meaning, that of external *mastery* over the environment, came to consciousness for the first human being. (Hegel knows this passage very well and often refers to it. It is hard to imagine why this *passage alone was not enough* to show him the error of his apprehension of Jewish religiosity).

NOTE
Words in brackets appear in the original translation.

Translated by Gershon Greenberg.

Other works by Hirsch: *Briefe zur Beleuchtung der Judenfrage von Bruno Butler* (1843); *Messiaslehre der Juden in Kanzelvortraegen* (1843).

Bonaventura Mayer
Dates Unknown

Born in Galicia, Bonaventura Mayer converted to Christianity to become a professor of languages at the University of Vienna. He subsequently proselytized, traveling throughout Eastern Europe in 1825 and 1826. During that trip, he encountered the Hasidic rebbe Israel Friedman of Ruzhin, whom he discusses in his work *Die Juden unserer Zeit*, which also describes the conditions of the Jews whom he met. He actively opposed Reform Judaism, and was attacked in the Jewish periodical press.

The Jews in Our Time
1842

They [the hasidim] study Kabbalah and Talmud diligently and successfully, and consequently they have among them excellent Talmud scholars. They also comprise three groups, each of them under one chief rabbi. We shall describe just one group.

This rabbi, Israel, lives in the town of Risen in the province of Volhynia, six miles from Zhitomir. He is a man lacking much scientific education, but of excellent natural intelligence. If he is still alive, he should today be in his middle forties. He married at fourteen and since then has been serving as chief rabbi. Several times a year, he journeys to places where his followers live and stays there over the Sabbath. Whoever has something against someone else comes to him with his complaint, and he delivers his verdict—not according to the Written Law but according to his natural intelligence. And his verdict is the law. His scribe writes the verdict, and he himself signs it with great difficulty. He is so illiterate that he is barely capable of signing his own name. His sentence is sacred and everyone must obey. People come to him for advice and help not only in legal matters but also in all other matters of life: if someone has a barren wife, or if his liquor business is not progressing well, if something has been stolen, or if he is not satisfied with his business dealings. In brief, they come to him in any situation and request his advice or his prayer. Sometimes, such a request succeeds; at other times—as indeed happens—things do not work out well.

His reputation is so great that even Russian noblemen come to consult with him, respect him, and love him. Thus, when I visited the rabbi in 1826, I met Field Marshal Wittgenstein. This nobleman accorded him every honor, even offering him his most beautiful palace in one of the towns in his dominion if he would agree to live there. He is indeed worthy of this general regard. Even important, complicated affairs do not escape his intelligence and are clear and obvious to him. His personality, too, has a good influence on his followers. One might say that he is a person of noble appearance. His face, except for a mustache, is smooth and beardless. He has the rare talent of being able to make everyone like him. His look has such magnetic power that even his enemy cannot withstand him.

Although his living quarters are built with royal splendor, he himself lives frugally and, unlike the other Jews of Russia, greatly values cleanliness. One might say, without exaggeration that during the week he eats no more than another person eats in a single meal. He sleeps no more than three of the twenty-four hours of the day. The other hours are devoted to his occupations. From early morning till eleven o'clock [in the morning], he receives the visitors. From twelve to one o'clock, he secludes himself to pray. During the afternoon hours, his chambers are again open to all. Each day he feeds many people, from all walks of society. They are all his guests. Sometimes, especially at festivals, the number of guests may be as much as a thousand. He himself does not attend the meal, except on Sabbaths and at festivals.

Eight years ago he had the misfortune to be implicated in a bad business, of which, as it later turned out, he was innocent. Among the Jews under him [i.e., the hasidim], there was an informer against his coreligionists, who informed about someone who was dealing in stolen goods. All this he testified in Russian courts. His followers were highly incensed at this, and they captured the informer secretly and set him afire. The affair did not remain a secret, and these people, to save themselves, accused the chief rabbi of having instructed them to do so. We do not know what the end of the legal process was.

NOTE

Words in brackets appear in the original translation.

Translated by David Louvish.

Other work by Mayer: *Das Judenthum in seinen Gebeten, Gebräuchen, Gesetzen und Ceremonien* (1843).

Grace Aguilar

Women of Israel, or, Characters and Sketches from the Holy Scriptures
1844

As the first and most beautiful relationship in which woman is undeniably necessary to man—the object of his first affections, to whom he owes all of cherishing, happiness, and health, from infancy to boyhood, and often from boyhood to youth; and who, in consequence, must be entwined with every fond remembrance of childhood, the recollection of which is often the only soother, the only light, in the darker heart of man—it is but just that we should examine, first, how the holy relationship of a MOTHER in Israel is guarded and noticed by our law.

The very first command relative to the duties of man towards man, marks out the position of children with regard to their parents, male and *female*, the representatives of God on earth. It was not enough that such position should be left to the natural impulses of gratitude and affection—not enough that the love and reverence of a child to his parent should be left to his own heart, although in the cases of both Isaac and Jacob such had been so distinctly manifested. No; the same tremendous voice which bade the very earth quake, and the fast rooted mountain reel—which spoke in the midst of thunders and lightnings, "Thou shalt have no other gods but me,"—also said, "Honor thy father and thy MOTHER," and added unto its obedience a promise of reward, the only command to which recompense is annexed, that its obedience might indeed be an obedience of love. And lest there should be some natures so stubborn and obtuse that the fear of punishment only could affect, we read in the repetition, and, as it were, enlargement on the ten commandments, "And he that smiteth his father or his MOTHER shall surely be put to death, and he that curseth or revileth his father or his MOTHER shall surely be put to death" (Exodus xxi. 15–17). "Ye shall *fear* every man his MOTHER and his father, and keep my sabbaths: I am the Lord" (Levit. xix. 3). "For every one that curseth his father or his MOTHER shall surely be put to death. He hath cursed his father or his MOTHER, his blood shall be upon him." And again, in Deuteronomy v. 16, we have the repetition of the fifth commandment, the reward attending its obedience still more vividly enforced: "Honor thy father and thy MOTHER, as the Lord thy God hath commanded thee, that thy days may be prolonged, and that it may go well with thee in the land which the Lord thy God giveth thee."

With laws like these, bearing on every one of them the stamp of divine truth, of a sacred solemnity which could come from God alone, how can any one believe in, much less assert, the Jewish degradation of woman, or call that JUDAISM which upholds it!

Jacob Ettlinger
1798–1871

One of the first German rabbis with academic training, Jacob Ettlinger was born in Karlsruhe and educated at the university in Würzburg. In 1826, he served as a rabbi in the Mannheim area. Ten years later, he was appointed chief rabbi of Altona; in this capacity, he was a prominent spokesman for German neo-Orthodoxy, a combination of adaptations to modernity, secular learning, and strict halakhic observance. He was a strong opponent of Reform Judaism; in 1844, he led a protest against the Brunswick Conference of Reform rabbis. He is known best for his work of Talmudic scholarship, *Arukh la-ner*. His disciples included other major German rabbis such as Samson Raphael Hirsch and Esriel Hildesheimer. (Excerpts of Ettlinger's major works appear in this volume.)

Rabbinic Reports on Circumcision
1844

Letter of Chief Rabbi Jacob Ettlinger in Altona

Altona, 24 Ab 5603
Chief Rabbi!
Messrs. Adler and Fuld, members of your congregation, asked for my opinion, from the Jewish-religious perspective, concerning the society that has formed in Frankfurt am Main in the midst of the Israelite community, regarding its basic principles. These are: the Mosaic law should be modified in accordance with the times and circumstances and should not be evaluated according to the word but according to the spirit; the Talmud, and thus the whole of the Oral Law, has no binding power over any Israelite; there is no hope of the coming of the Messiah, and the law of circumcision should be regarded only as Abrahamic, not Mosaic, and therefore has no validity for Israel.

Indeed, it might seem almost superfluous to waste words on characterizing the position taken by such a society within Judaism. It must be evident to every impartial person that this position is that of deception, lies, and apostasy. Every Israelite who knows his faith knows that those laws, whose validity is determined by time and circumstances, were decreed by the greatest divine lawgiver himself, and that therefore those legislative instructions, in which such a restrictive condition is not found, are given to the Israelites for all time, in all lands and circumstances. Every Israelite who cares about the truth knows that the law of circumcision was given by God to Abraham for him and his descendants as a covenant for everlasting time (1. B. M. 17) and that this was given by the Lord to Moses, as well—only briefly because it already existed, but because of its importance, it was repeated at Sinai (3. B. M. 12).

Before God, the omniscient, I hereby pronounce as my deepest conviction that whoever agrees with the corrupting principles of that already mentioned society, and specifically, he who neither himself fulfills the law of circumcision for the sons born to him, nor has it executed by the appropriate Israelite religious authority, is to be regarded as an apostate, irreligious Israelite, and is not acceptable as a witness, neither for oath nor in court testimony. But this does not require human testament. Judaism itself, as it has consistently existed for thousands of years in all corners of the inhabited world among the Israelites, bears witness to the inviolability of its content and its form, in order to reject the unscrupulous attacks of those who, to avoid seeing, press shut their eyes and those of others, and then want to believe that the sun has been extinguished. We, however, will ask the Lord God to open the eyes of the blind in Israel and return the lost to the bosom of faith, so that in the shadow of the Palms of Peace, all Israel will unite with him until the end of time.

Translated by Carola Murray-Seegert.

Zechariah Fraenkel
1801–1875

Rabbi and theologian Zechariah Fraenkel laid the ideological foundations of Conservative Judaism through a scholarly approach that balanced reform and tradition. Born in Prague, Fraenkel received a secular and rabbinical education. After earning his doctorate in Budapest, he held numerous Jewish public positions, including chief rabbi of Saxony and later president of the Rabbinical Seminary in Breslau. Supporting Jewish emancipation, his 1840 critique of antisemitic Jewish oaths in courts of law was pivotal in ending the practice in Saxony. Fraenkel developed the concept of "positive historical Judaism," advocating for the Jewish acceptance and pursuit of historical and scholarly research. Asserting that Jewish identity was grounded not only in religion, but also culture and history, he wrote a number of significant Jewish historical and theological texts.

The Symptoms of the Time
1845

By emphasizing religious activity, Judaism is completely tied to life and becomes the property of every individual Jew. A religion of pure ideas belongs primarily to the theologians; the masses who are not adapted to such conceptions concern themselves little with the particulars of such religions because they have little relationship to life. On the other hand, a religion of action is always present, demanding practice in activity and an expression of will, and its demands are reflected in the manifold life of the individual, with the result that the faith becomes the common property of every follower.

Thus we have reached the starting point for the consideration of the current parties in Judaism. The viewpoint of the Orthodox party is clear. It has grown up in pious activity; to it the performance of precepts is inseparable from faith, for to it, the two are closely and inwardly connected. Were it to tear itself away from observance and give up the precepts, then it would find itself estranged from its own self and feel as though plunged into an abyss. Given this viewpoint, the direction and emphasis of the Orthodox party is clear. Where else, save in the combination of faith and meticulous observance of the precepts, can it find that complete satisfaction which it has enjoyed in the heritage of the fathers? When it will reject that which it has so long kept holy and inviolable? No—that is unthinkable.

Against this party there has arisen of late another one [Reform] which finds its aim in the opposite direction. This party sees salvation in overcoming the past, in carrying progress to the limit, in rejecting religious forms and returning merely to the simple original idea. In fact, we can hardly call it a party in Judaism, though its adherents still bear the name Jew, and are considered as such in social and political life, and do not belong to another faith. They do not, however, belong wholly to Judaism, for by limiting Judaism to some principles of faith, they place themselves partly outside the limits of Judaism.

We will now turn to a third party which has arisen from the first party, and not only stands within the bound of Judaism, but is also filled with real zeal for its preservation and endeavors to hand it over to the descendants and make it the common good of all times.

This party bases itself upon rational faith and recognizes that the task of Judaism is religious action, but it demands that this action shall not be empty of spirit and that it shall not become merely mechanical, expressing itself mainly in the form. It has also reached the view that religious activity itself must be brought up to a higher level through giving weight to the many meanings with which it should be endowed. Furthermore, it holds that we must omit certain unimportant actions which are not inherently connected either with the high ideas or with the religious forms delineated by the revealed laws. We must, it feels, take into consideration the opposition between faith and conditions of the time. True faith, due to its divine nature, is above time, and just as the nobler part of man is not subjected to time, so does faith rise above all time, and the word which issued from the mouth of God is rooted in eternity. But time has a force and might which must be taken account of. There is then created a dualism in which faith and time face each other, and man chooses either to live beyond time or to be subjected to it. It is in this situation that the Jew finds himself today; he cannot escape the influence of the conditions of the time and yet when the demands of faith bring him to opposition with the spirit of the time, it is hoped that he will heed its call—find the power to resist the blandishments of the times. This third party, then, declares that Judaism must be saved for all time. It affirms both the divine value and historical basis of Judaism and, therefore, believes that by introducing some changes it may achieve some agreement with the concepts and conditions of the time. [. . .]

[The rabbis] established a rule which was intended as a guardian and protector against undue changes. It reads as follows: That which was adopted by the entire community of Israel and was accepted by the people and became a part of its life, cannot be changed by any authority.

In this fundamental statement there lies a living truth. Through it there speaks a profound view of Judaism which can serve for all times as a formula for needed changes and can be employed both against destructive reform and against stagnation. [. . .]

Only those practices from which it is entirely estranged and which yield it no satisfaction will be abandoned and will thus die of themselves. On the whole there is always a great fund of faith and religious activity to afford security against negation and destruction.

We have, then, reached a decisive point in regard to moderate changes, namely, that they must come from the people and that the will of the entire community must decide. Still, this rule alone may accomplish little. The whole community is a heavy unharmonious body and its will is difficult to recognize. It comes to expression only after many years. We must find a way to carry on such changes in the proper manner, and this can be done by the help of the scholars. Judaism has no priests as representatives of faith nor does it require special spiritual sanctimoniousness in its spokesmen. The power to represent it is not the share of any one family, nor does it pass from father to son. Knowledge and mastery of the law supply the sanctity, and these can be attained by everybody. In Jewish life, spiritual and intellectual ability ultimately took the place of the former priesthood which, even in early times, was limited in its function primarily to the sacrificial cult. Even in early days, Judaism recognized the will of the people as a great force and because of this recognition a great religious activity came into being. But this activity, in turn was translated into a living force by the teachers of the people through the use of original ordinances and through interpretation of the Scriptures. At times these actions of the sages lightened the amount of observance; at times they increased it. That the results of the studies and research of the teachers found acceptance among the people proves, on the one hand, that the teachers knew the character of their time, and, on the other hand, that the people had confidence in them and that they considered them true representatives of their faith.

Should Jewish theologians and scholars of our time succeed in acquiring such a confidence, then they will attain influence with the introduction of whatever changes may be necessary. The will of the community of Israel will then find its representatives and knowledge will be its proper exercise.

NOTE

Words in brackets appear in the original translation.

Translated by Mordecai Waxman.

Other works by Fraenkel: *Die Eidesleistung der Juden in theologischer und historischer Beziehung* (1847); *Darkhe ha-mishnah* (1859); *Entwurf einer Geschichte des Literatur der nachtalmudischen Responsen* (1865).

Solomon Judah Rapoport
1790–1867

Born in Lemberg (present-day Lviv) to a rabbinical family, Solomon Judah Rapoport (Shi"r) was a Talmudist and a moderate *maskil*, as well as a pioneering academic Jewish studies scholar. Son-in-law of Aryeh Leib Heller, he helped publish the latter rabbi's work, *Avne milu'im* in 1815 by adding indexes and marginalia. He became interested in the Haskalah and secular literature but was forced to earn a living as a kosher meat tax collector. He published articles for *Bikure ha-itim*, including biographies of medieval rabbinic figures. In 1837 he became a rabbi in Tarnopol, Galicia; subsequently the conservative community accused him of heresy. From 1840 until his death he lived in Prague, serving as a rabbinic court judge and as the city's rabbi.

Open Rebuke
1845

How, I ask you, could we have continued to be a nation until the present, and how could we have been able to walk such a great distance along the path of history without losing our unity or having our provisions run out, if we did not have the support to sustain us on the path and to breathe a pure and refreshing spirit into the weary. This support comes from the Sabbaths and holy festivals, the *zitzit* and the phylacteries, the house of prayer and the houses of religious study and together with all these the hope and solace of a better future. And so they have preserved us, guarding us from the danger that we might become too lazy to proceed forward, preferring instead to lie with our mouths open, becoming drunk upon the wine of the time and its pleasures and upon the delicacies of the land and its people. The guardians [of our unity] have isolated us and placed restrictions on all matters of food and marriage, militating against our assimilation among the peoples of the world. . . . All this you wish suddenly to annul and cast aside, and [yet you] still imagine that the name of Jeshurun will endure? These [customs and laws] that have sustained and guarded us have been tried out and have passed the test of time immemorial. Do you think that you can proceed without them and try a new course, without knowing what results it will bring?

NOTE

Words in brackets appear in the original translation.

Translated by S. Weinstein.

Other works by Rapoport: *Tekhunat ir Pariz* (1814); *She'erit Yehudah* (1827); *Yeri'ot Shelomoh* (1902).

Jacob Ettlinger

Arukh la-ner
1850

[Commentary to tractate Yevamot*]*

In this way, in addition, the statement in the Talmudic chapter *Ha-ro'eh* (*Berakhot* 56) can be explicated: "There are three types of peace—a river, a bird and a cooking-pot: a river, as it is written: 'Behold, I will extend peace to her like a river'; a bird, as it is written: 'Like birds in flight, so shall You, Almighty shield,' etc., 'with Your peace!'; a kettle, as it is written: 'O Lord, may You set peace for us like a cooking-pot set upon a fire.'" Now we need to provide a reason for our utilizing these three entities as symbolic allusions to peace, for, just as we have explained that peace has three beneficial effects for the Jewish nation as a whole insofar as observance of the Torah is concerned, there are similarly three beneficial effects of peace from the human perspective: 1) Man has multiple needs in respect of which he becomes weary and weak while engaged in the process of assembling them together and directing them to himself, and it is only when there is peace between a man and his neighbor, and each individual assists the other, that everyone will succeed in obtaining his full requirements in respect of which he is lacking. 2) Where there is no peace, all human goodness counts for nothing, as our Sages of blessed memory have declared: "If there is no peace, there is nothing, for each man would swallow his fellow man alive; but where peace exists, each individual will dwell alone in security under his vine and under his fig-tree, and will derive satisfaction from the good bestowed upon him." 3) Because man's entire life is full of obstacles opposing his desires and involves his being separated from the things he seeks, and as a result of this, enmity and a mutual separation of minds arise; but where there is peace, the various objectives being sought, and different people's minds, will unite together with a view to their becoming like a single individual, and human beings will thereby find repose for their souls. All this is alluded to by the three entities. In the first place, the river, which was formed from numerous sources and streams, none of which is, on its own, capable of providing human beings with any benefit on account of its puny size and its weakness, but when they unite and turn into a river upon which ships sail, they do indeed provide a benefit to mankind—so it is likewise in regard to peace. In the second place, the bird—for just as birds in flight hover over their nests to protect their fledglings so as to prevent injury befalling them at the hands of birds of prey, so too, in the same manner, does peace protect mankind. In the third place, the cooking-pot, for there are, within nature, no two opposing forces that are as powerful as fire and water, in relation to which our rabbis of blessed memory explained the significance of the biblical verse: "He makes peace in His high places"; but these two forces unite through the cooking-pot, which transmits the heat of the fire into the water contained within it to the point where fire and water become a single entity in the heated water. So too, it is through peace that all the opposing and separatist forces in life merge into a single unity.

Translated by David E. Cohen.

Fanny Neuda
1819–1894

The German-language writer Fanny Neuda (née Schmiedl) was born into a rabbinic family in Moravia (now the Czech Republic). She married the liberal rabbi Abraham Neuda and moved with him to Loštice, Moravia. After her husband died, Neuda wrote the first Jewish prayer book composed for women by a woman, *Stunden der Andacht* (Hours of Devotion; 1855), an updated version of the women's prayers known as *tkhines*. The book was immensely popular in

Eastern Europe and was translated into English in 1866. Neuda also wrote fiction inspired by Jewish domestic life.

On the Approach of Childbirth
1854

Before she labored, she was delivered;
Before her pangs came, she bore a son!
—Isaiah 66:7

Fear not, worm of Jacob,
O people of Israel,
For I will help you.
—Isaiah 41:14

The hard, painful hour of delivery draws near,
And in the midst of the pains and fears
That course through me
This fervent prayer rises from the depths of my soul—
May it ascend to you, Eternal Parent!
With every pain, with every pang that seizes me,
My words die on my lips.
Only your name, my God, remains alive on them.
They utter this cry alone: *God, my God!*
You who are my shield and my protector,
My comfort and my rescue,
The one who dampens my fears and my fright,
The one who embraces me in hope,
The one who is my strength—
Oh, as I raise my tearful eyes up to you, Parent of All,
May it draw your compassion down to me.

Let your mercy shelter me,
So these birth pangs do not overtake me,
So I am able to bear them with courage and strength.
Oh, that your parental grace
Might guide me safely and securely
Across this awesome threshold.
All-Compassionate One, shorten my suffering.
Let me soon achieve the joyous goal of this labor—
Let me soon enjoy a healthy, strong baby.
My God, do not now recall
All my sins and missteps in life!
Forgive me and pardon me now
For all my failings before you.
In your compassion and mercy, may it be your will
That I give life to a precious new being.
Preserve my life, and be with me,
For all my hope and trust rests in you. Amen.

Translated by Julia Watts Belser; Isaiah 66:7 from the Jewish Publication Society Tanakh: The Holy Scriptures; *Isaiah 41:14 adapted by Dinah Berland from the Stone Edition of the Tanach.*

Other work by Neuda: *Jugend-Erzählungen aus dem israelitischen Familienleben* (1856).

Isaac Mayer Wise
1819–1900

Rabbi Isaac Mayer Wise was a leader of American Reform Judaism, contributing to Jewish life through community organization and institutional development. Born in Steingrub, Bohemia (now the Czech Republic), he attended yeshiva and university before immigrating to America in 1846. He settled first in Albany, New York, and then Cincinnati, working as a Reform rabbi in both cities. Committed to unifying Jewish congregations and fostering Jewish life in America, Wise founded the Union of American Hebrew Congregations, the Hebrew Union College, the Central Conference of American Hebrew Rabbis, and the first American Jewish newspaper, *The Israelite*. Among his numerous publications was the first standardized American Jewish prayer book.

History of the Israelite Nation, from Abraham to the Present Time
1854

On this occasion a singular event occurred, which gave a new impulse to the piety and energy of Joshiah. The original copy of the laws, supposed to be written by Moses himself was found in the temple by the high priest, who delivered it to Shaphan, the king's scribe, by whom it was read to the king.

Since the hypercritics of our days attach so much importance to this event, drawing from it the conclusion that the kings, prophets and people of Israel previous to this date were altogether ignorant of the laws of Moses; and since some of them went even so far as to suppose the Pentateuch was then composed secretly, and published as the composition of Moses, we must stop here to make some remarks on the subject. We have proved that the style of the Pentateuch is imitated and whole sentences copied in all the books after Moses, that its laws, religious and political principles and institutions not only continually existed up to the reign of Menassah, but also inspired the prophets and psalmists as well as the historians. It can therefore only be asserted, that during the reign of Menassah and Amon, the Mosaic law was thus neglected, or burnt, as the ancient rabbins supposed, that no copy of it remained at court. For that no copy should have been left in the whole country, and among the Israelites in exile, is a matter of impossibility. But even granted that no copy of the Pentateuch existed at court, would not the governors of the people during the absence of Menassah, or would not Menassah himself, when he had returned from captivity, or would not the pious and popular Joshiah, so much influenced by Jeremiah, have endeavored to procure a copy of it? And if he had made such an attempt, would he not have been supported by the party then in favor of the administration who must have been in possession of numerous copies? From the words as they occur in the respective passages, it is plain, that the regret of Joshiah found its cause in the fact, that his predecessors have not observed EVERY THING AS WRITTEN IN THAT BOOK. The Mosaic laws were in force, but not every thing was done as those laws prescribed. We are also informed about the particular cases, which were not done in strict accordance with the laws. The symbols of foreign gods were not only suffered to be kept sacred in the country, but also occupied places in the temple, although idolatry was abolished; and the symbols introduced by Jerobeam still occupied their place at Bethel, and idolatry was practiced in the dependencies of Judah (II *Chron.* xxxiv, 33), all of which was against the Mosaic laws, which permitted only the introduction of such and of no other symbols, which the law specified. The groves in which idols were worshiped still existed, and places devoted to such worship were still considered sacred; the theraphim, or house gods, the wizards and the conjurers of the spirits also existed in private, all of which was opposed to the Mosaic laws. As regards the symbols of foreign gods, Solomon already laid the foundation to naturalize them even in the temple. Jerobeam introduced other symbols, which practice afterwards remained both in Israel and Judah. If a king abolished the idols, he did not think it sinful to deposit in the temple the vessels which bore the symbols of foreign gods, or other marks of art, which again led to idolatry.

The fact appears to be that the Mosaic laws in regard to the punishment set upon idolatry, and the practices connected with it, were amended in an early stage of this history, probably as early as the days of David, who found it impracticable to eradicate idolatry in the conquered provinces, as the law ordained; or in the days of Solomon, who introduced foreign symbols in the temple of God; if not so early certainly in the days of Jerobeam and Rehabeam and their immediate successors. It is a matter of impossibility, that the kings of Judah and of Israel could have so often introduced idolatry, or that the kings of Israel could have introduced an entire new set of symbols, in a land where the laws were considered the only safeguard of the people, and where every thing points so distinctly to the Mosaic laws, if such amendments had not been adopted by that body, which was entrusted with expounding the law to meet the exigencies of the age. The amendments were incorporated with the law, were copied and passed into the hands of the people, although many unadulterated copies of the law certainly were preserved, which most likely was one of the differences between the parties. Finally the amendments were considered of the same origin with the law, and those who protested against it had nothing to prove it. Therefore *Joshiah* left in the temple the altars of Menassah, the vessels and the works of art of different gods, although he had abolished idolatry; therefore the altar of Bethel was spared, although the place was in possession of King Hezekiah.

Other works by Wise: *Minhag America* (1857); *The First of the Maccabees* (1870); *A Defense of Judaism versus Proselytizing Christianity* (1889); *Reminiscences* (1901).

Fanny Neuda

For a Mother Whose Son Is in Military Service
1855

Almighty ruler of armies, you who reign mightily
In heaven and on earth, I raise my prayer to you
From the depths of a mother's heart.
Turn your presence toward me
And hear me in your mercy.

Following the call of duty,
My child has entered the ranks
Of those who fight on behalf of our country

To stand for what is right and proper,
To fend off threats to our nation's peace and
    security.
I thank you, Eternal Parent, for having given me
A child with strong, healthy limbs,
Capable of carrying out this valiant task,
But it shakes and terrifies my heart
To think of the many dangers that will surround
    him.
Young and inexperienced, far from the instruction
And admonitions of his parents,
How easily his heart might be tempted
To be unfaithful to his duties and to fall into sin.
Therefore I beg of you, Eternal Parent,
Take my son into your powerful protection.
Surround him with your all-encompassing grace.
Strengthen and invigorate every noble feeling
And every impulse toward good that is within him.
Strengthen and invigorate every memory
Of parental guidance and advice
That rises up in his soul—
That the teachings of virtue and fear of God
Never vanish from his sight,
That his soul not turn hard under the service of
    arms
And that no corrupting influences overcome
    him.

Translated by Julia Watts Belser.

Joseph Salvador

1796–1873

An eminent but controversial religious scholar, Joseph Salvador has been viewed simultaneously as proto-Zionist and assimilationist. Born in Montpellier to a Jewish father and a Catholic mother, he was raised in a liberal household. Antisemitic riots in Germany inspired Salvador to shift from his studies in medicine to Jewish antiquity, primarily as a means to uncover and disseminate historical reasons for Jewish pride. After graduation, he moved to Paris, where he briefly studied under the chief rabbi of Paris. Salvador theorized a new religion inspired by Enlightenment principles that fused Christianity and Judaism based on common roots in ancient Jewish faith and laws. He died in Versailles and was buried in a Protestant cemetery.

Paris, Rome, Jerusalem, or the Religious Question in the Nineteenth Century
1860

In all times of transition such as the one we are now undergoing, on every occasion when human society passes from one era to another era, from one way of doing things to another way of doing them, from one state to another state, innumerable hurdles will arise, with more than one knot to be untied or cut through. Signs and warnings accumulate, deserving to be carefully collected and reflected upon. Societies are required in such times of transition to pass many tests, in religion as well as in politics, before they will be able to unite the most blatant opposition forces. Still more is needed: in order for there to be a lasting solution, two conditions, contradictory at first glance, must be met. On the one hand, the society must evolve as a natural outgrowth of some great tradition of the past; on the other, it must effect a decisive break with that very past.

Consider the status quo, where we now stand. Thanks to the French Revolution—to use some of the beautiful words I have adopted as an epigraph to my letters—thanks to the French Revolution, a new direction, an obvious sequel has been providentially impressed upon one of the two poles around which human affairs revolve: upon politics, that is, taken in its most general sense, in its highest spirit of organization. Far from being limited to one state alone or to one area of the world—Europe—this sequel, this new movement has spread to the most disparate climes. If this first fact is recognized, and if, at the same time, a complete rupture has been effected between the present and the past, how can your soul feel any repugnance to hearing what I have to say? After I have invoked the spirit of French genius, which owes to its precision, to its clarity, the almost universal power it enjoys, will you find it strange to hear me assert that a corresponding change is coming sooner or later to the other pole around which human affairs revolve? Will you find it too extraordinary when I say that religion is destined to burst forth from the depths of its past, its roots, its entrails, a new spirit, a new transformation, an obvious sequel to its beginnings?

Many people, I know, think that one fine day religion fell from the sky perfectly formed, comparable to a statue created by Juno or Pallas, and that since then no human sculptor has added anything or taken anything away. But you do not share in this mistake, an idea, moreover, that crumbles upon the merest scrutiny. In spite of contrary assertions and appearances, nothing is less immutable than sacred dogma, nothing is more susceptible to taking or receiving, depending upon the circumstances, one name or title in place of another. In the history of religion, the idea of coming to terms with heaven or of forcing its gates by no means dates from today or yesterday; it has illustrious precedents and instigators.

Here, as in the whole course of my correspondence with you, I will therefore express myself without circumlocutions, for I will never hide behind oratorical reserve.

So long as the need for a new reconciliation shall not have been acknowledged between the two poles to which I have alluded; so long as a new kind of spirituality, or a new way of understanding the law of heaven shall not have enthusiastically ratified our new secular world, or the new way of determining the condition of peoples and individuals, all your efforts will be in vain. All efforts to reunite the political and social spirit of our new age with the religious structure of the old order will have the same result. In a hundred different ways, you will realize the biblical image of the new piece of cloth attached to an old garment, where only tears can stand out. From then on, whatever name you choose, whatever principle upon which you wish to stand, whatever external successes seem to promise new strength, the earth, at the slightest quake, will tremble under your feet, and if it is the sea, its chasms will open wide for you. The most capable men of our time, those who are most confident in the time-honored infallibility attributed to their opinions, will only succeed in introducing palliatives, the weakness of which will be only too evident. Never will they be permitted to hold in their hands the increasingly tangled thread of universal affairs; never will they be granted sufficient moral authority to disentangle them.

Translated by Michele McKay Aynesworth.

Other works by Salvador: *Loi de Moïse, ou, système religieux et politique des hébreux* (1822); *Histoire des institutions de Moïse et du people hébreu* (1829); *Jésus-Christ et sa doctrine* (1838); *Histoire de la domination romaine en Judé, et de la ruine de Jérusalem* (1847).

Samuel David Luzzatto
1800–1865

The poet, rabbi, and scholar Samuel David Luzzatto, also known as Shadal, was born in Trieste. He began writing poetry from a young age, and later penned academic works on Jewish history and the Bible. He translated the Ashkenazi prayer book into Italian in 1821–1822, and the Italian rite in 1829. Luzzatto joined the faculty of the Padua rabbinical college in 1829, where he taught until his death. A strong critic of Jewish mysticism, he upheld the value of Jewish traditions, believing that Judaism expressed universal humanist morals. Posthumously, Luzzatto's correspondence with other Jewish intellectuals, his early manuscripts, and varied writings were compiled and published by his son.

Lessons of Jewish Moral Theology
1862

These lessons (of which the first forty-seven paragraphs were already published in the *Rivista israelitica*) were written in 1832 for the use of those youth who, upon completing their primary and secondary education, attended this rabbinical institute in order to receive training that, one day, would enable them to become rabbis.

My soul was vividly penetrated by the urgent thought that future masters and pastors in Israel need access to a clear and just idea of the morality of Judaism in order to, in turn, teach that religion in its purity, which, in its primitive sources, sacred scripture, and tradition, is shown to be eminently social and a teacher of the most healthy civilization.

I observed that some Greek and Arabic schools that had become famous in the Middle Ages had great influence over the minds of many learned and famous Jewish writers and that the morality they taught was more ascetic than social and that in their excessive spiritual sublimity they were much less apt to educate and direct the common man toward the good and that which is biblical and Talmudic morality, in its divine simplicity.

You should, without excess verbosity, declare that any sentence that can be found in rabbinical writings that would seem opposed to these principles of universal charity and tolerance should be attributed to the unfortunate conditions of the times and places in which these rabbis lived and should, through us, the times having changed, abjure and recognize that which is contrary to Judaism, both biblical and traditional.

Translated by James N. Novoa.

Other works by Luzzatto: *Prolegomeni ad una grammatica ragionata della lingua ebraica* (1836); *Yesode ha-torah* (1880); *Igerot Shadal* (1882); *Discorsi storico-religiosi agli studenti israeliti* (1931).

Elijah Benamozegh
1823–1900

Orthodox rabbi and liberal scholar Elijah Benamozegh expressed an unlikely combination of traditional beliefs and modernizing practices in his theological and philosophical works. A lifelong inhabitant of Livorno, Italy, he received his Jewish education from his uncle, a Moroccan kabbalist. Benamozegh was a member of the rabbinical court and a professor at the rabbinical seminary. He published works in Hebrew, Italian, and French, seeking to expound a balance between religious traditions, modern scholarship, and science, and absorbing ideas from other religious and classical cultures.

Israel and Humanity
1863

The Jewish Idea of Progress

Judaism's approach to history is shaped by the fact that unlike other religions, it locates perfection not at the beginning but at the end of history. This, surely, is the meaning of its commitment to the coming of a messianic era, which we may define as faith in a future perfection of the human race—religious, moral, social, material—which must be achieved in the last days.

We know that rationalist criticism divides the development of the messianic doctrine into successive stages, according to which the complete idea dates only from a relatively recent time. It would be pointless to enter here into a debate on the antiquity of messianism. Whenever it first appeared, sooner or later Hebraism acquired it, and, most importantly, placed the realization of its hopes at the end of history. This feature of the Jewish faith is so characteristic, so essential, that although Christianity considers itself the realization of messianism, it has never ceased, as heir of Israel—and despite the contradiction between this idea and the body of its doctrines—to appoint the end of history for the accomplishment of its own promises of resurrection and rebirth.

Ecclesiastes is echoing traditional Israelite thought when it says: "The end of a matter is better than the beginning of it" (Eccl 7:8). And to show that it is no good being impatient, and that we must know how to await the course of events, it adds:

> Better a patient spirit than a haughty spirit. Don't let your spirit be quickly vexed, for vexation abides in the breasts of fools. (Eccl 7:8–9)

He [Moses] was able to lay the foundations of a system of law and a political constitution only by staying in harmony with the way of life of the men who surrounded him.

But Moses left unchanged not only Jewish doctrine but also Noachism, which remained for him and his successors, as for those who had gone before, the sole religious obligation of the Gentile. And we must add that the legislation which Moses gave Israel (and which was for Israel alone) addresses the particular needs of Israel's priestly calling.

Equality among Men

Generally speaking, Hebraism has preached and practiced civil and political equality among men, whether Israelites, proselytes, or ordinary Gentiles. It has been noted, quite accurately, that whereas the doctrine of force as its own justification prevailed everywhere in paganism, Judea was the first nation to exhibit respect for the rights of man.

In the vastness of the Roman Empire, on the one hand, we find selfishness and supreme faith in strength, on the other, in a tiny, little-known land, belief in the dignity of man, who knows no other master than God: such is the vivid contrast we find in the early years of our era.

And M. Laurent records in this connection that Christianity, unlike Judaism, preaches equality only on the religious plane, but has not been concerned with introducing its principles into the civil and political order, and that therefore, on this point, Mosaism goes further than Christian doctrine.

But if we wish to gain an accurate understanding of Judaism's conception of mankind, it is not enough to examine the Law, which is only its external aspect; we must also take account of ethics, which is an equally important expression of Jewish thought. We find that universalist tendencies are much more evident in the principles of ethical behavior developed by the sages of the Synagogue than in the Written Law. Here is perhaps not the place to undertake a detailed study of this matter. (See the author's *Morale juive et morale chrétienne*.) It is a field where the crop is so bountiful that one has only to glean in order to gather voluminous sheaves. We shall limit ourselves to a few precepts which illuminate the Jewish attitude toward the Gentile.

We are enjoined not to seek to gain his confidence by deceptive protestations of friendship, which the Talmud calls "stealing the mind of our fellow-men." That is not all. We must in fact behave in a kindly way toward him. The stranger must be allowed, just like Jewish widows and orphans, to gather up what falls from the reaper's hand, and to share with them the unharvested remains and the produce of that corner of the field reserved for the poor. We are commanded in general to look after the Gentile poor, to care for their sick, and to bury their dead, just as if they were Jews, for the sake of peace and good will.

These injunctions are not merely expressions of political or social expediency, rather than moral obligation, as might perhaps be imagined. The precepts are given without any consideration of time or place, and the examples which are cited in support of them are drawn from periods when Israel enjoyed complete national independence.

Translated by Maxwell Luria.

Other works by Benamozegh: *Emat mafgia al Ari* (1855); *Ta'am la-shad* (1863); *Storia degli Esseni* (1865); *Morale juive et morale chrétienne* (1867); *Teologia dogmatica e apologetica* (1877).

Akiva Joseph Schlesinger

1837–1922

Born in Pressburg (present-day Bratislava) and educated in Moravia, Akiva Joseph Schlesinger developed into an uncompromising foe of religious reform. His *Lev ha-Ivri*, in the form of an extended commentary on the last will and testament of his teacher Moses Sofer, was a passionate attack against any concession to the forces of modernity. Schlesinger advocated staunch pride in traditional Jewish culture, extending his hostility to all aspects of even modern Orthodox practices. A controversial figure, Schlesinger immigrated to Palestine in 1870, after having served as a judge and yeshiva lecturer in Hungary and Galicia. In the Land of Israel he advocated for a traditionalist protostate within Ottoman Palestine. When, in 1875, one of his pamphlets defended even such ancient practices as polygamy in the future settlement in the Land of Israel, he was denounced, banned, and marginalized. His efforts were instrumental in founding some of the earliest Jewish settlements of the late nineteenth century.

Lev ha-Ivri (The Heart of a Jew)
1864

What would our ancestors have done if they had seen a Jewish community appointing a prayer-reader and a rabbi for themselves dressed in the vestments of a Christian priest, and setting up an idol in the Temple of the Lord, by placing before the Holy Ark an alien individual, who raises his hand against the views of the Torah and whose throat speaks, in the presence of an open grave, in a foreign language to Jewish people, in the manner of a gentile priest coming to preach among the Jewish people? Even if we fall short of the spiritual level of our ancestors by not being prepared to sacrifice our lives on account of a minor sin, as they would do, even in regard to the current matter, where the legal obligation to sacrifice our lives is greater, as is made plain in tractate *Sanhedrin* 74—that at a time of anti-Jewish decrees made by the government, one must allow oneself to be killed rather than transgress even for a minor sin, and the Gemara proceeds to ask: "What is to be considered transgression of a minor precept?" to which the reply is given: "Even to change one's shoe-strap!"—and Rashi, of blessed memory, has explained this in reference to the type of shoe-strap worn by Jews—even in the case of a mere custom such as this, whereby Jews are distinguished from gentiles, where no precept as such is involved, but rather, merely a Judaic custom, an individual must sanctify the Name of the Almighty in public. See *ad loc.* "Said R. Jacob: 'The minimum definition of "in public" is ten Jews'"—and how much more so is this the case, then, where a change of language is involved. The entire pedigree and position of Israel was staked out by virtue of a Jewish custom, i.e., that they did not alter their language, and we may also invoke the case of the eighteen decrees [which the House of Shammai forced on Jewry] with the threat of being thrust through with a sword in the event of dissent, as cited by the Ḥatam Sofer Vol. II to *Even ha-ezer*; and how much more ought this to apply to customs relating to the religion and the synagogues that are in the public domain of Jewry! Now, praise be to God, blessed be He, there are currently no governmental decrees against us, as the Almighty has given us a ruler of kindly disposition—may his majesty be exalted; and we are able to stake out an affirmative position for ourselves, not through the sacrifice of our lives, but merely through inward efforts on our part. If we do not uphold our tradition even in this manner, but remain silent, our iniquity will be greater than we can bear—Heaven forbid—for presently, we can already see the results before us, when we regard all those countries in which they acted over-wisely against the views of the Torah and the words of our rabbis of blessed memory, and perceive what has befallen their descendants—and you are no different from them! The ancestors of these people hailed from Germany and from Prussia, France, and Italy, lands from which virtually the entire Torah and fear of God issued forth to Israel, and at the time of the decrees of the year 4856 [1096], one hundred and twenty holy communities sacrificed their lives in the German provinces alone; nonetheless, millions of ancestors such as these, who shed their blood for the sanctification of the Divine name, were unable, by reason of their merits, to shield their descendants, because they had gone astray from the way of Israel and the Jewish path and the landmarks set by the Torah, persisting in their deviation and adding to it, to the point where they have already introduced, in those communities in Germany which were great from ancient times, an organ in the synagogue with the image of a crucifix upon it.—Observe how other aspects of Torah, and the precepts and fundamental principles of the faith, have been forgotten and abandoned by them! They go about in an unrestrained manner, bereft of all faith, and, like a wild young ass, pursue their own desires, and their faith consists only of their financial gain. Thus, if such has been the fate of the seed of holiness on account of their altering the path of Israel and the customs of our ancestors of blessed memory, then, *a fortiori*, there is no need for concern in respect of our descendants coming after us, as their tragic destiny is a foregone conclusion. If we adopt a merely passive stance over this matter, that would constitute a sin too heavy to bear, and, *a fortiori*, this would apply to one who encourages or strengthens this path of wickedness; for if a person sins, he being in the class of "one rebelling on account of his own natural desires," even if this extends to all the prohibitions of the Torah, he has merely sinned against himself, and perhaps he will yet return to the Almighty; but one who causes others to sin and draw the seed of Israel along to destruction, is guilty of infinitely great evil; and anyone who causes the public to sin is not afforded the opportunity to repent. Indeed the Torah states that "You shall slay the animal too," since a human being has been involved in a sin on its account—even where it occurred unintentionally, and *a fortiori*, where it occurred intentionally. Should we claim that we are unaware of any such thing, i.e., that people are strengthening the hands of evil in this manner, can there possibly be upon earth someone so idiotic as not to have been affected by this matter? How did Berlin originally become launched on this path? They had a "preacher" named Solomon Plesner, who used to sit virtually all day long, enwrapped in a prayer shawl and tefillin, studying the Zohar, who performed deeds like one of the holy ones on High; but once the gate had already been opened to reform through one who was a very righteous individual in their estimation, they subsequently dismissed Solomon and hired for themselves another "preacher"; "when they were fed, they were sated," and Berlin, and likewise all the other places, acquired renown. Who is there so simpleminded as not to understand this matter—that the people will want only a Jeroboam and will not wish to hear of Jerusalem? Even a one-year-old child can understand the schemes and the snares of this evil; if, despite all this, they persist in such conduct, then undoubtedly those persisting in it are genuine disciples of Jeroboam, and all their bowings and prostrations are merely great outward symbols, but their interior is as forbidden food; their hearts turn aside to other gods, away from the Almighty; for true piety involves exercising caution in regard to a matter requiring investigation, and fasting and weeping; similarly, all the upright practices and the noble character traits are merely branches and leaves of the Tree of Life, and if the roots are lacking, and in particular, that root principle which the prophet Habakkuk came to encapsulate within one overarching principle: "And the righteous shall live by his faith"—if the heart is, in truth, distant from the Almighty, then a wind comes and uproots and overturns all these branches and leaves. Accordingly, as for anyone who strengthens, or draws himself close to, these so-called religious leaders, there can be no doubt that his heart is rooted in heresy, or in a lack of faith, or that there are seven abominations in his heart, or he is genuinely simpleminded and foolish, believing everything; for this too they will have to bear their sin, as they have become a stumbling-block unto the House of Jacob, both to our own generation and to those generations succeeding us.

Translated by David E. Cohen.

Other works by Schlesinger: *El ha-adarim* (1863); *Kol nehi mi-tsiyon* (1872); *Ḥevrah mahazire atarah le-yoshnah im kolel ha-ivrim* (1873); *Bet Yosef ḥadash* (1875).

Elissa Lisbonne
1806–?

Elissa Lisbonne, member of a Jewish family prominent in French political affairs, was the son of a rabbi in the Comtat Venaissin, one of the Papal States in southeastern France. This region around Avignon became a refuge for French Jews before they were emancipated during the French Revolution. Subsequent emigration led to the cultural decline of the Comtadin communities, though Lisbonne's periodical *La loi divine* stood out as an exceptional representative of literary activity in Avignon in the 1840s. His essay on the emancipation of women in Hebrew worship supported total equality of Jewish women in the rites of the synagogue.

On the Emancipation of Women in Jewish Worship
1865

Introduction

Theology teaches us that when God the Eternal formed man He gave him an extra rib. This rib was destined for the formation of woman in order that this creature, who was to become the rich ornament of humankind, had none of the dust God had used to create man.

Woman is thus a chosen being and the most remarkable one ever known.

In all religious societies there are prejudices, but there are some so entrenched in the minds of the faithful that one must be a practiced writer with a well-honed gift of persuasion to undermine and destroy them. I shall nevertheless make the attempt, however unavailing my pen, and hope that, by raising the serious issue of woman's emancipation in Jewish worship, I shall lead the eminent men of our faith to my way of thinking. Conclusive evidence will prove that woman, this divine emanation of the Eternal's breath, must return the faith to its former splendor through her participation, and, through her power of attraction, lead back to the Lord's temple those whose indifference has kept them away.

What ineffable joy one feels in the presence of woman: her delightful charm, her grace, her sensitivity, and her virtue endow her entire being with an aura of love that makes her resemble the Creator who made her and makes us love her, as one loves all that is charming and graceful, sensitive and virtuous! And you would have such a creature excluded from the Lord's house, isolated, and declared incapable of joining in our public adoration of the All-Powerful! This kind of thinking is an aberration that only the ancient prejudices of men could have engendered. Woman, with her keen sensitivity and infinitely receptive nature, should—even more so than man—participate in our religion's great acts of worship.

My father was a worship leader whose particular mission was to preside over the women's service. For thirty years he carried out his holy ministry. On Saturdays and solemn holy days, he recited the prayers and spoke the word of God in Provençale, the language of the people, for women at that time in the Comtat region knew no other language. Their only instruction was that of the family: cleaning house and feeding the children was all that their fathers and husbands required of them. They thus had no education at all, and religion—that pure religion full of love and spirituality—was, for them, entirely material.

My father officiated in a simple space adjacent to the temple. The women were so completely separated from the men that at the very moment of sanctification, the moment when the Book of Laws was elevated, they could only witness this great act of devotion on the other side of a partition purposely placed between their area and the men's synagogue.

This is the handiwork of those prejudiced men of old, this is how woman, who bore us in her womb, who nourished us with her milk, the most beautiful half of the human race, has been excluded from the Lord's temple, completely erased in Jewish worship, and viewed as a nullity, a slave at the command of man! And the prejudicial exclusion of women, making them incapable of participating fully in the worship service, still survives and prospers. We must now bring this custom to an end and emancipate woman, whose sweetness and sensitivity make her more suited than man for the holy acts of praise we offer up to the All-Powerful in His sacred temple.

Translated by Michele McKay Aynesworth.

Other work by Lisbonne: *Étude sur la religion d'Israël* (1865).

Penina Moïse

Hymns Written for the Use of Hebrew Congregations. Charleston, Congregation Beth Elohim 1867

Duties Towards Ourselves

1. SELF-KNOWLEDGE.

While man explores, with curious eye,
    The works of nature and of art,
He passeth *real* wisdom by,
    Nor cares to read the human heart.

A stranger to himself alone,
    He walketh forth in worldly guise;
Nor wouldst thou in his lofty tone
    The child of frailty recognise.

Yet pause, O man! in thy career,
    And search the chambers of thy soul;
For passions dark and deep are there,
    That spurn at reason's weak control.

A thirst for blood, for gold, for fame,
    Pollutes thee, yet thou know'st it not;
Because it borrows glory's name,
    And sheds false lustre on thy lot.

Seek piety—self-knowledge seek,
    Their guidance ask to virtue's road;
On thee will Heaven's light then break,
    And thou wilt know and bless thy God.

11. *Our Country*

Father of nations! Judge divine!
    From Thy blessed realms above
Thine ear to prayers and hymns incline,
    Breathed by patriotic love.
Is there one upon this earth,
    Who in welfare or in woe,
For the country of his birth,
    Feels not sympathy's strong glow?

Oh! may we not this feeling trace
    To creation's primal date?
When the great parent of our race
    Felt the exiles' bitter fate?
His first tears were not for toil,
    But for his lost flower-land—
Paradise, *his* native soil,
    Closed on him by God's command.

That pure sentiment was nursed
    When man's innocence had waned;
His progeny, where'er dispersed,
    Kept this virtue unprofaned.
Native to all human kind
    Is the sod of liberty!
Where no tyrant's law may bind
    Souls by nature's God made free. [. . .]

Passover

Oh! let us mingle heart and voice,
In unison let us rejoice,
    To one great God appealing;
The children of the Hebrew race,
Who, tho' divided now by space,
    Are linked by fate and feeling.
        Bondage hath ceased,
        And freedom's feast
        For souls released,
        By mem'ry kept,
        Each chord hath swept,
In which her sacred music slept.

The sword of vengeance flashed abroad!
The sceptre that became a *rod*
    Has by a rod been broken;

The child redeemed from Nile's great flood,
Has changed its waters into blood!
    A warning and a token
        Of plagues reserved
        For those who swerved,
        By power nerved,
        From laws humane,
        And dared constrain
God's witnesses to works profane!

The clime of darkness blacker grows,
No beam the worship'd sun-god throws
   Within the heathen's palace;
Regardless of the despot's prayer
Compell'd with trembling and with fear
   To drain the bitter chalice;
     Behold and praise
     God's wondrous ways
     Each hour displays!
     In contrast bright
     To Egypt's night
On Israel's home shines perfect light.

And thus with concentrated ray
On all who Heaven's will obey,
   Whate'er may be their station,
Through all the shadows cast by time,
Shall rise in lustrous grace sublime
   The blest star of salvation!
     The tyrant's doom
     In midnight gloom,
     From throne to tomb
     On freedom's spot
     It resteth not:
Light to man's *spirit there* is brought.

Creator! Liberator! Lord!
Let peace to us its palm accord,
   Twined with faith's pure evergreen;
Oh! bless the rulers of each land,
Who cause its branches to expand,
   Its rare fruitage to be seen.
     Most holy King!
     Let Judah cling
     To laws that spring
     From Mercy's seat,
     While at Thy feet
This day's memorial we repeat.

Judah Papo

d. 1873

Judah Papo was the son of Eliezer Papo, author of the 1826 Hebrew-language ethical (*musar*) tract *Pele yo'ets*, which Judah translated into Ladino in 1870, amending the work to reflect changes in Ottoman Jewish society. Judah Papo's encouragement of technological changes as a method of spreading Jewish knowledge is reflected in his words on the flourishing Ladino press.

Is the Printing Press Harmful? A Rabbi from Sarajevo Responds
1870

How great is the benefit of the printing houses, for thanks to the power of the printing press, the Torah is enhanced everywhere in the world. The rabbis are certainly making the effort to produce books, but nothing is gained because for the most part they do not have the means to have them printed. It is appropriate for the notables to support them in this [endeavor], and by virtue [of their support] they become the partners of the rabbi and gain most of [the benefit], for the one who enables [Torah study] is greater than the one who engages [in Torah study himself]. . . . When we consider this, we find that there is no better use of money than [supporting the publication of rabbinic books], for all expenses in fulfillment of a religious commandment are temporary, while this [act] lasts for generations. Furthermore, [the sponsor] is considered to be the one who sustains the hand of the rabbi, especially when his is a book of [religious] law or ethics, for its virtue is very great, as in each generation all those who acquire virtue on account of this book, [the sponsor] will share [in their merit]. The merit of the masses is dependent on him and will give him much enjoyment in the world to come, where he is sure to receive gifts. . . .

Furthermore, there is [another] great benefit from printing in that it enables the enhancement of understanding and perfection in the entire world. The newspapers that are printed, even though they carry much information that is of no importance, still have useful things in them that allow a person to educate himself. All the sciences and all kinds of knowledge and all the arts come off the printing press, and there is always a piece of wisdom or knowledge or art that one would not find elsewhere. If someone gathers all the wisdom from all of them, he surely will become a wise person, affirming what it says in the verse: "I have more understanding than my teachers." For the person who is learning from everyone educates himself, and this is what benefited people in Europe, where the sciences and knowledge and perfection continue to advance. Thank God that printing presses are now available everywhere and that there is [thus] a way for the Jewish people to derive much good from this.

NOTE
Words in brackets appear in the original translation.
Translated by Matthias Lehmann.

Simon Sofer
1820–1883

Simon (Shimon) Sofer was the second son of Moses Sofer and an illustrious rabbi and scholar in his own right. Sofer was born in Pressburg (present-day Bratislava), where, from an early age, he was regarded as an expert on rabbinic works and in Jewish poetry. At age twenty, he wrote a biography of his father. Simon, along with his brother Abraham Samuel Benjamin Sofer, also edited their father's responsa. In the mid-1840s, Simon served as rabbi in Mattersdorf. In 1861, he became the chief rabbi of Kraków, where he helped found Maḥzikey ha-das in an effort to combat the Haskalah then taking root among Galician Jewry; he also ruled on such issues as the suitable placement of the *bimah* in synagogues. He became a member of the Austro-Hungarian parliament in 1879.

Shem ha-gedolim ha-shalem (Names of the Great Ones, Complete)
ca. 1870

Although he himself would not recite "for the sake of the unification," in keeping with the ruling of the Gaon—the Noda bi-Yehudah [R. Ezekiel Landau]—he was occasionally jealous of those who say it.

Translated by Maoz Kahana.

Other works by Sofer: *Mikhtav Sofer* (two-volume collection of his responsa and commentaries; 1952–1955).

Jacob Ettlinger

Responsa binyan tsiyon (Responsa: Building Zion)
1874

No. 23

The Holy Community of Altona, Friday, 29 Marheshvan 5621 [14 November 1860]

To my dear friend, father of my son-in-law, the distinguished rabbi, our Teacher, R. Shemaryahu Zuckerman, may his light shine.

Regarding that which his exalted Honor in Torah—may his light shine—has written, to the effect that he has been accustomed to prohibit the drinking of wine which has been touched by a Jew who desecrates the Sabbath in public because he repudiates the entire Torah; and he has proved this from the responsa of the Mabit [R. Moses Trani], which he has cited, appearing in his work *Nekudat ha-kesef* 14 (para. 124) where he prohibits the drinking of wine that has been touched by Karaites, because they desecrate the Festive Seasons, and are like those who desecrate the Sabbath—but that there is an authority who dissents from his view—and he accordingly seeks my opinion in this matter:

In my humble opinion, he is halakhically correct, since one who desecrates the Sabbath in public is like one who repudiates the entire Torah, and he has the status of an idol worshiper; and it is possible that even the Maharshal [R. Solomon Luria], whom he cites in *Nekudat ha-kesef ad loc.*, who holds that Karaites do not create a prohibition for traditional Jews drinking wine touched by them, concedes that, though Karaites do not desecrate Sabbaths, they do desecrate the Festive Seasons, because they dissent from our computation of the calendar, albeit he does not hold that one who desecrates the Festive Seasons is comparable to one who desecrates Sabbaths. However, in regard to one who desecrates the Sabbath itself, who, according to all authorities, has the same status as one who repudiates the entire Torah, it is conceivable that even the Maharshal would agree that wine touched by such an individual is prohibited. One cannot legitimately argue that since the rabbinic decree prohibiting the drinking of their wine was made in order to prevent marriage with their daughters, and that the daughters of Sabbath desecrators are not prohibited to traditional Jews in marriage. This cannot be so, for if that were indeed the case, one who repudiated the Torah in favor of idolatry would not create a prohibition on our drinking it, yet, according to what is stated in Hullin (4), he *does* create such a prohibition; and we therefore have to say, as the Ran [Rabbenu Nissim Gerondi] writes in his novella *ad loc.*, and as his exalted Honor in Torah—may his light shine brightly—also cites, that since such an individual is like a fully fledged gentile, he is included within the rabbinic decree, despite the fact that there is no prohibition on marriage with his daughters—and that being

Maurycy Gottlieb, *Tańczący chasydzi (Dancing Hasidim)*, ca. 1875. The biography of Gottlieb appears in the Visual Culture section.

so, the same would apply to an apostate in respect of public desecration of the Sabbath. And so indeed has the *Rashba* [R. Solomon b. Adret] written in his responsa, cited by the *Bet Yosef* [R. Joseph Karo] (para. 119); namely, that the wine of an apostate in regard to public desecration of the Sabbath is like wine poured out in libations to idols. Now up to this point we have spoken from the strict perspective of the halakhah, as to how we are to regard one who desecrates the Sabbath in public; but insofar as the transgressors among Israel in our era are concerned, I do not know how I ought to judge them, considering that—on account of our many sins—the "bright spot" on the skin, indicative of leprosy, has spread so extensively that, in regard to the majority of them, desecration of the Sabbath is deemed tantamount to being permissible—if indeed the law applicable to one who maintains that a particular prohibited act is permitted—namely, that they are deemed to be merely *close* to willful transgression, is not actually applicable in their case. There are some among them who recite the Sabbath Eve prayers and make Kiddush, and afterwards desecrate the Sabbath by performing types of work prohibited both by the law of the Torah and by that of the rabbis. Now one who desecrates the Sabbath is regarded as simply an apostate, since one who repudiates the Sabbath effectively denies the Creation and the Creator—yet this type of person, by reason of his recitation of prayers and his Kiddush, accepts these beliefs! And what about their children, who have replaced them, who have never known and never heard the laws relating to the Sabbath, who are directly comparable to the Sadducees, who were not deemed to have the status of apostates, notwithstanding their desecration of the Sabbath, on account of the fact that they had adopted the practices of their ancestors, and accordingly were like a small child taken captive amongst idolators, as is explained (section 385); and the Mabit has written to the same effect (section 37), stating: "And it is also possible that Sadducees, who have not been accustomed to living among traditional Jewry, and have been unaware of the fundamentals of the faith, and do not conduct themselves with temerity against the Sages of their generation, are not to be regarded as willful transgressors," *etc.*—see above. And many of the transgressors of our generation are comparable to them, and preferable to them, in that, insofar as the Rash [R. Samson of Sens] adopted a stringent view in relation to the Karaites, to deem their wine as wine poured out to idols, that was not only on account of their desecration of the Festive Seasons—which are comparable to the Sabbath—but because they additionally denied the fundamentals of the faith, in that they circumcise but do not uncover the corona and pull the membrane down, and they have no laws in respect of bills of divorce and betrothals, as a result of which their children are bastards. But the majority of the transgressors in our own times have not committed breaches in relation to these matters, and therefore, in my humble opinion, one who adopts a stringent view in deeming the touching of wine by these transgressors as falling within the category of general gentile wine—may a blessing descend upon him. However, those adopting a lenient stance also have something of substance upon which to rely, unless it is clear to us that the person in question is aware of the laws of the Sabbath but nonetheless has the temerity to desecrate it in the presence of ten Jews assembled together—for such a person is like a fully fledged apostate, and his touching of wine makes it prohibited to drink. Such would appear to be the position, in the humble opinion of the junior and insignificant one, Jacob.

Translated by David E. Cohen.

Elimelech of Lizhensk and Zusya of Annopol (Hanipoli)

Elimelech of Lizhensk's biography appears earlier in this volume.

Zusya of Annopol, 1718–1800

Meshulam Zusya of Annopol was born in Poland and was the brother of Elimelech of Lizhensk. Zusya was a follower of Dov Ber, the Magid of Mezritsh, who also influenced Elimelech to become a Hasid. After Dov Ber's death in 1772, Zusya moved to Annopol, where he was instrumental in establishing Hasidism in Galicia. Zusya was one of the best-known heroes of Hasidic folk tales, portrayed as a humble and kind man who attained merit on account of his innocence and personal righteousness.

Menorat zahav (Golden Menorah)
1902

When Rabbi Zusya went to suffer the exile in Germany, he came to a city of Reform Jews. When they saw his ways, they mocked him and thought he was crazy. When he came into the synagogue, some of them poked fun at him, and when the children saw their parents ridiculing him, they thought he was crazy and began to pull at him, and tug at his belt. Then he beckoned to the children and said: "My dear children, gather round and I will tell you something." The children thought he would show them a trick. They all stood around him and he in the middle. And he said to them, "My dear children, look well at me, do not take your eyes off me." The children, because they thought he was going to show them something, looked steadily at him, and he also looked steadily at each child separately. After that he told them to go home.

When the children came home and were given their food, they refused to eat. One said that the meat had not been salted, and it must not be eaten. Another asked how one could eat unclean meat. And so all the children refused to eat. They said the dishes were unclean and the food was unclean.

Then, as women do, one went to another and told her that all of a sudden her son came home from the prayer house and refused to eat; whatever was given him, he said it was unclean. Then her neighbor said that her son too refused to eat and shouted that everything was unclean and that one could not pray in her house because her hair was uncovered. Then another neighbor came in and also told such things about her son—the whole town was amazed! Then they each learned that their sons were not the only ones who suddenly became pious. They said that the visitor whom they had ridiculed and thought crazy was none other than a saint. By looking at the children, he had instilled in them the idea of Judaism. The parents became afraid that they had shamed him and went to beg his forgiveness. And Zusya forgave them all.

Translated by Lucy Dawidowicz.

Uri of Strelisk
1757–1826

Uri of Strelisk, the son of a poor artisan, was a Hasidic leader who advocated asceticism and poverty. He was born near Janów, Galicia, and became the foremost disciple of Rabbi Solomon of Karlin. After the latter was murdered in 1792, Uri served as a rabbi in Lemberg (where he had studied earlier) and later in Strelisk (also in Galicia), though without formally establishing a court. He was famed for his lengthy, ecstatic prayer style, which led his followers to call him the Seraph, after the biblical six-winged creatures that sing praises to God. Uri also condemned the emphasis on miracles in Jewish traditions.

On the Seer of Lublin's Court
1911

When one comes to Lublin he should imagine to himself that Lublin is Eretz Israel, that the courtyard of the study house is Jerusalem, that the study house is the Temple Mount, that his apartment is the Porch, that the gallery is the Sanctuary, that his room is the Holy of Holies, and that the shekhinah speaks from his throat. Then he will understand what our rabbi is.

Translated by Dena Ordan.

Other work by Uri of Strelisk: *Imre kadosh* (1870).

Isaac Judah Yehiel Safrin of Komarno

Notser ḥesed to Avot (Preserving Mercy [Commentary to Ethics of the Fathers])
Date Unknown

For the Love of the Zaddik

As a general rule, however, the spirit and illuminating power of the zaddik affect and inspire only those of his generation who are favorably disposed toward him. They have no complaint against him, and his deeds are sweet to them. Which brings us back to the original meaning of the tanna's statement: Anyone, namely any zaddik of whom it is the case that the people are pleased with him, and hence become attached to him lovingly, with heart and soul, the spirit of God too is pleased with him, causing divine grace and light to rest on all those who cleave to him. But those people who are displeased with him, thus showing no inclination to bind themselves to him with heart and soul, may have no benefit from the divine spirit emanating through him, for it has no effect on those who are displeased with the zaddik and thus unwilling to bind themselves to him.

Translated by Norman Lamm.

Israel Salanter
1810–1883

Born in Zhagare, Lithuania, into a rabbinical family, Israel ben Ze'ev Volf Lipkin (widely known as Israel Salanter) was the founder of the Musar ethical movement, which stressed dedication to moral virtues along with strict adherence to religious commandments. In the early 1840s, Salanter established a Musar house in the Vilna area, where he taught moral and behavioral concepts to a generally middle-class society. In 1848, he declined an offer to teach at a government-created yeshiva in Vilna and moved to Kovno; then, facing opposition for allegedly separating the community into groups, he moved to Prussia, where he opposed the rise of modern Orthodoxy.

Be'ure ha-midot (Clarification of the Virtues)
Date Unknown

And Joshua said unto all Israel: "Draw near," etc.—Joshua 3:9.

In Midrash Genesis Rabbah, section 5 (Gen. Rabbah 5:7), it is stated: "Rav Huna said: 'He stood them up between the two staves of the Ark.' Said R. Aḥa, son of Ḥanina: 'He caused them to lean between the two staves of the Ark.' The rabbis said: 'He compressed them between the two staves of the Ark.' Joshua said to them: 'From the fact that the two staves of the Ark have supported you, you know that the Presence of the Holy One, blessed be He, is amongst you!' That is the meaning of that which is written there: And Joshua said: 'By this you shall know that the Living God is in your midst!'"

Before we start imbibing an inner spiritual meaning within the above statement (even if its authors did not have this in mind, and it is, perhaps, simply a case of the spiritual wind blowing in a straightforward direction, along the surface of the plateau), let us now express, in just a few words, the characteristics of the ways of human beings, as these differ from one another. There is a certain type of individual who is of good character and whose qualities are, by nature, desirable, and there is another type, whose character is the very reverse of this. Likewise, even in the case of a private individual, the various forces within his soul will, on occasion, not proceed along in an identical fashion; some of them will proceed on the correct path (without anyone pulling and directing them), while others will proceed on a crooked path; they will press on toward destruction unless one assists them with the power of one's understanding.

Let a man not say: "One cannot alter what God has made, and the blessed One has implanted the power of evil within me, so how can I hope to eradicate it?" This is not the case: the powers possessed by man are capable of being subdued, as well as altered, as we ourselves perceive in the nature of animals, in that mankind expends much of his energy in subduing them through his will, so as to prevent them from doing harm and causing destruction, and also in order to domesticate them—to alter their nature and to uproot their harmful traits. Similarly with man himself—he has the power to subdue his evil nature so that he does not implement it in practice; and also to alter his nature for the good through training and the force of habit (see *Ḥeshbon ha-nefesh*)—and this is in accordance with the statement of our rabbis of blessed memory (*Pirke avot* 4:1): "Who is mighty? He who can subdue his evil inclination, as it says: 'He that is slow to anger is better than the mighty, and he that rules over his spirit is better than he who captures a city'" (Proverbs 16:32). For the hallmark of might is to rise up against one's adversary with strength and power, to subdue him, and the hallmark of the conquest of a city is where the inhabitants of the city become inclined to obey their conqueror with love and esteem, where it is not burdensome for them to fulfill his orders, and where they rejoice in gladness and jubilation in the upholding of his desires. In this way, he who subdues his evil inclination is a mighty man simply by virtue of his fortifying himself so as to become one who restrains his lusts; this is the test for one who is "slow to anger"—that he does indeed possess anger, but restrains his temper so as to prevent it exploding; and from this stage he will slowly, slowly attain the level of "one who rules over his spirit"—where the disposition of his lusts is well and truly subjected to his intellect—to love justice and not to harbor a desire for its opposite. This is the whole purpose of man—to eradicate from his heart every harmful characteristic and trait; for so long as he is not cleansed from the ailments they create, albeit an individual prevails over his evil inclination on numerous occasions, he will eventually fall into their net (see *Sha‘are kedushah*, part I: 303). This was the supreme virtue of our father Abraham—peace be upon him—that he perfected all the forces of his soul which were conjoined to his body, as our Sages of blessed memory have stated (Gen. Rabbah 46:1): "Said the Holy One, blessed be He, to Abraham: 'There is no worthless element within you, except for your foreskin—remove it and eliminate the blemish!' 'Walk before Me and be perfect' (Genesis 17:1). See *ad loc.*—and in accordance with the Sages' statement (11:6): 'Everything that was created during the six days of creation requires some additional thing to be done with it; for instance, mustard requires a sweetener,' etc.—even man requires perfection." (And it is in this vein that the following Midrash (ibid., 30:10) may be explained: "Noah walked with God," etc. "R. Judah says: This may be compared to a king who had two sons, one big and one small. He said to the small one: "Walk with me!" and he said to the big one: "Come and walk in front of me!" Such was the case with Abraham, whose strength was of a worthy nature (Genesis 17)—hence he was told: 'Walk in front of Me and be perfect!' But in regard to Noah, whose strength was of a wobbly, infirm nature, scripture employs the phrase 'Noah walked *with* God.') For Noah (in accordance with his worth), because he was not commanded to circumcise himself, did not have it within his power to arrive at a level of genuine perfection, but could only attain the level of one capable of subduing his evil inclination—that being with the assistance of the Almighty, blessed be He, as our Sages of blessed memory have stated: 'The evil inclination of man prevails over him every day, and were it not for the fact that the Holy One, blessed be He, assists him, he would not be able to resist it' (Sukkah 52b). Accordingly, this is what is meant by the words 'With God,' etc. But as for Abraham, after removal of the blemish of his foreskin, all the powers within his soul were perfected, and of his own accord, he became as one who goes about singing and dancing merrily—happy to observe the way of the Lord. This is meant by the words 'Walk in front of Me!' (Genesis 17:1), and a similar notion is expressed in the *Tana' de-ve-Eliyahu,* chap. 25: 'Therefore, I used to say that every single individual within Israel is obliged to say: "When will my deeds attain the level of the deeds of my ancestors, Abraham, Isaac, and Jacob?"'" And it is in this manner that one can explain the Midrash (Gen.

Rabbah 46:1) on the verse (Hosea 9:10): "I saw your fathers as the first-ripe in the fig tree at her first season," on which R. Yudan observed: 'Just as the fig tree contains nothing valueless save for its stalk—so remove it and eliminate the blemish—in the same vein did the Holy One, blessed be He, say to Abraham: "You have no unworthy element within you," etc.'"

This is in accordance with the statement of the Midrash (Gen. Rabbah 1:4) "Six things preceded the creation of the world; some of them were actually created, while as to others, it merely entered the Divine mind to create them," etc. The Almighty entertained the thought of creating the Patriarchs. From where do we know this? From that which is stated (Hosea 9:10): "Like grapes in the wilderness" (the end of the verse being: "Like the first-ripe in the fig tree," as cited above). Now this matter may be explained as follows: it is acknowledged that the cause precedes the result, and the result (that is to say, the ultimate objective) follows in the wake of the causes preceding it. However, in regard to intent, the reverse is the case: the ultimate objective comes first, and in accordance with this (to establish it upon its foundation), the preparations for the causes are set in order for the sake of the essential ultimate objective. Now consider: in regard to the creation of the world (the earth and all that is upon it—see what distinguished authors have said about this) its ultimate purpose was to produce the perfect human being, who fears the Almighty and observes His commandments, as our rabbis of blessed memory have stated: "What is the meaning of the phrase: 'For this is the whole purpose of man' (Ecclesiastes 12:13)? Said R. Eliezer: The Holy One, blessed be He, declared: "The entire world was created only for this one" (Shabbat 30b)—see ibid. In accordance with the statement of the *Tana de-ve-Eliyahu* (cited above), it is manifestly evident that the essence of the creation is for the sake of mankind, that elevated species, who fulfills his obligation to ascend to the level of the Patriarchs.

This then is the meaning of the statement in the Midrash: "The Almighty entertained the thought of creating the Patriarchs"; namely, the ultimate purpose of the creation of the world in the thought of the Blessed One (which preceded the "cause"; i.e., the creation of the world) was the attainment of the spiritual level of the Patriarchs.

Accordingly, this is the meaning of the Midrash cited above (Gen. Rabbah 46:1) on the verse: "I saw your fathers as the first-ripe in the fig tree at her first season"—namely, that man was created for this ultimate purpose. And every man has it in his power to perfect all the forces within his soul that are conjoined with his corporeal matter, save for that part of him which Abraham was commanded to cut off.

Indeed, where the perfection of the evil inclination is concerned—and even within the context of merely subduing one's evil inclination, one ought not to relax one's efforts in pursuit of this goal, for even though the evil is eradicated from within an individual, nonetheless a font of mire remains concealed in his bosom to pour forth its waters, a phenomenon that will occur when prompted by a substantive cause that arouses them to reveal themselves from their hiding places, to extend themselves to go forth and cause destruction—like a man who has trained himself in regard to the character trait of patience, in that he will display no anger whatsoever in relation to anything done against his wishes and that is not to his benefit; notwithstanding all this, he is not guaranteed against developing a bout of anger in regard to some matter of great moment which, like the cumulative weight of sand, will become too burdensome to endure unless he delves into the depths of the great matter in question, even if this entails the demolition of his solid edifice, which he has acquired by virtue of his labor; and for such purpose he will require an extraordinary level of strength, to which he is not accustomed, to subdue his desires (since the habit of subduing in regard to this particular character trait of anger, which he previously acquired at a time when it was, from his perspective, within the context of mere subduing, has already been abandoned and eradicated by him, as he has made no use of it for a very lengthy period, ever since the time when he acquired it within the context of attaining "perfection"). And who knows whether, at a time like this, he will have the ability to attain the trait of "might," which is hard to acquire, without the prior force of habit?

To this end, how good it is for an individual possessed of worthy character traits to elevate them to lofty heights within the context of "subduing"; to acclimate himself to reverse his evil traits by force, to have a light shining in front of him for guidance in bad times—the time of trial, during which his solid pillars will be shaken—Heaven forbid! And how honorable it is for a man to deploy the trait of might to endure iniquity and incessant pain! To this end, an individual should seek out counsel and appropriate strategies as to how to perfect the character traits and the forces within his soul—

whether in small or in large measure—so that, at the very least, the corruption of his traits will be kept at a safe distance, and he will have no need to invoke the trait of might, save at infrequent intervals—at times of trial—in a manner commensurate with his situation, and his circumstances, and the qualities of his soul.

Translated by David E. Cohen.

Other works by Salanter: *Even Yisra'el* (1853); *Igeret ha-musar* (1857); *Imre binah* (1878); *Ets peri* (1880).

Shneur Zalman of Liady

Igrot ha-kodesh (Holy Epistles)
Date Unknown

The Limbs of One Body

It is written: *All the men of Israel . . . knit together as one man* (Judg. 20:11). Just as one man is composed of many limbs, and when they become separated it affects the heart—for "out of it are the issues of life"—so, since we are all truly as one man, the service [of God] will be established in the heart. Therefore it is said: *To serve Him with one consent* (Zeph. 3:9); only so.

Therefore, my beloved and dear ones: I beg of you to strive with all your heart and soul to implant in each one's heart the love for your fellow man, and not ever to consider a wicked thought about another, as it is written: *And let none of you devise evil in your hearts against his neighbor* (Zech. 8:17). If such a thought should ever arise, let him banish it from your heart, even as smoke is driven away, for this is truly like an idolatrous thought. [As the Rabbis taught:] Slanderous talk is as grave [a sin] as idolatry, adultery, and the shedding of blood all taken together. If this is so with speech [then it is surely so with thought]. For the advantage of proper thought over [proper] speech, whether for good or for better, is already known to the wise of heart.

NOTE

Words in brackets appear in the original translation.

Translated by Norman Lamm.

Haskalah and Pedagogy

Moses Mendelssohn
1729–1786

To the Jews of the West, Moses Mendelssohn was the figurehead of the Haskalah, the Jewish Enlightenment; to the German intellectuals of his day, Mendelssohn was a model Jew and a consequential philosopher and writer, later immortalized as the "Socrates of Berlin." Born in 1729 in Dessau, Germany, the son of a Torah scribe, Mendelssohn moved to Berlin in 1743, to follow his teacher, David Fraenkel. Educated in philosophy, the sciences, as well as classical and European languages, Mendelssohn developed a lifelong friendship with German Enlightenment figure Gotthold Ephraim Lessing, who modeled the hero of his drama *Nathan the Wise* on Mendelssohn. Mendelssohn championed Jewish civil rights and played a key role in securing certain religious freedoms for German Jews. Over the course of several decades, Mendelssohn wrote works on metaphysics and aesthetics, political theory and theology, exploring concepts such as the immortality of the soul, the validity of revelation, free will, and the relationship between religion and state. In 1783, Mendelssohn completed a translation of the Hebrew Bible into German (in Hebrew characters). His *Jerusalem, or On Religious Power and Judaism* stressed the uniqueness of Jewish law and argued for the rationality of the Jewish religion and its compatibility with modern life. (Several of Mendelssohn's works appear in this volume.)

The editor of this volume is indebted for this summary of his philosophical writing to Daniel Dahlstrom, "Moses Mendelssohn," in *The Stanford Encyclopedia of Philosophy*, Summer 2015 ed., edited by Edward N. Zalta, available at https://plato.stanford.edu/entries/mendelssohn/

On the Religious Legitimacy of Studying Logic (Commentary on Maimonides' *Milot ha-higayon*)
1761

There is no doubt, then, that the One Who Has Graced Man With Understanding has implanted in his heart the methods for becoming wise, and established for him upright rules and laws by means of which he can understand one matter from another, comprehend the hidden from the known, and arrive at the truth. Since He created man in His image, there is no doubt that He wished him to learn these methods, using them to discern the actions of the Eternal and the works of His hands, to study His Torah, and to understand its meaning and the depths of its secrets. Therefore, the individual who investigates these methods does the will of his Creator. Heaven forbid that he should be considered as someone who occupies himself with vanities or reads "external books"—may the Merciful One save us from such an opinion!

Of course, I know that the day is short and the work great. The few, distressed years of man's life barely suffice for him to occupy himself with Gemara, Rashi's commentary, and *Tosafot*, which we have been commanded to study, teach, observe, and perform. These are the most elevated matters: how, then, can a person turn his heart to occupy himself with adornments of wisdom such as [logic]? However, I have seen that these methods are very simple, and that a wise individual can learn them in their entirety in two or three days without any effort. It is proper, then, for youths who hang at the gates of the Torah to devote one or two hours a week to reflecting on these methods, especially since they are also of great use for the study of Gemara, Rashi's commentary, and *Tosafot*, as well as for dialectical Talmudic debate (*pilpul haverim*). For these methods straighten a person's intellect, guide him along correct paths, and even improve the external speech that is man's splendor and advantage over the beasts of the earth. How will someone who does not understand how to properly arrange his words comprehend the truth in the commentaries on the Torah and [the work of] the translators, may their memories be for a blessing? In truth, we see that most biblical commentators did not refrain from occupying themselves with these matters, and that some—such as Rashbam, Ibn Ezra, Re'em, and others—delved exceedingly deeply into these matters. Indeed, the author of *Middot Aharon* composed a commentary on the thirteen principles of rabbinic hermeneutics that is full of principles of logic. This should be sufficient to turn aside complaints regarding the gift that I have brought you today.

Moritz Daniel Oppenheim, *Lavater and Lessing Visit Moses Mendelssohn*, 1856.

NOTE

Words in brackets appear in the original translation.

Translated by Elias Sacks.

Other works by Mendelssohn: *Phaedon, or, On the Immortality of the Soul* (1767); *Letter to Lavator* (1769); *Bi'ur* (1780–1783); *Jerusalem, or, On Religious Power and Judaism* (1783).

Me'am Lo'ez
1730–1899

Me'am Lo'ez (From a People of Strange Language) is a multivolume popular biblical commentary and the most influential classic of Ladino literature. The main purpose of this series (1730–1899) was to provide basic Jewish education to Sephardim who were not fluent in Hebrew. *Me'am Lo'ez* follows the standard subdivision of biblical text into weekly portions that are accompanied by commentary, rabbinic writings on practical and legal aspects of Judaism, ethical teachings, and entertaining stories from rabbinic sources.

The project, begun in 1732 by Jacob Huli, was completed by Isaac ben Moses Magriso, on Exodus, Leviticus (1753), and Numbers (1764), all of them published by a prominent but impoverished press in Istanbul. Magriso shows interest in history, science, and etiquette, and also in miracles and supernatural phenomena.

Introduction to the Commentary on Numbers—Me'am Lo'ez, by Isaac Magriso
1764

To the Reader

The introduction to the first volume of this work,[1] which you already have, explains that one must know what mitzvot God commanded us to perform, and what he obliged us to avoid, to find out what sinful things one has done, unknowingly. We must learn more about the miracles God performed for our fathers, because in the weekly portions from the Prophets they are described very briefly, and, for the reason explained in the introduction to Exodus, many miracles are not related in the Law. One should also know about wars and battles that happened in the times of the kings of Israel and the prophets; the words they said to one another, why some people were killed, and what happened when. And one should also know the purpose of our holy and blessed Law, for you must not think that stories found in the Bible, and especially in the Torah, are there for the sake of telling tales, God forbid. Instead, it was the divine intention to couch all the secrets of the Law in the form of stories for the reason explained in that first introduction. Praise God, blessed be He, Jews, being children of a good father and sharing a good root, are great friends of our holy Law and eager to hear new things from it, because the sanctity of Abraham, Isaac, and Jacob is upon them. And thus every hour and every minute, they want to know when the rest of the Bible [*Me'am Lo'ez*] will be printed. Some wish to learn better the precepts of Judaism, while others want to know about the miracles God performed for our fathers. And you will see that with God's help, we will print an infinite number of books.

The reason we have not yet published the rest of the Bible [*Me'am Lo'ez*] is a lack of money. Our initial intention was to print Numbers after Leviticus, using the money made from its sales. But Leviticus was a financial failure. We lost a lot of money and many copies of the book, some of which, for our sins, perished because of fires, and others because of patrons who purchased a few installments[2] at first but then changed their minds and returned them. Those who returned their installments looking as if they had just been purchased did not cause much damage. But some brought back their installments ruined by rats, while others claimed they had lost theirs and wanted replacements. As a result, there were a great number of incomplete books that could not be sold and were sent to the genizah. But now—praise God, blessed be He—He inspired the hearts of some good people whose names will be listed in the introduction to this volume when it appears, with God's help. They made donations to support this endeavor, may God bless them. Since it involves great expense due to the high cost of printing, it is essential that everyone contribute a little each week for the two or three installments that will be printed and distributed weekly.

This is why I ask everyone, rich and poor, men and women, to make an effort and save two or three paras[3] from household expenses to pay for those installments each week. You must know that patrons participate in the mitzvah of publishing these books because without their weekly payments, this press would cease to print.

I also ask those who start buying these installments to continue doing so until the whole book is printed and to pay for them each week and not postpone till the following one, because it is difficult to pay five or six paras in one week, and because this way, the printer's expenses will be covered weekly. Do not think that buying these installments is a small mitzvah, for one does more than just read, gain knowledge of the world, learn the precepts of Judaism, and thus save one's soul from the pains of *gehenom*. In addition, one gets another great advantage: as a result of paying two or three paras per week, this person is marked as someone who "does virtue for many" [*Pirke avot* 5:21] during his whole life and after his death, since it counts as if he finished printing this book. When someone reads it, or learns about a precept of Judaism from it, or performs a mitzvah of which he did not know before, it is considered that this person who supported the printing participated in this mitzvah, because the Mishnah says: "If one does virtue for many, the virtue of many depends upon him" [*Pirke avot* 5:21]. This means that if one performs mitzvot for others, their mitzvot depend upon him, that is, count as if he performed them himself.

[. . .] In this world, everyone must strive to read what one is able to understand, the least of which is the weekly portion from *Me'am Lo'ez*, because reading it means reading all kinds of lessons, namely, the biblical verse, its interpretation, the Talmud, the halakhah, and the *agadot*,[4] because these are all compressed in this book. If in the other world you are asked whether you have read this or that lesson, you will be able to say that you have read all of them, because, as was already said, this book contains everything. Those who read and do everything as was explained here will receive the blessings of the Law. "He who listens to us will dwell in safety, untroubled by the terror of misfortune" [Proverbs 1:33]. Amen, may it be so.

NOTES

The diacritics for the words *Me'am Lo'ez* appear in the original this way.

1. [A reference to the Ladino introduction to the *Me'am Lo'ez* series, which appears in its first volume.—Ed.]

2. [Due to the poverty of Jewish printers in the Ottoman Empire, book production usually depended on donors or patrons. For this reason, many books were printed and distributed irregularly and by quire when presses received sufficient contributions.—Trans.]

3. [A small Ottoman coin.—Trans.]

4. [Nonlegal rabbinic writings.—Trans.]

Translated by Olga Borovaya.

Moses Mendelssohn

Phaedon
1767

Following the example of Plato, I have Socrates in his last hours relate the arguments for the immortality of the human soul to his students. The dialogue of the Greek author, which has the name *Phaedo*, has a multitude of extraordinary beauties, which deserve to be used—the best of the doctrine of immortality. I took advantage of its form, ordering, and eloquence, and have only tried to adapt the metaphysical proofs to the taste of our time. In the *first dialogue* I could stay somewhat closer to my model. Various of my arguments seemed to require only a minor change of the style, and other arguments seemed to necessitate a development from their fundamentals, in order to attain the convincing power which the dialogue of Plato lacks for a modern reader.

The long and intense declamation against the human body and its needs, which Plato seems to have written more in the spirit of Pythagoras than of his teacher, had to be moderated extensively due to our improved conceptions of the value of this divine creature [the human body]; and nevertheless it will sound strange to many of today's readers. I confess, that I have kept this section simply to pay homage to the winning eloquence of Plato.

From then on I found it necessary to diverge from Plato totally. His proofs for the immateriality of the soul seem, at least to us, so shallow and capricious, that they scarcely deserve a serious refutation. Whether this is due to our better philosophical insight, or stems from our poor insight into the philosophical language of the ancients, I am not able to decide. I have chosen a proof for the immateriality of the soul in the *second dialogue*, which the students of Plato gave, and some modern philosophers adopted from them. It seemed to me not only convincing, but also easiest, to be expressed according to the Socratic method.

In the *third dialogue* I had to take my refuge completely in the moderns, and allow my Socrates almost to speak like a philosopher from the eighteenth century. I would rather commit an anachronism, than leave out arguments, which can contribute something to convince the reader.

In such a way the following mean between a translation and my own composition arose. Whether I have also produced something new, or merely stated in a different way that which is often said, others may decide. It is difficult, in a matter about which so many great minds have reflected, to be thoroughly original, and it is ridiculous to want to pretend to do so. If I would have cited authors, then the names *Plotinus, Descartes, Leibniz, Wolff, Baumgarten, Reimarus*, et al. would often appear. Then perhaps it would be more obvious to the reader what I have added from my own thinking. But to the mere amateur, it is irrelevant, if he owes an argument to this person or that person; and the scholar knows well to differentiate the "mine" and "thine" in such important matters. [...]

I have deemed it expedient to write an introduction on the character of Socrates, who is the main person in the dialogues, in order to refresh my reader's memory of this philosopher. [...]

At that time in Greece, as at all times with the rabble, the kind of teachers stood in great esteem, who endeavor to encourage deeply-rooted prejudices and out-of-date superstitions, through all kinds of pretexts and sophistries. They gave themselves the noble name of *Sophists*, which due to their behavior was transformed into a name of disgust. They took charge of the education of the youth, and taught the arts, sciences, moral philosophy and religion, in both public schools and private houses, with general acclaim. They knew that in democratic government assemblies, eloquence was treasured above all, that a free man would gladly listen to mere chatter about politics, and that the appetite for knowledge of shallow minds prefers to be satisfied through fables. Hence, they never failed to skillfully weave together dissembling rhetoric, false politics and absurd fables in their speeches, such that the people listened with amazement, and rewarded them with extravagance. They were on good terms with the priests; for they mutually adopted the wise maxim: *live and let live*. When the tyranny of the hypocrites was no longer able to hold the free spirit of men under its yoke, these seeming friends of truth were commissioned to lead man's spirit astray on the false path, to confuse their natural conceptions, and to nullify all distinctions between truth and falsehood, right and wrong, good and evil, through blinding sophistries. The main principle in their theory was: *Everything can be proved, and everything can be disproved*; and in practice, *one must derive as much advantage from the folly of others, and from his own superiority, as he can*. Of course, they kept this last maxim secret from the public, as one can easily imagine, and entrusted it only to their admirers, who partook of their trade. But the morality which they taught publicly was just as corrupting to the heart of men, as their politics were for the justice, freedom, and felicity of mankind.

Since they were artful enough to entangle their own interests with the prevailing religious system, not only were decisiveness and heroism necessary to put an end to their frauds—even a true friend of virtue might not dare it without the utmost caution. There is no religious system so corrupt, that it does not give to at least some of humanity's duties a certain sanctification which the humanist honors. When he doesn't want to act contrary to his own purpose, he must leave it untouched. From doubt in religious affairs, to carelessness; from neglect of *religious rites*, to the contempt of *all* worship generally; the transition tends to be very easy, especially for minds which are not subject to the rule of reason, and which are ruled by avarice, ambitiousness, or lust. The priests of superstition rely on this deception and take refuge in it all too often, as an inviolable shrine, whenever there is an attack on them.

Such difficulties and obstacles stood in Socrates' way as he made the momentous decision to disseminate virtue and wisdom among his fellow men. On the one hand, he had to conquer the prejudices of his own upbringing, to enlighten the ignorance of others, to battle the Sophists, to suffer the malice, vulgarity, defamation, and abuse of his enemies, to endure poverty, to combat established authority, and what was the most difficult, to thwart the dark horrors of superstition. On the other hand, the weak minds of his fellow citizens were to be taken care of, scandal was to be avoided, and the good influence, which even the most absurd religion had on the morals of the simple-minded, was not to be squandered. He overcame all these difficulties with the wisdom of a true philosopher, with the patience of a saint, with the unselfish virtue of a friend of humanity, with the resoluteness of a hero, at the expense and loss of all worldly goods and pleasures. He sacrificed health, power, comfort, reputation, peace, and finally, life itself, in the most loving way, for the welfare of his fellow man. So powerfully did the love of virtue and justice and the inviolability of the duties to the *Creator* and *Preserver* of things whom he knew by the pure light of reason in the most vivid manner, operate in him.

NOTE

Words in brackets appear in the original translation.

Translated by Patricia Noble.

David Friedländer

1750–1834

David Friedländer was born in Königsberg and settled in Berlin in 1771. There he fashioned himself as a disciple of Moses Mendelssohn and became an advocate for the emancipation of Prussian Jews. In an infamous open letter to Probst Teller of the Lutheran Church in Berlin, he asked if Jews could join the Lutheran Church on the condition that they did not have to believe in the divinity of Jesus, as a means of gaining civic equality. The plan failed. He aimed at educational reforms and founded the Jewish Free School in 1778. He translated works by Moses Mendelssohn, translated a prayer book from Hebrew to German, and wrote textbooks to be used in liberal Jewish schools.

Reader for Jewish Children
1779

Fables

THE WOLF AND THE ANIMALS

The Lion's Chancellor, the Wolf, was taken to court by all the animals, who complained that no living being was safe from his predatory jaws. "This insatiable creature," they charged, "makes the forest a desert, our wives widows, and our children orphans." The King was angry, and forbade the Wolf his cruelty with firm words: "The past cannot be changed," he declared in royal manner, "but from now on, you must shun all violence. Satisfy yourself with the dead animals you find in the fields. Should you lose control of yourself, then swear to me that you will eat no meat for two whole years as a penalty for every living animal that you kill."

The Wolf swore this oath and departed. A few days later, when he saw a fat sheep in the meadow, a terrible hunger overcame him. He fought with himself: "Two years without enjoying meat!—This penalty is harsh! And I have sworn to it.—However, in every year there are 365 days. Day is when I see, and night is when I do not see. So, every time I close my eyes, it is night, and when I open them again, it is day."—Quickly, he closed his eyes and opened them again; so, out of evening and morning, the first day was made. In this fashion, he counted off two full years. "Now," he said, "I have paid in advance for my sin," he seized the sheep, and killed it.

A predator easily finds the means to thwart even the strongest oath.

Moral Sayings and Proverbs from the Talmud

Honest regret avails more than one hundred accidents.

The death of a wise man often teaches more than his life.

Conviviality or death!

To remain silent suits the wise man: the fool even more.

The man dignifies the title, not the title the man.

A genial countenance is a sign of inner godliness

Cast no stone in the spring where you have quenched your thirst.

The host provides the wine; the cupbearer receives the thanks.

He who does too much, does too little.

Translated by Carola Murray-Seegert.

Other works by Friedländer: *Reden der Erbauung gebildeten Israeliten gewidmet* (1815); *Moses Mendelssohn: Fragmente von ihm und über ihn* (1819); *Über die Verbesserung der Israeliten im Königreich Polen* (1819).

Baruch ben Jacob (Baruch of Shklov) Schick
1744–1808

Baruch ben Jacob (Barukh ben Ya'akov) Schick was a rabbinic judge and science scholar who settled in Minsk in 1760. Encouraged by the Vilna Gaon, who advocated the study of sciences as a tool for understanding the Torah, Schick translated Euclid's *Elements* into Hebrew. He also wrote texts on anatomy, preventive medicine, and mathematics, in the earlier part of his life drawing on sources from the Zohar. Schick was initially supported by Naftali Herts Wessely and other leaders of the Haskalah; later, they disparaged Schick for his uneven scholarship.

Introduction to Euclid
1780

The Gentiles abuse us and say that we are a foolish nation, not a wise one. They consequently slander the words of our sages, and say that whoever studies them becomes divorced from the norms of civility and from nature [*yibadel mi-ḥok ha-medini ve-teva 'olam*]. [. . .]

Such was not the way of our sages. No mystery, discipline, or science eluded them. This is evident from many statements in the Talmud, made in just a few words. Such as the statement in tractate *Berahot* [58b], "If comets passed through the galaxy of Orion, the world would be destroyed"; and the magnifying glass of Rabbi Gamliel [Eruvin 43b]; and all the matters of animal wounds (*trefot*) in which they were highly expert, such as the wound which, "if salves are applied, [the animal] will survive" [Hulin 54a], as opposed to those wounds which it would not survive.

NOTE

Words in brackets appear in the original translation.

Translated by David Fishman.

Other works by Schick: *Amude ha-shamayim* (1776); *Tiferet adam* (1777); *Keneh ha-midah* (1783).

Naphtali Herts Wessely

Words of Peace and Truth
1782

There is one people in the world alone who are not sufficiently concerned with "human knowledge" and who have neglected the public instruction of their youth in the laws of etiquette, the sciences and the arts. We, the children of Israel, who are dispersed throughout all of Europe and who live in most of its states, have turned our backs on these studies. Those among us who dwell in Germany and Poland have been especially negligent in this regard. Many among them are men of intelligence and great understanding, and many are also men of faith and piety, but from childhood their exclusive preoccupation has been God's laws and teachings. They have not heard of or studied "human knowledge." They are ignorant even of the grammar of the holy tongue, and they do not discern the beauty of its diction, the rules of its syntax and the purity of its style—which are wells from which spring wisdom and moral instruction. It goes without saying that they lack proper knowledge of the language of the peoples among whom they live. Many of them do not even know how to read or write the native language. Knowledge of the structure of the earth and the events of history are hidden from them, as are matters of civility, the sciences and the arts. They do not know or understand, for from the start nothing of all this was told to them, neither by their fathers nor by their teachers, who themselves were ignorant of these subjects. Even the fundamental principles of their faith were not taught systematically, so that all the youth might become conversant with them in an orderly fashion. Similarly, our youth were not taught ethics and psychology. Only some of the more outstanding students of God's Torah as they grew older perceived deficiency in matters of "human knowledge," and accordingly endeavoured to correct the fault committed by their teachers by gleaning knowledge either from books or from conversation, "here a little, there a little," but, alas, unsystematically and ineffectively. Their knowledge is like a lightweight coat on a cold day. Indeed, a clear knowledge in these subjects is not found except among individuals whose hearts and spirits moved them to listen to wisdom and pay heed to reason. They learned languages and read books with understanding and thus became like a fountain which replenishes and augments itself. They acquired this knowledge unassisted by their fathers and their superiors. They were driven solely by their love of truth. Such superior men, however, are few.

Translated by Y. S. Weinstein and S. Fischer.

Moses Mendelssohn

Light for the Path
1783

We, the entire assembly of the congregation of Israel, believe that the Torah that is in our possession today is exactly the same as was written by Moses our master, peace be on him. From then until now nothing in it has changed: it has been spared what befalls secular books, which scribes and copyists change over time through addition, subtraction, or alteration, sometimes accidentally because of laziness, and sometimes intentionally in their desire to correct the words of the author, with the result that after a time the true reading of the text is completely forgotten, and the book is reformulated. God who is faithful to His covenant promised us otherwise, as it is said: "It will never be forgotten from the mouth of His seed" (Deuteronomy 31:21). He repeated this promise through His holy prophets, saying, "this is my covenant with them, said the Eternal. My spirit that is on you, and my words that I have placed in your mouth, shall not depart from your mouths, nor from the mouths of your seed, nor from the mouths of your seed's seed, said the Eternal, from now and forever" (Isaiah 59:21). [. . .]

All languages differ from one another with respect to rhetorical style, and each one possesses unique qualities absent from the others. Therefore, if you translate a statement word for word into another language, there will be times when an individual who has mastered that language will completely fail to understand [what you produce]. And even if he might comprehend the basic intention, he will not sense the rhetorical pleasantness and graceful arrangement as they appear in the original language. [. . .]

You see, then, that the faithful translator must sometimes change a statement by adding to it, subtracting from it, or altering its order to make the speaker's intention understood. There is no one who contributes more to destroying and ruining that intention than an individual who preserves the words, translating word by word, even though, at first glance, he seems to be the most faithful [translator] and the most skilled at his art. For this reason, the sages, may their memories be for a blessing, condemned in many places the one who explains the verse "according to its form" [Babylonian Talmud, Kiddushin 49a; Tosefta, Megillah 3:41]. This refers to one who preserves the words by translating or elucidating [a text] word for word without making any changes or adjustments at all, even where linguistic usage makes it necessary to abandon the words in order to preserve the sense. Such a translator is called "a liar." For although he seems to be a faithful translator because he does not omit any word that he fails to translate, he deceives, since by means of such an approach the content is lost and the intended meaning is confused. Thus, the rabbis, may their memories be for a blessing, said in the second chapter of the tractate Kiddushin, as well as at the end of the Tosefta Megillah: "everyone who translates a verse according to its form is a liar" [ibid.].

As long as the children of Israel did not change their language, and as long as the multitude, young and old alike, was well-versed and fluent in the language of the land of beauty [that is, Hebrew], they did not need a translation of the Torah. Each person hearing the Torah recited by a reader who was precise in his vocalization, melody, and accents would understand the statement's intended meaning on his own according to its *peshat*, since he would have been accustomed to using similar expressions, sounds, and accents in all of his affairs and needs. And in a place where he did not comprehend the intended meaning of a verse, he would require an elucidation, which is an interpretation of the matter by means of different expressions in the holy language itself, rather than a translation into a foreign language. [. . .]

From then until now, no one has taken it on himself to fix the crooked and translate the holy Torah into the language that is proper, standard, and customary in our generation. Youths among the children of Israel who desire to grasp words of wisdom wander about, seeking the word of the Eternal from the translations of Christian scholars. For in every generation, Christians translate the Torah into their vernaculars according to the needs of the time, the requirements of proper language, and rhetorical pleasantness. Sometimes focusing on the words and sometimes focusing on the intended meaning, sometimes [by proceeding] word for word and sometimes by embellishing and adding an elucidation, they translate so that they do not lack an elixir for quenching the thirst of students, in accordance with the desire and need of each individual.

However, this path, which many members of our nation have followed, is lined with traps and stumbling blocks for those liable to slip, and great evil emerges from it. Since the Christian translators neither possess the rabbinic tradition, nor heed the words of the *Masorah*, nor even accept the vowels and accents that we possess, they treat the words of the Torah as a broken wall, before which each individual rises and which each individual treats as he desires. They add to, subtract from, and alter the Eternal's Torah, [changing] not only the vowels and accents, but sometimes even the letters and words (for who will restrain them?), according to their fancies and comprehension. By means of this, they sometimes read what occurs to their own minds, rather than what is written in the Torah.

However, I do not condemn these scholars for this, for what compels them to heed the tradition that they have not received from their ancestors, or the *Masorah* that has not been transmitted to them by individuals whom they deem trustworthy? Furthermore, they do not accept the words of the Torah in order to observe and perform all that is written there, but rather as a book of chronicles, to know the events of ancient times and to understand the ways of divine providence and governance in every generation. For these purposes, it does no harm if they sometimes alter details by adding or subtracting letters or words, just as they do with famous, well-known secular books, which every editor changes according to his wishes.

However, if this is possible for Christian scholars and their students, it is not possible for us, the house of Israel. For us, this Torah is an inheritance not only for the purposes mentioned above, but rather to know what the Eternal our God has commanded us to study, teach, observe, and perform: it is our life and the length of our days. In order that our lives not hang by the hairbreadth of reasoning and by the thread of reflection alone, our sages, may their memories be for a blessing, established the *Masorah* for us and set up a fence around the Torah, the commandment, the decree, and the law so that we would not grope like blind men in the dark. Consequently, we must neither move from their paved path nor weigh a path of life without proper scales and balances, based on the reasoning and conjecture of a grammarian or editor. We do not live from the mouth of such an individual, but rather according to what the Masoretes, whom we deem trustworthy, transmitted to us: so will it be and so will it be established. We will understand and give sense to scripture according to them; we will investigate and come to know what is written there, sometimes according to its *peshat* and sometimes according to the homilies of the sages, may their memories be for a blessing. For they are both correct, as I will elucidate later with the help of the Eternal.

When the Eternal graced me with male children and the time came to teach them Torah and instruct them in the words of the living God, in accordance with what is written, I began to translate the five books of the Torah into the polished, proper German that is customary in our times for the benefit of these young children. I provided them with the translation together with instruction in scripture, sometimes word by word and sometimes according to the intended meaning and context, in order to educate them in the intended meaning of scripture, the rhetoric of the language, and the purity of its lessons, so that they might grow up and understand it on their own. And behold, the Eternal sent me our teacher, the master Rabbi Solomon from Dubno, may his lamp be bright, to instruct the only son who then remained with me (may God strengthen his heart for His worship and reverence!) in the science of [Hebrew] grammar for one hour each day. When the aforementioned master saw my translation of the Torah, it found favor in his eyes and seemed proper to him, and he asked my permission to publish it for the benefit of the students to whom God had imparted an understanding of parables and rhetoric. I agreed, but on the condition that he would take care to comment on every instance in which I determined my translation according to one of the earlier exegetes or turned aside from all of their opinions, choosing for myself a different path that I thought fit with linguistic usage, the context of the matter, or the placement of the accents and their principles. He would inquire into and investigate all of this, discuss it with me, and write it up so as to elucidate the biblical writings in simple language, easily comprehensible to every reader. I also faithfully promised to aid him in composing and writing this elucidation, as far as I was able.

NOTE

Words in brackets appear in the original translation.

Translated by Elias Sacks.

Benedetto Frizzi
1756–1844

A physician and analytical scholar who published prolifically on a variety of topics from law, to medicine, to music, Benedetto Frizzi (Benzion Raphael Kohen) championed and critiqued Jewish life in Italy. Born in Ostiano, he was the first Jew to attend the local Jesuit public school. After receiving his medical degree in Pavia, he opened a practice in Trieste. It was there that he wrote *Difesa* in response to antisemitic attacks in Giovanni Battista d'Arco's writing. In 1790, Frizzi founded the first medical journal in Italy. His works on Jewish history, rabbinical practice, and Talmudic scholarship sought to arouse respect for the Torah while advocating modernization within the Jewish community.

Defense against the Attacks Leveled against the Jewish Nation in the Book Entitled On the Ghetto's Influence on the State
1784

Chapter IV. Demonstrates the Falsehood of the Alleged Evil Influence of Jews on the State, as Businessmen in Villages, and Also Shows Their Usefulness in the Points Omitted by the Refuted Writer as Well as Those to Which He Alludes

How can it be affirmed that the Jews live in villages without practicing professions or trades? As I indicated in chapter II, there are no professions or trades, either manual and liberal, that they do not practice. In every town in Italy doctors, lawyers, masters of various sciences, painters, musicians, tailors, carpenters, and teachers of every kind of craft abound. More abound in many islands of the archipelago, but we mention this as a passing comment as these are maritime cities, especially in the case of Corfu, where the famous Doctor Giuseppe Coen, who was named a military physician of the Most Serene Republic of Venice, lives in a fortress like every other person of the military profession. Many Jews still practice goldsmithery and every other art. In Germany and Poland, especially, there are many goldsmiths and tailors, and many work in agriculture. How many Jewish teachers are there, not only in France, Holland, and England but also in every other part of the universe? We have seen a Portuguese Jewish general and Jewish ambassadors to the kingdom of Fez and Morocco (CAM. Reg. Marocc. descriptio., p. 308, 341). In Ethiopia and Abyssinia, an Arab assured Signor Lodolfo that at the court there were some 60,000 of them (Lettre ou reflexions d'un minor, p. 63). Cardinal Commendoni (p. 64) relates that there were Jewish astronomers and doctors, even customs officers and warlords.

There is, then, a third source of constant and important profit, which is testimony to the influence of Jews in the state and which takes away the paradox of their subsistence. In this way, the malevolent consequences disappear when one speaks about their industriousness, which is called deceptive while in reality it is necessary.

Translated by James N. Novoa.

Other works by Frizzi: *Dissertazione di polizia medica sul Pentateuco in riguardo alle leggi e stato del matrimonio* (1788); *Dissertazione divisa in lettere sulla portata dei musicali stromenti con matematiche analoghe riflessioni* (1802); *Dissertazione di biografia musicale* (1805); *Petaḥ enayim*, 3 vols. (1815–1825).

Moses Mendelssohn

Letter to the Friends of Lessing (On the Spinoza Conversations between Lessing and Jacobi)
1786

Our friend's devotion to Spinozism is not to be seen as a mere hypothesis (as the Patriarch in *Nathan* puts it), postulated simply in order to discuss its pros and cons. Herr Jacobi, a man of established reputation in the Republic of Scholars, takes a public stand and asserts as fact: *Lessing was in effect and in actuality a Spinozist*. Proofs of this are supposedly to be found in correspondence between him, a third person, and myself, which, laid before the public in a court of inquisition, is to establish that fact beyond all shadow of doubt.

Indeed, this correspondence was the immediate occasion for me to publish, sooner than I intended, my *Morgenstunden or Lectures on the Existence of God* which I had outlined a few years ago. I made mention of that occasion in the Preface to the first Part of the *Morgenstunden*; not until the second Part was the correspondence to be made known. To be sure, it had been my original intent to initiate the philosophical debate immediately, and I even received permission from Herr Jacobi to make any use I wished of his letter. Yet so many considerations had to be taken into account. The substance of the issue appeared too delicate to me, the readers too unprepared, for me to introduce such a controversial investigation without preliminaries. I wished first to clarify the *issue* itself and only then to touch upon what concerns the *persons* involved; to reveal at the very start my concepts of Spinozism, of the noxious and innocuous qualities of this system, and subsequently to consider whether the one or the other person might be an adherent of that system, and in what sense they might have understood it.

All such questions as: Was Lessing a Spinozist? Did Jacobi hear the same from Lessing himself? What precisely was their state of mind when that confidence passed between them? All such questions could be put aside until we and the reader have come to an agreement on the issue as such, what, in fact, Spinozism is or is not. Hence I changed my original plan and decided to wait until the next Part to avail myself of the kind permission of my correspondent. Except that, as I now see, he has seen fit to steal a march on me. Casting all scruples aside, he throws down a bone of contention amongst the public, and for all posterity he brands as a Spinozist, an atheist, and a blasphemer our friend, *Gotthold Ephraim Lessing*, Lessing—the *editor of the Fragments, the author of Nathan*, that great and respected champion of theism and of the religion of reason. What is one to do now? Surely we ought to take up the defence of our friend? The most rigourous religious tribunal is not wont to begrudge even an indicted heretic such assistance. But I should think that we might perfectly well leave the author of *Nathan* to his own defence; even if I were a Plato or a Xenophon I would never have the temerity to make a speech in defence of *this* Socrates. *Lessing*, a *hypocrite*; the *author of Nathan*, a *blasphemer*; one would be thinking the impossible if one were to combine such contradictions; one could just as easily imagine *Lessing* and *blockhead* to be one and the same! For the present, since I am after all involved in the issue and Herr Jacobi is challenging me—first in personal letters and now in public—to take on our friend's cause, let us, dear reader, examine in concert the basis for the accusation. I shall go through the indictment before your very eyes, adding to the narrative what is to be added from my side, and supplying glosses wherever I deem the like to be necessary.

As Herr Jacobi tells it, he had heard from a friend [= Elise R.] that Mendelssohn was on the point of writing about Lessing's character; he enquired to what extent Lessing's religious views were known to Mendelssohn and added: *Lessing was a Spinozist*.

"My friend Elise," he said, "understood the point perfectly well; the matter seemed to her to be of extreme importance and she wrote Mendelssohn post haste in order to let him know what I had just disclosed to her."

"Mendelssohn," he continued, "was astonished, and his first reaction was to doubt the accuracy of my assertion."

The news of my astonishment is in no way a narrating of the facts but rather a supposition on the part of the narrator [= Jacobi]. What Herr Jacobi disclosed to our mutual friend, and what she in due course passed on to me, could not possibly have given rise to any such reaction on my part. My conviction as to the untruth of Spinozism can absolutely not be shaken, neither by Lessing's repute nor by that of any other mortal; neither could this report have the least effect on my friendship with Lessing; nor, by the same token, could my opinion of Lessing's genius and character be the lesser because of it. *Lessing, a follower of Spinoza?* Good Lord! What have a person's speculative views to do with the person himself? Who would not be delighted to have had Spinoza as friend, no matter how great his Spinozism? And who would refuse to give Spinoza's genius and excellent character their due?

As long as my friend still was not accused of being a secret blasphemer and a hypocrite to boot, the news of his being a Spinozist was a matter of complete indifference to me. I knew that there is also a refined Spinozism which rhymes very well with all that is practical in religion and morality, as demonstrated at length in my *Morgenstunden*; I knew that, in the main, this refined Spinozism can be easily reconciled with Judaism, and that Spinoza, irrespective of his speculative doctrine, could have remained an orthodox Jew were it not that in other writings he had called genuine Judaism into question and in so doing stepped outside the Law. Obviously Spinoza's doctrine would come much closer to Judaism than does the orthodox doctrine of the Christians. If I was able indeed to love Lessing and be loved in return where he was still a strict follower of Athanasius (or was at least considered so by me), then why not all the more where he approximated Judaism, and where I saw in him an adherent of the Jew, *Baruch Spinoza?* The label of Jew and Spinozist could be for me in no way so startling or so grating as it would seem to be for Herr Jacobi.

Finally, I had already been aware that in his earliest youth our friend had inclined to pantheism; and I knew that not only was he able to harmonize it with his religious system, but that he even sought, by means of it, to prove the Athanasian creed. A passage from a very early essay by this precocious writer, which I quote in the *Morgenstunden*, demonstrates this most clearly, and it was at the very outset of our acquaintance that he had given it to me for my perusal.

The news that Lessing was a Spinozist could in consequence neither astonish nor alienate me. But Jacobi's assertion I found most offensive; that, I must confess. After all, I had never made Herr Jacobi's acquaintance. I knew of his merits as a writer; but I had never read anything by him in the field of metaphysics. Neither did I know that he had enjoyed Lessing's friendship and personal company. Hence I took the report to be purely anecdotal, something which a visiting traveller might possibly have passed on to him. Everyone is familiar with this species of traveller in Germany, who totes an autograph album along from town to town, breathlessly retelling everywhere whatever they see of or ferret out from a man of merit, even hastening with it to the public press. Perhaps, I thought, someone like that picked up some garbled word of Lessing's or Lessing had written in his album the Greek motto: ONE AND ALL, and in a trice the monger of anecdotes made Lessing into a Spinozist. At the same time, I could well see that the intent was to convict Lessing without a hearing. The Germans have become accustomed, by studying natural history, to classifying everything. If they are at a loss as to what to make of someone's views and writings, they take the first opportunity to subsume him under a classification, making him into an "-ist," as though that settled the matter. Since I was in fact preparing to write about Lessing's character, I saw very well that this anecdote would carry me far off course, that it required discussions and investigations for which I had no heart, and that it would lead me astray into thorny subtleties and force me to rekindle a debate that should have been over long ago. Most unwelcome, then, this statement of Herr Jacobi's, and I pressed him for further clarification: how had Lessing demonstrated his Spinozism? on what occasion? with what words? The questions I put to Herr Jacobi are couched in terms somewhat too aggressive, but they are certainly appropriate to the issue; they were not said out of undue sensitivity on my part.

I received that added clarification I had requested—and in full measure. An epistle from Herr Jacobi addressed to me made it abundantly clear that I had not taken the true measure of my man; that Jacobi had penetrated the subtleties of the Spinozist doctrine more deeply than I had assumed; that he really had enjoyed Lessing's personal company; that he frequently had engaged him in intimate conversations, and that, finally, the news of Lessing's devotion to Spinoza was not to be seen as a mere retailing of anecdote but as the sum total of those same intimate conversations.

Anyone who knows such intimate conversations, anyone who has ever had the good fortune to enjoy them, would never question the sincerity and integrity of the conclusions reached in them. Within the sanctuary of friendship it is not simply a matter of mind opening itself to mind, but of heart to heart, disclosing its innermost secret folds and recesses. Friend unveils to friend all his most secret doubts, weaknesses, shortcomings, and flaws, that a kindly hand may touch, perhaps even heal them. Anyone who never tasted the bliss of such an hour of the heart's outpouring has never really known joy. But think for a moment of poor Rousseau when he, yearning with all his heart for that soul's balm, comes up instead against a granite-like soul that rejects him with all its strength!

Had this been the nature of the conversations Jacobi conducted with Lessing, then we would certainly have nothing to propose to exculpate our friend; we would have to accept the fact that Lessing was the most enigmatic character who ever lived, a peculiar combination of duplicity and arrogance; on the one hand, inflexibly close-mouthed; on the other, open to the point of childish frivolity. But if this were so, I should be sincerely sorry: for myself, for my friend Lessing, and for Herr Jacobi as well.

—*For myself*: I must confess, it would humble me greatly, had our friend Lessing deemed me, who so loved him and was so loved by him, to be unworthy of the confidence that another mortal was able to gain on such short acquaintance, and this after I had lived with him in intimate friendship for over thirty years, had unceasingly sought with him the truth, had conversed with him repeatedly, by letter and face to face, on those important matters. I confess my frailty. There is no creature on earth I would not begrudge such preferment.

—*For my friend Lessing*: how he must have been failing those last days of his life, if he did say in complete and heart-felt confidence all that he is reported to have said in that conversation. In that conversation he does not appear as the bold, resolute thinker who follows his reason and by that reason is led astray; there, he is a shallow-minded atheist, not a disciple of a Hobbes or a Spinoza but of some childish jokester who takes pleasure in booting aside anything his fellow man holds important and dear.

To be sure, Herr Jacobi admits to having abbreviated and summarized the conversations. Nevertheless, his well-known rectitude should permit us to assume that the chiefest point at issue has not suffered in the process, and that he has attributed to each person what each actually did. But in all that Lessing proposes there, not one single solitary thought can be found that is sane. All the reasonable arguments redound to Herr Jacobi's credit. He defends Spinozism with all the cleverness the system allows. Lessing does not offer even the slightest counter-proposition of any import; he accepts as correct and persuasive the very arguments the two of us had so often reflected upon in past conversations and had judged on their true merits; only from time to time does he interrupt his friend with an eccentric idea that as often as not is tantamount to blasphemy. Could Lessing, in a sincere, intimate outpouring of his heart, forget himself to such a degree?

And then to top it all: Lessing's evaluation of the *Prometheus* poem which Jacobi put in his hands, and was able to do so only because of the boldness of its content, certainly not because of any excellence in it; and Lessing found it so good! Thou wretched judge of art! how low must you have fallen that you find this paltry thing in earnest good! On his better days, I frequently saw him hand back to some poet much more acceptable verses, saying: "Not bad, my friend, not bad! but why in verses? Why don't you first see whether you would like these ideas in prose!" Herr Jacobi was reluctant to include those verses in his book without a disclaiming device: he enclosed a blank and blameless piece of paper which readers of tender conscience could insert between the pages in lieu of the corrupting verses. As I knew him, Lessing would have found the admonition more harmful than the poison. Anyone who can lose his religion because of bad verse surely has little to lose. In a word: if the dialogue is supposed to represent serious, intimate confidence, then I fail totally to discern the stamp of Lessing's character in anything he contributes; I miss his acumen, I miss his humour, I miss his philosophy, and I miss his critical sense.

NOTE

Words in brackets appear in the original translation.

Translated by G. Vallée, J. B. Lawson, and C. G. Chapple.

Jean-Pierre-Antoine Tassaert, *Bust of Moses Mendelsson*, 1785.

Benedetto Frizzi

Dissertation on Medical Policy Concerning Certain Foods Which Are Prohibited in the Pentateuch
1787-1790

All nations have been subject, in their authors, as in all other things, to significant important changes. Inclinations, needs, and the relations of their subjects change, as do the passions of the great. On account of this, even the pens of those who write must also change. In general, these serve to foment pride, to praise or combat the virtues or the vices of the people. Only the Jewish nation has always conserved the sole pleasure of writing, in the infinite number of its authors, from Maimonides to our day. Its only object, not to say the principal one, has been to illustrate the sacred scriptures, the Talmud and their commentators. But their observations were made from another point of view than that of philosophy based on reason. The captivity of this nation, its dedication to commerce, the uncertainty of its products, the scarce cultivation of true science, and a strange blindness on account of all of this, which began in antiquity, have made it always follow the paths of its predecessors in every century, without instituting an analysis of its laws or its customs.

Many of their writers have studied, yet they struggle to understand the value of the words of those who have already written a few of those items. Many read to write, but few dedicate themselves to topics that are more useful, to contributing to shaking up the spirit of the nation or to rendering it more advantageous to society.

The custom of writing in the Hebrew language is also an obstacle to advancement in all that is new. It is poor due to its antiquity, and this detriment could be easily corrected if people from outside the nation could have some influence on it; yet it remains in darkness because so few people understand the language.

The translation into Hebrew of the works of the most cultivated nations is not loved unless we count those of Avicenna and Averroes and other Arabic doctors, whose works were translated some time ago; the odd work by Ovid which has been translated by Marini of Padua; and those of Metastasio by the celebrated Luzatto of London. And yet the first steps toward literature among the most illuminated nations are through translations. The cultivated peoples are like elephants that require the example of the mother or nurse to follow, so that in progress their actions are spontaneous and their own. After observing all of this I conceived of a completely new plan for a work which was to be useful for the literary world in general and especially to my nation.

Inspired by the great example of my venerable master and predecessor, the illustrious Johann Peter Frank, who, with profound and vast erudition wrote a treatise on medical policy regarding the well-being of every nation, I took it upon myself to write about that which the Jewish people must do.

The incomparable Pietro Moscati of Milan, a royal professor and director of that great hospital, contributed to my courage and, after having written almost everything in Latin that could have to do with the healthiness of food, I induced myself to speak about everything else concerning the well-being of my nation in its own language, in a more universal manner. There will be two parts to my work: the carrying out of the Law of Moses based on the spirit of a legislative doctor, and the correction or approval of many contemporary customs introduced by rabbis or their use by Jews in relation to medical policy.

I will deal with pregnancy, childbirth, and midwives and all matters concerning infancy through puberty. Because a principal problem of my nation in this period is the education of its children, I will examine many aspects, combining the medical and philosophical spirit that, I believe, should always go hand in hand. I will examine the incomparable Mosaic legislation with regard to food and practices, priestly formalities, the marital state, cleanliness of houses, clothing, and the air, and of the dead. Afterward, the ailments named in the sacred scriptures will be dealt with, and all of this will lead to the perfection of a similar analysis.

I have not cited the importance of superstitions and systems, and I have followed, whenever possible, the voice of true philosophy. I have taken it upon myself to indicate sources and to point out the paragraphs that have guided me; however, I have presented these in the notes, thus simplifying the text.

Translated by James N. Novoa.

Naphtali Herts Wessely

Sefer ha-midot (Book of Virtues)
ca. 1780s

Noble-mindedness is a very fine character trait in the soul of man, and it extends in many directions: primarily in three, which are, noble-mindedness in wisdom, noble-mindedness in power, and noble-mindedness in wealth. The concept of noble-mindedness may be understood as follows: one who possesses one of these three fine traits, or two of them, or all three, or just one of their particular elements, and whose soul is desirous of assisting individuals other than himself, or the community as a whole, by making practical use of these, without seeking reward or monetary gain, or without obtaining honor from other human beings for what he has done save through just means; one who perceives that it is befitting and proper to act in this way, and appreciates that happy is the man who has the merit of helping and shielding the Almighty's creatures, or of performing a good deed desired by God—such a one may be described as noble-minded. Now the nobility of wisdom consists of acquiring other men's souls by the words of one's mouth, so as to bring them close to the Torah and to teach them knowledge and the ways of uprightness, to save their souls from destruction; and in similar vein, we find this in connection with those who gave instruction to the craftsmen in all the wisdom pertaining to the requisite practical skills employed when they were engaged in the sacred labor—i.e., in the construction of God's eternal temple—as it states in scripture: "For every willing man that has skill" (I Chronicles 28:21). Nobility in power consists of assisting others through one's strength and might—namely, one who will put his life at risk in fighting the battles of the Almighty on behalf of his people and on behalf of the cities of his God; and hence it is written in the Song of Deborah, concerning those men whose noble-minded spirit inspired them to do battle against Sisera and his camp: "They who offered themselves willingly among the people: bless the Lord!" (Judges 5:9). Nobility in regard to wealth consists of assisting others, or of donating to a good cause, from one's wealth and one's possessions, as scripture states in connection with the construction of the tabernacle: "Whosoever is of a willing heart, let him bring it," etc.,—"gold and silver and brass" (Exodus 35:5). Accordingly, the general principle is: any deed of substance that a person carries out, which he is not obliged to perform, and which many other people's natural disposition would lead them to shrink from performing—and he nonetheless performs it without hankering after any of the benefits which the inclination within a man's heart covets—such an individual may justly be described as noble-minded.

Translated by David E. Cohen.

Saul Ascher
1767–1822

Born Saul ben Anschel Jaffe in Berlin, Saul Ascher was an author, translator, editor, publisher, and philosopher. He sought social and civil reform for Jews, and fought against antisemitism; one of his works was burned in 1817 at a festival in Wartburg. Ascher was connected to other Haskalah figures, such as Solomon Maimon and Eduard Gans, and in secular thinking he followed the philosophy of Kant, vociferously rejecting the ideas of Fichte. Ascher's *Leviathan, oder über Religion in Rücksicht des Judentums* argues that Judaism's uniqueness comes from Maimonides' Thirteen Articles of Faith rather than from ritual commandments.

Leviathan
1792

Book II, Chapter 1: The Purpose of Judaism

Having laid out for the reader my thoughts about religion, revelation, and faith/belief, their manifold aim and their various components, I now consider myself competent to apply all this to Judaism.

First, I pose this question: What is the real purpose of Judaism? We view Judaism as something [of the] divine. According to His great plan, the creator inserted the seed of Judaism into the course of things, to break forth when opportune, blossom and remain standing in all its brilliance. Judaism was a vessel for the blessedness which God prepared for a portion of His creatures, while He created other vessels with other forms for other creatures. / Let us consider Judaism as a higher means provided by the creator to a human society, in order for it to partake in blessedness. We perceive that the human being already has enough inherent talent, in and for itself, for bringing happiness to the world. Accordingly, the primary intention of the creator with these higher means must have been to acquaint this human society with a level of blessedness, achievable only after a major revolution of its talents.

The unfathomable activities of the Highest for advancing His creatures in blessedness are as different as [the various] vessels for blessedness are according to climates and territories across the horizon. We can therefore assert that Judaism, above all, is given in a region where the main intent and ground principle of Judaism could contribute the most to the blessedness of [all] human beings. / Human beings were universally created according to a basic principle of blessedness. They deviate one from another only in terms of the form of blessedness, as conditioned by the climate. The creator had to select a form for the Jews which was appropriate in terms of climate-conditioned nature, to lead them to a path on which they found a level of blessedness—one which He showed to other people through His unfathomable decisions in other ways. / I can therefore find the real purpose of Judaism only in this: Judaism should be a means of making those human beings to whom it was designated live up to their spiritual talents, and as receptive as possible to the happiness of society. [. . .]

But our form of faith/belief must be displayed plainly and openly, like the book of nature before the world and future generations. No one should blame us for misusing faith/belief. Let us bring the witness to faith/belief forward.

1. I believe in one God.
2. In one single God who revealed Himself to our forefathers Abraham, Isaac and Jacob and promised them our salvation.
3. Who chose for Himself Moses and other men who pleased Him and bestowed upon them the gift of prophecy.
4. Who gave laws to our forefathers on Mt. Sinai.
5. We believe that the observance of the laws was holy to our forefathers. This kept them upon that path which we now walk upon with open faith/belief in God and His prophets.
6. We believe that this God is a God of love.
7. He will reward the good and punish the evil.
8. He governs the world through His foresight and omnipotence.
9. He will also direct our misfortunes towards the good.
10. We hope in redemption through His messiah in this life, and in our grave with those whom He will respectfully dignify at the resurrection.
11. We obligate ourselves to keep the covenant which the Eternal concluded with our fathers, through circumcision.
12. To celebrate the Sabbath as a day holy to God.
13. To renew the memory of His good deeds through festivals.
14. And implore grace and purification from Him, through atonement.

This is the *organon* of Judaism, and there is no other. [. . .]

To take the constitution of religion for its essence, for its function, engenders all sorts of harm, separating us away from all societies, hindering us from choosing professions in them, inducing us ultimately to concentrate all active powers upon a single point. Precisely because of this, religion itself became a motive to fixate our mind/spirit on a point about which we had more talent for speculation than for solid thinking according to principles. Withdrawn away from any acquaintance with humanity's progress in the arts and scientific studies, we slumbered dreamily.

Humanity let us sleep for a long time and meander around in our idealistic world. I do not know what good genius encouraged a Maimonides to bring Judaism back to sure principles. I do not know what evil genius let a Spinoza desert and transform Judaism into a nothing. I do not know what indifferent genius led a Mendelssohn to want to overcome his opponents, only to be overwhelmed himself. / This I do know: That I have these three men to thank for motivating me to take a step which is perhaps contrary to the entire direction of the human mind/spirit of our times. I therefore had to ascend to the exalted sources and descend again from there.

NOTE

Words in brackets appear in the original translation.

Translated by Gershon Greenberg.

Other works by Ascher: *Bemerkungen ueber die buergerliche verbesserung der Juden, veranlasst durch die Frage: Soll der Jude Soldat werden* (1788); *Eisenmenger der Zweite* (1794); *Die Germanomanie* (1815).

Solomon Maimon

Givat ha-moreh [Commentary to Maimonides' Moreh nevukhim, Guide for the Perplexed]
1792

The *telos* (*takhlit*) of man's activities, in the aspect (*behinah*) of having will and choice, is the ultimate human good (*ha'hatslahah ha'enoshi'it*). This excellence necessarily comes after the attainment of perfection. It is thus proper for us to research: What is the nature (*inyan*) of attaining this perfection? What are the means for possibly reaching (*nagia*) it? Let us say: The perfection of anything which exists consists of emerging from potentiality to actuality. The tree's perfection, for example, is that of bearing fruit. Man's perfection is intellection (*haskalah*). So it is in similar cases. In this respect, man is far from all the animals outside of himself. Each special (*me'yuhad*) species of animal has its necessarily special activity, in terms of its being of that respective species. Thus, the chameleon's perfection is digging into the earth; the spider's is weaving, etc. Moreover, the perfection of all the respective species of animals is not acquired through education and adaptation. Rather, the perfection exists (*nimtsah*) in each species with the onset of its being. It is also impossible for us to rob it of that activity which is special to it, or that it will acquire another [special] activity through education and adaptation.

This is not so for man. No special activity is imprinted upon him with the onset of his being (*heyoto*). Rather, he is prepared (*mukhan*) by nature for many and various activities. These are only potentially inherent to him at the onset of his being. They emerge gradually into actuality when causes challenge him. In addition, man's perfection is acquired by him through education and adaptation. Perfection is not imprinted upon him, as is the case with other living beings. We find that man's being is naturally prepared to acquire many kinds of perfection. Or, the being of man possesses many potentials (all disposition to perfection is called potential)—for example, the potential for feeling, for imagination, for memory, for understanding (*Verstand*), and so forth. Besides, it is proper for man [qua man] to direct all his aims towards actualizing all these respective potentials. This requires making efforts within various disciplines. While all the respective potentials extend to any sort of discipline, we will also apply the special sort of discipline to the potential special to it. As law is an allocation of activities (*Verteilung der Geschäfte*), it is also the foundation of the special discipline of politics. That is, it cannot be assumed that each member of the state satisfies his needs by himself—that he prepares his own food, weaves his clothing, and builds his house, etc. Rather, it is necessary for each and every one to specialize in one special activity.

From this ensues the perfection of each respective occupation. Each special man is prepared by nature for a special occupation. By concentrating on one occupation, it is possible for him to reach a great degree of perfection at it—something which is otherwise impossible. The single man, by himself, is analogous to a small town, where each special potential needs to become a special actuality. Then it is possible for him to reach a great degree of the [respective] perfection. For example, the potential of imagination needs to be special to the occupation of drawing or to [composing] a melody, etc. Reason (*tevunah, Vernunft*) needs to be special to logic. Intellect (*sekhel, Verstand*) combined with reason needs to be special to geometry and general philosophy. Man should not want to philosophize with imaginary drawings, or analyze the delight of the melody with his intellect. [. . .]

The venerable book, as its name indicates, is a *Guide to the Perplexed*. It includes principles of the discipline of metaphysics and its primary doctrines. This is followed by proofs (*perakim mofti'im*) for the reality of the Name, His unity, and negating His corporeality (*gashmiut*). Then, in general, what is needed for faith in Him. Or, what cannot be attributed to Him without impairing His perfection. The work also explains to us the nature of prophecy and interprets the books of prophecy. It shows us how theology does not contradict the human intellect, as the uneducated have thought. Rather, it fills the deficiencies of intellect. In addition to this, the *Guide* concerns itself with issues (*inyanim*) of great usefulness from other disciplines—natural science, astronomy and similar disciplines, in particular the science of the soul and its faculties. None of [what the *Guide* does] follows the learning-order of those respective disciplines; as it was not the intention of the teacher-author, may his memory be blessed, to copy the texts of those disciplines. [Rambam] himself, may his memory be blessed, explained that. He rather proceeds according to what follows from the nature (*teva*) of the issue (*inyan*), each issue in its proper place, in a manner suiting his intention. My essay (*ma'amar*) will be lengthy where Rambam, may his memory be blessed, dealt briefly. And it will fill the deficiencies in the disciplines of his age, judging by today's standards.

The treatise (*hibur*) [of Rambam] is an independent compendium of precious disciplines and lofty ideas (*yediot*) leading man to perfection. And it is proper that we give credit to the teacher-author, may his name be blessed, who left us a blessing which "might keep us alive, as it is today" [Deuteronomy 6:24]. This is after our long exile, with our becoming a disgrace [in the eyes of] our neighbors, an object of derision and mockery for those around us. The wisdom of our scholars was lost, and the reasoning (*binah*) of the insightful was hidden. Then the teacher, may his memory be blessed, shed light upon our vision with this venerable work. The treatise has its unique reality. Neither before nor after the teacher has anything like it been written. Anyone who studies it devoutly will recognize that, although we have been privileged to have the book for many centuries, we have not been worthy [enough to receive] its light. Our eyes [remain] dark in their sockets. They are so weak, that they cannot look at the resplendent light shining from the treatise.

There are several reasons for this: (1) The author, may his memory be blessed, was concise where he might have [expounded at] length. As will be explained, he himself, may his memory be blessed, composed his essay (*ma'amar*) only for those who philosophized and intellectualized (*hiskil*) about the disciplines. His words remain as a sealed volume for anyone else studying it. (2) The deficiency of the disciplines of his day, as measured by today's standards. This is especially so in natural science altogether, and its division established for astronomy, that is, for the concept of cosmic structure, in particular the order of the parts of the cosmos in relation to one another. The student will see this in my interpretations of the respective passages. (3) The [perceived] deficiency in the order—simply because Rambam composed the treatise with a special scope in mind. The principal intention is lost, namely to understand (*havanah*) his knowledge (*da'at*) at a single glance, outside of which everything could be doubted. To be sure, some later interpreters tried to supplement all of this. Let the intellectual (*maskil*) see for himself and judge whether or not they fulfilled their intention.

Since I have "great zeal" [I Kings 19:10] for the honor of the venerable author, I took it to heart to interpret this venerable text anew, elaborating where he, may his memory be blessed, was concise. I will explain by example every judgment which exists, adding to the example found in the essay; calling the students' attention to analogies between the views (*deot*) of Aristotle and his followers, and the views of outstanding contemporary philosophies. "Let me not be prejudiced to anyone or flatter anyone" [Job 32:21]. As the wise man said, "Love Socrates, love Plato, and love truth more than either" [Aristotle, *Nichomachean Ethics* 1096a:16].

NOTE

Words in brackets appear in the original translation.

Translated by Gershon Greenberg.

Solomon Maimon

The Autobiography of Solomon Maimon: Maskilic View of Heder
1792–1793

I must now say something of the condition of the Jewish schools in general. The school is commonly a small smoky hut, and the children are scattered, some on benches, some on the bare earth. The master, in a dirty blouse sitting on the table, holds between his knees a bowl, in which he grinds tobacco into snuff with a huge pestle like the club of Hercules, while at the same time he wields his authority. The ushers give lessons, each in his own corner, and rule those under their charge quite as despotically as the master himself. Of the breakfast, lunch, and other food sent to the school for the children, these gentlemen keep the largest share for themselves. Sometimes even the poor youngsters get nothing at all; and yet they dare not make any complaint on the subject, if they will not expose themselves to the vengeance of these tyrants. Here the children are imprisoned from morning to night, and have not an hour to themselves, except on Friday and a half-holiday at the Newmoon.

As far as study is concerned, the reading of Hebrew at least is pretty regularly learned. On the other hand, with the mastery of the Hebrew language very seldom is any progress made. Grammar is not treated in the school at all, but has to be learnt *ex usu*, by translation of the Holy Scriptures, very much as the ordinary man learns imperfectly the grammar of his mother-tongue by social intercourse. Moreover there is no dictionary of the Hebrew language. The children therefore begin at once with the explanation of the Bible. This is divided into as many sections as there are weeks in the year, in order that the Books of Moses, which are read in the synagogues every Saturday, may be read through in a year. Accordingly every week some verses from the beginning of the section proper to the week are explained in school, and that with every possible grammatical blunder. Nor can it well be otherwise. For the Hebrew must be explained by means of the mother-tongue. But the mother-tongue of the Polish Jews is itself full of defects and grammatical inaccuracies; and as a matter of course therefore also the Hebrew language, which is learned by its means, must be of the same stamp. The pupil thus acquires just as little knowledge of the language, as of the contents, of the Bible.

Translated by J. Clark Murray.

Lazarus Bendavid
1762–1832

Lazarus Bendavid was a prominent *maskil* in Germany and Austria. His intellectual activities ranged from critiques of Jewish traditionalism to Kant's philosophy. Born in Berlin, he practiced glass grinding before attending university and moving to Vienna, where he lectured on Kant. Returning to Berlin in 1797, he served as editor of *Spenersche Zeitung*. In 1806 he became director of the Jewish Free School, where he served until its closure in 1825. The School flourished during his tenure and became the first interfaith school by accepting Christian students.

Notes Regarding the Characteristics of the Jews
1793

I wish, then, to describe the four classes to which Jews today belong in order to derive therefrom the principal claim of this discussion, namely: to the extent that the Jews do not take advantage of [the opportunity] to abrogate the ceremonial laws, which are meaningless and inappropriate for our time; to the extent that they do not establish a purer religion, more worthy of God—the pure teaching of Moses—they will perforce remain, even if baptized, apathetic citizens who are harmful to the states [they inhabit].

The four classes are the following: The first class, which is still the largest, is that which retains its loyalty to and its belief in the entire immense conglomeration of Jewish traditions. This class considers it to be a sin if it is doubted that the distance between the heel and the ankle of the foot of Og, King of Bashan, is less than thirty cubits or that Moses received on Mount Sinai from God Himself the melody of several of the hymns sung on the Day of Atonement. This class will remain forever irredeemable and its extinction is the only hope for the coming generations. For this class of Jews baptism and the acknowledgement of the Christian faith are of value only in that the zeal for bread is no more injurious to their existence than it is to the Christian who wants to be accepted into a particular guild. Aside from this, they pray with the rosary with the heart of a superstitious Jew, harboring resentment toward the Jews and contempt for the Christians. One rich fellow belonging to this gang who was baptized—for what reason I know not—recently wrote to another baptized Jew and invited him, although he was poor, to marry his daughter since he did not want her to marry a Christian.

Among those who remain steadfast in the faith of their forefathers, they are not infrequently to be found—in spite of their superstitions—exceedingly worthy men who, with respect to their sincerity and to the ardent zeal of their efforts for the good of their co-religionists truly embellish this class. I knew a director of a hospital in Berlin who was willing to share his last shirt with anyone who needed it. I knew another, a very poor man, who made it his business to collect donations for people even poorer than himself and who would have thought it the greatest sin to have taken even a penny of the money placed in his hands for his own use, even at the time of his greatest need.

The second class of Jews is that dissolute mob who have abandoned the ceremonial laws because they were too much of a burden and because they prevented them from following unhindered their unbridled passions. Unfortunately, their number is still very great and will increase from day to day if a change does not soon take place. These, who in most cases were born to rich parents of the first class, were raised without a proper education and were led astray by love and wine. They consider themselves to be enlightened, but they merely arouse contempt. Their fathers are least at peace with themselves, while they must suppress the voice of conscience at every moment. They simulate enlightenment, but are incorrigible, uninformed vagabonds. These are the ones who, for the most part, are responsible for the bad opinion the Christians have of the Jews. These are the ones who through their immoral way of life cause the best of the first and third classes to abhor enlightenment in any form. The majority go over to Christianity the moment they meet a Christian maiden who is more cunning and more beautiful than she is clever and eloquent. After baptism, were it possible, they would be prepared to undergo a second circumcision were the acceptance of the Jewish religion to confer as many advantages as those attained through the acceptance of the Christian religion.

The third class seems to me to be always worthy of respect, even though my outlook in religion is far removed from theirs, for they are good men. Their intellect has not been cultivated by proper education, but their hearts are without blemish. [Consequently] their intellect is not sufficiently strong to elevate them to that level of enlightenment that makes a man moral even without such a religion that constantly reminds him of his [moral] duties. They are, however, cognizant of this weakness. Through fear of immorality, they remain [embedded] in an unrefined Judaism. With respect to themselves, they are suspicious of every innovation, but do not in principle disallow innovation for others. They are deemed to be stubborn and unbending Jews, but if the Jews of the first class could read what is in their hearts they would accuse them of heresy. For the most part they have a system entirely their own in matters of religion. They persecute no one and act charitably toward everyone. They are faithful husbands, loving parents, true friends and good citizens. The countries of Prussia and Austria benefit greatly from their devoted and indefatigable industry. In the majority of cases—though not without exception—the state can rely on the sons of these noble men to be loyal, useful men.

The fourth class is composed either of the sons of the third class or of men who, owing to fortunate circumstances, have been equipped by heaven with adequate mental powers and who have met with men of the better sort. This class, which combined all the virtues of the previous class with true enlightenment, is as removed from Judaism as it is from apathy [*Indifferentismus*]. They are disciples of the genuine natural religion. Sensing the necessity of the duty of believing with all the ardor that this religion instils in men of reason, they are nonetheless aware of the precarious pillars upon which civic security would rest and the superficial foundations upon which human happiness would lie were man prevented from believing in God, immortality or the advance toward further perfection after death. Their words are holy to them. A member of this class would be ashamed of himself were he to make a profession of faith—even if only *pro forma*—of that of which in his heart he was not convinced. He would think that such a profession of faith, such a mockery of man's most important possession, implies a different kind of belief, one which every upright man would abhor. He would in effect be saying: "Citizens and compatriots! I hereby betray my conscience for the sake of ephemeral happiness; I avow with my lips that which is not in my heart! Trust me not! Do not charge me with public office, for I have committed perjury and I could easily do so again were I to be prompted by equally powerful inducements!"

The men of this class cannot be very happy as long as they are considered by the Christians to be Jews because they are not Christians and they are considered by the Jews to be apostates because they are men [*Menschen*]. They cannot be very happy as long as their solicitude for the integrity of their own mode of life and for the upbringing of their children is beset by obstacle after obstacle.

NOTE

Words in brackets appear in the original translation.

Translated by Stephen L. Weinstein.

Other works by Bendavid: *Versuch über das vergnügen* (1794); *Vorlesungen über die Critik der reinen Vernunft* (1795); *Versuch einer Rechtslehre* (1802); *Über die Religion der Ebräer vor Moses* (1812).

Aaron Halle-Wolfsohn

Silliness and Sanctimony
1796

Act 2

YETKHEN: And how crude he was with me! He wants to arrange with Papa to marry me! How do you like that? I'd like to meet the man who'll force me to marry someone! No! No father can do that—I have a will of my own. Papa may do whatever he likes, but there's no way I'm going to marry that man.

SCENE 6

[REB HENOKH *furiously barges into the room as* YETKHEN *is finishing the previous line.*]

Reb Henokh: What? There's no way you'll have him? What do you think you're doing? Where do you get the nerve? You have the chutzpah to say that you won't have him? It's taking everything I've got to keep from tearing you to pieces! You spoiled brat! I'll teach you manners. You think I'm afraid to? I'll break every bone in your body. [*Runs around the room, grabs the music and books, tears them up, and flings the pieces at* Yetkhen.] I'm fed up with your nonsense!

Markus: Get a hold of yourself, for heaven's sake! You're acting like a raving lunatic!

Reb Henokh: Leave me alone, leave me alone. I'll tear her to pieces! [*Goes after* Yetkhen, *but* Markus *holds him back.*]

Teltse: Get him out of here, my dear Markus! Get him out, he doesn't know what he's doing—he'll make things even worse! [Markus *drags him out.*]

Scene 7

[Teltse *and* Yetkhen *are both crying. Pause.*]

Yetkhen: [*To herself.*] I'm in an extraordinary situation; I need to find an extraordinary solution. I'll use all my wits, risk everything—I've got nothing to lose. [*Aloud.*] Mama dear, crying will get us nowhere. We'll have to do something if we want to get out of this danger. I've read many stories, and Uncle has told me many others, about cruelty to children. But a father like this is unheard of! To persist so stubbornly—such a tyrant!

Teltse: [*Absentmindedly, having only heard the last few words.*] What do you know about his stubbornness? I can tell you stories! When an idea gets stuck in his head, God himself couldn't come knock it out of him. Get this: just yesterday afternoon . . .

Yetkhen: What if he comes back? I shudder at the very thought! Dear Mama!—go downstairs and make sure he doesn't come back up.

Teltse: How come? Markus is down there with him.

Yetkhen: He acts differently with you—you'll have more chance of detaining him than Uncle will, so please go, Mama dear! Talk to him, at least get him to calm down for a couple of days. In time, cooler heads will prevail. [*Pleading.*] Go to him!

Teltse: I'll do it if it makes you happy [*Going.*], even though I know that talking to him won't do any good. [*Exits.*]

Scene 8

Yetkhen: I am finally alone again, thank God! [*Locks the door.*] At least he will not take me by surprise, and I can think calmly about what to do. [*Thinks as she walks back and forth, stopping to contemplate the torn books and music.*] Look at all of this! He ruined everything! Is this any way for a father to behave? May a father do whatever he likes? Doesn't he have certain duties to his children? But if he does not feel obligated to anyone, I do not want to know about duties any more either! I will not even have a father any more! [*Pause.*] Yes, that's fine, but my mother? Oh well, that will probably be better for her than it is now—she is also suffering so much! [*In the process of picking them up, she finds a piece of the ripped up arias from Herr Von Schnapps. She picks it up, contemplating it sadly.*] You cannot escape his tyranny either! What behavior: forcing someone on me whom no maid would have, just because *he* is in love with him! [*Laughs wildly.*] Ha, ha! Imagine people's reactions on the promenade if I were to appear there with a man like that at my side! And Herr von Schnapps! He's asked for my hand countless times, and I would go to the ends of the earth for him. [*Pause.*] But what am I waiting for? I'm not accountable to my father any more—he is a tyrant! Yes, that's it, I have made my decision, and mustn't waver any more. I will leave this house today, I will throw myself into his arms today—today! I'll get everything together right away. [*Unlocks the door and exits.*]

Act 3

Scene 1

[*10 o'clock in the evening in* Reb Henokh's *living room.* Reb Henokh *sits at a table, his head resting in his hands. A volume of Talmud lies open in front of him. He frequently interrupts his studies with deep sighs.* Teltse *sits in a corner, sobbing. Pause.*]

Reb Henokh: I can't hear myself think; what good does all of this crying do? It's true, it is—because of our manifold sins—a great misfortune, but since we're Jews, we have to consider: *kol ma d'oved rakhmone l'tav oved*: everything that the Merciful One does, he does for good! It could have been even worse.

Teltse: What are you talking about? What do you mean, even worse? What could possibly be worse?

REB HENOKH: How should I know what could be worse? It could be worse—that's enough. And a Jew always has to find the silver lining in every cloud—a *gam zu letoyve*.

TELTSE: May God in his seventh heaven have mercy! A fine *gamzel letoyve* this is! The poor, poor child! Wherever she might be all of this time, she might even cause herself harm! The poor child! [*Cries.*] And such a husband! It's all because of you! All your insanity, you're driving me right into the grave, and yourself too, because of this craziness. May God have mercy! [*Cries.*]

REB HENOKH: I'm begging you to give it a rest—don't drive me completely out of my mind. [*Sighs.*] What should I do? God has clearly willed it to be so! Presumably, He knows what needs to be done! And what does that mean? I have to stay here silent while I'm terrified for my child? This is insane! Why would I think that she would run away? Who would think she would run away? Maybe if I was going to give her to some buffoon, some stripling, it would make sense, but as it is, what more could she possibly ask for? I know where all of this is coming from, though—I know it's for the sins, with which you and your brother ruined her!

TELTSE: [*Jumps up from her chair.*] Don't be so high and mighty; she also ran away from you. Divine decrees aren't solely to blame . . .

SCENE 2

[SHEYNDL *enters with a bowl of soup.*]

SHEYNDL: Won't you have a bit of soup? It's already so late, and you haven't eaten a thing today.

TELTSE: No, I can't. Just put it away. I don't want to eat; I've lost my appetite. [*Cries.*]

SHEYNDL: But what does all of this crying help? You're simply going to make yourself sick. You'll see, everything is going to work out; Herr Markus has sworn that he's going to do everything he can to bring her back.

TELTSE: Yes, yes . . . who knows where she is? She could really do something to herself, God protect us . . .

SHEYNDL: There's no need for you to get yourself in such a state; she is not going to hurt herself. Mam'selle Yetkhen is too much in love with herself for that.

REB HENOKH: And did you completely fail to notice the fact that she was leaving? How is it that you did not see who was going in and out to her?

SHEYNDL: I should know? How is that? Do you think that there's just the one visitor a day? It was a madhouse all day long. As soon as one *sheygets* arrived, there's another *sheygets* at the door. I didn't have a single minute to stay in the kitchen—it's a miracle that the food wasn't burned to a crisp! And had I said something, there would have been big trouble. [*Knocking is heard.*] I think someone's at the door; I'll go down and get it. [*Leaves.*]

SCENE 3

REB HENOKH: Did you hear that? Did you see what the girl said? The whole day, she was surrounded by goyim, and all of this was hidden from me—oy, the shame! How can I stand it all? What does this mean? My daughter's spending her time with goyim! Oy vey, oy vey! [MARKUS *enters.*]

TELTSE: [*Running over to him.*] Markus, dear Markus! What's happening? Still no news of her?

MARKUS: As of now I still haven't heard anything: I hope to receive some information soon, though.

TELTSE: So did you go to see Herr von Schnapps, did you ask the good-for-nothing if he knew anything?

MARKUS: Certainly I went there; I even did a little asking around among the servants, and I found out from them that last evening, he went riding around with some woman in a closed coach. Where exactly they were going, they didn't know.

TELTSE: That's a good sign already.

MARKUS: With this information, I went straightaway to one of my friends, revealed my suspicions to him, and asked him for his support in this risky affair. He's one of those friends who is an old enemy of Von Schnapps, and so I was fairly sure that he would make every effort, do everything possible in order to obtain detailed information and to bring the matter to light and make sure that the scoundrel gets his just desserts.

TELTSE: May God reward you, my dear Markus! I can't thank you enough—my gratitude is too meager. [*Cries.*]

MARKUS: What is all this for? Can an action which was merely my duty deserve such effusive thanks? Whatever I did, I was required to do as a brother, as a man.

REB HENOKH: But what does it help? Woe—for our manifold sins!—she has gone off with a goy, the dirty trollop! And she'll defile my whole house as well.

MARKUS: Now is not the time for speeches. What we need to do now is determine how we can free her from the clutches of these seducers. There's no way to change what happened in the past, and what happens in the future is up to each of us.

REB HENOKH: Why, do you think that maybe she'll come back? I would forgive her everything right away! I'll beg for atonement like a dog, God should forgive me all of my sins, I almost cursed her myself! But she's still mistaken. She'll have to marry Reb Yoysefkhe, if only for spite, and I don't care if she stands on her head.

MARKUS: You have to learn to speak more gently! All of your threats and curses are forgiven, but she is still not here. When we have her back home, God willing, I advise you as a friend to speak to her sternly but sensibly. If you ever try to keep her here by force, you shall regret it. You have seen how well strictness works; maybe you shall learn to bend a little now. To be perfectly open and frank with you, if I were your daughter, I would not marry this Reb Yoysef, and so she resists the idea of this marriage as well!

REB HENOKH: This doesn't come as any news to me; you're the only one she ever listens to! *Aval ko yihyeh*—But thus shall it ever be . . . [SHEYNDL *enters with a message, which she hands to* MARKUS, *and quickly exits again.*]

MARKUS: Everyone be quiet for a moment; this message may tell us something new! [*Reads.*] "With the greatest of friendship I hurry to write you that I am finally on the trail. The wolf has finally arrived, but the sheep is as of yet completely unharmed. Come to me as soon as possible; I wait for you at my house. Come whenever you wish; if you want, you can speak to your niece. More to follow." I have no time to lose; I will hurry there and soon I will have spoken with Yetkhen, and then I will return to you. [*Leaves.*]

TELTSE: God be praised and thanked! That that's all! A huge stone has been lifted from my heart, and I'll have a little soup now. Do you want some too?

REB HENOKH: If you like, but you know what, we'll set the table just like usual; I didn't have a proper lunch today. Come, Sheyndl will prepare something for us.

SCENE 4

[*In* LEMGIN's *lodgings.* YETKHEN, *her clothes disheveled, sits at the table crying, her head in her hands.*]

LEMGIN: When will you stop your crying? Silly thing! Laying it on a little thick, aren't you? After all, it's not as if you've been captured by a band of robbers. You're with decent people—no harm will come to you as long as you're good and play along! Come here, little fool—always be merry and cheerful. When you make faces like that, you'll scare people off. You'll never move a Christian soul that way. Here! Here's my glass of wine—drink, it gives you courage, and then we'll dance a little waltz! [*Goes to take her by the hand.*]

YETKHEN: Oh, let me go, I'm not in the mood for waltzing or drinking.

LEMGIN: Look here, you silly thing. How will you ever attract a lover that way? Let yourself be happy—you'll find more than enough lovers here. Only the finest clients come here; you can have your pick. But as I said, you have to behave differently, be very friendly, to entertain the young gentlemen so they'll fork over plenty. Play your cards right, and nothing will happen to you.

YETKHEN: [*Resisting.*] Then why are you keeping me here? I think you want to make a strumpet out of me. No, I haven't fallen so far, thank God—I still have parents, thank God, who will take me back.

LEMGIN: Yeah, yeah, I've heard that one before! I'm sure your parents are just great. Why did you run away from them, then? And why did the Mademoiselle spend time with that cream puff Von Schnapps? Heh! She's silent! [*Knocking is heard.*] Take my advice, really cheerful and happy! [*The knocking gets louder.*] Okay, okay—this one can't wait. [*Going.*] Put on something nice—take my advice, you hear? [*Exits.*]

Translated by Joel Berkowitz and Jeremy Dauber.

David of Makev

d. 1814 or 1815

Born in Rovno, Volhynia, David of Makev (Makov) served as a preacher and judge in Makow Mazowiecki,

Poland. At first a disciple of the Hasidic leader Menachem Mendel of Vitebsk, he grew disillusioned with Hasidism and became a follower of the Vilna Gaon. Indeed, after 1772 David blamed Hasidic courts for the spread of moral and religious anarchy, and he mocked the lighthearted revelry and emotionalism of their adherents, also criticizing the power of tsadikim and scorning what he regarded as their materialism. Among his most noteworthy anti-Hasidic works was the treatise containing *Shever poshe'im*, *Zot torat ha-kena'ot*, and *Zimrat ha-arets* (first written ca. 1798–1800).

Shever poshe'im: The Court of R. Ḥayim Ḥaykl of Amdur
ca. 1798

The communal treasurer stands on guard at the entrance to the rabbi's home to make inquiry concerning every invalid or cripple, and by what name he is called. One can hear the noise of the people as they are shouting—his own name and that of his family, the nature of his employment and from which country he hails and what religion he professes, whether he belongs to the Hasidim or to the Misnagdim. And each of them replies in a feeble tone of voice, whereupon the treasurer records it in a book, a flying roll. One says: "I come from such-and-such city, and by reason of my many sins, my throat has developed grunting sounds these past few years," and another says: "I come from a different city, and for these past few years, I have been called 'the blind one'"; while yet a third man declares that he has been seized by a raging fever and is now virtually at death's door; and from all of these, their creditors come to reclaim their respective loans, their homes are empty, they are falling by the wayside, with none to set them on their feet. And the treasurer says: "Greetings to you! Have no fear!" As they set up camp, so they journey on, they flee away and wander. I have given this scroll the title "The scroll of hidden things"—to reflect the shadow of death surrounding it and its lack of ordered arrangement. And this scroll is brought in secret—in the manner of spies—to the rabbi, to the chamber of the silent, and he exclaims: "Give it! Give it!"—and the treasurer informs him of the identity of the pauper and the wayfarer in question, and of the person leaning on a stick.

When the rabbi hears this, he becomes grieved at heart, but his snare is hidden within the stitches of his garments; and when he hears of any nobleman or wealthy individual, he then sings for joy, and all the people assemble early in the morning at his door; and the rabbi says: "Now is not the time to gather in the flock, as it is a time of divine wrath—tomorrow morning the Almighty will make known who the holy ones are, and He will draw them near unto Him, and each individual will eat in accordance with the fruit of his deeds." So the wayfarer lodges there overnight—behold, thus shall he surely be blessed! Throughout the night, the rains drip down upon them, and the fearsome ice descends upon their heads, and their knees knock one against the other—they seek death rather than life. Meanwhile, the rabbi lies stretched out upon his bed, with the attribute of divine judgment extended over his head, on a well-made bed, bereft of knowledge. Neither knowledge of Torah nor fear of the Almighty can come from boorish counsel, from such inspiration as stems from alien fire. And in the morning, he peruses the scroll and makes due investigation, carefully scrutinizing everything, and he exclaims: "Open the gates, and let the righteous nation, holding fast to the faith, enter, and I shall bestow upon them the priestly blessing!" And then he goes to the ritual bath until the time for prayer has passed, taking the scroll along with him, and there he directs the appropriate intents heavenward, and sets his eyes upon the monies and the gifts. And the treasurer says that the rabbi is creating ways and means to elicit the most propitious moments for his prayers, and meanwhile he urges: "Donate money by way of redemption for the soul, so as to secure a place of rest and repose for yourselves, and atonement monies; and he [the rabbi] will inform you of the solutions to your problems as unto one who would in ancient times make enquiry of the Urim. But give, right down to the last penny, for behold, now is the appropriate time and season when the donations pass under the shepherd's rod, and he will number and count, weighing out the monies in the balance, and distributing them to orphans, giving them a double portion; and the money has a further outlet, namely to bring out prisoners from the dungeon into the outside world; and anyone who counts monies in abundance is truly worthy of praise, and it will be accounted unto you in the sight of heaven as a sacrificial offering, and its owners will be assured that they will go on to enjoy long life. Do not say: 'What are we to eat?'—as the rabbi is most assuredly capable of doing all things, and he will pour out a blessing for you, and will remove from you sorrow and sighing. But if you do not donate as requested, you shall be accounted among those lacking in faith, and in lieu of gladness and exultation you shall experience mourning and lamentation; so have no concern for your monies, and thereafter, you may return to your homes." The treasurer collects up all the monies to be found in their hands, and they are left with nothing more than the corners of their garments. The treasurer counts up the monies with deliberation, be they utensils or coins, to ensure that he does not make an error, and he then brings the monies to the rabbi, who says: "Hand them over!"

The rabbi then begins to pray, and his heart is hollow; and his custom in prayer is that he shoots out the words like arrows, as the words of the King are pressing; and between each section of the prayers he sings lengthy chants, which can make the hair of a man stand on end. Now after he has recited the silent Amidah prayer in a state of trembling, he flees from the synagogue to relieve himself by urinating and emptying his bowels, whereafter he recites the benedictions *Asher yatsar* and *Rofe' holim*. The congregation is seated, and acknowledges the divine justice in respect of whatever misfortunes have befallen them before the pious, heretical rabbi, and the ears of the people are directed toward hearing the *Kedushah*—woe on account of the shame and reproach thereby generated! In the middle of the prayers he rubs wax on his fingers, and with his other hand he displays his wonders. These are but some of the matters in relation to him: at prayer times the flying roll is laid in front of him, a slip of paper containing a request for him to have in mind a certain beautiful woman who has turned aside from discretion, while praying for her in a thunderous voice; and at the moment when *Keter* [the first word of the sanctification prayer] is recited, they have already "made their arrow ready upon the string"—to have in mind one Moses, son of Gittel, who is in a state of nakedness and want. And at the moment of recital of "He who hearkens unto prayer," he focuses his mind, while shaking and trembling, yet in exultation and joy, upon one Samuel, son of Adah and Zillah; and at the time of the supplicatory prayers, he spreads his wings aloft, whereby the successful conclusion of the matter becomes doubly assured, wafted upon a pure wind on the bare heights. They draw near to the ark to pray for the women, either for the married ones or for the virgins, their eyes are bent upon obtaining redemption and ransom for their souls—to provide holiday clothes for their womenfolk, to be perfumed with myrrh and frankincense, so as to facilitate performance of the precept of giving one's wife her conjugal rights. After dealing with all the cases of sickness, he will, at the time of the morning prayer, endeavor to produce a compress and medicine for a betrothed maidservant; and they then expound *Vahev besufah* [the rabbinic notion that, where teachers and their students initially refuse to accept one another's halakhic interpretations and conclusions, their mutual hostility will ultimately melt away and turn into a close friendship]. And at eventide, the treasurer collects the donated gold and silver, equal to the booty seized by the Israelites at the Red Sea; and at prayer times, his wings are spread forth toward heaven, and there he will sing a new melody, and will ascend on high with joyful exultation.

Translated by David E. Cohen.

Other work by David of Makev: *Zamir aritsim* (1798).

David Friedländer

Open Letter
1799

Open Letter to His Most Worthy,
Supreme Consistorial Counselor and
Provost Teller at Berlin, from some
Householders of the Jewish Religion
But when the more perfect comes, the
imperfect will pass away. When I was a
child, I spoke like a child, I thought like a
child, I reasoned like a child; when I became a
man, I gave up childish ways.
1 Corinthians 13:10–1

Printed with approval of the censor after a question was addressed to me, and thus also with my permission. My response will similarly appear in print as soon as I have been able to think through and consider the matter in light of its importance amid many sorts of business and interruptions.—Teller

MOST WORTHY SIR,

Venerable Friend of Mankind

Permit us, most worthy Sir, who are not members of your church but are no less trusting than your most grateful pupils, to request from you instruction, counsel, and support in the greatest and most holy affair of man, which is religion. [. . .]

We were born of Jewish parents and reared in the Jewish religion. Our education had nothing distinguishing it from that of our comrades. Already in childhood the Talmud was put in our hands as a textbook, perhaps even earlier than sacred scripture. The religion that was taught to us, then, was full of mystical principles. The story of the primeval world was full of secrets, dark, incoherent; the events were foreign and, down to the last shades of meaning, so dissimilar to the occurrences of the world in which we lived that they seemed almost unbelievable. Characters, states of mind, and feelings of people who emerge in sacred scripture not only were puzzling for us in matters of expression but also, for the most part, stood in contrast to our feelings, expressions, and ways of acting. The ceremonial laws were observed with worrisome precision in the paternal household. These alienated us in the circle of everyday life; as empty customs without any further influence on our other preoccupations, they had no other effect than that their observation in the presence of persons of a different religious persuasion, even domestic servants, made us shy, embarrassed and often restless. [. . .]

In this labyrinth into which we have fallen through time and circumstances, we might almost say through our very virtue, we take refuge in you, venerable Sir. Teach us how we can find the way out. Tell us, noble friend of virtue, if we do decide to choose the great Protestant Christian community as a place of sanctuary: What kind of public declaration would you, and the men who sit with you on the venerable council, demand of us?

Or—the importance of the subject gives us the courage to express our question even more boldly: If providence, venerable Sir, had caused you to be born among us, and you had felt obliged to take a similar step for similar reasons, which confession would you, with your delicate conscientiousness, have signed or publicly declared?

Just a few words, and then we shall close.

The number of people who, full of trust, are sending this epistle to you is quite small. Yet unless we are mistaken there must be a sizable number of heads of families who find themselves in a similar position and who perhaps lack only an initial example to arrive at similar decisions. This is proven by several of the attempts, drafted by individuals of our religion, at how one might effect a religious reform. And although we are skeptical of the workability of these efforts, they nonetheless point unmistakably to the need of our householders who wish to throw off the shackles of ceremonial law and, one way or the other, to incorporate themselves into the great civil society. [. . .]

Without in the least seeking to anticipate your opinion, venerable Sir, we expect that the true spirit of Protestantism will shelter and protect us and our system within its wider circle. In this way we shall be able to attain the goal we have set for ourselves.

If the Protestant religion does indeed prescribe certain ceremonies, we can certainly resign ourselves to these as mere necessary *forms* that are required for acceptance as a member into a society. Let it be understood that we assume as a matter of principle that these ceremonies are required merely as *actions*, as *customs*, in order to attest: that the newly admitted member accepts the *eternal truths* out of conviction and that he submits to all the duties that result from this as a *man* and as a *citizen*. We do not regard this demand as a *sign* that he who performs the ceremonies is tacitly acknowledging that he accepts *in faith* the church *dogmas* of this community. We would be able to comply with and fulfill that demand with complete conscientiousness.

Translated by Richard Courter and Julie Klassen.

Menachem Mendel Lefin

Prayer against the Hasidim
1809

"Blessed are you, God, God of our ancestors, the great, awesome, and holy God. You have bequeathed *human understanding (da'at ha-enoshit)* to humanity. You have gifted us with the knowledge of your Written Torah and you have also bequeathed the Oral Torah to our ancestors. You gave us truthful teachers and just commentators to enlighten us with [their teachings]. Thus you elevated us above all life and brought us closer to your divine service. Your holy name called us. But because of our many sins and the vastness of our iniquities, many lengthy evil troubles befell us. We were exiled to the ends of the earth for thousands of years. We have nothing else except these precious gifts [the two Torahs], and were it not for them, I would have already lost all hope because of my misery. Indeed, now, in my old age, the seed of generations of liars has blossomed, a generation "who will curse its fathers" (Prov 30:11), a generation pure in its own eyes, but who will never be clean of its own filth, an "arrogant generation" (Ps 131:1 and Prov 30:13), "a generation whose sword-like teeth will eat the poor from the land" (Prov 30:14) has arisen to deceive your people, the House of Israel, and also to plunder this inheritance from their hands. For, behold, they will plot against your people to make them forget your Torahs and even to make them negate human understanding. Then Sabbatai Zevi, Nathan [of Gaza], Baruchiah [Russo], [Nehemiah] Hayon and [Jacob] Frank, may their names be blotted out, will come to fabricate never-ending names, secrets, and allusions in order to obligate the people to believe in them, in their divinity, and in their prophets, who abandon [the] paths of righteousness to walk in dark, crooked roads, saying, "We are gods and prophets and we may interpret and resolve [exegetical issues in] the Torahs as we desire." You, in your compassion, obstructed their design[s], destroyed their memory, and prevented the proliferation of their books from your people's midst. Now, in their stead, a culture of sinning, evil men, has arisen; they are the prophets of the Ba'al [Shem Tov], the sprouts of their thorns, the disseminators of the fruit of their filth. God and God of our ancestors, do not forsake us in [our] old age. Favor your remnant in Israel and [hear] their prayer to return your divine service to its dwelling place and your Torah to its rightful interpretation. May lies be wiped out from the earth, idolatry extirpated, and all of the evil be destroyed like smoke, and we, your people, will praise your name forever. We will sing your praise for generations.

NOTE

Words in brackets appear in the original translation.

[It is not clear who authored the prayer, although the handwriting is Joseph Perl's. The text makes specific reference to the writer's advanced age, but the second side of the page mentions the year 1818, when Lefin would have been sixty-nine years old and Perl only forty-six. Lefin's almost complete blindness led him to rely frequently on his disciples for writing, proofreading, and copyediting, in which case the prayer may be his in its entirety.—Professor Nancy Sinkoff, Rutgers University.]

Translated by Nancy Sinkoff.

Joseph Perl
1773–1839

Born in Tarnopol, Galicia, Joseph (Yosef) Perl was a satiric writer, educator, and proponent of the Haskalah. At first he was a follower of Hasidism, to the displeasure of his father, a wine and meat-tax merchant, who made him a partner in his business for a time. Perl later turned against Hasidism, and criticized it, including some of its leading figures, while remaining a follower of the teachings of the Vilna Gaon. In 1813, Perl founded a Jewish school in Tarnopol in the spirit of the Enlightenment. In response to the Austrian censorship of a German-language anti-Hasidic work, *Über das Wesen der sekte Chassidim*, which he wrote in 1814–1816, Perl wrote what some consider to be the first Hebrew novel, *Megaleh temirin* (1819), under the pseudonym Ovadiah ben Petaḥyah. There he satirized Hasidism, as the book pretended to be a collection of letters between Hasidic rebbes. He also composed a number of manuscripts in Yiddish.

Megaleh temirin (The Revealer of Secrets)
1819

Thus I went to all the *tsadikim* and I heard what they say in secret, and I also took the letters that they or those who serve them sent to one another and they didn't see, because by means of the cloud I went easily from one place to another when I put the manuscript in the corners of the *tsitsis*. I have reproduced some of their letters in this composition of mine in order to publicize them, so as to reveal to the public secret things that are of paramount concern. And I have named this composition *Revealer of Secrets*, because it really reveals secrets that hitherto were HIDDEN FROM EVERY HUMAN EYE. [. . .]

From Reb Zelig Letitchiver in Zalin to Reb Zaynvl Verkhievker in Kripen

Yesterday after evening prayers I stayed by our holy *rebe*, The Lamp of Our Generation, and listened to his words, which are SWEETER THAN HONEY OR THE HONEYCOMB. It was such a great pleasure for me because after the prayers, our holy *rebe*, his light should shine, was in total bliss and everything he said was with intense *dveykes*, as usual. During this time I learned from his talking and from his storytelling, thank G-d, more than what a HUMAN BEING can learn from the *toyre* of other *rebes*. I could go for days without eating or drinking to hear his holy speech.

But our holy *rebe* wanted to smoke his pipe and go to the outhouse. I gave him the pipe but I wasn't privileged to light it for him because while I was giving our *rebe* the pipe, another of our Faithful scrambled to light it. When I saw it wasn't our *rebe*'s wish to be accompanied to the outhouse, I went home overjoyed that I am worthy to be among our *rebe*'s people and that G-d gave me the privilege of hearing great things from our *rebe* that day.

When I got home, my wife gave me a letter brought by a visitor from your community, and my pleasure was doubled when I recognized your handwriting. But when I began to read your letter, IT SHOOK ME UP because I saw in it the news you bring me of a *treyf* travesty that was recently published against our Faithful and against the real *tsadikim*, and that this *bukh* was sent from Galicia to the prince of your community to read! According to your letter, it's full of wickedness, deceit and mockery aimed at the *tsadikim* and real *rebes*!

I wouldn't have believed it if anyone else had told me such a thing, because in my opinion it just isn't possible that in these times—when the generation is very near to the coming of the *meshiekh*, and when everyone sees plainly and openly the signs and the wonders that the *tsadikim* perform continuously—clearly, no secret is hidden from them, and who am I to tell of their praise?—for them PRAISE IS SILENCE; and the times—and there were many—are past when there were still those among our kinfolk who opposed us, but now, with G-d's help, THE WHOLE PEOPLE, SMALL AND GREAT, OLD AND YOUNG, MAN AND WOMAN, MALE AND FEMALE SLAVE, believe and know very well the power of the real *tsadikim* and all the opposition have already suffered an overwhelming public defeat and now all of them alike answer and speak respectfully, so that there is no one on earth but our Faithful; and when the *tsadikim* can do whatever their heart desires and compel G-d to do whatever they want; and when they perform the most extraordinary wonders, even just by their holy speech—if *this* is so, how could it be that someone could rise against them now of all times by composing a *bukh* and publishing it? The author himself must know that if our holy *rebe* wishes, he can do to him whatever his heart desires. Believe me, I would've fallen into deep melancholy because of your letter, but the pleasure I had before and the vodka I drank after I read your letter helped me push away melancholy with both hands, and with G-d's help, now I'm not the least bit melancholy.

But all the same, we got to see about doing something with regards to the *bukh*. For the time being, I'm afraid to inform our holy *rebe* of this news for two reasons. Because for the blink of an eye he'll be aggravated, G-d forbid! Even though our *rebe* must've already seen this in the higher worlds, all the same he might be aggravated, G-d forbid!, when he hears this in the lower world. And I'm also afraid maybe he'll instantly take some revenge against the writer of this here *bukh*, burning him by means of the Prince of the Toyre or some such thing, and we won't have the privilege of seeing this sinner and of getting sweet revenge—of hitting him, denouncing him, burning everything he owns and so forth. So I want to get your advice what to do, whether to tell our holy *rebe* and ask him not to take revenge against the author on his own but just through us, or not to tell him anything and do our part.

For right now, I'm informing you that first of all you should do whatever you can to get hold of this *bukh* so we can know what's written there and so we'll know the name of the *bukh*, so as to direct our Faithful to buy the *bukh* and burn it up and wipe it out, and also to find out who the author is so as to take revenge against him. In case the author's name isn't written in the *bukh*, maybe it contains the author's picture, the way the sinners print their picture at the beginning of their trashy books. Then, even if he's from another country, our *rebe* will look at his picture and punish him by looking. So don't be lazy about this! Be quick to get hold of the *bukh* and send it to me. A word to the wise. . . .

From me,

———

The main thing I forgot. Last *Shabes* there was here by our *rebe* a visitor from Galicia from the Lubliner's people and he brought our *rebe* greetings from the *tsadek* of Lublin with some *nigunim*. Our *rebe* added a few sections to them and made them whole. When you'll be by us, G-d willing, you'll have great satisfaction because you'll see from this that our holy *rebe* is the king among the *tsadikim*.

Translated by Dov Taylor.

Other works by Perl: *Katit la-ma'or* (1836); *Boḥen tsadik* (1838).

Anania Coen

1750–1834

Graziado Vita Anania Coen was born in Reggio nell'Emilia, a northern Italian town with a long history of notable rabbis and scholars, and Coen himself established a rabbinical school there. Besides his theological work, he published several treatises on the nature of the Hebrew language and Hebrew poetry, in addition to his own collections of poems. He also established the first Hebrew printing press in Florence, and became chief rabbi of this city in 1825, a position he held until his death.

An Essay on Hebrew Eloquence, Exposed in a Practical Lesson by Doctor Anania Coen, First Rabbi of the Jewish Community of Florence
1827

Lesson XIX. On the Means of Forming Good Taste

To truly form a sense of good taste, one must be in full command of the metaphysics of the sacred tongue, something which is so necessary (and which until now has never been dealt with) and about which I have considered, though my current duties do not allow me to pursue the topic at this time. Nonetheless, as we are in Europe and have successfully studied a European language and the rhetoric of that language, so with some example of figures taken from sacred scripture and some good poet of the Hebrew language by observing the nature of the language in the scriptures and its good writers one can easily achieve this even though any European language is very different from any oriental language, especially Hebrew.

For example *strength* indicates the internal force of man, the word *power* and the word *oz* designate strength and valor which are produced by internal force; hence, we find them in the Hebrew phrase *to wrap oneself or clothe oneself in strength* [Psalm 18:40] but not in force; hence, if one were to say *he is girded with strength* [Hebrew; from Psalm 93:1] it would not be in good taste because it is not in keeping with the nature of the language. This is why *I am robed with strength* [Hebrew] or *I am girded in strength* [Hebrew] is something known externally while it is only internal.

So all that is virtue or vice, as known from the outside, can be brought together by the verbs to clothe oneself, wrap oneself and thus *"You are clothed in glory and majesty"* [Hebrew; Psalm 104:1] and in similar expressions. In a sonnet from the year 1789 to his Excellence Manin, the last Doge of Venice that I came upon at his coronation, there was this verse, *"The wisdom of Solomon was for him a crowning intelligence"* [Hebrew] and hence it is said *"You have robed me in joy"* [Hebrew; Psalm 30:12] because joy is to be seen in facial expression and on the exterior of men. A biblical phrase taken from its sentiment and well applied to this case, and which serves as a worthy example, is "It is not in heaven; we have sinned" [Hebrew, Lamentations 3:42]. Thus, a fine Jewish poet says: *"My body is covered with maggots"* [Hebrew; Job 7:5]. Two biblical treatises brought together so well demonstrate the fine taste the three authors had. Hence Doctor Ephraim Luzzatto makes the husband speak to the bride in this way: *"Bring a veil; cover your face."*

All this shows that it is worth studying the nature of the Hebrew language assiduously in the sacred texts of the prophets and making observations based on the principles of rhetoric (of another language, because we are in Europe). This will contribute easily to cultivating good taste in modern Hebrew poetry and will advise a young beginner that he should not take the liberty to separate himself from the models of writing without first consulting those who know the nature of the language best, namely, the masters.

Translated by James N. Novoa.

Other work by Coen: *Della poesia rabbinica* (1828).

Lelio Della Torre
1805–1871

Born in the Piedmont in northern Italy, Lelio Della Torre was a prominent scholar in his day. In 1829 he helped found the Padua Rabbinical College, an important center of Italian Jewish education. Famed for his preaching, Della Torre taught homiletics. In addition to his sermons, Della Torre wrote nearly three hundred articles in Jewish publications alone, and also contributed to French, German, and Italian journals. For his efforts to integrate philosophical and theological studies, Della Torre was celebrated by both secular and religious intellectual organizations.

Five Orations Given in Padua by Lelio Della Torre
1834

On the Necessity of Combining Philosophical and Theological Studies: A Speech Read at the Grand Oratory of the German Rite on November 10, 1829, for the Inauguration of the Institute of the Rabbinical Seminary

It is undeniable that philosophy, or human reason, when left to itself, requires the celestial light of revelation, which saves it from the snares of any errors that all of us can easily fall into. Into how many pernicious snares do the leaders of philosophy fall, against their will or in their studies, despite the superhuman aid offered by revelation? This is especially so in the case of metaphysics. How many strange conjectures have these produced, and into how many empty opinions did these not lead us?

But, some will counter, the philosophical sciences, the spirit of research infused by those who practice them, can harm, as is evident to all, true belief in theological truth. It is unfortunately true that the excessive and negative freedom of judging everything, which some false philosophers of the past century introduced, has had detrimental consequences for religion and has caused grave harm to healthy philosophy, to customs and the social order, perverting every sacred principle, giving themselves the right to pass temerarious judgment on anything which they have barely meditated on nor understood. This, however, is not, nor is there anyone who ignores this, that castigated and true philosophy taught in public schools, especially those of the Austrian states, the only philosophy worthy of the name, which is the true knower of things and which gives to reason that which belongs to reason and to faith that which belongs to faith. In fact, I will say that it is important to religion that at least its pastors possess the true and healthy philosophical spirit so that to the degree that human intellect is capable of penetrating its recesses and knowing it better so as better to allow their brothers to know it and, not ignoring the travesties of human reason and knowing the arms of the impious, fighting in the wars of the Lord they can refute and contain them.

Translated by James N. Novoa.

Other work by Della Torre: *Tal yaldut* (1868).

Abraham Ber Gottlober

Pirḥe he-aviv (Spring Flowers)
1837

Introduction

This small volume which I now present to you, my fellow readers, is an offshoot of the numerous saplings that I have planted for myself over the course of many days, nay years; for ever since the time when I attained adulthood, I have toiled away and worn myself out so as to be of benefit to my younger brethren in every way I could; for who is there who cannot feel pain for this nation, the understanding of whose sages has remained concealed for so long? Like cast-out paupers, they gather gleanings and forgotten sheaves of corn in the corners of the fields of others. All this is on account of the transgression of those fools who bound themselves with a bond not to open their eyes to perceive the light of wisdom and of the sciences. They drive a wise man off their backs—they cry out against him as though he were a thief; and one who employs elegant language is deemed by them a great sinner!

But while I was still in my youth, and my soul yearned for the Hebrew language and its mellifluous expressions, I raised my hands unto the Most High God, and uttered a vow, as follows: "If Your right hand will assist me in assembling a full hand of ears of the grain of understanding plucked from the fields of discernment, I shall wave them as a sacred offering to the Almighty, and offer them in thanksgiving for acceptance by the young folk. Let them eat the flesh of the bulls and be sated from their fine taste, so that their souls may bless me when the time arrives for them likewise to take a vow to bring the first fruits of reason as an offering to future generations."

However, as I could not bring along to the publishing house all the poems and prose works that I had among my writings, so as to avoid adding to my expenses a burden that I would be unable to bear, I have chosen, for the time being, to publish the small quantity of material which is now before you, while the remaining mass of material, laid up in store with me, I shall publish in days to come if the Almighty will be with me, to preserve me in life as at this day. Now this little volume includes both poems and prose. Of the poems, some are the fruits of my reflections on various occasions, times when my thoughts meandered to and fro in exploration of the deeds of the Almighty and the spirit of the muse asserted itself within me, and some are translations from foreign languages; in regard to such poems as have been translated, I have recorded on the sheet below the names of the original authors. And as for the prose writings now presented to you, good reader, in the format of letters written by one man to another, do not imagine that they deal with business affairs and the like, for I have not set out with the objective of teaching the members of my nation the rules regarding the construction of letters pertaining to business affairs, but rather, my aim has simply been to improve linguistic style and raise moral standards, and to walk in the light of the intellect, which the fools—those who have regard for lying vanities—have rejected; or to clarify the meaning of a particular verse or idea appearing in the sacred writings or of an epigram of our rabbis of blessed memory. And since I have written the major part of the matters comprised in these compositions for the benefit of my friendly coreligionists, some of them with a view to offering them guidance, and others to inform them of my opinions and to elicit their opinions, they have inevitably emanated from me in the form of letters, and I had no desire to alter their format. In addition to this, there is the fact that this work does not, in its entirety, lead toward a single overriding purpose and goal, but rather, each letter is to be treated as an independent entity.

Now I will not deny, I fully acknowledge, that I will not escape the slander of many linguistic experts. Some of these will find fault with my poems, and others with my letters, for the following two reasons: a) with the poems, as I have not conformed to the rules governing syllables and have not trodden the path of those who have regard to the final product, to make the rugged parts level, so as to enable oxen to be placed there, and to substitute a donkey for a cow, to place it on a mountain of myrrh; for of what importance is the even metrical balance of syllables to the genuine interpreter, who will set his focus upon the merit of the idea being conveyed? What extra benefit can precision in the number of syllables employed confer upon him if the contents of the poem are totally lacking in spirit? The essence of a poem lies within itself, in its subject matter and in the lucidity of its expression—and as for the syllables and the rhyming stanzas, it is up to the poet to handle these at his discretion, one individual producing these in greater measure, and another in lesser degree, so long as he does not spoil the beauty of the style—on the contrary, the even balances of the syllables are in fact like gates and bars impeding access into the ideas of the composer of the poem; accordingly, I have not been particular over them, or over the metrical balance of the various stanzas in places where my hand grew short as it were, as I had seen that the overall style and mode of expression would be ruined because of them (as the reader may see in the middle of the poem entitled "Solitude"), so as to allow the wings of my ideas to soar to whatsoever destination the spirit of the poem had the desire to travel; and besides this, these conventions do not have their source within our sacred writings, but have been bequeathed to us from the languages of foreign nations; b) insofar as the prose writings are concerned, the critics' complaint will be that I have on numerous occasions employed words not found in the twenty-four sacred books of the Bible, but rather in the Mishnah, and sometimes in the Talmud. However, who is not aware of the poverty of our language, on account of the destruction of the works of antiquity, and that only a tiny fraction out of a great multitude of literary works have been left to us? Are not the twenty-four sacred books those which Divine Providence has preserved for us for a great deliverance, for it is they that constitute the essence of our religion, which has been set fully in order and preserved for eternity, while the remaining works, of a secular nature, perished by human hand, just like the works of the other nations of antiquity who suffered numerous exiles and enforced wanderings, as we did (and this constitutes a valid proof as to the Providence of the Almighty and of the sanctity of these books). It was as a result of the loss of our remaining literature that the vocabulary of our language became diminished. It became a dead language, one which was not spoken. Why, therefore, should we not supplement it with the numerous fresh words to be found in the books of the Mishnah and the Talmud, with a view to the enhancement of the Holy Tongue? Were the ancients not more familiar with the language than we are? Go forth and consider those nations whose languages are still living, how they are daily adding words from other languages. Should we, the Children of Israel, then be ashamed to accept what our ancestors, the Sages, had already established and accepted for themselves? Such a notion can only spring from an evil heart! In conclusion, then, I have written in a manner faithful to my ideas, and anyone wishing to accept them from me may gladly do so, and as for anyone who is not of similar inclination, let him act in accordance with whatever he may desire.

This small offering which I am now presenting to you was composed and completed while I was in my youth, in the springtime of my life, for I am now twenty-six years of age, and the majority of the things written here are already antiquated so far as I am concerned. It is for this reason that I determined, advisedly, to give this work the title *Pirhe he-aviv* (Spring Blossoms), to serve both as a memorial to me and as a pointer to the critic who, in case he comes along with a view to censuring me, will be able to take a look at the title of the book and say: "These are merely spring blossoms—let them be, and one may hope that their author will, in the fullness of time, bethink himself to increase the power of his literary abilities so that his next offering will be superior to this!" These are the words of him who loves all who seek the good.

18 Adar 5596 [1837]
Old Konstantinov
The Author

Translated by David E. Cohen.

Isaac Leeser
1806–1868

Born in Westphalia, Isaac Leeser immigrated to the United States in 1824 and became a pioneering figure in American Judaism and a staunch advocate for religious freedom. He was an author, educator, translator, publisher, founder of the first Jewish Publication Society, editor of America's first monthly Jewish periodical (*The Occident and American Jewish Advocate*), and cantor at Congregation Mikveh Israel in Philadelphia. Leeser was an observant Jew who opposed religious reform, yet sought to unify the American Jewish community. He popularized English-language sermons and created the first complete Hebrew Bible translation for American Jews.

Catechism for Jewish Children: Designed as a Religious Manual for House and School
1839

The Mosaic Religion in Particular

1. What religion do you profess?

I believe in the Mosaic Religion, which was revealed by the Lord; and I esteem the same as the true, pure, and unmixed word of God.

2. Are you firmly convinced of the truth of this belief?

I am firmly and completely convinced of the truth thereof, for the following reason: because the Mosaic Religion is based upon that celebrated revelation which God imparted in the immediate presence of a whole people, amidst extraordinary signs and wonders.

3. What is the peculiar distinguishing feature of the Mosaic Religion?

It teaches that there is but one God, and that He is incorporeal and indivisible; that is to say, that there exists no other being who has power to create any thing, or to destroy the least of those things which God has made. That this God does not possess a material figure like all those things which we can perceive by our senses, which are called corporeal or bodily substances; and that lastly, He cannot by any means be divided into different parts, being always the same, and not liable to change.

4. Whence is the name "Mosaic Religion" derived?

From Moses, the son of Amram, of the tribe of Levi, through whom God communicated his law to the people of Israel. So also teaches the Bible:

"Remember ye the law of Moses my servant, to whom I commanded on Horeb statutes and judgments for all Israel." Malachi iii. 22.

5. Was not the Deity known and worshipped already before Moses?

Yes; for the patriarchs, and even before them Enoch and Noah, acknowledged the Lord God, and worshipped Him.

"Enoch walked with God, and was no more here; for God had taken him away." Genesis v. 24.

"Noah was a righteous, upright man in his generation: Noah walked with God." Ibid. vi. 9.

6. Who were the Patriarchs?

The original fathers of the Israelitish people, now called the Jews: these were Abraham, Isaac, and Jacob or Israel.

"And He (God) spoke, I am the God of thy fathers, the God of Abraham, the God of Isaac, and the God of Jacob." Exodus iii. 6.

Other works by Leeser: *The Jews and the Mosaic Law* (1834); *Discourses on the Jewish Religion* (1867).

Isaac Erter
1791–1851

A Haskalah figure famous for his anti-Hasidic satires, Isaac (Yitsḥak) Erter was born in the Galician village of Koniuszek. Erter settled in Lemberg (present-day Lviv) and taught secular subjects for three years, beginning in 1816. In 1819, he was excommunicated for his maskilic activities by the chief rabbi of Lemberg, and he moved to Brody. From 1825 to 1829, Erter studied medicine at the University of Budapest; afterward, he practiced medicine in Galicia. His satiric stories were anthologized under the title *Ha-tsofeh le-vet Yisra'el*. He also cofounded the journal *He-ḥaluts*.

Ha-tsofeh le-vet Yisra'el: Tashlikh (The Observer of the House of Israel: Tashlikh)
1840

> *You will cast all their sins into the depths of the sea: You will show faithfulness to Jacob. . . .*
> —Micah 7:19–20

In the seventh month, on the first day of the month, while I was walking along the riverbank, I lifted up my eyes and I saw, and lo and behold! Samael was standing by the river, and evil angels were roaming around on both of its banks, and as for myself, fear of demons and satyrs had never terrified me all my life long, for I am a Jew, and I fear the Lord, the God of Heaven, alone. So I approached the Satan and enquired of him: "Why are you here, Samael? And what are you doing by this riverbed?" The Satan replied and said: "I am spreading a net over the river, to collect with the trawling net all the sins of the Children of Israel which they will cast away into the depths, into the tumultuous waves, so as to bring them up to Heaven; there will I spread them out in the midst of the divine camp, in order that all the heavenly hosts shall see, on High, the transgressions of this people, that they are mighty, and their sins, that they are exceedingly grievous." I replied: "You have acted foolishly, Samael, as you have chosen for yourself the waters of the land of Poland in which to hunt prey of iniquity and transgression! Make a detour to the rivers of Germany and of France; there the Children of Israel have their sidelocks cropped, there the Children of Israel go clean-shaven, there the Jews wear alien attire, in accordance with the fashion of the gentile nations in whose midst they dwell; whereas we, who are here, wear traditional Jewish garments, our beards are fully grown—not a single hair of them will fall to the ground—and each of the sidelocks of our heads is two-and-a-half cubits in length."

There was yet something further I had to say—and my words were upon my tongue—to recount all our righteous deeds, by virtue of which we are distinguished from the rest of the families of the House of Jacob, but lo and behold! A sound like that of thunder in the celestial sphere impacted on my ears, and I shut my lips, and I turned around to see what it was—and lo and behold! It was the voice of Samael, the Satan—the voice of his mocking laughter at my words. And he replied and said to me: "You have furnished me this day with cause for laughter by reason of your words and of the phrases issuing from your mouth! For you have stated today that it is the fullness of a man's beard and the length of his sidelocks that constitute the witnesses of his perfection of heart, and that the attire worn by him are a sign of righteous or wicked deeds. For it is from both the very hairs of their beards and the sidelocks of their heads that the iniquities of your brethren, the residents of this land, have grown mighty, and beneath the corners of their garments they conceal the foreskins of their hearts and the multitude of their transgressions. Look at the people emerging from the synagogues and the prayer houses! They will come, group after group, to the bank of this river, to seize hold of the corners of their garments and to shake out their sins into the water. Hasten, my satyrs! Gird yourselves with strength, my ministers! Station yourselves, each one of you upon his place! Make ready the net! Fasten its hooks! Strengthen its cords—so that the cord does not snap, or the hook shift, or the net descend to the depths of the riverbed on account of the weight of the burden it is bearing.

> But as for you, stand here together with me!
> Behold, your eyes are opened
> And you shall see the sins
> As they descend into the water" [. . .]

I turned my eyes toward the place to which they had been originally focused, and I saw, and lo and behold, from beneath the garments of the rabbis went forth: the image of jealousy; mockery of good families, mockery at those wise of heart. Mockery directed at everyone: quarrelling and strife, snares and nets, hearts of stone harder than rocks; and an inkwell belonging to scribes, and an image comprising many hands, and a wild boar of the forest, with its mouth polluted by the dung of human excrement bringing up the rear of the entire camp. The Satan said to me: "Do you see? All these have been born to the giant. It is the sin of pride! The image of this jealousy which you have seen is not the jealousy existing among learned men, which increases wisdom; it is that of the jealousy that loves the man who stirs up its spirit, and glorifies him, carrying him upon its hands, and he becomes a model for it: this jealousy, that sets its face against a man for evil, hates him, turns him into a reproach, and, if it could, would swallow him like a fish; this is the jealousy whose eye will be directed for evil objectives against one born at the same hour as oneself when people praise him in the gates, that will hate a resident of its city when people appoint him a rabbi, setting him upon a throne, and instead of according honor to his name, it scorns him. For this too is the fruit of the haughtiness in the hearts of the rabbis—to scorn every human being—to hold both nations and individuals alike in abhorrence. Only their own families are regarded as distinguished, and the families of the entire House of Israel are accounted merely as sheep. All the inhabitants of the world and the dwellers on earth are considered by them as vermin; *they* are giants, and all the wise of heart are mere grasshoppers in their sight. This man whose heart has elevated him heavenward, to devise skillful devices and to expose those who are dragging balls of fine dust along their pathways, is merely the largest of the grasshoppers, a cricket or a bald locust; however, out of the locust family, they alone are deemed giants; all the thoughts of these men are focused on their heads (they call someone of great discernment 'a head')—they live by their heads, they quarrel about their heads, and should one of them say: 'My head is upon me like Mt. Carmel!,' his fellow will speak about himself: 'My head is upon me like Mt. Lebanon!' That is the reason why the men compete, that is the reason why they quarrel, that is the reason why they ensnare souls; that is the reason for their imposition of bans of excommunication; it is not on account of fear of the Almighty, but on account of the pride and the haughtiness of their hearts. For fear of the Almighty causes the dispersed ones to return and brings near those who are distant, while as regards pride, it drives away with its arms everyone who is close to godliness, whereas those who are already distant from it, it disperses further still."

Now I had stood in silence until now, as I was astounded at the vision that I had just seen, to the point where I lacked the ability to find the words to express the inclination of my heart; but as soon as he had spoken, my spirit returned to me and my words came back to my tongue, and I called out: "What is the meaning of this polluted mouth of the pig that I saw? Ah, Lord! What is this unclean wild animal, an abomination for the Children of Israel, doing in the shadow of the wings of our teacher and our master?" The Satan replied and said: "It symbolizes the sin of those who utter unseemly words in their works of halakhic inquiries and responses, who speak in an obscene manner, employing lewd, detestable, and abominable expressions, as does one of those empty-headed individuals who make bodily incisions on themselves in the house of a prostitute, and the word of the Lord has become, in their works, an object of shame and abhorrence of the soul." I replied: "I am not aware, Samael, of any such enquiries concerning which you question me! Is it really your desire that the legislators of Israel should not offer guidance in the laws affecting women during their period of menstrual sickness, or when they have an issue of their blood not in the time of their menstrual ritual impurity? What ought the righteous judges do when arbitrating matters of strife within their gates? Where a women goes astray, and witnesses testify saying: 'She has committed harlotry while under her husband's roof,' should they make a blanket decree to prohibit her having continued marital relations with her husband before they have refined and clarified and sifted the words in question in accordance with statute and religious law? Do they possess the power to speak a word to this effect without creating disorder or concealing ethical laws?" The Satan replied and said: "There are different sorts of cases! For even the sages of the gentile nations, throughout all their dominions, record matters of strife such as these in a book, but their ears examine the words, and they refine their utterances so as to remove the abomination from their midst."

Translated by David E. Cohen.

Pinḥas de Segura

Dates Unknown

Pinḥas de Segura was the chief rabbi of Izmir (Smyrna) and a strong supporter of Western culture and interfaith relations.

A Sermon Delivered at the Great Synagogue of Smyrna on the Arrival of Sir Moses and Lady Montefiore in that City after His Successful Mission on Behalf of His Persecuted Brethren in Damascus
1840

> *Remember, I am with you: I will protect you wherever you go and will bring you back to this land.* —Genesis 28:15.[1]

From the Midrash *Shoḥer tov*.[2] "For the leader. Of the servant of the Lord, of David. I know what transgression says to the wicked." [Psalm 36:1–2.] As scripture says, "O happy Israel! Who is like you, etc." [Deuteronomy 33:29]. The Holy One, blessed be He, fights Israel's wars, but victory is theirs. And scripture says, "for the various signs and portents [. . .] that MOSES displayed" [Deuteronomy 34:11–12]. It does not say the Lord, but MOSES. The Holy One, blessed be He, sent him, but the victory belongs to MOSES. Deborah says, "Arise, O Barak, take your captives" [Judges 5:12]. David, when he went down to Goliath the Philistine, what did he say? "And all the kingdoms of the land shall know that there is a God in Israel" [I Samuel 17:46 reads similarly]. When the women responded, "the women sang as they danced, etc., and David [has slain] his tens of thousands!" [I Samuel 18:7]. David said to the Holy One, blessed be He, You gave me victory, and so I also give you victory.

It is our obligation to praise the infinite master of all, for the miracles and for the salvation, both revealed and hidden. It would not be enough, even if our mouths were filled with song about all of the good that He did for us in times of trouble. And each and every day, we are obligated to thank and praise our God in the heavens, God our salvation. "By Him whose understanding is perfect" [Job 37:16], this will never disappear from our eyes, that which God did for us and our children, like that which he did when the Israelites left Egypt. And He took us out from there by a strong hand, twice, by the hands of MOSES.

Here also, we saw that in every generation, they try to destroy us and our native land. And the Holy One, blessed be He, saved us and does wondrous things each and every day because of the love God has for His people. "Yet, even then, when they are in the land of their enemies" [Leviticus 26:44], it is true that everywhere, not a single nation or language rules over them. "The Lord can give victory without sword or spear" [I Samuel, 17:47]. When they are in distress, He "first afflicts, then pardons" [Lamentations 3:32]. God defends the Torah, which is "drawn up in full and secured," (2 Samuel 23:5), the Torah of MOSES.

[. . .] To thank God, "who delivered the people from under the hand"[3] of cruel peoples, from many peoples who thought to conspire about the whole nation, the Children of Israel, in all regions. They believed lies, killing for the sake of matzo for Passover.

[. . .] It will be for you as you were commanded by MOSES.

They put them, our brothers, in prison. In bitter and hard suffering, "cruel words" [Psalm 64:4]. "And there was a great outcry by the common folk,"[4] and it was bitter, [and] there was "wrath, indignation, and trouble" [Psalm 78:49]. And the leaders of the children of Israel were beaten, "strip her, strip her to her very foundations" [Psalm 137:7]. And they cried out to God, and their cry went up to Him. And God heard their cries, [based on Exodus 2:23–24] and gave the remedy before the plague. God prepared the path, the path of man, the man MOSES.

"Were it not for the Lord, who was on our side" [Psalm 124:1–2], God, "we perish, we are lost" [Numbers 17:27]. "As a father has compassion for his children, so the Lord has compassion for his people,"[5] the people of Israel he created in His world. "And God remembered His covenant" [Exodus 2:24], and provided for us ministers and deputies, heads of exile, noblemen and officers, [. . .] leaders of the House of Israel, the members of the exalted family of Sir ROTHSCHILD. [. . . they are] great and mighty, the wisest of the wise, in the Torah of MOSES. [. . .]

It is not only that He saved us from the hands of all of our enemies, but also that He made this a law for us, for our children, and our children's children, to sustain to this day. For you will no longer remember such as thing as this. MOSES went up before the great king, our master and crown of our head, and told him everything, the evil libels and wicked deeds. "He has given us light" [Psalm 118:27], and our eyes saw. Agreeing with him, the king went up, removed his ring from his hand, and wrote everything commanded by MOSES.

For this, we must pray for the peace of the kingdom "as the moon, established forever" [Psalm 89:38], "O king, live forever" [Daniel 2:4]. Forever we must bless and thank all of the mighty kings upon whom the Children of Israel rely, may their days and years be good. Especially the greatest of all queens, who rules in the city of London [. . .] may her kingdom never be destroyed forever and ever, as in the days of MOSES.

NOTES

1. [All English translations of the Bible come from *The Jewish Publication Society Tanakh*.—Trans.]

2. [*Shoḥer tov* is another name for the Midrash Tehilim, or Midrash on Psalms. This first paragraph is based on the midrash on Psalm 36.—Trans.]

3. [Exodus 18:10 reads "who delivered the people from under the hand of the Egyptians."—Trans.]

4. [Nehemiah 5:1 reads "There was a great outcry by the common folk and their wives."—Trans.]

5. [Psalm 103:13 reads "so the Lord has compassion for those who fear Him."—Trans.]

Translated by Dina Danon.

Isaac Bekhor Amarachi and Joseph ben Meir Sason

In Salonika in 1845–1847, Isaac Bekhor Amarachi operated a printing press that produced Hebrew and Ladino books. Among them were parts of the Zohar (1845) and a Ladino translation of Pinḥas Horowitz's *Sefer ha-berit* (1847). Amarachi also translated a Hebrew biography of Moses Montefiore into Ladino.

Nothing is known about Joseph Sason. In addition to *Sefer musar haskel*, Amarachi and Sason produced another text of *musar* (ethics), *Darkhe ha-adam*. Both works first appeared in Salonika in 1843 and were reprinted twice there.

Sefer musar haskel (Book of Moral Lessons)
1843

We translated *Musar haskel*[1] for the following five reasons:

The first is that our hearts have become so hardened that instruction does not easily penetrate them. This is why we wrote this educational book meant to be grasped by the mind for which it is intended.

The second reason is that last year more than one thousand children died of smallpox. This is why we relayed a lesson from *Sefer ha-berit*[2] to make sure the children are vaccinated against smallpox.

The third reason is that today our bodies are not as strong as they used to be. This is why we related here the fourth chapter of Rambam's *Laws of Behavior* [from *Mishneh Torah*], which rules that one must remain healthy to serve the Creator, and this ruling is not to be changed ever.

The fourth reason is that the verse says: "your wisdom and your understanding in the sight of the peoples" [Deuteronomy 4:6], and our sages of blessed memory say that the wisdom is the science of astronomy. This is why we included a bit of instruction in this science.

The fifth reason is that for our sins, many evils befell Israel because of false messiahs who came and killed millions of Jews. This is why at the end of this book we have a chapter about the Messiah, so that no one would be fooled if someone says that he is the Messiah, because the Messiah was born the day when the Temple was destroyed and is living in the Garden of Eden, as we will explain with God's help.

The author of *Seder ha-dorot*[3] writes that the first man was created on Friday, which was Rosh Hashanah. In the first hour of that day, God gathered dust from the four parts of the world. In the second hour, he molded it into the shape of a body. In the third hour, he made it grow arms and legs. In the fourth hour, he put a soul into it. In the fifth hour, he raised it to its feet. In the sixth hour, God brought all the animals of the sea and the field and all the birds and named them. In the seventh hour, he extracted Eve from Adam's rib. In the eighth hour, Adam and Eve went to bed. There were two of them when they went to bed, and four when they got up. In the ninth hour, God put Adam in the Garden of Eden and forbade him to eat from the Tree of Knowledge. In the tenth hour, Adam ate from the Tree of Knowledge. In the eleventh hour, God cursed him with ten curses. In the twelfth hour, he banished Adam from the Garden of Eden. We must ask why God did not create man by his word, the way he created the animals.[4] We must conclude that God had affection for man and made him his final creation, and that he created the world only for man, which is why he created him little by little. And since man is loved by God, he must protect himself from all kinds of dangers and perils. But because man is flesh and blood and, therefore, cannot live forever, God commanded him to be fruitful and multiply, so that the world may be replenished. For this reason, man is obliged to take care of his children and protect them from all kinds of accidents, because if man does not protect his children the world will be deserted. He is responsible for what God wanted him to do. In particular, it is necessary to vaccinate children to protect them from smallpox, because, for our sins, this year more than one thousand children who had not been vaccinated died of this disease.

NOTES

1. ["Instruction for the Mind." The work is attributed to Hai Gaon, an eleventh-century Jewish scholar in Pumbedita.—Trans.]

2. ["The Book of the Covenant," a compendium of scientific knowledge of the time produced by R. Pinḥas Elijah Horowitz (first published in 1797).—Trans.]

3. ["The Book of Generations," by the Lithuanian rabbi Yehiel Halperin (first published in 1768), is a chronological history from Creation to the author's time.—Trans.]

4. [According to the Bible, animals were created by God's word (Genesis 1:20, 24), while man was actually made by God (Genesis 1:26, 2:7).—Trans.]

Translated by Olga Borovaya.

S. Beilin

Dates Unknown

S. Beilin was a folklorist.

Heder Riddles and Puzzles among Lithuanian Jews
Second Half of the 19th Century[1]

2

A peasant was transporting a large cart of hay. He had to pass through a low gateway, but the cart couldn't pass under it. People advised the peasant to wear glasses with magnifying lenses, so that the gate would become larger, and the cartful of hay could easily pass through.

Even a small child can fully understand that this advice would lead to nothing and will, of course, explain that the growth is only an appearance. Meanwhile a quick-witted solver will immediately rebut the riddle teller with a more apt answer: "But the cartful of hay will also be magnified through the glasses!"

3

At the start of the Sabbath, a Jewish woman was in despair: what to do? She was supposed to say a blessing, as usual, over two burning candles, but she only had one. But she quickly regained her bearings with this solution: she put a mirror next to the burning candle and then two candles appeared before her eyes. Did she act wisely? asks the riddle teller.

Even a small child will understand that the woman's attempt is completely pointless, since the doubling is imagined, not real. However, a child who is presented with the riddle is still perplexed, for two candles are apparent to the eye. A bright child answers—or the adults lead him to answer—that if there are two candles thanks to the mirror, then simultaneously there will also be two women, so that each one of them will still have only one candle and the woman's predicament will not be reduced at all.

8

If the High Priest alone was allowed to enter the Temple's Holy of Holies, and if even he was allowed to enter only on Yom Kippur, then the question arises: what would people do on "Tishebov" (the Ninth of Av, the anniversary of the destruction of the Temple in Jerusalem)? According to the custom of this mournful day, one had to take off the luxurious covering hanging in front of the ark of the covenant. The answer is clear: while the Temple was still in existence, there could of course be no "Tishebov" day of mourning, and therefore there was no need to remove the covering.

9

If *Rosh-khoydesh* (the first of the month, a half-holiday) coincides with the fast of "Tishebov," is it necessary to read the portion of the festive psalms, *Hallel*, assigned for *Rosh-khoydesh*?

An attentive child will immediately point out to you the pointlessness of such a question. *Rosh-khoydesh* means the beginning of the month, while "Tishebov" literally means "the ninth day of the month of Av"; therefore, such an alignment is unthinkable.

11

Three travelers came to an inn. They had a shared treasure, which they gave to the innkeeper for safekeeping, with the condition that he return it to them when demanded not by one, but by all of them. Having given over the treasure, they sat down to eat. During dinner, they sent one of the companions to the innkeeper to ask for wine on behalf of all of them. But the sent man asked for the treasure instead of the wine, as if on behalf of the rest. The innkeeper, to make sure that he may give over the treasure, yelled to the other two companions a short question: "Gentlemen, may I?" They answered, "Yes, you may," assuming that he was speaking about the bottle of wine. The companion disappeared once the treasure was in his hands. When the other travelers learned of the hoax, they turned to a judge, with a complaint against the innkeeper, demanding he give them the treasure. Question: how could he have shielded himself from this responsibility? Answer: "Your Honor!" the innkeeper could have said, "we had an agreement about the return of the treasure upon the consensus and demand of all three companions. Let them, according to this agreement, bring to me their third companion. Then, I will give them the treasure."[2]

31

On one riverbank, there are three Jews and three muzhiks (peasants) with a boat, which can fit no more than two people at a time. They all had to go to the other side of the river, with the necessary condition that there would be no more muzhiks than Jews on either side of the river. That is, there shouldn't be on either riverbank two peasants with one Jew, three peasants with two Jews, etc., so as to avoid violence or insult from the "goyim." But, there can be on either riverbank an equal number of peasants and Jews, or more Jews than peasants, since there is no expectation of Jewish violence and insult against the "goyim."

One should do as follows. Two peasants take the boat to the other bank, one of them gets out, and the other comes back to the first bank and takes the third peasant. In this way, all three peasants are on the other bank. One peasant takes the boat to the first bank, and two Jews take the boat to the second bank, so that there are two Jews and two muzhiks there. Then, one Jew and one peasant go from the second bank to the first, so that there are two Jews and two peasants on the first riverbank. Then, two Jews take the boat from the first bank to the second bank, so that there are all three Jews and one peasant. The peasant takes the boat back to the first bank, so that all three peasants are back on the first riverbank with the boat, and all three Jews are on the second riverbank. Two peasants take the boat to the second bank and one of them comes back with the boat to get the third peasant from the first bank, and they both get off on the second bank.

This procedure can be simplified. From the beginning, one Jew and one muzhik can leave the first riverbank, the Jew comes back with the boat, two muzhiks take it to the second riverbank, and then one can proceed in the way already stated.[3]

NOTES

1. [This work was first printed in 1909. It is based on testimonies going back to the 1860s and forward.—Ed.]

2. Related by the physician Mrs. Raskin, in Tsarskoye Selo, in 1897.

3. This was related by R. S. Plotkiv from Verezino, Minsk area.

Translated by Alexandra Hoffman.

Isaac Samuel Reggio

1784–1855

Considered "the Mendelssohn of Italy," Isaac Samuel (Itsḥak Shemu'el) Reggio (also known as the Yashar) was a rabbi and philosopher. Born in Gorizia, near the Austro-Hungarian border, he mastered languages (including Hebrew) and studied mathematics. In 1819, inspired by Mendelssohn, he wrote an Italian translation of the Pentateuch with a Hebrew commentary. Mendelssohn's influence on Reggio can be felt, as well, in the latter's *Ha-torah ve-ha-filosofyah* (1827), which seeks to reconcile divine law and philosophy. He opened a rabbinical seminary in Padua in 1829. In 1846, following his father's death, he took over as the rabbi of Gorizia.

The Religious Instruction of Jewish Youth
1853

Thus there are two kinds of truths, equally ascertained, and therefore equally admissible; the one proceeding from intellect and called rational truth, the other formed in the heart, and called moral truth. The source of the latter might also properly be called *good sense*, which in fact acts, in many circumstances of life, in lieu of pure reason. A man endowed with good sense, and who has not yet become a slave to sensual appetites, will not doubt for a moment, even without having ever been acquainted with the proofs, that lying, calumniating, blaspheming, false swearing, robbing, murdering, betraying friendship, country or honour, are culpable and abominable actions. Other truths based on good sense are also the following: the faith we have in friendship, in the rectitude of those who administer justice, in the fidelity of a beloved object, in the tenderness of parents, in the excellence of virtue, and above all, in the wisdom, goodness, and providence of God; all these things we admit within our souls, not in consequence of a cold calculation of the intellect, but through an irresistible impulse of the heart. [. . .]

One of the features, which most enhances the value of religion, is precisely this, that it is the product, not of transcendental devices of the mind, but of faith in

God, itself springing from love, and that consequently, it is not originated by the intellect, but infused by a Divine grace. Thus we see every day, in our own experience, that the loftiest thoughts of virtue and heroism are not suggested to us by a long and laborious chain of syllogisms, but break upon us unexpectedly as inspirations of the heart; truly—considering the divine spirit dwelling within us, and which we have but to harbour carefully—they break upon us like inspirations of heaven.

Translated by M. H. Picciotto.

Other works by Reggio: *Ma'amar torah min ha-shamayim* (1818); *Ha-torah ve-ha-filosofyah* (1827); *Mafteaḥ el megilat Ester* (1841); *Beḥinat ha-kabalah* (1852).

Isaac Akrish
died ca. 1888

Isaac Akrish was a leading rabbi and *dayan* (judge) in Istanbul, who took a strong antimodernist stance on issues within the Jewish community. He opposed the teaching of European languages to Jewish youth, claiming that the ability to read Christian texts would lead to heresy. In 1862, he excommunicated Abraham de Camondo, a prominent member of the community, for founding a modern Jewish school in Istanbul. Akrish was almost imprisoned for this decision, but pressure from members of the Jewish community and the Ottoman government allowed him to remain free. Eventually he moved to Hebron, where he died.

Sefer kiryat arba
1858

There is a matter well known and widely publicized among all those who have come through the gates of our city, Constantinople [Istanbul], may God preserve it.... [I]t occurred about two years after the establishment of the school among us here in Constantinople, may God preserve it, that was to teach Jewish children, the youngest students in the school, the languages of the gentiles with their books.

A plague broke out among most of the children who studied there at that time; they went off into an evil way of life. They threw off the yoke of heavenly rule from themselves—from reciting the *Shema* declaration and from worshipping God (worship meaning [the *Amidah*] prayer). They mock the ritual washing of the hands and other things of this type. They say things to their mothers which we would not want to hear, all of which they have learned from their teacher there. [The teacher] was brought in from a distant land, a land of strange language, just as [the school was founded], in order to teach the children the languages of the gentiles. He would teach them from the books of religions of the nations of the world, the belief in that certain man and his mother,[1] may our ears be spared from hearing of it. Woe to the generation in which such things occur!

For this reason a committee of householders of our city, may God preserve it, has arisen to protest and complain to the Torah scholars (may God preserve them), saying that they are in the right in raising the flag of Torah and that such things may not be done among [the people of] Israel—to teach Jewish youngsters the languages of the gentiles while they still lack discernment, Torah knowledge, and fear of God because they are so young. This brings them to read books about the religions of the nations of the world, and [about] natural philosophy, which is forbidden because it contradicts knowledge of the Divine, God forbid, as well as [the doctrine of] the creation of the world, and similar things. These are the sorts of matters written in the books of the nations in their languages and according to their peoples, as is known. The fathers and mothers [of the students] understand nothing of this because they themselves are unfamiliar with the writings of those languages. This is how [students] end up throwing off the yoke and coming to heresies or the types of actions that occurred with some of the children, as was mentioned.

When a group of Torah scholars, may God preserve them, heard about all this they were deeply saddened. They asked themselves, "What can we do? The matter can only be solved by the greatest scholars of the generation, those rabbis, may God preserve them, upon whom the entire House of Israel rests!" The issue was very painful. Faith was almost lost entirely from the mouths of babies and infants, the youngest students in the school from whose mouths we derive life, as the sages say in various places.

For this purpose the Torah scholars, may God preserve them, acted with zeal and gathered together. There were about eighty rabbis, may God preserve them, and they determined together with God[2] not to allow any Israelite to send his son or his daughter to the school where they learn any one of the languages of the gentiles; rather [they must study] only our holy Torah and the language of Ishmael specifically and nothing else.³ The reason for this permission for the language of Ishmael is a secret, as is known. They announced this agreement in synagogue on the holy Sabbath, in all the synagogues in the city. Happy is Israel! Almost everyone accepted it gladly.⁴

NOTES

Words in brackets appear in the original translation.
1. A euphemism for Jesus and Mary.
2. I.e., in a legal decree.
3. Likely a reference to Ottoman Turkish in this case, although elsewhere the expression "Language of Ishmael" is employed by Jewish authors to refer to Arabic.
4. Although Akrish leaves off on a positive note here, later in the text he acknowledges that divisions on this issue continued to plague the Jewish community of Istanbul.

Translated by Matt Goldish.

Emmanuil Borisovich Levin
1820–1913

Emmanuil Borisovich Levin was a writer and public intellectual on Jewish political affairs in the tsarist empire. A proponent of secular education, Levin wrote a Russian grammar textbook for Jewish schools in the 1840s and taught in a Talmud Torah in his native Minsk as well as in the state-run rabbinical seminary in Zhitomir. He moved to St. Petersburg in the 1860s, where he became closely associated with the Gintsburg family of Russian Jewish financiers and communal activists. Levin was the first secretary of the Society for the Promotion of Culture among the Jews of Russia. With the support of Baron Goratsii Gintsburg, Levin published (sometimes anonymously) memoranda and other documents concerning the legal position of the Jews in Russia, their struggle for rights, and their collective plight in the effort to ensure legal emancipation.

Note on the Emancipation of the Jews of Russia
1859

For the purposes of preparing for this emancipation, *four* measures are proposed: 1) the establishment of a Jewish newspaper in Russian; 2) the establishment of a scholarly literary journal in Yiddish; 3) a reform of public Jewish schools; and 4) reform of the system of tax collection from Jews.

Sent to Evzel Gabrielovich Gintsburg in Petersburg, 13 July 1859

The goal, toward which all reasonable Jews in Russia at this time must strive, is undoubtedly to achieve *emancipation*, i.e., complete equality with Russians in terms of civic and political rights. In the rest of Europe, with the exclusion of France, Holland, and Belgium, emancipation of the Jews was achieved only through a long struggle in which famous writers and the most enlightened minds took a lively and active part. In spite of this, however, Jews in Western Europe are not everywhere emancipated. In our opinion, the reason for this lies, on the one hand, in centuries-old prejudice, constantly supported in the nations by hostile Christian writers who, consciously distorting Jewish religious teachings, strive to prove that the Jewish people are incapable of development and therefore are unworthy of regaining civic rights, which were taken away from them by the grim fanaticism of the Middle Ages. On the other hand, the reason lies in the constitutional form of government in many European states, where the passions and mentalities of parties have a freer playing field, and where the will of the monarch alone is not powerful enough to rein them in.

All this does not exist in Russia. Literature in our fatherland has up to this point, with few exceptions, touched on Jews minimally or not at all: Judaism was not considered important enough to be dealt with seriously. Some individual writers who were hostile to Jews fortunately did not exercise their authority. The newest journalism is currently saturated with a humanist spirit and relates positively to us. In this regard, our coreligionists throughout Germany can envy us. On the other hand, public opinion here in Russia is still in its infancy and is only *beginning* to form, while the autocratic government is not limited by any parliamentary politics. It is true that for the simple Russian folk, there is a certain antipathy toward Jews that is connected to some kind of ridiculous fear. But this antipathy is far removed from German hatred; it is irrational, not based on a firm understanding, and therefore it is easy to disturb it and transform it in due time into a brotherly agreement, if only we are able to take on the task in the proper way.

To achieve Jewish emancipation in Russia, it is necessary to influence the emerging public opinion, pre-empting the false judgment that our detractors, at the awakening of our civic life, will not hesitate to spread about us; we need to try to familiarize the Russian public with our three-thousand-year history, rich literature, true religious teachings, manners, customs, and qualities of the Jewish people. Do we have to prove that in Russia absolutely no one, not even the educated classes and the government itself, knows Jews? In a nation where there isn't even a Bible in the country's language, it is not surprising that no one has any knowledge of Jewish literature and religion, about their God-given holy mission to humankind. Everyone knows the kinds of murky sources from which those few are drawn, extremely fragmented and meager pieces of information about Judaism that force our government to descend from one mistake to the next. However, it is also necessary to act internally, i.e., toward educating the Jewish *masses*. It is necessary to prepare our coreligionists little by little for a great era and make them worthy and able to comprehend a higher good. Especially with the new spirit of the current government, we have reason to hope for the beginnings of such an era.

For the fulfilment of the two needs mentioned above, in our opinion three things are necessary: 1) a *public organ* in the Russian language, for the defense of Judaism from the outside; 2) a *scholarly literary journal* in the Yiddish language, for influencing the Jews themselves; and 3) *a radical transformation of Jewish schools*.

Translated by Alexandra Hoffman.

Other works by Levin: *Svod uzakoneni o yevreyakh* (1885); *Perechen ogranichitelnykh zakonov o yevreyakh v yevreyakh o rossii* (1890).

Grigory Bogrov
1825–1885

Born to a prominent rabbinical family in Poltava, Ukraine, Grigory Bogrov was a Russian-language writer, memoirist, and essayist on Jewish issues. Despite his traditional upbringing, Bogrov was sympathetic to maskilic ideals. In 1863, he began composing *Zapiski evreia* (Notes of a Jew), the three-volume memoir for which he is best known. Serialized over three years in Nikolai Nekrasov's journal *Otechestvennykh zapiskakh*, this was one of the first works by a Jewish author that seriously explored issues of contemporary Jewish life in Russia for a non-Jewish audience. Rich in thick ethnographic descriptions of Jewish life, the book was well-received and widely translated, although later critics accused the author of self-loathing for his harsh critique of Jewish life. Bogrov moved to St. Petersburg, where he was deeply involved with the circle of Russian Jewish intellectuals. He famously considered himself an "emancipated cosmopolitan," bound to the Jewish people through a sense of common fate and persecution, but not by much else. He converted to Russian Orthodoxy shortly before his death in order to marry a Christian woman.

Notes of a Jew
1863

Childhood Sufferings

PART 1, CHAPTER 2

However modestly my parents lived in the country, however little I was used to luxury and every comfort, at least at home I was used to cleanliness and order, to unbroken if simple pieces of furniture. Here I saw something completely different.

The room was fairly big and irregularly shaped. Two wide-open doors on the sides, leading into dark spaces, reminded me of the open mouths of toothless old men. The room was lit by a single tallow candle-end placed in a tall, dusty copper candlestick. The furniture consisted of a simple table, three or four unpainted chairs, and a low cupboard. In the eastern corner was a small ark covered by a faded brocade cloth.

A stooped old Jew sat at the table in front of an enormous open book. When we entered, he slowly lifted his head and lazily turned it toward us. I met his eyes meekly and was startled by his face. Under a pair of bushy gray brows, I saw gray eyes. Almost his whole face was covered by his long thick *peyes* and beard; what was not covered by growth was ashy yellow. Innumerable wrinkles traced his flat brow. A faded, soiled, velveteen yarmulke on the back of his head made a greasy, dirty spot on his bald skull.

"Well, sit down, Reb Zelman, you are welcome here," he greeted my father in a hoarse, guttural voice. "Ah, so this is your kid? Looks like a weak little thing . . . What has he been taught at home?"

"He can read the Bible a bit, but nothing else yet."

"That's very little, you'll have to work hard, kid! You can't be lazy here; I don't spoil anyone."

I kept quiet, but a sob caught in my throat. It took all my child's willpower not to start wailing. I would undoubtedly have failed but for another person who darted in through one of the side doors and caught my attention. I saw a stooped, wrinkled, small old woman with a face like a soaked apple, eyes small and black like thorns, no trace of eyelashes, and a nose like the beak of the most bloodthirsty bird of prey.

"There you are, Zelman! Thank God!" the old woman said in an unpleasant treble. "I'd already concluded that you changed your mind about bringing your little boy!"

"Why did you think so, auntie?" my father asked.

"God knows what kind of people you are! Your Rebecca is such a fashion plate that she may have decided it's not necessary to have her son educated." [. . .]

"My dear auntie," father said with a conciliatory smile, "let's not quarrel the first time we all meet."

During this whole unpleasant scene, I seemed not even to exist; they had completely forgotten about me. Finally, the nasty old woman noticed me, seemingly by accident.

"Aha! That's your son? He looks so delicate! He must have been raised on gingerbread! If I'd known he was so sickly, I'd never have agreed to take on such a burden. He could get sick and die, and I'll be held responsible. Come here, kid," Leah called me in the most commanding of tones.

I went to her unwillingly and timidly. She took my chin in her dry wrinkled hand and roughly raised my head.

"Are you spoiled? Huh? Tell the truth, kid. You watch out here . . . By God, I don't spoil anyone; I don't tolerate any nonsense around here." [. . .]

The reception we were given presaged nothing good. It was hard to sleep, but physical and emotional exhaustion brought me into that deep slumber that children attain after crying for an hour.

The next morning my father turned over my few belongings, gave me a few silver coins, said an unusually tender farewell, and left. I was now alone.

From that day I began to go to the *heder* (school), where my stern guardian and teacher ruled despotically. The heder was in a shack that my uncle rented from a poor Jewish woman. We studied in a low, dim room with sooty walls and a gigantic stove with a shelf on top. That shelf was our oasis in the desert: there we huddled in the dim light and rested; there we ate the provisions that each of us had brought; there we told frightening tales about dead people and witches; there we made merry. As soon as the thin one-kopeck tallow candle was lit and a light pierced the darkness of the shelf, we jumped down; the light was a signal to gather around the table and bend again threefold over our books until late at night. We followed this same routine every day. The numbing monotony lay on our souls like a dead weight, with no distraction, not a minute of rest during the entire day; how nice it would have been to run around, how we wanted to stretch our aching limbs!

There were about fifteen of us students. We lived more or less in harmony and friendship. The Jewish heder is an unusual kind of school, where all the students are equally intimidated, equally timid, equally scared, equally suffocated by the dreadful power of the teacher, who punished us at whim and was partial to no one. A kind of fellow feeling developed among the heder students, as among prisoners taken together to captivity and put in the same cell. The more the *melamed* (teacher) persecuted any one of the students, the more affinity the others felt for this student. Then again, the lucky one who was the teacher's favorite and suffered less from his cruelty would awaken envy, expressed in open enmity, from his classmates. This trait is so deeply etched into the Jewish character from childhood that it does not leave him even when he and his fellow heder students enter adult society. A Jew would give his last shirt to his suffering fellow, share his last piece of bread with him in a time of trouble, but is suffused with poisonous envy and malice when his fellow Jew succeeds. He is prepared to destroy the other's happiness with his own hand, at no benefit to himself, just to bring him down to the same level. For the Jew, fate is just such a vile, fickle *melamed*.

Translated by Gabriella Safran.

Other works by Bogrov: *Zapiski evreia* (1871–1873); *Evreiskii manuscript: Pered dramoi* (1876); *Maniak* (1884).

Mordechai Aaron Gintsburg
1795–1846

Born in Salantai, Lithuania, Mordechai Aaron Gintsburg spent his life in Kovno and Vilna. Gintsburg took a moderate position in contemporary debates about reconciling Judaism and modernity, arguing that enlightened ideals of reason were not in opposition to religion, but a means to counteract superstition. Perhaps with this effort in mind, he translated many secular histories (including stories about the discovery of the New World) into Yiddish and Hebrew, and was at the forefront of efforts to revitalize Hebrew as a modern language. Besides these translations, Gintsburg wrote widely, and together with Solomon Salkind, he founded the first Jewish secular school in Lithuania in 1841.

Aviezer
1863

Chapter 31

One day I came back from my synagogue and sat down in my room to take breakfast—a bowl of milk and some bread, instead of the compote juice and butter cake that had been my customary breakfast since the first days of my existence. And here comes my mother-in-law and shuts the door behind her, as if she has some secret to tell me. But I, who had begun to scorn her in the recesses of my heart, did not rise from my seat and ignored her until she took the lead and said: "Tell me, what is your interest in money?"

"And who has asked you for money?!" I proudly parried her question.

"If only you had asked," she replied angrily, "for it is better to ask than to st . . . st . . . steal, to steal."

The word had left her mouth, and streams of blood broke forth like a flash-flood to deluge my heart. An unnatural passion raised me forcefully from my seat and to my feet, and placed the following words in my mouth: "Is it a *theft* that you are asking me about?" I grabbed the bowl and poured the milk to the ground before her eyes, and who knows where my youthful fury would have led me had my mother-in-law not rushed out of my sight, and let me take out my wrath on the wood- and stone-work of the house. In short order I left in fury from the house and went to the house of R. Simhah, my teacher, to complain about my troubles. They kept silent and did not offer consolation, for they saw that my misery was too great for me to be consoled. I was still pouring forth my anguish to them when one member of my in-laws' household who liked me came and whispered in my ear that they had found the stolen object that I had been suspected of taking (based on my wife's slander). A stream of tears then gave relief to my distressed heart and calmed me a little.

The master of the house, R. Simhah, then gave vent to his wrath: through that servant he sent my mother-in-law angry words (of which the messenger kept nine measures to himself while transmitting only a tenth to her). Driven by his love of tranquility, my teacher expended much effort until he persuaded me to return to my in-laws' house and have lunch there. [. . .]

But the façade cast by my wife had also fallen from my mother-in-law's eyes. Her eyes no longer prejudiced by love of her daughter, she now saw and realized that her daughter had attempted to slander me and worried about the damage to her reputation should word get out in town about the plot against a son dear to his parents. She especially feared her husband, for she knew that he truly loved me. Her heart turned against her daughter, whom she punished with words and fierce blows. When I returned home at noon bitterly scowling, I found my mother-in-law greeting me with a smiling face and kind words. From that day onward I recovered my proper status and earlier semblance of dignity.

The anger on my face did not pass, and I did not inquire about my wife, whom I had not seen that entire day. She had secluded herself in her grandfather's house to ponder the shame that her mother had heaped on her. When I [later] went angrily and scowling to my bedroom, she slithered in, fell to my feet, and, with cheeks red from weeping and shame, took me by the hand and asked me if my anger over the insult had abated (for which her mother, with the fist, had taken her to account). If my desire for revenge was not sated, she added words that were a mixture of joking and desolation: she was now ready to suffer a second time at my hand, but I must not bring my case to her father in writing. Her words overcame my rage to the point where I promised to forget all her transgressions against me.

My mother-in-law repented with all her heart the ill she had done me, and resolved to behave really well toward me in order to atone for her previous maltreatment. She saw that so long as my bed was not complete, her daughter would not direct her love toward me. She had the idea of using medical means to arouse male potency in me. However, typical of her simple ways, she consulted not doctors but rather wise women, who cleverly discovered that the root of my halting powers was in some bewitched potion that an enemy of my in-laws had made me drink on my wedding day, and that I would never be able to have a proper erection until I had removed that spell.

This message from my mother-in-law was conveyed to me by one of the brothers of my father-in-law whom she knew had the power to bend me to his will. This man implored me to remove the charm within me by a vomit-inducing herb that one wise woman had prepared.

These words had a great impact on me. I told myself that, since a verbal spell was cast upon me by the casual utterance of a witch, a whisper from the lips of a holy magician (*baal shem*) would remove it. I therefore gave my nose to his incense and my ears to his vain whisperings, and now a *physical* magic lingers like a stone in my intestines—which I must eject by the force of violent and frequent vomiting. All this quite serious medicine was for an illness that I did not feel!

The marvelous result that the potion was to have [as the woman had promised] is effective only to the mind of someone who believes anything. She ordered that all the vomit that spewed from my throat was to be collected in a vessel, that it be poured onto a bonfire stoked for that purpose. And when the bewitched substance comes in contact with the fire, the heart of the sorcerer will burn; it was only extinguishable by waters drawn from the home of the victim of the witchcraft—an idea that the wise men of Egypt and the doctors of Gilead had never heard of! Although there is no counting and no cataloging the vast acts of madness that men commit for love of women (love has neither vision nor understanding), a man like myself not yet inflamed by the spirit of lust would be completely insane to wander after such inanities as these (all just to discover a lust unbeknownst to him!). All right-minded people, beware of such idiocy!

Nevertheless, my powers of resistance faded before the entreaties of my wife, who brought this love potion to me in my room, her cheeks scarlet from embarrassment, and forced me to take the potion if there was a single shred of love left in my heart for her. I reflected on my ways and found that I ought to do as she wished, if only out of decency. I shut my eyes tight, opened my mouth, and swallowed the entire contents of the cup.

Chapter 32

Running for its life, the terrified hare is chased by a ferocious dog that catches it and bites it once or twice vigorously and fiercely until it collapses unconscious. Then the dog loses its ferocity and hovers over its prey, calmly licking the blood running from its flesh. Oh leave me alone and do not kiss me, cries the hare, for your kisses hurt more than your bites.

I apply this fable impartially to my wife: her new love was worse than the hatred she had hitherto shown. The full effect of her animosity extended only to my exterior and clothing, but her cup of love penetrated to my very soul. When the contents of the mother-in-law's potion reached my innards, all my insides disintegrated, spilling out as water from this side and that; my heart raced and shook from its place; fountains of phlegm opened and spewed unceasingly—until my soul grew weak from the ailment.

The members of the household, rejoicing over the wonderful news that was soon to come, busied themselves with their labors of love for me: one built the fire, another got a vessel ready, and several stood armed with clubs and sticks waiting for the witch to arrive to extinguish the flames of his burning heart with waters from the house.

I imagine that if, at the moment they cast the vomit onto the fire, a neighbor had come by to ask for some water to quench his thirst, he would have received furious blows at their hands. However, the eye of fortune shone on them and did not penalize them for our idiocy; I alone—my teeth bent by the unripe fruit that I ate—was punished.

Into the afternoon the herb did its work deep in my innards. Afterward, it emerged from the holes in which it was hiding and acted brazenly, in full view: all my insides had turned into fountains of water and my throat into a fountain of vomit that flooded and filled all the vessels that the members of the household had sacrificed (until I had practically vomited up my mother's milk). Even when my mother-in-law relented and tried to stop the retching by a citron-fruit concoction, she only managed to shift its path from the upper exit holes to the lower ones—the intense medicine did not free me from its grasp until late at night. After that I slept a deep sleep—but not one of rest—until morning.

At dawn I suddenly awoke and tried to move my hands and feet, but my powers failed. I tried to regain my strength with the appetizing foods that my mother-in-law set forth copiously before me. But my lust for food failed to stimulate the lust for sex that they meant to enhance. I turned my head to the wall and lay down until noon. As the sun rose higher, my strength slowly returned. I rose from my bed to walk around the house a bit in fits and starts. I even tried to eat a light snack, but as soon as the food entered my throat, it was engulfed by the pain of swallowing; any pleasure from eating was outweighed by the pain of swallowing. Although to comply with the wishes of my mother-in-law (who verbally pressured me to eat to the full) I stuffed my mouth with food and forced myself to swallow some, the rest I turned around and covertly spit out, until I had emptied more than half my plate—not to restore myself but to calm the heart of my mother-in-law. Then I went back to bed and stayed there.

I slept badly that night, for I was beset by violent and frequent chills that wracked all my organs. I drew no heat from the multitude of blankets and pillows that the members of the household had showered on me. Nor could I see the light of the stove that they moved close to my bed. I rejected the hot drink they brought up to my mouth, concerned that it would further hurt my throat. In vain I carved out a "grave" in the depths of the pillows and blankets to protect me from the cold outside air, but the stormy chills coming from my insides could not be stopped.

Around midnight the grip of the chills had weakened, and an unnatural heat took me forcefully in its grasp and squeezed my marrow, like rivers of burning pitch twisting in my veins. A raging fire came out from my deepest innards to boil my blood; soon I shook off my blankets and clothes and rolled about naked in my bed as on burning coals. As all the members of the household were dozing, there was nothing to stop me from grabbing a pitcher of cold water and drinking it to the very last. Although my throat hurt from each mouthful of water, the pain burning in my belly was still worse than that in my throat. But just as before my clothes had lost their power to block out the cold, so now did the water lose its power to quench my blazing fire. Hence cold and heat kept changing their guard over my depleted body, until early morning, when a troubled sleep descended on me, I slept the sleep of the wicked in hell.

With daylight I awoke tired and oppressed: the fever had left me, but a dry and wracking cough exhausted me and the swelling kept growing in my throat. I looked in the mirror on the wall and beheld the illness had brought forth a white flag on my face to mark its territory. Through all this my mother-in-law did not deign to seek a doctor, but only the old ladies whose coals had already singed me were present. I fought with her as hard as I could and resisted taking medicines from them. My teacher took my side to keep me from being handed over to these ladies on matters of internal medications; only one external treatment, the washing of feet, was I persuaded to receive from their hands.

Chapter 33

But Oh! Even these waters of salvation drawn for me at the counsel of the women became waters of affliction: the first waters into which I put my feet were not hot enough for curative purposes. As they rushed to pour in the additional water that was beyond boiling, I did not manage to withdraw my feet quickly enough before some boiling water fell on my right foot and instantly scalded it. Soon I was ailing in all my organs inside as well as out, from my neck to the sole of my foot. Such is my reward for heeding my mother-in-law's follies!

Either this external pain or the fright it caused evidently hindered the illness from its intended course, so that that day the fever was late in coming; I even allowed myself to imagine that it would never return. Similarly, the household experts congratulated themselves that this external pain had rescued my soul from its inner torments; so they did not worry about me until the following night and kept firmly to their beds in a deep sleep. I alone could not find sleep in my eyes, I rolled about hurting from the bandaged foot and every few minutes alternately tied and untied my leggings to change the bandages they had placed on it, in order to dispel the heat. In the middle of the night the fever returned and burned my bones with greater fire and greater might—both the pain in my throat and the burns on my leg were forgotten in the distress of my soul. I melted in the fire of the fever; I tried to awaken the sleeping with calls and found that the throat roared but no one woke up. I thought of extinguishing the fire with cold water, but the experience of the previous night showed me water could not extinguish such a fire. And my damaged foot would not let me budge from my place; I lurched and moaned, I opened my mouth and inhaled a dragon's breath until I despaired of salvation. I uncovered my arms and legs and wrapped my head in my blanket and lay down as if comatose.

Oh, how I suffered that night and how exhausted I was from thirst! To this day I imagine that if I had then seen my brother (my mother's son) bleeding to death, I would have fallen upon him to quench my thirst with his blood. With the last shred of strength I managed to throw the blankets to the ground and fell crawling on hands and knees to beg for water. But my strength failed and I collapsed, my dry tongue sticking out of my mouth.

At the sound of my fall, my mother-in-law woke up and aroused the remaining household members who hastened to lift me up and put me back in bed. But I shouted in their ears: "Carry me and throw me into the water." But, following medical rules unbeknownst to me, they refrained from reviving me by filling my mouth with cold water! I begged them, wept bitterly, fought with them, cursed and screamed until despite themselves they relented and gave me some lukewarm water. To compensate, they forced me to drink large quantities of hot water to banish the internal heat with the external. A curse on you witchdoctors!

Before morning nature won out against all its foes internal and external, and cast me into a deep sleep. As the fever had left me before dawn, my sleep was uninterrupted until noon, when I woke up, rubbed my eyes, looked around at all my surroundings, and behold: my father-in-law too was standing above me, having returned from his travels in the morning! Then all the stones [that were sealing] my heart rolled away; I held his hand and kissed him; tears of joy dripped from my eyes. Not in vain did my heart swell, for his first words were: do not play around any more with home remedies. He sent for a doctor, who would address the matter of my illness with the diagnoses of medical science.

With all that, my cure was late in coming, and my soul found only a feeble voice, for the doctor took his time in relieving the power of the fever by his medications. In the goodness of his heart my father-in-law did not spare any expense. The eyes of the entire household were on me, their hands ready always to serve me all day. At night too they hourly changed guards in maintaining a vigil over me; only my wife, who had caused this tempest, did not share my troubles, despite the eyes of her mother; [instead] she turned her attention to her enjoyments and youthful games in her grandfather's house. Indeed, I was secretly grateful to her for this: just then she was a thorn in my side.

I had a few more sleepless nights, and several hours of fever that sent hot steam to my brain to the point where, at times, I became incoherent and spoke nonsense before nature gathered its powers to combat the illness and pushed it out through the pores of the skin by means of heavy sweat. The afflicting fever then passed.

Chapter 34

The impairments of this disorder linger in my memory. Here is one of the mysteries that I offer to scientists who study psychology to determine its solution. The mystery is as follows.

While the hand of the illness ruled over me, my soul detested all desirable foods, some seemed bitter and others acidic to me. Nothing tasted good except apple juice mixed with water and honey. In my youthful mind's eye I could only imagine the reason for this to be the spoilage of the food; but then a malicious spirit overtook me and made me conclude perversely that my wife in her hatred and evil heart was spoiling all the foodstuffs being prepared for me (rather like the suspicion that the common masses felt toward elites in the cholera days). As I was harboring this suspicion in my heart, my mind—burning with the flames of the fever—generated groundless ideas like this, to the point that the idea became anchored in my heart like a well-placed spike.

It was night, and the servant was preparing a pot of chicken soup in front of me. My wife came and tasted the concoction. At that moment the power of imagination took control of my eyes, and the force of illusion passed before me, and I saw my wife pouring vinegar into the pot! With my own eyes, not a stranger's, I saw this. My heart had not yet seduced me to judge based on what I saw; I waited for my palate to render the true verdict. But once I tasted it and my palate sensed something like vinegar, my thinking no longer equivocated since I possessed certification from two authorities—my eyes and my palate. In vain did all those then at home (including my faithful teacher) taste the pot of soup and swear that nothing was wrong with it: what were their beliefs worth compared to the direct evidence of my senses?

Will I ever again be surprised by the wondrous apparitions seen by the feeble-minded—terrifying pictures visible to those who believe in them? Let me never suspect that those who profess such visions are inventing them! Not so! They truly see ghouls and the spirits of the dead that they talk about. [. . .]

I had just begun to breathe the air of health when my father-in-law slipped away once more to his place of business. Just as I had wept tears of joy when he arrived, so I wept tears of sadness when he left. My heart feared that my wheel of fortune—turned toward the good by his hand—might be turned backward once his controlling hand was removed. [I worried that] my tears were offensive to my mother-in-law, who might consider them a silent rebuke, but on this occasion I was proven wrong: my mother-in-law's love truly returned to me, and she showed me pity after my days of illness as a woman pities the fruit of her own womb. She did not withhold from me any nourishment that the doctor had prescribed to help me, and in the course of six weeks the bloom of health again began to surface on my cheeks as of yore.

This [episode] was the first thorn that time had cast on my boyhood days; as it was a true not imaginary affliction, and my heart was soft and prone to unrestrained excitement, it impressed itself very deeply on the furrows of my heart, such that it would take a long time before I could efface it. I had the memory of those awful days, and the cause of them, before me always. Nor was I wrong to surmise that double trouble would yet arise: for what good was it that I loved my mother-in-law or father-in-law, if my wife's heart was not mine? So long as I do not win her affections I shall be considered a foreigner in this house, and how shall I be attractive to her and draw her to me with bonds of love? As my soul lacks the alluring gemstone that draws the hearts of maidens toward young men, such ideas pressed like stones upon my heart and did not permit a joyous spirit to return to me for many days after I had regained my strength.

Throughout all this it never occurred to me to call my parents to rescue me, as I knew they had enough troubles on their own. I took my private courage as my strength and relied on my patience; I said that either I shall save myself or I shall suffer what I cannot prevent. Therefore my letters to them contained nothing more than a brief "Hello" and "All is well." But one of father's faithful friends, who was living in my in-laws' town and who knew what I was enduring, did not act in this way: when he happened to go to my father's town, he told him in full that I was not lying in a bed of roses and revealed to him the illness that I had suffered. My parents heard this and took fright; my father soon resolved to come and meet me.

So one day, I was sitting on my seat lost in thought, my head in my hands, wondering what the Lord had in store for me, when a man dressed in traveler's garb came to the house. I lifted my eyes to the arriving visitor, and good Lord! "Father!" I called, and he answered, "Son!" and instantly we were wrapped in each other's arms. I stood astounded and stunned and could not bring a thing out of my poor lips, but my father kept greeting me. All my excitement, all my strength, my feelings, and my revived spirit came together at their proper destination—my heart, leaving almost no other trace of life in all my other limbs. This was the moment of ecstasy that forcefully overcomes years of pain and anguish!

NOTE

Words in brackets appear in the original translation.

Translated by Jay Harris.

Other works by Gintsburg: *Gelot ha-arets ha-hadashah* (adapted from Joachim Heinrich Campe's *The Discovery of America*, 1823); *Kiryat sefer* (1835); *Devir* (1844).

Mikhail Morgulis

1837–1912

Mikhail Morgulis was a Russian Jewish writer and activist. Educated as a rabbi at the state-run rabbinical seminary in Zhitomir, Morgulis later settled in Odessa, where he became deeply involved in projects related to Jewish Enlightenment, education, and reform as a member of the city's branch of the Society for the Promotion of Culture among the Jews of Russia. Morgulis wrote extensively on the "Jewish Question" and political matters in Jewish and general Russian periodicals, including *Rassvet* and *Den'*. While an early supporter of Jewish settlement in Palestine, he then opposed political Zionism. In his writings, Morgulis fought against antisemitism, encouraged the development of Yiddish literature and culture, opposed the Hebraization of Jewish schools, and promoted the synthesis of traditional Judaism with universalist principles. His memoirs were published in the journals *Voskhod* and *Evreiskii mir*.

Toward a History of the Education of Russian Jews
ca. 1863

Period III

In our first series of discussions, we explored the struggle between the government and the Jews, which was initiated by the former and ended with its triumph over the latter; in the second series, we talked about the same struggle, initiated by the Jews and ending, as we have seen, with a factual, though unofficial, victory for the latter. In this section, we explore the internal struggle within various Jewish elements who came to clash over their obvious diversity in their desires to realize the goal of educating Jews.

On the one hand, the government assumed that central religious injunctions, created in France by Napoleon, were highly instrumental in "eliminating former prejudices that alienated Jews from civic society." Therefore, the main goal of the government in terms of reforming the Jews was to establish a special institution called *crown rabbis*, who, having been educated in the spirit of the government, could serve as conduits to convey the state's ideas into Jewish civic life. Accordingly, the crown rabbis were to utilize the Jewish religion as a tool for reformation, since, in the view of the Jewish Committee, the Jewish religion was considered "the primary and only power influencing the social and familial conditions of this people." Later, however, this measure appeared one-sided because Jews could not trust the government organs and could not "accept civic authority as valid in matters of religion." This led to the conclusion that it was necessary to create a central institution, and to give it religious authority in the eyes of the Jews, since it, through its moral influence, could "give credence to all orders given by the government for the reformation" of the Jews and, under the closest supervision of the Ministry of Internal Affairs, could "direct *state rabbis* to gradually merge Jews into the general population, and to turn their activities to benefit the state." And so on 18 May 1848 the government formed the Rabbinical Commission. [. . .]

From the questions suggested by this second expanded rabbinical commission, two are significant for our discussion: 1) Jewish women's academies, and 2) the directive to rabbis to deliver model sermons.[1] With regard to the second of these questions, the rabbinical commission's investigation did not conclude with positive results, and we will discuss this in a different place when we deal with the influence of rabbinical schools on Jewish education. The first question, however, was initially resolved, but the measures suggested by the commission to achieve the goal of educating Jewish women appear to be more than naïve. The commission acknowledged that education of Jewish females, especially among the lower classes, is in a state of "relative neglect." Since this circumstance presupposes the existence among Jews of prejudice, based on faulty understanding, the commission was convinced of the need to investigate whether there are, in the teachings of the Jewish faith, places that, if interpreted literally, could have given rise to false understandings about the state of education of women among the masses. [. . .]

The commission learned that the Talmud has significance for both religious and civic affairs, and that the combination of Talmudic rules is called the Law (Torah), equal to the dogmatic teaching of Moses; according to Jewish religious convictions, the laws contain hidden wisdom, the understanding of which requires systematic and consistent study. Therefore, for females whose activities are limited to the domestic sphere, scholarly study of the law is completely useless and even, in many respects, harmful. Further, the Talmud contains a magnitude of laws, the fulfillment of which are not related to women's obligations and the study of which would be for them, according to Jewish understanding, simple "futile vanity." The commission thus concludes that the above-mentioned saying ["Anyone who teaches his daughter Torah teaches her *tiflut*" (frivolity) (b. Sotah 21b)], which forbids women to study the Law (Torah), has in mind Talmudic laws that cannot have any significant benefit for woman, and therefore it does not foreclose a way toward intellectual and moral development of the woman. [. . .]

Agreeing with the basic perspective of the 1857 commission that the Jewish religion does not forbid women's intellectual development, we cannot accept as expedient the measures chosen by the commission to achieve the goal of educating Jewish women. Having accepted a faulty base as the starting point for their assessment, the commission accordingly chose false measures for the achievement of the goal.[2]

NOTES

1. [The other questions included in the commission concern the prayer for the new moon (month); considering a type of oath for Jews; upholding bookkeeping standards; and establishing rules for selecting members of synagogue boards and prayer schools, as well as holding these governing boards accountable to procedures.—Trans.]

2. [The measures included ordering rabbis, preachers, and teachers to include in their teachings such phrases that would inspire both children and parents to

pursue education regardless of gender; instructing rabbis and preachers to let their audiences know ahead of time that the theme of a sermon would include the education of women; and instructing rabbis and preachers to convince parents to have their daughters visit communal houses of prayer and sermons, from the age of eleven or twelve.—Trans.]

Translated by Alexandra Hoffman.

Other works by Morgulis: *Sbornik po evreiskomu voprosu* (1869); *Voprosy evreiskoi zhizni* (1889); *Vopros, imenuemyi evreiskim* (1906); *Organizatsiia evreiskikh obshchin Rossii* (1910).

Isaac Ber Levinzon
1788–1860

Isaac (Yitshak) Ber Levinzon was born into a wealthy family in Kremenets, Ukraine. Although he received a traditional Jewish education, he also mastered Russian, German, French, and Latin, and was influenced by early Haskalah figures when he moved to Galicia, including Solomon Judah Rapoport, Isaac Erter, and Menachem Mendel Lefin. He made it his life's work to improve educational opportunities for Jews; his suggestions about publishing Hebrew books in the Russian Empire were adopted by governmental authorities; he also encouraged Jews to improve their lot by working in agriculture. Levinzon campaigned against blood-libel accusations and fought to discourage corruption and inequality within Jewish society over issues such as army recruitment. His works, in several genres including drama, often mocked Hasidism.

Emek refa'im (Valley of Giants)
1867

When I was still young, nineteen years of age, it entered my mind to fool the world (as was the practice of the "holy ones" in those days), and this was the scheme I adopted: I used to travel on Sabbaths, and in particular on the New Year, from one "holy man" to another, as was the custom of those who believed in "holy men" in those days. And when I returned home, I told stories of all their actions day and night—of their prayers, their dialogues, the manner in which they ate, their wealth and their greatness, and of their splendid journeys in carriages, and the like. In particular, I used to recount their wondrous deeds and their marvels and their prophecies, the like of which had never been heard of in all the earth. And lads and youngsters of about fourteen or fifteen years of age approached me to hear of the miracles and the wonders. And I said to them that these holy men had achieved this not by virtue of study of the Torah, but solely through their fear of the Almighty and through prayer, and as a result of the firm belief within their hearts.

But as for me, knowing, as I did, that in the large city of my birth I would not be able to comport myself in the glorious fashion of the Hasidic Masters, and in the rabbinic mode, first, because they knew me, from my youth, to be a total ignoramus and a perpetrator of evil deeds, and as one who hailed from a contemptible family [. . .], and second, because even if I had been of fine pedigree and conversant with sacred literature and the like, I would have been unable to fool the men of this city, as they had among them many students of Torah who were of fine pedigree, and that they moreover had among them numerous sages and literati, and such as were acquainted with various different branches of wisdom, as well as many intelligent businessmen who traveled around the entire globe and who were familiar with the realities of the world—and all of these types had no belief whatsoever in matters involving miracles and wondrous deeds. [. . .]

Accordingly, I chose to settle in a very small town, where there were neither students nor literati, neither men of wealth nor merchants, and whose inhabitants, owing to their poverty, were preoccupied with earning their livelihood, and lacked understanding even of mundane affairs; and, *a fortiori*, of deceit and fraud. And they believed, as had their forebears, in every vanity and falsehood—making enquiry of those divining by the clouds and of practitioners of magic, believing in the old women and their magical instruments. Hence, I said to myself: "It is here that I shall reside!"

So I rented a house close to the synagogue, and lived tightly closeted away, and recited my prayers in an exceedingly loud voice, chanting melodies and clapping my hands, and the entire town was astir at the sounds and commotion thereby generated. And from time to time I visited the lavatory, and proceeded from the lavatory to the ritual bath; and when, on occasion, I came to the synagogue, I used to make numerous pauses in my prayers, and in respect of all matters involving the precepts; and I invariably used to recount tales of miracles and wondrous deeds, and of the virtues of the "holy men" and the manner in which they comported themselves, to the point where the public perceived that my entire conduct corresponded exactly to that of the greatest personages among the holy ones, who were renowned as miracle workers. When I returned home after having traveled to a particular "holy man," all the townsfolk gathered around me, and I related to them whatever came to my mind concerning the deeds of this "holy man," and, one by one, the young men and those of tender years joined themselves to me and believed in me, to the point where I created a special prayer quorum for myself, and these young men formed a part of my privy council and of those who professed obedience to me, and they prayed alongside me. And with a view to creating a distinctive mark, we used to alter all the ancient customs, and adopted fresh customs, and recited our prayers in accordance with the Sephardic rite, incorporating all such usages as the "holy men" of our era have adopted; and everyone called our prayer quorum "the prayer-quorum of the Hasidim."

Then proceeding from one stage to the next, I came to introduce the general practice of bringing together a company of people for the third meal on the Sabbath, to sing, and to say a few words of Torah; after that, by virtue of their faith in me and in my uprightness, anyone who was the victim of any mishap, whether it was a sick wife, an internal ghost, a robbery, a theft, a lost object, or one who needed to make a request to the local rulers, and the like, came to me, and brought me ransom monies. After that, I donned white garments, and recited prayers from the prayer book of the Ari [R. Isaac Luria] of blessed memory; and they would refer to me by the title "Rebbe."

I then began traveling around the world and my initial trip was to the villages [. . .], and there were always two young men accompanying me, who approached every tenement-holder before I descended from my wagon, and publicized my name and the wonders I had wrought. I conducted myself in this manner for several years, until such time as I was well-known in all the villages and small towns close to the town in which I was living. When I came to a small town of this kind, the ritual slaughterer would bring me the knife for my inspection, and if he failed to do so, I would dismiss him from his post.

Subsequently, a number of young men would come to visit me, from time to time, on Sabbaths and on the New Year, as well as all those who were suffering from diseases or mishaps, and they would lodge with the householders of my town, and as a result of this, they obtained an abundance of benefits and financial support. A report circulated about in the small towns nearby that the Almighty had blessed the residents of the town in the merit of my dwelling among them. And the men of my town, when traveling, on occasion, on business affairs to towns both near and far, would praise my name and recount great miracles and wondrous deeds attributed to me, proclaiming that I could heal all the sick people throughout the world, and make poor people wealthy, free prisoners, cure the blind, and so forth.

Then people came to me from all over the world, and I became great. In addition, the residents of my own city became great and were exceedingly successful, and I accumulated money like the sands of the sea, and my name was very great throughout the world. [. . .]

Woe is unto me that I fooled the entire world, and was the cause of many and horrific evils both to private individuals and to the community of Israel as a whole! There is no end to the deceit and falsehood which I practiced during the course of my life.

Translated by David E. Cohen.

Other works by Levinzon: *Te'udah be-Yisra'el* (1827); *Efes damim* (1837); *Bet Yehudah* (1839); *Zerubavel* (1863); *Aḥiyah ha-shiloni ha-ḥozeh* (1864); *Or le-arba'ah asar* (1864); *Yemin tsidki* (1881).

Abraham Uri Kovner
1841/42–1909

Born in Vilna and yeshiva-educated around Minsk, Abraham (Albert) Uri Kovner was a *maskil* and literary critic who wrote initially in Hebrew and, after 1868, in Russian. Inspired to write critically about Haskalah Hebrew literature by what he considered its superficial preoccupation with subjects of little relevance, he was disturbed by the ignorance of science he found in his Jewish contemporaries. He was deeply influenced by the Russian literary critic Vissarion Belinsky. Later in life Kovner was arrested for forgery; while in prison he began an active correspondence with Dostoyevsky, discussing Jewish issues; Dostoyevsky published highlights of their discussions in several articles. Ultimately, Kovner converted to Christianity and took on the name

Arkadii Grigor'evich Kovner; he nonetheless continued to campaign against antisemitism.

Tseror peraḥim (A Bouquet of Flowers)
1868

A Brief Survey of the Situation of the Jews of Lithuania and Poland

I

I had recently published my work *Heker davar*, and for other reasons, I was compelled to seek out the city of my birth, Vilna, and the city of Warsaw—and a golden opportunity presented itself to me, during my journey, to cast a critical eye over the situation of our Jewish brethren in these places; whatever I witnessed personally, I have put into print, and it is this that I shall be presenting before you today, precious reader.

Now I am not about to travel with you from city to city and from district to district, as the sheets of my manuscript will be too few to incorporate it all, and the scribal pen will make heavy progress in depicting all the events in the lives of the Jews—those resident in the small towns—because these folk have not yet aroused themselves from their stupor of folly, which the lapse of more than a thousand years has cast upon them, and the soul of the writer is weary of the constant apparitions and sights of archaic customs that have undergone no change or alteration. The poverty and oppression that are weighing down the residents of those districts will cause the Jews to sink still further into the depths of folly, and will kill off within them that spirit of strength and might possessed by the residents of Walachia and of Bessarabia. In general, I will tell you: everything that you hear, by way of news every morning, from the informants in the newspapers to the effect that these places are now filled with understanding, that the Jews have cast off the "worn-out frying pans" with which they covered themselves for protection for so long—all such notions are but figments of the imagination; in reality, there is no change or alteration, there is no movement and sensation of a fresh way of life within the habitations of the Jews. As to those living in the small towns—they are in an eternal sleep, and who knows when they will awaken? [. . .] They lie there amid the filth and the mire, and their slumber is pleasant to them . . . however, in just a brief moment I shall transport you and bring you to the large cities: to Vilna, the capital of Lithuania, and to Warsaw, the capital of Poland, and we shall see how our Jewish brethren there are faring.

You will undoubtedly wish to know what the effects of the popular schools which the government set up for the Jews are—be silent then, and listen! It was entirely futile for the government to have ordered that all the Jewish people should seek out these schools, with no one being exempt; those rabbinic authorities arriving recently will endeavor, with all their might, that the feet of their children should not step into them; the deceitful ones will hunt their prey, with all the force at their disposal, so as to ensure that the laborious exertions of the government will remain a breach of faith. Admittedly, I cannot keep concealed under my tongue the fact that there are many who do attend the popular schools, but how these pale into insignificance against the vast number of Jews within this city! Not even one in a hundred goes there! The cause of this, in my view, is attributable to the teachers, who stand like a fortified wall between the Jews and the Enlightenment. This malignant plague of leprosy will destroy every goodly portion of ground among us, and who knows when we will escape the oppression of the enemies of the Enlightenment and of those who trouble the soul, as they do? In what way are we distinguished from all the nations on earth? Is there any nation or kingdom amid whom there is a root bearing gall and wormwood like us? And when did this plague commence among us? Is it not the case that the Jewish people had schools from time immemorial, so when was it, then, that the teachers increased so abundantly among us? We would be most reluctant to claim that these teachers are charlatans and base fellows, evil and sinful like the Jesuits, Heaven forbid! On the contrary, we know that the majority of them are straightforward and upright men and that all their activities and deeds are genuinely bound up with the feelings within their hearts and souls; but in spite of all this, they are as evil and destructive as the Jesuits, and indeed even worse than them; for once we lay bare the deceitfulness of the latter-day rabbinic authorities, we are surely able to be wary of them—but that is not the case with the teachers! Those who hate the Enlightenment not out of love for themselves, but out of a surfeit of false belief—such individuals are capable of causing harm at all times! Accordingly, what we are saying all boils down to the same thing! It would, however, be futile for the government to gird itself, with all its remaining strength, to breathe the spirit of Enlightenment into the Jews, but it should rather give the teachers the opportunity to lessen, within the hearts of the youth, the zeal and antagonism directed against all kinds of knowledge and wisdom. The worst form of distress that the government can cause us in its attempt to attract us to the Enlightenment would be keeping the teachers at a safe distance from the environs of Jewry. We would indeed have schools, at primary, intermediate, and high levels, but the feet of the teachers would not enter our domain; and without teachers, all hope would be lost.

Despite all this, the popular schools have brought no small benefit to the teachers, who have completed their fixed terms in the rabbinic *bet midrash* and are now among the guard of teachers in these schools; and had this governmental enactment only been made exclusively for the benefit of the teachers, that would have been sufficient—for, truth to tell, the lot of those who complete their fixed term in the rabbinic *bet midrash* in the capacity of teachers, and who do not subsequently seek out the academies of the secular sciences, is an evil and bitter one; and although they would not be amusing themselves with an abundance of luxuries at the present moment, they would nonetheless enjoy a modicum of support, though even there, a really horrific lack of proper gradation exists: those possessing the highest levels of intellect are at the bottom of the ladder, while those at the lowest intellectual levels find themselves at the top. By dint of this the small number of students who are present there are burdened and endure suffering . . .

II

[. . .] Here is the appropriate place to take note of numerous complaints which have been reiterated two or three times in various writings concerning the young *maskilim*, who have completed their fixed term of study in the rabbinic *bet midrash,* or who have sought out the academies of secular wisdom, to the effect that they have distanced themselves from the Hebrew language; in my view, they are doing the correct thing, for what is the lot of those who write in the Hebrew language, and what benefit accrues to them from their labor? Is it not poverty and deprivation, anger and pain, a lack of honor, and seven enemies in the soul for each sorrow they experience and for each step taken by them? How, therefore, can we blame these people, whose souls are precious in their estimation and who are seeking another form of livelihood, and aiming at a more solid goal? . . .

Besides all these factors, Hebrew literature, while affording a significant benefit to those who are in a state of stasis, is responsible for a great amount of harm to those who are moving up. How much worthy talent has gone to waste: how many days, nay years, have so many people lost as a result of their poetic compositions in the Hebrew language, the taste of which is that of the juice of mallows, and of works on grammar lacking any orderly arrangement, on researches and expositions, commentaries and interpretations, all of which are founded upon emptiness! And in all this, it was solely the Hebrew language that awakened their perception and thereby brought them to this pass. Men who were genuinely great, who were capable of doing a vast amount for the benefit of the Jews, wasted their supremely precious time on composition of flowery verses and poems bereft of any sound ideas, constructing a dialogue of vanity and delusion on the basis of the Hebrew language, and it was owing to this false dream of theirs—that they would be performing good deeds for the advantage of the nation—that they lived their whole lives in a state of error. On the other hand, the "little foxes" converted the Hebrew language into a tool whereby to demonstrate proficiency, and into a cause for boasting. These individuals, bereft, as they are, of all wisdom and knowledge, of any novel ideas and in understanding of the world, in their desire to be displayed as a banner at the entry gates, will read the Hebrew language as a token of victory, will beautify themselves with alien plumage, and the consensus view of the community, which does not know how to evaluate each thing in accordance with its worth, will be to welcome these elegant versifiers and poets with both hands, and to glorify itself in them. In order that you should be aware of, and appreciate, the extent to which the Hebrew language can destroy the intellect of the writers, I shall cite for you the words of a certain didactic individual, one Mr. [Ḥayim Tsevi ben Todros] Lerner (to whose name mentally deficient youth accord honor, as his name is lauded and blessed from the rising of the sun unto its setting) who, in the preface to his work *Moreh ha-lashon*, declared as follows: "Truly, all our labor is exclusively for the purpose of crowning it (the Hebrew language) with a priestly diadem. Albeit one writer comes along with his commentaries, another with his poems, another with his essays and yet another with his critique of the works of others, is not the name of the Hebrew language displayed upon the banner of them all? And all of them revere and sanctify the name of 'the Mistress,' and they all entreat her favor with a gift!" Precious reader, have you ever heard such empty words as these in contemporary literature? I swear by my life that this author, in composing words such as these, had no feeling whatsoever for what he had written—and authors of this kind are like machines, their hands writing out what their hearts do not understand. What is the Hebrew language per se? Is it indeed a "Mistress"? Surely it is comprised, as are all languages, of dead letters, with no inherent sanctity within them, and it is only the sacred *words* written in this language that can justly be called "sacred"—and that being the case, why should the name of the Hebrew language be displayed as a banner over all the authors, like the cover over the Holy of Holies, so as to prevent a visitor from presumptuously entering within?

Translated by David E. Cohen.

Other works by Kovner: *Ḥeker davar* (1865); *Iazyk faktov* (1908).

Rosa Gabbay
ca. 1850–ca. 1936

Rosa Gabbay was the daughter of Ezekiel Gabbay, founder of the Ladino newpaper *El jurnal israelit* and the personal banker of the Sultan Mahmud II. Rosa Gabbay's Ladino-language etiquette book reflects on courtesy and critiques the traditional role of Jewish girls, stressing the importance of modern education, and showing Western influences.

Courtesy, or Rules of Comportment
1871

As I write these words it occurs to me that, since it is the woman who runs the household, she must have wide knowledge and be a good manager. For many centuries our nation ignored women's education but the nation itself did not progress. Until now our leaders did not concern themselves about our women and, while they strove to advance men's education, they achieved nothing and there was no way to achieve it. But today we cannot deny that our leaders are exerting themselves to expand schools. The gentleman who occupies the presidency of the honorable Communal Council is not concentrating [any longer] on pointless business but rather on the development of schools, for here lies the prosperity of our nation. On his initiative a girls' school has been opened, as has been needed for many years. Finally the school has been opened, but there is not even a book in our language to begin teaching the youngest girls in order to give them some sort of start: at least five years are necessary to learn French and begin one's education, and it is not as easy for girls to learn foreign languages because there is no time for study.

We must concentrate on girls and educate them as soon as possible. On the basis of all these ideas and also as a reminder to my female coreligionists and perhaps also to the men who may read this book or hear it read, I have undertaken this task and collected these ideas from some books that discuss French manners. I have added some of what is appropriate for Jews and I have shown that most good manners are already required by our Holy Law, but unfortunately women are lacking in knowledge of that law. We hope that reading this book will heal the wound of ignorance and replace it with a desire for knowledge and civilization and that they will [consequently] read more advanced books than this one, since our book is no more than a door and entrance to education and manners.

And because this is the first time, we have taken a great deal of trouble to abandon proper Spanish in order that it should not be a hindrance to those who do not understand it. [Instead] we have sought to use Oriental Spanish [Ladino] in the hope that our work will find acceptance by ladies and gentlemen and that it will be, for me and other women, an encouragement to continue to translate and publish books for the progress of our nation, for this was the desire of my youth and that is what I have learned from my dear parents. My female friends! Let us awaken from the sleep in which we have been made to live! Let us seek our own advancement! Let us show that God created woman equal to men in cleverness and intelligence, and in a short time let us demonstrate our worth and put to shame those who do not appreciate women, and the God of Heaven will aid us.

NOTE
Words in brackets appear in the original translation.

Translated by Michael Alpert.

Eliezer Shem-Tov Papo
d. 1898

The teacher, rabbi, and religious writer Eliezer Shem-Tov Papo (not to be confused with Eliezer

Shem-Tov Papo, *musar* scholar and father of Judah Papo) was born and spent the majority of his life in Sarajevo, where he founded the Minḥat Eliyahu yeshiva, served on the rabbinic council, and was a member of the city's *hevrah kadisha*. In 1860, he moved to Belgrade, where he served on that city's rabbinic council between 1868 and 1884, and where he began to publish works in Judeo-Spanish. He immigrated to Palestine in 1896 and continued to publish books in Hebrew. Papo's publications reflect his goal of educating the Sephardic communities in which he lived through works in Judeo-Spanish on religious observance.

The Book of the Governing of My Household
1872–1874

31:1. Laws of Meat

The man should not purchase meat until he has taken counsel with his wife to see which type of meat she wants him to take, so that the wife cannot later say that it is dark meat, since she said that she wanted this meat.

But all of this applies well in a place where there is much meat, where each person can get the meat that they want; but in places where there is little meat, certainly each person cannot get the meat they want, as there are many who grasp onto every piece of meat, each one saying that he wants it, until they cause a huge dispute, and in the end it is he who is the strongest and knows how to fight, it is he who takes it for himself. It happens that the person who is honest or who can't fight, after all the labor and the struggle of waiting for three to four hours in the butcher shop, in the end they give him a "jewel" of meat that is more bones than meat. When he brings it home, his wife begins to yell, saying that this is a piece of meat like a black star: "I want you to see how good and fat the meat the neighbor took is, but now I say that he [referring to the husband] isn't good for anything, because he gives money for waste and mud," and things like this and even more, as women do, etc. So, in a way, he who does not fight in the butcher shop and steal good meat fights in the house that does not appreciate the meat.

The truth is that, on the one hand, she has reason to yell, since she does not know what she is going to cook with those bones, and above all, because the meat is lean and there is no fat in the house at all, what is she going to cook for the Sabbath or for the holidays; and especially when the Sabbath is followed immediately by a holiday or a holiday and then the Sabbath, what should she cook from this meat for three days, that for even among the poorest of the poor there should be three small meals for the night and three for the day, so that there are eighteen meals desired, and the blessed woman cannot make meals from bones: thus, she has much right to yell and to fight.

But with all of this, the woman who fears God (the Name, may it be blessed) should think of how many hours her husband waited in the butcher shop until he received that "jewel" of meat, and also how much suffering the blessed man endured until he gathered the money to pay for this meat, and in the good woman's thinking of the suffering that her husband went through until he brought this meat home, it is true that she has no right to yell or to cause a fight, God forbid, but rather, she should say to him: "My dear, do not feel sorry if there is no meat, or if it is dark or expensive; we will behead a small fowl and we will devise some other little dish and something of fish if there is some; and we will pass it as it will be." With this, "it is for her fear of the LORD that a woman is to be praised" [Proverbs 31:30] in speaking such phrases with her husband, that there will always be "well-being without your ramparts, peace in your citadels" [Psalm 122:7].

283:2. Laws of Coffee and of Not Going to the Coffeehouses on the Sabbath

1. Whoever has headaches, which are called migraines, and his medicine is to drink two or three coffees, and this malady strikes him on the Sabbath, and he summons a gentile to make him coffee, and after he drank a coffee the headache passed but more coffee remained, he who has this malady is permitted to drink the rest of the coffee.

2. It is permitted for the Jew to go to the coffeehouse of the gentile, even if they know him, and to drink the coffee that is already made. And this is exclusively in the coffeehouse that Jews are not accustomed to going to; but in the coffeehouse that Jews are accustomed to going to, even if the coffee is already prepared, they cannot drink it, for the reason that the gentile sees that the Jews are coming to him, I say it is certain that he prepared the coffee for the Jews and it is forbidden. According to the custom that is followed now, in which they make a coffee separately for each person who enters the coffeehouse, it is forbidden absolutely, as they made this coffee for a Jew.

And for the many sins that the drinking of coffee on the Sabbath in the coffeehouse of gentiles has already permitted, "there is none to take thought of them and none to seek them" [Ezekiel 34:6].

Suffering, because there are some who also drink coffee with milk of the gentile on the Sabbath and are hindered in many prohibitions. Woe upon us for the Day of Judgment! Therefore "he who values his life will keep far from them" [Proverbs 22:5]. Woe upon them and woe upon the souls of those who say: "Because the Name, blessed be He, commanded us to delight in the Sabbath, I have no greater delight than on the night of the Sabbath, after I have eaten my good fish, my good meat, my good wine, in the hour of eating fruit, to smoke three or four tobacco cigarettes; there cannot be a greater enjoyment of the Sabbath than this in the world." Woe upon him and woe upon his soul, that this enjoyment changes him for the worse, that many wounds are destined to come to him, whether in his body or in his soul. [. . .]

3. Those who, on the Sabbath evening, put a flask of coffee inside a pot full of sawdust or cinder and seal the flask well and put the pot inside the stove and the cinders or the sawdust is heated from the heat of the stove and the coffee boils, they do well. And I, the insignificant, my custom is in the winter to put the pitchers of coffee in a pot in the stove and the night of the Sabbath when it is desired, the coffee is already hot; and above all, that this hot water is very necessary for the privy and for washing the hands with it without any doubt.

Coffee—It is good that care is taken on the Sabbath to first pour the coffee into the cups and then to toss in the sugar.

To make coffee with milk on the Sabbath is forbidden and thus it is forbidden to make egg yolk beaten with sugar. [. . .]

A Jew can put to heat in front of the fire coffee that is already made on the eve of the Sabbath. And thusly one can heat it on the stove (as we are advised in the laws of *Hamin*, law 7). Those who are accustomed to tossing ground coffee in the cup and then pouring on top of it boiling water, there is a basis for their opinion, and he who is the strictest, blessings shall come to him.

Coffeehouse—Those who go to the coffeehouse even during the weekdays hinder themselves in many prohibitions and even more so those who go on the Sabbath. First is that coffee is forbidden and they drink it; and transgression results in transgression; it is certain that the gentile does not strain the water to make the coffee and it is possible that there are some worms, especially in the summertime.

And even more that they lagged in many forbidden things: be it things of commerce, and this is called profaning the Sabbath [. . .], be it gossip, be it jest, be it obscenity, as said the passage: "where there is much talking, there is no lack of transgressing" [Proverbs 10:19].

The people also say: "to talk much is to err much." This is the path of the evil inclination: first those are seduced who talk of the wheat and the cities and similar topics; then that they speak of the gentiles, of wars, of angels, of the *Tanzimat*; then, of Israel, of Reuben who is in this way, and Simon in that way, until they take up the esteemed rabbis and the rabbi of the city in their mouths. [. . .]

Woe upon them! those who waste the day of the holy Sabbath in the coffeehouse playing bingo, cards, checkers, billiards, chess, gambling, domino, etc. Is it not enough, for our sins, that during the whole week a book does not touch our hand, neither in the day, nor in the night, if still on the holy day on the Sabbath we waste it with games and perambulating, what are we and what are our lives? To waste lives in wheeling and dealing and playing games and perambulating—and the Torah, what will become of it?

Translated by Devi Mays.

Other works by Papo: *Sefer Damesec Eli'ezer*, 3 vols. (1862–1884); *Sefer ḥesed ve-emet* (1865).

Eliezer Zweifel
1815–1888

Born in Mogilev (present-day Belarus), Eliezer Zweifel was a *maskil* who worked as a rabbi, teacher, and writer in Hebrew and Yiddish. He wandered throughout Eastern Europe until 1853. He then taught at the government-run rabbinical seminary in Zhitomir, whose mission was to create rabbis with a modern outlook, a mission that Zweifel himself held in skepticism. Influenced by Nachman Krochmal's *Moreh nevukhe ha-zeman*, Zweifel treated Hasidim with much more respect than did other *maskilim* of the era; he aimed to resolve tensions among major Jewish factions.

Shalom al Yisra'el (Peace upon Israel)
1873

A Memorial to the Children of Israel, or The Guilt of Hasidim

Upon you, great ones, the rebbes of the Hasidim, who follow the path of the Ba'al Shem Tov, and of whose glorious name they boast and by whom they justify themselves, upon you, who are considered the righteous of the generation and those who sustain it, upon the men of holiness and of wondrous deeds spoken of in the mouths of thousands, nay myriads of our brethren, of those who sanctify you and revere you, and most especially upon you, the sons of the renowned tsadikim R. Mordechai of Chernobil, R. Israel of Ruzhin, and R. Menachem Mendel of Lubavitch—may the memory of them all be for a blessing—do I call with love and affection, with glory and honor, in supplication and with a plea, that you listen carefully and pay attention to my words, as they are words worthy of being uttered and heard, compelling words both for you and for us, words issuing from the depths of the heart, words from which, through their acceptance, much good and benefit will ensue. [. . .]

1. Issue an order, and announce in the synagogues and houses of study, with the force of a rabbinical decree, that no Hasid of any one tsadik may dare to speak erroneous and perverse words against the Hasidim of another tsadik, or against another sect, and that they are to refrain from falsely slandering one another in the gentile courts. [. . .]

2. To exhort your followers, by means of fearsome warnings, not to introduce any fresh custom, even of a trivial nature—not even a single word—into the prayers in the synagogue, since, as a result of things such as these, congregants frequently come to blows and descend to uttering abuse at prayer times. [. . .]

3. To remove from yourselves, and from all the charity collectors and all those engaged in the requisite distributions of the funds designated for the Land of Israel, all evil talk, slander, and mutual suspicion and to take care that all the monies donated by our brethren, the Jewish people, for the needs of the poor of the Land of Israel, should actually reach those persons on behalf of whom such donations were made. [. . .]

4. When those who are in your camp come to take counsel with you regarding traveling to the Land of Israel, and explain their arguments and their reasons compelling them to pursue this course, be deliberate in judgment, and make ample investigation and inquiry as to whether they are really sincere, as to whether they do not have another purpose and an alien objective lurking behind their desire and their proposal, since in the majority of cases, their primary motive is nothing more than a love of idleness and of throwing themselves upon the community for financial support. The sanctity of the Land of Israel, and their choice of the wholehearted worship of the Almighty, are nothing but a mask and a secret screen for facilitating the collection and assembling of donations both from private individuals and from the public to enable themselves to live without pain and struggle. [. . .]

5. To impose a strict prohibition upon the Hasidim not to make light of the sanctity of the Bible with the *Bi'ur* [of Moses Mendelssohn], and not to treat it with contempt, as is their normal regular practice. [. . .]

6. To distance yourselves from anything repulsive and the like when you prepare your letters for dispatch to your followers, by not employing phrases indicating that the keys of heaven have been delivered into your hands, and that you have been placed in charge of the hidden treasures of life and peace, and that you are meting out penalties and punishments by virtue of the power conferred upon you from above; for such words lead to laughter and scorn, to derision and mockery. [. . .]

7. Place a distance, little by little, between yourself and the rabble, they being the empty-headed and unstable individuals who strive after wind and pursue vanity, whose journeys and visits to you are not motivated by any good intentions, but, on the contrary, constitute a wasting of their time with emptiness and idleness, to assist with a portion of the singing and to excel in grabbing the leftovers of the rebbes' meals. But these men bring you no honor. [. . .]

8. Remove the "filthy garments" from yourselves—that is to say, the fattened and stuffed-up administrators, the fools, the gluttons and the drunkards, who suck the blood of the poor and the needy, and squeeze the last drop out of them, who treat all their days like festivals, who live a life of wealth and comfort by means of impudence and insolence, of rudeness and cruelty. They guard the entrances of their rebbe, but do not allow entry to God-fearing and wholehearted men, men who are

distressed and bitter of soul, whose entire motivation is for the sake of Heaven. [. . .]

9. Speak to the hearts of those close to you; exhort and urge those who listen to your voice, in regard to their learning the script and the language of the country in which you live, so that they should be entirely fluent in it, and that they should not stutter when speaking it, and that they should endeavor to teach their children, at least, that script and language:

a. Because it is the wish of the government, whose wishes must be deemed sacred in our eyes;
b. So that we do not bring harm and a grievous curse upon ourselves, for to sojourn and to mingle with a nation whose very language we cannot fathom and understand is one of the ninety-eight curses contained in the portion of "Rebuke," in Deuteronomy. [. . .]
c. That anyone who lacks knowledge of and familiarity with one of the living languages, lacks a double portion in his comprehension of the holy scriptures. [. . .]

10. There is a major halakhah applicable to every individual within Israel, a halakhah upon which the entire honor of the nation in exile is dependent, yet it is laid to rest in a corner, with no one enquiring or seeking information about it. [. . .]

And thus it is an obligation devolving upon all the great men of the generation that their words be listened to by the public, and specifically upon men who are like you, for your statements are deemed to possess the status of oral tradition, and are sanctified with the holiness of the divine mysteries, to proclaim and to inform and to publicize, and to emphasize, supported by several reasons based upon allusions and mystic lore, how severe is the prohibition against swindling a gentile, stealing his money, deceiving him, misleading him, or holding on to a lost object of his. Select for yourselves the most powerful sources to be found within our ancient authorities which speak earnestly about this, and which have their basis in the mountains of holiness—words which form part of the fundamentals of the requisite conditions of Jewish piety and saintliness, and discourse generously upon them with elegant expositions. [. . .]

My masters and my friends! My brethren and my companions! My beloved and my honored gentlemen! I have indeed made a great request of you, but—Heaven forbid—it is not a hard thing that I have imposed upon you. I am in no doubt that your opinion and mine are precisely identical on all of the ten points mentioned herein by me. [. . .]

Restore Hasidism to a state of wisdom, and wisdom will return to it! Behold, we are one people, we are the children of one Father, we are the children of one God—let there be no strife among us, and peace be upon Israel!

Translated by David E. Cohen.

Other works by Zweifel: *Minim ve-ugav* (1858); *Sefer haskel* (1862); *Tushiyah* (1867); *Ḥeshbono shel olam* (1878); *Sanegor* (1885).

Samuel Joseph Fuenn
1818–1890

The Vilna-born Samuel Joseph (Shemu'el Yosef) Fuenn was a leader of the Haskalah in Russia. Fuenn received a traditional Jewish education but was also educated in secular subjects, such as modern literature and foreign languages. As a *maskil*, he pushed for reforms in education and in rabbinical leadership among Russian Jews, a stance that had the support of the government. Upon the opening of the state-run Vilna Rabbinical Seminary in 1848, Fuenn was appointed to teach Jewish studies. In 1856, he resigned from that position and became the superintendent of Jewish government schools in the Vilna district; he was also the Vilna government's chief adviser on Jewish affairs. From 1860, he edited *Ha-karmel*, a Hebrew-language weekly (from 1871, a monthly) with a Russian supplement.

Dor ve-dorshav (A Generation and Its Seekers)
1879

Now when I was a young lad, sitting amidst the dust of the feet of those bound up with the houses of study, I would never hear them speaking anything sensible about the Hasidim, explaining and portraying the fundamental basis of the Hasidic system of thought, the reasons for it and its motivations, but only idle talk consisting of complaints about a few of their novel practices, which were not in accordance with the halakhah, and most of all, in relation to their practices, were their alterations in the fixed times for prayer and their recitation of the Shema outside its correct time. And insofar as this was concerned, although I was already diligent in my studies and in gaining an understanding of the works of those exploring the beliefs and opinions held among the Jewish people, it had never occurred to me to pay any special attention to Hasidism and to investigate its ways: however, the wife whom the Almighty had designated for me hailed from the daughters of the Hasidim, and she had two brothers belonging to the most Orthodox of the Hasidim of Chabad.

[. . .] There was also aroused within me a yearning to become acquainted with the researches into the pathways of the Hasidic system of thought—and in particular, when my brothers-in-law, my kinsmen, brought me the welcome news that the rebbe of Lubavitch was preparing to come in his honored person, to Vilna, to pay a visit to his community, to enlighten its eyes with the light of his Torah, and to revive its spirit with a spirit of knowledge and discernment. They even assured me faithfully that they would do everything within their power to bring me into his innermost sanctum of glory, and to arrange for me to be placed before him to enable me to speak with him face to face, and to present before His Honor my doubts, something which not even all the Hasidim succeeded in achieving. Those good tidings reached the assembly of Hasidim within our community at the end of Sivan or the beginning of Tammuz (5595), and from that time on, not even a few days elapsed without letters reaching them bringing good news, informing them on a daily basis of the stopping-places of the rebbe, while on his journey, for the purpose of visiting his well-wishers in every locale where they formed an association, and relating marvels, culled from his Torah teachings which he had expounded at his gatherings. And the joy of the anticipation of greeting the presence of their rebbe increased day by day, as he approached ever closer to Vilna. [. . .]

I too joined in their mirth, even though the Hasidic system of thought was still alien to me and I did not desire to sit in its shade. I was also genuinely furious with those who ridiculed them with contempt, without knowledge or sensitivity. After six or seven weeks (in the month of Av), the rebbe came to take up his abode, in all his glory, in our city. The men initiated into his mystic lore paid him great honor amongst us, the likes of which our brethren, the learners, and indeed the entire nation, never paid to any rabbi and illustrious genius, the wonder of the generation! The small community of the Hasidim found the wherewithal to turn over a special courtyard for hosting him, within which there were houses and rooms designated for his honor, and for his men who stood before him in the capacity of his aides and his servants; and there were large, spacious houses for the assembly of the Hasidim and of all those who desired to hear the expositions of his Torah teachings. The honor which the Hasidim pay to their rebbe is not just that of some extra adornment, but that of true glory and greatness, glory that involves them in a great deal of expense. [. . .] Accordingly my own desire also increased to see the face of the master whom they were seeking, and whose Torah teachings they were awaiting in anticipation.

On the second or third day after the honorable rabbi had come to Vilna, at the time of the afternoon service, I pressed through the crowd and entered the synagogue building to listen to Torah, and the house was filled, from one end to the other, with people standing closely pressed together, Hasidim who were Torah scholars learning Talmud among the people. The rabbi descended from his attic and came into the house, and swiftly passed through the assembly without turning to either side, until he reached the table and the chair which they had prepared for him. After a few moments, he sat as though deeply engrossed in thought, and after that he commenced his discourse. He spoke for about an hour; his head was on an incline, his eyes closed, his face awe-inspiring; he did not raise a hand, nor project a finger, nor did he modulate his voice, either by raising it or lowering it. Nor did he cease for a moment—it was as though a certain holy spirit was speaking from inside his throat. The content of this discourse, and his manner of speech, which were new to me, emboldened me to make my ears like a funnel, to hear and pay attention, and to focus my mind on acquainting myself with them. The rebbe concluded his discourse, and instantly returned to the chamber where he taught. He turned away, passed on, and was there no longer. The Hasidim stood up, astounded and trembling on account of the words of the Torah of their rebbe, as they were most elevating and uplifting. The discourses delivered by the Hasidic rebbes are not discourses of chastisement and reproof, for the purpose of bringing people back from sin and of stirring them to repentance, nor are they discourses of analytical dialectics, the themes of which are halakhah and logical reasoning, but rather, expositions of biblical verses and of statements of our Sages of blessed memory, based upon principles of the wisdom of the mystic lore, interpreted in accordance with the Hasidic system of thought, or, more correctly, they are explanations of basic principles of the wisdom of the mystic lore and of Hasidism, by way of allusions to and support from the biblical verses and statements of our Sages of blessed memory, which, for the sake of endowing them with additional worth, the Hasidim call Torah or Hasidism. Discourses of this type require Talmudic learning and mental acuteness, and to this end, men known as "reviewers" lodge as guests of the group of the rebbe, and they are men of perspicacity, who grasp and imbibe the words of Torah or of Hasidism emanating from the mouth of the rabbi, and then return and repeat them to their Hasidim just as the rebbe said them, and in like manner, get them to understand them explicitly with additional clarification. [. . .]

In order to save myself an unnecessary burden, I took up my pen to record the discourse of the rebbe in writing, and my wish came to fruition. I wrote it down in correct sequence, and did not abridge or omit anything. Armed with my composition, I came the next day to the reviewers of the rebbe, and showed it to them. They looked at it and were astonished, and did not believe what their own eyes had seen, that the rational power of a young man such as myself, belonging to the Misnagdim, who had never heard Hasidic teachings before, since the day of his birth, could succeed in understanding, imbibing, and recording in writing a great and profound discourse recalled from memory. After they had tested me by posing questions based upon the things said during the discourse and its subject-matter, and it had been demonstrated to them that I had understood and had come to an appreciation of its true quality, they drew me near to them with love and extended kindness to me; they entered into conversation with me, they explained various statements in accordance with their system of thought, they related great and wondrous events culled from the deeds of their great men and their holy ways. As their words flowed on, there also escaped from their mouths words of scorn and mockery directed against the Misnagdim who had placed them under the ban—those dry bones whose natural vigor had departed and who had no spirit within them.

[. . .] I was unable to extract from their mouths a single didactic principle or a single rational hypothesis set forth in a didactic manner, to the point where I mustered up sufficient fortitude within my soul to request and to beg: "My Masters, please do make known to me the ways of Hasidism. If I have now found favor in your sight, please teach me and enable me to understand a little of its general principles, so that I may know on what foundations the pedestals of its edifice have been sunk, for that is all that I desire!" Then they each marveled with one another, and they replied to me and said: "You are seeking great and wondrous things; Hasidism is the very body of the Torah—its measure is longer than the earth and broader than the sea, and you cannot learn it while standing on one leg!

[. . .] Out of all the words, the dialogues, the arguments, and the responses that had passed between me and the reviewers. [. . .] I could recall just two serious responses that I considered to be worthy of mention in this story of ours too. To my enquiry: "What is the difference between the mystical teaching of the Gaon of Vilna and that of the Baʻal Shem Tov?" they replied, saying: "The mystical teaching of the Gaon of Vilna is a desiccated tree, while the mystical teaching of the Baʻal Shem Tov is moist and juicy. [. . .] By way of response to my question: "Is the power of their rebbe sufficiently great as to perform miracles?" they replied pithily and by way of allusion: "Signs and wonders in the land of the children of Ham," and explained their statement, saying: "The performance of miracles in general is a small thing, and it pales into insignificance among those matters that are within the capability of the righteous. It is not on account of these that the rebbe is praised, nor is it in regard to this that his glory lies!" [. . .] The rebbe sat in the attic-chamber all day long, and it was there that the Hasidim went up to converse with him in private—as one went out, another went in. [. . .]

When I came into the room of the rebbe, the shadows of evening were already extended, and in the light of dusk, I could see him pacing about hither and thither, engrossed in thought, in a state of deep concentration, and his eyes were shut, his long and sloping eyelashes concealed with the shades of the forest. His face emitted dread, and his entire person bespoke glory and awe. I stood for a few moments on the threshold of the room; I did not move from my place so as not to disturb him, until he opened his eyes and turned toward me. The light in his eyes was like a flame of fire flashing up in the midst of the darkness. His eyes met mine, and I was seized with trembling. With a single gaze, he scrutinized me from the soles of my feet up to the crown of my head, and I felt just as is mentioned in scripture: "Who am I?" He said to me: "Come closer here, and tell me your request!" And as he spoke, he approached the table, sat on his chair, and beckoned to me to sit beside him, even though I was of tender years. I began presenting my request, saying: "I have already heard a great deal about Hasidism, and after we had had the merit of seeing the light of your countenance, which we had never expected, I request with all my soul: 'Teach me, I implore you, our Master, you who are the chief of the princes of Hasidism among us, a little of its fundamental principles—for who can teach as well as you?'"

"But why do you seek to know the ways of Hasidism?" asked the rebbe. "Is it to enable you to learn the ways of service of the Divine? Is there not sufficient information in all the sacred books of Israel? Are they not all replete with love of the Almighty and fear of Him? Even from within the commentaries of Rashi you are able to recognize your Creator and to gain knowledge of the ways in which to serve Him?—and there is no novel Torah whatsoever contained within Hasidism!"

"But, my Master and Teacher!" I replied in a supplicatory tone of voice: "Have I not been informed by, and heard from the mouths of the most discerning of the Hasidim, that Hasidism is the pathway leading up to an understanding of the spirituality of the Torah? And I, though but of tender years, have found sufficient strength within myself to delve deeply into the works of those investigating the beliefs and opinions of the Sages of Israel, and my eyes brightened with the light of their intellectual grasp of the internal aspects of the Torah, in accordance with their methodology. So for this, I implore you—magnify your kindness, to enlighten my eyes with the light of Hasidism, in order that I should have the merit to develop a discriminatory approach toward different ways of interpretation—for a young man such as I am cannot spiritually live off that which emerges from the plain meaning of things!" The rebbe remained silent for a few moments, after which he opened up with an explanation of the biblical verse: "His majesty is above the earth and the heavens, and He has exalted the power of His people, to the praise of all His loving ones"—and he presented a number of expositions by way of explication of the mysteries of *atsilut* [divine withdrawal]. And after obtaining permission from his exalted Honor, I presented my doubts and my arguments before him; and these matters stretched out for around half an hour. But when I also found strength within my soul to argue with force, he ceased speaking and responding, and said: "The time has arrived for the evening prayer." I understood that I had breached the bounds of etiquette and that the favorable moment had passed. I blessed the rebbe that he should enjoy peace, and took my leave of him. I had come into his presence full of anticipation of good things, but I departed from him empty-handed. I took mental stock of the situation, and knew that the reviewers had been correct in their assessment that my soul was not suited to imbibe Hasidism.

Translated by David E. Cohen.

Other works by Fuenn: *Darkhe ha-Shem* (manuscript, 1843); *Shenot dor va-dor* (1847); *Talmud leshon Rusyah* (1847); *Niḏḥe Yisra'el* (1850); *Kiryah ne'emanah* (1860); *Dor ve-dorshav* (1879–1880).

Scholarship and Science

Simhah Isaac ben Moses Lutski
1716–1760

Simhah Isaac ben Moses (Simḥah Yitsḥak ben Mosheh) Lutski, born in Lutsk (Łuck), Volhynia, was a writer, scholar, and spiritual leader who was known as "the Karaite Rashi." A student of rabbinical literature and Kabbalah, in 1754 his wealthy patron Mordechai ben Berakhah invited him to lead the *bet midrash* in the Crimean Karaite community of Chufut-Kale. Lutski wrote about Karaite halakhah, theology, philosophy, and Kabbalah; he analyzed the split between Rabbinism and Karaism.

Me'irat enayim (Light of the Eyes)
ca. 1750

Precepts 26 and 27

There is a severe admonition addressed to every individual within Israel not to add any precept on his own initiative onto those precepts which are written in the Torah, and likewise there is a severe admonition against removing/derogating from any of the precepts written in the Torah, but on the contrary, there is an obligation to take care to perform those precepts which are written explicitly in the Torah, without any addition or derogation—Heaven forbid—or those precepts that may be deduced from the words of the Torah by the similarity of words or phrases appearing in different passages and of *a fortiori* reasoning, which enjoy the same status as if they had been written in the Torah, and do not constitute additions to the written text—Heaven forbid!

And likewise, those precepts which have been permanently established as binding upon us by virtue of the "burden of the heritage" bequeathed to us by our ancestors, which enjoy some support from scripture, and all Israel—both Karaites and Rabbanites—unanimously accept their validity. But apart from this, it is forbidden to add to that which is written or to derogate from it—Heaven forbid! And this is what is meant by that which is written in the Torah: "You shall not add to the thing which I command you this day, nor shall you derogate from it." And it is further written: "You shall not add to it, neither shall you derogate from it."

Now these admonitions have been written just twice in the Torah, because addition to and derogation from the precepts of the Torah can come in two forms—either by way of adding an entirely fresh precept or removing an existing precept in its entirety, or merely by adding a little to the precept as written in the Torah, or by derogating in small measure from the precept as it is written—and both of these are equally bad.

Now the rabbinic sages have indeed erred greatly, and paid no heed to these admonitions, and have, of their own initiative, added to the precepts of the Torah, and have also derogated from them in respect of both types of addition and derogation. Either they have added novel precepts, such as, for example, the precept of lighting candles on the eve of the Sabbath, and the precept of waving the palm-branch on Sukkot, and many others besides these; or, alternatively, they have added a little to those precepts that are written in the Torah, such as, for example, they have added the obligation of uncovering the corona to that of plain circumcision, and they have invented an obligation to sanctify two days in respect of the festivals instead of one, and they have required seven "clean" days in respect of a menstruating woman, and a great number of other cases besides these.

And similarly, they have got rid of many of the precepts of the Torah. Either they have disposed of a precept in its entirety, such as, for example, they have abolished the notion of ritual impurity arising from contact with a corpse in the diaspora, and they have derogated from and in effect disposed of the notion of ritual impurity arising from contact of the contents of pots with the corpses of swarming creatures through [application of a rabbinic rule nullifying the impurity wherever the volume of such contents exceeds the volume of space occupied by the corpse by a factor of sixty], and they have set aside altogether the ritual impurity of a menstruating woman. Moreover, they have set aside the precept of attaching a thread of blue [to the obligatory fringes on four-cornered garments], and they have set aside the precept: "You shall kindle no fire" on the Sabbath; and there are numerous similar instances of this kind. Or, alternatively, they have set aside a part of the precepts written, such as, for example, the obligation to eat unleavened bread throughout all seven days of the Passover festival, and they have permitted the consumption of half of the prohibited fats. They have ignored many major divine utterances concerning incestuous relationships, and they have permitted a woman who has given birth to have marital relations with her husband after seven days in the case of a male, and after fourteen days in the case of a female child.

Apart from all these cases, there are numerous instances of their having added to and derogated from the precepts of the Torah, which is perfect, in accordance with the Sage, renowned for his expertise in this area, the Master, R. Solomon the Elder—may his soul rest in Paradise—author of the work "He Made a Palanquin," who assembled and compiled all the instances of their additions, and derogations from, and amendments to the divine precepts, and produced them in a scrolled manuscript, in the initial section of his book of disputation entitled "Fighting in the Gates," incorporated within his exposition included in that section, where these may be seen. In similar vein, the distinguished sage, our teacher, the Master, R. Abraham, son of the Master, R. Josiah Yerushalmi, performed a wonderful service in listing all their errors in his notable work, entitled "The Truth of Faith," where these may be seen.

What is vital for you to know and be bestirred by is that one who alters and varies the intent even of a single precept of the Torah, or who adds to it or who derogates from it, such a person is creating a defect in the perfection of the sacred and perfect Torah, and in the Truth of the One Who gave it, may His Name be blessed, and is limiting the knowledge of the Almighty, blessed be He, and His infinite wisdom, in that he is, from his point of view, setting straight that which Almighty God, blessed be His Name, has made crooked. Heaven forbid that we should believe such a thing; and accordingly the Almighty, blessed be He, has warned us against varying or altering the intent of the precepts, or adding to them or derogating from them, so as firmly to establish within us the truth of the belief in the perfection of the Torah, which is perfect and true, and in its duration and everlasting nature for all time.

For something which is absolutely perfect cannot admit of addition or diminution; and it is also intended for the purpose of firmly establishing within us the belief in the perfection of the One Who gave the Torah, blessed be His Name—that He is wholly and entirely perfect, without any defect, Heaven forbid! And accordingly it is forbidden for us to alter or add or remove a single word, or a single letter, or a single vowel point of the Torah of the Almighty, which is perfect and trustworthy, and *a fortiori* a single precept, Heaven forbid! Be aware of this accordingly, and appreciate it most profoundly.

Translated by David E. Cohen.

Joseph Vita Castelli
d. 1777

Joseph Vita Castelli, son of a prominent Livornese rabbi, received his medical degree from the University of Pisa in 1766, though, as a Jew, he had to pay his doctoral committee a double fee. Ironically, his strong humanist views led to another kind of discrimination toward the end of his short life: his application in 1770 to a Jewish medical society to be hired as a public doctor was denied. Castelli later criticized the poor understanding of religion as an obstacle to progressive use of the smallpox vaccine. Castelli's writings, composed in the vernacular, promoted Enlightenment ideals of reason and truth, as well as reliance on scientific methods in medical practice.

Medical-Critical Letter Written by Doctor Joseph Vita Castelli to His Friend, a Doctor, Regarding a Serious and Complicated Case of Acute Fever
1774

Art, which gives men the means to persevere and cure some sicknesses, seems nowadays to depend on philosophy, which is that great and clear source that produces all that is luminous and useful. I am not speaking about the haughty and fanatical philosophy that transports the intellect of certain men and claims to be able to explain and understand everything, and which is behind the primary essential causes of things, occupying itself completely to that end in useless investigations. Rather, I am speaking of that philosophy which regulates and corrects medical reasoning, and from which, as a solid trunk, the assiduous study of nature branches out, pointing to the correct use of criteria to discover the simple or true aspect, the circumspect and prudent expectation, in order to understand inclinations better, to support movements and continence in the end, and to find golden moderation in the use of so many celebrated remedies, only authorized by ignorance and by stupid credulity. This is, it seems to me, the most noble and most useful and worthy medical philosophy, and through its splendor people will be less likely to fall into error and allow themselves to be seduced by false opinions that in various periods in the past were either too much in favor or too much against the healing art that circulated among men.

The innocent nature of the philosophy of this luminous and felicitous century no longer leads the solitary thinker to revolt against the quarrelsome caprice of certain limited wits, nor to save himself from the fanatical ambition of those who are falsely wise; nor to admire, with a jealous quiver, the random, honored faith of illustrious yet ignorant people. Without these, the most noble and laudable reforms, truly worthy of the felicitous progress of the human spirit and of those marvelous lights, the eighteenth century can rightfully claim to flourish. It would seem to me that those cultivated nations that are able to counteract the vile and evil passions and satire with philosophical restraint are placed highly; they are those in which men mutually respect each other, showing a good example to their peers, and providing each other with an illustrious example to follow.

In fact, the method of suffocating those who suffer from acute sicknesses, through the use of many layers of clothes, and of keeping them enclosed in their own rooms as in a dark prison, of avoiding any contact with the air and making them putrefy in their own sordid feathers, is a method that nowadays is not only held in contempt by the most renowned writers and the most enlightened schools in Europe but is also abhorred and considered pernicious by those men who are distinguished by common sense, who are led to understand what truly is advantageous to their health.

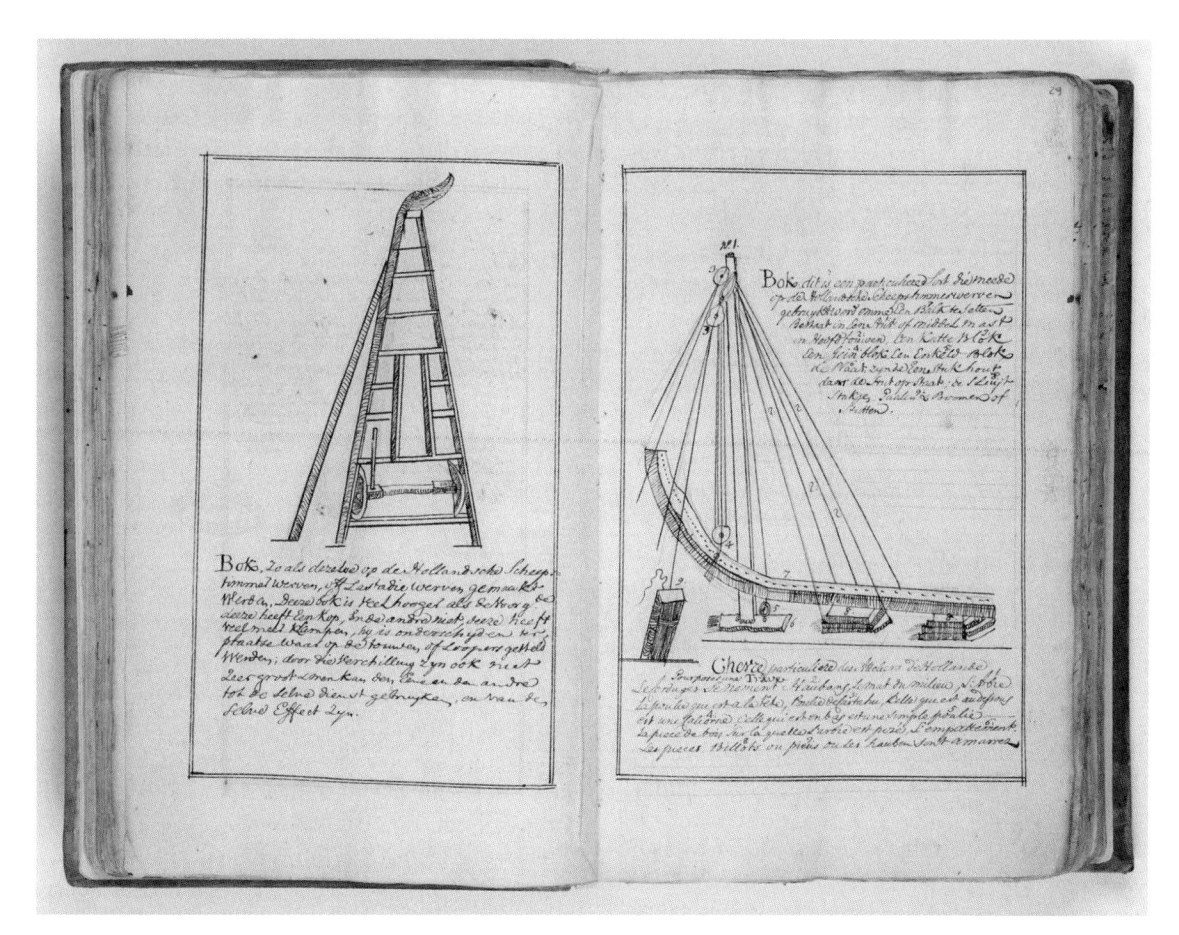

David Franco Mendes, *Dictionary of Maritime Terms*, ca. 1780. The biography of Mendes appears in the section Political Life and Thought.

Perhaps one day I might demonstrate the weak forces of my limited understanding and, desirous of the glories of the motherland and of those who are always famous and bestowed by the benevolent sovereign who sustains us, I will be able more openly to explain my ideas to the public. In this I will be accompanied by some particular story that can serve as an illustrious and eternal monument to the true, almost original Tuscan wisdom and to the honorable recognition of various sublime geniuses whom she can call, at various times, fecund mother and nurturer.

Translated by James N. Novoa.

Herz Homberg
1749–1841

Born near Prague, Herz Homberg served as supervisor of the German Jewish schools in Galicia, as well as a censor of Hebrew religious books in Vienna. A close friend of Moses Mendelssohn, Homburg was the first Jew in the Austro-Hungarian Empire to complete the University of Vienna's formal examination. Disliked by traditional Jewish leaders, Homberg's zeal to impose enlightened reforms was also seen as excessive by many of his fellow reformers. He founded some one hundred schools, stressing education in the German language.

Bene Zion: A Religious-Moralistic Textbook for the Youth of the Israelite Nation
1812

Ninth Section. Concerning the Duties of Mankind as Citizens

374. No man, in isolation, can gain for himself the means through which to satisfy his physical needs and develop his spiritual strength; he has almost no opportunity to practice the various virtues.

375. The instinct of self-preservation, therefore, forces the human being to join in society with others, to unite and increase his strength together with theirs, and so to achieve a serene position in life and to prolong his existence. [. . .]

393. The institutions that promote order and welfare and secure the nation's peace, and which cost immense sums, are borne by civil society; such costs are known as public expenditures. These expenditures are distributed among all members of society in relation to their fortune, and each individual must pay the amount he owes. All the payments together, known as the government revenue, flow into the state treasury, from which the expenditures are paid.

394. The collection of the contributions, the payment and remuneration of the state's requirements, the drafting and execution of laws, the foundation and maintenance of all necessary and useful institutions, the appointment of clergy to church service, the appointment of ministers, council members, judges, teachers, military commanders, etc., the determination of their duties and salaries, the declaration of war and peace, the signing of friendly pacts with other nations, etc., all together make up the duties of the state administration, which is entrusted to the highest-ranking person in the state. This person is called: emperor, king, duke, etc. The rightful leader of every civil society is appointed by God, so that, according to His will, the society is led with justice, gentleness, and love, and its good fortune is promoted.

> Daniel 4:22 "So that you (Nebuchadnezzar) convince yourself that the Highest (God) directs the rule over mankind, and entrusts it to one who pleases Him."

395. We should love our fatherland, meaning its constitution, laws, institutions, customs, and traditions, treasure it above all others, and support and promote the common public interest.

Translated by Carola Murray-Seegert.

Other works by Homberg: *Imre shefer* (1808); *Ben yakir* (1820).

Léon Halévy
1802–1883

Léon Halévy, born in Paris, worked toward the goal of European Jewish enlightenment. For Halévy, the emancipation and citizenship granted to Jews during the French Revolution made it possible for them to set aside religious superstition and embrace instead the arts and sciences. Although he suffered professionally from antisemitism, Halévy participated actively in French intellectual life, publishing literary translations, plays, and libretti. He was a follower of Henri de Saint-Simon, attracted by the latter's belief in the power of reason and science. Despite his early focus on

Judaism, Halévy kept his distance from Judaism, Christianity, and later distortions of Saint-Simonianism.

A Summary of Modern Jewish History
1828

The Jews are everywhere, in the old world and in the new. They can be found in Jamaica, in New England, in Washington's America as well as in Bolívar's, and even in Austral lands. If this people were not remarkable in so many other respects, it would still be so at the least for its universality and for the future-oriented spirit that governs its destiny. Though their true believers and their wives have longed for a return of the Jewish nation to that ancient land of Jerusalem, we do not think the Jews are destined to do so: we believe, however, that the day will come when men of all nations will have achieved such a harmony of morality and doctrine, of political and religious institutions, that this people, which is everywhere, will be able to feel part of one common nation. It is a long way, I realize, from the wretched quarrels reawakened among us by the ghosts of Loyola and Jansenius to that future of universal reform; but when a few obscure men proclaimed Christianity, a reform so quickly perverted by the Jewish religion, the whole universe was pagan. Paganism laughingly witnessed the quarreling orators, sophists, and philosophers wedded to their systems, when poor fishermen suddenly proclaimed a new faith, and the face of the world was changed.

Translated by Michele McKay Aynesworth.

Other works by Halévy: *Résumé de l'histoire des juifs anciens* (1825); *La Grèce tragique* (1846); *Vie de Fromenthal Halévy* (1862).

Isaac Markus Jost
1793-1860

Born in Bernburg, Germany, Isaac Markus Jost was an educator, historian, and community activist. After studying at the universities of Göttingen and Berlin, he settled in Frankfurt, where he taught for twenty-five years. In addition to his pedagogical works, Jost wrote histories of the Jews from the time of the Maccabees up to his own day. Jost contributed extensively to Jewish newspapers and periodicals and was known for actively defending Judaism against criticism and threats of legal encroachment. He devoted considerable time to charitable work, including aid to orphans.

The Rigors of Jewish Historiography
1832

The historiography of no people is so beset with the pretentious and condemnatory views of dilettantes as is that of the Israelites, which everyone fancies to know from the relevant sources. Thus, no matter how carefully even sober thinkers attempt gently to drive prejudice away, to cleanse imbibed conceptions, to classify and define often uncertain notions more precisely—striving to unchain the captives arouses the multitude to severe grumbling and often even violent opposition.

This is what frightens so many scholars, who would like to shed some light, from casting their beams into such an obscure domain. Instead of cultivating this thankless soil, the learned man finds sufficient fertile acreage in lovelier regions of science where the earth more generously rewards his labors, where with less effort he may hope for agreeable prospects, configurations, and sweeter fruits which will attract the spirit and mind of the multitude. For this reason the history of the Israelites—insofar as it does not appear as a necessary supplement to the history of religion—for the most part lies fallow. It is simply brushed off as inherently arid or else not worthy of development. Rarely is a critical spirit drawn to it, and even then mostly for secondary reasons. For some it serves as a guide while wandering among the sources of religion. For others it must supply from its arsenals weapons to defend Judaism against Christianity and Islam, to defend the latter two against the former, or each of these against the other. Individual sects even use Israelite history in putting forward their claims against all other sects. Thus, just as the Israelite people is scattered, subjugated to all, and freely esteemed by few, so too its history has been reduced to bondage. It seldom finds a friend or loving care.

But can there be a history of a slave? Asking the question reveals a mighty obstacle. It is commonly held that where independent activity has ceased, there too history has ceased. It is thought that history directs its attention to the development of forces, to a description of the origins, emergence, creativity, and circumstances of a people, its entanglements with other powers, its wars and clashes up to the point of its collapse. The older historical sources of the history of the Israelite people do indeed constitute rich mines of choice experiences of this kind; the mind's eye may here enjoy a highly manifold development of forces, and we may draw from these sources serious and boundless instruction. But as these same sources dry up, we must forego any further hope of new enjoyment. What pleasing pictures, one asks, can the lot of the slave still offer us? What henceforth makes up the variety in his life, aside from the exchange of masters?

In view of these considerations, everyone turns away his contemptuous or pitying glance. Only rarely does a friend of humanity linger to detect even among the humbled a certain power of spirit, to ponder carefully that power's opposition to the all-powerful force of external circumstances, and to recognize that it indicates more than a fossilized existence. But oh, how easily freedom of judgment is here led astray! The investigator is overcome with warm sympathy, which he is scarcely able to suppress before it comes to determine his historical judgment. It influences him more strongly in evaluating a subjugated people than in dealing with an individual slave. If this sympathy takes the form of attachment, the observer pours out his saddened heart in laments over the cruelty, injustice, and implacability of fate—over the lack of understanding, the malice, spite, and arrogance of those in power, who, misusing their chance predominance, shamefully trample upon mankind. If, on the other hand, he feels lively admiration for physical energy and contempt for human weaknesses, then he will regard the sufferings of the oppressed simply as deserved punishment for their misdeeds, the consequences of abnormality and of the calamitous renunciation of independence.

The Israelite people does not fail to recognize the great change which the God of Israel had determined shortly before the people's collapse. It is deeply affected by the change and clings ardently to its God, striving in vain to restrict Him. But it has been decided otherwise in the counsel of the Almighty. Knowledge and veneration of Him shall no longer be limited to a land, to a people. The hitherto favored nation collapses, its glory departs, its pride has vanished. Yet with an unending love it clings to its God; scattered and dispersed, it follows Him into all lands with greater faithfulness than before. It feels itself overwhelmed, but it does not acknowledge itself as vanquished. Its true fatherland—its God and its religion—has not been lost; it has become even more precious with the loss of worldly joys. Here the defeated people feels strengthened anew to enter the lists with all nations in the battle for truth. In the common struggle to attain that final reconciliation, the Israelites, regardless of all the misery which became their lot on that account, remain master of the field through nearly two thousand years—and they have never laid down their weapons.

It is the task of the historian to describe this spiritual struggle, especially during the second half of Israelite history. But the task requires both great caution and deep insight which, insofar as possible, penetrates to details. The historian must grasp precisely, not merely the general positions of the parties, which change in different periods, but also the positions held simultaneously but affected by locality and other circumstances. Otherwise he cannot understand, evaluate, or judge fairly the choice of weapons, the type of battle, and the opposing attacks. This understanding requires long preparation, highly comprehensive studies, and uncommon candor. The historical sources are scattered far and wide; in part they are already quite obscure; and often they deliver only fragments, isolated kernels. Many of them are inherently dull and vapid, worthy of attention more as evidence of their time and place than by virtue of their content. The gathering of testimony, which justice demands, wears upon one's patience because of the endless contradictions and absurdities, the expressions and references whose meaning can often only be surmised. One is confronted by an immense number of deeds, speeches, laws, disputes, opinions, stories, poems, legends, and other phenomena affecting the lot of the Israelites. This is to say nothing of the many different places, times, and thinkers. One must consider as well human inclinations, cultural variations, historical setting, and in general the prevailing circumstances of entire nations, districts, and individuals, to say nothing of natural predispositions, emotions, and intellectual movements. All this is necessary to arrive at a certain historical understanding and to derive fruitful results and just evaluations.

Historiography, at least in regard to the object of our concern, has not yet developed to the point where it can regard the evidence as complete and can proceed to issue a verdict. It still remains the duty of the historian of the Israelites to gather and to order, but to forego any general and reliable judgment. Even if in his opinion he is sufficiently familiar with individual segments of history to trust himself with an evaluation of the proceedings, this awareness must not delude him into arrogant condemnation. Rather, his judgment becomes totally impartial only when he subjects his view to the examination of similarly impartial experts. This consideration is our guiding principle. [. . .]

We consider the entire collection of Hebrew sacred literature a source of history although it was not all intended to be historical and even the actual historical books do not proceed from an historical point of view. Indeed, we are relatively more justified in drawing our subject matter from this literature to the degree that the historical material is only, as it were, included by chance, but does not constitute a book's sole contents. For such sources which contain only the account of events are much sooner subject to doubt than those in which historical data appear as known and acknowledged, and are unconsciously repeated and supplemented. In the former instance, we must examine the author, his level of culture, and his intent with utmost care before we trust him. In the latter, we need only apply inner criticism in order not to misunderstand the individual datum torn from its context; the fact itself lives before our eyes and weaves itself into the life of the people, appears in all manner of forms, inspires poetry, and proves to be indisputable truth. In this sense, the Holy Scriptures of the Hebrews become wholly excellent sources of history. They constitute a collection of popular accounts, thoughts, laws, speeches, poems, seldom separated into genres but rather meshed and interwoven, nearly always producing a clear portrait of the totality. In every book, in every paragraph—one is tempted to say in every expression—one sees the entire spirit of the people with its traditions and its relationships, a complete world of its own which manifests itself in every special form and whose specifics can be understood only by seeing the whole. The more this world appears locked in upon itself, the more closely is everything within it tied together; even what it received from the outside was forced to adapt itself to its forms and to fuse with it. This inner unity is its truth for the historian. [. . .]

But religious belief, as all previous attempts attest, does cast the historian in chains, and thus there must be some arrangement from the start to free him from either relating facts which he cannot justify because he all too obediently follows the text, or breaking with faith. An accommodation is achieved through sound criticism, which faith must allow the scholar. It is the critical method which must guide the historian through the realm of history, and although he continually follows particular authorities, it must nevertheless stand by his side, advising, warning, and showing him the way. True faith, which is located in the mind, is not threatened by the transformed appearances of externals; it cannot be true if it shrinks from criticism of historical data. Criticism no more does harm to religion than a closer examination of the laws of nature and their variability threatens to shatter belief in the Creator.

Translated by Michael Meyer.

Other works by Jost: *Geschichte der Israeliten seit den Zeit der Maccabaer*, 9 vols. (1820–1829); *Geschichte des Judenthums und seiner Sekten*, 3 vols. (1857–1859).

Leopold Zunz

The Liturgical Addresses of the Jews
1832

Scholarship and Emancipation

Permit me to preface the necessary information about the contents and the meaning of the book which is herewith presented to my readers with a few remarks about Jewish affairs in general and the problems to whose solution I should like to contribute in particular. In doing so I appeal the judgments of authorities which recognize prejudice and abuses to places where the verdict pronounced is truth and justice. For when all around us freedom, scholarship, and civilization are fighting for and gaining new ground, the Jews too are entitled to make claim to serious interest and untrammeled justice. Or shall the arbitrariness of club-law and of medieval madness retain a foothold only in the laws applying to Jews, at a time when clericalism and Inquisition, despotism and slavery, torture and censorship are on their way out?

It is high time that the Jews of Europe, particularly those of Germany, be granted right and liberty rather than rights and liberties—not some paltry, humiliating privileges, but complete and uplifting civil rights. We have no desire for stingily apportioned rights which are balanced by an equal number of wrongs; we derive no pleasure from concessions born of pity; we are revolted by privileges obtained in an underhanded manner. Any man should blush with shame whom a patent of nobility from the powers-that-be raises above his *brothers in faith*, while the law, with stigmatizing exclusion, assigns to him a place below the lowest of his *brothers in fatherland*. Only in lawful, mutual recognition can we find satisfaction, only irrevocable equality can bring our suffering to an end. However, I see no love or justice in a freedom which removes the shackles from the hand only to apply them to the tongue, in a tolerance which takes pleasure in our decline rather than our progress, in a citizenship which offers protection without honor, burdens without prospects. Such noxious elements can only produce serious sickness in the body politic, harming the individual as well as the community. [. . .]

The neglect of Jewish scholarship goes hand in hand with civil discrimination against the Jews. Through a higher intellectual level and a more thorough knowledge of their own affairs the Jews could have achieved a greater degree of recognition and thus more justice. Furthermore, much bad legislation, many a prejudice against Jewish antiquity, much condemnation of new endeavors are a direct consequence of the state of neglect in which Jewish literature and Jewish scholarship have been for about seventy years, particularly in Germany. And even though writings about the Talmud and against the Jews mushroomed overnight and several dozen Solons offered themselves to us as reformers, there was no book of any consequence which the statesmen could have consulted, no professor lectured about Judaism and Jewish literature, no German learned society offered prizes in this field, no philanthropist went traveling for this purpose. Legislators and scholars, not to mention the rabble among writers, had to follow in the footsteps of the 17th-century authorities, Eisenmenger, Schudt, Buxtorf, and others like beggars, or had to borrow from the dubious wisdom of modern informants. Indeed, most people frankly admitted their ignorance of this area or betrayed it with their very first words. The (supposed) knowledge of Judaism has not progressed beyond the point where Eisenmenger left off 135 years ago, and philological studies have made almost no progress in 200 years. This explains the fact that even estimable writers assume an entirely different character—one is tempted to call it spectre-like—when the subject of the Jews comes around: all quotations from the sources are copied from the subsidized works of the 16th and 17th centuries; statements that were successfully refuted long ago are served up like durable old chestnuts; and given the lack of any scholarly activity, or any up-to-date apparatus, the oracle of the wretches is consulted. Out of ignorance or malice, some people have blended an imaginary Judaism and their own Christianity into a sort of system of conversion or concluded that regressive laws were necessary. Although excellent men have already spoken out in favor of Jewish studies and worked for them, on the whole there has been little improvement in this regard. [. . .]

In the meantime, however, the Jews have not been completely idle. Since the days of Mendelssohn they have worked and written in behalf of civil rights, culture and reform, as well as their trampled-upon ancient heritage. A new era has revealed its strength in life and scholarship, in education and faith, in ideas, needs, and hopes; good seeds have been sown, excellent forces have been developed. But what is still needed is a protective institution which can serve as a support for progress and scholarship and as a religious center for the community. The physical needs and public safety of Jewish communities are being met by hospitals and orphanages, poorhouses and burial grounds. However, religion and scholarship, civil liberty, and intellectual progress require schools, seminaries, and synagogues; they must enlist the efforts of capable community leaders, competent teachers, well-trained rabbis. If emancipation and scholarship are not to be mere words, not some tawdry bit of fancy goods for sale, but the fountainhead of morality which we have found again after a long period of wandering in the wilderness, then they must fecundate institutions—high-ranking educational institutions, religious instruction for everyone, dignified religious services, suitable sermons. Such institutions are indispensable for the needs of the congregational totality of the Jews; but to establish them we need religious zeal and scholarly activity, enthusiastic participation in the entire project, benevolent recognition from the outside.

Free, instructive words are something not to be denied. Mankind has acquired all its possessions through oral instruction, through an education which lasts a lifetime. In Israel, too, the words of teaching have passed from mouth to mouth in all ages, and any future flourishing of Jewish institutions may derive only from the words that diffuse knowledge and understanding. [. . .]

Apart from all present-day efforts in this field and any personal connection I may have with them, the institution of the liturgical addresses of the Jews seemed to me to deserve and require a strictly historical investigation. The substance of my research on the origin, development, and fortunes of this institution, from the time of Ezra to the present, is now presented in this book. [. . .] I hope that in addition to their main purpose, the recognition of the right and the scholarship of the Jews, my investigations will stimulate interest in related studies and win for the nobler endeavors of our time the favor of the mighty, the benevolence of the prudent, the zeal of the pious. Such a reward will be sweeter to me than any literary acclamation.

Translator unknown; edited by Nahum N. Glatzer.

Adolphe Franck
1809–1893

Born in Liocourt, France, Adolphe Franck had a long career teaching philosophy and, later, natural and civil law. Author of one of the first critical histories of the Kabbalah, Franck published numerous works of philosophy. He took advantage of his early training in Hebrew studies to defend Judaism, whether through teaching, lectures, and journalism, or through work in organizations such as the Anti-Atheist League, the Society for Translation of the Scriptures, and the Society for Jewish Studies. He argued that the grounds for civil law and punishment derived from society's right to defend itself, rather than from the ancient tradition of retribution.

The Kabbalah, or The Religious Philosophy of the Hebrews
1843

At a time when the worship of the dead letter degenerated into idolatry; at a time when men passed their lives in counting the verses, the words and the letters of the Law, at a time when the official preceptors, the legitimate representatives of religion, saw nothing better to do than to crush the intellect as well as the will under an always increasing mass of external practices, that aversion for everything material and positive, and the habit of often sacrificing grammar and history to the interest of an exalted idealism, infallibly reveal to us the existence of a secret doctrine which has all the characteristics and all the pretensions of mysticism, and which, undoubtedly, does not date from the day it dared to speak in a clear language. Finally, without attaching too much importance to it, we cannot refrain from laying stress upon the following: We have already remarked, that in order to attain their aims and to introduce, in some manner, their own ideas into the very terms of the revelation, the Kabbalists resorted at times to more or less irrational means.

The Kabbalists' Conception of the Nature of God

The Kabbalists speak of God in two ways which in no wise impair the unity of their thought. When they attempt to define God, when they distinguish His attributes, and wish to give us a precise idea of His nature, they speak in the language of metaphysics, with all the lucidity permissible in matters of such nature and by the idiom in which they are expressed. But sometimes they represent the divinity as a being which cannot be comprehended at all, a being that lives always above all the forms with which our imagination may clothe it. In the latter case all their expressions are poetical and figurative, and then they combat, as it were, imagination with the weapons of imagination; then all their efforts tend to destroy anthropomorphism by giving it such gigantic proportions, that the frightened mind can find no term of comparison, and is compelled to rest in the idea of the Infinite. [. . .]

Finally, what is "Kingdom?" It is the permanent and imminent action of all the Sefiroth combined, the actual presence of God in the creation. This idea is fully expressed by the word Shekinah, one of the surnames of the "Kingdom." The true terms of this new trinity are, accordingly, the absolute, the ideal and the immanent face; or also, the substance, the thought and the life; that is, the uniting of the thought with the object. They constitute what is called "the middle column" (Amudah D'amtzissoh), because in all the figures customarily used to represent the Sefiroth they are placed in the centre, one above another, in the form of a vertical line or column. As may be expected of what we already know, these three terms also become so many "faces" or symbolical manifestations. The "Crown" does not change its name, it is always the "long face," the "Ancient of days," "the Ancient Whose name be sanctified" (Atikah Kadisha). "Beauty" is the "holy king," or simply the "King" (Malko), (Malko Kadisha), and the "Shekinah," the divine presence in things, is the "Matrona," or "Queen" (Matronitha).

When the one is compared to the sun, the other is compared to the moon; because the moon borrows all the light by which it shines from a higher place, from a degree immediately above her. In other words, real existence is only a reflection or image of ideal beauty. The "Matrona" is also called "Eve," "for," says the text, "Eve is the mother of all things, and everything that exists here below, nurses from her breast and is blessed through her." The "King" and the "Queen," commonly

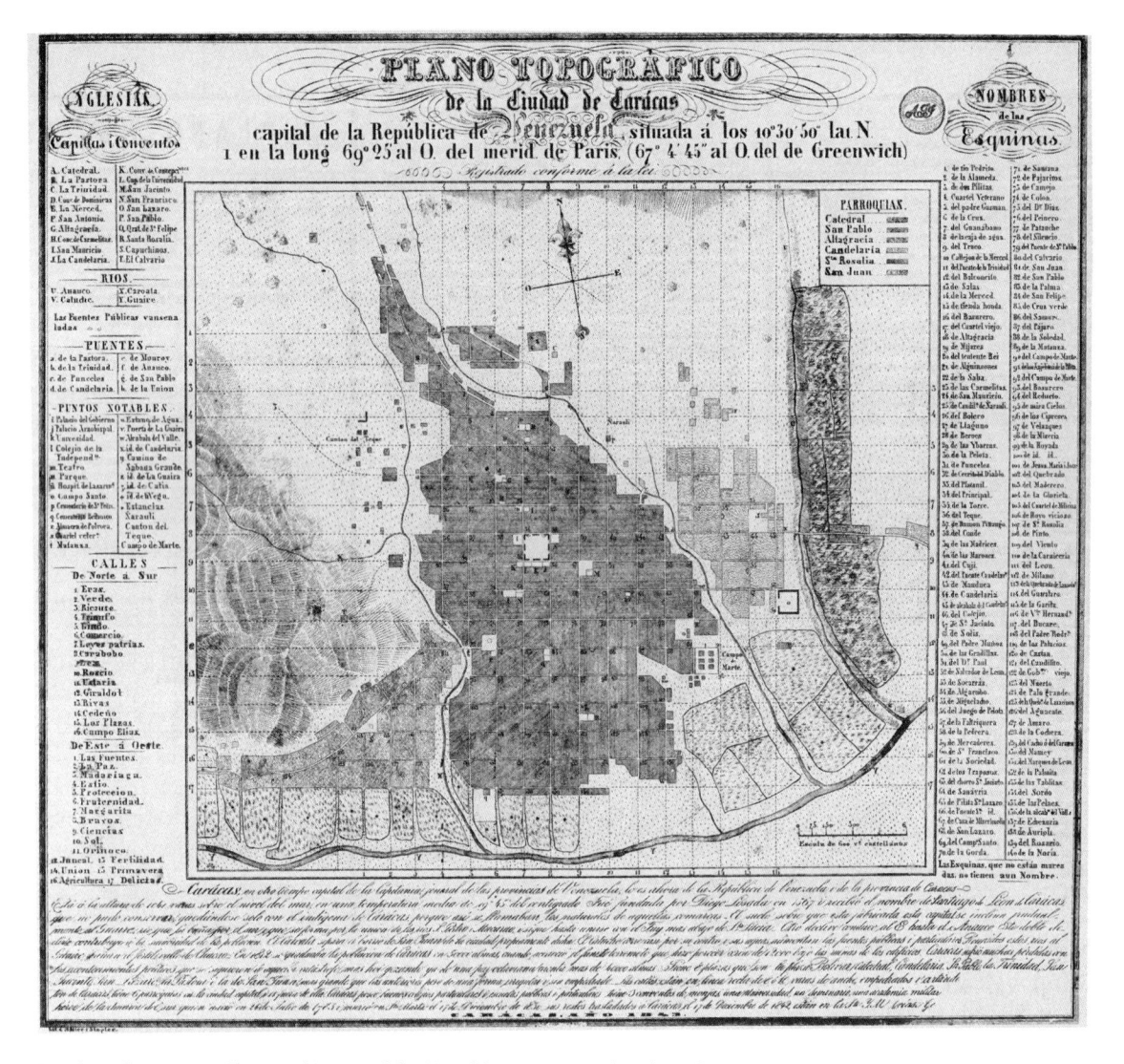

Angel Jacobo Jesurun, *Topographic Map of the City of Caracas, 1843*. Angel Jacobo Jesurun's topographical map of Caracas, with its geometric grid, is the first map after Venezuela's independence to be drawn and printed by a native of the city. After decades of war and an earthquake in the first decades of the nineteenth century, the city was depleted. Jesurun, an attorney by profession, also served as an advocate for the rights of Venezuela's Jews.

called also the "two faces" (Du Partsufin), form together a pair whose task is to pour forth constantly upon the world new grace, and through their union to continue the work of the creation, or, what is more, to perpetuate the work of the creation.

Translated by I. Sossnitz.

Other works by Franck: *Esquisse d'une histoire de la logique* (1838); *La religion et la science dans le Judaisme* (1883).

Leopold Dukes

1810–1891

Born in Pressburg (present-day Bratislava), Leopold Dukes was a historian and critic of Jewish literature. He was first educated in the traditional manner at Rabbi Moses Sofer's yeshiva in Pressburg; then he received a broader education in Würzburg, Germany. After a brief return to Pressburg, Dukes lived in Germany, France, and England (the latter for some two decades), where he researched Hebrew manuscripts and wrote about philology, rabbinic proverbs, aggadic literature, biblical exegesis, and medieval Hebrew-language Spanish Jewish poetry (especially that of Solomon ibn Gabirol).

Rabbinical Anthology
1844

Proverbs and Proverbial Sayings

1. In General

Proverbs are the wisdom of the people, the fruit of common sense, and in particular, are distilled from general experience. They are to the moral communication of men what coins are to the bourgeois. Through them alone, ordinary people obtain the wisdom brought to light by gifted men's persistent and mature contemplation, which they then use and transfer to their everyday affairs. Experience is the mother of proverbs, and they also lead back to it. They appear among all peoples and, in their generality, are universally intelligible precisely because they share a common soil—life itself—from which they all emanate. Only the native costume distinguishes one from another, and it is this alone that requires explanation.

The content of proverbs is very diverse; it encompasses a large sphere and includes the parable, which transforms a general idea into a structured picture; the maxim, which provides an actual rule of conduct; and the reflection, in which the maxim gleams only indirectly. The parable, or rather the comparison, is the basis for the proverbial mode of speech; it differs from the proverb in that it is not independent, is based on popular opinion, and defines the general with the clearest limits. Reflective proverbs are closest to maxims and differ from them merely by their particularity and by their specific nature, which also brings them into the vernacular and keeps them there. It is perhaps not unfounded to suppose that maxims, originating from wise men, seek unity in the manifold. Their soil is abstraction. The proverb proceeds from the particular; its soil is the perspective of the individual, whereby it is then elevated to the universal. A maxim embodies itself in the proverb; a proverb is spiritualized in the maxim. The more general a maxim, the better; the more specific a proverb, the more useful. The transition from the maxim to the proverb was perhaps represented by the fable, in which a general principle was expressed dramatically in a structured manner. The moral, as an extract from the fable, entered the vernacular as a proverb or a proverbial phrase.

Both the fable and the proverb, each reflections of ordinary life, at times contain much egotism. Practical wisdom places the ego at the center of the universe and makes everything else revolve around it. The fable should counteract egotism to some extent, but it does not always do so directly; it often presents a tableau and leaves it to the thinking man to abstract the message from it. The proverb, however, is more often presented in its complete nakedness. The maxim—the saying of the wise—makes a man consider something other than himself and his material advantage. The real purpose of all the maxims of the truly wise is to teach self-denial, which, in all honesty, is a lesson seldom freely adopted by the greater masses. As a rule, proverbs have only incorporated those maxims that aim at cleverness. It seems probable that most proverbs were initially the maxims of the wise and were afterward adopted by the people. The simpler and shorter a maxim, the more suitable it is for a proverb.

Translated by Carola Murray-Seegert.

Other works by Dukes: *Die Sprache der Mischnah: lexicographisch und grammatisch betrachtet* (1846); *Philosophisches aus dem zehnten Jahrhundert. Ein Beitrag zur Literaturgeschichte der Mohamedaner und Juden* (1868).

Heinrich Graetz
1817–1891

Historian and biblical scholar Heinrich (Hirsch) Graetz was born in Poznań (Posen) and received a yeshiva education. Strongly influenced by his friendship with Samson Raphael Hirsch, he studied at Breslau University (which did not give doctorates to Jews) and defended his dissertation (on Gnosticism and Judaism) at the University of Jena. Graetz began teaching Jewish history and Bible at the new Jewish Theological Seminary of Breslau in 1853, the same year that the first volume appeared of his comprehensive history of Jews, *Geschichte der Juden von den ältesten Zeiten bis zur Gegenwart*. It was the first work by a university-trained historian of the Jews to garner a widespread popular readership. His career and works, not without controversy, highlighted the growing rift between traditional and liberal Jewish forms of Judaism.

The Diaspora: Construction of Jewish History
1846

This is the eighteen-hundred-year era of the diaspora, of unprecedented suffering, of uninterrupted martyrdom without parallel in world history. But it is also a period of spiritual alertness, of restless mental activity, of indefatigable inquiry. In order to sketch a clear and appropriate picture of this period, one would have to draw a two-sided image. One aspect would show humbled Judah with the wanderer's staff in his hand, the pilgrim's bundle on his back, his features grave, his glance turned heavenward; he is surrounded by the walls of a dungeon, the implements of martyrdom, and the red-hot branding iron. The other aspect is of the same figure, bearing the earnestness of the thinker upon his luminous brow, the mien of a scholar in the radiant features of his face; he is in a study filled with a huge library in all the languages of mankind and dealing with all branches of divine and human knowledge. The external history of this era is a history of suffering to a degree and over a length of time such as no other people has experienced. Its inner history is a comprehensive *Literaturgeschichte*, a literary history of religious knowledge, which yet remains open to all the currents of science, absorbing and assimilating them; once again, a history unique to this one people. *Inquiring* and *wandering*, *thinking* and *enduring*, *studying* and *suffering*—these fill the long stretch of this era. Three times during this period world history changed its garb. Decrepit Rome languished and sank into the grave. Out of its decay the chrysalis of the European and Asiatic peoples took shape; these peoples in turn developed into the glistening, butterfly-like figures of Christian and Islamic knighthood; and, finally, from their incinerated castles arose the phoenix of civilized international relations.

World history was transformed three times, but the Jews remained the same; at most they merely altered their external appearance. Likewise the spiritual content of world history was transformed three times. From a developed but hollow state of civilization mankind submerged into barbarism and dismal ignorance, only to raise itself again from its ignorance into the bright spheres of a higher civilization. The spiritual content of Judaism remained the same: it only steeped itself in the substance and form of new ideas. While the Judaism of this era includes the most celebrated *martyrs*, compared to whom the persecuted sufferers of other nations and religions may almost be considered fortunate, it also produced towering thinkers who did not remain merely the pride of *Judaism* alone. There is likely no science, no art, no direction of the spirit in which Jews have not shared, in which they have not demonstrated equivalent ability. *Thinking* became as characteristic a feature of the Jews as did *suffering*.

On account of the largely forced, rarely voluntary, migrations of the Jews, the Jewish history of this era encompasses the entire inhabited earth: it stretches into the snowy regions of the north and into the blazing sun of the south; it traverses all oceans and establishes itself in the most remote corners of the world. As soon as a new part of the world is invaded by a new people, scattered Jews immediately appear, defying every climate and every hardship. If a new area of the world is discovered, Jewish communities are soon formed and grouped together here and there following an inner drive for crystallization which operates without worldly aid or external compulsion. Dispersed to all regions of the earth, the Jews form a huge circle that expands out of sight. Its periphery coincides with the ends of the inhabited world; at its center is the Temple, still sacred even in ruins. These migrations brought the Jewish people new experiences; homeless, they exercised and sharpened their gaze. Thus even the plenitude of their suffering contributed to broadening the horizons of Jewish thinkers. The Jewish history of this era witnessed, was affected by, and to an extent participated in all the overwhelming events of world history from the time when the full terror of the barbarians exploded upon the overrefined Roman Empire until the spark of culture was struck anew from the hard anvil of barbarism. Every storm upon the sea of world history also had an effect on Judaism, shaking it to its foundations without shattering it. The Jewish history of eighteen centuries presents a microcosm of world history even as the Jewish people has become a universal people; being nowhere at home, it is at home everywhere.

What prevented this ever-wandering people, these truly eternal Jews, from degenerating into brutish vagrants or a vagabond horde of gypsies? The answer is self-evident. During its desolate history of eighteen hundred years the Jewish people carried with it the Ark of the Covenant which placed an ideal striving in its heart and even transfigured the badge of shame on its garment with an apostolic radiance. The proscribed, outlawed Jew, pursued over the entire earth, felt an exalted, noble pride in bearing, and in suffering for, a doctrine which reflected eternity and by which the nations would eventually be educated to the knowledge of God and to morality, a doctrine from which the salvation and redemption of the world would go forth. The lofty consciousness of his glorious apostolic task kept the sufferer erect, even transformed his sufferings into an aspect of his exalted mission. Such a people for which the present meant nothing while the future meant everything, which seemed to exist by virtue of its hope, is for that very reason as eternal as hope itself. The Law and the messianic hope were two protecting and consoling angels at the side of the humbled Jews, saving them from despair, from stupefaction, and loss of identity. The Law for the present, the messianic hope for the future, both mediated by scholarship and the effusions of poetic art—these poured balm on the grieved hearts of the unfortunate people. Since for this subjugated nation the world at large was reduced to a gloomy, filthy dungeon in which it was unable to satisfy its urge to act, the more talented among its members retreated to the inner world of ideas which expanded proportionately as the restraints of the outside world were drawn more narrowly around its mangled body. Thus appeared a doubtless rare phenomenon: the persecuted proved more than a match for his oppressor, the tormented almost pitied his tormentor, the prisoner felt freer than his jailer.

Jewish literature reflects this serious intellectual life and was bound to become the richer as it not only served the needs of the highly talented, but acted as a salve for the entire suffering people. As the Jewish people made itself at home all over the inhabitable earth, Jewish literature became truly a world literature. It makes up the kernel of Jewish history which the history of suffering has surrounded with a bitter husk. The entire people has deposited its treasure of ideas and its inner being in this immense literature. The teachings of Judaism are contained in it, refined, glorified, visible to the weakest eye. Only someone accustomed to reducing a lofty, imposing wonder of the world to the category of an everyday phenomenon will regard it as of little ac-

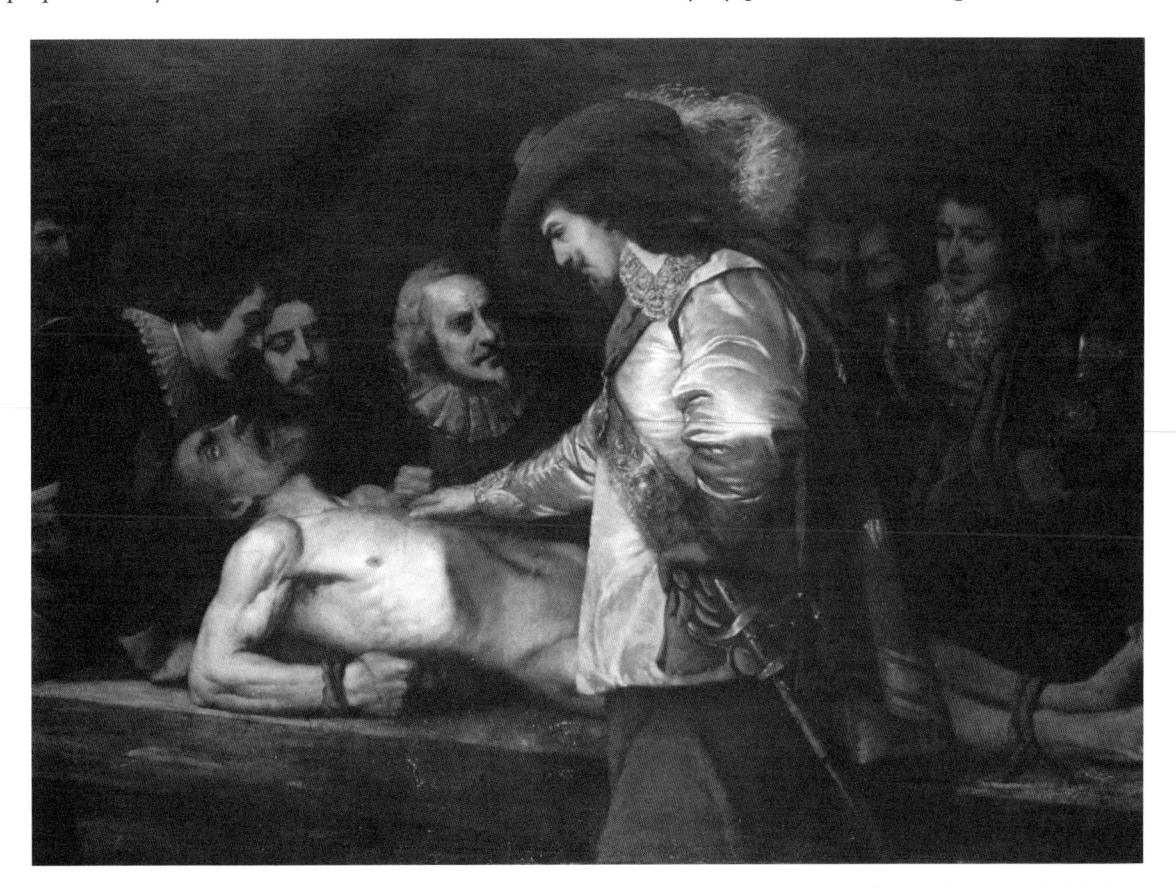

Benjamin-Eugene Fichel, *Harvey Demonstrating the Circulation of the Blood to Charles I, King of England,* 1850. Fichel depicts the seventeenth-century physician William Harvey demonstrating his discovery of blood circulation, a seminal moment in the history of modern medicine.

count. The consecutive data and events of Jewish history must be connected with the thread of this literature. It provides the pragmatic continuity and therefore must not be treated incidentally, as a mere appendix to the main history. The appearance of a new significant book is not just an interesting detail, but within its circle becomes a *deed* which has consequential ramifications. Jewish literature was born in pain and spasms of death; it is as manifold as the countries of its origin, variegated as the dress of the nations among whom it blossomed, rich and polymorphic as the recollection of its millennial experiences; it bears the unmistakable traces of a *single* progenitor, of Judaism. A single trait is imprinted upon all its configurations, every surface and edge reflecting the ideal whose rays they capture. Jewish literature thus constitutes the basic possession of this era which with regard to its active aspect can therefore justly be termed the *theoretical-religious* era. It stands in contrast to the era after the first exile, which had a *political-religious* character, and to the pre-exilic era, which was predominantly *political*.

Translated by Michael Meyer.

Other work by Graetz: *Die Verjüngung des jüdischen Stammes* (1863).

Nachman Krochmal
1785–1840

Born in Brody and living most of his life in Żółkiew (Zhovkve), Nachman Krochmal was a major, self-taught figure of the Haskalah in Galicia. He was a historian and biblical critic who emphasized the oral transmission of Jewish law. Studying Kabbalah and philosophical works by Maimonides, Nahmanides, and Ibn Ezra, he also embraced the teachings of Kant, Hegel, and other German thinkers. Krochmal's magnum opus was his *Moreh nevukhe ha-zeman* (Guide for the Perplexed of Our Time), which in the spirit of Maimonides addressed questions of the modern age. Despite his scholarship, Krochmal was not a prolific writer.

Moreh nevukhe ha-zeman (Guide for the Perplexed of Our Time)
1851

According to the workings of the natural order there are three periods through which each primordial nation passes from the time it comes into being until it passes from the scene and perishes:

1. The period of first growth, during which the spirit is born. [. . .] This spirit transforms the material parts of the nation into organic units, integrated through all manner of ordered relationships, and it holds them together as a single entity, ready to receive every excellence and perfection. This period is called: *the stage of the nation's germination and growth.*

2. Thereafter, the spirit becomes fully actualized, all those beneficial institutions and spiritual attributes to which we have alluded reach their apogee, and after a longer or shorter lapse of time, the nation moves forward in all of them, gaining fame and glory. This period will be called: *the stage of power and achievement.*

3. However, in the case of every living thing, the cause of its withering and death is already contained within it. Thus, even during the course of the second stage, the seeds of corruption and degeneration begin to appear in the nation. Thereafter, they sprout, proliferate, and grow, dissolving all bonds and corrupting every beneficial usage, until gradually the nation's glory dwindles away, the nation declines and diminishes to the point of nonexistence. We shall call this period: *the stage of decomposition and extinction.*

This is the pattern for all the nations which possess a limited manifestation of spirit, one of which is therefore finite and destined for extinction. But in the case of our nation, although we too have succumbed to the abovementioned natural course of events with regard to material and tangible externals, the fact is, in the words of the rabbis: "They were exiled to Babylon, exiled to Elam, and the Divine Presence was with them." That is to say, the universal spirit which is within us protects us and excludes us from the judgment that falls upon all mortals. And all this follows easily from what has been said above.

Even so, we have seen fit to mention the periods we have traversed since the nation's beginnings until this day in order to show clearly how the cycle of the three stages that we have mentioned repeats itself in our history, and how, when breakdown, decomposition, and decay have become complete, a new and reviving spirit always takes shape within us; though we fall, we arise invigorated—the Lord, our God, has not forsaken us.

Translated by Michael Meyer.

Samuel David Luzzatto

Igerot Shadal (Letters of Samuel David Luzzatto)
1851

I am a friend to all lovers of Torah and wisdom and my only desire and my complete salvation rest in disseminating the sources of the Torah in order that the earth will be full of the knowledge of God. Because of this, I teach and, in the process, I have learned that there are ancient books and especially manuscripts scattered around the whole Jewish diaspora, particularly in the countries of the East. No doubt there are valuable treasures that remain in darkness and there is no demand or request [for them]. I hope to God that you will be able to aid me and all lovers of the study of Jewish history by providing me with a list of the precious ancient books that are in your hands or those of your friends.

Above all, my soul has yearned to know the truth of the matter concerning what I have heard about your glorious city where there remain a few small [Jewish] communities that preserve their own special prayer book and rite whose liturgy is neither Sephardi nor Ashkenazi. I would like to know each and every one of these communities and the characteristics of their prayer books.

You should also know that I have seen a printed prayer book of the Romaniot rite (published first in Venice and later in Constantinople), which I showed to certain wise men from your country who told me that they had never seen such a thing and that this rite is no longer practiced anywhere.

And now, may God bless you, make me rejoice in your letters, either as a respondent or as an inquirer, and may God bless you with everything you do and may you know only happiness, along with your family and the household of your glorious and wise father-in-law, may he live long, and your soul as well, and the soul of the signatory here today in Padua, 12 Av 5611 [August 10, 1851].

Your friend, Shadal

NOTE
Words in brackets appear in the original translation.

Translated by Julia Phillips Cohen.

Samuel Joseph Fuenn

Kiryah ne'emanah (Faithful City)
1860

History of the City [of Vilna] from Its Original Foundation by Giedymin to Zygmund August I

1. Giedymin, the great prince of Lithuania, who dwelt in the fortress of the city of Troki, once went forth to hunt venison in the mountains surrounding the River Vilna. He shot with his bow and felled a huge wild ox on one of the mountains, where the crematoria for the princes of Lithuania and the house of worship for the idol Pieron were located; and he lodged there overnight. Giedymin had a dream, and lo and behold! A huge wolf was standing at the top of the mountain carrying an iron buckler, crying out in a loud voice equivalent to that of a hundred wolves; he trembled and awoke. He made inquiry of the chief priest, whose name was Lesdaika, to interpret his dream for him, and Lesdaika said to him: "The huge wolf that you have seen symbolizes a strong fortress and a great city which will one day stand on this place, and the sound of the hundred wolves symbolizes the renown and praise of the fortress and of the city, which will travel forth to the remotest portions of the earth." The prince Giedymin listened to what the interpreter had said, and commenced building the fortress and the city, which he called Vilna (in the year 1382 according to the Christian calendar—corresponding to 5082 in our calendar). This is the substance of the tradition hovering over the lips of the leading early writers of the Lithuanian nation. Whether it is true or merely allegorical, it attests to the greatness and the glory which became the heritage of the city in later times. It was a city of joy for the princes of Lithuania, the town where its sages and its great men resided, and besides this, it became the foremost of the settlements in which the Jews lived, a place for dissemination of Torah and wisdom to this day. While this prince was building the city and the fortress, he informed all the other cities, both near and far, about the city that he was building, and he invited anyone who so desired to acquire property in it. He apportioned fields and gardens to the agricultural laborers and granted them relief from all royal taxes for ten years; for merchants and workmen he announced exemption from all taxation, and he permitted them to do business and to pursue their crafts as they desired. On

hearing of this announcement, many Russians and Germans came, and the city was firmly established. And it is quite possible that, at that time, Jews too came to Vilna from the lands of Germany and Poland, which are close to Lithuania; and already from the year 1326 (corresponding to our year 5086) the Jews owned a special house for commercial purposes.

2. The early days of the inhabitants of Lithuania were an era in which idolatry prevailed, and except for those few of the citizens of Vilna who had accepted the Greek Christian faith (Greek Orthodoxy), the Lithuanians were the last of all the nations of Europe to accept that faith. However, when Jagiello, prince of Lithuania, sat on the throne of the Kingdom of Poland (in the year 1387, corresponding to 5147), and after he and all the noblest members of his family and the princes had converted to the Roman Catholic faith, he labored steadfastly to draw his people to the tradition of the covenant of his faith, and he began this process with Vilna.

This great event had the effect of bringing the position of the Jews of Lithuania into line with the position of the remainder of their Jewish brethren in all the lands of Christendom in that era. Indeed, the rulers of this country acted with greater benevolence toward the Jews than all the other rulers of Europe in those times, and they extended kindness to them in the early days, before the Jesuits arrived and created conflict in the land. When Jagiello entered into a pact with the rulers of Europe, he also took note of customary practices in their countries, and took up several of them and introduced them into his own country. He negotiated with Vilna with a view to conferring upon its citizens the right of the Magdeburg Law. This right, which raised the status of the citizens, on occasion demoted the status of the Jews, and became a stumbling block impeding every step they attempted toward progress for a lengthy period of time, as will become apparent.

3. When Jagiello ascended the throne of Poland, he handed Lithuania over to his brother, Skirgiello, and this country, and in particular the city of Vilna, were plundered as a result of the numerous wars waged by his brother's son, Witold, until such time as the Princedom of Lithuania, together with the city, became Witold's (1392, corresponding to 5152 of our calendar). It was then that the city of Vilna began to see the light of dawn. [. . .]

The terms of this charter of rights and privileges provide us with the following information:

That the Jews were already resident in the country from ancient times, that they had numerous occupations, and that most of them were engaged in moneylending in accordance with the practice of their coreligionists in other countries at this time.

That the enmity of the native inhabitants of the country toward the Jews had already inspired them to seek out false allegations against them, and in particular in relation to their moneylending, and that the Jews were found to be trustworthy and guiltless against their accusers, to the point where the prince regarded them as sufficiently trustworthy to afford them protection from the spirit of people's private hatreds, and to give credence to them, as trustworthy people, as against those making claims against them.

That they obtained the right to bring their lawsuits before the prince or his court, and the determination of their cases was not dependent upon the decrees of the courts of the city-governors; and this constituted a significant and notable right in those days, and it was this that stood them in good stead to liberate them from the yoke of the Magdeburg Law which the princes of Lithuania had instituted in Vilna.

That authority had been granted to the ecclesiastical judges of the Jews to judge their coreligionists in accordance with the law of Israel in respect of all matters, and thus the Jews would constitute a distinct community vis-à-vis the community of their neighbors, the Christians.

Translated by David E. Cohen.

Abraham Geiger
1810–1874

A central figure of Reform and liberal Judaism, Abraham Geiger was born in Frankfurt and served as a rabbi in Berlin and other cities. He studied at universities in Bonn and Marburg, associating with Samson Raphael Hirsch for many years until their ideological break. Geiger was influential in establishing the Jewish Theological Seminary in Breslau, though he did not receive an appointment there, and especially the Hochschule für die Wissenschaft des Judentums in Berlin. Best known for advocating that modernizing Jewish practice and encouraging humanism would both reinvigorate religious sentiment among Jews and resolve antisemitism among non-Jews, in 1835 he began to publish *Wissenschaftliche Zeitschrift für Jüdische Theologie* (Scientific Journal of Jewish Theology).

Judaism and Its History
1864

Revelation

There are facts of such an overwhelming power that even the most stubborn opinion must yield to them. Such a fact is the origin of Judaism in the midst of rude surroundings, like a vigorous growth out of a barren soil. We have essayed to draw, in a few scanty outlines, a comparison between the convictions, presentiments and assertions that prevailed in antiquity in general, and those presented by Judaism. Even that incomplete sketch must convince the unprejudiced mind that we behold an original energy which has preserved its significance for all times and has proven to be a creative force. [. . .]

They glorify that land as an especially favored and gifted one; and even when it has vanished from them, when it has been taken from them, their strength is not broken, they are not bound to its soil; their love for their earthly country rests upon their love for a higher one from which a ray descends upon the former. The poet, after bewailing the destruction of the city, the banishment of its inhabitants, after having indulged in lamentations, exclaims: "Thou, O God, remainest forever; Thy throne, from generation to generation" [Lamentations 5:19]—a thought which runs through thousands of years, even after the national life has disappeared. Can it be wondered that such a cheerful confidence exerted a powerful influence also on later generations? You hear the same words centuries thereafter. The state was destroyed a second time, every hope blasted, the last flickering light, kindled by Ben Koziba, was put out, and Roman oppression lay heavy upon the people. Rabbi Akiba with some friends visited Jerusalem, and they saw a jackal running out from where formerly the Holy of Holies had been standing. Akiba's companions wept and rent their clothes; Akiba remained silent, almost cheerful. His friends asked, "Since when have you become so indifferent to the misfortunes of our people? Do you not see the second fulfillment of the words: 'Yea, for this do we weep, because of the mountain of Zion, which is desolate, jackals walk about upon it?'" [*Ibid.*, 5:18]. "Well, my friends," replied Akiba, "indeed those words have again been verified; but the other will also come true: 'Thou O God, remainest forever, Thy throne from generation to generation.' I live in unshaken, firm confidence." [. . .]

Talent is an endowment with the ability of easily and quickly receiving, digesting, and reproducing with taste and skill; but talent leans upon something that has been achieved, upon results that are present before it, upon treasures already acquired—it creates nothing new. Genius works quite differently. It is independent, it creates, it discovers truths heretofore hidden, it discloses laws heretofore unknown; it is as though the forces that work in the depth of nature bared themselves to it in greater clearness according to their connection and legitimate co-operation; as though they presented themselves to it to be grasped, as though the mental and spiritual movements in the individual as well as in mankind as a whole, unveiled themselves before it, that it may behold the deepest foundation of the soul and may be able to dissect the motives and impulses hidden away there. Talent may be practiced, it may even be acquired by laborious application; genius is a free gift, a gift of grace, a mark of consecration stamped upon man, that can never be acquired, if it be not in the man. Talent, therefore, can not overcome impediments and obstacles if they present themselves with overwhelming force, it can not thrive under unfavorable circumstances. Genius, on the other hand, advances its conquering force against the most untoward conditions, it opens a way; it must expand its force, for it is a living impulse, a power that is stronger than its possessor, a touch of the energy dispersed into nature but condensed in him, linking him with the spirit of all spirits who manifests Himself to him by higher illumination. Talent propagates the knowledge which has been stored up, perfects it also now and then, and makes it the common property of all. Genius enriches humanity with new truths and perceptions, it gives the impulse to all great things that have come and are still to come to pass in this world.

When Columbus discovered the New World, he had not been specially prepared for it, nor fitted thereto by superior geographical knowledge, by greater experience gained on his voyages; nor could those justify any conclusion that India was to the west of Spain. It was the light of genius that caused him to see the surface of the earth, he was favored with a look into the nature of the globe and to feel that the land must be across the ocean which had been thought to be boundless; and thus what had been as knowledge, but imperfect, in him, turned into living conviction whose truth he made every effort to prove. Copernicus was probably not the greatest astronomer of his time; others may have made more correct calculations and may have been far superior to him in the science, but it was as if the whole working of the natural forces of attraction and repulsion and the entire movement of the world had been revealed to his vision; as though the veil which dark tradition had thickened, had been drawn aside from before him; as though he had looked with bold eye into the mechanism of the universe and held fast to what he had seen as a rapidly grasped truth which he afterwards with deep insight tried to substantiate, in which he did not fully succeed, because it had to be more clearly explained and more firmly established than he was able to do then. Newton is said to have been induced to establish the law of gravitation by the falling of an apple observed by him while sitting near an apple tree. Many people before him had seen apples falling, but not with the eye of genius; for that beholds in the single phenomenon the great, comprehensive law which causes that phenomenon; it looks through that external manifestation into the invisible working from which everything proceeds.

Such instances could be added to by others from every field. The historian who deserves the name as such, is not made by the profundity and care in research, the full knowledge of all incidents; he is perhaps often compelled to refuse a mass of burdensome material in order not to be perplexed and crushed by a crowd of details. But this affords him his favored position, that his vision is sharper and sees into the character of the time, that the entire working of the wheels of the ideas moving in the depths of the period, is laid bare before him. It is as if the period as a whole with its deepest foundations uncovered, stood before his mental vision, as if he had actually listened to the most secret intentions of its chief actors. [. . .]

Moses did his part of the work according to his great capacity as one of the whole people. Judaism arose within the people of revelation. And why then should we not use the word where we touch bedrock, an illumination proceeding from a higher mind and spirit, which can not be explained: which is not a compound produced by a process of development even if it is further developed afterwards; which all at once appears in existence as a whole, like every new creation proceeding from the original spirit? We do not want to limit and define the word in any dogmatic manner; it may be understood in different ways, but as to its essence it remains the same: the point of contact of human reason with the fundamental source of all things. High as the ancient teachers estimated revelation, they never denied that it is connected with human ability. The Talmud teaches: "The spirit of God rests only on a wise man, on a man possessing moral power, who is independent because he is frugal and contented by having conquered all ambition, greed, and desire"; a man who bears his importance within him, who feels the divine within him. Only such a one is capable of receiving the divine, not a mere speaking trumpet through which the spoken word passes without his being conscious of it; no, a man in the true sense of the word, who touches close upon the divine and is therefore susceptible to it. A deep thinker and great poet of the Middle Ages, Judah ha-Levi, emphatically designated revelation as a disposition that was present in the whole people. Israel, he says, is the religious heart of mankind which in its totality always preserved its greater susceptibility, and its individual distinguished men were the heart of that heart. Maimonides speaks of a flash-like illumination as which revelation must be regarded; to one the light lasted but for a short time, to another it occurred repeatedly, and with Moses, it was a lasting one, an illumination which lights up the darkness, affords man a look into the hidden recesses, which reveals to him what remains concealed for others.

Judaism is such a religion, has grown out of such divine visions and has connected into a whole all that it did behold; Judaism is a religion of truth, because the view into the essence of things is infallible, beholding the unchangeable and the everlasting: That is its everlasting message.

NOTE

Words in brackets appear in the original translation.

Translated by Charles Newburgh.

Other works by Geiger: *Was hat Mohammed aus dem Judentume aufgenommen?* (1833); *Urschrift und Uebersetzungen der Bibel* (1857).

Abraham Harkavy

1835–1919

Born to a wealthy family in the Minsk region, Abraham (Albert) Harkavy was a historian, activist, and librarian whose work concerned Jewish history and language in Eastern Europe, particularly in the ancient and medieval periods. After a traditional education, a stint at the Volozhin yeshiva and the state-sponsored Vilna rabbinical assembly, Harkavy received a

Western-style education in oriental studies at universities in St. Petersburg, Berlin, and Paris. He became the librarian of the Oriental and Semitic Department of the Russian Imperial Public Library in 1877. In his first monograph, *Ob iazyke evreev zhivushikh v drevnee vremia na Rusi* (On the Language of the Jews Who Lived in Ancient Russia), Harkavy advanced the influential if later disproven thesis that, on the basis of linguistic evidence, modern Russian Jews likely descended from Jews of Crimea and the Khazars. Writing in Russian and Hebrew, among other languages, Harkavy produced some four hundred books and articles on early interactions between Slavs, Muslims, and Jews; Jewish settlement in Eurasia; and the history of the Karaites. In 1880, he was appointed chair of the Society for the Promotion of Culture among the Jews of Russia.

On the Language of the Jews Who Lived in Ancient Russia
1866

In our previous studies[1] we attempted to prove that the first Jews in southern Russian were not Germanic, as is claimed by Graetz[2] and other German scholars, but rather Bosporan and Asian, as they came through the Kavkaz [Caucasus]. Let us now look at whether we can draw conclusions, based on historical data, about the language spoken by those first settlers. It is understood that we are speaking of the earliest period of settlement for which we have information, before the stream of Germanic Jews arrived at the time of the First Crusades. At that time, under the influence of Germanic Jews whose numbers highly exceeded those of their Slavic coreligionists, the mother tongue of the latter was gradually pushed out by the German dialect, as we will see below.

That the Bosporan Jews and their brothers in other Greek colonies of southern Russia spoke Greek in the first two centuries AD is evidenced by the writings of Jews in the Greek tongue about the liberation of captives found in Panticapaeum (Kerch), Anapa, and Olbia, which mention Jewish synagogues in these cities.[3] Additionally, these texts make it clear that scholars like Graetz[4] mistakenly suppose that the first Greek Jews in those environs arrived in the second decade of the eighth century, escaping persecution by the Byzantine emperor Leo the Isaurian. Furthermore, quite early on there were other Jews in Taurida who used the Hebrew language, as revealed in the burial stones with Jewish inscriptions discovered by Mr. Firkovich the Elder [Isaak-Boaz/Boguslav Firkowicz].[5] Knowledge of the Hebrew language by Crimean Jews continued, in some form at least, for a long time afterwards, until the Tatar tribes flooded Taurida and it fell to the rule of the Khazars. When the Slavic apostle Constantine the Philosopher (Cyril) headed to Khazaria around the middle of the ninth century (i.e., more than a century after some Khazars accepted the Jewish faith), to teach the Christian faith to the other part of this people, he passed through Korsun (Byzantine Chersonesus), where Jews lived.

In the same way that Greek Jews were using the Greek language, so, too, the Caucasian Jews, having arrived in southern Russia, undoubtedly spoke the languages of the countries from which they came. In general, before the settlement of Germanic Jews in Slavic lands and of Spanish Jews in Holland, Italy, and Turkey (at the end of the fifteenth century), there were no instances in Jewish history of Jews using a dialect different from the spoken language of the people among whom they lived. [. . .]

Again, we repeat, the question must be posed in this way: *did the Jews who arrived from Caucasian lands and Greek colonies to Slavic lands exchange the languages they brought with them for the Slavic language, or did they keep speaking those earlier languages until they were absorbed by Germanic Jews?*

Since researching any question requires knowing its status, i.e., what was done up to this point to arrive at its solution, we will present here those few studies that comprise the history of our problem.

NOTES

1. These studies originally appeared in Hebrew in the journal *Ha-karmel*, published in Vilna (year IV, issues 31 and 43, and year V, issues 2, 3, 9, 10). Since then, I have gathered many materials, and so I intend to begin this study anew and to publish them in the mother tongue. As a sample, I chose the current theme, which has a special interest for Russians.

2. *Geschichte der Juden*. VI. 1861, p. 69.

3. The most ancient of Jewish-Greek texts discovered and deciphered today belongs to the year 42; around this time (in the year 40), there is mention of Jews settling on the banks of the Black Sea/Pontus in the letter of the Jewish king Herod Agrippa to Caligula, in Philo's *Legatio ad Gajum*. For our purposes, it does not matter whether Agrippa wrote that letter, whether it

belongs to Philo's quill, or whether, finally, as Graetz assumes (III, note 24), it is written by someone else. About these texts, see our Appendix I.

4. *Geschichte der Juden*. V. pp. 188–189.

5. Some of these inscriptions were published in the *Bulletin of the Imperial Academy of Science* last year. See *Melanges asiatiques*, vol. V, pp. 119-164 and eight lithographs. On the same subject, currently in print is the work of Mr. Professor Khvolson in the memoirs of the Academy, which is the reason why we are not going into detail about these inscriptions.

Translated by Alexandra Hoffman.

Other works by Harkavy: *Ob iazykie evreev zhivushikh v drevnee vremia na rusi* (1865); *Skazaniia musul'man o slavianakh i russkikh* (1870); *O pervonachal'nom obitalishche semitov, indoevropeitsev i khamitov* (1872); *Skazaniia evreiskikh pisatelei o Khazarak i khazarskom tsarstvie* (1874); *Altjüdische Denkmäler aus der Krim* (1876).

Jacob Brafman
1825–1879

Born to a rabbinical family in the shtetl of Kletsk (present-day Belarus), Jacob (Yakov, Yuri) Brafman converted to Russian Orthodoxy at age thirty-four, around which time he began to teach biblical Hebrew in Christian seminaries and work as a censor of Hebrew and Yiddish texts for the Imperial government in St. Petersburg. Brafman also published widely on Jewish subjects in Russian periodicals, claiming from his position as a converted Jew that he could provide evidence of an international Jewish conspiracy led by the Society for the Promotion of Culture among the Jews of Russia and the Alliance Israélite Universelle. In 1869, Brafman published the first volume of his *Kniga kagala (The Book of the Kahal)*, a work that combined records of the Jewish community in Minsk with falsified materials that allegedly proved the existence of a secret Jewish "state within a state" or "Talmudic Republic" in the tsarist empire. The work was later translated into European languages, serving as propaganda for antisemites for decades. Despite the efforts of Jewish writers and activists to disprove the book's contents, it has had an unfortunate and enduring popularity in some circles.

Book of the Kahal: Materials for the Study of the Jewish Life
1869

Note I

An agent of the *kahal* who is charged with monitoring Jewish cases in the police and in giving gifts to officials is a Jewish middleman.

Jews utilize the art of the middleman not only in trade, but also in all aspects of life. That is why, in Jewish cities, the middleman is always alert: not only in the store, or the shop, or the inn, or other business and trade establishments, but also in administrative, juridical, and police institutions, and frequently even in the apartments of the persons belonging to these institutions.

These legions of middlemen—who are able to catch, so to speak, every movement in life and to extract from it substantial benefit for themselves, while also turning it into a communal Jewish goal—are divided into several classes. Each class has its own specialists: there are middlemen for trade, middlemen for contracts, middlemen who are engaged in procurement, and middlemen for issues that are legal, administrative, etc. [. . .]

Note III

There is no Jewish community, within or outside the empire, in which there aren't a few Jewish fraternal associations, and there is almost no single Jew who doesn't belong to some kind of fraternity.

The influence of these associations on the social and private life of Jews, both morally and materially, and on the social life of the country with a significant Jewish population, is very significant. Jewish fraternities are, so to speak, the arteries of Jewish society, and their heart is the *kahal*. Those who haven't first familiarized themselves with this powerful institution are unlikely to have a completely clear understanding of Jews as a whole and, in particular, of the organization of their communities and the internally engineered ties that link all Jews, scattered all over the entire world, into one powerful and unconquerable whole. But the most cursory investigation we dedicated to this subject amounted to a fairly bulky volume. It could not be contained here among the notes and we had to publish it separately.[1] [. . .]

Note V

The maxim "Jews form a state within a state," with which Schiller concludes and summarizes his description of Jewish life in Egypt 3,600 years ago, is quite justifiably applied by many to the life of the Jewish people in our time; but since a state without a territory is unthinkable, the above maxim was considered up to this point to be more of a poetic expression than a historical truth. In this book, which reveals for the first time the territory over which the Jewish *kahal* has always spread and currently spreads its laws, and which it actually subjected and continues to subject to its rule, the maxim gains the significance of irrefutable truth, and in this way it transforms from a question into an axiom. The territory of the Jewish kingdom is introduced to us in the law of the *kahal* regarding *ḥezkat yishuv*, that is, regarding the *kahal*'s control over the territory and population of its region. [. . .]

Note VII

In every Jewish society there are secure spaces that are constructed and supported by the *kahal* with community funds. These buildings are everywhere sizable, and located close to a synagogue or, more accurately, in the courtyard of a synagogue. To explain why such a community building is necessary right next to a synagogue, we must take a quick look at the general organization of the school or synagogue yard.

In cities and shtetls of the Jewish Pale, under the designation of the synagogue or school yard, we must understand a fairly small space, usually in the so-called Jewish quarter of the city, on which the following Jewish community buildings are constructed: 1) *bet ha-keneset* (the main synagogue), 2) *bet ha-midrash* (prayer house and school), 3) *bet ha-merḥats* with a *mikveh* (a public bath house with a ritual bath), 4) *ḥeder ha-kahal* (the chamber of the *kahal*), 5) *bet din* (Talmudic court), 6) *hekdesh* (infirmary and shelter for the poor), and others. The main synagogue's internal and external appearance is most impressive among the Jewish prayer houses. Nevertheless, since it is a cold building, it serves as the center for communal prayer only on the festivals of the new year and Yom Kippur, and on special occasions such as, for example, the appearance of a famous cantor in the city, or of a renowned preacher, or the case of some official's desire to visit a Jewish prayer house. At other times of the year, the main center for communal prayer is right next to the synagogue on the school yard, the *bet ha-midrash*. The *bet ha-midrash* has other names as well. It serves as the main center for the development of Talmud scholarship. In the morning and in the evening after prayer, different fraternities gather to listen to the wisdom of the Talmud from the lips of their teachers, and for many homeless people who dedicate themselves to the Talmud, the *bet ha-midrash* serves as a shelter which is never abandoned, day or night. Aside from this, the *bet ha-midrash* serves as a place for the discussion of the most important communal questions; in it are located the public and fraternity libraries. In the same place, next to the synagogue and the *bet ha-midrash*, there are always *kahal* baths with a *mikveh*.

Around this core center, placed closely together, are many private prayer houses—*kloyzes*, yeshivas, *talmudei torah*—which, similarly to the *bet ha-midrash*, serve as spaces for different learning establishments at which many Jews of different ages and social standing sacrifice their time and their moral and physical energies for the study of spiritual and civic Talmudic laws, and where every homeless wanderer and drifter can find a safe and unrestricted shelter. Aside from this, on the school yard there is always the *kahal*'s house, the character and dealings of which are introduced to us by all the *kahal*'s laws set out in this collection. Right next to this building, there necessarily must be the remainder of an ancient Sanhedrin, living to this day under the protection of the republic of the *kahal* and making up its legal department; this is the *bet din* (which will be discussed later), with its own rabbi, or *rosh bet din*, at the head, who has space for himself and his family here as well.

NOTE

1. This book was published under the title *Jewish Local and Global Fraternities*. By Y. Brafman. Vilnius, 1869.

Translated by Alexandra Hoffman.

Samuel David Luzzatto

Introduction to the Pentateuch
1870

It has been a belief universally shared by Israelites of all times that the Pentateuch was exclusively and entirely authored and redacted by the great prophet Moses; only the last chapter of Deuteronomy, the one describing the death of the holy writer, was questioned by the sages of the Talmud as to whether it should be attributed to Moses himself or to Joshua: "It is written,

'So Moses the servant of the Lord died there.' Now is it possible that Moses whilst still alive would have written, 'So Moses . . . died there'? The truth is, however, that up to this point Moses wrote; from this point Joshua the son of Nun wrote. This is the opinion of Judah, or, according to others, of Nehemiah."[1]

Against this universal and extremely persistent belief held by the entire Jewish, Christian, and even pagan antiquity, Father Riccardo Simon reacted, about a century and a half ago, by putting forward in his critical history of the Old Testament, the hypothesis that Moses may only be the author of that part of the Pentateuch which deals with laws and divine commands. On the contrary, the part of the book concerning history would have been redacted by certain Scribes, as he calls them, that is to say public writers or prophets as one may call them, who were nothing else, according to his hypothesis, than public officers charged with the task of writing history.

The nonsubstance of such a gratuitous supposition is evident through the simple consideration that the part dealing with precepts and legal provisions, and the historical part, are not in any way disjointed or detached, or even separated and distinct in the book, as they could not help but be if they had been redacted by two different authors: quite the opposite, on almost each page of the sacred code, we find the divine commandments in the course of the narrations themselves, inseparably nested and naturally snuggled. [. . .]

It is the second observation that our most ancient notables, with the rightful veneration that they always had for our arch prophet Moses, would never have tolerated . . . that the divine laws emanated through him could be united in a single body with narrations written by others than him. [. . .]

And it is my third observation, that the hypothesis of the scribes, charged by public authority with the task of writing history, is completely deprived of any foundation throughout the entire volume of the Pentateuch.

It would be difficult to infer the truth from our critic, especially from the apparent disorder that he thinks can be found in the Pentateuch; this too, much like the previous reason, is an argument that by wanting to prove too much, does not prove anything.

If the hypothesis that I have so far tried to refute seems to be revolting to you, beloved youth, the highly heterodox opinion that the most learned orientalists among the German theologians are presently daring to put forward will seem to you even more disgusting. It is therefore my duty to warn you against the impression that you may one day feel by reading works apparently dictated by much erudition and profound genius; it is my duty to share with you those weapons that my reflections were able to suggest in defense of the good cause.

Therefore, various modern linguists affirm that there exist no example of a language able to preserve itself so unchanged for the whole span of a thousand years as the Hebrew language appears to be from the first to the last writers of the holy canon, from Moses to Nehemiah. These personalities are, as we said, a thousand years distant from each other; from the pretended impossibility of such a durable uniformity in language, they infer that the Pentateuch could not have been written if not various centuries after Moses' times, for example at the time of David or even later.

This argument is only apparently sound, given the fact that the phenomenon under examination is really extraordinary, and without equal among the languages we know. If however one wants to go back to the causes of things, it is possible to observe that the main reason for the alteration of languages throughout centuries, is not the mere passing of time itself, but the influence of foreign people, be they enemies or friends.

It only remains to me, young scholars, to talk about the integrity of the holy book itself; this will be the longest, most instructive, and most enjoyable part of this introductory treatise. The absurd accusation moved against our nation by certain Christians in ancient times, such as Justin and Irenaeus the martyrs, and in less remote times, by Nicholas of Lyra and Pablo de Santa Maria (of Burgos), I mean the absurd accusation that the holy scriptures had been maliciously maimed and disfigured by us to displease the Christians: this theory is now recognized by modern scholars for what it is, that is to say as deprived of even a shadow of reason, while being on the contrary absolutely repulsive and opposite to reason, neither is it worth dwelling on its discussion.

However, my beloved youth, we should not be afraid to establish as a firm principle that the holy books did not in any way suffer from the dissolution of the kingdom of our fathers, that Ezra did not emend or in any way change the holy code, that he was not a scribe and that the holy text that is between our hands, must not be attributed as some critics would groundlessly like, to Ezra but only to Moses and God.

NOTE

1. [In Hebrew in the original (t. Menaḥot 30a).—Trans.]

Translated by Lucia Finotto.

Daniel Khvolson

The Semitic Nations
1872

With the same character, with which the individual human being is born, with the same he descends into the grave. The kindly disposed does not become ill-disposed, the judicious does not become thoughtless, the firm does not become instable, the stingy does not become benevolent, etc. By education one may acquire knowledge, good or bad views and opinions and prejudices, which will of course have their influence upon his actions, but his native character and inclinations, these can not change essentially. Age and education may, indeed, soften and modify also, to an extent, this or that trait of the character, but it itself they can not radically reconstruct. Social position may exert an influence upon the way the character manifests itself externally, but by no means can it change that character itself; for when the man of the lower class practices his cheating in the second-hand shop, or when he of the middle class swindles on the exchange, or as a director of a bank, or when he of the upper class, as governor of a province, or head of a cabinet, falsifies public opinion, deceives his monarch by false representation, then all these three do one and the same thing essentially, only under different forms, which are conditioned by their different social positions. [. . .]

We see, therefore, that the actions of men are determined chiefly by their native characters and inclinations, and that all other circumstances either have only a subordinate influence upon them, or operate only upon the manner how the human character shows itself externally. But a nation consists of single individuals, and who will deny, that every nation has a character peculiar to itself, more or less sharply pronounced. What is a nation but a great collective individuality. [. . .]

The character of a nation is as immutable as is that of an individual; the main characteristic traits of the modern nations, were peculiar to their ancestors a thousand and even two thousand years ago. [. . .]

From these qualities may be explained the various phenomena in the life of the Semites, their fortunes, institutions and spiritual productions.

1. The *soberness* of the spirit of the Semites manifested its influence upon their religion, their science, their poetry.

Upon their *Religion*.

a. The Semites produced sober, simple, easily understood religious views and conceptions; speaking generally, we may say, that the Semites, as long as they did not come in close contact with other nations, showed far less inclination to coarse superstitions than the Aryans. We find in the Pentateuch already, prohibitions against all manner of sorcery and witchcraft, as well as against the belief in the influence of the stars upon the fortunes of nations. Even those rabbis, who were not exposed to Persian influences, forbade every kind of incantation, the use of secret, magic-like remedies and talismans, the belief in good and evil days, good and evil forebodings. So also is the Arab of the desert, as the general testimony of travelers assures us, little accessible to superstitions, and is a far less strict Mohammedan than the Persian and Turk. [. . .]

2. The influence of Semitic soberness on *science*.

a. The philosophy of the Semites has a sober, one might almost say, a practical character; we call to mind only the Old Testament evidence of the existence of God. "Lift up your eyes," exclaims a great prophet, "to heaven and see who created all these!" Or as the Psalmist says: "The heavens declare the glory of God, and the expanse preaches of the works of his hands." Very simple, but I as a Semite, find it also very rational. The Semites occupy themselves almost exclusively with only such philosophical questions, which to a certain extent have an immediate significance for life, and never philosophise aimlessly about things that are unsearchable.

Translated by Ephraim M. Epstein.

Ignác Goldziher

The Zahiris
1883

Chapter One

It cannot be doubted that the two designations *ahl al-ḥadīth* and *ahl al-ra'y* originally referred to branches of legists occupied with the investigation of Islamic law: the former were concerned with the study of transmitted sources, and the latter with the practical aspects of the law. It is only later that the two terms indicate the contrast between the methods of legal deduction, a contrast which, as we have been able to observe, was quite common already in the second century.

The so-called orthodox schools (*madhāhib al-fiqh*) differ from each other in the earliest stages of their evolution in the extent to which they permit *ra'y* to be a determining factor in establishing Islamic law in a given case. The two extremes in this respect are Abū Ḥanīfah and Dāwūd al-Ẓāhirī. The former made considerable concessions to *ra'y* while the latter, at least in his early teachings, refutes any justification for this. Mālik b. Anas, al-Shāfi'ī, and Aḥmad b. Ḥanbal have taken the position between these two, not just chronologically, but also with respect to their recognition of *ra'y*. In the course of the development of these schools, this difference diminished through gradual concessions so that wide-spread confusion whether to consider a school as belonging either to *ahl al-ḥadīth* or to *ahl al-ra'y* dominates the historical literature. Ibn Qutaybah takes into account among the *aṣḥāb al-ra'y* all the founders of the legal schools with the exception of Aḥmad b. Ḥanbal, whom he does not mention, and Dāwūd, whom he could not have known yet; among the *aṣḥāb al-ḥadīth* he lists famous traditionists only. Al-Maqdisī considers Ahmad b. Ḥanbal's followers, together with those of Isḥāq b. Rāhwayhi, a famous Shāfi'ite, as *aṣḥāb al-ḥadīth* and not at all as belonging to the *madhāhib al-fiqh* to which Ḥanafites, Mālikites, Shāfi'ites, and Ẓāhirīs belong. [. . .]

First of all, it is necessary to make note of the position *ra'y* occupies in Islamic jurisprudence. This will enable us to define the position taken by Dāwūd and the school founded by him, and named after him, in the controversy between the rigid traditionalism and the sect whose adherents v. Kremer appropriately calls the speculative legists (*aṣḥāb al-ra'y*), a branch which was constantly gaining greater influence.

Chapter Two

The application of *ra'y* developed in Islamic jurisprudence as an inevitable postulate of the realities of practical legal affairs in the practice of judgeship. The theoretical canonist could quite easily dismiss the validity of *ra'y* as a justifiable source for legal affairs, for he studied the written and orally transmitted word and was not concerned with the turbulent affairs of daily life. But for a practising legist in Iraq or any other province under the dominion of Islam, it was not sufficient for the discharging of the obligations of his office to rely on sources from the Ḥijāz alone since these could not possibly give satisfactory answers to all sorts of problems arising daily in the different countries. Al-Shahrastānī's observation "that written texts are limited, but the incidents of daily life unlimited, and that it is impossible for something infinite to be enclosed by something finite" gave the initiative toward the introduction of speculative elements in the deduction of law. One example may suffice. In the newly conquered Islamic territories, there prevailed civil laws which differed considerably from those in the Ḥijāz; they were either rooted in the agrarian traditions of the country or created through the reality of the conquest. How could a code, derived from entirely different conditions, have given answers to legal problems which arose under these new circumstances? This and similar aspects—predominantly the problem that the existing sources of law were not complete and offered only occasional solutions which, however, were insufficient for all legal problems even for the country in which they originated—imposed the obligation on practising legists to consider themselves competent to exercise their subjective good sense, their insight, in the spirit of the existing sacred materials and in agreement with them, as legitimate instance for concrete cases for which the transmitted law provided no solution. How deeply the need for extending the legal bases was felt can be seen from the fact that even stern traditionists, unwillingly, but conforming under the pressure of realities, had to admit to *ra'y*.

However, they went to the utmost extremes of their system so that, in order to have ready for every concrete case a judgement from the traditions which was to be followed in practice, they often did not require the attestation of the tradition if it was a question of supplying an authority from the traditions for a legal decision. With this self-delusion, satisfaction was intended to be given, at least as a matter of form. Abū Dāwūd, so we learn, adopted the "weakest" tradition in his collection if for a certain legal paragraph there existed no better-attested tradition. Many a fabrication of traditions might have its origin in this fundamental endeavour to shun *ra'y*, at least ostensibly, for as long as possible. Yet those fabricated quotations from the traditions were nothing but *ra'y* clothed in traditions. The following saying is attributed to Sha'bī: "*Ra'y* is like a carcass; it is used as food in an extreme emergency only." Indeed, we notice, now and then, that even practising legists are obstinately opposed to applying *ra'y*. In any case, the number of people cannot have been large who, like Ḥafṣ b. 'Abd Allāh al-Nīshābūrī (d. 209), could claim to have held office as judge for twenty years without passing a single judgement on the basis of *ra'y*.

Translated by Wolfgang Behn.

Political Life and Thought

Shearith Israel

Congregation Shearith Israel was the first Jewish congregation established in North America. Between 1654 and 1730, it met in rented quarters, consecrating its first building in 1730 on Mill Street. To meet the needs of a steadily growing membership, the congregation moved into five different buildings over the centuries. The American Jewish architect Arnold Brunner designed Shearith Israel's present location, which it has occupied since 1897.

The Earliest Extant Minute Books of the Spanish and Portuguese Congregation Shearith Israel in New York, 1728–1786
1757–1758

The eve of New Year 5518 [September 14, 1757]

At a meeting of the Elders and Parnassim this day Mr Heyman Levy paid the fine for refusing serving Parnass Last year, it was at the same time voted by the Elders & Parnasseem that Mr Isaac Gomez Senr: serve as Parnas President for the ensuing year & Mr Samson Simson serve as Parnas Resident Mr Abrams Hatan Torah & Mr Samuel Judah Hatan Beresit

In the Name of the God of Israel

The Parnasim & Elders having received undouted Testimony That severall of our Brethren, that reside in the Country have and do dayly violate the principles our holy religion, such as Trading on the Sabath, Eating of forbidden Meats & other Henious Crimes, and as our Holy law injoins us to reprove one Another agreeable to the Commandments in Liviticus *Hocheach tocheach et 'ameetecha* thou shalt surely reprove thy Neighbour and not suffer sin upon him, the consideration of this Divine Precept has Induced the Parnasim & Elders to come to the following resolution in order to check the above mentioned growing evil & as our *Hachamim* observe *En 'onshin ela mazhero* That is no one is to be Punished unless First admonished, therefore whosoever for the future continues to act contrary to our Holy Law by breaking any of the principles command will not be deem'd a member of our Congregation, have none of the Mitzote of the Sinagoge Confered on him & when Dead will not be buried according to the manner of our brethren. But like Nehemiah who treated those of old that transgressed In the same manner he ordered the gates to be shut against Them, so will the Gates of our Community be shut intirely Against such offenders, but those that repent & obey the precepts of the Almighty, We beseech the Divine goodness to open to them the Gates of Mercy, & all their Enterprizes be attended with the Blessing of Haven. *Vechol hashomeang yabo elav beracha.*

At the meeting of the Parnasim & Elders of the Congration it was unanimously agreed that the foregoing should be read on the Holly day of Kipoor 5518. which was accordingly don in the Sinagog—and as Mr Benja Pereira our Hazan Declined serving it was agreed by said Parnassim & ajuntos to wright to the Parnassim & Elders of the Portogues Congration of London to send us one to whome wee ordred fifty Pounds Starling Salary pr anum to serve as a Hazan & teach the poor children Hebrew, English & Spanish the Letter being dated ye 4th Elul, in answer to which they wrote us that if any came they expected to have thire Expences and Passage paid by our Congregation which have agreed to do, as pr Coppy of the Letter dated March 13 1758 or 3 Veadar 5518.

Isaac Gomez Pte.

Mordecai Sheftall
1735–1797

Mordecai Sheftall was born in Savannah, Georgia, to Jewish British immigrants. Like his father before him, he was a merchant and an observant Jew. For several years the congregation of Mickve Israel held services in his home, as plans to build a proper synagogue for the congregation were stalled with the advent of the American Revolution. During the war he was the highest-ranking Jewish officer in the American army. Near the end of the conflict, he was captured and imprisoned by the British; he survived and remained a notable member of the American Jewish community.

In the Hands of the British
ca. 1778–1779

This day [December 29, 1778] the British troops, consisting of about 3,500 men, including two battalions of Hessians under the command of Lieutenant Colonel Archibald Campbell of the Seventy-first Regiment of Highlanders, landed early in the morning at Brewton Hill, two miles below the town of Savannah, where they met with very little opposition before they gained the height. At about three o'clock P.M. they entered and took possession of the town of Savannah, when I endeavored, with my son Sheftall, to make our escape across Musgrove Creek, having first premised that an intrenchment had been thrown up there in order to cover a retreat, and upon seeing Colonel Samuel Elbert and Major James Habersham endeavour to make their escape that way.

But on our arrival at the creek, after having sustained a very heavy fire of musketry from the light infantry under the command of Sir James Baird, during the time we were crossing the Common, without any injury to either of us, we found it high water. And my son not knowing how to swim, and we with about 186 officers and privates being caught, as it were in a pen, and the Highlanders keeping up a constant fire on us, it was thought advisable to surrender ourselves prisoners, which we accordingly did. And which was no sooner done than the Highlanders plundered every one amongst us, except Major Low, myself, and son, who, being foremost, had an opportunity to surrender ourselves to the British officer, namely, Lieutenant Peter Campbell, who disarmed us as we came into the yard formerly occupied by Mr. Moses Nunes.

During this business Sir James Baird was missing, but on his coming into the yard, he mounted himself on the stepladder which was erected at the end of the house and sounded his brass bugle horn, which the Highlanders no sooner heard than they all got about him, when he addressed himself to them in Highland language, when they all dispersed and finished plundering such of the officers and men as had been fortunate enough to escape their first search. This over, we were marched in file, guarded by the Highlanders and [New] York Volunteers who had come up before we were marched, when we were paraded before Mrs. Goffe's door on the Bay, where we saw the greatest part of the army drawn up.

From there, after some time, we were all marched through the town to the courthouse, which was very much crowded, the greatest part of the officers they had taken being here collected and indiscriminately put together. I had been here about two hours, when an officer, who I afterwards learned to be Major Crystie, called for me by name and ordered me to follow him, which I did, with my blanket and shirt under my arm, my clothing and my son's, which were in my saddlebags, having been taken from my horse, so that my wardrobe consisted of what I had on my back.

On our way to the white guardhouse we met with Colonel Campbell, who inquired of the major who he had got there. On his naming me to him, he desired that I might be well-guarded, as I was a very great rebel. The major obeyed his orders, for, on lodging me in the guardhouse, he ordered the sentry to guard me with a drawn bayonet and not to suffer me to go without the reach of it, which orders were strictly complied with until a Mr. Gild Busler, their commissary general, called for me and ordered me to go with him to my stores, that he might get some provisions for our people, who, he said, were starving, not having eat[en] anything for three days, which I contradicted, as I had victualled them that morning for the day.

On our way to the office where I used to issue the provisions, he ordered me to give him information of what stores I had in town and what I had sent out of town, and where. This I declined doing, which made him angry. He asked me if I knew that Charlestown [South Carolina] was taken. I told him: "No." He then called us poor, deluded wretches, and said: "Good God! how are you deluded by your leaders!" When I inquired of him who had taken it, and when, he said, General [James] Grant, with 10,000 men, and that it had been taken eight or ten days ago, I smiled and told him it was not so, as I had a letter in my pocket that was wrote in Charlestown but three days ago by my brother.

He replied we had been misinformed. I then retorted that I found they could be misinformed by their leaders, as well as we could be deluded by ours. This made him so angry that when he returned me to the guardhouse, he ordered me to be confined amongst the drunken soldiers and negroes, where I suffered a great deal of abuse and was threatened to be run through the body or, as they termed it, "skivered" by one of the York Volunteers, which threat he attempted to put into execution three times during the night, but was prevented by one Sergeant Campbell.

In this situation I remained two days without a morsel to eat, when a Hessian officer named Zaltman, finding I could talk his language, removed me to his room and sympathized with me on my situation. He permitted me to send to Mrs. [Abigail] Minis, who sent me some victuals. He also permitted me to go and see my son, and to let him come and stay with me. He introduced me to Captain Kappel, also a Hessian, who treated me very politely.

In this situation I remained until Saturday morning, the second of January, 1779, when the commander, Colonel Innis, sent his orderly for me and [my] son to [go to] his quarters, which was James Habersham's house, where on the top of the step I met with Captain Stanhope, of the "Raven," sloop of war, who treated me with the most illiberal abuse and, after charging me with having refused the supplying of the King's ships with provisions, and of having shut the church door, together with many ill-natured things, ordered me on board the prison ship, together with my son. I made a point of giving Mr. Stanhope suitable answers to his impertinent treatment and then turned from him and inquired for Colonel Innis. I got his leave to go to Mrs. Minis for a shirt she had taken to wash for me, as it was the only one I had left except the one on my back, and that was given me by Captain Kappel, as the British soldiers had plundered both mine and my son's clothes.

This favour he granted me under guard, after which I was conducted on board one of the flatboats and put on board the prison ship "Nancy," commanded by Captain Samuel Tait, when the first thing that presented itself to my view was one of our poor Continental soldiers laying on the ship's main deck in the agonies of death, and who expired in a few hours. After being presented to the captain with mine and the rest of the prisoners' names, I gave him in charge what paper money I had, and my watch. My son also gave him his money to take care of. He appeared to be a little civiller after this confidence placed in him, and permitted us to sleep in a stateroom, that is, the Rev. Moses Allen, myself, and son. In the evening we were served with what was called our allowance, which consisted of two pints and a half [of water?], and a half gill of rice, and about seven ounces of boiled beef per man. We were permitted to choose our messmates, and I accordingly made choice of Capt. Thomas Fineley, Rev. Mr. Allen, Mr. Moses Valentonge, Mr. Daniel Flaherty, myself, and son Sheftall Sheftall.

NOTE

Words in brackets appear in the original source document.

Ezekiel Landau

Eulogy for Empress Maria Theresa
1780

Today is the eighth day since the evil tidings came that the crown has fallen from our head (Lam. 5:16). It was my obligation to see that we should immediately have arranged a great memorial service, following the biblical text, *In every square there shall be lamenting, in every street cries of "Ah, woe!" The farm hand shall be called to mourn, and those skilled in waiting to lament* (Amos 5:16). We should have fulfilled the verse, *I was bowed with gloom, like one mourning for his mother* (Ps. 35:14). For the mother of the realm has fallen, our sovereign, pious, humble and righteous, the Queen and Empress Maria Theresa, may her soul rest in the Garden of Eden. She was indeed the mother of the realm; from her loins royalty has gone forth (cf. Gen. 35:11).

However, I delayed until now, not out of laziness, God forbid, but because of several reasons. First, because of the intense grief that overwhelmed me when I heard the news, I had no strength to speak, and I knew not what to say. In me was fulfilled the verse that applies to the friends of Job: *They sat with him on the ground seven days and seven nights. None spoke a word to him for they saw how very great was the suffering* (Job 2:13). So with me: so great was the pain of my grief that I could not collect my thoughts to speak coherently for seven days, until today.

[. . .] Thus so long as Joseph was alive—and by "alive" I mean ascending from one level to the next, all because of the influence of Jacob who guided him properly—Jacob continued to ascend, even after his death, and was called "alive." Therefore R. Johanan replied, "I am interpreting a biblical verse." The meaning is, indeed the wailers and the embalmers and the buriers performed their tasks, but so long as his offspring is alive, he thereby remains alive.

Let us now look at our gracious sovereign the Empress Maria Theresa, may she be remembered for good. She was worthy of leaving a son like this: our sovereign, who excels in all virtues and achievements, the Emperor Joseph, may His Majesty be exalted. It was his mother who guided him from his youth in every fine virtue. She therefore should not be called dead, for even though she has departed from us, her subjects, her splendor and majesty have not departed. They are her son, this esteemed emperor. He is her splendor, he is her majesty, about him it is fitting to say, *in the light of the king's face there is life* (Prov. 16:15), for in the light of his face is the life of his gracious mother after her death. [. . .]

How shall I begin? Time does not suffice to express even a minute portion of praise that is due. Well known is the splendor of this great dynasty, the House of Austria, from the day when its radiant majesty began to shine. How many Emperors reigned, one after the other, each one exalted, each one a gracious monarch who dealt beneficently with all. We Jews as well have always found refuge in their realms. May God reward the goodness and graciousness of each one in the world of truth. Thus for the honor of the dead we should indulge in deep lamenting and grief.

Translated by Marc Saperstein.

Moses Mendelssohn

Preface to *Vindiciae Judaeorum*
1782

It is remarkable to observe how prejudice changes its form in every century in order to oppress us and to pose difficulties for our admission to civil society. In former, superstitious times, it was holy wafers that we wantonly defiled; crucifixes that we stabbed and made bleed; children whom we secretly circumcised and delighted to tear to pieces; Christian blood that we used at our Passover festival; wells that we poisoned; etc. We have been reproached with unbelief, stubbornness, witchcraft, and Satanism. On these accounts we have been tormented, our property has been stolen, and we have been driven into misery when we have not been put to death. Now times have changed. These calumnies no longer make the desired impression. Now we are just charged with superstition and stupidity; lack of moral feelings, taste, and fine manners; unfitness for the arts, sciences, and useful professions, especially those in the service of warfare and the state: and an insurmountable propensity for deceit, usury, and lawlessness. These have taken the place of those coarser accusations in order to exclude us from the multitude of useful citizens and drive us out of the maternal bosom of the state. Formerly, every imaginable effort was made and various measures were taken to turn us not into useful citizens, but into Christians. And since we were so stiff-necked and stubborn as to not allow ourselves to be converted, this was reason enough to regard us as a useless burden to the world and to attribute to such depraved monsters all the horrors that could only subject them to the hatred and contempt of all people. Now the zeal for conversion has subsided, and we are completely neglected. People continue to distance us from all the arts and sciences as well as the other useful professions and occupations of mankind. They bar us from every path to useful improvement and make our lack of culture the reason for oppressing us further. They tie our hands and reproach us for not using them.

Translated by Curtis Bowman.

Moses Mendelssohn

Jerusalem
1783

I recognize no eternal verities save those which not only can be comprehended by the human intellect but can also be demonstrated and confirmed by man's faculties. It is, however, a misconception of Judaism if Mr. Moerschel were to assume that I cannot take this position without deviating from the religion of my fathers. On the contrary, I consider this view an essential aspect of the Jewish religion and believe that this teaching represents one of the characteristic differences between Judaism and Christianity. To sum it up in one sentence: I believe Judaism knows nothing of a *revealed religion* corresponding to the way Christians define the meaning of this term. The Israelites possess a *divine legislation*: laws, commandments, statutes, rules of conduct, instruction in God's will and in what they are to do to attain temporal and eternal salvation. Moses, in a miraculous and supernatural way, revealed to them these laws and commandments, but not dogmas, eternal verities or self-evident propositions. These the Lord reveals to us as well as to all other men at all times through nature and events, never through the spoken or written word. [. . .]

One applies the term "eternal verities" to those principles which are not subject to time and remain eternally unchanged. [. . .] Besides these eternal verities, there exist also temporal, historical truths—events which occurred at a certain point in time and may never recur, or principles which, by the processes of cause and effect, became accepted as truth at a certain time and place and whose claim to be truth is relative to this point in time and space. To this category belong all truths in history—events of former times which once took place, of which we were told by others but which we ourselves can no longer observe.

[. . .] I do not believe that man's intellect is incapable of perceiving those eternal truths which are indispensable to man's happiness and that God, therefore, was compelled to reveal them in a supernatural way. Those who cling to this notion deny the omnipotence or the goodness of God. [. . .] They think that He was good enough to disclose to men those truths on which their happiness depends but that He was neither omnipotent nor good enough to grant them the capacity of discovering these truths for themselves. [. . .] If the human race, without revelation, cannot be but depraved and miserable, why should by far the larger part of mankind have been compelled to live without the benefit of true revelation from the beginning? [. . .]

According to the tenets of Judaism, all people can attain salvation; and the means to attain it are as widespread as mankind itself, as liberally dispensed as the means of satisfying one's hunger and other natural needs.

[. . .] Judaism does not claim to possess the exclusive revelation of immutable truths which are indispensable to salvation. It is not a revealed religion as this term is commonly understood. Revealed religion is one thing; revealed legislation, another. The voice that was heard on that great day at Sinai did not proclaim, "I am the Eternal, thy God, the necessary self-evident Being, omnipotent and omniscient, Who rewards men in a future life according to their deeds." This is the universal religion of reason, not Judaism. This kind of universal religion was not, and in fact could not have been, revealed at Sinai; for who could possibly have needed the sound of thunder or the blast of trumpets to become convinced of the validity of these eternal verities? [. . .] No, all this was supposed to be already known or taught and explained by human reason and certain beyond all doubt. [. . .] The divine voice that called out, "I am the Lord thy God who led thee out of the land of Egypt" (Exodus 20:2)—this is a historical fact, a fact on which the legislation of that particular people was founded; laws were to be revealed here, commandments and judgments, but no immutable theological truths.

[. . .] Among the precepts and statutes of the Mosaic law there is none saying "Thou shalt believe" or "Thou shalt not believe"; all say "Thou shalt do" or not do. Faith accepts no commands; it accepts only what comes to it by way of reasoned conviction. All commandments of the divine law are addressed to the will, to man's capacity to act. In fact, the original Hebrew term [*emunah*] which is usually translated as "faith" means in most instances merely "trust" or "confidence," e.g., "And he trusted in the Lord, and He counted it to him for righteousness" (Genesis 15:6); "And Israel saw . . . and trusted the Lord and His servant Moses" (Exodus 14:31). Whenever the text refers to eternal verities it does not use the term "believe," but "understand" and "know." "Know this day and meditate upon it in thy heart that the Lord is God . . . there is none else" (Deuteronomy 4:39).

Nowhere does a passage say, "Believe, O Israel, and thou wilt be blessed; do not doubt, Israel, lest thou wilt be punished." Command and prohibition, reward and punishment apply only to acts of commission or omission which depend on a man's will power; and these are governed by his notions of good and evil and affected by his hopes and fears. Beliefs and doubts, however, intellectual assent or dissent, are governed neither by our wishes or desires, nor by our fears or hopes, but by what we perceive to be true or false.

For this reason, ancient Judaism has no symbolical book, no articles of faith. No one had to be sworn to credal symbols or subscribe by solemn oath to certain articles of faith. We do not require the affirmation of religious doctrines by oath and consider this practice incompatible with the true spirit of Judaism.

NOTE

Words and ellipses in brackets appear in the original translation.

Translated by Alfred Jospe.

Jonas Phillips

1736–1803

The German-born Jonas Phillips immigrated to America in 1756. Settling first in Charleston, he worked as an indentured servant to pay off his passage. In 1759 he moved north, first to Albany, then to New York City, and eventually to Philadelphia. After initially failing in business, Phillips enjoyed considerable success. Intensely active in Jewish religious life in New York and Philadelphia, he was, at the same time, a fervent revolutionary patriot who served in the Philadelphia militia.

Letter to Federal Constitutional Convention
1787

> 7 September 1787
>
> Sires
>
> With leave and submission I address myself to those in whom there is wisdom and understanding and knowledge, they are the honourable personages appointed and Made overseers of a part of the terrestrial globe of the Earth, Namely the 13 united states of america in Convention Assembled, the Lord preserve them amen—
>
> I the subscriber being one of the people called Jews of the City of Philadelphia, a people scattered & dispersed among all nations do behold with Concern that among the Laws in the Constitution of Pennsylvania, there is a Clause Sect 10 to viz—I do believe in one God the Creatur and governor of the universe and Rewarder of the good & the punisher of the wicked—and I do acknowledge the Scriptures of the old & New testament to be given by divine inspiration—to swear & believe that the new testament was given by divine inspiration is absolutely against the Religious principle of a Jew, and is against his Conscience to take any such oath—By the above law a Jew is deprived of holding any publick office or place of Government which is a Contridictory to the bill of Right Sect 2 viz
>
> That all men have a natural & unalienable Right to worship almighty God according to the dictates of their own Conscience and understanding & that no man ought or of Right can he Compelled to attend any Religious Worship or Creed or support any place of worship or Maintain any minister contrary to or against his own free will and Consent, nor can any man who acknowledges the being of a God be Justly deprived or abridged of any Civil Right as a Citizen on account of his Religious sentiments or peculiar mode of Religious Worship, and that no authority can or ought to be vested in or assumed by any power whatever that shall in any case interfere or in any manner Controul the Right of Conscience in the free Exercise of Religious Worship.—
>
> It is well known among all the Citizens of the 13 united states that the Jews have been true and faithful whigs, & during the late Contest with England they have been foremost in aiding and assisting the states with their lives & fortunes, they have supported the cause, have bravely fought and bled for liberty which they can not Enjoy.—
>
> Therefore if the honourable Convention shall in their Wisdom think fit and alter the said oath & leave out the words to viz—and I do acknowledge the scripture of the new testament to be given by divine inspiration, then the Israelites will think themself happy to live under a government where all Religious societys are on an Equal footing—I solicit this favour for myself my children & posterity, & for the benefit of all the Israelites through the 13 united states of America.
>
> Your Most devoted obed. Servant
>
> JONAS PHILLIPS
>
> PHILADELPHIA 24th *Ellul* 5547 or *Sepr* 7th 1787.

David de Isaac Cohen Nassy
1747–1806

A champion of Jewish emancipation, David de Isaac Cohen Nassy belonged to a leading family in the Dutch colony of Suriname. In 1792 he moved for a short time to Philadelphia, where he was elected to the American Philosophical Society in recognition of his work as a physician. A man of contradictions, he owned a plantation and held slaves although he saw himself as a proponent of Enlightenment ideals. Upon his return to Suriname, he was active in promoting the enlightenment of the Portuguese Jewish community, cofounding a learned society as well as a college of letters. Over his career he played a variety of roles, including pharmacist, journalist, and historian.

History of the Colony of Suriname
1788

We will briefly mention several of his more important military expeditions. In the year 1731, Mr. Boeyé, Officer of the Christian Citizens Militia, received an order from the Council to carry out a military expedition against the Maroons,[1] and Captain Nassy was charged with having a detachment of his Citizens ready to reinforce Boeyé in the event of fighting or apprehension. Nassy mobilized, accompanied by his Indians, according to the orders that he had received, and along the way he met Boeyé, who was retreating with all possible haste, because he had had the misfortune along the way of encountering by chance a group of fugitives who had killed one of his men. However much Nassy pleaded with him to continue on the campaign, insisting that he would meet up with the Maroons within two or three days and engage them, Boeyé would not listen to him and persisted in his refusal to join in. Nassy therefore took on the campaign for his own account, went to confront the enemy with his detachment, and had the good fortune to encounter them in their houses, to capture several of them, and to kill a considerable number of them. Meanwhile criminal charges were brought against Officer Boeyé on account of his dilatory behavior; yet he in turn accused Captain Nassy; as a result of which charges were brought against both of them by the public prosecutor; with the result that Boeyé was found guilty and was punished. The truth of this is evident in several eulogies and popular ballads that have been composed in Spain by a Jewish poet with the name *Bien Venida del Monte*, in honor of Captain Nassy.

In the year 1738 there was a rebellion on a plantation in Sarua belonging to the Jew Manuel Pereyra, in which the Negroes were for the most part from Kormantine, these being the most formidable of all these Africans, and they killed their master, as we have already mentioned above. Mr. Is. Arrias, former Commander of the Jewish Citizens Militia, who had two large residences close to the location where the rebellion had taken place, sent out a contingent of volunteer Citizens against them, under the command of two Subordinate Officers, Isaac Nassy and Abr. de Britto: Mr. Arrias provided this military expedition with everything that the detachment needed at his own expense, as well as sending along all the good Negroes that he had at his plantations. This campaign was so fortunate that the detachment that had been sent out, after being away for 6 months, during which time no one had received word concerning the fate of these volunteers, returned with 47 prisoners and 6 hands of those whom they had killed. The council, more than a little pleased with this outcome, paid out according to our archives 75 guilders to each Officer, 36 to each Citizen, each armed Negro 20, and each Negro porter 5 guilders; but the noble Mr. Arrias, whose plantations had suffered very greatly as a result of this campaign, received, as far as we know, not the least reward; he was not even thanked in writing by the council.

Mr. Hartsinck also recounts that a certain village of rebels, who are known by the name Creoles, as one commonly names those born in this country and who are the most formidable of all enemies, because of both their cunning and their skillfulness that they have attained through their association with the Whites since childhood, was attacked in the year 1731 by Captain Bley and was turned upside down; meanwhile it is known that this band of Negroes always went around committing every manner of hostilities against the Whites, and that this village first in the year 1743, in the time of Governor Mauricius, was destroyed to the extent that one no longer knew the village by the name that it carried before, and this as a result of the unflinching courage of Captain D. C. Nassy. Already an elderly man, he set out in the Harvest Month of the year mentioned, with 27 Civilians, 12 Soldiers, 15 Indians, 165 Negroes, and 60 Canoes (or boats made of hollowed-out trees) according to a plan that he had devised and presented to the council on the 10th of the Hay Month of 1743. After traveling up the Surinam River and having come upstream of various waterfalls that one encounters in navigating the river, he marched his detachment and attacked the enemies on the day of *Kippur*, or *atonement of the Jews*; and without any consideration of the holiness of that day, he pursued the enemies, set their cabins afire, destroyed the village, tore the roots of their staple crops out of the ground, took 14 captives, and killed very many villagers. The entire colony was very surprised by this campaign, yet the envy that had long been expressed with respect to the actions of this captain found support in some of the mistakes he had made, and teeth were sharpened against him, even though the outcome of his campaign had very greatly exceeded every expectation.[2]

The fact of the matter is: the orders of the captain were such that he was to march into the village of these Creoles, fight against them, destroy everything, and without delay to inform the council without leaving the place before receiving further orders; but instead of following these orders, his band, that included one of his brothers as well as one of his sons, having been told by the Indians and Negroes that the Maroons had poisoned the creeks and that in the present drought they would not be able to find water to drink, began to grumble so much that he found it necessary, against his will, to turn back with his prisoners and bring on his own the news of the victory he had achieved. Upon his arrival, which fell on the 14th of the Wine Month of the same year, his friends informed him of the mistake that he had made and furthermore that he must therefore prepare to defend his innocence, at least with plausible reasons, while his enemies and those envious of him were prepared to speak ill of him before the council; but, flattering himself that the fortunate outcome of a campaign that was considered well-nigh impossible would gain him some lenience with the council, he did not hesitate, several days after his arrival, to represent himself in the proceedings with all possible confidence. The council, and Governor Mauricius in particular, heaped a thousand accusations upon him, among these that he had appropriated the spoils that the Negroes belonging to the Christians had taken from the Maroons in order to give them to the Negroes of the Jews; and also that he had brought too many supplies into the forest and had wasted them; upon which he was ordered, without hearing his defense, to compensate the Negroes and several Indians for the detriment they had supposedly suffered; while steps were taken to further involve him in a criminal trial. This unexpected treatment, which brought about the collapse of the edifice of his glory, had such a frightful influence on the spirit of this good man that he contracted a strong fever that ended his days at the age of nearly 67 years. After his death, Mr. Is. Carilho was chosen as Captain in his place, according to his act of commission, signed in the Winter Month of that same year 1743.

NOTES

1. [Maroons were descendants of African slaves and native Americans who formed bonds and rebelled against white plantation owners.—Ed.]

2. To find confirmation of all these things that one can read on p. 766 of Hartsinck, one can ask the Negroes of Juka, our new allies, about the truth of all this, and one will then find out that they have given two names to this village of the Creoles that was demolished by Nassy: *Gri-Gri* and *Nassy-Broko*. In the rural gibberish or Negro English, *Gri-Gri* means the sound that one makes when walking quickly over the ground with bare feet; *Dem ron gri-gri* is a way of saying *when fleeing they ran very quickly*. *Nassy Broko* means *Nassy demolished it or tore it down*, as *Broko* means nothing other than to demolish, to tear down, to smash up, to break into pieces, to destroy, etc.

Translated by Piper Hollier.

Other works by Nassy: *Observations on the Cause, Nature and Treatment of Yellow Fever* (1793); *Lettre politico-theologico-morale sur les juifs. Dans laquelle on développe le principe de l'egalité parmi les hommes, le vrai sens de la liberté, et l'esprit de plusiers dogmes réligieux et rabiniques* (1798).

Zalkind Hourwitz

1751–1812

Born near Lublin, Poland, Zalkind Hourwitz left his village for Berlin, ultimately settling in Paris in 1774. He initially knew no French and barely avoided starvation, yet he studied Ovid, Molière, Voltaire, and Rousseau in his free time. He won praise and renown for his essay "Apologie des juifs" (1789), which helped frame the debate about Jewish emancipation in France. Hourwitz served as interpreter of oriental languages at the Bibliothèque royale, and enthusiastically supported the French Revolution. As a political activist, journalist, and author, he fought tirelessly for the rights of French Jews.

Vindication of the Jews
1789

The means of making the Jews happy and useful? Here it is: stop making them unhappy and unuseful. Accord them, or rather return to them the right of citizens, which you have denied them, against all divine and human laws and against your own interests, like a man who thoughtlessly cripples himself. . . .

To be sure, during times of barbarism, there was no shortage of ways of oppressing the Jews. Yet we are hard pressed even in an enlightened century, not to repair all the evils that have been done to them and to compensate them for their unjustly confiscated goods [hardly to be hoped for], but simply to cease being unjust toward them and to leave them peacefully to enjoy the rights of humanity under the protection of general laws. . . .

The simplest means would be therefore to accord them throughout the kingdom the same liberty that they enjoy in [Bordeaux and Bayonne]; nevertheless, however simple this means appears, it is still susceptible to greater perfection, in order to render the Jews not only happier and more useful but even more honest in the following manner.

1. They must be accorded permission to acquire land, which will attach them to the fatherland, where they will no longer regard themselves as foreigners and will increase at the same time the value of the land.

2. They must be permitted to practice all of the liberal and mechanical arts and agriculture, which will diminish the number of merchants among them and in consequence the number of knaves and rogues. [...]

4. To make their merchants more honest, they must be accorded the freedom to exercise every sort of commerce, to keep their stores open, to carry any product, and to live among the other citizens. Then being more closely allied with the other citizens, more at their ease and with their conduct more exposed to the inspection of the police, having moreover to manage their credit, their reputation and especially their regular customers, they will have in consequence less inclination, less necessity, and less facility in cheating and buying stolen goods.

5. To better diminish this facility in cheating, they must be forbidden, on pain of annulment of the transaction, the use of Hebrew and German [Yiddish] language and characters in their account books and commercial contracts, whether between themselves or with Christians.

6. It is necessary therefore to open the public schools to their children, to teach them French, which will produce a double advantage: it will make it easier to instruct them and to make them familiar from earliest infancy with Christians. They will establish with the Christians bonds of friendship which will be fortified by living near to each other, by the use of the same language and customs, and especially by the recognition of the freedom that they will be accorded; they will learn from these bonds that the Christians worship a Supreme Being like themselves, and as a result the fraud that the Talmud authorizes in dealings with pagans will no longer be permitted.

7. To better facilitate these bonds, their rabbis and leaders must be severely forbidden from claiming the least authority over their coreligionists outside of the synagogue, from prohibiting entry and honors to those who cut their beards, who curl their hair, who dress like Christians, who go to the theater, or who fail to observe some other custom that is irrelevant to their religion and only introduced by superstition in order to distinguish the Jews from other peoples. [...]

We could add that the freedom of the Jews is the best means of converting them to Christianity; for, once putting an end to their captivity, you will render useless the temporal Messiah that they expect, and then they will be obliged to recognize Jesus Christ as a spiritual Messiah in order not to contradict the Prophets, who predicted the arrival of some kind of Messiah. [...]

Are so many verbiages and citations necessary to prove that a Jew is a man, and that it is unjust to punish him from his birth onward for real or supposed vices that one reproaches in other men with whom he has nothing in common but religious belief? And what would the French say if the Academy of Stockholm had proposed, twelve years ago, the following question: "Are there means for making Catholics more useful and happier in Sweden?"

NOTE

Words in brackets appear in the original translation.

Translated by Lynn Hunt.

Other works by Hourwitz: *Origine des langues* (1808); *Lacographie ou écriture laconique, aussi vite que la parole* (1811).

Moses Seixas
1744-1809

Moses Seixas was a first-generation American of Portuguese Jewish stock, his parents having emigrated from Lisbon. The family settled in Newport, Rhode Island, where Seixas was later to distinguish himself in civic, religious, and mercantile affairs. A Freemason, Seixas was grand master of his Masonic lodge. He was also warden of the Touro Synagogue. A banker by profession, Seixas was the cofounder and first cashier of the Bank of Rhode Island. His congratulatory letter of 1790 to George Washington expresses his deep concern for the future of religious liberty in the new American republic.

Letter to George Washington
1790

Deprived as we heretofore have been of the invaluable rights of free citizens, we now (with a deep sense of gratitude to the Almighty disposer of all events) behold a government erected by the Majesty of the People—a Government which to bigotry gives no sanction, to persecution no assistance, but generously affording to All liberty of conscience and immunities of Citizenship, deeming every one, of whatever Nation, tongue, or language, equal parts of the great governmental machine.

In His Reply, President Washington Echoed Seixas's Words

It is now no more that toleration is spoken of as if it was the indulgence of one class of people that another enjoyed the exercise of their inherent natural rights. For happily, the government of the United States, which gives to bigotry no sanction, to persecution no assistance, requires only that they who live under its protection should demean themselves as good citizens, in giving it on all occasions their effectual support.

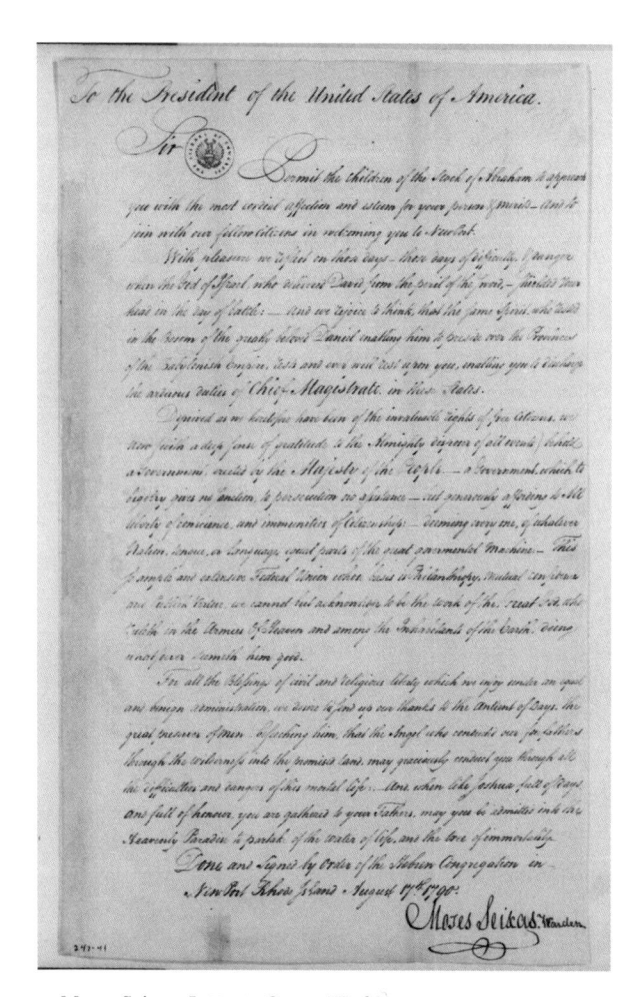

Moses Seixas, *Letter to George Washington.*

David Franco Mendes
1713–1792

David Franco Mendes was a Dutch-Portuguese businessman born into a prominent Sephardic family of Amsterdam. A prolific writer, he had a gift for languages, of which he knew seven, and wrote his poetry in Hebrew. His best-known literary work is the drama *Gemul Atalyah*, influenced partly by Jean Racine's play *Athalie*. Franco Mendes was also a highly regarded Judaic scholar. In the latter part of his life, a crisis in the Dutch economy ruined his business, obliging him from 1778 on to earn his living by copying manuscripts.

Note of Royalty Who Visited the Sephardic Synagogue of Amsterdam between 1642 and 1781
1792

> THE VOICE OF PRAYER AND THE VOICE OF SONG
> GIVEN IN
> THE HOUSE OF THE LORD ELOHEI YISRAEL
> THE HOLY CONGREGATIONS OF THE SEPHARADIM
> MAY THE LORD COMFORT US
> IN THIS GREAT CITY OF AMSTERDAM
> FROM THE DAY THEY SETTLED IN IT IN THE YEAR 1597
> UNTIL THIS DAY [1792]
> A MEMORIAL FOR THE CHILDREN OF ISRAEL
> WRITTEN BY DAVID FRANCO MENDES
> MAY HIS MAKER WATCH OVER HIM AND GRANT HIM [LONG] LIFE

In Memory of the Kings, Princes & Noblemen Who Came to Our Synagogues on 22 May 1642

His Excellency, Frederick Henry, Prince of Orange & Nassau, Stadtholder of the United Provinces, with the Most Illustrious William, his son, accompanied by the Royal Infanta, Maria, & the most serene Queen Henrietta Maria, Consort of the most august Charles the first, King of Great Britain.

In the year 1668,
His Highness Cosimo the Third, Prince of Toscana, later Grand Duke.

His Majesty William III, King of Great Britain, Prince of Orange, Stadtholder and Captain General of Sea & land of these Provinces

In the year 1731,

His Serene Highness Francisco the First, Grand Duke of Lorena, who, in 1729, was elected Duke of Toscana & in 1765, Emperor.

In the year 1768,

His Serene Highness William the 5th, Stadtholder, Captain General & Admiral of the United Provinces & Her Royal Highness, Frederika Sophia Wilhelmina, Princess of Prussia, His Consort.

On July 1st.

His Majesty, Christian the 7th, King of Denmark & Norway. Incognito, under the name of the Prince of Travendal.

On September 3.

His Royal Highness, Henry, Prince of Prussia.

On 21 August 1772.

His Royal Highness, Czartorinsky, Prince of Poland, Lieutenant General of the Kingdom, accompanied by the Princess, his Consort and Daughters.

David Franco Mendes, cover of *Kol tefila ve-kol zimra*, "David Dancing before God and Being Annointed as King," 1792.

On 12 July 1781

His Imperial Majesty Joseph the Second, Emperor of Germany and King of Bohemia & Hungary & of the Romans.

NB. incognito, using the name of the Count of Falkenstein

Translated by Marvin Meital.

Other work by Mendes: *Gemul Atalyah* (1770).

Isaac Sasportas

d. 1799

A Haitian-born Sephardic Jew of Portuguese descent, Isaac Sasportas made his living as a trader in textiles, operating in South Carolina and among the Caribbean islands. Infected by the revolutionary fervor so widespread in France, America, and the Caribbean in the late eighteenth century, Sasportas first became involved in a failed attempt to liberate the slaves of Curaçao. He later tried to promote a slave rebellion in Jamaica, hoping to do what Toussaint Louverture had done in Saint-Domingue (modern Haiti). But Sasportas was betrayed to British officials on the island, who sentenced him to be publicly hanged.

Plan for the Invasion of Jamaica to Emancipate Slaves and Interrogation Testimony to British Authorities Following His Arrest for the Plan to Emancipate Slaves in Jamaica
1799

1. Initial Proposal for an Invasion of Jamaica Submitted by Isaac Sasportas to Toussaint Louverture.

"When the genie of liberty inspired me the noble project to carry to the English, our natural enemies, all the devastating plagues that we have endured due to their unjust and eternal war on us, I swore on my honor, on the manes of our unhappy brothers robbed by them of their spirit, to perish or avenge them. An opportunity has arisen, so I am avidly putting before your eyes, citizen General [Toussaint Louverture], a quick sketch. . . . of the means to employ to ensure that the holy insurrection takes place.

Here are the motives that shall lead us to put this project in practice.

1st motive: for a long time, English knavery provoked heaven's wrath. Their unprecedented cruelty against their wretched slaves forced them to raise the holy flag of revolt [during the 1795 Maroon War]. . . . Despite the courage of the oppressed, their oppressors re-enslaved them through yet another crime. They bought in Havana big dogs accustomed to eating flesh and had the rebels devoured by these animals. . . . [Forced to sign a peace treaty, the maroons] are awaiting a favorable occasion to renew their struggle for their rights. . . .

2nd motive: the profound security in which the English have lulled themselves, their arrogance and their insolence. . . .

3rd motive: accustomed to trample underfoot honor and sacred promises, the English feigned to extend a helping hand to the French émigrés [who fled the Haitian Revolution and settled in Jamaica], only to victimize them by their Machiavelism. . . .

During the first insurrection in Jamaica [1795 Maroon War], I learned that one of the chiefs was a black to whom my father had given his freedom (his name is Charles). I set out to meet him. . . . He spoke to me with the vehemence that characterizes a free man, but the weakness of the insurgents would force them to sign a treaty with the superior council of the governor of Jamaica.

I met him again in early 1797. . . . He said a lot to me about you, citizen general, thanking heaven that you were leading the government of Saint-Domingue. He was hoping to see his wishes fulfilled one day. . . . I went to Cap . . . to present my project to you. . . .

First I will leave from here [Cap-Français in Saint-Domingue] to Santiago de Cuba, where I will embark on a Spanish smuggler to Port Antonio [in Jamaica]. From there I intend to travel to Kingston, stopping in Negro Town [a maroon camp] . . . where I will go in cahoots with Charles, who will introduce me to the main chiefs of the Blue Mountains. There I will do all that is necessary to facilitate the landing of the army [of Saint-Domingue]. . . .

I will then go to Kingston, where I will see what citizen Dubuisson [entrusted with enrolling French refugees in the conspiracy] has done on his side. . . . I will decide on all the measures that need to be taken, I will draw precise maps, I will conduct my business, and I will take the same road back to Port Antonio. On the way back I will meet the insurgent leader *Cadjo* and ask him for a trusted man who will follow me back to Cap [Français] to present a petition from all the men who deserve to be free.

[A detailed description of the main fortified points in Jamaica follows].

After reaching Kingston, a strong [French force] can easily seize the fort of Twelve Apostles. . . . Once it is seized, one can easily force the warships of Port Royal to surrender. . . .

You should also know that five hundred [French] prisoners of all colors are kept on board two pontoons [prison ships]."

2. Isaac Sasportas, Scribbled Notes on an Invasion of Jamaica (c. 2 October 1799).

"First, proclaim a general emancipation.

Second, appoint [the maroon chiefs] Charles and Tom as generals. We already have their appointment certificates.

Third, confiscate all property to the benefit of the [French] republic.

Fourth, give Mr. Dubuisson and myself full latitude to do what is necessary.

Fifth, elect town councils in this country [Jamaica] and organize everything according to the principles of the French Revolution."

3. "Proceedings of a Court Martial Held by Virtue of a Special Commission . . ." (16–17 December 1799)

"I dare to take the quill to continue my defense, and prove 1. that I am not guilty of the crime of espionage and 2. that I have not come to the island to get the negroes to rise up. . . .

The only witness, the only alleged proof, which is presented before me is Mr. Dubuisson, who told lies to protect himself. He told you an endless story, filled with contradictions. He alone devised the project to get the negroes to rise up and to invade the island, and he says it was I who gave the plan of attack. . . . So many lies! How easy it is to disprove them!

I will tell you first that I only came to Jamaica twice, the first time against my will since I was taken by the privateer *The Sprightly* and only spent three days in Kingston. The second time (the present time) I came to Kingston from Santiago de Cuba with 2,000 gourdes to buy goods and a ship and trade, as the Spaniards of Cuba often do in this island. Before that, I had never set foot in any part of Jamaica. . . . Throughout my [second] stay, until my arrest, I could not have done what I am being accused of, as proved by the witnesses Simon, Lafargue, Louis Dalest, Nicolas, who prove that I never left Kingston, since I was with them almost at all times. . . . This proves that I am not a spy. . . .

I now have to prove that I had no communication with any type of negro. I have not seen Charles since the year 1790 or 1791 and I know not what has happened to him since . . . as witnessed before you by Mr. Garcia. . . .

So, after you carefully weigh the truth with the scale of impartiality, you will find that I am no criminal."

4. Isaac Sasportas to the Earl of Balcarres (20 December 1799)

"In prison.

I shuddered inside when I learned that I would soon be destroyed. I was not made for crime, no, my heart was never in it. Mr. Dubuisson only gave you vague details, of little use to you. I don't ask you for my life, but to please listen to me and allow me to speak to you. Postpone the death sentence by a few days, I ask you in the name of everything you hold dear. *In a word, Mister Governor, I can save the island of Jamaica from a great calamity* that my death might not preclude. . . .

I await your patience impatiently. Please lower yourself to my level."

[The signature bears three dots, a sign often associated with membership in a Freemason lodge].

NOTE

Words in brackets appear in the original translation.

Translated by Philippe Girard.

Lev Nevakhovich
1776–1831

An author, playwright, translator, and philosopher, Lev (Yehudah Leib) Nevakhovich was one of the first *maskilim* in the Russian Empire. He was employed by the government as a translator of Hebrew documents and as an expert on Jewish affairs. Nevakhovich sat on Tsar Alexander I's so-called Jewish Committee, a body that sought to regulate and define the place of the Jews within the empire. For the purposes of this committee, Nevakhovich penned his famous *Vopl' dshcheri iudeiskoi* (Lament of the Daughter of Judah). In typical Enlightenment fashion, this work sought to prove the Jews' utility in society as loyal citizens while in turn arguing for religious tolerance. Dismayed by the direction of Russian policies toward Jews, Nevakhovich later left Jewish topics behind and focused his writing on philosophy and drama. He converted to Christianity in 1806, a move that did much to discredit the Haskalah among the Russian Jewish public. He later moved to Warsaw, where he worked as a civil servant and translator.

Lament of the Daughter of Judah
1803

O Russians, you who love your fellow men! You would shudder from the bottoms of your kind hearts if you saw the effect of that terrible accusation which Jews who were eyewitnesses to the unjustified deaths of fellow members of their race cannot call to mind without trembling. More than once during my childhood my tears mingled with those of my mother, who used to tell me, with grief in her voice, of the terrible events that broke the nation's heart. Almost the whole world knows how many thousands of victims this unjust accusation cost.

The festival of Pesach just mentioned is that in which Jews remember the time of their forefathers' exodus from Egypt, a time that they revere as a memorial of the first era of their free existence. During this festival, they mentally share in the joy of their forefathers.

Noble children of the north! Your mild monarchs have taught you to look with a calm and impartial eye upon the rites of worship of the different nations living under your shield, upon the various festivities that make up their happiness—and you do not disturb this! But in those days Jews did not yet have the good fortune to be Russia's subjects; in those days hatred, that hellish Fury, managed to convince many that Jews supposedly have need of this horrific evil on the day of that festival. Then the credulous and simpleminded were incited by cunning and wily souls to place a dead and mutilated infant surreptitiously by night beneath some house of a Jew, which malice was pleased to designate. The next morning that house is surrounded by a crowd of people demanding vengeance. A grizzled patriarch is plucked in the most contemptuous and violent manner from the circle of his innocent family; the rabbi (teacher of the law) and the most venerable of the Jews are taken; and finally, without further investigation, without the acceptance of any protestations of innocence from the victims, they are subjected to the most brutal executions. Children are robbed of a father, the wife of a husband, the brother of a brother . . . The joy and festivity they had hoped to enjoy at that time gave way to lamentation, sobbing, and despondency. And so afterward, as this festival approached, each of them was seized by a terror that some sort of similar misfortune would descend on his house. But when this terrible lot was drawing to a close and some of the persecuted had fallen victim to the fury of the misguided plotters devoted to their devilish delight, the rest, with grief-stricken hearts, counted themselves safe for that year. What a pitiful solace! What a sorrowful comfort!

The Polish king Augustus Poniatowski of blessed memory, a wise and benevolent ruler, was moved to tremble at such inhuman outrages and through his wisdom brought them to an end. At last the dead bodies of infants ceased to be found beneath the houses of Jews, which still further demonstrated the absurdity of the past calumnies. Alone the mighty hand of Empress Catherine the Great of Russia was able to ease the lot of this nation, which had previously been the plaything of arbitrary deeds. Under the peaceful protection of Russian power, those hounded by fate found respite from earlier oppressions and began to feel to the full extent their former woes, the recollection of which even now forces whole floods of tears from their eyes. Alas! Now that the blows have ceased, these people begin to feel the pain of their wounds, which previously in their fever-like suffering they could not feel!

Oh, Christians! You who live in community with them, you must know that virtue is just as sacred to them as it is to you—just look! But how do you look upon them? . . . Do you look for the Jew in the human being? No. Look for the human being in the Jew, and you will find him without a doubt. Only look. You will see among them many people who keep their word sacredly. You will see many compassionate people who give alms to the poor, not only of their own tribe but of other tribes too. You will see that many of them magnanimously pardon wrongs. You will see in them gratitude, restraint, and respect for the old. Likewise you will see with what feeling they revere those people of other faiths who show them kindness and do good to them—and with what veneration they bethink themselves of the sovereign. Lessing puts it splendidly this time: "Are a Christian and a Jew really first and foremost a Christian and a Jew rather than human beings?" I do not doubt that there are many among you who, in having dealings with Jews, have witnessed the generosity of their behavior and their sentiments of gratitude. The trouble is, the only trouble is, that no one discloses observations of this kind. And if anyone happened to observe something repugnant in certain of them, you still cannot form an opinion about the generality of people on this basis, just as I, if I see many depraved people among Christians, similarly cannot make a judgment about all of their coreligionists.

I also make so bold as to say this to you: If you have observed depravity in some Jews close to you, take a

Abraham Abramson, *Medal Commemorating the Enfranchisement of the Jews of Westphalia by Jerome Bonaparte*, 1808. Jerome Bonaparte, brother of Napoleon, was appointed to rule the short-lived Kingdom of Westphalia which Napoleon established in North Germany. The medal celebrates his grant of emancipation to Jews of this model kingdom in 1808.

good look at yourselves and do not be upset that I am going to ask, "Are you yourselves not perhaps the cause of it?" Forgive the Jews if the torments inflicted upon them over several centuries have given them an unfavorable opinion of the Christian nations. Might it be that a Jew of upright principles will in fact not establish close ties with you but will seek to distance himself, just as the Americans avoided the Spanish? In those close to you, then, you do not for the most part see the image of the real Hebrew but only the depraved one. Have a long hard look at yourselves. I say, do you yourselves perhaps support their outrages with your patronage? . . . So you live with a nation without knowing its heart. I swear that a Jew who observes his religion faithfully cannot be a wicked person, or a bad citizen!

Translated by Brian Cooper.

Other works by Nevakhovich: *Vopl' dshcheri iudeiskoi* (1803); *Sulioty, ili Spartantsy XIX stoletiia* (1809); *Mysli, otnosiashchiesia k filosoficheskoi istorii chelovechestva* (1829).

Benjamin Disraeli

Utilitarian Follies
1835

A political sect has sprung up avowedly adverse to the Estates of the Realm, and seeking by means which, of course, it holds legal, the abrogation of a majority of them. These anti-constitutional writers, like all new votaries, are remarkable for their zeal and activity. They omit no means of disseminating their creed: they are very active missionaries: there is no medium of the public press of which they do not avail themselves: they have their newspapers, daily and weekly, their magazines, and their reviews. The unstamped press takes the cue from them, and the members of the party who are in Parliament lose no opportunity of dilating on the congenial theme at the public meetings of their constituents.

Chapter II. Of the Utilitarian System—Its Fallacies

The avowed object of this new sect of statesmen is to submit the institutions of the country to the test of UTILITY and to form a new Constitution on the abstract principles of theoretic science. I think it is Voltaire who tells us that there is nothing more common than to read and to converse to no purpose, and that in history, in morals, and in divinity, we should beware of EQUIVOCAL TERMS. I do not think that politics should form an exception to this salutary rule; and, for my own part, it appears to me that this term, UTILITY, is about as equivocal as any one which, from the time of the Nominalists and Realists to our present equally controversial and equally indefinite days, hath been let loose to breed sects and set men abrawling. The fitness of a material object for a material purpose is a test of its utility which our senses and necessities can decide; but what other test there is of moral and political utility than the various and varying opinions of mankind I am at a loss to discover; and that this is utterly unsatisfactory and insufficient, all, I apprehend, must agree.

Indeed, I have hitherto searched in vain in the writings of the Utilitarian sect for any definition of their fundamental phrase with which it is possible to grapple. That they pretend to afford us a definition it would be disingenuous to conceal, and we are informed that Utility is "the principle which produces the greatest happiness of the greatest number." Does this advance us in comprehension? Who is to decide upon the greatest happiness of the greatest number? According to Prince Metternich, the government of Austria secures the greatest happiness of the greatest number: it is highly probable that the effect of the Austrian education and institutions may occasion the majority of the Austrian population to be of the same opinion. Yet the government of Austria is no favourite with the anti-constitutional writers of our own country. Gross superstition may secure the greatest happiness of the greatest number, as it has done in Spain and Portugal: a military empire may secure the greatest happiness of the greatest number, as it has done in Rome and France: a coarse and unmitigated despotism may secure the greatest happiness of the greatest number, as it does to this day in many regions of Asia and Africa. Every government that ever existed, that has enjoyed any quality of duration, must have been founded on this "greatest happiness principle," for, had not the majority thought or felt that such were its result, the government could never have endured. There have been times, and those too not far gone, when the greatest happiness of Christian nations has been secured by burning men alive for their religious faith; and unless we are prepared to proclaim that all religious creeds which differ from our own are in fact not credited by their pretended votaries, we must admit that the greatest happiness of the greatest number of mankind is even now secured by believing that which we know to be false. If the greatest happiness of the greatest number, therefore, be the only test of the excellence of political institutions, that may be the plea for institutions which, according to the Utilitarians especially, are monstrous or absurd: and if to avoid this conclusion we maintain that the greatest number are not the proper judges of the greatest happiness, we are only referred to the isolated opinions of solitary philosophers, or at the best to the conceited conviction of some sectarian minority. UTILITY, in short, is a mere phrase, to which any man may ascribe any meaning that his interests prompt or his passions dictate. With this plea, a nation may consider it in the highest degree useful that all the statues scattered throughout the museums of Christendom should be collected in the same capital, and conquer Christendom in consequence to obtain their object; and by virtue of the same plea, some Iconoclastic enemy may declare war upon this nation of Dilettanti to-morrow, and dash into fragments their cosmopolite collection.

Viewed merely in relation to the science of government, the effect of the test of utility, as we have considered it, would in all probability be harmless, and its practical tendency, if any, would rather lead to a spirit of conservation and optimism than to one of discontent and change. But optimism is assuredly not the system of the Utilitarians: far from thinking everything is for the best, they decidedly are of opinion that everything is for the worst. In order, therefore, that their test of utility should lead to the political results which they desire, they have dovetailed their peculiar system of government into a peculiar system of morals, in connection with which we must alone subject it to our consideration. The same inventive sages, who have founded all political science on UTILITY, have founded all moral science on SELF-INTEREST and have then declared that a system of government should be deduced alone from the principles of human nature. If mankind could agree on a definition of Self-interest. I willingly admit that they would not be long in deciding upon a definition of Utility. But what do the Utilitarians mean by the term Self-interest? I at once agree that man acts from no other principle than self-interest, but I include in self-interest, and I should think every accurate reasoner must do the same, every motive that can possibly influence man. If every motive that can possibly influence man be included in self-interest, then it is impossible to form a science on a principle which includes the most contrary motives. If the Utilitarians will not admit all the motives, but only some of the motives, then their science of government is not founded on human nature, but only on a part of human nature, and must be consequently and proportionately imperfect. But the Utilitarian only admits one or two of the motives that influence man; a desire of power and a desire of property; and therefore infers that it is the interest of man to tyrannise and to rob.

The blended Utilitarian system of morals and politics, then, runs thus: Man is only influenced by self-interest: it is the interest of man to be a tyrant and a robber: a man does not change his nature because he is a king; therefore a king is a tyrant and a robber. If it be the interest of one man to be a tyrant and a robber, it is the interest of fifty or five thousand to be tyrants and robbers; therefore we cannot trust an aristocracy more than a monarch. But the eternal principle of human nature must always hold good. A privileged class is always an aristocracy, whether it consists of five thousand or fifty thousand, a band of nobles or a favoured sect; therefore the power of government should be entrusted to all; therefore the only true and useful government is a representative polity, founded on universal suffrage. This is the Utilitarian system of morals and government, drawn from their "great works" by one who has no wish to misrepresent them. Granting for a moment their premises, I do not see that their deduction, even then, is logically correct. It is possible to conceive a state of society where the government may be in the hands of a favoured majority; a community of five millions, of which three might form a privileged class. Would not the greatest happiness of the greatest number be secured by such an arrangement? and, if so secured, would or would not the Utilitarian, according to his theory, feel justified in disturbing it? If he oppose such a combination, he overthrows his theory; if he consents to such a combination, his theory may uphold tyranny and spoliation.

But I will not press this point: it is enough for me to show that, to render their politics practical, they are obliged to make their metaphysics impossible. Let the Utilitarian prove that the self-interest of man always leads him to be a tyrant and a robber, and I will grant that universal suffrage is a necessary and useful institution. A nation that conquers the world acts from self-interest; a nation that submits to a conqueror acts from self-interest. A spendthrift and a miser alike act from self-interest: the same principle animated Messalina and Lucretia, Bayard and Byng. To say that when a man acts he acts from self-interest is only to announce that when a man does act he acts. An important truth, a great discovery, calling assuredly for the appearance of prophets, or, if necessary, even ghosts. But to announce that when a man acts he acts from self-interest, and that the self-interest of every man prompts him to be a tyrant and a robber, is to declare that which the experience of all human nature contradicts; because we all daily and hourly feel and see that there are a thousand other motives which influence human conduct besides the idea of exercising power and obtaining property; every one of which motives must rank under the term Self-interest, because every man who acts under their influence must necessarily believe that in so acting he acts for his happiness, and therefore for his self-interest. Utility, Pain, Power, Pleasure, Happiness, Self-interest, are all phrases to which any man may annex any meaning he pleases, and from which any acute and practised reasoner may most syllogistically deduce any theory he chooses. "Such words," says Locke, "no more improve our understanding than the move of a jack will fill our bellies." This waste of ingenuity on nonsense is like the condescending union that occasionally occurs between some high-bred steed and some long-eared beauty of the Pampas: the base and fantastical embrace only produces a barren and mulish progeny.

Chapter III. Of Abstract Principles in Politics, and the Degree of Theory that Enters into Politics

We have before this had an *a priori* system of celestial mechanics, and its votaries most syllogistically sent Galileo to a dungeon, after having triumphantly refuted him. We have before this had an *a priori* system of metaphysics, but where now are the golden volumes of Erigena, and Occam, and Scotus, and Raymond Lully? And now we have an *a priori* system of politics. The schoolmen are revived in the nineteenth century, and are going to settle the State with their withering definitions, their fruitless logomachies, and barren dialectics.

I should suppose that there is no one of the Utilitarian sages who would not feel offended if I were to style him the Angelical Doctor, like Thomas Aquinas; and I regret, from bitter experience, that they have not yet condescended sufficiently to cultivate the art of composition to entitle them to the style of the Perspicuous Doctor, like Walter Burley.

These reflections naturally lead me to a consideration of the great object of our new school of statesmen in general, which is to form political institutions on abstract principles of theoretic science, instead of permitting them to spring from the course of events, and to be naturally created by the necessities of nations. It would appear that this scheme originated in the fallacy of supposing that theories produce circumstances, whereas the very converse of the proposition is correct, and circumstances indeed produce theories. If we survey the career of an individual, we shall on the whole observe a remarkable consistency in his conduct; yet it is more than possible that this individual has never acted from that organised philosophy which we style *system*. What, then, has produced this consistency? what, then, has occasioned this harmony of purpose? His individual character. Nations have characters as well as individuals, and national character is precisely the quality which the new sect of statesmen in their schemes and speculations either deny or overlook. The ruling passion, which is the result of organisation, regulates the career of an individual, subject to those superior accidents of fortune whose secondary influence is scarcely inferior to the impulse of his nature. The blended influences of nature and fortune form his character; 'tis the same with nations. There are important events in the career of an individual which force the man to ponder over the past, and, in these studies of experience and struggles for self-knowledge, to ascertain certain principles of conduct which he recognises as the cause of past success, and anticipates as the guarantee of future prosperity: and there are great crises in the fortunes of an ancient people which impel them to examine the nature of the institutions which have gradually sprung up among them. In this great national review, duly and wisely separating the essential character of their history from that which is purely adventitious, they discover certain principles of ancestral conduct, which they acknowledge as the causes that these institutions have flourished and descended to them; and in their future career, and all changes, reforms, and alterations, that they may deem expedient, they resolve that these principles shall be their guides and their instructors. By these examinations they become more deeply intimate with their national character; and on this increased knowledge, and on this alone, they hold it wise to act. This, my Lord, I apprehend to be the greatest amount of theory that ever enters into those political institutions, which, from their permanency, are alone entitled to the consideration of a philosophical statesman; and this moderate, prudent, sagacious, and eminently practical application of principles to conduct has ever been, in the old time, the illustrious characteristic of our English politicians.

Isaac Leeser

The Claims of the Jews to an Equality of Rights
1841

Letters on the Equal Rights of Jews

LETTER 1. TO WILLIS G. CLARK, ESQ.

We will admit, that, during the ages of superstition and darkness, silence was often imposed upon us by the terrors of persecution, by the executioner's axe and the rack of the inquisitor. Works designed to exhibit the wrongs we had to endure, and to perpetuate the history of our sufferings were surrendered to the destroying flames, depriving us thus of the melancholy privilege of the sympathy of posterity for fallen greatness. Nevertheless, enough has been left to the Jews to teach unto others what is their opinion of the Creator and of his laws, and of the glorious hope of salvation which awaits all mankind. Why then, let me ask, are *we* not more consulted when we are the subject of discussion? Why will men spread false views when the truth is accessible?

This unphilosophical proceeding may claim some extenuation in countries where one class of the inhabitants has a legal superiority over the other, as in England and Germany, and Spain and Italy, in short in nearly all Europe; for then the privileged class may have a personal interest in keeping up a state of ignorance, in order to sustain the prejudice under which the legally oppressed labour, and to prevent a removal of the burden of odium and disqualification already established by law and custom. In countries like those, selfishness may claim such a cause as a reason for pardonable ignorance, when the Jews are represented as enemies to the common welfare, and their doctrines as hostile to the public security; there the bigot may feel himself justified by special pleas, when he seeks to wipe away the name of Israel from the roll of nations. But how ought the case to stand in this country, where there exists no legal disqualifications against us, at least not in those states where we are most numerous? Why should we be looked upon with distrust in this happy land—happy because possessed of freedom and blessed with the knowledge of that heavenly Revelation which was first given to us—where we are permitted under the protection of equal laws to call on our Maker in our ancient language after our own manner, undisturbed by the dread of the tyrant or the fear of the inquisitor? Here, therefore, it is indeed surprising that the crudities of foreign journals, and the false inventions of interested travellers, should find such implicit belief, and that works of men evidently prejudiced should obtain currency: whilst the only sources of real information are not suffered to see the light; as though the anathema pronounced against us in the middle ages, and retained in tyrannical countries to this day, was to be transplanted and cherished also in this land against the Sons of Jacob, as the only exception to the benefits of equal rights.

Were this illiberal spirit residing only in the bosom of the ignorant multitude, who are often swayed by ideas imperfectly understood, and led astray by clamour artfully fomented by wily demagogues: I would be content to submit to it with silence, as being the fate which the minority upon every question of expediency has to suffer, even in the freest country. The majority must rule; and if this majority has had no means of obtaining correct knowledge, it is but too apt to look with suspicion and distrust upon the opinions and doings of the minority, however respectable and virtuous this minority may be. But, unfortunately, it is not the great multitude alone who act so unworthily; it is not the ignorant mass solely who wrongly suspect Israel's descendants, who speak falsely concerning our character and our religious hopes. Men, who from their position are the makers of public opinion, the preachers and the conductors of the press lend themselves, not rarely, I trust unwittingly, to the propagation of unsound views concerning us, and are thus instrumental in keeping alive a prejudice which ought long since to have been buried in the tomb of oblivion. It were time indeed that each society should do its utmost to improve the condition, both spiritual and temporal, of its own members, without interfering with that of others, mindful that where equality is the law of the land, there is no privileged class (a). Liberty precludes the idea of *toleration*, and the majority, no matter how large, have no right to claim any merit (b) for leaving the minority undisturbed in the enjoyment of equal rights; and surely there exists no equitable rule to render odious the opinions and to restrain the actions of an individual or of a body of men, unless their opinions and conduct might become injurious to the public weal (c). This being the case, we utterly deny the right of our Christian neighbours to bring up our people and our religion as a constant topic of discussion; and what is more, to raise funds to bring about a defection of our members. If there exists such a right in the majority, the same right is inherent in us; and if we should exercise it, as exercise we might, would it not cause a great degree of just indignation and discontent in the minds of the majority? [. . .]

I will rest here for the present, but I may address you again on this subject at a future day if you will permit me to do so.

Yours, respectfully, I. L.
Philad. Dec. 12th, 1839

Jacques-Isaac Altaras and Joseph Cohen

Altaras, 1786–1873

Cohen, 1817–1899

Isaac Altaras, a shipbuilder and head of the Marseilles consistory, and Joseph Cohen, a lawyer, coauthored an influential report on the "moral and political state" of Algerian Jews. Altaras and Cohen argued that Algerian Jews were sympathetic to France and capable of being "civilized" as French citizens. They advocated such emancipatory reforms as the establishment of new schools and consistories that would favor those wanting emancipation. Cohen eventually became head of the newly formed Algerian consistory and in 1860 founded *La vérité israélite*, a weekly journal focused on Jewish history and culture.

Report on the Moral and Political State of the Israelites of Algeria and on the Means to Improve It
1842

Among the diverse races of Algeria, the Jewish population merits special attention.

At first glance, one sees a mass of people who comprise approximately one-fifth of the total civilian population, consisting of individuals who have long been accustomed to the African environment, active middlemen living alongside indigenous tribes whose language they speak and with whom they alone maintain extensive relations. The Jews seem destined by these various means to serve as a liaison between the French and the former masters of the land. But if one enters further into the secret of their existence, one finds among them an admirable aptitude for assimilating the principles of civilization imported from abroad; an intelligence that, spurred on by the persecution and hardships of surviving under the Arabs' iron yoke, has almost always developed in remarkable ways; and finally, a lively and deep appreciation for the nation that has liberated them and invited them to share in the benefits of civil equality.

Along with these auspicious characteristics, however, one finds vices that result primarily from the debased condition in which the Jews have lived for such a long time and from the abrupt transition from slavery to freedom brought about by the French victory. The customs of the lower classes are riddled with depravity; there is also poverty, the inevitable consequence of a more complicated state of civilization and of the war that for the last twelve years has caused continuous upheaval in our colony.

This sudden contact between two civilizations as different as those of the Arabs and the French has in turn resulted in rather dangerous organizational problems; the persistence of certain ancient powers has only with some difficulty combined with the power of the new authorities. As the extent of these powers has been poorly defined by French law, administrative action has often been completely halted, resulting in a lack of order, of hierarchical subordination, and of serious indirection in the civil and religious organization of Algerian Jews.

In the end, the lack of unity has led to the creation among them of coteries whose antagonism is a further hindrance to the rare steps taken by an already shaky authority.

The Jews in our colony thus constitute one of those races that, having been grafted onto a new society with their own customs and originality, must be initiated into the principles of that civilization in order that morality, which is always fragile in periods of transition, be strengthened in their souls, and that their minds be developed along the path of political and moral progress.

This noble mission of strengthening the morals of a population that for eighteen centuries has suffered in a state of degrading servitude would doubtless be a rather powerful incentive for the philosopher and the philanthropic economist, and we are convinced that

France's wise government, which is constantly working to improve human morality, would not hesitate to pursue this glorious goal.

But if, alongside these purely moral considerations that have such an immediate influence on the happiness and tranquility of nations, we place the political results that the Jewish element can, if well guided, bring about for the prosperity of our African possessions, one must recognize that it is not merely a question of philanthropy, but rather a serious matter of national power and greatness.

It is not just from this point of view that Algerian Jews seem destined to play an important role in the future of our colony. One may foresee with certainty that, at a not-so-distant time, they will constitute the only indigenous group.

Translated by Michele McKay Aynesworth.

Other work by Cohen: *Les déicides* (1861).

Karl Marx
1818–1883

Philosopher, economist, sociologist, and journalist, Karl Marx became one of the most influential thinkers in history. Born in Trier, Prussia, into a German Jewish family who had converted to Christianity, he spent most of his life in London. Publication of his *Communist Manifesto*, written with Friedrich Engels, coincided with the European revolutions of 1848. Its closing statement, "Working men of all countries, unite," became a war cry of class struggle, and Marx's own role in promoting revolution led to his permanent exile in London. Marx was especially concerned with ideas of property, social justice, and human rights inherited from the Enlightenment via the French Revolution. In *On the Jewish Question*, Marx writes of Jewish "hucksterism" as emblematic of humanity's universal need to be emancipated from greed and self-interest.

On the Jewish Question
1843

The German Jews seek emancipation. What kind of emancipation do they want? *Civic, political* emancipation.

Bruno Bauer replies to them: In Germany no one is politically emancipated. We ourselves are not free. How then could we liberate you? You Jews are *egoists* if you demand for yourselves, as Jews, a special emancipation. You should work, as Germans, for the political emancipation of Germany, and as men, for the emancipation of mankind. You should feel the particular kind of oppression and shame which you suffer, not as an exception to the rule but rather as a confirmation of the rule.

Or do the Jews want to be placed on a footing of equality with the *Christian subjects?* If they recognize the *Christian state* as legally established they also recognize the régime of general enslavement. Why should their particular yoke be irksome when they accept the general yoke? Why should the German be interested in the liberation of the Jew, if the Jew is not interested in the liberation of the German?

The *Christian* state recognizes nothing but *privileges*. The Jew himself, in this state, has the privilege of being a Jew. As a Jew he possesses rights which the Christians do not have. Why does he want rights which he does not have but which the Christians enjoy?

In demanding his emancipation from the Christian state he asks the Christian state to abandon its *religious* prejudice. But does he, the Jew, give up *his* religious prejudice? Has he then the right to insist that someone else should forswear his religion?

The *Christian* state, *by its very nature*, is incapable of emancipating the Jew. But, adds Bauer, the Jew, by his very nature, cannot be emancipated. [. . .]

The *formation of the political state*, and the dissolution of civil society into independent *individuals* whose relations are regulated by *law*, as the relations between men in the corporations and guilds were regulated by *privilege*, are accomplished by *one and the same act*. Man as a member of civil society—*non-political* man— necessarily appears as the *natural* man. The rights of man appear as natural rights because *conscious* activity is concentrated upon political *action*. *Egoistic* man is the *passive, given* result of the dissolution of society, an object of *direct apprehension* and consequently a *natural* object. The *political revolution* dissolves civil society into its elements without *revolutionizing* these elements themselves or subjecting them to criticism. This revolution regards civil society, the sphere of human needs, labor, private interests and civil law, as the *basis of its own existence*, as a self-subsistent *precondition*, and thus as its *natural basis*. Finally, man as a member of civil society is identified with *authentic man*, man as distinct from citizen, because he is man in his sensuous, individual and *immediate* existence, whereas *political* man is only abstract, artificial man, man as an *allegorical, moral* person. Thus man as he really is, is seen only in the form of *egoistic* man, and man in his *true* nature only in the form of the *abstract citizen*.

The abstract notion of political man is well formulated by Rousseau: "Whoever dares undertake to establish a people's institutions must feel himself capable of *changing*, as it were, *human nature* itself, of *transforming* each individual who, in isolation, is a complete but solitary whole, into a *part* of something greater than himself, from which in a sense, he derives his life and his being; [of changing man's nature in order to strengthen it;] of substituting a limited and moral existence for the physical and independent life [with which all of us are endowed by nature]. His task, in short, is to take from *a man his own powers*, and to give him in exchange alien powers which he can only employ with the help of other men."

Every emancipation is a *restoration* of the human world and of human relationships to *man himself*.

Political emancipation is a reduction of man, on the one hand to a member of civil society, an *independent* and *egoistic* individual, and on the other hand, to a *citizen*, to a moral person.

Human emancipation will only be complete when the real, individual man has absorbed into himself the abstract citizen; when as an individual man, in his everyday life, in his work and in his relationships, he has become a *species-being*; and when he has recognized and organized his own powers (*forces propres*) as *social* powers so that he no longer separates this social power from himself as *political* power.

NOTE

Words in brackets appear in the original translation.

Translated by T. B. Bottomore.

Other works by Marx: *The Poverty of Philosophy* (1847); *Writings on the U.S. Civil War* (1861); *Capital: Critique of Political Economy*, vol. 1 (1867).

Anonymous

This Ladino-language community document describes the difficulties experienced by the Jews of Izmir, who felt unfairly burdened by sales taxes imposed on them by their community to cover the costs of kosher items, rabbinic salaries, and maintenance of Jewish institutions.

The Cry of the Poor Jews of Izmir
1847

We, the poor of Israel, inhabitants of the city of Izmir, may God protect it, slaves of our lord and king, Sultan Abdülmecid, may his name be praised and long live his reign, [are] oppressed and humiliated by the wealthy communal leaders, may God protect and keep them, many of whom are *francos*. For many years we have been dishonored and abused by their governance and rule over the city, which has always been in their hands. If a poor or middle-class person rejects their rule, no matter how minor the issue, he is excommunicated, or turned over to the authorities and arrested or beaten. When one of them violates the law, he is never brought to justice. The poor, believing that it was [the leaders] who were covering the expenses of the community, such as the sums due to the government, [as well as] those for charitable institutions and those dedicated to caring for the sick and the cemetery, tolerated this, as one who relies on another becomes subservient to him.

Now the poor and middle classes have realized that as a result of the *Tanzimat-i Hayriye* [Beneficial Reforms] that our merciful king has applied to all of his reign, there are no longer any additional taxes or fines apart from the poll tax and the profit tax that each person must pay individually. All of the expenses of the city, [including the cost of the] Society for Visiting and Tending to the Sick, the Burial Society, the Society for Clothing the Poor, the Talmud Torah [school], the *asara batlanim*, the chief rabbi, and the rabbinic court are covered by the *gabela* on wine, meat, and cheese. Of the 25,000 arayot yielded every year by the wine *gabela*, the poor and middle classes pay twenty thousand arayot, while the wealthy communal leaders pay five thousand. The same is true for meat. The poor cover the payments that are due to the ritual slaughterers along with additional sums for the expenses of the city, nearing forty thousand arayot. The ritual slaughterer receives his payment right away, [which means that] the poor pay double the price for meat while the rich eat meat with no tax or payment to the ritual slaughterers. As has been made known across the whole city, of the ninety thousand [arayot] yielded by the meat *gabela* per year, the poor and middle classes pay at least seventy thousand. Such is the administration and rule of the wealthy communal leaders, who treat the poor as slaves, taking no pity on them and abusing them much more than [we were abused during] our enslavement in Egypt.

NOTE

Words in brackets appear in the original translation.

Translated by Dina Danon.

Karl Marx

Manifesto of the Communist Party
1848

A spectre is haunting Europe—the spectre of communism. All the powers of old Europe have entered into a holy alliance to exorcise this spectre: Pope and Tsar, Metternich and Guizot, French Radicals and German police-spies.

Where is the party in opposition that has not been decried as communistic by its opponents in power? Where is the opposition that has not hurled back the branding reproach of communism, against the more advanced opposition parties, as well as against its reactionary adversaries?

Two things result from this fact:

I. Communism is already acknowledged by all European powers to be itself a power.

II. It is high time that Communists should openly, in the face of the whole world, publish their views, their aims, their tendencies, and meet this nursery tale of the Spectre of Communism with a manifesto of the party itself.

To this end, Communists of various nationalities have assembled in London and sketched the following manifesto, to be published in the English, French, German, Italian, Flemish and Danish languages.

I. Bourgeois and Proletarians[1]

The history of all hitherto existing society is the history of class struggles.

Freeman and slave, patrician and plebeian, lord and serf, guild-master and journeyman, in a word, oppressor and oppressed, stood in constant opposition to one another, carried on an uninterrupted, now hidden, now open fight, a fight that each time ended, either in a revolutionary reconstitution of society at large, or in the common ruin of the contending classes.

In the earlier epochs of history, we find almost everywhere a complicated arrangement of society into various orders, a manifold gradation of social rank. In ancient Rome we have patricians, knights, plebeians, slaves; in the Middle Ages, feudal lords, vassals, guild-masters, journeymen, apprentices, serfs; in almost all of these classes, again, subordinate gradations.

The modern bourgeois society that has sprouted from the ruins of feudal society has not done away with class antagonisms. It has but established new classes, new conditions of oppression, new forms of struggle in place of the old ones.

Our epoch, the epoch of the bourgeoisie, possesses, however, this distinct feature: it has simplified class antagonisms. Society as a whole is more and more splitting up into two great hostile camps, into two great classes directly facing each other—Bourgeoisie and Proletariat.

From the serfs of the Middle Ages sprang the chartered burghers of the earliest towns. From these burgesses the first elements of the bourgeoisie were developed.

The discovery of America, the rounding of the Cape, opened up fresh ground for the rising bourgeoisie. The East-Indian and Chinese markets, the colonisation of America, trade with the colonies, the increase in the means of exchange and in commodities generally, gave to commerce, to navigation, to industry, an impulse never before known, and thereby, to the revolutionary element in the tottering feudal society, a rapid development.

The feudal system of industry, in which industrial production was monopolised by closed guilds, now no longer sufficed for the growing wants of the new markets. The manufacturing system took its place. The guild-masters were pushed on one side by the manufacturing middle class; division of labour between the different corporate guilds vanished in the face of division of labour in each single workshop.

Meantime the markets kept ever growing, the demand ever rising. Even manufacture no longer sufficed. Thereupon, steam and machinery revolutionised industrial production. The place of manufacture was taken by the giant, Modern Industry; the place of the industrial middle class by industrial millionaires, the leaders of the whole industrial armies, the modern bourgeois.

Modern industry has established the world market, for which the discovery of America paved the way. This market has given an immense development to commerce, to navigation, to communication by land. This development has, in its turn, reacted on the extension of industry; and in proportion as industry, commerce, navigation, railways extended, in the same proportion the bourgeoisie developed, increased its capital, and pushed into the background every class handed down from the Middle Ages.

We see, therefore, how the modern bourgeoisie is itself the product of a long course of development, of a series of revolutions in the modes of production and of exchange.

Each step in the development of the bourgeoisie was accompanied by a corresponding political advance of that class. An oppressed class under the sway of the feudal nobility, an armed and self-governing association in the medieval commune:[2] here independent urban republic (as in Italy and Germany); there taxable "third estate" of the monarchy (as in France); afterwards, in the period of manufacturing proper, serving either the semi-feudal or the absolute monarchy as a counterpoise against the nobility, and, in fact, cornerstone of the great monarchies in general, the bourgeoisie has at last, since the establishment of Modern Industry and of the world market, conquered for itself, in the modern representative State, exclusive political sway. The executive of the modern state is but a committee for managing the common affairs of the whole bourgeoisie.

The bourgeoisie, historically, has played a most revolutionary part.

The bourgeoisie, wherever it has got the upper hand, has put an end to all feudal, patriarchal, idyllic relations. It has pitilessly torn asunder the motley feudal ties that bound man to his "natural superiors," and has left remaining no other nexus between man and man than naked self-interest, than callous "cash payment." It has drowned the most heavenly ecstasies of religious fervour, of chivalrous enthusiasm, of philistine sentimentalism, in the icy water of egotistical calculation. It has resolved personal worth into exchange value, and in place of the numberless indefeasible chartered freedoms, has set up that single, unconscionable freedom—Free Trade. In one word, for exploitation, veiled by religious and political illusions, it has substituted naked shameless, direct, brutal exploitation.

The bourgeoisie has stripped of its halo every occupation hitherto honoured and looked up to with reverent awe. It has converted the physician, the lawyer, the priest, the poet, the man of science, into its paid wage labourers.

The bourgeoisie has torn away from the family its sentimental veil, and has reduced the family relation to a mere money relation.

The bourgeoisie has disclosed how it came to pass that the brutal display of vigour in the Middle Ages, which reactionaries so much admire, found its fitting complement in the most slothful indolence. It has been the first to show what man's activity can bring about. It has accomplished wonders far surpassing Egyptian pyramids, Roman aqueducts, and Gothic cathedrals; it has conducted expeditions that put in the shade all former Exoduses of nations and crusades.

The bourgeoisie cannot exist without constantly revolutionising the instruments of production, and thereby the relations of production, and with them the whole relations of society. Conservation of the old modes of production in unaltered form, was, on the contrary, the first condition of existence for all earlier industrial classes. Constant revolutionising of production, uninterrupted disturbance of all social conditions, everlasting uncertainty and agitation distinguish the bourgeois epoch from all earlier ones. All fixed, fast-frozen relations, with their train of ancient and venerable prejudices and opinions, are swept away, all new-formed ones become antiquated before they can ossify. All that is solid melts into air, all that is holy is profaned, and man is at last compelled to face with sober senses his real conditions of life, and his relations with his kind.

The need of a constantly expanding market for its products chases the bourgeoisie over the entire surface of the globe. It must nestle everywhere, settle everywhere, establish connexions everywhere.

NOTES

Words in brackets appear in the original source document.

1. By bourgeoisie is meant the class of modern capitalist, owners of the means of social production and employers of wage labour. By proletariat, the class of modern wage labourers who, having no means of pro-

duction of their own, are reduced to selling their labour power in order to live. [Engels, 1888 English edition.]

2. This was the name given their urban communities by the townsmen of Italy and France, after they had purchased or conquered their initial rights of self-government from their feudal lords. [Engels, 1890 German edition.]

Translated by Samuel Moore in cooperation with Friedrich Engels.

Reuben Kulisher
1828–1896

Educated in both a European and a traditional Jewish fashion, Reuben (Ruvim) Kulisher was one of the first Jewish students to graduate from a Russian university. A physician, he served in the Russian army medical corps and, from 1860, was on the staff of the Kiev Military Hospital. He also published widely in the Russian and Hebrew press on medical topics, Jewish history, communal living, and education. While still a student, Kulisher penned the famous poem "Otvet slavianinu" ("An Answer to the Slav"), a work that circulated in manuscript form for decades before being published in 1911. There he expresses the alienation of the Jew in Russian society, demands equality, and condemns Slavic antisemitism. His memoirs were serialized in the Russian Jewish journal *Voskhod* (1892–1894) and published in expanded book form in 1896.

An Answer to the Slav
1849

Introduction

I hesitate to sound immodest,
So I must warn you in advance,
If you will listen now in earnest,
Then please excuse my stance.

More startling than other words,
And I will use this frightening word—
It is as novel to your ears
As the whistle of steam that I first heard.
Perhaps your ears are all too tender,
Unused to terrifying sounds.
Then you'll immediately consider
My speech so spitefully unbound.

Not ancient ghosts or petty demons,
Nor the old mounted wicked witch,
Nor even Satan's evil sermons
Contribute to the subject which
I wish to talk to you about:
Those themes have long since been portrayed,
And even cannibals no doubt,
To some will seem a bit too staid.
I wish to introduce the *Jew*.
Please don't be scared, I beg of you,
Oh, how you trembled, turning pale—
I'll either smash the frightening tale
Or for a time put it aside
So fragile souls can feel no fear
While those with moral strength decide,
To love the truth with hearts sincere. [. . .]

III

In exile I was given shelter,
For loads of money, by the Pole;
My sufferings grew manifold
With wild assaults by Polish *szlachta*[1]
Beholding my endless torments
How many times the Pole rejoiced:
His crops were watered by the torrents
Of Jewish blood upon his fields!
From Little Russia came the raids
By Cossacks threatening to erase me,
And for my gold the Pole repaid me
With nothing but profound contempt.

Those people had no God, although
They wanted to appease him so;
And knowing neither Faith nor Love
They sought those virtues in my blood.
And though the people have improved
And they no longer torture Jews,
We still cannot sigh with relief,
The road to peace is long and steep.
It's been my lot to stand there waiting
At Russia's still unopened gate.
For bread and salt upon a plate
In vain I stood anticipating.
I'm just allowed to share the pain
Of this vast empire and its nation:
Your brother in war and desperation,
In peace you treat me with disdain.
Enlightenment brings me only torment,
I see without any adornment:

With others enjoying naught but bliss
What misery for me exists.

NOTE

1. *Szlachta* (Pol.) = Polish rank-and-file landed gentry.

Translated by Maxim Shrayer.

Other works by Kulisher: *Itogi, Nadezhdy i ozhidaniia russkikh evreev za poslednie 50 let, 1838–1888* (1896).

Ernestine Potovsky Rose
1810–1892

Born in Piotrków, Russian Poland, into a rabbinic family, Ernestine Potovsky Rose was much better educated than most girls of her time. Her discontent with the legal subjugation of women to men motivated her to leave home at age seventeen. Living briefly in Berlin and Paris before going to England, Potovsky joined a circle of enlightened, reform-minded people who included William Rose, whom she married in 1836. The couple immigrated to New York, where she became deeply involved in the movements for women's rights, suffrage, the abolition of slavery, and temperance.

An Address on Women's Rights
1852

October 19, 1851

[E]ven here, in this far-famed land of freedom and of knowledge, under a republic that has inscribed on its banner the great truth that all men are created free and equal and are endowed with inalienable rights to life, liberty, and the pursuit of happiness—a Declaration wafted like the voice of Hope on the breezes of heaven to the remotest parts of earth, to whisper freedom and equality to the oppressed and down-trodden children of men—a Declaration that lies at the very foundation of human freedom and happiness, yet in the very face of that eternal truth, woman, the mockingly so-called "better half of man," has yet to plead for her rights, nay, for her life; for what is life without liberty? and what is liberty without equality of rights; and as for the pursuit of happiness, she is not allowed to pursue any line of life that might promote it; she has only thankfully to accept what man, in the plenitude of his wisdom and generosity, decides as proper for her to do, and that is, what he does not choose to do himself.

Is woman then not included in that Declaration? Answer, ye wise men of the nation, and answer truly; add not hypocrisy to your other sins. Say she is not created free and equal, and therefore, (for the sequence follows on the premises) she is not entitled to life, liberty, and the pursuit of happiness. But you dare not answer this simple question. With all the audacity arising from an assumed superiority, you cannot so libel and insult humanity as to say she is not; and if she is, then what right has man, except that of might, to deprive her of the same rights and privileges he claims for himself? And why, in the name of reason and justice, I ask, why should she not have the same rights as man? Because she is woman? Humanity recognizes no sex—mind recognizes no sex—virtue recognizes no sex—life and death, pleasure and pain, happiness and misery recognize no sex. Like him she comes involuntarily into existence; like him she possesses physical, mental, and moral powers, on the proper cultivation of which depends her happiness; like him she is subject to all the vicissitudes of life; like him she has to pay the penalty for disobeying nature's laws, and far greater penalties has she to suffer with her country. Yet she is not recognized as his equal. In the laws of the land she has no rights; in government she has no voice, and in spite of another principle recognized in this republic, namely, that taxation without representation is tyranny, woman is taxed without being represented; her property may be consumed by heavy taxes, to defray the expenses of that unholy and unrighteous thing called war, yet she cannot give her veto against it. From the cradle to the grave, she is subject to the power and control of man, father, guardian and husband. One conveys her like some piece of merchandise over to the other.

At marriage she loses her entire identity. Her being is said to be merged in her husband. Has nature there merged it? Has she ceased to exist or feel pleasure and pain? When she violates the laws of her being, does he pay the penalty? When she breaks the laws of the land, does he suffer the punishment? When his wants are supplied, is it sufficient to satisfy the wants of her nature? Or when, at his nightly orgies, in the grog-shop, the oyster cellar, or the gaming table, he spends the means she helped by her co-operation and economy to accumulate and she awakens to penury and destitution, will it supply the wants of her children to tell them, that owing to the superiority of man she has no redress by law?—and that as her being was merged in him, so also ought theirs to be?

But it will be said that the husband provides for the wife, or in other words, he is bound to feed, clothe, and shelter her. Oh! the degradation of that idea? Yes, he keeps her, so he does his horse. By law both are considered his property; both can, when the cruelty of the owner compels them to run away, be brought back by the strong arm of the law; and according to a still extant law of England, both may be led by the halter to the market place and sold. This is humiliating indeed, but nevertheless true, and the sooner these things are known and understood the better for humanity. It is no fancy sketch. I know that some endeavor to throw the mantle of romance over the subject, and treat woman like some ideal existence not subject to the ills of life. Let those deal in fancy that have nothing better to deal in. We have to do with sober, sad realities, with stubborn facts.

But again it will be said, the law presumes the husband would be kind, affectionate, that he would provide for and protect the wife; but I ask, what right has the law to presume at all on the subject? What right has the law to entrust the interest and happiness of one being to the power of another? And if this merging of interests is so indispensable, then why should woman always be on the losing side? Turn the tables; let the identity and interest of the husband be merged in the wife, think you she would act less generous towards him than he towards her?—that she would be incapable of as much justice, disinterested devotion, and abiding affection as him? Oh! how grossly you misunderstand and wrong her nature. But we desire no such undue power over man. It would be as wrong in her, as it now is in him; all we claim is our own rights—We have nothing to do with individual man, be he good or bad, but with the laws that oppress woman. Bad and unjust laws must in the nature of things make man so too. If he acts better, if he is kind, affectionate, and consistent, it is because the kindlier feelings instilled by a mother, kept warm by a sister, and cherished by a wife, will not allow him to carry out the barbarous laws against woman; but the estimation she is generally held in is as degrading as it is unjust.

Not long ago, I saw an account of two offenders brought before a Justice in New York; one, for stealing a pair of boots, for which offence he was sentenced to six months imprisonment; the other, for an assault and battery on his wife, for which offence he was let off with a reprimand from the Judge! With my principles I am entirely opposed to punishment. I hold to reforming the erring, and removing the causes, as being much more efficient as well as just than punishing; but the Judge showed the comparative value he set on these two kinds of property. But you must remember that the boots were taken by a stranger, while the wife was insulted by her legal owner. Yet it will be said that such degrading cases are few. For the sake of humanity, I hope they are; but as long as woman is wronged by unequal laws, so long will she be degraded by man.

We can hardly have an adequate idea how all-powerful law is in forming public opinion, in giving tone and character to the mass of society. To illustrate this point, look at that inhuman, detestable law, written in human blood, signed and sealed with life and liberty, that eternal stain on the statute books of this country, the Fugitive Slave Law. Think you, that before its passage you could have found any in the free States, except a few politicians in the market, base enough to desire such a law? No, no! Even those that took no interest in the subject, would have shrunk from so barbarous a thing; but no sooner is it passed, than the ignorant mass, the rabble of the self-styled Union Safety Committee, found out we were a law-loving and law-abiding people. Such is the magic power of law; hence the necessity to guard against bad ones, hence also the reason why we call on the nation to remove the legal shackles from woman.

Set her politically and civilly free, and it will have a more beneficial effect on that still greater tyrant she has to contend with, public opinion. Carry out the Republican principle of universal suffrage, or strike it from your banner, and substitute freedom and power to one half of society, and submission and slavery to the other. Give women then the elective franchise. Let married women have the same right to property that man has; for whatever the difference in their respective occupations, the duties of the wife are as indispensable and far more arduous than the husband's. Why, then, should the wife at the death of her husband, not be his heir to the same extent that he is to her?

In this legal inequality there is involved another wrong. When the wife dies, the husband is left in the undisturbed possession of all, and the children are left with him. No change is made, no stranger intrudes on his home and his affliction; but when the husband dies, not only is she, as is too often the case, deprived of all, or at best receives but a mere pittance, but strangers assume authority denied to the wife and mother. The sanctuary of affliction must be desecrated by executors, every thing must be ransacked and assessed, lest she should steal something out of her own house, and to cap the climax, the children are taken from her and placed under guardians. When he dies poor, no guardian is required, the children are left with the mother to care and toil for them as best she may; but when any thing is left for the maintenance and education of the children, then it must be placed in the hands of strangers for safe keeping, lest the mother might defraud them. The whole care and bringing up of the children are left with the mother, and safe they are in her hands; but a few hundred or thousand dollars cannot be entrusted with her. [. . .]

To achieve this great victory of right over might, woman has much to do. She must not sit idle and wait till man inspired by justice and humanity will work out her redemption. It has well been said, "He that would be free, himself must strike the blow." It is with nations as with individuals, if they do not strive to help themselves no one will help them. Man may, and in the nature of things will, remove the legal, political, and civil disabilities from woman, and recognise her as his equal with himself, and it will do much towards her elevation; but the laws cannot compel her to cultivate her physical and mental powers, and take a stand as a free and independent being. All that, she has to do. She must investigate and take an interest in every thing on which the welfare of society depends, for the interest and happiness of every member of society is connected with that of society. She must at once claim and exercise those rights and privileges with which the laws do not interfere, and it will aid her to obtain all the rest. She must, therefore, throw off that heavy yoke that like a nightmare weighs down her best energies, viz., the fear of public opinion.

It has been said, that "The voice of the People is the voice of God." If that voice is on the side of justice and humanity, then it is true, if the term God means the principle of Truth and of Right. But if the public voice is oppressive and unjust, then it ought to be spurned like the voice of falsehood and corruption; and woman, instead of implicitly and blindly following the dictates of public opinion, must investigate for herself what is right or wrong—act in accordance with her best convictions and let the rest take care of itself, for obedience to wrong is wrong itself, and opposition to it is virtue alike in woman as in man, even though she should incur the ill will of bigotry, superstition, and priestcraft, for the approval of our fellow-being is valuable only when it does not clash with our own sense of right, and no further.

The priests well know the influence and value of women when warmly engaged in any cause, and therefore as long as they can keep them steeped in superstitious darkness, so long are they safe; and hence the horror and anathema against every woman that has intelligence, spirit, and moral courage to cast off the dark and oppressive yoke of superstition. But she must do it, or she will ever remain a slave, for of all tyranny that of superstition is the greatest, and he is the most abject slave who tamely submits to its yoke. Woman, then, must cast it off as her greatest enemy; and the time I trust will come when she will aid man to remove the political, civil, and religious evils that have swept over the earth like some malignant scourge to lay waste and destroy so much of the beauty, harmony, and happiness of man; and the old fable of the fall of man through a woman will be superseded by the glorious fact that she was instrumental in the elevation of the race towards a higher, nobler, and happier destiny.

Other works by Rose: *Mistress of Herself: Speeches and Letters of Ernestine L. Rose, Early Women's Rights Leader* (2008).

Alliance Israélite Universelle

The Alliance Israélite Universelle was established in Paris in 1860 to improve the legal and cultural status of Jews in Asia Minor, the Middle East, and North Africa. It promoted the gallicization and Westernization of Sephardi and Mizrahi Jews in the Mediterranean world largely through an extensive network of elementary and vocational schools. By 1900, it was operating one hundred schools, primarily in Turkey, Tunisia, and Morocco, with a total enrollment of twenty-six thousand students. Highly centralized, like the French government itself, its programs to transform traditional Jewish life often created tensions between the Paris headquarters and the traditional communities in which it established its schools.

Proclamation of the Alliance Israélite Universelle
1860

Israelites! If, scattered over the whole surface of the earth and intermingled with all nations, you remain attached to the old religion of your ancestors, however weak be the bond that unites you therewith:

If you do not deny your religion, if you do not hide your worship, if you do not blush at being Israelites;

If you abhor the prejudices still entertained against us; the reproaches raised against us; the slanders, continually repeated, the lies, perpetually renewed; the injustice done us; the persecutions, which are either tolerated or excused;

If you hold, that the oldest and most simple of spiritual religions ought to maintain its place, fulfil its mission, proclaim its right, and manifest its vitality amid the new theories that agitate modern society;

If you believe, that the sublime idea and the vigorous worship of the One and Indivisible God, of which we are the oldest heirs and persistent defenders, ought to be guarded against the insinuations of doubt or indifference;

If you maintain, that religious liberty, this life of the soul, is nowhere better guarded, for the common good of all, than in those countries in which the Jews enjoy it fully and without any restriction whatsoever;

If you believe, that the creed, inherited from his ancestors, is for every one a sacred patrimony, that our firesides and our consciences are inviolable sanctuaries, which ought not to be invaded again as they lately have been;

If you hold, that unity is strength: that, although we are members of various nations, we may still be one nationality in sentiments, hopes and expectations;

If you think, that by legal means, by the invincible power of right and reason—without exciting any trouble, without frightening any power, without raising the indignation of any party, except that of ignorance, bigotry and fanaticism—you would obtain much and impart much by your zealous and intelligent action;

If you agree, that a large number of your co-religionists, still under the yoke of the sufferings, proscriptions and insults of twenty centuries, could regain their dignity as human beings, their rights as citizens;

If you believe, that those who are blind, ought to be enlightened, and not forsaken; and that those who are afflicted, ought to be assisted, and not merely pitied; that we should defend those who are calumniated, and not look on with silent compassion: that we ought to give material aid to those who are persecuted, and not simply cry and lament at their persecution;

If you hold, that the resources, hitherto isolated; the good intentions, one detached from the other, the aspirations, started without any definite object—could be united for higher purposes, so that the united action may be felt all over the globe;

If you hold, that it would be an honor to your religion, a lesson to the nations, a progress of humanity, a triumph of truth and reason, to see concentrated all the forces of Judaism, though small in number, but great by the innate love for the common good;

If you hold, that the influence, which the principles of 1789 exercise all over the world, is paramount; that the law taught by these principles is a law of justice, that it is desirable that this spirit may pervade all nations and that the example of religious liberty is an absolute power;

If you hold all these points to be true and correct then, Israelites of the whole world, come listen to our appeal and grant us your aid and your assistance. The work is a great and blissful one. We are establishing the Alliance Israélite Universelle!

Translator unknown.

Morris Jacob Raphall
1798–1868

Morris Jacob Raphall was born in Sweden to a banking family and was educated in Copenhagen and England. A university lecturer, translator, and secretary to the chief rabbi of Great Britain, he published translations of parts of the Mishnah and defended Judaism against the blood libel in Damascus in 1840. In 1849 Raphall moved to New York City and served as rabbi of B'nai Jeshurun congregation. Raphall's treatise on slavery, published in 1861, shocked Jews especially in the North during the Civil War. His defense was based on his analysis of biblical laws concerning slaves.

Note to reader: Raphall's article is placed logically here before the response by David Einhorn's; all other works in this volume follow alphabetical order within a chronological year.

The Bible View of Slavery
1861

New York, Jan. 15th, 1861

The subject of my investigation falls into three parts:—

First, How far back can we trace the existence of slavery?

Secondly, Is slaveholding condemned as a sin in sacred Scripture?

Thirdly, What was the condition of the slave in Biblical times, and among the Hebrews; and saying with our Father Jacob, "for Thy help, I hope, O L-rd!" I proceed to examine the question, how far back can we trace the existence of slavery?

It is generally admitted, that slavery had its origin in war, public or private. The victor having it in his power to take the life of his vanquished enemy, prefers to let him live, and reduces him to bondage. The life he has spared, the body he might have mutilated or destroyed, become his absolute property. He may dispose of it in any way he pleases. Such was, and through a great part of the world still is, the brutal law of force. When this state of things first began, it is next to impossible to decide. If we consult Sacred Scripture, the oldest and most truthful collection of records now or at any time in existence, we find the word *evved*, "slave," which the English version renders "servant," first used by Noah, who, in Genesis ix. 25, curses the descendants of his son Ham, by saying they should be *Evved Avadim*, the "meanest of slaves," or as the English version has it "servant of servants." The question naturally arises how came Noah to use the expression? How came he to know anything of slavery? There existed not at that time any human being on earth except Noah and his family of three sons, apparently by one mother, born free and equal, with their wives and children. Noah had no slaves. From the time that he quitted the ark he could have none. It therefore becomes evident that Noah's acquaintance with the word *slave* and the nature of slavery must date from before the Flood, and existed in his memory only until the crime of Ham called it forth. You and I may regret that in his anger Noah should from beneath the waters of wrath again have fished up the idea and practice of slavery; but that he did so is a fact which rests on the authority of Scripture. I am therefore justified when tracing slavery as far back as it can be traced, I arrive at the conclusion, that next to the domestic relations of husband and wife, parents and children, the oldest relation of society with which we are acquainted is that of master and slave. [. . .]

And if you answer me, "Oh, in their time slaveholding was lawful, but now it has become a sin," I in my turn ask you, "When and by what authority you draw the line?" Tell us the precise time when slaveholding ceased to be permitted, and became sinful?" When we remember the mischief which this inventing a new sin, not known in the Bible, is causing; how it has exasperated the feelings of the South, and alarmed the conscience of the North, to a degree that men who should be brothers are on the point of embruing their hands in each other's blood, are we not entitled to ask the reverend preacher of Brooklyn, "What right have you to insult and exasperate thousands of G-d-fearing, law-abiding citizens, whose moral worth and patriotism, whose purity of conscience and of life, are fully equal to your own? What right have you to place yonder grey-headed philanthropist on a level with a murderer, or yonder mother of a family on a line with an adulteress, or yonder honorable and honest man in one rank with a thief, and all this solely because they exercise a right which your own fathers and progenitors, during many generations, held and exercised without reproach or compunction. [. . .]"

This, indeed, is the great distinction which the Bible view of slavery derives from its divine source. The slave is a *person* in whom the dignity of human nature is to be respected; *he has rights*. Whereas, the heathen view of slavery which prevailed at Rome, and which, I am sorry to say, is adopted in the South, reduces the slave to a *thing*, and a thing can have no rights. The result to which the Bible view of slavery leads us, is—1st. That slavery has existed since the earliest time; 2d. That slaveholding is no sin, and that slave property is expressly placed under the protection of the Ten Commandments; 3d. That the slave is a person, and has rights not conflicting with the lawful exercise of the rights of his owner. If our Northern fellow-citizens, content with following the word of G-d, would not insist on being "righteous overmuch," or denouncing "sin" which the Bible knows not, but which is plainly taught by the precepts of men—they would entertain more equity and less ill feeling towards their Southern brethren. And if our Southern fellow-citizens would adopt the Bible view of slavery, and discard the heathen slave code, which permits a few bad men to indulge in an abuse of power that throws a stigma and disgrace on the whole body of slaveholders—if both North and South would do what is right, then "G-d would see their works and that they turned from the evil of their ways"; and in their case, as in that of the people of Nineveh, would mercifully avert the impending evil, for with Him alone is the power to do so. Therefore let us pray. [. . .]

And above all things, L-rd merciful and gracious, avert the calamity of civil war from our midst. If in Thy supreme wisdom Thou hast decreed that this vast commonwealth, which has risen under Thy blessing, shall now be separated, then we beseech Thee let that separation be peaceable; that no human blood may be shed, but that the canopy of Thy peace may still remain spread over all the land. May we address our prayers to Thee, O L-rd, at an acceptable time; mayest Thou, O G-d, in Thy abundant mercy, answer us with the truth of Thy salvation. Amen.

Other works by Morris Jacob Raphall: *The Festivals of the Lord: As Celebrated by the House of Israel in Every Part of the World* (1838); *Jewish Dogmas: A Correspondence between Dr. Raphall . . . and C. N.* (1849); *Post-Biblical History of the Jews; from the Close of the Old Testament, about the Year 420 BCE* (1856).

David Einhorn
1809–1879

David Einhorn, a leading American Reform rabbi born in Bavaria, became the first rabbi of Har Sinai Congregation in Baltimore. Before his emigration, he had challenged the religious authority of the Talmud, supported holding synagogue services in German, and sought to omit references to biblical sacrifices. His rendering of a new prayer book was a model for the Union Prayer Book published by the Central Conference of American Rabbis in 1894. In response to a political sermon delivered by American rabbi Morris Jacob Raphall in 1861, Einhorn strongly disputed the latter's proslavery stance, leading to Einhorn's violent dismissal and his move to Congregation Keneseth Israel in Philadelphia and later to Congregation Adas Jeshurun in New York City.

Note to reader: see the selection by Morris Jacob Raphall, immediately preceding this essay.

Response to "A Bible View of Slavery"
1861

The question simply is: Is Slavery a moral evil or not? And it took Dr. Raphall, a Jewish preacher, to concoct the deplorable farce in the name of divine authority, to proclaim the justification, the moral blamelessness of servitude, and to lay down the law to Christian preachers of opposite convictions. The Jew, a descendant of the race that offers daily praises to God for deliverance out of the house of bondage in Egypt, and even today suffers under the yoke of slavery in most places of the old world, crying out to God, undertook to designate slavery as a perfectly sinless institution, sanctioned by God [. . .]

If a Jewish theologian distorts truth in such a way, and drags slavery into our innermost sanctuary and seals this with the eternal word—enlightening "ten flaming Commandments of Sinai," then the pen threatens to drop from our hands, as we exclaim: "Woe to the ears that have to hear this!" [orig. of this phrase printed in Hebrew] [. . .]

And now, a word to you, dear co-religionists, and particularly to you, members of my Congregation! At the moment that I am writing this down, January 9th, the thunder-cloud still hangs heavily over our head, and hides the future of our beloved land in dense mist. Perhaps some of you in our midst may consider it unjustifiable that at such a time I have thus unequivocally expressed my conviction in the foregoing regarding the law of Moses about slavery. The Jew has special cause to be conservative, and he is doubly and triply so in a country which grants him all the spiritual and material privileges he can wish for, he wants peace at every price and trembles for the preservation of the Union like a true son for the life of a dangerously sick mother. From the depth of my soul, I share your patriotic sentiments, and cherish no more fervent wish than that God may soon grant us the deeply yearned-for peace. Still—no matter which political party we may belong to—the sanctity of our Law must never be drawn into political controversy, nor disgraced in the interest of this or that political opinion, as it is in this instance, and with such publicity besides, and in the holy place! The spotless morality of the Mosaic principles is our pride and our fame, and our weapon since thousands of years. This weapon we cannot forfeit without pressing a mighty sword into the hands of our foes. This pride and renown, the only one which we possess, we will not and dare not allow ourselves to be robbed of. This would be unscrupulous, prove the greatest triumph of our adversaries and our own *destruction*, and would be paying too dearly for the fleeting, wavering favor of the moment. Would it not then be justly said, as in fact it has already been done, in consequence of the incident referred to: *Such* are the Jews! Where they are oppressed, they boast of the humanity of their religion; but where they are free, their rabbis declare slavery to have been sanctioned by God, even mentioning the holy act of the

Revelation on Sinai in defense of it. Whereas Christian clergymen even in the Southern States, and in presence of the nation's Representatives in part, though admonishing to toleration—openly disapprove of it and in part *apologize* for it, owing to existing conditions!

Translated by Johanna (Einhorn) Kohler.

Other works by Einhorn: *Das Princep des Mosaismus und dessen Verhaltniss zum Heidenthum und rabbinischen Judenthum* (1854); *David Einhorn Memorial Volume: Selected Sermons and Addresses* (1911).

Moses Hess
1812–1875

Born in Bonn, Moses Hess received a traditional Jewish education from his grandfather and no further formal schooling. However, Hess taught himself French and German and became active in socialist circles, often writing for the *Rheinische Zeitung*, edited by his friend Karl Marx. Though he was initially uninterested in Jewish concerns, the 1840 Damascus affair (a blood libel against notable members of the city's Jewish community) inspired in him a new belief in the necessity of a Jewish homeland, leading him to become an early leader of Labor Zionism.

Rome and Jerusalem
1862

What we have to do at present for the regeneration of the Jewish nation is, first, to keep alive the hope of the political rebirth of our people, and next, to reawaken that hope where it slumbers. When political conditions in the Orient shape themselves so as to permit the organization of a beginning of the restoration of a Jewish state, this beginning will express itself in the founding of Jewish colonies in the land of their ancestors, to which enterprise France will undoubtedly lend a hand. You know how substantial was the share of the Jews in the subscriptions to the fund raised for the benefit of the Syrian war victims. It was Crémieux who took the initiative in the matter, the same Crémieux who twenty years ago traveled with Sir Moses Montefiore to Syria in order to seek protection for the Jews against the persecutions of the Christians. In the *Journal des Debats*, which very seldom accepts poems for publication, there appeared, at the time of the Syrian expedition, a poem by Léon Halévi, who at the time, perhaps, thought as little of the rebirth of Israel as Crémieux, yet his beautiful stanzas could not have been produced otherwise than in a spirit of foreseeing this regeneration. When the poet of the *Schwalben* mournfully complains:

Where tarries the hero? Where tarries the wise?
Who will, O my people, revive you anew;
Who will save you, and give you again
A place in the sun?

The French poet answers his query with enthusiastic confidence:

O'er your banks where our colors have fluttered!
Come again a call supreme!
Au revoir is not *adieu*—
France is all to those she loves,
The future belongs to God.

Alexander Weill sang about the same time:

There is a people stiff of neck,
Dispersed from the Euphrates to the Rhine,
Its whole life centered in a Book—
Ofttimes bent, yet ever straightened;
Braving hatred and contempt,
It only dies to live again
In nobler form.

France, beloved friend, is the savior who will restore our people to its place in universal history.

Allow me to recall to your mind an old legend which you have probably heard in your younger days. It runs as follows:

"A knight who went to the Holy Land to assist in the liberation of Jerusalem, left behind him a very dear friend. While the knight fought valiantly on the field of battle, his friend spent his time, as heretofore, in the study of the Talmud, for his friend was none other than a pious rabbi.

"Months afterward, when the knight returned home, he appeared suddenly at midnight, in the study room of the rabbi, whom he found, as usual, absorbed in his Talmud. 'God's greetings to you, dear old friend,' he said. 'I have returned from the Holy Land and bring you from there a pledge of our friendship. What I gained by my sword, you are striving to obtain with your spirit. Our ways lead to the same goal.' While thus speaking, the knight handed the rabbi a rose of Jericho.

"The rabbi took the rose and moistened it with his tears, and immediately the withered rose began to bloom again in its full glory and splendor. And the rabbi said to the knight: 'Do not wonder, my friend, that the withered rose bloomed again in my hands. The rose possesses the same characteristics as our people: it comes to life again at the touch of the warm breath of love, in spite of its having been torn from its own soil and left to wither in foreign lands. So will Israel bloom again in youthful splendor; and the spark, at present smoldering under the ashes, will burst once more into a bright flame.'"

The routes of the rabbi and the knight, dear friend, are meeting today. As the rabbi in the story symbolizes our people, so does the knight of the legend signify the French people which in our days, as in the Middle Ages, sent its brave soldiers to Syria and "prepared in the desert the way of the Lord" [Isaiah 40:3].

Have you never read the words of the prophet Isaiah: "Comfort ye, comfort ye, my people, saith your God. Speak ye comfortably to the heart of Jerusalem, and cry unto her, that the appointed time has come, that her iniquity is pardoned; for she hath received at the Lord's hand double for all her sins. The voice of one that crieth in the wilderness, prepare ye the way of the Lord, make straight in the desert a highway for our God. Every valley shall be exalted, and every mountain and hill shall be made low, and the crooked shall be made a straight place, and the rough places a plain. And the glory of the Lord shall be revealed, and all flesh shall see it together: for the mouth of the Lord hath spoken it" [Isaiah 40:1–5].

Do you not believe that in these words, with which the second Isaiah opened his prophecies, as well as in the words with which the prophet Obadiah closed his prophecy, the conditions of our own time are graphically pictured? Was not help given to Zion in order to defend and establish the wild mountaineers there? Are not things being prepared there and roads leveled, and is not the road of civilization being built in the desert in the form of the Suez Canal works and the railroad which will connect Asia and Europe? They are not thinking at present of the restoration of our people. But you know the proverb, "Man proposes and God disposes." Just as in the West they once searched for a road to India, and incidentally discovered a new world, so will our lost fatherland be rediscovered on the road to India and China that is now being built in the Orient.

Do you still doubt that France will help the Jews to found colonies which may extend from Suez to Jerusalem, and from the banks of the Jordan to the Coast of the Mediterranean? Then pray read the work which appeared shortly after the massacres in Syria, by the famous publisher, Dentu, under the title *The New Oriental Problem*. The author hardly wrote it at the request of the French government, but acted in accordance with the spirit of the French nation when he urged our brethren, not on religious grounds, but from purely political and humanitarian motives, to restore their ancient State.

I may, therefore, recommend this work, written, not by a Jew, but by a French patriot, to the attention of our modern Jews, who plume themselves on borrowed French humanitarianism. I will quote here [. . . from . . .] this work, *The New Eastern Question*, by Ernest Laharanne.

"In the discussion of these new Eastern complications, we reserved a special place for Palestine, in order to bring to the attention of the world the important question, whether ancient Judea can once more acquire its former place under the sun. [. . .]"

NOTE

Words in brackets appear in the original translation.

Translated by Meyer Waxman.

Other works by Hess: *Die heilige Geschichte der Menschheit* (1837); *Sozialismus und Kommunismus* (1842).

Judah Scheindling of Shkudy
Dates Unknown

In 1827, Tsar Nicholas I issued a statute that effectively made Russian Jews liable to military service, as part of a policy that sought to transform the Jewish population into integrated subjects who would be useful to the interests of the monarchy. While serving in the army, many Jewish soldiers maintained a sense of community by collectively participating in religious practices. A minute book, or *pinkas*, kept by a group of Jewish soldiers between 1864 and 1887, serving in Skudas, Lithuania, details the activities of a psalms society, or *ḥevra tehilim*, organized among Jews serving in the Fourth Infantry Regiment of the Russian Army. The scribe is said to have been Judah

(Yehudah) Scheindling of Shkudy. Psalms societies comprised voluntary groups of Jewish worshipers who would recite psalms in connection with specific occasions and rituals.

Excerpts from the Minute Book of a Psalms Society in the Russian Army
1864–1867

This minute-book belongs to the members of the Psalms-Society formed here, at Aleksat, of the honorable Jews serving in the army of His Imperial Majesty Alexander, may His glory be exalted, at the camp of the Saxony regiment, in the year 5624. [. . .]

Servants of the ruler of the land, our magnificent Emperor Alexander, holy king forever: Heed the call of the king of Israel, the august and sublime David, our delighted savior, conquer your souls with his honey-laden holy songs, go forth in courage and strength to follow the orders of your honorable commanders and ruler, listen to the voices of the officers whom you serve first and foremost; and then, in your hours of peace and quiet, seek out and obey the duties of every soul in Israel, the law of Our God, to praise His holy name with prayers to our holy Creator, which have given hope to our nation. May your spirits be exalted in joy by these holy words, to praise His magnificence in the sweet phrases of the Psalms composed for ever and ever. Amen.

The Members of the Society

ABRAMOVITCH, Abraham ben Samuel: drummer in third battalion; born 1840 in Koigorad (Kopoigorad?), Volhynia province; inducted as a Cantonist into the Kiev Cantonist Battalion (no date given); no Russian literacy; carpenter; single; *gabbai sheini* of Society in 1864–5 and 1866–7.

ARONOVITCH, Kadish ben Aryeh: private in second battalion; born 1841 in the city of Mogilev, Mogilev province; inducted in 1858; no Russian literacy or trade; single.

BILETSKI, David ben Jacob: in regimental headquarters; from Vil'ki, Grodno province; *shamash* of Society in 1864–5 and 1866–7; no other information.

EICHEN, Isaac ben Abraham Jacob: first battalion; no other information.

FURMAN, Aryeh Leib ben Israel Isaac: drummer in third battalion; born 1834 in Bluden', Grodno province; inducted in 1853; no Russian literacy or trade; single.

GOTLIB, Israel Dov ben Jacob: bugler in first battalion; born 1835 in Gandomir, Radom province; inducted in 1855; no Russian literacy or trade; single.

HUREVITZ, Abraham ben Jacob Mordecai: bugler in first battalion; born 1835 in Prianitsy, Radom province; inducted in 1852; no Russian literacy or craft; single.

KHOYKER, Simḥah ben Jacob: no other information.

KLARNET, Isaac ben Samuel Moses: private in regimental headquarters; born 1834 in Kikol, Plotsk province; inducted 1853; no Russian literacy; carpenter; married to Sarah, two daughters, family lived with him; *shomer tikkunim* and *borer* of Society 1864–5.

KLEIN, Shraga ben Isaac: no other information.

KVITKOVSKI, Isaac ben Aryeh: company bugler, first battalion; born 1830 in Sopotskin, Augustow province; inducted 1849; no Russian literacy or craft; single.

LEVIN, Me'ir ben Abraham: private in first battalion; born 1831, Tel'shi, Kovno province; inducted as Cantonist in 1851; reads and writes Russian; tailor; single.

LIPMAN, Isaac ben Eliezer: in regimental headquarters, from Nevel', Vitebsk province; no other information.

MORDEKHELEVICH, Jacob ben Moses: private in third battalion; born 1841 in Bialystok, Grodno province; inducted as Cantonist in 1854; no Russian literacy; tailor; single; *gabbai* of Society in 1866–7.

NEIMAN, Isaac ben Ze'ev: no other information.

ORANOVSKI, Zvi Hirsh ben Aryeh: private in third battalion; born 1841, Troki, Vilna province; inducted as Cantonist (no year given); no Russian literacy; cobbler; single; *ro'eh ḥeshbon* and *borer* of Society, 1864–5.

PECHIN, Nathan ben Isaac: barber in third battalion; born 1835 in Volkovyshki, Augustow province; inducted 1852; reads and writes Russian; no trade; single.

PEDIS, Daniel ben Mordecai: private in second battalion; born 1841 in Bialystok, Grodno province; inducted as Cantonist in 1854; no Russian literacy; tailor; single; *ne'eman 'al ha-ma'ot* and *borer* of Society, 1866–7.

PEISKOVITCH, Hayim Nathan ben Pesah: company bugler in first battalion; born 1835 in Makov, Plotsk province; inducted 1853; no Russian literacy or craft; single.

PRITIKIN, Mordecai ben Moses: private in regimental headquarters; born 1843 in Loev, Minsk province; inducted as Cantonist in 1853, released to mother in 1859, returned to service in 1863; reads and writes Russian; no trade; married to Feiga Haya; *gabbai rishon* of Society in 1864–5 and *shomer tikkunim* in 1866–7.

SHAFIR, Efraim Zvi ben Ezekiel: drummer in first battalion; born 1836 in Ilusa (possibly Ilza), Radom province; inducted 1855; no Russian literacy or craft; single.

SHMULOVSKI, Zvi Hirsh ben Shalom: no other information.

SKURNITSKI, Yerahmi'el ben Judah: barber in second battalion; born 1836 in Plogovits, Radom province; inducted 1855; reads and writes Russian; cobbler; single; *borer* of Society 1866–7.

STAMETSKI, Jacob ben Judah: voluntarily hired tailor to regiment; no other information.

STARK, Samuel ben Zvi: bugler in third battalion; born 1836 in Skrishlina, Radom province; inducted 1855; reads and writes Russian; no craft; single; *ro'eh heshbon* of Society 1866–7.

VAKHMAN, Israel Eliezer ben Zvi: barber in second battalion; born 1837 in Kazmina, Lublin province; inducted 1855; no Russian literacy; tailor; married to Liba, daughter and son, family lived with him.

VERBLOVSKI, Moses ben Zalman: drummer in third battalion; born 1832 in Kireki Ostrov, Augustow province; inducted 1852; reads and writes Russian; no craft; single.

VOLFMAN, Moses ben Hayim Aryeh: private in second battalion; born 1837 in Zvolen, Radom province; inducted 1855; reads and writes Russian; no craft; single.

ZESLER, Moses Zalman ben Jacob: private in regimental headquarters; born 1838 in Vykhovolsk (probably Volkovysk), Grodno province; inducted as Cantonist (no date given); no Russian literacy; smith; single; *ne'eman 'al ha-ma'ot* and *borer* of Society in 1864–5; *borer* in 1866–7.

[Surname unknown]: the child Israel ben Efraim Zvi: in first battalion; no other information.

[Surname unknown]: the child Me'ir Leib ben Abraham: musician in regimental headquarters; no other information.

[Surname unknown]: Efraim ben Simhah: in first battalion; from Granitsa, Radom province; no other information.

Translated by Michael Stanislawski.

Journalism

Jacob Samuel Bick
1772–1831

A journalist, satirist, biographer, and translator from a wealthy commercial family in Brody, Galicia, Jacob Samuel (Ya'akov Shemu'el) Bick was initially a follower of the Haskalah. He advocated changes in education and business, and initially satirized Hasidic practices (apparent in his "Ḥezyone hitul," published in the 1820s), and encouraged the promotion of Yiddish. Though initially critical of Hasidism, Bick ultimately abandoned the Haskalah. He died in a cholera epidemic in Brody, and many of his manuscripts did not survive the Brody fire of 1835.

Letter to Tuvie Feder
1815

"You are angry about the language into which my book has been translated? You sound like chirping birds and clattering animals and wild beasts in the forest! Kindly recall, my dear friend! What language did our fathers, and our fathers' fathers, speak in Poland for about the past four hundred years? It was in that language that our most illustrious geniuses, the author of the *Bayit ḥadash* [R. Joel Sirkes]; R. Moses Isserles; author of the *Sefer Me'irat enayim*; and the Shakh [R. Shabetai ben Meir ha-Kohen]—of blessed memory, spoke and thought and delivered discourses. We indeed heard the Gaon of Vilna, of blessed memory, speaking in this language. The sage Faber might be overly struck by this in his work *Yedi'ot gelilot ha-arets*, ch.1, p. 274 in the Halle edition [published in 5575/1815], reckoning this language as one among the derivatives of German. So, if the language of Germany, the 'first-born,' is so dear to you, why have you not assessed the translation of the Bible by the Magid—the translations *Tsene-rene* and the *Naḥalat Tsevi*? In those works (which were essential for their times and for their communities), the language is replete with errors, and one finds in them no great wealth of pronouns and verbs, nor does one experience any active sensation of elevation therein that would make an impression on any individual with fine literary taste, such as are all to be found in the translation of R. Mendel of Satanov, whose wisdom will lead him onto the pathways of the purest kind for translators, even with regard to phrases that have not yet undergone correction [. . .]

Now the languages of France and of England, which are also included among the languages of 'Ashkenaz,' Gaul, Rome and Greece, have, by virtue of the efforts of the savants of successive generations, become most distinguished over the past three hundred years! While they still contain the aforesaid admixture of other languages, they have become vehicles for lofty poetry and flowery speech, of a most elevated and rarefied kind! About a hundred years ago the German language had lowly status; about eighty years ago, the Russian language was that of peasants; even the ancient tongues, Greek and Latin, were lowly at the beginning of their history until such time as their savants came along, who refined and clarified their vocabulary, created structures, and invented linguistic rules, until they attained that great state of perfection that so astounds us. It is the masses who establish the language of each nation; when initially established, there is no difference between one language and another from the perspective of their worth, save that in one language, the consonants exceed the vowels in number, as is the case with the languages of the northern regions, while in another language, the vowels are greater in number than the consonants, as is the case with the languages of the south! But they are all of a halting nature at the start—possessing neither form nor beauty. It is, however, only the philosophers who will create a lovely vessel and a wondrous form out of raw material and shapeless matter. . . . Put an end to your words! You have not done well, my brother! You will inherit neither honor nor glory when your taunts come to light; send your statements to the sage R. Mendel of Satanov with a view to seeking his forgiveness for having insulted him . . . this is my considered advice to you, tendered by your friend, who desires your welfare, who seeks your good at all times!"

Jacob Samuel Bick

[This note appears in the original *Kol mevaser*.] Editorial Note: Many readers of *Kol mevaser* will not understand the above letter which is written in Hebrew; hence, we feel that it is appropriate to translate it; and in particular, because it was written by a very great man, R. Jacob Samuel Bick of blessed memory, of Brody, a great Talmudic scholar and cultured individual, and a religious Jew. The letter may usefully serve as a riposte to all those who mock simple Yiddish. R. Jacob Samuel Bick wrote this letter to R. Tuvie Feder, who had made fun of the renowned R. Mendel Levine, or alternatively, R. Mendel of Satanov, for having translated the Book of Proverbs into simple Yiddish, and he by way of response justified himself.

Translated by David E. Cohen.

Löw Schwab
1815–1891

Löw Schwab was a controversial Hungarian rabbi, the first rabbi in Moravia to preach in German. He advocated both for moderate reforms of Jewish practice and of Austro-Hungarian law, with the dual goals of reviving of the Jewish faith and state emancipation. Schwab's reformist desires were narrow: he stressed modernization while hoping that educated, increasingly assimilated Jews would stay within the fold. He worked tirelessly to close the radical Reform congregation in Budapest, succeeding in 1852.

The Jews
1840

An Enlightening Treatise and Correction to the Article of the Same Title Written by Mr. Kilit Gasparich and Published on 7 June in Csarnok

A RESPONSE TO MR. G

In the supplement of *Sürgöny*, a certain Mr. Gasparich published an article about the Jews; in it, following numerous impressive sentences, sanctimonious admonitions and heartbreaking sighs over the viciousness of the miserable Jews, and after some *fabricated quotations from the Talmud,* he concludes that Jews should not, must not, be granted civil rights unless they become completely Christian or abandon the Talmud and its "horrible" principles.

My religion and the Talmud (*Pirke avot* 1:6) so condemned by Mr. G. oblige me to assume that everyone has favorable intentions; I thus must accept as true Mr. G.'s declaration that he was inspired to write this article not by hatred, hostility, or some other impure motivation but by the pure love of humanity and noble aims for the benefit of our Christian friends. Additionally, Mr. G. states this declaration and others like it so many times and so seriously, and repeats the teachings of his master so often, talking about his love of humanity and all individuals—not excluding Eskimos, Hottentots, and even Jews—with such interest and such deeply moving words that one would have to have an iron heart to cast doubt over his noble, humane intentions, even though every one of his lines present a bitter challenge to our faith.

Thus, no matter how hard it is for us not to be irritated about the kind of dishonorable nonsense that has been presented and refuted a hundred times before this, no matter how superfluous it is to retaliate seriously and powerfully when we have been attacked by such outdated and rusty weapons of long-refuted prejudices, still, exercising great self-restraint, I would like to call Mr. G's speech a clever argument and subject it to a calm and serious examination. Maybe I will succeed in teaching him something and can correct his views on the "miserable Jewish people" and their religious texts, lessening to some degree the thick darkness of ignorance that surrounds him.

Mr. G. starts off with the observation that *according to the will of fate, the Jewish people have been dispersed among the nations of the world in order to be living proof that internal strife leads to the downfall of a country.* It is quite a clumsy and hackneyed ethic that fate would want to teach people in this manner. There was no need to go so far and to involve such great preparations. The entire history of the world resounds with this message and imbues every nation with the belief that *every country that suffers internal strife will go under.* Moreover, fate could not have found anything less suitable to demonstrate this truth with than the example of the dispersion of the Jews. In the days when it happened, it was the most natural consequence of existing circumstances and the nations were not compelled to attribute moral reason to it. Countries far larger and mightier were also forced to bow to the world power of Rome and subjected themselves to slavery. How could tiny Judea—no matter how brave and heroic—have attempted to shake off the yoke of the tyrant without retribution? The fact that this tiny country subsisted for so long while several world monarchies came and went one after the other is more of a miracle than its demise in the end. Wouldn't the example of Rome, the judge of the world, or artistic and learned Greece, or any other country brought down by internal strife be more suitable for hammering this doctrine into the heads of the nations? But from the point of view of revealed faith, the dispersion of the Jewish people appears in a completely different, much more important light for the objective observer.

The mission of the people of Israel for the nations of the earth relates to its dispersion as well as its chosenness. We can go so far as to say that their dispersion fulfills the mission of chosenness. What we mean is that after the period when Israel was safeguarding the fire of pure knowledge of God that gave light to other nations in its own home, fate ordered them to be dispersed among strangers in order to test their faithfulness to their calling again and again, with the task of serving as a living fountain from which the nations, whose pure knowledge of God had been awakened, could draw good insights in order to strengthen and expand their faith. Israel's duty was to stand among the nations, holding the teachings, their lives embodying the teachings, with miraculous events, with their sturdy faith that defeats even death and humiliation, serving as living proof of God's existence and authority, as an eternal reminder of God's extraordinary acts to provide them with guidance and enlightening, as a living religious certificate that preaches the eternal salvation-truth of God and of fate to every person and every nation in a language intelligible to all. This remains Israel's mission today.

Translated by Vera Szabó, from a translation by Mór Ballagi from German into Hungarian.

Other work by Schwab: *Emlékeztetés vallásban nyert oktatásra az iskolából kilépizraelita ifjúságnak ajándék gyanánt* (1846).

Godchaux Baruch Weil (Ben-Lévi)

The March 17th Decree
1841

> Laws are always tainted by the passions and the prejudices of the legislator.
> —Montesquieu, *The Spirit of the Laws*

In 1807, Mordecai Blum, his wife Rebecca, and his son David were living in a village in Alsace. As in all Jewish families of the time, the father engaged in trade, the son studied Talmud, and the mother took care of the house. Though not very rich, Mordecai Blum was energetic and industrious enough to earn a living and, thanks to the good credit he enjoyed, he even managed to make a profit from his difficult labors. Like others of his kind, he dealt in everything. He bought goods, sold them, and lent money on occasion. Honest in business, trustworthy and charitable, he was generally liked and esteemed—as much as an Israelite could be in that period in Alsace, where a popular prejudice, too old to be uprooted, had established in principle that all Jews were usurers.

David Blum was a tall and handsome young man of twenty, with a calm and reflective nature. Beneath his reserved and timid surface, however, lay original ideas and noble sentiments. He had not limited himself to the study of rabbinical literature but also could read German and French, and he had gained some notions of history from old books bought cheaply off an aristocrat fleeing the revolution. He had thus come to be regarded in the area as a scholar. All the local girls envied Sarah, his fiancée, a young Jewish girl with black hair and bright eyes, who brought him a nice dowry.

Awaiting the time appointed for the union of the young couple, the Blum family lived peacefully and contented until the promulgation of an imperial decree caused the seemingly solid edifice of their happiness to crumble. This decree, which tarnishes the reign of Napoleon with its intolerance, injustice, and disregard for rights, ordained that from March 17, 1808, all French Jews would be forced into military service, without the right to hire a replacement. It contained other draconian measures as well, including the suspension of all obligations, promises, and loans made by a Jew to a non-Israelite unless the lender could prove that he had furnished the full amount of the loan. It's easy to see what havoc such exceptional laws wreaked in Alsace, where nearly all commerce—especially that of money—was in the hands of Israelites.

Among the numerous victims of this iniquitous decree, none was so violently affected as the Blum family. The time to join the army had come for David; his number drawn, he was obliged to leave his parents. As he was leaving, his face burning beneath the tears that his desperate mother spilled on him under the pretext of giving him a goodbye kiss; he received a visit from the father of his fiancée, who informed him—coldly and not without embarrassment—that Sarah couldn't wait for his return and would look for another husband. When poor David had joined his regiment and had begun to adapt to military life, he received terrible news from his family: Mordecai Blum's debtors, immorally profiting from the tyrannical decree against the Jews, were refusing to pay what they owed him unless he could prove he had given them the full sum of the loan. And since such proofs were impossible to give, Mordecai found himself completely ruined overnight. Moreover, since his credit was lost, his lenders, who didn't have to prove anything because they weren't Jews, called in their loans. Because he couldn't pay immediately, he panicked and was declared insolvent. And since of course he didn't keep records, he was condemned to two years in prison for bankruptcy.

As he didn't complain, no one will ever know what Mordecai suffered. A mournful sadness, dull eyes, and hair turned suddenly white were the only signs of his despair until the morning that he was found dead on the foul mattress of his prison. His wife Rebecca had faced everything with a religious resignation, and had even managed to stifle her tears during the hour every day that it was permitted for her to spend at the prison. But once she lost her husband, she gave way to cries of sadness, as well as to threatening curses and fits of rage, which were soon recognized as the symptoms of madness. She became so violently deranged that she had to be locked up in a mental institution, from which God, out of pity, quickly called her to Him.

It would be impossible to describe David Blum's stupor when he received this fatal news in Spain, where he was stationed with his regiment. Constrained by military discipline, he couldn't give full rein to his righteous suffering. He would have surrendered his life to go and defend his father or console his mother, but imprisoned by his uniform, he was not even allowed the sad consolation of crying on their tomb. He cursed the emperor, exhaling his rage in vain threats and his hatred in useless oaths, while his eyes burned with the dark fire of despair and his heart boiled over with the fiery lava of vengeance. Soon he seemed dead to the world. He did his duty with exactitude, but mechanically. He shot and marched with the same inert indifference. A cruel memory had taken over his very being and life became for him a series of lethargic intervals. One day, however, at an inspection, General Guilleminot, struck by the wasted appearance of the young soldier, asked a fellow officer the cause. The latter responded with disdain: "He's an Alsatian Jew and a rather bad soldier. He lacks nerve and courage." At these words, blood rushed to David's head. He stood up straight and grabbed for the handle of his sword. But that flash of animation soon calmed and the pale face of the orphan once again returned to its habitual blankness.

From this time forward, nothing managed to trouble the leaden sleep that weighed down David Blum's senses. When, four years later, he witnessed the burning of Moscow and the sacking of the Kremlin, his calm and indifference did not give away even for an instant amid the dangers that surrounded him. A few days later—it was October 24, 1812—he found himself on the banks of the Luga River with a division of the French army beating a retreat, hotly pursued by the Russians under the command of Kutusoff. The French general, seeing his division getting crushed by the Russian artillery, stationed a hundred of his grenadiers in a church overlooking the road. David was among the hundred brave men who, using the church as cover, fought with such valor that they managed to break the enemy columns five times with their well timed and well aimed fire. They provided the French division the opportunity to regroup in the bottom of a ravine, where, though only eighteen thousand strong, they held out against, and ultimately defeated, fifty thousand Russians. After this brilliant battle, General Guilleminot, the French commander, received the survivors among those valiant grenadiers who had saved the day. David was designated as having been especially intrepid.

"What is your name?" the general asked him.

"David Blum, Alsatian Jew, whom you designated four years ago in Spain as a bad soldier."

"You are a brave man, David Blum, and I am making you an officer."

"Thank you, general, but I want nothing. I fought in order to defend the lives of my comrades and not for your emperor who ruined, dishonored, and caused the death of my family. . . ."

A few weeks later, the French army, in total chaos, was attempting its disastrous retreat across the Beresina. Cold and hunger had strewn the countryside with the dead and dying. Stopping to warm himself at a bivouac, Napoleon was astonished at the morale that one group of soldiers had managed to maintain amid the terrifying disorder of the rest of the army.

"We owe our lives to our comrade David Blum," they told him. "His energy has sustained ours. His courage has saved us from skirmishes with the Cossacks. And his prudence has always provided us with food and fire."

"David Blum," the emperor said in the voice that made all the thrones of Europe tremble, and that, when he wanted to, he could make so sweet and appealing. "You are a good soldier and I offer you a place in my Old Guard." Removing a silver cross that adorned his uniform, he gave it to the Jewish soldier. Overcome by the old hatred that was fermenting in him, but at the same time fascinated by the respectful fear that everyone else felt in the presence of the emperor, David responded with firmness, although his face betrayed the emotions that agitated his soul:

"Sire! I am an Alsatian Jew and cannot accept either advancement or decoration, because to do so would be to accept blood money for my family who were dishonored by the odious decree of March 17th . . ."

"Ah!" responded the displeased emperor, "I have been told of that." He added in a curt tone: "They deceived me yet again in this matter, but we will take it under consideration." A cloud passed over his features, a deep ridge crossed his large brow. Then, as if he wanted to shake off an unpleasant thought, he jumped onto his horse and galloped away, followed by his silent general staff.

Translated by Maurice Samuels.

Die Allgemeine Zeitung des Judentums
1842

This announcement appeared in a German Jewish periodical on July 23, 1842, welcoming what was going to be the first Ladino periodical, *La Buena Esperansa*, projected to appear in Izmir in 1842. The project failed; however, the announcement contains two garbled lines in square Hebrew-Ladino print, all that survives of the prospectus prepared by the prospective editor, Rafael Uziel.

La Buena Esperansa (The Good Hope)
1842

Hamburg, July 7. (Personal communication) In Smyrna, a newspaper will now be published in the Jewish-Spanish language commonly spoken there, entitled *La Buena Esperansa*. We have the prospectus dated 12 Sivan, which announces the subscription price of 100 piasters per annum (approximately 12 thalers) and a weekly publication. The contents will contain commercial news, current commodity prices, exchange rates, shipping port traffic reports, auction and sales announcements, as well as political news from all parts of the world, and finally articles aimed at spreading light and knowledge among the Jews of the Turkish Empire. [Here follows an approximate reconstruction of the two Ladino quotations from Uziel's prospectus.] "And we will often publish things necessary for success with which few people of our nation in these parts are familiar. . . . But the sages in our parts of Turkey do not waste or employ their time on such things, nor do they study, and this is so because of the great poverty and a great lack of money in these parts."

Translated from German by Carola Murray-Seegert; translated from Ladino by Olga Borovaya.

David Kuh
1818–1879

David Kuh was born in Prague, studied in Vienna, and helped to found German-language newspapers in Budapest and Pécs. Though in his youth he was a proponent of Czech nationalism, antisemitic rhetoric and riots during the 1840s led him to reverse his position and support German political parties. In addition to his career as a journalist he was also a politician (he founded the Deutsche Freiheitliche Partei and also served on the Bohemian Diet and the Imperial Diet) and a poet, and in his final years he founded a publishing house in Prague. A legal case against the scholar Václav Hanka, whom Kuh accused of forgery, led to Kuh's libel conviction, a case that brought out anti-Jewish sentiments.

A Word to Jews and Slavs
1844

Conclusion

But you, West Slavic Jews, you who are so proud of your intelligence and education, you who are so proud of the sciences that you tend like exotic plants [. . .] I ask whether you are so weighed down by oppression that you must wait until someone elevates you and approaches you!

I ask whether you are also proud to be almost the last among your coreligionists in Europe to firmly, closely and joyfully affiliate with a European nationality! While the blame for this lapse is only in small part yours, and the obstacles you must overcome are great, very great, then so much greater must be your efforts and endurance, in order to reach such a glorious goal.

Among the members of your faith, you are known for being witty and perceptive. Because of that, it is not so long ago that the vast majority of Europe's Israelite communities appointed their teachers and rabbis from your midst. Does your heart not swell when, in awareness of your power, you realize that your art and science could be nurtured and cultivated in the language and the ethos of your countrymen, and that men of yours could also be leaders among their learned and wise and, through their blessed gifts, spread light, drive away darkness, and with that the prejudice against you?

Does your heart not swell, when you realize that apart from your great missions and tasks, which you regard as unfinished, you could be called upon to implement the highest and most noble ideals? Called to transmit the spirit from Western and Eastern Europe and called, like the other Western Slavs, to the spiritual dominion over those people who will be the flag-bearers of European education for the people of the Orient?

Your brethren in Germany thought this way and proceeded accordingly; you however—you could accomplish ten times more than they. Others would not view the benefits and advantages you might so acquire with hostility or envy: no, they would bless you for joining in the effort and helping to reach the lofty goal. Ha! What a benefit for art and science, what a benefit for both Jewish and Christian Slavs, if you, almost to a man, would pursue Slavic literature with the same zeal as you now apply to the Talmudic, one that is presently so little known and one-sided.

Unlike all the other harshly oppressed, of whom not one has suffered comparably, you have not surrendered yourselves to uncontrolled sensual pleasures in order to find comfort and numbness in misfortune; unlike all the other slaves, you did not become dull and insensitive: no, your spirit is serene and alert, your heart remains warm and sensitive because you have conquered and preserved a realm, although elsewhere excluded and confined to a narrow *Judengasse* [Jewish lane] in which you can freely joust.

And so you, you who would be respected, unlike animals and those deprived of human rights, you have always esteemed and protected the divine spark in men, the spirit, and have never let it be suppressed: the greatest hero of Slavic literature, one of the most exalted poets and noblest combatants for justice and truth, is thought to be one of your blood. May he be a bright star who illuminates a new path for you, and may he provide brilliant evidence to your Christian compatriots that your blood, too, is a knightly and noble one.

His forefathers were oppressed and scorned like you. But in your case, here and now, idle words will not suffice. You must become actively involved, sacrifice much and tear down much in order to achieve more greatly, to build more splendidly. You must put aside and slough off everything that is foreign in your appearance. If the honorable costume of the ancient Sarmatians makes their descendants objects of mockery, then you must cast it off; why should you, of all people, cling to it so faithfully? If the man's beard, as an emblem of Judaism, has become a cause for laughter, then you must cut it off. Nothing from your side, including your appearance, can be allowed to separate you from your Christian brethren, to impede socialization.

The wish that Slavic languages be taught in your schools is one that some of you share: you must now try to make this a reality. The time will then come when you must no longer go begging to your brethren in Germany to quench your oft stirring thirst for European knowledge and culture. Then you, as well as your far less numerous brethren in Holland, Belgium, Denmark and North America—as it is in France, England, and especially in Germany—would have your own publications for your religious and social settings, for all academic faculties, and for the branches of your history and literature.

If, presently, it also came to pass that in your synagogues your rabbis and preachers would let the word of God ring out each week in the language of the country, this too might play a part as an exceptional element that would stimulate some national and spiritual interests, bring you esteem and prestige, and promote a convergence that would be of equal, mutual benefit to both parties.

Translated by Carola Murray-Seegert.

Other work by Kuh: *Album der Erinnerungen* (under the pseudonym Emil Dornau; 1856).

Rafael Uziel
1816–1881

Rafael Uziel was a merchant, journalist, and publisher of the first Ladino periodical. A Tuscan subject, he was born in Izmir, where his ancestors had moved from Livorno in the seventeenth century. In 1842, Uziel attempted to publish a Ladino newspaper, *La Buena Esperansa* (The Good Hope), but did not succeed because he could not garner enough subscriptions. In 1845, however, he began to publish *Sha'are mizraḥ/Las puertas de Oriente* (The Gates of the East). Printed by an English Protestant press, the first Ladino newspaper appeared through November 1846, when it closed for financial reasons. Later, Uziel moved to Gallipoli and the Dardanelles, where he represented the Alliance Israélite Universelle and served as a correspondent for the Paris Ladino periodical *El verdadero progreso israelita*.

Editor's Note in Sha'are mizraḥ (Gates of the East)
1846

We gratefully acknowledge the signs of munificence shown to us by His Majesty's government which has officially licensed our periodical, *Sha'are mizraḥ*. We understand that this benevolence of His Majesty's government toward us shows that he wants us, as well as the other nations subjects of His Majesty, to be informed and developed in all things, because he is sure that the benefits of the press are so great that we can become as knowledgeable in all sciences as the most civilized nations of Europe. Let us respond to this benevolence by making every effort to instruct our sons and relatives in all fields of knowledge encouraging everything that serves public good so that we can prosper in everything and be united in everything as worthy subjects of such a gracious and just sovereign as His Majesty, *yod-resh-he* [May he be exalted].

Translated by Olga Borovaya.

Rafael Uziel

On the Discords among the Jews of Izmir
1846

Gentlemen, having received incorrect information in the last column of the previous issue, we reported that the discords in our community had been settled. We also promised to give a detailed account of this much-desired peace, which is what we hoped for. "We hoped for good fortune," etc.,[1] "when they heard how I was sighing."[2] As if it were not enough that we endure afflictions everywhere else, now we suffer seeing the disarray and poor administration in the Jewish community of Izmir. . . . "Because of this our hearts are sick, because of these our eyes are dimmed."[3]

The same controversy and nearly the same disputes that we see today occurred in our community in 5599 [1839]. Everybody already knows about the great harm they caused as well as about the two parties' mutual insults and resentment, and especially about the amount of money both parties spent [to further their cause]. But the worst thing was the great desecration of God to which it led: we were scorned and shamed by the nations.[4] And so many storms have erupted around us that it is impossible to recount even one percent of those troubles. Finally, after two years of continuous controversies, on II Av 5601 [July 29, 1841], great fire descended from heaven and burned down two thirds of Izmir, our beautiful and illustrious city. Two thirds, I tell you. Ninety percent of Jewish houses were destroyed in this great disaster. Within sixteen hours the city of Izmir was destroyed and desolate. All people, men and women, young and old, were crying out loudly and bitterly, weeping, and begging God for mercy. Those who had died of hunger and thirst were lying in the middle of the streets, as the prophet said [of those] "who faint for hunger at every street corner."[5] Day and night we pray to the great and merciful God that this shall not happen to us again. "Nevermore shall you be called 'Forsaken,' nor shall your land be called 'Desolate.'"[6]

What was the cause of the disaster that befell us? The great animosity that reigned among us, the great hatred between us. Why was our Temple destroyed? Why was our Jerusalem desolate? "Fair Jerusalem; 'Is this the city that was called perfect in beauty?'"[7] "The crown has fallen from our head; Woe to us that we have sinned!"[8] Why did we become slaves among the nations? Why are we in this sad and despondent condition? Finally, why do we live in such misery? All of this is because of our terrible crimes, unwarranted hatred, speaking evil of others, desecration of God, and murder. May he who in his mercy and grace forgives crimes and absolves sins forgive us our crimes and absolve us and all sinners in his great name. . . . "Turn from Your blazing anger, and renounce the plan to punish Your people."⁹ "Look and save the sheep of your flock,"¹⁰ "because you are a compassionate and merciful king."¹¹

After all these troubles and misfortunes had passed, "the land had peace for four years."¹² For about four years there was some peace in the city. Three or four months ago, one could notice that a new upheaval threatened to emerge in the community, but nobody tried to prevent it from spreading. A great fire inflamed the Jewish community in all parts of the city. Thus the controversy of 5599 [1839] returned. As we explained in the previous issue, the community is split into two parties: one seems to have forgotten what that infamous controversy led to four years ago; the other does not remember the past [at all]. After two years of upheaval, neither of the parties gained anything, [and] there was no improvement. And thus one party lost as much as the other. There was no time of healing,¹³ and the upper classes lost the reputation and influence they had enjoyed in the community. And nothing has been gained. Brothers, "Let us search and examine our ways, and turn back to the Lord."¹⁴ Now we are humbly begging our esteemed rabbis, highly revered shepherds of this flock, filled with zeal and love of God and the people, to embrace peace¹⁵ and step in between the two parties. Gentlemen, take on the work of Aaron, the High Priest. Find a reasonable agreement that would suit both parties. Let peace and love dwell in our community. Wake up, gentlemen, act like fathers toward their children. "He cares about the poor and the needy; He brings the needy deliverance. He redeems them from fraud and lawlesness; the shedding of their blood weighs heavily upon him."¹⁶ Help the people to achieve abundance and prosperity. All our misery is caused by these terrible controversies, hatred, and animosity. Therefore, do your best to conciliate them, so that a worse disaster may not occur. We are sure that in the next issue, with God's help, we will report on the agreement and complete peace that will [soon] reign in our community.

"May the Lord grant strength to His people! May the Lord bestow on His people wellbeing!"¹⁷

NOTES

Words in brackets appear in the original translation.

1. Jeremiah 8:15. The full verse reads: "We hoped for good fortune, but no happiness came; for a time of relief—instead there is terror!"

2. Lamentations 1:21.

3. Lamentations 5:17.
4. Non-Jews.
5. Lamentations 2:19.
6. Isaiah 62:4.
7. Lamentations 2:15.
8. Lamentations 5:16.
9. Exodus 32:12b.
10. From the *Tahanun*, or supplication, which forms part of the morning and afternoon prayers.
11. From the Arvit le-Shabat prayer.
12. Judges 3:11, but replacing "forty" with "four," a reckoning that better suited Uziel's account.
13. A paraphrase of Jeremiah 8:15.
14. Lamentations 3:40.
15. Paraphrase of Psalm 132:9: "Your priests are clothed in triumph."
16. Psalm 72:13–14.
17. Psalm 29:11.

Translated by Olga Borovaya.

Giuseppe Levi and Esdra Pontremoli

Levi, 1814–1874

Pontremoli, 1818–1888

Giuseppe Levi and Esdra Pontremoli were the editors of *L'educatore Israelita: Giornale di letture per le famiglie israelitiche* (The Israelite Educator: Newspaper of Readings for Jewish Families), the first Italian Jewish monthly periodical, founded in 1853, distributed widely across the emerging nation, and published in fifty volumes. As Italy was formed over the course of the century, Levi and Pontremoli, both rabbis, held out hope that the nascent nation would offer new opportunities and recognition of Italian Jews. The newspaper changed its name upon the death of Levi, and continued publication until 1922.

L'educatore Israelita: A Newspaper of Readings for Jewish Families. Compiled by the Teachers Giuseppe Levi and Esdra Pontremoli
1853

Preface

We have already offered a glimpse, in our program, into the nature of this publication. Yet the desire to open our heart, especially to those benevolent people who have looked favorably upon our initiative, induces us to begin this volume with a fuller explanation of our thoughts.

In this publication we do not propose to create or present things that are out of the ordinary or new, or to present ourselves as messengers or apostles of new religious ideas. Even a genius in our century would possibly fail in such a mission, as it is beyond our capacity and far from our intention. We seek only to follow the paths of the teachers, to repeat what is known to the sages, that which all the teachers know how to teach to their students, and to complete that humble task with youth who are far away, a task which throughout the year we carry out with the youth who are entrusted to us.

We are not unaware that by adopting an idea that is not ambitious but rather humble and simple, especially well known and old, without the trappings of the kind of novelty that in so sweet a fashion tickles the fancy of the soul, we run the risk of stirring up at the very outset in many of our coreligionists, the various characters and affections not always apt to encourage us in our endeavor. Among our coreligionists, as in all the other confessions, there are numerous levels with respect to faith, from the most rigorous and blind Orthodoxy, [. . .] to the most reckless Philosophy. In this diverse spectrum of thinkers and believers, how few indeed will greet this publication with joy and hope! The indifferent, that class of people who are largely destructive because they are numb and bereft of strong feelings, barely move their pallid lips in a faint snicker and go on. The incredulous people look down from the height of their astonishment and, between scorn and disdain, turn their gaze away from us after looking upon us with great indifference. The believer himself, as with regard to something that is good yet useless and dangerous, shrugs warily, between suspicion and hope.

Even though we suppose that there will be so little interest on the part of many of our coreligionists, we would like to hope that, once we have begun some steps in this direction, little by little these clouded expressions will grow serene, harsh faces will be calmed, and hostile, suspicious and uncertain people will become friendly and open. The first reaction is mired in uncertainty and suspicion, but through drawn-out conversations friends are made and they explain things to each other and arrive at an understanding.

In order to hastily bring about this reconciliation we want to open our hearts and make our idea known in its entirety.

It is the bad habit of some (for reasons that are more or less unjust and which I do not want to discuss) to associate the idea of religion with a divorce from all forms of human progress, from the marvels of the human mind. For them religion entails a return to the past, a repudiation of the present and the future.

We wish to protest this by showing that we do not accept this divorce between religion and progress. As sons of this century, we admire its glories and creations and feel their greatness. We do not look back to past centuries, the images of which we are fleeing but which we regret. We fully embrace the progress of the present and the hope of the future, and we irrevocably desire to leave behind those centuries of strife and blood and recognize the sublime law made by God for man to explain in an ever greater way the power of the mind and the heart, as a testimony to that infinite science of which it is but a pallid reflection.

Yet if the needs of the material presented find easier and fuller satisfaction in the new wealth that is made available thanks to human industriousness, if the mind is sublimated in the marvelous creations of science, if the heart itself opens with trust and joy to the mildest customs of the present, there are nonetheless, in the soul, secret, indistinct and powerful aspirations, needs, desires and hopes for which science has no words and for which all the miracles of the century do not suffice to satisfy or satiate.

Translated by James N. Novoa.

Ezekiel Gabay
1825–1898

Ezekiel (Yeḥezkel) Gabay, born in Baghdad, was a Jewish community leader, Ottoman government official, and journalist. He served as secretary of the Meclis Pekidim, the lay council of notables in charge of communal affairs, which was established in Istanbul in 1860 with the goal of reforming the community administration. This council, which consisted of members of the Sephardic pro-Western elite, propagated its ideas through the first long-lived Ladino periodical, *El Jurnal israelit* (1860–1873), edited by Gabay, and eventually banned by the rabbis. In 1869, Gabay became a government official and, subsequently, president of the supreme criminal court. An expert in Islamic law, in 1865 he wrote "The Organic

Statute of the Jewish Nation in Turkey" (*Hahamhane Nizamnamesi*) in Ottoman Turkish, which was later incorporated into the Ottoman civil code; he also created syllabi for Jewish schoolchildren.

From the Editor, El Jurnal israelit
1860

From the Editor:

With God's help, the time has come for our newspaper to appear before the community, and I am sure that at first our esteemed subscribers will not judge us for its errors, because all beginnings are difficult, and little by little we will correct these errors. And I thank my patrons at the Meclis Pekidim,[1] who decided to establish this newspaper, so much needed and required by the community and even more so by the government, whose goal is to do everything possible so that the people would not lack any knowledge.

Until now, many newspapers were founded and began to come out, but none of them managed to survive, because nobody supported them except for their publishers, and nobody appreciated their significance. Now that many other good and important things have been introduced in our nation, the Meclis Pekidim established *El Jurnal israelit*.[2] We must first of all ask the pure and almighty God on High to give a long and brilliant life to our ruler, our king, the source of our life, king of the earth and master of the seas, a king who is son of a king who was son of another king, Sultan Abdulmecid, may He exalt his majesty, may his glory and power extend from one end of the earth to the other. In his time, the world saw the light and brilliance of science, and many implements were invented to facilitate knowledge and inquiry and to ensure that we would not miss anything. Our nation has taken similar measures and is trying to promote progress.

I hope that with the help, first of all, of the almighty God and also of the Meclis Pekidim, our newspaper will succeed and, even though it starts as a weekly, will grow to a daily. I am asking my esteemed subscribers in all parts to welcome and encourage this periodical, so that it can develop and continue to appear. May it be favorable before Him, may it be according to His honor that the Messiah come and reveal himself, he "who announces peace, who brings good news, who announces salvation, who says to Zion, 'Your God reigns'" [Isaiah 52:7].

Ezekiel Yeḥezkel Gabay
El Jurnal israelit, 27 December 1860

NOTES

1. [Lay council of notables in charge of communal affairs established in Istanbul in 1860.—Trans.]
2. [It came out in Istanbul between 1860 and 1873 and was edited by Ezekiel Gabay.—Trans.]

Translated by Olga Borovaya.

Other works by Gabay: *El Kanun name de penas: Letras de nuestro senyor El rey* (1860); *El Buen Dotrino* (1861); *El kateshizmo por Menester de las Eskloas Yisraelitas en la Turkiya* (1879).

Daniel Neufeld
1814–1874

An educator who was born in Praszka, Poland, and attended a Catholic secondary school, Daniel Neufeld advocated for reform in the language, dress, and customs of Polish Jews. As a Polish patriot, he was affiliated with the Polish-language Jewish newspaper *Jutrzenka* and was sent into exile in Russia for his views. Although not sympathetic to Hasidism, he argued for gentle persuasion toward modernity. In addition to writing biblical commentary and translating Hebrew prayer books into Polish, he wrote poetry in both languages.

Editorial about Jews in the American Civil War
1861

Warsaw, August 15, 1861 [in the weekly journal Jutrzenka (Dawn), August 16, 1861]

Everyone knows the reason behind the fratricidal war between secessionists and unionists in the United States. We touch upon the war in this weekly, to the extent that the subject falls into our sphere of interest.

We previously communicated a short message about the war zeal that has overwhelmed our fellow-believers in America and about how everybody is flocking under the banner of the unionists (no. 2, p. 15). We cited this as proof that Jews always and everywhere unite with the nation that does not restrict them in the enjoyment of civic rights, as proof that they can be fit for military service just like any other race; and we were glad to see our American coreligionists who, not by futile declamations but with weapons in their hands, defended humanity's cause to abolish the bondage of Negroes, connected to the cause of the nation of which they are a constituent part. To complement that message, we moreover add that among the men who, after the ghastly scenes of murder committed on the 19th and 20th in Baltimore, had to seek refuge in flight, was a local rabbi Dr. Einhorn [Rabbi David Einhorn] who edited a pamphlet in which he challenged the hypocritical statement of Rabbi Raphael [Rabbi Morris J. Raphall], in New York, that slavery was permissible according to Divine Law: a statement that would be more typical of a cruel plantation owner than of a rabbi professing the thoroughly humane teachings of Moses.[1]

Lack of bias requires that we do not pass over in silence the acts of our American coreligionists, who oppose the abolition of slavery, all the more because such acts are occasionally supported by armed action. The New York German commercial daily of May 8th reports as follows: In Westpoint, Georgia, a company of Jewish insurgents was formed, who have sworn the oath: "Erect the banner of slavery on the Capitol in Washington, or die!" With love toward our coreligionists, adds our editor, Mr. Mayer, who is a Jew, we wish that the second part of this oath be fulfilled. Reporting on these occurrences, a reporter with the *Journal of Judaism* states, inter alia: "Were those people willing to identify with Judaism, they would better remember that their conduct deviates from the religion that binds them to act against bondage, and betrays the union that was the first on the globe to utter and announce equal rights in religion not only as domestic law but as a natural law of humankind, and that this very fact marked a turn toward our better fortune. *Every Jew who raises his hand against the union should be regarded as participating in patricide.*"

For us, unbiased judges of the American cause, the events—although we are indignant to the quick at the sight of the downtrodden prestige of sanctity of the Divine Law, which is used and abused by a rabble of impudent empty-hearted people as a pretense to oppress their fellow-creatures—what I am saying is that for us, these sorrowful events are consoling in that, at least, they offer us new proof that confutes the old charge that Jews, dispersed all around the world, form a homogeneous force of personal views that are inimical to all nationalities.

And so we can see a part of this formidable power, with which reactionaries are wont to frighten us, in a country where personal liberty has reached the remotest edges of possibility, and where, therefore, such power could develop with the least restraint: it is there that we can see it divided into two hostile camps, each of which, with the Bible in one hand and a sword in the other, is defending the cause of the province to which it belongs, not even being forced to do so by the law of military conscription, which is unknown in the United States. Each of them, following the traces of their fellow-citizens of other denominations, demonstrates the reasonableness of his cause out of Moses himself, and both support these demonstrations with the strength of weaponry; and we can see the followers of Judaism fighting against one another regardless of the community of faith, as we have every so often seen Christians of diverse nationalities standing up to fight in opposing ranks despite their religious identity.

Where is, therefore, the conjectured solidarity among all the Jews in the world? Such phantasms and such suspicions could only have been hatched in the morbid brain of fanatics. As for us, we hold it as a sacred obligation toward our country to confute such extravagancies of fantasy at every single opportunity, and, remaining mindful of the importance of the subject, we shall incessantly repeat, and incessantly demonstrate, repeat and demonstrate ad nauseam, that Jews, merely forming a religious association that is less permanent, less cemented and less organized, as is the case with all associations of this sort, cannot be a nation within the other nation, in no country and upon no condition, whatsoever!

NOTE

1. [Both Raphall's and Einhorn's words on slavery can be found in this volume.—Ed.]

Translated by Tristan Korecki; edited by Marian Krzyzowski.

Other works by Neufeld: *Pięcioksiąg Mojżesza dla Żydów-Polaków* (1863); *Modlitewnik dla Żydów-Polaków* (1865).

Daniel Neufeld

The Hebrew Crusading Newspaper
1861

We [of the Polish weekly journal *Jutrzenka* (Dawn), October 25, 1861] have already had the opportunity to mention a number of periodicals devoted entirely to

Jewish affairs. We have also named three similar Hebrew-language journals, among which the oldest is *Ha-Magid,* published in Ełk (no. 4, p. 28).

By and large, we consider Hebrew folk periodicals to be of necessity a temporary measure for Israelites who do not yet have command of the language of the country in which they are citizens. The goals of such journals were outlined almost a century ago by the Mendelssohn school, which in its journal titled *Ha-Me'asef* (The Collector), published in Hebrew and in German, established a school for reform both inside and outside civilization.

Aside from its religious writing, *Ha-Magid* offers mainly political news, analyzing it like a born diplomat privy to all-and-any European affairs, and resolves the most burning questions: Roman, American, or Danish; digs up the Isthmus of Suez; dismantles Turkey; and even sets off on expeditions to China and Siam.

In one of these political excursions, mind you, *Ha-Magid* drops in on Poland, sits in the editor's chair, and, with no knowledge of our relations in ancient or in contemporary Poland, assumes the amusing role of denunciator, repeating threadbare charges, and, finally, apostrophizing us *brethren* in Poland, saying: "Who is it that has robbed, killed, tormented us—it is the Poles! . . . Remember this, O my brothers! We have been told in truth, that Poles and Jews have reconciled, but we don't believe in this love: the age-long mutual hatred betwixt the two nations does not turn into love overnight. A Pole will bond with a Jew only out of self-interest; such is the age-old truth. . . ."

We are not surprised at *Ha-Magid's* ignorance of national history and politics, for this often occurs: nor are we surprised that it objects to our reconciliation, which has been rapturously applauded by Jewish journals all over the world, not even excluding the journal *Zion,* issued *in the Russian language in Odessa,* since the sobriquet of our people, throughout the ages, states that this people is a *magid pesha* (fabricator); but what we nonetheless cannot comprehend is how they have so deeply not appreciated the spirit of their readers in Poland. Reconciliation, the effects of which are deservedly feared by *Ha-Magid* (in respect to itself), is an accomplished fact: *blind is he who cannot see it!* No solicitation nor endeavor in this world will ever sever the ties of this unity, not betwixt the two nations, as *Ha-Magid* words it, for nowhere are Jews a nation within a nation (why would the politicizing *Ha-Magid* not be aware of this truth?) but between the two tribes that now find it so convenient to have concord that they *jointly* offer thanks to the Eternal God in their temples every day.

Let us avoid further remarks with respect to the sagacious ideas of Polish history as elaborated upon in *Ha-Magid,* as these fall beyond our weekly's scope; the political press is capable of defending itself from the slander shamefully cast at our past: we would nevertheless advise *Ha-Magid* to replace the *ha-emet ve-ha-shalom* (Truth and Peace) as its motto, with *ha-sheker ve-ha-medanim* (Lies and Dissension), and instead of quoting the prophet Zechariah, may it call upon the false prophets of its prototype, the Crusading Newspaper [*Gazeta Krzyżowa*]!

Translated by Tristan Korecki; edited by Marian Krzyzowski.

Al. K.

Newspaper correspondence points to the class divisions within the Polish Jewish community, and to the question of methods considered unsuited for calling attention to such issues.

Response to a Writer's Letter in *Jutrzenka,* January 3, 1862
1862

Correspondence
Warsaw, 15 December 1861

Mr. Medard's reply to our letter dated 15 November has not, in the least, surprised us; we had indeed expected it, exactly in the form in which it is composed. The excuse of the author in response to the charges presented against him is one more piece of evidence that goodwill is always the driving force behind what our writers pronounce; even when pointing out the faults of our fellow-believers, they don't look at the means but only aim confidently to achieve their goals.

Therefore, it is our turn today to explain the reasons behind our somewhat acrid commentaries against Mr. Medard in our previous letter, because somebody might conjecture, especially after having read the author's defense, that we have challenged the freedom to highlight the flaws of the lower classes of our coreligionists, whether in a novel or on the stage, and that thereby, holding *noli nos tangere* as our motto, we consider ourselves independent of the laws of satire.

Such thoughts have always been, and remain, remote from us.

We know all too well the imperfections of our lower-class fellow-believers; we know that their glaring distinction in attire, speech, and mores from the progressive class should be subject to radical measures of reform; but is it appropriate, as it were, to mimic their mannerisms and language in novels and on the stage to achieve these measures? We do not think so.

The class against which the missiles of satire are delivered is, regretfully, unenlightened to such an extent that it cannot benefit from the satire; in turn, one who is involuntarily condemned to read such pieces feels painfully affected by the insinuations that exceed the limits of satire. Why, therefore, acquiesce to the uncertain if, leaving the resolution of such an issue of social importance to time, one may expect a far quicker result?

Instead of mocking the speech of street peddlers, had the authors of social satire respectfully admonished those of our coreligionists who have sealed themselves off into their own "selves," and forgotten their duties toward their impoverished brethren, and for whom there is nothing sacred on this earth save for wealth; then, not only would we not feel offended but, indeed, we would be grateful to them for their willingness.[1] Yet, alas! the role of satire has hitherto been confined to mimicry of the language of those strata of society that, doomed by fate to be isolated within the nation, have *proven incapable* of accepting this cardinal foundation of progress and civilization. A detail so important, justifying the existing state of affairs, has been completely neglected by the writers of social satire: they took things as they appeared to them in nature . . . and hence, their satirical pieces could not inspire confidence and propitiate adherents: every instance of their appearance was regarded, although unfairly, as a symptom of their being part of a coterie, malice, *et inde irae*.

Today, with such vehement attempts to improve the behavior of all strata of our society, there is no way for satire not to achieve a position corresponding to its vocation; today, I am saying, we ought to maintain a watchful eye on it, so that it may never deviate, even for a moment, from its designated track, and instead of being a proselytising master, turn into a caustic crank.

We have come out against Mr. Medard's tale for the sole reason that it has again brought before our eyes those traditional figures who speak in a weirdly distorted language; for we suspect underlying malevolence in this somewhat overly passionate representation of them that is seemingly betrayed by the astringent tone in a few of the sections. But the author's defense has convinced us that we prejudged this story, and considered as animosity that which apparently ensued from the author's intent to render the presented picture conspicuously as an accurate photograph . . . therefore, now changing our previous presumption, we must remind Mr. Medard that what we look for in a novel is, primarily, beauty, and that even realism clothed in a vestment of fantasy ought not to dazzle with its bareness; otherwise, apart from being a Flemish picture, a given story could have no other advantage.

NOTE

1. Considering these flaws not as a characteristic attribute of one stratum of the populace but rather as a universal law of human infirmities, would obviously be the primary condition for such satire.

Translated by Tristan Korecki; edited by Marian Krzyzowski.

Shiye Mordkhe Lifshits
1829–1878

Shiye Mordkhe Lifshits, who spent most of his life in Berdichev, was a pioneering linguist and lexicographer, and an exponent of modern Yiddish culture and the idea of political Yiddishism. In contrast to other *maskilim* who denigrated Yiddish as a backward, mongrel tongue, Lifshits believed that the language could be utilized to spread Enlightenment values to a mass audience. In this regard, he helped Sholem Yankev Abramovitsh, the great fiction writer, to switch to Yiddish as his main form of literary expression. Lifshits was also likely instrumental in pushing Alexander Zederbaum to publish *Kol mevaser*, Russia's first Yiddish periodical. Lifshits's lexicographical work, particularly on his native Volhynian dialect, and in his multilingual dictionaries, was groundbreaking.

Yudl and Yehudis
1862

Meaning the Jews and Their Yiddish Language

YEHUDIS: Yidele—a question. Hear me out.
  And please don't interrupt and start to shout.

YIDELE: I'm not exactly in the mood, my dear,
   But go ahead and ask me and I'll hear.
YEHUDIS: That's the very problem that I face:
   The way you treat me is a big disgrace.
   You think you are so lofty, great and wise.
   But as for me—you just avert your eyes.
   You're full of smiles for everyone but me,
   But I'm belittled, as the world can see.
YIDELE: I don't enjoy this life of ours, you see.
   Each time you speak it makes me want to flee.
   And what about your looks? They're even worse!
   I look upon our marriage as a curse.
YEHUDIS: Oh, alas, how tragic is my fate,
   That Yidele should end up as my mate!
   You look at others full of admiration
   To bow to them is then my obligation.
   You envy all the others without measure
   And looking just at strangers is your pleasure.
YIDELE: I wish that from this life I could be freed:
   The truth is that I live it out of need.
   Others bring some beauty to my life.
   I'll bow to them, but never to my wife!
   Their pearls of wisdom are my greatest joys
   But when you talk it simply sounds like noise.
YEHUDIS: That sad, unhappy story is quite old:
   How often has it tearfully been told!
   Someone else's wife looks good to you,
   She's beautiful and wise and charming too.
   But once these wives were uglier than me,
   They wrote and spoke just like a child of three.
   But they had better luck—and better goals
   So now they're fit to play important roles.
   They were dressed with elegance and flair
   They danced and laughed and didn't have a care.
   And if you'd dressed me up in lavish style,
   And pampered me and loved me all the while . . .
   It might at first seem difficult to do
   But later you'd have pleasure from me, too.
YIDELE: I must admit, your argument rings true.
   But there's one thing that I'll forever rue.
   I miss my former wife—why did we part?
   That causes me such pain inside my heart.
   To lose a brilliant diamond is so cruel!
   The whole wide world believed she was a jewel.
   Her charm and virtue never could be faulted,
   Her ancestry was noble and exalted.
   Your ancestry is murky and in doubt
   Your origins are scattered all about.
   Her name inspires worshipers far-flung:
   No Yiddish jargon, she. She's "Holy Tongue"!
YEHUDIS: I know the Holy Tongue as well as you,
   I honor her and love her beauty too.
   And what I hope her future fate will be
   Is just the same as what I wish for me.
   Do not think I hate her, wish her ill,
   Instead I hold her dear, and always will.
   But don't forget that in this present day
   She's in the past, and I am here to stay.
   Your visits may be formal and polite,
   But I'm the one you need both day and night.
   She's beautiful and charming, I've no doubt,
   But I'm the one you cannot do without.
   Her standing in the world is truly high,
   But who has borne your children—she or I?
   You can't go back to her, you foolish man,
   It's just a waste of time to think you can.
   Go see some other ladies—I won't balk.
   Go stroll with them and chat and talk.
   But even as their company you keep,
   Beware, I say, of getting in too deep.
   They'll only turn your head, but in the end
   You'll see you'll never be their friend.
   You hope to be accepted by the best?
   You'll have to treat your wife as do the rest.
   So why not dress me up and make me pure?
   I soon will have great beauty and allure.
   In no time flat you'll see how I have grown
   I'll soon possess a greatness of my own.
   My lovely songs for you are sure to please,
   Like nightingales that warble in the trees.
   I'll learn to read, I'll write what books you need.
   Wisdom for the masses is my creed!
   You'll see—my mind is nimble like a hare
   And it will give you pleasure, I declare.
   The end result will benefit us both.
   I pledge it and I swear a holy oath.
   But do you fear to send your wife to school?
   Then I'm afraid you're acting like a fool.
   I'm sorrier for you much more than for me
   You're dirtying your face but cannot see.
   That's not the way for decent folk to act:
   I won't put up with it for long, and that's a fact!

Ha-melits's editors have heard and read
Each word Yehudis plaintively said.
And so we answer in our journal's name:
"All this squabbling really is a shame:
Creating peace and love in place of strife

Between a Jewish husband and his wife—
A virtue that our learned sages bless.
So, Yidele, be honest and confess:
Yehudis is not ugly. Just rejoice
In all her folk songs and her lovely voice;
In the way she translates Holy Writ
And Talmud, with such subtle wit;
Her proverbs and her sayings—pure delight!
You look away, but laugh with all your might.
It's true she is neglected, it's well known
Her garden is completely overgrown.
But we will clean her and pull up the weeds,
And teach her what it is her husband needs.
We'll tutor her and soon she'll teach in turn
All the arts the people need to learn.
So both of you will live in peace and love
And Yudl won't feel looked down from above."
Yehudis has a newspaper—her own!
Her knowledge of the world has quickly grown.
Of politics and science she writes much,
She even has a literary touch!
Her speech is now so clear and wordly-wise,
That Yudl has no grounds to criticize.
She tells him lovely tales from long ago,
And also what a modern man should know.

She fills him in on Jews in every land,
And tells him what means more than cash in hand.
Gaps within her wisdom still remain—
There are some things she cannot well explain.
But time's a splendid teacher, that's for sure
It's what enables children to mature.
So go ahead and laugh you foolish clown.
Some day you'll surely hear of her renown.
And even now the skeptics who at first
Rejected her, now quench their thirst
With *Kol mevaser*, so of course,
Yudl and Yehudis won't divorce.
Instead he'll show her honor and display
His high esteem forever and a day.
He may have other friendships now and then
But will not be untrue to her again.
Maybe he will make her, who can tell,
Respected by all other folk as well.
Yidele, your idle dreams must cease:
Remember who it was that brought you peace!
—Lifshits of Berdichev

Translated by Solon Beinfeld.

Other works by Lifshits: *Rusish-yidisher verter-bikh* [*sic*] (1869–1886); *Yidish-rusisher verter-bikh* [*sic*] (1876).

Urye Kahan and Alexander Zederbaum
Unknown

Kahan, Dates Unknown

Urye Kahan wrote articles for the early Yiddish weekly *Kol mevaser*, on topics such as education reform and popular science. He also provided biographies of famous figures in Jewish history. Writing under his own name or under the pseudonym "Ish ployni vekoyen" (approximately "John Doe ha-Cohen"), Kahan wrote on the need to educate girls as well as boys, and on the need to reform and expand traditional heder education to include grammar, logic, reading, writing, and arithmetic.

Zederbaum, 1816–1893

Born in Zamość, Poland, Alexander Zederbaum was a journalist, editor, and a champion of the Haskalah. Settling in Odessa in 1840, Zederbaum became a central figure in maskilic circles through his role as editor and newspaper publisher. In 1860, he founded *Ha-melits*, the first Hebrew weekly in the Russian Empire, a paper that he published until the end of his life. In 1862, he established *Kol mevaser*, a hugely influential Yiddish weekly—the first of its kind in Russia—that provided a space for the development of writing in Yiddish by writers such as Sholem Yankev Abramovitsh and Sholem Aleichem. Zederbaum also established the Russian Jewish newpaper *Razsvet*. Zederbaum moved to St. Petersburg in 1871; in his later years, he took a more overt political stance in his papers, speaking out against antisemitism and advocating for the early Zionist movement. He also wrote several books of fiction in Hebrew and Yiddish.

A Few Remarks Regarding the Education of Women
1863

So, is it not an injustice for girls to be so neglected that the refined feelings which are God's gift to all mankind are often destroyed in them? But if you speak to Jewish parents they will tell you that a girl does not need to be taught anything. They say that even if some day she has to write down a laundry list or carry on a conversation, she will learn that on her own when she becomes a housewife. The question of bringing up children does not even occur to them. Thus a girl grows up rough and crude. Every year she gets better at plucking feathers. She sees no one except the water carrier and the dairymaid. Then she gets married and goes out into the world, dealing with people in exactly the same manner she did in her mother's kitchen.

At the same time, she has a good memory and recalls accurately all the stories of demons and ghosts she heard from the old maidservant while sitting on the stove during the long winter nights. She passes them on to her children down to the last detail. She has no notion of prayer; she merely knows how to repeat every morning the words of the *modeh 'ani* ["I thank," prayer said upon awakening]. But she does not understand what she says and to whom she is saying it. Can one hope that such a mother will be a good raiser of children, a good mistress of the house, and a devoted wife who will be of benefit to her husband? Just look at the children of such a mother and you will see how coarse they are, what bad habits they have, how their understanding of higher things suffers from the superstitions that she has unfortunately instilled in their hearts. Their great natural talents have been ruined by the foolishness they listen to all day long in the heder from their mentor—the *behelfer* [assistant] who teaches them respect—and from the ignorant and foolish *melamed* [traditional teacher].

It is certainly not pleasant for any educated person to contemplate how Jews damage their children. But it is even worse when you see how some parents, who belong to the so-called educated classes, bury their children so deeply they will never be able to rise again. It breaks my heart when I remind myself of the wretched education they give them. For them, education is just a matter of fashion, like a big crinoline gown and the like. But the truth is they know nothing about education. And these idle people boast and pride themselves that they are European. They call themselves *aristocrats* and want to be considered the upper crust. But let us look at how such fathers guide their daughters. Up to the age of fifteen she grows up without any learning. But when she is a bit older and begins to meet people, she suddenly learns that she is an educated mademoiselle! Now her life begins. Of course when a *shadkhen* [marriage broker] arrives and starts to arrange a match, the parents start to say that it is not refined for their daughter to speak plain Yiddish and then they hire a tutor to teach her to play the piano and speak a smattering of French. You can imagine what kind of education a girl receives whose studies began with her engagement and ended on her wedding, but who thinks that she has in this short time learned the entirety of knowledge. Where does all this lead for such educated young ladies? Do they reach the goal that education is supposed to provide? No! It is quite the opposite. They are even more ruined than those girls who have not studied at all. Why is that? Because they have in fact received no education and because the parents thought that by providing their daughter with a big wardrobe they have discharged their duty to her in full. Afterwards, not only is she ignorant, but she starts to take on airs. And since she once read novels—though she doesn't really understand them—she would like to find in her future husband an extraordinary man who is exactly as depicted in the exaggerated novel from which she has derived her entire education. And if she does not see in the future husband all those fine qualities which in her opinion are indispensible, then he isn't the right man for her. [. . .]

Afterword by the Editors

Ever since *Kol mevaser* began appearing there has been an uproar over the question of the education of girls among Jews. Everyone sounds the alarm demanding only education and yet more education. All make fun of our grandmothers. Yes, it is indeed right to educate daughters, but how and by what means? It is easy to shout: "I don't like this building—it must be torn down." But a wise man asks: "Show me your plan and tell me how the new structure will be better." Our dear correspondent indeed speaks wisely. But his eagerness for education has led him astray. He ought to describe the issue from both sides and not in such a simple way. He sets up the women of the past merely as fools and the women of today as coquettes. The only difference is that he makes no distinctions among the women of the past—they are all worthless. Today's women, however, are only bad if they study between their engagement and their wedding. It follows therefore that those who have studied since childhood are fine. We, however, because we are editors and know that the world takes some notice of our words, are required to express our opinions impartially. Our grandmothers should not be so easily dismissed. It is thanks to them that our Jewish identity survived those difficult times when Jews throughout the world had to suffer greatly for their faith. What other nation in the world can boast of such honest and faithful wives? It was not love that tied the Jewish wife to her husband. When she married at an early age she knew nothing of love and desire. Religion was the tie that bound her to her husband. [. . .]

We, today's enlightened children of those simple, old-fashioned mothers, ought not to be ashamed of them. We are nourished to this day by the spiritual fruit of the tree of faith that our mothers planted in our hearts.

Translated by Solon Beinfeld.

Other works by Zederbaum: *Bein ha-metsarim* (1867); *Keter kehunah* (1868); *Di geheymnise fun Berditshev* (1870).

Shiye Mordkhe Lifshits

The Four Classes
1863

The Yiddish Language?

The Yiddish language is our mother tongue. But is it the language of education, by means of which we can best understand each other?[1] Does anyone even make the suggestion that our education should be conducted in our own language? On the contrary, I only hear the language being abused and ridiculed. People constantly say: it is corrupt! I confess that I do not understand with what justification one can say of a language, in which many thousands of people—a whole nation—live their daily lives, that it is corrupt. "Corrupt" can properly be said of something that once was better, but has become spoiled. Can one say of other languages that they were once better? Were they handed down from Mount Sinai in their present form? They arise, just like our language, from various other languages. Why are they not considered corrupt? The truth of the matter is that it is not appropriate to say of any language that it is totally corrupt, because a language is only the symbol of thought. Therefore, a nation can create whatever symbol it wishes, so long as people can thereby understand one another!

A corrupt idea means something that is truly corrupt. The corrupt use of the very term *corrupt* has unfortunately led the Jews astray! No sooner does one of us start to learn a foreign language than he becomes an expert on the corruptness of our language and begins to ridicule it. In time, he begins to ridicule us as well. Later, his ridicule leads to self-hatred. He senses that he remains a Jew. Awkwardly, he exerts himself to create the impression that he is no longer a Jew. That grants him all the more right to mock and despise the Jews. Thereby he unfortunately becomes hopelessly entangled and confused regarding the concepts of Jewishness and humanity. He tries to cease being a Jew and ends up ceasing to be a man! He tortures himself for days on end wrestling with the difficulty of pronouncing foreign languages, all in order to forget Yiddish. Yet unfortunately he speaks only Yiddish in his sleep and when he is suddenly frightened he cries out in plain Yiddish. He will never be able to make a foreign language his own, because he was not brought up in it. Yet he makes fun of his own language and tries as much as possible to distance himself from it. Such educated Jews cannot even become good friends among themselves. Each of them despises Jews, yet each of them is still called a Jew, with his own "jargon" on his tongue in spite of everything. [. . .]

The uneducated and devout sector of our Jewish population likewise abuses our mother tongue. They believe they can take pride only in their true mother tongue, the one in which God created the world and gave us the holy Torah. They are ignorant of the languages of the world and at the same time Yiddish is for them a kind of stepmother-tongue. For that reason there can be no unity among us. [As it is written in Bereshit Rabbah:] "Between the grandmother and the woman in labor the child suffocates." Each one raises his child as he understands—or does not understand—and things get worse, not better.

Why should it upset us that any coarse boor can mockingly parody the way we speak? Why should it be a surprise? As the master treats his dog, they say, so the whole household will be treated. Thus in truth all other nations despise our language and us at the same time. Well, my dear readers, we see how much trouble *one* corrupt idea can bring with it! Of course! The most important task that our reason has to accomplish is to distinguish and compare. What is most essential to distinguish is truth from falsehood, cause from effect, essential matters from secondary matters, good from evil. Now we know what is corrupt and what is not.

[. . .] Some might ask me: wouldn't it be better if we forgot our jargon and instead became accustomed to the educated language of the nation among which we live? My reply would be that there is no point in looking at what would be better but rather at what *is*. Perhaps it would also be better if the whole world spoke one language, if there were only one country, one faith. Or that it would be better if there were everywhere one currency and one system of weights and measures and if there were.... There is no end to what might be better! For the time being we speak Yiddish and it appears that we Polish Jews will not so soon be speaking to one another in Russian, in German, and not even in Hebrew! Therefore we must look at what *is* and if we cultivate the Yiddish language, with God's help the fruits of our labor will arrive most quickly and most surely and be of the best quality.

My belief in the great benefit that will result for the Jewish community inspired in me a strong desire to do something about it. I was unable to talk myself out of it and since then have spent some time preparing a first draft of a German–Yiddish and Yiddish–German dictionary—though I know people may laugh at me.[2] But, my dear readers, one swallow does not make a summer! Therefore whoever has goodness in his heart, who loves all people in general and Jews in particular, is urged to join me in this holy work!

NOTES

1. Who can deny that education makes the strongest impression in a person's life?

2. That would be a very useful thing and the author ought to complete it and have it published. But it seems to us that it might be better to create a Yiddish–Russian and Russian–Yiddish dictionary and include in it all the Yiddish words and expressions from different regions. [Editor of the journal]

Translated by Solon Beinfeld.

Daniel Neufeld

Progress: The Meaning of Passover
1863

Once again, following our custom of addressing readers [of the weekly journal *Jutrzenka* (Dawn), April 3, 1863] in view of the upcoming celebrations, we open the book of books, our holy Torah, in order to draw from it one of the great principles by which the world has hitherto been ruled.

The forty centuries that have elapsed since it was composed have not yet covered the book with the dust of archaeology, with the mildew of antiquity. It retains a modern freshness and contains almost contemporary facts, principles of all societies, reflections of the laws and institutions from all countries of the world.

We are celebrating Passover this evening, the memorable day commemorating the passage of the eastern tribe from a nomadic state into one of nationhood. The journey claimed many victims, not only due to external obstacles that hindered the forging nation from acquiring land for eternity, but also because of a lack of inner perfection in a tribe of shepherds, who had for centuries been under the subjection of the Pharaohs.

Oh how much superhuman effort, how many ways of incentivizing through miracles, instigation, and examples was Moses forced to employ before he succeeded in convincing this unfortunate people that they could become a structured society, before they believed his words that he would lead them to the Promised Land. [. . .]

Move forth, children of Israel, we still repeat today; Israel only lives through progress, every halting of it is backwardness; "Forward!" is the motto of Israel. [. . .]

Life awakens across the nation, as all the Christian youth are gathering under the banners of enlightenment, all the estates [i.e., social classes], civic, artisan, noble, and even quiescent peasants. Scientific institutions are sated with Christians, while we—we still have our dark heders, and in them, fanaticism is clogging up all the crevices through which, despite the tightly closed doors and windows, a ray of enlightenment might have squeezed; the rags it uses to tamp these crevices are the poor brethren, erring impulsive dreamers—we are constantly discoursing about enlightenment, while the entire country has merely ten elementary schools, and merely three nurseries—and we fill the columns of periodical magazines with braggadocio about our commitment and we boast with a drop of water that we offer to our brethren when they are truly in need of an ocean. Yet, the spirit of the time says to us: What's the yelling for! What's the prattle for! Take up, instead, the work of enlightenment, the act of eradicating fanaticism. . . . Tell the sons of Israel: "Move forth!"

The dark cavern of fanaticism, with sinister ghosts performing ludicrous gesticulations, growling meaninglessly; in the darkest recess of this dungeon sits a vampire, with a pair of wide black wings, his snout still soaking in blood sucked out of his victim, dormant under the waft of his wings [. . .] and at his call, the poor, emaciated sons of Israel gather from the towns and hamlets of the Polish countryside, everyone carrying a bundle with a tribute for the vampire in one hand, the heavy sweat of the haggard wife doing toilsome labor, and in the other, a mug that fills now and then with an abominable intoxicant that is called, apparently mockingly, *aqua vitae* and not *aqua mortis*; from the mug, the distressed are drinking the oblivions of their wretchedness and their humiliation, fomenting artificial joviality on their foreheads, artificial blushes on their pale faces— from all the towns and hamlets there are gathering the unfortunate pariahs of Polish society, who exclude themselves from the gaieties of the world, suicidally pushing away the generous hand of their brethren in the faith, who would wish to lift them up from the muck, closing their eyes for fear of ceasing to be blind, covering their ears in fear of a voice of conscience—they gather from all the Polish towns and hamlets at the call of the vampire from the cavern of obscurantism, at the voice of the prophets of Ba'al, who base their mission upon a falsified mandate, allegedly obtained from the hands of the God of Israel, which centuries ago sounded in the Arabian wilderness: Tell the sons of Israel: "Move forth!" "Arrive with the redemption!"

But we turn again to address those false prophets; speaking to them once again in the words of Isaiah: "Why are you harassing my people?" What are these unfortunate ones guilty of, for you to set on their annihilation, on their humiliation? What is this hospitable country guilty of, so that you deprive it of the agricultural labor of the talented part of the nation, whom you hold back on its way to progress? Before whom do you close the gate of the temple of science? For whom do you obstruct the path to agriculture, to the crafts, to worthy work? Whom do you imbue with a toxin for daydreaming about things ridiculous, harmful?

We have divined your ignoble designs. The progress of the populace is your downfall. Social enlightenment will open these people's eyes and they will cease worshiping you like a deity, once they have recognized your nothingness. Farm work, manual work, doesn't provide those better-than-expected profits that speculation may offer; the agricultural populace would not be able to bring gifts to you from their fixed but quite modest incomes. This is why you hold back the people from enlightenment; this is why you withhold farming from them; and this is why the spirit of the time speaks to us in the words of Moses: Tell those unworthy sons of Israel: "Move forth!" "Get out of this country!"

Half a million of our population, half a million talented, assiduous, and artful people languish in towns large and small, feeding on a piece of dry pabulum for the whole of the week, dressing themselves in tatters picked up from rubbish pits, and, being a burden to themselves and the society, smothering, pushing each other off, wilting ignominiously.

Take a look at the other countries of Western Europe, at Germany, France, at the inconspicuous small Flemish land, which look entirely like a delightful Eden, like a meticulously cultivated vegetable garden, where you do not find a span of ground not verdant with lush vegetation, where the people, densely concentrated, live in abundance and happiness, with no jaundice or competition, attached to the country and the family thatch.

In our place, areas impenetrable to the eye lie fallow: sandy dunes, where no vegetation delights the eye, quagmires and whirlpools exhale venomous miasmas, pestilence to human health, uninhabited steppes clad with useless weeds.

For there is no satisfactory number of hands to do the labor, there is no necessary discretion and reasonableness to utilize these unserviceable and noxious areas to the benefit of those who work and for the good of the country, since these hands and these heads are preoccupied with abject commerce, industry, and begging, which barely provide the exigencies of life, exposing industrious citizens to scorn. [. . .]

Abandon the cubit and the scales, Israel; abandon the city with its dust storms and fumes; quit the spoiled atmosphere of industry and petty trade, unknown to our great lawgiver, condemned by our seer-bards, who saw the prospect for developing national life only in agriculture, knowing that true nationality is based only on the cultivation of land that demands attachment and sacrifice for it.

Translated by Tristan Korecki; edited by Marian Krzyzowski.

Alexander Zederbaum

A Great Announcement
1863

God be praised, it is now a year since we began printing our supplement to *Ha-melits*, the *Kol mevaser*, the world's first newspaper in plain Yiddish. At first, many people ridiculed us, but time has shown us that we did the right thing. It is a useful thing for *all classes*. Whoever examines the articles that have appeared this year in the *Kol mevaser* will recognize that it has done much good. It has delighted many people who up to now have had no possibility to find out exactly what is happening in the world concerning things they urgently need to know—as merchants, as citizens of the country, or as property owners in the city. Today it is simply a pleasure to see that an artisan, a simple family man, a woman, or whoever wishes to, can read a newspaper every week and learn all sorts of things—about the world: about war and peace among the nations, about everything that is happening among Jews all over the world. He can read stories from ages past, about new and useful inventions and the most difficult ideas, all written in a language and in a style that everyone can understand. Is that not a good thing? And can anyone find fault with the newspaper? We can say that quite openly, and it will not mean that we are boasting, since men of great wisdom have already said so in their letters to us. The fact that so-called enlightened people cry out that we are making the speech of the silent masses respectable and that therefore these masses will not want to try to learn Russian or German. That is utterly false. First of all, the language is strong enough even without us, and millions of people speak it. Secondly, Yiddish is not nearly as unattractive as they make it out to be. There are expressions in the language that are full of charm, not to mention Yiddish witticisms that have a worldwide reputation. Who are the greatest humorists in the foreign newspapers? Are they not Jews? And do they not tell Yiddish jokes that make the whole world roll on the floor laughing? Thirdly, it's really the other way around. From the newspaper Jews will become aware that while among themselves Yiddish is enough, in the wider world you cannot manage with it. And what about all the many new words those who diligently read the *Kol mevaser* have absorbed this year, the many new ideas they have received, and how much more experienced they have become? And this is just the beginning. We have many more good correspondents who can write and spell just as we have started doing, so as not to confuse the public.

Translated by Solon Beinfeld.

Abraham Harkavy

A Few Words Concerning Literary Criticism
1864

Admittedly, it is true that all our hearts will be filled with feelings of astonishment when we recall the giant steps that the new generation has taken upon the peaks of the sciences and forms of technology; we will universally be impressed when contemplating the profound inventions that the people of our generation have revealed out of the dark, which attest that the spirit of man is not akin to that of the beasts that descends ever downward, that human spirit which bursts forth to ascend ever higher toward the hollow of the pit from which its refined soul was dug, and which raises itself above the heights of the mountains of those exalted elements of knowledge and sublime branches of wisdom that distinguish him, and elevate him to the status of a son of God! All our eyes will shed tears of joy when we consider that all this is the handiwork of the "daughter of God"—the soul dwelling within us, which allows no sleep to the eyes of the intellect nor slumber to the eyelids of discernment, and which, on occasion, arouses and bestirs them, with a loud voice, crying out with strength: "Arise, do your work, for it was for this purpose that you were created!" Let us all give thanks to our own generation, as it has achieved great things by openly demonstrating that it is through the various branches of wisdom and the sciences that the feeble human being is capable of having dominion over nature and drain it to its foundations. For who had ever heard of anything like this before, that a man could dispatch his message to his brother living at the end of the earth, and faraway beyond the seas, and send his words to the end of the world, and his friend would be able to listen, and hear them, and even reply to him within an instant (i.e., the telegraph)? And who had ever seen such things as these, that a man should be able to fly by means of a "flying vehicle" over the entire expanse of the world, as one of the heavenly angels and the holy seraphim without becoming tired and weary (i.e., the railway)? And a human being, weak in body and puny in strength, can now proclaim to the ends of the earth and the distant isles: "Approach here, for I have brought you close"; to the inhabitants of the east: "Embrace the men of the west with loving arms!" and to those dwelling in the south: "Fall lovingly upon the necks of your brethren, the inhabitants of the north!"

But despite all this, let us not be guilty of falsehood by boasting and saying that we have already attained the goal which we designated for ourselves, and for which the Supreme Wisdom directed the creation of man; indeed, on the contrary, the more the secrets of nature and its power become revealed to us, the more the abundance of understanding scatters its rays of light over the dark places of the entire globe, the more it appears that we are intellectually naked, and that a veil of thick darkness is spread over all that is governed by the human eye, and that a mask of thick mist, like the heavenly firmament, is spread out over our heads, and that, like blind men, we are groping about at noonday.

The same also appears to be the case in the field of Hebrew literature, as we cannot deny that it has vastly extended its borders during the past eighty years or so (from the time of the publication of the first edition of *Ha-me'asef*, in 5544 [1784])—and then, not long thereafter, the holy tongue started to compete with the languages in parlance in Europe when three weekly journals (*Ha-magid, Ha-melits,* and *Ha-karmel*) and two or three annual journals (*Kokhve Yitzhak, Yeshurun,* and *Otsar Ha-ḥokhmah*) were published; albeit that each year, numerous works in the pure Hebrew tongue were published, which amply attested to the fact that our brethren, the Jewish people, had bestirred themselves and awoken from the mighty trance of darkness into which they had sunk, as though into mighty waters, for a thousand years. Although the eye of anyone bearing affection for his people will delight greatly and laugh when seeing how the thistles and the nettles that have sprung up upon them are slowly, slowly vanishing ever since the day their teachers and parents—their crown—were removed from them, nonetheless we will find thorns too among these lilies, and dark clouds will blacken the purity of the skies of the Hebrew language, for the field of critical appraisal of the works of the sages of Israel has until now, to our sorrow, lain waste and desolate, with neither pruning nor hoeing being carried out in it. Instead of what we see in respect of the gentile languages, critical reviews of a novel quality, fresh as the dawn over the mountains, and the phenomenon of seven critics seizing hold of the corner of the garment of a single writer to tear his work to pieces, leaving no matter, either of a major or a minor nature, intact, without being subjected to the rod of critical appraisal; and not a single book or author avoids receiving either a generous handful of honor and praise, or, alternatively, of shame and disgrace. In contrast to this, among us, the Jews, every reviewer maintains silence, every critic is struck dumb; and from the day that *Ha-me'asef* ceased publication, no one subscribes to any journal containing genuine literary criticism; there is no trustworthy critic who will openly present his verdict, without showing favoritism, in the Hebrew language, on the works published in that tongue, and only on infrequent occasions can the voice of a man shouting out be heard, filling his mouth with praises for an author and a work of scientific character, notwithstanding that all those familiar with literature and language will cry out in protest against him, as though he were a thief; we hear the sound of words—words of praise—but we do not see the image of a sound and faithful review, which advises each writer of both his good and his bad points; and even if we were to meet someone who took the task of review seriously and declared that it was his wish powerfully to arouse the slumbering object of his review, to raise it from the abyss of oblivion and to infuse the spirit of life into the nostrils of this unconscious entity, which we regard as already deceased, upon but a little reflection, we shall discover that that individual comes not for the purpose of distinguishing between the good and bad material, but only to uproot and to destroy—and he will gouge out the eye of the writer, he will seek occasion against him and fall upon the author like an enemy and an adversary to smite his work with a ban, as though he were unaware that the time has passed when sages and writers would break each other with the staff of injury, by uttering words with a stream of fury and a torrent of rage, and that, now that the time has arrived for the words of the wise to be heard when spoken in quiet, every sage and writer has the staff of Pleasantness in his hand; no one will strike another, nor will he rule through the rod of his wrath—he will pronounce only an upright judgment, with a view to removing any thorns from the work and to repairing any breaches in it. I find most beautiful the elegant tale of the British savant John Russell, related when he came to submit Louis the Fourteenth, the king of France, to the bar of historical judgment. He tells us what one of the travelers saw with his own eyes: "In an Eastern land, excavators found a certain grave, in which there was the corpse of an unknown individual; all of a sudden, a certain man proclaimed that this deceased person had been known during his lifetime as a saint and miracle worker. Masses of the people who, like fools, believe everything without exposing it to the smelting furnace of scrutiny, instantly erected a glorious edifice, pleasant to the sight (a mausoleum), in honor of the saint over the grave, and a huge crowd of men and women, both old and young, from all the cities and provinces both near and far, assembled to pray at fixed times at the grave of the man of miracles; a few days later, another individual spread a report that the grave actually contained within it the bones of an accursed villain known for his multiple abominations, who, during his lifetime, had become a curse. The men of the East, whose opinions swayed as a reed sways in the water, fell upon the glorious edifice, which their own hands had established just a short while before, with a mighty rage, and destroyed it down to its foundations, not leaving one stone on top of another; they then took out the carcass from its grave, and dragged it through the mire of the streets, after which they cast it away, as food for the birds of the heavens and the beasts of the field. A few months later, a wise man came along, and as a result of inquiries and research, gave out that the deceased man was neither an upright individual who was able to perform miracles, nor a wicked and base fellow, but simply a man who conducted himself in a straightforward fashion, keeping to the middle path, in whose lifetime people had neither expressed wonder at his righteousness and holiness nor cursed him with a grievous curse on account of his violence and wickedness." "In a manner corresponding to this 'vision,'" the aforementioned sage went on to say, "We may perceive that whenever those who recount the events of the times wish to pass judgment on the character and actions of a famous figure from history, half will glorify and elevate the figure being assessed, and will praise him in excess of the measure required to establish the truth, while the other half will spread a garment of contempt and shame over him to the point where his name is used as a proverb and a byword of reproach. If we investigate thoroughly, and truth serves as a lamp to our feet, we will discover that, in the majority of instances, both sides have missed the mark and have fabricated things that are incorrect." Something of this kind is happening now in regard to the assemblage of critical reviewers of the literary works of the sages of Israel: some of them mete out to each writer a *se'ah*'s measure of praise, in overflowing measure, and turn a blind eye to his errors, whereas others thrust him forth with enmity, and procure horns with which to gore him with full strength—they will seek out a pretext, and unbridle their mouths and their tongues to revile and insult him, contrary to the norms of ethical conduct, and in a pressurizing manner.

O you of perfect faith within Israel! Why has no eye been raised to see, in relation to the leading nations in Europe, how gentle and genuine criticism, founded upon the pedestals of peace and truth, has come to be the mother of modern literature and the origin of the most lofty and powerful ideas? Make inquiry of the savants of each nation as to whether it was not literary criticism that first taught them to distinguish between the good and the bad, between truth and falsehood, and between something beautiful and of good taste and something ugly and of repugnant taste!

As for the British—a mighty nation—no science or form of knowledge was beyond their ken, and they were the first who presumed to ascend to the loftiest heights of the sciences—it was in that nation where, in the eighteenth century, the journals *The Spectator* and the *Edinburgh Review* started being published. They went forth armed with the following type of weapons: logic and attractive reasoning, against every author, to point out his errors to him, even where he was someone who was acknowledged as worthy of praise, and whose renown was great among the nations. The *Edinburgh Review* was not afraid to come out against the distinguished poet Byron, to chastise him openly wherever he deviated from the accepted norms governing the composition of poetry; and the other nations saw this practice adopted by the English and followed suit accordingly. The Germans, at the end of the last century, founded the journals *Thalia, Deutscher Merkur, Bibliothek für die schoenen Kunste*,[1] and the greatest writers, Lessing, Schiller, Goethe, Wieland, Bürger, Mendelssohn, and Nicolai, were not embarrassed to review even a minor work to ascertain whether it was of fine or of poor quality, and to present their verdict to the general public.

In our native land of Russia too, a new light appeared upon the horizon ever since the time when the great literary critic, Belinsky, started berating every author and every book that had not succeeded in joining the "communal assembly" of books and writers. We still recall the verbal blows he inflicted and the rod administered by him to the back of fools in the columns of *Molva, Moskoviskiy*, and similar journals. All the writers of his era could attest that it was only from that time on that the Russians began moving forward, rather than backward, over the field occupied by writers. Therefore, sages of Israel, listen to the advice of a man of tender years like me, for happy is the generation in which the seniors listen to their juniors; assemble together as friends, in unison, with a view to founding an "association of critics," which, like a shepherd inspecting his flock, will examine all Jewish literary works published each year, whether good or bad; you are not to respect the person of any man nor favor the person of any individual, but rather, your path is to be guided exclusively by the power of truth; you are to do battle against the enemies of the truth wielding neither the sword of victory nor the spear of enmity, but only the sword of genuine criticism and the element of soundly based review; and who can assess the immense benefit that will accrue from this to the Hebrew language and to those composing literature in it, as there are currently many young writers who do not know how to read literature in the languages of the gentile nations and who have not experienced the sunlight of critical review. If they should obtain a mere whiff of its scent, they will feel themselves insignificant by reason of the honor accorded to other writers, for which their soul lusts—should they perceive that, instead of glory, they inherit only a double portion of shame; though this is not the case at present, where the Hebrew language is like a city that has been breached, without a wall, and anyone wishing to assume the title of "author" is at liberty to do so. And to the Jewish writers whose names are renowned and lauded, the sunlight of critical review of their works will bring healing in its wings, for error is like a net spread forth to ensnare all living creatures, and sin crouches at the door of the writers. Who has ever succeeded in composing a work free from errors?

Would that the words of a figure of minor importance such as myself were to find a place in the hearts of the great sages of Israel, for then, truth would extend the curtains of its tent, and firmly affix its peg so that it can never be shifted, and the earth would be filled with knowledge as the waters cover the seas!

At the conclusion of my letter, I have seen fit to draw the attention of R. Jacob Ezekiel Levia to the fact that, in his explanation of the statement of R. Ḥanina in tractate *Sanhedrin*: "What is the meaning of *Amen*? It stands for 'God, the faithful King'"—that this is to teach us about the three fundamental principles of our faith (*Ha-melits* 82, p. 577), he had already been preceded in this exposition by my relative, the rabbi and sage, the bookseller Judah Idel Shereshevskii, in his work *Kur la-zahav*, see p. 150; and I have seen fit to "restore the lost object to its owner," in accordance with what we have been commanded by our Sages: "Anyone who cites a statement in the name of the person who said it brings redemption to the world."

It is well known to all those who are acquainted with the work composed by the savants Masser, Bodek, Fishman, and the band of their associates in their *Sefer ha-ro'eh*, that they subjected the names of the leading sages of Israel, i.e., Rapaport, Tsoren, Luzzatto, and Reggio, to derision and abuse—we have accordingly seen fit to draw the attention of the sage and rhetorician R. Sholem Abramovitsh, the fruits of whose wisdom we consume and from the clarity of whose language in *Ha-melits* and *Ha-karmel* we obtain satisfaction, to the fact that, in our view, he did not act well in heaping contempt and shame upon R. Eliezer Zweifel. In his essay "Kilkul ha-minim," printed in his work *Mishpat shalom* last year, his enmity for Zweifel exceeded the bounds of acceptability. The sage R. Sholem Abramovitsh will forgive me if I speak out against him invoking the words of the prophet Micah the Morashite: "They who bite with their teeth and cry 'Peace!'" And indeed, how great are the words of our Sages of blessed memory: "There are some people whose names are beautiful but whose deeds are ugly," for the reviewer gave his book the title *Mishpat shalom* [Judgment of Peace], while in reality it contains neither justice nor peace, but merely a spirit of enmity and hatred, hovering over the surface of the entire critique. Even before he began to review the book *Minim ve-ugav*, anger issued forth from his mouth and the expressions emanating from his lips were like piercings of a sword, declaring as he did: "Not so are those who halt between two opinions, but rather, they make a noise like dogs, etc. To what can this be compared? To the thief found breaking in with stealth." However, here is not the appropriate place to demonstrate that, as a result of the reviewer arriving in anger when starting to review a work, he will be bound to reach erroneous conclusions! Even after he has completed the review, not even half of the reviewer's fury is yet spent; he still fails to return his sword to its sheath, just as our Sages comment on the biblical verse: *Et va-hev besufah*—"his spear is still outstretched in his hand to devour and to destroy!" Once more he directs his face towards R. Eliezer Zweifel to dogmatize that he pretends to be wise, claims to be pious, but that he is in fact a hypocrite and a deceiver (p. 42). Has anyone heard words like these emanating from the mouth of an honest reviewer in our times? Surely not!

NOTE

1. *Bibliothek der schönen Wissenschaften und der freyen Künste.*

Translated by David E. Cohen.

Berish Rozenblum and Menashe Margolis
Rozenblum, Dates and Life Details Unknown

Margolis, 1837–1912

Born in Berdichev, Ukraine, Menashe Margolis received a traditional religious education and training in secular studies, eventually working as a lawyer in Odessa. He assumed a leadership position among that city's Jews and became a prominent figure in the development of the Jewish press in Hebrew, Yiddish, and Russian. In addition to his active involvement in periodicals such as *Kol mevaser*, *Ha-melits*, *Voskhod*, and serving as a founding editor of the Odessa Russian Jewish paper *Den'*, Margolis also translated works into Russian and Yiddish. He wrote Russian-language books on Jewish history and on educational reform and contributed to the Russian-language *Evreiskaia entsiklopediia* (The Jewish Encyclopedia).

A Story about a Rabbi, Followed by a Letter (in Kol mevaser)
1864

A Story about a Rabbi, by Berish Rozenblum

One of the most important things that the government has introduced in Russia to improve education among Jews is the decree that each community must choose a learned rabbi who has studied in a rabbinical seminary. It would truly be excellent if among Jews there were to be found educated rabbis who knew how to speak with people and knew how to get along in the world. Unfortunately, such rabbis do not yet exist and even if they did, they would be distrusted. The blame for that falls on both sides—on the common people and on the new rabbis. Yet if you think about it, the common people may have more of an excuse. It is a common saying that an older person will always defer to a younger one, and there is truth to it. If the common people were a bit more educated, they would understand what kind of rabbis they need and would no doubt treat them better. But those rabbis that have already had a bit of education and take great pride in it, often behave badly. Many of them do things that it is a shame to talk about. By now the Jewish population is unfortunately so fed up that people don't even want to take the trouble to choose a rabbi with a higher diploma and a certificate of good behavior from his school. As a result, no candidate wants to go through the drudgery of studying. What good does it do him? If he is learned, he will get little respect for it. If he has little learning, he knows for certain that nobody cares about that and it will not be an obstacle for him. If someone does come to a city and wishes to become the rabbi there, all he has to do is to come to an understanding with certain people—highly esteemed persons whose path to heaven consists of busying themselves with communal needs and with virtuous actions on behalf of the common good. One word from them, and the candidate can rest easy. No need to worry about the shoemakers and tailors—the views of people of that class is not an issue. It is easy to understand that where money plays the chief role, nothing good will come of it. Understandably, such rabbis cannot carry out the mission that the government has entrusted them with. They do not dare raise their voices at an assembly of the leaders of the community and state that in communal affairs there should be new arrangements that are more in harmony with our times. It is after all only recently they came to these same leaders seeking their votes in the selection process. They do not dare explain to the common people that it is time to get rid of the old rags and not continue to pursue the former ways. They are afraid that if they do that, they will anger the community leaders and thereby lose their favor—which for many reasons they cannot afford to do. Can anything new be expected from such people, whom money has misled to the point where they forget that their obligation is to expand education among the common people and to explain eloquently what a good thing it is? They are supposed to lead the blind onto the right path, not constantly to think about themselves and do everything only for their own benefit. When this will all end, we do not know. We can only hope that education, which these days has accomplished such wonders, which encompasses all things and changes everyone for the better, will also change the rabbis, so that the ugly things that happen now will cease. But for now it is hard to console oneself with hopes for the future. Educated people have become accustomed to hearing and seeing rabbis in other countries who are truly great men. Their lofty words touch everyone. They delight their communities with their splendid sermons. They earn the respect of all with their piety, their kindness, their education, their religious learning, their honesty, their truthfulness and the work they perform for the common good. But the educated person who loves the Jewish people will suffer great pain when he sees that in our largest Jewish communities the position of rabbi is filled with nonentities unworthy of such a noble title. Many of them—can you believe it?—have almost no understanding of our sacred Hebrew tongue!!!

(To be continued)
Berish Rozenblum, Berdichev

Letter (in Kol mevaser*), by Menashe Margolis*

The readers of *Kol mevaser* need to be told, first of all, that the new rabbis have already been written about everywhere. They have been denounced and defended and reasonable people understand what the new rabbis are, what they need to do and what they cannot do. We are pleased that they are already being discussed in *Kol mevaser.* We do not agree with Reb Aaron Rozenfeld who says in Number 15 of *Ha-melits* that Reb Berish Rozenblum should not have written about it in *Kol mevaser* because the common people do not need to know about such things. On the contrary: it is precisely the common people, for whose sake the new rabbis have been appointed, who need to know who their leaders are. The common people have enough sense and experience to understand these matters. So while Reb Berish did nothing wrong by writing, he was mistaken in what he said about the new rabbis—that they are just interested in the money. That is too strong, because the majority of them truly love Jews, have defended them and written good things about them. They come forward when it is necessary to put in a word in favor of the Jews. We wouldn't have cared if Reb Berish had said that there are some bad people among them, some who are not versed in Jewish religious texts, don't know Hebrew well and do little for the community—there is a disgrace in every family. In that case we would have seen that he is serious. He could have pointed out serious flaws and examined things from all sides. But to denounce them all and say they are all swindlers is unworthy. Reb Berish wanted to prove that for the sake of the money, the new rabbis do not even venture to tell their fellow-townsmen to get rid of their traditional "old rags." We have already seen what resulted when they are told that: there is an outcry, a clamor, a meeting is called and the outcome is—the rabbi "can't get along with the public," that the new rabbis want to enlighten the people by force, and so forth. It seems to us that even Reb Berish himself cannot have intended that. Everyone understands the words *get along with the world* to mean knowing how to deal with ordinary people, not to incite them against themselves. And even if he did intend that, he would not ask for tearing off "rags." Secondly, let us not fool ourselves—do you really think that a rabbi has the power with his words to order people to cast off their traditional clothing? That is a mistake: people who since childhood have believed deep in their hearts that it is holy, cannot be helped by anyone, not even foreign rabbis with their fine phrases. It would be a transgression for a rabbi to tear away from people what they consider sacred. Have you not felt what it means to take from someone what his life is centered on—for example to take a boy away and send him to a Hasidic rebbe? You would struggle, wouldn't you? Yet you demand that the common people should tear off the "old rags" and who of all people is supposed to do it? The new rabbis! We have already seen how a new rabbi who allowed himself to be led by such Reb Berishes to denounce "old rags" in his sermon: they wanted to drag him down from the pulpit. Luckily for him, the governor was present. If our new rabbis want to be useful, let them not preach about such things—let them live in such a way as to prove to the people that education is useful for a person. Let them help the masses with whatever they can. Let them enlighten the young, in whose tender hearts good seeds can still be sown. Let them get it out of their heads that old people can be made over. [. . .]

Now we want to ask the editors: after Reb Berish's text, they commented that "as a whole" the article is too strong, "although it is true." Presumably the words "it is true" refer to the article "as a whole." In other words, you thought it over and decided that it was true. Later, when Reb I. Shur wrote to you that it could not be true, you added that you accept his letter, though it doesn't quite claim that the article is a lie. Then you add: "after all we ourselves certainly don't know the truth." So the question is: how is it that you already doubted what you at first claimed to be certain of? We want to ask something else. Under Reb I. Shur's letter in Number 14 you note that "we have to accept it and not make too many inquiries." We were pleased with that. One or the other: if someone writes the truth, then let the world know about it. If he writes a lie, it won't be passed over in silence and the writer will be ridiculed. That will make certain that other writers will think twice before they write something. That is what other editors do as well.

A week later, in *Ha-melits*, you state that Reb Berish's article sat on your desk for several months and you didn't have the stomach to publish it. It would appear that you are not obliged to accept everything that you don't care for. Afterwards you got a letter that informs you that such and such people are offended because you didn't print their article. So you printed it. At this point we don't understand it at all. If you believe that it's not necessary to make inquiries, why did you have to wait until they wrote to you? If you believe that it is necessary to make inquiries, why didn't you make them? Why did you remain stuck in the middle? Only when someone came along and slandered Rabbi P. did you declare the matter closed.

We ask you, if you really are concerned with the truth, to print this letter and provide us with answers to all our questions. If you clearly tell the truth, we will admit that you are right. If we do not admit it, it will mean that we rely on the judgment of the readers of *Kol mevaser*. The public knows where the truth lies. In order to show that we are not ashamed of *Kol mevaser* and mean it seriously, we sign our name:

Kiev, April 21, 1864, Student M. Margolis

Translated by Solon Beinfeld.

Other work by Margolis: *Der period fun bildung in Rusland* (1910).

Sholem Yankev Abramovitsh (Mendele Mokher Sforim)

The Association "Concern for the Needy"
1865

When Berdichev, that famous commercial city, began, in the last few years, to fall from its high estate and the number of newly impoverished but respectable inhabitants kept increasing, I started to think about whether some means could be found to assist the needy in their straitened circumstances. By doing so, we could at the same time prevent envy, hatred, disputes, and all manner of evils that could eventually arise in the city as a result of unalleviated poverty. When poverty begins to appear in a place, it usually brings many other ills with it. People become a bit more hard-hearted. They bend the rules of fairness. One individual trespasses on another. Each man tries to snatch the food from the other man's mouth. "What of it," they say. "He's got enough, believe me. We're people too, we want to eat too." What is the outcome of all this? People dispute, they quarrel, they fight over a bone. Poverty is no joke! May no one have to endure it, dear God!

All of this went through my mind, until God in his wisdom sent me the wonderful idea of founding the association Maskil el Dal—that is, "Concern for the Needy," whose goal is twofold: 1) to help respectable but impoverished people in a way that will enable them to climb back up a little—for instance by helping them to earn a living. It would not, however, simply distribute alms, which would only increase the number of idle recipients of charity; 2) to support decent people and employ all possible legitimate means to see to it that they are not wronged and to guard them against all misfortunes. To this end we have established strict rules. In particular, whoever wishes to join the association must deposit dues of at least 3 rubles for the reserve fund and contribute at least 50 kopecks each month. Another important requirement is to create a committee of five people, one of whom shall be the *rosh ha-vaad* (president), the second the *mashgiach* (inspector), and the third the *mucher* (treasurer), and two more candidates.

The committee is obligated to lead the association according to its rules and in keeping with its goals. The names of those they help with money must be kept strictly secret, so that even the members of the association will not know about it nor will they be allowed to look at the book of expenses. At the end of the year, however, the committee will select from among the member of the association one man to whom they will have to submit an account of income and expenses. He can even discreetly investigate whether the committee has fully carried out its obligations.

Once the whole plan had been committed to paper, I turned to two respected and wealthy young men from among the enlightened *maskilim* of Berdichev, Mr. Chaim Scheinberg and Mr. Frenkel. They were soon joined by another fine and worthy gentleman, Mr. Peisach Shper. When we had all examined the entire plan, we turned to the celebrated wealthy philanthropist, Reb Moses Isaac Hurvitz. He liked the plan and on one evening at the home of Mr. Moses Isaac Sheinman, *rosh khoydesh* [first day of] Tevet 5624 (December 11,

1863), we inscribed our names in the *pinkas* [chronicle] of the association. On that day it began to function. That, gentlemen, is the story of the origins of the Maskil el Dal Association. *(Kol mevaser)*

Translated by Solon Beinfeld.

A. Grodner
Dates Unknown

Appearing in *Kol mevaser*, the author provides a satirical description of a *besmedresh* (house of study), titling it the equivalent of "Jewish Good Deeds."

Yidishe Mitsves (Jewish Good Deeds)
1866

The synagogues where older and more modest congregants pray are spared to some extent. It is a good thing that they are closed all day and all night and are opened only for early morning prayers and reciting of Psalms, then closed and reopened for the late afternoon and evening prayers. Even so, there is no lack of disorder. People quarrel over who should be the *gaboim* [sextons] of the synagogue, over who should be called to read from the Torah portion. People talk and carry on whole conversations. On Purim you could be driven to distraction by the *gragers* [rattles] and on Simches Toyre by the noise and the disputes over the procession with the Torah scrolls. In many places brandy is drunk and honey-cake eaten after the Simches toyre service. But that is nothing compared to the *besmedresh*, which is holier than a synagogue, for it is where "prayer and study exist in one place." It's true that older, pious Jews go there before prayer, sit and study and after that recite the chapter from the Mishnah and Gemara and then go home. That's all very well. But middle-aged and young men, unmarried or recluses separated from their wives, carry on in ways that would be inappropriate in a decent private home. After prayer, still in their tefillin, they sit down to study, which might seem proper, but in the meantime they feel like having a nap, so they put their elbows on the open Talmud and sleep contentedly, truly a "significant sleep" [requiring prayer on awakening]. In Hasidic prayer houses, they even have a drink. As they chant the traditional melody while reading the Gemara, they pluck hairs from their beards and sidelocks and leave them in the pages of the Gemara or *Shakh*,[1] and what was hanging in those hairs finds its grave therein. Afterwards they start talking, gossiping, and discussing what's going on in heaven, as if they were standing right there. They deliberate about what the tsar eats—diamonds or gold coins under his sauce; how much he spends a year. They deride the dead and the living, tell stories about evil spirits, ghosts, demons, imps, and phantoms; recount how the dead climb to heaven every night on a fiery ladder; how they immerse themselves ritually in the well of the cemetery; how they gather at midnight in the synagogue and if a living person happens to wander in they call him to read from the Torah, after which he dies; how the dead come and choke and pinch, leaving black-and-blue marks; how the Angel of Death tugs at the soul and smites the dead body with red-hot iron combs, how the demons lie in wait for the woman in childbirth and only the knife that lies by the bedside with [. . .] written on a slip of paper with Psalms written on it, can save the baby; they tell of the River Sambatyen which throws stones all week long but on the Sabbath it rests and then you can cross over to the land of the Red Jews; of the clay golem who acted as a servant on the Sabbath, of dreams and magicians; some tell of miracle workers, Hasidic rebbes who raise the dead, grant wealth, provide children and perform other miracles; of an invisible man and other such exaggerations—the same gossip that the Hasidim exchanged in the *mikve* in the morning. The difference is only that in the *besmedresh* they drink a little liquor accompanied with something to eat, just like in a tavern. After that they lie down to have a nap on the bare bench across from or next to the ark of the Torah. No one is responsible for what he does in his sleep. Not to mention the studious recluses and the yeshiva *bokherim* [students] who are even more privileged. They are allowed to undress down to their shirts and using the candles by which they had studied, they hunt down the little beasts that dwell in the folds of the shirt. You often hear sounds from the sleepers that leave a smell afterwards. For that reason the enlightened say: "It stinks like in a *besmedresh*." And if they hear a story they can't believe, they say "that's *besmedresh* gossip—those buffoons, what do they know?" During the whole year no shovel is used on the floor, not to mention water to wash the boards. May heaven protect us from what gets smeared on the tables, benches, and windows. That's why in the *besmedresh* you walk on clods of earth (but that doesn't hinder the ecstatic running back and forth during prayer). The tables and benches are covered with dried-out mud so thick it's black and wrinkled.

The surfaces are scratched up, in part by fingernails, in part by carving simple notches, or a rose, or a Star of David, or a few letters. The window panes are green. On the pulpit, all year long, there is written in chalk: "When Adar [the month of Purim] approaches, joy increases." The walls are smoky-black, just like in the New Synagogue in Prague, where tradition maintains they should not be whitewashed. The lectern is covered with candle wax, but nobody cares. The slop pail near the door is overflowing so there's a flood up to your ankles. The towel is wet and dirty. The door-handle has broken off.

Often a dispute, a fight, breaks out between two yeshiva *bokherim* over some trifle they are arguing about—not God forbid having to do with their studies, but over some worldly matter. They evaluate someone's lavish way of life and wealth. One says more, the other says less and suddenly they start to slap each other, to tear at each other's sidelocks. They rush around the whole *besmedresh* and then down the steps. The whole street comes running to see. And that is the daily corruption of a holy place, before the ark where the Torah scrolls and religious books are stored.

NOTE

1. [Acronym for *Sifte Kohen,* Sabbatai Kohen's (1621–1622) authoritative commentary on the *Shulḥan arukh*.—Ed.]

Translated by Solon Beinfeld.

Alexander Zederbaum

Keter Kehunah: On the Seer's Fall
1867

On the night of Simhat Torah 5575 [1814], the Seer[1] closeted himself in his room on the second story of his home. The one window overlooking the wide Jewish street was open; it was very near to the ground. When the spirit of ecstasy settled upon him, he ran to and fro in the room. Moving in haste to look skyward, he lost his balance and fell full-length on the ground. The perpetual uncleanliness of that street saved him from sudden death, for had he fallen on the paving stones he would have smashed his skull and broken his neck, but to his delight there was a mound of refuse there on which he landed. In a flash, the hasidim who were rejoicing on a full glass of wine made a commotion, hurriedly bringing expert physicians to restore him for he had fainted. The fall and the fright set his bones atremble, so that he tossed and turned in pain for nine months, until he died and was gathered unto his fathers on Tisha be-Av 5575 [1815]. The hasidim said that the zaddik had put his head out the window in order to grab hovering angels by their robes as a means of hastening the end of days, but Satan succeeded in confusing him and pushing him until he fell through the lattice. Miraculously, they recount, there was a row of empty glass bottles on that windowsill but when he fell he neither broke nor overturned a single bottle.

NOTE

Words in brackets appear in the original translation.

1. [The Seer is Ya'akov Yitsḥak Horowitz, hasidic leader in Poland known as the Seer of Lublin.—Ed.]

Translated by Dena Ordan.

Fabius Mieses
1824–1898

Fabius Mieses, a poet, writer, and scholar of philosophy born in Brody, Galicia, was exposed to the Haskalah as a youth and studied Hebrew literature. In 1840, he moved to Kraków, where he taught himself several languages as well as mathematics and astronomy. Returning to Brody and then living in Breslau and Leipzig, he wrote for Hebrew and German periodicals, including *Ha-melits* in which his *Milḥemet ha-dat* was published. His *Korot ha-filosofyah ha-ḥadashah* (History of Modern Philosophy) dealt with German philosophers; he also wrote poetry, including a piece on Darwin.

Milḥemet ha-dat (Religious War)
1868

Second Article, Chapter One

In the previous article, I presented you, dear reader, with the essence of the three different approaches existing within our religion, to which I have respectively referred by the names: "The Enlightened Ones, the Godly Ones, and the Group of the New Rabbis," and in the three chapters of this article I shall subject their respective views to scrutiny, and in so doing, I shall not be laying one handbreadth bare while concealing two!

[. . .] Let us suppose for a moment that the approach of the Enlightened Ones is correct, and that the objective of the Torah was, in their view, merely to teach philosophical expositions such as the following: the Unity of God, and that whatever is written in the Torah is within the realm of philosophy; if that were the case, the philosophical investigators amongst the gentile nations, who acknowledge these truths as a result of their own contemplation, ought to be regarded as fully fledged Jews, or perhaps as "saints on earth," despite their not having been circumcised and immersed in a ritual bath, and notwithstanding that, throughout their lives, they have never engaged in performance of the practical precepts. Is this not a really foolish proposition, to which no intelligent person would give his assent?

[. . .] Let not a stubborn person think that the exhortation contained in many places in our Torah against idol worship logically implies, through its repudiation, the notion of divine unity, for in reality, the intent of these exhortations is not directed against the perceptions and notions which are opposed to the spirituality of contemplative science involved in divine wisdom. Rather, it is intended as a repudiation, expressed in the form of a Torah-based statute, of the service of and reverence for the acts of idolatry and the secondary matters associated with it, and of the making of images and fashioning them with one's own hands, the reasons underlying which you will hear about in our explanation in the third article; and also, the reason mentioned in the Torah in connection with the exhortation against idolatry is by no means capable of teaching us the necessity of distancing ourselves from materialization of the deity, as it is written (Exodus 20:5): "You shall not bow down to them," etc., "for I, the Lord, am a zealous God, Who visits the sins of the fathers," etc. Those who oppose our nation and our religion would be able to imagine, because of this (and in fact, many among them *have* so thought) that the Lord, the God of Israel, feels jealousy and rivalry, loves dominion and honor and the like, being possessed of the attributes of a ruler of flesh and blood. They further claim that the verse: "Hear O Israel, the Lord our God, the Lord is One" (Deuteronomy 6:4) is not a principle of faith, as the belief of Israel in the Unity of the Almighty, blessed be He, and the like, is not clearly outlined in this phrase—but rather, the word "Hear" simply means "Know" or "Pay attention," in the way that such an expression is employed in casual conversation or as an established hypothesis, and it is not used by way of a command and decree. Moreover, the precise parameters of and the exclusive meaning that may be derived from this exalted teaching are not so plainly delineated therein as to preclude it being expounded in other ways, or even in a manner contrary to its original intent; only once in the Torah is its meaning clarified, to a minor degree and very briefly (in Deuteronomy 4:39), albeit as a secret matter, and merely by way of allusion intended for the one who discerns, and is aware of, and has penetrated into, its true meaning. It is not a plain exposition, inscribed explicitly upon the tablets of the Torah in such manner as to enable the masses to run through it at speed, and as to permit every individual not belonging to the special elite, or who has not delved sufficiently deeply into Divine wisdom as to be conversant with the mysteries of existence, to understand it.—

(Continuation to follow)

Fabius Mieses

Translated by David E. Cohen.

Other works by Mieses: *Ha-kabalah ve-ha-hasidut* (1866); *Korot ha-filosofyah ha-ḥadashah* (1887); *Sefer kevutsat shirim* (1891).

Sholem Yankev Abramovitsh (Mendele Mokher Sforim)

Fishke the Lame
1869

Fishke started to narrate in his lisping, stammering way.

"You seem to know I married the blind orphan girl, and after the wedding we lived well, like a Jewish couple should. I think I kept my part of the bargain right enough. Every morning I took her, as is fitting, out to her spot by the old cemetery. She'd sit there on a bit of straw and beg alms with a melody from Lamentations that touched everyone who passed. Plenty of shopkeepers only dream of earning like her—they can sit whole days in the store, crying their wares and shouting themselves hoarse, haggling with customers and not bringing in a cent. And still there's rent to pay plus interest on the money they borrowed for stock. Whereas my wife had no expenses and brought in a pretty penny—enough to live on. But people's never satisfied, and when they have potatoes they want meat.

"'Y'know what,' my wife started to say, 'people like you an' me, such a couple as the both of us, never run afoul in the world. In this trade, our flaws is pure advantages. So listen to your wife who's a bit older an' a little wiser'n you: take me out in the world with folks of the better sort, and you'll see, we'll haul in a fortune. In this place there ain't much more to be done. I sit for hours 'til someone has pity and gives a groschen. People been talking about Lekish, the cholera groom what went out into the world with his wife Perl—how he struck it rich. After the wedding they lit out an' their luck's steady ever since! Motl the pauper met up with 'em making the rounds of houses in Kishinev—he says their sacks was stuffed with scraps of meat, loaves of bread, smoked lamb, sausage, sheep's tail, and Perl's face shone so bright you'd go blind just lookin' at her. People coming back from Odessa say they seen Yontl, our other cholera groom, draggin' hisself around the shops on his buttocks—God sends him everything he needs. An' God won't forsake us neither. While it's still summer let's get moving, because each day we're here is a waste of time.'

"So we headed out. What should I say? We had it good. Whenever we come to a town or a city, we hit the jackpot. Everybody stared at us and not a single person turned us down. Wherever we went, the poorhouse stood open, and for a few pennies the synagogue attendant got the both of us invited to supper at a decent house. My ol' lady taught me the rules of beggary—I was out of touch with the real world and didn't know the ropes when it come to making the rounds of the houses. She was an expert in such things and taught me all I know: how to peer into a house, how to pretend to cough, moan an' groan, how to beg for mercy with a pathetic look, how to beg for alms, how to hang on like a leech, how to haggle or wish people well, and how to swear at 'em with curses that make the blood run cold. I learned all of this in no time.

"We was foot paupers—that is, draggin' ourselves around on foot. Like soldiers, poor folk is divided into infantry and cavalry—them that walks and them that gets around in wagons. Apart from these is also city poor folk, born somewheres in a city, what don't have nothin' to do with people born in the country. And then there's wagon poor folk, born on the road in caravans, whose ancestors always been on the move. These paupers is all like gypsies: day and night they wander from one end of the world to the other—born, bred, wed, and soon enough dead along the way. They's free men and beholden to no one: never pay no taxes, don't carry no papers, don't say no prayers, and don't mind leaving Judaism behind. Nothin' sticks to 'em. They's another type of creature altogether, neither fish nor fowl. My wife and I was infantry paupers, so you can imagine how, with me an' my bad legs, we used to crawl along real slow, like crabs. Little by little, because of this my wife started to scold, curse me, and make nasty remarks. She done give me nicknames, blamed me for my bum legs, said I'd turned her into a fool from top to bottom. To hear her tell it, she'd made a man of me and taken me out in the world to be with proper folks, but I wasn't true to her, I played dirty tricks on her. I used to keep quiet and swallow all she said, I swear!

"Until we come to the city of Balta we'd already gone and dragged ourselves along for a couple months. There we missed the great fair, which is famous round the world—an' she was sick over it, like as if she'd lost a fortune. When we left Balta, on the road we met up with a large band of country paupers, cavalry. The entire group was riding in three wagons. Among 'em was old and young, all kinda women, girls, and boys. For some reason they liked us and welcomed us onto one of the wagons, so after that we traveled around with the troupe. What should I tell you? A new world popped open to me at first, and I was very happy. I'd see an' hear amazing things I can't hardly describe. I learned how they'd slander people and mock the whole world, like when everyone told about stunts they pulled—how they filched loaves of bread or swiped a hen from a nitwit. They'd curse out rich folk for all they was worth, just like that, for no reason. I can tell you for a fact, they all hate the rich a heap more than the rich hate them. I used to hear boys chatting with girls, jokin' around and pairing up; one whole wagon hitched itself up with another. But it ain't decent to talk about that. I saw how they was able to disguise themselves, when they come to a city. One person pretended to be hunchbacked and another lame, one pretended he was blind, another mute, and another crippled. As soon as they left town the crooked were made straight, the lame man was healed, the blind could see, the mute could talk, and the cripple could walk. Just me and my wife was stuck with our flaws. Later I got the notion that they'd taken to us because of this, we was plain useful to 'em. More than once they blurted out that defects like ours, for paupers, ain't nothin' but gifts from God, 'cause they bring in good wages. My wife's blindness was several notches higher'n my limping. On top of that, when she opened her mouth, which flapped open like it was on hinges, people stopped in their tracks and their hair stood on end. One healthy redhead on our wagon kissed up to her like he was in love, made jokes, and talked with her 'til dawn. Whenever he hustled up a scrap of white bread, a slice of meat, a cake, or cooked peas, he'd hand it over to her. I didn't give it a second thought. What did I care about him feeding her, clowning around, admiring her, and—for all it mattered to me—turning her into a Turk? But they finally took to mocking me, taunting me, making my life bitter as the gall from a rotten liver, 'til I was the butt of all jokes. Every minute someone played a trick on me, every second I had another nickname. I was always to blame and everybody did whatever he wanted with me. If I started to get upset, they just rubbed salt in my wounds. 'Listen how our fine man moans an' groans, soon he's gonna bust out crying.' They beat me to death, and when my face was wet with tears, they used to say: 'Fishke, what you so happy 'bout? You grinning like a idiot! Look, everybody, lookit him laugh!' Then someone'd say, 'Give 'm a kick in the shins, or a smack on the back, that's a cure for laughing. If that don't work, we'll slap down the hair on his head or twist his ear and whisper a secret. That should get him started, sure 'nough as bitter herbs at a Passover Seder. After all, we got to take care of our own kind!'

"Sometimes they would throw me off the wagon and—while I limped along struggling to keep up, the best I could—clap their hands, laughing: 'Bravo, Fishke! That's it—dance, Fishke, dance! Hey, everybody, just look at the way Fishke lifts his feet, dancin' along so fine an' dandy. He could dance at any wedding, knock on wood!' Once the redhead who was messin' around with my wife—the devil take him—said: 'Fishke's no cripple! The bastard is putting us on, just pretending to be lame. We ought to straighten him out—jab him hard in the leg and you'll see him kick!' That's how they tortured me. I'd think back on the good years when I sat like a prince in the bathhouse, living like God in Paris. What else did I need? The devil gave me the idea to get married. I wanted to find buried treasure and ended up buried with no treasure."

Translated by Ken Frieden.

Israel Leon Grosglik
1851–1904

Israel (Izrael) Leon Grosglik was born into a Hasidic family in Warsaw. He learned Polish on his own and at age eighteen began to write for the Polish-language Jewish newspaper *Izraelita*. In the early 1870s, Grosglik preached regularly at a progressive synagogue, and began working for the Jewish community board, eventually becoming secretary. Despite his efforts to assimilate, Grosglik remained friendly with the Orthodox community in Warsaw, and advocated for meetings between Hasidic and progressive Jewish youth as a means to promote integration and secular education.

Letters of a Young Ex-Hasid
1869

We live in a time of a universal striving for science and civilization, and the spirit of the time warms the hearts of everyone alike with its breath. It permeates the depths of the soul and reason, taking no notice of the barriers and Chinese walls that attempt to dam its advance; it knows no barriers, and paves the way for itself even where it would be least expected, in the bosom of backwardness and fanaticism . . . in the bosom of Hasidism. And there it embraces *young* minds, stirring up in them the lust to become acquainted with the external world, and incites people to partake in the triumphant parade of the human spirit. Despite the obstacles set against it, the sensitive minds of these young *bet midrash* (house of learning) captives cannot remain indifferent to what is occurring beyond what is circumscribed for them. Indeed, traditional *youth* desire secular knowledge; the science with which they were hitherto fed, an education that revolves around a tight circle of mystical inquiries that they regard as inadequate, is no longer satisfactory to them; but they are not yet in a position, or rather have had no opportunity, to speak out about this.

At this point, I should more clearly explain my reasons for the very sake of clarifying things, in particular with regard to the present mental conditions of young Hasidim, and otherwise to avoid an objection that I might easily encounter on this occasion, of which I do not consider myself deserving.

It is very wrong to claim that I am condemning the learning of Talmud and am presenting it in an unfavorable light because it is the only subject of study among traditional youth, particularly the Hasidim. I am far from advocating such nonsense. He who is more or less acquainted with the contents of the Talmud knows that, contrary to what some may think, it is not exclusively a collection of theological teaching, fabulous allegories, and unpractical investigations, nor is it "full of superstitious notions, ignorance, and fanaticism," as the respectable author of *The Christian-Jew* has idealized in her imagination; rather, it is something far superior to this. In our time, many people agree with the view that the Talmud is easily classified among the most celebrated and most enduring monuments of human spirit and reason. What the Talmud required of its authors, as scholars and commentators of Mosaic jurisprudence, was, on the one hand, immensely gifted abilities and mental brilliance, while also, on the other hand, to possess an enormous reservoir of comprehensive knowledge, spiritual and insofar as was possible at the time, positivistic, experiential; this is proven by their work, the Talmud, where on almost each page we encounter views that reflect all branches of secular study known at the time. [. . .]

The thing is, namely, that this state of affairs no longer satisfies young Hasidim, that is to say, those who already have had occasion to learn that apart from the rebbe, Hasidim, and mysticism in the world, there are other people, and other areas of study that may and should be of interest to us. These young minds finally want to extricate themselves from the circumscribed circle within which they are almost forcefully kept. A few days ago I myself witnessed two young Hasidim, who instead of going to welcome the rebbe, who had arrived on that very day in our town, and after being preoccupied with the Talmud all day, stealthily endeavored to leave the procession of their elder colleagues and made their way to their own home. When I asked one of them why he was staying at home, he replied to me: "We have more worthwhile tasks for the time being"—and they sat down to study a book whose content was not at all Talmudic but was a Polish grammar. I could recount hundreds of such examples for you; unfortunately, however, they are not yet in a position to speak about this, and even then, how could a pronouncement like this be helpful to them? For in whom could a young Hasid confide his thoughts? His parents, kinsmen, or other Hasidic acquaintances?—they would have him stoned. A colleague who shares this line of thinking? But how can such a person help him? "So, why could he not go talk to another progressive person of his religious persuasion"—many a reader would naïvely exclaim—so that he could offer the young man advice, and perhaps something more. Lastly, why could he not go to his *young* progressive fellow believers, who would support him with action, sharing with him a portion of their own knowledge? Young hearts, they can easily understand one another."—Hah! that's true, the young progressive, if he were willing to listen to the young Hasid, the latter being willing, in turn, to go and talk to the former, then they would probably understand each other with ease. But by means of what miracle could this ever happen?

For one has to realize that the youth of these two classes of our coreligionists tend to avoid one another to an even greater extent than their fathers have done; they are not brought closer to one another by affairs of the mind, nor by monetary affairs. . . . A young Jew, with a more or less secular education, shuns Hasidim like a pariah, and is ready to repudiate any trace of tribal commonality that makes him related to the latter—almost hating him. Albeit the young progressive would give excuses for this antipathy, but what a weak and inane argument he employs! In the first place, he says, I am offended by his outer appearance. "How could one,["] he says, ["]approach a man who is weird, in his attire as well as his entire composition; and, what is central, a dull-witted man, a fanatic?" And what is it that repulses a young Hasid from a European Jew, so to name him? There are certain justified reasons, perhaps! Namely, he can't find anything in this Europeanness that he would characterize as Jewishness, and this is what a Hasid, even if thoroughly rational (for they exist as well), very much cares about. He first and foremost wants to be a Jew, and to find a Jew in a Jew; or else, he would never enter into any confidential relationship with another [i.e., such a Jew], fearing that he himself may suffer because of this. Is he himself, the Hasid, wanting to be a Jew, one that he ought to be? This is another matter; but it is partially not his fault. Let us enlighten him, and he will become a European Jew, one that Judaism wants to have, one that Mendels[s]ohn wanted to have in Germany, and one we all want presently. If a Hasid is not yet one, then this is only because he has a perverted idea of what he actually should be.

This is how the youth of the two streams interact with each other. Yet, all the same, their rapprochement, while offering enormous benefits to one party, would probably not remain without a redemptive influence upon the other. Let us, however, leave this reciprocity aside for now, since our young progressives might readily impute that my intention is to turn them into Hasidim. The point here is, the benefit would mainly go to the traditional youth. But, how to reconcile such two extreme elements? Let us try to intercede.

Understandably, I do not at all intend to address Hasidic youth at present. First, because these words will probably not reach them, and second, because the matter concerning them is not in fact so difficult to tackle. Let me confine myself, for the time being, to asking our young progressives whether, having somewhat reconsidered what it is that, in their own words, repulses them from approaching their backward fellow-brethren, would they not recognize the unfoundedness of their accusations? Above all else, is it seemly to hate, almost to despise a man considered spiritually backward? Would it not be right, rather, to extend the hand to those whose rescue remains within our potential and who will not despise our relief, which is sincere and salvific, instead of indifferently gazing at them standing at the edge of the abyss and calling in vain for help? Rather than avoiding them, let us appear keen in respect of them, let them become convinced that we don't want to foist alien convictions upon them, and before long, we will see that they will not be avoiding us.

Translated by Tristan Korecki; edited by Marian Krzyzowski.

Moritz Hartmann

1821–1872

Although Moritz Hartmann was the grandson of Eleazar Fleckeles, an influential rabbi in Prague, Hartmann abandoned religion as a young man, choosing a career in politics, editing, and creative writing. He was born in Dušnik, Bohemia, and studied philosophy and medicine, spending time in Breslau and Leipzig. During the turbulent political events of 1848, he was elected to the parliament in Frankfurt and affiliated with one of the most radical factions. When the parliament was dissolved, he worked as a journalist in Geneva, Paris, England, Italy, and Stuttgart, ultimately ending up in Vienna, where he served as editor of the *Neue Freie Presse*. His poetry and journalistic pieces stressed revolutionary themes.

Impressions of the Prague Revolution
1874

But I want to go on recounting how the Prague movement developed, and what made the revolution, which brought so many impressive, great, and noble things to light everywhere, made everything in Prague wretched, vulgar, and disgusting.

The heroic mood of the Prague rabble, with its desire for freedom, first turned against some bakeries. Encouraged by this triumph, the rabble then turned against the Jews.

The rumor that there was to be an attack on the Jews had been circulating for several days. The authorities took precautions, but they and the national guard were helpless. *Svornost*,[1] the Czech newspaper, which could have done something, did nothing. The Jews who had been attacked several times in the Flea Market closed their shops and withdrew into the Jewish Quarter. One day, walking with two friends near the theater, we heard a loud noise coming from the Flea Market—shouting and banging, as if planks and beams were crashing on top of each other. We hurried in that direction and saw a wild crowd pulling down the Jews' stalls. When they had finished they shouted, "Get the Jews! To the Jewish Quarter!"

I hurried home and collected my weapons, then went to the Karolinum, the Prague university building. I met a number of students, among whom several were ready to go to help the Jews. We formed a little troop, and brave Schiller, lieutenant of the students, headed the procession. Professor Johannes Spielmann, assistant director of the insane asylum, marched next to me. Having arrived at the Old Town Square, we found the part of the square that adjoins the Jewish Quarter packed with a huge crowd of people. They shouted, cursed, and made up accusations against the Jews so as to encourage each other to violence and to attack.

Our good leader ordered us to advance, and we marched in close formation through the angry mob. All its fury was vented against us as it realized we were going to help the Jews. But the people did not dare attack us. Had a single one of them found the courage to attack our little troop, we would have been lost. But they contented themselves with raging at us with words and gestures. I shall never forget the face of a head mason, pale with fury; he was one of the leaders of the crowd. He ran alongside us, snorting with rage, almost foaming at the mouth, repeating, "I'm an educated man, too, but I've never heard of anyone protecting the Jews!" We safely reached . . . the narrow street leading into the Jewish Quarter and the Three Fountains Square. It had been a difficult journey.

We found a group of students there, including several who belonged to the Czech party. We formed a chain, leveled our bayonets, and closed the street leading to the Jewish Quarter. The mob pressed so close, cursing and shouting, that we frequently had to pull back our bayonets so as not to impale those in front. We stood like this for hours.

It is remarkable that we did not find the Jewish Quarter already in the hands of the rabble, and that they did not attack. But there was a good reason—the crowd had already been beaten back that morning in an amazing, truly Biblical way. With cries of rage they had advanced as far as the Three Fountains Square, certain of plunder. Most of the Jews fled, and the women and children had gone into hiding. It seemed as if the mob would be able to satisfy its base cravings.

But a single man frustrated their hopes and rescued the Jews from their predicament. This man, a former circus rider who had returned to his home in the Jewish Quarter after numerous travels, hurled himself, alone and unarmed, at the crowd charging toward the narrow entrance to the quarter, where once there had been a gate. In this narrow, high, and dark street, he grabbed a large armoire standing in front of a second-hand furniture shop, lifted it high above his head, and rushed forward like Samson against the Philistines with the gates of Gaza. The attackers were seized with terror when they saw this huge man with his massive weapon advancing toward them like a moving mountain. They must have felt as if they were seeing a miracle. Those in front fell to their knees, crying, "Jesus, Mary, and Joseph!" The others fled.

It was probably the memory of this event that kept the cowardly and superstitious crowd from making a decisive attack and that helped our little group. Gradually our troop grew, as students and members of the national guard joined us through other entrances. Among the students who courageously stood fast with us was young Prince Rohan, a boy of about 16 or 17 years of age at the time.

Finally, after a long wait, several companies of grenadiers arrived led by General Serbelloni, a man with a very likable soldier's face. With a smile, he quickly made his way through the crowd. Together with the grenadiers we cleared the square. The crowd dispersed into the wide streets adjoining the Jewish Quarter where some Jews were allowed to live and threw stones through the windows. But the danger was not yet over and we patrolled the streets all night. This was not in vain, for at midnight we prevented a small boat from landing that was trying to let looters disembark at the back of the Jewish Quarter near the bank of the Vltava.

Since on this and following days the seizure of the Jewish Quarter was prevented, an attempt was made to persecute the Jews in a different way. It was Easter, and suddenly the old story resurfaced that a Christian child had disappeared and had surely been sacrificed by the Jews as an Easter lamb. The Jews trembled in terror. But this time everyone was on guard, and the thunderstorm that threatened to drench the city in blood passed by.

Bearing such events in mind, is it not right to say that the Prague Revolution was repulsive? But it was more than repulsive. Its mood was also immensely sad for the Germans, who were no better liked than the Jews, and Czech partisans spoke as openly and with as much conscious hatred against them as the rabble did against the Jews. At about the same time I heard Petr Faster, an innkeeper and patriot, Arnold, and other soap-box orators preach in this way. Frau Jenny Lutzer-Dingelstedt, who had been born in Prague, came to make a guest appearance. She was to sing the "Huguenots" and use the occasion to sing a few national songs, as was the fashion. A Czech demonstration was expected, and, though I was not interested in the theater, I went to see it.

The demonstration was confined to fanatical applause for the Czech songs. But something else made a greater impression on me. During the performance it occurred to me how similar our situation was to that of the Huguenots. The Germans in Bohemia were surrounded by equally fanatical enemies. I was overcome by an unbearable sadness, and could have cried when a well-known Czech writer (who also wrote in German) walked past me, touched my shoulder, and pointing to the stage said half seriously, half jokingly (as if he had guessed my thoughts), "The same could happen to you." I laughed in his face.

NOTE

1. The word *svornest* means unity or solidarity.

Translated by Wilma Abeles Iggers, Káča Poláková-Henley, and Kathrine Talbot.

Other works by Hartmann: *Kelch und Schwert* (1845); *Reimchronik des Pfaffen Maurizius* (1849); *Erzählungen eines Unsteten* (1858); *Tagebuch aus Languedoc und Provence* (1858); *Bruchstücke revolutionärer Erinnerungen* (1861).

Isidoro Epstein
1827–1894

Isidoro (b. Isaac) Epstein was born into an Ashkenazic family in Hofgeismar, a city in Hesse-Kassel, part of the German Confederation. A mathematician and engineer, he emigrated to Mexico in the wake of the 1848 revolutions in Europe. He was a founder of the German press in Mexico and in 1872 began publishing *Vorwärts* (Forward), a periodical named after the official newspaper of the Social Democratic Party of Germany, which advocated the emancipation and assimilation of Jews. Epstein never renounced his Jewish identity or his German heritage, but he became a Mexican citizen, taking an active role in the country's civic and political life. In articles designed to loosen the power of the Catholic Church there, Epstein satirized the Bible, believing that education would pave the way to a modern society. As a Jew serving in prestigious posts, he became an important symbol of progressive secularism in Mexico and worked to combat antisemitism.

Why Our Forefather Adam Had to Bite the Apple
1875

Dear reader, take out a sheet of paper and a pen and follow my calculations. This measure will not be pointless, as the numbers we will be dealing with are rather enormous, and mistakes can be easily made.

Let us suppose, then, that each couple that has descended from the house of Adam and has lived on this beautiful planet had only three children (a not at all unrealistic supposition); let us further suppose that only 6,000 years have passed from the time of Adam's birth to today, and that human beings' ability to bear children begins only at 30. All of these suppositions are perfectly reasonable, given what realistically occurs in the world. If, then, we allow that the human race has passed through only 200 generations, with three children allotted to each couple (husband and wife), the result is a geometric progression whose first term is 2, the exponent $3f2$, and the number of terms of the progression is 200. The following formula will serve to summarize this progression:

$$S = \frac{a(e^n - 1)}{e - 1}$$

Plugging in the respective values of the present case, we get:

$$S = \frac{2[(1,5)^{200} - 1]}{199}$$

According to this formula, the value of S—that is to say, the number of people on earth if no one from Adam on had died—would be a trifling 1,661 quintillion.

I see you are smiling, dear reader, asking me, "And so?" But, do you perhaps have any idea of what this immense number means?

I shall demonstrate it with a few practical examples.

The entire surface of the Earth measures approximately 506 ¼ million square kilometers, or 5,347 trillion square feet. Supposing, then, that no one had died since Adam, the question would be how to fit all these people on the planet. How much space must we allot each individual? Maybe a square foot? That is very little, and yet if we were to arrange people in this manner, their shoulders would be touching. Even if the surface of all the seas were used for this purpose, would there be enough room on Earth? If you believe that, dear reader, you are sadly mistaken. Only 5,347 trillion could fit; so what would we do with the rest? Even if we placed 10 individuals per square foot, we could only fit in 53,470 trillion of them. In order to place all 1,661 quintillion people on the planet, we would have to crowd in 310,680 trillion people per square foot.

Translated by Michele McKay Aynesworth.

Other work by Epstein: *Tratado de la mecánica aplicada* (1888).

Sa'adi Besalel a-Levi

How Does a Newspaper Survive?
1877

In order to survive, a newspaper needs numerous subscribers, the help of the community, paid publications, the aid of the friends of education, the generosity of the nation, and the support of the societies whose duty is to sustain it. Our newspaper,[1] however, does not enjoy the privilege of having any of these things.

1. The number of our subscribers, instead of growing, is diminishing. In Salonica, we believe 10 percent of the Jewish population is registered in our book as subscribers, but in reality, it is no more than 1 percent.

2. As for our community on whose support we had counted, we did not have the fortune of the periodicals

in Constantinople, Izmir, and other places [. . .] we hope that our esteemed community will find these arguments convincing and will not resent us any longer.

3. Until now, people did not pay to have their articles printed, unless these publications served their own interests.

4. How are we going to earn the right to get support? While there is never a shortage of things to be printed, for some reason they are sent to another press. As the Alliance[2] pays to have its bulletin printed every month or every other month, we propose to publish in a separate column in *La Epoka* its materials that have not yet appeared there [. . .] and at the end of every month or every two months we will print its bulletin—and all of this for the same price it pays that other press.

As for our subscribers in the provinces, unfortunately, because of the war,[3] we have lost many of them, together with the payments they owed us.

In Monastir [Bitola], not only did three people refuse to pay what they owed us for last year and cancelled their subscriptions because we had asked them to pay postage, but now our agent informs us that subscribers who continue to receive the newspaper want to pay us in banknotes instead of silver.[4]

We hear the same thing from Constantinople. [. . .] Even though we are charging such a tiny sum, seventy *gurush* per year, they want to pay us in paper money! If they realize that the cost of printing fifty issues per year includes postage, stamps, workers' wages, our own labor, money exchange fees, price of the equipment, rent, etc., they will not dare pay in paper instead of silver! [. . .]

How does a periodical survive? We are sustained only by the small support that we receive from some people who know and appreciate the value of education. And their kind encouragement gives us hope that our endeavor will succeed in the future.

—*Editorial Staff*
(*La Epoka*, 10 December 1877)

NOTES

1. [This newspaper came out in Salonica between 1875 and 1911. Its founder and first editor in chief was Sa'adi a-Levi.—Trans.]

2. [Alliance Israélite Universelle, a Paris-based philanthropic organization, which established a network of schools in the Ottoman Empire.—Trans.]

3. [The Russo-Turkish war of 1877–1878.—Trans.]

4. [During the war, the Ottoman government issued banknotes that had very little value. For this reason, many periodicals began to indicate the subscription price in silver.—Trans.]

Translated by Olga Borovaya.

Anonymous

This letter reports on a conference held by the Alliance Israélite Universelle in Istanbul on the situation of Eastern Jews; it was written in December 1876 and published by a leading Ladino periodical, *El Tiempo*, on January 19, 1877.

Letter Addressed to the Conference of Constantinople in Favor of the Jews of the Orient
1877

Paris, December 1876
To Mr. President and Members of the Conference of Constantinople
Sirs,

You were nominated to discuss the interests of a great number of people in the Orient, and to accomplish a work of peace and justice.

In coming before you today, we are not addressing your generous power for ourselves. Given the goodness we enjoy in the different governments where we were born and amongst the populations of which we form a part, we are deputies amongst you on behalf of the Jews of Germany, England, Austria, Belgium, France, Holland, Italy, and Switzerland, all united by belief in the same faith. We pray that your initiative will complement the work of humanity with which you are charged, and which promises so many important results.

You are meeting to arrange the civil and political status of diverse populations in the Orient. We Jews, citizens of liberal nations, came to ask that you make no distinction between peoples of different religions, and to ensure that our coreligionists have the same rights as other inhabitants of these areas.

The events happening in the Danubian provinces are painful proof that clearly demonstrates the danger of inequality of rights between the diverse populations of the same country, as was done through the Treaty of Paris in 1856 and the Convention of Paris in 1858. Every privilege given to one race or faith gives way to persecution, as the persecutions taking place in Romania or Serbia have shown Europe for so many years. We hope that the hour has come to put an end to these persecutions.

In Turkey, equal treatment of all of the non-Muslim populations has always been guaranteed. At present, Jews are mentioned in all of the laws that were given to advance the empire and improve the status of the *reayas*, as did the Hatti Sherif of Gulhane of 13 November 1839 and the Hatti Humayun of 1856.[1] Ottoman civil law gave equality to all people without distinction of race or faith in the eyes of the law. These precedents promise that the Jews as well as all non-Muslim subjects will equally enjoy the improvements that will be introduced by the governance and policies of Turkey.

NOTE

1. The book appended to this letter, entitled *The Status of the Jews in Serbia and in Romania*, pp. 1–31. [The Hatti Sherif of 13 November 1839 and the Hatti Humayun of 1856 are decrees central to the Ottoman *Tanzimat*, or "Reorganization." Among the many reforms introduced by these edicts was equal treatment of all of the empire's subjects regardless of religion.—Trans.]

Translated by Dina Danon.

Ilya Orshanski
1846–1875

Born in Ekaterinoslav (present-day Dnipro, Ukraine), Ilya Orshanski (Il'ia Orshanskii) was an author, journalist, and lawyer involved with Jewish intellectual circles in Odessa. An active writer for the Hebrew and Russian Jewish press, he was openly critical of the Russian government and its treatment of Jews. In 1871, for example, he boldly and publicly accused the government of supporting the pogroms that had ravaged Odessa that year. In response, the government shut down *Den'* (The Day), the paper in which Orshanski's editorial had been published. Orshanski's essays—later collected and published posthumously—on the legal, economic, and social history of Jews of Russia were noted for their impartial, objective erudition and deep understanding of legal scholarship. His more general work on jurisprudence in Russia was held in high regard. Orshanski was an early advocate for the establishment of secular Jewish schools in the Yiddish language.

The Russification of Jews
1877

A major issue within the internal politics of the Russian government concerns the Russification of populations in our remote regions who follow different religions and are of other ethnic backgrounds. Everyone among us currently agrees that disunity and animosity toward diverse elements within Russia's population cannot and should no longer be tolerated. Serious measures must be taken to unite the Russian body politic into one harmonious whole and, at the same time, give the actually Russian element of the population the place of privilege that, according to justice and the indisputable logic of history, it should occupy. The consensus among the Russian people, no matter which party they belong to, ends there. As to the immediately subsequent question—in what way can one reach this desired goal of national unity for Russia's people?—opinions vary significantly. [. . .]

Only the freedom and equality of citizens—regardless of their foreign descent and religious orientation, which are of no significance to the state—create unity of social interests, and consequently, political unity for the population. Meanwhile, the ruling element, by virtue of its magnitude and superior spiritual development, is to be elevated, in contrast to those who artificially promote and support themselves by external means. [. . .]

Moving on from these general thoughts to the application of the principle of Russification to the Jews specifically, it is not difficult to note that the currently dominant views among the best elements of our society and in our press, regarding the character and direction of Russian politics with regard to foreigners in the western provinces, fully apply to the Jews as well. In comparing Russian Jews of today to what they were just fifteen years ago, we notice the following curious phenomenon. Over these fifteen years, Jews went very far to achieve citizenship and, alongside this, Russification. While formerly—neither among Russian society, nor among the Jews themselves—there was not even a thought about the possibility of Jews being considered Russian citizens, a fairly large class of Jews now exists who insistently assert the privilege and right to be considered Russian people and citizens of Russia; and Russian society itself is becoming increasingly accustomed to the thought that Jews should carry all the obligations and utilize all the rights of Russian citizenship. But to what do we owe this positive change? Is it to the general liberal beginnings, lying at the basis of fundamental reforms that were carried out in Russian life by the current tsarist regime, or to the Russification of the western provinces? To this question, one can definitively answer that the main factor in the civilization of

Jews and their merging with the ruling population is the impulse in the Russian state and society, which should justly be called not "narrowly national" but "generally humanist." Even before the Polish revolt affected current views about the question of Russification, at a time when the intention was to satisfy the constantly growing intellectual and material needs of Jews, as well as other classes of the Russian population, Jews were the first to consider themselves not only people and citizens, but also Russian people and citizens of Russia. And this should come as no surprise.

Translated by Alexandra Hoffman.

Other works by Orshanski: *Russkoe zakonodatelstvo o evreiakh* (1877); *Issledovania po russkomu pravu* (1892).

Sholem Yankev Abramovitsh (Mendele Mokher Sforim)

The Brief Travels of Benjamin the Third
1878

Hurrah! The Lost Tribes!

"Hey, hey, out of my way!" shouted a driver from the seat of his coach as he nearly ran into two women standing in the middle of the busiest street in Glupsk, both carrying baskets of foodstuffs—meat, radishes, onions, and garlic—under their arms. The two were exchanging confidences in voices that could be heard a mile away, each hastening along on opposite sides of the street, so that by the time they finished their conversation they were shouting operatically above the din of coaches, cabs, wagons, and carts piled high with firewood, which formed a long, impassable column of traffic.

"Hasya-Beile! Will I see you at the gypsy fortune-teller's tonight? I'll be there with my boyfriend, and he told me that yours will be there too. We'll have a grand time. Come on, you goose, you'll enjoy it! Won't you come, Hasya-Beile?"

"My missus, drat her, has given me the honor of making farfel and sourdough bread tonight, but I'll try to slip away. Please, though, Dobrish, not a word of it to anyone!"

"Listen here, Hasya-Beile! Your missus won't croak if she has to wait another hour for her dinner. If she gets hungry, tell her to eat worms. And Hasya-Beile, don't sift your flour so well, because all you'll have left is the bran. How much did you manage to pocket from your market money today?"

"The rascal! The rascal! Somebody grab that sneak! What the Devil does he think he's doing? He should be strung up from a lamppost!"

"Why, what happened, Hasya-Beile? What are you screaming for?"

"A thief, Dobrish! He very nearly made off with my basket. It's a lucky thing I had my eyes open."

"Then look up ahead, Hasya-Beile! What's that crowd doing there? There must be a fire. That's the second one today, and I'll bet it's not the last!"

"But there are no fire bells, Dobrish. We'd be hearing them if there was a fire."

"Wait, here comes Sima-Dvosse the market-woman, I'll ask her. Sima-Dvosse! Sima-Dvosse! What's all that commotion?"

"I don't know and I'm not sure I care to. Maybe Nehame-Nisa does. Nehame-Nisa, sweetheart! What are all those people standing in a circle for? Tell your ducks to pipe down, because I can't hear you. I'll bet Hodl will buy them all for the feast. Didn't you hear she gave birth this morning? Ooh, my, what fat ducks! There wasn't an egg to be had in the market today. What's going on there?"

"How should I know? I suppose it's the lost tribes. I heard someone shout something about them."

"What, lost tribes in Glupsk? Ai ai ai! We'd better go take a look!"

With a cry the women ran to join the circle. In it a large gang of drifters was hooting:

"Hurrah, sea monsters! Hurrah, basilisks! Hurrah, the lost tribes!"

The lost tribes were none other than our two heroes, Benjamin and Sendrel, who, shortly after the incident of the bridge, arrived in Glupsk and within a few weeks were quite famous. The town's leading Jews were as excited about them as they were about the local shoemaker who was discovered in those days to be a hidden miracle worker. First to come across the two was a pair of proper old ladies, Toltze and Treine, whose well-known habit it was to don their best Sabbath jackets and kerchiefs every evening and sally forth from town to greet the Messiah. One day as the sun went down, it fell to their happy lot to encounter our worthies, freshly arrived from Teterevke, on the hither side of the tollgate and to escort them into Glupsk. It did not take long for the old women to find out everything about the two strangers entrusted by fate to their care. Toltze and

Treine exchanged wondering glances and poked each other smilingly in the ribs. "Well, Toltze?" "Well, Treine?" they whispered, yielding quickly to their premonition that the travelers were no ordinary mortals. So overcome with joy were they that, hearing of the two men's journey, they seemed to grow younger on the spot. "Well, Toltze?" "Well, Treine?" they whispered again, staring at the heaven-sent figures and nudging each other once more.

In the days that followed, Toltze darned the newcomers' socks while Treine patched their shirts and made new laces for their shoes, and both were as blissful as a pair of young brides. Nor were our heroes well received just by them. Where else but in Glupsk, indeed, could they have been so appreciated? Yea, get ye Glupskward, Jewish children! Why languish in loafery by the stoves of small-town synagogues when you can be in Glupsk, blast it all! There you will meet your true equals, your Toltzes, your Treines, and your thousands of other Jews, fine, reputable folk every one; there you will prosper and be made whole again; there you will find favor, there you will gain merit, there you will begin at last to live . . .

Glupskward ho and the Devil take the hindmost!

Here is Benjamin's description of the place:

"Arriving by the Teterevke Road, you must indulgently cross a large bog, then a second, and then the third and largest, into which, to put it baldly, empty the sewers and chamberpots of Glupsk, bringing with them all the town has to offer. Each day has its own items, colors, and smells and can easily be guessed by what comes along. If, for instance, you encounter an effluvium yellowed by scrubbing sand and mixed with fish scales, the heads and toes of chickens, animal hairs, and charred bits of hoof, you may, confident that it is a Friday, reach for your bucket and birch rod and run straight to the bathhouse. On the other hand, if floating your way is a solution of eggshells, onion peels, radish stems, herring tails, the gristle of calves' livers, and empty marrow bones, it is time to wish your fellow Jews a good Sabbath and hasten home to eat your weekly noodle pudding. Sundays, the tide slows to a bare trickle; now it carries bits of burned kasha, dried lumps of dough, torn dishrags, and an occasional scouring pad; the water carrier has not begun his weekly rounds and there is barely enough in the bilges of the barrels to wash out the Sabbath stew pots. And so it goes throughout the week, no two days of which bear the same sludge or stench.

"Once you have safely passed the slop bogs, you will come, gentle reader, to a small mountain of debris that is the remains of a burned house. On top of it, looking like an itinerant preacher on his soapbox, generally stands a cow, serenely chewing her cud while staring bemusedly at the throng of Jews below running back and forth like drugged ants with their walking sticks, canes, and umbrellas. Now and then she lets out a bovine sigh or exhalation, as if in pity for the world, and also, alas, for her own wretched fate at having fallen into the clutches of such a people.

"Putting the burned house behind you, you may now proceed straight ahead, and if, as I most sincerely hope, you do not slip and break a leg on any of the treacherous cobble stones that lie somewhat oddly distributed, but rather regain your footing each time, you will reach a kind of square, in which you will find the true life of Glupsk. Indeed, if there is reason to call the Teterevke Road Glupsk's guts, this square can rightly be considered its heart, which beats without stopping day and night. Here are the shops with their shelves of goods, and especially, with their odds and ends of cloth, lace, ribbons, satins, and furs that are Glupsk's famous discount fabrics, so called because its tailors disdain to count them as the customer's when they are left over from what he has paid for. Around them noisily swarms a solid mass of Jews, pushing, pushed, and poked by carts and wagons; but although it is claimed by Glupsk's doctors that the average autopsy of your local Jew turns up at least one wagon shaft in his body, little credence can be put in their statistics, most of the town's medicine being practiced by its barber-surgeons.

"Among the familiar voices in the town square of Glupsk are those of its little ragamuffins, who go about shouting in a peculiar singsong: 'Hot kasha cakes! Hot pudding! Come and get it! Get your onions! Get your Jewish garlic!' Vying with them are the sounds of outdoor prayer, a group for which can always be found before sunset, while loudest of all are the cries on nights of the Sanctification of the Moon, when passersby are accosted with the call of 'Yes sir, come and bless 'er!' Porters, their bodies coiled in thick rope, wait for work; retired veterans stand about in their puttees and tattered greatcoats; rag ladies hawk old underclothes, caftans, jackets, and other wear; and in the midst of all this stands the town watchman, a Gentile munching on a piece of Jewish challah given him for snuffing out the Sabbath lights in houses and guarding its crumbs as zealously as if it were the Passover afikoman.

Pickpockets are hard at work; out of nowhere springs a grimy, wild-haired beggar girl and shrieks in a practiced voice while grabbing your lapel, bawling as if she meant to kill you for your money; scamps run jeering after a madman in a crumpled cap who is crooning a sad ballad; and a young man stands by a chest with a peephole, into which Jews peer while he mimes and chants:

"'That's London that you're looking at . . . There goes the Pope in red breeches—see how people doff their hats . . . Here are Napoleon and his Frenchies fighting the Prussians. The Prussians are running like roaches!. . . And now see the Sultan with a fine lady in his carriage. The man holding the whip and reins is his grand vizier. No, the horses are rearing! The carriage has turned over! The Sultan has taken a spill! They're trying to free themselves. . . All right now, that's enough! How much do you expect for a copper farthing?'["]"

Translated by Hillel Halkin.

James Sanua
1839–1912

James Sanua, born Yaqub Sanu in Cairo, was a journalist and playwright whose family was connected professionally to the royal family in Egypt. Sanua studied in Italy and then taught in Egypt. In 1877, Sanua founded the satiric journal *Abou Naddara*, and was consequently banished to France for his subversive writing. He continued to write in nonliterary Arabic, publishing the journal series *Rehlat Abou Naddara Zar'a* (Travels of the Man in the Blue Glasses from Egypt to Paris), which contained cartoons as well as prose.

The Journey of the Holy Man Abou Naddara Zarqa from Cairo the Victorious to Paris the Glorious
1878

A Conversation between Abou Khalil *and* Abou Naddara Zarqa *at Café Riche, Boulevard des Italiens, on the Night of the 14th of July 1878, Paris*

[. . .] Abou Khalil: Good Lord, I've missed your banter, old man *[1] Thank goodness you made it here safely, and what a blessed day your arrival brings * What took you so long, anyway? * I left Cairo the same day as you, but in the afternoon, and took leave of you in Alexandria where you were strolling and taking the air in the agreeable company of the youths of the City of Alexander the Great, who adore you, or so I'm told, whilst I set off, my boy, and boarded the Brindisi ship, as they call it, only to arrive here quicker than a bolt of lightning. So here I am—and I've been waiting for you for more than a fortnight. How many days did you spend in Alexandria, and how many in Malta and Marseilles? Tell me everything at length, and don't be sparing with your anecdotes. I can't get over your witty repartee—after all, it's the reason why I left my dear homeland and came to these parts. Well come on then, what are you waiting for? Give me all you've got, and delight the ears of your good friend Abou Khalil *

Abou Naddara: Nothing would give me more pleasure, my good man. Who better to tell my tales to than you? [. . .]

Abou Khalil: *Khawaga*[2] Yusif Ramla wrote to me from Alexandria to inform me you'd left on the first of this month on a French ship via Malta, so tell me in detail everything that happened to you from the moment you left Alexandria up until this evening *

Abou Naddara: Luckily, the ship wasn't too full, and the captain was one of our brothers, so once he'd greeted me and worked out what was what, he immediately asked the maitre d', the butler, and the crew to look after me, and introduced me to the ladies from first and second class, telling them, "This here is Abou Naddara, who's opened the eyes of the world, revealing to people both lofty and humble, the tyranny of rulers most cruel; who's roused the slumbering fellah [peasant], and told him of his rights and his power!" *

Abou Khalil: Good gracious, how marvellous! I bet you couldn't believe your luck when you found yourself sitting amongst the madames—you must have whipped out your pipe, treated them to a tune or two, and had them wiggling their behinds in no time at all. You really are charmed, Abou Naddara, when it comes to that sort of thing *

Abou Naddara: Thanks be to God! But after a wonderful few days, things went sour on the final day and night *

Abou Khalil: Why's that? Did something unfortunate happen, God forbid?

Abou Naddara: You don't know the half of it! Just thinking about it gives me goosebumps and makes my hair stand on end *

Abou Khalil: A storm must have got up, and the sea roiled and the waves crashed, and the ship been tossed back and forth, and the passengers trembled and hit the deck *

ABOU NADDARA: As it happens, you're spot on; to hear your description, anyone would think you'd been there. I was fast asleep when I heard a screaming and a wailing and a terrible fuss, and water pouring into my cabin, so I leapt from my bunk, and found the water up to my knees. I said to myself "There's no doubt about it, the Sheriff[3] must have summoned the shrewdest astrologers and had them incite the spirits of the sea against us, so that the ship will be smashed to pieces and Abou Naddara will end up a fish's turd!"

ABOU KHALIL: But the Lord saved you, for you have the finest men of religion in the Land of Egypt at your side, praying for your good fortune *

ABOU NADDARA: May God preserve them and accept their prayers, and lift the burden of oppression and tyranny from the shoulders of Egypt's children, and bless them instead with a ruler who is just and sage, for surely the oppression of our country can get no direr than this. To see the people here in France, so jolly and gay, and so prosperous—what's it all down to?

ABOU KHALIL: Freedom * If everything that happened at home were to happen here, d'you think this lot would just put up with it? They've done away with many a king *

ABOU NADDARA: The time's run away with us, Abou Khalil, and between you and me, I'm getting peckish, so let's eat and then I'll tell you about the rest of my journey.

A Conversation between ABOU KHALIL *and* ABOU NADDARA ZARQA *at Café L'Américaine in Paris on the night of the 14th of July 1878*

ABOU KHALIL: Praise the Lord. I say, Abou Naddara, God certainly takes good care of us; may he always do so and never let our enemies rejoice on our account. The world's your oyster; only good things lie ahead. That was a meal to end all meals, the like of which our forefathers never savored; the meat here tastes quite different—it's simply delectable, no two ways about it—and the delicious stuffed vegetables, and magnificent kebabs, and fresh greens, and salads that whet your appetite, and peppered pickles, and incomparable fruit, and pastries that revive the soul, and the wine—dip a finger in it and it comes out looking like it's dripping blood... Dear me, what a feast. And how much did the whole dinner come to, you drunkard?

ABOU NADDARA: Two francs, my good man *

ABOU KHALIL: A snip at the price! In that case, we swindled the owner of the establishment as well as disgracing the table by devouring our food like crows. Those two francs scarcely pay for the bread each one of us ate. I tell you what, life here is cheap for someone who knows their way around, but even the shrewdest of strangers is clueless. What's the name of the place we dined at? From now on I shan't eat anywhere else *

ABOU NADDARA: It's called the Restaurant des Quatre Drapeaux, which means the Four Banners Inn.

ABOU KHALIL: It certainly deserves a banner of its own. You must write me the street name and number *

ABOU NADDARA: Rue Montmartre, number 142 *

ABOU KHALIL: Thank you kindly, or *merci monsieur* as they say.

ABOU NADDARA: And where did you eat before I arrived? *

ABOU KHALIL: In the street. You can't imagine how the bastards took me for a ride, old man. I'd spend seven or eight francs at a time on meals, I swear to goodness. Honestly, if you'd arrived a month later I'd be bankrupt, it would have been the end of me, and I'd have been a scandal for all to see. Whoever said that visiting a country without knowing its language is more like school than holiday had it quite right *

ABOU NADDARA: Indeed. See, Abou Khalil, philosophers have likened this life to a book, and they say that those who never leave their country of birth have only read its first page *

ABOU KHALIL: What a delightful thought. It's certainly true, and all the more so these days, when a person simply has to travel, otherwise they'll never see for themselves the results and benefits of human progress, the merits of the sciences and arts, the advances of industry and the wonders of technology *

ABOU NADDARA: But the thing is, when one of us does, and then reflects on the matter, he grieves over his country and the ignorance of its children, though that ignorance be the result of the injustice of their ruler, who intends his subjects' eyes never to be opened so that they'll obey his commands without complaint, and continue to recite nonsense like "God works in mysterious ways," and give him every last para they possess until finally they starve to death, saying "Praise be to you O Lord, this is Your will!"

ABOU KHALIL: And to come here and see fine government, justice and integrity—but that's enough of this gloomy subject; let's return to your journey. Now where were we?

ABOU NADDARA: You tell me *

Abou Khalil: Enough joking about, my man. This is Paris, in the land of seriousness. So, you were struck by a storm at sea the night before you reached Malta?

Abou Naddara: Indeed we were, but the good Lord saved us and we entered Malta on Saturday night. We didn't go ashore until the next day, however—but at any rate, those few words of Maltese I learnt from the late Salvo the cobbler came in handy *

Abou Khalil: Good Lord, how brilliant! And what kind of place is this Malta?

Abou Naddara: Malta is a splendid island, a drawing of which you will find in the seventh issue of my *Journey*, and the finest fortified citadel in the Mediterranean; those Englishmen you know so well have spruced it up and got it looking quite lovely. Yet its inhabitants, poor things, are quite innocent of civilization, and most of them can neither read nor write—though as they say, a fool is always contented—and you see them walking around barefoot, wearing tattered trousers and grubby hats. But they take religion very seriously, and are fanatical and zealous to the utmost degree *

Abou Khalil: Are they all like that, I wonder?

Abou Naddara: No, only the lower classes *

Abou Khalil: So they also have people of high standing *

Abou Naddara: Certainly; there, the rich are rolling in money and the poor are paupers *

Abou Khalil: Go on then, give us a few words in Maltese *

Abou Naddara: With pleasure. Now, I wanted to disembark and take a look around the town, so I waved to a young boatman and immediately he came up on deck and said to me in his curious tongue, "*Sinjur, ara l-barka tiegħi, il-barka tiegħi sabiħa ħafna, hejja miegħi nurik Malta. Malta ħanina, fjur mtagħ il-mondo*"—meaning "Sir, look at my boat, she's a beauty. Come with me and I'll show you around Malta. Malta's the flower of the world" *

Abou Khalil: Good gracious, you speak Maltese fluently! And what did he say to you on the way?

Abou Naddara: He wanted to take me for a trip, as you've gathered, and when I protested that I was an old man, he replied "*Mintix xiħ u oħti Maria tisbaħ tfajl ta' Malta, u int sinjur lissa ġoven, il-leħja tiegħek sewda!*" ["You're no old man, or my sister Maria's the prettiest girl in Malta. You're still young, sir, your beard is quite black!"].

Abou Khalil: That boatman sounds savvy, and a charming lad too. Tell me the rest then, come on *

Abou Naddara: Another man, who wanted to get me to buy a pair of earrings to give to my sweetheart, said to me "*Ixtri il-imsielet għarusa tiegħek, di mhix għalja di rħisa ħafna*" ["Buy these earrings for your bride—they're not expensive, they're very cheap"], and when I told him that I "*jiena ma nridx*" ["I don't want them"], he flew into a rage and started yelling "*Haqq il-Madonna u s-Sagrament!*" ["By the Madonna and the sacrament!"] and a great deal more in that vein, and so I was obliged to buy the earrings. On Saturday at noon we set sail for Marseilles, arriving on Tuesday morning; it was a magnificent crossing, with a calm sea, a radiant sun, and a limpid sky, and wonderful food and drink—why, those few days were a veritable pleasure-trip *

Abou Khalil: Thanks to the Lord for your safe arrival *

Abou Naddara: As for Marseilles, there's plenty to say about that city, so tomorrow after lunch I'll tell you all about it and the places I saw there *

Abou Khalil: God reward you. [. . .]

NOTES

[This text is written in the colorful, stagey mix of Egyptian and literary Arabic that Sanua employed throughout his humorous journals. The phrases of Maltese, written in Arabic script in the original, are in large part genuine, augmented by a hefty dose of pastiche and a few errors; in any case, they would almost certainly have been comprehensible to readers. With thanks to Michael Cooperson for his assistance with the Maltese.—Trans.]

1. [The punctuation in the original contains images of stars (sitting lower on the line than asterisks) marking major breaks in the flow of speech, and between them no punctuation at all, only larger-than-usual spaces that function similarly to commas or periods. The stars are preserved in the translation because they clearly mark the text as classical Arabic.—Trans.]

2. [A term of polite address used in Egyptian dialect for foreigners and non-Muslims.—Trans.]

3. ["Sheriff" is a very free translation of *shaykh al-ḥāra*, a title referring to a small-time local notable in charge of an urban neighbourhood—implying nosiness, self-importance and subordination to higher powers—which Sanua used to lampoon the Khedive of Egypt.—Trans.]

Translated by Katharine L. Halls.

Visual and Material Culture

This section contains three subdivisions: material culture, synagogue architecture, and fine art. The objects in each section are presented in chronological order. This arrangement provides some jarring juxtapositions as well as remarkable pairings. See, for example, the Jewish women depicted on page 403, or the contrasting images of mothers and children on page 452. Material culture allows us to see the continuity of traditional forms of Jewish art, including a rich variety of ritual objects from around the world. Each of the examples reflects the intersection between Jewish tradition and local craftsmanship, style, and materials. Synagogues commissioned (and sometimes designed) by nineteenth-century Jews bear witness to the emergence of the modern synagogue and the search for a new architectural identity.

The fine arts represent even more of a sharp break, as Jews had been excluded from participation in them for much of their history. In fields such as painting and sculpture, artists required training and patronage in order to succeed. While scholars have long put to rest the notion that premodern Jews eschewed figural art, it is nevertheless the case that Jewish participation in the formal fine arts was exceedingly rare. The extraordinary achievements of Jews (among them converted Jews) who took to the fine arts once the academies, salons, and exhibit spaces were opened to them is one of the signal developments in this period. It is notable that no sooner was photography invented than Jews quickly embraced it as an expressive and transformative artistic medium. We can trace as well the emergence of Jewish subjects as touchstones for a wholly modern artistic sensibility.

As creators, but also as patrons, collectors, commissioners, critics, and popularizers of the visual arts, Jews made significant and notable contributions to the arts and to their appreciation in the emerging public spheres.

Material Culture

Amulet for the Protection of Pregnant Women and Newborn Children (Artist Unknown)

Amulets were crafted to protect pregnant women and newborn children from the powers of the evil Lilith, Adam's mythical first wife. Mystical texts surround this image, written in Hebrew, Aramaic, and Judeo-Spanish.

Amulet for the Protection of Pregnant Women and Newborn Children
Eighteenth Century

Museum purchase, Bernard Kimmel Collection, Magnes Collection of Jewish Art and Life, Bancroft Library, UC Berkeley.

Omer Calendar (Artist Unknown)

This omer calendar, marking the days between the holidays of Passover and Shavuot, is still used at Congregation Mikveh Israel in Philadelphia. The letters stand for H=Homer (Ladino for Omer); S=Semana, the number of weeks in the counting; D=Dia, the days in the counting to be added to the weeks.

Omer Calendar, Designed for Counting the Omer in Mikveh Israel
Eighteenth Century

Courtesy Congregation Mikveh Israel, Philadelphia.

Huppah (Artist Unknown)

This depiction of the huppah (wedding canopy as well as ceremony), is from Georg Bodenschatz, *Kirchliche Verfassung der heutigen . . . Juden* (Frankfurt/Leipzig, 1748/49). Note the Treustein or wedding stone, against which the groom broke the glass, on the synagogue wall near the right corner of the huppah.

Huppah
1748

Picture Collection, the New York Public Library, Astor, Lenox and Tilden Foundations.

An inventory of the household goods, etc., of N. Levy, deceased....

In the closet in the front parlour...

2 Vollumes Chambers's Dictionary [Cyclopaedia]...
History of England by Rapin [Paul de Rapin-Thoyras]...
Carkess Book Rates [Charles Carkesse, The Book of Rates]...
Cowley's Law Dict....
Merchant's Map of Commerce...
Laws of Massachusetts...
2 Religion [of Nature] Delineated by Wolasten [William Wollaston]...
Stevensen's Spa[nish] Dict....
3 Old Bibles in English...
Lingua Franca Dict....
Coles [Elisha Coles, the Younger] Lattin and Eng. Dict....
Dutch and French Dict....
[Nathan] Bailey English Dict....
Newhouse on Navigation...
Mathematical Tables...
11 Historical Registers...
4 Lock[e] on Human Understanding...
3 [Humphrey] Prideaux Connect [Old and New Testament Connected]...
Mathematick Lessons...
Jure Maritimo...
3 Plutarch's Lives...
4 Statutes Abridged...
Voyage Round the World...
2 Gazetteers...
Arithmetick...
Magistrate's help...
Eng. and Dutch Grammer...
Confession of Faith...
Treasury of Mathematicks...

Inventory of Household Goods of Nathan Levy

Nathan Levy (1704–1753) was a merchant and a founder of the Jewish community of Philadelphia. The inventory of his goods and library includes a number of religious books in Judeo-Spanish, as well as numerous secular classical books and musical instruments.

Inventory of Household Goods of Nathan Levy
1753

Jacob Rader Marcus. *American Jewry Documents, Eighteenth Century*. Cincinnati, Ohio: Hebrew Union College Press, 1959, p. 9.

Ketubah (Artist Unknown)

The ketubah can take myriad forms, although in essence it is a religious and legal contract of marriage. Traditionally, ketubot outline the conjugal and economic conditions of a marriage and are written in Aramaic. This ketubah, or wedding contract presented to the bride, was written and illustrated in Rome.

Ketubah

1754

Courtesy of the National Library of Israel, Jerusalem.

Snuff Box (Myer Myers)

Myer Myers (1723–1795) was a renowned gold- and silversmith who was born in colonial New York. The son of Dutch immigrants, Myers became one of America's foremost craftsmen of the late eighteenth century by creating works for elite non-Jewish clients alongside his production of Jewish ritual objects. As the number of synagogues in New York and Philadelphia increased, there was a growing need for ceremonial objects, which encouraged artisans like Myers to take up smithing. Myers completed a seven-year apprenticeship, registering as a goldsmith in 1746, at which point he was the first American-born Jew to become an established retail silversmith within the British Empire. He became the president of the New York Silversmiths Society in 1786.

Snuff Box
1760–1770

The Metropolitan Museum of Art, Purchase, Mr. and Mrs. Marshall P. Blankarn Gift, 1966.

Torah Finials (Myer Myers)

Torah finials are a pair of ornaments used to decorate the upper ends of the rollers on which the Torah scroll is wound. The Hebrew term *rimonim*, which means "pomegranates," references the traditionally spherical shape of the finials.

Pair of Torah Finials (Rimonim)
1765–1776

Courtesy of Kahal Kadosh Mikveh Israel, Philadelphia. Photography by Rick Echelmeyer.

Torah Shield (Ze'ev, Son of Abraham [?])

This Torah shield contains a rare example of a personal inscription by the silversmith, stating, "This is the work of my hands in which I take pride, Ze'ev [son of Abraham?], silversmith from Piotrków in the year 1766."

Torah Shield
ca. 1766

The Jewish Museum, New York/Art Resource, NY.

Hanukkah Lamp (Rötger Herfurth)

Rötger Herfurth (1722–1776) was a Christian silversmith who worked in Frankfurt. Herfurth became a master silversmith in 1748, joining the Leschhorn family workshop, which was active for about a century. Herfurth produced numerous ceremonial objects for Jewish clients, following a fire in Frankfurt's Jewish ghetto in the early eighteenth century that claimed much of the community's existing Judaica. As a result of restrictions imposed on Jews prior to Emancipation that restricted their access to entering the silver-working trade, ceremonial objects were commissioned from Christian artisans. Herfurth created menorahs, candlesticks, spice boxes, Torah finials, and other objects for ritual use.

Hanukkah Lamp
ca. 1769–1776

The Jewish Museum, New York. Gift of Adele Ginzberg, F 5237.

Wedding Riddle (Artist Unknown)

This wedding riddle from Italy is written in Hebrew and Judeo-Italian.

Wedding Riddle for Mazal Tov, Daughter of the Late Yekutiel Tagliacozzo and Moses Jacob, Son of the Late Mordecai Rossello
ca. 1770

Courtesy of the Library of the Jewish Theological Seminary, New York.

Curtain and Valance for Torah Ark (Jacob Koppel Gans)

Jacob Koppel Gans was the son of an embroiderer, born in the Bavarian town of Hochstadt. Following in his father's footsteps, Gans was himself a master embroiderer, active in the second half of the eighteenth century. Although few examples of his work remain, Gans is best known for a Torah ark curtain and valance dating to 1772–1773, made of velvet and embroidered with metallic and silk thread. The repetition of motifs on the valance and curtain, serving to visually integrate both pieces, is a stylistic detail original to Gans's work. The artist's curtain and valance are a rare example of signed Jewish ceremonial art, as Jewish artists of the period were not permitted to join guilds in German cities.

Curtain and Valance for Torah Ark
1772–1773

The Jewish Museum, New York. Gift of Dr. Harry G. Friedman.

Torah Crown (Wilhelmus Angenendt)

The purpose of the Torah crown is to augment visually the status of the Torah scroll, further emphasizing its importance and centrality to Jewish life. These magnificent guilded ornaments are placed over the upper ends of the rollers of a Torah when the scroll is closed. Wilhelmus Angenendt (1737–1817), the crown's creator, was a Dutch silversmith active in the workshop of Swedish goldsmith Johannes Schiotling. Prior to Emancipation, it was common for Christian artisans to fulfill commissions from Jewish patrons, who were barred from entering the metalworking trades. This crown was among several ritual objects that Angenendt produced for Jewish clients.

Torah Crown
1775

Collection Jewish Historical Museum, Amsterdam. On loan from the Portuguese Jewish Community, Amsterdam.

Sukkah Decoration (Israel David Luzzatto)

Working in Trieste toward the end of the eighteenth century, Israel David Luzzatto (1746–1806) is best known for a micrographic drawing designed for a sukkah decoration. Micrography, a form of drawing originally created by scribes whereby miniature lines of text form an image, has been employed by artists to establish a connection between an image and a textual reference. In Luzzatto's sukkah decoration, the artist uses the text of Ecclesiastes to delineate the form of an astrolabe, an instrument used to measure the altitude of the sun, which in turn alludes to the references of solar movement in Ecclesiastes. Such paper decorations were popular among Italians Jews of the eighteenth century.

Sukkah Decoration
ca. 1775

The H. Ephraim & Mordecai Benguiat Family Collection, S 256. The Jewish Museum, New York/Art Resource, NY.

Henriette Herz as Hebe (Anna Dorothea Lisiewska-Therbusch)

Henriette Herz was a famous Berlin salon host, translator, and memoirist. Her iconic portrait, in which she posed at age fourteen as Hebe, the goddess of youth, was painted by Anna Dorothea Lisiewska-Therbusch (1721–1782), one of the few female court painters active in the eighteenth century. Biographical details on Herz appear in the section on Literature, in this volume.

Henriette Herz as Hebe
1778

Image courtesy of bpk, Berlin/Nationalgalerie, Staatliche Museen, Berlin, Germany/Joerg P. Anders/Art Resource, NY.

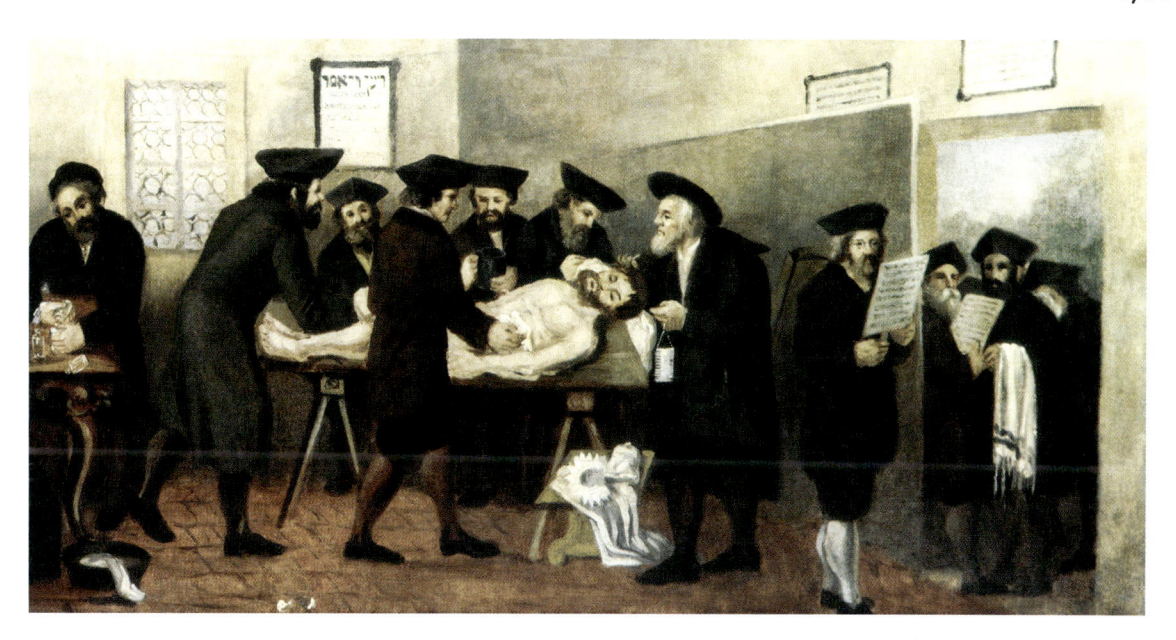

Jewish Burial Society (Artist Unknown)

These images from a series depict acts of loving-kindness to the dead performed by members of the Jewish burial society, or *ḥevrah kadisha*, in Prague. Participation in this voluntary society, for men and women, was considered a great honor and an act of ultimate generosity.

(Above) *The Washing of the Body*
ca. 1780

Jewish Museum in Prague.

(Below) *Sewing the Shrouds*
Date Unknown

Jewish Museum in Prague.

Portrait of Benjamin S. Judah (Ralph Earl)

Benjamin S. Judah (1761–1831) was an influential businessman in New York City and Philadelphia who built his wealth on shipping contracts to and from the West Indies. Judah was bankrupted when Great Britain imposed a naval embargo against the United States during the War of 1812. Ralph Earl's portraits of Jewish sitters attest to the various roles played by Jews in the establishment of American society throughout the colonial and Federal periods, as well as their desire to negotiate a cultural identity in relation to both place and religion.

Portrait of Benjamin S. Judah
1794

Wadsworth Atheneum Museum of Art, Hartford, CT. Photo by Allen Phillips.

Cup and Saucer with Portrait of Isaac Daniel Itzig and His Residence (Artist Unknown)

This cup and saucer pictures an image of Jewish German banker Isaac Daniel Itzig and his home, in Berlin.

Cup and Saucer
1795

Jewish Museum Berlin, photo: Hans Joachim Bartsch (digital copy: KGK 85_14_0c).

Oldest Jewish Cemetery in America (Photographer Unknown)

The oldest Jewish cemetery in the United States is located in New York City; the grave of Cantor Gershom Mendes Seixas can be seen here in the burial grounds of Congregation Shearith Israel.

Oldest Jewish Cemetery in America
1798

American Jewish Historical Society, New York, NY, and Boston, MA.

Torah Ark Curtain, Gördes, Turkey (Artist Unknown)

This Torah ark curtain was designed in Turkey.

Torah Ark Curtain
Late eighteenth–early nineteenth century

The Jewish Museum, New York. Gift of Dr. Harry G. Friedman.

Hand-Washing Basin (Artist Unknown)

This hand-washing basin, for Jewish ritual purposes, comes from Bursa in the Ottoman Empire.

Hand-Washing Basin from Mayor Synagogue
ca. 1800

Israel Museum, Jerusalem, Israel/Bridgeman Images.

Portrait of Giacomo Meyerbeer as a Boy (Friedrich Georg Weitsch)

Friedrich Georg Weitsch (1758–1828) spent much of his career working as a court painter in Berlin. He produced portraits for German nobles, was appointed court painter of Karl Wilhelm Ferdinand, Duke of Brunswick, as well as court painter and rector for the Berlin Academy of Art. Weitsch painted portraits for prominent Jewish clients, including the opera composer Giacomo Meyerbeer.

The public display of Weitsch's portrait of Meyerbeer caused a controversy that highlights the challenges faced by Jews seeking to take their place in civil society and forced the Beer family to carefully negotiate the relationship between the private and public spheres.

Portrait of Giacomo Meyerbeer as a Boy
1802

bpk, Berlin/Musikinstrumenten-Museum/Art Resource, NY.

Portrait of Amalie Beer (Johann Karl Kretschmar)

Amalie Beer (1767–1854) was a philanthropist and preeminent *salonnière* known for hosting Berlin's foremost musicians and intellectuals in her home. She hosted reformed Jewish prayer services in her home on Sabbaths and holidays, attracting throngs to the dignified manner and elegant setting. Beer was also the mother of the composer Giacomo Meyerbeer (born Jacob Mayer Beer), the writer and poet Michael Beer, and the astronomer Wilhelm Beer. Her portrait was painted by Johann Karl Kretschmar (1769–1847), a German painter who specialized in historical painting and portraiture. He studied with landscape painter Johann Friedrich Weitsch and later taught at the Berlin Art Academy. Kretschmar painted portraits of several prominent Berliners, including Beer.

Portrait of Amalie Beer
1803

© Stiftung Stadtmuseum Berlin/Hans- und-Luise-Richter-Stiftung. Reproduktion: Hans-Joachim Bartsch, Berlin.

Circumcision Bench (Artist Unknown)

This ritual circumcision bench was crafted in Údlice, Bohemia. The text of the circumcision service is inscribed on the seat back.

Circumcision Bench
ca. 1805

Jewish Museum in Prague.

Medal in Honor of the Grand Sanhedrin of Napoleon (Alexis Joseph Depaulis and Augustin Dupré)

French engravers Alexis Joseph Depaulis (1790–1867) and Augustin Dupré (1748–1833) collaborated on a remarkable Napoleonic-era medal that honored the Grand Sanhedrin, a representative body of seventy-one rabbis and Jewish leaders established by Napoleon to develop Jewish legal principles that would reconcile their religious beliefs and practices with those of modern French society. In exchange for political and military support, Napoleon offered French Jews religious freedom and state protection.

Medal in Honor of the Grand Sanhedrin of Napoleon
1806

The Jewish Museum, New York/Art Resource, NY.

Torah Binder (Koppel ben Moses Heller)

Koppel ben Moses Heller, of Bretzfeld, Germany, designed this Torah binder (wimple) in Munich, stating that it was "made for Menachem, called Mendl, ben Judah Loeb Schnaidack (Schnaittach), born under a good sign on Thursday, 3rd of Marheshvan 5575 (Oct. 17, 1814)." Wimpels made from the cloth covering a baby boy at circumcision were brought later to the synagogue in a celebratory manner to bind the Torah scroll.

Torah Binder
1814

Accession no. 80.83, Gift of Mr. and Mrs. Theodore Lilienthal, Magnes. Collection of Jewish Art and Life, Bancroft Library, UC Berkeley, Berkeley, California.

Alms Container (Artist Unknown)

This alms container from Charleston, South Carolina, is made of silver, cast and engraved.

Alms Container from Kahal Kadosh Beth Elohim Synagogue, Charleston, South Carolina
ca. 1819

Private collection New York. Image courtesy of Special Collections, College of Charleston.

Illustrated Daily Prayer Book (Hijman [Ḥayim ben Mordecai] Binger, with Marcus and Antonie Binger)

Born in Amsterdam in the mid-eighteenth century, Hijman Binger (1756–1830) worked initially as a bookkeeper, and then in a clothing rental business. Following his retirement, Binger endeavored to create a daily prayer book, drawing its texts from well-known sources and illustrating the manuscript with the help of his children. Completed in 1820, the prayer book is a striking example of a handwritten, illuminated Hebrew manuscript from the early nineteenth century.

Illustrated Daily Prayer Book
1820

Bibliotheca Rosenthaliana, Special Collections of the University of Amsterdam.

Grace Mendes Seixas Nathan (Mrs. Simon Nathan) and Her Son Seixas Nathan (William James Hubard)

Grace Mendes Seixas Nathan was born in Connecticut in 1752 to a patriotic, literary Jewish family. In 1780, she married the British merchant Simon Nathan, a supporter of the American Revolution who arrived in colonial America in 1773. Their son Seixas, born in 1785, was one of the signers of the New York Stock Exchange's constitution and the president of Congregation Shearith Israel, the first Jewish congregation established in North America. Their portrait was done by William James Hubard, an English painter who specialized in silhouettes, portraits, and miniatures. Hubard found success in both Britain and the United States, where he spent the majority of his career.

Grace Mendes Seixas Nathan (Mrs. Simon Nathan) and Her Son Seixas Nathan
ca. 1824

Private collection.

Medal from Dedication of the Munich Synagogue in 1826 (I. W. Loewenbach)

I. W. Loewenbach was a Jewish medalist in Munich who was active from the 1820s through the 1860s. He created medals on Bavarian nationalist themes including the inauguration of the statue *Bavaria* in Munich (1850), the Seventh Centenary of Munich (1858), and the fiftieth anniversary of the October Festival in Munich (1860). Loewenbach's medal commemorating the dedication of the new synagogue in Munich (1826) is among the earliest German synagogue medals. It became customary for Jewish communities to issue medals to commemorate new synagogues or other Jewish public buildings.

Medal from Dedication of the Munich Synagogue in 1826
1826

Photo © The Israel Museum, Jerusalem by Yair Hovav, Israel Museum, 754/86.

Torah Curtain (Artist Unknown)

This Torah curtain originates from Ankara, Turkey.

Torah Curtain
1826

The Israel Museum, Jerusalem, Israel/Bridgeman Images.

Jewish Women from Izmir Whitewashing (Artist Unknown)

Hand-colored lithograph.

Jewish Women from Izmir Whitewashing
1830

The Israel Museum, Jerusalem, Israel/Bridgeman Images.

Portrait of Cecilie Freiin von Eskeles (Friedrich von Amerling)

Cecilie Freiin von Eskeles (1760–1836) was noted for her salon, which attracted leading musical, literary, and intellectual figures. Daughter of the noted court Jew Daniel Itzig, she brought the Berlin-style salon to Vienna. She was a noted harpsichordist. Friedrich von Amerling (1803–1887) was a Viennese painter in the court of Emperor Franz Josef.

Portrait of Cecilie Freiin von Eskeles
1832

Germanisches Nationalmuseum Nuremberg. Photo by J. Mosolf.

Saada, the Wife of Abraham Benchimol and Preciada, One of Their Daughters (Eugène Delacroix)

Eugène Delacroix is one of the best-known French romantic painters. Following the French conquest of Algeria, Delacroix traveled to North Africa in 1832, creating a series of Orientalist paintings and drawings that exoticized scenes of daily life in Algeria and Morocco. While in Tangier, his delegation was accompanied by Abraham Benchimol, a translator with the French consulate who also acted as a guide and adviser to Delacroix. Benchimol introduced the artist to Tangier's Sephardic culture, taking him to a synagogue and a Jewish wedding. Delacroix later painted Benchimol's wife and daughter, Saada and Preciada, in a bridal portrait on the day of Preciada's marriage.

Saada, the Wife of Abraham Benchimol and Preciada, One of Their Daughters
1832

Image copyright © The Metropolitan Museum of Art. Image source: Art Resource, NY.

Feuchtwanger Cent (Lewis Feuchtwanger)

Lewis Feuchtwanger (1805–1876) was a German doctor and metallurgist who immigrated to New York City, where he opened a pharmacy. In addition to his work as a pharmacist and medical practitioner, Feuchtwanger attempted to introduce a metal alloy known as "German silver" into U.S. coinage, promoting this nickel silver as a less-expensive alternative for coins of small denomination. Feuchtwanger privately minted his own coins and brought his idea to Congress, although his proposal was ultimately rejected. He also published several treatises on his scientific pursuits, including an important work on gemology, *Popular Treatise on Gems*, which is also excerpted in this volume.

Feuchtwanger Cent
1837

Courtesy of the American Numismatic Society.

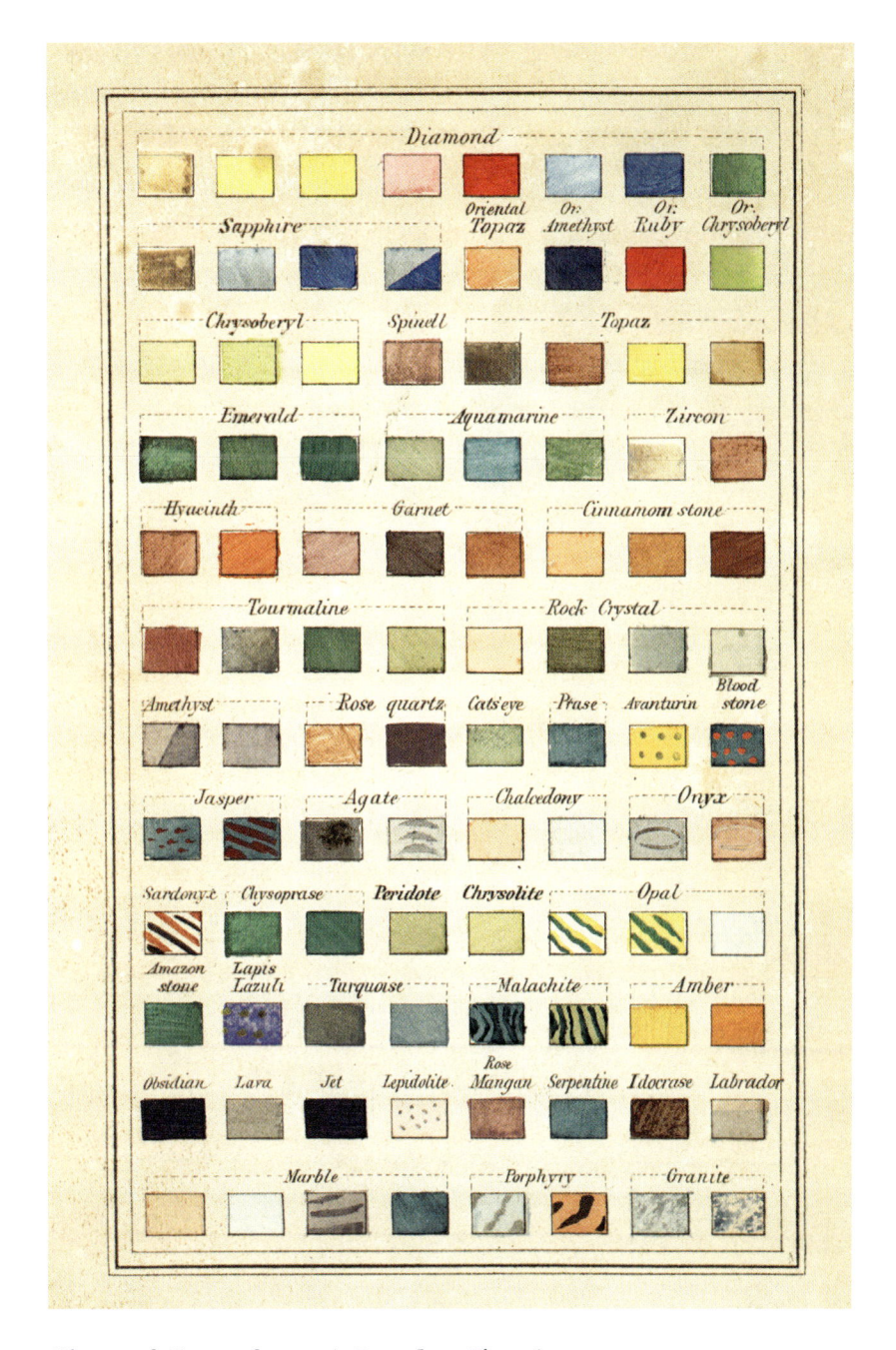

Chart of Gems from *A Popular Treatise on Gems* (Lewis Feuchtwanger)

Chart of Gems from A Popular Treatise on Gems
1838

Courtesy of the Smithsonian Institution Libraries, Washington, DC.

Wedding Sofa (Artist Unknown)

This Biedermeier-style sofa from Danzig, consisting of a birch veneer over pine, may have been commissioned on the occasion of a marriage. The oval contains an image of clasped hands, and the text in Hebrew reads: "This is the donation of the valued and exalted R. Shlomo Friedländer with his partner, the modest M. Daubr, may she live. 5598" (1838).

Wedding Sofa
1838

Photo by Malcolm Varon. Photo Credit: The Jewish Museum, New York/Art Resource, NY.

Shiviti (Moses Ganbash)

Moses Ganbash (active first half of the nineteenth century) was a scribe working in Turkey during the first half of the nineteenth century. He is best known for a remarkable illustration made in 1838–1839 combining a *shiviti*—traditionally, a decorative plaque bearing the verse, "I am ever mindful of the Lord's presence"—with a topographic map of Israel. Panoramic maps featuring holy sites of Judaism were popular during the nineteenth century, although the artist's conflation of a map with a *shiviti* was a unique achievement, linking the metaphysical omnipresence of the Lord with the physical spaces central to Jewish liturgy. That much of the map's border is made from paper collage speaks to Ganbash's skill as an artist and a scribe.

Shiviti, *Topographic Map of the Land of Israel*
1838–1839

The Jewish Museum, New York. Gift of Dr. Harry G. Friedman, F 5855.

Medal Commemorating Sir Moses Montefiore (Artist Unknown)

Medal Commemorating the Trip Made by Sir Moses Montefiore of England and Adolphe Crémieux of France to Stop Anti-Jewish Measures against the Jews of Damascus
1840

Image courtesy of the Jewish Museum, New York/Art Resource, NY.

Ewer and Basin (Artist Unknown)

From Turkey, this ritual object was used by the Benguiat family, a large and prominent Sephardic family in the Ottoman Empire.

Ewer and Basin Used on Passover
ca. 1845

The Jewish Museum, New York/Art Resource, NY.

Ketubah (Artist Unknown)

This ketubah is from Oran, Algeria.

Ketubah

1847

Courtesy of the Library of the Jewish Theological Seminary, New York.

Paper Cut—*Mizraḥ* (Moses Michael Rosenboim)

Paper cuts have long been a popular Jewish folk art. Given the widespread availability of paper in Europe by the mid-nineteenth century and the simplicity of the tools required in making paper cuts, this craft could be practiced even by those with little means or few skills. In addition to being aesthetic objects, paper cuts also fulfilled a religious purpose and were often connected to a particular festival, event, or ritual. Paper cuts have been a tradition of Jewish folk art, with the earliest record dating to the fourteenth century. Within Eastern and Central Europe, several extant examples dating from the eighteenth century onward illustrate the development of the art form in its use for interior decoration. An 1848 *mizraḥ* created by the artisan Moshe Michael Rosenboim, located in Schönlanke (Trzcianka, Poland) is a masterful example of a Judaic paper cut. *Mizraḥim* are decorative objects that are hung on the eastern walls (facing toward Jerusalem in European areas) of Jewish homes and are used as an aid to prayer as well as a symbol of divine protection.

Paper Cut—Mizraḥ
1848

Property of Sidie Weiskopf. Image courtesy of University Press of New England, photo by Robert E. Mates, Englewood, NJ.

H. M. King Leopold I Stamp, Belgium (Jacques Wiener)

Jacques Wiener (1815–1899) was the eldest of three brothers who were successful Jewish Flemish medalists and engravers. His innovation was the idea of precisely engraving the exterior and interior of a building on the two sides of a medal, an approach that he employed for notable Belgian churches as well as a series of forty-one medals depicting Europe's most important buildings. Jewish subjects included the *Opening of the Jewish Home for the Aged in The Hague* (1841) and the *Opening of the Synagogue in Cologne* (1861). Wiener also engraved the first Belgian postage stamp, an image of King Leopold I that was the first stamp issued on the European continent.

H. M. King Leopold I Stamp, Belgium
1849

Courtesy of Postbeeld, Haarlem, The Netherlands.

The Music Room of Fanny Hensel (Julius Helfft)

Noted composer and *salonnière*, Fanny Hensel (1805–1847) may have used this room to compose and to play her music to intimate circles of family and friends. Biographical details on Hensel appear in the section on Performing Arts, in this volume.

The Music Room of Fanny Hensel
1849

Thaw Collection, Gift of Eugene Victor Thaw Art Foundation, 2007-27-41. Photo: Matt Flynn © Smithsonian Institution Cooper Hewitt, Smithsonian Design Museum Photo Credit: Cooper Hewitt, Smithsonian Design Museum/ Art Resource, NY.

Esther Scroll (Artist Unknown)

This scroll for the holiday of Purim originates from Baghdad.

Esther Scroll (Megilat Ester)
ca. 1850

Braginsky Collection Megillah 75. Braginsky Collection, Zurich. Photography by Ardon Bar-Hama, Ra'anana, Israel.

Tombstone (Artist Unknown)

This tombstone of a Torah scholar from Sieniawa, Poland, adopts a folk-art style.

Tombstone
1855

Photograph by Marcin Wodziński (courtesy of the photographer).

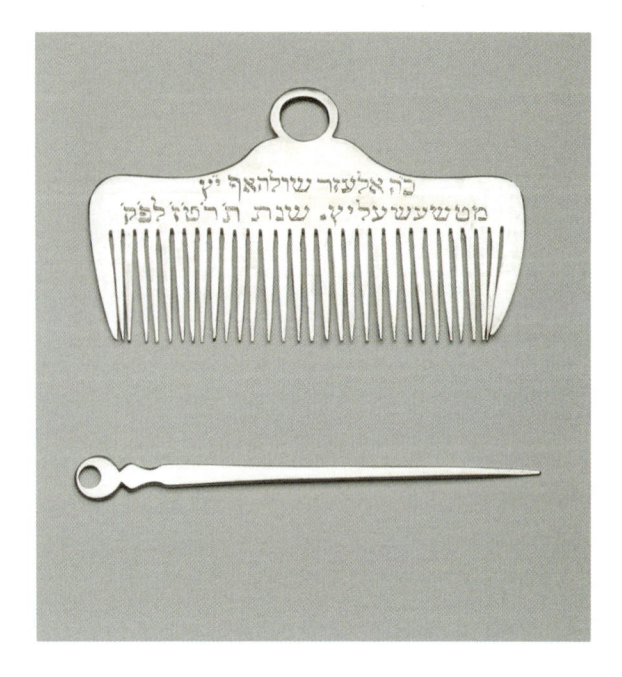

Burial Comb and Nail Pick of the Bischitz Burial Society

The process of purification of the body, known as *taharah*, involves a ritual cleaning of the corpse according to Jewish rites. Prior to being dressed in a white cotton shroud, the body of the deceased is washed, the nails are cleaned using a ritual nail pick, and the hair is combed using a special burial comb. These objects vary greatly in design, although they are often made from silver or copper and feature engravings of Judaic motifs and Hebrew inscriptions. The comb and nail pick shown here are likely to have been crafted by Johann Nowotný, who was active from 1853 to 1881; Bischitz (Byšice) is in present-day Czech Republic.

Burial Comb and Nail Pick of the Bischitz Burial Society
1855–1856

The Jewish Museum, New York, NY. Gift of Frances and Hubert J. Brandt, 2012-91.1-2. Photo by Richard Goodbody, Inc. Image courtesy of the Jewish Museum, NY/Art Resource, NY.

Paper Cut—*Shiviti* Sign (Artist Unknown)

This paper cut comes from Izmir in the Ottoman Empire.

*Paper Cut—*Shiviti *Sign*
1858–1859

The Israel Museum, Jerusalem. B85.0612, 168/054. Photo © The Israel Museum, Jerusalem by Yair Hovav.

Ketubah (Artist Unknown)

This ketubah was designed in Bucharest, Romania.

Ketubah
1859

Gross Family Collection.

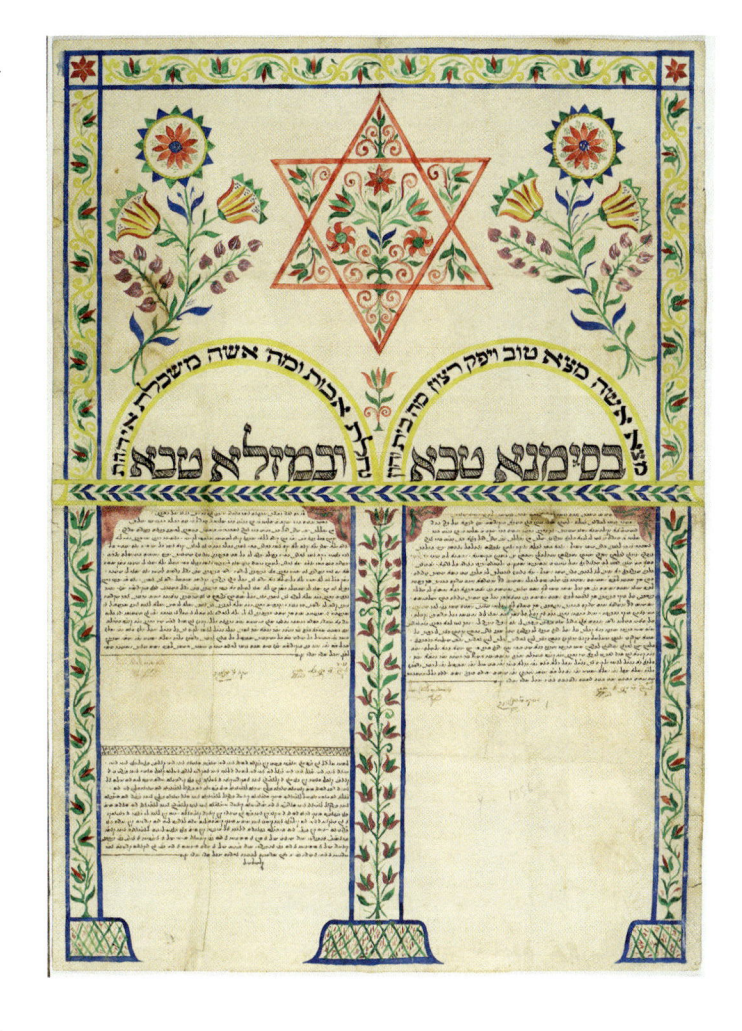

Medal of Appreciation (Wenzel Seidan)

In 1860, the Austrian Jewish community commissioned a medal of appreciation for Franz Joseph to commemorate the emperor's granting to Jews the right to own property within the Austrian Empire. It was created by Wenzel Seidan (1817–1870), a Czech medalist and engraver. Seidan studied at the fine art academies of Prague and Vienna, ultimately settling in the Austrian capital after also working in Italy and France.

Medal of Appreciation from the Austrian Jewish Community to Emperor Franz Joseph for Granting the Right to Own Property
1860

Gift of the Samuel Freidenberg Collection, FB/600-1860-1. Photo by Richard Goodbody, Inc. The Jewish Museum, New York. Image courtesy of the Jewish Museum, New York/Art Resource, NY.

Torah Scroll and Case (Artist Unknown)

The origin of this Torah scroll is in Turkey. It was donated by the Camondo family, one of the most important Jewish families in Istanbul, many of whose members settled in Paris and greatly contributed to French cultural life.

Torah Scroll and Case
1860

© RMN-Grand Palais/Art Resource, NY.

Kiddush Cup and Wine Carafe (Daniel Henriques de Castro)

Daniel Henriques de Castro (1806–1863), a member of one of Amsterdam's prominent Portuguese Jewish families, was a pharmacist, art collector, and glass engraver. He executed works for use in Jewish rituals as well as items for non-Jewish clients. Castro took after the master engraver known as Wolf, carrying on the technique of stippling, whereby numerous small dots are made upon a glass surface with the use of an etching needle and a small hammer. A painstaking process, the stipple method produces a particularly delicate, filmlike design that cannot be achieved through the more common technique of acid etching. In 1883, Castro's son published an article about glass engraving, "Een en ander over glasgravure," in a Dutch quarterly, detailing the processes of his father's art.

Kiddush Cup and Wine Carafe
ca. 1860

Collection Jewish Historical Museum, Amsterdam.

Postage Stamp (Jacob Abraham Jesurun)

The descendant of Portuguese Jews who emigrated from Holland to the Caribbean in the seventeenth century, Jacob Abraham Jesurun (1806–1875) was a merchant in Curaçao, where his company owned several ships as well as a wharf, dockyard, and coal depot. The Jesurun firm also obtained a contract for mail delivery within the Caribbean in 1867, and in 1869 had its own stamps printed featuring the firm's initials, J.A.J.&Z. (Jacob Abraham Jesurun & Zoon), and the firm's home port of Curaçao.

Postage Stamp
1861

Courtesy of American Sephardi Federation.

416 VISUAL AND MATERIAL CULTURE

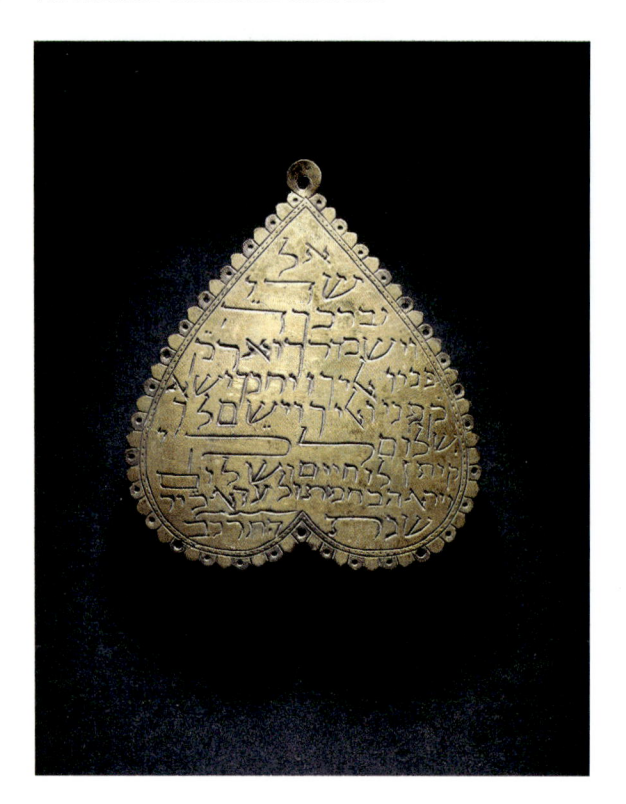

Amulet for Bitoul Ada (Artist Unknown)

This unusual heart-shaped amulet from Morocco is inscribed with the words "God Almighty," followed by the priestly blessing (Numbers 6:24–26) and an individualized text: "May God give him life and peace, and fear of God, the youth Bitoul Ada, son of Y——, in the year 5622."

Amulet for Bitoul Ada
1861–1862

The Jewish Museum, New York.

Medal—St. Stephanskirche (Jacques Wiener)

Medal of St. Stephen's Cathedral, Vienna
1862

Courtesy of the American Numismatic Society.

Paper Cut—Brit Milah (Nachman ha-Kohen Bialsker)

The paper cut made by Nachman ha-Kohen Bialsker commemorates a circumcision, or *brit milah*.

Paper Cut—Brit Milah
1862

Courtesy of Yad Chaim Weizmann, the Weizmann Archives, Rehovot, Israel.

Ketubah (Zemah Davidsohn)

Artist and calligrapher Zemah Davidsohn created this marriage contract for a Jewish couple who married in New York in 1863.

Ketubah
1863

Courtesy of the Library of the Jewish Theological Seminary, New York.

Alms Plate (Artist Unknown)

Alms Plate
1864

Israel Museum, Jerusalem, Israel/Bridgeman Images.

A Jewish Tailor (Mark Antokolski, sculptor)

Born in Vilna, Mark Antokolski (1843–1902) studied at the Imperial Academy of Fine Arts in St. Petersburg, where he won the Great Silver Medal for *A Jewish Tailor* in 1864. Other early sculptures on Jewish themes were *The Miser* (1865), *The Kiss of Judah Iscariot* (1867), *The Talmudic Debate* (1869), and *Inquisition* (1869). Turning his attention to Russian history, Antokolski's *Ivan the Terrible* (1871) impressed Emperor Alexander II, who acquired it for the Hermitage. Other Russian subjects included Peter the Great, Tolstoy, and Turgenev. Antokolski won first prize in sculpture at the Paris Exposition of 1878.

A Jewish Tailor
1864

State Russian Museum, St. Petersburg. © 2014, State Russian Museum, St. Petersburg.

Medal with the Image of Judith and Moses Montefiore (Charles Wiener)

Charles Wiener (1832–1888) had an illustrious career as a medalist in Belgium. His output featured architectural medals (many of which were collaborations with his brother Jacques) as well as royal portrait and exhibition medals. Notable pieces included a portrait of Prince Albert (Queen Victoria's consort), the city of London, and a medal commemorating the visit of Tsar Alexander II to London in 1874. Jewish subjects included a medal of E. A. Astruc, chief rabbi of Belgium, and a double portrait of Sir Moses and Lady Judith Montefiore.

Medal with the Image of Judith and Moses Montefiore
1864

Photo © The Israel Museum, Jerusalem by Peter Lanyi.

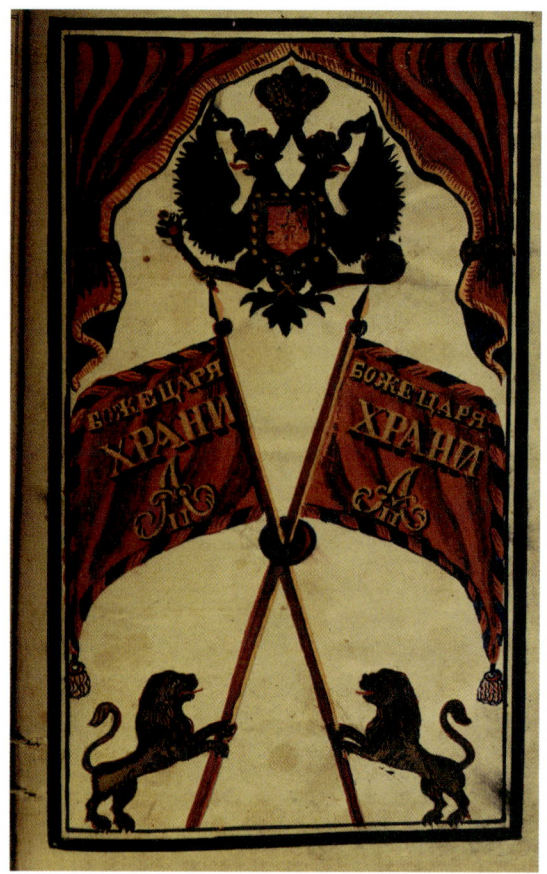

Minute Book of Psalms Society Serving in the Russian Army

In 1827, Tsar Nicholas I issued a statute that effectively made Russian Jews liable to military service, as part of a policy that sought to transform the Jewish population into integrated subjects who would be useful to the interests of the monarchy. While serving in the army, many Jewish soldiers maintained a sense of community by collectively participating in religious practices. A minute book, or *pinkas*, kept by a group of Jewish soldiers between 1864 and 1887, serving in Shkudy (Skuodas, Lithuania), details the activities of a Psalms Society, or *ḥevra tehilim*, organized among Jews serving in the Fourth Infantry Regiment of the Russian Army. The scribe is said to have been Judah Scheindling of Shkudy. Psalms Societies comprised voluntary groups of Jewish worshipers who would recite psalms in connection with specific occasions and rituals.

Minute-Book of Psalms Society Serving in the Russian Army
1864–1867

The Mendel Gottesman Library, Yeshiva University, MS. 1150.

Medal Commemorating the Opening of the Dutch Jewish Orphanage in Amsterdam (Jacques Elion)

The medalist Jacques Elion (1842–1893), from a Dutch Sephardic family, was introduced to his craft by his father, Samuel Jacob Cohen Elion (1812–1880), a medalist and gem cutter. After studying at the Royal Academy of Fine Arts in Amsterdam, Jacques Elion had a successful career making portrait medals honoring members of the Dutch royal family as well as governmental and cultural figures. He also designed medals to commemorate the openings of social welfare institutions (e.g., orphanages, homes for the aged), public buildings (the City Theater, the Palace of Industry), and events (the International Agricultural Exhibition) in Amsterdam.

Medal Commemorating the Opening of the Dutch Jewish Orphanage in Amsterdam
1865

The Jewish Museum, New York. Gift of the Samuel and Daniel M. Friedenberg Collection, FB/600-1865-1. Photo by Richard Goodbody, Inc. Image courtesy of the Jewish Museum, New York/Art Resource, NY.

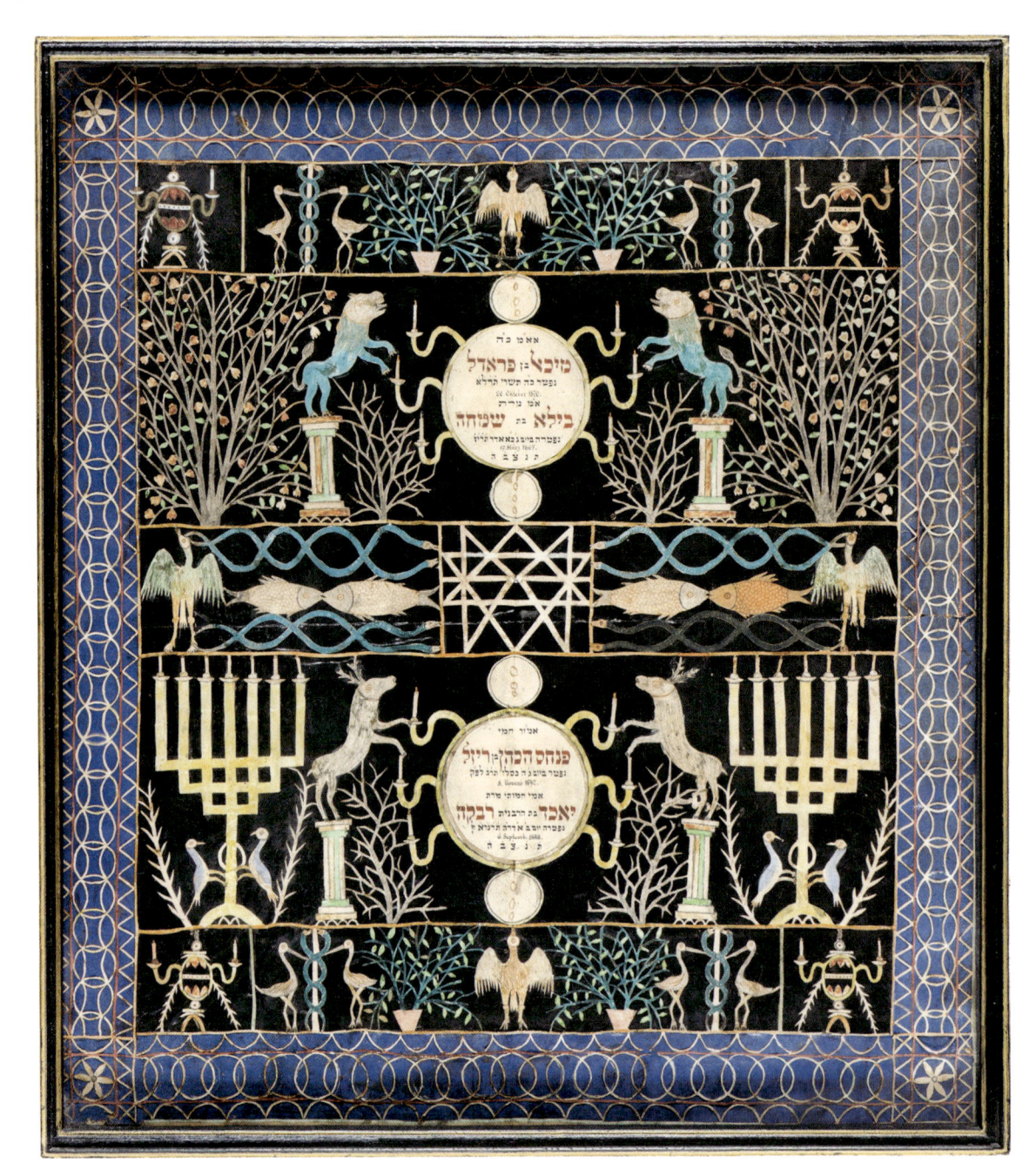

Paper Cut—Yortsayt (Artist Unknown)

This paper cut, commemorating the anniversary of a date of death, originates from Galicia.

Paper Cut—Yortsayt
1867–1880

Anonymous owner, Haifa. Photograph by Noam Feiner.

Ivan the Terrible (Mark Antokolski)

Ivan the Terrible
1871

State Russian Museum, St. Petersburg. © 2014, State Russian Museum, St. Petersburg.

Religious Liberty Monument (Moses Ezekiel)

Born in Richmond, Virginia, Moses Ezekiel (1844–1917) was a soldier-turned-sculptor whose time in the military greatly influenced many of his works. Ezekiel, who entered the Virginia military in 1862, became known for his Civil War memorials, monuments, and portraits. In addition to his military sculpture, Ezekiel was the first Jewish sculptor in America to make monuments for the Jewish community. Following the end of the Civil War, he studied sculpture in Ohio, but soon moved to Berlin to attend the city's art academy. While in Berlin, Ezekiel was awarded the prestigious Michel Beer Prix de Rome, which provided the artist a stipend to study in Rome for two years. Finding success and renown in Rome among local and international audiences, Ezekiel spent his career working and traveling between Italy and America.

Religious Liberty Monument
Marble
1876

Courtesy of National Museum of American Jewish History, Philadelphia, The City of Philadelphia, Fairmount Park Commission. Photo by Jeff Goldberg/Esto.

Ketubah (Artist Unknown)

This ketubah was created in Isfahan, Iran.

Ketubah

1887

Courtesy of the Library of the Jewish Theological Seminary, New York.

Synagogue Architecture

Shearith Israel Synagogue

Congregation Shearith Israel was the first Jewish congregation established in North America, and the only Jewish congregation in New York City from 1654 until 1825. Between 1654 and 1730, it met in rented quarters, consecrating its first building in 1730 on Mill Street. To meet the needs of a steadily growing membership, the congregation moved into five different buildings over the centuries. The American Jewish architect Arnold Brunner designed Shearith Israel's present location, which it has occupied since 1897.

Shearith Israel
1730 and 1818

Image courtesy of the YIVO Institute for Jewish Research. Permission from the rights holder: Drawings by Esther Oppenheim, used by permission of Congregation Shearith Israel.

Built 1730, rebuilt 1818, a synagogue stood on Mill Street for over a century

With the Crosby Street Synagogue, 1834, Shearith Israel began its northward march

Touro Synagogue, Newport, Rhode Island

The Touro Synagogue in Newport, Rhode Island, is home to the second-oldest congregation in the United States. As Sephardic Jews began emigrating from the Caribbean to colonial America in the seventeenth century, the Jewish population of Newport grew and eventually established the Nephuse Israel Congregation, which later became the Congregation Jeshuat Israel toward the end of the 1600s. By the mid-eighteenth century, the community had acquired sufficient financial support to build a synagogue and began construction in 1759. Designed in the European Palladian style that was popularized in colonial architecture, the synagogue was completed in 1763. Later named after Isaac Touro who kept watch over the institution during the American Revolution, the building was designated a National Historic Site in 1946.

Touro Synagogue
1763

Courtesy Touro Synagogue.

Synagogue in the Park at Wörlitz, Germany

Designed in the German neoclassical style, the Wörlitz synagogue was modeled on Rome's Temple of Vesta, featuring a circular building with a conical roof. A cemetery and house for *taharah*, ritual purification of the dead, were constructed in 1795. The synagogue remained open until 1910. Its architect, Friedrich Wilhelm von Erdmannsdorff (1736–1800), was an eminent German architect and artistic adviser to Prince Leopold Friedrich Franz von Anhalt-Dessau, who commissioned Erdmannsdorff to design the building in 1789. The synagogue was constructed a year later in Wörlitz's main park, replacing its predecessor, which was torn down to accommodate the construction of a town hall in the city's market square.

Synagogue in the Park at Wörlitz, Germany
1789–1790

Photo: akg-images/Schütze/Rodemann.

Janów Sokólski Synagogue

Janów, Poland, was home to a unique wooden synagogue. The town was settled by Jews toward the end of the seventeenth century, and by 1739 the Jewish population formed the majority of the town's residents. In 1719, the local diocese permitted the construction of a synagogue, which was completed in 1740. In keeping with the Polish–Lithuanian architectural tradition, the Janów synagogue drew on local wooden building traditions and featured a painted and carved interior. Prior to World War II, the synagogue was restored and conserved by the State Office for Historical Buildings; however, like most wooden synagogues in Poland, it was burned and destroyed by Nazis during the war.

Janów Sokólski Synagogue
Eighteenth Century

Art Institute of the Polish Academy of Sciences, Warsaw, negative number 18691.

Óbuda Synagogue

The Óbuda Synagogue in Budapest is the oldest functioning synagogue in Hungary. The building, designed by Hungarian architect András Landherr, was inaugurated in 1821. Its restrained, neoclassical aesthetic was consistent with popular architectural trends in nineteenth-century Hungary, distinguished only by Hebrew inscriptions on the outer façade of the building.

Óbuda Synagogue
1820–1821

Gross Family Collection.

Interior of the Beth Elohim Synagogue, Charleston, South Carolina (Solomon Nunes Carvalho)

1838

Collection of Kahal Kadosh Beth Elohim. Photo courtesy of Special Collections, College of Charleston Library.

Dohány Street Synagogue

The Dohány Street Synagogue in Budapest is the largest synagogue in Europe, and the second largest in the world, capable of accommodating three thousand people. The German-born Austrian architect Ludwig Förster designed the Moorish- and Byzantine-inspired synagogue, which was built between 1854 and 1859. A Jewish museum flanking the synagogue was built between 1930 and 1931, constructed upon the former home of Theodor Herzl, founder of the Zionist movement. The synagogue remains open to worshipers and visitors, as do the museum and a Holocaust memorial park.

Dohány Street Synagogue
1854–1859

Sergii Korshun © 123RF.

Grand Synagogue of Lyon (Abraham Hirsch)

Born to a family of embroiderers, Abraham Hirsch (1828–1913) studied architecture at the École des Beaux-Arts in Lyon, France. Because the traditional apprentice system was often closed to Jews who faced endemic antisemitism, the burgeoning academic system offered more opportunity for aspiring Jewish architects. Hirsch was the first known Jew to have attended a Western school of architecture, and he went on to become the chief architect of Lyon. He designed numerous buildings in the city, including the Grand Synagogue of Lyon, which was completed in 1864. Designed in the neo-Byzantine style, the synagogue is now designated an official historic monument.

Grand Synagogue of Lyon
1863–1864

Image courtesy Bibliothèque municipale de Lyon. Photographer: Nicolas Daum.

Grand Synagogue of Paris (Alfred-Philibert Aldrophe)

A leading Jewish architect of the late nineteenth century, Alfred-Philibert Aldrophe (1834–1895) studied at the National School of Design in Paris. Aldrophe worked with prominent Jewish clients, including the Rothschilds, the wealthy family of bankers for whom he designed a private residence in Paris, the Rothschild Orphanage, and the Synagogue at Versailles. Aldrophe was also selected as the architect for the monumental Synagogue de la Victoire, in Paris. Designed in the neo-Romanesque style of many contemporaneous French churches, the synagogue complemented the prevailing architectural aesthetic in France, integrating the architectural and social structures of Jewish spiritual life into a predominantly Christian city. Aldrophe took part in the French international exhibitions of 1855 and 1867, and he was appointed as a judge on the awards committee for the London Exhibition of 1862. Following his distinction as an officer of the Legion of Honor in 1867, he became the official architect of the eleventh arrondissement of Paris in 1871.

Grand Synagogue of Paris (*Synagogue de la Victoire*)
1867–1876

Photo courtesy of Grand Synagogue of Paris.

Fine Art

Theresa Concordia Mengs
1725–1808

Theresa Concordia Mengs was the daughter of the Dresden court painter Ismael Israel Mengs (1688–1764), who had converted to Protestantism before her birth, and the elder sister of the renowned artist Anton Raphael Mengs (1728–1779). She spent most of her life in Rome and was known for her miniature portraits in pastel and paint on enamel, as well as miniature copies after Renaissance masters. Mengs also worked in Dresden as court painter to the Electors of Saxony. She was elected a member of the Accademia di San Luca in Rome in 1765.

Self-Portrait
1745

Image courtesy of bpk, Berlin/Staatliche Kunstsammlungen, Dresden, Germany/Art Resource, NY.

Martha Isaacs (Attributed)
ca. 1755–1840

An Anglo-Jewish miniature painter, Martha Isaacs was likely the daughter of the embroiderer Levi Isaacs. She studied under the British landscape painter Thomas Burgess, prior to traveling to Calcutta, where she painted portraits of British subjects. There, Isaacs married a prominent English official, Alexander Higgins, following her conversion to Christianity. Isaacs exhibited her work with the Free Society of Artists in London, a group of artists who organized annual exhibitions of contemporary British art in the 1760s.

Portrait of David Tevele Schiff, Chief Rabbi of London
ca. 1765–1771

On loan from the United Synagogue. © Jewish Museum London.

Anton Raphael Mengs
1728–1779

Anton Raphael Mengs, son of Ismael Israel Mengs (1688–1764), a Dresden court painter who had converted to Protestantism, was a pioneer of the neoclassical style. In his time he was celebrated as the greatest living painter. Among Anton Raphael Mengs's most notable works are the ceiling fresco *Parnassus with Apollo and the Muses* (1759) in the Villa Albani in Rome and the frescoes he painted for Charles III at the Palacio Real in Madrid (1762–1769 and 1774–1775). Mengs published a number of volumes on art, including the influential handbook for painters *Thoughts on Beauty and Taste in Painting* (1762).

Annunciation
1767

Image courtesy of Alfredo Dagli Orti/Art Resource, NY.

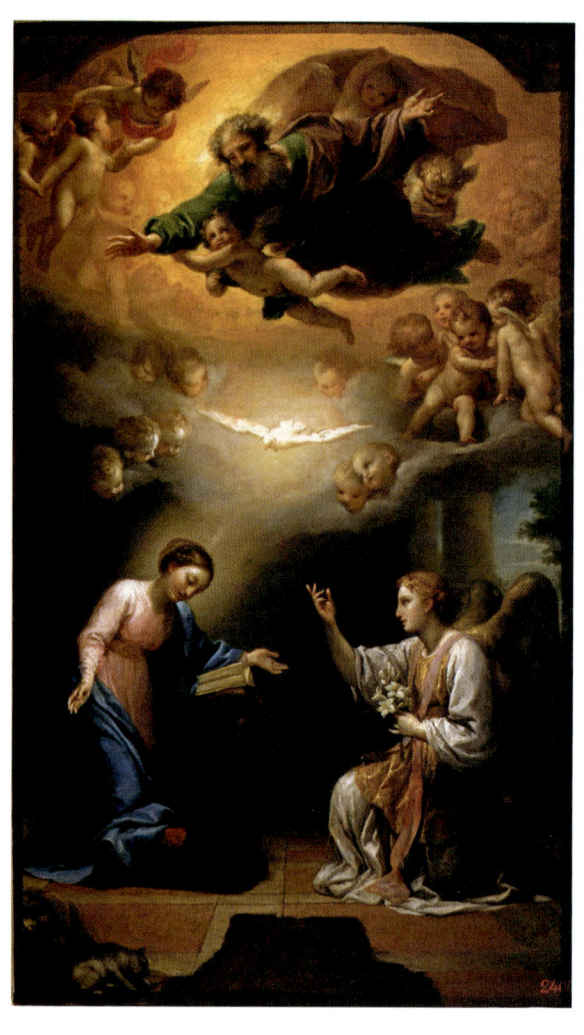

Anton Raphael Mengs

Portrait of the Marquesa de Llano
1770

Real Academia de Bellas Artes de San Fernando, Madrid, Spain. Image courtesy of Scala/Art Resource, NY.

Charles Towne
1781–1854

Charles Towne, the son of the painter Francis Town (also known as Isaac b. Benjamin Thun; 1738–1826), was known for his portrayals of English country life in the first decades of the nineteenth century. His depictions of landscapes and animals have affinities with the Norwich School; prominent among these works are Towne's *The Boat Builders, Norwich* (1811) and *Cattle Fair* (1826), which portrays the marketplace in Norwich. Beginning in 1806, Towne exhibited his works at the Royal Academy of Arts and the British Institution.

Landscape with Figures
1812

Towneley Hall Art Gallery and Museum, Burnley, Lancashire/Bridgeman Images.

Triumph des Jahres 1813.
Den Deutschen zum Neuenjahr.

Henschel Brothers (Gebrüder Henschel)

Friedrich (1781-1837); August (1783-1828/1829); Wilhelm (1785-1865); and Moritz (1788-1862)

The Henschel brothers were four Breslau-born Jewish artists who collectively signed their work "Gebrüder Henschel" (Henschel Brothers). Working in Berlin from around 1806 to 1829, they became widely known for their popular engravings "Scenes from the Life of Goethe," as well as portraits of celebrities (including the philosopher Johann Gottlieb Fichte and the soprano Angelica Catalani), theatrical scenes, patriotic illustrations, and series depicting the military costumes of the Prussian and French armies. The image depicted here is a caricature of the victory over Napoleon at the Battle of Leipzig, December 1813.

Triumph des Jahres 1813 (*Triumph of the Year 1813*)
1813

Deutsches Historisches Museum, Berlin/S. Ahlers.

Philipp Veit
1793–1877

Philipp Veit was the grandson of the philosopher Moses Mendelssohn and the stepson of the poet and critic Friedrich von Schlegel. He studied with the great romantic painter Caspar David Friedrich in Dresden. Veit converted to Catholicism in 1810 and went on to paint many Christian subjects. From 1815 to 1830, he lived in Rome, where he was a leading figure in the Nazarenes, a group of German romantic painters. From 1830–1843, Veit served as director of the Städel Institute in Frankfurt, where he painted the fresco *The Introduction of the Arts to Germany through Christianity* (1832–1836).

Religion
1819

Photo credit: bpk, Berlin/Nationalgalerie, Staatliche Museen, Berlin, Germany/Klaus Göken/Art Resource, NY.

Jeremiah David Alexander Fiorino
1797–1847

Born in Kassel, Germany, Jeremiah David Alexander Fiorino was a prominent miniaturist who painted portraits on porcelain and ivory. He studied at the Kassel Academy, where he won a grand prize. Fiorino decorated a famous Meissen service for the Saxon royal family and served as court painter in Dresden, where he made notable portraits, including medallions of King Albert, Prince Maximilian, and Prince Ernest of Saxony.

Portrait of a Girl with a Red Belt
ca. 1820s

Fine Art Gallery Alte Kunst, Vienna.

Moritz Daniel Oppenheim
1800–1882

Moritz Daniel Oppenheim, an observant Jew born in Hanau, Germany, became the first Jewish member of the Frankfurt Museum Society in 1825. Early in his career, he painted religious subjects and portraits, including of the Rothschild family and Heinrich Heine. Oppenheim's *The Return of the Jewish Volunteer from the Wars of Liberation to His Family Still Living in Accordance with Old Customs* (1833–1834) explored Jewish acculturation in the face of modernity. He published this painting, along with nineteen other works, in *Scenes from Traditional Jewish Family Life* (1866), which was widely distributed in several portfolios and bound editions.

The Return of the Jewish Volunteer from the Wars of Liberation to His Family Still Living in Accordance with Old Customs
1833–1834

The Jewish Museum, New York. Gift of Richard and Beatrice Levy. Photo by John Parnell. Image courtesy of the Jewish Museum, New York/Art Resource, NY.

Solomon Alexander Hart
1806–1881

Solomon Alexander Hart entered the Royal Academy of Arts in 1823 and was elected the first Jewish member of the academy in 1840. He was known for Jewish subjects including *Interior of a Polish Synagogue at the Moment When the Manuscript of the Law Is Elevated* (1829–1830) and *The Feast of the Rejoicing of the Law at the Synagogue in Leghorn, Italy* (1850). Hart also painted many historical subjects, frequently drawn from Shakespeare's plays and Walter Scott's novels.

An Early Reading of Shakespeare
1838

© Royal Academy of Arts, London. Photographer: John Hammond.

Charlotte von Rothschild
1807–1859

Charlotte von Rothschild was born into a prominent Jewish banking family, growing up in London prior to moving to Frankfurt later in life with her husband. Having long taken an interest in art, Rothschild studied under the French painter Baron François Gérard, as well as the painter and art dealer Moritz Oppenheim, who painted her marriage portrait. One of Rothschild's most outstanding works is a Haggadah she illuminated for her uncle, Amschel Mayer Rothschild, completed in 1842. Containing eighteen text illustrations in addition to decorated initials, the Haggadah is remarkable for its conflation of Jewish and Christian motifs, interpreted through a nineteenth-century aesthetic sensibility. It is the only known Hebrew manuscript to have been illuminated by a woman.

Passover Haggadah with German Translation
1842

Braginsky Collection No. 314, title page. Braginsky Collection, Zurich. Photography by Ardon Bar-Hama, Ra'anana, Israel.

Solomon Alexander Hart

The Feast of the Rejoicing of the Law at the Synagogue in Leghorn, Italy
1850

© The Jewish Museum, New York/Art Resource, NY.

Rudolf Lehmann
1829–1905

Rudolf Lehmann was born into a Jewish family of artists near Hamburg. The son of Leo Lehmann, a painter, Lehmann undertook his artistic training in Paris, Munich, and Rome, alongside his brother Henry. After winning a gold medal at the Paris Salon 1843 for one of his paintings, the artist was commissioned by the French government to produce a number of religious paintings for provincial churches. Lehmann became a talented and sought-after portraitist, whose sitters included English nobles, as well as the poet and playwright Robert Browning. Having married in London and spent much of his career in the city, Lehmann frequently exhibited at the Royal Academy. Later in his life Lehmann also wrote his autobiography.

Portrait of Leo Lehmann
1851

The Cleveland Museum of Art, Bequest of Noah L. Butkin 1980.268. © The Cleveland Museum of Art.

Salomon Leonardus Verveer
1813–1876

Salomon Leonardus Verveer was a Dutch artist, born in The Hague, who specialized in townscapes rendered in a romantic style. While he traveled through France and Germany, the cities and villages of his homeland were his primary subjects. Verveer depicted harbor views, river scenes, and occasional genre scenes, as well as Jewish neighborhoods. He received awards in Brussels in 1842 and 1851, and in his native land Verveer was named a knight of the Order of the Netherlands Lion (1863) and was appointed to the Order of the Oak Crown by King William III (1874).

Townview with Bell Tower in the Background
1851

Collection Simonis & Buunk, Ede, The Netherlands.

Solomon Nunes Carvalho
1815–1897

Solomon Nunes Carvalho, the son of a prominent Sephardic family in Charleston, South Carolina, had a career as both a painter and a photographer. While he was a distinguished portraitist, he also painted other subjects including his childhood synagogue, Kahal Kadosh Beth Elohim. In the 1840s, Carvalho made daguerreotypes, and in 1853–1854, he accompanied General John C. Fremont as the official photographer for an expedition through the territories of Kansas, Colorado, and Utah. Carvalho subsequently had studios in New York, Philadelphia, Baltimore, and Charleston and was active in the Jewish communities of those cities.

Portrait of Wakara
1854

Gilcrease Museum, Tulsa, OK.

Abraham Solomon
1824–1862

Abraham Solomon was from a prominent Ashkenazic family that came to Britain in the late eighteenth century. He studied at the Royal Academy and showed there regularly beginning in 1841. Solomon was known for his paintings of literary genre subjects and socially conscious themes of contemporary life. Early in his career he painted Jewish subjects, including *Rabbi Expounding the Scriptures*, shown at the Society of British Artists in 1840. Solomon's painting *First Class: The Meeting—And at First Meeting Loved* (1854) prompted a scandal, leading Solomon to paint a second more respectable version (seen here). Two of Abraham Solomon's siblings—Rebecca and Simeon—also had notable artistic careers.

First Class—The Meeting
1855

National Railway Museum, York, Great Britain. Image courtesy of SSPL/National Railway Museum/Art Resource, NY.

Abraham Solomon

Waiting for the Verdict
1857

Tate Gallery, London, Great Britain. Image courtesy of Tate, London/Art Resource, NY.

Friedrich Friedländer
1825-1901

A Bohemian-born artist, Friedrich Friedländer was a celebrated genre painter who studied at the Vienna Academy. Friedländer began his career as a history painter—the most prestigious genre of academic painting at the time—creating the sensationalized *The Death of Tasso*, prior to devoting the majority of his oeuvre to genre scenes. As a more democratic outlook on subjects worthy of aesthetic consideration began to take root in painting of the period, Friedländer drew inspiration from scenes of military and everyday life in Vienna. He was awarded several orders of knighthood, including the Order of Francis Joseph and the Bavarian Order of Michael in 1865, and the crown for merit in 1867. He later was elevated to noble status with the suffix *von Mahlheim* appended to his title.

People Pouring out of a Public Building into the Street
1859

Österreichische Galerie Belvedere.

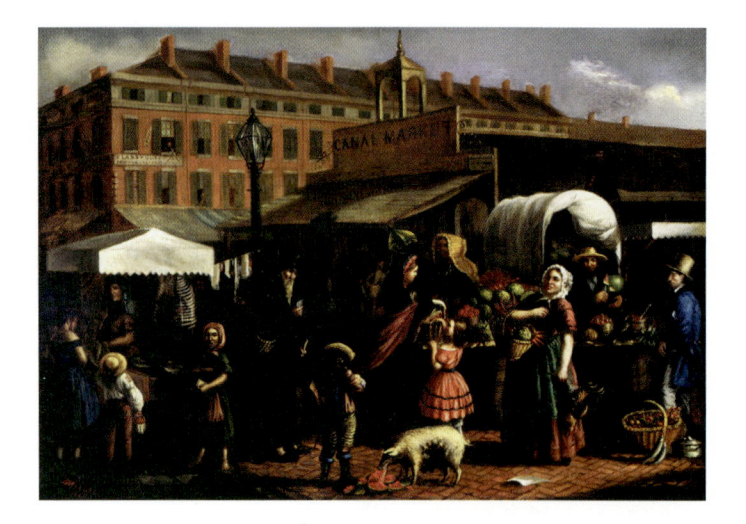

Henry Mosler
1841–1920

The German-born, American-raised painter and printmaker Henry Mosler worked as an artist and correspondent for *Harper's Weekly* during the Civil War. In his home city of Cincinnati, he painted *Plum Street Temple* (ca. 1866), representing the synagogue of the leading Reform Rabbi Isaac Mayer Wise, as well as portraits of the local Jewish community. Mosler subsequently settled in Paris, where he showed his works in the Salon from 1878 to 1897. His 1879 entry, *Return of the Prodigal Son*, was awarded an honorable mention and acquired for the Musée du Luxembourg, making it the first painting by an American artist that the French government purchased.

Canal Street Market
1860

Cincinnati Museum Center–Cincinnati History Library & Archives.

Aleksander Lesser
1814–1884

Born into a wealthy family of Warsaw bankers and merchants, Aleksander Lesser studied in Warsaw, Dresden, and Munich. He made his reputation as a painter of Polish historical and Christian religious subjects. In the 1860s, Lesser became one of the first artists to depict scenes from the history of Polish Jewry. He is most known for his painting of a contemporary event: *The Funeral of the Five Victims* shows a cross section of Polish society (Catholics, Protestants, and Jews) at the funeral for protesters who were shot by police during a patriotic demonstration in Warsaw on March 2, 1861.

The Funeral of the Five Victims
1861

From the collection of the National Museum in Kraków. Image courtesy of Photographic Studio of the National Museum in Kraków.

Rebecca Solomon
1832–1886

Rebecca Solomon painted works based on seventeenth- and eighteenth-century dramas as well as contemporary genre scenes that often touched on issues of class, ethnicity, and gender. As a woman, Solomon was unable to study at the Royal Academy (unlike her brothers Abraham and Simeon), but she trained elsewhere and regularly exhibited her work at the Academy starting in 1858. While Solomon secured important private commissions and was well regarded by critics, she had to supplement her income by working as an artist's assistant and making illustrations for magazines.

The Arrest of the Deserter
1861

The Israel Museum, Jerusalem. Gift of Stella Permewan, Liverpool, through the British Friends of the Art Museums of Israel, B58.08.0347. Photo © The Israel Museum, Jerusalem by Elie Posner.

Maurits Leon
1838–1865

The Dutch genre painter Maurits Leon was born to a distinguished Sephardic family in The Hague. Following his studies there and at the Royal Academy in Antwerp, he settled in Amsterdam, where he became known for his genre paintings and received the Royal Medal in 1861. In the 1860s, his focus shifted to painting Jewish religious services in an Amsterdam synagogue as well as subjects related to the history of Sephardic Jews in Holland. Unfortunately, the whereabouts of all but a few of Leon's paintings are unknown. The image of *Spinoza before His Judges* is of a lithograph by Johannes Heinrich Rennefeld (1832–1877).

Spinoza before His Judges
ca. 1865–1870

Lithograph after a painting (no longer extant) by Maurits Leon. Collection of Jewish Historical Museum, Amsterdam.

Jacques-Émile-Édouard Brandon
1831–1897

Born into a Spanish Portuguese family in Bordeaux, Jacques-Émile-Édouard Brandon studied at the École des Beaux-Arts in Paris and initially made his reputation with Christian subjects, particularly his series on the life of Saint Bridget. He later focused on Jewish themes, notably synagogue and classroom scenes, the Sabbath, and portrayals of rabbis with children. While Brandon's style was academic, he did show *Scene in a Synagogue* and other works in the first impressionist exhibition in 1874.

Sermon of the Fast of Av (Synagogue of Amsterdam)
1867

Musée d'art et d'histoire du Judaïsme, Paris, France. On deposit from the Louvre. Inv. RF1116: D.94.511. Photo by Hervé Lewandowski. ©RMN-Grand Palais/Art Resource, NY.

Édouard Moyse

1827–1908

Édouard Moyse was born in Nancy and raised in Paris, where he studied at the École des Beaux-Arts. He became one of the first artists in France (along with Édouard Brandon) to represent Jewish subjects. Moyse painted biblical themes; scenes of Jewish life and ritual, significant historical events for French Jewry; and portraits of rabbis. He first showed at the Salon in 1850 and was awarded a second-class medal in 1862.

The Grand Sanhedrin
1867

Musée d'art et d'histoire du Judaïsme, Paris. Photo: Michèle Bellot. © RMN-Grand Palais/Art Resource, NY.

Simeon Solomon
1840–1905

Simeon Solomon attended the Royal Academy at age fifteen and was the youngest artist whose work was ever shown there. Early in his career, he painted Old Testament and Jewish religious subjects. Inspired by the Italian Renaissance, Solomon increasingly turned to religious mystical subjects and classical pagan themes painted in a pre-Raphaelite style. Much of Solomon's work was homoerotic, and in 1871 his prose poem on the theme of same-sex male love, "A Vision of Love Revealed in Sleep," was attacked. His arrest and conviction for gross indecency in 1873 destroyed Solomon's career and led to years of social condemnation, alcoholism, and poverty.

Carrying the Scrolls of the Law
1867

The Whitworth Art Gallery, the University of Manchester/Bridgeman Images.

Moritz Daniel Oppenheim

The Bar Mitzvah Discourse
1869

The Jewish Museum, New York. Gift of the Oscar and Regina Gruss Charitable and Educational Foundation, Inc., 1999. Photo by Richard Goodbody. Image courtesy of the Jewish Museum, New York/Art Resource, NY.

Alberto Henschel
1827–1882

Born in Berlin, Alberto Henschel was the son of Moritz Henschel, of the Gebrüder Henschel (Henschel Brothers). In 1866, he emigrated to Brazil, where he opened photographic studios in Recife, Salvador, Rio de Janeiro, and São Paulo. His studios produced thousands of *cartes de visite* portraying all classes of Brazilian society: nobility, merchants, white middle class, black free, and enslaved people. In 1874, Emperor Dom Pedro II appointed Henschel as a photographer of the Imperial House.

Negersklavin Bahia (*Black Slave Bahia*)
ca. 1869

Leibniz Institute for Regional Geography, Archive for Geography, SAm21-0064.

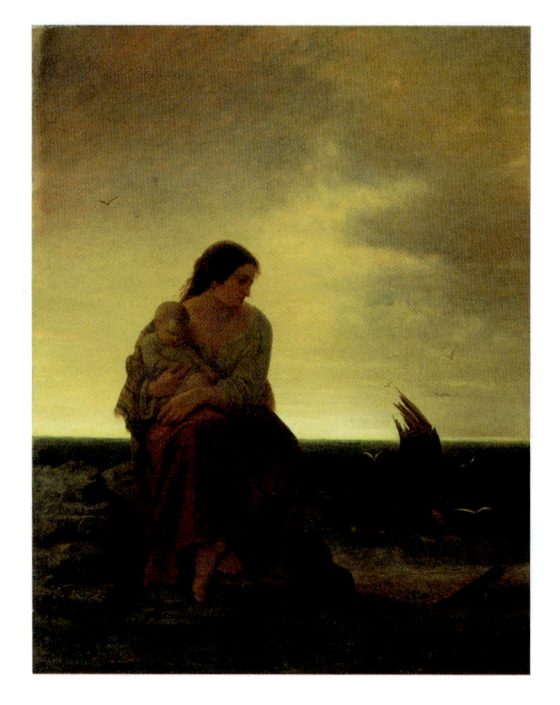

Julius Muhr
1819–1865

The genre painter Julius Muhr, born to a Central European Jewish family, studied at the royal art academies in Berlin and Munich. From 1847 to 1854, he worked on Wilhelm von Kaulbach's suite of murals for the grand staircase at the Neues Museum in Berlin. While primarily known for his genre paintings, Muhr also painted portraits, including one of Leopold Zunz, a founder of *Wissenschaft des Judentums* ("science of Judaism"). Muhr converted to Protestantism when he married in 1860.

Fisherman's Wife Mourning at the Shore
ca. 1860s

Hamburger Kunsthalle, Hamburg, Germany. Photo by Elke Walford. Image courtesy of bpk, Berlin/Hamburger Kunsthalle, Hamburg, Germany/Art Resource, NY.

Jacques-Émile-Édouard Brandon

Heder (Jewish Children's School)
1870

Israel Museum, Jerusalem. B48.09.0399. Photo © The Israel Museum, Jerusalem.

Alphonse Lévy

1843–1918

Born in Alsace, Alphonse Lévy moved to Paris, where he studied academic painting with the French painter and sculptor Jean-Léon Gérôme. Beginning in the mid-1860s, and extending through the years of the Franco-Prussian War and the Paris Commune, he published his political cartoons (under the pseudonym Saïd) in a number of Parisian journals, including *Monde comique*, *Journal amusant*, and *L'éclipse*. Lévy's interest turned to Jewish subjects in the mid-1870s, and his caricatures of rural Alsatian Jews illustrated Léon Cahun's *La vie juive* (1886) and Sacher Masoch's *Contes juives* (1888). In 1902, he published his own volume, *Scènes familiales juives*.

"L'aigle déplumé!..." (*The Bald Eagle!*)
Satirical print of the emperor Napoleon III as an eagle chained to a perch.
1870–1871

© Victoria & Albert Museum, London.

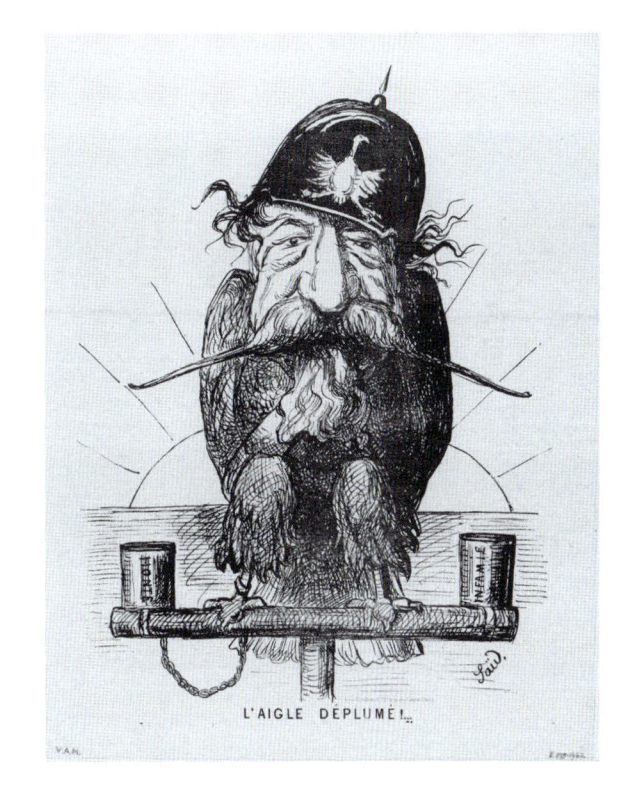

Eduard Julius Friedrich Bendemann
1811–1889

The son of a Berlin Jewish banker and his wife, Eduard Julius Friedrich Bendemann converted to Protestantism as a young man. He gained early recognition for paintings of Jewish historical scenes, notably *Jews Mourning in Exile* (1832) and *Jeremiah at the Destruction of Jerusalem* (1836). Bendemann taught at the Dresden Academy of Fine Arts from 1839 until 1855, during which time he painted a series of monumental frescoes of historical figures and events for the Royal Palace. He served as director of the Düsseldorf Academy from 1859 to 1867, and in his later years returned to Old Testament themes as well as commissioned portraits.

Jeremiah and the Fall of Jerusalem
1872

Nationalgalerie, Staatliche Museen, Berlin, Germany. Image courtesy of bpk, Berlin/Nationalgalerie, Staatliche Museen, Berlin, Germany/Art Resource, NY.

Jozef Israëls
1824–1911

The son of an observant Jewish family in Groningen, Holland, Jozef Israëls became one of the foremost Dutch artists of the nineteenth century. After initially painting portraits and historical subjects, in the 1850s Israëls turned to painting genre scenes in a powerful realist style, particularly depictions of the hard lives of fishermen and their families. In the 1870s, Israëls became a leader of the Hague school and achieved international renown. Late in his career, Israëls portrayed Jewish subjects, notably *The Son of an Ancient People* (1889) and *The Jewish Wedding* (1903), as well as biblical subjects.

The Last Breath
1872

Gift of Ellen Harrison McMichael in memory of C. Emory McMichael, 1942. Philadelphia Museum of Art, Philadelphia, Pennsylvania, USA. Image courtesy of the Philadelphia Museum of Art/Art Resource, NY.

Camille Pissarro
1830–1903

Factory near Pontoise
1873

Camille Pissarro was raised in a French Sephardic family on the Caribbean island of St. Thomas. In 1855, he left for Paris, where he studied at the École des Beaux-Arts and began exhibiting in the Salon in 1859. In the 1870s, Pissarro became a founding member of the impressionists and became known for his luminous landscapes and cityscapes. Often considered the "father" of the impressionist movement, Pissarro was the only artist who showed in all of the group's eight exhibitions (1874–1886).

Photo credit: Kharbine-Tapabor/The Art Archive at Art Resource, NY.

Camille Pissarro

Self-Portrait
1873

Musée d'Orsay, Paris, France. Photo credit: Erich Lessing/Art Resource, NY.

Tina Blau
1845–1916

Born in Vienna in 1845, Tina Blau was the daughter of a physician who enthusiastically supported her artistic development through education and travel. Like many women artists of the period, Blau was not permitted to attend a formal art academy and therefore studied privately. After traveling in Europe and living in an artist colony in Hungary, Blau returned to Vienna, where she shared a studio with the landscape painter Emil Jakob Schindler. Although their relationship was often characterized as one of pupil and teacher, the two were in fact colleagues. Blau moved to Munich in 1883 and married the painter Heinrich Lang following her conversion to Protestantism. In Munich, she taught still life and landscape painting at the Münchner Künstlerinnenverein, a fine arts academy exclusively for women. After her husband's death, Blau returned to Vienna.

Jewish Street in Amsterdam
1875–1876

Eisenberger Collection, Vienna, Austria. © Vera Eisenberger, KG, Vienna.

Max Liebermann
1847–1935

Max Liebermann, the son of a Berlin Jewish family, was a dominant figure in the German art world in a career that spanned many decades. He initially painted Dutch peasants in a realist style, led the antiestablishment naturalist movement in the 1880s–1890s, and after 1895 worked for many years in an impressionist style. Liebermann helped found and served as the president of the progressive Berlin Secession from 1898 to 1910 and was president of the Prussian Academy of Arts from 1920 until Hitler's rise to power in 1933, when Liebermann was forced to resign his position.

The Dutch Sewing School
1876

Von der Heydt-Museum Wuppertal.

Camille Pissarro

A Road in the Woods in Summer
1877

Photo by Hervé Lewandowski. Musée d'Orsay, Paris, France. © RMN-Grand Palais/Art Resource, NY.

Maurycy Gottlieb
1856–1879

Born to an Orthodox family in Drohobych, Galicia (now Ukraine), Maurycy Gottlieb studied art in Lemberg (now Lviv, Ukraine), Vienna, Kraków, and Munich. Important early works on Jewish themes included *A Jewish Wedding (1876)*, *Self-Portrait as Ahasuerus (1876)*, and *Shylock and Jessica* (1876), inspired by Shakespeare's *Merchant of Venice*. Gottlieb is most well known for the large Rembrandtesque paintings that he made in the last three years of his short life, most notably *Jews Praying in the Synagogue on Yom Kippur* (1878) and the unfinished works *Christ before His Judges* (1877–1879) and *Christ Preaching at Capernaum* (1878–1879).

Jews Praying in the Synagogue on Yom Kippur
1878

Tel Aviv Museum of Art Collection. Gift of Sidney Lamon, New York, 1955.

Ernst Josephson
1851–1906

Born in Stockholm to a family that had immigrated from Prussia in the late eighteenth century, Ernst Josephson settled in Paris in 1879. In his early paintings, he primarily focused on historical and biblical subjects inspired by the Old Masters. In the 1880s, influenced by Gustave Courbet and Édouard Manet, his style became more realist and impressionist. Josephson became a leader of the Opponents, a Paris-based group of modernist Swedish artists who rebelled against the artistic conservatism of their native land. While suffering from mental illness during the last two decades of his life, Josephson was extremely productive in an innovative expressionist mode.

David and Saul
1878

Nationalmuseum, Stockholm, Sweden/Bridgeman Images.

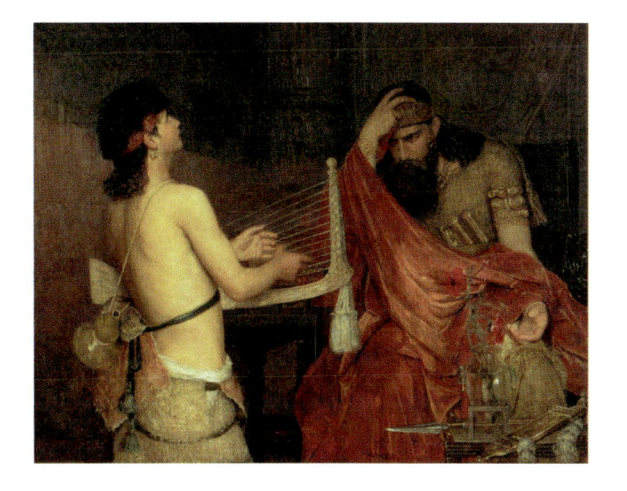

Maurycy Gottlieb

Christ Preaching at Capernaum
1878–1879

Muzeum Narodowe w Warszawie, Warsaw.

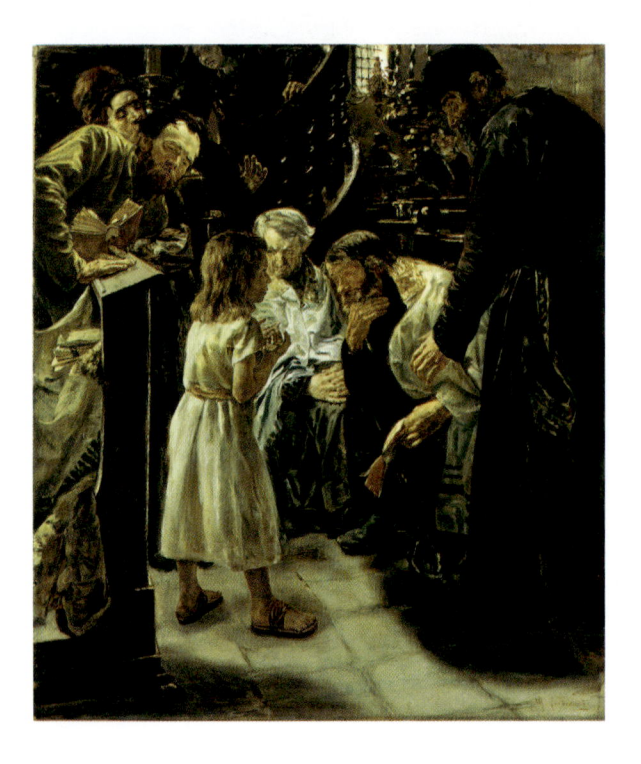

Max Liebermann

The Twelve-Year-Old Jesus in the Temple with the Scholars
1879

Photo Credit: bpk Bildagentur/Hamburger Kunsthalle, Hamburg, Germany/Art Resource, NY.

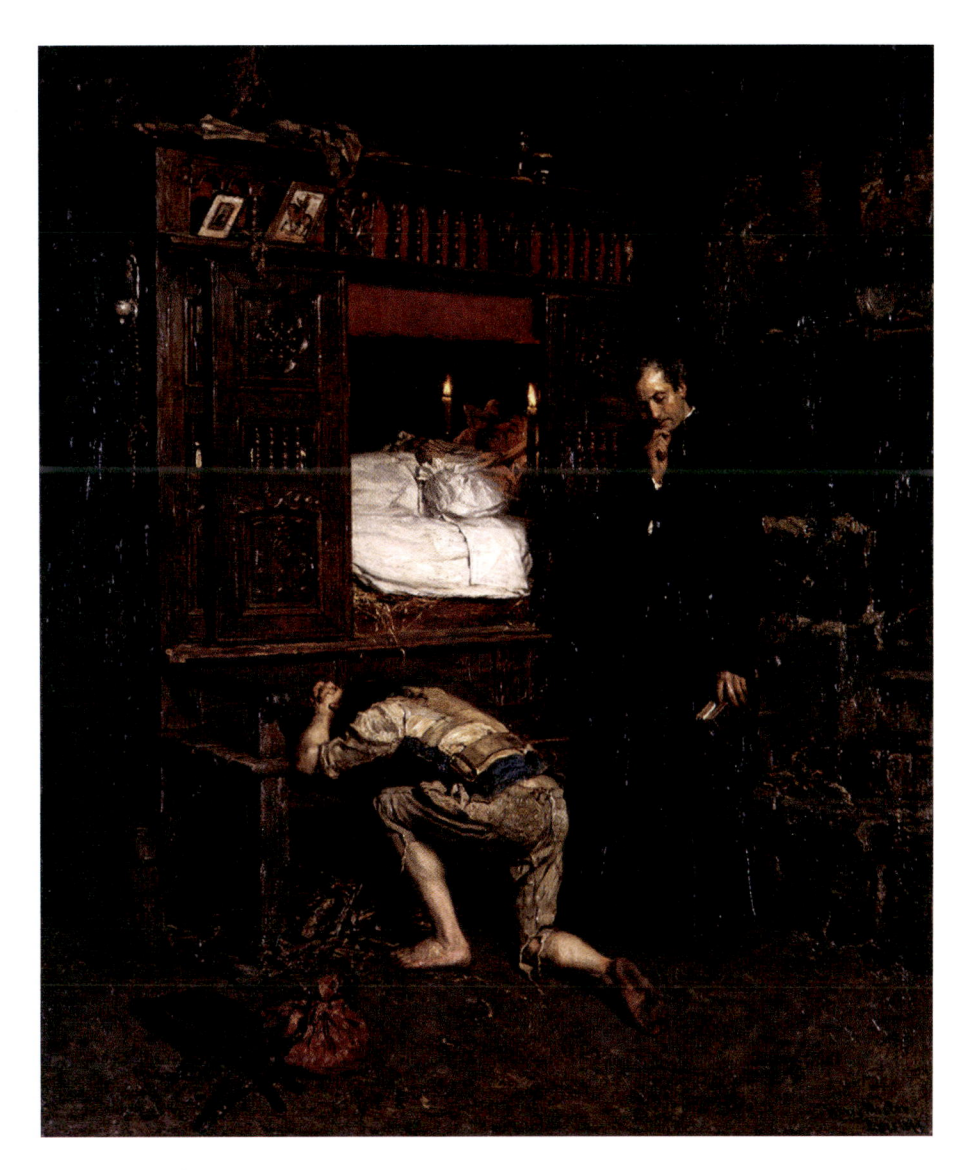

Henry Mosler

Return of the Prodigal Son
1879

Collection Musée départemental breton, Quimper, dépôt du Musée de Cholet—© Cliché Musée départemental breton/Serge Goarin.

Camille Pissarro

The Avenue de l'Opéra, Sunlight, Winter Morning
ca. 1880

Musée Saint-Remi, Reims, France. Photo credit: Erich Lessing/Art Resource, NY.

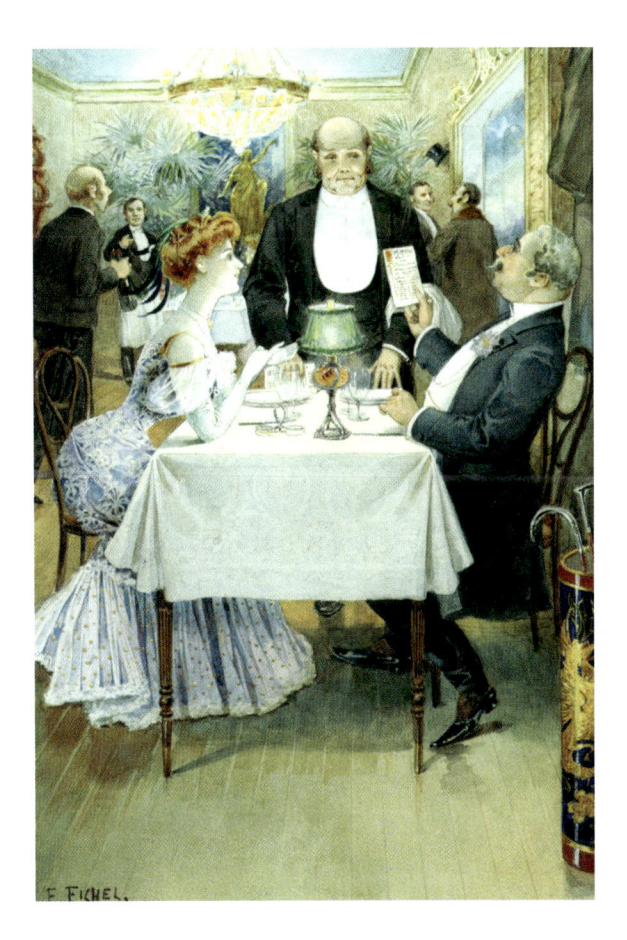

Benjamin-Eugène Fichel
1826–1895

Benjamin-Eugène Fichel was a French artist of small historical and genre paintings who worked in the style of Ernest Meissonier. Like the elder master, Fichel specialized in eighteenth-century themes, and his work was esteemed for its highly refined technique and exactitude of historical details. Fichel attended the École des Beaux-Arts and showed regularly at the Salon, where his paintings won medals in 1857 and 1869. He was named a chevalier of the Legion of Honor in 1870.

At the Restaurant
Date Unknown

John Noott Galleries, Broadway, Worcester, Great Britain. Photo Credit: Fine Art Photographic Library, London/Art Resource, NY.

Friedrich Friedländer

The Death of Tasso
Date Unknown

Österreichische Galerie Belvedere.

Henry Mosler
Date Unknown

***Drawings Published in* Harper's.**
Library of Congress Prints and Photographs Division
Washington DC., 20540. LC-USZ62-124302.

Geskel Salomon
1821–1902

Born and raised in Denmark, Geskel Salomon attended the Royal Swedish Academy of Arts and settled in Sweden. Known for his portraits, he also painted historical events and genre pictures. An observant Jew, Salomon painted scenes of Jewish religious practices in Scandinavia, including *Lighting the Sabbath Candles* (1900). He also published books on the Venus de Milo and the Apollo Belvedere. Salomon became a member of the Academy in 1872.

Ferdinand II, 1810–1859 Bourbon King of Two Sicilies
Date Unknown

Royal Palace Caserta Italy. Image courtesy of Gianni Dagli Orti/The Art Archive at Art Resource, NY.

The Performing Arts

The ritual cycle of Jewish life had always contained a performative aspect. The Passover Seder provided a dramatic ritual around the family table while everyone told the Exodus story, sipped wine, dunked herbs, and counted off the ten plagues. The Torah was read weekly in public with precise cantillation, and cantors led prayer services in joyful or mournful tunes as the occasion demanded. Purim set the scene for carnival-style revelry, costumed antics, and a *purimshpil* (Purim play) capping the merriment of that day. These traditional channels of the performance of Jewishness continued into the modern period, often with some alterations.

The novelty in Jewish performing arts in the later eighteenth and early nineteenth centuries involved the adaptation of traditional materials into new forms, as well as a turn to performing arts that were unconnected to religious life. Jews flocked to theaters and became ardent subscribers, performers, and producers of plays, operas, and music. Some of the most renowned libretti and music of nineteenth-century opera were composed by Jews; some were prolific writers of operettas. Every manner of support for the performing arts could be found within the Jewish world. Jews made their mark as creators and consumers of world-class art music. Remarkably, many artists made a transition within a generation or two from plying their skills within the traditional Jewish ambit to playing them on the greatest stages in the world.

Theater

Isaac Harby
1788–1828

Isaac Harby, from a Sephardic family, was an early leader of the Reform movement in the United States. In the 1820s he helped to found the Reform Society of Israelites in Charleston, working with congregants at Congregation Beth Elohim to petition for changes in the format of the service, introducing English-language prayers and commentary. Harby was also a playwright, critic, and journalist who edited several newspapers in the American South. President James Monroe was in the audience when Harby's dramatic work *Alberti* was performed.

Alberti: A Play in Five Acts
1819

[From] Dramatis Personae

As Performed at the Charleston Theatre

Alberti, *Commander of the Florentine Army*
Lorenso D'Medici, *surnamed the Magnificent*
Ippolito, *betrothed to Antonia*

Scene—Florence, in Italy

Time—A Night and Day, 1480, A.D.

An objection is made against this piece, which I readily admit. It has neither thunder, lightning, assassination, banditti, battles, scenery, nor song to recommend it. Probably my aim was higher, or my taste not exactly conformable to the admirers of Melo-Dramatic extravaganza. Another objection has been started, namely, that to have rendered the catastrophe completely striking, Antonia should have destroyed herself in the second scene of the fifth act. I am aware that *suicide*, (dramatically speaking) is quite the fashion; and that a species of atheistico poetical refinement has lately usurped the place of many of our vulgar notions. But—if I am allowed to know any thing concerning beings of my own creation—I can assure the reader, (who is of course a critic) that Antonia happened to be brought up religiously and morally; and, however unhappy she might have been, she reflected too correctly to have ever contemplated such an act. It is hoped that the reader will take my word for this.

The last objection against "Alberti"—is the most formidable—*it is an American production!* To this charge, (as I do not know how to get over it) I must plead guilty. I have even the hardihood openly to acknowledge, nay, be proud of the accident of birth, which has placed me under the protection of laws that I revere, and in the bosom of a country that I love. It is surely time for transatlantic critics to borrow the assistance of "sweet oblivion," and allow her to soften down those feelings and prejudices which have grown out of past hostilities. To regard the place of an author's birth as necessarily connected with the merits or demerits of his production—to view him through that medium alone, in which smoky war—not cheerful literature—presents her votaries—may be very spirited and very national; but it would be rather difficult to convince the world, that *Criticism*, under such banners, can be either just, useful, or liberal. [. . .]

Alb: And since I find
   This hateful passion wrought within thee thus,
   That nothing else can pluck it from thy soul,
   But to unloose my deep and dreadful secret;
   Prepare to hear the cause—
Ippo: Aye, speak it out!
   Lot forth this dread intelligence, though it blast me!
Alb: I would have kept it from thee, all in mercy,
   But thou thyself compellest me to speak—
Ippo: O! give it utterance;—though every word
   Stab to my heart, that were some ease, compar'd
   To this dark horrible uncertainty.
Alb: Meet me at noon.
Ippo: Where?
Alb: In Count Ridolpho's gardens.—Thou dost start
   That I should mention that forbidden spot—
   But meet me there—for there I must unfold
   A tale will make thee feel how much thy peace
   Is dear to this sad heart. Mark me, at noon.
   Until that hour arrive I am call'd hence
   On a soul-trying purpose. Fare thee well. [*Exit.*]
Ippo: What darkling horrors swim above my head,
   And cloud the heavens from me! Can it be—

My father love Antonia! He, my rival!
Yes, yes; her beauty—her all-conquering beauty
Melts even his adamant—O, fatal beauty!
O, grief illimitable! Can it be?
No, no, I plague myself with horrid dreams—
He love another! he whom I have heard
Speak of my mother as one enshrin'd
And lock'd up in his heart! O, no, my father,
I wrong thy constancy. Two hours hence he said,
Would that the time were come; but he has said it,
And he makes good all pledges. [. . .]

Lor: My Alberti, then—
    For by that name I found thee, Ferdinand—
    Say, of thy son——
Alb: Alas!
Lor: Ridolpho had a son too by that marriage.
Alb: He had—Ippolito——
Lor: Aye, thy son, Ippolito;
    There is another mystery; the youth
    Who saved my life——
Alb: Is count Ridolpho's son, Cesario.
Lor: Ridolpho's!
Alb: Now thou seest the sacred bar
    Which keeps him from Antonia.
Lor: Antonia is his sister!
Alb: By the same father; but another wife
    Had sooth'd Ridolpho's grief—Antonia's mother.
Lor: How came Ippolito with thee? knows he—
Alb: This very hour I will make clear to thee,—
    To thee and to the world—my conduct pest.

Other work by Harby: *The Gordian Knot, or, Causes & Effects* (1807).

Mordecai Manuel Noah

She Would Be a Soldier, or, the Plain of Chippewa; An Historical Drama in Three Acts 1819

Act I.

Scene I. *A Valley with a neat Cottage on the right, an Arbour on the left, and picturesque Mountains at a distance.*

Enter from the cottage, Jasper *and* Jenkins.

Jenkins: And so, neighbour, you are not then a native of this village?
Jasper: I am not, my friend; my story is short, and you shall hear it. It was my luck, call it bad or good, to be born in France, in the town of Castlenaudary, where my parents, good honest peasants, cultivated a small farm on the borders of the canal of Midi. I was useful, though young; we were well enough to live, and I received from the parish school a good education, was taught to love my country, my parents, and my friends; a happy temper, a common advantage in my country, made all things easy to me; I never looked for to-morrow to bring me more joy than I experienced to-day.
Jenkins: Pardon my curiosity, friend Jasper: how came you to leave your country, when neither want nor misfortune visited your humble dwelling?
Jasper: Novelty, a desire for change, an ardent disposition to visit foreign countries. Passing through the streets of Toulouse one bright morning in spring, the lively drum and fife broke on my ear, as I was counting my gains from a day's marketing. A company of soldiers neatly dressed, with white cockades, passed me with a brisk step; I followed them through instinct—the sergeant informed me that they were on their way to Bordeaux, from thence to embark for America, to aid the cause of liberty in the new world, and were commanded by the Marquis de la Fayette. That name was familiar to me; La Fayette was a patriot—I felt like a patriot, and joined the ranks immediately.
Jenkins: Well, you enlisted and left your country?
Jasper: I did. We had a boisterous passage to America, and endured many hardships during the revolution. I was wounded at Yorktown, which long disabled me, but what then? I served under great men, and for a great cause; I saw the independence of the thirteen states acknowledged, I was promoted to a sergeancy by the great Washington, and I sheathed my sword, with the honest pride of knowing, that I had aided in establishing a powerful and happy republic.
Jenkins: You did well, honest Jasper, you did well; and now you have the satisfaction of seeing your country still free and happy.
Jasper: I have, indeed. When the army was disbanded, I travelled on foot to explore the uncultivated territory which I had assisted in liberating. I purchased a

piece of land near the great lakes, and with my axe levelled the mighty oaks, cleared my meadows, burnt out the wolves and bears, and then built that cottage there.

JENKINS: And thus became a settler and my neighbour; thanks to the drum and fife and the white cockade, that lured you from your home.

JASPER: In a short time, Jenkins, everything flourished; my cottage was neat, my cattle thriving, still I wanted something—it was a wife. I was tired of a solitary life, and married Kate, the miller's daughter; you knew her.

JENKINS: Ay, that I did; she was a pretty lass.

JASPER: She was a good wife—ever cheerful and industrious, and made me happy: poor Kate! I was without children for several years; at length my Christine was born, and I have endeavoured, in cultivating her mind, and advancing her happiness, to console myself for the loss of her mother.

JENKINS: Where is Christine? Where is your daughter, neighbour Jasper?

JASPER: She left the cottage early this morning with Lenox, to climb the mountains and see the sun rise; it is time for them to return to breakfast.

JENKINS: Who is this Mr. Lenox?

JASPER: An honest lieutenant of infantry, with a gallant spirit and a warm heart. He was wounded at Niagara, and one stormy night, he presented himself at our cottage door, pale and haggard. His arm had been shattered by a ball, and he had received a flesh wound from a bayonet: we took him in—for an old soldier never closes his door on a wounded comrade—Christine nursed him, and he soon recovered. But I wish they were here—it is growing late: besides, this is a busy day, friend Jenkins.

JENKINS: Ah, how so?

JASPER: You know Jerry Mayflower, the wealthy farmer; he has offered to marry my Christine. Girls must not remain single if they can get husbands, and I have consented to the match, and he will be here to-day to claim her hand.

JENKINS: But will Christine marry Jerry? She has been too well educated for the honest farmer.

JASPER: Oh, she may make a few wry faces, as she does when swallowing magnesia, but the dose will go down. There is some credit due to a wife who improves the intellect of her husband; aye, and there is some pride in it also. Girls should marry. Matrimony is like an old oak; age gives durability to the trunk, skill trims the branches, and affection keeps the foliage ever green. But come, let us in. [. . .]

Enter CHRISTINE *and* LENOX *from the cottage.*

JASPER: Christine, here is farmer Mayflower and his friends, who have come to visit our cottage, and you in particular.

CHRISTINE: They are all welcome. Good morning, Jerry—how is it with you?

JERRY: Purely, Miss Crissy, I'm stout and hearty, and you look as pretty and as rosy as a field of pinks on a sunshiny morning.

JASPER: Come here, farmer—give me your hand—Christine, yours—[*Joins them.*]—there; may you live long and happy, and my blessings ever go with you.

CHRISTINE: [*Aside in amazement*] Heavens! what can this mean? [LENOX *is agitated—pause—*JASPER *and group retire—*LENOX *remains at a distance.*]

JERRY: Why, Miss Crissy, your father has consented that I shall marry you, and I've come with my neighbours to have a little frolic, and carry you home with me.

CHRISTINE: And am I of so little moment as not to be consulted? Am I thus to be given away by my father without one anxious question? [*With decision.*] Farmer, pardon my frankness; on this occasion, sincerity alone is required—I do not like you, I will not marry you—nay, do not look surprised. I am a stranger to falsehood and dissimulation, and thus end at once all hopes of ever becoming my husband.

JERRY: Why, now, Miss Crissy, that's very cruel of you—I always had a sneaking kindness for you, and when your father gave his consent, I didn't dream as how you could refuse me.

CHRISTINE. My father has ever found me dutiful and obedient, but when he bestows my hand, without knowing whether my heart or inclinations accompany it, I feel myself bound to consult my own happiness. I cannot marry you, farmer.

Michael Beer

1800-1833

Poet and dramatist Michael Beer was born near Berlin to a wealthy German Jewish family. From age seventeen, he traveled extensively in Italy, visiting his brother, the composer Jacob (Giacomo) Meyerbeer. Beer's first plays were influenced by his Italian journeys, Goethe's classicism, and a desire for Jews to be accepted into European society. At nineteen, Beer was a founding member of the Verein für Kultur und Wissenschaft der Juden, along with Heinrich Heine, Eduard Gans, and Leopold Zunz, and advocated for the recognition of both Jewish peoplehood and Jewish artistic tradition. His play *The Paria* may be the first to have universalized a term for an outcast class in India.

The Paria: A Tragedy in One Act
1823

Dramatis Personae
    GADHI, A Paria
    MAJA, his Wife
    BENASSAR, Indian Attendant

    SCENE—THE PARIA'S HUT

GADHI: [. . .] I have no fears for nature's usual horrors
  Impartial threatening each created being.
  An exile from the reign of social life,
  Cast from the world's thronged current on the shore,
  My home the forest and my friends its tenants,
  Fearless for daily life's support I tread
  The tiger's jungle and the serpent's brake.
  Yet I can tremble when the shrill Naquarrah
  Proclaims the fearful neighborhood of man;
  And by the track, marked with the panther's footstep,
  Turn from his human rival's dreaded den,
  The Brahmin temple. Soon some hunter's arrow
  To check my flight may reach this beating heart.
  Then swells the chorus, then the shout arises;
  For Bramah triumphs when a Paria falls.
MAJA: Oh! Gadhi.—Thunder not, all-powerful God!
  Thy voice is fearful.
GADHI: Weep, my Maja, weep
  Unhappy wife, and give thy thanks to Heaven
  That it has left thee tears; for me, the Paria,
  No memory wakes their long exhausted fountain.
  But thou hast gazed on life in all its splendor,
  And happier days thy earlier childhood knew.
MAJA: Not for those days, nor all their bliss, I pine;
  The life 'twas thine to save is thine for ever.
  And when I see thee cheerful, canst thou deem
  That such low griefs could cloud thy Maja's brow?
  What are the sensual goods of life to me?
  A woman's bosom knows one bliss on earth,
  The bliss to love, and feel that love requited.
GADHI: An outcast's love is but a sad requital.
MAJA: An outcast thou!
GADHI: And is not such thy husband?
  Will not the babe which hangs upon thy bosom,
  Will not his offspring, with shame-sunken head,
  His blood, his race, his whole succession weep,
  Weep the hot tears oppression strains from misery,
  That our affection ever gave them birth?
  Speak, if thy voice be thunder. If thy name
  Be justice and forbearance. Mighty Bramah,
  Hear and give answer. Tell me why thy hate
  Pursues for aye the race from whence I spring,
  Because forsooth, in ages wrapt in fable,
  A Paria once withheld his worship due;
  Your priests proclaim, where'er the Ganges rolls,
  That still our presence spreads pollution round.
  Preach that the brow, whence mercy streams for others,
  Turns in averted anger from a race
  Which calls thee by the common name of father.
MAJA: Ah no! The master work of him who made us
  Is such an heart as thine. The great Creator
  On his best labours never stamped his curse.
  Their doctrine is a lie.
GADHI: It is, my Maja.
  Did I not deem it such, my faith would waver
  In him to whom their guilty offerings rise.
  Bramah is kind to all. Flows not from him
  The light that vivifies a fruitful world?
  Has not his hand, to shield us from his tempests,
  Wreathed o'er our heads the broad banana's vault?
  Is he not sire of all embracing nature,
  Who never drove the Paria from her bosom? [. . .]
  Man only, with presumptuous hand, confounds
  The general order, and repels his neighbor,
  Boasts of his crimes, and calls his phrensy [frenzy] faith.

Translated by Francis Egerton Ellesmere.

  Other works by Beer: *Klytemnestra* (1819); *Struensee* (1827).

Joseph Ha-Efrati

1770–1804

Born in Troplowitz, Silesia (now Opawica, Poland), Joseph (Yosef) Ha-Efrati (Joseph Troplowitz) was a Hebrew poet and playwright. Although his most significant play, *Melukhat Sha'ul* (*The Kingdom of Saul*; it was also translated into Yiddish), was based on biblical tales, Ha-Efrati often wrote on contemporary subjects, in the form of eulogies for important *maskilim*, traditional rabbis, and statesmen, as well as poems to commemorate historical events. He was influenced by other writers of the Haskalah as well as non-Jewish Enlightenment authors including Goethe, Schiller, and Rousseau. Ha-Efrati lived in Ratibor (Racibórz) and Prague.

Melukhat Sha'ul (The Kingdom of Saul)
1826

Act One

 Saul [*upon returning from smiting the Amalekites*]. Jonathan *and his other sons.*
Saul: My fury still burns within my heart like a flame of fire!
Even after I have smitten him, I have found no place of rest;
An adversary of the children of my people when they went up from Egypt,
This day, I have felled him with an avenging sword,
Almighty God, already from that time, admonished us: "Destroy his memory for eternity!"
Jonathan: Just as you have subdued this Amalekite,
So too, my father, the king, will you humble all your foes;
The seed of Israel will once more live under your scepter,
Every man securely beneath his vine and his fig tree.
Saul: Joy, fear, exultation, sadness, rage within me—
What is strength and salvation to me on this day?
O my delightful children, I can still vividly recall
The day on which I prophesied and was turned into another person!
Within my soul was poured out a spirit of grace, mixed with salvation.
My soul still experiences the pleasantness of the words of the Seer,
For they have dripped wine onto my palate sweeter than honeycombs.—
That I would rule over Israel I knew full well,
To save them from the hands of evildoers, filled with violence.
But will I, as the years wear on, also go forth in royal apparel before the men of the army?
Will I once more overpower the enemy and subdue him,
As I did unto those who were fighting over Jabesh?— This I do not know!
Jonathan: See, my father, that you have saddened my heart with your words.—
Strengthen yourself and tend the flock, the flock of your inheritance!
These scattered sheep, the sheep that have been driven away—
Saul [*holding* Jonathan's *hand*]: Behold, you are the man who delights my heart! You are a mighty man of valor—
This day too, if I should cease to rule over Israel
Jeshurun will not perish, Jacob will not be obliterated,
If you, Jonathan, are to lead this nation.—
But from me has been taken the majesty, the glory of the crown.
From the day I returned from battle, I have found no repose,
And from time to time I see an image from afar
Frightening and awesome, clothed in the king's suit of armor,
A trampled crown cast beneath his feet.—
I have not ceased being king; I have ceased to rule—
The majesty of kingship is not with me; the heart of kingship too is nonexistent,
Like a lily torn to pieces in the vulture's mouth
Shall it be cast away into one of the valleys in the wilderness.—

Translated by David E. Cohen.

Solomon Ettinger

Serkele
1839

Reb Shmelke: Well, I can see that you are a clever man, so I will tell you the whole story in brief. [*He takes a drink.*] As you see me before you, I'm called Reb

Smelke [*Shmelke*, as pronounced by a Litvak—Trans.]. My "German" name is Smelke Traunichts. But the people here, most of whom are my enemies, call me "The Litvak." Why? Because I am from Lithuania—I'm a native of Vilna. I tell you—Vilna, a Holy Community! You've undoubtedly been there, haven't you?

STRANGER: Once upon a time.

REB SHMELKE: How did you like the big chandeliers and the rooms for midnight prayers [in the Great Synagogue]? Beautiful, aren't they? Real gems, I tell you! My ancestors were always community councilors there, and rich men. My late father, that saintly man—may he put in a good word for us in heaven—used to do business with Lemberg, sometimes with cowhide, sometimes with tallow, sometimes with anise. Once he came here with hog-bristles and decided that while he was at it he should affiance me with the daughter of the owner of the place where he used to stay. [*He takes a drink.*] To make it short, I got married and the Lord, may his name be blessed, smiled upon me: I became a very wealthy man. I own a fine inn, a fine wine-cellar, a nice collection of silver. And there's enough money, too. But then God afflicted me with a great misfortune—namely, that my wife Feygele suddenly fell down the stairs and alas, died young. I wept, I fainted, I moaned. But, what's the use of moaning? Deceased remains deceased and I had to take care of things by myself. [*He takes a drink.*] She left me quite a bit of jewelry, too. In short, not to drag things out—I'm a well-regarded and wealthy man . . .

STRANGER [*impatiently*]: Well, make it short!

REB SHMELKE: Well, so be it. I won't spin it out. [*He empties his glass and refills it.*] So a few weeks later I sent a *sadkhen* [=*shadkhen*, marriage broker], a certain Reb Smerele [=*Shmerele*], a *koser* [kosher, respectable] Jew to Serkele. She has a daughter, in fact a very nice girl, to tell the truth a bit of a "fine lady" and worldly, but in an inn, especially in an inn like mine, you need that sort of person. You never can tell, maybe sometimes she'll have to chat with a high official and receive him graciously. Or on the other hand to get angry and yell, you know how it is in inns like mine.

STRANGER [*impatiently*]: Well, go on, but make it short.

REB SHMELKE: Yes, I'll make it short. I don't want to wear you out. You're tired from the road. So where was I? Aha! You see, I'm losing track of what I'm saying. The point is, why did I send for Serkele in the first place? Because I had heard from a trustworthy person that she wants to add 1400 rubles to the girl's dowry in addition to gifts and sundry items and she's an only daughter too, after all. In any case, to make it short: how can someone like Serkele, who only a few years ago was sitting with her foodstuffs and flour and whose father was no Hebrew calligrapher either. . . . So what if, as people say, he could study the Talmud, what's so special about that? I've seen a lot of learned Jews begging from door to door!

STRANGER [*in German, to himself: Alas, it is all too true!*]: Well, tell me more, but make it short.

REB SHMELKE: Yes, I'll make it extremely short. What's the pedigree of this wretched woman? Her brother was perhaps a somewhat respectable person, but even he a few years ago he had to run away because of some affair or other and has never come back. How can a misfortune, an affliction, like this Serkele give orders to me, a local wealthy man [*he pats himself on the belly*], affluent, if I may say so, with these words: "My only daughter will first have to learn to measure [Lithuanian] oats and to speak the Litvak language and then maybe she can become Smelke Litvak's bride." A vulgar flour-woman can give me orders like that! I was ashamed for the *sadkhen*, for Reb Smerele. Well, so what if I do speak the Litvak language? Here in Lemberg they make fun of the Litvak language and we in Vilna make fun of how they speak here. One thing's for certain: I didn't create all these languages!

Translated by Solon Beinfeld.

Abraham Daninos
Dates Unknown

Abraham Daninos, a Sephardic Jew native to Algiers, was a pioneer of modern Arabic drama. His works fused European and Arabic dramatic styles, and were written in a mixture of colloquial and literary Arabic. In addition to writing plays, Daninos was a translator for the Civil Court of Justice in Algiers, and when the French arrived in 1830, he acted as a guide and translator. For this service he was awarded the order of chevalier in the Legion d'honneur.

The Pleasure Trip of Sweethearts Reunited after the Agonies of Love Unrequited in the City of Tiryaq in Iraq
1847

An Explanation of the Plot of this Book[1]

Naʿma is the daughter of a *caïd* of one of the regions in Iraq, and Nuʿman is her paternal first cousin, whom she married while her father was still alive. When her father died, Nuʿman was seized with a desire to go abroad; he became captain of a pirate ship in the service of the Pasha and sailed to India with his friend Captain Damanhur. When his expedition returns, Naʿma's feelings toward him have changed: she wants to divorce him, take her wealth and property, and marry Caïd Rabih, her maternal cousin (it is her mother's scheming that has put her in this frame of mind). On their travels, the Pasha orders them (Nuʿman and Damanhur) to go to the Islands of Waq to collect taxes and tithes, and from there to continue on to the Land of Kafur to collect birds and parrots with feathers of every strange hue, trees with leaves of gold and silver and seeds of emerald and ruby, and whales the color of gold and silver. The Pasha also sends with them a magnificent present for Maghrib the Wise, ruler of the Land of Kafur, renowned throughout the Mashriq and the Maghrib. Throughout their absence, Captain Damanhur's wife Amnaʾ is sorrowful, and is struck with anguish when she sees all the boats returning without her husband Damanhur; Naʿma's heart softens, too, toward her cousin Nuʿman, and when they return she reconciles with him and they get back together. Damanhur also returns, and so, to celebrate, they set out on their pleasure trip.

Dramatis Personae

[. . .]
Naʿma, Captain Nuʿman's Wife
Fiyyala, Lalla Naʿma's Maidservant

Act One

Scene Three

Naʿma and Fiyyala

Naʿma: What took you so long, Fiyyala? It's been two hours now since I sent for you!

Fiyyala: It was Sidi Nuʿman and his ranting that held me up, honest. Don't blame me, Lalla!

Naʿma: Tell me, then, what's that fool been saying to you?

Fiyyala: He said, His breast is consumed with passion,
His head is enraptured too,
And if you don't show him compassion
He'll lose his mind over you.

Naʿma: Poor idiot, God forgive us both. He's no good for me and I'm no good for him.

Fiyyala: Sidi Nuʿman is a kind and charming man, I swear. Just listen to his sweet words and you'll adore him, you'll even say there's no one in the world that compares!

Naʿma: Oh, but that Nuʿman of yours is a sailor and a rogue—what good's that? Caïd Rabih is an important official, and he has the ear of our ruler.

Fiyyala: Prestige and importance are all very well, Lalla, but ask yourself whom your heart truly loves.

Naʿma: You're right, Fiyyala, just look what fate has written . . .

Act One

Scene Four

Naʿma alone

Naʿma: Fiyyala's right, Nuʿman is a kind and charming man; I've been infatuated ever since I laid eyes on him. My mind beguiled and my heart afflicted, I'm constantly distracted by thoughts of him. I cannot forget my love for him, and no naysayer can dissuade me.

To the words of detractors I pay little heed,
And as for my secret, my lips remain sealed.
My beloved's departure has torn us asunder,
I toss and I turn while he peacefully slumbers.
From friends and companions I feel I've grown distant
Whilst loving him dearly's become my one constant.
Pure in intention, my ardor sincere,
I wander alone in the hope he'll appear.
My heartache earns only my fellows' disdain;
They cannot perceive the extent of my pain.
My beloved's good name never passes my lips;
In extremis, a pronoun is all I'll admit.
Try asking my secret; you'll see I decline—
So hold your tongue, meddler, and leave me to pine.
My heart's confidences I shall not betray
I'm not wont to gossip, so what would I say?

Whoever says I have but myself to blame
Is lying, for we are all pawns in love's game.
But compulsion entails no dishonor or shame
And the tales of past lovers will tell you the same
So call it both pleasure and pain, if you will,
Butterflies in the stomach or a blow that could kill,
Or a blessing, misfortune or fervent desire
Which in seeking, the soul will despair or expire.

NOTE

1. [*Lalla* and *Sidi* are titles of respect (feminine and masculine respectively), *Lalla* in particular being typically North African. The title *caïd* (from Arabic *qaʾid*, commander) designated a native governor appointed by the French colonial administration. The plot summary and the dialogue between Fiyyala and Naʿma are written in the mix of Algerian dialect and literary Arabic which characterizes much of this work, while Naʿma's poetic soliloquy is in literary Arabic. Daninos employs four different meters here, and Shmuel Moreh and Philip. C. Sadgrove, in *Jewish Contributions to Nineteenth-Century Arabic Theatre: Plays from Algeria and Syria : A Study and Texts* (Oxford: Oxford University Press, 1996) identify a number of the lines as quotations from other works, a common practice in Arabic literature. In the final line, "blessing" (*niʿma*) is the same as the heroine's name, the different vowel in Naʿma representing the local pronunciation.—Trans.]

Translated by Katharine L. Halls.

Rachel Félix
1821–1858

Born near Mumpf, Switzerland, Rachel (born Elisa-Rachel) Félix was a prominent French actress. Her parents worked as peddlers, and as a child, she performed music alongside her sister Sophie-Sarah on the streets. After her family moved to Paris in 1831, Félix attended school to train as a musician and actor, eventually entering the Conservatoire de Paris. She joined the Comédie Française, then the premier stage in France, in 1838. By the 1840s, Félix achieved renown. Alongside her acting, she is known for having sustained romantic relationships with several prominent figures in France, including Napoléon III.

Poster of Rachel Félix (see p. 474)
ca. 1848

Moses Samuel Konfino
Unknown

It is believed that Moses Samuel Konfino's play *Pyesa di Yaʿakov Avinu kun sus izus* (The Song of Our Forefather Jacob and His Sons) is the oldest extant Judeo-Spanish play. It was published in Bucharest, and it is thought by Judezmo studies scholar David M. Bunis that the work was adapted from an earlier Hebrew version. The play was clearly written for a children's performance; Konfino included an introduction stating that he aimed to illustrate the value of familial harmony.

The Song of Our Forefather Jacob and His Sons
1862

I want to recount a beautiful tale. I ask that the men relax. Listen, and see how marvelous it is how merciful God restores justice for us.

JACOB: He said to his son, I wanted to send you to find out about the tribulations of your brothers. At your service, Joseph said to him, and wished "good day" to his brothers.

They responded to him, "Good health and long life." Come now, take off the silk coat. The brothers said, let us eat. Here come the *moros*,[1] let us sell him.

The brothers took him and lifted him out of the pit. The Ishmaelites took him to Potiphar and sold him. Bring him to his master, with everything in hand. In addition, he conducted himself as a good man.

His mistress was an evil character. She plotted to seduce him. He responded, I will not do that. Because God is watching me and it is not right.

She put him in prison because he said he would not do it. He was content because God saw it fit. Pharaoh dreamed about cows and sheaves. He said to Joseph, please tell me the meaning.

The meaning of this is abundance and famine. See to collecting all sorts of grains. He told him his intention to make him second-in-command, so that the latter did not happen in Egypt.

Word went out from the king in Egypt. Joseph would do everything he intended. Joseph collected grain during the time of abundance, to protect his city from all wrong.

Unknown Artist, Poster of Rachel Félix, ca. 1848.

He responded to them, I also see a very big sign that you are spies. If you want to be released without a single fault, may your younger brother be present.

Then his brothers came to buy grain. They bowed down to the ground at the sight of Joseph. From where did you come, Joseph asks them. From the Holy Land, they answer.

Then the nine brothers go to the father, telling him everything that happened. The father said to them, Why are you doing this? Why did you tell the king that you have another brother?

Judah said to him, Give him to me. Allow me to look after Benjamin my brother. Then Judah came with his brother, with gifts and a document in hand.

When Joseph saw his brother Benjamin, he said to his son, Free the prisoner. And set a fine table. Because today, I want to celebrate as I please.

They ate and drank and got drunk, and everyone gave presents to Benjamin. And they put the goblet in his sack. The brothers did not realize what they had done.

Benjamin realized all that had happened. Joseph had told him the whole story. To see if Judah was going to stand by his word. Joseph was going to test him through this.

Joseph said to his son, Leave and catch them quickly. They did something dishonest. They took my precious goblet. See to getting it back and find out who did it.

When he caught them, he said, Why did you do this, this inappropriate thing? And the king divined all of this. You should know, I am arresting whoever did this.

His brothers return to Joseph's home. He also asks them, Why did you steal this? We cannot answer you, we have no reasonable answer. We were guilty in the eyes of God, who took vengeance on us.

Judah jumped and said, I will not allow it. I, your servant, guarantee my father's honesty. I would be more content if you would arrest me instead of the rest. Instead of seeing what would happen to my honest father.

When he heard this, Joseph's tears flowed. I wanted to make you realize, and you did not understand. I called you my brothers and you did not answer. They saw him with their own eyes did not recognize him.

When Benjamin heard this, he jumped on him. He hugged and kissed him with much esteem. When his brothers saw him they ran to him. He also hugged them with much esteem.

Joseph said to his brother, I went up to my father. For it must be five years that he has been hungry. Here, there can be found all sorts of vegetables, he should make haste and come down and not delay.

The brothers went up to their father. They said to one another, Who will tell him this? They found Serah, and asked her to tell him in song so that he wouldn't be shocked.

Serah heard this and took a tambourine. She said to Jacob, I want to sing a beautiful song for you. To make you happy, which is very pleasing.

Jacob responded, Sing my dear, because my heart is filled with pain. By the time you finish the song, God will allow my sons to return in peace.

She began, Joseph my uncle is alive. He was sold to the Ishmaelites and was captive in Egypt. And he is master now in all of Egypt.

Jacob responded, What is this that you say, because these words have revived my soul. Because of what you did for me, I beg God that you will not know death.

They spoke about this. The sons came back from Egypt to their father. They gave him good news, that Joseph had been made king in Egypt.

Jacob said to them, Let us go and see him. If God will perform a miracle in allowing me to see him. For I have been crying for him for so long. I do not mind if I die, as long as I see him.

Jacob went down from the Holy Land. To be with his son and embrace him. Joseph also went out with his two sons to be with his father and the eleven tribes.

When Jacob saw him, so prestigious, he hugged him, kissed him and cried. And gives thanks to mighty God, who performed this miracle, and allowed him to find his son in good time.

This is, for the men, a nice gift. And we beg that God forgives us. If we made a mistake, please forgive us, as this is the first time we have come out [before an audience].

NOTE

1. [Literally "Moors." Denotes the Ishmaelites in Genesis 37:28.—Trans.]

Translated by Dina Danon.

Adah Isaacs Menken
1835–1868

Adah Isaacs Menken achieved celebrity first as an actress, later gaining some literary following for her poetry. Uncertainty surrounds Menken's family history, as she claimed various ancestries and racial identities, and her true birthplace remains obscure. Perhaps best known for her role in a staging of *Mazeppa* in which she seemed to appear nude and also for her challenges to dominant social mores, Menken came to be among the most popular social figures of mid-nineteenth-century American life. While it is unclear whether or not she was born to Jewish parents or ever formally converted to Judaism, she studied classical Jewish texts and wrote on Jewish themes in her poetry. Napoleon Sarony (1821–1896) was famed for his photography of people from the theater world.

Portrait of Adah Isaacs Menken
1866

Napoleon Sarony, *Portrait of Adah Isaacs Menken*, 1866.

Anonymous

El médico jugetón (The Fake Doctor) is a Ladino-language adaptation of Molière's play *Le médecin volant* (The Flying Doctor). Modified to appeal to its readers, the play was published in Constantinople's *El Tiempo* and was advertised as a drama to encourage morality.

The Fake Doctor
1873

A Play by Molière in One Act of Sixteen Scenes[1]

SCENE 1

[CARLO, ESTERINA]

CARLO: Is there any news, Esterina? Do you have any advice for me?

ESTERINA: Why do you want advice? I have a lot of news for you. Do you know that my uncle is forcing Laurita to marry Hananiá? You can be sure that if she did not love you so much, the marriage contract would already have been signed. But because my cousin and I are such friends, she has shared her secret with me. And because my uncle's stinginess drove us to total despair, we thought of a trick that would destroy this marriage plan. My cousin pretended to fall ill, and the wretched old man who believes it sent me to fetch a doctor. If you have a friend who knows our secret, let him see her and recommend that she be sent to the country because she needs a change of air. The old wretch will do as he is told and will put her in the little cottage at the edge of our garden. This way, he will remain in his house, while the two of you enjoy yourselves until the wedding.

CARLO: Sounds very good, but where am I going to find this kind of doctor who would make such sacrifices for my sake? I can assure you that I do not know where to look for a charlatan of this sort.

ESTERINA: It has just occurred to me that you could dress your valet as a doctor, because there is nothing easier than fooling our old man.

CARLO: My valet is stupid and will ruin everything. But since there is nobody else, good or bad, we will have to use him. Goodbye. I am going to look for him. But where the hell am I going to find this fool? Oh look, here he comes!

Scene 2

[Carlo, Shelomo]

Carlo: [*To* Shelomo] Hello, my unfortunate friend, Shelomo! You can't imagine how delighted I am to see you! You came exactly at the moment when I needed you most. But since you are not capable of doing this . . .

Shelomo: What am I not capable of doing? Senior, give me any task! Ask me to find out what hour the bell has sounded, or how much oil costs, or tell me to put shoes on a horse and you will see what I am worth and what I am capable of. Do you hear me?

Carlo: Very good, but this is not what I want from you.

Shelomo: And what do you want? Tell me quickly, there is nothing I am unable to do. Tell me, let's see. What do you need?

Carlo: Can you be a doctor?

Shelomo: Be a doctor? I can do everything except this. If this is about medicine, I can't do anything for you. How the hell do you want me to become a doctor? Are you making fun of me?

Carlo: I don't know how, but if you do it, I will give you ten ducats.

Shelomo: Ah! If you give me ten ducats, I won't say I can't become a doctor. Don't look at me now. Believe me, as soon as I dress like a doctor, even those who know me will not recognize me and call for me. But you will see. Where do you want to send me?

Carlo: To Frederico, whose daughter is ill. But you are so dumb that instead of helping you will [. . .]

Shelomo: Enough, have faith in me. I assure you that I can kill a person better than all the doctors, and nobody will say anything to me, because doctors' mistakes are fixed by graves. But I won't deny it, it is very difficult to be a doctor. But what if I can't cure anyone?

Carlo: What a fool you are! Don't worry, this is very easy. Frederico is an ignorant man and so vain that it is easy to dupe him. Just mention Hippocrates, Galen, and Rambam and some diseases. Show your education and tell him that you are considered first among physicians.

Shelomo: Got it. I will speak about philosophy, mathematics, and other things where he can't notice my blunders. Since this man is so vain and ignorant, I will do better than you expect. But first of all, get me some doctor's clothes, because the way I am dressed now, I look like someone who sleeps under bridges.

[Shelomo *and* Carlo *exit.*]

Scene 3

[Frederico, Mercado]

Frederico: Go quickly, bring a doctor because my daughter is very ill. Run!

Mercado: You think she is ill? Of course, you want to marry her off to an old man. Don't you think this illness comes from thinking too much of some game? Look at the difference between the two![2]

Frederico: Go quickly, because I worry that this illness may delay the wedding.

Mercado: He is driving me crazy. When I tell him something, he responds as if he has not heard me. I can't take it anymore. I need a doctor as much as she does.

Scene 4

[Esterina, Frederico, Shelomo]

Esterina: Oh uncle, I am so glad to see you! I have good news for you. I have brought you the most knowledgeable doctor. He has come from foreign lands, where he studied. He has many books and will certainly cure your daughter. I was told about him at just the right time. He is so knowledgeable that I would also like to fall ill so that he would cure me.

Frederico: Where is he?

Esterina: He was following me. Here he is!

Frederico: I am at your service, Senior doctor. I sent for you because I wanted you to see my daughter who is ill, and you are our only hope.

Shelomo: Rambam and Galen said, with reason, that one is not well when ill. You are right to place your hopes in me, because I am the greatest and most talented physician and the most knowledgeable in medicine, herbs, and ways of using them.

Frederico: I am amazed!

Shelomo: You must not think that I am an ordinary doctor, some charlatan. Compared to me, all other doctors are apprentices. I know the secrets and mysteries of life. I know Latin. Listen, senior: *Per omnia saecula saecularium.*[3] But I am wasting my time, you don't understand anything. Let me check your pulse. I will see what you have.

Esterina: But it is not he who is ill, it is his daughter.

SHELOMO: It does not matter, the father's blood is the same as the daughter's. By checking the father's blood, I can tell what the daughter's illness is. Senior Frederico, can you show me your daughter's urine?

FREDERICO: Yes, of course. Esterina, bring me my daughter's urine. [ESTERINA *exits*.] Senior doctor, I worry that my daughter may die.

SHELOMO: Oh no! She must not die without doctor's orders. [ESTERINA *enters*.] This urine shows fever, high temperature, and inflammation, but don't worry, this is not dangerous.

FREDERICO: What are you doing, Senior doctor? Why are you touching it?

SHELOMO: Don't be surprised, ordinary doctors just look at it. But being an extraordinary one, I touch it and thus determine the cause of the disease, its development, and the way to cure it. Now, it is necessary to make her bleed, as is recommended by our old and venerable system.

ESTERINA: [*Exits and comes back.*] I tried hard to make her bleed.

SHELOMO: What? Make her bleed profusely. *Medicinus multus sangus*.[4] If everyone bleeds like this, I will regret having become a doctor.

ESTERINA: [*Exits and enters.*] Here, this is all the blood I was able to get from her.

SHELOMO: What? Senior Frederico, your daughter is in delicate health, but the art of medicine is going to cure her. Now I am going to prescribe her a diuretic, but before this, I would like to see the patient.

ESTERINA: She is up already. I can bring her here, if you want.

SCENE 5

[ESTERINA, LAURITA, FREDERICO, SHELOMO]

SHELOMO: Seniora, it seems you are ill?

LAURITA: Yes, Senior.

SHELOMO: That's exactly what I thought. The great physician Aristot [*sic*] in the chapter on animals relays a curious secret, which explains many diseases. For example, when a person's gall expands all over his body, he becomes yellow. I can tell you another secret from the scholarly books: the worst thing for one's health is illness. And the enemy of gladness is melancholy. It follows from all of this that your daughter is ill and that I must prescribe her treatment.

FREDERICO: Quickly. Bring a table, an inkpot, ink, paper, and a pen.

SHELOMO: Can anyone here write?

FREDERICO: What? You cannot write?

SHELOMO: My mind is so busy with various things that I have forgotten how to do it. Your daughter needs to spend some time in the country.

FREDERICO: We have a beautiful garden with a nice house. If you want, I will send her there.

SHELOMO: I must see this place. [*They exit.*]

SCENE 6

[NOTARY]

NOTARY: They say that Senior Frederico's daughter is ill. I must inquire about her health and offer my services as a family friend.
Hello! Hello!
Is Senior Frederico here?

SCENE 7

[FREDERICO, NOTARY]

NOTARY: I heard that your daughter was ill and came to offer my services in case you need them.

FREDERICO: I have been here with the wisest man.

NOTARY: Would it be possible for me to talk to him for a minute?

SCENE 8

[FREDERICO, NOTARY, SHELOMO]

FREDERICO: This is a very wise and capable man, a friend of mine, and he would like to talk to you.

SHELOMO: I am very busy, Senior Frederico. I need to see my patients. Forgive me, Senior Notary, for not being able to stay.

NOTARY: Senior, after what Senior Frederico has told me about you, your merits and wisdom, it has been my greatest desire to have the honor and privilege of meeting and greeting you. I hope you don't have anything against this. Men engaged in sciences should be venerated, and especially those who study medicine, because this requires studying other sciences. This is why Hippocrates said in his book: *Vita brevis, ars vero longa* (Science is long, life is short).[5]

SHELOMO: Of course! *Vinum lactificatum cor humanum* (Wine gladdens the human heart).[6]

NOTARY: You are not one of those physicians who is attached to one branch or school of medicine, and I think that you base your art on experience and reasoning. I disapprove of those who despise a doctor because he did not cure a patient, since life does not depend on him, and his goal is to help nature. Let me assure you,

Senior doctor, that I like your views very much, because your profession is an honorable one, and in antiquity people like you were treated as gods. Forgive me for keeping you for so long. I am leaving you in the hope that we shall meet again. Goodbye. [*Exits.*]

FREDERICO: What do you think of this man?

SHELOMO: He knows a couple of things, but he left very quickly, or else I would have asked him a few questions about the subjects I have learned during my two years at school and from the books that I have at home, and you would have seen how confused he would have been. Forgive me for leaving now because I have to do a few things. [FREDERICO *gives him money.*] Oh, Senior, what are you doing?

FREDERICO: I know how much I owe you.

SHELOMO: Are you joking? I won't accept it, I am not an ordinary man. [*Takes the money.*] Why trouble yourself with this? [*They exit.*]

NOTES

1. [An adaptation of Molière's *Le médecin volant.*—Trans.]

2. [Mercado's words make no sense, because the rewriter changed the French text for the sake of decency. In the original, the servant says: "Why do you want to give your daughter to an old man? Don't you think this [illness] comes from her desire to have a young man to work on her?"—Trans.]

3. [For ever and ever.—Trans.]

4. [A nonsensical word combination.—Trans.]

5. [Translation in the Ladino original.—Trans.]

6. [Translation in the Ladino original.—Trans.]

Translated by Olga Borovaya.

Abraham Goldfaden

1840–1908

Considered the "father of Yiddish theater," Abraham (Avrom) Goldfaden was a poet, playwright, and director. Born in Starokostiantyniv, Ukraine, Goldfaden was first introduced to Yiddish theater while a student at the state-sponsored Zhitomir rabbinical seminary, where he performed in a student production of Solomon Ettinger's *Serkele*. After a decade as a teacher, Goldfaden became an impresario and writer for the nascent Yiddish stage. In 1877, he moved to Iaşi, Romania, where he created sketches, plays, and songs for the stage. His early plays drew upon a variety of European traditions, including vaudeville, operetta, and comedy, through a Jewish angle that stressed education, self-improvement, romantic love, social responsibility, and shtetl life. As his troupe toured the Russian Empire in the early 1880s, Goldfaden's content became more serious, emphasizing politics, Jewish fate, nationalism, and tragedy and melodrama. In the final decades of his life, Goldfaden was forced by various circumstances to move from city to city, and he flirted briefly with Zionist politics. He eventually settled in New York. The year 1906 in the illustration below appears to be a misprint.

Shulamis

1881

Characters

MAENOYAKH, an old citizen of Bethlehem
SHULAMIS, his daughter
AVISHOLOM, a young hero descended from the Maccabees.

FOURTH SCENE

AVISHOLOM: I shall not leave here until I have rested
Jerusalem is still such a long way to go.
Here I have water, that's certainly good
And raisins and almonds, that too isn't bad.
[*He unties his bundle*]
Raisins and almonds—it reminds me of the little song
With which Bas-Tsion, the Daughter of Zion,
Sang her son, Yidele, softly to sleep:

I

Inside the Temple in a corner room,
Sits the poor widow Bas-Tsion alone.
She rocks her son Yidele gently to sleep
And this is the song that she sings all the while:

"Under Yidele's cradle tonight
Stands a kid with a coat of pure white,
The kid goes to market to buy.
That is the trade you will ply—
Raisins and almonds to eat,
Yidele, sleep now, my sweet!"

II

The song is a prophecy, Yidele mine:
You'll be dispersed all over the world

Abraham Goldfaden, Music from "Rozhinkes mit Mandlen," from his play *Shulamis*, 1881.

And be a merchant of grains of all kinds.
You will grow wealthy and prosper in time.
And when you are wealthy, a prosperous man,
You should remember the song that I sang:

"Raisins and almonds to eat,
That is the trade you will ply.
Yidele will sell and will buy,
Yidele, sleep now, my sweet!"

III

Times will be coming of stocks and of bonds,
With markets all over the world.
You'll be greatest of bankers on earth,
And you will grow richer than ever before.
And when you are wealthy, a prosperous man,
You should remember the song that I sang:

"Raisins and almonds to eat
That is the trade you will ply.
Yidele will sell and will buy,
Yidele, sleep now my sweet!"

IV

Times will be coming of fast railway trains,
They will soon cover the earth like a flood.

You will lay roadways of iron and steel,
Growing much richer than ever before.
And when you are wealthy, a prosperous man,
You should remember the song that I sang:

"Raisins and almonds to eat,
That is the trade you will ply.
Yidele will sell and will buy,
Yidele, sleep now, my sweet!"

[*He finishes singing, puts down his bundle and picks up his water-bottle.*]

I've eaten a bit, not as much as I'd like,
But washing it down with some water is good.

[*He gets up to go to the well, and as he bends down to fill up with water, he hears a scream from the well. Out of fear he drops the bottle and jumps back from the well. He sings:*]

What is that I hear?
A devil's voice, I fear!

SHULAMIS [*from the well*]:
 I will bless this unknown man—
 Oh, please, Sir, save me if you can!

Translated by Solon Beinfeld.

Other works by Goldfaden: *Di kishef-makherin* (1878); *Der fanatik oder beyde Kuni-Lemls* (1880); *Bar Kokhba* (1883).

Israel Aksenfeld

Recruits
Date Unknown

AARON: It's all a plain lie. It's because our Jews throughout the land in the little villages are so primitive, so stupid, they can't even read. Anyone will tell them the most absurd things and they believe it. The most pathetically ignorant of them believe in the Rabbi; they call him the Good Jew—he's neither good nor devoutly Jewish. As a matter of fact, he's probably more ignorant than they are. Yet they listen to him as though each word comes directly from on High. If they could only read Russian, read anything, they'd be able to see in the newspapers that all this is no calamity but really a blessing from the Czar. If the Czar proclaims that a girl less than 18 and a boy less than 20 shouldn't be allowed to marry, shouldn't we thank him for this? When the ukase becomes official it may be 16 and 18, just like in the Torah. But these dumb animals see everything as a calamity. They're like the ignorant Russian muszhiks who think it a calamity when the government insists they build chimneys so they shouldn't smother in their hovels from the smoke. They have to have some sense beaten into them before they allow the government to save their lives, or save them from being blinded or die from gas poisoning. The German peasants reacted the same way when they were told to plant potatoes and alternate their crops. This was to make their lives easier and more productive. But no, they all act like ignorant beasts when wiser heads try to do them a favor. Because our Jews are poor, they marry off their children when they are 13. When the former Polish senate wanted to pass a law to make the marriage age 18 and 20, the dumb boobs, yes, our stupid Jews, quickly started to marry off tiny little children only 8 years old.

PERELE: But when they start to take Jewish boys to be recruits, isn't it a terrible calamity? What a misfortune!

AARON: No. Our Czar, bless him, wants all his subjects to become equal citizens. To live and trade wherever they wish, not the way it has been until now, that in only 15 provinces are the Jews allowed to live and trade. If we want equal rights with the Russians, we must also have equal responsibilities. Because the Jews weren't allowed to offer recruits, the Czar now wants that they should. From this will come the rights to the Jews to live and trade on an equal footing with all Russians. Only after you buy a pew in the synagogue do you have a right to occupy it. It's the same thing. If we supply recruits, we'll have the right to move about freely and trade where we wish.

PERELE: What a bitter pill it is to a mother and father when her child is taken—for twenty-five years! I would die a thousand times, God forbid, if a child of mine were taken. I find no comfort that they take another mother's child. Her woe does not diminish mine. We are both cursed with the worst misfortune in the world. [AARON *rises, kisses her.*]

AARON: My darling, what a silly notion that a child of ours would be taken if we had a son. As upper-class citizens, we have special privileges from the Czar. He exempts our class from this obligation. This is natural and everyone understands it. [*He is near the window.*] I'll have to cut this short. Here comes Yisroelik der Ukrainer. He never comes around on a Sabbath. Look how he is hurrying. There must be trouble. [YISROELIK *enters.*]

YISROELIK: A peaceful Sabbath. I hurried before the crowd gets here. Yes, they're all on their way here. You ought to know why they are coming. They'll be here any minute.

AARON: What happened?

YISROELIK: They sent for me right in the middle of the Sabbath dinner that I should rush to Reb Shloime Spyuche for the Council meeting. It was no use, I just couldn't get out of it. When I got there, not only was the Council in session, but the whole village together with all the poor Jews from the neighbouring hamlets were there, hollering and screaming. You won't believe what went on there when I tell you. A guardian angel must have brought Reb Pinchus there—if he had not got there in time we would really be in trouble. Gavriel Shed, that drunk, stole a third of the money from the alms cup and guzzled a tank of whiskey, and as stinking drunk as he is, they made him the official messenger of the Council. Reb Shloime is in charge; he has no beard, but a behind to sit on he has, and his head—I don't think he knows which end is which. It was a black day for the Jews when he became the head councilor . . . and his wife, that deaf snake . . . she's our first lady! And another Council member is Velvel "for example," with his idiotic sayings that make as much sense as the man in the moon. To join this great cabal, there descended from every back alley and rathole in the village the "big brains." What went on! You would have had plenty to laugh and cry about. Everyone believes that the Ukase demanded that the Council supply a recruit at once. The soldiers who brought the document only asked the Council to sign a receipt—just a receipt. The poor Jews believed that if the Council would not sign then the Ukase would not be in effect. You should have heard the shrieking and howling from inside and outside, from all over the town. Everyone was yelling, "Don't sign! Don't sign!" And the deaf First Lady, Shloime's Bruche, she kept cursing him; under no circumstances was he to sign: "Don't sign, Don't sign!" Even Velvel Gelyevater was screaming like a wild one, "Don't sign; then they won't take a recruit."

AARON [*Sadly wiping a tear.*]: It's a pity, a dreadful pity. Blind. They are so blind, so ignorant. It's a lucky thing this is not a big city. There they would be grabbed away or thrown out.

YISROELIK: Such screaming, wailing, "Don't sign, don't sign!" Then Pinchus the Redhead, God bless him, explained that the ukase is a ukase whether they sign it or not. And if they don't supply recruits, then the Council members would be drafted and maybe even sent to Siberia. Then they really became frightened.

AARON: So what did Reb Pinchus accomplish?

YISROELIK: Did he accomplish something! Did he, just! The dumb cows were frightened out of their wits, and that miserable deaf sow almost went out of her mind. Now she started to scream . . . [*Mimics* BRUCH.] "Sign—for God's sake, sign!"

PERELE: You don't mean to say they signed on the Sabbath? It's impossible.

YISROELIK: No, God forbid. But they were all pretty scared by what Pinchus told them. Then they sent Gavriel the drunk to get the soldiers so they could ask them to wait till after sundown, the end of Sabbath. Then the fireworks started. The workers came in and demanded that they be given rights. They started a fight. At that point I got the idea to tell them to come to see you.

AARON: Till they come, I will try to explain something to you. We're living here in comfort, and we have been blessed with a few rubles—it is ours. No one,

God forbid, has the right to take it away or the villain will be punished. Now, why is this? Because we have a just land, with police, with a magistrate, a governor, and so on. They protect us from robberies, from all injustices so that no one takes advantage of anyone. And do you know who protects them and us, and everybody? The soldiers. If we didn't have so many soldiers, so many battalions, so many generals, then some barbarians like the French would take away all of us together with our possessions, the police, the magistrates, and the governors. That's why we have to have war, not to let the enemy into our country. Comes the question, who should go and fight for us? Actually, all of us should fight the enemy. But we don't need so many people. Only a few hundred thousand soldiers are enough to defeat the enemy. That's why it is fated that some should remain at home and some should serve in the army. Each village draws lots, and through the lottery it is decided who shall be a recruit. That's why we must look upon our soldiers as the precious chosen ones who go to fight for all of us. The fathers and mothers must realize that their sons go to war in their place, otherwise everyone would have to go.

Translated by David S. Lifson.

NOTE

This translation is a twentieth-century version of Aksenfeld's nineteenth-century work.

Opera

Lorenzo Da Ponte
1749–1838

Born Emmanuele Conegliano in Ceneda, Venetian Republic, the man known as Mozart's librettist began life as a poet, scribbling verse during tedious school lessons. Those teenage experiments, plus a solid grounding in Hebrew, Latin, and Greek, primed him for the writing life ahead. When a young Mozart, already famous, requested his assistance, Da Ponte agreed; thus began their illustrious collaboration.

Between librettos, Da Ponte lived adventurously, gambling, living in brothels, and writing seditious poetry, for which he was twice tried and convicted. Da Ponte settled in America, selling Italian books and writing a long, lively autobiography.

Così Fan Tutte
1790

Music: Wolfgang Amadeus Mozart

Wolfgang Amadeus Mozart, composer and Lorenzo Da Ponte, librettist, *Così Fan Tutte, Image of Libretto*, 1790.

First Act

FIRST SCENE

[*A coffee-house*
Ferrando, Don Alfonso and Guglielmo]
No. *i* TRIO
FERRANDO
 My Dorabella couldn't
 Do such a thing:
 Heaven made her
 As faithful as she's fair.
GUGLIELMO
 Fiordiligi simply
 Couldn't betray me: I
 believe her
 constancy equals her
 beauty.
DON ALFONSO
 My hair is already grey, I
 speak with authority; But
 let's have done with
 argument.
FERRANDO and GUGLIELMO
 No, you've told us
 They could be faithless; If
 you're honest
 You will prove it.
DON ALFONSO
 Let's not trouble with proof.
FERRANDO and GUGLIELMO
 [*setting their hands to their swords*]
 No, no, we demand it:
 Or out with your sword
 And we'll break up this friendship.
DON ALFONSO
 what folly to try
 to discover
 The wrong which will make us
 wretched when we've found it!
FERRANDO and GUGLIELMO
 He strikes at my honour
 Who allows his lips to
 utter a word which does
 her wrong.

Translated by Lionel Salter.

Giacomo Meyerbeer
1791–1864

A pathbreaking composer, Giacomo Meyerbeer surprised and delighted generations of opera fans in Europe and around the world. To the staid formula of live performances, he added sound effects, electric spotlights, and an erudite conception of history, making opera at once smarter and more spectacular. Meyerbeer was born Jacob Liebermann Beer, in Prussia, to a wealthy Jewish family. He studied piano and composition before finding success with the Paris Opera. Condemned by the antisemitic Wagner, Meyerbeer's reputation suffered, though he is today credited with transforming his chosen medium, making opera more attractive to its audiences.

Robert le diable
1831

From Giacomo Meyerbeer, *Robert le diable*, title page.

486 THE PERFORMING ARTS

Edgar Degas, Ballet scene from Meyerbeer's opera *Robert le diable*, 1876.

Alexandre-Marie Colin, *Cornélie Falcon as Rachel in the opera* La juive *by Halévy*, 1835.

Jacques-François-Fromental-Élie Halévy
1799–1862

Born in Paris, composer Jacques-François-Fromental-Élie Halévy (known more widely as Fromental Halévy) greatly influenced French grand opera. Halévy entered conservatory at age nine, winning awards and attention in his youth before gaining tremendous popularity in the early 1830s. His 1835 masterpiece *La juive*, with a libretto by Eugène Scribe, secured his status in French opera. In 1851, Halévy became a full professor of composition at the Conservatoire de Paris, where he taught several important composers of the next generation of French music, including Georges Bizet and Camille Saint-Saëns.

La juive
1835

Jacques-François-Fromental-Élie Halévy, Libretto cover for *La juive*, 1835

Jacques-François-Fromental-Élie Halévy

La reine de Chypre
1841

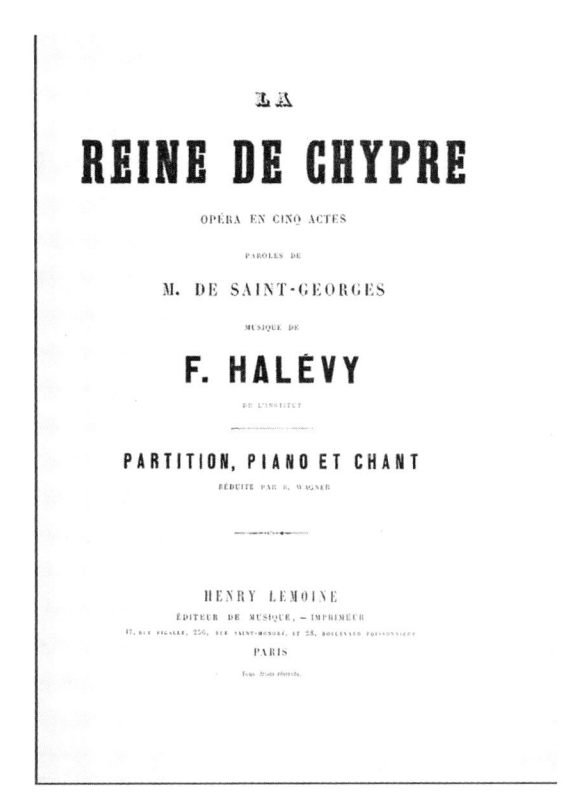

Jacques-François-Fromental-Élie Halévy, *La reine de Chypre, Libretto*, title page, 1841.

Eduard Magnus

The prominent portraitist Eduard Magnus was born in Berlin, his father a wealthy trader. Magnus received an education in several fields, eventually settling on art. During Magnus's early career as a painter, styles and sensibilities shifted as romanticism developed and neoclassicism faded among the bourgeoisie of central Europe. The painter's oeuvre fits squarely in this context, his best-known portraiture utilizing realist conventions to evoke romantic ideals. His portrait of Swedish singer Jenny Lind, who gathered an enormous, international following after a promotional tour of the United States in partnership with P. T. Barnum, remains a prime example of his work.

Portrait of the Singer Jenny Lind (the "Swedish Nightingale")
1846

Portrait of the Singer Jenny Lind (the "Swedish Nightingale"), 1846.

Giacomo Meyerbeer

Le prophète
1849

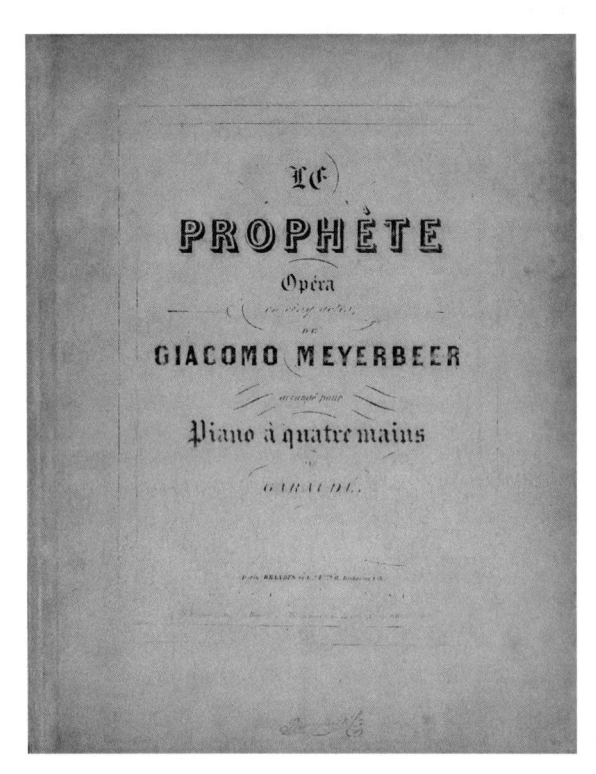

Giacomo Meyerbeer, *Le prophète*, title page, 1849.

Jacques Offenbach
1819–1880

A prolific composer with a light comic touch, Jacques Offenbach produced scores of operettas, a lasting musical legacy. Born in Cologne, a cantor's son, Offenbach mastered the cello at an early age, confounding his instructor. Performances in Parisian salons led, eventually, to renown, French citizenship, and a successful streak of operettas, begetting him more fame in the mid-1860s. Maturity conferred a more serious perspective, and his impish style yielded to a more sober, sensitive approach. By the time of his death, Offenbach was a national hero, worthy of the state funeral he was given.

The Brazilian's Song from the Opera *La vie parisienne*
1866

> Brazilian, I'm rich, I've got dough
> There's plenty of gold in my sack
> Paree, here I am, I've come back
> And richer than ever before!
>
> Two times was I here in the past
> My suitcases bulging with gold
> And diamonds too bright to behold
> How long did it last, do you ask?
>
> Time for 200 girlfriends and me
> With mistresses waiting in line
> Six months full of pleasures divine
> Then nothing, Paree, my Paree
>
> In six months you'd emptied my bags
> And sent me back home to Brazil
> I bore you no grudge or ill will
> Though going from riches to rags
>
> But under Rio's savage skies
> I raged at fortune to return
> And oft repeated as I burned
> Another sack of gold or die
>
> I didn't die, I earned my share
> Of princely sums, but let's be real,
> I'm here again so you can steal
>
> The loot I've stolen over there
> The loot I've stolen over there
> The loot I've stolen over there

Ooooh
Brazilian, I'm rich, I've got dough
There's plenty of gold in my sack
Paree, here I am, I've come back
And richer than ever before!

Brazilian, I'm rich, I've got dough
There's plenty of gold in my sack
Paree, Paree, my gay Paree
Paree, here I am, I've come back!

Hurrah, hurrah, hurrah!
I've just got off the ship
Let down your hair, my honey pots,
Hurrah, hurrah, hurrah!
You'll soon be drawing lots
To take your turn and kiss these lips
This pigeon's ready to be plucked
So take my dollar bills, my gold
My watch, my rings, my whole bankroll
Just tell me you're my buttercup

I'll be merry and carefree
Chivalrous and debonair
On the town in gay Paree
We'll go dancing in Asnières

Get this straight, I'm telling you
Before you say adieu
I'm going to get my money's worth
I promise you

I'm going to get my money's worth
I'm going to get my money's worth
Come on, come on,
Come on, come on!

Translated by Michele McKay Aynesworth.

Jacques Offenbach

La Grande-Duchesse de Gérolstein
1867

Jacques Offenbach, *La Grande-Duchesse de Gérolstein*, cover, 1867.

Anton Rubinstein
1829–1894

Among the most renowned pianists of the nineteenth century, Anton Grigoryevich Rubinstein was born in Podolia (now in Moldova) and debuted as a prodigy in Moscow at age ten. He went on to tour several important European cities afterward, gathering fame for his performances and compositions and eventually settling in St. Petersburg in 1848. His first opera, *Dmitry Donskoy*, premiered in 1852, and by the end of the decade, he had attracted the patronage of Yelena Pavlovna, Grand Duchess of Russia. In 1862, under the auspices of the duchess, Rubinstein established the St. Petersburg Conservatory, serving as its director until 1867 and again from 1887 to 1891. Rubinstein's contribution to music was prolific, including dozens of large-scale compositions alongside his work as an educator and performer.

Der Thurm zu Babel (The Tower of Babel)
1870

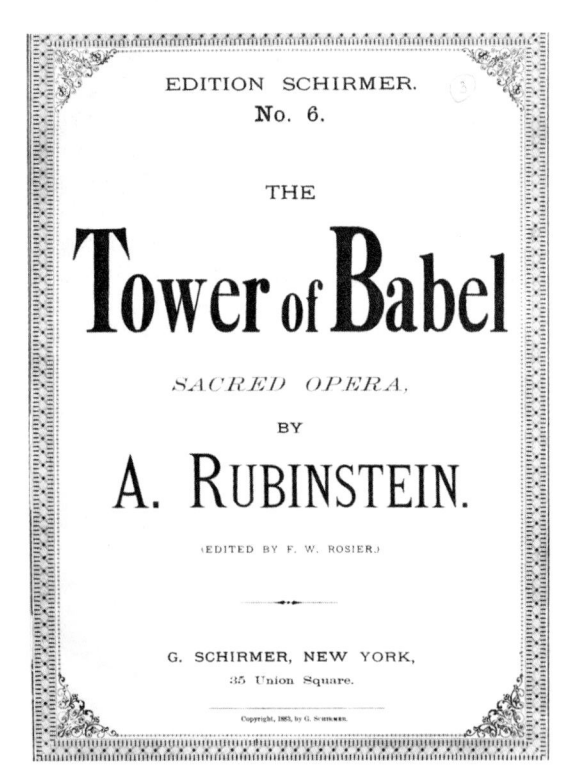

Anton Rubinstein, *Der Thurm zu Babel (The Tower of Babel)*, title page, 1870.

Adolf Gustaw Sonnenfeld
1837–1914

Born in Breslau, Adolf Gustaw Sonnenfeld studied music in Germany before settling permanently in Warsaw in 1857. Sonnenfeld composed music for popular theaters and dance halls in Warsaw, and in 1867, he formed the Warsaw Orchestra, which toured the region performing popular music. In addition to his significant body of popular music, he composed five operas, six operettas, and the ballet *Pan Twardowski* (1874).

Kantorzysta: Polka na fortepiano, op. 68
ca. 1870

Adolf Gustaw Sonnenfeld, "Kantorzysta: Polka na fortepiano, op. 68," ca. 1870.

Karl Goldmark
1830–1915

Hungarian-born Karl Goldmark was a composer who overcame poverty and lack of formal training to achieve critical and popular renown. Though hardly prolific, Goldmark produced several important operas, symphonies, and concertos, finding fame in Vienna, his adopted city. A cantor's son, born into an enormous and nearly destitute Jewish family, Goldmark learned the piano and violin before turning to orchestral music. On the whole, he rejected the avant-garde for the traditional, finding original variations within classic musical forms.

The Queen of Sheba
1875

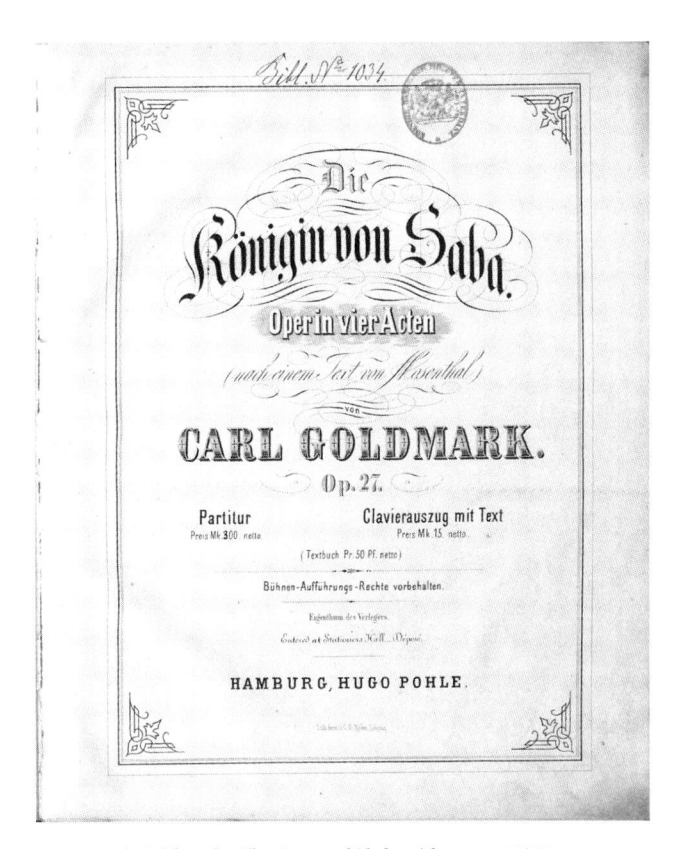

Karl Goldmark, *The Queen of Sheba*, title page, 1875.

Jacques Offenbach

Tales of Hoffmann
1880–1881

Jacques Offenbach, *Tales of Hoffmann*, title page, 1880–1881.

492 THE PERFORMING ARTS

Geskel Salomon

Biography of Salomon appears in the Visual and Material Culture section of this volume.

Drawing of Costume for Vitka in the First Production of the Opera Dalibor by Bedřich Smetana

Date Unknown

Drawing of Costume for Vitka in the First Production of the Opera Dalibor by Bedřich Smetana, date unknown.

Music

Levi Isaac of Berdichev

A Din Toyre mit Gott/Der kadish fun rabi Levi Yitshok (A Court Case with God/The Kaddish of Rabbi Levi Isaac)
ca. 1790

> "Good morning, Master of the universe!
> I, Levi-Yitzchok of Berdytschev, have come to hold
> Judgment with You concerning Your people Israel.
> What have You against Israel?
>
> Why have you imposed Yourself upon Your people Israel?
> Everywhere you say: "Command the children of Israel."
> Everywhere—"Speak to the children of Israel."
> "Father of mercy, how many nations are there in the world
> Persians, Babylonians, Romans.
> The Russians—what do they say?
> That their emperor is ruler.
> The Germans—what do they say?
> That their Kaiser is king.
> The English—what do they say?
> That their king is ruler.
> But I Levi-Yitzchok of Berdytschev say?
> Magnified and sanctified be the Great Name.
> And I Levi-Yitzchok of Berdytschev say:
> I will not move from this place, from this very spot,
> Until there will be an end,
> Until there will be an end to this exile.
> Magnified and sanctified be the Great Name . . ."

Translated by F. Doppelt.

Anonymous

Several versions of this anonymous poem about the life of the biblical Abraham exist, composed in Judeo-Spanish.

La vocación de Abraham
ca. 1800

> Terah's wife is pregnant
>   day after day she turned pale,
> she already knew what she had
>   but she did not reveal it to her husband.
>
> One day she went out to fields and vineyards,
>   she found a cavern and went in there
> where Abraham our father was going to be born,
>   Abraham our father, may he rest in peace.
>
> The Lord of Abraham shall be,
>   when he started to implore.
>
> Look to the son born to us,
>   to the altar he took him.
>
> Lord of one-hundred-years-old Abraham,
>   he [Abraham] will [still be able to] seduce at ninety.

Translated by Edwin Seroussi.

Shneur Zalman of Liady

Niggun of Four Stanzas
ca. 1800

Shneur Zalman of Liady, "Niggun of Four Stanzas," ca. 1800. A notated version of a wordless hasidic *niggun*, melody.

Isaac Nathan
1790–1864

Born in Canterbury, England, Isaac Nathan studied Italian musical traditions and was a friend of Lord Byron, for whom Nathan set poetry to music, including Byron's *Hebrew Melodies*. Nathan moved in 1841 to Australia, where he is credited with having composed the continent's first opera.

Song Settings for the Poet Lord Byron's *Hebrew Melodies*
1815

Isaac Nathan, "Song Settings for the Poet Lord Byron's *Hebrew Melodies*," 1815.

Michael Joseph Guzikov
1806–1837

Born in Shklov (now Sklou, Belarus) to a family of musicians, Michael Joseph (Mikhl Yosef, also Yekhiel Mikhl) Guzikov made inroads for traditional klezmer musicians into broader European music with his performances on the *tsimbl*, a variety of xylophone. The instrument remained popular in itinerant bands in Europe from the High Middles Ages until the early nineteenth century, when it caught on among bourgeois composers for use in symphony orchestras. Guzikov himself attracted the attention of Felix Mendelssohn and other renowned composers on his tours of the Russian Empire and Europe.

Shir hama'alot (Song of Ascents)
1827

Michael Joseph Guzikov, "Shir hama'alot (Song of Ascents)," 1827.

Artist Unknown

The illustration accompanying this march depicts three Polish Jewish soldiers taking part in the Polish uprising of 1830–1831. The rendering of an "Israelite National Guard in Warsaw" alongside solemn, patriotic music constitutes a visual and aural representation of Jewish belonging to the Polish national cause prior to 1863. It is found in various forms, including in an 1860 reprint as a piece of published sheet music in Germany.

Marsch der Israelitischen national Garde in [zu] Warschau
ca. 1831

"Marsch der Israelitischen national Garde in Warschau," ca. 1831.

Fanny Mendelssohn Hensel
1805–1847

Fanny Hensel, the granddaughter of the philosopher Moses Mendelssohn and financier Daniel Itzig, and sister of the composer Felix Mendelssohn Bartholdy, was born in Hamburg into a wealthy family. A composer of numerous songs, piano compositions, cantatas, and other musical works, Hensel was pressured by her brother Felix (who claimed sole title to many of her works) and the general social attitude not to publish her music. She was married to the painter Wilhelm Hensel.

Fanny Mendelssohn Hensel, with Wilhelm Hensel, Duette: Mein Liebchen, wir sassen beisammen (Duet: My Sweetheart, We Sat Together)
1841

Fanny Mendelssohn Hensel, with Wilhelm Hensel, "Duette: Mein Liebchen, wir sassen beisammen (Duet: My Sweetheart, We Sat Together)," 1841.

Charles-Valentin Alkan
1813–1888

Charles-Valentin Alkan (born Charles-Henri-Valentin Morhange) was raised in Paris, receiving instruction in music from an early age. Alkan entered the Conservatoire de Paris as a child and by early adulthood was a well-respected pianist. Known almost entirely for his piano compositions, Alkan wrote technically difficult music that largely defied conventions of the day. He associated with influential figures of the romantic movement such as Frédéric Chopin and Victor Hugo, though his music generally avoids the more bucolic themes of romanticism in favor of the grotesque. Alkan retired relatively young, spending much of his life studying Talmud and other literature, withdrawn from urban life.

Ancienne melodie de la synagogue
1844

Charles-Valentin Alkan, "Ancienne melodie de la synagogue," op. 31, no. 6, 1844.

Giacomo Meyerbeer

Hallelujah: Eine Cantatine für 4 Männerstimmen mit begleitung einer obligaten orgel und des chores ad libitum
1847

Giacomo Meyerbeer, "Hallelujah: Eine Cantatine für 4 Männerstimmen mit begleitung einer obligaten orgel und des chores ad libitum," p. 1, 1847.

Samuel Naumbourg
1815–1880

Born near Ansbach, Bavaria (now in Germany), Samuel Naumbourg was raised in a family connected to a long lineage of cantors. After receiving musical training in Munich, Naumbourg settled in Paris in 1843, establishing himself as an influential choirmaster among the city's synagogue choirs. Over the course of his career, Naumbourg compiled and published synagogue music for a broad audience, drawing on both his southern German heritage and conventions of opera popular in France at the time to give his music wide appeal.

Seu Shearim (Lift Up Your Heads, O Gates)
1847

Samuel Naumbourg, "Seu Shearim (Lift Up Your Heads, O Gates)," in *Z'mirot Yisrael*, 1847.

Moses L. Penha
Dates and Details Unknown

Esther's Triumph
1847

Friends, let's celebrate this day—Viva!
Purim, occasion to be gay—Viva!
Safe and free from Haman's wrong,
Let's shout in unison this song—Viva, viva, viva . . .

Esther, brilliant as the sun—Viva!
Grand Sultana, king's loved one—Viva!
Pleaded mercy for her race,
The wish was granted, by his grace—Viva, viva, viva . . .

Esther wants Haman condemned—Let him die!
So Ahasuerus has him hanged—Let him die!
Putting faithful Mordecai
In the two-faced villain's place—Viva, viva, viva . . .

Protected by her loving hand—Viva!
Avenged of the infernal man—Viva!
An end was put to the tyrant's reign,
Again and again, sing this refrain—Viva, viva, viva . . .

Together we rejoice today—Viva!
With feasts and dancing, glorify—Viva!
Our grand defender Mordecai
And immortal Esther the brave—Viva, viva, viva . . .

Translated by Michele McKay Aynesworth.

Israel Moses Ḥazan
1808–1862

Israel Moses Ḥazan, born in Smyrna and raised in Jerusalem, was from a rabbinic family of Spanish and Turkish origin. He was appointed as a jurist in Jerusalem in 1842 and became an emissary in London for the Jewish community of Jerusalem in 1844. While in London, he condemned the reforms issued by the Brunswick rabbinical conference, in the form of a pamphlet, *Kin'at tsiyon* (1846). In 1847, he became chief rabbi of Rome, and later served in Corfu and Alexandria. He also composed religious poetry. In 1862, he moved back to the Land of Israel but died in Beirut.

Kerakh shel romi (City of Rome)
1850

Passage I (Folio 1A)

The Baḥ (Bayit Hadash) was asked concerning the practice in synagogues of using music which is sung in the houses of worship (of non-Jews).[1] It is only forbidden regarding melodies which are unique to the non-Jews, since then (these melodies) are practices of idolatry, analogous to their altar which is completely forbidden (for us to use). . . . But if the music is not unique (to non-Jewish worship) then it seems to me that there is no prohibition, since we certainly do not learn from them the non-Jewish way of worship.

. . . Concerning the ruling of the Baḥ on the matter of music, since it is at hand, we shall say something about it. With all due respect to him, the matter of music, even music unique to non-Jewish worship, is not analogous to (the laws pertaining to) an altar.

Passage II (Folio 2a)

And if this tune (*Qol*) which the non-Jews sing in their houses of worship is one of submissiveness that penetrates the heart according to the art of music and according to what one was accustomed; and lacking it, the hearts and minds of the congregation will not be in a proper mood—can it be believed that because fools went astray and established this music in their houses of worship, that we should also forbid something our nature demands? This is one of the five senses which gives pleasure to the body. Why should there be a difference between (the sense of hearing) and the sense of taste and the sense of smell? (It is permitted in the Torah) for Jews to taste sacrifices and smell the incense (even though non-Jews taste offerings and smell incense in their houses of worship). Isn't this because a person cannot overrule his natural spirit, common to all humans? The same law and the same reason applies to the sense of hearing and music, which relates equally to all people. . . . Can the Italian Jew, for example, overturn his natural (feelings) acquired in his homeland? (He is obviously influenced by the music he hears every day in the theatres, circuses and streets.)

According to the reasoning of the Baḥ, why isn't it forbidden to say Habdalah on a cup of wine next to the *tebah* (reader's desk), since also in the churches they make a blessing over their wine? Thus, the conclusion is as we have stated. In a matter which is natural and needed to all people, each according to its own laws and faiths, it is not relevant to make a prohibition. Otherwise, people could not live in peace (since there would be so many prohibitions).

I have a great proof that everything that has a good reason—whether because of pleasure or honor or because nature demands it by virtue of the customs of the various lands—even if that thing is unique to the religious service of some churches of whatever national background, not only is this thing permissible to Jews and there is no prohibition of following in the ways of non-Jews; but quite to the contrary, it is a mitzvah to follow in their ways to beautify our synagogues with all types of beauty and honor which are equally (appreciated) by all human beings of that land—even if this practice is unique to the (non-Jewish) places of worship.

Passage III (Fol. 4a)

There is a great difference between the Moslems and the Christians in this matter. The Christians never considered our prayer and our rituals to be heretical and shameful, as the Radbaz wrote about the Moslem (attitude towards Jewish worship). On the contrary (the Christians) praise and glorify our recognition of God's oneness. Since we are valued respectfully in their eyes, the Radbaz would admit that we should improve our religious services and especially our synagogues so that they (Christians) will not scuff at us saying: a beautiful Torah in an ugly vessel. This is because (the Christians) know the value of our Torah and mitzvot and prayer, which have been translated into the languages of their lands, as is known. Returning to the words of the Baḥ, let us say that if the Baḥ had studied the details carefully and had distinguished between music—which has its own reason—and an altar (which is purely for their worship and is considered as) a practice (law) without a reason—he would not have written as he did. . . .

I call into witness heaven and earth that when I was in the great city of sages and scholars, Izmir, I saw among the illustrious sages those who were great singers according to the art of music. At their head was the illustrious Rabbi Abraham Ha-Cohen Arias. For the musical form for the High Holy Days, which requires great submissiveness which is called among them *hizun*, they used to go to the Christian churches on their holy days, (and would stand) behind the wall (so that they could hear the church music) in order to learn from the [sic] (the Christians) the submissive tone which deeply moves the heart. From those melodies, they arranged wondrous *kadishim* and *kedushot*. And this is a great proof to all I have said and explained above; and this is enough. And I have found another support (for my position) in the responsa of the Geonim *Qobetz Gadol*, number 152 . . . who conclude that . . . it is forbidden for a hazan of a synagogue to sing in a language other than Hebrew; but as far as the melody itself is concerned when singing the Hebrew words, it does not matter (whether they derive from non-Jewish sources).

NOTE

1. Baḥ is an acronym for Bayit Hadash, title of the responsa collection of Polish rabbi Yo'el Sirkis (1561–1640).

Translated by Edwin Seroussi.

Other works by Hazan: *Naḥalah le-Yisra'el* (1851); *She'erit ha-naḥalah* (1862); *Iyye ha-yam* (1864).

Louis Gottschalk
1829–1869

The pianist Louis Gottschalk was a musical magpie, collecting influences from around the world and stitching them together into singular compositions. Few other composers, before or since, have embraced influence with such zeal. Gottschalk borrowed eagerly from Caribbean, Latin American, and Creole traditions as he meandered through Cuba, the West Indies, Puerto Rico, and elsewhere, giving concerts and sampling local customs. Born in New Orleans, introduced early to the piano, Gottschalk was anointed by Frédéric Chopin, who recognized his nascent genius. Gottschalk achieved early success in Europe, and during his life, fame followed him in every direction.

The Water Sprite—Polka
1853

Louis Gottschalk, "The Water Sprite—Polka," 1853.

Charles-Valentin Alkan
Super flumina Babylonis
1859

Charles-Valentin Alkan, *Super flumina Babylonis*, 1859.

Mikhl Gordon
1823–1890

Shuttling between worlds—Yiddish and Hebrew, religious and secular—came naturally to Mikhl Gordon, the Vilna-born poet and songwriter. A proud *maskil*, he championed modern, secular ways of thinking and prodded religious Jews, especially Hasidim, to evolve with the times. Yet Gordon never abandoned Judaism, and his articles, poems, and songs reflected his deep engagement with traditional Judaism. For most of his life, Gordon's fame rested on his music. Writing under a pseudonym, he expressed deep sympathy for married Jewish women saddled with large families and capricious husbands—an extraordinary act for a Jewish male writer at the time.

Whisky
ca. 1868

So let's drink whisky, brothers—
let's hope we live to drink again.
Let's drink now—enough of eating.
How can you forget about whisky for so long!
If we didn't have whisky,
how would we live in this world?

I must treat whisky honorably.
I stand before it as before an old person,
for it knew my great-grandmother,
and my grandmother used to like it.
From her I inherited the good trait
of draining the whole flask constantly.

When the matchmaker came to my grandfather
to discuss a match between my mother and father,
they talked and talked and nothing came of it,
till whisky entered the picture.
Through whisky the match was agreed on—
my father became my mother's groom.

The marriage took place right away—
they drank whisky all night.
Everyone drank out of big glasses
in honor of the groom and bride.
Through whisky my father married my mother—
through whisky I came into the world.

I still remember that at my circumcision
the whisky never left the table.
Everyone cried *Mazl Tov!*
May the child live and become a rabbi!
That's why I drink most of a glass,
usually without stopping.

As soon as I was weaned from the breast,
I developed a lust for whisky.
I didn't want my mother's cereal,
I just wanted a little whisky.
I used to take it from a bowl with a spoon
and scream: Mama, give me a little bit more!

At my bar mitzvah, they told me
to drink as much as I wanted.
Of all *mitzvahs* the greatest
is to drink only the best whisky.
When I drink three glasses of whisky,
I forget about all the mitzvahs.

Whenever whisky incites me,
I can commit all kinds of sins;
They can't ever punish me for them
because I've never had enough sleep;
I have no shame, no respect—
I've drunk whisky, and that's an excuse for everything.

When they brought me to the marriage canopy,
I thought: What do I need this kind of trouble for?
But right away they brought in whisky
to say the Seven Blessings with it.
If I hadn't encountered whisky there,
I would have fled right away.

The whisky then said wise things to me:
just stand there quietly, don't suffer—
your wife will eat your heart out,
but just don't forget whisky.
You'll hear your wife's curses,
but through whisky they'll become blessings.

And when your wife makes a face,
drink up a big glass right away.
When she screams at you,

drink up one-two-three.
Let her scream endlessly,
and you just up-end the glasses.

That's what happened in ancient times:
the Tree of Knowledge was a grapevine.
Eve talked Adam into
drinking whisky—it's no sin.
If Adam hadn't loved whisky, he would have driven
   Eve away.

When you feel up or down,
just drink whisky and feel merry;
when times are not good for you,
drink whisky—don't lose your courage.
Through whisky, everyone gets proud and happy—
an underling becomes a king.

I love whisky with its sweet voice.
True, it costs me my last penny;
I don't have any money any more—just a bit of faith.
True, I have very good security,
and as long as I am merry and don't want to worry,
why should I care today about what will happen
   tomorrow?

When I come to the end of my few years,
I want them to put whisky with me in my grave—
a flask of whisky next to the wall
and a big glass in my right hand.
When the resurrection comes, I'll be here again
and I'll drink whisky right away, in the first hour.

May God just hear my prayer
that the excise tax be repealed soon.
It's my ancestors and their sins that are responsible
for whisky's being subject to such cruel laws.
Our ancestors were saintly people—
they knew nothing of excises and bar payments.

I have heard from pious people
that things will be good when the Messiah comes:
There'll be much whisky for rich and poor
and all the rivers will be full of whisky.
I'd like to live to see the Messiah come—
I'd swim like a fish in the river.

But be that as it may,
I drink my whisky and pay taxes.
Let water run in the rivers—
I can buy my whisky in a tavern.
I constantly fulfill the mitzvah of drinking whisky,
and keep saying: *l'chaim, l'chaim*!

Translated by Barnett Zumoff.

Pesach-Elijah Badkhn
Dates Unknown

Dubbed the "Genius of Jesters," Pesach-Elijah Badkhn was a playful troubadour who traveled to Minsk, Vilna, and elsewhere performing his funny, nervous Yiddish melodies. Like the characters in his songs, he straddled worlds: religious and secular, serious and comic. For years, he avoided publishing his lyrics, though he finally grew tired of rival singers stealing his songs and decided to claim credit for them in print. Pesach-Elijah performed around the Pale of Settlement, traveling widely as his fame and songbook expanded.

Songbird, or Six Folk Songs
1871

(*The songs*)
It frightens us so,
With our poor wares to go
And face the wide world and its scorn.
We have lived many days,
But know only the ways.
Of the villages where we were born.

(*The author*)
You've got nothing to fear,
Just go straight out from here—
You'll find friendship in towns big and small.
The villager's art,
If it's clever and smart
Won't be looked down on at all.

(*The songs*)
Still, we fear to depart:
Who will have the kind heart
To provide us with lodging and rest?
The learned, we know,
Will tell us to go.
We'll be lodged with poor *badkhns* at best.

(The author)
If only you knew:
Books more foolish than you,
Belong to the rich upper class.
Their spines, I am told,
All have letters of gold
And their bookshelves have doors made of glass.

(The songs)
Yet we fear we'll be shamed;
By Hasidim—defamed,
And denounced where *maskilim* hold sway.
For the one—not *Hasidish*,
For the other—too Yiddish.
So they'll both want us out of the way.

Translated by Solon Beinfeld.

Other work by Gordon: *Di bord, un dertsu nokh andere sheyne yidishe lider* (1868).

Samuel Naumbourg, "Aggudat Shirim" (*Recueil de chants religieux et populaires des Israélites*), cover, 1874.

Samuel Naumbourg
Aggudat Shirim
1874

Elyokum Tsunzer
ca. 1836–1913

Elyokum Tsunzer was born in Vilna and became "the father of Yiddish poetry," a prolific and widely revered versifier. He wrote before, after, and even during his conscription in the Russian army, jotting poems in the soldiers' barracks. Poetry aside, he was a well-known singer, in high demand at Russian weddings and other public occasions. Tsunzer's unflinching and faintly lugubrious melodies chronicled the plight of Jews under tsarist rule.

Song of the Railway
1875

A whole world of railways appeared in our time
They carry their passengers—poor men and rich.
Admire the wonder, but bear this in mind:
It's really a parable, meant just for you.
It is we who are seated in passenger cars.
Locomotives are time: as they rapidly move
And pull many millions of people along
And fly like a bullet shot out of a gun.
Every rail on the line is a second of time.
Every station you pass is a year that's gone by.
The hours fly past like a railwayman's booth,
The train is a whole generation of man.
The ticket you hold in your wallet or purse—
That is your fortune, your whole travel plan.
How far you will ride and in what class you sit
Is decided by God, the Director of Trains. . . .

The conductors inspect every ticket in turn
And seat all the passengers, each in his class.
Who's in First Class, in upholstered divans,
And who is in Third, with its crowding and damp.
Conductors are messengers sent from above,
Carrying out the decisions of God:
Who shall have comfort, and prosper in life,
And who shall be wretched in narrow confines;
Who shall enjoy both good health and good luck,
With children like apples that fall from a tree.

And who, with affliction and sorrow in life,
May even some day be thrown out of his home.
You can look at conductors, but don't say a word—
The world, after all, has to follow a plan.
The ticket determines where everyone sits
As God, the Director of Trains, has ordained.

At every station, as soon as bells ring,
Conductors jump down to the platforms in haste.
The passengers run, each with baggage in hand.
Very many get on, very many get off.
The stations, you see, are the years of our lives.
On Rosh Hashanah, on the holy New Year
The tickets are issued. Some travel far,
While others, alas, must depart from the train.
The true ticket-window's the heavenly court
Which issues the tickets and sets all the rules—
Who will ride long, who just for a while,
Or who just missed his train and will not travel at all.
When you're told to get off, do not haggle and plead,
No matter if you're not at all an old man—
Your ticket expired, your cry is in vain.
God has decided—the Director of Trains.
The motorman stands at the engine in front,
Its cylinder steaming with burning hot coals.
One slip of his hand and it goes off the rails
And wagons of people are in danger of death.
Our motorman—that is our reason, our brain.
It leads us in life, just as he leads a train.
But reason itself can mislead and derail,
So we must have a cylinder—Torah from God.
Where things become difficult, Torah will help.
If you have reason, but also belief
You will move safely along in your life.
But if you just lead with your weak, foolish brain,
And laugh at the cylinder, scoff at God's plan,
See! You will certainly go off the rails
And suffer the wrath of Director of Trains!

Translated by Solon Beinfeld.

Louis Lewandowski

1821–1894

Born in Wreschen, Prussia (now Września, Poland), Louis Lewandowski remains among the most influential mid-nineteenth-century composers of synagogue music. Lewandowski was appointed musical director and choirmaster of the New Synagogue in Berlin upon its opening in 1866. Incorporating Eastern European *nusaḥim* and the romantic style of Felix Mendelssohn into the canon of German *ḥazanut*, Lewandowski's compositions appealed widely, both during his life and for decades after it. In addition to his career compos-

Louis Lewandowski, undated sheet music of composition Psalm 92, "Od yenuvun" ("They Shall Still Bring Forth"), 1876.

ing, Lewandowski taught vocal music at various Jewish schools in Berlin. The composer's influence reached as far as the many Conservative and Reform congregations taking root in the United States around the time.

Samuel Naumbourg, "Title Page for His Version of Salamone de Rossi's *Hashirim asher le-Shelomoh* (The Songs of Solomon)," 1876. De Rossi (1570–1630), singer, violinist, and musician in the Gonzaga court in Mantua, is best known for his innovation of introducing polyphony into synagogue music. Naumberg recovered his score by dint of great effort and printed it as *Cantiques de Salomon Rossi*. This edition aroused new interest in De Rossi's music in synagogues throughout the Western world.

Psalm 92, Od yenuvun (They Shall Still Bring Forth)
1876

Samuel Naumbourg

Title Page for His Version of Salamone de Rossi's Hashirim asher le-Shelomoh
1876

Abraham Baer

1834–1894

Abraham Baer, "Baal T'fillah: Oder, Der practische Vorbeter (Prayer Leader: Or the Practical Litanist)," 1877.

Born in Filehne, Prussia (now Wieleń, Poland), Abraham Baer worked as a teacher and cantor in various communities in the Prussian province of Posen, eventually settling in Gothenburg, Sweden. Baer became the city's chief cantor in 1860, thereafter publishing works for choir and organ. His collection *Baal T'fillah* remained the principal repertoire for generations of European cantors, compiling the yearly synagogue liturgy arranged according to various rites.

Baal T'fillah: Oder, Der practische Vorbeter (Prayer Leader: Or The Practical Litanist)
1877

Salomon Sulzer
1804–1890

Salomon Sulzer was dubbed the "father of modern synagogue music" thanks to his influence on nineteenth-century Jewish liturgy. Born in Austria, trained from a young age as a cantor, and given his first cantorial appointment in his hometown of Hohenems, Sulzer recast music for holy days, Sabbath services, and non-Jewish events, adding harmony, organ sounds, and special flourishes to beloved traditional songs. Sulzer's influence was immense and widespread, and it carried over into the century after his death. In life, he published two major volumes of synagogue melodies and was lauded by Franz Schubert, Franz Liszt, and other famous European composers.

Statement upon the Publication of* Denkschrift an die hochgeehrte Wiener israelitische Cultus-Gemeinde *(Memorandum to the Esteemed Viennese Israelite Religious Community)
1886

In the first place, it behoves us to fight the opinion that the regeneration of the service can be achieved only by a complete break with the past, by abolishing all traditional and inherited historically evolved liturgy. . . . To me it appeared that the confusion in the synagogue service was a consequence of the need for a restoration, but one based on historical ground; and that we might discover the original, noble forms to which we should anchor ourselves, developing them in artistic style. The older generation would recognise the familiar and beloved element, while the younger generation should be educated to the appreciation of it. Jewish liturgy must satisfy all musical demands while yet remaining Jewish: it should not be necessary to sacrifice Jewish characteristics to artistic forms. [. . .]

I thought it my duty to consider, as far as possible, the traditional tunes bequeathed to us, to cleanse the ancient and dignified ones of the later accretions of tasteless embellishment, to bring them back to their original purity, and to reconstruct them in accordance with the text and the rules of harmony.

Translator unknown.

Elyokum Tsunzer

The Flower
Date Unknown

> Where everyone travels, in the middle of the road,
> there is a wonderful flower.
> It's been lying there and rotting for several days now.
> The wind blows it around,
> and it cries out and weeps a great plea:
> "Slowly—watch where you're going!
> Have mercy—see, you're trampling
> a flower with a beautiful blossom!
> Someone have pity—
> just come here
> and pick up a flower that sparkles!
> Carry me back
> to where I came from,
> to where they first planted me.
>
> "For when I see flowers now on every side,
> I cry a river of tears.
> I remember my previous happiness—
> I was the equal of any other flower.
> When I blossomed in the emperor's garden
> and the sun shone brightly,
> dozens of servants tended to me.
> Just see what has become of me now:
> stepped on and trampled,
> soaked,
> my flowers deprived of their color;
> I lie in the garbage,
> the rain pours,
> there is no pity for me."

As the flower weeps there and cries out,
every man's heart is moved.
An angel comes from far away
and hears its wailing and pain.
"Tell me, flower, tell me the story—
you move my heart tremendously.
Where did you grow? What's that place called?
How do you come to be here on the road?"
The flower shrieks:
"Oh woe is me, woe!
Don't you remember me at all from before?
I'm from Jerusalem—
'Jew' is my name—
at least *you* should have pity on me!

"For two thousand years, if you had seen me
when I had my kingdom,
you yourself would have marveled at me,
at the beauty of my every petal.
Priests, Levites, innumerable generals—
I boasted of my blossoms then.
Then they suddenly tore me out of my place,
and I have been wandering for nearly two thousand
    years.

"Wherever I've been,
I've seen murderousness:
they tore me limb from limb,
burned me, cut me, and inflicted other indignities,
and only because I am a Jew!"

Thus did the Jew wander once,
like the flower on the road with its blossom.
One takes his honor, one calls him *zhid*,
one tramples him.
And now he's lost his courage and boldness,
his power and strength.
He has only his faith—that's still his consolation
in the long dark night.
Ah, my heart breaks with pain,
for you too once blossomed!
Such a beautiful flower,
and everyone tramples it.
How can you not have pity?

As soon as the angel hears it mention
its ancient pedigree in Zion,
he places it amid all the flowerpots
and it begins to blossom again.
And he consoles it with his sympathy:
"Wipe away your tears—the sun will soon start to
    shine for you.
I won't disrupt your faith, God forbid—
I'll just spruce you up!"
So the flower asks him:
"Tell me your name,
let's know your name."
He answers it:
"My name is Alexander,
Czar of Russia."

Translated by Barnett Zumoff.

Credits

Sholem Yankev Abramovitsh (Mendele Mokher Sforim), "The Little Man; or, Portrait of Life" and "Fishke the Lame," from *Classic Yiddish Stories of S. Y. Abramovitsh, Sholem Aleichem, and I. L. Peretz*, trans. and ed. Ken Frieden (Syracuse, N.Y.: Syracuse University Press, 2004), pp. 3–5, 44–47. Translation copyright © 2004 by Ken Frieden. Used with permission of the publisher; "The Brief Travels of Benjamin the Third," from *Tales of Mendele the Book Peddler: Fishke the Lame and Benjamin the Third*, ed. Dan Miron and Ken Frieden, trans. Hillel Halkin (New York: Schocken Books, 1996), pp. 359–64. Used with permission of Dan Miron.

Abraham Abramson, *Medal Commemorating the Enfranchisement of the Jews of Westphalia by Jerome Bonaparte*, obverse and reverse. The Israel Museum, Jerusalem, 754/001B. Photo copyright © The Israel Museum, Jerusalem, by Yair Hovav.

Isaac Akrish, "A Rabbi of Istanbul Condemns the Teaching of European Languages," trans. Matt Goldish, from *Sephardi Lives: A Documentary History, 1700–1950*, ed. Julia Phillips Cohen and Sarah Abrevaya Stein (Stanford, Calif.: Stanford University Press, 2014), pp. 124–25. Copyright © 2014 by the Board of Trustees of the Leland Stanford Jr. University. All rights reserved. With the permission of Stanford University Press, www.sup.org.

Yisroel Aksenfeld, *Recruits*, from *Epic and Folk Plays of the Yiddish Theatre*, trans. and ed. David Lifson (Rutherford, N.J.: Fairleigh Dickinson University Press, 1975), pp. 171–73. Used with permission of Associated University Presses; "The Headband," from *The Shtetl*, trans. Joachim Neugroschel (New York: Overlook Press, 1979), pp. 49–50, 61–62. Copyright © 1979 by Joachim Neugroschel. www.overlookpress.com. All rights reserved. Used with permission of the publisher.

Sa'adi Besalel a-Levi, from *A Jewish Voice from Ottoman Salonica*, ed. Aron Rodrigue and Sarah Abrevaya Stein, trans. Isaac Jerusalmi (Stanford, Calif.: Stanford University Press, 2012). Copyright © 2012 by the Board of Trustees of the Leland Stanford Jr. University. Reprinted in *Sephardi Lives: A Documentary History, 1700–1950*, ed. Julia Phillips Cohen and Sarah Abrevaya Stein (Stanford, Calif.: Stanford University Press, 2014), pp. 108–9. Copyright © 2014 by the Board of Trustees of the Leland Stanford Jr. University. All rights reserved. With the permission of Stanford University Press, www.sup.org.

Yom Tov ben Israel Jacob Algazi, Authorization of Receipt of Donation by "Eretz Israel Contribution Fund" of Ferrara (Italy) Congregation. By "Emissaries of the Holy City of Jerusalem." Courtesy Kedem Auction House, Jerusalem.

Judah Alkalai, "Hoping for Redemption: Anticipating the Messianic Year," trans. Olga Borovaya, from *Sephardi Lives: A Documentary History, 1700–1950*, ed. Julia Phillips Cohen and Sarah Abrevaya Stein (Stanford, Calif.: Stanford University Press, 2014), pp. 39–40. Copyright © 2014 by the Board of Trustees of the Leland Stanford

Jr. University. All rights reserved. With the permission of Stanford University Press, www.sup.org, and the translator. Published in Ladino as *Yehudá Alcalay y su obra "La paz de Jerusalén" (Ofen, 1840): En los orígenes del sionismo y en lengua sefardí*, ed. Pilar Romeu (Barcelona: Tirocinio, 2011), pp. 65–66.

Charles-Valentin Alkan, *Ancienne melodie de la synagogue*, 1844, from *25 Préludes dans tous les tons majeurs et mineurs*, op. 31. Berlin: A. M. Schlesinger, n.d. (ca. 1847). Plate S. 3336; from Charles-Valentin Alkan, *Super flumina Babylonis*, op. 52 (Psalm 137 paraphrase). Paris: Richault, n.d. [1859]. Plate 13296 R. Reprint—Paris: Billaudot, ca. 1971. *Super flumina Babylonis*, op. 52 (Psalm 137 paraphrase), 1859. Paris: Richault, n.d. [1859]. Plate 13296 R. Reprint—Paris: Billaudot, ca. 1971.

Anonymous, "Class Conflict amidst the Jews of Izmir: A Rebellion of the Jewish Poor," trans. Dina Danon, from *Sephardi Lives: A Documentary History, 1700-1950*, ed. Julia Phillips Cohen and Sarah Abrevaya Stein (Stanford, Calif.: Stanford University Press, 2014), pp. 43–44. Copyright © 2014 by the Board of Trustees of the Leland Stanford Jr. University. All rights reserved. With the permission of Stanford University Press, www.sup.org. Published in Ladino as *Shav'at aniyim* (Izmir, 1847), copyright © The British Library Board, 1938.g.2. Used with permission of The British Library.

Anonymous, from *In Praise of the Baal Shem Tov (Shivhei Ha-Besht)*, ed. and trans. Dan Ben-Amos and Jerome Mintz (Bloomington: Indiana University Press, 1970), pp. 11–13, 34. Used with permission of the translators.

Oro Arieh, "'The Sorrows of a Woman': A Jewish Widow Faces Eviction," trans. Yali Hashash, from *Sephardi Lives: A Documentary History, 1700–1950*, ed. Julia Phillips Cohen and Sarah Abrevaya Stein (Stanford, Calif.: Stanford University Press, 2014), pp. 59–60. Copyright © 2014 by the Board of Trustees of the Leland Stanford Jr. University. All rights reserved. With the permission of Stanford University Press, www.sup.org. Translated from the Hebrew in "Oro Arieh to Moses Montefiore (1866)," The Jewish National and University Library, Jerusalem, Institute of Microfilmed Hebrew Manuscripts, F-6159. Used with permission of The Jewish National and University Library.

Fanny von Arnstein, from Hilde Spiel, *Fanny von Arnstein*, trans. Christine Shuttleworth (New York: New Vessel Press, 2013), pp. 116–17. Used with permission of the publisher.

Michael Joseph Edler von Arnstein, from Hilde Spiel, *Fanny von Arnstein*, trans. Christine Shuttleworth (New York: New Vessel Press, 2013), p. 48. Used with permission of the publisher.

Saul Ascher, from *Leviathan*, trans. Gershon Greenberg, from *Modern Jewish Thinkers: From Mendelssohn to Rosenzweig*, ed. Gershon Greenberg (Boston: Academic Studies Press, 2011), pp. 322–23, 330–32. Used with permission of the publisher.

David Attias, *The Golden Garden*, trans. Olga Borovaya, from *Sephardi Lives: A Documentary History, 1700–1950*, ed. Julia Phillips Cohen and Sarah Abrevaya Stein (Stanford, Calif.: Stanford University Press, 2014), pp. 36–38. Copyright © 2014 by the Board of Trustees of the Leland Stanford Jr. University. All rights reserved. With the permission of Stanford University Press, www.sup.org. First published in Ladino as *La güerta de oro* (Livorno: Giovanni Vincenzo Falorni, 1778).

Hayim Yosef David Azulai, "Extracts from the Diary of Haim David Azulai in Holland, England, and France," trans. Elkan Nathan Adler, from *Jewish Travellers: A Treasury of Travelogues from 9 Centuries*, ed. Elkan Nathan Adler (New York: Routledge, 2014), pp. 363–65. Copyright © 1930, first published by RoutledgeCurzon. Reproduced by permission of Taylor & Francis Books UK.

Abraham Baer, *Baal T'fillah: oder, Der practische Vorbeter*, 1877. Musik- och teaterbiblioteket, Stockholm.

Samuel Siegfried Karl von Basch, from *Memories of Mexico: A History of the Last Ten Months of the Empire*, trans. Hugh McAden Oechler (San Antonio, Tex.: Trinity University Press, 1973), pp. 24–25. Used with permission of the translator.

Peter Beer, "The Childhood and Youth of a Man of the Enlightenment," from *The Jews of Bohemia and Moravia: A Historical Reader*, ed. Wilma Abeles Iggers, with translations by Wilma Abeles Iggers, Káča Poláčková-Henley, and Kathrine Talbot (Detroit: Wayne State University Press, 1992), pp. 38–43. Translated from *Die Juden in Böhmen und Mähren*, ed. Wilma Abeles Iggers (Munich: C. H. Beck Verlag, 1986). Copyright © C. H. Beck'sche

Verlagsbuchhandlung (Oscar Beck), Munich 1986. English translation © 1992 Wayne State University Press. Reprinted with the permission of Wayne State University Press.

Elijah Benamozegh, excerpts from *Elijah Benamozegh: Israel and Humanity*, from Classics of Western Spirituality series, trans. and ed. and with an introduction by Maxwell Luria (New York: Paulist Press, 1994), pp. 166, 258–59. Copyright © 1995 by Maxwell Luria. Used with permission of Paulist Press. www.paulistpress.com.

Lazarus Bendavid, "Notes Regarding the Characteristics of the Jews," trans. Stephen L. Weinstein, from *The Jew in the Modern World*, 3rd edition, ed. Paul Mendes-Flohr and Jehuda Reinharz (New York: Oxford University Press, 2010), pp. 111–13. Used with permission of the translator.

Jonah ben Gabriel, "Selections from the Chronicle of Jonah ben Gabriel," from *The Folk Literature of the Kurdistani Jews: An Anthology*, trans. and ed. Yona Sabar (New Haven, Conn.: Yale University Press, 1982), pp. 132–34. Used with permission of the publisher.

Elijah ben Solomon, "Ethical Will," from *Hebrew Ethical Wills: Selected and Edited by Israel Abrahams, Volumes I and II* (Philadelphia: Jewish Publication Society of America, 1926), pp. 312–16, 320–25. Copyright © 1926, 1954 by the Jewish Publication Society of America. Reprinted by permission of the University of Nebraska Press.

Besht (Israel Ba'al Shem Tov), "Tsava'at ha-Rivash," in "Defining Katnut and Gadlut," from *The Religious Thought of Hasidism*, ed. and trans. Norman Lamm (New York: Yeshiva University Press, 1999), pp. 405–6. Used with permission of the translator.

Ber Birkenthal of Bolechów, from *The Memoirs of Ber of Bolechow*, trans. Mark Vishnitzer (London: Oxford University Press, 1922; New York: Arno Press, 1973), pp. 77–79. Used with permission of the translator's estate.

Grigory Bogrov, *Notes of a Jew*, from "From Notes of a Jew: Childhood Sufferings," trans. Gabriella Safran, from *An Anthology of Jewish-Russian Literature: Two Centuries of Dual Identity in Prose and Poetry*, vol. 1, edited, selected, cotranslated, and with introductory notes by Maxim D. Shrayer (Armonk, N.Y.: M. E. Sharpe, 2007), pp. 63–65. English translation copyright © by Gabriella Safran. Reprinted by permission of Maxim D. Shrayer. All rights reserved. Not for reproduction.

Samuel Nunes Carvalho, attributed, *Self-Portrait of S. N. Carvalho*, ca. 1850. Courtesy of the Library of Congress.

Alexandre-Marie Colin, Cornélie Falcon as Rachel in the opera *La juive* by Halévy, 1835. Bibliothèque nationale de France.

Lorenzo Da Ponte, "Così Fan Tutte," libretto, music by Wolfgang Amadeus Mozart, from *Le nozze di Figaro: Così fan tutte*, trans. Lionel Salter, ed. Dennis Drew Arundell (London: Cassell, 1971). English translation by Lionel Salter, © the Lionel Salter Library. Used with permission of the translator's estate; Wolfgang Amadeus Mozart, composer and Lorenzo Da Ponte, librettist, *Così Fan Tutti, Image of Libretto*. Harvard Library, Loeb Music Library.

Edgar Degas, Ballet scene from Meyerbeer's opera *Robert le diable*, 1876. Victoria & Albert Museum, London, UK/Bridgeman Images.

Ayzik-Meir Dik, "The Panic or The Town of Hérres," from *No Star Too Beautiful: An Anthology of Yiddish Stories from 1382 to the Present*, ed. and trans. Joachim Neugroschel (New York: W. W. Norton and Co., 2002), pp. 162–65. Translation Copyright © 2002 by Joachim Neugroschel. Reprinted by permission of Georges Borchardt, Inc., on behalf of the translator; from *The Women Shopkeepers, or, Golde-Mine, the Abandoned Wife of Brod by Ayzik-Meir Dik: A Bilingual Yiddish/English Edition*, trans. and ed. Paul Azaroff and Lillian Schanfield (Lewiston, N.Y.: Edwin Mellen Press, 2008), pp. 27–28, 62–63. Used with permission of the publisher.

Dov Ber of Mezritsh, "Tzimtzum: An Act of Love," from *The Religious Thought of Hasidism*, ed. and trans. Norman Lamm (New York: Yeshiva University Press, 1999), pp. 44–45. Used with permission of the translator.

Zerah Eidlitz, *Or la-Yesharim* [Light for the Righteous], from *Jewish Preaching, 1200–1800: An Anthology*, trans. and ed. Marc Saperstein (New Haven, Conn.: Yale University Press, 1989), pp. 421–24. Used with permission of the publisher.

Elimelech of Lizhensk and Zusya of Annopol, "Introduction and Edited Version of 'The Proselytizer, Zuysa of Annopol,'" from *The Golden Tradition: Jewish Life and Thought in Eastern Europe*, ed. Lucy S. Dawidowicz (New

York: Holt, Rinehart, and Winston, 1967), pp. 93–94. Copyright © 1967 by Lucy S. Dawidowicz. Reprinted by permission of Georges Borchardt, Inc., on behalf of the Estate of Lucy S. Dawidowicz, and by permission of Henry Holt and Company, LLC. All rights reserved. Elimelech of Lizhensk, "The Relationship of Love and Fear," from *The Religious Thought of Hasidism*, ed. and trans. Norman Lamm (New York: Yeshiva University Press, 1999), pp. 110–11. Used with permission of the translator.

Jacob Emden, from *Megillat Sefer*, trans. Jacob J. Schacter, manuscript pp. 142a–b. Used with permission of the translator.

Kalonimos Kalman Epstein, "Leah and Rachel, the Hidden and Revealed Worlds," from *The Religious Thought of Hasidism*, ed. and trans. Norman Lamm (New York: Yeshiva University Press, 1999), pp. 599–601. Used with permission of the translator.

Shloyme Etinger, "The Assembly," from *No Star Too Beautiful: An Anthology of Yiddish Stories from 1382 to the Present*, ed. and trans. Joachim Neugroschel (New York: W. W. Norton and Co., 2002), pp. 156–58. Translation copyright © 2002 by Joachim Neugroschel. Reprinted by permission of Georges Borchardt, Inc., on behalf of the translator.

Jonathan Eybeschütz, "Sermon of Ethical Rebuke Preached . . . during the Penitential Period Preceding the New Year's Day, 5505 [1744], to the Congregation of Metz," from *Jewish Preaching, 1200–1800: An Anthology*, trans. and ed. Marc Saperstein (New Haven, Conn.: Yale University Press, 1989), pp. 329–46. Used with permission of the publisher.

Afanasy Fet, "Sheltered by a crimson awning . . ." trans. Alissa Dinega Gillespie, from *An Anthology of Jewish-Russian Literature: Two Centuries of Dual Identity in Prose and Poetry*, vol. 1, edited, selected, cotranslated, and with introductory notes by Maxim D. Shrayer (Armonk, N.Y.: M. E. Sharpe, 2007), p. 25. English translation copyright by Alissa Dinega Gillespie. Reprinted by permission of Maxim D. Shrayer. All rights reserved. Not for reproduction.

Benjamin-Eugene Fichel, *Harvey Demonstrating the Circulation of the Blood to Charles I, King of England, 1850*. Copyright © Bibliothèque de l'Académie nationale de Médecine (France).

Eugénie Foa, "Rachel; or, the Inheritance," trans. Maurice Samuels, from *Nineteenth-Century Jewish Literature: A Reader*, ed. Jonathan M. Hess, Maurice Samuels, and Nadia Valman (Stanford, Calif.: Stanford University Press, 2013), pp. 294–97. Copyright © 2013 by the Board of Trustees of the Leland Stanford Jr. University. All rights reserved. With the permission of Stanford University Press, www.sup.org.

Salomon Formstecher, "The Stolen Son: A Contemporary Tale," trans. Jonathan Hess, from *Nineteenth-Century Jewish Literature: A Reader*, ed. Jonathan M. Hess, Maurice Samuels, and Nadia Valman (Stanford, Calif.: Stanford University Press, 2013), pp. 336–40. Copyright © 2015 by the Board of Trustees of the Leland Stanford Jr. University. All rights reserved. With the permission of Stanford University Press, www.sup.org.

Zechariah Fraenkel, "On Changes in Judaism," from *Tradition and Change: The Development of Conservative Judaism*, ed. and trans. Mordechai Waxman (New York: Burning Bush Press, 1958), pp. 44, 46–50. Reprinted with permission from The Rabbinical Assembly.

Adolphe Franck, from *The Kabbalah, or The Religious Philosophy of the Hebrews*, rev. and trans. Isaac Sossnitz (New York: Kabbalah Publishing Co., 1926), pp. 74, 145, 167–68. Copyright © Isaac Sossnitz. Used with permission of the translator's estate.

Jacob Frank, *Collection of the Words of the Lord*, trans. Harris Lenowitz, in "Yakov Frank and His Daughter Ewa," from *The Jewish Messiahs* by Harris Lenowitz (New York: Oxford University Press, 1998), pp. 176–77, 186, 192. Copyright © 1999 by Harris Lenowitz. Used by permission of Oxford University Press, USA.

Ludwig A. Frankl, "Vaterlandische Sagen und Legenden IV (Ancestral Tales and Legends IV)," trans. Edan Dekel and David Gantt Gurley, from Edan Dekel and David Gantt Gurley, "How the Golem Came to Prague," *Jewish Quarterly Review*, vol. 103, no. 2 (Spring 2013), pp. 247–48. Reprinted with permission of the University of Pennsylvania Press.

David Friedländer, "Open Letter," from *A Debate on Jewish Emancipation of Christian Theology in Old Berlin*, ed. and trans. Richard Crouter and Julie Klassen (Indianapolis, Ind.: Hackett Publishing, 2004), pp. 41–42, 76–78.

Copyright © 2004 by Hackett Publishing Company, Inc. Reprinted by permission of Hackett Publishing Co., Inc. All rights reserved.

Rosa Gabbay, "An Etiquette Handbook for Sephardi Women," trans. Michael Alpert, from *Sephardi Lives: A Documentary History, 1700–1950*, ed. Julia Phillips Cohen and Sarah Abrevaya Stein (Stanford, Calif.: Stanford University Press, 2014), pp. 63–64. Copyright © 2014 by the Board of Trustees of the Leland Stanford Jr. University. All rights reserved. With the permission of Stanford University Press, www.sup.org.

Eduard Gans, "A Society to Further Jewish Integration," trans. Jakob Hessing, from *The Jew in the Modern World: A Documentary History*, 2nd ed. ed. Paul Mendes Flohr and Jehuda Reinharz (New York: Oxford University Press, 1995), pp. 216–17. Used with permission of the translator.

Mordechai Aaron Gintsburg, "Aviezer," trans. Jay M. Harris and Saadya Sternberg, from *Everyday Jewish Life in Imperial Russia: Select Documents, 1772–1914*, ed. Chaeran Y. Freeze and Jay M. Harris (Waltham, Mass: Brandeis University Press, 2013), pp. 308–13. Copyright © 2013 Brandeis University. Reprinted with permission of University Press of New England.

Abraham Goldfaden, Music from "Rozhinkes mit Mandlen," from his play *Shulamis*. Musical arrangement by Jerry Silverman. Used by permission. All rights reserved. From Jerry Silverman, ed., *The Yiddish Songbook* (1983). Image courtesy of YIVO Institute for Jewish Research.

Karl Goldmark, from *The Queen of Sheba*, 1875. Leipzig: Hugo Pohle, n.d. Plate 348.H.P.342.

Ignác Goldziher, from *Ignaz Golziher and His Oriental Diary: A Translation and Psychological Portrait*, trans. and ed. Raphael Patai (Detroit: Wayne State Universty Press, 1987), pp. 88–90. Used with permission of the translator's estate; from *The Zahiris: Their Doctrine and Their History: A Contribution to the History of Islamic Theology*, trans. and ed. Wolfgang Behn, ed. Alexander Scheiber (Leiden: E. J. Brill, 1978), pp. 3–5, 7. Used with permission of Koninklijke Brill NV.

Mikhl Gordon, "Whiskey," trans. Barnett Zumoff, from Joseph and Chana Mlotek, *Pearls of Yiddish Poetry* (Jersey City, N.J.: Ktav Publishing, 2010), pp. 6–12. Used with permission of the publisher.

Yehudah Leib Gordon, "Awake My People!" trans. Deborah Goldman, from *The Jew in the Modern World: A Documentary History*, 2nd ed., ed. Paul Mendes-Flohr and Jehuda Reinharz (New York: Oxford University Press, 1995), p. 384. Used with permission of the translator; "The Tip of the Yod," trans. Rachel Seelig, from *The Jew in the Modern World: A Documentary History*, 2nd ed., ed. Paul Mendes Flohr and Jehuda Reinharz (New York: Oxford University Press, 1995), pp. 362–64. Used with permission of the translator.

Maurycy Gottlieb, *Tańczący chasydzi* (*Dancing Hasidim*), ca. 1875. From the collection of the Emanuel Ringelblum Jewish Historical Institute in Warsaw.

Louis Gottschalk, *The Water Sprite—Polka*, 1853. Courtesy of the Library of Congress.

Heinrich Graetz, "Construction of Jewish History," in "The Diaspora: Suffering and Spirit," trans. Michael Meyer, from Michael Meyer, *Ideas of Jewish History* (Detroit: Wayne State University Press, 1987), pp. 229–30. Copyright © 1974 by Michael A. Meyer. Copyright © 1987 by Wayne State University Press. Reprinted with the permission of Wayne State University Press.

Francis Grant, *The Right Hon. B. Disraeli M.P. Chancellor of the Exchequer*, 1852. Photo: John Hammond. Hughenden Manor, High Wycombe, Buckinghamshire, Great Britain. Photo credit: National Trust Photo Library/Art Resource, NY.

Simon Gratz and Samuel Hays, "Letters to Richea Gratz, 1793," Jacob Mordecai Papers, Rare Book, Manuscript, and Special Collections Library, Duke University, from *American Jewry: Documents; Eighteenth Century; Primarily Hitherto Unpublished Manuscripts* by Jacob Rader Marcus, trans. unknown (Cincinnati, Ohio: Hebrew Union College Press, 1959), pp. 66–67. Reproduced with permission of Hebrew Union College Press in the format Book via Copyright Clearance Center.

Sara Hirsch Guggenheim, "Aurelie Werner," trans. Jonathan Hess, from *Nineteenth-Century Jewish Literature: A Reader*, ed. Jonathan M. Hess, Maurice Samuels, and Nadia Valman (Stanford, Calif.: Stanford University Press, 2013), pp. 431–34. Copyright © 2013 by the Board of Trustees of the Leland Stanford Jr. University. All rights reserved. With the permission of Stanford University Press, www.sup.org.

Michael Joseph Guzikov, *Shir hama'a lot*, 1827. Image courtesy of the YIVO Institute for Jewish Research.

Jacques-François-Fromental-Élie Halévy, *La juive*, 1835. Paris: Brandus, Dufour & Cie., n.d. [1857]. Plate B. & Cie. 9198. Reprinted Paris: Henry Lemoine, n.d. (after 1878). Plate 4304.HL; *La reine de Chypre*, libretto by Eugène Scribe, 1841. Richard Wagner, piano reduction, Paris: Henry Lemoine, n.d. [1875]. Plate 7813 HL.

Aaron Halle-Wolfsohn, "Silliness and Sanctimony," from *Landmark Yiddish Plays: A Critical Anthology*, ed. Joel Berkowitz and Jeremy Dauber (Albany: State University of New York Press, 2006), pp. 98–103. Copyright © 2006, State University of New York. All rights reserved. Reprinted by permission of the publisher.

Aaron Hart, "Aaron Hart to Mo," Seminaire du Saint Joseph, Hart Papers, from *American Jewry: Documents; Eighteenth Century; Primarily Hitherto Unpublished Manuscripts* by Jacob Rader Marcus, trans. unknown (Cincinnati, Ohio: Hebrew Union College Press, 1959), p. 49. Reproduced with permission of Hebrew Union College Press in the format Book via Copyright Clearance Center, and permission of Seminaire du Saint Joseph.

Moritz Hartmann, "Hartmann's Impressions of the Prague Revolution of 1848," from *The Jews of Bohemia and Moravia: A Historical Reader*, ed. Wilma Abeles Iggers, with translations by Wilma Abeles Iggers, Káča Poláčková-Henley, and Kathrine Talbot (Detroit: Wayne State University Press, 1992), pp. 139–41. Translated from *Die Juden in Böhmen und Mähren*, ed. Wilma Abeles Iggers (Munich: C. H. Beck Verlag, 1986). Copyright © C. H. Beck'sche Verlagsbuchhandlung (Oscar Beck), Munich 1986. English translation copyright © 1992 Wayne State University Press. Reprinted with the permission of Wayne State University Press.

Israel Moses Ḥazan, "Kerakh Shel Romi" [City of Rome], in Edwin Seroussi, "Rabbi Israel Moshe Hazzan on Music," from *Haham Gaon Memorial Volume*, ed. Marc D. Angel (New York: Sepher-Hermon Press, 1997), pp. 183–95. Used with permission of Edwin Seroussi.

Heinrich Heine, "A Seder Night," trans. Elkan N. Adler, from *Yisröel, the Jewish Omnibus*, ed. Joseph Leftwich (London: James Clarke and Co., 1945), pp. 242–44. Used with permission of the publisher; "Farewell, You Cheerful Folk of France," from *Songs of Love and Grief*, trans. Walter W. Arndt, ed. Jeffrey L. Sammons (Evanston, Ill.: Northwestern University Press, 1995), p. 129. Copyright © 1995 by Northwestern University Press. All rights reserved. Used with permission of the publisher.

Fanny Mendelssohn Hensel, with Wilhelm Hensel, *Duette: Mein Liebchen, wir sassen beisammen* (Duet: *My Sweetheart, We Sat Together*), 1841. Mendelssohn-Archiv/MA Ms. 163, S. 83. Staatsbibliothek zu Berlin, Stiftung Preussicher Kulturbesitz bpk Bildagentur/Staatsbibliothek zu Berlin, Stiftung Preussicher Kulturbesitz/Art Resource, NY.

Moses Hess, from *Rome and Jerusalem: A Study in Jewish Nationalism*, trans. Meyer Waxman, PhD (New York: Bloch Publishing, 1918), pp. 145–50. Used with permission of the translator's estate.

Samuel Hirsch, from *The Religious Philosophy of the Jews*, trans. Gershon Greenberg, from *Modern Jewish Thinkers: From Mendelssohn to Rosenzweig*, ed. Gershon Greenberg (Boston: Academic Studies Press, 2011), pp. 187–88. Used with permission of the publisher.

Zalkind Hourwitz, "Vindication of the Jews," from *The French Revolution and Human Rights: A Brief Documentary History*, 1st ed., trans. and ed. Lynn Hunt (Boston: St. Martin's, 1996), pp. 49–50. Copyright © 1996. Used with permission of Bedford, Freeman and Worth Publishing Group, LLC.

Aaron Isaac, "Pioneer in Sweden," from *Memoirs of My People: Through a Thousand Years*, ed. and trans. Leo W. Schwarz (Philadelphia: Jewish Publication Society, 1943), pp. 166–71, 180–81.

Jacob Joseph of Polonoy, "The Other Man's Faults," from *The Religious Thought of Hasidism*, ed. and trans. Norman Lamm (New York: Yeshiva University Press, 1999), pp. 433–34. Used with permission of the translator.

Angel Jacobo Jesurun, *Topographic Map of the City of Caracas*, 1843. The Lionel Pincus and Princess Firyal Map Division, The New York Public Library, Astor, Lenox and Tilden Foundations.

T. Johnson, *Portrait of Emma Lazarus*, 1852. Courtesy of the Library of Congress.

Isaac Markus Jost, "The Rigors of Jewish Historiography," from *Ideas of Jewish History*, ed. and trans. Michael Meyer (New York: Behrman House, 1974), pp. 178–80, 181–83, 184, 185–86. © Behrman House, Inc., included with permission http://www.behrmanhouse.com.

Siegfried Kapper, "Ben-Oni (Son of Sorrow)," trans. Roderick A. Ginsburg, from *In Search of Freedom*, ed. Guido Kisch (London: E. Goldston, 1949), p. 208. Used with permission of the translator's estate.

Daniel Khvolson, "Daniel Khvolson to Heinrich Leberecht Fleischer," from Ismar Schorsch, "Converging Cognates: The Intersection of Jewish and Islamic Studies in Nineteenth Century Germany," *Leo Baeck Institute Year Book*, vol. 55 (September 2010), p. 19. Used by permission of Oxford University Press/Leo Baeck Institute.

Vincenz Georg Kininger, *Portrait of Fanny von Arnstein*. Jewish Museum, Vienna.

Abraham Kohn, "A Jewish Peddler's Diary," trans. Abram Vossen Goodman, *American Jewish Archives*, vol. 3 (1951), pp. 96, 98, 100, 102, 105. Used with permission of American Jewish Archives.

Leopold Kompert, "The Death of the Tavern Keeper's Wife," from *The Jews of Bohemia and Moravia: A Historical Reader*, ed. Wilma Abeles Iggers, with translations by Wilma Abeles Iggers, Káča Poláčková-Henley, and Kathrine Talbot (Detroit: Wayne State University Press, 1992), pp. 107–9. Translated from *Die Juden in Böhmen und Mähren*, ed. Wilma Abeles Iggers (Munich: C. H. Beck Verlag, 1986). Copyright © C. H. Beck'sche Verlagsbuchhandlung (Oscar Beck), München 1986. English translation copyright © 1992 Wayne State University Press. Reprinted with the permission of Wayne State University Press.

Alexander Kraushar, frontispiece to *Frank i frankiści polscy 1726–1816*, v. 2 (Kraków, 1895), Portrait of Eva Frank. Image courtesy of the Library of the YIVO Institute for Jewish Research.

Nachman Krochmal, "The Cycles of Jewish History," trans. Michael Meyer, from Michael Meyer, *Ideas of Jewish History* (Detroit: Wayne State University Press, 1987), pp. 202–3. Copyright © 1974 by Michael A. Meyer. Copyright © 1987 by Wayne State University Press. Reprinted with the permission of Wayne State University Press.

Ruvim Kulisher, "An Answer to the Slav," trans. Maxim D. Shrayer, from *An Anthology of Jewish-Russian Literature: Two Centuries of Dual Identity in Prose and Poetry*, vol. 1, edited, selected, cotranslated, and with introductory notes by Maxim D. Shrayer (Armonk, N.Y.: M. E. Sharpe, 2007), pp. 28–29. English translation copyright by Maxim D. Shrayer. Reprinted by permission of Maxim D. Shrayer. All rights reserved. Not for reproduction.

Yehezkel (Ezekiel) Landau, "Eulogy for Empress Maria Theresa," from Marc Saperstein, *Your Voice Like a Ram's Horn* (Cincinnati, Ohio: Hebrew Union College Press, 1996), pp. 455, 460, 461, 463. Used with permission of the publisher; "Sermon for the Sabbath Preceding Passover," from *Jewish Preaching, 1200–1800: An Anthology*, trans. and ed. Marc Saperstein (New Haven, Conn.: Yale University Press, 1989), pp. 364–66, 368–69. Used with permission of the publisher.

Raphael Laniado, "From Spain to Syria: A Jewish Scholar from Aleppo Studies His Family History," trans. Yaron Ayalon, from *Sephardi Lives: A Documentary History, 1700–1950*, ed. Julia Phillips Cohen and Sarah Abrevaya Stein (Stanford, Calif.: Stanford University Press, 2014), pp. 389–90. Copyright © 2014 by the Board of Trustees of the Leland Stanford Jr. University. All rights reserved. With the permission of Stanford University Press, www.sup.org.

Menachem Mendel Lefin of Satanow (also Mendel Lefin Satanower), "Prayer against the Hasidim," trans. Nancy Sinkoff, from *Out of the Shtetl: Making Jews Modern in the Polish Borderlands* (Providence, R.I.: Brown Judaic Studies, 2004), pp. 274–75. Used with permission of the publisher. Translated from manuscript from the Joseph Perl Archive, JNULA, 4 1153/5.

Lev Levanda, "Seething Times," excerpts, trans. Maxim D. Shrayer, from *An Anthology of Jewish-Russian Literature: Two Centuries of Dual Identity in Prose and Poetry*, vol. 1, edited, selected, cotranslated, and with introductory notes by Maxim D. Shrayer (Armonk, N.Y.: M. E. Sharpe, 2007), pp. 45–59. English translation copyright © by Maxim D. Shrayer. Reprinted by permission of Maxim D. Shrayer. All rights reserved. Not for reproduction.

Levi Isaac (Yitzhak) of Berdichev, "A Din Toyre mit Gott/Der kadish fun rabi levi yitshok" [Kaddish of Rebbe Levi Isaac], trans. F. Doppelt in Avraham Zvi Idelsohn, "Songs of the Chassidim," #104, from *Thesaurus of Oriental Hebrew Melodies*, vol. 10 (Berlin and Jerusalem: B. Harz, 1932). Used with permission of the Estate of Avraham Zvi Idelsohn; "Women and the Miracles of Purim and Hanukkah," from *The Religious Thought of Hasidism*, ed. and trans. Norman Lamm (New York: Yeshiva University Press, 1999), pp. 589–90. Used with permission of the translator.

Emanuele Levi, *Journal*, trans. Alberto Cavaglion, in Alberto Cavaglion, "Judaism and Children's Literature: Emanuele Levi's Giornale (1822–1823)," from *The Jews of Italy: Memory and Identity*, ed. Bernard D. Cooperman and Barbara Garvin (Bethesda: University Press of Maryland, 2000), pp. 361, 364–65, 367, 370–71. Used with permission of the publisher.

Louis Lewandowski, Psalm 92, Od yenuvun, 1876. Courtesy of Sacred Music Press, Hebrew Union College-Jewish Institute of Religion, New York.

Moshe Leyb Lilienblum, "The Sins of My Youth," from *Everyday Jewish Life in Imperial Russia: Select Documents, 1772–1914*, ed. Chaeran Y. Freeze and Jay M. Harris (Waltham, Mass: Brandeis University Press, 2013), pp. 353–67. Copyright © 2013 Brandeis University. Reprinted with permission of University Press of New England.

Isaac Joel Linetski, from *The Polish Lad*, trans. Moshe Spiegel (Philadelphia: Jewish Publication Society of America, 1975), pp. 29–33. Copyright © 1975 by the Jewish Publication Society of America. Reprinted by permission of the University of Nebraska Press.

Aaron Lopez and Benjamin Gomez, "Letters between Aaron Lopez and Benjamin Gomez," from *American Jewry: Documents; Eighteenth Century; Primarily Hitherto Unpublished Manuscripts* by Jacob Rader Marcus, trans. unknown (Cincinnati, Ohio: Hebrew Union College Press, 1959), pp. 4–6. Reproduced with permission of Hebrew Union College Press in the format Book via Copyright Clearance Center.

David Hisquaiu Baruch Louzada, "Old Hebrew Prayer in Time of Revolt of Negros," in Zvi Loker and Robert Cohen, "An Eighteenth-Century Prayer of the Jews of Surinam," from *The Jewish Nation in Surinam: Historical Essays*, ed. and trans., and with an introduction by, Robert Cohen (Amsterdam: S. Emmering, 1982), p. 78. Translated from manuscript in Lyons Collection, Box 3, No. 205, American Jewish Historical Society; David Hisquiau Baruch Louzada, "Hebrew Prayer at the Time of Revolt of the Negroes," probably in Surinam, ca. 1790. Papers of Jacques Judah Lyons (1813–1877) [Collection number P-15, Box 3, Folder 205], American Jewish Historical Society, New York and Boston.

Joseph Solomon Lutski, *Epistle of Israel's Deliverance*, from *Karaite Separatism in Nineteenth-Century Russia: Joseph Lutski's Epistle of Israel's Deliverance*, ed. and trans. Philip E. Miller (Cincinnati, Ohio: Hebrew Union College Press, 1993), pp. 74, 76, 112, 156, 158. Used with permission of the publisher.

Ephraim Luzzatto, "The Doctor Who Fell Prey to Love," from *The Penguin Book of Hebrew Verse*, ed. and trans. T. Carmi (New York: Viking Press, 1981; London: Allen Lane, 1981), p. 506. Copyright © T. Carmi, 1981. Reproduced by permission of Penguin Books Ltd.

Samuel David Luzzatto, "An Enlightened Exchange across the Mediterranean," trans. Julia Phillips Cohen, from *Sephardi Lives: A Documentary History, 1700–1950*, ed. Julia Phillips Cohen and Sarah Abrevaya Stein (Stanford, Calif.: Stanford University Press, 2014), pp. 391–92. Copyright © 2014 by the Board of Trustees of the Leland Stanford Jr. University. All rights reserved. With the permission of Stanford University Press, www.sup.org.

Eduard Magnus, *Portrait of the Singer Jenny Lind (the "Swedish Nightingale")*, 1846. Nationalgalerie, Staatliche Museen, Berlin. Image courtesy of bpk, Berlin/Nationalgalerie, Staatliche Museen, Berlin, Germany/Klaus Göken/Art Resource, NY.

Solomon Maimon, "Introduction," from *Givat ha-Moreh*, trans. Gershon Greenberg, from *Modern Jewish Thinkers: From Mendelssohn to Rosenzweig*, ed. Gershon Greenberg (Boston: Academic Studies Press, 2011), pp. 129–31, 135–36. Used with permission of the publisher.

Avraham Mapu, from *The Love of Zion*, trans. Joseph Marymount, from *The Love of Zion & Other Writings*, ed. David Patterson (New Milford, Conn.: Toby Press, 2006), p. 33. Originally published as *The Sorrows of Naame*, trans. Joseph Marymount (New York: National Book Publishers, 1919). English translation copyright © 1919 Joseph Marymount; from *The Hypocrite*, trans. David Patterson, from *The Love of Zion & Other Writings*, ed. David Patterson (New Milford, Conn.: Toby Press, 2006), pp. 309–10. Translation copyright © 1964 David Patterson. Both reprinted by permission of The Toby Press.

Karl Marx, "On the Jewish Question," from *Karl Marx: Early Writings*, ed. and trans. T. B. Bottomore (New York: McGraw-Hill, 1964), pp. 3–4, 29–31. Used with permission of the translator's estate; "Manifesto of the Communist Party," trans. Samuel Moore in cooperation with Frederick Engels, 1888, from *Marx/Engels Selected Works*, vol. 1 (Moscow: Progress Publishers, 1969), pp. 98–137, as found on Marx/Engels Internet Archive (marxists.org), transcription/markup Zodiac and Brian Baggins, proofed and corrected against 1888 English edition by Andy Blunden. Copyleft Marx/Engels Internet Archive (marxists.org) 1987, 2000. Permission is granted to copy and/or distribute this document under the terms of the Creative Commons Attribution-ShareAlike License www.marxists.org/admin/legal/cc/by-sa.htm.

Bonaventura Mayer, excerpt from *Die Juden unserer Zeit* [The Jews in Our Time], trans. David Louvish, from David Assaf, *The Regal Way: The Life and Times of Rabbi Israel of Ruzhin* (Stanford, Calif.: Stanford University Press, 2002), pp. 82–83. Copyright © 2002 by the Board of Trustees of the Leland Stanford Jr. University. All rights reserved. With the permission of Stanford University Press, www.sup.org.

Menachem Mendel of Vitebsk, "An Immortal Pleasure," from *The Religious Thought of Hasidism*, ed. and trans. Norman Lamm (New York: Yeshiva University Press, 1999), p. 165. Used with permission of the translator.

Moses Mendelssohn, "Jerusalem," from *Jerusalem and Other Jewish Writings*, trans. and ed. Alfred Jospe (New York: Schocken Books, 1969), pp. 61–65. Used with permission of the translator; "From the Preface to *Vindiciae Judaeorum* (1782)," trans. Curtis Bowman, "From Light for the Path" and "On the Religious Legitimacy of Studying Logic," trans. Elias Sacks, from *Moses Mendelssohn: Writings on Judaism, Christianity and the Bible*, ed. Michah Gottlieb (Waltham, Mass: Brandeis University Press, 2011), pp. 43–44, 190–93, 196–98, 239–40. © 2011 Brandeis University. Reprinted with permission of University Press of New England; "Letter to the Friends of Lessing/Morfenstunden," from *The Spinoza Conversations*, trans. Gerard Vallee (Lanham, Md.: University Press of America, 1988), pp. 127–32. Copyright © 1988. Used by permission of Rowman & Littlefield Publishing Group. All rights reserved; "Phaedon," from *Phaedon, or On the Mortality of the Soul*, trans. Patricia Noble (New York: Peter Lang, 2007), pp. 42–43, 46–47. Used with permission of the publisher.

David Franco Mendes, Cover to *Kol tefila ve-kol zimra*, David Dancing before God and Being Annointed as King, 1792. Ets Haim–Livraria Montezinos, Amsterdam; *Dictionary of Maritime Terms*. David Franco Mendes: 1713–1792, Nieuw Zeevaarts woordenboek met de uitlegginge van dien, in de NeederDuytsche, Fransche, Spaansche & Portugeesche Taalen (Dictionary of maritime terms), image 29, Ets Haim—Livraria Montezinos, Amsterdam.

Abraham Mendes de Castro, "Personalia," from Isaac S. Emmanuel and Suzanne A. Emmanuel, *History of the Jews of the Netherlands Antilles*, vol. 2 (Cincinnati: American Jewish Archives, 1970), pp. 1096–99. Used with permission of American Jewish Archives.

Daniel Mendoza, from *The Memoirs of the Life of Daniel Mendoza* (New York: Arno Press, 1975), p. 65. Image courtesy of the YIVO Institute for Jewish Research.

Giacomo Meyerbeer, from *Hallelujah: Eine Cantatine für 4 mäNnerstimmen mit begleitung einer obligaten orgel und des chores ad libitum*, 1847. Image provided courtesy of the Library of Congress, Music Division; *Le prophète*, 1849. Paris: Brandus, n.d. Plates B. et Cie. 5191, 5111; *Robert le diable*, 1831. Johann Peter Pixis (1788–1874), piano reduction. Paris: Maurice Schlesinger, d. [1831]. Plate M.S. 1157.

Relle Morschene, "Introduction to a Letter from Relle Luzzatto Morschene to Chief Rabbi Raffael Natan Tedesco of Trieste," trans. Lois Dubin, from *Early Modern Workshop: Jewish History Resources*, vol. 3: Gender, Family, and Social Structures (Middletown, Conn.: Wesleyan University Press, 2006), pp. 154–55. Copyright © 2006 by Relle Luzzatto Morschene. Reprinted with permission of Wesleyan University Press. www.wesleyan.edu/wespress.

Nachman of Bratslav, recorded by his scribe Nathan of Nemirov, "Tiku Emuna," *Likute Moharan II*, Homily 5, in Zvi Mark, *Mysticism and Madness: The Religious Thought of Rabbi Nachman of Bratslav* (London: Continuum Publishing, 2009), pp. 17, 20. Copyright © Zvi Mark, 2009. Used with permission of Bloomsbury Publishing plc; "The Rabbi's Son," excerpts from *Nahman of Bratslav: The Tales*, from *The Classics of Western Spirituality Series*, translated, introduced, and edited by Arnold Band (New York: Paulist Press, 1978), pp. 135–38. Copyright © 1978 by Arnold J. Band. Used with permission of Paulist Press, in the format Book via Copyright Clearance Center. www.paulistpress.com.

Isaac Nathan, from Song Settings for the Poet Lord Byron's *Hebrew Melodies*, 1815. London: J. Fentum for the Proprietor, n.d., plates 102–5.

Samuel Naumbourg, *Aggudat Shirim (Recueil de Chants Religieux et Populaires des Israélites)*. 1st ed., Paris: S. Naumbourg, n.d. [1874]; *Seu Shearim*, 1847. Courtesy Sacred Music Press, Hebrew Union College–Jewish Institute of Religion, New York; Title Page for His Version of Salamone de Rossi's *Hashirim asher le-Shelomoh*, 1876. Courtesy YIVO/Center for Jewish History.

Fanny Neuda, "For a Mother Whose Son Is in Military Service," from *Hours of Devotion: Fanny Neuda's Book of Prayers for Jewish Women*, ed. and adapted into verse by Dinah Berland, trans. Julia Watts Belser (New York: Knopf, 2008), pp. 169–70. Used with permission of the editor; "On the Approach of Childbirth," from *Hours of Devotion: Fanny Neuda's Book of Prayers for Jewish Women*, ed. and adapted into verse by Dinah Berland, trans. Julia Watts Belser (New York: Knopf, 2008), pp. 144–45. Used with permission of the editor. Includes Isaiah 66:7, from Jewish Publication Society, *Tanakh: The Holy Scriptures: The New JPS Translation to the Traditional Hebrew Text* (Philadelphia: Jewish Publication Society, 1985). Copyright © 1985 by the Jewish Publication Society, Philadelphia. Includes Isaiah 41:14, adapted by Dinah Berland, from the *Stone Edition of the Tanach—The Torah/Prophets/Writings: The Twenty-Four Books of the Bible Newly Translated and Annotated*, ArtScroll Series, ed. Rabbi Nosson Scherman (New York: Mesorah Publications Ltd., 2003), p. 1025. Used with permission of the publisher.

Lev (Judah Leyb) Nevakhovich, "Lament of the Daughters of Judah," trans. Brian Cooper, from *An Anthology of Jewish-Russian Literature: Two Centuries of Dual Identity in Prose and Poetry*, vol. 1, edited, selected, cotranslated, and with introductory notes by Maxim D. Shrayer (Armonk, N.Y.: M. E. Sharpe, 2007), pp. 7–9. English translation copyright by Brian Cooper. Reprinted by permission of Maxim D. Shrayer. All rights reserved. Not for reproduction.

Jacques Offenbach, from *La Grande-Duchesse de Gérolstein*, 1867. Paris: Brandus & Dufour, n.d. (ca. 1867), reprinted Paris: Ph. Maquet, n.d. (after 1887); from *Tales of Hoffmann*, ca. 1880–1881. Paris: Choudens Père et fils, n.d. [1881]. Plate A.C. 5100.

Moritz Daniel Oppenheim, *Lavater and Lessing Visit Moses Mendelssohn*, 1856. Gift of Vernon Stroud, Eva Linker, Gerda Mathan, Ilse Feiger, and Irwin Straus in memory of Frederick and Edith Straus, Magnes Collection of Jewish Art and Life, Bancroft Library, UC Berkeley; *Portrait of Heinrich Heine*, 1831. Hamburger Kunsthalle, Hamburg, Germany. Image courtesy bpk, Berlin/Hamburger Kunsthalle, Hamburg, Germany/Elke Walford/Art Resource, NY.

Judah Papo, "Is the Printing Press Harmful? A Rabbi from Sarajevo Responds," trans. Matthias Lehmann, from *Sephardi Lives: A Documentary History, 1700–1950*, ed. Julia Phillips Cohen and Sarah Abrevaya Stein (Stanford, Calif.: Stanford University Press, 2014), pp. 61–62. Copyright © 2014 by the Board of Trustees of the Leland Stanford Jr. University. All rights reserved. With the permission of Stanford University Press, www.sup.org.

Moses L. Penha, "El triumfo de Esther" [Esther's Triumph], from Isaac S. Emmanuel and Suzanne A. Emmanuel, *History of the Jews of the Netherlands Antilles*, vol. 2 (Cincinnati: American Jewish Archives, 1970), p. 1089. Used with permission of the publisher.

Joseph Perl, from *Revealer of Secrets: The First Hebrew Novel*, trans. Dov Taylor (Boulder, Colo.: Westview Press, 1997), pp. 15, 21–23. Used with permission of the translator. Dov Taylor's newly revised translation of Joseph Perl's *Revealer of Secrets* and its sequel, *Testing the Righteous*, will be published together in a single forthcoming volume.

Ludwig Philippson, "The Three Brothers," trans. Jonathan Hess, from *Nineteenth-Century Jewish Literature: A Reader*, ed. Jonathan M. Hess, Maurice Samuels, and Nadia Valman (Stanford, Calif.: Stanford University Press, 2013), pp. 225–26. Copyright © 2013 by the Board of Trustees of the Leland Stanford Jr. University. All rights reserved. With the permission of Stanford University Press, www.sup.org.

Osip Rabinovich, "The Penal Recruit," trans. Brian Horowitz, from *An Anthology of Jewish-Russian Literature: Two Centuries of Dual Identity in Prose and Poetry*, vol. 1, edited, selected, cotranslated, and with introductory notes by Maxim D. Shrayer (Armonk, N.Y.: M. E. Sharpe, 2007), pp. 41–42. English translation copyright by Brian Horowitz. Reprinted by permission of Maxim D. Shrayer. All rights reserved. Not for reproduction.

Shelomo Yehudah (Shi"r) Rapoport (Salomon Jehuda Leib), "Open Rebuke," trans. Stephen L. Weinstein, from *The Jew in the Modern World: A Documentary History*, 2nd ed., eds. Paul Mendes Flohr and Jehuda Reinharz (New York: Oxford University Press, 1995), p. 191. Used with permission of the translator.

Samuel Romanelli, from *Travail in an Arab Land*, ed. and trans. from the Hebrew with introduction and notes by Yedidah K. Stillman and Norman A. Stillman (Tuscaloosa: University of Alabama Press, 1989), pp. 28–29, 48–49. Copyright © 1989 The University of Alabama Press. Used with permission of the publisher.

Abraham Rosanes, "'A Lone Jew among All Those Christians': A Bulgarian Jewish Devotee of Classical Greek," transcribed by Zvi Keren and translated by Matt Goldish, from *Sephardi Lives: A Documentary History, 1700–1950*, ed. Julia Phillips Cohen and Sarah Abrevaya Stein (Stanford, Calif.: Stanford University Press, 2014), pp. 46–48. Copyright © 2014 by the Board of Trustees of the Leland Stanford Jr. University. All rights reserved. With the permission of Stanford University Press, www.sup.org, and the translator. Translated from the unpublished memoir of Abraham Rosanes of Rusçuk (Ruse), Private Collection of Sivan Toledo.

Roza, wife of Leyzer ben Moses Judah, *Title Page of the Register of a Jewish Midwife*. Bibliotheca Rosenthaliana, Special Collections of the University of Amsterdam.

Anton Rubinstein, *Der Thurm zu Babel (The Tower of Babel)*, 1870. Julius Rodenberg, author of libretto; Fitz William Rosier, English text. New York: G. Schirmer, No. 6, 1883. Plate 2792.

Isaac Judah Yehiel Safrin of Komarno, trans. Dena Ordan, from David Assaf, *Untold Tales of the Hasidim: Crisis & Discontent in the History of Hasidism* (Waltham, Mass.: Brandeis University Press, 2010), p. 98. Copyright © 2010 Brandeis University. Reprinted with permission of University Press of New England; "For the Love of the Zaddik," from *The Religious Thought of Hasidism*, ed. and trans. Norman Lamm (New York: Yeshiva University Press, 1999), p. 310. Used with permission of the translator.

Geskel Salomon, Drawing of Costume for Vitka in the First Production of the Opera *Dalibor* by Bedřich Smetana, date unknown. Photo credit: Alfredo Dagli Orti/The Art Archive at Art Resource, NY.

Napoleon Sarony, *Portrait of Adah Isaacs Menken*, 1866. American Jewish Historical Society, New York and Boston.

Isaac Sasportas, "Proceedings of a court martial held by virtue of a special commission . . ." (16–17 December 1799), CO 137/103, British National Archives, Kew, trans. Philippe Girard; "Projet de la descente à l'isle Jamaïque ct les moyens d'y parvenir" (2 October 1799), in "Robert Liston to William Grenville" (3 January 1800), CO 137/103, British National Archives, Kew, trans. Philippe Girard; "Scribbled notes on an invasion of Jamaica" (ca. 2 October 1799), Crawford Muniments, Acc. 9769, Personal Papers, 23/10/1176-1188, National Library of Scotland, trans. Philippe Girard; "Isaac Sasportas to the Earl of Balcarres" (20 December 1799), Crawford Muniments, Acc. 9769, Personal Papers, 23/10/1176-1188, National Library of Scotland, trans. Philippe Girard. All used with permission of the translator.

Judah Scheindling of Shkudy, from Michael Stanislawski, *Psalms for the Tsar: A Minute-Book of a Psalms-Society in the Russian Army, 1864–1867*, trans. Michael Stanislawski (New York: Yeshiva University Library, 1988), pp. 14–15, 31–33.

Barukh Schick (Shklov), "Introduction to Euclid," trans. David Fishman from David Fishman, *Russia's First Modern Jews* (New York: NYU Press, 1995), p. 41. Reprinted with permission from NYU Press copyright © 1995.

David Schornstein, "The Tithe," trans. Maurice Samuels, from *Nineteenth-Century Jewish Literature: A Reader*, ed. Jonathan M. Hess, Maurice Samuels, and Nadia Valman (Stanford, Calif.: Stanford University Press, 2013), pp. 95–98. Copyright © 2013 by the Board of Trustees of the Leland Stanford Jr. University. All rights reserved. With the permission of Stanford University Press, www.sup.org.

Moses Seixas, *Letter to George Washington*. Courtesy of the Library of Congress.

Sheftall Sheftall, Sheftall Sheftall Papers, MS 726, Georgia Historical Society, Savannah, Georgia, from *American Jewry: Documents; Eighteenth Century; Primarily Hitherto Unpublished Manuscripts* by Jacob Rader Marcus, trans. unknown (Cincinnati, Ohio: Hebrew Union College Press, 1959), pp. 238–40. Reproduced with permission of Hebrew Union College Press in the format Book via Copyright Clearance Center.

Samuel Mendes de Sola, "Licence Authorizing Daniel da Costa Gomez to Be a Ritual Slaughterer, . . ." from Isaac S. Emmanuel and Suzanne A. Emmanuel, *History of the Jews of the Netherlands Antilles*, vol. 2 (Cincinnati, Ohio: American Jewish Archives, 1970), p. 1012. Used with permission of the publisher. Original source: Ms. Ets Haim Library (Amsterdam), Doc. No. 51.

Adolf Gustaw Sonnenfeld, *Kantorzysta: polka na fortepiano, op. 68*, ca. 1870. Courtesy Warsaw Public Library.

Solomon Sulzer, Statement upon the Publication of *Denkschrift an die hochgeehrte Wiener israeleitische Cultus-Gemeinde* [Memorandum to the Esteemed Viennese Israelite Religious Community], in Peter Gradenwitz, "Jews in Austrian Music," from Josef Fraenkel, *The Jews of Austria* (London: Vallentine Mitchell, 1967), p. 19. Used with permission of the publisher.

Jean-Pierre-Antoine Tassaert, *Bust of Moses Mendelssohn*, 1785. Photo Reinhard Friedrich, Nationalgalerie, Staatliche Museen, Berlin, Germany. Photo credit: bpk Bildagentur/National Galerie, Staatliche Museen, Berlin, Germany/Reinhard Friedrich/Art Resource, NY.

David Tevele, "A Sermon contra [Naphtali Herts] Wessely," trans. Saul Fischer and Paul Mendes-Flohr, from *The Jew in the Modern World*, 3rd ed., ed. Paul Mendes-Flohr and Jehuda Reinharz (New York: Oxford University Press, 2010), pp. 78–79. Used by permission of Oxford University Press, USA.

Eliakum Tsunzer, "The Flower," trans. Barnett Zumoff, from Joseph and Chana Mlotek, *Pearls of Yiddish Poetry* (Jersey City, N.J.: Ktav Publishing, 2010), pp. 18–22. Used with permission of the publisher.

Unknown, Epitaph from the tombstone of Rebecca Henriquez da Costa, trans. Aviva Ben-Ur, from Aviva Ben-Ur and Rachel Frankel, *Remnant Stones: The Jewish Cemeteries of Suriname* (Cincinnati, Ohio: Hebrew Union College Press, 2009), p. 89. Used with permission of the authors.

Unknown, *Marsch der Israelitischen national Garde in Warschau*, 1831. JCS Universitätsbibliothek Frankfurt am Main/Digitale Sammlung Judaica.

Unknown artist, *Eva Frank's house in Offenbach during the visit of Tsar Alexander I, November 1813*. Haus der Stadtgeschischte, Stadt Offenbach am Main.

Unknown artist, *Humphreys and Mendoza; Their Third Public Contest for Superiority, on Sept. 29; 1790*. Image courtesy of the YIVO Institute for Jewish Research.

Unknown artist, *Moroccan Peddler in London*. The Jewish Museum, New York/Art Resource, NY.

Unknown artist, *Portrait of Fromet Guggenheim* (1867), Mendelssohn-Archiv. bpk, Bildarchiv/Staatsbibliothek zu Berlin, Stiftung Preussischer Kulturbesitz, Berlin, Germany/Art Resource, NY.

Unknown artist, *Portrait of Rahel Levin Varnhagen*. Varnhagen Collection, Biblioteka Jagiellońska, Kraków.

Unknown artist, *Portrait of R. Akiva Eger*. Courtesy of The National Library of Israel, Jerusalem.

Unknown artist, *Poster of Rachel Félix*. Copyright © Coll. Comédie-Française.

Unknown author, "The Calling of Abraham," lyrics trans. Edwin Seroussi, from Bienvenida Aguado and Loretta Gerassi, *Chants judéo-espagnols de la Méditerraneé orientale/Judeo-Spanish Songs from the Eastern Mediterranean*, W 260054 (Paris: INEDIT/Maison des Cultures du Monde, 1994). Lyrics translated from the Spanish, from Elena Romero, *Coplas sefardíes: Primera selección* (Córdoba: El Almendro, 1991). Used with permission of the translator.

Unknown photographer, *Ignaz Goldziher Speaking at His Bar Mitzvah, 1863*. Copyright © Hungarian Jewish Museum and Archives, Budapest.

Uri of Strelisk, "On the Seer of Lublin's Court," trans. Dena Ordan, from David Assaf, *Untold Tales of the Hasidim: Crisis & Discontent in the History of Hasidism* (Waltham, Mass.: Brandeis University Press, 2010), p. 98. Copyright © 2010 Brandeis University. Reprinted with permission of University Press of New England.

Rafael Uziel, "The Sins That Started the Fire: A Journalist's View from Izmir," trans. Olga Borovaya, from *Sephardi Lives: A Documentary History, 1700–1950*, ed. Julia Phillips Cohen and Sarah Abrevaya Stein (Stanford,

Calif.: Stanford University Press, 2014), pp. 40–43. Copyright © 2014 by the Board of Trustees of the Leland Stanford Jr. University. All rights reserved. With the permission of Stanford University Press, www.sup.org; "Editor's Note," from *Sha'are mizraḥ* (June 11, 1846), no. 65, trans. Olga Borovaya in *The Sephardi Studies Project*, ladino.stanford.edu. Used with permission of the translator.

Rahel Levin Varnhagen, "Letters 1799–1800," New York Public Library, Schwarzman Building–Dorot Jewish Division Rm 111 *PWZ (Varnhagen, R.) 99-1468, selected in *Rahel Varnhagen: The Life of a Jewess*, ed. Hannah Arendt (London: Leo Baeck Institute, 1957), pp. 197–99.

Voleti, *Prayers at the Tomb of Rabbi Isaac ben Sheshet at Algiers*, ca. 1870. The Jewish Museum, gift of Dr. Harry G. Friedman; The Jewish Museum, NY/Art Resource/Scala.

Godchaux Baruch Weil (writing under pseudonym Ben-Lévi), "The March 17th Decree," trans. Maurice Samuels, from *Nineteenth-Century Jewish Literature: A Reader*, ed. Jonathan M. Hess, Maurice Samuels, and Nadia Valman (Stanford, Calif.: Stanford University Press, 2013), pp. 304–7. Copyright © 2013 by the Board of Trustees of the Leland Stanford Jr. University. All rights reserved. With the permission of Stanford University Press, www.sup.org.

Alexandre Weill, "Braendel," trans. Maurice Samuels, from *Nineteenth-Century Jewish Literature: A Reader*, ed. Jonathan M. Hess, Maurice Samuels, and Nadia Valman (Stanford, Calif.: Stanford University Press, 2013), pp. 87–93. Copyright © 2013 by the Board of Trustees of the Leland Stanford Jr. University. All rights reserved. With the permission of Stanford University Press, www.sup.org.

Naphtali Herts Wessely, "Words of Peace and Truth," trans. Stephen L. Weinstein and Saul Fischer, from *The Jew in the Modern World: A Documentary History*, 2nd ed., ed. Paul Mendes-Flohr and Jehuda Reinharz (New York: Oxford University Press, 1995), p. 71. Used with permission of the translators.

Auguste Widal (wrote under the name Daniel Stauben), from *Scenes of Jewish Life in Alsace*, ed. and trans. Rose Choron (Malibu, Calif.: Joseph Simon/Pangloss Press, 1991), pp. 3–8. Used with permission of the translator's estate.

Shneur Zalman of Liady, *Niggun of Four Stanzas*, ca. 1800. From Raffi Ben-Moshe, *Experiencing Devekut. The Contemplative Niggun of Habad in Israel* (Yuval Music Series 11, Jerusalem: Jewish Music Research Centre, 2015, p. 123); "Tzimtzum: An Infusion of Light" and "The Limbs of One Body," from *The Religious Thought of Hasidism*, ed. and trans. Norman Lamm (New York: Yeshiva University Press, 1999), p. 41–43, 421. Used with permission of the translator.

Aleksander Zederbaum, *Keter kehunah*, trans. Dena Ordan, from David Assaf, *Untold Tales of the Hasidim: Crisis and Discontent in the History of Hasidism* (Waltham, Mass.: Brandeis University Press, 2010), p. 114. Copyright © 2010 Brandeis University. Reprinted with permission of University Press of New England.

Leopold Zunz, "The Liturgical Addresses of the Jews," from *The Dynamics of Emancipation: The Jew in the Modern Age*, ed. N. Glatzer (Boston: Beacon Press, 1965), pp. 11–14. Used with permission of the editor's estate.

Index of Authors and Artists

Biographical information about each author or artist appears at the beginning of the person's first selection. The reader may search by subject in the web-based version of the *Posen Library of Jewish Culture and Civilization.*

Aaron Worms of Metz, 186
Abramovitsh, Sholem Yankev (Mendele Mokher Sforim): *The Little Man; or, Portrait of a Life,* 111; "The Association 'Concern for the Needy,'" 360; "Fishke the Lame," 363; *The Brief Travels of Benjamin the Third,* 372
Aguilar, Grace: "The Escape: A Tale of 1755," 89; *Women of Israel, or, Characters and Sketches from the Holy Scriptures,* 196
Akrish, Isaac, 255
Aksenfeld, Israel: "The Headband," 106; *Recruits,* 481
Aldrophe, Alfred-Philibert, 434
a-Levi, Sa'adi Besalel: *Memoir,* 65; "How Does a Newspaper Survive?," 369
Algazi, Yom Tov ben Israel Jacob, 169
Al. K., 346
Alkalai, Judah, 192
Alkan, Charles-Valentin: "Ancienne melodie de la synagogue," 496; *Super flumina Babylonis,* 499
Allgemeine Zeitung des Judentums, Die, 339
Alliance Israélite Universelle, 327
Altaras, Jacques-Isaac, 319
Amarachi, Isaac Bekhor, 252
Amerling, Friedrich von, 403
Angenendt, Wilhelmus, 388
Anonymous: *In Praise of the Ba'al Shem Tov,* 77; "A Story of What Happened to Rav Moshe Danon and the Elders of the Jewish Community of Sarajevo on 20 October 1819," 123; "A Dirge for the Ninth of Av," 125; "The Cry of the Poor Jews of Izmir," 321; "Letter Addressed to the Conference of Constantinople in Favor of the Jews of the Orient," 370; *The Fake Doctor,* 476; "La vocación de Abraham," 493. See also Artist Unknown
Antokolski, Mark: *A Jewish Tailor,* 418; *Ivan the Terrible,* 423
Arieh, Oro, 56
Arnstein, Fanny von, 19
Arnstein, Michael Joseph Edler von, 11
Artist Unknown: *Amulet for the Protection of Pregnant Women and Newborn Children,* 378; *Omer Calendar,* 379; *Huppah,* 380; *Inventory of Household Goods of Nathan Levy,* 381; *Ketubot:* 382, 408, 413, 417, 425; *Wedding Riddle,* 386; *Jewish Burial Society,* 391; *Cup and Saucer with Portrait of Isaac Daniel Itzig and His Residence,* 393; *Oldest Jewish Cemetery in America,* 394; *Torah Ark Curtain,* 395; *Hand-Washing Basin,* 396; *Circumcision Bench,* 399; *Alms Container,* 400; *Torah Curtain,* 402; *Jewish Women from Izmir Whitewashing,* 403; *Wedding Sofa,* 406; *Medal Commemorating Sir Moses Montefiore,* 407; *Ewer and Basin,* 407; *Esther Scroll,* 411; *Tombstone,* 411; *Burial Comb and Nail Pick of the Bischitz Burial Society,* 412; *Paper Cut—Shiviti Sign,* 412; *Torah Scroll and Case,* 414; *Amulet for Bitoul Ada,* 416; *Alms Plate,* 418; *Minute Book of Psalms Society Serving in the Russian Army,* 420; *Paper Cut—Yortsayt,* 422; *Poster of Rachel Felix,* 473; *Marsch der Israelitischen national Garde in Warschau,* 495. See also Anonymous
Ascher, Saul, 231
Attias, David, 9
Azulai, Ḥayim Joseph David, 72

Ba'al Shem Tov: "Igeret aliyat ha-neshamah" ("Epistle on the Ascent of the Soul"), 143; *Tsava'at ha-Rivash (Testament of Rabbi Israel Ba'al Shem Tov),* 164
Badkhn, Pesach-Elijah, 501
Baer, Abraham, 504
Baruch of Shklov, 223
Basch, Samuel Siegfried Karl von, 58
Beer, Michael, 468
Beer, Peter, 40
Beilin, S., 253
Benamozegh, Elijah, 205
Bendavid, Lazarus, 235
Bendemann, Eduard Julius Friedrich, 454
ben Gabriel, Jonah, 88
Berlin, Saul: *Ketav yosher (Epistle of Justice),* 162; "Besamim rosh" ("Scent of a Bitter Spice"), 164
Ber of Bolechów, 15
Bet Din of Hamburg, 182
Bialsker, Nachman ha-Kohen, 417
Bick, Jacob Samuel, 335
Binger, Hijman [Hayim ben Mordecai], 401
Blau, Tina, 457
Bogrov, Grigory, 257
Brafman, Jacob, 296

INDEX OF AUTHORS AND ARTISTS

Brandon, Jacques-Émile-Édouard: *Sermon of the Fast of Av (Synagogue of Amsterdam),* 449; *Heder (Jewish Children's School),* 453

Carvalho, Solomon Nunes: *Travel Journal,* 70; *Interior of the Beth Elohim Synagogue, Charleston, South Carolina,* 431; *Portrait of Wakara,* 444
Castelli, Joseph Vita, 278
Chorin, Aaron, 181
Coen, Anania, 244
Cohen, Joseph, 319

Daninos, Abraham, 471
Da Ponte, Lorenzo, 484
David of Makev, 239
Davidsohn, Zemah, 417
Delacroix, Eugène, 404
de la Motta, Jacob, 183
Della Torre, Lelio, 245
Depaulis, Alexis Joseph, 399
Dik, Isaac Meyer: *The Women Shopkeepers, or, Golde-Mine, the Abandoned Wife of Brod,* 112; *The Panic, or, The Town of Hérres,* 116
Disraeli, Benjamin: *Vivian Grey,* 82; *The Wondrous Tale of Alroy,* 84; "Utilitarian Follies," 315
Dohány Street Synagogue, 432
Dov Ber of Mezritsh, 159
Dukes, Leopold, 286
Dupré, Augustin, 399

Earl, Ralph, 392
Eger, Akiva: "Statement of Mourning," 22; "Letter of Rabbinic Appointment to the City of Posen," 30
Eidlitz, Zeraḥ, 152
Einhorn, David, 330
Elijah ben Solomon, Gaon of Vilna: "Epistle against the Hasidim," 153; "Ethical Will," 166; *Bi'ur ha-Gra: Glosses to Shulḥan arukh,* 173
Elimelech of Lizhensk: *No'am Elimelekh (Pleasing Qualities of Elimelech),* 163; *Menorat zahav (Golden Menorah),* 213
Elion, Jacques, 421
Emden, Jacob: *Megilat sefer (The Scroll of the Book),* 6; *Mor u-ketsiyah (Myrrh and Cassia),* 150; *Sefer hitavkut (Book of Struggle),* 151
Epstein, Isidoro, 369
Epstein, Kalonimos Kalman, 193
Erter, Isaac, 248
Ettinger, Solomon: "The Assembly," 136; *Serkele,* 470
Ettlinger, Jacob: "Rabbinic Reports on Circumcision," 197; *Arukh la-ner,* 200; *Responsa binyan tsiyon (Responsa: Building Zion),* 211
Euchel, Isaac: *Toldot rabenu he-ḥakham Mosheh ben Menaḥem (Biography of Our Wise Teacher, Moses, Son of Menachem),* 13; *Igrot Meshulam (Epistles of Meshulam),* 74
Eybeschütz, Jonathan: "Sermon of Ethical Rebuke Preached . . . ," 140; *Sefer luḥot edut (Tablets of Testimony),* 144; *Urim ve-tumim (The Urim and Thummim),* 156; *Tiferet Yonatan (The Splendor of Jonathan),* 184
Ezekiel, Moses, 424

Fet, Afanasy, 130
Feuchtwanger, Lewis: *Feuchtwanger Cent,* 404; *Chart of Gems from A Popular Treatise on Gems,* 405
Fichel, Benjamin-Eugène, 463
Fiorino, Jeremiah David Alexander, 439
Fleckeles, Eleazer, 168
Foa, Eugénie, 85
Fonseca, Salomón López, 135
Formstecher, Salomon, 100
Fraenkel, Zechariah, 197
Franck, Adolphe, 285
Francolm, Isaac Asher, 192
Frank, Jacob, 148
Frankl, Ludwig A., 86
Franks, Rebecca, 10
Franzos, Karl Emil, 119
Friedländer, David: *Reader for Jewish Children,* 222; "Open Letter," 241
Friedländer, Friedrich: *People Pouring out of a Public Building into the Street,* 445; *The Death of Tasso,* 463
Frizzi, Benedetto: *Defense against the Attacks Leveled against the Jewish Nation in the Book Entitled* On the Ghetto's Influence on the State, 226; *Dissertation on Medical Policy Concerning Certain Foods Which Are Prohibited in the Pentateuch,* 230
Fuenn, Samuel Joseph: *Dor ve-dorshav (A Generation and Its Seekers),* 273; *Kiryah ne'emanah (Faithful City),* 291

Gabay, Ezekiel, 343
Gabbay, Rosa, 269
Ganbash, Moses, 406
Gans, Eduard, 185
Gans, Jacob Koppel, 387
Gaon of Vilna: *See* Elijah ben Solomon, Gaon of Vilna
Geiger, Abraham, 292
Gintsburg, Mordechai Aaron, 259
Goldfaden, Abraham, 479
Goldmark, Karl, 491
Goldziher, Ignác: *My Oriental Diary,* 61; *The Zahiris,* 299
Gomez, Benjamin, 3
Gordon, Judah Leib: "Awake My People!," 132; "The Tip of the Yod," 133
Gordon, Mikhl, 500
Gottlieb, Maurycy: *Jews Praying in the Synagogue on Yom Kippur,* 459; *Christ Preaching at Capernaum,* 460
Gottlober, Abraham Ber: *Zikhronot u-masa'ot (Memoir and Journeys),* 64; *Pirḥe he-aviv (Spring Flowers),* 246
Gottschalk, Louis, 499
Graetz, Heinrich, 287
Grand Sanhedrin (France), 176
Gratz, Richea (Family of), 20
Grodner, A., 361
Grosglik, Israel Leon, 365
Guggenheim, Fromet, 7
Guggenheim, Sara Hirsch, 108
Guzikov, Michael Joseph, 494

Ha-Efrati, Joseph, 470
Halévy, Jacques-François-Fromental-Élie: *La juive,* 486; *La reine de Chypre,* 487
Halévy, Léon, 280
Halle-Wolfsohn, Aaron: *Siḥah be-erets ha-ḥayim (A Conversation in the Afterlife),* 75; *Silliness and Sanctimony,* 236
Harby, Isaac, 466
Harkavy, Abraham: "On the Language of the Jews Who Lived in Ancient Russia," 294; "A Few Words Concerning Literary Criticism," 354
Hart, Aaron, 15
Hart, Solomon Alexander: *An Early Reading of Shakespeare,* 440; *The Feast of the Rejoicing of the Law at the Synagogue in Leghorn, Italy,* 442
Hartmann, Moritz, 367
Ḥayim of Volozhin, 172
Ḥazan, Israel Moses, 497
Heine, Heinrich: "A Seder Night," 80; "Donna Clara," 124; "Farewell, You Cheerful Folk of France," 128
Helfft, Julius, 410
Heller, Koppel ben Moses, 400
Henriques de Castro, Daniel, 415
Henriquez da Costa, Rebecca, 7
Henschel, Alberto, 452
Henschel Brothers (Gebrüder Henschel), 438
Hensel, Fanny Mendelssohn, 495
Herfurth, Rötger, 385
Herz, Henriette de Lemos, 47
Hess, Moses, 331
Hirsch, Abraham, 433
Hirsch, Samson Raphael, 188
Hirsch, Samuel, 194

Homberg, Herz, 280
Hourwitz, Zalkind, 308
Hubard, William James, 401

Isaac, Aaron, 26
Isaacs, Jorge, 113
Isaacs, Martha (attributed), 435
Israel ben Samuel of Shklov, 190
Israëls, Jozef, 454

Jacob Joseph of Polnoye, 159
Janów Sokólski Synagogue, 429
Jeitteles, Judah, 37
Jesurun, Jacob Abraham, 415
Joel, J. A., 56
Josephson, Ernst, 459
Jost, Isaac Markus, 281

Kahan, Urye, 349
Kapper, Siegfried, 130
Katzenellenbogen, Pinchas, 4
Khvolson, Daniel: "Letter on His Conversion," 48; *The Semitic Nations*, 299
Kohn, Abraham, 43
Kompert, Leopold, 94
Konfino, Moses Samuel, 473
Kovner, Abraham Uri, 266
Kretschmar, Johann Karl, 398
Krochmal, Nachman, 290
Kuh, David, 339
Kulisher, Reuben, 324

Landau, Ezekiel: *Derushe ha-tselah* (*Sermons* [of Landau]), 147; *Noda bi-Yehudah* (*Known in Judah*), 158; "Sermon for the Sabbath Preceding Passover," 160; "Eulogy for Empress Maria Theresa," 303
Landau, Jacob, 180
Laniado, Raphael, 12
Lazarus, Emma: *Epochs*, 134; "The New Colossus," 137
Lazarus, Rachel Mordecai, 32
Lebensohn, Abraham Dov (Adam) ha-Kohen: "Lament of the Daughter of Judah," 128; "Seeker of Truth," 129
Leeser, Isaac: *Catechism for Jewish Children: Designed as a Religious Manual for House and School*, 248; *The Claims of the Jews to an Equality of Rights*, 318
Lefin, Menachem Mendel: *Sefer ḥeshbon ha-nefesh* (*Book of Moral Accounting*), 177; "Prayer against the Hasidim," 242
Lehmann, Rudolf, 443
Leon, Maurits, 448
Lesser, Aleksander, 446
Levanda, Lev, 117
Levi, Emanuele, 38
Levi, Giuseppe, 342

Levi Isaac of Berdichev: *Kedushat Levi* (*Sanctity of Levi*), 168; "A Din Toyre mit Gott/Der kadish fun rabi Levi Yitshok" ("A Court Case with God/The Kaddish of Rabbi Levi Isaac"), 493
Levin, Emmanuil Borisovich, 256
Levinzon, Isaac Ber, 265
Lévy, Alphonse, 453
Levy, Esther, 60
Lewandowski, Louis, 503
Liebermann, Max: *The Dutch Sewing School*, 458; *The Twelve-Year-Old Jesus in the Temple with the Scholars*, 460
Lifshits, Shiye Mordkhe: *Yudl and Yehudis*, 347; "The Four Classes," 351
Lilienblum, Moses Leib, 62
Linetski, Isaac Joel, 115
Lisbonne, Elissa, 208
Lisiewska-Therbusch, Anna Dorothea, 390
Loewenbach, I. W., 402
Lopez, Aaron, 3
Louzada, David Hisquiau Baruch, 163
Lutski, Joseph Solomon, 68
Lutski, Simhah Isaac ben Moses, 277
Luzzatto, Ephraim, 122
Luzzatto, Israel David, 389
Luzzatto, Samuel David: *Lessons of Jewish Moral Theology*, 204; *Igerot Shadal* (*Letters of Samuel David Luzzatto*), 291; *Introduction to the Pentateuch*, 297

Magnus, Eduard, 487
Magriso, Isaac, 219
Maimon, Solomon: *Solomon Maimon: An Autobiography*, 17; *Givat ha-moreh* [Commentary to Maimonides' *Moreh nevukhim*, Guide for the Perplexed], 233; *The Autobiography of Solomon Maimon: Maskilic View of Heder*, 234
Mapu, Abraham: *The Love of Zion*, 97; *The Hypocrite*, 99
Margolis, Menashe, 358
Markel-Mosessohn, Miriam, 58
Marx, Karl: *On the Jewish Question*, 320; "Manifesto of the Communist Party," 322
Mayer, Bonaventura, 195
Me'am Lo'ez, 219
Menachem Mendel of Vitebsk, 180
Mendele Mokher Sforim. See Sholem Yankev Abramovitsh
Mendelssohn, Moses: *On the Religious Legitimacy of Studying Logic* (*Commentary on Maimonides' Milot ha-higayon*), 218; *Phaedon*, 220; *Light for the Path*, 224; "Letter to the Friends of Lessing (On the Spinoza Conversations between Lessing and Jacobi)," 226; "Preface to *Vindiciae Judaeorum*," 304; *Jerusalem*, 304

Mendes, David Franco, 310
Mendes de Castro, Abraham, 2
Mendes de Sola, Samuel, 146
Mendoza, Daniel: *The Art of Boxing*, Preface, 14; *Memoirs of the Life of Daniel Mendoza*, 33
Mengs, Anton Raphael: *Annunciation*, 436; *Portrait of the Marquesa de Llano*, 436
Mengs, Theresa Concordia, 435
Menken, Adah Isaacs, 476
Meyerbeer, Giacomo: *Robert le diable*, 485; *Le prophète*, 488; "Hallelujah: Eine Cantatine für 4 Männerstimmen mit begleitung einer obligaten orgel und des chores ad libitum," 496
Mieses, Fabius, 362
Moïse, Penina: "Miriam," 127; *Hymns Written for the Use of Hebrew Congregations. Charleston, Congregation Beth Elohim*, 209
Montefiore, Judith Cohen, *The Jewish Manual of Practical Information in Jewish and Modern Cookery with a Collection of Valuable Recipes & Hints Relating to the Toilette*, 45; *Private Journal of a Visit to Egypt and Palestine*, 67
Mordecai, Emma, 53
Morgulis, Mikhail, 263
Morpurgo, Rachel Luzzatto, 131
Morschene, Relle Luzzatto, 21
Mosler, Henry: *Canal Street Market*, 446; *Return of the Prodigal Son*, 461; *Drawings Published in Harper's*, 464
Moyse, Édouard, 450
Muhr, Julius, 452
Myers, Myer: *Snuff Box*, 383; *Torah Finials*, 383

Nachman of Bratslav: "The Tale of a Rabbi and His Only Son," 79; "Tiku emunah," 179
Nassy, David de Isaac Cohen, 306
Nathan, Isaac, 494
Naumbourg, Samuel: "Seu Shearim (Lift Up Your Heads, O Gates)," 497; *Aggudat Shirim*, 502; Title Page for His Version of Salamone de Rossi's *Hashirim asher le-Shelomoh* (*The Songs of Solomon*), 504
Neuda, Fanny: "On the Approach of Childbirth," 200; "For a Mother Whose Son Is in Military Service," 202
Neufeld, Daniel: "Editorial about Jews in the American Civil War," 344; "The Hebrew Crusading Newspaper," 345; "Progress: The Meaning of Passover," 352
Nevakhovich, Lev, 313
Noah, Mordecai Manuel: "Ziprah Nunez's Account of the Family Escape," 45; *She Would Be a Soldier, or, the Plain of Chippewa; An Historical Drama in Three Acts*, 467

INDEX OF AUTHORS AND ARTISTS

Óbuda Synagogue, 430
Offenbach, Jacques: The Brazilian's Song from the Opera *La vie parisienne*, 488; *La Grande-Duchesse de Gérolstein*, 489; *Tales of Hoffmann*, 491
Oppenheim, Moritz Daniel: *The Return of the Jewish Volunteer from the Wars of Liberation to His Family Still Living in Accordance with Old Customs*, 440; *The Bar Mitzvah Discourse*, 451
Orshanski, Ilya, 371

Paneth, Ezekiel, 174
Paperna, Abraham Jacob, 131
Papo, Eliezer Shem-Tov, 269
Papo, Judah, 210
Pascheles, Wolf, 93
Penha, Moses L., 497
Perl, Joseph, 243
Philippson, Ludwig, 98
Phillips, Jonas, 305
Pissarro, Camille: *Factory near Pontoise*, 455; *Self-Portrait*, 456; *A Road in the Woods in Summer*, 458; *The Avenue de l'Opéra, Sunlight, Winter Morning*, 462
Pontremoli, Esdra, 342

Rabbis of Schwerin, 154
Rabinovich, Osip, 102
Raphall, Morris Jacob, 328
Rapoport, Solomon Judah, 199
Reggio, Isaac Samuel, 254
Romanelli, Samuel, 66
Rosanes, Abraham, 51
Rose, Ernestine Potovsky, 325
Rosenboim, Moses Michael, 409
Rothschild, Charlotte von, 441
Rothschild, Salomon de, 49
Roza, Wife of Leyzer ben Moses Judah, 22
Rozenblum, Berish, 358
Rubinstein, Anton, 490

Safrin, Isaac Judah Yehiel of Komarno: "Account of His Visit to Lublin," 33; *Notser ḥesed to Avot (Preserving Mercy* [Commentary to *Ethics of the Fathers*]), 214
Salanter, Israel, 214
Salomon, Geskel: *Ferdinand II, 1810–1859 Bourbon King of Two Sicilies*, 464; *Drawing of Costume for Vitka in the First Production of the Opera Dalibor by Bedřich Smetana*, 492
Salvador, Joseph, 203
Samuel, Rebecca, 16
Sanua, James, 374
Sason, Joseph ben Meir, 252
Sasportas, Isaac, 311
Scheindling of Shkudy, Judah, 332
Schick, Baruch ben Jacob (Baruch of Shklov), 223
Schlesinger, Akiva Joseph, 206
Schornstein, David, 109
Schwab, Löw, 336
Segura, Pinḥas de, 250
Seidan, Wenzel, 413
Seixas, Moses, 309
Shearith Israel (synagogue), 301, 426
Sheftall, Mordecai, 301
Sheftall, Sheftall, 39
Shneur Zalman of Liady: *Tanya*, 166; *Igrot ha-kodesh (Holy Epistles)*, 217; "Niggun of Four Stanzas," 493
Sofer, Moses: *Sefer ha-zikaron (The Book of Memory)*, 28; *Derashot Ḥatam Sofer (Sermons of Ḥatam Sofer)*, 179; "Responsa Ḥatam Sofer: *Oraḥ ḥayim* 154," 180; *Ḥut ha-meshulash (Threefold Cord)*, 186; "Responsa Ḥatam Sofer: *Oraḥ ḥayim* 51," 188; "Responsa Ḥatam Sofer: *Oraḥ ḥayim* 36," 191
Sofer, Simon, 211
Solomon, Abraham: *First Class—The Meeting*, 444; *Waiting for the Verdict*, 445
Solomon, Rebecca, 447
Solomon, Simeon, 451
Sonnenfeld, Adolf Gustaw, 490
Soria, Angelo (Mordechai) de, 142
Sulzer, Salomon, 505
Synagogue in the Park at Wörlitz, Germany, 428

Tevele, David, 161
Touro Synagogue, Newport, Rhode Island, 427
Towne, Charles, 437
Tsunzer, Elyokum: "Song of the Railway," 502; "The Flower," 505

Uri of Strelisk, 214
Uziel, Rafael: "Editor's Note in *Sha'are mizraḥ (Gates of the East)*, 341; "On the Discords among the Jews of Izmir," 341

Varnhagen, Rahel Levin, 24
Veit, Philipp, 439
Verveer, Salomon Leonardus, 443

Wasserzug, Moses, 35
Weil, Godchaux Baruch (Ben-Lévi): "The Rise and Fall of a Polish Tallis," 87; "The March 17th Decree," 337
Weill, Alexandre, 103
Weisel, Leopold, 91
Weitsch, Friedrich Georg, 397
Wessely, Naphtali Herts: "Shire tiferet" ("Songs of Glory"), 122; *Words of Peace and Truth*, 223; *Sefer ha-midot (Book of Virtues)*, 231
Widal, Auguste (Daniel Stauben), 95
Wiener, Charles, 419
Wiener, Jacques: *H. M. King Leopold I Stamp*, 410; *Medal of St. Stephen's Cathedral*, 416
Wise, Isaac Mayer, 201

Zederbaum, Alexander: "A Few Remarks Regarding the Education of Women," 349; "A Great Announcement," 353; "Keter Kehunah: On the Seer's Fall," 362
Ze'ev, Son of Abraham, 384
Zunz, Leopold: "My First Lessons in Wolfenbüttel," 47; "The Liturgical Addresses of the Jews," 283
Zusya of Annopol (Hanipoli), 213
Zweifel, Eliezer, 271